DATE DUE

PRINTED IN U.S.A.

CLASSICAL AND MEDIEVAL LITERATURE CRITICISM

Guide to Gale Literary Criticism Series

For criticism on	Consult these Gale series
Authors now living or who died after December 31, 1959	*CONTEMPORARY LITERARY CRITICISM (CLC)*
Authors who died between 1900 and 1959	*TWENTIETH-CENTURY LITERARY CRITICISM (TCLC)*
Authors who died between 1800 and 1899	*NINETEENTH-CENTURY LITERATURE CRITICISM (NCLC)*
Authors who died between 1400 and 1799	*LITERATURE CRITICISM FROM 1400 TO 1800 (LC)* *SHAKESPEAREAN CRITICISM (SC)*
Authors who died before 1400	*CLASSICAL AND MEDIEVAL LITERATURE CRITICISM (CMLC)*
Authors of books for children and young adults	*CHILDREN'S LITERATURE REVIEW (CLR)*
Dramatists	*DRAMA CRITICISM (DC)*
Poets	*POETRY CRITICISM (PC)*
Short story writers	*SHORT STORY CRITICISM (SSC)*
Black writers of the past two hundred years	*BLACK LITERATURE CRITICISM (BLC)*
Hispanic writers of the late nineteenth and twentieth centuries	*HISPANIC LITERATURE CRITICISM (HLC)*
Native North American writers and orators of the eighteenth, nineteenth, and twentieth centuries	*NATIVE NORTH AMERICAN LITERATURE (NNAL)*
Major authors from the Renaissance to the present	*WORLD LITERATURE CRITICISM, 1500 TO THE PRESENT (WLC)*

ISSN 0896-0011

Volume 30

CLASSICAL AND MEDIEVAL LITERATURE CRITICISM

Excerpts from Criticism of the Works of World
Authors from Classical Antiquity through the
Fourteenth Century, from the First Appraisals
to Current Evaluations

Jelena O. Krstović
Editor

The Gale Group

DETROIT • SAN FRANCISCO • LONDON • BOSTON • WOODBRIDGE, CT

This book is printed on acid-free paper that meets the minimum requirements of American National Standard for Information Sciences—Permanence Paper for Printed Library materials, ANSI Z39.48-1984.

Library of Congress Catalog Card Number 88-658021
ISBN 0-7876-2409-8
ISSN 0896-0011
Printed in the United States of America

10 9 8 7 6 5 4 3 2 1

Contents

Preface vii

Acknowledgments xi

Preface

Since its inception in 1988, *Classical and Medieval Literature Criticism* has been a valuable resource for students and librarians seeking critical commentary on the writers and works of these periods in world history. Major reviewing sources have assessed *CMLC* as "useful" and "extremely convenient," noting that it "adds to our understanding of the rich legacy left by the ancient period and the Middle Ages," and praising its "general excellence in the presentation of an inherently interesting subject." No other single reference source has surveyed the critical reaction to classical and medieval literature as thoroughly as *CMLC*.

Scope of the Series

CMLC is designed to serve as an introduction for students and advanced readers of the works and authors of antiquity through the fourteenth century. The great poets, prose writers, dramatists, and philosophers of this period form the basis of most humanities curricula, so that virtually every student will encounter many of these works during the course of a high school and college education. By organizing and reprinting an enormous amount of commentary written on classical and medieval authors and works, *CMLC* helps students develop valuable insight into literary history, promotes a better understanding of the texts, and sparks ideas for papers and assignments. Each entry in *CMLC* presents a comprehensive survey of an author's career, an individual work of literature, or a literary topic, and provides the user with a multiplicity of interpretations and assessments. Such variety allows students to pursue their own interests; furthermore, it fosters an awareness that literature is dynamic and responsive to many different opinions.

CMLC continues the survey of criticism of world literature begun by Gale's *Contemporary Literary Criticism (CLC), Twentieth-Century Literary Criticism (TCLC), Nineteenth-Century Literature Criticism (NCLC), Literature Criticism from 1400 to 1800 (LC),* and *Shakespearean Criticism (SC).* For additional information about these and Gale's other criticism series, users should consult the Guide to Gale Literary Criticism Series preceding the title page in this volume.

Coverage

Each volume of *CMLC* is carefully compiled to present:

- criticism of authors and works which represent a variety of genres, time periods, and nationalities

- both major and lesser-known writers and works of the period (such as non-Western authors and literature, increasingly read by today's students)

- 4-6 authors or works per volume

- individual entries that survey the critical response to each author, work, or topic, including early criticism, later criticism (to represent any rise or decline in the author's reputation), and current retrospective analyses. The length of each author or work entry also indicates relative importance, reflecting the amount of critical attention the author, work, or topic has received from critics writing in English, and from foreign criticism in translation.

An author may appear more than once in the series if his or her writings have been the subject of a substantial amount of criticism; in these instances, specific works or groups of works by the author will be covered in separate entries. For example, Homer will be represented by three entries, one devoted to the *Iliad,* one to the *Odyssey,* and one to the Homeric Hymns.

Starting with Volume 10, *CMLC* will also occasionally include entries devoted to literary topics. For example, *CMLC*-10 focuses on Arthurian Legend and includes general criticism on that subject as well as individual entries on writers or works central to that topic—Chrétien de Troyes, Gottfried von Strassburg, Layamon, and the Alliterative *Morte Arthure*. Presocratic Philosophy is the focus of *CMLC*-22, which includes general criticism as well as essays on Greek philosophers Anaximander, Heraclitus, Parmenides, and Pythagoras.

Organization of the Book

An author entry consists of the following elements: author heading, biographical and critical introduction, principal English translations or editions, excerpts of criticism (each preceded by a bibliographic citation and an annotation), and a bibliography of further reading.

• The **Author Heading** consists of the author's most commonly used name, followed by birth and death dates. If the entry is devoted to a work, the heading will consist of the most common form of the title in English translation (if applicable), and the original date of composition. Located at the beginning of the introduction are any name or title variations.

• A **Portrait** of the author is included when available. Many entries also feature illustrations of materials pertinent to the author or work, including manuscript pages, book illustrations, and representations of people, places, and events important to a study of the author or work.

• The **Biographical and Critical Introduction** contains background information that concisely introduces the reader to the author, work, or topic.

• The list of **Principal Works** and **English Translations** or **Editions** is chronological by date of first publication and is included as an aid to the student seeking translated versions or editions of these works for study. The list will focus primarily on twentieth-century translations, selecting those works most commonly considered the best by critics.

• **Criticism** is arranged chronologically in each entry to provide a useful perspective on changes in critical evaluation over the years. All titles by the author featured in the critical entry are printed in boldface type to enable the user to ascertain without difficulty the works being discussed. Also for purposes of easier identification, the critic's name and the publication date of the essay are given at the beginning of each piece of criticism. Anonymous criticism is preceded by the title of the journal in which it appeared. Publication information (such as publisher names and book prices) and parenthetical numerical references (such as footnotes or page and line references to specific editions of works) have been deleted at the editors' discretion to provide smoother reading of the text. Many critical entries in *CMLC* also contain translations to aid the users. Footnotes that appear with previously published pieces of criticism are reprinted at the end of each essay or excerpt. In the case of excerpted criticism, only those footnotes that pertain to the excerpted text are included.

• A complete **Bibliographic Citation** provides original publication information for each piece of criticism.

• Critical excerpts are also prefaced by **Annotations** providing the reader with information about both the critic and the criticism, the scope of the excerpt, the growth of critical controversy, or changes in critical trends regarding an author or work. In some cases, these notes include cross-references to excerpts by critics who discuss each other's commentary. Dates in parentheses within the annotation refer to a book publication date when they follow a book title, and to an essay date when they follow a critic's name.
• An annotated bibliography of **Further Reading** appears at the end of each entry and lists additional secondary sources on the author or work. In some cases it includes essays for which the editors could not obtain reprint rights. When applicable, the Further Reading is followed by references to additional entries on the author in other literary reference series published by Gale.

Topic Entries are subdivided into several thematic rubrics in which criticism appears in order of descending scope.

Cumulative Indexes

Each volume of *CMLC* includes a cumulative **author index** listing all authors who have appeared in Gale's Literary Criticism Series, along with cross references to such biographical series as *Contemporary Authors* and *Dictionary of Literary Biography*. For readers' convenience, a complete list of Gale titles included appears on the page prior to the author index. Useful for locating an author within the various series, this index is particularly valuable for those authors who are identified with a certain period but who, because of their death date, are placed in another, or for those authors whose careers span two periods. For example, Geoffrey Chaucer, who is usually considered a medieval author, is found in *Literature Criticism from 1400 to 1800* because he died after 1399.

Beginning with the tenth volume, *CMLC* includes a cumulative index listing all topic entries that have appeared in the Gale Literary Criticism Series *Classical and Medieval Literature Criticism, Contemporary Literary Criticism, Literature Criticism from 1400 to 1800, Nineteenth-Century Literature Criticism,* and *Twentieth-Century Literary Criticism.*

Beginning with the second volume, *CMLC* also includes a cumulative nationality index. Authors and/or works are grouped by nationality, and the volume in which criticism on them may be found is indicated.

Title Index

Each volume of *CMLC* also includes an index listing the titles of all literary works discussed in the series. Foreign language titles that have been translated are followed by the titles of the translations—for example, *Slovo o polku Igorove (The Song of Igor's Campaign).* Page numbers following these translated titles refer to all pages on which any form of the title, either foreign language or translated, appears. Titles of novels, dramas, nonfiction books, and poetry, short story, or essay collections are printed in italics, while those of all individual poems, short stories, and essays are printed in roman type within quotation marks. In cases where the same title is used by different authors, the author's name or surname is given in parentheses after the title, e.g. *Collected Poems* (Horace) and *Collected Poems* (Sappho).

Critic Index

An index to critics, which cumulates with the second volume, is another useful feature of *CMLC*. Under each critic's name are listed the authors and/or works on whom the critic has written and the volume and page number where criticism may be found.

A Note to the Reader

When writing papers, students who quote directly from any volume in the Literary Criticism Series may use the following general forms to footnote reprinted criticism. The first example pertains to material drawn from a periodical, the second to material reprinted from books.

Rollo May, "The Therapist and the Journey into Hell," *Michigan Quarterly Review,* XXV, No. 4 (Fall 1986), 629-41; excerpted and reprinted in *Classical and Medieval Literature Criticism,* Vol. 3, ed. Jelena O. Krstovic (Detroit: Gale Research, 1989), pp. 154-58.

Dana Ferrin Sutton, *Self and Society in Aristophanes* (University of Press of America, 1980); excerpted and

Suggestions Are Welcome

Readers who wish to make suggestions for future volumes, or who have other comments regarding the series, are cordially invited to write or call the editors (1-800-347-GALE, Fax: (248) 699-8049).

Acknowledgments

The editors wish to thank the copyright holders of the excerpted criticism included in this volume and the permissions managers of many book and magazine publishing companies for assisting us in securing reproduction rights. We are also grateful to the staffs of the Detroit Public Library, the Library of Congress, the University of Detroit Mercy Library, Wayne State University Purdy/Kresge Library Complex, and the University of Michigan Libraries for making their resources available to us. Following is a list of the copyright holders who have granted us permission to reproduce material in this volume of *CMLC*. Every effort has been made to trace copyright, but if omissions have been made, please let us know.

COPYRIGHTED EXCERPTS IN *CMLC*, VOLUME 30 WERE REPRODUCED FROM THE FOLLOWING PERIODICALS:

Cahiers des Études anciennes, n. 20, 1987. Reproduced by permission.—*Echos du Monde Classique/Classical Views*, v. XXXII, 1988. Reproduced by permission of the University of Calgary Press.— *Éire-Ireland*, v. 10, 1975. Copyright © 1975 by the Irish American Cultural Institute. Reproduced by permission of the publisher.—*The Classical Bulletin*, v. 66, 1990. Copyright © 1990 *The Classical Bulletin*. All rights reserved. Reproduced with permission of Ares Publishers, Inc., 7406 N. Sheridan Rd., Chicago, IL 60626. Reproduced by permission of the publisher via Copyright Clearance Center, Inc.—*The Classical Journal*, v. 81, February-March, 1986. Reproduced by permission of the publisher.—*The Mankind Quarterly*, v. XXIII, Fall, 1982. Reproduced by permission.

COPYRIGHTED EXCERPTS IN CMLC, VOLUME 30, WERE REPRODUCED FROM THE FOLLOWING BOOKS:

Bamberger, Bernard J. From *The 'Torah': A Modern Commentary*. Union of American Hebrew Congregations, 1981. © Copyright, 1981 by the Union of American Hebrew Congregations. Reproduced by permission.—Baroody, Wilson G. and William F. Gentrup. From "Exodus, Leviticus, Numbers and Deuteronomy" in *A Complete Literary Guide to the Bible*. Edited by Leland Ryken and Tremper Longman III. Zondervan Publishing House, 1993. Copyright © 1993 by Leland Ryken and Tremper Longman III. All rights resevered. Reproduced by permission of Zondervan Publishing House, A Division of HarperCollins Publishers.—Boer, W. Den. From *Some Minor Roman Historians*. E. J. Brill, 1972. Copyright 1972 by E. J. Brill. All rights reserved. Reproduced by permission.—Breuer, Mordechai. From "The Study of Bible and the Primacy of the Fear of Heaven: Compatibility or Contradiction?" in *Modern Scholarship in the Study of Torah: Contributions and Limitations*. Edited by Shalom Carmy. Jason Aronson Inc., 1996. Copyright © 1996 Rabbi Isaac Elchanan Theological Seminary. All rights reserved. Reproduced by permission.—Bruford, Alan. From "Cú Chulainn - An Ill-Made Hero?" in *Text und Zeittiefe*. Edited by Hildegard L. C. Tristram. Gunter Narr Verlag T bingen, 1994. © 1994 Gunter Narr Verlag T bingen. Reproduced by permission.—Crusemann, Frank. From "The Pentateuch as Torah: The Way as Part of the Goal" in *The Torah: Theology and Social History of Old Testament Law*. Translated by Allan W. Mahnke. Fortress Press, 1996. English translation copyright © 1996 Augsberg Fortress. All rights reserved. Reproduced by permission—Erasmus. From "Dedicatory Letter to Erasmus' Edition of St. Jerome" in *Collected Works of Eramus: Patristic Scholarship The Edition of St. Jerome*. Edited, translated and annotated by James F. Brady and John C. Olin. University of Toronto Press, 1992. © University of Toronto Press 1992. Reproduced by permission.— Eskenazi, Tamara Cohn. From "Torah as Narrative and Narrative as Torah" in *Old Testament Interpretation: Past, Present, and Future; Essays in Honor of Gene M. Tucker*. Edited by James Luther Mays, David L. Peterson and Kent Harold Richards. Abingdon Press, 1995. Copyright © 1995 by Abingdon Press. All rights reserved. Reproduced by permission.—Friedman, Richard Elliott. From "Sacred History and Theology: The Redaction of Torah" in *The Creation of Sacred Literature: Composition and Redaction of the Biblical Text*. Edited by Richard Elliott Friedman. University of California Press, 1981. © 1981 by The Regents of the University of California. Reproduced by permision of the author.—Gray, Cecile Crovatt Gay. From The *'Táin Bó Cualnge' and the Epic Tradition*. University of Dallas, 1979. © 1983 Cecile Crovatt Gay Gray. All rights reserved. Reproduced by permission of the author.—Habel, Norman C. From

PHOTOGRAPHS AND ILLUSTRATIONS APPEARING IN *CMLC*, VOLUME 30 WERE RECEIVED FROM THE FOLLOWING SOURCES:

Eutropius

fl. c. 320-c. 387

Roman historian.

INTRODUCTION

A high-ranking official in the governments of several Roman emperors, Eutropius wrote what was for centuries considered one of the standard Roman histories. Written for the emperor Valens in 369 or 370, Eutropius's *Breviarium ab Urbe Condita (Compendium of Roman History)* summarizes the history of Rome, particularly chronicling its military and political concerns from its founding in 753 B.C. to 364 A.D. Although the book has been somewhat neglected in the twentieth century, it has influenced generations of historians and is still used today to supplement Roman republican and imperial history.

Biographical Information

Most of what can be constructed of Eutropius's biography has been garnered from secondary references to Eutropius, for he says very little about himself in the *Breviarium.* While critics disagree on the accuracy of these secondary attributions, it is generally accepted that he was born in Italy or in the province of Asia soon after 320, for he was a contemporary of the Emperor Valens (b. 328?) and Julian (b. 331). Eutropius's parents were probably quite wealthy but not of senatorial rank, for although Eutropius was well-educated, service in the imperial secretariat was generally pursued by *curiales,* members of the middle class. His career in the Eastern bureaucracy makes it likely that he studied Greek and law, probably in Rome, where students from throughout the empire gathered.

Soon after 340 he gained entry into the imperial secretariats, beginning his career as a clerk under Constantius in the eastern section of the Secretary of State for Correspondence *(magister epistularum).* When Constantius died in 361, Julian became sole emperor; he shortly afterward formed an investigatory committee that led to the banishment of six high government officials and the execution of five others. Eutropius must have been cleared of any wrongdoing, for he later accompanied Julian on the Persian campaign in 363 and was among the military and court officials to choose Julian's successor when he died in that same year. Julian was succeeded by Jovian and later Valentinian, during which time Eutropius continued to serve as a senior official. Some time afterward Eutropius was taken on in the administration of the Eastern

Emperor Valens, brother of Valentinian; in his *Breviarium* he claims to have accompanied Valens in 367-69 in his campaign against the Goths.

A promotion to the senior post of Secretary of State for General Petitions *(magister memoriae)* under Valens followed in 369. Eutropius wrote the *Breviarium* in that year or the next, possibly to show his gratitude to Valens for his promotion to the most important of the three Secretariats. Eutropius then became proconsul of Asia from 371 to 372, a position through which he had direct access to the Emperor; while in this position, Eutropius received a constitution on the restoration of the cities to Asia of part of their civic lands and restored buildings at Magnesia. Although he was later implicated in a plot against Valens, for which he was brought to Antioch on the charge of complicity, Eutropius probably was exonerated, for he escaped the many executions—of guilty and innocent alike—that followed. Nonetheless, he was removed from the proconsulship.

When Valentinian died in 375, followed by Valens in 378, the succession of Gratian and Theodosius marked Eutropius's return to political life. Sometime after 372 Eutropius travelled to Rome and was accepted in the court of Gracian; he was installed as prefect of Illyricum under Theodosius from 380 to 381, during which time Eutropius influenced the establishment of many laws, some of which lessened the punishment for various crimes. After concluding his prefecture in late 381, he moved to Constantinople, continuing to enjoy the approval of the Emperor Theodosius, who elected him Eastern consul in 387.

Major Works

Eutropius's only extant work is the *Breviarium.* Working primarily from source materials, including an abridgement of Livy's *Epitome, Suetonius auctus,* and what is known as Enmann's *Kaisergeschichte,* the book covers the whole of Roman history "from the founding of the city" *(ab urbe condita)* in 753 B.C. to the death of Jovian in 364 A.D., and was probably commissioned by Valens so that he, Valentinian, and the military commanders could acquire a sound knowledge of Roman history, which was demanded of them by the senatorial aristocracy. The history may also have been intended to bolster support of Valens's aggressive foreign policy against the Persians, which he undertook in order to recover the land surrendered by Jovian. Although the *Breviarium*'s ten short books are primarily concerned with the most important events in the lives of the emperors and with wars and their importance in the expansion and contraction of the empire, Eutropius reveals both a pro-senatorial bias—praising emperors who are on good terms with the senate—and a disdain for unnecessary conflict.

Critical Reception

The popularity of the *Breviarium* is attested to by its translation into Greek a mere ten years after its composition; indeed, Paeanius's translation of 380 was followed by two other Greek translations: in the sixth century by Capito of Lycia, and in traces of the *Chronographia* of Theophanes the Confessor, an eighth-century Greek author. The *Breviarium* became a common textbook in the Middle Ages, both in its original form and in the expanded versions of Paul the Deacon (c. 800) and Landolfus Sagax (c. 1000). Later historians—including Peter Damiani *(Historia Remensis),* Henry of Huntingdon *(Historia Anglorum),* Vincent de Beauvais *(Speculum Doctrinae),* Saint Jerome, Ammianus Marcellinus, Saint Augustine, and Bede— would draw on Eutropius heavily in their own work. Editorial interest increased in the sixteenth century, when various editions of the *Breviarium* appeared; Daniel Nathan Erickson conjectures that the popularity of the *Breviarium* grew because it could be copied quickly due to its brevity, thus making it both attractive to manuscript copyists and less expensive for the public. Numerous editions appeared throughout the eighteenth and nineteenth centuries, when the *Breviarium* was used as a Latin textbook in Germany, Britain, and elsewhere. Although interest in the book has waned somewhat in the twentieth century, it continues to be used to supplement Roman republican and imperial history. The appearance of two new English translations in the last ten years also attests to a renewed interest in Eutropius and his work, which, as H. W. Bird has written, "for several hundred years after its composition . . . played a major role in transmitting knowledge of Rome to later generations."

PRINCIPAL WORKS

Breviarium ab Urbe Condita (history) c. 369-70

PRINCIPAL ENGLISH TRANSLATIONS

A Briefe Chronicle, where in are described shortlye the originall, and the successiue estate of the Romaine weale publique, the alteratyon and chaunge of sondrye offices in the same . . . from the . . . foundatyon of the city of Rome, vnto the M.C. and xix. yeare there of [translated by Nicolas Haward] 1564

Eutropius's Compendious History of Rome [translated by John Clarke] 1722

Eutropius's Epitome of the Roman History [translated by N. Thomas] 1760

Eutropius' Abridgement of Roman History [translated by John Selby Watson] 1853

The Breviarium ab Urbe Condita of Eutropius [translated by H. W. Bird] 1993

CRITICISM

W. Den Boer (essay date 1972)

SOURCE: "Eutropius" in *Some Minor Roman Historians,* E. J. Brill, 1972, pp. 114-72.

[*In the following excerpt, Den Boer examines the possible source materials for Eutropius's works, what his histories reveal about ancient topography and chronology, and his attitudes toward Roman politics, especially domination of the barbarians, deification of emperors, and Constantine's conversion.*]

Eutropius the Man

There are many gaps in our knowledge of Eutropius which will be impossible to fill. Modern scholars tend to identify him with a number of high-ranking officials of the same name who worked between the years 360 and 390. Caution must still, however, be observed. According to his *praefatio,* a dedication to emperor Valens, he was a *magister memoriae.* The dedication gives the emperor the titles Gothicus Maximus, so that 369 or 370 would seem to be the most likely date.

The validity of the identification of the historian with the proconsul of Asia in 371, who bore the same name, is most important.[1] If this official is the same man as the historian,[2] a *terminus ante quem* is set for the *breviarium.* After all, had he already been installed in this post, the author would not have failed to mention the fact in his dedication to the emperor. But some doubt remains as to whether the Eutropius known to have been *Asiam proconsulari tunc obtinens potestate* is the same man as the historian. If we assume this to be the case, many of our uncertainties are removed. We are then in a position to know that the historian was suspected of treason and acquitted, but held no more offices until the accession of Gratian. He then held the office of *praefectus* of Illyricum[3] in 380 and 381, and that of Eastern consul in 387. In that case, he should also be identified with Eutropius the friend of Symmachus, who was among the most successful imperial servants of his time.

Marcellus Empiricus mentions a Eutropius who is sometimes, though without a shred of evidence, identified with the historian. The reference to this man states that 'aliique nonnulli etiam proximo tempore illustres honoribus viri, cives ac maiores nostri, Siburius Eutropius atque Ausonius' wrote about medical matters; this Eutropius was a *Burdigalensis,* and lived in the middle of the fourth century.[4]

It is amazing how easily modern scholars are tempted to draw far-reaching conclusions from an instance of identical names. One should realize that there is insufficient support in the sources both for Seeck's proposed identification of Eutropius with Symmachus' correspondent,[5] and for that with a nephew and pupil of the rhetor Acacius of Caesarea. Hence the modern scholar who portrays Eutropius as in the following quotation oversteps the limits of what can be justified by reasonable arguments. However, his summary is sufficiently interesting to merit our attention, since it reflects the *communis opinio* of many modern students. 'One of these highly placed contacts was Eutropius, the historian and medical writer of Bordeaux. Earlier he had held the proconsulship of Asia, but he had gone into retirement when he was suspected of involvement in a plot against the Emperor Valens. He then re-emerged under Gratian, to take his place with so many of his Aquitanian countrymen at the Court. At some time in this period, Eutropius met Symmachus at Rome, but soon, after the accession of Theodosius in early 379, he returned to the East with the new Emperor, and became prefect of Illyricum in the crucial years of campaigning 380 and 381.'[6] How fortunate it would be if we could accept this biographical sketch as correct. But it is impossible to be sure. As far as Eutropius is concerned, we still have little other to go by than his work—the few scraps of external information carry very little weight.

Sources

Eutropius' sources involve the same problems as Eutropius the man. Most of the time we simply do not know where he gets his information. The same uncertainty, moreover, arises when Eutropius is discussed as a source for later historians.[8] There are two passages which require particular attention in discussing Ammianus Marcellinus, for instance, and the extent of his borrowings from Eutropius.

(1) Diocletian's *adoratio* is described by both authors in roughly similar detail.[9] Eutropius says: 'Diligentissimus tamen et sollertissimus princeps et qui imperio invexerit adorarique se iusserit, cum ante eum cuncti salutarentur'.

If we compare this passage with Ammianus, we see that the latter places the statement in an entirely different context. He is concerned not so much with court ceremonial, as with the fact that Ursicinus must submit to it when he appears before Constantius; he goes on to relate the origin of this custom, which was probably known to the entire civil service. The possibilities of handing down certain spectacular facts to succeeding generations are often underestimated. Diocletian's *adoratio* was such a spectacular fact. Ammianus has the following to say: 'Diocletianus enim Augustus omnium primus, externo et regio more instituit adorari, cum semper antea ad similitudinem iudicum salutatos principes legerimus'.

(2) Ammianus' account of Diocletian's attitude towards Galerius, after the latter's defeat by the Persians, is likewise sometimes thought to be derived from Eutropius. However, the facts were familiar enough, and are mentioned by Jerome and Festus besides Ammianus and Eutropius.

> Hieron. *Chron.* 227c:
>
> Galerius Maximianus victus a Narseo ante carpentum Diocletiani purpuratus cucurrit

> Eutr. IX 24:
>
> pulsus . . . tanta insolentia a Diocletiano fertur exceptus, ut per aliquot passuum milia purpuratus tradatur ad vehiculum cucurrisse

> Festus 25,1:
>
> pulsus . . . tanta a Diocletiano indignatione susceptus est, ut ante carpentum eius per aliquot milia passuum cucurrerit purpuratus

> Ammianus 14,11,10:
>
> Augusti vehiculum irascentis per spatium mille passuum fere pedes antegressus est Galerius purpuratus

The main point of the description is that Galerius has to submit to this humiliation wearing full ceremonial dress, *purpuratus,* an emphasis that is characteristic of civil servants, who live in a world of insignia. This, in all likelihood, is the source of the four above passages, all of which stress the word *purpuratus*.[10]

At first sight one tends to link Jerome with Festus on account of the words *ante carpentum,* which they have in common. It would be as incorrect, however, to attach too much importance to this as a mark of 'derivation', as it would be to draw a similar conclusion from use of the word *vehiculum,* which occurs in both Eutropius and Ammianus.

It is significant that Helm, according to whom Jerome used Eutropius as a source on many other occasions, dismisses any connection between Jerome and Festus on this. His reasoning, unfortunately, is weak: he maintains that Jerome did use Eutropius, and that no-one could therefore believe that he also consulted Festus as well. To my mind, the other solution, namely, that Jerome's use of the word *carpentum* is fortuitous, is quite possible. Helm's dismissal of this idea, however, obliges him to assume the existence of a 'source' of which, incidentally, nothing is known. I feel that, in this case, the use of a single word should not be considered decisive. All the stories in circulation at the time mentioned a waggon, i.e. *carpentum* or *vehiculum*. The thread tracing both words to a single written source is somewhat tenuous. And if one persists in one's theory of derivation it seems odd that no-one defends the theory that Jerome derived his rendering directly from Festus.[11] Helm is against this, because he does not expect a man working as hurriedly as Jerome to consult the possible sources thoroughly. This realistic attitude is praiseworthy, but should be taken still further. Considering the situation in civil service circles everywhere and in every age, one should assume that there was a lively oral tradition—certainly as regards facts as well-known as Diocletian's *adoratio* and the humiliation of Galerius.

Galerius' victory in the East was equally well known, and could not but affect all those who desired to write edifying histories. Galerius was, of course, extremely suitable as an example of deed humiliation followed by great honours.[12]

> Hieron.:
>
> Galerius Maximianus superato Narseo et uxoribus ac liberis sororibusque captis a Diocletiano ingenti honore suscipitur
>
> Eutr.:
>
> pulso Narseo castra eius diripuit: uxores sorores liberos cepit . . . ad Diocletianum . . . regressus ingenti honore susceptus est
>
> Festus: superato rege Narseo, uxore eius ac filiabus captis . . .

I feel that these passages permit of no definite conclusions as to Jerome's dependence, either on Festus or on Eutropius.

The same futile textual comparison has been applied to the *Epit. de Caes.* One example must suffice,[13] the death of the emperor Julian.

> Hieron.:
>
> Iulianus in Persas profectus. . . . a quodam simulato perfuga ad deserta perductus . . . ab obvio forte hostium equite conto ilia perfossus.
>
> *Epit.:*
>
> in Persas proficiscitur . . . a transfuga quodam in insidias deductus . . . ab uno ex hostibus et quidem fugiente conto percutitur
>
> Festus: . . . ab obvio hostium equite conto per ilia ictus.

We have here a certain degree of 'correspondence' (Helm), which I propose to analyse. The authors of rhetorical school textbooks took great pains to describe the death of Julian in resounding periods. These were learned by heart and often declaimed at school. The correspondence in the above descriptions is paralleled in Continental history textbooks: 'Philippe le Beau took a cool drink and died.' The only connection this has with the use of any particular source is that at some point a school master expressed the facts in terms that subsequently became popular. The terms presumably used at court and in religious circles to describe the death of Julian were taken over by the Establishment a generation later.

It is so easy to be misled by similarities of expression, even when they correspond word for word. In the following instance the phrasing is identical and the facts are mentioned in the same order, but, even so, there is no reason whatsoever to consider direct derivation. This is the description of the death of Caesar Gallus and the insurrection of Silvanus.[14]

> Hieron.:
>
> Gallus Caesar sollicitatus a Constantio patrueli, cui in suspicionem ob egregiam indolem venerat Histriae occiditur.
>
> Silvanus in Gallia res novas molitus XXVIII die occisus est.
>
> Eutr.:
>
> Gallus Caesar occisus est, vir natura ferus et ad tyrannidem pronior, si suo iure imperare licuisset.
>
> Silvanus quoque in Gallia res novas molitus ante diem tricesimum extinctus est.

Even a casual glance at the above shows a number of differences. In the first place, Eutropius does not tell us where Gallus died; secondly, he does not give the exact number of days of Silvanus' reign; and thirdly and, in my opinion, most important, Jerome's opinion of Gallus is decidedly favourable, as opposed to that of Eutropius. Here we have a good example to show how little word-for-word correspondence or the same order of presentation of the facts sometimes helps to establish interdependence. The twenty-eight days are also given by Aurelius Victor (42,16) and the *Epit.* (42,10). There is as little reason to consider derivation here as in the case of Napoleon's hundred days, which no school textbook fails to mention.

Ab uno disce omnes: the many studies of Eutropius' sources are listed by Schanz, among others. They are seldom relevant to an understanding of the author as an individual.[15]

Topography

Eutropius provides at least one complex of data not found in any other summary of Roman history. He repeatedly mentions the number of milestones *(miliaria)* that indicate the distance to Rome.

Very frequently these details are regarded as derivations from some handbook, which assumption is then used to explain away the phenomenon.[16] Now we know absolutely nothing of the existence of such a handbook, but this, of course, does not necessarily mean that there never was one. However, even if it were true that Eutropius used conveniences of this kind, the question remains why he is the only one to supply these details. The answer is most probably that since at this time the barbarian threat to the peace and security of Rome was increasing, a lively interest developed in other situations and periods in which Rome was threatened, and by enemies much nearer to the City. Eutropius catered to this interest. The following nine passages, all of which are concerned with the history of Rome prior to Hannibal,[17] will illustrate this.

I 8,3 Ita Romae regnatum est per septem reges annis ducentis quadraginta tribus, cum adhuc Roma, ubi plurimum, vix usque ad quintum decimum miliarium possideret.

I 15,2 (Coriolanus) Romanos saepe vicit, usque ad quintum miliarium urbis accessit, oppugnaturus etiam patriam suam.

I 17 Sequenti tamen anno cum in Algido monte ab urbe duodecimo ferme miliario Romanus obsideretur exercitus, L. Quintius Cincinnatus dictator est factus.

I 19 Fidenae sexto, Vei octavo decimo miliario (absunt).

I 20 Statim Galli Senones ad urbem venerunt et victos Romanos undecimo miliario a Roma apud flumen Alliam secuti etiam urbem occupaverunt.

II 5 T. Quintius dictator adversus Gallos, qui ad Italiam venerant, missus est. Hi ab urbe quarto miliario trans Anienem fluvium consederant.

II 8 Iam Romani potentes esse coeperunt. Bellum enim in centesimo et tricesimo fere miliario ab urbe apud Samnitas gerebatur, qui medii sunt inter Picenum, Campaniam et Apuliam.

II 12,1 Postea Pyrrus coniunctis sibi Samnitibus, Lucanis, Brittiis Roman perrexit, omnia ferro ignique vastavit, Campaniam populatus est atque ad Praeneste venit, miliario ab urbe octavo decimo.

III 14,1 Decimo anno postquam Hannibal in Italiam venerat, P. Sulpicio Cn. Fulvio consulibus Hannibal usque ad quartum miliarium urbis accessit, equites eius usque ad portam.

As we know, under the kings, Roman territory extended up to the fifteenth milestone. If we bear this in mind, the importance of Coriolanus' treachery becomes quite clear: he came up to the fifth milestone, and was therefore almost as dangerous as the Gauls and Hannibal, who later pushed as far as the fourth milestone. When the Cincinnati defended Rome, the enemies first came as far as the twelfth (the Aequi) and later to the fourth milestone (the Gauls). Similarly, readers are reminded that Rome was saved on various occasions by members of one and the same family. The Quintii set an example for the emperors of the author's own time. The threats presented by Fidenae and Veii were serious, as their geographical nearness will confirm. When Rome first became mistress of Italy, one severe military threat remained within the peninsula itself: the Samnites.[18] After the Samnite Wars, the power of Rome extended up to the hundred-and-thirtieth milestone. Even temporary disasters such as the wars against Pyrrhus could not overthrow her, even though the king advanced up to the eighteenth milestone; immediately afterwards, 'terrore exercitus qui eum cum consule sequebatur, in Campaniam se recepit'.[19] The war against Hannibal ended almost as well. After Cannae, no distance from Rome is mentioned until eight years later, ten years after the beginning of the war.[20] By that time the danger had waned somewhat, as the following sentence shows: 'mox consulum cum exercitu venientium metu Hannibal ad Campaniam se recepit'.[21]

References to the *miliaria* are a striking characteristic of Eutropius' **Breviarium** and not of others, such as that of Festus. There are a number of reasons for this, for instance, the fact that Festus had a more restricted task.[22] There is more to it than this, though. Eutropius first mentions the *miliaria* when he wishes to indicate the modest extent of Roman territory under the kings.[23]

Here speaks the proud Roman, who knows how powerful Rome eventually became. Herein, too, lies the point of departure for the discussion of those periods in which the existence of Rome was threatened. A description of such dangerous times might arouse a sense of danger in the mind of both writer and reader of the **Breviarium.** Eutropius projects the tensions of his own time onto the earlier history of Rome, and even onto the time of the kings. Topographical indications by means of *miliaria* in historiography can not, of course, have antedated the use of these stones in road construction. The oldest surviving milestone dates from the first Punic War,[24] while the first reference to such stones in historical literature is to be found in Polybius (III, 39,8) in his account of the construction of the via domitia by Cn. Domitius Ahenobarbus in 118 B.C.[25] Nevertheless, this does not mean that Eutropius introduces an anachronism in order to give an historially ignorant public a certain impression of the past. After all, this, the presentation of a certain point of view, became the objective of historians such as Livy, and of Florus with Justin in his wake.[26] Increased activity in the field of road construction probably stimulated their use, as did the erection of the *miliarium aureum*[27] by Augustus in 29 B.C. From Augustus onwards the use of *miliaria* became widespread, distances were usually indicated in 'miles', notably for the main roads running through the Empire. The custom thus developed of reckoning distances almost exclusively according to the number of milestones: *ad lapidem primum, secundum,* etc.[28]

This clear and useful retrospective method of indicating distances did not always have the same connotations. When Livy mentions distances from Rome, he usually has a straightforward piece of information to impart which very rarely directly concerns Rome herself. He merely wishes to give a relative indication of the distance between places A and B, which are so many *miliaria* apart. Eutropius, however, in discussing barbarians or rebellious citizens[29] threatening the city, almost always mentions their distance from Rome. Florus before him also did so with some emotion: 'Quid ergo miramur moventi castra a tertio lapide Hannibali iterum ipsos deos—deos inquam, nec fateri pudebit—restitisse?' Although this emotion also occurs in Livy, it is exceptional.[30]

We did Eutropius no injustice when we said that he projects the tensions of his own time (in 369 Valens defeated the Goths) onto an earlier period in the history of Rome, in this case the time of the kings. His contemporary, Aurelius Victor, is not free from such fears either. Their study of the history of the past century had taught these officials to recognize the dangers constantly threatening the Danubian and far Eastern borders of the Empire. Victor refers to a *commune Romani malum orbis,* a wide-spread evil, threatening

the Roman world.[31] Their own career must also have awakened these two civil servants to the fear that a catastrophe might take place. Indeed, they did not have to wait for the battle at Adrianople, where Valens fell, for the temporary nature of apparently permanent political and military institutions such as the Roman Empire to be brought home to them.

In discussing this matter I should like to present the question of *Quellenforschung* in an entirely new light. It must have been evident to writers in the third century, whose writings have not survived, that the very existence of Rome was, to say the least, assailable. Indeed, this must have become clear to many when Valerian was taken prisoner by the Persians. Now if writers like Eutropius were familiar with these older writings, as we may assume with some confidence, it is to be expected that something of the third-century mentality, of its insecurity, doubts and disquiet, coloured their own work. It is curious, to say the least, that for more than a century scholars have been diligent in attempting to trace verbal derivation from writings that are no longer extant, whereas derivation of moods, which is plausible enough where the events in question are sensational, is ignored. Then as now, man had the ingrained habit of comparing the present to the past. This common human tendency alone is enough to lead us to expect derivation of moods. In the second century A.D., Florus' history quotes distances that come very close to Eutropius' alarming reports.[32] This work, written two centuries earlier, had become a standard textbook in the course of time, which suggests yet another possible influence: the rhetorical stories taught at school. These had perhaps as important an effect as the authors' personal experiences in the imperial service, or comparisons with whatever dreadful events had taken place a century earlier. Reading, personal experience, and the desire to find a reflection of the past in the present are three of the factors that influenced Eutropius in writing as he did.[33]

Chronology

The chronology in Eutropius' **Breviarum** is not entirely consistent, but it is practical. It is also entirely conventional.

To start with I shall give a list of the various dating methods used. (A): Triple datings, dates calculated from or for the time of the kings; (B): Double datings based on the consular years and a.u.c.; (C): A.u.c. datings (the relatively large number of datings based exclusively on the years of consuls are not included); (E): Three passages in (C), indicated by an asterisk, which will be discussed separately; (D): Datings according to the month calendar, and one synchronism (with Alexander the Great); these will also be discussed separately.

A.

I 1,2 Is (Romulus) cum inter pastores latrocinaretur, decem et octo annos natus urbem exiguam in Palatino monte constituit, XI Kal. Maias, Olympiadis sextae anno tertio, post Troiae excidium, ut qui plurimum minimumque tradunt, anno trecentesimo nonagesimo quarto.

IV 10,1 Tertium deinde bellum contra Carthaginem suscipitur, sexcentesimo et altero ab urbe condita anno, L. Manlio Censorino et M. Manilio consulibus, anno quinquagesimo primo postquam secundum Punicum transactum erat.

I 11,1 Secundo quoque anno iterum Tarquinius ut recipereretur in regnum bellum Romanis intulit, auxilium ei ferente Porsenna, Tusciae rege, et Romam paene cepit. Verum tum quoque victus est.

I 11,2 Tertio anno post reges exactos Tarquinius cum suscipi non posset in regnum neque ei Porsenna, qui pacem cum Romanis fecerat, praestaret auxilium, Tusculum se contulit, quae civitas non longe ab urbe est, atque ibi per quattuordecim annos privatus cum uxore consenuit.

I 15,1 Octavo decimo anno postquam reges eiecti erant expulsus ex urbe Q. Marcius, dux Romanus, qui Coriolos ceperat, Volscorum civitatem, ad ipsos Volscos contendit iratus et auxilia contra Romanos accepit.

B.

II 15 C. Fabio Licino C. Claudio Canina consulibus anno urbis conditae quadringentesimo sexagesimo primo legati Alexandrini a Ptolomaeo missi Romam venere et a Romanis amicitiam, quam petierant, obtinuerunt.

X 18,3 Is status erat Romanae rei Ioviano eodem et Varroniano consulibus anno urbis conditae millesimo centesimo et octavo decimo.

IV 22,1 Anno sexcentesimo vicesimo septimo ab urbe condita C. Cassius Longinus et Sex. Domitius Calvinus consules Gallis transalpinis bellum intulerunt.

IV 23,1 M. Porcio Catone et Q. Marcio Rege consulibus sexcentesimo tricesimo et tertio anno ab urbe condita Narbone in Gallia colonia deducta est.

VI 6,1 Anno urbis conditae sexcentesimo septuagesimo sexto L. Licinio Lucullo et M. Aurelio Cotta consulibus mortuus est Nicomedes, rex Bithyniae, et per testamentum populum Romanum fecit heredem. Mithridates pace rupta Bithyniam et

Asiam rursus voluit invadere.

VI 8,1 Sexcentesimo octogesimo primo anno urbis conditae, P. Cornelio Lentulo et Cn. Aufidio Oreste consulibus duo tantum gravia bella in imperio Romano erant, Mithridaticum et Macedonicum.

VI 15 M. Tullio Cicerone oratore et C. Antonio consulibus, anno ab urbe condita sexcentesimo octogesimo nono, L. Sergius Catilina, nobilissimi generis vir, sed ingenii pravissimi, ad delendam patriam coniuravit cum quibusdam claris quidem, sed audacibus viris.

VI 16 Sexcentesimo nonagesimo anno urbis conditae D. Iunio Silano et L. Murena consulibus Metellus de Creta triumphavit, Pompeius de bello piratico et Mithridatico. Nulla umquam pompa triumphi similis fuit. Ducti sunt ante eius currum filii Mithridatis, filius Tigranis et Aristobulus, rex Iudaeorum; praelata est ingens pecunia et auri atque argenti infinitum. Hoc tempore nullum per orbem terrarum grave bellum erat.

VIII 1,1 Anno octingentesimo et quinquagesimo ab urbe condita, Vetere et Valente consulibus res publica ad prosperrimum statum rediit bonis principibus ingenti felicitate commissa. Domitiano enim, exitiabili tyranno, Nerva successit.

C.

X 17,2 Annis mille centum et duobus de viginti fere, ex quo Romanum imperium conditum erat.

* V 4 Anno urbis conditae sexcentesimo sexagesimo secundo primum Romae bellum civile commotum est, eodem anno etiam Mithridaticum.

* II 18,1 Anno quadringentesimo septuagesimo septimo, cum iam clarum urbis Romae nomen esset, arma tamen extra Italiam mota non fuerant . . . census est habitus.

III 10,1 Quingentesimo et quadragesimo anno a condita urbe L. Aemilius Paulus P. Terentius Varro contra Hannibalem mittuntur.

* VI 7,1-2 Anno urbis Romae sexcentesimo septuagesimo octavo Macedoniam provinciam Marcus Licinius Lucullus accepit . . . Et in Italia novum bellum subito commotum est. Septuaginta enim quattuor gladiatores ducibus Spartaco Crixo et Oenomao effracto Capuae ludo fugerunt, et per Italiam vagantes paene non levius in ea quam Hannibal moverat paraverunt.

* VI 17,1 Anno urbis conditae sexcentesimo nonagesimo tertio Gaius Iulius Caesar qui postea

imperavit cum Lucio Bibulo consul est factus.

VI 18,1 Anno urbis conditae sexcentesimo nonagesimo septimo M. Licinius Crassus . . . contra Parthos missus est.

VII 1 Anno urbis septingentesimo fere ac nono interfecto Caesare civilia bella reparata sunt.

D.

II 27,1-2 Numquam in mari tantis copiis pugnatum est . . . Contra Lilybaeum civitatem Siciliae pugnatum est ingenti virtute Romanorum . . . Pugnatum est VI Idus Martias.

X 16,2 (Iulianus) hostili manu interfectus est VI. Kal. imperii anno septimo, aetatis altero et tricesimo.

X 18,2 (Iovianus) decessit imperii mense septimo, tertio decimo Kal. Mart., aetatis, ut qui plurimum vel minimum tradunt, tertio et tricesimo anno.

II 7,3 (Latini . . . superati sunt; ac de his perdomitis triumphatum est) Statuae consulibus ob meritum victoriae in Rostris positae sunt. Eo anno etiam Alexandria ab Alexandro Macedone condita est.

A

Very important dates are given in three forms (cf. Thucydides, whose system of dating is to give the year of office of the Athenian archons, Spartan ephors and of Hera's priestess in Argos).

The date of the foundation of Rome (I 1,2) is given as follows:

a. XI Kal. Maias. According to the monthly calendar, in keeping with tradition (21 April);

b. the third year of the sixth Olympiad, i.e. 753 B.C.;

c. 394 years after the fall of Troy (1148 B.C.), i.e. 754 B.C.

The point is that Varro's reckoning of 753 is retained here. Eutropius or his source was aware that there were various systems of time-reckoning in use *(ut qui plurimum minimumque tradunt),*[34] and that these yielded different dates. Those best known for the fall of Troy are 1184/83 or 1148/47. The latter is that used by Eutropius. If we count from the fall of Troy up to (and excluding) the foundation of Rome, then we arrive at the date 754. It was the vivid Greek imagination, shared by historians, that insisted on bridging the gap of four centuries between Aeneas (whose dates are known from the date of the conquest of Troy) and the year of the foundation of the city. However, if we base our calcu-

lations on the history of Alba Longa with its thirteen kings, at a rate of three kings per century (Herodotus similarly counted in generations) we arrive at a total of 430 years, which means that Troy fell in 1184 and not in 1148.

For the Third Punic War (IV 10,1) he also gives three dates, but these are not established in the same way as the dates for the foundation of Rome:

a. ab urbe condita;

b. consular year;

c. number of years between the Second and Third Punic Wars.

He has learned from experience. Method c. is most suitable for a *breviarium,* and, indeed, a quite obvious one to use. His relative dating from the Second War, is emotive in effect: 'Thus long did our forefathers tolerate Carthage!' In terms of formal calendars, however, one might say that only two systems, that of the *fasti consulares* and that which reckoned a.u.c., were employed.

Up to I 15 he follows a different, equally practical, system: the dates traditionally assigned to the kings. He continues to use this method for the eight years following their expulsion. From I 16 onwards, he uses the consular years. Throughout the history of the republic, this method of dating was, of course, generally followed, but it was still used in imperial times. In adhering to it, Eutropius follows the example of such illustrious predecessors as Tacitus.

B

We often find the use of consular years and dates a.u.c. combined. The beginnings of overseas relations: the first embassy to Rome from Ptolemy II, and the request for a treaty. Rome, represented as the mightier power, complies (II 15) (273 B.C.).

The end of the **Breviarium** is also marked by a double dating (X 18,3) and these two examples would seem to indicate that other double datings may have a particular significance.

The beginning of the conquest of Gallia Transalpina (IV 22,1) and the foundation there of Narbo as a colony six years later (IV 23,1). In the first case he gives, though not as part of his dating method (perhaps an irrelevant distinction) the names of the consuls in office (124 and 118 B.C.). This civilian colony is mentioned with remarkable emphasis.[35] Eutropius might have spoken in the words of Cicero, 'specula populi Romani ac propugnaculum istis ipsis nationibus oppositum et obiectum'[36] and he must have remembered Postumus' Gallic Empire and others who had saved the Imperium Romanum (in spite of their rebellion).[37]

Another year of sufficient importance to merit double dating is that marking expansion in the East: the year 74 B.C., when Bithynia fell to Rome (after the death of the Bithynian king) and the last Mithridatic War began (VI 6,1); this was to last much longer owing to the events that took place three years later (VI, 8,1).[38] The degree of interest aroused by Mithridates is shown a third time in VI 16, which in a way rounds off the account of Roman overseas expansion: 'Hoc tempore (62 B.C.) nullum per orbem terrarum grave bellum erat'.

Events within the country had meanwhile taken a less favourable turn. To Eutropius, the conspiracy of Catilina was of sufficient significance to merit double dating (VI 15). One should not, however, infer that the single dating method is reserved for minor events. Rather, the writer applies more than one method of dating when he introduces a break in the composition of the narrative or for particular emphasis.[39]

C

It is apparent from those places where the author uses only dates a.u.c. that events which are given no more than a single date can be of historical importance, even though they receive no particular emphasis within the framework of the **Breviarum:**

> X 17: It was necessary, though humiliating, for Jovian to abandon his plans for further expansion. The year of this decision deserved to be remembered as a warning, and is here expressed, most fittingly, a.u.c.: 'pacem cum Sapore, necessariam quidem, sed ignobilem, fecit multatus finibus ac nonnulla imperii Romani parte tradita. Quod ante eum annis mille centum et duobus de viginti fere, ex quo Romanum imperium conditum erat, numquam accidit';

> V 4 the civil war between Marius and Sulla;[40]

> VI 7 the war against Spartacus, a *novum bellum;*

> VI 17 Caesar's consulship;[41]

> VI 18 Second consulship of Crassus and Pompey (55 B.C.).

The inclusion of the latter two circumstances is important, for, after mentioning Carrhae, Eutropius says, 'Hinc iam bellum civile successit exsecrandum et lacrimabile, quo praeter calamitates, quae in proeliis acciderunt, etiam populi Romani fortuna mutata est' (VI 19). This ominous date is in perfect accord with the civil war that broke out after the death of Caesar, counting from the foundation of the city; but how long would she continue to exist? The date of the civil war is indicated a.u.c., as was the year of disasters, 216 B.C. (III 10,1). In one other instance does an a.u.c. dating mark the conclusion of a period of war within Italy (dated fairly arbitrarily as 477 a.u.c.): this was the first war outside Italy (II 18).[42]

It is a notorious fact that not all historians have given the date of the foundation of Rome the same place in their chronological systems. We find, for instance, 751/0 (Cato-Polybius), 753 (Varro), 752 *(Fasti Capitolini).*[43] Judging by the frequency of correspondence, we may assume that Eutropius' source, or sources, follows the *Fasti.*

D

Now and then he dates an event according to the month calendar, but these instances are largely, to my mind, a matter of chance. For instance, the battle of Lilybaeum, VI Idus Martias (II 27,1-2), and the death of Julian and Jovian which were, perhaps, still fresh in people's memories (X 16,2 and 18,2). Furthermore, the latter date marks the conclusion of the **Breviarum,** as XI Kal. Maias, the foundation of Rome, marked its beginning (I 1,2).

There are seventeen dates for which Eutropius used the fasti consulares, naturally for the history of the Republic. In doing so he followed the example set by the old histories, and presumably also oral tradition.[44] He proves himself a worthy heir of a tradition of writing senators, in that he does not refer to the regnal years of the emperors[45] except in connection with their death, and not even always then. He never indicates an event as having taken place during a particular regnal year. It is typical of him that when he does wish to date an event occurring during the reign of Augustus, he does so with reference to his consulship (VII, 8,1: 'duodecimo anno quam consul fuerat').

Synchronisms, i.e. dating by events occurring other than in Rome, play a very minor part. Eutropius gives only one (II, 7,3): the Latins were defeated in the same year as that in which Alexander the Great founded Egyptian Alexandria. For the sake of completeness, it should be observed that, in recounting a series of events, he sometimes dates subsequent occurrences from the beginning of Hannibal's invasion (III 14,1; 23).

The following conclusion may be drawn from the chronological data. The practice of double dating, of dating according to the persons in consular office, and the use of dates a.u.c., point to a system (introduced either by Eutropius himself or by his source) which he followed quite deliberately. This method is conventional in its adherence to the Fasti Capitolini and is not influenced by the custom of placing events according to regnal years. Eutropius was a conventional historian, but he was, first and foremost, a senator. As regards the accuracy of his dates, considering that this concise **Breviarium** covered more than 1000 years of Roman history, one can only agree with what has been said of a historian much greater than he: 'Exact chronology was often impracticable—and often superfluous.'[46] The division into periods is comparatively easy to follow. Only one point marking such a period remains ambiguous (II 18,1), unless one assumes that the words *arma . . . extra Italiam mota non fuerant* contain an allusion to a fact considered of such importance as to be regarded as a turning point in the history of Rome.

E

There are a number of dates that are difficult to place within the chronological framework. For instance, the year 477 a.u.c. (II 18,1), in which a census was held. The only explanation that will fit the latter piece of information is that Eutropius held the date of the foundation of Rome to be 752 B.C.; we then arrive at 275 B.C., a census year.[47] Subsequently, in 18,3, he mentions the opening of hostilities against the Carthaginians: *Ap. Claudio Q.* (this should be *M.*) *Fulvio consulibus.* Again, if the year 752 is taken to mark the beginning of the Roman era, then the census presents no problems, but we do find ourselves in difficulties as regards the end of the wars that were previously restricted to Italy. Now Eutropius does not in so many words connect these two facts, but the words *arma . . . extra Italiam mota non fuerunt* suggest that the Romans were soon after waging war outside Italy. The passage continues, *et contra Afros bellum susceptum est* (§ 3), which could point to activities outside Italy before 264 B.C.[48] Hence the idea that the census in question is that of 265/4 B.C. It must be admitted that this year would be satisfactory for two reasons. Firstly, because it would meet the requirement that, as Eutropius' text implies, this census took place just before the beginning of the First Punic War, and secondly because in this year C. Marcius Rutilus enjoyed the unique honour of a second term of office as censor. Nevertheless, this unprecedented honour is not mentioned in the *breviaria,* and if it had been a reason for mentioning this census, then surely Eutropius would at least have hinted at it.[49]

The census of 275 B.C., however, would seem the most likely in the light of other events given special attention in the *breviaria.* If in the entire book only one census is mentioned at all, there must be a special reason why it was remembered. For the year 275 B.C. such a reason is not hard to find. It was noted for the actions of the plebeian censor C. Fabricius Luscinus. He it was who had proved incorruptible in the struggle against Pyrrhus; consul in 282, wounded at the battle of Asculum, consul again in 278, twice *triumphator,* he was eminently suitable for the office of censor. He it was who expelled the patrician P. Cornelius Rufinus

from the senate—although opinions differ as to his motives. In any case he was considered the censor *par excellence.*[50] As early as the second century A.D. he was being mentioned in the *breviaria.*[51]

V 4: the year 662 a.u.c. was remarkable for a number of events:

a. the outbreak of the first Civil War;

b. the outbreak of the Mithridatic Wars;

c. Marius' sixth consulship.

If we take the foundation of Rome to have occurred in 752 B.C., which dating is given in Eutropius' chronology somewhat more frequently than any other, 662 years a.u.c. would correspond to the year 90 B.C. Yet this date cannot be regarded as the year of outbreak of the Civil War, or of the Mithridatic Wars, or indeed of Marius' sixth consulship, which we know him to have held in 100 B.C. Nor would it help to consider the years 663 or 664 a.u.c. If we are to make any sense of the information given (though it should always be borne in mind that the minor historian did not necessarily select his material with due care, so that any attempt at coordination is to overrate him) then we should read, 'Anno urbis conditae sexcentesimo sexagesimo *sexto*', instead of *secundo* and ' . . . C. Marius *septiens*', instead of *sexiens.* For 666 years a.u.c. is in our terms 86 B.C., the year of Marius' seventh consulship, and a year to which both the *bellum civile* and the *bellum Mithridaticum* may plausibly be dated.[52] The events in question are already sufficiently involved, and, to add to the confusion, the readings are inconclusive, to say the least, the word *sexagesimo* being lacking in FGLO, only occurring in PD. Presumably his failure to find this word prompted Paianios to conduct his own research. Unfortunately, his conclusion was incorrect. His calculations resulted in a dating of 672 a.u.c., i.e. 80 B.C., which is impossible.

VI 7 taken together with VI 8 and 10 contains information about M. Licinius Lucullus, known after his adoption as M. Terentius Varro Lucullus. He was the younger brother of L. Licinius Lucullus, who is here erroneously referred to as his *consobrinus.* M. Lucullus was consul in 73 and proconsul of Macedonia in 72 and 71. In 71 he was ordered to help Crassus in the war against Spartacus.

VI 7 gives 678 a.u.c. as the date of the beginning of his proconsulship. This would place it in the year 74, which is two years too early, unless we accept a chronolgy starting from 750 B.C.—which is unlikely in view of VI 8.

VI 8 gives 681 a.u.c. which, if we take 752 as the year of foundation, tallies with 71 B.C. and the consuls mentioned, P. Cornelius Lentulus and Cn. Aufidius Orestes.

The most likely explanation of the discrepancies in these chapters is that Eutropius' account of the Luculli as military commanders places their generalship between the years 74 and 70 B.C., and that no further chronological specification within that period was considered necessary.

Ut qui plurimum minimumque tradunt

The expression 'ut qui plurimum minimumque tradunt' occurs twice, in I 1,2 and X 18,1. We can find the former, but not the latter, in Paianios' Greek translation . . . . This rendering, 'as those historians (say, who) recount the longest and shortest time', needs an explanation. Is it the author's intention to indicate a mean? Or should the sentence be understood as follows: *ut (eos praeteream) qui . . . tradunt?*[53] A third possibility is that Eutropius is saying that both parties, those who assign the earliest and those who assign the latest possible date to the fall of Troy, agree that a period of 394 years elapsed between the fall of Troy and the foundation of Rome. If the latter interpretation, which comes closest to the text, is correct, then Eutropius was guilty of a very serious blunder, for in that case there must have been a tradition stating that Rome was founded in 790 (1184 – 394 = 790). In fact, he probably subscribed to the view that Troy fell in 1148 and Rome was founded (394 years later) in 754. The third interpretation could then be paraphrased as follows: 'as regards the time from the destruction of Troy to the foundation of Rome, I am inclined to compromise, and to find a position between the two extremes'. But this still does not help us to find the correct translation of the above phrase.

One could try to find a parallel for the words *plurimum minimumque* in Greek usage, though this is not a very profitable line of approach, either. . . . This must be a case of two groups of people holding different opinions: one considers the Araxes to be larger, the other thinks it is smaller than the Istros. The explanation given by Ed. Meyer, that this indicates a 'median', is unsatisfactory.[54]

. . . If we follow the text as it has survived rather than Wil.'s reconstruction, 'both less and more' means 'able to cope with'. According to Meyer this is 'eine durchaus unanstössige, dem fünften Jahrhundert geläufige Redensart'. This is undoubtedly putting it too strongly, for he cannot name a single parallel.

However interesting such speculations may be, common Greek usage of the fifth century B.C. still proves nothing for common Latin usage of the fourth century A.D. I could not find a single Greek parallel for Eutropius' words. Comparing them with the expression *uno mense aut altero,* 'hardly (or 'at most') two months' in A.V. *de Caes.* 37,10, merely confuses the issue. Perhaps, however, A.V. *de Caes.* 41,22 can be of use: *Statimque triennium post minimum fatali bello Constantinus cadit.* This can only mean '*about* three years later'.

X 18,2 concerns the age at which Jovian died. Eutropius says that he was 33 years of age, but we know that there was at least one other account according to which he died at the age of 40: *annos gerens proxime quadraginta* (*Epit.* 44,4). It does not seem likely that Eutropius went to such lengths to establish a median from among varying accounts of Jovian's age at his death to arrive at the age of 33, even in speaking of contemporary history.[55] It is much more probable that he wrote down his own estimate of the emperor's age. Six or seven years' difference between the emperor's actual age (if the Epitomist is right) and Eutropius' estimate of his age is still, after all, a possible margin of error. Thirty-three as a median age means that some people thought that he died at 26 years of age, and others at 40. A difference of as much as fourteen years, if the emperor was never considered to have lived past forty, is a very curious margin even for a fragmentary traditional history to leave.

It would therefore seem most likely that the words *ut qui plurimum minimumque tradunt* in both cases indicate no calculated median but an estimate.

NOTE

On p. 131, note 42, I noted that Eutropius' a.u.c. dates are not reliable. Apparently he cannot make up his mind when Rome was founded. A list of the dates he uses, converted into dates B.C., follows below.

Year of the foundation of Rome

750 B.C.: VI 6,1.[56]

751 B.C.: IV 22,1; 23,2.

752 B.C.; VI 7; 8,1; 15; 16; 17,1; 18; VII 1. V 4 probably also belongs in this group.[57]

753 B.C.: I 1,2

754 B.C.: X 17,2; 1118 years a.u.c. corressponds to 364 A.D. I.e., the date of the foundation of Rome is here 754 B.C.

756 B.C.: III 10,1.

Personal Experience

References to contemporary events are to be found in various places. The best known is that in which

Eutropius recounts that he took part in Julian's expedition in the East (X 16,1): 'hinc Iulianus rerum potitus est ingentique apparatu Parthis intulit bellum, cui expeditioni ego quoque interfui.' However, he seldom mentions himself even when he refers to his own time. IX 13,2: 'Zenobia autem posteros, qui adhuc manent, Romae reliquit.' The term used has become stereotyped, e.g. for the reconstruction of Carthage: 'quae nunc manet' (IV 21). The general knowledge of his audience was apparently such that they knew Mogontiacum, but had difficulty in distinguishing the various Drusi of the Julio-Claudian dynasty. He therefore mentions that Claudius was the son of Drusus, *qui apud Mogontiacum monumentum habet.* This is no *flosculus* culled from Suetonius, but a helpful reference to a monument that was apparently still extant.[58]

Inevitably he addresses the emperor in the introduction. He addresses him on one other occasion, and it is no coincidence that he does so in comparing emperorship and dictatorship. Moreover, this is the only point (I, 12,2) at which he interrupts his own narrative: 'Neque quicquam similius potest dici quam dictatura antiqua huic imperii potestati, quam nunc tranquillitas vestra habet, maxime cum Augustus quoque Octavianus, de quo postea dicemus, et ante cum C. Caesar sub dictaturae nomine atque honore regnaverint.' It seems a curious way of explaining this republican office. Is this 'aside' evidence of abysmal ignorance or didactic ingenuity? Perhaps both: the ignorance is then mainly the readers' or the listeners', the ingenuity Eutropius'. The divided emperorship was, in his own time and immediately before, a controversial military and political issue, to which he alludes in his discussion of Marcus Aurelius and Lucius Verus. XIII 9,2: 'Tumque primum Romana res publica duobus aequo iure imperium administrantibus paruit, cum usque ad eos singulos semper habuisset Augustos.' One can well imagine that the writer was longing to produce better work, though forced to mention these trivial details. The end of his *Breviarium* may be read as an expression of his desire to write a greater historical work, although perhaps too much importance has been attached to this statement.[59]

On a number of occasions Eutropius makes good use of his knowledge of contemporary military affairs. One of the best examples of this is his treatment of war-elephants, particularly as used by Pyrrhus and Hannibal.

Florus had already paved the way with an obviously rhetorical discursiveness quite different from, for instance, Appian's sober account. Although he knew and used Florus' work, Eutropius imposed certain limitations on his own work, which is perhaps why he does not refer to the greatest battles. In a way, he was fortunate in that his patron, the emperor himself, had no time to read extensive rhetorical accounts *à la* Florus. Eutropius thus avoids falling into the same pitfalls as his predecessor, who knew the elephant only as big

game. In Florus' time the elephant was no longer used in battle; in Eutropius' age the Romans were once again confronted with these awe-inspiring animals in the wars against the Persians, so this subject was sure to be of general interest. Eutropius knew what was expected of him; the elephant had become part of the stock repertoire of history and Eutropius could not therefore leave him out. But his account is sober, as is that of Appian—with whom, incidentally, he has little else in common. The explanation for his matter-of-fact rendering is obvious. He could not afford to speak of a well-known phenomenon with high-flown rhetoric. He is restrained because he and his contemporaries, officers and civil servants alike, know all about battle elephants. Ammianus Marcellinus uses the same technique, and for the same reasons, in his exposé of Julian's expedition against the Persians.[60] On the other hand, if one compares the relevant passages in Florus and Eutropius, the differences are quite unmistakable.

Florus I 13,8-10.

Actum erat, nisi elephanti, converso in spectaculum bello, procucurrissent, quorum cum magnitudine tum deformitate et novo odore simul ac stridore consternati equi, cum incognitas sibi beluas amplius quam erant suspicarentur, fugam stragemque late dederunt. In Apulia deinde apud Asculum melius dimicatum est Curio Fabricioque consulibus. Iam quippe terror beluarum exoleverat, et Gaius Numicius quartae legionis hastatus unius proboscide abscisa mori posse beluas ostenderat. Itaque in ipsas pila congesta sunt, et in turres vibratae faces tota hostium agmina ardentibus ruinis operuerunt.

I 13,12

Nam provectis in primam aciem rursus elephantis, unum ex eis pullum adacti in caput teli gravis ictus avertit; qui cum per stragem suorum recurrens stridore quereretur, mater agnovit et quasi vindicaret exiluit, tum omnia circa quasi hostilia gravi mole permiscuit. Ac sic eaedem ferae, quae primam victoriam abstulerunt, secundam parem fecerunt, tertiam sine controversia tradiderunt.

I 13,28

Sed nihil libentius populus Romanus aspexit quam illas, quas ita timuerat, cum turribus suis beluas, quae non sine sensu captivitatis summissis cervicibus victores equos sequebantur.

Eutr. II 11,3

Commissa mox pugna, cum iam Pyrrus fugeret, elephantorum auxilio vicit, quos incognitos Romani expaverunt. Sed nox proelio finem dedit; Laevinus tamen per noctem fugit, Pyrrus Romanos mille octingentos cepit et eos summo honore tractavit, occisos sepelivit. Quos cum adverso vulnere et truci vultu etiam mortuos iacere vidisset, tulisse ad caelum manus dicitur cum hac voce: se totius orbis dominum esse potuisse, si tales sibi milites contigissent.

II 14,3

Curius in consulatu triumphavit. Primus Romam elephantos quattuor duxit.

II 24

L. Caecilio Metello C. Furio Placido consulibus Metellus in Sicilia Afrorum ducem cum centum triginta elephantis et magnis copiis venientem superavit, viginti milia hostium cecidit, sex et viginti elephantos cepit, reliquos errantes per Numidas, quos in auxilium habebat, collegit et Romam deduxit ingenti pompa, cum (CXXX) elephantorum numerus omnia itinera compleret.

IV 27,3

(Q. Caecilius Metellus) Iugurtham variis proeliis vicit, elephantes eius occidit vel cepit . . .

As we said, Ammianus Marcellinus does not need many words to weave the war-elephants into his story. Nevertheless, there are lingering echoes in his words of the fear this awesome weapon inspired: 'Post hos elephanti gradientium collium specie, motuque immanium corporum, proprinquantibus exitium intentabant, documentis praeteritis formidati' (24,6,8).

Appian's account of the battle at Thapsus is entirely different.[61] Scipio took the field against Caesar with sixty elephants, provided by King Juba. The news of the presence of these animals made a great impression on Caesar's soldiers, even before the battle . . . . When Juba subsequently withdrew, leaving only half his elephants with Scipio, 'Caesar's men plucked up courage to such a degree that the fifth legion begged to be drawn up opposite the elephants, and it overcame them valiantly. From that day to the present this legion has borne the figure of an elephant on its standards'.[62] Is is easy to understand why, after this historic event, elephants held no more terrors for the Roman legions for several centuries.

Rome and the Barbarians[63]

The writers of *breviaria* write about foreign policy under the republic with intense national pride, as when Egypt actually requests an alliance (II 15). Eutropius refuses to be intimidated by the past glory of famous adversaries; the way in which Athens is referred to as a *civitas Achaiae* (V 6) is simply insulting to this glorious city: *ab Aristone Atheniensi Mithridati tradita est.* Jerusalem, though also conquered, fares better: *quae*

fuit urbs nobilissima Palaestinae (VII 19,3). It goes without saying that this official favoured the city of Rome, but it must have made many people bitter (though probably not Eutropius) to think that the eternal city, like other cities, had become dependent on the whims of the emperor: *Alexander Severus Romae quoque favorabilis fuit* (VIII 23). Athens, Jerusalem, even Rome, whatever their past fame, had ceased to present any political or military problems.

The foremost contemporary problem was Rome's relationship to the 'barbarians'. Eutropius, as a typical member of the senatorial class, combines humanity with a profound conviction of the rightness of Roman domination. He was apparently, or preferred to seem, oblivious of the fact that this situation gave rise to tension among the subjected peoples. His manner of taking Rome's power for granted sometimes strikes us as cynical, although it probably springs rather from a naive consciousness of superiority. He is entirely unaffected by the doubts that plagued Tacitus, as the following two passages show.

Samnites (II 9,1-3):

Postea Samnites Romanos T. Veturio et Sp. Postumio consulibus ingenti dedecore vicerunt et sub iugum miserunt. Pax tamen a senatu et populo soluta est, quae cum ipsis propter necessitatem facta fuerat . . . Neque ullus hostis fuit intra Italiam, qui Romanam virtutem magis fatigaverit.

Corinth (IV 14,1):

Corinthiis quoque bellum indictum est, nobilissimae Graeciae civitati, propter iniuriam legatorum Romanorum.[64]

Moreover, criticism of the murder of the enemy commander Viriathus is implied rather than stated: 'Et cum interfectores eius (sc. Viriathi) praemium a Caepione consule[65] peterent, responsum est numquam Romanis placuisse imperatores a suis militibus interfici' (IV 16,3).

The behaviour of Q. Servilius Caepio certainly did not live up to this hypocritical assurance.[66] One can scarcely imagine that Eutropius did not know the true story of how Caepio bribed Viriathus' men to betray him. The writer of *De viris illustribus* certainly did know what happened, which shows that the perfidious part played by the Roman commander must have been familiar to many, indeed that the popular history books had helped to make the facts common knowledge.[67] Livy's *periocha* also exposes the betrayal and its instigator, and devotes some words of praise to the brave opponent, for whom Eutropius feels nothing but contempt ('pastor primo fuit, mox latronum dux').[68] Valerius Maximus termed the deed a *perfidia* on both sides, the Spanish traitors and Caepio.[69] Even Velleius Paterculus could not pass over it in silence, and wrote that Viriathus was killed *fraude magis quam virtute Servili Caepionis*.[70]

It would seem that Eutropius is alone in his opinion. Yet the Christian authors also remain unmoved by the perfidy of the Roman commander. Orosius has only a glancing reference to the murder of Viriathus,[71] and, like Eutropius, creates the impression that the Romans had dissociated themselves from the murder. Nevertheless, it would oversimplify the case to assume that the two versions arise from different sources. Eutropius despises the *latrones*.[72] His attitude can be traced back to that of Florus, which need not necessarily entail direct derivation: 'vir calliditatis acerrimae, qui ex venatore latro, ex latrone subito dux et imperator'.[73] And here lies the reason for the Romans' lack of chivalry and implacable hatred: Viriathus had indeed constituted a serious threat, and might well have become the Romulus of Spain. As always, magnanimity towards the enemy petered out as soon as this enemy became, or seemed to have become, a serious threat to the safety of Rome. Eutropius' humaneness, like Florus', is severely limited.

The author took great pleasue in detailing the numbers of soldiers mobilized and the booty amassed in the wars of conquest. Sometimes, as in the case of the size of the fleet in the First Punic War, such information is fairly reliable; compared to Polybius' numbers, those given by Eutropius are 'slight variants due to careless transmission'.[74] Sometimes, too, the information supplied by Eutropius (and Florus, for that matter) is more or less fictitious.[75] One may well ask to what purpose, then, these figures are included in a *breviarium*. Eutropius tells us, I think, in his introduction. He sees his task as a *per ordinem temporum brevis narratio*. The story is told, recited, in order to please the emperor ('ut . . . possit . . . laetari'). He has no intention of providing the emperor with a piece of scholarship that he would have to read attentively ('cognoscerat lectione').

Every time major decisions are mentioned, numbers serve to illustrate the *narratio*. When Rome goes to Africa during the First Punic War, when she subsequently wages war with Hannibal, when the Empire is torn by the civil war between Caesar and Pompey, the numbers of troops and details of the losses bring home the gravity of the situation.[76]

Plunder is taken completely for granted, as it was at the time the wars of conquest were conducted,[77] but it is only after the Third Macedonian and the Third Punic Wars that booty is mentioned frequently. The emphasis placed on the honesty of the Romans after the latter war is most significant (IV 12,2): 'Spolia ibi inventa, quae variarum civitatum excidiis Carthago collegerat, et ornamenta urbium civitatibus Siciliae, Italiae, Africae reddidit, quae sua recognoscebant.'

The richest booty of all was that gained by Aemilius Paullus after Pydna,[78] but Eutropius shifts the emphasis to accentuate the magnanimity of the conqueror towards King Perseus: 'nam et volentem ad pedes sibi cadere non permisit et iuxta se in sella conlocavit.'[79]

The benevolence of the conqueror had two main aspects. On the one hand he liberates the oppressed (IV 7,3): 'Macedonibus et Illyriis hae leges a Romanis datae: ut liberi essent et dimidium eorum tributorum praestarent, quae regibus praestitissent, ut appareret, populum Romanum pro aequitate magis quam avaritia dimicare.' It is no coincidence that Eutropius adduces this particular task of the Romans whilst placing Macedonia and Illyria, which had gained prominence by his own time, in historical perspective. The *breviarium* thus disseminates propaganda to discourage desertion to the barbarian side, and the imperial conquests in Pannonia were represented as having liberated the inhabitants from slavery.[80]

On the other hand, the Romans acted in a humane manner towards those they had conquered, as the example of Perseus was supposed to prove. Rome's mildness was all the more remarkable seeing that Perseus' activities could be construed as a rebellion.[81] Nor, after the First Punic War, did the Carthaginians have any cause to complain of the harshness of their Roman conquerors (II 27,2): 'Etiam Carthaginienses petiverunt, ut redimi eos captivos liceret, quos ex Afris Romani tenebant. Senatus iussit sine pretio eos dari, qui in publica custodia essent; qui autem a privatis tenerentur, ut pretio dominis reddito Carthaginem redirent atque id pretium ex fisco magis quam a Carthaginiensibus solveretur.'

The Second Punic War is used to illustrate the high standard of Roman military honour and the difference between the morality of the Romans and that of the Carthaginians (III 11,1): 'Hannibal Romanis obtulit, ut captivos redimerent, reponsumque est a senatu eos cives non esse necessarios, qui cum armati essent, capi potuissent.' The difference between the Romans, who refused to recognize their countrymen as citizens once they had been taken prisoner by the enemy, and the Carthaginians, who were glad to take back their men after the first war, is characteristic. The Roman's humaneness is limited, particularly towards his own fellow soldiers; he knows no greater bitterness than when confronted with what he considers cowardice. Yet this attitude is not consistent, as we see when Hannibal takes the proud Romans at their word, and feels at liberty to treat his prisoners accordingly (III, 11,2): 'ille omnes postea variis suppliciis interfecit et tres modios anulorum aureorum Carthaginem misit, quos ex manibus equitum Romanorum, senatorum et militum detraxerat.' This reaction of Hannibal's was always severely condemned by the Romans even though, according to the Roman code of honour, soldiers who surrendered were disgraced. Now, however, the Roman code of honour was conveniently ignored—naturally. The fact that the Romans had certain standards of permissible military behaviour did not mean that they would overlook the offence if another party, and the enemy at that, put the dishonoured soldiers to death.

We shall not discuss the accuracy of Eutropius' account, although it was probably not far from the truth. But if we try to analyse the personality of the historian as revealed in his work, we are struck by the curious combination of the stern morality (which is much praised) of the Roman republican leaders on the one hand, and its Carthaginian repercussions, which can only be seen as wanton cruelty, on the other.[82] Both the story and the dual attitude are characteristic of Eutropius, and perhaps also of his time. The solidarity of imperial subjects had to be perfect, in the fourth century A.D. as in other times; anyone who did not live up to these standards was condemned to be cut off from society. Nevertheless, the enemy who took this to mean that he could with impunity kill those who were no longer welcome in Rome, was the cruel barbarian and always would be, in harsh contrast to Rome's humane attitude in Spain (III 17): 'regem Hispaniarum magno proelio victum in amicitiam accepit et primus omnium a victo obsides non poposcit'.

In III 21-22, Eutropius makes it quite clear what he means by Carthage's *perfidia.* The actual terms of the peace are immaterial here.[83] The estimated cost of a war often increases as protracted negotiations drag on, to the irritation of the victor. In this case, the length of the negotiations is interpreted as a *nova perfidia,* for which the Carthaginians were made to pay.[84] Here again our investigation is not concerned with the accuracy of the account, but with the information considered relevant for his *breviarium* by an official who likes to see quick results. Eutropius must have known what wars cost, but in his time no barbarian nation was as rich in spoil as were the wealthy Carthaginians centuries before. He was well aware of the fact that, in his own time, wars were an expensive business, and he deplores the civil war waged against Magnentius ten years earlier (X 12,1): 'ingentes Romani imperii vires ea dimicatione consumptae sunt, ad quaelibet bella externa idoneae, quae multum triumphorum possent securitatisque conferre.'

Time and again we see that what he admires in the terms for peace set by previous generations of Romans is the self-restraint which governed their treatment of a conquered enemy. He notes this attitude in discussing the conditions of the peace set Antiochus III, *quamquam victo* (IV, 4,3). His accounts of conquests of barbarians are therefore seldom if ever provocative.

The enemies of old, now members of the Imperium Romanum, cannot have taken exception to this textbook, which perhaps partly explains its popularity. Moreover, the retailing of honours accorded generals in the past must have gratified the upper classes. Here again, Eutropius knew what would interest his public: military distinctions, and the triumph as ultimate ideal. Indeed, triumphs are described in disproportionate detail. In the case of the Syrian war, Scipio's triumph *(Scipio Romam rediit, ingenti gloria triumphavit)* had long lost its sting, even for Syrian Roman readers.

As we have seen, there are limits to mildness when the interests of the state are at stake. The historian decides for himself if *clementia,* which he believes should be the rule, is rightly abandoned. It is likewise his personal opinion if he says that the behaviour of individual Roman citizens is not consonant with the interests of the state. Indeed, it is with surprising severity that he condemns the Civil War, thus also censuring C. Julius Caesar[85] (IV 19,1): 'hinc iam bellum civile successit exsecrandum et lacrimabile, quo praeter calamitates, quae in proeliis acciderunt, etiam populi Romani fortuna mutata est.' The tears that Caesar later wept at the news of Pompey's death (V 21,3) do not, however, absolve him from his grave responsibility. Eutropius' attitude towards Caesar is nevertheless ambiguous. He refers to Caesar's return from Gaul, yet without taking sides in the conflict between the general and the senate (VI 19,2): 'Caesar enim rediens ex Gallia victor coepit poscere alterum consulatum atque ita, ut sine dubietate aliqua ei deferretur.' At the same time, the opposition of Marcellus and others is termed *iniuria;* this is in connection with the senate's demand that Caesar disband his troops, which Eutropius, consciously or unconsciously following the lead of his source, apparently considers an 'injustice'. Yet Eutropius makes no attempt to exonerate the man who *adversum patriam cum exercitu venit.* He also criticizes Caesar's last years: 'agere insolentius coepit et contra consuetudinem Romanae libertatis' (VI 35).

Of all kinds of wars, he considers civil war the most reprehensible. Eutropius was the first fourth-century writer to blame Constantius II for causing such a war. Later, Ammianus, Orosius and the Epitomist were to agree with him.[86]

The Romans themselves had realized this early on, and their historians followed a fairly general mode of thought. Therefore, even if a war had started inside the country, it had to look as if it were waged outside. The struggle against Sertorius had to be a foreign war, which it was certainly not. Nevertheless, it would be incorrect to attribute this attitude to the war in Spain to moral disapproval of civil war. It had to be comouflaged as a hostile encounter with Spaniards, no doubt because the Roman conqueror could celebrate a triumph only if he were the victor in a foreign war.[87]

The writings of Florus and Eutropius have one element in common. They have no illusions, either about the republican senators during the civil war, or about the enormous significance of the battle of Actium,[88] though Florus surpasses Eutropius by far in that he sometimes tries to trace the causes of a war, a refinement which one need not expect of Eutropius.[89]

The views of Eutropius and of his contemporaries on the limits of imperial tolerance are perhaps best summed up in the paragraph on the actions of Titus, which he describes with apparent approval. Rebellions by conquered nations are effectively and severely countered, but he turns a blind eye to criticism of the emperor in high places in Rome itself, which was likewise a form of rebellion (VII 21,2): 'in oppugnatione Hierosolymorum sub patre militans duodecim propugnatores duodecim sagittarum confixit ictibus. Romae tantae civilitatis in imperio fuit, ut nullum omnino punierit, convictor adversum se coniurationis dimiserit vel in eadem familiaritate, qua antea, habuerit.'

It was the tolerant emperors, especially Augustus and Trajan, who enjoyed the highest esteem. Their conquests are listed, their failures practically ignored. Augustus' good fortune (VII 9-10) is not so highly praised as Trajan's goodness. This has often been overlooked, because the best-known expression in the *breviarium, felicior Augusto, melior Traiano* (VIII 5,3), has stuck in people's memories and given the impression that the emperors were equally appreciated. This impression, however, is incorrect. Trajan is the favourite. The four chapters in his praise (VII 2-5) are unique in Eutropius' work.

This is what he had in mind when he promised Valens that he would tell his tale plainly and concisely, but 'additis etiam his, quae in principum vita egregia extiterunt'. It has been said,[90] in my opinion erroneously, that he writes in greater detail of these, his two favourite emperors, in order to explain and justify the expression 'more fortunate than Augustus, better than Trajan'—a phrase with which the senate later greeted emperors at their investiture. If such had been his intention, he would not have created so obvious a distinction in his account of their periods of rule. There is no doubt that Eutropius preferred Trajan even to Augustus. Moreover, the policy of conquest adhered to by the former was of greater relevance than ever in the fourth century.

The *breviarium* is a book about people. Names are given, but issues are seldom explained; as he promised the emperor, his inspiration was to be the *inlustrium virorum facta*. He rarely describes battles, except those of the Second Punic War, and even then he omits all reference to Zama, to name but one. Marius and Metellus, and later Sulla *(ingentem virum)* are mentioned in connection with the war against Jugurtha.

The causes of the conflict, or the course of the military undertakings, enter the picture very briefly, if at all. It may well be true that, to us, Roman history is *sine nominibus,* but the fourth-century senator at any rate went to some trouble to avoid this situation. Unfortunately his efforts were not crowned with success. His work was too short—indeed, it had to be, after all, its chief objective was brevity. Meanwhile, the imperial biographies (including, surely, the *Historia Augusta*), which are roughly contemporary with the *breviaria,* were eagerly read. They provided the reading public with material which was not to be found in the *breviaria.*

The biographies were also better qualified than any *breviarium* to satisfy the public demand for exciting anecdotal detail. However, this is not to say that such anecdotes are lacking in Eutropius' work.

For instance:

II 5,1: How L. Manlius acquired the cognomen Torquatus; and

II 6,2-3: How Valerius acquired the cognomen Corvinus. The account of the wars against Pyrrhus is enlivened by much circumstantial detail:

II 11,3: Pyrrhus' well-known comment on the courage of the Romans;

II 12,3 and 14,1: C. Fabricius Luscinus;

II 13,3: Cineas, Pyrrhus' envoy, and his opinion of the Romans;

II 21-25: The customary account of the heroism of M. Atilius Regulus in 256 B.C. brightens the discussion of the First Punic War;[91] and

IV 8,1: Perseus' ship.

It has been wrongly suggested that Eutropius adopted the fashion of including anecdotes in his narrative specifically for his account of imperial times,[92] i.e., in only five instances: VII 18,3: Vitellius' banquet; VII 21: Titus; IX 13,1: Aurelian and Tetricus IX 18,2: the removal of the body of Numerian, a detail that is also to be found elsewhere; X 18,1: particulars about Jovian's death. The above list, however, disproves this suggestion.

Senate and Emperor[93]

Eutropius was a conscientious, restrained writer, who was by no means indifferent to the problems of his time. One burning political issue was that of the influence of the senate, to which he himself belonged. In his preoccupation with this matter, he is at one with

Aurelius Victor. Both quote the year 235 as marking the end of the collaboration between emperor and senate. They describe Maximinus Thrax in almost identical terms:[94] the military proclaim him emperor 'cum nulla senatus intercessisset auctoritas'. Eutropius, a prouder man than Victor, keeps silent on the pusillanimity of the senate; nor does he refer to the humble origins of this emperor, although he often does so in other cases. To my mind, there is no doubt that the extreme brevity with which Eutropius writes of Maximinus is inspired by contempt. His ideal of co-operation between senate and emperor is that achieved by Trajan: 'In my position as emperor, I treat the common citizen as I should wish to be treated by an emperor if I were a common citizen.'[95] What he admired in Trajan was the fact that he respected the prerogatives of the senate, the most important of which was the *consecratio* of the deceased emperor. It is of great interest to note that Eutropius is alone in recording the *consecratio* (or its omission) of nearly all the emperors.

The passages in which he mentions the *consecratio* of deceased emperors may be placed in five categories. The first category (A) contains straightforward statements of the usual course of events. The second is an isolated case; in C, as we shall see, the wording has been varied intentionally. In the fourth group, it was not, if Eutropius' phrase is taken literally, the senate who carried out the consecration. The last group (E) lists the names of emperors who were not thus honoured.

Once again, the accuracy of Eutropius' statement whether an emperor was or was not consecrated is not here at issue.[96] The point is to see what he says about the events in question.

. . . . .

The terminology used in this context is most revealing, and has never, to my knowledge, been studied thoroughly.[97] There is a large group of emperors whom the senate deified as a matter of course. The terms customarily employed by Eutropius are 'Divus apellatus est' or 'inter Divos relatus est'.[98] He goes on to give a meticulous account of deviations from the usual ritual of deification. Trajan, whom he admired so much, was accorded the honour of having his remains buried within the city; Diocletian was consecrated even though, having abdicated, he was no longer emperor at his death; Claudius II was further honoured with the erection of a golden statue and shield.[99] Where Eutropius himself was particularly strongly in favour of the honour conferred, for instance, in the cases of Antoninus Pius and Marcus Aurelius, he says so.[100] He also tells us if there were any difficulties attendant upon the consecration, as in the case of Hadrian, Gordian I and Jovian.[101] The well-known instances in which this honour was with-

held are also mentioned: Tiberius, Caligula, Nero and Domitian;[102] Eutropius further states that Commodus and Geta were not consecrated either. His statement about Commodus is in conflict with Victor, who recounts that this emperor was finally consecrated thanks to the efforts of Septimius Severus, and on account of his father's merits.[103] Here again Eutropius (if, that is, he agreed with Victor) proves rather uncommunicative: he makes no reference to this occasion on which the senate was overruled. Geta never was consecrated; his *damnatio memoriae* was never repealed, despite his brother and murderer Caracalla's witticism, 'sit divus, dum non sit vivus': let them deify him, as long as they do not revive him.[104] Eutropius is equally reticent about the deification of Gallienus. The earliest surviving version of this event, which was most humiliating for the senate, is Victor's: Claudius II compelled the senators to consecrate his predecessor: *subacti a Claudio*.[105] Eutropius suppresses the event altogether; coming from this emperor it was too profound a mortification to be borne. He does, however, mention the fact that Antoninus Pius also demanded his predecessor's *consecratio*.[106] Another notable omission in Eutropius' account is a story of Victor's to the effect that, towards the end of his life, Hadrian had a number of senators imprisoned in order to have them put to death. This rumour was proved false after the emperor's death. And the senators were so happy about their return that they were swayed by the request of the new emperor.[107]

Eutropius is incapable of demeaning himself by providing history with a happy ending.[108] Perhaps the fact that he does not subscribe to Victor's oblique praise of Caesar underlies his bluntness, which sometimes makes him appear implacable. Like the anonymous author of *De viris illustribus*, Victor is filled with admiration for Octavian's 'magnus avunculus'.[109] Eutropius' tone is different—he speaks of Caesar's 'shameless conduct, that contravened the traditional Roman idea of freedom'.[110] Brutus the assassin was in his eyes a hero inspired by his great ancestor, L. Iunius Brutus, who drove out Tarquinius Superbus.[111]

Both Bruti, ancestor and descendant, were laid to rest in a mausoleum of harmless rhetorical verbiage. There was no question of republican, let alone revolutionary, aspirations among officials like Eutropius. He was a loyal servant of his emperor. Yet it is significant that in the decade in which Victor and Eutropius were writing, it was possible for the central figure of the Roman revolution, Gaius Julius Caesar, to inspire two interpretations as different as theirs. A study of the sources that equates these two abbreviators and assumes their dependency on a single source, as is so often done, defeats its own purposes. *Quellenforschung* is useless in this connection, and what is more, it obstructs our view of two personalities—both admittedly 'minor' historians, but nevertheless entirely dissimilar in all other respects. Their personality is revealed, more than anywhere else, in their attitude to Caesar. Caesar's consecration, described in many surviving sources, is omitted by Eutropius. Once again, his silence is significant.

The most interesting cases are those in which Eutropius is in favour of the consecration, but where the ritual of apotheosis could not be observed because, for instance, the body could not be found. This happened in the case of Decius. Aurelian managed to arrange his consecration, but there are indications that his name was often erased from inscriptions. The Christian emperors, such as Constantine the Great and Constantius II, also presented difficulties, in that the pagan rites could not be performed in their entirety. It is quite clear why the *consecratio* of both Constantine and his son were incomplete according to pagan beliefs: the body had not been burned, and the apotheosis was thus not carried out in accordance with the prescribed ritual.[112] It is understandable that a pagan senator, who respected tradition, cannot in such cases say that an emperor *inter Divos relatus est*.

It is thus no coincidence that Eutropius uses a different terminology for each of these four emperors, preferring to say *meruit inter Divos referri*. I am inclined to feel that this is an unusually subtle instance of senatorial theology; *mereo* means to deserve; it also means to be rewarded, to be given a claim to, to be promised.[113] This ambiguous term was most convenient for the senate. I think it probable, although it is not capable of proof, that the terminology is not Eutropius' own, but that it originated in senatorial practice. The subtlety of the phrasing employed in connection with precisely these four emperors, all of whom should have been consecrated, but for some circumstance that made regular deification impossible in each case, can be no accident. Such subtlety of expression occurs nowhere else in Eutropius.

These nuances escaped his Byzantine translators. They cannot be blamed for this, since the *consecratio* was a pre-Byzantine and pre-Christian custom.[114] Eutropius did not restrict the use of the second phrase, 'meruit inter Divos referri', to the Christian emperors, he also uses this expression for Decius and Aurelian. As a rule, he handles the controversy between paganism and Christianity with the utmost restraint. Many scholars have been surprised to note that he does not even mention Constantine's conversion to Christianity. His only reference to Christianity is when he condemns Julian for his persecution of Christians, even though the persecution was bloodless.[115] Generally speaking, this may be a diplomatic silence; on the other hand, his repugnance to bloody persecution bears out the humanity characteristic of Eutropius, though very Roman in type.[116]

Before imperial times, apotheosis was an exceptional distinction. Tradition has it that Romulus was honoured in this manner (I 2,2): 'ad deos transisse creditus est et consecratus'. Camillus, who had saved the city from the Gauls, was regarded as a second Romulus 'quasi et ipse patriae conditor' (I 20,3), and was consequently deemed worthy of the same honour as Romulus (II 4): 'honor ei post Romulum secundus delatus est'. But these were the only two to be consecrated, for such honours accorded ill with the spirit of the Republic. In imperial times, however, *consecratio* was a matter to be handled by the senate, and thus constituted a problem with which Eutropius was also confronted.

The Emperor during his Lifetime

There was a connection between the living, reigning emperor and his successor, which sometimes led the successor to insist on deification against the will of the senate. This is said even of Antoninus Pius (VIII 7,3), and Victor says the same of Claudius II with respect to Gallienus (*De Caes.* 33,27). Although the senators must have resented imperial interference as undermining their own authority, it did not affect the general principle that Victor expressed as follows (33,30): 'adeo principes atque optimi mortalium vitae decore quam quaesitis nominibus atque compositis, quantum coniciatur, caelum adeunt seu fama hominum dei celebrantur modo.'

The policies of the living nearly always affected the honours accorded the dead. This need not surprise us. The form of worship granted after his death was a continuation of the homage the living emperor enjoyed in Eutropius' time; and it is an established fact that the living emperor was worshipped as a god. The historian proclaims this worship, in a sense, in his dedication to Valens: 'tranquillitatis tuae . . . mens divina'. Scipio Africanus was another who was already considered a privileged being who spoke with the gods during his lifetime (III 20,2): 'cui viro divinum quiddam inesse existimabatur, adeo ut putaretur etiam cum numinibus habere sermonem'. Augustus was considered almost divine, even before his death (VII 8,4): 'vir, qui non inmerito ex maxima parte deo similis est putatus'. Trajan, too, was granted near-divine status before he died (VIII 4): 'per orbem terrarum deo proximus . . . et vivus et mortuus'.

The honours showered on the emperor did not, however, mean that the historian did not feel at liberty to pass value judgements on many emperors, based on their deeds. If we compare Eutropius' approach with the usual historical view, determined chiefly by Tacitus, of the Julio-Claudian dynasty, we see that his attitude is only in part conformist. Tiberius (VII 11,1), Caligula (VII 12) and Nero (VII 14 and especially 15) are treated unfavourably. It would seem as if subtlety were out of the question: the 'simple' listener did not want subtlety.

All the more surprising, then, the chapter on Claudius (VII 13). Admittedly, Eutropius does not conceal *quaedam crudeliter et insulse,* but it is abundantly clear that he admired the emperor's moderation as a ruler. The question inevitably arises, where this view originated, for it is completely opposed to the traditional view of the despot dominated by his wives and freedmen. The answer is not hard to find. In spite of Tacitus, there was a flourishing senatorial tradition that remembered past honours bestowed on its class. Eutropius draws on this when he says, 'tam civilis autem circa quosdam amicos extitit, ut etiam Plautium, nobilem virum, qui expeditione Brittanica multa egregie fecerat, triumphantem ipse prosequeretur et conscendenti Capitolium laevus incederet' (§ 4). The importance Eutropius attached to this imperial honour emerges from the fact that he had just (§ 2) called Cn. Sentius and A. Plautius (*illustres ac nobiles viros.* The two references to Plautius as a *vir nobilis* (repetition is unusual in a *breviarium*) underline both his importance and that of Claudius' gesture. It is the senator who speaks here.

The same senatorial sense of honour determines the historian's valuation of many emperors in yet another way. Finance and territorial expansion are tasks of the greatest importance in which Vespasian excelled and for these he is highly praised; but he is also praised for his restraint—which should always be interpreted to mean being on good terms with the senate (cf. VII 19,12).

Those who transgress the code of values set forth by Eutropius come to a bad end. This happened to Domitian, who committed the major sins of *libido, iracundia, crudelitas, avaritia* and *superbia,* besides the murder of senators, arrogation of divine honours, financial excesses (a golden statue), and almost consistently unsuccessful attempts at territorial expansion. No other fate was possible for an emperor who thus became the exact opposite of his father and brother than to be murdered by his own servants and be buried like a dead cur or beggar. He has gone down in history as a prime example of the *exitiabilis tyrannus* (VII 23; VIII 1).[117] Conversely, the example of liberality is Titus whose life, described in two chapters (VII 21-22), is in sharp contrast with that of his younger brother. The words used to characterize his rule are *familiaritas, facilitas* and *liberalitas*—terms that reflect the emperor's relationships with highly-placed men in his direct surroundings. Eutropius probably stresses this particular case quite deliberately, having learned, during his term of office, how important was a satisfactory relationship between the emperor and his government officials. The very fact that neither Vespasian nor Titus allowed themselves to listen to *delatores* restored the atmosphere of co-operation between the emperor and the upper *ordines.*

The events of the year 68/69 are also discussed in unexpected detail, perhaps in view of later usurpations, such as those in the third century. He is particularly interested in the origins of the emperors. For Galba, *antiquissimae nobilitatis senator* suffices. Otho's background requires more extensive treatment, in itself no good sign.[118] Vitellius needs still more space—and all this serves as a prelude for Vespasian, *obscure quidem natus sed optimis comparandus.*[119] His interest in the emperors' origins, lively though it is, is not as intense as that of Aurelius Victor.[120] Not for nothing were the emperors who succeeded the Julio-Claudian dynasty often scrutinized as to their background, and frequently judged on that basis. The emperors of 68/69 are no exception. Nerva: *nobilitatis moderatae;* Trajan: *familia antiqua magis quam clara,* with a description which also serves to 'place' Hadrian, *consobrinus suae filius;* Antoninus: *genere claro sed non admodum vetere;* Marcus Aurelius is the first about whose background he has no reservations: *haud dubie nobilissimus, quippe cum eius origo paterna a Numa Pompilio, materna a Solentino rege penderet.*[121] The next interesting case, much later, is Septimius Severus, whose humble origins we have seen pointed out by Victor. The fact that he was a self-made man also emerges clearly enough from Eutropius' account: he tells us that the emperor came from Africa and gives details of his career, but he does not mention the humble social position of the family. The military anarchy produced a long series of family trees notable chiefly for their obscurity: *obscurissimo genere* (Maximinus Thrax), *obscurissime natus obscurius imperavit* (Aemilius), *obscurissime natus* (Postumus), *vilissimus opifex* (Marius), *obscurissime natus* (Diocletian), *villissime natus* (Carausius).[122] Eutropius does not allow such considerations to cloud his judgement of their rule. Postumus and Diocletian come off particularly well, as does Carausius.

The closer a historian gets to his own time, the more cautiously must he proceed. Yet even Constantine the Great's origins are weighed in the balance when Eutropius says that he succeeded his father, *ex obscuriore matrimonia eius filius* (X 2,2).

The emperor's *acclamatio* by the senate was an important occasion. If it did not take place, the author does not fail to say so (IX 1: Maximinus, IX 7: Valerian, IX 11,1: Claudius II). The senate was deprived of this 'right' by the soldiers. Of Pertinax the author says, 'ex senatus consulto imperare iussus' (VIII 16), nor is the fact omitted that Tetricus was a senator, and had to put up with many mutinies on the part of the soldiers who elected him (IX 10). The hostility between soldiers and senate largely determined Eutropius' view of the past, and particularly of the previous century. He must have agreed with Victor (37,5): 'abhinc militaris potentia convaluit ac senatui imperium creandique ius principis ereptum ad nostram memoriam, incertum, an ipso cupiente per desidiam an metu seu dissensionum odio'.

According to the Suda, Eutropius was an Italian.[123] His origin did not, however, preclude Eutropius' acceptance of emperors from elsewhere. Sometimes he even gives the impression that he regards the non-Italic origins of many leaders as a symbol of the universality of the Empire. He displays not a trace of dissatisfaction with Trajan's background, although he does stress the fact that the emperor's father was the first of his line to achieve the heights of consular dignity (VIII 2,1). No more is Severus' African origin held against him. Nevertheless, the author likes to include information of this nature: *Decius, e Pannonia inferiore; Aurelianus Dacia Ripensi oriundus; Carus Narbone natus in Gallia; Maximianus Galerius in Dacia haud longe a Serdica natus; Licinius Dacia oriundus*.[124] These little details must have been important to Eutropius. We can understand him better if we assume, and there are ample grounds for such an assumption, that his readers and listeners liked to read about a fellow-countryman who succeeded in becoming the leader of the empire. It must be admitted that a painful contrast is thus created between the insignificant details supplied and the important facts he sometimes omits. Constantine may serve as an example. His rule is praised, but our pagan author makes no reference whatsoever to the emperor's conversion to Christianity.

Eutropius' high opinion of the emperor deserves further analysis. He points out that Constantine was very popular in the provinces, mainly because of his military successes; the author refers more particularly to the conquests in Gaul, where Constantine defeated the Alamanni and the Franks. Chapters X 4-8 are decidedly unequal in their appreciation of the emperor and his deeds. Good deeds and bad are placed side by side, with no attempt at unification. The emperor's origins, of interest to Eutropius, are also pointed out here.[125] There are evil deeds, committed for political reasons: the death of Licinius was *contra religionem sacramenti;* Crispus' name is avoided, the murders neither concealed nor condoned (X 6,3): 'verum insolentia rerum secundarum aliquantum Constantinus ex illa favorabili animi docilitate mutavit. primum necessitudines persecutus egregium virum filium et sororis filium, commodae indolis iuvenem, interfecit, mox uxorem, post numerosos amicos'. However, the following chapter appears to have been designed to eliminate the unfavourable impression: it is a continuous flow of praise.

Constantine's reign most clearly shows the degree to which an abbreviator's working methods were influenced by politics. As we have seen, Eutropius did not succeed in shaping the relevant chapters into a coherent whole, a failing to be attributed, not to his sources, but to the delicate nature of the subject. Christian tradition had rendered this emperor's position unimpeachable, and had become a force which the pagan had to take into account. Nevertheless, he was quite at liberty to criticize the emperor's conduct in matters upon which he, an experienced civil servant, was an expert: the emperor's legislation (X 8,1) included unnecessary details and severe decrees for which Eutropius could apparently muster no admiration, though we do not know exactly at which measures his criticism was directed.[126] The struggles for the succession, both before and after Constantine, are discussed in greater detail than we would expect from a *breviarium*. His discursiveness is understandable if we remember the importance the senator-historian attaches to legitimacy. The *acclamatio* had always, after all, been essentially a matter for the senate. It would be foolish to attack Eutropius on the score of his diplomatic treatment of the greatest of Christian emperors. His analysis is more than capable of standing comparison with the efforts of others. Victor also refers to the death of Crispus, but he also glosses over the fact that he was murdered with the words *incertum qua causa* (*de Caes.* 41,11). Although this smacks of servility, we should not underestimate Victor. Having mentioned the execution of Crispus and the punishment of a vulgar rebel on Cyprus, he goes on to say: 'quo excruciato, ut fas erat, servili aut latronum more, condenda urbe formandisque religionibus ingentem animum avocavit, simul novando militiae ordine'. Eutropius was incapable of such masterly irony, which casually mentions the transfer of the capital, conversion to Christianity and military reforms all in one breath.

In this summary of Roman history women are virtually ignored. Of course, the Sabine virgins, Lucretia and Virginia, are part of the stock repertoire, even for those who do no more than summarize the earliest history of Rome (I 7,8-10, 18); no historian writing about Hadrian's accession could ignore Plotina's influence (VIII 6); no more could Cleopatra (VI 22, VII 6,7) or Zenobia (IX 13) be disregarded. But this is the sum of the abbreviator's interest in the subject. Those who stress Suetonius' influence on Eutropius will not find a trace of it here, at any rate.[127] No Livia, no Aggripinas, no Julias. The *magister memoriae* had no time for frivolous matters.

One thread that runs throughout the book, whether the author is discussing the time of the Kings, the Republic or the Empire, is the dignity of war. War was always better than peace without honour. Hence the open criticism of Jovian (X 17,1): a necessary but dishonourable peace. So much, at least, he could afford to say soon after the emperor's death—it goes without saying that it would have been impossible while the emperor was still alive.[128]

Economic Problems

Eutropius barely touches upon economic problems. Slaves are mentioned only on the occasion when they were used for the defence of Rome during the Second

Punic War (III 10). Roman politicians often argued that the conquests in the provinces enabled the Roman legions to 'liberate' the people from slavery to their previous masters. Eutropius interprets the facts in this manner only once (VIII 13,1): '[Marcus Aurelius] Pannoniis servitio liberatis . . . triumphavit'.[129]

One particular passage (IX 14) is always quoted in connection with the debasement of the coinage which took place in Imperial times: 'hoc (Aureliano) imperante etiam in urbe monetarii rebellaverunt vitiatis pecuniis et Felicissimo rationali interfecto'. Victor also mentions this event (35,6): 'neque secus intra urbem monetae opifices deleti, qui, cum auctore Felicissimo rationali nummariam notam corrosissent, poenae metu bellum fecerant'. Its gravity illustrates the independence and power attained by the *monetarii;* it also shows the extent to which the process of devaluation, which had been going on for a long time, was aggravated by these officials.[131] The full-scale war that it precipitated claimed seven thousand victims among the imperial troops. To be sure, the abbreviators did not mention events such as these for their economic interest, but because of their serious military repercussions. Their interest in the provinces was likewise determined by other than economic considerations.

The fact alone that an emperor came from the Danubian territories was enough to stimulate an interest in that province. Eutropius caters to this interest, but in moderation.[132] We are told no more about specific measures in the Danube region (except, of course, for military exploits) until Probus, who repealed Domitian's prohibition of viticulture in Gaul and Pannonia.[133] In comparing Eutropius and Victor, we find that the latter sometimes takes slightly more interest in economic matters, such as the reclamation of virgin soil in Pannonia, in which connection he refers to Galerius (*de Caes.* 40.9). Eutropius does not mention this project, but he does tell us of the dangers that threatened the area in the form of marauding bands of Sarmatians and Quadi (IX 8,2).

Abridged histories have always been spiced with particularly picturesque details. Here we see Marcus Aurelius faced with the realization of the gravity of the rebellions at the Danube front. In order to combat these difficulties he made a personal sacrifice: the sale of his most precious possessions (VIII 13,2). Such incidents look well in a textbook. Nevertheless, it would be unfair to think that the author is quite oblivious of economic considerations. Aurelian's reform of the coinage (IX 14) was certainly no picturesque detail, but an extremely serious undertaking. However, one would not expect the hasty reader of a *breviarium* to go to the trouble of gathering all the relevant information. Besides, it is doubtful whether Eutropius himself had access to these particulars.[134] Economics were not his strongest point, nor of other classical historians. This is linked with the

fact that economic history has little popular appeal; the few economic measures that did catch the fancy of the public, such as Probus' measures for the advancement of viticulture in Gaul and Pannonia, are infallibly recorded (IX 17,2). Of the details of Aurelian's monetary reforms, little is known; at any rate, they met with scant enthusiasm in Gaul and Britain. There are indications that Eutropius was told of the matter by Gallic informants who were more than likely to contrast Aurelian's attempted reforms with Julian's successful financial measures. These had been all the more welcome after the devastation and complete exhaustion left in the wake of Magnentius' insurrection (X 10,2), in which Gaul, too, had been deeply involved.[135] Julian is praised for his provincial policies on account of his deeds in Gaul—his economic reforms as well as his military exploits (X 16,3). It even looks as if Eutropius is rather vague about the difference between *aerarium* and *fiscus* (X 16,3; 1,2). He does not mention the Gracchi; their socio-economic importance did not interest him. No more, it seems, was he interested in the political and constitutional significance of their activities, even though it is precisely in these matters that he sometimes wishes to educate his readers.[136]

A study of his comments on provincial administration shows that Gaul, Africa and Asia are referred to most frequently; his information about Gaul is in general of greater importance than that given for the two other provinces. However, this need have no connection with Eutropius' alleged Gallic origin,[137] but rather with the dramatic course of events in Gaul in the third and fourth centuries.

There is little point in searching for written sources of his information on provincial affairs. Schanz,[138] though apt to be somewhat dogmatic, is right in assuming that this modest work owed little to extensive study of the available sources. Every conquest had its legend, and scraps of the story, correct or otherwise, were passed on, usually by word of mouth, in official circles.

Christianity

Eutropius does not mention Constantine's conversion. A possible reason for this omission is that he did not wish to sow or to aggravate religious dissension, an explanation that accords well with his disapproval of Julian's handling of religious matters (X 16,3): 'religionis Christianae nimius insectator, perinde tamen, ut cruore abstineret'. These words may be interpreted as a denunciation only of Julian, but they certainly also contain an indirect criticism of all Christian rulers who stooped to violence. Nevertheless this passage (and, indeed, his treatment of Constantine generally), in spite of its somewhat haphazard composition, bears the stamp of a considered opinion, which has allowed the emperor's many excellent qualities to outweigh other consideration. The passage in question is directly followed by the remark that Julian modelled himself on Marcus Aurelius, a choice which must have satisfied Eutropius, who greatly admired this emperor (VIII 11).

It is no coincidence, I feel, that many people were dissatisfied with the end of the *breviarium*. Nor does it seem hazardous to venture the hypothesis that the Anonymus Valesiani was among them, and that he himself supplied an ending which in his opinion placed the facts in a more accurate historical perspective than did Eutropius' account. Julian's words (6,33, ed. Moreau) reveal the *Anonymus* to be a Christian, indeed a fanatic, whose severe criticism is elsewhere derived from Orosius. It is worth investigating the differences between Eutropius and the Anonymus.

(1) An. Val. is hostile to barbarians. He credits Constantine with an heroic action which Eutropius would never have recognized as such and indeed does not even consider worth mentioning (1,3): 'ferocem barbarum capillis tentis raptum ante pedes Galerii imperatoris adduxerat'.

(2) As a corollary, their description of Constantine's character is based on different material. Both, indeed, represent him as ambitious, but the striking particulars adduced by An. Val. are lacking in Eutropius (X 5; 7). The killing of the post horses in order to avoid capture by Severus (2,4) is one example; Victor also mentions this incident (40,2).

(3) The tradition that Philippus Arabs was a Christian (6,33) may throw some light on An. Val.'s sources. Orosius (7,28) also refers to Philippus Arabs as a Christian, which is not to say that An. Val. based his writings on Orosius, though this is likely. The tradition itself owes its existence to primitive retrospective wishful thinking: Would it not be wonderful if Rome's thousandth anniversary had been celebrated under a Christian emperor? No doubt this pipe dream gave rise to the crude historical fabrication. Be this as it may, and though no direct dependence of the one on the other can be proved, An. Val. and Orosius must have had a common source. That there is at least a link between the two is confirmed by the following.

(4) An. Val. and Orosius condemn Licinius in the same terms[139] for expelling the Christians from court—another incident not mentioned by Eutropius, who prefers to avoid referring to the persecutions as much as possible.

(5) Eutropius actually condones Licinius' action. The agressor was Constantine (X 5): 'Licinio bellum intulit, quamquam necessitudo et adfinitas cum eo esset; nam soror Constantia nupta Licinio erat' and again (X 6): 'postremo Licinius victus apud Nicomediam se dedidit et contra religionem sacramenti occisus est'. The feeble excuse given by An. Val., 'ne iterum depositam

purpuram in pernicie rei publicae sumeret', is unsatisfactory. Hence his reiteration of the arguments set forth in 5,20; this persecutor was another who deserved no better: 'quamvis omnibus iam ministris nefariae persecutionis extinctis, hunc quoque in quantum exercere potuit persecutorem digna punitio flagitaret'. In this character, and similarly denounced by Orosius, Licinius went down in Christian history. Understandably, since passions ran so high, Eutropius' moderate opinion lost its effect. He did not take sides clearly enough, it was thought, and it was tempting to exaggerate matters even more. 'Licinius scelere avaritia libidine saeviebat, occisis ob divitias pluribus, uxoribus eorum corruptis' (5, 22).

(6) It is not surprising that Galerius (3,8) was also unpopular with An. Val., and that the dreadful suffering accompanying his sickness is interpreted as a divine punishment.[140] Eutropius takes a very different view, 'vir et probe moratus et egregius re militari', and also speaks of his humiliation at the hands of Diocletian. An. Val. passes over this matter in silence, and has nothing to add to the *breviarium* in this respect.[141]

(7) An. Val. also has the professed aim of presenting edifying information, albeit for a different section of the public—the Christians. They were no doubt most satisfied with what he said of Constantine: 'iusto ordine et pio vicem vertit. edicto si quidem statuit citra ullam caedem hominum paganorum templa claudi'.

(8) Thus the reign of Constantine can be made to look as if it had known no bloodshed. But this it is only possible to do if one suppresses the fact of Crispus' death, as does An. Val. He is nevertheless obliged to mention the military successes of Constantine's discredited son. Eutropius cuts a good figure in the face of this hypocrisy: although he does not mention Crispus by name, he does tell us that he was murdered by his own relatives. Furthermore, his previously quoted favourable opinion of this unfortunate prince implies condemnation of Constantine (X 5,3): 'primum necessitudines persecutus egregium virum filium et sororis filium, commodae indolis iuvenem, interfecit, mox uxorem, post numerosos amicos.'

We need not go into further, less striking, differences, for these are not matters of principle. The chief divergences are based on the Christian and pagan points of view. Victor and the *Epit. de Caes.* are on the side of Eutropius. The eight points mentioned above exemplify an essential disparity. A world of difference lies between the pagan and the Christian idea of what was relevant and necessary for the edification of an historically ignorant public. An. Val. did not, however, succeed in ousting Eutropius. Perhaps, after all, he was too common, whereas Eutropius maintains his dignity as a senator throughout. His observations about Constantine's legislative labours are extremely suggestive: some laws were good, others severe, but very many were superfluous. He immediately proceeds to refer to the foundation of Constantinople, 'ut Romae aemulam faceret' (X 8,1). It remains uncertain whether the author considered this a good or a superfluous move. An. Val. (6,30) is more effusive.[142]

'Miserable epitomes', says one modern author.[143] Perhaps so, but there are degrees of 'miserableness', and there is integrity besides, which has survived, for once, to become an historical exception. Eutropius' summary became the textbook of the Middle Ages, of the Byzantine world, and of the humanists.

Appendix

The whole work is very logical in composition and lacks the artificial links created by Victor. Now and then, the connection between three passages is somewhat tenuous, but even then the reader is scarcely ever led astray. For instance, VI 18 has been interpolated between 17 and 19, and 'hinc' (19,1) should, strictly speaking, follow the fighting in Gaul (17, especially the end of § 3). Nevertheless, these passages do not present any problems; indeed, the work as a whole is remarkably straightforward.

Renewed study of the text does not add much to our knowledge of historical events. Of the various editions, that of H. Droysen (1879) is the most valuable in its treatment of the philological aspects. The editions of C. Wagener (1884) and F. Ruehl (1887) are decidedly less satisfactory: of the two the latter, though not as good as the other, is the more widely used.[144] In places where the text is incomplete, the Greek translation can occasionally be used to provide complementary or alternative readings.[145] Unfortunately, though, Paianios is not always equally helpful, as we see in IV 27. Here the Greek is a literal translation of the Latin text as we have it, and thus of little use. The text cries out for improvement, most editors preferring *corruptum* to *correctum*.[146]

Various passages could be cited which Ruehl's edition approaches with exaggerated caution. One passage in particular merits individual attention, since it had historical consequences of some significance.

In IX 8,1 Ruehl gives the following text: 'Nam iuvenis in Gallia et Illyrico multa strenue fecit occiso apud Mursam Ingenuo, qui purpuram sumpserat et † Trebelliano'. Victor (*de Caes.* 33,1) refers to Regalianus besides Ingebus (= Ingenuus[147]). The credit for amending Eutropius' text belongs to that 'illustre savante', Anne le Fèvre.[148] A certain amount of significant evidence (including numismatic material) pertaining to the rebellions of Ingenuus and Regalianus has also been preserved.[149]

Ruehl's caution in refusing to substitute 'Regaliano' for 'Trebelliano' is undoubtedly (although he does not say so in so many words) inspired by *Tyr. trig.* 26,2: '[Gallienus acted ruthlessly] in Trebellianum factum in Isauria principem, ipsis Isauris sibi ducem quaerentibus.' Ruehl probably thought that the author of this *vita* might well have influenced Eutropius in this respect. However, once we know that Eutropius did not come after the *Historia Augusta* but preceded it, this view is rendered untenable.

In order to explain 'Trebelliano' in Eutropius' text, scholars early adduced the fact that the author of the *vita* calls himself 'Trebellius Pollio', and assumed that Eutropius' use of the name derives from him. As we have seen, this is chronologically impossible. It is more satisfactory to assume that the *Historia Augusta* got his name from Eutropius,[150] but that does not solve all our problems. For it is not certain whether this error originated with Eutropius, or whether it dates back to an earlier stage of textual tradition. W. Schmid has put forward a strong case for the latter possibility. As we see, these minor historians were often unjustly criticized for errors for which they themselves were not even responsible. There will always be captious critics who refuse to be convinced and who accuse those who rectify Eutropius' text of tampering with it.[151] However, since there is no other passage in Eutropius where a fictitious ruler is introduced into the history of Rome, there is every reason to acquit Eutropius of this charge. The *Historia Augusta,* on the other hand, has a habit of introducing imaginary rulers. Eutropius certainly deserves the benefit of the doubt.

List of Abbreviations

AHR: American Historical Review

ALL: Archiv für lateinische Lexikographie und Grammatik

ARW: Archiv für Religionswissenschaft

Bull. Comm.: Bollettino della Commissione Archeologica Communale di Roma

Bull. Inst. Cl. Stud. (London): Bulletin of the Institute of Classical Studies of the University of London

BSAF: Bulletin de la Société nationale des antiquaires de France

CAH: Cambridge Ancient History

Class. et Med.: Classica et Mediaevalia

CPh: Classical Philology

CQ: The Classical Quarterly

CR: The Classical Review

Ec. Hist. Rev.: Economic History Review

Fleckeis. Jahrb.: Jahrbücher für Classische Philologie herausgegeben von Alfred Fleckeisen

Heidelb. Jahrb.: Heidelberger Jahrbücher

HZ: Historische Zeitschrift

Jahrb. f. A. u. Chr.: Jahrbuch für Antike und Christentum

JHS: Journal of Hellenic Studies

JRS: Journal of Roman Studies

Mnem.: Mnemosyne

P.I.R.: Prosopographia Imperii Romani

Proc. of the Cambr. Philol. Soc.: Proceedings of the Cambridge Philological Society

RAC: Reallexikon für Antike und Christentum

RE: Paulys Realencyclopädie der classischen Altertumswissenschaft

REA: Revue des Études Anciennes

REL: Revue des Études Latines

Rev. Hist.: Revue Historique

Rev. Phil.: Revue de Philologie, de Littérature et d'Histoire anciennes

RFIC: Rivista di Filologia e di Istruzione Classica

RhM: Rheinisches Museum für Philologie

TLL: Thesaurus Linguae Latinae

ZNum.: Zeitschrift für Numismatik

Notes

[1] Ammianus Marcellinus 29,1,36.

[2] See A. Chastagnol in Rev. Phil. 41 (1967), 85, in which the older literature is listed. Cf. J. Matthews, 'Continuity in a Roman Family; The Rufii Festi of Volsinii', Historia 16 (1967), 484-509; esp. 494-5; M. Hauser-Meury, Prosopographie zu den Schriften Gregors von Nazianz, 1960, 80, opposes this view.

[3] A. H. M. Jones, 'Collegiate Prefectures', JRS 54 (1964), 78-89; esp. 79, about this particular prefecture; cf. Matthews, art. cit., 495.

[4] Marcellus, De Medicamentis, pref. (ed. Helmreich, Teubner 1889,1); cf. RE 6, Col. 1520, 'Eutropius' 3. K. F. Stroheker, Der senatorische Adel im spätantiken Gallien (Tübingen 1948), no. 136 (p. 170), rightly does not identify this Eutropius with the historian, either.

[5] See O. Seeck, Die Briefe des Libanius zeitlich geordnet (Leipzig 1906), 434, 151 ff.; H. F. Bouchery, Themistius in Libanius' brieven (Antwerp 1936), 253 ff.

[6] Matthews, art. cit., 494-5; R. Syme, Ammianus Marcellinus and the Historia Augusta, 105, note 3, agrees. . . .

[8] We agree with W. Seston (Dioclétien et la tétrarchie, Paris 1946, 23) when he says, 'Il y a trop de conjecture dans les remarques de quiconque étudia les sources des compilateurs du IVe siècle, et le plus souvent les conclusions de la Quellenforschung sont trop absolues'. Comparison of a modern discussion of the sources and the survey given by M. Petschenig in Bursians Jahresberichte 72 (1892), 20, shows that nothing has changed in the course of eighty years. This is hardly surprising: research on sources involves too many unknown factors. The student should be prepared to admit that derivations in the breviaria are likely to remain highly speculative.

[9] See R. Syme, op. cit., 105, with reference to Eutr. IX 26 and Amm. Marc. 15,5,18.

[10] For legislation on the purple, see RE 23 (1959), col. 2013 ff. (K. Schneider).

[11] R. Helm, 'Hieronymus und Eutrop', RhM 76 (1927): 'Der Ausdruck ante carpentum und die stärker die Tatsache betonende Ausdrucksweise stimmt zu Festus; aber niemand wird annehmen wollen, dass H. dazu neben E. auch F. eingesehen habe oder dass er zufällig auf dieselbe Fassung gekommen sei'.

[12] For the following see Hieron. 227 ff; Festus 14,6; Eutr. IX 25,1. Also Jordanes, Rom. 301; Oros. VII 25,9; Chron. min. I 643.

[13] Hieron. 243b; Epit. 43,2. See also Helm, art. cit., 301.

[14] Hieron. 239cd; Eutr. X 13. See also Helm, art. cit., 300.

[15] M. Schanz, Geschichte der römischen Literatur, IV^2 (1914), 77 ff. Eutropius' significance for later generations need not concern us here. His importance for the SHA has been rightly emphasized once more by W.

Schmid, 'Eutropspuren in der Historia Augusta', *Bonner Historia-Augusta Colloquium* 1963 (1964), 123-133. Cf. T. Damsholt, 'Zur Benutzung von dem Breviarium des Eutrop in der Historia Augusta', *Class. et Med.*, 25 (1964), 138-150.

[16] E.g. Schanz, *op. cit.*, 78: 'Angaben über Ortsentfernungen von Rom und chronologische Daten können leicht aus Handbüchern entnommen werden'.

[17] Cf. *Mnem.* 21 (1968), 270.

[18] See for these wars E. T. Salmon, *Samnium and the Samnites* (Cambridge 1967), which does not, however, discuss the treatment of the wars against the Samnites in the later *breviaria* (cf. my review in *BIOR* 27 [1970], 396-397).

[19] II 12,2.

[20] III 14,1. In fact, eight years. The year in question is 211 B.C., *P. Sulpicio Cn. Fulvio consulibus.*

[21] Contradicted by the defeat of Cn. Fulvius, which the author does not fail to mention; cf. Liv. 26, 9-11.

[22] See below, p. 173 ff.

[23] I 8,3: *adhuc . . . usque ad quintum decimum miliarium possideret.*

[24] See Kroll, *s.v.* 'miliarium', *RE,* Suppl. VI, Col. 399. The stone was erected by the aediles P. Claudius Pulcher and C. Furius Paulus, presumably in 253 B.C. (see Broughton, *Magistrates* I, 211). *ILS* 5801.

[25] F. W. Walbank, *Commentary on Polybius* I (1957), *ad. loc.;* Kroll *(loc. cit.),* Col. 400, line 46 ff.

[26] E.g. the anachronisms in Livy II 11,17; III 6,7; 69,8; V 4,12; Florus I 22,44; Justin XXII, 6,9.

[27] *Miliarium aureum,* see *RE,* Suppl. IV, Col. 499.

[28] The only exceptions, which are not, however, of importance in this case, are VIII 8, 4 and IX 2,3.

[29] Useful information in D.S., *Dict. des ant., s.v.* 'Miliarium'. Cf. Varro, *RR.* III 2; Plin. *NH.* 23,159; Quintil. IV 5,22; Plin. *Epist.* X 24; Tac. *Ann.* XV, 60; *Hist.* II 24, 45; IV 11; Amm. Marc. XIX 8.5; XXXI 3,5; and elsewhere.

[30] E.g. V 4,12: *intra vicesimum lapidem in conspectu prope urbis nostrae . . .*

[31] *De Caes.* 33,33. In this connection see C. G. Starr, *art. cit.,* 585, on the third century: 'an era in which the Mediterranean world was rent by internal war and grounded by invasions from without'.

[32] Florus I 22,44.

[33] Only then can one proceed to ask whence he derived his topographical indications. Schanz' theory that they were taken from a 'handbook' seems acceptable. See above, note 16.

[34] For an explanation of these words, see below, p. 135.

[35] Cf. for instance Vell. I 15; II 7,8 and Cic. *Brut.* 43, 160.

[36] Cic. *pro Font.* V 13.

[37] IX 9; 11. For Postumus, see N. Jankowski, 'Das gallische Gegenreich (259-274 n. Chr.) und seine soziale Basis im Spiegel der *Historia Augusta*', *Helikon* 7 (1967), 125-194.

[38] For the *bellum Macedonicum* and M. Lucullus' activities there between 72 and 70 B.C., see Cic. *Verr.* II 23 ff., Plut. *Caes,* 4,1. Besides Eutr. VI 7;8,10, see also Fest. 9,3-4; Amm. Marc. 27,4,11.

[39] E.G. VIII 1,1, Nerva.

[40] This war and the *bellum sociale* are described as *bella funestissima* (V 9,2).

[41] VI 17 is indirectly a double time indication, for besides the date a.u.c. Eutropius has written 'C. Iulius Caesar, qui postea imperavit, cum L. Bibulo consul est factus'.

[42] If the year of foundation is taken to be 752 B.C. here, as it is often elsewhere, the year meant in II 18 is 275, and the census referred to is that of that year. Nevertheless, we may not take Eutropius too literally in this matter since the years a.u.c. do not always tally. (However, 275 B.C. remains the most likely date for this census, see p. 133). For the various dates for the foundation of Rome to be reconstructed from Eutropius' text, see the list on p. 137.

[43] See *Lexikon der alten Welt* (1965, *s.v.* 'Zeitrechnung', col. 3321 [H. Kaletsch]). E. J. Bickerman, *Chronology of the Ancient World* (London 1968), 77.

[44] Odd as it may seem, until far into the present century classics students at one of the Dutch universities were expected to know the names of the consuls for the period 200 B.C. to 200 A.D.!

[45] Cf. R. Syme, *Tacitus* (1958), 390 ff.: 'The Roman senator could not bear to use the regnal years of emperors.'

[46] Syme, *op. cit.,* 390.

[47] Broughton, *op. cit.,* gives 479 a.u.c.

[48] We do not know whether Paianios deliberately took a different line from Eutropius; he has, 470 a.u.c. instead of 477 a.u.c. In any event, the year 282 B.C. is unlikely to be historically correct as a date marking the beginning of expansion beyond Italy.

[49] For C. Marcius Rutilus, see Broughton, *op. cit.,* 179 and 202.

[50] J. Suolahti, *The Roman Censors. A Study on Social Structure* (Helsinki 1963), 256 ff., esp. 258-9: 'The mythical glow which formed about him later was such that he was held up as the ideal and model of Roman qualities. He was thus well adapted to become the ideal of censor.'

[51] Florus I 13,22; Liv. *Per.* 14.

[52] In general, it is impossible to correct all Eutropius' errors, but I have made an exception in the case of his chronology, for which the systems used are normally readily traced.

[53] This interpretation was first suggested by seventeenth-century editors, and was included, for instance, in the Leiden edition of Henricus Verheyk in 1793, and even in 1935, in Q. O. Polenta's edition: 'per non parlare di quelli che di più e di quelli che di meno tramandano'.

[54] B. G. Niebuhr, *Kl. Schr.* I 154; Ed. Meyer, *Forsch.,* II 404.

[55] This opinion was held by many early commentators; it is summed up as follows by Verheyk in his 1793 edition: 'Sunt enim qui plures annos Joviano tribuant. Velut ipse Victor in Epitome. *Interiit,* inquit, *annos gerens proxime quadraginta.* Sunt etiam qui pauciores: mediam inter utrosque viam insistit Eutropius.' Not surprisingly, however, Verheyk fails to specify the sources which refer to Jovian as having been still younger, for no such source has ever existed. Amm. Marc. 25,10,13; Eutr. *loc. cit.,* and Socrat. 3, 26.5, all give his age as 33 years, whereas only *Epit.* 44,4 gives it as 40 years.

[56] For the dating of L. Licinius Lucullus' activities, see Broughton, *op. cit.,* 106 ff., to whose conclusions I have nothing to add. Cf. also Broughton's *Supplement to the Magistrates of the Roman Republic* (1960), 34-35.

[57] See above, p. 134.

[58] Erected by Tiberius after 9 B.C. See Suet. *Claud.* I; Cass. Dio LV 2,3. For its present state, see M. Besnier

in *RE* 30 (1932), col. 2423.

[59] X 18,3 (See p. 189): 'Nam reliqua stilo maiore dicenda sunt. Quae nunc non tam praetermittimus, quam ad maiorem scribendi diligentiam reservamus.'

[60] For Florus' account, see above, p. 16. See also *Mnem.* 18 (1965), 384; 21 (1968), 272. In addition to the classical evidence listed there, see also the more recent studies quoted in *RE* 5, Col. 2248/57 (Wellmann); *RAC* 4, Col. 1001 ff. (Opelt), esp. 1022-3.

[61] B.C. II 96.

[62] The translation is that of H. White in the Loeb edition of Appian, III, 405. Cf. *b. Afr.* 83-85.

[63] Even before the battle of Adrianople, Rome's relationship with the barbarians betrayed traces of a type of patriotism that was to contribute to developments ensuing immediately after Eutropius. This patriotism has been brilliantly described by F. Paschoud, *Roma Aeterna, études sur le patriotisme romain dans l'occident à l'époque des grandes invasions.* Inst. suisse de Rome, 1967, 20. Paschoud discusses high-ranking pagans and Christians, but the seeds of their feelings about Rome had already been sown in the widely-read *epitomes,* and particularly in Eutropius. M. Fuhrmann's brilliant study, 'Die Romidee der Spätantike' (with its excellent bibliography), *HZ,* 207 (1968), 529-561, continues Paschoud's work in a discussion on the veneration accorded Rome at a later period.

[64] Cf. Liv. *Perioch.* 52. Florus I 32: 'facinus indignum'. See above, p. 7.

[65] Caepio, consul in 140, proconsul in 139 B.C. See Broughton, *Magistrates,* 477 ff.

[66] Esp. App. *Ib.* 70, 74-75.

[67] *De vir. ill.* 71,3.

[68] *Perioch.* 54: 'Viriathus a proditoribus consilio Servili Caepionis interfectus est ab exercitu suo multum comploratus ac nobiliter sepultus; vir duxque magnus et per quattuordecim annos, quibus Romanis gessit, frequentius superior'.

[69] 'Viriathi etiam caedes duplicem perfidiae accusationem recepit, in amicis, quod eorum manu interemptus est, in Q. Servilio Caepione consule, quia in sceleris huius auctor inpunitate promissa fuit victoriamque non meruit, sed emit.'

[70] See Vell. 2, 1,3 and the commentary by F. Portalupi (Turin 1967).

[71] V 22,15: 'percussores Sertorii praemium ne petendum

quidem a Romanis esse duxerunt, quippe qui meminissent antea Viriati percussoribus denegatum.'

[72] *Latrones* are well described in R. MacMullen, *Enemies of the Roman Order* (1956), 255 ff., 351, note 4; id., *Historia* 14 (1965), 102, n. 33.

[73] Florus I 33,15. Cf. *Mnem.* 18 (1965), 377 note 1. The facts are also given in P. Jal's edition of Florus I, 1967, p. 138.

[74] Walbank, *Commentary on Polybius* I 28,6 on Eutropius II 21,1.

[75] See for instance Florus I 18,7. Cf. W. W. Tarn in *JHS* 27 (1907), 50, note 17.

[76] II 22; III 8; 9; 10; 11,4-5; VI 20.

[77] A complete list of the conquests mentioned, numerous as they are for a *breviarium,* is not necessary. II 21,2-3 and 22,2 discuss the First Punic War. The conditions of the peace with Antiochus III are given in IV 4,3.

[78] Cf. J. H. Collins, *Propaganda, Ethics, and Psychological Assumptions in Caesar's Writings,* thesis, Frankfurt a.M. 1956, 43.

[79] See Liv. 45,34,5 for the booty (cf. Eutr. IV, 8). Eutr. IV 7,2 on the magnanimity of Aemilius Paullus.

[80] Defection to the enemy: see MacMullen, *op. cit.,* 362, note 29, which gives the relevant passages (cf. *ibid.,* 351, note 5). Pavel Oliva, *Pannonia and the Onset of Crisis in the Roman Empire* (Prague 1962) 287. For the Roman emperors as liberators, see Eutr. VIII 13,1 (under Marcus Aurelius); *vita Marci* 19,3; Oliva, *op. cit.,* 47,287.

[81] *Rebellavit* should be interpreted as a mutiny (IV 6,1); Florus' expression *se erexit* is somewhat clearer (I 28,1). Cf. *Mnem.* 1965, 375.

[82] For the distinction between runaway slaves and deserters, see Walbank's *Commentary on Polybius* XV 18,3 (p. 468).

[83] In any case, Polybius XV 18 differs in certain details from Liv. 30,37 and App. *Lib.* 54. Cf. Walbank, *Comm., loc. cit.*

[84] III 21,3: 'ut quingenta milia pondo argenti darent.' III 22,2: 'additis quingentis milibus pondo argenti centum milibus librarum propter novam perfidiam.' The surviving texts do not agree, which has led to desperate attempts to make the figures correspond to those given by Livy and Pliny the Elder (33,51); commentators in classical times also went to great lengths to try

to solve this infinitely complex problem. See the edition of Verheyk, *loc. cit.*

[85] See also p. 15.

[86] Eutr. X 15,2; Amm. Marc. 21,1,2; *Epit.* 42,18; Oros. 7,29,18. Cf. P. Jal, *La guerre civile à Rome* (Paris 1963), 460.

[87] Florus II 9,6; Eutr. VI 5,2. Jal, *op. cit.,* 440.

[88] Eutr. V. 7,4; Jal, *op. cit.,* 157 (senators). Actium: Florus II 21,11; Eutr. VII 7.

[89] Causes of war: Florus II 9,6. Jal, *op. cit.,* 361.

[90] Pichon, *Histoire de la littérature latine,* 788.

[91] References, s.v. 'Atilius' (51) in *RE* (v. Rohden) and Broughton, *Magistrates* I, p. 209.

[92] Schanz, *Geschichte der römischen Litteratur,* IV², 78.

[93] A summary of the following arguments was given by the present author in 'Rome à travers trois auteurs du quatrième siècle', *Mnem.* 21 (1968), 273 ff.

[94] *De Caes.* 25; Eutr. IX 1. I do not share the negative opinion of Syme, *Emperors and Biography,* (Oxford 1971), 189. The passage that to my mind best illustrates the importance Eutropius attaches to a thorough cultural grounding is X 10,2, where he judges Vetranio favourably, although he cannot refrain from mentioning his lack of cultural background: 'quem grandaevum iam et cunctis amabilem diuturnitate et felicitate militiae ad tuendum Illyricum principem creaverunt, virum probum et morum veterum ac iucundae civilitatis, sed omnium liberalium artium expertem adeo, ut ne elementa quidem prima litterarum nisi grandaevus et iam imperator acceperit.'

[95] VIII 5; see J. H. Thiel, 'Trajanus', *Kon. Akad. v. Wetenschappen, Akademiedagen* no. 8 (1955), 20.

[96] It is difficult, even for modern historians, to be sure about this. In *L'Imperatore Probo* (Rome 1952), G. Vitucci, for instance, on the basis of the knowledge available at that time, rightly assumed that Probus was not consecrated. An inscription in honour of L. Caesonius Ovinius Manlius Rufianus Bassus, which was found not long ago, tells us that he was 'electo a *divo Probo* ad pre(side)ndum iud(icio) mag(no)'. See G. Barbieri in the *Acta des IV. Intern. Kongresses für griechische und lateinische Epigraphik* (1962) (Vienna 1964). However, it would exaggerate the reliability of the epigraphical material to draw the conclusion that this definitely confirms Probus' deification. Eutropius, after eulogizing the emperor, states (IX 17,3)

'interfectus tamen est Sirmi tumultu militari in turri ferrata'. Cf. Victor 37,4; *Epit.* 37,4; *vita Probi* 21,4. I cannot subscribe to Syme's conclusion (*op. cit.,* 225): 'Clearly drawing on KG'.

[97] The best summary of Eutropius' treatment of consecration, even though it does not point out the differences in terminology, is that of F. Taeger, *Charisma* II (1960), 633.

[98] See the list given above.

[99] VIII 5,2 (Trajan), cf. VIII 4: 'ob haec per orbem terrarum deo proximus nihil non venerationis meruit et vivus et mortuus'; IX 28 (Diocletian); IX 11,2 (Claudius II).

[100] VIII 8,4 (Antoninus Pius); VIII 14,2 (Marcus Aurelius).

[101] VIII 7,3 (Hadrian); IX 2,3 (Gordian); cf. S. J. Oost, 'The Death of the Emperor Gordian III' in *C. Ph.* 53 (1958), 106-7; X 18,2 (Jovian).

[102] VII 11,3 (Tiberius); VII 12,4 (Caligula); VII 15,1 (Nero); VII 23,1 and 6 (Domitian).

[103] Victor *De Caes.* 20,30. Cf. Cassius Dio 75,7; Herodian 2,10,3. For further information see J. A. Straub art. 'Commodus' in *RAC* III, col. 255.

[104] *Vita Getae* 2,9.

[105] *De Caes.* 33,27; 30.

[106] Eutr. VIII 7,3: 'Cum . . . vehementer exigeret'.

[107] *De Caes.* 14, 13-14.

[108] This attitude is reflected, later, in the *H.A.: vita Hadriani* 25,8; *vita Antonini Pii* 6,3. It has been convincingly demonstrated that Eutropius precedes that SHA, e.g. by W. Schmid, 'Eutropspuren in der Historia Augusta', *Bonner Historia-Augusta Colloquium* 1963 (1964), 123-133. For Hadrian's *consecratio* see F. Vittinghoff, 'Der Staatsfeind in der römischen Kaiserzeit', *Neue deutsche Forschungen,* Bd. 84 (Berlin 1936), 87-89; more recently G. W. Clarke, 'The Date of the Consecratio of Vespasian', *Historia* 15 (1966), 318-327, esp. 320 ff.

[109] *De viris illustribus* 78; Aurelius Victor, *De Caes.* 1,1.

[110] Eutr. VI 25 (cf. p. 15, above).

[111] *Ibid.*

[112] Cf. the excellent summary by L. Koepp, 'Die Konse-krationsmünzen Kaiser Konstantins und ihre religionspolitische Bedeutung', *Jahrb. f.A.u. Chr.* 1 (1958), 94-104, esp. 95.

[113] For *mereo* in the sense of 'to show oneself to be worthy of something' and hence 'to lay a claim to something', see VIII 4 and IV 12,4. This meaning of course occurs frequently on funerary inscriptions: b.m.f. = *bene merenti fecit* (e.g. C.I.L., VI, 7778, 16450). It is not inconceivable that Eutropius derived his use of *mereo* from the terminology used on tomb inscriptions.

[114] IX 4 (Decius); IX 15,2 (Aurelius); X 8,2 (Constantine the Great); X 15,2 (Constantius II). Unfortunately Paianios, the translator, says nothing about the consecration of Constantius II. . . . See also 'Consecration' *RAC* III, col. 284 (L. Koepp-A. Herrmann). G. Herzog-Hauser 'Kaiserkult' in *RE* Suppl. IV, 806-853 gives the history of the *consecratio* of each emperor. The best study of the ritual is by E. Bickermann, 'Die römische Kaiserapotheose', *ARW* 27 (1929), 1-31. For the Christian emperors, especially Constantine the Great, see A. Kaniuth, *Die Beisetzung Konstantins des Grossen. Unters. zur religiösen Haltung des Kaisers* (1941).

[115] X 16,3; cf. Ammianus Marcellinus 22,10,7; 25,4,20. Aurelius Victor does mention Christianity (but only in passing) in connection with Constantine (41,12). For Festus see below, p. 178.

[116] For other expressions of this sentiment, see: II 27,4; III 17; IV 16,3.

[117] Not even Commodus is so thoroughly despised (VIII 5), probably because he also had a number of military successes to his credit, notably against the Germans. In modern works he is also sometimes more favourably judged than formerly, e.g. Oliva, *op. cit.,* 299-300.

[118] For Otho, whose ancestry was in fact most distinguished, see F. Klingner, 'Die Geschichte des Kaisers Otho bei Tacitus', *Sächsische Akad. der Wiss.,* 92 (1940), 3-27 (= Wege der Forschung 97 (1969), 388-412).

[119] The year of the three emperors: Otho: 'materno genere nobilior quam paterno, neutro tamen obscuro' (VII 17,1). Vitellius: 'familia honorata magis quam nobili. Nam pater eius non admodum clare natus tres tamen ordinarios gesserat consulatus' (VII 18,1). For the actual ties of the emperors with their social environment, see Syme, *Tacitus* (1958), 150 ff. (Galba), 205 (Otho), 386 (Vitellius).

[120] See above, p. 21, note 7.

[121] VIII 1,1; 2,1; 6,1; 9,1.

[122] IX 2,1; 6,1; 9,1; 9,2; 19,2; 21,1. Sometimes these comments are notoriously erroneous. For Septimius Severus see T. D. Barnes, 'The family and career of Septimius Severus', *Historia* 16 (1967), 87 ff. I should like to stress once more that Eutropius' blunders have been pointed out time and again. My present concern, however, is with his personality and his enormous success.

[123] See p. 115.

[124] IX 4 (cf. *RE* 29, col. 1250); 13,1 (cf. *RE* 9, col. 1351); 18,1 (cf. *RE* 4, col. 2456: including the emperor's wish to have been born a Roman); 22,1 (cf. *RE* 28, col. 2517); X 4,1.

[125] Constantine, *obscurus* on his mother's side, was nevertheless the son of an Augustus, as was Maxentius, and hence of better lineage than Licinius and Maximinus Daia, who were *homines novi* (X 4,2).

[126] Some scholars feel that the words *plerasque superfluas* apply to his religious reforms as described in Sozomen. I 8-9 (Verheyk). *Nonnullas severas (leges)* implies an evaluation presumably of financial measures, cf. *De Caes.* 41,20. Praise of his military policy is differentiated by means of the words 'fortuna in bellis prospera fuit, verum ita, ut non superaret industriam' (X 7,1).

[127] E.g. J. Wight Duff, *A Literary History of Rome in the Silver Age* (London 1927), 643.

[128] This makes X 17,1 a *terminus post quem* for publication.

[129] An ideological controversy has developed around this subject. For instance, Oliva, *op. cit.,* 286, reproaches Alföldi for adopting the point of view of the emperor's biographer (sc. *vita Marci* 17,3). . . .

[131] See *RE* 9, col. 1373-4. L. Homo, *Essai sur le règne de l'empereur Aurélien* (Paris 1904), esp. 79, 155 ff., for Eutropius 164; K. Gross in *RAC* I (1950), col. 1006. R. Tuncan, 'Le délit des monétaires rebellés contre Aurélien', *Latomus* 28 (1969), 948-959.

[132] Oliva's book is most enlightening on this point. See also 'Illyricum in the Epitomators', in R. Syme, *Emperors and Biography,* 221-236; also 'Emperors from Illyricum', *ibid.* 194-207.

[133] Already referred to in Victor *de Caes.* 37,3. Eutr. IX 17,2, later in *vita Probi,* 18,8 Cf. Oliva *op. cit.,* 171, 315-6, with references to modern studies. T. D. Barnes' 'Three notes on the *vita Probi',* *CQ* 20 (1970), 198 ff. represents an attempt to indicate sources for Probus as the promotor of vineyards; cf. Syme, *op. cit.,* 224.

[134] Even though modern research is full of gaps, the general lines are relatively clear. See A. H. M. Jones, *Ec. Hist. Rev.,* Second Series, vol. 5 (1952-53), 297-8; C. H. V. Sutherland, *JRS* 51 (1961), 94-5; Jones, *Later Roman Empire* (Oxford, 1964), 26.

[135] Ammianus Marcellinus 16,5 14-15; *Epit.* 48, 4-8. Ammianus describes the campaign against Magnentius as an 'insuperabilis expeditio' (14,1,1). See Jones, *op. cit.,* I, 120. For the significance of Magnentius' rebellion (X 9,3) see S. Mazzarino, *Aspetti sociali del quarto secolo* (Rome 1951), 121.

[136] The position of Egypt in the Empire as a whole is discussed in VII 7: 'Aegyptus per Octavianum Augustum imperio Romano adiecta est praepositusque ei C. Cornelius Gallus. Hunc primum Aegyptus Romanum *iudicem* habuit'. In his own way, he explains the office of dictator in Republican times in I 12, 1-2 (his phrasing is extremely cautious), the people's tribune in I 13, and the military tribune in II 1 and 3; the joint emperorship of Marcus and Verus clearly means something new in his work (VIII 9,2). He appears to have heard vaguely of the struggle to get a plebeian elected consul, but places it in the wrong context (II 7,1) and finally refers twice to censorship without offering any explanation of the office of censor (I 16 and II 6,1).

[137] See above, p. 115.

[138] *Geschichte der römischen Literatur,* IV², 77: 'Für die Abfassung des Schriftchens konnte natürlich ein ausgewähltes Quellenstudium nicht in Frage kommen'.

[139] An. Val. 5,20, 'repentina rabie suscitatus'. Cf. Oros. 7,28,18. For further similarities between An. Val. and Orosius, see Moreau's *Excerpta Valesiana* (Teubner 1968²), 5,29 and 5,33-35.

[140] Cf. Lact. *de mort.* 33 and Eus. *HE* 8, 16,3 ff. See p. 101 ff.

[141] Eutr. X 2,1; IX 24 (cf. Amm. Marc. 14,11,10). See p. 117.

[142] Zosimus' attitude is quite different: 111,2, Julian as the great benefactor of Constantinople; cf. Amm. Marc. 22,9,2; *Paneg. Lat.* XI 24. The question is whether pagan *breviaria* could be as readily transformed into Christian as some modern historians think. I feel that there is a world of difference between An. Val. and Eutropius, but in point of fact we know next to nothing about this anonymous Christian writer. Cf. Momigliano, *Conflict,* 87. However, it is doubtful whether we may say that the Christian passages are interpolations derived from Orosius and leave it at that. There is more than an interpretation at stake. For further differences to the pagan *breviaria* see An. Val. 2,4; 3,7; 4,10;

4,12; 6,30; 6.33.

[143] Syme, *op. cit.,* 144 and 105 (on Victor, Eutropius and Festus): 'poor and scrappy productions, all three' ' . . . the three epitomators betray the low standard still prevalent in the days of Julian and Valentinian (and an abysmal ignorance about the past history of imperial Rome). Otherwise, who would have made the effort of writing, who would have read these meagre compilations?' Cf. A. Cameron, *Hermes* 92 (1964), 375-6.

[144] See the review of these three editions by M. Petschening in *Bursian,* 72 (1892).

[145] III 7 (end); cf. K. Duncker, *De Paianio Eutropii interprete,* Progr. Greiffenberg 1880.

[146] Petschenig, however, considers this change 'viel zu gewaltsam' (*op. cit.,* 27). I noted excessive caution in V 9; furthermore in IX 7, where the asterisk after *Norico* is unnecessary, and where one should not assume a *lacuna* of two words, as Ruehl suggests. In XI 34, it is unnecessary to add the word *civitatem.*

[147] See W. Schmid, 'Eutropspuren in der Historia Augusta', *Bonner Historia-Augusta Colloquium* 1963 (Bonn 1964), note 10.

[148] See especially the important article by Schmid (esp. 126), who demonstrates that it is Salmasius who suggested this change.

[149] J. Fitz, *Ingenuus et Régalien,* Collection Latomus, 81 (1966), 49 ff., tacitly assumes, without discussing the text, that IX 8,1 is about Regalianus.

[150] Syme, *Ammianus,* 48.

[151] E. Hohl, most recently in *Klio* 27 (1934), 157 ff; cf. (against Hohl) Schmid, *art. cit.,* 127. The matter was taken up once more, using Hohl's arguments, by J. Rougé, 'L'Histoire Auguste et l'Isaurie au IVe siècle, *REA* 88 (1966), 282, esp. 288 ff., 315.

H. W. Bird (essay date 1986)

SOURCE: "Eutropius on Numa Pompilius and the Senate," *The Classical Journal,* Vol. 81, No. 3, February-March, 1986, pp. 243-48.

[*In this essay, Bird contends that the* Breviarium*'s treatment of Roman rulers reveals that "what was primarily important for Eutropius was how they interacted with the senate."*]

Eutropius was the Emperor Valens' *magister memoriae* in A.D. 369/370 and had accompanied the Emperor Julian on the ill-fated expedition against the Persians in 363. His **Breviarium** of Roman history from Rome's foundation to the death of Jovian in 364, written in clear, unaffected Latin, quickly become popular. It was soon translated into Greek and in its original Latin form became a school textbook for the middle ages and beyond. One of my own copies was published in Glasgow in 1783 and presented as a school prize to Moses Brown, a student in the fourth grade of Glasgow Grammar School in 1796.

In his preface Eutropius informs the reader of his general plan of composition: to arrange briefly from the foundation of Rome to his own day those particulars in war or peace most worthy of note with the concise additions of such matters in the lives of the emperors that were remarkable. The present article focuses upon Eutropius' repeated use of Numa Pompilius as an *exemplum* and his attitude towards the senate and certain republican personages who affected its status.

Numa Pompilius

Among the kings, and despite his obvious interest in Rome's early expansion, Eutropius seems to have been particularly fond of Rome's second ruler, Numa Pompilius. According to the breviarist Numa waged no wars but was of no less service to the state than Romulus. He established laws and customs among the Romans, who, because of their frequent hostilities, were until that point regarded as semibarbaric *latrones.* Furthermore, he divided the previously unregulated years into *ten months (sic)* and founded numerous sacred rites and temples at Rome (Eutrop. 1.3). Such a description might not be unusual in itself, as a comparison with *De Viris Illustribus* 3, *De Caesaribus* 14.2 or *Historia Augusta, Carus* 2.6 demonstrates, but subsequently Eutropius tells us that after the First Punic War and the triumph over the Sardinians Rome had no war on its hands for the first time since the reign of Numa Pompilius (3.3). More striking is his chapter on Antoninus Pius, "a remarkable man, deservedly compared with Numa Pompilius":[1]

> Ergo Hadriano successit T. Antoninus Fulvius Boionius, idem etiam Pius nominatus, genere claro. sed non admodum vetere, vir insignis et qui merito Numae Pompilio conferatur, ita ut Romulo Traianus aequetur. vixit ingenti honestate privatus, maiore in imperio, nulli acerbus, cunctis benignus, in re militari moderata gloria, defendere magis provincias quam amplificare studens, viros aequissimos ad administrandam rem publicam quaerens, bonis honorem habens, inprobos sine aliqua acerbitate detestans, regibus amicis venerabilis non minus quam terribilis, adeo ut barbarorum plurimae nationes depositis armis ad eum controversias suas litesque deferrent sententiaeque parerent. hic ante imperium ditissimus opes quidem omnes suas stipendiis militum et circa amicos liberalitatibus

minuit, verum aerarium opulentum reliquit. Pius propter clementiam dictus est.

(Eutrop. 8.8)

This whole section reads more like a list of necessary imperial virtues than anything else.

Again, in the very next chapter (8.9), Eutropius mentions Numa as the agnate ancestor of that imperial paragon, Marcus Aurelius,[2] ostensibly deriving this information from Marius Maximus. No other king, including Romulus, is accorded such treatment.

In a similar vein, the *Historia Augusta* (*Pius* 2.2) also lists Pius' many good qualities, then states that he was well deserving of comparison with Numa in the opinions of all good men. Even more telling is the last section of the same *Vita* (*Pius* 13), which is a eulogy of the emperor. It concludes: "qui rite comparetur Numae, cuius felicitatem, pietatemque et securitatem caerimonias semper obtinuit."

Numa was likewise an object of admiration to Ammianus Marcellinus. The king's reign was legendary for its tranquility (14.6.6), and he and Socrates are cited as models of truthfulness (16.7.4). He is set among such figures as Socrates, Pythagoras, Scipio the elder, Marius and Octavius, who had gained fame through reliance on their guardian spirits (21.14.5). Finally Numa is mentioned as a man of principle like Cato and contrasted with that utter scoundrel, Maximus, the *praefectus praetorio* executed by Gratian in 376 (28.1.39). It should cause no surprise, therefore, that Eutropius, like his fourth-century contemporaries, found Numa extremely useful as an *exemplum*. The king enjoyed a remarkably high reputation in the fourth century, and by his repeated reference to Numa in the **Breviarium** Eutropius seems to have been intent on transmitting to the emperor Valens those essential qualities of a good ruler which go beyond being successful in war.[3] Eutropius apparently hoped that Valens would see Numa (and Pius) as examples to follow.

The Senate

In 1972 it was pointed out by den Boer that "one burning political issue [of Eutropius' day] was that of the influence of the senate,"[4] and subsequently Momigliano remarked that what defined a man writing in Latin at Rome in the fourth century was what he thought about Christianity, the Germans and the senate.[5] Any reader of the **Breviarium** will quickly notice that Eutropius was certainly preoccupied with the senate. He discussed many domestic affairs, social, political or economic, and those responsible, often with balanced judgements. Nonetheless he completely omitted mention of those two important second-century figures, the Gracchi. One has to question this glaring omission. Den Boer (p. 166) believes that the author

was not interested in their socioeconomic importance or the political and constitutional significance of their activities. That is, of course, possible, but I am convinced that the main reason was Eutropius' disapproval of their anti-senatorial stance. This is borne out by his treatment of Marius, Sulla and Q. Caecilius Metellus, the one-time patron and subsequent enemy of Marius. In the post-Gracchan period the Caecilii Metelli were one of the dominant families at Rome, and its members are frequently mentioned by Eutropius prior to his discussion of the Jugurthine War.[6] The campaigns of L. Calpurnius Bestia and Sp. Postumius Albinus had been ignominious for the Romans in the opinion of Eutropius (4.26). He then gave the credit to Q. Caecilius Metellus (cos. 109) for restoring the Roman army to its former discipline "with great severity and restraint but without cruelty to any one" (4.27). Metellus, after defeating Jugurtha in various battles, killed or captured his elephants and caused many towns to surrender. He was, it would seem, just on the point of putting an end to the war *(finem bello positurus esset)* when he was succeeded by Marius. The latter actually finished the war through his quaestor, Cornelius Sulla, "ingentem virum," who had Bocchus betray Jugurtha. Both Metellus and Marius celebrated triumphs over Jugurtha, even if it was before the chariot of the latter that Jugurtha was led (4.27). Eutropius' favour for Metellus and implicit depreciation of Marius is evident later at the beginning of Book Six, where he writes of "Quintus Caecilius Metellus, the son of that Metellus who had subdued Jugurtha."

This bias is even more manifest at the beginning of Book Five. Marius was made consul a second time after the victory over Jugurtha and the imminent threat of the Cimbri and the Teutones. A third and fourth consulship were granted him as the wars were protracted.

> But in the fourth consulship he had as a colleague Quintus Lutatius Catulus. Consequently [*itaque*] he joined battle with the Cimbri and in two battles killed 200,000 of the enemy, took 80,000 prisoners with their general Teutobodus and for this service he was elected consul a fifth time in his absence (5.1.4)

The *itaque* seems to be deliberately inserted to enhance the role of Catulus, as we shall see. Immediately afterwards Eutropius describes a second battle against the Germans fought by Marius and Catulus. The author emphasizes the greater success of Catulus. Their armies were of equal size, but Marius took only two standards, while Catulus captured thirty-one (5.2). Absolutely no mention is made of Marius' momentous army reforms, which helped to bring about the victories over the German invaders and, in the long run, to transform the history of the Late Republic.[7]

In the Social War, which Eutropius discusses next, it is Sulla who is on prominent display. Among other outstanding exploits he so thoroughly routed Cluentius' numerous forces that he allegedly lost only one man of his own. The conflict lasted four years; in the fifth it was terminated by Sulla, who had greatly distinguished himself on many occasions as praetor in the same war (5.3).

In the Civil War which followed, Marius, then in his sixth consulship, is charged with instigating the conflict through his ambition to be appointed commander against Mithridates. Sulla, the first to enter the city in arms, is exonerated because he was driven by Marius to take that action (5.4).

We then find Sulla fighting in Greece, having killed Sulpicius and driven Marius out of Rome. At the Piraeus Sulla defeated Archelaus, Mithridates' general, and his army of 120,000. Only ten thousand were left, while the Romans had only fourteen men killed (5.6). Sulla next proceeded to reduce some of the Dardanians, Scordisci, Dalmatians and Maedi and won over the rest. Peace with Mithridates was granted on Roman terms, after which Sulla was compelled to hasten to Rome because, while he was busy winning victories over Mithridates in Greece and Asia (i.e. over a foreign foe), Marius and Cinna had recommenced hostilities at Rome, put to death the noblest of the senate and various ex-consuls and proscribed many. The rest of the senate quit Rome and fled to Sulla, begging him to save his country. He defeated Norbanus near Capua, killed seven thousand of Norbanus' men, captured six thousand and lost only 124 himself. Scipio's army came over to him without a fight (5.7). Against Marius junior he killed 15,000 and lost only 400. At the battle of the Colline Gate he cut down 58,000 and captured the remaining 12,000 (5.8). Eutropius accords Sulla the honour of having composed the troubles of the state, namely those two most lamentable wars, the Social and the Civil (5.9 and 6.1), in which more than 150,000 men had been killed, 24 consulars, 7 praetorians, 60 of aedile rank, and nearly 200 senators. Marius, by implication, is left as the villain of the piece. By contrast a brief, eminently fairer synopsis of the careers of Marius and Sulla is given by the unknown author of the *De Viris Illustribus* (67 and 75). Another fourth-century writer, the author of the *Historia Augusta,* compares Commodus with Sulla as a mass-murderer and stigmatizes Septimius Severus as a Punic Sulla or a Punic Marius for putting countless senators to death.[8]

Den Boer (151) is probably correct in taking Eutropius' statement regarding Trajan (8.4.5), "In my position as emperor I treat the common citizen as I should wish to be treated by the emperor if I were a common citizen," to imply his ideal of cooperation between the senate and emperor. There can be little doubt that Eutropius' sympathies were entirely pro-Sullan and decidedly pro-senatorial.[9] It is most unlikely that he was ignorant of the Gracchi and their activities: the author of the *De Viris Illustribus* has chapters on both (64-65), the author of the *H.A.* drags them in as alleged ancestors of the Gordians (*Gord.* 2.2), and Ammianus Marcellinus plainly knew of them (30.4.19). It appears that Marius and the Gracchi were, even in the fourth century, accepted as opponents of the senate, and the senatorial Eutropius deliberately chose to belittle the former while totally ignoring the latter. Sulla emerges as the hero of those difficult days with decidedly positive roles assigned to Q. Caecilius Metellus and Q. Lutatius Catulus, both members of the Roman nobility. In fact Catulus had been badly beaten by the Cimbri near Tridentum in 102 and had been compelled to give up the Po valley to the invaders. Marius joined him the following year and together they won the great victory over the Cimbri at the Raudine Plain.[10] Metellus, as censor in 102, tried to expel Saturninus and Glaucia from the senate; but this merely resulted in mob violence, and his colleague, Caprarius, would not back him. In 100 he was exiled for refusing an oath to observe Saturninus' agrarian law. Recalled soon afterwards, he never regained his political prominence. Neither Catulus nor Metellus were as significant in Roman history as the Gracchi or Marius, but to Eutropius they represented "the right stuff," the proper exemplars to set before the emperor Valens and other fourth-century readers.

Caesar also comes in for a good deal of criticism. In 6.19 Eutropius observes that the Civil War caused by Caesar's demand for a second consulship was truly execrable and deplorable, for, besides the havoc occurring in the various battles, the very fortune of the Roman people was changed: *Romani populi fortuna mutata est.* This phrase was regularly used when the state of things changed for the worse, as can be seen in Sallust and Velleius.[11] The consuls and the whole senate, according to Eutropius, left Rome and joined Pompey. At Pharsalus in 48 B.C. Eutropius tells us:

> Never before had a greater number of Roman forces assembled in one place or under better generals, forces which would easily have subdued the whole world, had they been led against barbarians. (6.21)[12]

Once again den Boer seems to be correct in observing (155) that Eutropius does not subscribe to Victor's oblique praise of Caesar or share the admiration felt for him by Victor and the author of the *De Viris Illustribus.* Indeed, according to Eutropius, Caesar, after terminating the civil wars, returned to Rome and began to conduct himself with excessive arrogance, contrary to the usages of Roman liberty. He personally disposed of those positions of honour which the people had previously conferred, did not even rise when the Senate approached him, and exercised regal and almost tyrannical powers. The natural consequence of this was the conspiracy led by the two Bruti, of the family of that Brutus who had expelled the kings—a conspiracy which culminated with the assassination of Caesar. Book Seven begins with the renewal of the civil war because the senators favoured the assassins and Antony attempted to crush them. The Republic was thrown into confusion: Antony, of Caesar's party, committed many crimes, and the senate declared him a public enemy (7.1). All this, we are led to infer, was the legacy of Caesar.

Eutropius throughout his work demonstrates a horror of civil wars and a repugnance for those who, like Marius and Caesar, cause wars because of their ambition. He probably did little research for his **Breviarium**[13] and preferred, instead, to write his abbreviated history according to his own personal predilections. One of the major issues of his day was the influence of the senate, and like his contemporary, Aurelius Victor, he is preoccupied with this matter.[14] Indeed, as den Boer has argued (159), it seems reasonable to assume that whenever Eutropius writes that an emperor acted with restraint we should interpret this to mean that he was on good terms with the senate. We have already noted that Trajan's proper relationship with his fellow citizens and the senate is heavily stressed (8.2-5). Both Augustus (7.8) and Nerva (8.1) are described as *civilissimi,* which implies acceptance by the senate, and Vespasian (7.20) and Titus (7.22) are said to have been loved and respected by that body. This is also the case with Nerva (8.1), Antoninus Pius (8.8) and Marcus Aurelius (8.11-14), and even with the ephemeral and practically unknown emperor Quintillus, who allegedly reigned but seventeen days (9.12). The tradition which carefully recorded the attitude of every emperor towards the *patres* had long been in existence, and Eutropius was heir to that tradition. So he diligently records any imperial mistreatment of the senate as well as the reverse,[15] and it is merely an extension of this attitude when he harks back to republican times and singles out such notables as the Gracchi, Marius and Caesar for omission or criticism and others like Q. Caecilius Metellus and Sulla for exaggerated praise. What was primarily important for Eutropius was how they interacted with the senate.

The **Breviarium,** because of its conciseness and readability, may well have been the most popular history of Rome in the middle ages and beyond. Nevertheless, it gave its readers a singularly slanted and senatorial perspective.

Notes

[1] The Epitomator (*Epit.* 15.3) also compares Pius to Numa.

[2] So does the *Historia Augusta* (*M. Aur.* 1.6).

[3] Eutropius writes of Trajan, "Gloriam tamen militarem civilitate et moderatione superavit" (8.4).

[4] W. den Boer, *Some Minor Roman Historians* (Leiden 1972) 150.

[5] A. Momigliano, *Essays in Ancient and Modern Historiography* (Oxford 1977) 134.

[6] Eutrop. 4.13, 4.14, 4.16, 4.21, 4.23, 4.25. On their importance *vid.* E. Gruen, *Roman Politics and the Criminal Courts 149-78* B.C. (Cambridge, Mass., 1968), ch. IV.

[7] E. Gabba, "Le origini dell'esercito professionale in Roma: i proletari e la riforma di Mario," *Athenaeum* 27 (1949) 173-209; *id.* "Ricerche sull'esercito professionale romano da Mario ad Augusto," *Athenaeum* 29 (1951) 171-272; R. E. Smith, *Service in the Post-Marian Roman Army* (Manchester 1958) 9 ff.; G. R. Watson, *The Roman Soldier* (Bristol 1969) 21-22; H. Last, *C.A.H.* IX (1932) 133-37 and 146-47.

[8] *H.A. Comm.* 8.1, *Pesc. Nig.* 6.4. For other negative impressions of Sulla in the *H.A. vid. Carac.* 2.2, 4.10, 5.4.

[9] For emphasis on the bad treatment of the senate *vid.* Eutrop. 7.2, 7.3, 7.14, 9.1, 9.14, 10.11. Cf. 8.4, 8.8, 8.13.

[10] *Vid.* T.F. Carney, "Marius' Choice of Battle-field in the Campaign of 101," *Athenaeum* 36 (1958) 229-37.

[11] Sallust, *Cat.* 2, *Jug.* 17; Vell. Pat. 2.57.118; cf. Aur. Victor, *De Caes.* 24.11.

[12] Cf. 10.12, where the battle of Mursa in A.D. 351 is similarly described.

[13] M. Schanz and C. Hosius, *Geschichte der römischen Literatur* IV² (Munich 1914) 77; den Boer 167.

[14] Den Boer 150-51; H. W. Bird, *Sextus Aurelius Victor: A Historiographical Study* (Liverpool 1984) 24-40.

[15] *Vid.* note 9.

Harry Bird (essay date 1987)

SOURCE: "Eutropius: In Defence of the Senate," *Cahiers des Études anciennes,* No. 20, 1987, pp. 63-72.

[In the following essay, Bird explores Eutropius's treat-

ment of Roman governments as a response to the then-strained relations between the Emperor Valentinian and the senate.]

When Eutropius was composing his **Breviarium** of Roman history in ca. A.D. 369 he held senatorial rank[1]. It seems likely that he had attained this status ten years or so earlier when Constantius II promoted him to the post of *magister epistularum*[2]. His rank is important because it would significantly affect his point of view and one of the main political issues of the day was the influence of the senate[3] Although this had long been a major concern, the accession of Valentinian and Valens in 364, both military men from Pannonia, exacerbated the situation. Apparently Valentinian "hated the well-dressed, the learned, the rich and the high-born[4]". Pannonians and others of humble origin were promoted to positions of power[5] as Valentinian reorganized Italy and Rome. Senators, on the other hand, were excluded from many of their customary offices, especially the vicariate and prefecture of Rome, while most of the consulships went to generals and senior administrative posts were generally assigned to tried and trusted professionals. Consequently relations between Valentinian and the senate grew strained and in the later years of his reign, amid a series of investigations and trials, many senators were exiled or even executed[6].

In the late sixties it seems that Eutropius was with Valens in the area along the lower Danube as the emperor battled against the Visigoths. Indeed, he demonstrates precise knowledge of the tribes who inhabited the region, the Thaiphali, Victohali and Thervingi. He also knew that the old province of Dacia was a thousand miles in circumference and that Aurelian was killed on the old paved road between Constantinople and Heraclea[7] Evidently, as *magister memoriae,* he enjoyed the emperor's favour, but he could still sympathize with the plight of his fellow senators at Rome.

From the time of Augustus the emperor had become the focal point of all state activities and accordingly the political importance of the senate had dwindled. Nevertheless, it continued to play a significant role under the Julio-Claudians, Flavians and Antonines until 193. In that momentous year various contingents of the Roman army supported four contenders for the throne and thereafter it was generally the army which selected the emperor. The point was missed by both Eutropius and his contemporary, Aurelius Victor.

By the fourth century, following the autocratic tendencies of Diocletian and his successors, the emperor was no longer *primus inter pares* but rather the *orbis totius dominus* (or *regnator*), the *rector gentium*[8]. He had become responsible for whatever befell the state, good or ill, and the history of the empire had consequently become the history of the emperors. Nevertheless the senate of the fourth century still regarded itself as the

pars melior humani generis[9]; its prestige and power continued to be potent factors which successive emperors could not ignore. It, in turn, accepted autocracy as inevitable, the only means of ensuring stability. None the less the conduct of the emperor towards it was crucial. As a senatorial spokesman, then, Eutropius endeavoured to demonstrate what the relations between the emperors and the senate should be[10]. His deceptively simple account of republican history underlined the senate's significant role in overseeing Rome's emergence as a world power. In the imperial period he diligently noted its good relations with the army and the popular emperors down to the reign of Quintillus. The material he selected was frequently chosen with a purpose and not simply copied slavishly from the sources. Its inclusion was intended to persuade an emperor, who was not particularly perspicacious or well-read[11], of the role of the senate in Rome's history and to plead its cause for the future.

Eutropius' preoccupation with the senate is evident throughout the first four books which end with the triumphs of Metellus and Marius over Jugurtha. The senate is mentioned fifteen times[12], but only once (1.13) negatively:

> Sixteen years after the expulsion of the kings, the people of Rome rebelled on the grounds that they were being oppressed by the senate and consuls. Then they created for themselves tribunes of the people as their own particular judges and defenders, by whom they might be protected against the senate and the consuls.

Otherwise Eutropius emphasizes the way the senate governed the growing state with wisdom, honour and patriotism. He especially notes that the senate repudiated the ignominious peace treaties with the Samnites, Numantines and Numidians[13], a theme to which he will revert in his penultimate chapter of Book Ten, when he indignantly denounces Jovian's shameful peace with the Persians in 363.

Throughout his description of the republican period Eutropius discusses many social, political or economic affairs, often with balanced judgement. Nonetheless, he completely omitted mention of those two important second-century figures, the Gracchi. One has to question this glaring omission. Den Boer believes that the author was not interested in their socioeconomic importance or the political and constitutional significance of their activities[14]. That is, of course, possible, but I am convinced that the main reason was Eutropius' disapproval of their anti-senatorial stance. This is borne out by his treatment of Marius, Sulla and Q. Caecilius Metellus, the one-time patron and subsequent enemy of Marius. In the post-Gracchan period the Caecilii Metelli were one of the dominant families at Rome, and its members are frequently mentioned by Eutropius prior to his discussion of the Jugurthine War[15]. The campaigns of L. Calpurnius Bestia and Sp. Postumius Albinus had been ignominious for the Romans in the opinion of Eutropius (4.26). He then gave the credit to Q. Caecilius Metellus (cos. 109) for restoring the Roman army to its former discipline "with great severity and restraint but without cruelty to any one" (4,27). Metellus, after defeating Jugurtha in various battles, killed or captured his elephants and caused many towns to surrender. He was, it would seem, just on the point of putting an end to the war *(finem bello positurus esset)* when he was succeeded by Marius. The latter actually finished the war through his quaestor, Cornelius Sulla, *ingentem virum,* who had Bocchus betray Jugurtha. Both Metellus and Marius celebrated triumphs over Jugurtha, even if it was before the chariot of the latter that Jugurtha was led (4.27). Eutropius' favour for Metellus and implicit depreciation of Marius is evident later at the beginning of Book Six, where he writes of "Quintus Caecilius Metellus, the son of that Metellus who had subdued Jugurtha".

This bias is even more manifest at the beginning of Book Five. Marius was made consul a second time after the victory over Jugurtha and the imminent threat of the Cimbri and the Teutones. A third and fourth consulship were granted him as the wars were protracted.

> But in the fourth consulship he had as a colleague Quintus Lutatius Catulus. Consequently *(itaque)* he joined battle with the Cimbri and in two battles killed 200,000 of the enemy, took 80,000 prisoners with their general Teutobodus and for this service he was elected consul a fifth time in his absence (5.1.4).

The *itaque* seems to be deliberately inserted to enhance the role of Catulus, as we shall see. Immediately afterwards Eutropius describes a second battle against the Germans fought by Marius and Catulus. The author emphasizes the greater success of Catulus. Their armies were of equal size, but Marius took only two standards, while Catulus captured thirty-one (5.2). Absolutely no mention is made of Marius' momentous army reforms, which helped to bring about the victories over the German invaders and, in the long run, to transform the history of the Late Republic[16].

In the Social War, which Eutropius discusses next, it is Sulla who is on prominent display. Among other outstanding exploits he so thoroughly routed Cluentius' numerous forces that he allegedly lost only one man of his own. The conflict lasted four years; in the fifth it was terminated by Sulla, who had greatly distinguished himself on many occasions as praetor in the same war (5.3).

In the Civil War which followed, Marius, then in his sixth consulship, is charged with instigating the conflict through his ambition to be appointed commander against Mithridates. Sulla, the first to enter the city in arms, is exonerated because he was driven by Marius to take that action (5.4).

We then find Sulla fighting in Greece, having killed Sulpicius and driven Marius out of Rome. At the Piraeus Sulla defeated Archelaus, Mithridates' general, and his army of 120,000. Only ten thousand were left, while the Romans had only fourteen men killed (5.6). Sulla next proceeded to reduce some of the Dardanians, Scordisci, Dalmatians and Maedi and won over the rest. Peace with Mithridates was granted on Roman terms, after which Sulla was compelled to hasten to Rome because, while he was busy winning victories over Mithridates in Greece and Asia (i.e. over a foreign foe), Marius and Cinna had recommenced hostilities at Rome, put to death the noblest of the senate and various ex-consuls and proscribed many. The rest of the senate quit Rome and fled to Sulla, begging him to save his country. He defeated Norbanus near Capua, killed seven thousand of Norbanus' men, captured six thousand and lost only 124 himself. Scipio's army came over to him without a fight (5.7). Against Marius junior he killed 15,000 and lost only 400. At the battle of the Colline Gate he cut down 58,000 and captured the remaining 12,000 (5.8). Eutropius accords Sulla the honour of having composed the troubles of the state, namely those two most lamentable wars, the Social and the Civil (5.9 and 6.1), in which more than 150,000 men had been killed, 24 consulars, 7 praetorians, 60 of aedile rank, and nearly 200 senators. Marius, by implication, is left as the villain of the piece. By contrast a brief, eminently fairer synopsis of the careers of Marius and Sulla is given by the unknown author of the *de Viris illustribus* (67 and 75). Another fourth-century writer, the author of the *Historia Augusta,* compares Commodus with Sulla as a mass-murderer and stigmatizes Septimius Severus as a Punic Sulla or a Punic Marius for putting countless senators to death[17].

There can be little doubt that Eutropius' sympathies were entirely pro-Sullan and decidedly pro-senatorial[18]. It is most unlikely that he was ignorant of the Gracchi and their activities: the author of the *de Viris illustribus* has chapters on both (64-65), the author of the *Historia Augusta* drags them in as alleged ancestors of the Gordians (*Gord.* 2.2), and Ammianus Marcellinus plainly knew of them (30.4.19). It appears that Marius and the Gracchi were, even in the fourth century, accepted as opponents of the senate, and the senatorial Eutropius deliberately chose to belittle the former while totally ignoring the latter. Sulla emerges as the hero of those difficult days with decidedly positive roles assigned to Q. Caecilius Metellus and Q. Lutatius Catulus, both members of the Roman nobility. In fact Catulus had been badly beaten by the Cimbri near Tridentum in 102 and had been compelled to give up the Po valley to the invaders. Marius joined him the following year and together they won the great victory over the Cimbri at the Raudine Plain[19]. Metellus, as censor in 102, tried to expel Saturninus and Glaucia from the senate; but this merely resulted in mob violence, and his colleague, Caprarius, would not back him. In 100 he was exiled for refusing an oath to observe Saturninus' agrarian law. Recalled soon afterwards, he never regained his political prominence. Neither Catulus nor Metellus was as significant in Roman history as the Gracchi or Marius, but to Eutropius they represented "the right stuff", the proper exemplars to set before the emperor Valens and other fourth-century readers.

Caesar also comes in for a good deal of criticism. In 6.19 Eutropius observes that the Civil War caused by Caesar's demand for a second consulship was truly execrable and deplorable, for, besides the havoc occurring in the various battles, the very fortune of the Roman people was changed: *Romani populi fortuna mutata est*. This phrase was regularly used when the state of things changed for the worse, as can be seen in Sallust and Velleius[20]. The consuls and the whole senate, according to Eutropius, left Rome and joined Pompey. At Pharsalus in 48 B.C. Eutropius tells us:

> Never before had a greater number of Roman forces assembled in one place or under better generals, forces which would easily have subdued the whole world, had they been led against barbarians (6.21)[21].

Here den Boer seems to be correct in observing that Eutropius does not subscribe to Victor's oblique praise of Caesar or share the admiration felt for him by Victor and the author of the *de Viris illustribus*[22]. Indeed, according to Eutropius, Caesar, after terminating the civil wars, returned to Rome and began to conduct himself with excessive arrogance, contrary to the usages of Roman liberty. He personally disposed of those positions of honour which the people had previously conferred, did not even rise when the Senate approached him, and exercised regal and almost tyrannical powers. The natural consequence of this was the conspiracy led by the two Bruti, of the family of that Brutus who had expelled the kings—a conspiracy which culminated with the assassination of Caesar. Book Seven begins with the renewal of the civil war because the senators favoured the assassins and Antony attempted to crush them. It was on that account *(ergo)*, Eutropius asserts, that the Republic was thrown into confusion and Antony, who was committing many crimes, was declared a public enemy. Unfortunately Octavian was reconciled to Antony through Lepidus and the three proceeded to proscribe the senate and put to death Cicero and many others of the nobility (7.2). Even more, including Cassius and Brutus, perished subsequently at Philippi and the republic was divided up among the conquerors (7.3). In effect that battle signified the end of the republic and of the senate's dominant role in politics. Eutropius was well aware of the fact; he makes no further mention of the senate until the reign of Nero and henceforth it is only its relationship with the emperors which is discussed.

Two of Rome's most "unpopular" emperors, Nero and Domitian, were guilty of putting to death many of the senators, and came to sticky ends[23]. In fact the senate went so far as to declare Nero a public enemy (7.15). "Good" emperors, however, such as Vespasian and Titus, were beloved and respected by the senate (7.20; 7.22), and Trajan, who stands preeminent in this list, did nothing unjust to any senator (8.4). Marcus Aurelius refused to lay taxes on the provinces or the senate, preferring to auction off his own and his wife's property (8.13). All were naturally deified[24]. Eutropius thereafter notes the senate's role in acclaiming several of the succeeding emperors, adding brief comments in a few instances[25]. The comments themselves are intriguing. Elagabalus arrived in Rome amid the great expectations of *both the army and the senate*. He behaved with such obscenity and utter shamelessness, however, that he was killed in a military revolt together with his mother (8.22). Aurelius Alexander succeeded him, acclaimed Caesar *by the army,* Augustus *by the senate* (8.23). This linkage of the army and the senate appears deliberate, though historically inaccurate in the latter case, since the senate actually proclaimed him Caesar in June, 221[26]. Indeed, the *Historia Augusta* criticizes and corrects Eutropius on this point[27]. Eutropius' objective here seems to be an attempt to show Valens that the army and the senate could and should work together.

The author then commences Book Nine with the telling statement that Maximinus succeeded Alexander:

> The first emperor who was elected from the military solely by the will of the soldiers since no authorization of the senate had been given and he himself was not a senator[28].

Eutropius' disapproval is evident, though not as explicit as that of Aurelius Victor[29].

Finally Eutropius informs his readers that Claudius succeeded Gallienus, chosen *by the soldiers* and declared emperor *by the senate* (9.11)[30]. Upon his death two years later the senate accorded him extraordinary honours, by deifying him and erecting a gold shield to him in the senate house and a gold statue on the Capitol. This felicitous harmony between the army and the senate continued into the next reign when *the army* elected an emperor Quintillus, Claudius' brother, *vir unicae moderationis èt civilitatis* (9.12). It was with the consent of *the senate* that he was acclaimed Augustus. Unfortunately, at least for Eutropius (and Aurelius Victor), the co-operation between the army and the senate was not to recur and Eutropius probably assumed that at this juncture the senate lost its role in conferring legitimacy on the appointees of the army[31]. At any event the author makes no further mention of the august body, although he continues to register the consecration of the emperors down to Jovian, and this, according to den Boer[32], was the most important senatorial prerogative. One can only presume that Eutropius felt that he had made his case in the earlier chapters for the harmonious co-operation of the emperor, the army and senate, the three essential elements of the empire. Den Boer has also observed that Eutropius, unlike Victor, "keeps silent on the pusillanimity of the senate[33]". This is to be expected. The political climate had changed in the decade since the appearance of the *de Caesaribus* and by 369 the senate was more in need of support than criticism. Six years later, with the accession of Gratian to the throne, the pendulum had swung again. Within a brief period the supporters of Valentinian had been removed (some were even executed) and the senate became reconciled with the court. Its members once more served in their accustomed offices of state and criminal cases involving them now went before the urban prefect and his special court, the *iudicium quinquevirale*. The following year *clarissimi* were no longer subject to torture. No wonder Symmachus could rejoice over the beginnings of a new *saeculum*[34].

Under such circumstances the carefully crafted defence of the senate in the **Breviarium** would not have been necessary and the work may have been quite different. The Emperor Gratian had by then reassured the senatorial aristocracy of its three points of concern: the protection of property, personal security and social standing.

Notes

[1] In the dedication of his work he describes himself as *vir clarissimus*.

[2] For the evidence *vid. the Prosopography of the Later Roman Empire,* Cambridge, 1971, 317.

[3] W. den Boer, *Some Minor Roman Historians,* Leiden, 1972, 150; A. Momigliano, *Essays in Ancient and Modern Historiography,* Oxford, 1977, 174.

[4] Ammianus, 30.8.10; cf. *Epit.* 45. According to Procopius, Valens was a *Pannonius degener* (Ammianus, 26.7.16).

[5] A. H. M. Jones, *the Later Roman Empire,* Oxford, 1964, 141; J. Matthews, *Western Aristocracies and the Imperial Court* A.D. *364-425,* Oxford, 1975, 35-41.

[6] A. Alfoldi, *a Conflict of Ideas in the Late Roman Empire; the Clash between the Senate and Valentinian I,* Oxford, 1952, 48ff; E. A. Thompson, *the Historical Work of Ammianus Marcellinus,* Cambridge, 1947, 101-102; C. Schuurmans, "Valentinien I et le senat romain", *Antiq. class.,* 18, 1949, 25. But cf. Matthews, *loc. cit.*

[7] Eutrop., 8.2; 9.15.

[8] Ammianus, 15.1.3; 29.5.46; Victor, *de Caes.,* 5.4; 8.8; Festus, 26; 28.

[9] Symm., *Ep.,* I, 52.

[10] *Vid.,* the telling statement in the dedication: "that your Serenity's divine mind may rejoice to learn that it has followed the actions of illustrious men in governing the empire . . ."

[11] Ammianus describes Valens as *"subagrestis ingenii, nec bellicis nec liberalibus studiis eruditus"* (31.14.5) and *"inconsummatus et rudis"* (31.14.8).

[12] Eutrop., 1.2; 1.6; 1.13; 2.5; 2.9; 2.23; 2.25; 2.27; 3.10; 3.21; 4.4; 4.17; 4.20; 4.21; 4.24.

[13] Eutrop., 2.9; 4.17; 4.24.

[14] *Op. cit.,* p. 166.

[15] Eutrop., 4.13; 4.14; 4.16; 4.21; 4.23; 4.25. On their importance *vid.* E. Gruen, *Roman Politics and the Criminal Courts 149-78* B.C., Cambridge, Mass., 1968, ch. IV.

[16] E. Gabba, "le Origini dell'esercito professionale in Roma: i proletari e la riforma di Mario", *Athenaeum,* 27, 1949, 173-209; *id.,* "Ricerche sull'esercito professionals romano da Mario ad Augusto", *Athenaeum,* 29, 1951, 171-272; R. E. Smith, *Service in the Post-Marian Roman Army,* Manchester, 1958, 9ff; G.R. Watson, *the Roman Soldier,* Bristol, 1969, 21-22; H. Last, *C. A. H.,* IX, 1932, 133-137, 146-147.

[17] *H. A. Comm.,* 8.1; *Pesc. Nig.,* 6.4. For other negative impressions of Sulla in the *Historia Augusta, vid., Carac.,* 2.2; 4.10; 5.4.

[18] For emphasis on the bad treatment of the senate *vid.* Eutrop., 7.2; 7.3; 7.14; 9.1; 9.14; 10.11. Cf. 8.4; 8.8; 8.13.

[19] *Vid.,* T. F. Carney, "Marius' Choice of Battlefield in the Campaign of 101", *Athenaeum,* 36, 1958, 229-237.

[20] Sallust., *Cat.,* 2; *Jug.,* 17; Vell. Pat., 2.57.118; cf. Aur. Victor, *de Caes.,* 24.11.

[21] Cf. 10.12, where the Battle of Mursa in A.D. 351 is similarly described.

[22] *Op. cit.,* p. 155.

[23] Eutrop., 7.14-15; 7.23.

[24] For the consecration of the emperors *vid.* den Boer, *op. cit.,* 151-158. He observes that Eutropius is unique "in recording the *consecratio* (or its omission) of nearly all the emperors".

[25] Eutrop., 8.16; 8.23; 9.7; 9.11; 9.12.

[26] *Fer. Dur.,* II, 16/17; *H. A. Alex.,* 1.2; *Heliog.,* 1.5; S. Dusanic, "Severus Alexander as Elagabalus' Associate", *Historia,* 13, 1964, 487-498.

[27] *H.A. Heliog.,* 64.4-5; T.D. Barnes, the Lost Kaisergeschichte and the Latin Historical Tradition", *B.H.A.C. 1968/69,* 1970, 38.

[28] Cf. Victor, *de Caes.,* 25.1; *H.A. Max. Duo,* 8.1.

[29] *De Caes.,* 25.2.

[30] Cf. Victor, *de Caes.,* 34.1; *H. A. Gall.,* 15.3; *Claud.,* 1.1-2; Zos., 1.46; *Oros.,* 7.23.1; Syn Sathas, p. 39. Victor here applauds what he considers to be the one positive action of a generally corrupt and venal army.

[31] Victor (*de Caes.,* 36) believed that the senate won back from the army its right to select emperors when it chose Aurelius' successor, Tacitus. The *H. A.* concurred; *"quam gravis senatus auctoritas fuit"* (*Tac.,* 2.2).

[32] *Op. cit.,* p. 151. Den Boer also suggests (p. 161) that "the hostility between the soldiers and senate largely determined Eutropius' view of the past and particularly of the previous century. He must have agreed with Victor . . .".

[33] *Ibid.*

[34] *Ep.,* I.13. For a sound account of this period *vid.* Matthews, *op. cit.,* 64-87.

H. W. Bird (essay date 1988)

SOURCE: "Eutropius: His Life and Career," *Echos du Monde Classique/Classical Views,* Vol. 32, n.s., No. 7, 1988, pp. 51-60.

[*In the essay that follows, Bird attempts to reconstruct the details of Eutropius's life, particularly his career as a Roman administrator.*]

In spite of the confident assertions of many modern scholars,[1] what we know for certain about the life and career of Eutropius, the author of the once popular **Breviarium ab urbe condita,** is extremely limited. What follows, therefore, is a considered, but tentative, reconstruction.

Eutropius, like his contemporary and fellow-abbreviator, Sextus Aurelius Victor, was born soon after A.D. 320,[2] for he is called a contemporary of the Emperors Valens (b. 328?) and Julian (b. 331)[3] and must have been at least in his mid- to late thirties when he was *magister epistularum* of Constantius prior to 361,[4] and somewhat older in 369 when he served in the senior position of *magister memoriae* under Valens.[5] It is possible that he was born in Italy,[6] but his name and the fact that he owned estates in Asia[7] and certainly spent most of his career in the East may indicate that his family had connections in Asia. At any rate, it is highly unlikely that he was a medical man from Bordeaux, as some modern scholars believe.[8]

His family was apparently well-to-do but not of senatorial rank for, although Eutropius must have received a good education to gain entry into the *sacra scrinia,* these offices were not regarded as fashionable by senatorials. As a consequence, they attracted men of the middle classes.[9] Furthermore, it seems likely that Eutropius knew Greek reasonably well in view of his prominent position in the Eastern bureaucracy. Indeed, although this may have been common knowledge, he realized that Julian was extremely well-versed in Greek literature.[10] There are three other possible indications. He notes that Hadrian and Marcus Aurelius were very learned in Greek, describes how Lucius Verus was "struck with a rush of blood which the Greeks call *apoplexis*" and informs us that Constantine's death was foretold by a "*crinita stella* which the Greeks call a comet."[11] He would also have studied law since his posts entailed much legal work, he shows a distinct fondness for Numa Pompilius, Rome's first lawgiver,[12] and he was able to give a concise but shrewd critique of the laws enacted by Constantine.[13]

At least part of Eutropius' education probably took place at Rome. In 370 Valentinian enacted a law which put the urban prefect in charge of students at Rome.[14] The prefect was responsible for maintaining order among the students, for ensuring that they did not evade their responsibilities in their home towns, and for drawing up a list of the best students for the emperor, so that they might have suitable employment found for them in the administration.[15] A similar system almost certainly existed under Constantius II when Eutropius was completing his education, and the future historian was presumably among those bright young students at Rome who gained entry into the *sacra scrinia* in ca. 345.

His first post may well have been that of clerk *(exceptor)* in the *scrinium epistularum,* which was under the *magister epistularum* and employed, at least under Leo I (456-474), thirty-four clerks all told.[16] Promotion was strictly by seniority, each clerk rising step-by-step until he became *melloproximus* and finally *proximus,* the senior member of his *scrinium.* Progress at first must have been slow as the *proximi* served three years.[17] On the other hand, death, early retirement and the fluctuating political scene between 340 and 355 may have accelerated the process. At any rate, it seems reasonable to accept that Eutropius had risen to be *magister epistularum* by 361. Among his various functions in the *scrinium,* he would have handled judicial petitions and *relationes* and drafted rescripts, checked the judicial records of provincial governors, received all manner of petitions and read out in the consistory the requests of provincial and diocesan delegations. He would also have dealt with military and grain supply reports and issued *probatoriae* to officials of the praetorian and urban prefects, proconsuls and vicars.[18] During this period he would presumably have become acquainted with Constantius II and a number of his officers, for his curt description of the emperor's defeats by the Persians, especially the one in 348 near Singara, gives the impression that it derived from the account of an eyewitness.[19]

When Constantius died at Mopsucrenae, the last station in Cilicia between that province and Cappadocia, on November 3, 361, Eutropius was, in all likelihood, still on the imperial staff. His statement that Constantius "enriched his friends and allowed none whose active service he had experienced to go unrewarded" (10.15) has the distinct appearance of a personal comment. Furthermore, Ammianus maintains that under Constantius "no one who was to hold a high position was appointed to a post at the palace suddenly or untried, but a man who after ten years was to be *magister officiorum* or *comes largitionum* or appointed to any similar position, was thoroughly known."[20]

Julian reached Constantinople on December 11, 361 and soon afterwards set up an investigatory committee, comprising Mamertinus, Arbitio, Agilo, Nevitta and Jovinus, under his new praetorian prefect, Salutius Secundus. The committee met at Chalcedon, in the presence of the commanders and tribunes of Joviani and Herculiani, and ultimately banished Palladius *(exmagister officiorum),* Taurus (ex-praetorian prefect), Florentius (the *magister officiorum*), Saturninus *(ex cura palatii),* Euagrius *(comes rei privatae)* and Cyrinus *(exnotarius),* and ordered the execution of another Florentius (consul and expraetorian prefect), Ursulus *(comes largitionum),* Apodemius *(ex-agens in rebus),* Paulus *(notarius)* and Eusebius *(cura thalami).*[21] Eutropius was probably also investigated, but clearly was exonerated of any wrong-doing or antipathy towards Julian, for he informs us that he was with Julian on the Persian campaign in 363 (10.16), probably as a senior administrator and perhaps even as *magister epistularum.* Whenever any emperor died his administrators went on with their business unless replaced.

The new emperor would invariably have to keep the government functioning, reward his friends and supporters, and try to conciliate those who could be won over, in addition to retaining the support of the army. Julian did, indeed, make numerous attempts to improve the bureaucracy, cutting out many notaries and *agentes.* His appointments were made on the grounds of proven competence and his senior officials were generally professional administrators and intellectuals from whom Julian demanded honesty and hard work. As Browning put it: "None pursued this policy as systematically as Julian."[22]

Eutropius was perhaps also among the military and court officials who met after Julian's death in June, 363 to choose his successor. He would have belonged to the *residui e palatio Constanti* under Arintheus and Victor who vied with the military faction of Nevitta and Dagalaifus in selecting a new emperor.[23] In view of his subsequent career, however, it seems hardly likely that he did or said anything to offend either party. Nevertheless Eutropius may not have been with Jovian when that emperor died suddenly at Dadastana on the Bithynian-Galatian border on February 17, 364. Three differing accounts of the emperor's death are given, yet the author comes to no personal conclusions (10.18). Eutropius was perhaps left at Antioch in early 364 to deal with administrative matters there when Jovian decided to hurry back to Constantinople.

At the end of February, 364 Valentinian, also a Pannonian officer like Jovian, and recently promoted by the latter to be tribune of one of the *scholae,* was unanimously elected emperor by the chief civil and military leaders. In view of the argument above, it would appear that Eutropius did not take part in the election, but he does observe that Jovian "was deified through the kindness of the emperors who succeeded him, for he was inclined to equity and liberal by nature."[24] These positive remarks about Jovian and the implicit praise of Valentinian and Valens, in addition to the statement by Ammianus that Jovian made few promotions and was rather selective,[25] probably indicate that Eutropius had served as a senior official in the administration of Jovian and had been kept on by Valens.

Valentinian had little liking for the men of letters favoured by Julian or for Roman aristocrats.[26] Two successive *magistri officiorum* of Valentinian, Remigius and Leo, both of humble origins, began their careers as financial clerks in the office of one of the *magistri militum.* Maximinus, son of a *cohortalis,* practiced at the bar, became *praeses* of Corsica and of Sardinia, *corrector* of Tuscia, *praefectus annonae* at Rome, vicar of Rome and *praetorian prefect.*[27] Valens, the Eastern Emperor, had less to do with the Roman aristocracy, and seems to have enjoyed a better reputation than his brother.[28] He was loyal to his friends, rarely changed his officials and was strict in maintaining discipline in the army and in civil life.[29] Eutropius' dedication of his work to Valens is itself a sign of the author's gratitude and loyalty to the emperor. He presumably expected favourable treatment from the emperor in return. In addition, Eutropius refers several times throughout the *Breviarium* to those notable Roman generals or emperors who restored or maintained military discipline.[30] This, too, would have flattered Valens. Finally, the statements of both Ammianus and the Epitomator, that Valens was slow to replace his officials, also indicate that Eutropius was probably kept on by Valens. If so, where did Eutropius meet Valens? It has been suggested that in 364 Eutropius was at Antioch, the imperial residence from 362 when Julian was mounting his Persian expedition. Valentinian and Valens parted company at Sirmium in August, 364 and Valens spent the winter at Constantinople. At the end of winter, possibly in March 365, Valens hastened to Antioch, and it was probably here that he made the acquaintance of Eutropius. In the meantime Procopius had seized the opportunity offered by Valen's departure from Constantinople to make a play for the throne.[31] He won over Constantinople, Thrace, Nicaea Chalcedon and Bithynia, but by mid-winter of that year he had been deserted by his followers and executed by Valens.[32] Many of his followers or suspected followers were put to death, exiled or demoted.[33] Clearly Eutropius was not among them, so he could hardly have been at Constantinople or in any of those areas controlled by Procopius. He had been fortunate.

In the period 367-369 Valens was fighting in the region of the lower Danube against the Goths who had sent aid to Procopius.[34] It appears that Eutropius had accompanied the emperor, for he demonstrates items of precise information about the region. He knew the names of the tribes living there in 369 (the Thaiphali, Victohali and Thervingi), as well as the fact that the old province of Dacia was a thousand miles in circumference (8.2). In addition, he seems to have seen the exact place where Aurelian was assassinated, on the "old paved road between Constantinople and Heraclea, in a place which is called Caenophrurium" (9.15). Thus it was during these years (367-369) that Eutropius was promoted to the position of *magister memoriae* of the East, since he held this position in 369 when he dedicated his work to the emperor. Indeed, it is quite possible that the writing of the *Breviarium* was Eutropius' way of expressing his gratitude to Valens for his promotion to the largest and most important of the three *scrinia*.[35] Valens clearly held Eutropius in high esteem even prior to the composition of the *Breviarium.* The careful wording of the dedication (i.e., "that your Serenity's divine mind may rejoice to learn that it has followed the actions of illustrious men in governing the empire") and some of the contents of the work will have given the emperor further cause to favour its author. There are also hints throughout the Imperial section of the work that Eutropius regarded the emperors' loyalty and generosity towards their friends as very significant imperial virtues.[36] As a corollary to this he emphatically criticizes Maximian and Constantine for their cruelty and faithlessness towards their friends and, in the case of Constantine, even towards his relatives.[37] Eutropius' own loyalty and competence had paid off. He had successfully served these emperors and could look forward to further service and even further promotion.

This apparently occurred soon afterwards, in 371, when Ammianus informs us that a Eutropius was proconsul of Asia.[38] It would be reasonable to assume that Valens' loyal administrator (and eulogizer in the *Breviarium*) had been suitably rewarded with a senior Eastern position for which he was clearly well-equipped.[39] Asia, like Africa, was a special province, standing outside the official hierarchy inasmuch as it was not under the disposition of the Vicar of Asiana or of the praetorian prefect.[40] This gave Eutropius direct access to the emperor, yet another privilege for the author. While governing his province, he received a constitution on the restoration to the cities of Asia of part of their civic lands and he restored buildings at Magnesia on the Maeander.[41] Unfortunately his proconsulship was not to have a happy ending. Caught up in a vast web of deceit when a plot against Valens was discovered, Eutropius was summoned to Antioch on the charge of complicity. Although the philosopher Pasiphilus was cruelly tortured to force him falsely to implicate Eutropius, he bravely refused to do so, and Eutropius escaped the mass of executions of both innocent and guilty alike.[42] His career, however, suffered as a result. He was replaced as proconsul of Asia by Festinus of Tridentum, who may probably be identified with Festus, the author of yet another and even shorter *Breviarium* dedicated to Valens in ca. 370. Festus had also succeeded Eutropius as *magister memoriae*.[43]

In 375 the emperor Valentinian I died of apoplexy and his position in the West was taken by his elder son, Gratian. The latter drove the Alamans out of Gaul and re-established the Rhine frontier. Meanwhile, the Huns had forced the Goths from their homes north of the Danube. Some of the Thervingian Goths were transported into Thrace by Valens in 376, while another group of Greuthungian Goths crossed the Danube by themselves. Thrace became a battleground and the Romans suffered considerable losses, which caused Valens to leave Antioch for Thrace and Gratian to march to his assistance. Before the latter could arrive, however, Valens attacked a force of Goths outside Adrianople on August 9, 378. It was a disaster: the Roman army was cut to pieces and Valens perished, his body vanishing in the mêlée. Still, the Goths failed to capture Adrianople and, though joined by bands of Huns and Alans, were equally unsuccessful when they attacked Constantinople. Gratian swiftly chose as coruler Theodosius, who was proclaimed Augustus in

January, 379 at Sirmium. Four years of fighting and negotiating ensued, but finally a peace treaty was struck with the Goths in October, 382. They were settled in vacant lands south of the Danube, retaining their own ruler and laws but bound to Rome by an alliance. In return for annual food subsidies they provided the empire with soldiers.

It appears that sometime after 372 Eutropius travelled to Rome and here he made the acquaintance of Q. Aurelius Symmachus, a distinguished aristocrat and one of the most notable orators and writers of the period, who held the prefecture of Rome in 384 and the consulship in 391.[44] Again the evidence depends entirely on the coincidence of names, but the historian possessed those necessary qualifications which would permit access to Symmachus' circle. He was a writer whose work was becoming well-known since it was soon to be used by Ammianus, Jerome and Orosius and translated into Greek by Paeanius. Furthermore, he had held senior positions in the civil administration (obtaining thereby the *clarissimate*), and must have retained powerful and influential friends. Finally, he was a pagan, which would have endeared him to Symmachus (who was the most prominent champion of paganism at that time), and, as his work demonstrates throughout, a convinced supporter of the senatorial cause.

Gratian's court, packed with the friends and relatives of the professor and poet Ausonius, was more kindly disposed towards the aristocracy and those of a literary background. Eutropius evidently benefitted from the new dispensation and found himself in favour with Theodosius. In 379 Symmachus wrote to Eutropius to enlist his support for a friend, Postumianus.[45] Symmachus would hardly have made such a request if Eutropius had not possessed influence. Postumianus profited from his friend's assistance. He held offices in the Eastern administration before obtaining the Eastern prefecture in 383.[46] Theodosius followed the precedent of Valens and other eastern emperors in employing as praetorian prefects those who had proved their efficiency in lower offices.[47] Eutropius was also to benefit further from the death of Valens in 378. In early January 380, a year after Theodosius had been installed as Augustus of the East, the historian was appointed prefect of Illyricum. Eutropius presumably spent the two years of his tenure at Thessalonica and Constantinople while Theodosius fought and negotiated with the Goths to the north.[48] During his tenure of office he possibly influenced the enactment of a substantial number of laws, some of which lessened the severe punishment for various crimes.[49] This conforms with what we know of Eutropius' disposition from his work, for there are numerous indications throughout the **Breviarium** which indicate that Eutropius was vehemently opposed to cruelty and severity and esteemed justice and moderation.[50] For example, Maximian's cruelty is twice castigated very sharply,[51] and Constantine is criticized for enacting many superfluous laws, some of them severe.[52]

After concluding his prefecture in late 381 Eutropius probably stayed on in Constantinople, and certainly continued to enjoy the approval and esteem of the emperor Theodosius and other notables. Symmachus wrote to him in 387 and Libanius in 390.[53] Indeed, the crowning achievement of his career came in 387 when he was elected Eastern consul, with the emperor Valentinian II as his Western counterpart.[54] This was a signal distinction, for the ordinary consulship was still "the one ancient Republican office which retained its glamour untarnished."[55]

Eutropius' outstanding career, spanning the reigns of the emperors Constantius II to Theodosius, is a clear indication that he was extremely competent and loyal, and probably a shrewd survivor. He must have earned the respect not only of a succession of emperors of diverse character and interests, but also of military leaders, senior civilian officials and leading senatorials, a remarkably difficult task given the nature of the times. Moreover, his successful career, together with that of his close contemporary, Sextus Aurelius Victor, demonstrates that the bureaucracy of the second half of the fourth century contained men of integrity and moderation despite the well-founded strictures of Ammianus. How much the publication of the **Breviarium** assisted him we cannot say, but it is highly likely that Valens, Gratian, Theodosius, Libanius, Symmachus and others were suitably impressed. Modern critics, such as Sir Ronald Syme, may indeed scorn the work as "a poor and scrappy production."[56] Nevertheless, it certainly helped to promote the career of a decent and efficient administrator who apparently lived up to the meaning of his name: he was both versatile and of a gentle disposition.[57]

Notes

[1] E.g., A. H. M. Jones, J. R. Martindale, J. Morris, *The Prosopography of the Later Roman Empire* (Cambridge 1971) 317 (henceforth cited as *PLRE*); J. Matthews, "Continuity in a Roman Family: The Rufii Festi of Volsinii," *Historia* 16 (1967) 494-495; *id., Western Aristocracies and the Imperial Court* A.D. *364-425* (Oxford 1975) 8, 9, 73, 96, 97, 107. For some inconsistencies and errors in the *PLRE* see T. D. Barnes, *Phoenix* 26 (1972) 140ff.; *Phoenix* 27 (1973) 135ff. W. den Boer (*Some Minor Roman Historians,* [Leiden 1972] 114-115) has some sensible words of caution about drawing "far-reaching conclusions from an instance of identical names."

[2] H. W. Bird, *Sextus Aurelius Victor: A Historiographical Study* (Liverpool 1984) 5.

[3] Nicephorus Gregoras, *Or. in Constant. Magn.* (in Lambecius, *comm. de bibl. Vindob.* VIII.136ff.).

[4] *Scr. Orig. Cpl.* II.144. The author mistakenly identifies him as *epistolographos* of Constantine, but this is clearly improbable since Constantine died in 337, his son Constantine II in 340.

[5] Eutrop. *Brev. dedicatio.* This and the fact that he was with Julian on the Persian campaign in 363 (Eutrop. 10.16) are the only pieces of totally incontestable evidence for Eutropius' life and career.

[6] *Suda* s.v. Eutropius, where he is called an Italian sophist.

[7] Symm. *Ep.* III.53.

[8] *PLRE, loc. cit.;* Matthews, *loc. cit.;* R. Syme, *Ammianus Marcellinus and the Historia Augusta* (Oxford 1968) 105, agrees with Matthews. Cf. the strong warning of den Boer, *loc. cit.*

[9] A. H. M. Jones, *The Later Roman Empire,* vol. II (Oxford 1964) 577-578.

[10] Eutrop. 10.16.

[11] Eutrop. 8.7; 8.10; 8.12; 10.8. *Epit.* 16.5 probably derives from Eutrop. 8.10. There are twenty-two other indications that the Epitomator borrowed material from Eutropius.

[12] H. W. Bird, "Eutroius on Numa Pompilius and the Senate," *CJ* 81 (1986) 243-244, emphasizes this.

[13] Eutrop. 10.8. He also notes that Diocletian made many judicious arrangements and regulations still in effect in 369/370 (Eutrop. 9.23), and that Ulpian was the *conditor iuris* (Eutrop. 8.23).

[14] *Cod. Theod.* XIV.9.1.

[15] H. I. Marrou, *A History of Education in Antiquity,* trans. G. Lamb (London 1956) 310-311.

[16] See n.4 and Jones, *LRE,* vol. II, 576.

[17] Jones, *loc. cit.*

[18] *Ibid.* Hence presumably his precise knowledge of many geographical locations throughout the empire, e.g., 10.5; 10.8; 10.9; 10.12.

[19] Eutrop. 10.10. Cf. Ammianus, 18.5.7; *Chron. min.* 1.236; Festus, 27; Jerome, *Chron.* 236. See T. D. Barnes, *Phoenix* 34 (1980) 163-164.

[20] Ammianus 21.16.3.

[21] Ammianus 22.2.4ff.

[22] R. Browning, *The Emperor Julian* (Berkeley 1976) 128.

[23] Ammianus 25.5.1ff.

[24] Eutrop. 10.18.2.

[25] Ammianus 25.10.15.

[26] Jones, *LRE,* vol. I, 141-142; E. A. Thompson, *The Historical Work of Ammianus Marcellinus* (Cambridge 1947) 102ff.; A. Alföldi, *A Conflict of ideas in the Late Roman Empire; the Clash between the Senate and Valentinian II* (Oxford 1952) *passim.*

[27] Jones, *loc. cit.* The similar careers of others are also listed.

[28] Jones, *LRE,* vol. I, 147, citing Ammianus and Themistius; the Epitomator (*Epit.* 46.3) concurs.

[29] Ammianus 31.14.2ff.; *Epit.* 46.3.

[30] Eutrop. 4.19; 4.27; 8.7; 8.23; 9.14.

[31] Ammianus 26.6.10ff.

[32] Ammianus 26.9.1ff.

[33] Ammianus 26.10.1ff.

[34] Ammianus 27.5.1ff.

[35] For their relative size, functions and importance see Jones, *LRE,* vol. II, 576.

[36] Eutrop. 7.8; 7.13; 7.19; 7.21; 8.4; 8.5; 8.8; 8.12; 9.7; 10.7; 10.15; 10.16.

[37] Eutrop. 10.5; 10.6.

[38] Ammianus 29.1.36; Lib. *Or.* 1.159; Greg. Naz. *Ep.* 71.

[39] Despite the reasoned scepticism of den Boer *(loc. cit.),* I find it much less likely that Valens would have chosen an otherwise unknown Eutropius for this position at this particular juncture so soon after the appearance of the *Breviarium.*

[40] Jones, *LRE,* vol. I, 275.

[41] Bruns, *Fontes*[7], 97; *Hell.* IV.63, cited in *PLRE,* 317.

[42] Ammianus 29.1.1ff., esp. 29.2.36; Lib. *Or.* 1.159.

[43] Ammianus 29.2.22; Eunapius 7.6.6-13; Syme, *loc.*

cit. in n.8; *PLRE*, 317, 334-335; cf. den Boer, *op. cit.* , 178, 181; J. W. Eadie, *The Breviarium of Festus, A Critical Edition with Historical Commentary* (London 1967) 1ff.

[44] Symm. *Ep.* III.46-51; Greg. Naz. *Ep.* 70-71. For Symmachus see *PLRE*, 865-870.

[45] Symm. *Ep.* III.48.

[46] Matthews, "Continuity in a Roman Family" (see n.1) 495.

[47] A. H. M. Jones, "Collegiate Prefectures," *JRS* 54 (1964) 79; *LRE*, vol. I, 161. Presumably Theodosius appointed him, though perhaps on the recommendation of Gratian. Eutropius' continued appointments in the East, particularly this one, lead me to conclude that he was not an Aquitanian: cf. Matthews, *loc. cit.* in n.46.

[48] Jones, *LRE*, vol. I, 156.

[49] *PLRE*, 317. His influence with Theodosius is demonstrated by the posts to which the emperor appointed him.

[50] E.g., Eutrop. 1.3; 1.13; 4.17; 4.27; 7.12; 7.13; 7.16; 7.19; 7.20; 7.21; 8.1; 8.4-5; 8.8; 8.14; 9.14; 9.17; 9.23; 9.27; 10.3; 10.6.

[51] Eutrop. 9.27; 10.3.

[52] Eutrop. 10.8.

[53] Symm. *Ep.* III.52-53; Lib. *Ep.* 979.

[54] For the evidence see *PLRE*, 317.

[55] Jones, *LRE*, vol. II, 531-532. S. Dill (*Roman Society in the Last Century of the Roman Empire* [London 1899], 145) describes the consulship of the fourth century A.D. as "one of those dignified fictions by which the Romans distinguished the vastness which separated them from the days of freedom."

[56] Syme, *loc. cit.* in n.8.

[57] Regarding the date of the dedication, it seems likely to me that Eutropius would present his work to Valens as a special gift when the emperor celebrated his triumph over the Goths and assumed the title Gothicus Maximus. This probably took place in late 369 at Constantinople. I should like to thank the anonymous referee for several helpful hints.

H. W. Bird (essay date 1990)

SOURCE: "Structure and Themes in Eutropius's *Breviarium*," *The Classical Bulletin*, Vol. 66, Nos. 3-4, 1990, pp. 87-92.

[*In the following essay, Bird contends that Livy's* Epitome *provided Eutropius with a model by which to organize the book-divisions and themes of the* Breviarium.]

When Eutropius came to write his abridged history of Rome in A.D. 369 he must have had a plan of composition, some idea of how long he wished to make his work, which sources he would utilize. He may even have discussed some of the particulars with his emperor, Valens, as the first words of the *proemium* seem to indicate, and the emperor's suggestions would not have been lightly disregarded. What Valens apparently wanted was a concise, straightforward but comprehensive history of Rome from its foundation down to the death of Jovian some five years earlier, when Valentinian and Valens had come to power. One major reason is manifest. According to Ammianus, Valens was somewhat lazy, *subagrestis ingenii . . . nec liberalibus studiis eruditus.*[1] He is also described as a *cessator et piger, inconsummatus et rudis.*[2] This was the emperor for whom Eutropius was writing, consequently the history in order to be palatable, would have to be clear, concise and simple in both design and language. Eutropius complied. There would be no need of documentation or a multiplicity of sources and it appears that Eutropius generally followed only three or four major sources (including Fabius Pictor[3] and an *Epitome* of Livy) for the republican period, and only the *Kaisergeschichte* for the imperial period.

Eutropius certainly computed with care the number of years he would be covering, for he is quite precise, if not totally accurate, in his dating of Rome's foundation, the twenty-first day of April in the third year of the sixth Olympiad and the three hundred and ninety-fourth after the destruction of Troy,[4] and he concludes his work by twice stating that in the year when Jovian made his shameful peace with Persia and died, Rome was one thousand, one hundred and eighteen years old. But how was he to separate that vast period into manageable sections? Not by centuries, that is abundantly clear. Livy's monumental history had been divided by copyists into pentads and decads, and the *Epitome* of his work would conveniently conform, whereas Tacitus' *Annals* and *Histories* appear to have been composed in hexads.[5] The consular historian, however, was not popular in antiquity and Eutropius, unlike Ammianus, probably never even considered emulating him in any way.[6] For such a circumscribed work as the ***Breviarium*** that would have proven tedious and otiose. Recourse to Livy's *Epitome* for source material would cause Eutropius to consider that format as a model, and for that reason he may have decided to structure his work in ten books. At any rate Eutropius' first book dealing with Roman history from the city's foundation to its destruction by the Gauls in 390 B.C., coincides with the material covered by Livy (and his *Epitome*) in books one to five. Livy then described the course of Roman history from the aftermath of the Gallic invasion to the conclusion of the First Punic War in his next fifteen books. Eutropius condenses this material into his second book, incorporating in ten chapters (18-27) the all important First Punic War, which Livy had covered in five books (16-20), but appending, almost as an afterthought, a brief note on Rome's success against the Falisci. This may well indicate recourse to a different source, with Eutropius following the Livian *Epitome* for his outline but not for all of his material, as Pirogoff argued in 1873.[7] Nevertheless both Livy and Eutropius concur in emphasizing the importance of the Gauls' sack of Rome and the Romans' victory over Carthage in the First Punic War.

Livy's next decad, books twenty-one to thirty, is occupied with the narrative of the Second Punic War and contains a large number of exciting incidents and vivid descriptions. It begins (21) with a character description of Hannibal, the siege of Saguntum and Hannibal's crossing of the Alps, and ends with the Battle of Zama. Eutropius also spends three quarters of Book Three (7-23) on the Second Punic War and concludes it with the Romans' victory at Zama. Nonetheless Eutropius had other things in mind at the beginning of Book Three: he realized and was at pains to emphasize that the Romans' defeat of Carthage in the First War had made Rome an international power for the first time. Accordingly the Romans offered assistance to Egypt against Antiochus of Syria and entertained Hiero of Syracuse, who came to the city with a substantial gift of wheat. It was natural that both Livy and Eutropius should follow their accounts of the conclusion of the Second Punic War with descriptions of the Macedonian and Syrian Wars. Livy, as it would appear to Eutropius, covered these events in pentads in his next fifteen books (31-45), but here Eutropius seems to have discovered that he could no longer adhere to a modified Livian format and he pushed his fourth book down to the end of the Jugurthine War, adding, in his final paragraph, almost as an afterthought, the Romans' early victory against the Cimbri in Gaul, and other successes against the Scordisci, Triballi and Lusitani. Another noticeable distinction between the two authors at this point is that whereas Livy described at length the Third Punic War and the destruction of Carthage (Book 51), and also the careers of the Gracchi (Book 57ff), Eutropius was content with a brief report of the former (4.10 and 4.12) and deliberately omitted all mention of the latter. For Livy and Sallust[8] the destruction of Carthage (and Corinth) in 146 B.C. marked a watershed in Roman history. Such appears not to have been the case with Eutropius. Furthermore, the fourth century senator preferred to bury in oblivion those two assailants of the Senate's powers and prerogatives, the Gracchi.[9]

Eutropius' Book Five is significantly shorter than the other nine. The general length of each book is between six-and-a-half and eight pages, though Book One is slightly shorter, but Book Five is only three-and-a-half pages long. It commences with the Romans' losses to and eventual victories over the Cimbri and Teutones, then covers the Social War, the beginning of the Civil War and the Mithridatic War, and ends with the Sullan party's success in the Civil War and Sulla's triumph for his victory over Mithridates. Sulla is the real hero of this book, Marius is the villain. Eutropius introduces Sulla at the end of Book Four as Marius' distinguished quaestor who was responsible for Jugurtha's capture, and again mentions him, at the very beginning of Book Six, as the man who *rem publicam composuisset*. But the tremendous historical significance Eutropius attributes to this period is best demonstrated by the final few lines of Book Five:

> *This was the end of the two most destructive wars, the Italian, which was also called the Social War, and the Civil War, which together lasted for ten years. Nevertheless they destroyed over a hundred and fifty thousand men, twenty-four ex-consuls, seven ex-praetors, sixty former aediles and almost two hundred senators.*

For Eutropius it was a series of destructive civil wars which sounded the death knell of the Republic and for these he held Marius and Caesar chiefly responsible. Accordingly, just as Book Five was the book of Sulla and Marius, Book Six is really the book of Pompey and Caesar, the former acting as hero, the latter as villain. Pompey is introduced in a very positive manner at the end of Book Five for his successes in Sicily and Africa and his triumph at the age of twenty-three, something totally unprecedented at Rome. Thereafter much of Book Six is devoted to his exploits. Caesar is introduced as consul half-way through the book. After the description of his Gallic campaigns Caesar is blamed for starting:

> *bellum civila—exsecrandum et lacrimabile. Quo praeter calamitates, quae in proeliis acciderunt, etiam populi Romani fortuna mutata est.*[10]

What Eutropius means by that is explained at end of the book. After terminating the civil war throughout the world Caesar returned to Rome and began to act *insolentius . . . et contra consuetudinem Romanae libertatis*. He assigned offices at his own discretion which the people had previously conferred, did not even rise to greet the senate, and did other things of a regal or almost tyrannical nature.[11] Consequently a conspiracy was formed against him and he was assassinated. There can be no doubt that Eutropius felt that Caesar had destroyed the republic and created a different form of government, for when he introduced Caesar in chapter seventeen Eutropius writes *C. Julius*

Caesar, qui postea imperavit, using the verb *imperare* in its imperial sense.

Eutropius now had to decide how to divide up the imperial period from Caesar's death to that of Jovian when he sensibly decided to end his **Breviarium.** Having already determined, so I believe, to structure his work in ten books, he had to choose suitable *termini* for Books Seven through Ten. Not a difficult task. Not only had Suetonius, whom he had surely read, and Tacitus ended their *Lives of the Emperors* and *Histories* respectively with Domitian, that emperor was conveniently the last of the Flavian dynasty, Nerva the beginning of the new deal. Furthermore, the consuls of the year of Nerva's acclamation were Vetus and Valens, and it was for the Emperor Valens that Eutropius was writing. Thus Eutropius could end his seventh book with another conspiracy and assassination and start Book Eight by writing that in the consulship of Vetus and Valens the empire was restored to a most prosperous condition by being entrusted *ingenti felicitate* to the rule of good emperors. A murderous tyrant was dead, succeeded by a man of moderation and noble descent, who provided for the welfare of the state by adopting Trajan, Eutropius' favourite emperor.

It is also at Book Seven that Eutropius is forced to leave his republican sources, the *Epitome* of Livy, Fabius Pictor and others, and switch to what appears to have been his sole open source for the imperial period, the *Kaisergeschichte,* a series of brief biographies of the emperors from Augustus to Constantine or Constantius II.[12]

Book Eight describes the lives and exploits of the emperors from Nerva, through the Antonines to the Severan dynasty, and ends with the last of the Severi, Alexander Severus. His reign clearly marked a watershed in Roman history for not only did it signal the end of two lengthy and, so it was thought, successful dynasties, it also ushered in a period of half-a-century of confusion. That this was, indeed, a critical juncture is stated most forcefully by Eutropius' contemporary, Aurelius Victor:

> *Although he (Alexander Severus) governed for more than thirteen years he left the state strengthened in all respects. From Romulus to Septimius it evolved gradually and stood at its summit, so to speak, through the policies of Bassianus. To prevent its sudden collapse was the task of Alexander. Thereafter, as long as its leaders were more concerned to dominate their fellow citizens than to subjugate foreign peoples and took up arms against each other, they cast down the Roman state headlong, as it were, and good men and bad, the noble and the lowly, even many of barbarian background, were indiscriminately put in power. Indeed, where there is universal chaos and affairs are not conducted in their accepted manner, all*

> *think it right, in the manner of the mob, to seize the offices of others which they cannot manage, and they foully corrupt knowledge of the liberal arts. Thus the violence of fortune, once it has acquired uncontrolled licence, drives men on with destructive lust. It was, indeed, kept in check for a long time by virtue, as if by a wall, but, after almost all had been broken by criminal acts, it entrusted the state even to men of lowly birth and inadequate training.*[13]

Eutropius, therefore, had a ready-made ending for Book Eight and beginning for Book Nine.

Maximinus, with whom Book Nine commences, was the first emperor to come to the throne chosen solely by the troops without the senate's approval, as Eutropius, Victor and the *Historia Augusta* all state.[14] The notice was certainly carried by the *Kaisergeschichte.* But where was he to conclude the book? Two possibilities lay before him, a) the ending of the fifty years of chaos when Diocletian seized power, pacified the Roman world and reorganized the imperial system, or b) when Diocletian resigned office and Constantius, Constantine's father, became one of the two senior emperors. He chose the latter, apparently for two reasons. First, he could thereby honour Diocletian at the end of Book Nine, and second, he could pay special respect to the founder of the Flavian dynasty, Constantius, and devote his final book to Constantius' successors. Accordingly he closes his penultimate book with the following statement:

> *Diocletian grew old in honourable retirement as a private citizen in a villa which is not far from Salonae and showed extraordinary virtue inasmuch as he alone, of all men since the founding of the Roman empire, returned, of his own accord, from so lofty a position to the status and circumstances of private life. What happened to him, therefore, was what had happened to no one since the creation of mankind, namely that, although he had died as a private citizen, he was nevertheless enrolled among the gods.*[15]

Victor is similarly kind regarding Diocletian's resignation and retirement, though he notes that not all shared that opinion.[16]

Eutropius was able to commence his final book, dealing with recent and contemporary events, at the point where Constantius and Galerius became *Augusti.* It is no accident that Constantius, theoretically the senior emperor, is named first and that Eutropius presents us with a lengthy and extremely warm and laudatory description of him, whereas he merely states that Galerius was *vir et probe moratus et egregius re militari.*[17] Nevertheless it was Galerius who actually dominated the second tetrarchy: Constantius died a year after his elevation to Augustus. There were several reasons for Eutropius to paint a rosy picture of Constantius. The latter was essentially a popular emperor because of his moderation, especially towards the Christians, and no one under Constantine and the Flavian dynasty, which he unknowingly founded, would have dared publish anything pejorative about his memory, that is, if anything negative could be found. Furthermore, like Titus, his reign as Augustus was short-lived, and his prior imperial activities were mainly restricted to Britain, a political backwater, and Gaul, where he was successful in both civil and military spheres.

Eutropius did not, however, feel restrained when he came to deal with Constantine. His description of the latter is carefully balanced if rather fragmented. Thus, on the negative side he is charged with insolence and the bloody persecution of members of his own family, in the latter part of his reign, he could only be likened to princes of middling character and, regarding his laws, some were good but most were superfluous and some were downright severe.[18]

Jovian's death, on February 17th, A.D. 364, made for a natural conclusion to the **Breviarium.** His brief reign of seven-and-a-half months was notable for only one act: the disgraceful peace he made with the Persians, whereby Rome ceded the great fortresses of Nisibis, Singara and Castra Maurorum in Mesopotamia, and five provinces and fifteen fortresses beyond the Tigris.[19] This caused Eutropius to make his most passionate personal statement: the Romans had never before, in 1118 years, given up territory, even after humiliating defeats at the Caudine Forks, Numantia and Numidia.[20] The Wars were immediately renewed with the Samnites, Numantines and Numidians and peace was never ratified with Numantia and Numidia until the Romans were victorious. Thus it was only through the kindness of the emperors who succeeded him that Jovian was deified.

This sentiment is essentially that of Livy. In an exhortation given by Scipio Africanus, Livy writes that in most of her wars Rome had won through only after suffering dreadful losses inflicted by the Etruscans, Gauls, Samnites and, of course, Hannibal:

> Amid this wreckage of her fortunes, one thing remained intact and immovable, the virtus of the Roman People.[21]

That is to say not only courage, but also perseverance. Livy's twenty-second book narrates Rome's terrible defeats at the hands of Hannibal, but ends on a defiant note, like that of Eutropius above:

> Yet all these disasters and defections never made the Romans so much as mention peace, either before the consul returned to Rome, or after his return had renewed the remembrance of the terrible loss sustained. On this latter occasion, indeed, such was the high spirit of the country, that when the consul

returned after this great disaster of which he himself had been the chief cause, all classes went in crowds to meet him, and he was publicly thanked because he had not despaired of the republic.

What distinguished Rome from her enemies was her often demonstrated ability to recover from catastrophe, a proposition stressed by Livy, Eutropius and subsequent authors such as Ammianus, Claudian and Rutilius Namatianus.[22]

Another common theme is that of military discipline. The most obvious example is where Manlius Torquatus had his son flogged to death in 340 B.C. for disobeying his orders:

> Nevertheless the brutality of the punishment made the soldiers more obedient to their general; and not only were guard-duties, watches, and the ordering of outposts, everywhere more carefully observed, but in the final struggle also, when the troops had gone down into battle, that stern act did much good.[23]

Livy had earlier told a similar story about the dictator Postumius Tubertus, who had his son beheaded for leaving his post to fight a brave single action.[24] In addition he narrates the attempt by L. Papirius Cursor to execute Q. Fabius Rullianus, his *magister equitum,* for engaging in battle contrary to his express orders.

This theme proved engaging to Eutropius, probably because he was himself a strong advocate of strict military discipline. Certainly his emperor, Valens, was, if we are to believe Ammianus, who describes him as *severus militaris et civilis disciplinae corrector.*[25] But Eutropius appears even-handed in his assessment of the army. When it abandoned Tarquinius Superbus at Ardea the implication is that it behaved well in supporting the people against a tyrannical king. A similar case is made for the army's support of Virginius in 450 B.C. against Appius Claudius and the Decemvirs: Virginius was performing an honourable military service, Claudius was on a campaign of an entirely different kind. Again, when Eutropius recounts the Livian story of Papirius Cursor and the army's intervention to save Q. Fabius, the tone is positive. Military disaffection could be justified.[26] In other instances, though, Eutropius notes the lack of discipline of various Roman armies and the successes attendant upon the restoration of such discipline, e.g. by Scipio Africanus at Numantia[27] and by Q. Caecilius Metellus in Africa against Jugurtha.[28] Further references to military discipline occur throughout the imperial period, involving Vespasian, Alexander Severus, Aurelian, Probus, Galerius and Constantius II.[29]

Conclusion

Livy's *Epitome,* which Eutropius, in all likelihood, used

as a major source for the first six and a half books of his **Breviarium** seems not only to have provided him with a structural model for his work, but also with material for two of his chief themes which were of importance in A.D. 369 and later. First, Rome had always suffered military catastrophes, but through her pertinacity had survived to triumph. This reflected Eutropius' and Valens' aspirations *vis-a-vis* Persia and the recovery of the lost provinces in the East. Second, military discipline was essential if those aspirations were to become reality and Valens was to repeat the success of Trajan, Eutropius' paragon emperor.

Notes

[1] Ammianus, 31.14.5.

[2] *Ibid.,* 31.14.7-8. Cf. 21.10.8 where Ammianus describes Nevitta the Frank, whom Julian made consul in A.D. 361, as *inconsummatus et subagrestis.*

[3] Eutrop. 3.5.

[4] *Ibid.,* 1.1. For a thorough discussion of Eutropius' chronology *vid.* W. den Boer, *Some Minor Roman Historians.* (Leiden, 1972), pp. 124-137.

[5] R. Syme, *Tacitus* (Oxford, 1958), p. 253.

[6] H. W. Benario, *An Introduction to Tacitus* (Athens, Georgia, 1975), p.159.

[7] W. Pirogoff, *De Eutropii Breviarii Indole ac Fontibus* (diss. Berlin, 1873).

[8] Sallust, *Cat.* 10.1

[9] H. W. Bird, "Eutropius in Defence of the Senate," *Cahiers des Etudes Anciennes* XX (1987), p.65.

[10] Eutrop. 6.19.

[11] *Ibid.,* 6.25.

[12] T. D. Barnes, *The Sources of the Historia Augusta* (Brussels, 1978), p.91ff., H. W. Bird, "Further Observations on the Dating of Enmann's *Kaisergeschichte,*" *C.Q.* n.s. 23 (1973), p. 375.

[13] *De Caesaribus,* 24.7-11. Cf. *H. A. Alex.* 64.1.

[14] Eutrop. 9.1; Victor, *De Caes.* 25.1; *H. A. Max. Duo,* 8.1.

[15] Eutrop. 9.28

[16] *De Caes.* 39.48.

[17] Eutrop. 10. 1-2.

[18] *Ibid.,* 10.5, 10.6, 10.8: H. W. Bird, "The Roman Emperors: Eutropius' Perspective," *Ancient History Bulletin* 1 (1987), pp. 147f.

[19] Ammianus, 25.7. 1-9.

[20] *Ibid.,* 31.16.9, *H. A., Carus,* 21.

[21] Livy, 26.41.12.

[22] Ammianus, 31.5.11-17; Claudian, *Bell. Get.* 145ff., *Still. III,* 144 ff.; Rutilius, *de reditu suo* I. 121ff.

[23] Livy, 8.7.15-19. For a brief summary *vid.* G. Webster, *The Roman Army* (Chester, 1956), pp. 22f.

[24] Livy, 4.29.5.

[25] Ammianus, 31.14.1.

[26] Eutrop. 1.18; 2.8.

[27] *Ibid.,* 4.17.

[28] *Eutrop.,* 4.27.

[29] *Ibid.,* 8.7; 8.23; 9.14; 9.17; 9.24; 10.10.

FURTHER READING

Bibliography

Bird, H. W. "Select Bibliography." In *The Breviarium ab urbe condita of Eutropius,* by Eutropius, translated by H. W. Bird, pp. 168-74. Liverpool: Liverpool University Press, 1993.

   Select bibliography of secondary sources on Eutropius and the late Roman Empire.

Müller, Friedhelm L. "Literaturverzeichnis." In *Eutropii Breviarium ab urbe condita,* by Eutropius, translated by Friedhelm L. Müller, pp. 311-18. Stuttgart: Franz Steiner Verlag, 1995.

   Bibliography of bibliographies, editions of Eutropius's work, and secondary sources in German, Italian, French, and English.

Criticism

Claudianus, Claudius. *The In Eutropium of Claudius Claudianus,* translated by Alfred Carleton Andrews. Philadelphia: University of Pennsylvania, 1931, 135p.

   Claudius Claudianus's invective against Eutropius, presented in Latin with Andrews's English translation on facing pages.

Erickson, Daniel Nathan. *Introduction to Eutropius's "Compendium of Roman History": Introduction, Trans-*

lation, and Notes, pp. 1-18. Ph. D. dissertation, Syracuse University, 1990.

Evaluates the literary and historical merit of Eutropius's history in comparison with three other fourth-century Roman compendia.

St. Jerome

346/47-419/20

(Full name Sophronius Eusebius Hieronymus.) Roman translator, historian, exegete, and letter writer.

INTRODUCTION

Named a Doctor of the Church primarily for his Latin translation of the *Bible,* St. Jerome is also noted for his scriptural interpretations, church histories, and satiric commentaries on the moral culture of his day. Jerome's scholarly monasticism was interlaced with a wide-ranging knowledge of non-Christian literature and Hebrew exegitical works, reflecting the complex and resilient link between the Classical world and early Christianity.

Biographical Information

Born in Stridon, near Aquileia, around 346 or 347, St. Jerome observed the violent disintegration of Greco-Roman civilization. His family was Catholic and fairly wealthy, and Jerome was well educated at home and in Rome, primarily in grammar and rhetoric. Although he describes his early life as one of idleness and lack of scholarly ambition, his increasing interest in ecclesiastical literature and scriptural studies was stimulated by his interaction with a close group of friends who lived in Aquileia and included Chromatius (the future bishop of Aquileia), Jerome's foster brother, Bosonus, and Heliodorus (the future bishop of Altinum).

In 373 Jerome left his companions to travel to Antioch, where he fell into ill-health; in a famous letter to Eustochium Jerome described his feverish experience of being transported to the throne of God and accused of neglecting religious works for secular literature. In response, Jerome vowed never to study secular literature, but it was a promise he kept imperfectly. Although he read Classical literature for the rest of his life, Jerome devoted himself to studying the *Bible* and other religious writings. He also resolved to lead an ascetic life, and the following year began a monastic life in the desert of Chalcis. Jerome's tendency to incite feelings of enmity eventually led him to leave Chalcis in 379 for Antioch and then Constantinople; during this period he studied under church scholars and began translating the *Chronicle of Eusebius* (382).

In 382 Jerome returned to Rome, where his reputation as a Biblical scholar grew, and where, observing the last, decadent stages of the Roman Empire, Jerome reaffirmed his commitment to monasticism and asceti

cism. Some biographers of Jerome have claimed that he assisted Pope Damascus, and that, in the Roman hierarchy, he was to have directly succeeded him. However, Jerome's own writings suggest that he played a less prominent role in the ecclesiastical council. Much of his attention during this period was devoted to translation and commentaries of the *Bible,* in particular the *Psalms* and the entire *New Testament.* Despite the respect Jerome's scholarly works earned him, he proved an unpopular figure in Rome, and in 385 he left Rome for Antioch and then Bethlehem, where he established a monastery. For the next several decades he continued to translate religious works, compile an immense church history, catalogue the lives of "illustrious men," document ecclesiastical controversies, write scriptural commentaries, and correspond with many leading Christian scholars of the day. Of particular theological interest is Jerome's correspondence, beginning in 404, with Augustine. Although the first letters concern somewhat antagonistic disagreements regarding scriptural interpretation, most of the subsequent ones chronicle their serious and friendly discussions of religious issues and controversies. Jerome's increasingly bad health and the numerous military invasions of Bethlehem from the East during that time contributed to the sporadic nature of his work after 406. St. Jerome died in 419-20 in Bethlehem, where a shrine to him wa erected; his body was subsequently transported to Rome.

Major Works

Jerome is best known for his translation of the Hebrew *Bible* into Latin; originally requested by Pope Damascus, Jerome's version of the *Vulgate* (finished in 404) was affirmed as the "authentic" *Bible* of the Roman Catholic Church by the Council of Trent in the sixteenth century, due to its widespread and long-standing use within the church. Heralded as the most literary as well as the most faithful of the existing Latin translations, Jerome's *Vulgate* was profoundly animated and informed by Jerome's exegetical work in scripture and scriptural commentaries. During his years in Palestine, Jerome had worked to perfect his knowledge of Hebrew, which gave him access to a larger range of Biblical commentaries and interpretations. An example of his incorporation of Hebrew texts is his *Commentary on Ecclesiastes* (389), which uses both the Latin translation and the Hebrew version as its basis. In addition, Jerome published *Quaestiones hebreicae in Geneism (Hebrew Questions*; 390), short interpretive essays on the book of *Genesis*; in these essays, Jerome considers rabbinical interpretations in order to provide justification for his corrections to the Old Latin *Bible*. His exegetical work also includes commentaries on the twelve minor prophets (finished 406) and on the four major prophets (begun 407, unfinished); these works are collected in *Opus Prophetale*. Jerome contributed several treatises to the recording of church history, including the *Book of Illustrious Men* (392), which includes not only church leaders but several non-Christian writers and scholars such as Seneca and Philo, and writings on church controversies. Jerome's *Epistulae (Letters*; 371-418) reflect his caustic wit and austere moral sense; they are written to a wide range of correspondents, including friends, church leaders, and counsel-seekers. In these epistles Jerome is at his most candid and his most critical, particularly of the corrupted morality of Rome.

Critical Reception

Jerome's work in translation and interpretation was well recognized during his lifetime, so much so that his Latin translation of the *Bible* has become the standard version of the Roman Catholic Church and has formed the basis of his historical importance. The *Vulgate Bible* remains at the center of critical acclaim for Jerome's accomplishments for the sensitivity and lyricism of its style as well as the breadth of his research into scriptural interpretation. Yet beyond his well-documented understanding of religious writings and in direct con-

tradition to Jerome's own anti-Ciceronian vision, Jerome demonstrated an appreciation, familiarity, and skill with secular literature; some critics have claimed that he deserves the title of the "Christian Cicero" for the clarity and realism of his prose. In a sixteenth-century essay explaining his "rescue" of Jerome from incompetent transcribers and editors, Erasmus praises Jerome's scholarly achievements: "If you demand learning, I ask you, whom can Greece produce with all her erudition, so perfect in every department of knowledge, that he might be matched against Jerome? . . . Who ever became so equally and completely at home in all literature, both sacred and profane?" Jerome's letters and accounts of Church controversies reflect his sharp and often wry criticisms of the mores of Roman society, of corrupted faith and morality within the Church, and of inept interpretations of scripture. Although he is not remembered for generating original theological ideas, his translations, commentaries, and compilations have proved invaluable for religious and secular historians. Many modern scholars consider Jerome representative of the intertwining and sometimes contradictory tendencies of early Christianity: steeped in classical literature, Jerome advocated strict monastic and ascetic practices. In addition, the strength of his spirituality existed alongside a sometimes strained relationship with the Church hierarchy, caused by Jerome's staunchly critical attention to the interpretative problems and moral conflicts of his age.

PRINCIPAL WORKS

Epistulae (letters) 371-418

Vita Sancti Pauli Primi Eremitae (biography) 380

Altercatio Luciferiani et Orthodoxi (dialogue) 382-83

De perpetua Virginitate B. Mariae; adversus Helvidium (treatise) 382-83

*Vulgate [translator] (history) 382-85, 391-404

Chronicon Eusebii Caesariensis of Eusebius [translator; from the *Chronicon* of Eusebius] (history) 382

De interpretatione nominum hebraicorum [translator; from the *Onomasticon* of Eusebius] (history) 389-90

Commentary on Ecclesiates (commnetary) 389

De Spiritu Sancto [translator; from the *De Spiritu Sancto* of Didymus of Alexandria] (treatise) 390

Quaestiones hebraicae in Genesim (commentary) 390

Vita Malchi, monachi captivi (biography) 391

*Jerome translated the *Old Testament* from Hebrewand the *New Testament* from Greek.

PRINCIPAL ENGLISH TRANSLATIONS

CRITICISM

Erasmus (letter date 1516)

SOURCE: Excerpt from "Dedicatory Letter to Erasmus's Edition of St. Jerome" in *Collected Works of Erasmus,* Vol. 61, edited and translated by James F. Brady and John C. Olin, University of Toronto Press, 1992, pp. 4-14.

[*In the following excerpt, written in 1516, Erasmus evaluates the historical importance of Jerome's writings and describes the difficulties he had in restoring Jerome's corrupt texts.*]

. . . [Now if] honour was paid even to works of superstition like the books of Numa and the Sibyl, or to volumes of human history as was customary in Egypt, or to those that enshrined some part of human wisdom such as the works of Plato and Aristotle, how much more appropriate that Christian princes and bishops should do likewise by preserving the writings of men inspired by the Holy Spirit, who have left us not so much books as sacred oracles! And yet somehow it happened that in that field our ancestors did singularly little. We may not think much, I grant you, of the loss of pagan authors, the only result of which is that we are less well informed or less eloquent, but not less virtuous. But think of the admirable and really saintly authors bequeathed to us by Greece, that seat of learning, or its rival Italy, by Gaul, once such a flourishing home of culture, or Africa with all its originality, or Spain with its tradition of hard work. How impressive was their recondite learning, how brilliant their eloquence, how holy their lives! And yet, I ask you, how few of them survive, preserved more by accident than by any help from us! And those survivors, how foully mutilated, how badly adulterated, how full throughout of monstrous errors, so that to survive in that condition was no great privilege! For my part, far as I am from despising the simple piety of common folk, I cannot but wonder at the absurd judgment of the multitude. The slippers of the saints and their drivel-stained napkins we put to our lips, and the books they wrote, the most sacred and most powerful relics of those holy men, we leave to lie neglected. A scrap of a saint's tunic or shirt we place in a gilded and bejewelled reliquary, and the books into which they put so much work, and in which we have the best part of them still living and breathing, we abandon to be gnawed at will by bug, worm, and cockroach.

Nor is it hard to guess the reason for this. Once the character of princes had quite degenerated into a barbaric form of tyranny, and bishops had begun to love their lay lordships more than the duty of teaching bequeatheds to them by the apostles, the whole business of instruction was soon abandoned to a certain class, who today claim charity and religion as their private trademark; sound learning began to be neglected, and a knowledge of Greek, still more of Hebrew, was looked down on; to study the art of expression was despised, and Latin itself so much contaminated with an ever-changing barbarism that Latin by now was the last thing it resembled. History, geography, antiquities, all were dropped. Literature was reduced to a few sophistic niceties, and the sum of human learning began to be found only in certain summary compilers and makers of excerpts, whose impudence stood in inverse proportion to their knowledge. And so they easily allowed those old classic authors to fall out of use or, what is more like the truth, they deliberately contrived their disappearance, for they now read them in vain, lacking all things necessary for their understanding. They did, however, make a few haphazard extracts from them which they mingled with their own notes; and this made it even more in their interest that the old authors should disappear, to save them from the charge of plagiarism or ignorance. It was worth their while for Clement, Irenaeus, Polycarp, Origen, Arnobius to fall out of use, that in their stead the world might read Occam, Durandus, Capreolus, Lyra, Burgensis, and even poorer stuff than that. So under their long and despotic rule such was the holocaust of humane literature and good authors that a man who had meddled even slightly with sound learning was expelled from the ranks of the doctors.

The result of this was the total loss of so many luminaries of the world, whose names alone survive and cannot be read without tears; and if by some chance any have escaped destruction, they are damaged in so many ways and so much mutilated and adulterated that those who perished outright might seem fortunate. Now this seems to me a perfectly monstrous fate for all learned authors, but far more monstrous in Jerome than anywhere else, whose many outstanding gifts deserved that he, even if no one else, should be preserved complete and uncorrupted. Other authors have each a different claim upon us; Jerome alone possesses, united in one package, as the phrase goes, and to a remarkable degree, all the gifts that we admire separately in others. Distinction in one department is a great and rare achievement; but he combined overall excellence with being easily first in everything separately, if you compare him with other authors, while if you compare him with himself, nothing stands out, such is his balanced mingling of all the supreme qualities. If you assay his mental endowments, where else would you find such an enthusiastic student, such a keen critic, such prolific originality? What could be more ingenious or diverting, if the subject should call for something entertaining? If however you are looking for brilliance of expression, on that side at least Jerome leaves all Christian authors so far behind him that one cannot compare with him even those who spent their whole time on nothing but the art of writing; and so

impossible is it to find any writer of our faith to compare with him that in my opinion Cicero himself, by universal consent the leading light of Roman eloquence, is surpassed by him in some of the qualities of a good style, as I shall show at greater length in his life. For my part, I have the same experience with Jerome that I used to have with Cicero: if I compare him with any other author, however brilliant, that man suddenly seems as it were to lose his voice, and he whose language has no rival in my admiration, when set alongside Jerome for comparison, seems to become tongue-tied and stammers. If you demand learning, I ask you, whom can Greece produce with all her erudition, so perfect in every department of knowledge, that he might be matched against Jerome? Who ever so successfully united every part of the sum of knowledge in such perfection? Was there ever an individual expert in so many languages? Who ever achieved such familiarity with history, geography, and antiquities? Who ever became so equally and completely at home in all literature, both sacred and profane? If you look to his memory, never was there an author, ancient or modern, who was not at his immediate disposal. Was there a corner of Holy Scripture or anything so recondite or diverse that he could not produce it, as it were, cash down? As for his industry, who ever either read or wrote so many volumes? Who had the whole of Scripture by heart, as he had, drinking it in, digesting it, turning it over and over, pondering upon it? Who expended so much effort in every branch of learning? And if you contemplate his lofty character, who breathes the spirit of Christ more vividly? Who has taught him with more enthusiasm? Who ever followed him more exactly in his way of life? This man, single-handed, could represent the Latin world, either for holiness of life or for mastery of theology, if only he survived complete and undamaged.

As it is, I doubt whether any author has had more outrageous treatment. A good part of all he wrote has perished. What survives was not so much corrupted as virtually destroyed and defaced, and this partly by the fault of illiterate scribes whose habit it is to copy an accurate text inaccurately and make a faulty text worse, to leave out what they cannot read and to corrupt what they do not understand—for instance, the Hebrew and Greek words which Jerome often brings in; but in a much more criminal fashion by sacrilegious men, I know not whom, who have deliberately cut down very many passages, added some, altered many, corrupted, adulterated, and muddled almost everything, so that there is hardly a paragraph which an educated man can read without stumbling. What is more (and this is the most pestilential way of ruining a text), as though it were not enough to have put together so many idiotic blunders, showing equally ignorance and inability to write, under the name of one who is equally a great scholar and a geat stylist, they have mixed in their own rubbish into his expositions in such a way that no one can separate them. Ascribe a book to the wrong author, and there are many indications that this is wrong; but if scraps are intermingled, like darnel in wheat, where is the sieve that can screen them out? That all this has happened I shall shortly demonstrate in the catalogue of Jerome's works, and in the two prefaces and critical introductions of the second volume.

I was roused therefore, partly by this insufferable ill-treatment of so eminent a Doctor of the church, on whose immortal works these worse than Calydonian boars have wreaked their fury unpunished, and partly by thoughts of the general advantage of all who wish to learn, whom I saw debarred by these outrages from enjoying such a feast—I was roused, I say, to restore to the best of my ability the volumes of his letters, which were the richest in learning and eloquence and proportionately the worst corrupted, although I well knew how difficult and arduous was the task I took in hand. To begin with, the labour of comparing together so many volumes is very tedious, as they know who have experience of working in this treadmill. Often too I had to work with volumes which it was no easy business to read, the forms of the script being either obscured by decay and neglect, or half eaten away and mutilated by worm and beetle, or written in the fashion of Goths or Lombards, so that even to learn the letter-forms I had to go back to school, not to mention for the moment that the actual task of detecting, of smelling out as it were, anything that does not sound like a true and genuine reading requires a man in my opinin who is well informed, quick-witted, and alert. But on top of this far the most difficult thing is either to conjecture from corruptions of different kinds what the author wrote, or to guess the original reading on the basis of such fragments and vestiges of the shapes of the script as may survive. And further, while this is always extremely difficult, it is outstandingly so in the works of Jerome. There are several reasons for this. One is that his actual style is far from ordinary, starred with epigrams, highlighted with exclamations, rich in devious and cunning artifice, in pressing close-packed argument, in humorous allusions, sometimes seeming to use all the tricks of the rhetorical schools without restraint, and everywhere exhibiting the highly skilled craftsman. As a result, the further his style is from the understanding of ordinary people, the more blunders it is defiled with. One man copies not what he reads but what he thinks he understands; another supposes everything he does not understand to be corrupt, and changes the text as he thinks best, following no guide but his own imagination; a third detects perhaps that the text is corrupt, but while trying to emend it with an unambitious conjecture he introduces two mistakes in place of one, and while trying to cure a slight wound inflicts one that is incurable.

Besides all this, there is the astonishing way in which Jerome mixes material of the most varied kinds. He even went out of his way to do this, but with complete success. It was a kind of ambition and ostentation, if you like, but of a pious and holy kind: to display his own resources with the object of shocking us out of our lethargy and awaking his drowsy readers to study the inner meaning of the Scriptures. There is no class of author anywhere and no kind of literature which he does not use whenever he likes—sprinkling here and there, pressing harder, ramming it home: Hebrew, Greek, Latin, Chaldaean, sacred and profane, old and new, everything! Like a bee that flies from flower to flower, he collected the best of everything to make the honey stored in his works, he plucked different blossoms from every quarter to adorn his chaplet; he put together his mosaic out of tesserae of every colour. And of all these it was the most recondite materials that he habitually wove in with the greatest readiness. There is nothing so obscure in the meaning-within-meaning of the Prophets, in the hidden senses of the whole Old Testament, in the Gospels or the Epistles, that he does not use as though it were familiar, sometimes with such a sidelong glance that only a well-instructed and attentive reader will catch the allusion. What is there in the literature of the Hebrews or Chaldaeans, in rhetorical or geographical textbooks, in poetry and medicine and philosophy, and even in books written by heretics, from which he does not draw thread to weave into his book? To understand all this, encyclopaedic learning is essential, even if the texts were faultless; and what happens, do you suppose, when everything is so damaged, so mutilated, so muddled that, if Jerome himself came to life again, he would neither recognize his own work nor understand it?

And then there was a further handicap. The greatest part of the authors upon whom Jerome drew as his sources have perished, and with their support it might have been possible to repair somehow the results of repeated damage or even loss: for this is, as it were, the sheet-anchor in which scholars normally take refuge in their greatest difficulties. For since I did not undertake this labour to secure either reputation or reward, I at least was not so much moved by something that might perhaps have deterred another man from setting his hand to any business of the kind. What is that? you will ask. I mean this: no other work brings a man more tedium and weariness, and equally no work brings its author less repute or gratitude, because, while the whole advantage of one's exertions is enjoyed by one's reader, he fails to appreciate not only how hard one has worked for his benefit but even how much he has gained, unless someone by chance were to compare my work with the texts in current use. The reader wanders at leisure over smiling fields; he plays and runs and never stumbles; and he never gives a thought to the time and tedium it has cost me to battle with the thorns and briars, while I was clearing that land for his benefit. He does not reckon how long a single brief word may sometimes have tormented the man trying to correct it, nor does he bring to mind how much I suffered in my efforts to remove anything that might hold him up, how great the discomforts that secured his comfort, how much tedium was the price of his finding nothing tedious.

But I shall be tedious myself if I recount all the tedium I have endured in this affair; so let me say just one thing, which is bold, but true. I believe that the writing of his books cost Jerome less effort than I spent in the restoring of them, and their birth meant fewer nightly vigils for him than their rebirth for me. The rest any man may conjecture for himself. Why need I mention here the ingratitude and ignorance of some men I could name, who would rather have no changes whatever in the text of the best authors? They do nothing themselves, and object noisily to the distinguished efforts of others; men whose judgment is so crass that they find errors in what is perfectly preserved and stylish elegance in the foulest corruptions, and (what is worse) of such perversity that, while they do not grant scholars the right to correct a faulty text by hard work, they allow some worthless fellow to befoul and stultify and ruin the works of the greatest authors at his own sweet will without a protest. And so it is inevitable that one should earn no gratitude from the majority and win the resentment of this last class of men even for the service one has done them. You may say that profit means nothing to the noble soul, and that honour and glory are easily despised by the good Christian. Yes: but even men of the highest character look for gratitude if they have deserved it. Who can tolerate scandal and abuse in return for doing good?

Of all this I was well aware; but I was moved by a great desire to rescue Jerome, by the thought of being useful to those who have the Scriptures at heart, and last but not least because your Highness approved and would have it so, and you above all others gave me the impulse and unflagging encouragement to undertake this. And so I despised all the difficulties, and like a modern Hercules I set out on my most laborious but most glorious campaign, taking the field almost unaided against all the monsters of error. I cannot think that Hercules consumed as much energy in taming a few monsters as I did in abolishing so many thousand blunders. And I conceive that not a little more advantage will accrue to the world from my work than from his labours which are on the lips of all men. To start with, by comparing many copies, early copies especially, and sometimes adding my conjectures as the traces of the script suggested, I have removed the blunders and restored the correct reading. The Greek words, which had been either omitted or wrongly supplied, I have replaced. I have done the same with the Hebrew also; but in this department what I was less able to manage for myself I have achieved with the assistance of others, and especially of the brothers Amerbach, Bruno, Basilius, and Bonifacius, whom their excellent

father Johannes Amerbach equipped with the three tongues as though they were born expressly for the revival of ancient texts. And in this they have even outstripped their father's wishes and expectations, thinking nothing more important than the glory of Jerome and for his sake sparing neither expense nor health. For my part I was very grateful for their help, having only dipped into Hebrew rather than learnt it. And yet I saw to it that the keen reader should find nothing lacking even if I lacked it myself, and what fell short in my own capacity has been fully supplied out of the resources of others. Why should I be ashamed to do in the defence of such an author what the greatest monarchs do without shame in the recovery, and even the destruction, of paltry towns?

I have added a summary to each treatise or letter, opening the door, as it were, to those who wish to enter. And then, since not everyone is blessed with such wide linguistic and literary knowledge, I have thrown light on anything that might hold up a reader of modest attainments by adding notes, hoping to achieve a double purpose: first, to make such an eminent author, who hitherto could not be read even by men of great learning, accessible to those whose learning is but small, and second, that it may not be so easy in future for anyone to corrupt what other men have restored. Not content with this, the pieces wrongly circulating under Jerome's name, many of them such that their author is clearly not Jerome but some botcher as witless as he is impudent, I have not cut out, in order that a reader whose appetite is greater than his taste might run no risk of disappointment (to put it more bluntly, so that every donkey may find its thistle), but exiled to a suitable place, although in themselves they deserve no place at all. Next, I divided the whole corpus (I speak of the section which I took for my own province) into four volumes. In the first I have grouped together his pieces of moral instruction by exhortation and example, because what deals with the ordering of life deserves attention first. The second I have divided into three classes, into the first of which I have put certain things that show some degree of culture and are worth reading, but are falsely ascribed to Jerome; into the next, things which are not his, but carry an author's namè in their headings; the third class is a kind of cesspool into which I have thrown the supremely worthless rubbish of some impostor, I know not whom, of whom it may fairly be doubted which is the greater, his inability to write, his ignorance, or his impudence. At least, whoever he was, he seems to me to deserve public execration for the rest of time; and he must have had a very low opinion of the intelligence of posterity if he hoped that there would never be anyone who could distinguish the ravings of a half-witted noisy fellow from the works of a man of the highest eloquence, learning, and sanctity. The third volume I have allotted to his works of controversy and apologetics, those, that is, which are devoted to refuting the errors of heretics and the calumnies of his opponents. The fourth I have kept for the expository works, I mean the explanations of Holy Scripture.

With something of the same zealous intentions I have lately produced a New Covenant equipped with my annotations, and I decided that the dedication of that work should be shared by Leo the supreme pontiff and your Highness, that my new undertaking might come before the public protected and recommended by the names of the whole world's two greatest men. But Jerome, recalled to the light from some sort of nether region, I prefer to dedicate to you alone, either because I owe you without exception everything I have, or because you always have a special concern for Jerome's reputation, perceiving with your usual wisdom that after the writings of the evangelists and apostles there is nothing more deserving of a Christian's attention. For my part I would gladly believe that Jerome himself takes some pleasure in the thought that his restoration to life in the world has the authority of your most favourable name, for he is no more the greatest of theologians than you are second to none among bishops whom all admire. He mastered to such good effect the whole cycle of knowledge in its completeness, and you likewise have blended in a wonderful harmony the full circle of a bishop's virtues.

In all other respects the agreement is admirable. I have one anxiety, that my limited powers may fail to do justice to Jerome's importance or to your eminent position; for nowhere do I feel more clearly how small my talent is than when I am striving to make some sort of response to your exalted virtues and your unbounded goodness to me. But what was I to do, bound to you as I am by so many and such great obligations that if I sold myself into slavery I should not be in a position to repay any part of my debt? I have done what bankrupts often do, making a token payment to bind themselves yet more irrecoverably, and thus proving that it is the means and not the will they lack; they are ill-starred rather than dishonest debtors, and for this very reason often secure the good will of a jury, because they are not so much ungrateful as unfortunate. In such cases the only means of showing gratitude is to be a frank and cheerful debtor, and to acknowledge one's debt is the first step towards paying it. Or rather, to compare a situation even more like mine, I have followed the example of those who would rather raise a fresh loan than go to prison for nonpayment, and have borrowed from Jerome the wherewithal to repay you. Though why should it any longer look like something borrowed rather than my own?—real estate often passes from one ownership to another by occupation or prescriptive right. In any case, in this line of business Jerome himself has laid down a principle for me in his preface to the books of Kings, repeatedly calling that work his, because anything that we have made our own by correcting, reading, constant devotion, we can

fairly claim is ours. On this principle why should not I myself claim a proprietary right in the works of Jerome? For centuries they had been treated as abandoned goods; I entered upon them as something ownerless, and by incalculable efforts reclaimed them for all devotees of the true theology.

It is a river of gold, a well-stocked library, that a man acquires who possesses Jerome and nothing else. He does not possess him, on the other hand, if his text is like what used to be in circulation, all confusion and impurity. Not that I would dare assert that none of the old corruptions, no traces of his previous ruined state, remain; I doubt if Jerome himself could achieve that without the aid of better manuscripts than I have yet had the chance to use. But this with all my zeal I have achieved, that not many now remain. And if I have done nothing else, at least my attempt will spur on some other men not to accept hereafter indiscriminately whatever they may find in their books, however badly corrupted by one impostor after another or masquerading under some false title, and read it and approve it and cite it as an oracle. I only wish that all good scholars would devote all their forces to the task of restoring as far as possible to its original purity whatever in the way of good authors has somehow survived after such numerous shipwrecks! But I should not like to see anyone enter this field who is not as well equipped with honesty, accuracy, judgment, and readiness to take pains as he is with erudition; for there is no more cruel enemy of good literature than the man who sets out to correct it half-instructed, half-asleep, hasty, and of unsound judgment. . . .

Henry Hart Milman (essay date 1860)

SOURCE: An excerpt from *History of Latin Christianity; Including That of the Popes to the Pontificate of Nicholas V,* Vol. 1, Sheldon and Company, 1860, pp. 117-18.

[*In this excerpt, Milman briefly discusses the importance of the* Vulgate *to incorporating Eastern religious thought into the development of Christianity in the West.*]

. . . [Of both] the extension of monasticism, and the promulgation of the **Vulgate** Bible, Jerome was the author; of the former principally, of the latter exclusively. This was his great and indefeasible title to the appellation of a Father of the Latin Church. Whatever it may owe to the older and fragmentary versions of the sacred writings, Jerome's Bible is a wonderful work, still more as achieved by one man, and that a Western Christian, even with all the advantage of study and of residence in the East. It almost created a new language. The inflexible Latin became pliant and expansive, naturalizing foreign Eastern imagery, Eastern modes of expression and of thought, and Eastern religious notions, most uncongenial to its own genius and character; and yet retaining much of its own peculiar strength, solidity, and majesty. If the Northern, the Teutonic languages, coalesce with greater facility with the Orientalism of the Scriptures, it is the triumph of Jerome to have brought the more dissonant Latin into harmony with the Eastern tongues. The **Vulgate** was even more, perhaps, than the Papal power the foundation of Latin Christianity. . . .

William Henry Fremantle (essay date 1882)

SOURCE: An excerpt from "Hieronymus (4) (Jerome), St." in *A Dictionary of Christian Biography, Literature, Sects and Doctrines; during the First Eight Centuries, Being a Continuation of "The Dictionary of the Bible,"* Vol. III, edited by William Smith and Henry Wace, John Murray, 1882, pp. 48-50.

[*In the following excerpt, Fremantle critically appraises Jerome as translator, expositor, theologian, church and general historian, and letter writer.*]

. . . 1. As a translator, Jerome deserves the highest place for his clear conviction of the importance of his task, and the perseverance against great obstacles which he displayed. This is shewn especially in his prefaces, which are of great value as shewing his system. For the most part he took very great pains, but not with all alike. The Chronicles, for instance, he went over word by word with his Hebrew teacher; Tobit he translated in a single day. His method was, first, never to swerve needlessly from the original; second, to avoid solecisms; third, at all risks, even that of introducing solecisms, to give the true sense. These principles are not always consistently carried through. There is sometimes undue laxity, which is defended in the treatise *De Optimo Genere Interpretandi;* sometimes there is an unnecessary literalism, which arises from a notion that some hidden sense lies behind the words, but really deprives the words of sense. His versions were during his lifetime both highly prized and greatly condemned. His friend Sophronius translated a great part of them into Greek, and they were read in many of the Eastern churches in Jerome's lifetime. After his death his versions gradually won their way to universal acceptance in the West, and were finally, with some alterations (mostly for the worse), stamped with the authority of the Roman church at the council of Trent. . . .

2. As an expositor, Jerome lacks originality. His Commentaries are mostly compilations from others; and he gives their views at times without any opinion of his own. This, however, gives these works a special value as the record of the thoughts of distinguished men, such as Origen. His derivations are puerile. His interpretation of prophecy is the merest literal application of it to events in the church. He is often inconsistent, and at times seems to veil his own opinion under that of another. His allusions to the events of his own time as illustrations of Scripture are often of great interest. He wrote in great haste (Pref. to b. ii. of **Comm. on Eph.** and Pref. to b. iii. of **Comm. on Gal.**), and from this reason, as well as from his frequently weak health and weak eyes, and also from his great self-confidence, he trusted to his memory too much. His strength and his weakness may be seen in his correspondence with Augustine. He is strong in all that relates to the necessity of translating from the Hebrew, in verbal criticism, and in the quotation of the Greek commentators, but weak in the more philosophical and historical faculty required for the interpretation of such a passage as Gal. ii., which formed the chief subject of controversy between them.

3. The books on Hebrew names, **Questions on Genesis,** and the site and names of Hebrew places shew a wide range of interest, and are useful contributions to Biblical knowledge, especially the latter, which is often appealed to in the present day. But even here Jerome was too ready to take in the tales of the Jews rather than to exercise an independent judgment.

In theology, properly so called, he is weak. His first letter to Damasus on the Trinitarian controversies at Antioch, while it shews a clear perception of what the church taught, shews also a shrinking from dogmatic questions and a servile submission to episcopal authority. He accepted without question the damnation of all the heathen. His dealings with Origen shew his weakness; he surrendered his impartial judgment as soon as Origen's works were condemned. In the Pelagian controversy the slight sense shewn by him of the importance of the questions at issue contrast markedly with the deep conviction expressed in the writings of Augustine. In some matters, which had not been dealt with by church authority, he held his own; as in the question of the origin of souls, as to which he is decided as a creationist. He puts aside purgatory and scoffs at millenarianism. His views on the Apocrypha and on the orders of the Christian ministry have become classical.

4. For church history he had some considerable faculty, as is shewn by the dialogue with a Luciferian. His knowledge was great, and his sympathies large, when there was no question of church condemnations. His book *De Viris Illustribus* is especially valuable, and his defence of it against Augustine's criticism shews him a man of wider culture and greater knowledge than his opponent. But the lives of the hermits shew a credulity which would incorporate legend into history. In matters of controversy his ordinary method is to take as absolute truth the decisions of bishops and even the popular feeling in the church, and to use all his powers in enforcing these. His own life and the docu-

ments in which its details are imbedded are his best contributions to church history.

5. His knowledge of and sympathy with human history generally was very much like that of the monks of later times. He had much curiosity and considerable knowledge. His translation of the Chronicle of Eusebius shews his interest in history; but it is very uncritical. The mistakes of Eusebius are not corrected but aggravated by the translator; and his own additions shew that his critical faculty was not such as to guard against the admission of considerable errors; and his credulity constantly reveals itself. There is nothing in his writings which shews even the rudiments of a philosophy of history. He knew both the events of his time and facts lying beyond the usual range. He was acquainted, for instance, with the routes to India, and mentions the Brahmans (*Ep. xxii. lxx.* &c.) and Buddha (*Adp. Jov.* i. 42). Events like the fall of Rome made a deep impression upon him; but he deals with these very much as the monks of the Middle Ages dealt with the events of their time. He is a recluse; he has nothing of political sagacity, and no sense of human progress.

6. His letters are the most interesting part of his writings, and will always continue to be read with interest. They are very various; they are vivid in their expression of feeling and graphic in their pictures of life. The letters to Heliodorus (14) on the praise of hermit life; to Eustochium (22) on the preservation of virginity in the mixed life of the Roman church and world; to Asella (45) on his departure from Rome; to Nepotian (52) on the duties of the presbyters and monks of his day; to Marcella from Paula and Eustochium (46), giving the enthusiastic description of monastic life among the holy places of Palestine; to Laeta (107) on the education of a child whose grandfather was a heathen priest, whose parents were Christians, and who was herself to be a nun; to Rusticus (125), giving rules which shew the character of the monastic life in those days; all these are literary gems; and the Epitaphia of Blesilla (39), Fabiola (77), Nepotianus (60), Paula (108), and Marcella (127) form a hagiography of the best and most attractive kind.

Style.—His style is excellent, and he was rightly praised as the Christian Cicero by Erasmus, who contrasts his writings with the monkish and scholastic literature. It is vivid, full of illustrations, with happy turns, such as "lucus a non lucendo," . . . , "fac de necessitate virtutem," "Ingemuit totus orbis et Arianum se esse miratus est." The scriptural quotations and allusions are often overdone and forced but there is no unreality or cant in this; and he never loses his dignity except in the case of controversial personalities.

Character.—A few words must be added on Jerome's character and influence. He was vain, and unable to bear rivals; extremely sensitive as to the estimation in which he was held by his contemporaries, and especially by the bishops; passionate and resentful; but at times becoming suddenly placable; scornful and violent in controversy; kind to the weak and the poor; respectful in his dealings with women; entirely without avarice; extraordinarily diligent in work, and nobly tenacious of the main objects to which he devoted his life. There was, however, something of monkish cowardice in his asceticism, and his influence was not felt by the strong.

Influence.—His influence grew through his life and increased after his death. If we may use a scriptural phrase which has sometimes been applied to such influence, "He lived and reigned for a thousand years." His writings contain the whole spirit of the church of the middle ages, its monasticism, its contrast of sacred things with profane, its credulity and superstition, its subjection to hierarchical authority, its dread of heresy, its passion for pilgrimages. To the society which was thus in a great measure formed by him, his Bible was the greatest boon which could have been given. But he founded no school and had no inspiring power; there was no courage or width of view in his spiritual legacy which could break through the fatal circle of bondage to received authority which was closing round mankind. As Thierry says in the last words of his work on St. Jerome, "There is no continuation of his work; a few more letters of Augustine and Paulinus, and night falls over the West."

Arthur Stanley Pease (essay date 1919)

SOURCE: "The Attitude of Jerome towards Pagan Literature," *Transactions and Proceedings of the American Philological Association,* 1919, pp. 150-67.

[*In the essay that follows, Pease discusses the influence of pagan literature on Jerome's writings and concludes that Jerome realized that the "complete acceptance of the new faith did not necessarily involve total rejection of what was of value in the old literature."*]

The student of classical literature can hardly be indifferent to the question how his favorite authors have been in various ages regarded. While at present the attitude of individuals towards the classics may, in view of the wide distribution of printed texts, be a matter of less concern, it is obvious that, when manuscripts were few, not merely the accurate text tradition of an author but even the bare preservation of his works must often have depended upon the esteem in which they were held by the few persons who possessed them. Again, the pagan literature depended for its existence upon the sufferance of Christian transmitters, and it was thus a matter of no little moment whether their disposition towards it was apprehensive, contemptuous, indifferent, or friendly. It seems, therefore, worth while to reëxamine[1] the attitude in this regard of St. Jerome, a Christian of distinction and influence in a period of transition, during which the pagan culture was yielding to the Christian—himself a man thoroughly trained in the secular education and yet consistently devoted to the new faith. This combination will assure us that his feelings would not have been those of a narrow and unsympathetic bigot,[2] nor yet of a superficial rather than a sincere Christian.

Jerome's life extended from between 340 and 350[3] to 420, and included the reign of Julian[4] and the pagan revivals of the fourth century,[5] as well as the period of such severe blows against paganism as the destruction of the temple of Sarapis at Alexandria and the prohibition of pagan worship in 392.[6] But it is significant that Jerome wrote no works directed specifically against the old faith, and seldom mentions contemporary pagan opponents of Christianity.[7] The absence of vigorous pagan opposition doubtless made it easier to consider the classical literature on its own intrinsic merits, rather than as the vehicle of religious propaganda.

It is now my intention to trace briefly some of the influences which determined Jerome's attitude towards the classics. And first, both in chronology and importance, was his education, a subject so fully treated by Grützmacher[8] in his biography that I need merely summarize his results. Becoming in 354 a pupil of Donatus,[9] he studied the classical writers, including Plautus and Terence, Sallust, Lucretius, Horace, Virgil, Persius, and Lucan, with commentaries upon them by Donatus and others,[10] as well as many points on figures of speech and grammatical matters.[11] In addition he acquired a sense for literary style, which made him extremely sensitive to works of unrhetorical composition, and in his own writings, though by no means approaching the perfection of his classical models, he became a follower of Ciceronian traditions, and one of the better stylists of the Latin fathers.[12] His study of rhetoric, including the declaiming of *controversiae*,[13] left traces upon him which he later tried in vain to eradicate.[14] In his philosophical studies he appears to have come into little first-hand contact with the great Greek philosophers, for though he mentions Plato, Aristotle, Theophrastus, Carneades, and others,[15] it is clear that nearly all quotations from them are through the medium of Cicero, Seneca, or other Latin writers.[16] Indeed it appears that he did not learn Greek at all until he went to Antioch in 373.[17]

That the early rhetorical interests of Jerome should have influenced his later thought is not surprising. Despite aspersions upon the childish vanity and insincerity of rhetorical and philosophical studies[18] as compared with the simple truth of the Scriptures,[19] and occasional assertions of revolt from the established rules of the rhetoricians,[20] he remained very sensitive to

criticisms against his style, and apologized for its defects on the grounds of absence from Latin associations,[21] the corrupting influence of his Hebrew studies,[22] hasty composition, and frequent dictation.[23] Again, like the Italian humanists, with their fondness for classical models and antipathy to the barbarous diction of the theologians,[24] Jerome's tastes were offended by the stylistic rudeness of the early Christian writings. He tells of his original dislike for the Hebrew language and its sounds—the *stridor lectionis Hebraicae*,[25]—and how, after reading Quintilian and Cicero, he passed to the study of the book of Daniel in the original, with which he was so much disgusted that had it not been for the encouragement of his teacher he would have abandoned the study altogether.[26] He was also acutely aware of the harshness of the Greek and Latin versions of the Old Testament,[27] and explained this as due to their being translations,[28] declaring that not even Homer or the authors translated by Cicero[29] sound well in Latin, and that Cicero himself, in a single work based on Greek sources, had coined more Latin terms than are found in all the Latin Scriptures.[30]

We must now discuss Jerome's vision, perhaps the best known incident in his life. In his twenty-second letter, written in 384[31] to the nun Eustochium and discussing the preservation of virginity, he warns against the enticements of secular interests and exclaims: "What agreement have Christ and Belial? What has Horace in common with the Psalter? Virgil with the Gospels? Cicero with the Apostle?"[32] And he continues by relating his own experience.[33] Ten or eleven years before,[34] when on his way to the East, he could not bear to leave behind the library he had collected.[35] And so, after Lenten fasts and vigils, after reading Cicero and Plautus, he was seized by a fever and rapt in the spirit before the tribunal of the Judge; where there was such a flood of light, and such resplendence from the glory of the angel spectators, that, prostrate on the earth, he dared not uplift his eyes. Asked about his state, he answered that he was a Christian. "Thou liest," answered the Judge; "thou art a Ciceronian, not a Christian; for where thy treasure is, there is thy heart." After flogging and torture Jerome took solemn oaths never to possess or read secular manuscripts, and thereupon, with shoulders dark with weals, returned to consciousness. Thenceforth he read divine books more zealously than previously he had read secular writings.

In regard to this vision two points must be noted. First, it was but a dream, though vivid and highly colored, and no doubt with a great impression, as such nightmares often have, upon a mind overwrought by asceticism.[36] And secondly, Jerome tells it for a definite moralizing purpose, in a very rhetorical fashion.[37] Indeed, the dream might be found, could one study its antecedents, to be based upon rhetorical models. At any rate it is significant that later Christians were by dreams somewhat similarly diverted from secular reading.[38] Let us now observe how Jerome's vision was regarded. A few years after describing it he thus addresses Eustochium and Paula:[39] "You yourselves know that it is more than fifteen years since Tully or Maro or any of the secular authors has been taken into my hands, and if by chance any influence from them creeps into my citations, such cases are but misty recollections, as it were of a dream long past."[40] Fifteen years or more later[41] he feels it necessary[42] to defend himself against charges of Rufinus that he had had a monk at Bethlehem copy dialogues of Cicero, had taught the classics to young pupils, and had proved false to the promises made in his vision.[43] His defence is based upon several grounds: that Rufinus himself read Cicero;[44] that the promise was made in a dream,[45] and that dreams are notoriously unreliable;[46] also that Rufinus has probably himself not kept absolutely his baptismal and monastic vows.[47] This defence is long and sophistical,[48] and one feels that Jerome "doth protest too much," for the habits of Rufinus are irrelevant, since he had had no such vision, and the argument that dreams are not binding, though sound,[49] is here weakened by being coupled with that drawn from the lapses of Christians from other obligations.

So far as I am aware no definite attempt has been made to discover how far the dream affected Jerome's attitude toward literature. It has been observed[50] that he asks Paul of Concordia for a copy of Aurelius Victor, and that many classical quotations—in fact the bulk of those which he makes—fall in works subsequent to the vision.[51] I have tried the experiment of dividing the letters into groups, following the chronological arrangement of Pronberger,[52] making the first group include letters 1-4, dating from 370 to 374, and closing at about the probable date of the vision, and the second group letters 5-46, dating from 375 to 386 (the approximate date of the *Commentary on Galatians*).[53] The first group covers, in Hilberg's edition, 20 pages; the second, 324. In the first group Hilberg indicates at 12 places reminiscences of secular writers, or an average of once in 1.6 pages; in the second, following the vision, at 42 places, or once in 7.7 pages. But since the first group is so small as to vitiate comparisons, I have made a third, immediately following and equal in length to the second, that is, of 324 pages, containing 118 allusions or one in 2.7 pages. A subsequent group of 324 pages[54] contains 63 cases, or one in 5.1 pages, while the remaining 231 pages of Hilberg's second volume[55] show 49 cases, or one in 4.7 pages. These figures are subject to modifications here and there,[56] and the groups are of course somewhat arbitrary. Yet it is of interest to observe the diminished frequency of citation immediately following the vision, and again, the increase subsequent to the period of the *Commentary on Galatians.* Could we be more precise as to the dates of letters we might make these groups correspond more exactly to differing periods in his attitude.[57]

Jerome, as I have said, explained to his lady friends that what classical quotations occurred in his works were due to reminiscence, not to renewed consultation of the originals, and this statement Lübeck[58] accepts, save as applied to the Greek historians, a necessary tool for Biblical studies. That the authors of his youthful training were those most frequently quoted—especially Cicero, Horace, and Virgil[59]—need occasion little surprise, and that many passages, particularly of the poets, clung to his memory was but natural, and is indicated by the number of times some particular lines are repeated in his works.[60] Frequently a quotation is inexact in such a way as to suggest that Jerome was trusting to his memory.[61] That he seldom cites exact references is hardly significant, for, despite his scholarly interests, he is commonly negligent about this even in the case of works of Christian scholarship,[62] where a reader might desire to verify references, while Biblical texts are constantly quoted, even as proof-passages, without mention of their exact source. Important in this connection are Jerome's dictated works,[63] which show no marked reduction in the frequency of classical allusions.[64] How largely these reminiscences go back to his boyhood and to what extent they were refreshed by renewed reading[65] we shall never know.

In the light, then, of Jerome's statements and practice it is likely that the vision had some effect for fifteen years or so, but that after that he regarded it as in no way binding. One is tempted to suggest that the interruption in his ascetic life in the Orient caused by his stay in Rome in 382-385 might have been responsible for this backsliding, but his references in the *Commentary on Galatians* to the fifteen years during which he had not read pagan authors do not favor this theory. More likely is it that the change was gradual and that its full effects were not felt till after he was settled in 386 for his long stay at Bethlehem. Again, the unnatural ascetic exaltation in which he had been at the time of the dream, as a young man of twenty-five or thirty, had yielded to the maturer judgment of age,[66] which saw matters in truer proportions.

All his life, however, was passed with books, and they allowed little room for interest in contemporaneous events. Civil wars,[67] barbarian invasions in the East[68] and the West,[69] and the capture of Rome[70] by Alaric are, indeed, mentioned, and to defects in the social fabric of his time he often alludes,[71] but economic, military, and political questions interested him but little.[72] The slight degree of his feeling for the historic tradition of the Roman state is due to his non-Roman birth, his long residence in the Orient,[73] and a constant sense of the contrast between worldly and spiritual glory.[74]

A second factor affecting Jerome's attitude towards the classics is, not unnaturally, the mental outlook of those for whom he wrote.[75] In his homilies and tractates for the "simpler brethren" of the monastery at Bethlehem, classical references are naturally infrequent.[76] On the contrary, in writing to a profligate deacon,[77] he scathingly assumes that, except for mental dulness, the man would be only too familiar with comedians, lyric writers, and mimes. But in addressing cultivated readers the pearls of classical allusion are more lavishly cast. In letters to Pope Damasus, himself an imitator of Virgil,[78] he quotes from the *Aeneid* to illustrate a principle of scansion,[79] and includes other reminiscences of Augustan poets.[80] Addressing Pammachius he uses many classical allusions and compares Pammachius to Aeneas,[81] while in the *epitaphia* on distinguished Roman ladies,[82] where the rhetorical element is prominent, such allusions are frequent.[83] In a letter to Theophilus, bishop of Alexandria,[84] Jerome commends him for not having, in a paschal letter, inserted phrases from secular writers, and elsewhere he considers it more proper to cite Christian than pagan views.[85] Yet he was, in general, greatly influenced by the character, and still more by the culture, of those to whom he wrote, and to the sophisticated he allowed himself a freedom from which he abstained when addressing the more easily scandalized simplicity of the monks at Bethlehem.[86]

But apart from morals or propriety, there was another determining factor, namely, the theological one. Pagan literature (especially the epics)[87] was permeated by references to pagan gods, and to such unbecoming ethical examples he was, like Plato, opposed,[88] just as to those elements in the society of his time which he recognized as relics of paganism.[89] But as he saw matters, from the standpoint of a scholar rather than a preacher, the dangers were more those of wrong belief than of wrong conduct, of heresy rather than of worldliness. Now of Christian heresies the roots lay in pagan philosophy,[90] and heretics were regarded as natural successors of the philosophers.[91] Consequently the passages in which philosophers, as sources of error, are mentioned with disparagement, are many, the objections against them being sometimes that they intentionally deceive,[92] more often that they wander from the truth,[93] that they clothe their thoughts in difficult language,[94] or that their lives and teachings are inconsistent with Christian standards,[95] while the positive dogmas of all schools are frequently attacked.[96] Yet we must note a striking passage in the **Commentary on Daniel,** in which he says:[97] "If you read all the books of the philosophers you cannot help finding in them some part of the vessels of God. In Plato, for instance, God as the fashioner of the world; in Zeno, the chief of the Stoics, the departed and immortal souls, and virtue as the sole good," etc. And elsewhere he praises the Platonic view of philosophy as practice for death,[98] the cardinal virtues of the Stoics,[99] the philosophic doubt of Carneades,[100] and the views of Cicero on friendship, similar in content to those of the Christians.[101]

It was, then, practical considerations which influenced Jerome's attitude, both towards philosophical literature and towards other types as well.[102] In a letter to Magnus,[103] explaining why he so often quotes the classics, he cites the precedent of many ecclesiastical writers, beginning with St. Paul. His practical justifications were chiefly the following. First, the need of studying the classics in order to be educated at all,[104] and to have models upon which to found the gradually developing Christian literature.[105] Secondly, the desire to meet pagan adversaries on their own ground,[106] a method particularly employed in assertions to infidels that if miracles were performed and laudable works done by pagans, similar miracles and merits must be allowed to Christians;[107] and, *per contra,* to convince Christian readers that they must at least prove themselves equal in these virtues to the pagans whom they despise.[108] Thirdly, he finds it desirable to make much use of history, and this in two ways: (1) as necessary for interpreting allegories, particularly those in the prophets,[109] and (2) as containing examples of virtues and vices useful for study,[110] though this latter method was obviously in need of severe restriction.[111] Finally, almost all literature contains information of value. In the spirit of Pliny the Elder[112] and Quintilian[113] he remarks[114] that "almost all the books of all writers—except such as with Epicurus have not learned letters—are replete with learning." In scientific matters, accordingly, in so far as they do not conflict with ecclesiastical dogmas, he freely uses pagan writers.[115] Great use is also made of proverbial expressions, some literary[116] and some from everyday life, and the satirists, especially Persius, are favorites, doubtless because of their moral earnestness and their dissatisfaction with the social conditions of paganism.[117]

I have attempted, then, briefly to trace the influence upon Jerome of his education, the mental outlook of his correspondents, his theological beliefs, and the practical necessities arising in the life of a scholar and controversialist. In a long life, full of critical activity, it is but natural that the picturesque dream of his youthful asceticism should have lost its force, even had it had at first a greater effect than the rhetorical character and hortatory purpose of its description would indicate.[118] Indeed, we may say that the subsequent world, more deeply impressed by one dramatic incident than by many years passed in modification or contradiction of it, has ascribed to the vision of Jerome altogether too much importance. But, making all due allowance for the dream, his attitude, like that of others, appears, if not absolutely consistent, at least easily intelligible. It was that of a man classically trained, seeing the strong points but also the weaknesses of the secular literature; in his youthful enthusiasm led first to admiration and then to strong, though temporary, aversion to the classics; and, finally, with the sanity of maturer life and the influence of the culture of the Greek East, able to walk with a surer step, realizing that complete acceptance of the new faith did not necessarily involve total rejection of what was of value in the old literature. In other words, his progress was the familiar succession of narrowly conservative and unquestioning upbringing, radical disillusionment and revolt, and true and ripe liberalism.

Notes

¹ Cf. Zöckler, *Hieronymus* (1865), esp. pp. 325, ff.; Lübeck, *Hieronymus quos noverit scriptores et ex quibus hauserit* (1872)—a useful but very incomplete work (cf. Grützmacher, *Hieronymus,* I [1901], 114, n. 6; Traube, *Vorlesungen und Abhandlungen,* II [1911], 66, n. 2); Comparetti, *Virgilio nel medio evo,* I², (1896), 109-111; Grützmacher, I, 113 ff.

² Like Tertullian; cf. Farrar, *Lives of the Fathers,* I (1889), 120.

³ On the date of his birth see Grützmacher, I, 45-48.

⁴ Cf. *in Abac.* II, p. 660.

⁵ References to Q. Aurelius Symmachus are lacking in Jerome (Grützmacher, I, 276), but to Vettius Agorius Praetextatus he refers in *Ep.* 23, 2, 1; cf. *Ep.* 39, 3, 7; *contra Ioann. Hieros.* 8.

⁶ Cf. *Ep.* 107, 2, 3; *in Is.* VII, p. 279; *Tract. de Ps.* 96 (*Anecd. Mared.* III, 2, 142); also *Ep.* 92, 3, 2 (translated by Jerome). On the neglect of pagan worship cf. *Ep.* 107, 1-2, written in 401 (Grützmacher, I, 100) or 399-400 (Pronberger, *Beiträge zur Chron. der Briefe des hl. Hier.* [1913], 68-69). Cf. *adv. Iovin.* II, 38.

⁷ Cf. Grützmacher, I, 275 ff.

⁸ I, 113 ff.

⁹ *Chron.* ann. Abr. 2370; *in Eccl.* p. 390; *adv. Rufin.* I, 16.

¹⁰ *Adv. Rufin.* I, 16: cf. Grützmacher, I, 114, n. 6. These authors, at least, it seems fair to select from those quoted by him as probably having been studied in his school days (Lübeck, 5, to the contrary). To the list should be added some *sententiae* of Publilius Syrus—both genuine and spurious; cf. Wölfflin, *Publilii Syri sententiae* (1869), 14-15; Lübeck, 115; *Ep.* 107, 8, 1. To the few cases from Lucretius cited by Lübeck, 116-117, should be added that noted by Hilberg in *Ep.* 77, II, 2; cf. Grützmacher, I, 114, n. 6.

¹¹ Grützmacher, 114, and nn. 3-4; Lübeck, 175, n. 3. On the borrowings from Donatus to be detected in Jerome see Grützmacher, I, 115, n. 2, and especially Lammert, "De Hier. Donati discipulo" (1912), in the *Comment. philol. Ienenses,* IX, 2. In spite of his re-

spect for Donatus Jerome could view the *grammatici* and their interests with a little humor, as may be seen from *in Ionam,* p. 426.

¹² Grützmacher, I, 117 classes him second only to Lactantius. Cf. Zöckler, 323: "So hat . . . erst Hieronymus die lateinische Sprache christlich und die christliche Theologie lateinisch gemacht," and he quotes Ozanam (*Hist. de la civil. chrét. au V'siècle,* II, 100) as calling Jerome "le maître de la prose chrétienne pour tous les siècles suivants." Cf. Erasmus as quoted by Zöckler, 340, n. 1. On the stylistic peculiarities of Jerome cf. Goelzer, *Étude lexicogr. et gram. de la latinité de S. Jérôme* (1884), and the works of Paucker cited by him, *op. cit.* VII, n. 1; Schanz, *Gesch. röm. Lit.* IV, I², (1914), 494-495; Pease in *Journ. Bibl. Lit.* XXVI (1907), 107 ff.

¹³ *Adv. Rufin.* I, 30; *in Galat.* II, 2, p. 408.

¹⁴ Grützmacher, I, 121-122; *adv. Rufin.* I, 30.

¹⁵ Lübeck, 57 ff.; Grützmacher, I, 122-123.

¹⁶ *Adv. Rufin.* III, 39, p. 565; cf. Lübeck, 58, n. 1. Also *Praef. in lib. Iob* (quoted in *adv. Rufin.* II, 29); cf. Rufin. *Apol.* II, 29. Porphyry, however, Jerome cites at first hand (cf. Lübeck, 64-86; also the reproaches of Rufinus, *Apol.* II, 9, p. 362; II, 10 bis, p. 365; II, 29; II, 42), and other lesser philosophers, *e.g.* Alexander of Aphrodisias (Lübeck, 96, n. 1; Grützmacher, I, 124, n. 3).

¹⁷ Rufin. *Apol.* II, 9, p. 362; Hier. *adv. Rufin.* I, 30. Cf. Grützmacher, I, 151, and n. 1; *adv. Rufin.* II, 22; III, 6. On the dislike of Augustine and Ausonius for Greek see Lockwood in *T.A.P.A.* XLIX (1918), 120.

¹⁸ Cf. the preface to his translation of Origen's homilies on Jeremiah (pp. 741-742); also *Ep.* 52, 4, 1; 66, 9, 1; 120, praef. 4; *adv. Helvid.* 2; *in Ezech.* IX, p. 360; *contra Lucif.* 14.

¹⁹ Contrasts of worldly wisdom and Christian simplicity are frequent; *e.g., Ep.* 48, 4, 3; 57, 12, 4; 133, 12; *in Is.* VII, p. 311; *in Galat.* III, pp. 485-486; 487-488; *Tract. de Ps.* 132 (*Anecd. Mared.* III, 2, 245); *Homil. in Ioann.* I (*Anecd. Mared.* III, 2, 388). Accordingly, as we learn in *Tract. de Ps.* 77 (*Anecd. Mared.* III, 2, 63), ecclesiastici . . . rustici sunt et simplices; omnes vero haeretici Aristotelici et Platonici sunt; cf. *Tract. de Ps.* 83 (*Anecd. Mared.* III, 2, 84). For Augustine's condemnation of rhetoric see Farrar, II, 304-305. But the other side of the story is seen in *Comm. in Galat.* III, pp. 487-488; with which cf. *Tract. de Ps.* 86 (*Anecd. Mared.* III, 2, 104). These passages suggest I Cor. 1, 23-28. Jerome's admiration for Demosthenes and Cicero was great, and their names often appear as types of oratory; *e.g., Ep.* 26, 14, 1; 29, 1, 3; 57, 13, 2; 84, 6,

1; 85, 1, 1; 99, 2, 1; 125, 12; 126, 2; 130, 6; 147, 5; *conira Ioann. Hieros.* 4 and 12; *adv. Pelag.* III, 16; *de Vir. Ill.* prol.; *in Is.* VIII, pp. 327-328; *in Ionam,* p. 419; *in Naum,* pp. 538-539; *in Galat.* III, pp. 485-486; *Praef. in lib. Is.; Praef. in lib. Dan.*

[20] Cf. *Ep.* 60, 8, 1.

[21] Cf. *Ep.* 50, 1, 2; 50, 2, 3; 85, 1, 1.

[22] Cf. *in Galat.* III, pp. 485-486.

[23] Cf. *Ep.* 117, 12; 118, 1; 119, 1; 128, 5; 129, 8; *in Is.* (in the different prologues); *in Ezech.* XIV, pp. 239-240; VIII, 283-284; *in Mich.* prol. pp. 431-432; *in Agg.* p. 774; *in Zach.* prol. pp. 777-778; II, p. 826; *in Matt.* prol. pp. 7-8. For the difficulties of dictation cf. *in Galat.* prol. pp. 369-370; III, pp. 485-486; *in Abd.* p. 386.

[24] Cf. Moore, *Hist. of Relig.* II (1919), 293.

[25] *In Galat.* III, pp. 485-486; cf. *Ep.* 26, 14, 1; 125, 12.

[26] Cf. *Praef. in lib. Dan.* (pp. 1291-1292 Migne).

[27] *In Is.* praef. pp. 5-6.

[28] *Chron.* praef.; *Ep.* 29, 1, 3.

[29] *Chron., l. c.; Praef. in Pentateuch.*
[30] *In Galat.* 1, p. 387.

[31] Grützmacher, 1, 58; Pronberger, *op. cit.* 25-26.

[32] *Ep.* 22, 29, 7; cf. Tert. *de Praescr. adv. Haeret.* 7.

[33] *Ep.* 22, 30, 1-6; repeated by Rufin. *A pol.* 11, 6.

[34] *Annos plurimos;* but the event fell in 373 or shortly thereafter; cf. Grützmacher, 1, 61.

[35] On his library see *Ep.* 5, 2, 2-4. It apparently included both ecclesiastical and secular books (cf. Grützmacher, 1, 128-129), and it is of interest to note that Jerome, with a scholar's natural instincts, later encouraged the writing of books, for he writes to a monk (*Ep.* 125, 11; dating, according to Grützmacher, 1, 88, after 410; according to Pronberger, *op. cit.* 77-78, about 409): Texantur et lina capiendis piscibus, scribantur libri, ut et manus operetur cibum et animus lectione saturetur. This advice, anticipating by more than a century a like provision in the Rule of St. Benedict, is probably the first instance of encouragement to monks to copy books; cf. Wattenbach, *Das Schriftwesen im Mittelalter*[3] (1896), 428; Norden in *Die Kultur der Gegenwart,* 1, 8[2] (1907), 409. For the carrying out of Jerome's principles by monks see Rufinus, *A pol.* 11, 8 bis, p. 363.

[36] In *Ep.* 22, 7, 1-2 we have proof of the unwholesome condition into which Jerome's imagination had been brought as a result of prolonged fastings.

[37] Schöne, *Die Weltchronik des Eusebius* (1900), 240, calls the vision "eines der ärgerlichsten Musterstücke verlogener Rhetorik, mühsam ausgesonnener Begeisterung und unechter Frömmigkeit." But, as Grützmacher (1, 153) says, a real experience undoubtedly underlies the account.

[38] Cf. Sandys, *Hist. of Class. Scholarship,* I[2] (1906), 618; also Traube, 11 (1911), 66: "In ähnlicher Art durch eine Vision—auch das ist zum rhetorischen Kunstgriff geworden—wird unzählige Male nach Hieronymus die Stellung des Christentums zur Beschäftigung mit den Klassikern fixiert, der Unwert dieser Beschäftigung eingeschärft"; and *ib.* n. 4.

[39] *In Galat.* III, pp. 485-486. For the date see Grützmacher (1, 60-62), who puts it in 386-387. This conflicts, however, as Grützmacher recognizes, with the "fifteen years" in the present passage, for 373 + 15= 388. Perhaps *plus quam quindecim anni* is not exact.

[40] Cf. *Ep.* 70, 3, 2.

[41] Grützmacher, 1, 68, dates the book against Rufinus in 402.
[42] *Adv. Rufin.* 1, 30-31.

[43] Rufin. *A pol.* 11, 7-8, pp. 359-360; 11, 8 bis, p. 363.

[44] *Adv. Rufin.* 1, 30.

[45] *Ib.* 31.

[46] *Ib.*

[47] *Ib.*

[48] Cf. Zöckler, 325, n. 1.

[49] Farrar, 11, 185, n. 3, considers his account in this passage very unlike what he had previously written to Eustochium (cf. *Ep.* 22, 30, 6). But Farrar underestimates the rhetorical character of the twenty-second letter, and hence is over-concerned with Jerome's failure to live in accordance with it. Norden, *op. cit.* 408, thinks that Jerome's compromise did more honor to his *"Wissensdrang und Formensinn"* than to his *"Wahrhaftigkeit und Gewissenstreue."*

[50] Zöckler, 48, n. 2; Farrar, 11, 185. The passage is *Ep.* 10, 3, 2.

[51] This had been noted by Magnus, to whom, in *Ep.* 70 (written between 399 and 403, according to

Grützmacher, 1, 100; or in 398, according to Pronberger, *op. cit.* 56) he explains the reason for his many classical quotations. He appears to have suspected that Magnus had been instigated by Rufinus to make this inquiry; cf. *Ep.* 70, 6, 2, and Pronberger, *l.c.*

⁵² Cf. *op. cit.* pp. 95-96; the results according to Grützmacher's table (1, 99-100) differ in an almost negligible degree. Josephus I exclude from the list of secular authors because of his indispensability for ecclesiastical scholars.

⁵³ Either before or after *Ep.* 46 Grützmacher and Pronberger indicate a break of about seven years in the correspondence.

⁵⁴ Running into Hilberg's second volume.

⁵⁵ Through *Ep.* 120 (408-409 A.D.).

⁵⁶ Due to differences in dating the letters, in deciding what constitutes a classical reminiscence, and to unlikeness in the contents of the letters.

⁵⁷ I have selected for comparison the letters rather than other works falling in these years, partly because the allusions in them have been more completely noted (though even to Hilberg's gatherings additions can be made), and partly because they are less specialized in contents and more truly representatives than either commentaries or controversial works. Grützmacher (1, 133) thinks that about the year 399 a change in Jerome's attitude set in, basing his belief on *Ep.* 70, but I doubt if the change was a sudden one, and the reason for the decisive tone of *Ep.* 70 is that Jerome's previous practice had been then called in question.

⁵⁸ P. 9. Traube, 11, 66, characterizes this view of Lübeck as *"ganz kindisch."* The truth probably lies between these extremes. Rufinus (*A pol.* 11, 8, p. 361) is contemptuous of Jerome's defence of himself on the ground of reminiscence. Noteworthy exceptions to Lübeck's view as stated are the lengthy quotation in *Ep.* 57, 5, 2-4 from Cic. *Opt. Gen.* 13-14 (cf. the reproaches of Rufinus in *A pol.* 11, 8, p. 360) and the rather long quoted passages in *adv. Rufin.* 111, 39. Cf. also n. 65 *infra.*

⁵⁹ Cf. Lübeck, 5; Zöckler, 326.

⁶⁰ Cf. in Lübeck's work such lines as Virg. *Aen.* IV, 298; VI, 625 ff., 724 ff., 733 ff.

⁶¹ Many cases are noted by Lübeck: *e.g.,* misquotation of Cicero (*in Is.* XII, p. 504); of *Aen.* 1, 743 (*adv. Rufin.* 111, 28); of *Aen.* 11, 329 (*Praef. in Esdram,* p. 1525); of *Aen.* IV, 379 (*in Ezech.* 111, p. 99); of *Aen.* V, 89 (*in Ezech.* 1, p. 22); reversal of the order of lines of Hor. *Epist.* 1, 1, 99-100 (*in Eccl.* p. 409). Augus-

tine, who also does not always quote correctly (*e.g., de Doctr. Christ.* 11, 31), sometimes recognizes his fallibility by such phrases as *si bene recolo* (*e.g., de Doctr. Christ.* 111, 11). In some instances Jerome adapts the quotation to fit its new context; in others he doubtless bases his readings on different text traditions from those commonly employed to-day.

⁶² Of course many exceptions may be found; *e.g., in Dan.* prol. pp. 617 ff.

⁶³ Cf. n. 23 *supra.*

⁶⁴ *E.g., Ep.* 117 and 118 (both dictated) contain, in 23 pages, 9 allusions, or one in 2.5 pages. Letters 119 and 129 (also dictated), despite unfavorable subject-matter, are not free from allusions.

⁶⁵ On Jerome's habits of reading compare the outside testimony of Sulpicius Severus, *Dial.* 1, 9, 5. The extent to which works studied in youth might affect one's later thought is recognized by Augustine, *C. D.* 1, 3; cf. Cassian, *Collat.* 14, 12; and n. 58 *supra.*

⁶⁶ Cf. Farrar, 11, 185. But see Mollweide in *Wien. Stud.* XXXIII (1912), 280-283. Perhaps his temporary desertion of classicism may have had the result, as Zöckler, 324, suggests, of making his later style less imitative.

⁶⁷ Cf. *Ep.* 60, 15, 1 ff.; 60, 17, 1; 77, 8, 4.

⁶⁸ Cf. *Chron.* praef.; *Ep.* 60, 16, 1-5; 66, 14, 1-2; 77, 8, 1-4; 114, 1-2; 118, 2, 2; 126, 2; *in Ezech.* VIII, pp. 283-284.

⁶⁹ *Ep.* 123, 16.

⁷⁰ *Ep.* 123, 17; 127, 12-13; 128, 5; 130, 4-7 (where Jerome's excitement leads him into frequent classical reminiscence); in *Ep.* 142, 1 Rome and Alaric are perhaps to be understood under the names of Jerusalem and Nebuchadnezzar.

⁷¹ Especially in hortatory letters. Sometimes his work approaches the field of Juvenalian satire; cf. Weston, *Latin Satiric Writing Subsequent to Juvenal* (1915), 82-100; also n. 117 *infra.*

⁷² Mention of emperors and civil officials is rare.

⁷³ There his outlook was largely Greek; cf. *Ep.* 50, 2, 3.

⁷⁴ He numbered, however, among his friends several of aristocratic lineage; *e.g.,* Furia (*Ep.* 54, 1, 2; 54, 6, 3), Paula (*Ep.* 108, 1, 1; 108, 3, 1; 108, 33, 2), Marcella (*Ep.* 127, 1). But some of these references to ancestry would very likely not have been made had it not been

for rhetorical usage; cf. *Ep.* 130, 3.

[75] *E.g.* cf. *Ep.* 49, 1.

[76] Even there he twice quotes Persius, 1, 1 (*Anecd. Mared.* III, 2, 130; III, 3, 83). Plato and Aristotle are also several times vaguely disparaged, indicating that these were names of which his fellow-monks had heard; cf. *adv. Pelag.* 1, 19.

[77] *Ep.* 147, 3.

[78] Cf. Schanz, *Gesch, röm. Lit.* IV, I² (1914), 215 and 217.

[79] *Ep.* 20, 5, 2. But Lübeck, 176, n. 1, points out that Jerome is perhaps here following Victorinus.

[80] With *Ep.* 21, 2, 5 cf. Virg. *Ecl.* 4, 61; with *Ep.* 21, 42 perhaps cf. Hor. *Epist.* 11, 1, 123.

[81] *Ep.* 66, 11, 1.

[82] Cf. n. 74 *supra*.

[83] *E.g. Ep.* 108; 127; 130. Cf. also *Ep.* 107 to Laeta, on the education of her daughter.

[84] *Ep.* 99, 2, 1. Is this perhaps an implication that in other letters of Theophilus quotations from classical sources were to be expected? A paschal letter of Theophilus, included in Jerome's letters because translated by him, contains (*Ep.* 100, 15, 2) reminiscences of Horace and Publilius Syrus!

[85] Cf. *in Is.* XVI, p. 665; *Ep.* 52, 2, 1; 60, 5, 3; 105, 3, 3. The view of Augustine is (*de Doctr. Christ.* II, 63) that pagan evidence is less valuable than scriptural.

[86] The tractates in the *Anecdota Maredsolana*, III, give most welcome glimpses into the society by which Jerome was there surrounded. His adaptation to his audience and correspondents was perhaps based upon I Cor. 9, 22.

[87] Cf. *Ep.* 21, 13, 4.

[88] Cf. *Ep.* 21, 13, 8; *adv. Iovin.* II, 38.

[89] With *Ep.* 21, 13, 3-9 cf. Paulinus in *C. S. E. L.* XVI, 506, ll. 76 ff. Of such intrusions of paganism Jerome (*Ep.* 27, 2, 1) asserts himself innocent.

[90] Cf. *Ep.* 133,2 (quoting Tert. *adv. Hermog.* 9). The characteristically Roman attitude of Tertullian (cf. Taylor, *Classical Heritage of the Middle Ages* [1901], 110) is in contrast to that of Justin, Clement, and Origen, who regarded philosophy as a guide to Christianity (cf.

Taylor, *op. cit.* III; 116-117; also Clem. *Strom.* 1, 5, 28). The philosophical learning of Clement and Origen is noted by Jerome in *Ep.* 70, 4, 3; 120, 10, 2; 124, 6-7; *adv. Pelag.* 1, 19; *contra Ioann. Hieros.* 19 and 32.

[91] The literal meaning and pagan use of *haeresis* are discussed in *Comm. in Titum,* p. 737, and in *Comm. in Is.* V, p. 227, Zeno is called *Stoicae sectae haeresiarches*. Philosophers and heretics are combined in lists of those of mistaken views (*in Eccl.* p. 475; *in Naum,* pp. 538-539, 582; *in Is.* III, p. 105; VI, p. 272; *in Hierem.* IV, p. 994); Marcion is even worse than Epicurus (*in Is.* VII, p. 285). The heretics largely rely on Plato and Aristotle; *Tract. de Ps.* 77 (*Anecd. Mared.* III, 2, 63); 140 (*Anecd. Mared.* III, 2, 272); 143 (*Anecd. Mared.* III, 2, 284). In *adv. Rufin.* III, 39 Jerome excuses himself for having mistakenly in his youth taken over into Christianity certain beliefs from his training in pagan philosophy.

[92] In *Tract. de Ps.* 115 (*Anecd. Mared.* III, 2, 215) he quotes Col. 2, 8, advising against the casuistry of philosophers; cf. *in Ezech.* IX, p. 360. To their contentiousness he applies a phrase of Tertullian (*de Anima,* 1), *philosophus animal gloriae* (quoted in *Ep.* 66, 8, 3; 118, 5, 2).

[93] *Ep.* 53, 4, 2; 65, 21, 2; *in Ezech.* I, p. 10; *in Is.* XII, p. 530; *Tract. de Ps.* 83 (*Anecd. Mared.* III, 2, 84); *de Ps.* 106 (*Anecd. Mared.* III, 2, 177); *Tract. in Marc.* 8 (*Anecd. Mared.* III, 2, 350); *Homil. in Ioannem,* I (*Anecd. Mared.* III, 2, 388).

[94] Cf. *in Amos,* II, p. 283; *in Is.* XII, p. 492; *in Naum,* p. 582; *in Eccl.* p. 475; *adv. Helvid.* 2.

[95] *E.g., Ep.* 69, 3, 6; *in Is.* I, p. 35.

[96] Cases are too numerous to recount. Cf. the errors of the Epicurean cosmogony (*Tract. in Is.* 6, in *Anecd. Mared.* III, 3, 110) and doctrine of pleasure (*in Is.* XI, p. 473; cf. XIX, p. 788), though in *adv. Iovin.* I, 4 he asserts that Pythagoras, Plato, Aristides, Aristippus, Epicurus, and others preferred virtue to pleasure. In *Comm. in Eccl.* p. 461 he condemns the Epicurean and Cyrenaic denial of immortality. Other cases of disparagement of philosophers are *Ep.* 33, 3; 133, 2; *contra Lucif.* 14; *adv. Iovin.* II, 7; *in Is.* X, p. 425; *in Ezech.* VIII, p. 290; *in Ionam,* p. 419; *in Eccl.* p. 495.

[97] P. 624; cf. *in Tit.* p. 709. With Jerome's view compare Aug. *de Doctr. Christ.* II, 60.

[98] *Ep.* 127, 6; but cf. *Ep.* 60, 14, 2, where this principle pales in comparison with that of I Cor. 15, 31.

[99] *Ep.* 66, 3, 1.

[100] *Contra Ioann. Hieros.* 35.

[101] *In Mich.* II, p. 517. In *Ep.* 79, 9, 4, pagan agreement with Christian views is noted.

[102] Cf. the sensible words of Augustine, *de Doctr. Christ.* II, 28.

[103] *Ep.* 70, 4, 1 ff.

[104] In *Ep.* 21, 13, 9, he admits that such study *in pueris necessitatis est,* though this may refer only to the compulsion applied to boys by their elders. Basil, *ad Adulescentes,* 2 (Migne, *Patr. Gr.* XXXI, 565-568), observes that in youth we are unprepared for the mysteries of the sacred writings and therefore practice ourselves on others, as soldiers drill first in athletics. On the impossibility of an education without study of pagan subjects cf. Grützmacher, 1, 131 and 134; Taylor, *op. cit.* 108 ff. To refrain from such training would force the Christians to accept an intellectual equipment inferior to that of the pagans; cf. *Ep.* 70, 6, 2. Hence the objection of the Christians to the edict of Julian forbidding them to teach grammar and rhetoric; cf. Comparetti, I² (1896), 106, and n. I; Aug. *Conf.* VIII, 10.

[105] Thus he acknowledges imitation in his *de Viris Illustribus* of the homonymous work by Suetonius (*Ep.* 47, 3, 2; 112, 3, 2; *Vir. Ill.* prolog.), and, in his translations, of Cicero and other translators (*Ep.* 57, 5, 2; 106, 3, 3; *in Mich.* II, p. 480; *in Galat.* I, p. 387); and Weston (*op. cit.* 98-99) would detect in *Ep.* 50, 5, 2 a similar recognition of kinship with Horace and Juvenal.

To express imitation of pagans by Christians Jerome often uses a form of epithet doubtless familiar at his time. Thus in *Ep.* 57, 12, 2 Pammachius is *nostrorum temporum Aristarchus* (cf. *adv. Rufin.* I, 17; III, 30); in *Ep.* 22, 35 Josephus is *Graecus Livius;* Virgil (*in Mich.* II, p. 518-519) is *poeta sublimis* (*non Homerus alter, ut Lucilius* (1189 Marx) *de Ennio suspicatur, sed primus Homerus apud Latinos*); with which compare *Ep.* 121, 10, where Virgil is *alter Homerus apud nos;* David (in *Ep.* 53, 8, 17) is *Simonides noster, Pindarus et Alcaeus, Flaccus quoque, Catullus et Serenus;* Lactantius (*Ep.* 58, 10, 2) is *quasi quidam fluvius eloquentiae Tullianae;* Jovinian (*adv. Iovin.* I, 1) the *Epicurus Christianorum;* Vigilantius (*Ep.* 61, 3, 3; ironically) is the *solus . . . Cato;* cf. *contra Ioann. Hieros.* 39: *Hippocrates Christianorum* (and *ib.* 38); also *in Is.* XII, 492-493: *noster Luscius Lanuvinus.*

I might here note, in connection with this sophistical etiquette of indirect reference (cf. Wright's *Julian* [Loeb Classical Library], I, xi), that Jerome commonly employs such expressions as *gentilium fabulae* (*Ep.* 117, 6, 4; *contra Ioann. Hieros.* 19; *in Is.* VI, pp. 236 and 240; X, p. 444; *in Galat.* I, p. 418), *fabulae poetarum* (*Ep.* 130, 7; *in Is.* IV, p. 159; *in Hierem.* III, pp. 923-924; *in Ezech.* VI, p. 197; *in Dan.* pp. 652-653; *in*

Osee, II, pp. 53-54; *in Naum,* p. 549), *fabulae* (*contra Ioann. Hieros.* 35; *adv. Iovin.* I, 7; *in Amos,* II, p. 289; *in Galat.* II, p. 619; *in Ephes.* III, p. 651), or *in saeculari litteratura legimus* (*in Amos,* III, p. 313). The following epithets are frequent: *insignis poeta* (Virgil, *in Is.* XVI, p. 680; Ovid, *in Osee,* I, p. 24); *illustris poeta* (Virgil, *Ep.* 140, 10, *in Zach.* I, p. 792); *poeta gentilis* (Virgil, *Ep.* 7, 4, 1, and 17, 2, 1, *in Eccl.* p. 448; Horace, *Ep.* 16, 2, 1); *ethnicus poeta* (Virgil, *Ep.* 79, 7, 8); *poeta saecularis* (Persius, *Tract. de Ps.* 93, in *Anecd. Mared.* III, 2, 130); *ardens poeta* (Lucan, *Ep.* 123, 17, *in Is.* XV, p. 657; called *ardentissimus poeta* in *Comm. in Ezech.* XIII, p. 545); *poeta doctissimus* (Oppian, *in Ezech.* XIV, p. 595); *philosophus et poeta* (Virgil, *in Eccl.* p. 469); *poeta* (Virgil, *in Eccl.* pp. 452 and 460, *in Ezech.* IX, p. 357); *quidam poeta* (Claudian, *in Is.* VIII, p. 361); *lyricus* (Horace, *in Mich.* II, p. 517); *Latinus . . . historicus* (Sallust, *in Galat.* I, p. 416; cf. III, p. 500); *historicus* (Sallust, *adv. Iovin.* II, 10); *nobilis historicus* (Sallust, *in Eccl.* p. 430).

[106] As St. Paul quoted from Aratus, Epimenides, and Menander; cf. *Ep.* 70, 2, 2 ff.; 70, 2, 4; 130, 18; *in Tit.* pp. 706-707; *in Ephes.* III, p. 648; *in Galat.* II, p. 471. Other examples are given in *Ep.* 70, 3, and Jerome says that Cyprian was criticized for failure thus to meet pagans on their own ground. An example of Jerome's own method will be found in *Comm. in Osee,* I, p. 5.

[107] Thus the incredible youth of Ahaz when he became, at what Jerome reckons as eleven years of age, the father of Hezekiah, is paralleled by Greek and Roman prodigies (*Ep.* 72, 2, 1-3); the story of Jonah and the whale is defended by the even more improbable tales which pagan readers of Ovid accept (*in Ionam,* p. 406); that of Nebuchadnezzar eating grass is more worthy of credence than many tales from mythology, such as Scylla, the Chimaera, the Hydra, the Centaurs, and ancient metamorphoses (*in Dan.* p. 645); if Apollonius of Tyana could mysteriously disappear, why could not Jesus?—*quid magis licet hoc Domino non licet?* (*contra Ioann. Hieros.* 34; cf. 35). But elsewhere (*ib.* 32) he condemns the use of pagan arguments by Christians and heretics; cf. *ib.* 19 and *Ep.* 133, 3.

[108] Cf. *Ep.* 66, 8, 3; *adv. Iovin.* II, 14. Similar *a fortiori* arguments are drawn from pagans who preferred virtue to pleasure (*adv. Iovin.* I, 4), respected virginity (*ib.* I, 41 ff.), avoided remarriage (*Ep.* 54, 1, 2; 79, 7, 8; 123, 8), and maintained peaceable dispositions (*Ep.* 17, 2, 1).

[109] A good example is found in *Comm. in Dan.* praef. pp. 621-622. Josephus is, of course, constantly employed as testimony for the truth of Scripture. On the importance of history cf. Aug. *de Doctr. Christ.* II, 44; and for philosophy as ancillary to scriptural exegesis, Taylor, 112. Jerome, in spite of fondness both for Virgil and for the detection of allegory, did not consider the

fourth Eclogue as prophetic; cf. *Ep.* 53, 7, 3. In fact, though recognizing that the pagans themselves employed allegory in explaining secular writers (*in Ezech.* III, p. 89), he was not himself inclined to do so.

[110] Instances will be found in *Ep.* 52, 3, 5-6; 57, 3, 2; 58, 5, 2; *adv. Iovin.* II, II; etc.

[111] In *Ep.* 77, 2, 3, however, he derives the greatness of Fabiola not from her Fabian ancestry, *sed de ecclesiae humilitale.* Augustine in the *de Civitate Dci* similarly belittles pagan *exempla virtutis,* for if it were too freely admitted that worthy characters might be produced outside Christianity, dangerous results might follow. Cf. Litchfield in *Harv. Stud.* XXV (1914), 67-70.

[112] Plin. *Ep.* III, 5, 10.

[113] X, 1, 40; X, 1, 57.

[114] *Ep.* 70, 6, 1. So Gregory of Nazianzus favored gathering roses among the thorns of paganism (*Carm.* 1, 2, 10, 214 ff. in Migne, *Patr. Gr.* XXXVII, 695-696), and similar advice is found in Basil, *ad Adulescentes,* (Migne, *Patr. Gr.* XXXI, 563 ff.). The works of Gregory, a teacher of Jerome (cf. Grützmacher, 1, 177 ff.), abound in classical quotations for which he makes no apology (though he upbraids Gregory of Nyssa in *Ep.* II for abandoning Christian books for the trade of a rhetorician; cf. *Ep.* 235), and Basil takes for granted that the young will study secular writings. For the greater tolerance of the Eastern Church see Comparetti, 1², 105, n. 1.

[115] *E.g.* in explaining eclipses (*in Is.* VI, p. 240). In *Ep.* 121, 6 Xenophon's *Oeconomicus* is praised; elsewhere medical writers are employed (cf. Pease in *Harv. Stud.* XXV [1914], 81-82).

[116] Here is probably one explanation of Jerome's fondness for comedy (another being the influence of Donatus), for the New Comedy is primarily description of life; cf. *Ep.* 54, 9, 5. He recognizes, like Arnobius (*adv. Gent.* IV, 35) and others, the unbecoming nature of many comedies and mimes; *e.g., Ep.* 52, 5, 7 and 147, 3; *in Ezech.* X, p. 404; *in Ephes.* III, p. 666. But the New Comedy is also as free as any form of pagan literature from corrupting theological doctrines. For Jerome's quotations from comedy and mimes see Lübeck, 106-115, to which several additions might be made. Tragedy was nearly negligible; for a few references to Euripides—indirectly borrowed—cf. Lübeck, 17-18, and Zöckler, 328. The witnessing of tragedies and comedies is condemned (*in Ezech.* X, p. 404).

[117] For Horace see Lübeck, 162-167; for Persius, *id.* 195-198; for Juvena¹, *id.* 198-199, to which add *Vit. Hilar.* 12 (cf. Juv. 10, 22) and *Ep.* 52, 5, 4 (perhaps cf.

Juv. 13, 242). Persius even makes his way into Jerome's sermons: *Tract. de Ps.* 93 (*Anecd. Mared.* III, 2, 130; cf. III, 3, 83). Horace's contempt for gods that were the work of men's hands (*Sat.* 1, 8, 1 ff.) is welcomed (*in Is.* XII, p. 528). For the popularity of Persius and Juvenal cf. Sandys, *Hist. of Class. Scholarship,* 1² (1906), 644-645.

[118] Traube well remarks (II, 66): "Trotz der Vision, trotz seine Schwüre blieb Hieronymus, was er war: Grammatiker, Philolog, Klassizist, Zitatenjäger, der christliche Aristarch, der es nie aufgegeben hat die Alten zu lesen und zu zitieren. Für die lateinische Literatur des Mittelalters, für die Entwicklung der Sprache ist das von dem gewaltigsten Einfluss gewesen. Er will die Bibel nicht nur *fideli sermone,* sondern *puro sermone* übersetzen."

Harrison Cadwallader Coffin (lecture date 1923)

SOURCE: "The Influence of Vergil on St. Jerome and on St. Augustine," *The Classical Weekly,* Vol. 17, No. 22, April 7, 1924, pp. 170-75.

[*In the following essay, originally delivered as a lecture in 1923, Coffin explores the deep influence of Vergil on Jerome's writings and claims that, through his knowledge of Vergil, "Jerome really constitutes a link between the classical times and the Middle Ages."*]

It is impossible to read the works of the Christian Latin writers without being impressed by the extent to which they were influenced, both in language and in ideas, by the works of Vergil. This influence is shown through all periods of the Christian Church; indeed, a convenient index of the classicism of any Church writer is the use which he makes of Vergil. Since Jerome and Augustine represent the best in ecclesiastical prose of the first five centuries, it will be convenient to indicate the extent of the Vergilian tradition in the Christian Church by showing how these two great writers were affected by the works of the great pagan poet.

Eusebius Hieronymus—or Jerome, as he is more usually called—was born in Stridon, on the borders of Dalmatia, about 340. His parents were Christians, so that early in life he imbibed the spirit of Christianity both by precept and by example. While still a young man, he went to Rome, where he studied under the celebrated grammarian Donatus. After completing his studies under Donatus, he studied theology at Treves, and then returned to Rome to become the confidential adviser of Pope Damasus. After that Pontiff's death, Jerome adopted a rigorously ascetic mode of life, and founded a monastery at Bethlehem, where he spent the remainder of his days.

As an author Jerome was both prolific and versatile. Perhaps his best known work is his translation of the

Bible, a monument of learning and studious application. Besides this magnificent piece of erudition he composed several commentaries on the Scriptures, some controversial works, a work entitled **De Viris Illustribus,** and a number of letters, more than one hundred of which have been preserved.

As a writer Jerome stands among the first of the Christian Fathers. His style is clear and vivid, not too much tainted by rhetorical exaggeration. Indeed, it is so good that, in the estimation of some critics, he, rather than Lactantius or Ambrosius, deserves the title of 'Christian Cicero'. He was a strongly original writer. His style served as a model for succeeding generations of patristic authors, and yet that style depends for much of its beauty and effect upon reminiscences of the Classics. These reminiscences show that Jerome's knowledge of the classical authors was most extensive. Vergil and Horace, Sallust and Suetonius, Cicero and Quintilian, Terence, Lucan, Persius, not to mention lesser personages such as Valerius Maximus, are all as familiar to him as the books of the Bible. His acquaintance with the Greek authors was not so wide, but one finds traces of Aristotle, Homer, Hesiod, Plutarch, and Plato. Almost on every page of Jerome one finds citations from the pagan writers, quotations to establish some point of fact, or simply a phrase from one of the poets woven into the thread of his discourse. Much of the richness of Jerome comes from these classical echoes.

Chief among his classical models was Vergil. Here we are confronted by the same strange contradiction which we meet in other writers, especially in Tertullian. In spite of his profound knowledge of the pagan writers, in spite of his dependence upon them for all sorts of stylistic ornaments, nevertheless Jerome cannot quite reconcile the study of the pagans with true Christianity, and therefore decries the reading of the pagan authors, especially Vergil.

The ancient writers had been rebuked because they were pagans, and yet their works were carefully studied, and they must have been regarded by the educated Christians as men of great enlightenment. The patristic writers were obliged to study the pagan authors, partly to refute them, partly because they were the basis of all culture. Again and again the pagans are quoted as authorities even on matters of theological dogma. Jerome had said of Vergil (**Commentarius in Micheam:** see Vallarsi's edition of Jerome, 6.518 [Venice, 1766]), that he was 'not the second but the first Homer of the Romans', and yet, in a letter to Damasus (Epistle 21, page 123, Hilberg), he censures those priests who lay aside the Gospels and the prophets and read comedies, who recite the amorous words of bucolic poetry, and have Vergil ever in their hands, and take a sinful delight in that study which for children is a matter of necessity. But his own frequent

reminiscences of Vergil show that it was impossible to dispel the words of the poet from his mind. For example (**Commentarius in Ezechiel,** Chapter 40: compare Migne, Patrologia Latina, 25, Column 375), in describing the darkness of the catacombs where many of the martyrs were buried, he says, 'Here one can move only step by step, and in the gloom one is reminded of Vergil's phrase Horror ubique animos, simul ipsa silentia terrent'. And yet, when excited by emotions of reverence and piety, he exclaims (**Epistula ad Eustochium** 1.12), 'What has Horace to do with the Psalter, or Vergil with the Gospel, or Cicero with the Apostle?' Some of Jerome's adversaries, in their eagerness to catch at any excuse for discrediting him, reproved him for this inconsistency. When he established a school in which grammar and rhetoric were taught, with Vergil as a background, his opponent Rufinus, casting Jerome's own words in his teeth as a rebuke, attacked him viciously for being so derelict in his duty as to allow young students to read pagan authors.

Of all the pagan authors, Vergil affected Jerome most deeply. For instance, we find Vergil quoted in a discussion of the rhetorical figure aposiopesis; as an authority for the fact that incense came from Sheba; and on the subject of placating gods that they might not injure men. Parallelisms are noted between a Scriptural expression and a Vergilian phrase. So, for instance, in the **Commentary on Jeremiah** 6.4, Vae nobis, quia declinavit dies, quia longiores factae sunt umbrae vesperi, he quotes as a parallel Vergil, Ecl. 1.82-83 et iam summa procul villarum culmina fumant, maioresque cadunt altis de montibus umbrae. Similarly, in commenting on Jeremiah 18.14, Nunquid deficiet de petra agri nix Libani? aut evelli possunt aquae erumpentes frigidae et defluentes?, he quotes Vergil, Ecl. 1.59-60, 63, Aen. 1.607-609.

Besides these examples, there are dozens of instances, especially in the Letters, where Vergil is quoted to fill out a phrase; in these he is sometimes referred to by name, sometimes characterized as *poeta gentilis,* or by some equally general appellation. Frequent, too, are the instances where the Vergilian phrase appears without any hint that a quotation is being used: iterum iterumque monebo, numero deus inpare gaudet, non omnia possumus omnes, dux femina facti, and many others. Sometimes the Vergilian idea is repeated in different words, as etiam quae tuta sunt pertimescam, an evident reflection of omnia tuta timens, Aeneid 4.298.

One important fact must, however, be remarked here. Vergil is quoted as an authority on literature, art, science, prosody, mythology; in these fields his ideas are freely borrowed, and his phrases are generously used, but he is never quoted on questions specifically pertaining to the Christian faith. Indeed, Jerome girds at those Christians who quote pagan writers in support of Christian doctrines. Jerome really constitutes a link between the classical times and the Middle Ages; he is thoroughly saturated with profane learning, but for religious authority he relies exclusively on sacred sources. We have his unequivocal statement that he did not believe in Vergil as a Messianic prophet. In a letter to Paulinus (Epistle 63, page 454, Hilberg), he throws ridicule upon those who look upon Vergil as a Christian without Christ, and treats the whole matter as childish:

> . . . Quasi non legerimus Homerocentonas et Vergiliocentonas ac non sic etiam Maronem sine Christo possimus dicere Christianum quia scripserit
>
> iam redit et virgo, redeunt Saturnia regna,
> iam nova progenies caelo demittitur alto,
>
> et matrem loquentem ad filium
>
> nate, meae vires, mea magna potentia solus,
>
> et post verba salvatoris in cruce
>
> talia perstabat memorans, fixusque manebat.
>
> Puerilia sunt haec et circulatorum ludo similia, docere, quod ignores, immo, ut cum Clitomacho loquar, ne hoc quidem scire, quods nescias.

The Vergilian tradition in Jerome is quite evident and easy to trace. He had been trained in the schools of rhetoric where Vergil was the great model, the consummation of all that was best in Latin style. Hence it is that Vergil appeals to him first of all as a literary figure. The belief in Vergil's universal knowledge is not evident in Jerome, as it is in some of the other ecclesiastical writers, but there does appear some hint of his authority in secular matters, whether in poetry or prose, grammar or rhetoric, mythology or science, that is to say, in all the first elements of culture. Jerome mocks at the belief in Vergil as a Messianic prophet, and never mentions him as a worker of wonders, and yet he is so profoundly influenced by him, that, Churchman as he was, he did not hesitate to quote the pagan poet as casting light even on the Holy Scriptures. He seems to be in doubt just how far a Christian can use the pagans and still be a Christian, and consequently invokes the authority of Vergil only on secular matters, but even so there may be detected in him a shadowing forth of that universal authority which Vergil was later to have in matters both secular and sacred. Jerome will not admit the infallibility of Vergil; his ascetic Christian spirit felt a repugnance toward some of the expressions of pagan sentiment: hence it is that in his writings the tradition of Vergil is not so fully rounded as it later became[1]. It must also be observed that Jerome does not inveigh against the pagan writers

as such; he does not deny their educational value; what he does oppose is the tendency of some of the priests to let themselves be influenced by the pagans to the exclusion of everything else. In the development of his philosophy and his theology he was chiefly influenced by the Scriptures, but in matters outside this domain, in the field of general knowledge, of art, science, mythology, polite learning generally, he was powerfully influenced by the pagan Classics, and chief among his models was Vergil, the most influential figure in the history of poetry.

In considering the influence of Vergil on Augustine, we are met by different conditions. Augustine's experience of life was different from Jerome's, and their theological notions were not the same; it is therefore not surprising that they should show in a different degree the influence of the classical authors whom they had both studied.

Augustine is one of the mightiest figures in the history of the Church. Three of his predecessors, Lactantius, Ambrosius, and Jerome, had been decorated with the title of 'Christian Cicero', *honoris causa,* but here we have one who has been deemed worthy of the name of 'Christian Plato'. He was born at Tagaste, in Numidia, in 354. His father had been a pagan and his mother a Christian, but he for some time belonged to the sect of the Manicheans. While still a young man he went to Rome, and was from there called to Milan to teach rhetoric. While in Milan he fell under the sway of Ambrosius, and in 387 he allowed himself to be baptized. After leaving Milan he returned to his native town, and remained there until called to the priesthood at Hippo, where in 395 he became bishop.

Such was the unflagging industry of Augustine that, in spite of his exacting duties as bishop, he was the most prolific of all the Christian writers. There are more than one hundred titles of works, chiefly theological, which belong to Augustine, besides a considerable number of letters. Of these works it will be sufficient to emphasize two, which are important not only as theology, but as world literature, the Confessiones, and the treatise on The City of God, De Civitate Dei. The Confessiones, one of the earliest autobiographies of which we have any trace, gives a moving description of his spiritual unfolding from his early youth to his episcopate[2]. The City of God, on the other hand, is a more philosophical work. It was composed as a rejoinder to those of the pagans who had asserted that the evils which had sapped the strength of Rome, and humbled her empire to the dust before the unkempt hordes of Alaric, were the result of Christianity and nothing else. In this book, a universal defence of his faith, Augustine concentrated all the vast stores of his learning and his eloquence. Professor Mackail (Latin Literature, 276) has called the book "the epitaph of the ancient civilizations".

As a stylist, Augustine is a notable figure, far surpassing those patristic writers who preceded and followed him[3]. In those of his works which are addressed to the learned world he uses, so far as was then possible, the classical speech, while in the discourses intended for the people he modifies his language to adapt it to a popular audience. All of Augustine's writings are characterized by passionate expression, and by originality of style.

Like most of the other Church writers, Augustine was profoundly influenced by his intensive study of the Classics. He drew material from the following authors: Claudian, Ennius, Horace, Lucan, Persius, Terentianus Maurus, Terence, Valerius Soranus, Vergil, Homer, Apuleius, Cicero, Aulus Gellius, Justinus, Labeo, Livy, Plato, Pliny, Plotinus, Pomponius, Porphyry, Sallust, L. Annaeus Seneca, Tertullian, and Varro. This list indicates on his part the possession of a truly formidable body of learning. Indeed, he had read and stored away in his vast memory all that was best in the literary productions of Greece and Rome, and he used the material freely in the composition of his own works. One thing that Augustine had in common with Jerome was that chief among his classical models was Vergil.

For example, in the De Civitate Dei Vergil is quoted about seventy times, more frequently than all the other writers combined. Augustine must have had by heart the whole of the Vergilian corpus. He quotes from all of Vergil's works, but the quotations from the Aeneid are the most numerous. In the De Civitate Dei he quotes Vergil for Roman history and mythology, for the grandeur and importance of Rome, for the impotence of the gods to defend their worshippers, and the need of the worshippers to protect the gods. He quotes him with satiric reference to the fact that the gods are troubled by the morals of mortals, and for the decadence of the moral spirit in Rome. For the dangers and laxity of the pagan religions he quotes the favorite poet of the Romans against themselves, where those who died by their own hand are represented as suffering in the underworld. He also quotes Vergil in a spirit of reproof in a discussion of magic arts. He quotes him to show that the Brutus who slew his own son was *infelix*. A Vergilian line is used to describe perfect composure of mind, and another is introduced to show how Porphyry had refuted one of the doctrines of Vergil in regard to the necessity imposed upon purified souls to taste of Lethe. He quotes from the Fourth Eclogue as prophetic of the coming glories of the kingdom of Christ. He rebukes Vergil for declaring that all the evils of the mind come from the body. On the same topic he quotes the words of Aeneas to his father on the possibility of men's souls returning to their bodies. He quotes Vergil, calling him *nobilissimus eorum poeta,* in a discussion of the stature of the men of former times. In a discussion of the message which God sent through the angels, Vergil is quoted together with the Bible. Lines of Vergil are adduced in a discussion whether Saturn was a man or not; and in another place Vergil's authority is invoked on the history of the early kings of Rome. On the subject of the end of the world and the falling stars he cites the Vergilian line *facem ducens multa cum luce cucurrit.* In a discussion of miracles he says that, if it were possible for the priestess of the Massylian race to stop the flow of water, change the course of the stars, and call up the spirits of the departed, as Vergil declares in the Aeneid (4.487), how much more probable is it that God can perform miracles, which, though well within His power, are nevertheless incomprehensible to the heathen? In treating of the views of the Platonists, who declared that there were no sins without punishment, but that penalties were established for all sins, either during life or after death, he quotes Vergil, though only to refute him. He quotes him also on technical matters, such as etymology. Frequently, too, the same quotation is used more than once[4].

The condition just reviewed in the De Civitate Dei obtains also in the rest of Augustine's work, though the number of actual quotations is not so large. All through his varied writings he quotes Vergil more than he does any other author; and just as he knew the pagan authors better and used them more often than any other ecclesiastical writer knew them or used them, so his use of Vergil is more extensive than that found anywhere else in the history of Christian Latin literature.

Augustine's acquaintance with Vergil had begun early. In speaking of his early education he says (Confessiones 1.20), *cogebar tenere Aeneae nescio cuius errores.* For a long time he was in the habit of reading Vergil every day, but, when he was forty-three years old, a sudden access of asceticism caused him to deplore the days in which he let himself 'weep for Dido because she slew herself for love, though at the same time I was ummoved to tears when dying to Thee, O God, my life, ah, wretched man that I was' (Confessiones 1.20).

He is so entranced with the Trojan story that he says (Confessiones 1.22) . . . esset dulcissimum spectaculum . . . equus ligneus plenus armatis et Troiae incendium "atque ipsius umbra Creusae" (compare Aeneid 2.772). He says in another place (Confessiones 1.27) that he was obliged to declaim Vergil—a regular exercise in the Schools. Proponebatur enim mihi negotium animae satis inquietum praemio laudis et dedecoris vel plagarum metu, ut dicerem verba Iunonis irascentis et dolentis, quod non posset "Italia Teucrorum avertere regem". He describes there the school exercises in which 'we were forced to follow in the footsteps of the poets, and to tell in prose what the poet had said in his verses; and that one excelled who pretended to be affected by wrath or grief like the character whom he was impersonating, and clothed his thoughts in the most fitting words'. Augustine says that he was accounted very skilful at this exercise, and indeed we can tell from his works that he was a singularly penetrating and consistent student of the great classic writers.

Augustine not only believed thoroughly in Vergil as a Messianic prophet, but even went so far as to declare that there were among the pagans several prophets who foretold the coming of Christ. This declaration appears in a general form in several places, notably in his work, Contra Faustum, Book 13, Chapters 1, 2, 15, 17. In the Epistulae ad Romanos Incohata Expositio, Chapter 3, he says:

> Fuerant enim et prophetae non ipsius, in quibus etiam aliqua inveniuntur, quae de Christo audita cecinerunt, sicut etiam de Sibylla dicitur; quod non facile crederem nisi quod poetarum quidam in Romana lingua nobilissimus antequam diceret ea de innovatione saeculi, quae in Domini nostri Jesu Christi regnum satis concinere et convenire videantur, praeposuit versum, dicens "Ultima Cumaei iam venit carminis aetas". Cumaeum autem carmen Sibyllinam esse nemo dubitaverit.

With this compare the statement in De Civitate Dei 10.27:

> De quo <i. e. Christo> etiam poeta nobilissimus poetice quidem, quia in alterius adumbrata persona, veraciter tamen, si ad ipsum referas, dixit <here he quotes Ecl. 4. 13-14> . . . scelerum tamen manere vestigia, quae non nisi ab illo Salvatore sanantur, de quo iste versus expressus est. Nam utique non hoc a se ipso se dixisse Vergilius in eclogae ipsius quarto ferme versu indicat, ubi ait "Ultima Cumaei iam venit carminis aetas", unde hoc a Cumaea Sibylla dictum esse incunctanter apparet.

In Epist. 258.5, he has much the same thing:

> Nam omnino non est, cui alteri praeter dominum Christum dicat genus humanum <here he again quotes Ecl. 4. 13-14>. Quod ex Cumaeo, id est ex Sibyllino carmine, se fassus est transtulisse Vergilius.

Lactantius had made considerable use of the Sibylline books in discussing the tangled question of the Fourth Eclogue, but in no other author do we find such continued insistence on that Eclogue with its supposed prophecy of the Christ as we find in Augustine.

Augustine not only believed in Vergil as a prophet, but he believed him to have imitated certain passages of the Bible. This was not a new theory. Tertullian had declared that all the poetical and philosophical ideas of Greece and Rome were either borrowed or adapted from the Old Testament, and Jerome had in several

instances indicated a supposed parallel between Vergil and the Bible. Similarly Augustine, in De Civitate Dei 15.19, definitely says that Vergil had imitated the Scriptures: Imitatus namque est poeta ille litteras sacras, in quibus dicitur domus Jacob iam ingens populus Hebraeorum (compare Aen. 1.284; 3.97). Again, in De Civitate Dei 21.27, we find this:

> Mirari autem soleo etiam apud Vergilium reperiri istam Domini sententiam, ubi ait: "Facite vobis amicos de mammona iniquitatis ut et ipsi recipiant vos in tabernacula aeterna" <Luke 16.9>. Cui est et illa simillima: "Qui recipit prophetam in nomine prophetae, mercedem prophetae accipiet; et qui recipit iustum in nomine iusti, mercedem iusti accipiet, <Matthew 10.41>. Nam cum Elysios campos poeta ille describeret, ubi putant habitare animas beatorum, non solum ibi posuit eos, qui propriis meritis ad illas sedes pervenire potuerunt, sed adiecit atque ait: "Quique sui memores alios fecere merendo" <Aen. 6. 664>, id est, qui promeruerunt alios, eosque sui memores promerendo fecerunt. Prorsus tamquam iis dicerent, quod frequentatur ore Christiano, cum se cuique sanctorum humilis quisque commendat et dicit "Memor mei est", atque id ut esse possit promerendo efficit.

In addition to these direct quotations from Vergil, there are numerous instances where Augustine has used Vergilian imitations or allusions in discussing questions of mythology, natural phenomena, and scientific subjects. For instance, Vergil is referred to on the subject of Jupiter and his place in the pantheon, on Juno as sister and wife of Jove, and on the subject of her hatred for Aeneas. Neptune is, according to Vergil, the ruler of the seas, and the builder, with the aid of Apollo, of the walls of Troy. Pluto is king of the underworld, and his dominions are guarded by Cerberus; in this connection is also brought in the Vergilian picture of the Elysian Fields. The Vergilian version of the legend of Proserpina is also adduced; so are the legends of Mars, Rhea Silvia, Venus and Adonis, Mercury as the inventor of letters and the messenger of the gods, Minerva in her various aspects of Tritonia, Diana, or Luna, and patroness of the arts and creator of the olive tree, of Cybele, of the Fates, and of Janus. The demigods, such as Proteus, Hercules, and Rhadamanthus, appear in Augustine as they do in Vergil, and the picture of the Homeric heroes is also drawn from him. Other subjects, the knowledge of which Augustine may have derived from Vergil, are the functions of the rivers Phlegethon and Lethe, the spontaneous generation of bees, and the use of the celebrated incense from Sheba. These last named references are hardly in the nature of direct quotations, but the Vergilian idea is incorporated with a very slight change of wording.

In addition to these direct or indirect adaptations of Vergil, there are hundreds of instances where only the use of a rare or poetic phrase betrays the Vergilian origin. Such phrases as *manibus cruentis, tam dira cupido, ortus et obitus, preces et vota, aspera et dura,* the list of which could be extended almost indefinitely, show that Augustine's mind was so thoroughly saturated with the words of Vergil that the Vergilian phrases had become an integral part of his own vocabulary.

To recapitulate, Augustine makes the widest use of Vergil of any of the Christian writers. To Augustine, Vergil is a universal and omniscient authority. He is quoted not only on questions of fact, but on questions of doctrine. The poet's testimony is accepted on matters of mythology, geography, science, art, indeed on all questions of general knowledge. In addition to all this, the Messianic prophecy plays in Augustine a much larger rôle than in the other ecclesiastical writers; indeed Augustine extends the doctrine to include others than Vergil. The only phase of the Vergilian tradition which Augustine does not mention is that which assigned to the poet magical powers, and this tradition does not appear in the literature until the twelfth century. The Aeneid is quoted or referred to more often than any other single work, but the Eclogues and the Georgics play a by no means insignificant part. The poems of the Appendix Vergiliana are never referred to; whether this omission is due to accident or to design it is impossible to say.

Augustine does not indulge in heated denunciation of the pagan writers as did so many of his predecessors. It is true that twinges of conscience had brought him to the point of regretting his early studies in the pagan Classics. We find him using such terms as *fumus et ventus . . . inania nugarum* to describe these studies; once he speaks of *poetica falsitas,* and even goes so far as to say (De Civitate Dei 1.4) *Vergilius poetarum more mentitus est,* but this is only a transient sentiment, for Augustine continued to read Vergil. These few adverse comments by no means express his real opinion of the great Roman poet. What he really thought of him is indicated by the fact that he openly calls him *nobilissimus poeta,* and still more by the fact that he used him more than he did any other ancient author.

Notes

[1] On the later tradition of Vergil see e.g. the article by Professor K. F. Smith, THE CLASSICAL WEEKLY 9.178-182, 185-188.

[2] On this autobiography see Professor Charles J. Goodwin, THE CLASSICAL WEEKLY 17.134-135.

[3] Compare E. Norden, Die Antike Kunstprossa (1898), 2.621.

[4] Compare S. Angus, The Sources of the First Ten Books of Augustine's De Civitate Dei (Princeton University Dissartation, 1906).

L. Hughes (essay date 1923)

SOURCE: "Conclusion" in *The Christian Church in the Epistles of St. Jerome,* Society for Promoting Christian Knowledge, 1923, pp. 107-09.

[*In the essay that follows, Hughes contends that Jerome's writings express the unique character of medieval Christianity.*]

Dean Fremantle in his "Prolegomena to Jerome" says (p. xxxiii.) truly enough:

> His writings contain the whole spirit of the Church of the Middle Ages, its Monasticism, its contrast of sacred things with profane, its credulity and superstition, its value for relics, its subjection to hierarchical authority, its dread of heresy, its passion for pilgrimages.

But after all it is the **Vulgate** which was his crowning achievement and his greatest contribution to the Church of Christ. In it his varied gifts are seen to most advantage, for, as a translator of the Bible, he shows a capacity, a caution, a patience, an independence of judgment, a diligence and a critical acumen which he nowhere else displays. For evidence of some of these qualities the famous **"Prologus Galeatus"** is sufficient where he defies the "mad dogs who bark and rave" at his work; so also is his firm and clear discrimination between the Old Testament and the Apocrypha and his unflinching resolve in spite of the Council of Nicaea, to class the book of Judith in the latter. The **Vulgate** is indeed his masterpiece, between which and his epistles there is a great gulf fixed as regards literary and spiritual worth. It is impossible to read even a few pages of his correspondence without realising its highly rhetorical character and that the writer is allowing to run riot that forensic training which he, like so many other fathers of the Church, had received.

An artist in words must be necessarily scrutinised with strictness and suspicion, and his sonorous sentences must be critically sifted and compared with other trustworthy testimony before they can be accepted at their face value. Jerome's love of literary effect, his brusque Johnsonian dogmatism, his unscrupulous invective (*e.g.* against Vigilantius or Onasus of Segeste (xl. 3)), his credulity and superstition (*e.g.* 1 "de muliere septies percussa"), all impress the reader with the need of caution and reserve. He has the nervous sensitiveness and irritability of the scholar-recluse, and the monk's tendency to flights of imagination.

There can be little doubt, *e.g.,* that his account of the fall of Rome is much exaggerated: "Urbs inclyta et

Romani imperii caput uno hausta est incendio . . . in cineres ac favillas sacrae quondam ecclesiae conciderunt" (cxxviii. 4); whereas we know from Orosius' History vii. and other sources, that Alaric refrained from destroying churches. As Sir S. Dill conjectures (p. 307): "The warm imagination and vehement rhetoric of St. Jerome have probably deepened the colours of the tragic tales of massacre and sacrilege which reached him." Yet he has bequeathed, to later generations, portraits of contemporary life both pagan and Christian, but especially Christian, which no student of the period can presume to ignore. His vivid pictures of the fashionable clerical fop with his lusts and his legacy hunts, of the real and nominal monks and virgins, are evidently drawn from life; his description of the learned ladies on the Aventine immortalises a unique chapter in the history of the Church, while his sketches of the ascetic movement are essential to any record of the fourth and fifth centuries. Jerome, in fact, shows in their beginnings three institutions on which the Christianity of the Middle Ages took its stand, viz. the **Vulgate,** the Monastery, the Papacy, a triumvirate which reigned and ruled for more than a millennium; he shows, too, a Church which, outwardly victorious over heathenism and heresy, was still sowing the seeds of internal corruption and needing continually to pray: "In all time of our wealth, good Lord deliver us."

Mary Elizabeth Pence (essay date 1941)

SOURCE: "Satire in St. Jerome," *The Classical Journal,* Vol. 36, No. 6, March, 1941, pp. 322-36.

[*In the following essay, Pence explores Jerome's satirical style, focusing primarily on his letters.*]

I.

Sophronius Eusebius Hieronymus Sanctus was born between A.D. 340 and 350 into a world of bloodshed and destruction—the last age of the old Graeco-Roman civilization. In the span of his life came the final destruction of paganism and the crumbling of Rome under not only the attacks of barbarians from without, but also the lowered standards of morality within her boundaries. The date of his birth[1] fell in the troubled times after the death of Constantine in 337, but before Constantius, by shedding the blood of nine of his near relatives, made himself sole emperor in 353. He saw the long succession of emperors and puppet emperors, a few of them able and patriotic, but on the whole weak men, whose reigns were marked by murder and intrigue.

The opening of the fifth century was accompanied by the ravaging of the whole of the Roman world by barbarians. In 401 and again in 403 Alaric invaded Italy with his Visigoths. In 405 a great host of Ostrogoths, Vandals, Suevi, and Burgundians under the leadership of Radagaisus swarmed through Italy, plundering as they went, until finally their leader was caught near Florence and put to death. In 409 Alaric entered Italy for the third time, and in August of the year 410 his army besieged Rome and sacked it. The destruction and suffering in the city were horrible. Jerome, from his retreat in Bethlehem, uttered a cry of anguish at the fate of his beloved Rome. To his friend Principia he wrote:[2]

> A terrible rumour has come from the West that Rome has been besieged and that the safety of the citizens' lives had to be bought by gold, and that then they were besieged again, so that after having lost their property they also lost their lives. My voice sticks in my throat, and sobs choke my words as I dictate. The city has been taken, which once took captive the whole world.

One by one Roman provinces passed into the hands of the barbarians. In 419 and 420, at the time of Jerome's death, the Empire was practically wholly overwhelmed, although sixty years more of havoc and destruction were to pass before its final collapse.

The fall of Rome was imminent, however, long before Alaric and Radagaisus invaded the Italian peninsula. Grave economic wrongs, a lack of feeling of duty and citizenship among true Romans everywhere, low moral standards among nobles and clergy alike, had for a long time been breaking down the Empire from within. St. Jerome, for one, was fearless in denouncing the moral evils which existed in the world of his day and in his *Letters,* especially, he appears as another Juvenal.

The saint cannot be called a satirist in the formal sense of the word, perhaps, for he did not write in verse, but except for that one detail he has all the earmarks of one. Even in his own day his critic Onasus called him a "writer of satires in prose."[3] J. Wight Duff, in his book on Roman satire, says:[4] "What gives satire its vital importance in Latin literature is not poetic charm, for, though in verse, it is not poetry of the highest order; it is rather its faithful representation of contemporary life and its comments thereupon." By this criterion Jerome is a satirist of the first rank. With scathing sarcasm, as well as with some exaggeration, he rails against all classes of society—patricians, plebeians, and even slaves. He denounces the chattering through of slaves who surround noble ladies and decries the influence for evil which they exercise.[5] "Slaves," he says, "are always complaining, and whatever you give them, it is never enough. For they do not consider how much you have, but how much you give, and they console their vexations as only they can—by finding fault."

Again and again he pointed a finger of shame at the woman of the world who painted her face and showed off in a robe of shining silk.[6] "Nowadays," he writes his pupil Eustochium, "you see many women filling their closets with fine clothes, changing their dresses every day, and so they never can get rid of the moths."

He has much to say about widows. In a letter to Principia he describes pagan widows thus:[7]

Such women always paint their faces with rouge and powder, they strut about in silk dresses, actually glitter with jewels, wear gold necklaces galore, and hang from their pierced ears the most expensive pearls from the Persian Gulf, to say nothing of reeking with perfume. They rejoice that at last they have escaped from a husband's supremacy, and look about for another, not intending to obey him, according to the law of God, but rather to command him. With this in mind they even choose poor men, so that they will have husbands in name only, who will have to endure rivals patiently, or, if they grumble, will be cast out then and there.

This smacks of the sixth satire of Juvenal! In that famous poem the first-century satirist also describes the woman who is a busybody, running about town like *Fama* herself, gleaning every scandal to be learned, and passing on her tales to each man and woman she meets. Now hear Jerome.[8]

Rumors and lies reach the ears of matrons and, fanned by their racing tongues, reach into all the provinces. You can see many of these women who, with painted face and frenzied tongue, their eyes like those of snakes and their teeth polished with pumice-stone, foam at the mouth when they carp at Christians. One of them [and here he quotes directly from the first satire of Persius; as Rand says, "Jerome often smears his barbs with a little of the ancient virus."[9]]—One of them, with a purple mantle about her shoulders, talking through her nose, shouts out some ridiculous nonsense and minces her words on her dainty palate."[10] Then the whole chorus of gossiping women joins in and every one of them begins to snarl.

Jerome's barbs, however, were especially aimed at those who called themselves Christians and yet lived wicked lives. He bitterly attacked the . . . s, "dearly-beloved sisters," who, under guise of seeking spiritual consolation, lived in the same house with their male friends:

Why, even noble ladies of the best families, [laments Jerome] desert their husbands to live in sin, and in the name of religion. Many a Helen follows her Paris about, and has not the slightest fear of Menelaus.

Oh for shame, for shame, the world is hastening to destruction, but our sins flourish and increase. The glorious city, heart of the Roman Empire, is consumed by one great fire. There is no region in the world which does not harbor her exiles. Churches once sacred have now fallen into heaps of dust and ashes, but we still strive for money and for power. We live as if we were going to die tomorrow, and yet we build as if we were to live forever in this world. Gold gleams in our walls, our ceilings, the capitals of our pillars, and yet when we allow our poor to die, Christ too dies, naked and hungry, before our doors.[11]

We are reminded here again of Juvenal. In his second satire he attacks the false philosophers who, while in public, show the stern looks and righteous manners of the Stoics, but in private practice the worst vices.

Jerome found many a hypocrite to ridicule. In a letter to Eustochium he tells about one very noble lady whom he has seen on her way to church.[12]

Recently I saw a very noble Roman lady—I'll not mention any names lest you think this a satire—in the basilica of St. Peter's. She was preceded by her own band of eunuch couriers, and she was actually giving out money to the beggars—a penny apiece—to make people consider her extremely pious. Then, as usually happens in such a case, one old woman, weighed down with years and rags, ran up to her again to get another penny, but when her turn came, she got a blow instead of a coin, and the poor culprit paid with her blood for such a crime. Verily, avarice is the root of all evils. . . . Peter the Apostle said: "Silver and gold have I none, but such as I have, give I thee." . . . But nowadays many say, in deed if not in word, "faith and pity have I none, but such as I have, silver and gold, that I do not give to you either."

And in the same letter he describes holy women who practice piety merely in order to attract attention to themselves.[13]

Some women [he writes] even disfigure their faces so that men will be sure to know they have been fasting. As soon as they spy anyone, they begin to groan, to lower their eyes and cover up their faces—that is, except for one eye, which they leave uncovered to see if their actions are being observed. They wear a black dress and a girdle of sackcloth, their hands and feet are always dirty; only their stomachs, because they can't be seen, are seething with food. Others dress in goats' hair, and returning to their infancy, make themselves babies' hoods, and look just like owls.

The church of Jerome's day was far removed from the early years of Christianity when simple men lived according to the spirit of the Gospels. By the end of the fourth century the Bishop of Rome was a great potentate surrounded by wealth and luxury and worldly pomp. There was also much corruption among all classes of the clergy. Jerome had a great deal to say about these ecclesiastics. For example, he describes those who, when they ought to have been going about their duties, spent their time visiting the merry widows of Rome:[14]

> They kiss the heads of their patrons [writes the saint] and then hold out their hands—to say a benediction over them, you would think, if you did not already know that they were receiving a reward for that blessing.

> There are other men, [he continues][15] and I speak of members of my own order, who seek to become presbyters and deacons only to be able to visit women more freely. The only thought of such men is their clothes—do they have a pleasant odor, do their shoes fit smoothly? Their hair is crimped up by a curling-iron, you can tell, their fingers shine with rings, and if the path they walk on is even a little damp, they walk on tiptoe so as not to spot their shoes. When you see such as these, consider them men betrothed rather than men ordained. Some, indeed, spend all their zeal and their whole lifetime in learning the names and households and characters of married ladies.

> I will describe briefly to you one who is the master of this art in order that you may more easily recognize the pupils when you know their teacher. He gets up in haste—with the sun. The order of his morning calls is fixed. He thinks he must take short cuts, and the importunate old man almost walks into the very bedrooms of ladies still asleep. If he sees a little pillow, or an elegant table-cloth, or any little bit of household furniture, he praises it, he admires it, he fingers it, and complaining that he needs just such a thing as this, does not beg it so much as he extorts it, because all the women are afraid of offending the town gossip. Chastity, yes, and fasting are not for him. What he approves of is a savory dinner, with a big fat bird, for instance. He has a cruel and impudent tongue, ever ready for insult. Wherever you go, he is the first one you see. Whatever news is whispered about, he either started the tale, or exaggerated it. His horses are changed hourly, and are so sleek and spirited that you might think he was the brother of the king of Thrace himself. [A reference to Diomede, another barb taken from the Classics!]

The *Letters* of Jerome abound in such flagellations of his fellow-churchmen.

But to turn from clergymen to a more general field, Jerome also holds forth brilliantly against the way everyone tries to expound the Scriptures:[16]

> Everyone, nowadays, [he writes] thinks he can interpret the Bible! But you can't possibly make any progress without a guide to point out the way. Grammarians, rhetoricians, philosophers, . . . yes, musicians, astronomers, and astrologers have to learn from qualified teachers. Why, even farmers, and masons, and carpenters cannot be what they want to be without training. As Horace says:[17]

> Quod medicorum est
> promittunt medici; tractant fabrilia fabri.

> The art of interpreting Scripture is the only one which everyone everywhere thinks he can do best.

And again Jerome emphasizes his point by quoting Horace:[18]

> Scribimus indocti doctique poemata passim.

> The gossipy old woman, the old man in his dotage, the long-winded sophist all consider themselves masters of the art; they tear the Scriptures to pieces, and then teach them before they themselves have learned them. Some, with knit brows and big words, philosophize about Sacred Letters to groups of women. Others—oh, the shame of it!—learn from women what they teach to men. And, as if this were not enough, with a certain glibness of tongue they boldly declaim to others what they themselves do not understand. I say nothing about those who, like myself, came to a knowledge of the Scriptures after the study of secular literature. Such men, when they charm popular audiences by the polish of their style, think that whatever they say is the word of God. They do not deign to find out what the prophets, the apostles, have meant, but fit incongruous passages to suit their own meaning, as if it were a splendid method of teaching, and not the worst, to corrupt the real meaning and to make the Holy Scriptures do their own bidding. As if I had never read centos from Homer and Vergil! and yet I know that it is impossible to call Vergil, who did not know Christ, a Christian simply because he wrote:[19]

> And now the Virgin returns, now the kingdom
>   of Saturn returns;
> Now a new race descends from heaven on
>   high.

Here Jerome shows himself a scholar as well as a satirist. He realized, although many learned men of his day did not, that neither Vergil, nor the Sibyl in the fourth eclogue, was foretelling the coming of Christ.

> But all this, [continues Jerome] is childish and like a mountebank's trick. It is bad enough to teach what you do not know, but much worse not even to know that you know nothing.

Apparently Jerome had no fear of arousing long-lasting hatred against himself. In fact, he expected it, for he wrote thus to Furia in 394:[20]

> I am putting my hand into the fire knowingly and with my eyes wide open. Eyebrows will be raised,

fists shaken at me, and [he concluded, quoting from the *Ars Poetica* of Horace] "With a booming voice will angry Chremes rage."

Angry Chremes did rage, and on all sides. Rufinus, for one, said:[21]

> Jerome wrote a certain treatise while he was in Rome which all pagans and enemies of God, all apostates and persecutors, and indeed all who hated the name of Christians, vied with each other in copying down; for in that work he defamed with the most foul reproaches every rank and class of Christians, every group of the clergy, and indeed the Universal Church. And that man further said that the crimes laid to us by the pagans were true, and even that much worse things were done by our people than those ascribed to them.

Such charges, however, did not baffle Jerome. He answered them with scathing irony and became more and more the champion of Christian sanctity, against the luxury and vice of the day.

II.

Jerome resembles the Republican satirist Lucilius, however, rather than Juvenal, when he rails against his enemies. Juvenal, as a rule, attacks men only if already dead, and his satire is aimed at actions rather than individual men. Often the individuals whom he does single out for abuse are fictitious, representing a type. Not so Jerome! In vigor of expression and bitterness of tongue against his contemporaries he is a true descendant of Lucilius.

In an early letter he speaks thus of Lupicinus, a priest of his native Stridon:[22]

> In my own country the household god is the stomach and men live for the day alone. The richer a man is, the holier he is considered. Well, according to the old proverb, the cover is worthy of the dish, since the priest there is Lupicinus. He proves that the popular adage is true which Lucilius said made Crassus laugh the only time in his life: *Similem habent labra lactucam asino cardus comedente.* In other words, at Stridon a crippled pilot steers a leaking boat, a blind man leads the blind into a deep pit, and, as the ruler is, so are the ruled.

But those who suffered most from the pen of Jerome were the ones who had dared to criticize him—the poor monk, for instance, who opposed his stand against the heretic Jovinian, and in public. Vividly he pictures for his friend Domnio the poor churchman who spent his time loitering about the streets, at the crossroads, and in all the public places. He was a gossip, an ignoramus, why, he didn't even know Aristotle or Cicero!

It is a good thing [remarks Jerome] that he decided to become a monk instead of a lawyer, for no one could be proved innocent if he did not so please. No wonder that such a master of the Latin tongue and of eloquence should overcome me, far away, and out of practice in speaking Latin, when he could vanquish even Jovinian in person. *Jesu bone,* Jovinian, *qualem et quantum virum,* whose writings no one can understand and who sings for himself alone, and for the Muses![23]

To Riparius, a presbyter, he attacks Vigilantius, who was preaching in southern Gaul against the worship of relics.[24] He begins by remarking that the heretic was inappropriately named. He should be called not Vigilantius but Dormitantius. The rest of the paragraph is just as well left untranslated. But he goes on to say:[25]

> His tongue ought to be cut out by doctors, or better still, his head should be treated—for insanity. And as he does not know how to speak, may he learn some day to keep quiet. I myself saw the monster once, and I wanted to bind the madman with Scripture texts, like the chains of Hippocrates, but he had gone, departed, escaped, flown—*sed abiit, excessit, evasit, eripuit.*

Here Jerome uses Cicero's invective against Catiline, and with great effect.[26] "But whatever the fool says," concludes our satirist, "it should be considered just so much talk and noise."

And Onasus, the priest, poor Onasus! Our ecclesiastic pokes fun at his disfigured nose, his manner of speech, his name. Onasus, apparently, did not hold with Swift, who writes in *The Battle of the Books:* "Satire is a sort of glass, wherein beholders do generally discover everybody's face but their own."[27] On the contrary, he had the unfortunate idea that all Jerome's satires were directed against him, and furthermore, he aired his grievances round about. But he learned, and a bitter lesson it was, what it meant to cast aspersions on the pitiless censor. In the fortieth epistle to Marcella, Jerome plays on the word O-Nasus to ridicule the priest's homely nose, and he adds:[28]

> What, is Onasus of Segesta the only one who puffs out his cheeks like bladders and balances hollow words on his tongue? It pleases me to make fun of ghosts, of owls, of monsters of the Nile. But whatever I say you take it as meant for you. At whatever vice the point of my pen is turned, you cry out that it's aimed at you alone!

And he continues in still another vein:

> And so you think that you are handsome simply because you are called by a lucky name (Onasus is a form of Onesimus, and means "lucky" or "prof-

itable").[29] Not at all! A thicket is called a *lucus* because it gets no light, and the Fates *Parcae* because they never spare, and even the Furies go by the name *Eumendies.* . . . But if you always become angry when your faults are mentioned, I'll make you feel handsome again by singing to you the poem of Persius.[30] "The king and queen want you for their son-in-law; the girls run after you; and whatever you tread upon becomes a rose."

Persius is here deriding the foolish prayers of old women who make such wishes for new-born children.

However [Jerome continues],[31] I shall give you some advice, on what you should hide to appear more handsome. Don't show your nose on your face, don't say a word, and then you can be both handsome and eloquent.

As we have already seen in Jerome's satirical pictures of the times and in his raillery against his enemies, the saint often made reference to the ancient classics, especially in his later works. There was a time in his youth when his burning enthusiasm for the monastic movement and biblical study made him feel that all secular literature must be rejected. "What similarity is there between light and darkness?" he had demanded, in a letter to Eustochium.[32] "What agreement between Christ and Belial? What has Horace to do with the Psalter? Vergil with the Gospels? Cicero with the apostles? . . . We ought not to drink from the chalice of Christ and of devils at the same time." He even had a dream in which he was severely rebuked by Heaven for reading too much Cicero, and he vowed that never again would he read a pagan book.[33] But he loved the classics. He had studied them eagerly in his school-days at Rome under the guidance of Marius Victorinus and Aelius Donatus, both great classical scholars. Even the rigorous discipline of his life as an ascetic in the Chalcidian desert could not make him forget his early training in Vergil and Horace and the satirists. And as time went on, the memory of the dream faded ever more into the past and quotations from the classics occurred more and more frequently, even in works where we should expect them least of all.[34] For example, in the very letter in which he rebukes himself for the flowery eloquence of his youth and emphasizes the superiority of the Christian simplicity of language over pagan rhetoric, he refers to Vergil six times, citing the *Aeneid,* the *Georgics,* and the *Eclogues,* to Petronius once, and to Cicero six times, including a long passage from an oration which has been lost.[35]

III.

Most of the classical references in the *Letters* of Jerome are to Vergil, but it is interesting for us to note that our ecclesiastic, a writer of satire himself, quotes the earlier Roman satirists in one out of every five citations.

Lucilius, Horace, Persius, Juvenal are quoted many times, and also Petronius and Martial. A few examples will show how Jerome continually introduces words from pagan classical satire into his own writings.

He especially loves to identify himself with Horace. In 394 he complains to his friend Domnio of the invidious gossip directed against him by some obscure enemy; he declares that he could retaliate in kind if he so wished—that his opponents could be warned of him just as men once were of Horace:[36]

Faenum habet in cornu, longe fuge.

Jerome indicates in several passages, moreover, that he feels a similarity of injustice between the charges brought against him for a leaning toward the heretic Origen and the accusations made against Horace for unfavorable criticism of Lucilius.[37]

Letter L is a bitter attack against an ignorant monk who had criticized his book *Against Jovinian.* It contains five quotations from the satires of Horace, Persius, and Juvenal. Jerome contemptuously describes his opponent as an emptyheaded, overeloquent public speaker, whose sayings were held up as models of rhetoric to curly-headed schoolboys. He echoes here the first satire of Persius, which, directed against the corruption of literature of the day, describes with scorn the man who says:[38] "Ah, it's a grand thing to have people point you out and say, 'that's the man.' Who wouldn't like to have his poems assigned to a hundred curly-headed schoolboys?"

In this letter Jerome also identifies himself with Juvenal. He states that he, too, could give an eye for an eye, a tooth for a tooth. His ability to retaliate is as great as that of his enemy; he, too, has been to school and has written themes. With the first century satirist and in similar application he exclaims:[39]

Et nos saepe manum ferulae subtraximus.

In a later epistle this line from Juvenal is used caustically against an opponent who has criticized his method of translation from Greek into Latin:[40] "What do you say, O pillar of learning, the Aristarchus of our times? You who come to an opinion after perusing all the writers! I guess I have studied all this time in vain, and in vain *saepe manum ferulae subduximus.*

To Rusticus Jerome describes the wrong kind of monk thus:[41]

Some monks shrug their shoulders to the sky and croaking I don't know what nonsense to themselves, with their glaring eyes fastened on the ground, they balance swelling words on their tongues, so that if you add a herald, you would think that His Honor the Mayor was coming.

Both the spirit and the expression of Persius are reflected here, although the poet is not directly quoted. Persius writes *nescio quid . . . cornicaris*[42] and Jerome, *nescio quid cornicantes;* the poet, *trutinantur verba,*[43] and the saint echoes, *verba trutinantur.*

In the same letter[44] Jerome advises the young monk to beware of flatterers,

> who will fawn upon you with loud praises and in some way or other make powerless your judgment. But if you suddenly look behind you, you will find that they are mocking you with their gestures, either curving their necks at you like storks, or wiggling their hands at their ears like donkeys' ears, or sticking out at you the thirsty tongue of a dog.

This is an imitation of Persius, who, with similar advice for the writers of his day, exclaims:[45]

> O lucky Janus, no human stork can peck at you behind your back; no hand, mimicking white donkeys' ears, will make fun of you. No, nor can any tongue stick out at you as far as a thirsty Apulian dog's!

Jerome also quotes from the satirists to express his own feelings, often in an application which is not at all satiric. For example, in one letter he apologizes to a friend because he has not written much sooner—but his present wordiness will make up for past sins. For, as Horace says in his satire:[46] "This fault all singers have; if asked to sing among their friends they never will, but if not asked, they never stop."

In a letter to Rufinus, dated 398, Jerome excuses its poor style by explaining that illness had compelled him to dictate the epistle. He says:[47] "I cannot dictate with the same charm with which I write because when I write I often turn my stylus over to erase, for anything worth reading must be written again and again" These are almost exactly the words of the poet Horace, who warns in his *Satires* that what is worth writing must have cost much effort.[48] These passages are further evidence that Jerome liked to compare himself to Horace and to the other Roman satirists.

Quotations from Roman satire are also made as important authority for the support of Jerome's own opinions. In regard to original sin he cites Paul and Vergil to the effect that passions are innate in human lives, and he continues:[49] *Quam ob rem et gravissimus poeta Flaccus scribit in satira:*

> Nam vitiis nemo sine nascitur; optimus ille est
> qui minimis urgetur.

Again in **Letter LXXIX** these words are quoted to emphasize to Salvina the fact of the essential sinfulness of man.[50] Horace is also produced along with Cicero as a model for the right method of translating. After quoting from the *De Optimo Genere Oratorum* the indignant monk continues thus.[51] "And Horace, too, a man both intelligent and learned *(acutus et doctus),* in his *Ars Poetica* teaches the same thing I do concerning the right way to translate:

> Nec verbum verbo curabis reddere fidus
> interpres.

But it is the ethical precepts of the earlier satirists that Jerome especially loves to quote. As Duff aptly points out, satirists are always preachers, and Jerome no less than Horace, Persius, and Juvenal. By depicting the vice and corruption in an evil world they think they can show men the better way. Horace, through his verses, gives his philosophy of life. Persius was ever ardent in preaching the ideals of Stoicism. Juvenal was more bitter than the others, but he too had a doctrine—to trust the gods and do the right.[52] It is easy to see why these poets appealed to Saint Jerome! The monk advises Eustochium in **Letter XXII** not to be too pious, nor yet too humble, lest she seek glory in avoiding it. "Desire for praise," he writes,[53] "is a fault which only a few avoid, and that man is best whose character, like a beautiful body, is disfigured by the fewest blemishes." The words he uses are Horatian: *qui quasi in corpora rara naevorum sorde respergitur.* The well-known passage in the sixth satire of Book I reads:[54]

> velut si
> egregio inspersos reprehendas corpore naevos.

This passage of Horace is often quoted by Jerome.

Paulinus of Nola is advised in the year 395 to persevere in his study of the Scriptures.

> Nil sine magno
> vita labore dedit mortalibus,

warns Jerome, quoting the maxim of "the Bore" from Horace's famous ninth satire.[55]

The ethical precepts of Persius are also given a Christian application. For instance, in a letter to St. Augustine, Jerome tells his friend that a difference of opinion between them should not lead to injured feelings.[56] But that is a just reproof for friends, "if," as Persius says, "we think so much about another man's wallet that we cannot see our own." So, too, in a letter to Principia, he praises the virtues of their mutual friend Marcella, who lived ever mindful of death, extolling the *disertissimique praeceptum satirici:*[57]

Vive memor leti, fugit hora, hoc, quod loquor, inde est.

Therefore, the satirists not only provided the monk with epigrams to hurl against his foes, but they also upheld ideals which were Christian in spirit and in application.

St. Jerome's personality was made up of opposites, and although for the most part we have looked at one side of his nature only, he combines the most excellent qualities with grave faults. He was ever sensitive and impulsive, capable of great friendships, as well as equally great enmities. His attitude toward pagans was often tolerant, and yet he fought bitterly and long against heretics; unjust and violent in his attacks, and, as we have seen, not above insulting his opponents and giving them nicknames. In his moral attitude he was rigorous to the extreme—Wright speaks of him as "the pious puritan"[58]—and yet he was kindly and generous, wholly without avarice. As a scholar, his devotion to his work, his tremendous industry, his erudition call for our deep admiration. In his own day he was loved as well as hated. Countless numbers of men and women, laymen and monks, traveled to Bethlehem from all parts of the world—to visit the birthplace of Christianity, it is true, but especially to see Jerome.[59] Sulpicius Severus, a contemporary of the saint, writes his impression of the great scholar. This quotation I take from E. S. Duckett's excellent book, *Latin Writers of the Fifth Century.*[60]

> The heretics hate him because he is always attacking them; the clergy hate him because he rebukes their way of life and their sins. But all good men admire and love him. He is read through all the world.

His works remain a monument of lasting value. The Church did well indeed to honor his name.

Notes

[1] Scholars are not agreed on the date of the birth of St. Jerome. It is usually placed at about 345. For a discussion of this matter cf. Ferdinand Cavallera, *Saint Jerome, Sa vie et son oeuvre:* Louvain (1922), II, 3f., who places the date near 347; and Georg Grützmacher, *Hieronymus:* Leipzig (1901-1908), I, 41-43. Cf. also *Classical Journal* XXXIII (1937-1938), 4.

[2] *Epist.* CXXVII, 12. The edition of the *Epistulae* referred to throughout is by Isidorus Hilberg, "Corpus Scriptorum Ecclesiasticorum Latinorum" Vols. LIV-LVI: Vienna (1910-1918).

[3] *Epist.* XL, 2.

[4] J. Wight Duff, *Roman Satire: Its Outlook on Social*

Life: Berkeley, University of California Press (1936), 6.

[5] CXVII, 8.

[6] XXII, 32.

[7] CXXVII, 3.

[8] LIV, 5.

[9] Edward Kennard Rand, *Founders of the Middle Ages:* Cambridge, Harvard University Press (1928), 113.

[10] *Persius* I, 32 f., 35.

[11] CXXVIII, 4 f.; cf. XXII, 14.

[12] XXII, 32.

[13] *Ibid.,* 27.

[14] XXII, 16.

[15] *Ibid.,* 28.

[16] LIII, 6 f.

[17] Horace, *Epist.* II, 1, 115 f.

[18] *Ibid.,* 117.

[19] Vergil, *Ecl.* IV, 6 f.

[20] LIV, 2; Horace, *A.P.* 94.

[21] *Apologia in S. Hieronymum* II, 5 (Migne, *P. L.* XXI, 357).

[22] VII, 5; cf. Cicero, *De Fin.* V, 92; *Tusc.* III, 31.

[23] L, 1-2.

[24] CIX, 1.

[25] *Ibid.,* 2.

[26] Cicero, *Orat. in Catil.* II, 1.

[27] Swift, Preface to *The Battle of the Books,* ed. Temple Scott: London (1919), I, 160.

[28] XL, 2.

[29] Cf. W. H. Fremantle, trans., *Principal Works of Saint Jerome,* "Nicene and Post-Nicene Fathers": New York (1893), VI, p. 55, n. 1.

[30] Persius, *Sat.* II, 37 f.

[31] XL, 3.

[32] XXII, 29.

[33] For Jerome's account of the dream, cf. *Epist.* XXII, 30.

[34] Cf. Arthur Stanley Pease, *The Attitude of Jerome towards Pagan Literature, T.A.P.A.,* L (1919), 150-167.

[35] *Epist.* LII.

[36] L, 5; Horace, *Sat.* I, 4, 34. In this satire Horace speaks thus of the fear men have of his barbs.

[37] Cf. *Epp.* LXXXIV, 2; CXVII, 1.

[38] Persius, *Sat.* I, 28 f.

[39] Juvenal, *Sat.* I, 15. Juvenal's verse is, *Et nos ergo manum ferulae subduximus.*

[40] LVII, 12.

[41] CXXV, 16.

[42] Persius, *Sat.* V, 12.

[43] *Ibid.,* III, 82.

[44] CXXV, 18.

[45] Persius, *Sat.* I, 58-60.

[46] VI, 2; Horace, *Sat.* I, 3, 1-3.

[47] LXXIV, 6.

[48] Horace, *Sat.* I, 10, 72 f.

[49] CXXXIII, 1; Horace, *Sat.* I, 3, 68 f.

[50] LXXIX, 9.

[51] LVII, 5; Horace, *A.P.,* 133 f.

[52] Duff, *op. cit.,* 8 f.

[53] XXII, 27.

[54] Horace, *Sat.* I, 6, 66 f.

[55] LVIII, 11; Horace, *op. cit.,* I, 9, 59 f.

[56] CII, 2; Persius, *Sat.* IV, 24.

[57] CXXVII, 6; Persius, *Sat.* V, 153.

[58] Wright, F. A. and Sinclair, T. A., *A History of Later Latin Literature:* London (1931), 49.

[59] Cf. *Epist.* LVIII, 4 for Jerome's account of the large numbers who crowded to the little monastery in Bethlehem: *De toto huc orbe concurritur; plena est civitas universi generis hominibus et tanta utriusque sexus constipatio, ut, quod alibi ex parte fugiebas, hic totum sustinere cogaris.* Cf. also *Epist.* LXVI, 14, in which he complains that he can get no work done because of his many visitors.

[60] Duckett, Eleanor Shipley, *Latin Writers of the Fifth Century:* New York (1930), 124 f.

Valery Larbaud (essay date 1946)

SOURCE: Excerpt from *An Homage to Jerome, Patron Saint of Translators,* translated by Jean-Paul de Chezet, The Marlboro Press, 1984, pp. 39-41.

[*In this excerpt from a work originally published in French in 1946, Larbaud discusses the inventive effort that Jerome invested in his translation of the* Vulgate.]

Hieronymopolis is encircled by two concentric lines of fortifications: one low, much damaged, almost collapsed: Jerome's revision of the ***Itala,***[1] one of the first Latin versions of the Bible; the other tall, thick, powerful, awe-inspiring: the **Vulgate.** Two high towers overlook these walls: the ***Gallican Psalter*** and the ***Roman Psalter.*** It is generally through them, from without, that one approaches Jerome's achievement: these towers and ramparts, visible from afar, at the same time announce and hide the city. All the critics and scholars who have studied Jerome have said that his "masterwork," his greatest title to glory, *laus praecipua,*[2] was the **Vulgate.** And this opinion, often accepted with too much docility, is the reason why the personal works of Jerome have been neglected in favor of his work as a translator. "In conclusion, his most important work was the translation of the Scriptures, an immense task rather than a work of genius," writes the French author quoted above. An "immense task" *and* "a work of genius" one ought rather to call it; and one should also define the words "his most important work." The importance of the **Vulgate** has no need of demonstration; it is one of our civilization's cornerstones, and both St Peter's in Rome and New York's skyscrapers partly rest on it. One might object that this role could have devolved on the ***Itala***—whether reviewed by Jerome or not—in the absence of his **Vulgate.** But in that case, the Catholic Church would have a Book less faithful to the original texts, and less well translated, of the great classics of Hebrew literature; one may also wonder whether such an anthology would have had the same success and the same influence (particularly from a linguistic standpoint) as

Jerome's **Vulgate.** However, this so to speak practical or secondary importance of Jerome's "main work" must not prevent us from seeing the intrinsic value of his original work. There exists here a deliberate neglect, and its unfairness is of the same order as for example paying attention to Charles Baudelaire only insofar as he was the translator of Edgar Allan Poe. Whoever reads something of Jerome's own realizes at once that in the **Vulgate** he has before him a great book or rather a great body of literature translated by a great writer.

And that the **Vulgate** is truly a work of genius is confirmed by the qualities we discern there: that solidity, that grandeur, that majestic simplicity of style and expression. And the crumbs from this feast in which the Orient was served to the West have nourished and will continue to nourish generation upon generation of readers, writers, and poets to come. Would the *Itala* or *Vetus Romana* have been capable of doing the same? At any rate, it is in the wellsprings of Jerome's **Vulgate** that various literatures have found their inspiration, and, for our specific part, Bossuet, Racine and Claudel are all steeped in the vitalizing glow of those deep and living waters.

One must also take into account the prodigious inventive effort behind such a creation, and consider as well how the translator, having little by little, in his own works, got beyond the rules of rhetoric, the literary twists and conceits that he inherited from his masters, and forging constantly ahead—like Cervantes—toward greater freedom and simplicity, ended up by inventing a syntax, a style, an idiom, both popular and noble, that Latin—so different from the Latin of his *Letters*—which heralds the Romance languages, and which surely played a large role in their formation; or that "ecclesiastical interpretation which is intended," Jerome declares, "not for the prattling students of philosophers, nor for a few disciples, but for mankind as a whole" *(Letter XLIX).*

A greater effort, this, than the one needed to lift the bronze sphere in Athens! Particularly if one considers the distaste that Jerome had to overcome at the start of his exegetic career: a sort of horror when confronted by the language, the form, the novelty of Scriptural writing, whether he read the Septuagint or the Hebrew text. We too feel some of that surprise when we switch suddenly from the Greek classics to the Bible. Let us give it a try. Even if we have almost completely forgotten our Greek, let us take in the Septuagint a passage that is familiar to us thanks to various translations in one or several modern languages: a chapter from Job or Esther, or from the Song of Songs, for instance. We shall have little trouble understanding it; but how odd, we say to ourselves, for whom "Greek" is the Greek of Demosthenes or Thucydides. How strange, outlandish, scandalous this Greek is! Unheard-of constructions, juxtapositions serving in lieu of logical deductions, an endless phosphorescence of images, the magical and splendid desolation of some unknown ocean bottom: a new planet with its craters, its crevices, its valleys, suddenly visible to the naked eye, and with their earthen color that is not of this earth—the moon only a hundred yards away! Now we begin to have a faint idea of what Jerome must have felt when he was still imbued with Donatus' lessons and Cicero's and Quintillian's prose. But the day was to come when this strangeness would cease to shock him, and when he would see the beauty in this simplicity; the day when he would formulate his admirable and celebrated judgment of St Paul as a writer, a judgment worthy of Paul himself, and which concludes thus: " . . . *sed quocumque respexeris, fulmina sunt.*"[3]

Notes

[1] According to modern specialists (A. D'Alès in his work on Novatius) one ought not to say the *Itala* but the *Romana* or *Vetus Romana*. It is this version, made or received in Rome in the third century, that Jerome calls *Vulgata,* the name subsequently given to his own version.

[2] A. Ficarra, preface to *Florilegium Hieronymianum,* published on the occasion of Jerome's fifteenth centenary (1920).

[3] " . . . but wherever you turn, there are flashes of lightning." (Tr. note.)

George E. Duckworth (essay date 1948)

SOURCE: "Classical Echoes in St. Jerome's *Life of Malchus,*" *The Classical Bulletin,* Vol. 24, No. 3, January, 1948, pp. 28-29.

[*In the following essay, Duckworth cites Jerome's allusions to classical source materials in the* Life of Malchus.]

Professor Mierow has . . . published a new text and a translation of St. Jerome's **Vita Malchi monachi captivi,**[1] thus making this entertaining biography more available to the general reader. The biography contains two striking reminiscences from Roman poetry and seems rich in passages which may also be echoes from classical authors. It is well known that Jerome studied classical writers, including Plautus, Terence, Horace, Vergil, Lucan, and many others, and that his knowledge of Roman literature was extensive. The echoes and reminiscences of earlier authors in his works have been known for three-quarters of a century, ever since they were collected and published by Luebeck in 1872.[2] Van den Ven praises the collection by saying that Luebeck "a réuni tous les emprunts faits par S. Jérôme aux écrivains profanes,"[3] but the estimate of Pease is less favorable; he calls Luebeck's work "a useful but very incomplete work."[4]

The only passage which Luebeck cites as an echo of pagan literature in the **Life of Malchus** is the famous simile of the ants in Vergil's *Aeneid*, IV, 402-407, which Jerome reworks in lines 166-176. Here, as Van den Ven says, "il y a réminiscence, emprunt de mémoire, non emprunt direct, mais la réminiscence est remarquable, car outre la similitude de la construction, certain expressions de Virgile ont passé textuellement dans le latin de S. Jérôme."[5] Van den Ven proves conclusively that the Latin version of St. Jerome is the original text of the **Life of Malchus** and that the Greek and Syriac versions are translations from the Latin,[6] and one of his decisive arguments is the fact that the Vergilian expressions in this passage of Jerome are amplified in the Greek and Syriac versions in such a way that their relationship to Vergil can come only through the Latin text.

Jerome's phraseology in the **Life of Malchus** is of especial interest to students of early Latin; it is rich in alliteration and asyndeton, and often recalls the language of Plautus and Terence, both of whom Jerome knew well. The following instances are noteworthy: 43 f., *quantis pater minis, quantis mater blanditiis persecuti sunt ut pudicitiam proderem;* 86 f., *non enim ad pugnandum sed ad praedandum venerant;* 87 f., *rapimur, dissipamur, in diversa distrahimur;* 130 f., *quid prodest parentes, patriam, rem familiarem contempsisse;* 206 f., *mens mali praesaga putare dominum, meditari mortem.*[7] A striking instance of word-play occurs in 141 f.: *habeto me martyrem potius quam maritum.* Colloquial expressions are found e.g. *quid multa?* (49, 176), *vae mihi misero!* (69), *quid agimus, anima?* (134). But when we read a passage with five short sentences in eleven words (86 f.: *Audit causas. Hortor ad fugam. Non aspernatur. Peto silentium. Fidem tribuit.*), we realize how far we have come from the Latin of the Ciceronian age. On the other hand, a passage such as the following seems definitely Plautine: *Exite furciferi, exite morituri! Quid statis? Quid moramini?* (229 f.), and there are two passages which sound like echoes from Terence's *Adelphoe:* 129 f., *ut incanescente iam capite virgo maritus fierem?* cf. *Ad.* 938 f.: *ego novos maritus anno demum quinto et sexagensumo fiam atque anum decrepitam ducam?* 218 f.: *quid putas nobis fuisse animi?* cf. *Ad.* 665: *quid illi tandem creditis animi misero?*

Among the most important of Jerome's classical models was Vergil.[8] In addition to the passage listed by Luebeck and cited above, it is possible that there may be a Vergilian echo in 124 f.: *duco in speluncam semirutam novam coniugem, et pronubante nobis tristitia;* this recalls the passage in *Aen.* IV, 165 f., in which Dido and Aeneas enter the cave with Juno as *pronuba.* Jerome gives the main theme of the **Life of Malchus** in his final sentence (266 ff.): *vos narrate posteris, ut sciant inter gladios, inter deserta et bestias, pudicitiam numquam esse captivam, et hominem Christo deditum posse mori, non posse superari.* This is good Christian doctrine, but there are also numerous parallels in earlier pagan literature; e.g., Horace, *Odes,* I 22: *integer vitae scelerisque purus non eget Mauris iaculis,* etc., and Seneca, *Troades,* in which Andromache is willing to undergo torture and death rather than reveal the hiding place of Astyanax; cf. especially her words in 577 *(nam mori votum est mihi)* and in 582-588. Likewise Jerome in 221 f. *(O multo gravior expectata quam inlata mors!)* expresses an attitude towards death that is not unlike that of many characters in Seneca's tragedies. Furthermore, the epigrammatic neatness of the phrase in 215 f. *(ne, dum mortem fugimus, incurramus mortem)* is reminiscent of Seneca's tragic style.[9]

Many of the thoughts cited above are commonplaces, and Jerome may not have had in mind any particular passage from classical literature. The situation is very different, however, with the following passage—the second of the two certain reminiscences from earlier authors. As Malchus and the woman flee into a cave to escape capture by their former master, they think thus in their hearts (217 f.): *si iuvat Dominus miseros, habemus salutem; si despicit peccatores, habemus sepulcrum.* . . . Van den Ven includes this passage among those which show that the Latin version is better than either the Greek or the Syriac, and says of the Greek version of this passage, "l'harmonie de la phrase a disparu,"[11] but he fails to give the true origin of Jerome's sentence. The origin of the passage, I believe, is undoubtedly Seneca, Troades, 510-512, spoken by Andromache to Astyanax as she conceals him from Ulysses by hiding him in the tomb of Hector:

> fata si miseros iuvant,
> habes salutem; fata si vitam negant,
> habes sepulchrum.

There is an amazing similarity between these two Latin passages. The Stoic fatalism of Seneca has been restated in Christian terms, but the balanced phraseology, the repetition of the verbs *iuvare* and *habere,* of the nouns *miseros, salutem, sepulchrum,* prove without question that Jerome has the passage of Seneca in mind. The similarity is all the more interesting since Luebeck has no references whatsoever in his collection of classical authors to the tragedies of Seneca. The close relationship between the passage in Jerome and Andromache's speech in Seneca (1) gives added proof that Pease is correct in his belief that Luebeck's collection of material is far from complete, (2) provides additional support, if such support be needed, for Van den Ven's conclusion that Jerome's **Life of Malchus** is the original text and that the Greek version is a translation from the Latin, and (3) makes it more likely that Jerome may well have had Seneca's tragedies in mind when he wrote other passages, e.g., 215 f. and 221 f. Although Luebeck listed only echoes and reminiscences from Seneca's prose works, the influence of the tragedies of Seneca upon St. Jerome cannot be denied, at least in his **Vita Malchi.**

Notes

[1] C. C. Mierow, "Sancti Eusebii Hieronymi *Vita Malchi Monacki Captivi*," in *Classical Essays presented to James A. Kleist, S.J.* (Saint Louis University, 1946). pp. 31-60. References to the *Life of Malchus* in this paper are to lines in Mierow's edition.

[2] A. Luebeck, *Hieronymus quos noverit scriptores et ex quibus hauserit* (Leipzig, 1872). See also A. S. Pease, "The Attitude of Jerome towards Pagan Literature," *Transactions and Proceedings of the American Philological Association* L (1919), pp. 150-167.

[3] P. Van den Ven, *S. Jérôme et la vie du moine Malchus le captif* (Louvain, 1901), p. 90, n. 2.

[4] Pease, *op. cit.,* p. 150, n. 1.

[5] Van den Ven, *op. cit.,* p. 90; see also J. Plesch, *Die Originalität und literarische Form der Mönchsbiographien des hl. Hieronymus* (München, 1910), pp. 10 f.

[6] *Op. cit.,* pp. 43-93; cf. H. C. Jameson, "The Latin Manuscript Tradition of Jerome's *Vita Sancti Malchi*," in *Studies in the Text Tradition of St. Jerome's Vitae Patrum,* edited by W. A. Oldfather (Urbana, 1943), pp. 449 f.

[7] Cf. also 98, 128, 143, 157 f., 194.

[8] For Vergilian passages in Jerome, cf. Luebeck, *op. cit.,* pp. 167-191; see also H. C. Coffin, "The Influence of Vergil on St. Jerome and St. Augustine," *Classical World* 17 (1923-4), pp. 170-175.

[9] Cf. e.g., Seneca, *Troades,* 55 f.: *caret sepulchro Priamus et flamma indiget ardente Troia;* 233: *et tanta gessit bella, dum bellum parat. . . .*

[11] *Op. cit.,* p. 66, n. 1.

Mary Dorothea Diederich (lecture date 1950)

SOURCE: "The *Epitaphium Sanctae Paulae:* An Index of St. Jerome's Classicism," *The Classical Journal,* Vol. 49, No. 8, May, 1954, pp. 369-72.

[In this essay, originally delivered as a lecture in 1950, Diederich explores Jerome's letter 108—the Epitaphium Sanctae Paulae—*in an effort to cite evidence of Jerome's classicism.]*

Among the many interesting letters of Saint Jerome which I believe give striking evidence of his classicism is the **Epitaphium Sanctae Paulae, Letter CVIII** in the collection. This epistle is addressed to Eustochium, the daughter of the saintly Paula, to console her for the loss of her departed mother. Written in the form of a *laudatio funebris,* the letter contains many of the elements of this particular type of literature. Jerome begins his eulogistic tribute with an expression of admiration of Paula's nobility of lineage and of her holiness of life. She was a descendant of the family of the Gracchi, says Jerome; a descendant of the Scipios, the heir of that Paulus whose name she bore, the true and legitimate daughter of Martia Papyria, who was mother to Africanus.[1] In true Ciceronian style, Saint Jerome concludes this genealogical introduction with a rhetorical flourish alluding to Paula's preference of Bethlehem to Rome, "leaving her palace of gleaming gold to dwell in a poor cottage of clay."[2] True to the form of the exordium of the classic consolatory address, Saint Jerome declares that he does not grieve over the loss of this perfect woman, but that he is thankful to have known her.[3] He admits the inadequacy of his words in praising so admirable a woman, whose praises, he says, are sung by the whole world, who is admired by bishops, regretted by bands of virgins, and wept for by crowds of monks and by the poor. The saint thereupon resumes the narrative presenting in detail the immediate line of ancestry of Paula's parents, of her mother Blesilla and of her father Rogatus. The former, he repeats, claims descent from the Scipios and from the Gracchi; the latter comes from a line of distinguished ancestry in Greece, in fact, "the blood of Agamemnon coursed through his veins."[4] However, he takes up again the laudation of Paula's own merits, expressing the perfection of her virtue in a striking simile, comparing her with a perfect gem and with the brilliance of the sun.[5] Echoing throughout the several passages following are the thoughts and words of Cicero, Seneca and Pliny. In the first book of the *Tusculan Disputations,* Cicero declares that no one has lived too short a life who has discharged the perfect works of virtue.[6] He says that there is nothing in glory that we should desire it, but that none the less it "follows virtue like a shadow." The saint says of Paula that by shunning glory she earned glory; for glory follows virtue as its shadow and, deserting those who seek it, it seeks those who despise it. It is here that the Ciceronian *virtutem quasi umbra sequitur* is employed to express the reward of virtue. Saint Jerome then continues the life history of Paula, her marriage to Toxotius, "in whose veins flowed the noble blood of Aeneas and the Julii," and becomes reminiscent of a phrase of his favorite poet. The daughter of Toxotius, he says, is called Julia, as he is called Julius; cf. *Iulius a magno demissum nomen Iulo* (*Aen.* 1.292).

After an account of the noble lady's family, of her husband and five children, the panegyric stresses in eloquent and moving lines the subject of social service among the poor. In a series of rhetorical questions, he alludes to her far-reaching kindnesses even to those whom she had never seen, to her charity to the poor man, to the bedridden person supported by her, and the hungry and sick sought out by her throughout the city. The letter continues with the story of Paula's social success, her entertainment of two most admirable gentlemen and Christian prelates, by whose virtues she was influenced to forsake her home for a life of asceticism.

It is in this pathetic account of her separation from her loved ones that we find Vergilian and Horatian reminiscences interspersed in thought and diction. To single out one instance, richly typical; in the farewell to the youngest child, the boy Toxotius, Jerome utilizes perhaps unconsciously the Vergilian *supplex manus ad litora tendit.* (*Aen.* 3.592) with inflectional variations, it is true, and a parallel Vergilian expression *oculos aversa tenebant* (*Aen.* 1.482). The Horatian *siccis oculis* (*Carm.* 1.3.18) is also employed in the description of Paula's heart-rending leave-taking of her children.

The journey across the sea is minutely described, the phrase *sulcabat navis mare* harking back to Vergil (*Aen.* 10.197), and Pliny 12 *N.H.* 1, 2. Allusion to the passage of Scylla and Charybdis seems to be an incentive for additional quotations from the *Aeneid* 1.173 and 3.126-7. Paralleling the journey of the Trojans and their stop to refresh and restore their wearied limbs, Saint Jerome says Paula stopped a short time at Methone to recruit her wearied frame. The travelog, Vergilian in its terminology, contains in addition to the many geographical references of the journey, a copious outpouring of biblical and historical data. The travelers sail past Malea, Cythera's island, and the scattered Cyclades.[7] The entire itinerary is detailed by Saint Jerome giving the complete series of stopping places up to the time of Paula's retirement from the world to a life of seclusion in her cell in Bethlehem. On mentioning Joppa in the course of travel, the port of Jonah's flight, he cannot refrain from introducing half apologetically the fable of Andromeda bound to the rock.

Ore lambebat, a graphic depiction of Paula's ardent faith in licking with her mouth the very spot on which the Lord's body had lain, shows close verbal resemblance to Vergil's *Aeneid* 2.21 and 6.873. Then follows an abundance of scriptural references in the description of Paula's ecstatic appreciation of the Holy Places in Palestine, classical poetic phraseology interspersed throughout. Paula's exclamation on her arrival in Bethlehem is a reminder of the Roman poet's trans-

port of admiration for Italy, hailing it as the land of Saturn, great mother of earth's fruits. (*Georg.* 2.173) Vergil exclaims: *Salve, magna parens frugum!* and Saint Jerome: *Salve, Bethlehem, domus panis . . . Salve, Ephrata, regio uberrima, atque karpophoras, cuius fertilitas deus est.*

The account of the journey made by Paula and her companions through the Holy Land terminates with the travelers reaching Egypt where they are welcomed by the ecclesiastics and religious men of the region. Not long afterwards, in the words of Saint Jerome, determined to dwell permanently in holy Bethlehem, she took up her abode for three years in a miserable hostelry, till she could build the cells and monasteries for her daughter and the maidens accompanying her, to say nothing of a guest-house for passing travelers where they might find the welcome which Mary and Joseph missed.

Having assimilated so thoroughly the works of the classical authors, Saint Jerome, it seems, finds it difficult not to incorporate occasionally the fables of poets by way of appropriate application. In defending his extravagant praise of the subject of the epitaphium he says his carping critics must not insinuate that he is drawing on his imagination or decking Paula like Aesop's crow, with the fine feathers of other birds.[8]

In the enumeration of the extraordinary virtues of humility, modesty, liberality, and benevolence, Saint Jerome draws from the Scriptures so copiously as to leave little occasion for use of pagan authors: however, all of a sudden alluding to the vice of envy that follows in the track of virtue, he quotes the well known line from Horace (Carm. 2.10.) *feriuntque summos fulgura montis* to be followed again by a series of Scriptural allusions which descrie Paula's attitude in her frequent sicknesses and infirmities.

In the succeeding chapter where Saint Jerome minutely describes the order of Paula's monastery and the method of direction of her community, ther is an echo of Sallust[9] in the comment on avarice and covetousness. In the words of Sallust: "Avarice is ever unbounded and insatiable, nor can either plenty or want make it less,"— *neque copia neque inopia minuitur.* Saint Jerome, in exactly the same words, relates how Paula restricted her Sisters in order that covetousness might not take hold of them. She was afraid lest the custom of having more should breed covetousness in them, an appetite which no wealth can satisfy, for the more it has, the more it requires, and neither opulence nor indigence is able to diminish it. Then mindful it appears of the oft repeated Vergilian *Quid memorem* (*Aen.* 6.123, 601; 8.483) the Saint bursts forth again in praise of Paula's clemency and attention towards the sick and the wonderful care and devotion with which she nursed them. At the conclusion of the rehearsal of the rigid regimen

Paula imposed upon herself, Saint Jerome utilizes his knowledge of the Greek philosophers when he mentions that, difficult though it be to avoid the extremes, the philosophers are quite right in their opinion that virtue is a mean, and vice an excess, or as we may express it in one short phrase, *Ne quid nimis.*[10]

Continuing to weave into the thread of his discourse Biblical citations to establish his point of fact, Saint Jerome discloses the manner in which Paula avoids the captious questions of the heretics, concluding with the words—*globos mihi Stoicorum atque aeria quaedam deliramenta confingis,* "bubbles, airy nothings of which the Stoics rave."[11]

As the *epitaphium* moves on, the Saint must needs again revert to Paula's lofty character. It is in this portion of his description of her that we read a most delightful and interesting account concerning the brilliant mind of Jerome's talented disciple. He declares that Paula knew the Holy Scriptures by heart; that she and her daughter Eustochium would by no means rest content until he had solved for them the many different solutions to their questions. The learned Doctor of the Church confesses that as a young man he had only with much toil partially acquired the Hebrew tongue, but that Paula succeeded so well that she could chant the psalms in Hebrew and could speak the language without a trace of the pronunciation peculiar to Latin. Eustochium, too, could boast of this same accomplishment.

Saint Jerome is reluctant, it seems, to come to the end of the *epitaphium,* but finally approaches the subject of the death of Paula with a rhetorical flourish, employing a metaphor Vergilian in color to be suddenly followed by the Horatian *siccis oculis.* The devotion of Eustochium to her mother is then touchingly described as also the last moments of the saintly matron. An allusion to the classic "conclamatio" which appears in this description reads as follows: *Cumque a me interrogaretur, cur taceret, cur nollet respondere inclamanti, an doleret aliquid, Graeco sermone respondit nihil se habere molestiae, sed omnia quieta et tranquilla perspicere.*

The dramatic scene of the funeral procession, the chanting of the psalms, now in Greek, now in Latin, now in Syriac by the ecclesiastics and virgins present and her sepulture, the final eulogistic tribute emphasizing again Paula's great charity to the poor, is followed by Saint Jerome's **Consolatio** to the dear daughter of the noble Roman lady.

As practiced in the ancient consolatory address, Saint Jerome now concludes his *epitaphium* with the classic farewell to his dear departed protégée. Recalling the familiar line by which the Venusian poet predicts his own immortality, the devoted saint says: *Exegi monumentum aere perennius quod nulla destruere possit uetustas* (Hor. *Carm.* 3.31).

The Titulus Sepulchri, the epitaph which Saint Jerome had inscribed on Paula's tomb, the only poetry of Saint Jerome that has come down to us, again bears witness to the noble lineage of his friend Paula, and to his appreciation of the classic authors whom he knew so well.

> *Scipio quam genuit, Pauli fudere parentes*
> *Gracchorum suboles, Agamemnonis inclita proles*
> *Hoc iacet in tumulo, Paulam dixere priores*
> *Eustochiae genetrix, Romani prima senatus*
> *Pauperiem Christi et Bethlemitica rura secuta est.*

Notes

[1] Matris Africani (sc. Minoris) vera et germana progenies. cf. Plutarch, *Vit. Aemilii Pauli* c. 5; Plin. *Nat. Hist.* 15. 126.

[2] Auro tecta fulgentia informis luti vilitate mutavit; cf. Cic. *Par.* 1. 3. 13.

[3] Non maeremus, quod talem amisimus, sed gratias agimus, quod habuimus. V. C. 1.11

[4] Rogatum proferant patrem—quorum altera Scipionum Graecorumque progenies est, alter per omnes Graecias usque hodie et stemmatibus et diuitiis ac nobilitate Agamemnonis fertur sanguinem trahere, qui decennali Troiam obsidione deleuit. V. C. 108. 3.11.

[5] Et sicut inter multas gemmas pretiosissima gemma micat et iubar solis paruos igniculos stellarum obruit et obscurat, ita cunctorum uirtutes et potentias sua humilitate superauit minimaque fuit inter omnes. V. C. 108. 3. 11. (Cf. Lucr. 3.1044 [Ed.])

[6] cf. Cic. *Tusc. Disp.* 1.109; Sen. *Epist.* 79.13; Plin. *Epist.* 1.8. 14.

[7] Inter Scyllam et Charybdim Adriatico se credens pelago quasi per stagnum uenit Methonen ibique refocilato paululum corpusculo. . . et *sale tabentis artus in litore ponens,* per Maleas et Cytheram sparsasque *per aequora Cycladas et crebris . . . freta concita terris. cf Aen.* 1.173: *Aen.* 3. 126-7.

[8] Phaed. 1.3; Hor. *Epist.* 1.3.

[9] Sall. *Bell. Cat.* 11.

[10] Ter. *Andr.* 61.

[11] cf. Chrys. *ap. Eustath. ad Hom. Iliad* 23. 66.

Louis N. Hartmann (essay date 1952)

SOURCE: "St. Jerome as an Exegete" in *A Monument to Saint Jerome: Essays on Some Aspects of His Life, Works, and Influence,* edited by Francis X. Murphy, Sheed & Ward, 1952, pp. 37-81.

[*In the following essay, Hartmann discusses and critically evaluates Jerome's method as a scriptural interpreter, especially as evidenced in his commentaries.*]

For many reasons the writings of St. Jerome have won just fame for their author. He is renowned as a master of Latin prose, a vigorous controversialist, an ardent advocate of Christian asceticism, and as a source of much useful historical information. But it is especially as a Scripture scholar that Jerome has won immortal laurels, and earned for himself not only the title of "Doctor of the Church" but that of *Doctor Maximus sacris Scripturis explanandis*—its greatest doctor in interpreting Sacred Scripture. This honor has been conferred upon him primarily because of his great masterpiece, his *monumentum aere perennius,* the translation of the Hebrew Bible into Latin, which not only became the "commonly accepted," or **Vulgate,** Bible in the Western Church, but was solemnly proclaimed by the Council of Trent as the "authentic" Bible of the Latin Church, "because it was approved by centuries of use in the Church itself."[1]

Dealing with Jerome as an exegete, as we are in this essay, we are not directly concerned with the Latin **Vulgate.** Yet after all, we cannot do full justice to St. Jerome as an exegete if we ignore his translation of the Sacred Scriptures. For every translation, unless it is a merely mechanical word-for-word rendering of the original, must be based on and include an interpretation of the mind of the original author. A translation is essentially a condensed form of exegesis. It sets forth the result of a process of reasoning about the mind of the author, without discussing the critical reasons for this conclusion. Jerome himself, as an expert translator, was fully aware of this truth. Thus in the preface to his translation of the Book of Job from the Hebrew, he tells us that he hired a Jewish rabbi to give him an exegesis of this difficult Book, and adds, "I do not know if I gained anything from his instruction. I only know that I cannot translate anything unless I first understand it."[2]

I. Jerome's Exegetical Works

Before undertaking a critical judgment of the nature and value of Jerome's achievements as an exegete, it seems well to enumerate his principal works in the field of Biblical studies. By treating them in the chronological order of their production we can note a certain progress in his aims and methods.

It is hard to say what external influences may have first led the young Roman scholar into this particular field of ecclesiastical studies, for which he was so eminently qualified by natural talents and disposition.[3] At any rate, shortly after he finished his course in the profane classics at Rome, he set out to apply his newly acquired literary skill to the composition of an exegesis of Abdias, the shortest Book of the Old Testament. Published surreptitiously by one of his friends, this juvenile production, which indulged in the then very popular allegorical style of interpretation, won for its youthful author no little notoriety. But no trace of it now remains, except perhaps inasmuch as parts of it may be incorporated in the saint's later commentary on this Prophet. In fact, it is only from the prologue of this much more mature work, written about a quarter of a century later, that we learn of the opuscule of his early years. "In my youth," he there confesses to his shame, "led by an ardent love for the study of the Scriptures, I made an allegorical interpretation of the Prophet Abdias, the historical sense of which I did not then understand."[4]

Only after several years of preparatory study in the East did Jerome again produce a work on Sacred Scripture. But this time he followed the safer course of confining himself to translating the works of others. At Constantinople in 380-381, while attending the lectures of St. Gregory of Nazianzus, and no doubt under the influence of this great admirer of the Alexandrian school of exegesis, Jerome translated several homilies of Origen into Latin: fourteen on Jeremias and fourteen on Ezechiel,[5] nine on Isaias,[6] and two on the Canticle of Canticles.[7]

Apparently not fully satisfied with Origen's explanation of Isaias's vision of the Seraphim (Is. 6:1-8), Jerome published his own treatise on this passage.[8] This is his earliest Biblical work, apart from translations, that has come down to us, and it already shows the exegetical method that he was to follow more or less closely in all his subsequent work: a large dependence on previous commentators combined with a certain independent judgment of his own. Here, for instance, he borrowed freely from Origen; yet, at least in one important point (the interpretation of the two Seraphim as signifying God the Son and the Holy Ghost), he rejected the exegesis of the Alexandrian sage. This rejection was to prove very useful to him when, some years later, he was accused of being a blind follower of Origen (cfr. *Ep.* 84, 3). It is also to be noted that, although Jerome already possessed a good working knowledge of Hebrew, and used it occasionally in discussing the meaning of certain words, still his interpretation in this as well as in his other writings of the next few years is based not on the Hebrew text but on the Greek Septuagint, in the form of the Old Latin Version. To this he often adds a Latin translation of the later Greek versions—of Aquila, Theodotion and Symmachus.

During his stay in Rome from 382 to 385 Jerome produced no major work on the Scriptures. Yet several interesting little treatises, in the form of letters, show that during this time he was not occupied solely with the spiritual direction of pious ladies or with secretarial work for his good friend Pope St. Damasus. These minor works treat of the meaning of certain foreign words that had been left untranslated in the Latin Version, such as *Hosanna* (*Ep.* 20), *Alleluja, Amen, Maran Atha* (*Ep.* 26), *Diapsalma* (*Ep.* 28), *Ephod, Theraphim* (*Ep.* 28), and of the letters of the Hebrew alphabet in connection with the Alphabetic Psalms (*Ep.* 30). To this period also belongs his interpretation of the Parable of the Prodigal Son (Luke 15:11-32; *Ep.* 21), of Psalm 126 (*Ep.* 36), as well as his adverse criticism of the commentary of St. Reticius of Autun on the Canticle of Canticles (*Ep.* 37). This last-mentioned epistle is noteworthy as one of the earliest examples, in the field of Biblical studies, of a "book review" (in quite a modern sense) by an eminently qualified critic. Here Jerome likewise states his own views on what constitutes good exegesis. After giving some examples of the absurd interpretations contained in this book under review, Jerome concludes with this remark: "Innumerable are such defects, which, it seems to me, make his commentary worthless. It is indeed written in an ornate style, fluent with Gallic pomposity. But what has this to do with exegesis? The prime concern of an exegete is not to show off his own eloquence but to help the reader understand the sense of the original author."[9]

It was also during this period that Jerome undertook, at the request of Pope Damasus, a work which was destined to have a profound influence upon all the following generations in the Western Church and, at the same time, no small influence upon the type of his own subsequent work. This was his revision of the Old Latin Version of the New Testament, which he made in accordance with the best Greek manuscripts at his disposal. Even though his zeal in correcting the *Vetus Latina* seems to have gradually slackened, so much so that it is uncertain whether his revision reached beyond the four Gospels, still this work—our present **Vulgate** New Testament—is on the whole based on an excellent critical text of the original Greek Gospels and is rightly considered one of the glories of the Latin Church. His first revision of the Old Latin Psalter, made at this time, following a few Septuagint manuscripts, proved less successful and never gained much popularity outside the Eternal City. It is now used only at St. Peter's, Rome, and in a few odd texts of the Roman

Missal and Breviary. Hence it is usually referred to as "the Roman Psalter."[9a]

These labors on the text of the Bible gave Jerome a deeper realization of the value of textual criticism and the importance of getting back to the original texts. Therefore, when he left Rome shortly after the death of Damasus and became a voluntary exile in Palestine for the rest of his life, he spent his first years there in perfecting his knowledge of Hebrew and in preparing a better Latin edition of the Old Testament. Apparently because he did not yet feel competent to make an original Latin translation direct from the Hebrew, or at least because he did not yet wish to run the risk of meeting with opposition to so novel a translation, he at first undertook only a revision of the Old Latin Version of the Old Testament, made in accordance with Origen's Hexaplar Text. This latter he thought to be superior to the common Septuagint text from which the Old Latin had been made. How far he proceeded in this work it is difficult to say, but he seems to have published the revised text of only Paralipomenon (lost, except the Preface[10]), the so-called Books of Solomon—Proverbs, Ecclesiastes, Canticle of Canticles (the Preface[11] and a few fragments preserved), Job[12] and the Psalms. This second revision of the Psalms, now usually called "the Gallican Psalter" from its early popularity in Gaul, is still the Psalter of the official Latin **Vulgate.**[13] Despite its many defects, it has been used in the Roman Breviary up to the present, although now the new, much better Latin Psalter, recently made directly from the original texts and issued by the Holy See in 1945, may be used in its place.

During these first years in Palestine, 386-390, Jerome was still so faithful a follower of Origen that he interrupted his Hebrew studies in order to translate, at the request of Paula and Eustochium, thirty-nine Homilies of Origen on certain passages in St. Luke's Gospel.[14] Shortly before doing this work, and likewise as a favor for these same ladies, he composed his only commentaries on the Pauline Epistles, in the order of Philemon, Galatians, Ephesians and Titus.[15] These commentaries also depend to a large extent on Origen's work and, except for the one on Philemon, abound in allegorical interpretations.

A much more original work is the ***Commentary on Ecclesiastes,***[16] which Jerome published about the year 389. It marks an important milestone in the history of exegesis, inasmuch as it is the first original Latin commentary to take cognizance of the Hebrew text. The text which Jerome here comments on is not indeed his definitive translation of Ecclesiastes that is now found in our Vulgate. This final rendering of the text he had not yet made at this date. The text of this commentary is basically that of the Old Latin Version (an early translation made by an unknown author from the Greek Septuagint) but corrected according to the Hebrew text.

"St. Jerome in the Wilderness," by Joos Van Cleve.

"I must briefly note," says the exegete in his Preface, "that here I am not following any authority [*i.e.,* any standard text] but, while making use of the Hebrew, I am accommodating myself rather to the customary readings of the Septuagint [*i.e.,* the Old Latin], at least in those passages which do not differ too much from the Hebrew. Sometimes I also record the readings of Aquila, of Symmachus and of Theodotion, in order not to scare away the reader's interest by too novel a text of my own, although on the other hand I would not want to go against my conscience by following up these rivulets of conjectures at the cost of thereby abandoning the source of truth [*i.e.,* the Hebrew text]."

About this time, probably in 390, Jerome published his very interesting **Liber Hebraicarum Quaestionum in Genesim.**[17] The title "Hebrew Questions" hardly gives an adequate idea of the nature of this valuable work. We might describe it as a series of notes made on various short passages of the Book of Genesis while the author was studying the Hebrew text of this Book in preparation for his new Latin version direct from the original. These notes, therefore, are intended partly to show where and why the Old Latin needed correction, and partly to explain the meaning of those proper names which could not well be translated, but whose etymology is alluded to in the text. But besides this, these "Hebrew Questions" also record the current Jewish exegesis of various passages of this Book. This work therefore forms a veritable treasure-house of curious Rabbinical interpretations. Many of these were later on preserved in the Talmud, but others are not recorded elsewhere. It is a pity that Jerome did not complete and publish his "Hebrew Questions" on the other Books of the Old Testament.[18]

While engaged on this task, he issued two other works which he hoped would prove useful to Latin readers of the Bible: his **Book on Hebrew Names** and his **Book on the Sites and Names of Hebrew Places.**[18a] The former, which was the main source whence the Latin writers of the Middle Ages drew their knowledge of the meaning of Hebrew proper names, has now not much more value than a museum curio. It attempts to give the meaning of almost all the proper names occurring in the Old and the New Testament, but, based largely on the works of Philo and Origen, it offers in most cases mere fanciful and popular etymologies devoid of scientific exactness.

On the other hand, his work on Biblical place-names will always retain a certain scientific value. Many of the identifications with modern sites are indeed somewhat inexact, and a few are far from correct. But they represent the traditions of the fourth-century Christians and Jews who lived in Palestine, and as such they must be taken into consideration by any modern author who would write on the topography of ancient Palestine. This work is, of course, essentially a translation of the Greek *Onomastikon* of Eusebius of Caesarea. But Jerome, who was well acquainted with Palestinian geography from his long sojourn and many journeys in the Holy Land, added his own corrections, additions and observations to a fairly appreciable degree.[19]

The next fifteen years, from 391 to 406, formed the most productive period in the industrious life of Jerome. During these years he published his new Latin translation of all the Books of the Hebrew Bible, besides writing numerous commentaries and shorter treatises.

This is not the place to treat either of the great merits or the small defects of this justly famous version of the Sacred Scriptures, which had such a profound influence on all later ages in the Latin Church. It is sufficient to point out here, in passing, that this work won its subsequent popularity not merely because of the illustrious name of its author, but more particularly because of its own intrinsic value. We must not forget that it was undertaken without any official authorization on the part of the Church, and even in the face of no slight opposition from high-standing ecclesiastics who, like St. Augustine,[20] feared that it would undermine the value of the Septuagint—which, after all, had the approval of the Apostles. Augustine felt that it would, at the same time, disturb the simple faith of ordinary Christians, whose Old Latin Version seemed to them the *ipsissima verba Dei*. Others, from less sincere motives, even accused Jerome of wanting to Judaize the Church of Christ.[21] Yet within a few centuries his new translation gradually succeeded in supplanting all the Protocanonical Books of the *Vetus Latina* Old Testament, with the sole exception of the Psalms. The "Gallican Psalter" still remains the Psalter of the Vulgate, while the superior translation of the Psalms which Jerome made directly from the Hebrew has come down to us in only a few manuscripts.[22] Of the seven Deuterocanonical Books—those not found in the Hebrew Canon of the Sacred Scriptures—he translated only two; the other five have been carried over into our Vulgate just as they were in the Old Latin Version. Even the translation of the two, Tobias and Judith, which Jerome made from the Aramaic merely to satisfy the request of his friends, was done in a halfhearted and hasty manner.

While Jerome was engaged in the publication of this new translation of the Scriptures, he also composed commentaries on each of the twelve minor Prophets.[23] These commentaries, in which his new Latin Version is used as the basic text to be explained, are rightly reckoned among the most valuable of his exegetical works. The numerous difficulties in these short but often very obscure Prophetical Books offered the exegete of Bethlehem a broad field on which to display his vast erudition. Of much less worth is his **Commentary on St. Matthew's Gospel.**[24] It is rather a series of brief notes on the Gospel than a commentary in the strict sense. According to its prologue, this work was written at the urgent entreaty of his friend Eusebius of Cremona, in the short space of two weeks while Jerome was recuperating from a three-months illness.

Of a similar nature of brief notes, or *scholia,* are his *Commentarioli in Psalmos,* which he wrote sometime before 402.[25] This long-lost work was discovered by Dom G. Morin and published by him in 1895.[26] To the same learned Benedictine we owe our knowledge of St. Jerome as a homilist; he published seventy-four of his homilies on the Psalms, ten on St. Mark's Gospel, and ten on other passages of the Bible.[27] These homilies were preached to the monks at Bethlehem in the years 392-401.

During these same fifteen years Jerome wrote, in the form of epistles, many smaller treatises on Biblical subjects, such as **"On the Study of Sacred Scripture"** (*Ep.* 53), in which he not only exhorts Paulinus to devote himself to a deeper knowledge of the Bible but also rejects with no little vehemence the pretensions of rank amateurs and dilettantes to usurp the authority of specialists in Scripture. Another valuable opuscule of his is his essay **"On the Right Way to Make a Translation"** (*Ep.* 57), in which he justifies the sane use of free translation as long as it is faithful to the thoughts of the original author. Of less value, because of the excessive use of allegorical interpretations, are his treatises **"On the Vestments of the High Priest"** (*Ep.* 64), **"On the Judgment Rendered by Solomon"** (*Ep.* 74), and **"On the Forty-two Stations of the Israelites in the Desert"** (*Ep.* 78). Some of the questions he treats sound very odd: **"How could Solomon and Achaz beget children while still mere boys themselves?"** (*Ep.* 72), and **"Was Melchisedech an ordinary mortal or was he an apparition of the Holy Ghost?"** (*Ep.* 73).

To several of his friends Jerome sent interpretations of various passages of Scripture which they had asked him to explain. Thus, for Amandus (*Ep.* 55) and for Marcella (*Ep.* 59) he explains certain difficulties in the New Testament. Even two Goths, Sunnia and Fretela, send him their Scripture doubts, and for their benefit he writes a long and interesting discussion of the textual differences between the Septuagint-Old Latin and the Hexaplar-"Gallican Psalter" in 178 places of the Psalms (*Ep.* 106).[27a]

We are all the more astonished that Jerome could produce so much in the field of Scripture studies during these fifteen years (391-406), when we recall that most of his controversial writings on other subjects likewise fall in this same period. Thus, his well-known dispute with Rufinus over the accusation of Origenism, which began in 393, covers roughly this same time.

It is sometimes asserted that, on account of this controversy, the year 393 forms an important turning-point in Jerome's attitude toward the great Alexandrian theologian. It is true that his ardent admiration for Origen's exegetical writings did cool off considerably during this period of his life. No doubt the anti-Origenist controversy had something to do with this. But this point can be easily exaggerated.[28] Even before 393 Jerome was not an entirely uncritical follower of Origen's exegesis, and at least on one fundamental principle of interpretation he never followed him at all: on the Alexandrian's strange notion that certain passages of Scripture are devoid of any literal meaning, having only an allegorical or spiritual sense.[29] On the other hand, Jerome continued to employ Origen's allegorical method of interpretation to the very end of his life, albeit with ever decreasing frequency.

During the last fifteen years of his life (406-420) Jerome's Biblical works are much less numerous. This is only in part due to the aged scholar's failing health and to the disturbed circumstances of the time, when his monastery at Bethlehem fell victim to the fury of the Pelagians and the ravages of several waves of barbarian invasions. The main reason why his published works are comparatively few during these years is that they are mostly of much greater length and more carefully written. It was at this time that he crowned his exegetical masterpiece, the *Opus Prophetale,* as he himself calls it, with his great commentaries on the four major Prophets: Daniel[30] in 407, Isaias[31] in 408-410, Ezechiel[32] in 410-415, and Jeremias[33] in 415-420. This last commentary had covered only the first thirty-two of the fifty-two chapters of Jeremias when the hand of death wrote "Finis."

Likewise, relatively few of Jerome's minor works date from this last period of his life. We have only his discussion of the textually disputed passage in I Corinthians 15:51, on the resurrection of the body (*Ep.* 119), his answers to various questions on the New Testament proposed by Hedibia (*Ep.* 120) and Algasia (*Ep.* 121), his allegorical interpretation of "The Promised Land" (*Ep.* 129), and his eloquent exposition of Psalm 89 (*Ep.* 140). This last opuscule, written about a year before his death, forms a fitting close to his long laborious life, for this magnificent Psalm contemplates the brevity and misery of human life, and when our septuagenarian exegete writes here so touchingly of the sorrows and troubles of "decrepit old age," he may well be speaking from personal experience.

II. Influences that Affected Jerome's Exegesis

That the writings of St. Jerome exercised a far-reaching influence on all subsequent generations in the Church is generally recognized and need not be elaborated here. But it is perhaps not so well known how deeply he himself was affected by the Biblical scholars of the preceding ages as well as of his own age. It is sometimes said that Jerome was a self-educated man.[34] This is no doubt true enough in the sense that he received his Biblical education more from private reading than from oral instruction. But he also attended the lectures of various experts in the Scriptures, and he himself insists that he was not a "self-taught" man. In *Ep.* 84, 3 he gives us such a detailed account of his schooling in the Biblical sciences that this passage is well worth quoting here in its entirety.

When Rufinus and others, who "loved him so much that they could not even be heretics without him," accused him of having had teachers who were themselves of dubious orthodoxy, Jerome (about the year 400) wrote this *apologia* of his education:

> As a young man, I was carried away with a wonderful zeal for learning, but I did not teach myself, as certain ones presume to do. At Antioch I frequented the lectures of Apollinaris of Laodicea and I was much devoted to him. But, even though he instructed me in the Holy Scriptures, I never accepted his contentious doctrine about the mind. Later on, though my hair was already becoming gray, which is more becoming in a professor than in a pupil, I nevertheless journeyed to Alexandria and attended the lectures of Didymus. In many respects I gratefully acknowledge my debt to him. What I did not know I learnt; what I already knew I did not lose under his instruction. Then, when people thought I would finally call a halt to my schooling, I came back again to Jerusalem and Bethlehem, and there had Bar-anina teach me at night. With what trouble, too, and at what a cost! For he was afraid of the Jews and used to come to me like another Nicodemus.

> All of these men I frequently refer to in my works. The tenets of Apollinaris are, of course, opposed to those of Didymus. Should each faction, therefore, pull me to their own opposing side because I admit that both of these men were my teachers? Moreover, if it is right to hate any men and despise any race, I am certainly a bitter enemy of the circumcised. For even to the present day they persecute our Lord Jesus Christ in their synagogues of Satan. Why then should any one throw it up to me, that I had a Jew as my teacher? Or will this certain someone be bold enough to quote the letter I addressed to Didymus as to a master? What a great crime for a pupil to call a learned old man "Master"!

Jerome had other instructors besides these whom he mentions in this letter, particularly "the very eloquent" St. Gregory of Nazianzus, of whom he says, "He was my teacher, and I learnt from his explanations of the Scriptures."[35] But the Nazianzene, like the two other great Cappadocians, Basil and Gregory of Nyssa, was more of an orator and theologian than an exegete. The chief lesson that Jerome learnt from him was probably

that Origen's allegorical interpretations were indeed to be used and imitated, but with prudence and sobriety.

However, the other three teachers mentioned above were representatives of the three great exegetical schools of that time: Apollinaris (c. 390) of the Antiochian school, Didymus (c. 398) of the Alexandrian school, and Bar-anina of the Rabbinical school of the Palestinian Jews. Almost every page of Jerome's commentaries shows the influence of these three schools on his own type of exegesis. Hence, in order to have a full appreciation of his commentaries, it is necessary to know something of the aims and methods of these masters who taught him both by their words and by their writings. We will, therefore, first give a brief account of the main tenets of the two famous Patristic schools of exegesis, the Alexandrian and the Antiochian, and show the extent of Jerome's indebtedness to each of them; then we will treat of the part which the Palestinian rabbis played in molding his attitude towards the Scriptures.

Influence of the Alexandrian and Antiochian Exegetes.

All the ancient writers on the Bible, whether orthodox or heretical, Christian or Jewish, considered the Sacred Scriptures to be the word of God. The only exceptions were a few pagan adversaries, such as Celsus and Porphyry. This is, of course, an incontrovertible fact. But in our own age of rationalism it is often overlooked. Only within the last century or two have men who are otherwise not hostile to the Bible and its teachings treated this Book as if it were a merely human document. Modern rationalistic exegesis, therefore, is concerned solely with the investigation of what the human authors of the Bible meant by their words. It denies any Divine influence on them. Even the practice of some modern exegetes who still believe in the inspiration of the Scriptures has at times been tainted by this viewpoint.

On the contrary, all ancient exegetes laid great stress on the Divine message contained in the Sacred Scriptures. They held that God employed the human authors as His instruments, for the purpose of revealing to men His will and the knowledge of supernatural truths. Therefore, since God, as well as man, is the author of this Book, the concern of the exegete is to search out beneath the more or less obvious sense of the human author's words the deeper meaning intended by the divine author. Following the example of St. Paul, who often distinguished between the "letter" and the "spirit" of Holy Writ, Christian exegetes commonly called these two senses of Scripture the "literal" and the "spiritual." It is only in regard to the relationship between these two senses and in the method of deducing the spiritual from the literal sense that exegetes differed among themselves. This difference forms the chief distinction between the two famous schools of exegesis that had their headquarters respectively at Alexandria in Egypt and at Antioch in Syria.[36]

At the risk of oversimplification, we may sum up this difference by means of modern terminology by saying that, according to the Antiochians, whatever God wished to reveal to us in the Scriptures was also understood in some way or other by the inspired authors, and therefore any higher meaning given to a passage must be solidly based on the direct, literal meaning of this passage. According to the Alexandrians, on the other hand, God's message to us in the inspired Books often surpassed the understanding of the human author of these Books; and therefore, since God's meaning need not be tied down too rigorously to the direct sense as intended by the human authors, a passage may often be interpreted in a figurative way ("tropologically" or "allegorically" they called it), so that we may arrive at the fuller, higher meaning intended by God. Hence, while the Alexandrians did not entirely neglect the literal sense and in fact often made useful contributions to Biblical philology, grammar, etc., their special emphasis was on the elaboration of the allegorical or mystical interpretations. This art they developed to an astounding degree of ingenuity and beauty.

The Antiochians also admitted in many passages a meaning deeper than that contained in the superficial sense of the words. But they protested that this higher or "typical" sense, as they called it, must either be derived from the primary, obvious sense by a strict process of reasoning, or must be proved through the testimony of some other passage of Scripture to have this higher meaning. Even here, where, for instance, the New Testament interprets some event in the Old Testament as a "type" or prefigurement of something in the New Testament, they held that the Old Testament author himself foresaw this deeper meaning in his words through a certain vision, or *theoria,* granted him by God.[37] Thus, the typical sense was for them just as much the literal sense as was the direct, obvious meaning of the words. The latter, as distinct from the typical sense, they usually called *historia,* or the historical sense. But both senses they considered as the "literal" or true sense of Scripture, inasmuch as both are founded on the *words* of the inspired author *in the meaning intended by him.* Hence, they were opposed to the Alexandrian practice of reading into an earlier Book of the Bible ideas explicitly stated only in a later Book. They thus laid the base for the doctrine of the Development of Revelation, and so distinguished the Old Testament from the New, and older Books of the Old Testament from more recent Books.

Both schools had certain advantages as well as disadvantages. The Alexandrian method served admirably the purpose of edification, for it gave spiritual import to many parts of the Bible, especially of the Old Testament, which otherwise could hardly be distinguished from profane literature. But it also gave too much room to the free play of the imagination, and where a brilliant genius like Origen was deceived by some erroneous opinion of Neo-Platonic philosophy, he could too easily be misled into drawing certain heretical conclusions from what he believed to be the allegorical sense of the Scriptures.

The Antiochian method, on the other hand, was much more scientific. It was really based on the solid principles of sound reason. But here too, where there is question of the super-rational truths of a Divine revelation, mere unaided reason can be as dangerous as free imagination. Overemphasis on rational arguments can make a man a rationalist. Of course, none of the Antiochian exegetes, not even Theodore of Mopsuestia, the most erratic of them all, was a rationalist in the modern sense of one who denies the supernatural. But several of them did go astray. The excessive rationalism of Antioch begot the Nestorians, just as the exaggerated piety of Alexandria produced the Monophysites.

St. Jerome, as we have seen, came in contact with both methods of exegesis and was influenced by both. As a wise eclectic, he endeavored to draw the best from each school while avoiding the excesses of both.

To the Antiochians he owed, at least in part, his theoretic principle that the direct, literal sense of Scripture is first to be investigated and explained, and only then, with this clear, literal sense serving as a basis, is the higher, spiritual interpretation to be developed. His dependence in this regard is shown by his employment of the terminology of Antioch, since he usually speaks of the literal sense as that which is *secundum historiam,* or the *historiae veritas*—or, most often, simply *historia.* But actually, in practice, he often forgets to carry out this principle.

For, on the whole, his exegetical method is much closer to that of the Alexandrians. After explaining the literal sense, or even without this explanation, when he judges the obvious sense to be clear enough, he hastens to expound the spiritual message of the passage, and this he does almost always in the style of the Alexandrian exegetes, in fact, frequently in their very words, even where he does not explicitly state the source of his quotation. Only rarely does he develop the deeper meaning of Scripture according to the more exact method of the Antiochians. He leaves no doubt where his own preferences lie: his citations from the works of the allegorical interpreters of Alexandria are far more numerous than are those from the more cautious exegetes of Antioch. However, this preponderance is in part due to the fact that the latter school was still in its youth during Jerome's life-time and had as yet produced only a comparatively small collection of commentaries to quote from, whereas the exegete of Bethlehem had at his disposal a much more voluminous library from the older school at Alexandria.

An examination of almost any of Jerome's commentaries will show this eclectic method, whereby he combined the literal interpretation, as favored by the Antiochians, with the spiritual interpretation of the Alexandrians, so that the former served, at least in theory, as the basis of the latter. But we also have several statements of his own to prove that this was his avowed purpose. The quotation of a few of these may not be out of place.

In his earliest extant exegetical work, on Isaias's vision of the Seraphim,[38] Jerome begins as usual by quoting the passage to be explained ("In the year that king Ozias died, I saw" etc.), followed by this comment: "Before we speak of the vision itself, it seems well to consider who Ozias was, how many years he reigned, and who were his contemporaries in the other countries." Then, after answering these questions, he continues, "Having thus first treated of this matter of history [*praemissa historia,* which might also be translated, "Having prefixed this literal interpretation"], it remains to give the spiritual interpretation, for the sake of which the history itself [or, the "literal interpretation"] has been unfolded *(spiritalis sequitur intellectus, cujus causa historia ipsa replicata est)."* The exegete then goes on to show, by a rather fanciful comparison with other similar temporal clauses, that the prophet could not have had a vision as long as the leprous king was alive.

Again, in his **Commentary on Ezechiel 42:13f.,**[39] a passage about the north and south Temple-chambers reserved for the priests, Jerome says: "The north and south chambers are, I think, either what they merely were in history [*i.e.,* the literal sense], or they symbolize the secrets of spiritual understanding *(quae vel historiae continent simplicitatem, vel spiritualis intelligentiae sacramenta),* so that through the *Aquilonem* [the dark clouds of the north] we should come to the *Meridiem* [the high point of the south]. For the *littera* [the literal sense] is not so to be read, nor the foundations of the *historia* [the historical sense, the explanation of passed events] so to be laid, that we may not come to the *culmina* [the top of the building, the highest sense of Scripture]. Yet neither is a most beautiful edifice to be built up to the roof, when the foundations beneath it are by no means solid."

Finally, we may quote Jerome's **"Eulogy on Paula,"** for what is here[40] approved in the disciple is clearly the master's ideal also. "The Holy Scriptures she knew by heart. Although she loved their literal meaning *(historia)* and used to say that this was the basis of truth, she was still more concerned with their spiritual understanding,

and with this high roof *(culmen)* she protected the edifice of her soul."

Influence of the Jewish Exegetes.

While it is generally admitted that Jerome owed much to the Christian exegetes who preceded him, it is not so widely known that he was likewise profoundly influenced by the Jewish scholars whom he eagerly sought as his teachers. We have already referred to Bar-anina, his *nocturnus praeceptor* at Jerusalem and Bethlehem. But there were several other erudite Jews, usually left unnamed in his works, whom he hired as his teachers—"for a goodly sum of money," as he complains in more than one place. He studied under these rabbis primarily for the purpose of being able to translate the Hebrew Bible into Latin, but their explanations were not limited to a merely grammatical exposition of the text. Jerome would have unconsciously absorbed a certain amount of rabbinical exegesis from them, even if he had not intentionally set out, as he really had, to find out what their traditional interpretations were.

In several of the Prefaces to his revisions or translations of the Old Testament Books he speaks of the help he received from these Hebrew scholars in preparing his Latin version. A quotation from one of these Prefaces—that prefixed to his lost revision of the Old Latin Paralipomenon[41]—will let him show in his own words, how and why he enlisted the aid of these Jewish scholars. At the same time this will give a fair sample of his interesting style, as far as it can be reproduced in another language.

This Preface, written about the year 389, begins as follows:

> Just as those understand Greek history better who have visited Athens, and appreciate better the Third Book of Virgil who have sailed from Troy, passed Leucates and Acroceraunia, to Sicily, and from there to the mouth of the Tiber, so also will he have a clearer perception of the sense of Holy Writ who has gazed on Judea with his own eyes, and recalled at their own sites the stories of its ancient cities, whose names are either still the same or have been changed. For this reason we also took special care to undertake this labor in company with the most learned men of the Hebrews,[42] and likewise to travel all over this province, whose name resounds throughout the whole Church of Christ.
>
> For I must admit, to you my dearest Domnion and Rogatian, that, in regard to the divine volumes, I have never trusted in my own ability, nor have I let my own opinion be my teacher. Even in those things which I thought I already knew, my custom has been to make inquiries, and I have done so all the more in those matters about which I was uncertain. Hence, when you recently wrote to me and begged me to translate the Book of Paralipomenon into

Latin, I procured a former teacher of the Law from Tiberias, who was held in high esteem among the Hebrews, and I conferred with him "from top to toe," as they say. Only thus fortified, have I been bold enough to do what you asked of me.

In a similar way, he speaks of the assistance he received in preparing his translation of the difficult Hebrew text of Job:[43] "In order to understand this Book, I hired, for no small sum of money, a certain teacher of the city of Lydda who had the reputation of being 'A 1' *(primus)* among the Hebrews." He tells us likewise how he made his Latin version of the Aramaic Book of Tobias:[44] "Since Chaldaic (i.e., Aramaic) is related to Hebrew, I found a man who could speak both of these languages very well. So, devoting one day's work to it, I dictated in Latin to my secretary whatever he translated for me into Hebrew." Apparently the Hebrew translation was oral, not written. This interesting little scene, then, of Jerome acting as interpreter between his Hebrew-Aramaic friend and his Latin secretary shows us that he possessed a good *speaking* knowledge of Hebrew, something which is lacking in most of the modern philologists who presume to criticize him.[45] If he had wished, Jerome could have translated this Book directly from Aramaic himself, although he never fully mastered this language as well as he had Hebrew.

The first one, however, to teach him Hebrew was not a rabbi but a converted Jew. It was clearly an act of Divine Providence that led the young ascetic, who was destined to provide the Church with its authentic version of the Bible, to come in contact with this Hebrew-speaking monk in the desert of Chalcis. To this settlement of anchorites in eastern Syria, Jerome had retired in 376, after spending several months at Antioch, and here he stayed until 380. No doubt the principal motive that made him welcome this opportunity to learn the sacred language of Moses and the Prophets was his ambition to be an expert in the Biblical sciences. But, writing to the monk Rusticus in 411, he attributes a more pious motive to his initiation into the secrets of Hebrew grammar. His purpose was, of all things, to rid himself of impure temptations! This precious autobiographical notice (*Ep.* 125, 12) deserves to be quoted in full.

> As a youth, even while I was hemmed in by the solitude of the desert, I could not bear the stimulation of the passions and nature's ardor. Though I tried to overcome it by frequent fasts, my imagination was still aflame with impure thoughts. So, in order to bring my mind into control, I made myself the pupil of a certain fellow monk who had been converted from Judaism to Christianity. And thus, after studying the acumen of Quintilian, the eloquence of Cicero, the majesty of Fronto, and the suavity of Pliny, I learnt the Hebrew alphabet and exercised myself in its hissing and aspirate words.

> What labor I then underwent! What difficulties I had to bear! How often I quit in despair, and how often I began again through my ambition to learn! This can be vouched for not only by the memory that I myself have of what I then suffered, but also by the memory of those who lived that life with me. But I thank the Lord that from this bitter seed of study I can now gather the sweet fruits.

We are told here of the almost superhuman efforts that Jerome made to master this Semitic tongue which was so different from the type of languages he already knew. We learn also how he, who began so many other scientific projects with great enthusiasm and yet failed to bring them to completion, stuck to this dry and discouraging task until he carried it to a successful end, because he realized far more than did any other Christian scholar of antiquity, how useful, or even necessary, a knowledge of Hebrew was for a thorough understanding of the Bible. But he does not tell us what methods he used in learning Hebrew. Certainly he had none of our modern aids in grammars and dictionaries. His only textbook was the sacred text itself. By reading the text with his Hebrew teacher, he learnt the meaning of the words together with the rules of inflection and syntax. Naturally, as he made progress in this, he could check for himself the correctness of the explanation that his teachers gave him, by comparing one passage with another, or by consulting the various translations of the Hebrew Bible that had already been published. But in many cases he had to rely solely on the traditional meaning that the Jews attached to difficult words or passages.

It is obvious, therefore, that Jerome depended on the authority of his Hebrew teachers to a considerable extent, first of all in his translation of their Bible. When his critics objected to some novel interpretation in his new Latin version, he would retort by saying, "Ask any Hebrew and he will tell you."[46] In his commentaries, too, he would at times justify his translation by saying, "The Hebrew who gave me instructions in the Sacred Scripture told me this."[47] But even where we have no direct testimony to this fact, we may rightly presume that, wherever his version departs from all or most of the older versions, especially in the meaning of Hebrew words which occur only once or twice in the Bible, such as the names of rare animals, birds, plants, etc., he is simply following the current interpretations among the Jews. A comparison between his translation and the Targums (the Aramaic translations made by the Jews of that period) will show a surprising number of striking resemblances.

One of the other examples will suffice to show how our Latin Vulgate still bears the effect of this tradition, even in passages where there is nothing rare or obscure about the Hebrew words in question. Thus, our Douay Version, which was made from the **Vulgate,** reads in Genesis 2:8: "And the Lord God planted a paradise of pleasure from the beginning." The Septuagint-Old Latin has: " . . . a paradise in Eden towards the east." Jerome's comment on this in his ***Hebrew Questions on Genesis***[48] is as follows: "Instead of 'paradise' the Hebrew has *gan,* that is, 'garden.' Moreover, the Hebrew word *eden* means 'pleasure.' Likewise, the following, 'towards the east' is written in Hebrew, *mekedem,* which Aquila translated. . . as we would say, 'from the start.'. . . From this it is perfectly clear that before God made heaven and earth, He first founded paradise." In confirmation of this current Jewish interpretation Jerome could also have cited 4 Esdras 3:6. The Targums likewise understand the phrase in the same way, and the equivalent of Jerome's conclusion is found in this statement of the Talmud:[49] "Seven things were created before the world was created; among these, the garden of Eden, of which it is written: 'And the Lord God planted the garden of Eden from the beginning.'" Yet almost all modern exegetes agree that the older Hebrew tradition, as represented by the Septuagint, is correct.[50]

Again, in Isaias 22:17 we have this strange comparison in the **Vulgate:** "Behold, the Lord will cause thee to be carried away, as a cock *(gallus gallinaceus)* is carried away." In his commentary on this passage (*PL,* 24, 273D) Jerome says simply, "All others have translated the word *geber* as 'man *(vir)*'; but the Hebrew who instructed us in the reading of the Old Testament translated it as *gallus gallinaceus.*" The word *geber* is indeed used in Neo-Hebrew for "cock," but in all the dozens of places where it occurs in the Old Testament, it is used solely for the male of the human species, and it should be so understood in this passage also.

While the number of passages in the Vulgate that have been influenced by the rabbinical teachers of St. Jerome may not be so great, there are scores, or rather hundreds, of places in his commentaries where the exegete refers to the current Jewish interpretations of Scripture. Nor need we attribute all of these to the oral instruction received from the rabbis. We have a valuable statement of his about his acquiring copies of certain Hebrew books which were certainly not the Books of the Hebrew Bible, for these he already had. They were most probably certain commentaries, similar to the *midrashim* which have come down to us in the Talmud. This statement of his is contained in a letter written at Rome in 384 to Pope Damasus (*Ep.* 36).

Incidentally, this letter also gives us an insight into Jerome's enthusiastic love for Biblical learning, which caused him to postpone the answer to a letter from the Pope, who was his personal friend and benefactor. Damasus had written to him and asked him for the solution of certain Biblical difficulties. Failing to get a

reply, the Pope then sent a deacon to see why Jerome "had fallen asleep." Finally this answer was written:

> Jerome to the Most Blessed Pope Damasus. When I received the letter from your Holiness, I called at once for my secretary and told him to take my dictation. While he was getting ready for the task, I was figuring out ahead of time what I was about to dictate. But just as I was beginning to move my tongue, and he his hand, there suddenly came in on us a certain Hebrew carrying not a few volumes which he had borrowed from the synagogue under the pretext of reading them himself. "Here is what you have been asking for," he said; "take them right away." And while I was hesitating and wondering what to do, he so frightened me by insisting on haste in the matter, that I laid everything else aside and flew to the transcription of these volumes. In fact, I am still engaged on this work. But yesterday you sent a deacon to me to say that you were still waiting for what you call a "letter" from me, but which I think would be more like a regular Commentary.

Jerome then goes on to say that for the time being he can give only a short and "off-hand" reply to the Pope's difficulties. Later on, when he has finished copying the Hebrew volumes, he will send him a longer letter.

Besides this reference to the written traditions of the Jews, we have several other statements of Jerome to show that he was acquainted with the opinions of the rabbis who lived long before his time. Traditional exegesis among them was very conservative. It consisted largely in repeating what earlier rabbis had said. Thus, concerning a peculiar interpretation of Ecclesiastes 4:13-16,[51] Jerome reports: "When my Hebrew friend, whom I often refer to, was reading Ecclesiastes with me, he told me that Barakiba, whom alone they hold in the very highest esteem, gave this interpretation of the present passage." This Bar-akiba is also mentioned by Jerome's contemporary, St. Epiphanius, who says (*Haer.* 15) that he was known both as Bar-akiba and just Akiba, and in another place (*Haer.* 33) calls him "Rabbi Akiba." In fact, Jerome himself calls him simply "Akiba" in his commentary on Isaias 8:14, where he gives an impressive list of the names of the leading rabbis of the first two centuries.[52] There can be no doubt, therefore, that Jerome is referring here to the renowned Rabbi 'Aq ba ben Joseph, who organized a very influential school of Jews shortly before their last futile rebellion against Rome in A.D. 132-135, and is rightly regarded as one of the main founders of Rabbinical Judaism. Jerome mentions him again in *Ep.* 121, 10:[53] "The Jews say, 'Barachiba and Simeon and Hellel, our masters, have handed down to us that we may walk two miles on the sabbath,' and other such things, preferring the teachings of men to God's teaching." A few lines further on he says, "Their teachers are called . . . 'wise men,' and, whenever they set forth their traditions, they have the custom of telling their disciples, . . . 'the wise men teach these traditions'." The Greek phrase used here is the literal translation of the common Talmudic expression . . . . Shortly before this, in the same letter, Jerome informs us that the Jews call their tradition . . . [by] the exact equivalent of the Hebrew word *mishn h,* meaning "repetition." Similarly, in his commentary on Habacuc 2: 15ff,[54] we read: "At Lydda I once heard a certain one of the Hebrews, who was called 'a wise man' . . . among them, tell this story." The story is too long and unbecoming to repeat, but it should be noted that the Greek title, given here to the teacher, corresponds precisely with the Aramaic word *tann '* (plural, *tann ' m*), which is the title given in the Talmud to the rabbis of the first couple of centuries of the Christian era.

These examples, many more of which could be given, are sufficient to show that St. Jerome was well acquainted with rabbinical writings and their oral traditions. But from this, one should not conclude that he accepted all their interpretations with blind docility. On the contrary, he has made it perfectly clear in his commentaries, which interpretations he found reasonable and useful, which ones he considered merely interesting and harmless, but of little or no value, and which ones he rejected vehemently, as opposed to the true, Christian interpretation of the word of God.

First of all, the rabbis laid great stress on the literal sense of Scripture. To establish this sense correctly, they had sound, rational principles. The so-called "Seven Rules of Hillel" are, on the whole, very sensible and still quite useful. Although Jerome does not mention all these rules as such, their general influence can often be discerned in his literal interpretation of the text. Occasionally he seems to refer to one or the other of these rules themselves, *e.g.,* the "rule of context" in his commentary on Matthew 25:13. However, in this matter of the basic importance of the literal interpretation, it is often difficult to judge how much he owes to the Jewish exegetes and how much to the Fathers of the Antiochian school.

Besides this investigation of the direct sense of the text, the rabbis also sought for a deeper meaning hidden beneath the more obvious one. They did so, however, in a manner quite different from that of either the Antiochian or the Alexandrian Fathers. Their purpose was partly to find a Scriptural basis for their peculiar religious customs, and partly to draw moral lessons from the pious legends that they thus added to the Biblical stories. The former class of comments are known as *halaka,* "way, conduct," the latter, as *haggada,* "exposition," or *midrash,* "explanation." Although the bulk of the Talmud is devoted to the *halaka,* Jerome seems to have taken comparatively little interest in these minutiae of Jewish observances. But many of the stories told as *midrashim* struck his fancy, and

he thought that these curious tales would likewise interest his readers. He merely gives them for what they are worth. After narrating one of these legends,[55] he adds, "Just as this has been told us by the Hebrews, so we also have repeated it for the men of our own tongue, but as far as the reliability of these stories is concerned, we can only refer to those who have told them to us. For the rest, we who are enrolled under Christ's name, leave the letter that kills, and follow the spirit that gives life." Whereupon he interprets the passage in a "deeper sense" from the Christian viewpoint.

However, he does not pass on to his readers all the Jewish traditions he has heard of, for he considers many of them worthless or even scandalous. Thus he writes to Algasia (*Ep.* 121, 10): "I could not recount all the traditions of the Pharisees, . . . nor their old-womanish tales. For the size of this book would not permit it, and moreover, many of them are so improper that I would be ashamed to tell them."

Here, as in many other passages of his works, Jerome speaks so harshly of the traditions of the Jews that, if he were alive today, he would surely be called "anti-Semitic," even though he could say that many of his best friends were Jews. This is especially the case whenever he treats of the Old Testament prophecies which foretell the happiness of the Messianic age. According to the Christian interpretation, which the Church received from the Apostles, these prophecies are usually to be understood in a figurative sense, that is, under the image of an astounding material prosperity the prophets were describing the spiritual blessings brought by the Messias. Hence, in these cases the metaphorical sense is really the literal sense. But the Jews interpreted these obvious metaphors in a grossly literal sense, and therefore refused to accept Jesus of Nazareth as the Messias, since he clearly failed to live up to their fantastic expectations. Likewise castigated by Jerome's stinging ridicule were those Christian heretics, known as "chiliasts" or "millenarians," who indeed acknowledged Jesus as the Christ but believed that He would reign on earth with His saints in wonderful terrestrial pleasures for a thousand years at the end of the world—at the "Millennium." For Jerome these heretics were just "semi-Jews" and "Judaizers," because they followed the Jewish custom of interpreting the Scriptures in this "carnal" way.

Dozens of such passages in Jerome's commentaries could be cited, but just one or the other sample must here suffice. Commenting[56] on the words of Isaias 60:1-3, our exegete says:

> The Jews and our own semi-Jews, who expect a golden and bejewelled Jerusalem from heaven, claim that these things will take place in the thousand-year reign, when all the Gentiles are to serve Israel, and when the camels of Madian and Epha and Saba

come there, bearing gold and incense. . . . From the islands, too, and especially on the ships of Tharsis, her daughters will fly like doves, bringing wealth in gold and silver. The walls of Jerusalem will be built up by the foreigners, with the kings of the Gentiles acting as foremen. . . . This is what they say who long for earthly pleasures, who seek beautiful wives and numerous children, and whose god is their belly, as they glory in their shame. This error of theirs is also followed by those who under a Christian name admit they are like the Jews.

Or again, on the words of Jeremias 31:23f., he says, "This prophecy was only partially accomplished under Zorobabel and Ezra. Its complete fulfilment is reserved for the times of Christ—either in His first coming, when these things have taken place spiritually, or in His second coming, when, according to our idea, they are entirely fulfilled in a spiritual sense, but, according to the idea of the Jews and of our own Judaizers in a carnal sense."

Jerome sums up this matter very well by saying:[57]

> Following the authority of the Apostles and the Evangelists, and especially that of the Apostle Paul, we demonstrate that, that which for the Jews is carnally promised, has been and is now being fulfilled spiritually among us. Nor is there any other difference between Jews and Christians except this, that, while both they and we believe that the Christ, the Son of God, has been promised, we hold that the things foretold of the Messianic age have already been fulfilled, whereas they hold that these things are still to be fulfilled.

We cannot dwell longer on the individual interpretations that Jerome heard of from his Hebrew teachers.[58] We must still mention the most important influence that the Jews exercised on him, an influence which affected his whole attitude toward the text of the Bible. This is the exaggerated esteem that they instilled in him for their own current Hebrew text. One of the most striking expressions which occur over and over again in all his writings is "*Veritas Hebraica*—the Hebrew truth." If he had meant by this that the original documents, as they left the hands of the inspired Hebrew authors, were the very words of God, he would have been entirely right. But he seems hardly ever to have considered the possibility that during the long manuscript history of the text before his time, innumerable accidental and even intentional changes may have crept into it. That he got this idea from his Hebrew teachers seems certain, for even the ordinary Jews of today never doubt but that their present Hebrew Bible is an exact copy of the very words of Moses and the Prophets. Of course, Jerome's Hebrew text, like the present Massoretic text, was substantially the same as the original and was, on the whole, probably more like the original than was the Hebrew text which the Septuagint translators employed six hundred years

before. But it had unquestionably suffered many corruptions in the course of the centuries, and in numerous places had a poorer reading than that preserved in the Septuagint.

The principal results of Jerome's excessively high regard for his particular variety of the "Hebrew truth" were these. First of all, he drew from it the conclusion that any Book or any part of a Book that was not in his Hebrew Bible was therefore not a part of the Sacred Scriptures. This question, however, of his views on the Canon is treated elsewhere in this volume and need not detain us here.

Secondly, although Jerome was eclectic in borrowing from other commentators, in his translation of the Old Testament he limited himself solely to the current Hebrew text, and this despite the fact that he shows himself elsewhere an expert in textual criticism.[59] Departures from this principle, that is, instances when he follows the Septuagint-Old Latin readings where these are at variance with the Hebrew text before him, are comparatively rare and can usually be explained either as an indeliberate lapse due to haste, or a misunderstanding of a difficult Hebrew passage. Hence, on the whole, his Latin version is a very faithful but by no means slavish reproduction of the current Hebrew text. He would be perfectly justified in saying of his whole translation what he said in his Preface to the Books of Samuel and Kings:[60] "I am not at all conscious of having changed anything from the Hebrew truth." We can therefore make use of his version to ascertain the nature of the Hebrew text at the end of the fourth century. As far as the consonants are concerned, his was almost identical with our present Hebrew text, but quite different from the one on which the Septuagint is based. In regard to the vowels, however, it is certain that Jerome used a purely consonantal text with no visual aids for the pronunciation of the vowels except the *matres lectionis*.[61] Moreover, the vowels which his teachers told him to join to the consonants, differed in some respects from the "vowel-points" that were added a few centuries later by the Massoretes, not merely in regard to inessential differences in sound (as far as this can be shown from his inadequate Latin transcriptions) but even at times in a variant sense which a change of vowels gives to a word.

Thirdly, Jerome's infatuation with the current Hebrew text brought about in him a change of attitude toward the Septuagint. At first, like the other Christian writers of his time, he also regarded this Greek version as a supernatural production. Its translators were considered as divinely guided in their work. Hence, when he first noticed the great difference in the spelling of personal names between the Septuagint and his Hebrew text, and at the same time presumed that both texts were originally the same in this regard, he concluded that all the variant readings in the current copies of the

Septuagint-Old Latin version were due to the errors of copyists. (Actually, most of the differences were original, each text being partly right and partly wrong.) Thus, in his **Praef. in lib. Paral. juxta LXX,**[62] written in c. 389, he says, "In the Greek and Latin codices this Book of names is so corrupt, that one would think it was compiled less of Hebrew than of barbarian and Sarmatian names. This, however, is not to be ascribed to the Seventy *(Septuaginta)* Translators, who, *filled with the Holy Spirit,* transcribed the true text correctly, but to the fault of the copyists." In his essay, **"On the Right Way to Make a Translation"** (*Ep.* 57, 7-11), written in 395, he observes that the New Testament authors often quote the Old Testament according to readings which differ somewhat from those of the Septuagint. This difference he attributes chiefly to the "free translations" made by the Apostles and Evangelists, although by this time he is willing to admit that even the original Septuagint was often in error. Finally, in his **Praef. in Pent.,**[63] written between 398 and 406, he has lost all faith in the supernatural origin of the Septuagint, which, according to pious legend, had been the work of seventy men working separately in seventy cells, each one producing independently of the others, yet in perfect agreement with them, the whole Pentateuch.

> I know not (he says) who was the first author to fabricate with his lie those seventy cells at Alexandria. For neither Aristeas, the *hyperaspistes* of Ptolemy, nor Josephus, who wrote a long time after, mentions any such thing. These, on the contrary, say that the Seventy met in one basilica and translated, not prophesied. It is one thing to be a prophet, and quite another thing to be a translator. In the former case the Spirit reveals future events, in the latter, by mere erudition and a good vocabulary, a man renders into another language what he understands the original to mean. Unless, of course, we should hold that Cicero translated Xenophon, Plato, and Demosthenes under the inspiration of the rhetoric spirit.

It is very seldom that Jerome doubted the truth of his *veritas Hebraica.* Thus, in his commentary on Galatians 3:10, he notes that St. Paul quotes Deuteronomy 27:26 according to Septuagint, with which, our erudite scholar observes, the Samaritan Pentateuch agrees, whereas the later Greek translators and his own Hebrew text have a slightly different reading. Here he is inclined to suspect the latter reading. Again, in Galatians 3:13 the Apostle quotes Deuteronomy 21:22 as "Cursed is everyone who is hung on a tree," although all the texts, including even the Septuagint, have, "Cursed by God. . . ." Jerome feels that the latter phrase is unbecoming to Christ. After trying vainly to give it a favorable interpretation,[64] he concludes that either the Apostle quoted the passage somewhat freely, "or, as seems more likely, after Christ's Passion someone added the words, 'by God,' not only in the Hebrew codices but also in ours, in order that we might be branded with infamy for believing in a Christ who was cursed by God." But surely, this latter hypothesis is absolutely untenable.

Therefore, even though he was not entirely justified in the almost unbounded trust he placed in his Hebrew text, still his new version is so much superior to the Old Latin that we must be grateful for his bold assurance, which caused others to have confidence in his new version and thus helped to win the acceptance of this better Latin text.

III. Jerome's Merits as an Exegete

The account of Jerome's works and of the influence of other scholars upon him, as described above, has already given a fairly good idea of his importance as an exegete. It only remains to sum up his chief merits, and to answer certain objections which have been raised in depreciation of his worth.

There can be no doubt about the judgment which the men of his own time passed on him. Long before his death he was held by all, both in the East and in the West, to be the greatest authority on the Sacred Scriptures. In this field where he was supreme, and in a certain sense unique, everyone listened to his words as to the utterances of an oracle. His contemporary, Sulpicius Severus, has one of the disputants in his *Dialogus*[65] (written in c. 405) say to the other two, "I would be surprised if he [Jerome] were not already known to you through his writings, since he is read throughout the whole world." Even the great Augustine seems to have stood in awe at Jerome's immense knowledge of things Biblical. Although the zealous Bishop of Hippo felt obliged in conscience to disagree with the learned monk of Bethlehem on one or the other point, still he always expresses himself in remarkably humble tones. Thus, he writes to him, not in false humility but in simple honesty, "I have not as great a knowledge of the divine Scriptures as you have, nor could I have such knowledge as I see in you."[66] In fact, it is precisely because Augustine realized the great authority Jerome enjoyed, that he feared the mischief which could be done by even one wrong interpretation made by him on an important point of doctrine.

During the following centuries Jerome was universally acknowledged as the prince of Christian Scripture scholars—not only during the Middle Ages, but also among the savants of the Renaissance and the great commentators of the Golden Age of Catholic Exegesis, the sixteenth and seventeenth centuries. The first doubts were cast on his reputation only in modern times, when Biblical science was divorced from theology and began to be studied merely for the sake of science, solely from the viewpoint of philology, archaeology, history, and the like.

In keeping with this well-merited popularity, the Church in her Oration on his feastday (September 30th), calls St. Jerome her "Greatest Teacher in setting forth the Sacred Scriptures—*Doctor Maximus in exponendis Sacris Scripturis.*" It is commonly agreed on that this title, which apparently goes back to the fifteenth century,[67] is meant by the Church in a truly comparative sense and not merely in the sense of "a very great Doctor." Indeed, in comparison with all the other Doctors and Fathers of the Church, not only of the West but also of the East. But, understood in this meaning, Jerome's title has given rise to some discussion. For, if we take "exegesis" in its strictest sense, as signifying that penetrating investigation of the mind of the inspired author which seeks to fathom the logical sequence of his thoughts, it can hardly be denied that in this regard Jerome was really surpassed by several other exegetes, especially those of the Antiochian school, including another Doctor of the Church, St. John Chrysostom.

Murillo would take the qualifying phrase *"in exponendis Sacris Scripturis,"* to mean, "in translating the Sacred Scriptures."[68] Certainly, Jerome is the greatest Doctor of the Church in this respect. But such a statement is so obviously true that it seems rather ridiculous to insist on it. Why should the Church call him who alone of the Fathers made any Bible translation at all, her "greatest translator of the Sacred Scriptures"? To us, therefore, it appears more probable that this phrase is to be taken in a broad and general sense, embracing all forms of Biblical science, such as philology, textual criticism, history and archaeology, as well as exegesis and interpretation (or translation). If we make the comparison on this wide basis, we can well affirm that there has been no other ancient writer in either the Eastern or the Western Church who was greater than St. Jerome as a "Biblical scholar."

The only writer of the Latin Church before the sixteenth century who could be brought forth as a possible rival of Jerome's exegetical laurels is St. Augustine. But a comparison between these two might be unfair to both. Each is a specialist in his own particular field. In philosophy and speculative theology Augustine, of course, far outstrips Jerome. Hence, when it comes to the subtle study of certain theological texts of Scripture, the former Doctor usually excels the latter. Yet the eminent theologian of Hippo was seriously handicapped in his use of the Sacred Scriptures. He had to take his Old Latin Version just as he found it, and ran the risk of drawing serious conclusions from what was merely a wrong translation of some passage. He had but little knowledge of the history that lay behind the text he used, and still less ability in having recourse to the original texts, at least of the Old Testament.

But here Jerome was right at home. What he lacked in speculative talents and philosophical training he made up in critical acumen and in a vast positive knowledge of the Bible and the allied Biblical sciences. He shows clearly where the preference of his own genius lay. When Sunnia and Fretela offer him the opportunity of discussing numerous textual questions on the Psalms, he responds with obvious satisfaction (*Ep.* 106, 2), "You ask of me a work . . . in which not the ingenuity but the erudition of the writer is put to the test." Therefore, these two contemporary Doctors of the Church were in no sense rivals, neither subjectively nor objectively. They complemented each other's great work in laying the solid foundations on which later scholars were to erect the magnificent edifice of Catholic theology. It is really a pity that Augustine never saw the realization of his oft-expressed wish that he and Jerome might meet and work together.

In comparing St. Jerome with other famous exegetes of the fourth and fifth centuries, there is a certain matter that is not to be overlooked. Each of these men had his own special field of preference. Augustine's commentaries on the words of our Lord or on St. John's Gospel, and Chrysostom's commentaries on the Epistles of St. Paul do indeed surpass anything that Jerome wrote on the New Testament Books. But this was not Jerome's special field. His unique knowledge of Hebrew and Aramaic induced him to devote his talents to the study of the Old Testament. In this part of the Bible he chose the most difficult Books, the writings of the Prophets. Here he is *facile princeps.* He is the only ancient writer who commented on *all* the Books of the major and minor Prophets. And he did this extremely well.

Jerome, no doubt, would have admitted that Christians are naturally and rightly more interested in the New than in the Old Testament. But he felt that there was a danger of their neglecting the divine revelation made before the time of Christ. Thus, to Algasia, who had sent him several New Testament difficulties for solution, he complains good-humoredly of her failure to ask him about the Old Testament. "I notice," he writes to her (*Ep.* 121, Praef.), "that your questions which are all on the Gospels and the Epistles, show that either you do not read the Old Testament enough or you do not understand it well enough, for it is involved in so many obscurities and types of future things that it all needs explanation."

St. Jerome's outstanding characteristic, wherein he easily surpassed all other Christian writers of antiquity, is his enormous erudition. He was very well informed. As Sulpicius Severus says,[69] "In universal knowledge no one would dare to compare himself with him." God may not have endowed him with an intellectual capacity for deep speculation, but He did give him two precious talents which Jerome invested at Evangelical usury: an insatiable thirst for learning, and a phenomenal memory for retaining all that he learnt. Augustine, who was himself well-read in Latin literature, both ecclesiastical and profane, testifies[70] that Jerome "had read all or almost all the authors of both parts of the world who had written anything before his time on the teaching of the Church."

In like manner, we must still marvel at the frequency with which he makes the most apt quotations from the classics as well as from the Patristic writings. His own works are often brilliant mosaics of skillfully employed references to and citations from other authors. But nowhere is his prodigious memory so much in evidence as in his use of the Bible itself. He must have known most of the Scriptures by heart. For in those days there was no such thing as a concordance to help a faulty memory locate a pertinent text. Yet Jerome can pile on one quotation after another from various parts of the Bible whenever such references have some connection with the passage under discussion.

His encyclopedic knowledge, however, was not a mere accumulation of other men's ideas. Despite the efforts of his humility to present the truth through another's words, he cannot conceal the fact that he has made no mean independent contribution to the general fund of knowledge. Many a statement of his, for instance, about the critical reading of a certain passage or about its meaning, is quite original. His powers of observation were finely developed. He viewed the world with a keen eye and knew the faults and foibles of his fellow men as well as their virtues. Well-travelled especially in Palestine, he took note of its natural history, its physical features, its flora and fauna. Remarks on these interesting topics, often combined with a peculiar droll humor, enliven many a page of his commentaries.[71]

In order to have as much time as possible for the acquisition of new knowledge, Jerome usually worked very fast on his commentaries and translations. No doubt, some of his works would have been better if he had spent more time on their production. But the accusation of undue haste is generally overstressed. Indeed, Jerome himself is partly to blame for this false impression. Much given to rhetorical language, he makes a generous use of the licit figure of speech known as hyperbole, or in ordinary language, exaggeration. But he presumes that sensible readers, unlike literal-minded moderns, would not take his statements too strictly. Thus, when he says that his translation from the Hebrew of the three "Solomonic" Books—Proverbs, Ecclesiastes and Canticles—was "the work of three days"[72] he is obviously speaking hyperbolically. The mere dictation of even the final draft of these Books in so short a time would have been almost a physical impossibility. Since we still have practically the same Hebrew text as that on which he worked, a comparison between this and his excellent translation of it shows that he must have spent weeks, if not months, on his preliminary drafts. Therefore, even though he calls his Latin Tobias the outcome of "one day's labor,"[73] and his Latin Judith the result of "one short burning of the midnight oil,"[74] we should not draw the conclusion, as is so often done, that these are careless productions, because here we no longer have the original with which to compare his version.

Nor are we justified in saying that "another defect of Jerome, possibly more blameworthy than the hurry of his work, is a lack of hermeneutical method, an uncertain and inconsistent attitude towards the fundamental principles of scriptural exegesis."[75] On the contrary, Jerome had a very definite method in all his commentaries, and he carried it out quite consistently. His method, as shown above, was essentially eclectic: to borrow what is good from all three schools of exegesis, the Alexandrian, the Antiochian, and the Rabbinical. When he quotes the divergent opinions of these different schools he may seem to be inconsistent. But he is not necessarily making all these opinions his own.

In several places he states explicitly what his method was. We can cite only a few examples here. Thus, in the Prologue to his **Commentary on Osee,**[76] after enumerating all the previous commentaries written on this Book, he says to Pammachius, "I mention these that you may know what predecessors I have had in the field of this Prophet. However, to you, who are sensible, I admit in all sincerity and not from pride (as certain friends of mine forever insinuate) that I have not followed these commentators in all their opinions. I am acting as a judge rather than as a mere translator of their work. I state what I think is probable in each, and what I have learnt from one or the other of the Hebrew masters." In the Prologue to his **Commentary on Zacharias**[77] he speaks of having studied the previous works of Origen, Hippolytus and Didymus on this Prophet, and adds, "All their exegesis, however, is allegorical. They hardly ever treat of the literal sense *(historia)*. So, desiring to imitate the 'householder who brings forth from his storeroom things new and old,' and the bride of the Canticle of Canticles who says, 'The new and the old, my beloved, I have kept for thee,' I have combined the literal interpretation *(historia)* of the Hebrews with the figurative interpretation *(tropologia)* of our own scholars, in order that I might build upon the rock and not upon sand, and might thereby lay a firm foundation, such as Paul, the wise builder, wrote that he had laid." Jerome, therefore, could well say (*Ep.* 61, 1), "Since it is my earnest purpose to read many authors, in order to gather different flowers from as many fields as possible, with the intention not of approving of everything but of choosing what is good, I do indeed use many books, but only that from these many I may learn much."

The complaint that Jerome often fails to keep his promise of showing which of the many cited interpretations he approves of and which one he disapproves of, is quite common and is not limited to modern critics. Even his devoted friend Paula seems to have found this difficulty in his commentaries, as he himself admits in his Eulogy on her (*Ep.* 108, 26):

> She persuaded me to give her a running commentary as she read through the Old and the New Testament together with her daughter [Eustochium]. Though from modesty I would have refused this, yet, on account of her repeated and persistent pleas, I consented to teach her what I myself had learnt, that is, not my own ideas, for such presumption is a bad teacher, but what I had learnt from the illustrious men of the Church. Whenever I was in doubt and frankly admitted my ignorance, she would never accept my excuses but would always force me by her unremitting questioning to tell her which of the many weighty opinions I considered the more probable.

Nevertheless, there is this to be said in defence of Jerome's habit of presenting various opinions without indicating which ones he makes his own. He generally does this only when he is quoting different *allegorical* interpretations. Now, although several such interpretations on one and the same passage may often seem to contradict one another, they can really be all more or less justified. For none of them pretends to give the genuine literal sense of the passage. Hence, when Jerome finds one Father making a spiritual application of a text in one way, and another Father accommodating the same text in quite a different way, there is no reason why he should feel himself obliged to praise the one and condemn the other. Instead, he rightly leaves it up to his readers to choose any of these ingenious interpretations that may seem the more appropriate.

At least one practical advantage that we have from his habit of making numerous citations in his commentaries is that he has thus preserved for us large parts of the writings of older exegetes whose works would otherwise have been completely lost. In fact, the writings of St. Jerome formed one of the main channels through which much of the erudition of the Greek Fathers reached the Latin-speaking Church. In the same way, his commentaries as well as his version of the Scriptures have enriched all Christendom with much of what was good in the Biblical lore of the Jewish scholars. "I have made it my resolve," he states expressly,[78] "to make available for Latin readers the hidden treasures of Hebrew erudition and the recondite teachings of the masters of the Synagogue, as long as these things are in keeping with the Holy Scriptures."

The last adverse criticism of Jerome's exegesis that we shall consider is the assertion that he indulges far too much in allegorical interpretations, either of his own concoction or borrowed from others. We readily grant that in this respect a great deal of his exegesis is not written in the manner of a modern commentary. But first of all, we must note that even in his own works there is a steady progress from his earliest commentaries, which abound in allegorical interpretations, to his mature works on the Prophetic Books, where much more restraint is shown in the use of such farfetched accommodations. "We do not at all deny," says Pope Benedict XV in his Encyclical on the occasion of the fifteenth centenary of the death of St. Jerome,[79] "that Jerome, in imitation of the Latin and Greek exegetes who preceded him, made use at first of allegorical interpretations to perhaps an excessive degree. But his love of the sacred Books and his unceasing toil in constantly reading them and in weighing their meaning, led him ever on to a right appreciation of their literal sense and to the formulation of sound principles regarding it."

Jerome, however, never completely abandoned the allegorical method, not merely because it was in vogue in those days and was expected of him by his readers, but also because he himself was convinced of the utility or even necessity of such exegesis. For him the Bible was not meant to be the plaything of men's minds; it was a heaven-sent manna for men's hearts and spiritual nourishment for their souls. He never forgot the truth, always taught by the Church and recently again enunciated by Pope Pius XII,[80] that "the Sacred Books were not given by God to men to satisfy their curiosity or to provide them with material for study and research, but, as the Apostle observes, in order that these Divine Oracles might 'instruct us to salvation, by the faith which is in Christ Jesus' and 'that the man of God may be perfect, furnished to every good work.'" Therefore, in those passages where the literal sense would merely be of historical interest, Jerome never hesitated to add to his literal interpretation a spiritual or allegorical interpretation, more or less founded on the direct sense, and thus "interpret so that the Church might receive edification" (1 Cor. 14:5).

In all this, Jerome showed himself a true "Father and Doctor of the Church." Immeasurably far above his fame as a scientific exegete is his immortal glory as a Saint of God. He was, as Sulpicius Severus says,[81] "a man above all else Catholic—*vir maxime Catholicus.*" Except for his mistaken and quite understandable attitude on the Canon, his orthodoxy has never been questioned. The mind and sense of the Catholic Church he made his own. Before all else he was guided by tradition: "the men of old who have preceded us in the Faith." It is this spirit of his, inspiring every line he wrote, that makes his writings so dear to all true Catholics and so disliked by many outside the Church. He had no need to submit his works to the subsequent approval of the Church; he made sure that there would be nothing in them that could offend her. "I made it my resolve," he said (*Ep.* 119, 11), "to read all the men of old, to test their individual statements, to retain what was good in them, and never depart from the faith of the Catholic Church."

His love for the Church sprang from his love for Christ, whose Mystical Body she is. And it was his love for the Incarnate Word of God that enkindled in him his ardent love for the written word of God. For him "every single page of both Testaments seems to center around Christ."[82] "Ignorance of the Bible means ignorance of Christ," he would say,[83] "for 'Christ is the power of God and the wisdom of God,' and he who does not know the Scriptures does not know God's power and wisdom." "What other life can there be without the knowledge of the Scriptures," he wrote (*Ep.* 30, 7), "for through these Christ Himself, who is the life of the faithful, becomes known!"

We, who in the midst of our modern pagan civilization still cherish the precious heritage bequeathed us by our Fathers in the Faith, have need to listen again to Jerome's message of enthusiastic love for God's word in the Sacred Scriptures. To us also he addresses the words that he wrote to Paula (*Ep.* 30, 13):

> What, pray, can be more sacred than this sacred mystery [of the Scriptures]? What can be more delightful than the pleasure found therein? What food, what honey can be sweeter than to learn of God's wise plan, to enter into His sanctuary and gaze on the mind of the Creator, and to rehearse the words of your Lord, which, though derided by the wise of this world, are really full of spiritual wisdom! Let the others, if they will, have their wealth, and drink from jewelled cups, be clad in silk, and bask in popular applause, as if they could not exhaust their riches in all kinds of pleasures. Our delight shall be to meditate on the Law of the Lord day and night, to knock at His door when it is not open, to receive the bread of the Trinity, and, with our Lord going before us, to walk on the billows of the world.

Notes

[1] "Haec ipsa vetus et vulgata editio (sacrorum librorum), quae longo tot saeculorum usu in ipsa Ecclesia probata est . . . pro authentica habeatur" (*Enchiridion*, Denz.-Banw.-Umberg n. 785).

[2] "Cujus doctrina an aliquid profecerim nescio; hoc unum scio, non potuisse me interpretari nisi quod ante intellexeram" (*PL,* 28, 1081). It is to be noted that Jerome uses both the word *interpretari* and the word *exponere* somewhat interchangeably in both the sense of "to translate" and the sense of "to explain, to expound, to give an exegesis"; *e.g.,* in the Preface to his translation of Tobias (*PL,* 29, 26) *"exposui"* means simply "I translated."

[3] One might be tempted to attribute this to the example of Victorinus, who taught rhetoric at Rome while Jerome was studying there and who wrote certain commentaries (now lost) on the *Apostolum* (the Acts and Epistles). But two facts militate against this hypothesis: Jerome says, at least according to the better manuscripts, merely that "Victorinus taught rhetoric in Rome while I was a boy *(me puero),*" and not that he "taught me as a boy *(me puerum)*" and secondly, in his later life Jerome despised the commentaries of Victorinus, as containing more rhetoric than Biblical knowledge. Cfr. *Prolog. in Comment. in Gal.* (*PL,* 26, 308), *De vir illus.,* 101 (*PL,* 23, 701), and *Chronic. an. Dom.* 358 (*PL,* 27, 687).

[4] *PL,* 25, 1097. In this later work, written in 395, he seems to imply that the early work was composed some thirty years before: "Nec diffiteor per hosce triginta annos in ejus (= Domini) opere me ac labore sudasse." But the "thirty" is perhaps to be taken as a somewhat exaggerated round number. The first commentary was probably written not much before 370, that is, after rather than before his journey to "the semi-barbarous banks of the Rhine."

[5] *PL,* 25, 583-786.

[6] *PL,* 24, 901-936.

[7] *PL,* 23, 1117-1144.

[8] *Ep.* 18. (The more recent editions of St. Jerome's Epistles are in *PL,* 22 and in Vols. 54-55-56 of the Vienna *Corpus Scriptorum Ecclesiasticorum Latinorum.*) For the date of this composition, cfr. Jerome's statement in his Commentary on Isaias, written in 408-410 (*PL,* 24, 91): "I admit that about thirty years ago, while I was at Constantinople and was receiving instructions there in Scriptural studies from that very eloquent man, Gregory the Nazianzene, who was then bishop of that city, I wrote a short treatise on this vision (*i.e.,* Is. 6: 1ff.) without adequate preparation." In *Ep.* 84, 3, written in 399 or 400, he says that this little treatise had been composed some twenty years before.

[9] *Ep.* 36, 3: " . . . sed quo eum, qui lecturus est, sic faciat intelligere, quomodo ipse intellexit qui scripsit."

[9a] This has been the traditionally accepted explanation of the fate of Jerome's first revision, and this opinion is still widely held. But D. DeBruyne (*Revue Bénéd.,* 1930, 101-126), has apparently proved that Jerome had nothing to do with the "Roman Psalter"; this would be merely one of the variant forms of the unrevised Old Latin Psalter; Jerome's first revision, accordingly, would now be completely lost except for some quotations from it preserved in Jerome's earlier works.

[10] *PL,* 29, 401.

[11] *PL*, 29, 403.

[12] *PL*, 29, 61-114; P. de Lagarde (Göttingen, 1887); C. P. Caspari (1893).

[13] Together with Origen's critical marks it is published in *PL*, 29, 117-398, where the "Roman Psalter" is given in a parallel column. According to D. De Bruyne (*Revue Bénéd.*, 1929, p. 299) the name "Gallican Psalter" is due originally not to its early use in Gaul but to the widespread use of manuscripts made in the monastery of St. Gall, Switzerland, bearing the title, *"Psalt. Gall."*

[14] *PL*, 26, 219-306. This work was probably issued in 389.

[15] *PL*, 26, 507-618. These works were written in 386-387.

[16] *PL*, 23, 1009-1116.

[17] *PL*, 23, 935-1010.

[18] In the Preface to this work he speaks of "the books of 'Hebrew Questions' which I have decided to write on *all* the Sacred Scriptures." Several times in his *Onomasticon* he refers the reader for further information to these books which he hoped soon to publish.

[18a] These two works are published in *PL*, 23, 771-928.

[19] Jerome himself says in his Preface that he "omitted some items that do not seem to merit recording and changed many other items." Actually his omissions are very few and his changes and additions are not too numerous; cfr. E. Klostermann, *Das Onomasticon von Eusebius* in the Berlin Corpus of the Greek Fathers (Leipzig, 1904), pp. xxiv f.

[20] *PL*, 22, 833, 952. Augustine, however, later on acknowledged the worth of Jerome's new translation, and in his later writings often cited it with praise; cfr. Vaccari, *Institutiones Biblicae* (Rome, 1929), 288.

[21] Rufinus, for instance, who maliciously changed the name of Jerome's Hebrew teacher, Baranina, into Barabbas (*PL*, 21, 611-616).

[22] Published in *PL*, 28, 1125-1240; and in a more critical edition by P. de LaGarde (Leipzig, 1874), and by J. M. Harden (London, 1922).

[23] *PL*, 25, 815-1578. These commentaries were not written in their present order, which is that of the Vulgate; but *Nah.*, *Mich.*, *Soph.*, *Ag.*, and *Hab.* appeared in 392; *Jon.* and *Abd.* in 396; *Zach.*, *Mal.*, *Osee*, *Joel* and *Amos* in 406.

[24] *PL*, 26, 15-218. This work was written shortly before Easter in 398. The only other commentary on the New Testament, besides the ones on the Pauline Epistles, mentioned above, in which Jerome had a hand is his revision of the Commentary on the Apocalypse by Victorinus of Pettau; ed. *CSEL*, 49.

[25] Cf. *Apol. adv. Ruf.*, I, 19 (*PL*, 23, 413).

[26] *Anecdota Maredsolana*, 3, 1. These *scholia* were used by the compiler of the *Breviarium in Psalmos* (*PL*, 26, 821-1378) which was once falsely attributed to St. Jerome.

[27] *Anecd. Mareds.*, 3, 2-3.

[27a] According to De Bruyne (*Zeitschr. f. d. neutest. Wiss.* 28 [1929], 1ff.), these two Goths and their learned letter is a mere fiction, invented by Jerome as a literary device whereby he could refute the common objections raised against his second revision of the Psalms. Cf. however, A. Zeiller, "La lettre de S. Jérôme aux Goths, Sunnia et Fretela," *Comptes rend. Acad. Inscript. et Bel.-Let.* (Paris, 1935), 238-250.

[28] As is done, for instance, by L. Schade in his "Inspirationslehre des hl. Hieronymus" (*Bibl. Stud.*, XV, 4-5.[1910], 119).

[29] Cfr. A. Vaccari, "I fattori della esegesi geronimiana," in *Biblica* I (1920), 466ff.

[30] *PL*, 25, 491-584.

[31] *PL*, 24, 17-678. The Fifth Book of this Commentary, explaining only the literal sense of the "Ten Visions" of Isaias (Is. 13:1-23, 18), was first published as a separate opuscule in 397.

[32] *PL*, 25, 15-490.

[33] *PL*, 24, 679-900; *CSEL*, 59.

[34] So L. Schade, who says simply, "Er war Autodidakt" (*Bibliotek der Kirchenväter: Hieronymus*, 1914, p. lxii).

[35] *De vir. illus.*, 117 (*PL*, 23, 707).

[36] Hence, we speak here of the "Alexandrian" and the "Antiochian" exegetes chiefly in the sense that the basic principles of their exegesis were derived from one or the other of these two schools, even though many of these men actually lived in various other parts of the Roman Empire. The Alexandrian school was the older. Among its outstanding exegetes were Pantaenus, its founder († c. 200), Clement († c. 215), Origen, the greatest of them all († 254), Dionysius († 265), Pierius († c. 300), Eusebius of Caesarea († 340), Athanasius († 373), Didymus († c. 398), and Cyril of Alex. († 444). The chief exponents of the Antiochian school

were Lucian, its founder († 213), Theodore of Heraclea († 355), Eusebius of Emesa († c. 359), Apollinarius (or, Apollinaris) of Laodicea († c. 390), Diodorus of Tarsus († c. 393), John Chrysostom († 407), Theodore of Mopsuestia († 428), Polychronius of Apamea († c. 430), and Theodoret († 458).

[37] Cfr. A. Vaccari, ". . . nella scuola esegetica di Antiochia," *Biblica* I (1920), 3-36.

[38] See footnote 8.

[39] *PL,* 25, 412.

[40] *Ep.* 108, 26.

[41] *PL,* 29, 401.

[42] In Jerome's writings, as in ancient Christian literature generally, "a Hebrew" *(Hebraeus)* is a respectful term which regards merely the man's race or language, whereas "a Jew" *(Judaeus)* is a term of reproach, emphasizing the man's religion, which from the Christian viewpoint is worthy of reprobation.

[43] *Praefatio in Job secundum Hebraeum (PL, 28, 1081).*

[44] *PL,* 29, 25f.

[45] Jerome admits, however, that the Jews used to laugh at his quaint accent and faulty pronunciation of the strange sibilants and gutturals of Hebrew; cfr. his *Comment. in Tit.* 3:9 *(PL,* 26, 594f.).

[46] This appeal to the authority of the Hebrews backfired on Jerome in the rather comical dispute with Augustine about the name of the ephemeral plant that sheltered Jonas (Jon. 4:6f.). When a certain North African bishop had Jerome's new version publicly read in church, the people raised such a hubbub at hearing the old "cucumber-vine" of Jonas now changed into "ivy," that the bishop had the choice of either restoring the old reading or finding himself without a congregation. The Jews of those parts, who were asked about it, said that the change was no improvement. Augustine admits that they might have said this from ignorance or malice, but they were really quite right. Cfr. *PL,* 22, 833f., 929ff. Actually, Jerome's description of this plant in his Commentary on Jonas *(PL,* 25, 1147f.) shows that his teachers correctly identified it with the castor-oil plant, but the Latin word for it, *ricinus,* had apparently slipped his memory.

[47] Cfr. his Commentary on Amos 3:11 *(PL,* 25, 1019C).

[48] *PL,* 23, 940.

[49] *Pessachim* 54a; *Nedarim* 39; *Jalkut* 20.

[50] The Hebrew phrase *miq-qedem* means literally, "from the front," but by usage it means either "of old" or "in the east." The Septuagint was also correct in taking "Eden" for a proper name. Jerome, as usual, likes to show its popular Hebrew etymology.

[51] *PL,* 23, 1048f.

[52] *PL,* 24, 119. This passage mentions, among others, the well-known Scribes: Shammai, Hillel, Johannan ben Zakkai, and Meir. Unfortunately, the text here, as published by Migne, seems to be rather corrupt.

[53] *PL,* 22, 1033f.

[54] *PL,* 25, 1301B.

[55] *Comment. in Zach.* 11:11 *(PL,* 25, 1496).

[56] *PL,* 24, 587f.

[57] *PL,* 24, 865D; *CSEL,* 59, 367. This statement occurs in the introduction to the last part of the last Commentary that Jerome wrote.

[58] Many good studies have already been made on the relationship between Jerome's Commentaries and the Rabbinical literature. But this mine of research has not yet been exhausted. Among the more valuable studies are the following:

H. Grätz, *Monats. f. Gesch. u. Wiss. d. Jud.,* 1854, 1855.

M. Rahmer, *ibidem,* 1865, '67, '68, '97; also, *Die Commentarii zu d. 12 kl. Proph.* (1902).

M. J. Lagrange, *Rev. Bibl.,* 1898.

V. Aptowitzer, *Zeits. altt. Wiss.,* 1909.

A. Condamin, *Rech. de science relig.,* 1914.

F. M. Abel, *Rev. Bibl.,* 1916, '17.

[59] *E.g.,* in his revision of the Latin Gospels, and in his knowledge of the Septuagint MSS. Even modern textual critics still divide the Septuagint MSS into three main families according to Jerome's statement in his *"Praef. in lib. Paral. juxta Heb."* (PL, 28, 1324f.): "In regard to the recensions of the Septuagint, in Alexandria and Egypt they use the edition of Hesychius, from Constantinople to Antioch they approve of the copies edited by Lucian, the martyr, while in the regions between these two provinces they read the Palestinian codices prepared by Origen and published by Eusebius and Pamphilus. Thus the whole world is divided by this threefold form of the text."

[60] *PL,* 28, 557f.

[61] Several times he speaks of the ambiguity of Hebrew words because they were written with consonants only; *e.g.,* in his *Comm. in Jer.* 9:22 (*PL,* 24, 745B; *CSEL,* 59, 126—his last major work!), he says, "The Hebrew word which is written with the three letters, *daleth, beth,* and *res*—for it has no vowels between them—, if, according to the context and the judgment of the reader, it is read as *dabar,* it means 'word,' if as *deber,* it means 'death,' if as *dabber,* it means 'speak.'" However, even in his time the text already had the marks now known as "extraordinary points"; *e.g.,* in Gen. 19:33 (on Lot's daughter lying with him) the Massoretic text still has a seemingly meaningless dot over the phrase, "and in her rising"; Jerome says (*Quaest. in Gen., PL,* 23, 973), "They put a point over it, as if it were something unbelievable and beyond nature to have intercourse and not know it." So also the Talmud (*Rabba in Gen.* 51): "Why is there a point here? To show that he did not know it when he was asleep, but that he did know it when he got up."

[62] *PL,* 29, 402A.

[63] *PL,* 28, 150f.

[64] *PL,* 26, 361ff. One of his attempts to explain the phrase, "Cursed by God," is of special interest. "The Hebrew who gave me some instructions in the Scriptures used to say that it could also be read as, 'Because with reviling God was hung up.'" Jerome rightly doubts the possibility of the Hebrew words having such a meaning. But it is to be noted that this *Hebraeus qui me in Scripturis aliqua ex parte instituit* was most probably the converted Jew who gave Jerome his first Hebrew lessons, for no other Jew would have tried to give such a Christian interpretation to the passage.

[65] *Dial.* 1, 8 (*PL,* 20, 189; *CSEL,* 1, 161).

[66] *PL,* 22, 912; 33, 247; *CSEL,* 34, II, 269.

[67] Cfr. L. Murillo, "S. Jerónimo, el 'Doctor Máximo,'" in *Biblica* 1 (1920), 434, n. 3; 442, n. 1.

[68] Murillo, *l.c.,* pp. 447ff.

[69] *Dial., l.c.*

[70] *Contra Julianum,* 1, 34 (*PL,* 44, 665).

[71] Cfr. Leop. Fonck, "Hieronymi Scientia naturalis exemplis illustratur," in *Biblica* 1 (1920), 481-499.

[72] "Tridui opus": *PL,* 28, 1241.

[73] "Unius diei laborem arripui": *PL,* 29, 26.

[74] "Huic unam lucubratiunculam dedi": *PL,* 29, 39.

[75] O. Bardenhewer, *Patrology* (T. J. Shahan's translation, 1908), 463. Essentially the same statement is repeated in Bardenhewer's last German edition, III (1912), 628.

[76] *PL,* 25, 820.

[77] *PL,* 25, 1418.

[78] *Comment. in Zach.* 6:9ff. (*PL,* 25, 1455D).

[79] *Encycl.* "Spiritus Paraclitus," Sept. 15, 1920, *Acta Apost. Sedis* 12, 410.

[80] *Encycl.* "Divino Affante Spiritu," Sept. 30, 1943, par. 49; quoted here from the "English Translation Provided by the Vatican," N.C.W.C., 23.

[81] *Dial.* 1, 7 (*PL,* 20, 188; *CSEL,* 1, 160).

[82] *Encycl.* "Spir. Parac.," *Acta Apos. Sedis* 12, 418.

[83] *Prol. in Comment. in Is.* (*PL,* 24, 17B).

Francis X. Murphy (essay date 1952)

SOURCE: "St. Jerome as an Historian" in *A Monument to Saint Jerome: Essays on Some Aspects of His Life, Works and Influence,* edited by Francis X. Murphy, Sheed & Ward, 1952, pp. 115-41.

[*In the essay that follows, Murphy describes the development of Jerome's interest in history alongside a chronological investigation of his life and writings. Murphy notes how that interest expresses itself in Jerome's writings that are not overtly historical.*]

The seventy-odd years that form the Age of St. Jerome—from 347 to 420—were hardly an era of great historical writing. As F. Lot and Professor Laistner have pointed out, but for the productions of the pagan Ammianus Marcellinus and the Christian Sulpicius Severus, the fifth century finds the West bereft of any true historian. But the situation might easily have been different. For, several times in the course of his long, eventful career, the most erudite man of the age, Jerome of Stridon, had promised himself and posterity that he would get round to writing a first-class history of the Christian era. Thus, in the opening chapter of his *Life of Malchus,* written in 390 or 391, Jerome says:

> I have purposed—if the Lord gives me life and my detractors cease to persecute me, who am now a fugitive and shut off from the world—to write a history from the coming of the Savior down to our own times, from the Apostles to the dregs of this

age, and to describe how and through whom Christ's Church came into being; how, growing up, it waxed by persecutions and was crowned with martyrdoms; and how, after reaching the Christian Emperors, it became yet greater in power and wealth, but declined in virtue.[1]

A decade earlier, when finishing his translation of the *Chronicle* of Eusebius of Caesarea (381), he had also promised:

> I have been content to reserve for a much broader history *(latiori historiae)* the remainder of the reigns of Gratian and Theodosius, not because I hesitate to write freely and truthfully about the living—for the fear of the Lord dispels the fear of men—but because, with the barbarians roving about wildly on our very own soil, all things are uncertain.[2]

Jerome was actually haunted by an historical sense. It permeates his Scriptural commentaries. It is continually betraying itself in his letters and controversies. It was due unquestionably to the classical training to which he had been subjected as a boy—to his familiarity with Tacitus and Livy, with Suetonius, Herodotus and Xenophon. But it was just as certainly due to the influences of Christianity thrust upon him in Rome, as an impressionable youth coming into contact with the recently recognized ecclesiastical authorities, as well as wandering through the catacombs, and meditating upon this new spiritual force that "in the fulness of time" was found gradually growing upon Imperial Rome.

An early indication of such historical awareness is given in his preoccupation with the work of Hilary of Poitiers, *On the Synods,* when he arrived in Treves in 367, having completed his classical studies in Rome.[3] It is equally evident in his appeal to the Pope in Rome a few years later, when in the desert of Chalcis he is called upon by the contentious monks there to take a stand with regard to the Antiochian schism and the Trinitarian controversy then raging: "Now indeed, *proh dolor!* After the faith of Nicea, after the decree of Alexandria joined in by the West, a new expression for the three hypostases is demanded by the Arian offspring, by these peasants, of me, a man of Rome!"[4] It is fully apparent, once he has been through the "postgraduate" Scripture course at Constantinople under (among others) St. Gregory Nazianzen. For almost immediately thereafter, Jerome set about the translation and revision of Eusebius' *Chronicle* of world history.

But even before turning his hand to the *Chronicle,* Jerome had betrayed a considerable historical interest and insight in his *Dialogue against the Luciferians*[5]—disciples of Bishop Lucifer of Calaris, who had gone into schism over the question of receiving back into the Church the bishops guilty of defection at the Council of Rimini. Writing the *Dialogue* at Antioch in 378, Jerome utilizes the conversation between an orthodox Catholic and a Luciferian named Helladius to refute, one after another, the objections brought against granting pardon to the bishops who had already been admitted to penance at the Council of Alexandria in 362. He displays at once a complete mastery of the historical narratives of the Gospels, and in particular of the Acts of the Apostles. He manifests a thorough familiarity with the Acts of the councils of Nicea and of Rimini, as well as with the writings of Cyprian, Hilary and Tertullian.

Though this dialogue is an early work of St. Jerome's, it demonstrates at once his clear-cut appreciation of the role of tradition in explaining and supporting the Scriptures. In it he witnesses to the ecclesiastical patterns that go back to the very origins, concerning the sacraments, the role of the Church and of the episcopate, as well as to numerous liturgical practices.[6] He likewise displays a concern for the history of heresy, from the days of the Jewish religion down through the earliest Christian heretics to his own day—a preoccupation that will be characteristic of all his future writings. And everywhere he points to historical sources, to trustworthy evidence, in support of his contentions. Thus he advises:

> If anyone desires to learn further about these matters, let him consult the Acts of the Synod of Rimini, whence we ourselves have drawn these facts. . . . Should anyone think these things to have been made up by us, let him consult the public records. The archives of the Church are complete. And indeed, the memory of these things is still fresh. There are still men living who were present at this Synod [Rimini]. And, what decides the matter, the Arians themselves do not deny that these things happened as we report them. . . . [7]

It seems really as a result of his stay in Constantinople (c. 380-381) that, along with his Scriptural interests, Jerome caught sight of the real meaning and indispensability of historical studies for the Scripture scholar. It was as a result of his contact with men like Apollinaris of Laodicea and Gregory Nazianzen, as well as of his wide reading in Origen, Irenaeus, and above all in Eusebius of Caesarea.[8]

Jerome had been brought up in the West in an age when historical writing had reached a low ebb. The pagan productions of the day, with the already mentioned exception of Ammianus Marcellinus, were a few epitomes and biographical surveys—the works of men like Eutropius, Aurelius Victor and Rufius Festus, along with the so-called *Historia Augusta:* mainly abridgements of Livy and conventional pictures of the Roman emperors, traceable to the imitation of Suetonius and Tacitus. For the most part, the age had lost the concept of the historian as a literary artist who gives a well-rounded picture of an epoch "in which the importance of individual persons and episodes are justly appraised as larger or smaller parts of a whole, and in which certain broad philosophic concepts serve as a guide through a maze of history and as an aid for the reader towards a true interpretation."[9]

In coming upon Eusebius' *Chronicle,* Jerome had been immediately struck by the vast sweep of its accomplishment. For Eusebius had published a résumé of universal history from Adam down to the reign of Constantine, complete with chronological tables and references. It was really part of his *Preparatio Evangelica,* a vast work of synthesis that was to form a complete apology for the Christian religion.[10] Jerome at once perceived the immensity and the utility of the résumé. Before him, Hilary of Poitiers, Eusebius of Vercelli and Chromatius of Aquileia had been exposed to this Greek ecclesiastical learning, but had apparently failed to appreciate its full significance. Jerome grasped its indispensability in permitting the Western Christian to orientate himself in the course of world history, and thus facilitate his study both of the Scriptures and of the milieu of profane knowledge. Hence his determination to translate the *Chronicle,* without, however, also doing into Latin the chronological tables which were really an adaptation from the chronographer, Julius Africanus (c. 240).

By way of preparation for his task, Jerome seems to have familiarized himself with his own Latin authors, in particular with Suetonius and Tacitus, and perhaps also with the epitome of Pompeius Trogus' *Philippic History* made by M. Junius Justinus in the third century. For the translation, while faithful to the original, contains numerous references introduced by Jerome as of interest to his Western readers. He begins his own preface to the translation by some remarkably sensible observations with regard to translation methods. He then set forth part of the difficulty of the task:

> And to this difficulty [the unreality of a strictly literal rendition] which is common to all translation work, this further affects us, that this history is so complicated, having strange-sounding names, things not known to Latins, inexplicable numbers, critical marks intertwined with text and numerals, so that it is almost more difficult to explain the method of reading than it is to proceed to a notice of the reading.[11]

He then explains his critical apparatus in which, while following the pattern set by Eusebius, he makes use of several columns in recording contemporary reigns, but marks each with a different type of ink, so that the brief text of commentary on each particular event or personage may be lined up with the proper year to which it belongs. He concludes his preface with the remark:

> I would rather have my readers satisfied, so that they may assign to its proper author the truth of the Greek [original], and may realize that those things which we have inserted on our own have been culled from the most reliable authors. It should be known that I have used in part both the assistance of a translator and of an amanuensis, so that I have given exact expression to the Greek, and have also injected into the story a good deal of Roman history, which Eusebius, the original author of this book, did not do, not so much because he was ignorant of the latter—for he was a most learned man—but because, writing for a Greek audience, he did not feel it necessary.

> Thus, from Ninus and from Abraham down to the fall of Troy, it is a simple translation from the Greek. From Troy to the twentieth year of Constantine, many things have been added and changed round, which I have taken most carefully from Suetonius and from other illustrious historians. From the above-mentioned year of Constantine [325] down to the consulate of the august Caesars, Valentinian II and Valens [378], the whole is my own.[12]

In the beginning of his preface, Jerome makes some remark regarding the translation as an *"opus tumultuarium"*[13]—but he is certainly exaggerating. For the complexity and the ingenuity with which he has the various tables of parallel reigns worked out belie any such thing as haste. However, as Helm has remarked of the interpolations regarding the literary figures of Latin antiquity in particular, Jerome must have jotted down annotations from Suetonius and the other authors on the margin of his copy of Eusebius' text.[14] Then, under the confusion of his own revisions and rearrangement, a number of these additions tended to get misplaced. However, Jerome had no certain chronology regarding these ancient authors that he could follow without fear of error. There simply was no good Latin tradition dating these various writers. Thus are explained certain inconsistencies and apparent indecisions that Jerome is attempting to cover with his *"tumultuarium."*

In translating the *Chronicle,* Jerome, as he says, added much new material for the period beginning with the Trojan war. It has been recently suggested that he was following, in his arrangement, Justinus' epitome of the *Philippic History* of Pompeius Trogus:[15] so that while Jerome appears to be definitely paralleling his history to fit in with a philosophy of the *Four Empires,* he is influenced much more particularly by the secular current of thought than by the Biblical commentaries of Hippolytus, Tertullian and Origen upon the Prophets of the Old Testament, and in particular upon the Book of Daniel. This presupposes a thorough familiarity upon Jerome's part with Trogus, and with the current of Latin thought he represents, which indeed goes all the way back to Ennius, and is reflected in the chronographers and in Claudian. But although Jerome does point with scorn to the evils inherent in the Roman Empire, there seems to be lacking in his observations the definitely anti-imperial spirit and condemnatory approach that is characteristic of Trogus. Likewise, there is serious question as to Jerome's familiarity with this particular historian. He does not mention him until he is writing his own ***Commentary on the Prophet Daniel*** in 407,[16] some twenty-seven years after his translation of the *Chronicle*. Then he is definitely influenced by the parade of authorities cited by Porphyry in his attack upon Daniel.

What seems to point to the influence of Trogus, however, is the fact that Jerome, departing from Eusebius' arrangement, outlines his history with the four great empires of Assyria, Persia, Greece and Rome succeeding each other in the second, or "guide," column of his manuscript. Like Trogus, he seems to have had considerable difficulty placing the Medes, whom, at this period, he did not consider one of the four principal imperial nations.[17] Eusebius, not following this pattern, had left one hundred and eleven years after the fall of Assyria free, before beginning an account of the Persians. Jerome fills in the gap with the names of eight kings of the Medes, only four of whom Eusebius had mentioned in his text, though he had named the other four in the chronological preface to the work. In his own preface, Jerome merely mentions Suetonius and "other illustrious historians" as the source of his additions.[18] Thus, though he is obviously conforming to a pattern other than that set by the original, it is still an open question as to whether he is being guided by his Biblical knowledge of Daniel and the commentators, or whether he is drawing from Trogus and the anti-imperial literature of the Augustan age.

The third section of Jerome's ***Chronicle,*** covering the period from A.D. 325 to 379, Jerome claims as his own, though here he leans heavily on Eutropius, the *magister memoriae* under Valens.[19] In general, he follows the previous pattern, and is thus little more than a recorder of the principal happenings in the political world, following up the detailed accounts of the Roman kings, the evolution of the Republic and Empire, the dealings of the Roman legions with various frontier tribes and legions, as well as anecdotal and geographic material, that had characterized Jerome's additions to Eusebius' original. Considerable attention is naturally paid to the series of bishops and important religious events, a listing of the main Christian and pagan authors of the age, and a recording of such phenomena as earthquakes, famines, battles, and monstrosities.

The whole work is thus a prodigious storehouse of historical lore, not well integrated nor properly proportioned, it is true. Towards the end, Jerome indulges a number of personal judgments on men such as Basil, Cyril of Jerusalem, and Peter of Alexandria that are far

from the spirit of impartiality. But it did furnish both Jerome and his readers in the West with a magnificent opportunity to locate themselves in regard to world history. And it is written with considerable verve and attention to style, no matter how short the item or notice being set down. As Père Cavallera remarks:

> By relating the present to the past, it allowed for a continuous feeling of solidarity between generations. In linking sacred and profane history, it presented a double advantage. It confirmed the faithful in their conviction that their religion was the most noble, the most ancient and the most pure of all those creeds then cluttering the world; but, at the same time, in arousing, or in at least continuing, a sympathetic approach to profane history, it recalled for the reader the fact that, while a citizen of heaven, he was still a citizen of the Roman Empire, an heir to that ancient civilization of whose history the principal facts were here recalled for him. Hence it helped to prevent a loss of interest in the world, or a narrow isolationism from the things of the present.[20]

The popularity of Jerome's translation of the ***Chronicle*** is well attested by the number of manuscripts in which it was circulated, and in its numerous continuations down through the centuries, beginning with that of Prosper of Aquitaine. Along with Augustine's *City of God*—which, incidentally, owed much to Jerome's translation—the ***Chronicle*** was the staple of world history upon which the Middle Ages were nourished for over a thousand years.

Jerome had spoken of a "broader history" of the Christian age that he was contemplating, as he brought his translation of Eusebius to a close. But his Scriptural and controversial activities from now on would preclude any such strictly historical undertaking. His sojourn in Rome from 382 to 385 was the occasion for his applying himself to issuing a new Latin version of the four Gospels, collated from various Greek manuscripts, along with the older Latin versions. The evidence thus afforded of Jerome's interest in textual problems has been well set forth by K. Hulley in his study of the "Principles of textual criticism known to St. Jerome,"[21] wherein he ranges up and down the avenues of both lower and higher criticism, and, by copious quotation from the prefaces and commentaries, demonstrates Jerome's genuine competence in these fields.

Jerome, of course, from his earliest days had been a great bibliophile. Particularly under the influence of his experiences at the great Christian library center of Caesarea, where he seems first to have actually examined Origen's *Hexapla,* his interest and his efforts in obtaining correct texts of the Scriptures, properly attributed and attested to, is paramount in all his endeavors. He became extremely aware of the necessity of coping with the original languages, and of using them properly—thus his own rather painful mastery of Hebrew, his excursions into Syriac, Coptic and Aramaic.

Jerome seems to have been particularly sensitive about the matter of knowing a language thoroughly, not only hiring, at considerable cost, a rabbi for lessons in Hebrew, but keeping an observant ear ever open to particularities and similarities in idiom and dialect, and between languages themselves, in the course of his travels and his association with peoples from all over the then known world. Thus, as a young man travelling through Gaul, he declares that he has paid close attention to the Celtic languages spoken by the several barbarian peoples settled round about Treves and Normandy. Years later, when writing his **Commentary on the Epistle to the Galatians,** he mentions how closely the tongues of the numerous tribes in the Near East resembled the speech of the Gauls:

> Whence we infer that the Galatians . . . have their own language, which is practically the same as that of the peoples round Treves. Nor does it matter that they have corrupted it to a certain extent, for the Africans have changed the Phoenician language in good' part, and Latin itself is modified in each age and clime. . . . [22]

It is possible, of course, that Jerome, knowing a good deal about the history of these tribes and their wanderings, claims a trifle too much for his own general experience—but at least he betrays a considerable interest in the subject.

Jerome too notes the wealth of historical detail afforded by monuments and other relics of the past, of various types and proveniences. Thus his early interest in the Roman catacombs; but likewise, his awareness of the "Pythagorean Monuments" scattered up and down the coast of Italy, witnessing to the prevalence of that particular philosophy and superstition in the pre-Christian ages, as Jerome points out for Rufinus.[23] In the matter of geographical detail, of place names, and of origins, he does not hesitate to correct his own opinions, garnered from his reading, by the actual state of affairs, as he came to see it in his travels.[24] Jerome was thus very well equipped as an historian, not only well-travelled, but supremely aware of the useful arts that contribute to the truth and accuracy of any attempt to capture and delimit what has taken place in the past. On the whole, he manifests a critical eye and an ability to evaluate data that are well beyond the stature of his age—with the sole exception, perhaps, of his contemporary chronicler, Sulpicius Severus.

In Jerome's controversial works, for example, historical references, appeals to tradition, citations of ancient authors abound, as well as the dramatic interest arising from story sources, and frequent attempts are made at clearing up involved problems and difficulties through the exercise of critical judgment. He exhibits great care in quoting his adversaries verbatim before smothering them under an avalanche of facts, figures and vituperation. In his **Adversus Helvidium,**[25] he devotes the main sections to the problems of the virginity of the Blessed Mother and the subsidiary questions of the "brothers of the Lord." In ferreting out parallel references and cases by way of proof, supplementary to his main argument, he roams all over the Old Testament, demonstrating at once his mastery of that great document and his recognition of its value as an historical source. He appeals then to profane literature and history. His final decision is rendered with reference to "the whole series of ancient writers: Ignatius, Polycarp, Irenaeus, Justin Martyr, and many another apostolic and eloquent man who wrote volumes full of wisdom on these same matters against Ebion, Theodotus, Byzantius and Valentine . . ."[26]

In his defense of virginity against the attacks of Jovinian, having exhausted his Scriptural references, Jerome turns to secular literature, exclaiming: "I will now run briefly through the Greek, Latin, and barbarian historians, and will prove that virginity has always been held to be the chief glory of chastity . . ."[27] And he reels off a host of fables, stories and anecdotes culled from Porphyry and Josephus, wherein he cites Herodotus, Strabo, Xenophon, Ovid, Virgil, etc., and reaches from Diana of the Ephesians and Dido of Carthage to the Milesians and the Gymnosophists of India (Ethiopia). He finishes with a catalogue of the evils of married life that is really staggering in its mounting vulgarity, but, as always, he calls upon Plutarch, Seneca, Plato, Aristotle and, in particular, the *De nuptiis* of Theophrastus—again via the *De abstinentia* of Porphyry—for the testimony and justification.[28]

In the second part of the **Adversus Jovinianum,** Jerome presents a myriad of parallels and contrasts between the customs, laws, eating habits and peculiarities of every nation and people then known to mankind, a feat that would bear comparison with the work of one of our modern sociological encyclopedists, though again, for the most part, Jerome is quoting from Porphyry without benefit of citation.[29]

Jerome was engaged in two other historical tasks during the course of his earlier career: the composition of several *Vitae patrum* and of the eulogies of a number of his friends. The former—the lives of Paul the Hermit, of Malchus and of Hilarion—are in the nature of edifying stories built in good part upon legend and hearsay that Jerome gathered from among the desert fathers, but having certain bases in fact. Jerome shows himself quite insistent as to the historical character of

Paul, whom he nominates as the first hermit and the predecessor of St. Anthony, though he admits that Anthony is properly venerated as the Father of Monasticism as such.

In writing his preface to the Life of Hilarion, Jerome says explicitly:

> In attempting this work, I contemn the words of my evil-wishers who, having once quarrelled with my Paul, will now try to detract from my Hilarion. To the former they objected on the score of his "solitary life"; against the latter, they will bring complaint that he was "too socially inclined"—maintaining that he who was never seen simply never existed; and he who was seen often did not amount to anything. . . . [30]

Despite the fact that Jerome follows closely the Quintilian-prescribed form of encomium, and that he refers to centaurs and other monsters in his *Vita Pauli*, he does place the "first hermit" in a strictly historical setting. Throughout the work he strives to give the impression that what he is relating is for the most part factual, though obviously intended as an edifying advertisement for the monastic state in which Jerome is so primarily concerned.[31] The same can be said for his *Vita Hilarionis*, based, as he maintains, upon conversations with St. Epiphanius, who knew the hermit intimately.[32]

In regard to the *Vita Malchi,* there is some appearance of verisimilitude, it being the story of an incident in the life of a monk captured by the Saracens, and finally saved through the instrumentality of a lion guarding the entrance to a cave in which he had taken refuge from pursuit—this latter incident, or course, being a most unfortunate circumstance as far as historical criticism is concerned. But it is really capable of being lived down.[33]

These *Vitae* are extremely well-written narratives. They pay close attention to geographical detail and give evidence of being linked to the history of the times. Shot through as they are with demons and monsters, they present a problem with which Weingarten and Winter, Dölger and Schiweitz have wrestled at considerable length. The outcome of their studies seems to be that there was a hyperconsciousness of demonology among the early desert fathers and, at the same time, a tendency towards overcredulity in regard to these and other such phenomena.[34] It gravely affected even such realists as Jerome and Augustine. But Jerome had set out to write true biographies in keeping with the standards of the times. From a literary viewpoint, from a monastic-propagandist viewpoint, and from an historical viewpoint, he succeeded, despite the rigidity of form imposed by convention and the distraction of bizarre episodes.

Of a more reliable historical character are Jerome's eulogies of a number of his friends, written by way of consolation to their loved ones, but also as a record and testimonial of their saintly lives. This is particularly true of his "Letters" concerning Blesilla and Paula, Eustochium, Fabiola and Marcella, Nepotianus and Nebridius. While outlining the main historical facts, and apparently eschewing the *loci communes,* Jerome lays great stress upon the practice of Christian virtue to which these heroes and heroines of his were wholly committed—in the case of Nepotianus, swinging into a characterization of the ideal young priest; and utilizing the life of Paula as a model for the Christian maiden. All is done very elegantly, and with sufficient detail to render posterity an exceptionally clear picture of the life of these well-to-do, ascetically inclined devotees and acquaintances of his.[35]

That Jerome was still thinking in terms of a full-scale historical work shortly after his permanent settlement in Bethlehem in 386 or 387 is evident from his preface to the *Vita Malchi,* wherein he spoke of the "larger history" he was then contemplating. Despite his good intentions, however, this projected history never saw the light of day. In its place, Jerome found himself more and more absorbed in Scriptural studies.

Writing to Paulinus in 395, Jerome expatiated at length upon the preparation necessary for a proper appreciation of the "word of God." He describes the pains taken by secular authors to obtain a proper understanding of the world about them:

> We read in the older histories how men wandered over whole provinces, approached new peoples, crossed the seas, in order that they might see for themselves what they had read in books. . . . Thus Pythagoras, to see the sages of Memphis; thus Plato laboriously traversed Egypt . . . and, for the sake of Archytas of Tarentine, the coast of Italy formerly called Magna Graecia, that he who was a master and a power in Athens . . . might become a foreigner and disciple, preferring in a modest fashion to learn, rather than impudently to pour forth his own. . . . We read that a man came from the ends of the earth to see Titus Livy. . . . And Apollonius, whether the magician, as it is commonly thought, or the philosopher, as the Pythagoreans maintain, entered Persia, crossed the Caucasus, the lands of the Scythians and Massagetes . . . penetrated India . . . and came to the Brahmins, that he might listen to Hiarcas, seated on a throne of gold, drinking the waters of the Tantalus and expatiating upon nature, morals and the course of the stars. . . . He travelled thence by way of Babylonia, Chaldea, the land of the Medes, Assyrians, Parthians, Syrians, Phoenicians, Arabs and Palestine to return to Alexandria and enter Ethiopia, that he might there see the Gymnosophists. . . . [36]

Thus making a vivid résumé of the *Life of Apollonius of Tyana* written by Philostratus,[37] Jerome hurries on to discuss St. Paul and the Christian heroes. He continues:

> I have run through these things briefly, that you may understand that one cannot embark upon the Sacred Scriptures without preparation and a guide pointing out the way. I will not pass over the grammarians, rhetoricians, philosophers, geometricians, dialecticians, musicians, astrologers and medical men, whose knowledge is most useful for us mortals, and is divided into three disciplines: evidence, method and practice.

> I will take up the minor arts, which are controlled not so much by "word" as by the hand. Farmers, bricklayers, builders, the hewers of metals and wood, wool-makers, clothiers, etc., who put together various furnishings and meaner products, just cannot become what they desire to be without the aid of an instructor.

> *Quod medicorum est*
> *promittunt medici, tractant fabrilia fabri.*

> Alone the art of the Scriptures is one that all indiscriminately claim for themselves:

> *scribimus indocti doctique poemata passim.*[38]

Then, pausing briefly to lacerate the fabricators of the centos of Homer and Virgil, Jerome proceeds to outline the nature and intent of the various books of the Old and New Testament.

For some time, then, Jerome had been determined to retranslate the Old Testament, at first by a revision of the Septuagint, but then directly from the Hebrew, and to provide commentaries and emendations for the whole body of the Scriptures. In so doing, his prefaces to the different books provide a course in lower and higher criticism, in paleography, diplomatic and heuristic, whereby he proves himself master of many of the disciplines ancillary to the competent historian.[39]

In the midst of this new Scripture work, Jerome paused once more for a strictly historical exercise. Ever since his translation of Eusebius' *Chronicle* he had felt the need of a good *nomenclator,* or handbook of Christian authors, that would at once parallel Suetonius' and the other secular manuals, and serve as an inspiration and justification of the Christian coming-of-age in the literary field.

For an Imperial official and friend of his, Flavius Dexter by name, Jerome drew up his ***De viris illustribus,***[40] a list of 135 authors, from the Apostles down to himself, whose works or reputations had been preserved as part of the Christian tradition, including several pagans and heretics whose productions held a special interest for the Christian scholar: Philo, Josephus, Seneca and Justin of Tiberias.

There is nothing particularly original about the ***De viris.*** As both Sychowski and Bernouilli were at great pains to show, Jerome takes the first seventy-eight authors almost verbatim from Eusebius' *Ecclesiastical History,* filling in but a few minor details on his own.[41] As a matter of fact, he has read very few of these authors, though he gives the impression that he is familiar with most of them at first hand. But Jerome had to get the information from somewhere! And he is tremendously more self-reliant for the authors of his own times, including such contemporaries as Basil, Ambrose, Rufinus, and Hilary.[42] It is very easy to be overcritical of such apparent "plagiarizing," if the historian of today fails to realize that Jerome's procedure was not only in keeping with the temper of his age, but was also about the only thing he could do, lacking the tremendous facilities at the disposal of the critical historian of modern times. The copious use of footnotes today is, after all, hardly more than a mechanism to cover up a procedure that in its essentials differs from Jerome's but little.

The last of Jerome's 135 notices is given over to his own literary productions down to the year 392—and shows him off at the age of forty-five as a man who has already definitely made his way in the Christian literary world, and who felt considerably conscious of that fact.

Historically speaking, the book is most valuable for its effect upon the Christian consciousness of the day—the literary notices for the men of the fourth century are, of course, invaluable—but the main impact of the work was the fact that it demonstrated the coming of age of Christian scholarship. It was actually the first handbook of Christian literature, and served as a model throughout the ages from Gennadius and Isidore down to Trithemius, Cave and St. Robert Bellarmine—a guide and a reservoir for the current of literary awareness from the sixth to the sixteenth century.

The question as to what historians Jerome had actually read is a most interesting and complex one. Pierre Courcelle maintains that as far, at least, as the Greek authors are concerned, he had read only those that would be directly useful to him in the study of the Scriptures; and that, therefore, when Jerome lines up a list such as: Hermippius the Peripatetic, Antigonus of Carystos, Satyrus, Aristexenes the musician, Apollonius, etc., he is really citing them from the now lost preface to Suetonius. Even Thucydides and Polybius were hardly more than names to him. However, he had read a great deal of Herodotus. Xenophon he knew both in Cicero's translations and in the original, at least for the *Cyropedia.* He had first-hand knowledge of Philo. But his real picture of the world from an historical view-point comes from Josephus, whom he must have known in good part by heart. He was also well acquainted with the works of Porphyry, mainly, of course, through Origen and Methodius. But he makes such frequent and complete use of the *De abstinentia* of that great anti-Christian antagonist that he simply must have read it.[43] As far back as 1872, of course, Luebeck indicated most of this.[44] And Jerome's own contemporary friend and foe, Rufinus of Aquileia, had long previously blurted out a similar accusation: "Indeed he [Jerome] sprays Aristides and Chrysippus, Empedocles and other names of Greek authors like smoke or clouds before his readers' eyes, that he may appear learned and of wide reading. . . . "[45]

As for the Latin historians, it is quite certain that Jerome had first-hand acquaintance with most of them—*e.g.,* Sallust, Livy, Caesar, Suetonius, etc.—for they were used as school texts, along with the poets. He seems to have used Pompeius Trogus and his epitomist, Justinus; he certainly had an acquaintance with Eutropius, upon whom he bases most of his continuation of Eusebius' *Chronicle.* Hence he should also have known the lesser chronographers and court historians, such as Sextus Aurelius, Rufius Festus, and the "Epitomes" of the Caesars.[46] Jerome can be very frank with regard to his own testimony concerning these things, as he is in the prologue to the second book of his *Commentary on Galatians:*

> Marcus Varro, a most diligent observer of all antiquity, and others who have imitated him, have handed down much about this people [the Galatians] that is worthy of being recalled. But because we have proposed not to introduce into the temple of God the uncircumcised—*and as I may simply confess, it is now many years since I have ceased to read these things*—I will merely quote the words of our own Lactantius. . . . [47]

In his preface to book three, he likewise assures Paula and Eustochium, for whose benefit he is writing:

> You yourselves know that for more than fifteen years [*i.e.,* since the famous dream mentioned in his Letter to Eustochium #22] I have never had in my hands a copy of Cicero, Virgil, or of any other author of pagan letters. And if indeed while I talk, something of these authors slips out, it is due to a recalling as through a cloudy dream of the past. . . . [48]

Thus it becomes most difficult to decide when Jerome is really quoting from among his Latin authors—for his memory was really prodigious. "Dye the wool once purple," he had chided Rufinus, "and what waters will wash it clean?"[49]

It is, however, in his Scriptural works that Jerome gives clearest indication of his historical talents and critical

tastes. Beginning with his *Hebraic Questions in Genesis*[50] he manifests a complete, fairly well-integrated, and comprehensive picture of the past. It is shot through with mistakes, of course, owing to the faulty state of historical knowledge and studies of the day. It stems from Josephus, Origen, Philo, Porphyry, and Eusebius, although Jerome not infrequently tries to give the impression that it is coming directly from Thucydides, Berosus, Plutarch, Dichaearchus, Alexander Polyhistor, Callinicus, Suetonius, etc. But the fact is that, in itself it manifests what was evidently a rather clear picture in Jerome's mind. It begins with the origins of various peoples scattered over the farthest reaches of the then known world, and stretches from the outposts of the Caucasus and India to the fastnesses of Africa, and the northernmost outposts of Britain. Thus Jerome amplifies Josephus on Genesis:

> To Japhet son of Noah, were born seven sons who possessed the land of Asia from Amanus and Taurus to Syria Coeli, and the mountains of Cilicia down to the river Tanain; in Europe, as far as Gadira, leaving their names upon both places and people. Of these latter, very many changed; yet many also remained as they were. The Galatians are of Gomer; the Scythians of Magog; the Medes of Madai; of Iavan are the Iones or Greeks, whence the Ionian sea. Of Thubal are the Iberians, also called Spaniards. . . . Of Mosoch, the Cappadocians: whence one of their cities is called Mazeca to this day. . . . Of Thiras, the Thracians. . . . I know that a certain man [St. Ambrose of Milan] has narrated the history of the Goths, who have been recently bacchanalizing in our lands, as of Gog and Magog, thus characterizing them by their present activities, and as they are referred to in Ezechiel. Whether this is a true interpretation or not will soon be seen by the finish of their war. But certainly the learned Goths themselves have in the past rather referred to themselves as of the Getes than of Gog and Magog. . . . [51]

The *Hebraic Questions in Genesis* is really part of a trilogy, made up of a translation of Eusebius' *Book of Place Names,*[52] together with his *Onomasticon,* or "Book of Hebrew Names,"[53] originally attributed to Philo and Origen. Unfortunately, all three books are vitiated to a certain extent by the ancient pseudoscience of etymology, in which Jerome is an especially great offender. But, at the same time, they represent a considerable amount of personal erudition on his part, particularly in the elaborations on the geography of Palestine and its environs supplied by his own personal knowledge—information that is still useful, and that, incidentally, proved most timely for the pilgrims then beginning to resort to the Holy Land in such great numbers.

Jerome's commentaries, beginning with those on Abdias and Ecclesiastes, running through the attention he gives to St. Paul in Galatians, Philemon, Ephesians and Titus, as also his Matthew, along with the minor Prophets, and Ezechiel, Isaias, Jeremias and Daniel are a great amalgam of historical and Scriptural lore. He hesitates to begin a commentary unless he has Origen at his side—he was accused even in his own day, particularly in regard to the Twelve Minor Prophets, of having lifted from Origen bodily[54]—yet, to say there is little that is original in his work would be simply false. For Jerome paints vivid pictures, using his immense knowledge as a background. Frequently he is quoting verbatim, without mention of his source; but, as likely as not, having once made a passage completely his own, he could not then distinguish between his own thoughts and those of his reading. Yet you cannot read through these commentaries without being struck with the man's tremendous historical consciousness, no matter whence he may be garnering his material.

Thus in the **Commentary on Isaias,** Jerome insists over and over again, particularly in the first six chapters, that Isaias vividly foretold the tragic events that would come upon Judea under Titus and Hadrian.[55] He maintains that he is not unaware that the city of Jerusalem had undergone other sieges in the course of the centuries. "But under the Romans, the whole of Judea was devastated, its cities put to the torch, and to this day the foreigner exploits the land." And he turns to Josephus to demonstrate that it is with this last spoliation that the prophecy has been carried out to the minutest detail. He is likewise insistent that all interpretation begin with history: "And we say this, not condemning the tropological sense, but because the spiritual interpretation must follow the order of history, which, many forgetting, they wander off into the most obvious errors against the Scriptures."[56] But as history is made up of many facets which succeed one another in the course of time, it belongs to the ingenuity of the commentator to discover the actual burden of events that carried out a particular prophecy.

When treating of a warning addressed to the king of Assyria, for example, Jerome insists upon remaining in the domain of ancient history: "From the context," he writes, "it is obvious that this applies to Sennacherib, king of the Assyrians." Several authors thought that Isaias 17:7, pertaining to the oracle uttered against Damascus, had received its realization in the time of Christ, when the Kingdom of the Savior replaced the already destroyed realm of Damascus. "A pious wish of the interpreters," is Jerome's comment, "but not in accordance with historical actuality." "We ourselves will follow the historical order, in the endeavor to cap off with historical fact an edifice begun on historical foundations."[57]

Jerome was really the first author of antiquity to question the story of the origin of the Septuagint, at least thrice expressing more than polite doubt and annoyance at the credulity of his contemporaries:

> For I know not who was the first author to construct out of a falsehood the seventy cells at Alexandria, in which they [the translators] were supposed to have all written the same things, though separated from each other, since neither Aristeas, one of the coterie around Ptolemaus himself, nor, much later, Josephus makes mention of any such things. But rather, they tell us that these men, gathered in a large basilica, wrote down a translation, not a prophecy . . . unless perchance we are to believe that Cicero translated the *Oeconomicon* of Xenophon, the *Protagoras* of Plato, and the *Pro Ctesiphon* of Demosthenes under the influence of the "rhetorical spirit. . . ." Do we then condemn these older writers? Not at all. . . . For they translated before the coming of Christ; and what they did not under-stand, they translated in dubious phrases. But we are writing after His passion and resurrection . . . hence are handling not prophecy but history. It is one thing to describe what you have merely heard, and quite another what you have actually seen. . . . [58]

Jerome approaches the Scriptures as a strictly historical document, a fact which he makes clear in the following passage, where he is quoting almost verbatim from Origen:

> Does anyone believe in God the Creator? He cannot believe unless he first believe that those things are true which are written about His saints, viz.: Adam was made of plasma by God; Eve, fabricated from a rib in his side; Enoch translated; Noah alone saved from amidst a shipwrecked world. . . . These and the rest that is written in Scriptures, unless one believe the whole of it, he cannot believe in the God of the saints. Nor can he be brought to the faith of the Old Testament unless he can prove to his own satisfaction all these facts which history records regarding the patriarchs, prophets, and other outstanding men. . . . [59]

He insists, again and again, that the Scriptures cannot be understood unless one start from an historical foundation. He knows, however, that

> Many things are spoken of in the Scriptures in accordance with common opinion at the time when they took place, and not according to the real truth of the matter. Thus, Joseph is spoken of in the Gospel as the "father of the Lord," Mary herself, who knew she had conceived of the Holy Ghost, telling her Son, "Behold! Thy father and I have sought thee sorrowing."[60]

As has been seen, Professor Swain recently maintained that Jerome took at least part of his approach to the over-all picture of history from the anti-imperial literature represented by Pompeius Trogus' *Philippic History,* rather than from the commentaries on the Apocalypse and on Daniel by Hippolytus, Irenaeus and Origen. But there is great difficulty in admitting that he was being so immediately influenced by an historian who was for Jerome but an obscure author. This is particularly true when one reflects that running through Jerome's thought there is a definite idea of progress in history that is bound up with a strictly Jewish concept of divine providence. For all the philosophical bent of Thucydides, Herodotus and Polybius, there was no real over-all plan to their idea of fate, certainly no integrated philosophy giving a spiritual as well as a cosmic meaning to the rise and fall of empires and kingdoms.[61] This latter was strictly the creation of the Jewish Scriptures, beginning with the story of the creation in Genesis, and being elaborated in set terms by the major and minor Prophets.[62] It is Eusebius who first appears to feel the tremendous swing of this trend of thought; and it is from Eusebius primarily that Jerome gathers his principal ideas, however much Trogus may have been on his mind.

Much of the burden of Jerome's **Commentary on Daniel** is in reality an attack upon Porphyry. The latter maintained that the book of Daniel was written not earlier than the time of the Machabees, about 165 B.C., and that, instead of being a prophecy, it was really a description of events up to the reign of Antiochus, of which there remained an historical record. Jerome makes use of all his predecessors—Origen, Methodius, Eusebius[63]—and hammers away at the position taken by the great pagan adversary of Christianity, not without some effect, though he finds the learning of Porphyry formidable. Thus, in his preface:

> To understand the latter parts of Daniel, a multiple history of the Greeks is necessary, namely: Sutorius, Callinicus, Diodorus, Hieronymus, Polybius, Poseidonius, Claudius, Theonis and Adronicus called Alypius, whom Porphyry declares he is following; in like manner also, Josephus and those whom Josephus quotes, and particularly our own Livy and Pompeius Trogus and Justinus, who narrate the whole history of the final vision. . . . [64]

But he gives Porphyry fair play throughout the commentary, juxtaposing his interpretation to that of the general run of Christian commentators:

> Thus far the historical order has been followed, and between Porphyry and ourselves there is no quarrel. The rest, continuing down to the end of the volume, he regards as of Antiochus. . . . Our commentators . . . refer all this to the anti-Christ. . . . [65]

But let this all be said of Antiochus. Wherein does that harm our religion? . . . Let them then say, Who is this "stone which is cut from the mountain without hands; which has grown into a great mountain and filled the earth, and assumed a fourfold form"? Who is this son of man, who is to come with the clouds, and to stand before the ancient of days, and to be given a kingdom to which there will be no end,

while all the people, tribes and tongues shall serve him? Porphyry avoids these things which are quite obvious, and asserts that they are prophesied about the Jews, whom we know to be in servitude to this day. . . . [66]

Jerome himself, of course, refers this prophecy directly to Christ, the Light of the World.[67]

On the larger question of a pattern or direction in history, Jerome feels there is evidently a close connection between divine providence and the paths of human history, and that this is discernible through the fulfilment of events foretold by the prophets of old. But he seems to preserve a fairly open mind in his interpretations.[68] While his concept of the sweep of the historical process subsumes the rise and fall of the four great empires, there is not a deterministic nor an apocalyptic tinge to his thinking, least of all a millenarian twist. He maintains that the corruption and downfall of these great states has been due to pride and rapacity on the part of their rulers and people. Hence he is not surprised to see signs of disaster coming upon the Rome of his day.[69]

Yet in his **Commentary on Isaias,** speaking of the section where the prophet describes the "wolf lying down with the lamb, and the leopard with the goat" (11:16) Jerome says:

> And this we see in our own day in the Church, where the rich and the poor, the powerful and the humble, kings and private people, mingle together, and are governed by young men whom we call apostles, and apostolic men, unskilled in speech but not in wisdom.[70]

Again, in his comment on the famous sixtieth chapter of Isaias (I off.), Jerome says:

> This can be taken either in a material or in a spiritual sense. If in a material, we see the Roman Caesars bending their necks to the yoke of Christ, building churches at the public expense, and leveling the fiats of law against the persecutions of the gentiles and the attacks of heretics. . . . Although we now see these things coming to pass in the Church of today, they will be more fully carried out upon the consummation of the world, in the second coming of the Savior.[71]

As an historian, then, Jerome did have well in mind the necessity of possessing a vast sweep of the knowledge of antiquity. Insofar as his main interests were governed by the Sacred Scriptures, he confined his immediate endeavors to keeping himself abreast of works needful in that field—not, however, without at least making pretense of being well acquainted with all the literature of antiquity. In the long run he makes fairly critical use of most of his material, and he is as honest as any man of the deep past in acknowledging his borrowings—or failing to do so. But he did have a magnificent grasp of the history of civilizations as known to his day. He had even figured out for himself an entire *Weltanschauung,* completed by a chronological analysis of his world. Thus he ends his supplement to Eusebius' *Chronicle:*

> Up to the consulate of Valentinian and Valens II [A.D. 378], all the years:
>
> a) From the 15th year of Tiberias and the preaching of our Lord Jesus Christ amount to 351;
>
> b) From the second year of Darius, King of the Persians, at the time when the temple of Jerusalem was rebuilt, equal 899;
>
> c) From the first Olympiad, the time when Isaias was preaching among the Jews, amount to 1,155;
>
> d) From Solomon and the first building of the Temple, amount to 1,411;
>
> e) From the capture of Troy, at which time Samson was alive among the Jews, amount to 1,161;
>
> f) From the time of Moyses and of Cecrops, first king of Attica, equal 1,890;
>
> g) From Abraham and the reign of Ninus and Semiramidis, equal 2,395.

Thus the whole course of time, from Abraham to the above-mentioned date, contains 2,395 years; and from the Flood until the time of Abraham, there are thought to have been 942 years; and from Adam to the Flood, 2,242 years. Thus from Adam down to the fourteenth year of the reign of Valens . . . the whole course of years amounts to 5,579.[72]

Notes

[1] *PL,* 22, 53.

[2] *Chronici canones* (ed. J. Fotheringham, London, 1923), 5.

[3] Jer., *Ep.* 5, 2.

[4] Jer., *Ep.* 15, 3.

[5] *PL,* 23, 155-82.

[6] Cf. P. Batiffol, "Les sources de l'Altercatio Luciferiani et Orthodoxi," *Miscel. Geronimiana* (Rome, 1921), 97ff.

[7] *PL,* 23, 172.

[8] F. Cavallera, *Saint Jérôme, sa vie et son oeuvre* (Paris, 1922), I, 55-62; cf. P. Courcelle, *Les lettres grecques en Occident* (Paris, 1943), 84-86 (Irenaeus), 88-100 (Origen), 103-105 (Eusebius), 38 and 104 (Gregory Nazianzen).

[9] Cf. M. Laistner, "Some Reflections on Latin Historical Writing in the V Century," *Class. Phil.* 35 (1941), 241-58.

[10] *Ibid.,* 243.

[11] Cf. F. Foakes-Jackson, *Eusebius Pamphili* (Cambridge, 1933), 142ff.

[12] *Chronici canones,* 2.

[13] *Ibid.,* 4-5.

[14] R. Helm, *Hieronymus Zusätze in Eusebius Chronik* [*Philologus,* Supplem b. 21, Heft II] 92, 95.

[15] J. Swain, "Theory of the Four Monarchies: Opposition History under the Roman Empire," *Class. Phil.* 35 (1940), 1-21.

[16] Jer., *Comm. in Dan.,* Prologus (*PL,* 25, 494).

[17] Cf. Swain, *op. cit.,* 19.

[18] *Chron. canon.,* 5.

[19] Cf. R. Helm, "Hieronymus und Eutrop," *Rhein. Museum* 76 (1927), 138.

[20] F. Cavallera, *Saint Jérôme,* I, 66.

[21] *Harv. Stud. in Class. Phil.* 55 (1944), 87-109; id., "Light cast by St. Jerome on certain paleological problems," *ibid.,* 54 (1943), 83-92.

[22] *PL,* 26, 357; cf. V. Sofer, "Das Hieronymus Zeugnis über die Sprachen der Galater und Trevirer," *Zeit. f. Klas: Phil.* 55 (1937), 148-158.

[23] Jer., *Adv. Ruf.,* III (*PL,* 23, 485).

[24] Cf. F. Stummer, "Corvallis, Mambre und Verwandtes," *Jour. Pal. Or. Soc.,* 1932, 6-21; id., "Die Berwertung Palästinas bei Hier.," *Oriens Christ.,* 1935, 60-74.

[25] *PL,* 23, 183-206.

[26] *Ibid.,* 17 (*PL,* 23, 202); cf. P. Courcelle, *op. cit.,* 79-81.

[27] *Adv. Jov.,* I, 41 (*PL,* 23, 270).

[28] P. Courcelle, *op. cit.,* 60-62, where he points out the studies proving Jerome's main sources to be the *De matrimonio* of Seneca, the *Gamika Paraggelmata* of Plutarch, and a lost tract of Porphyry whence Jerome drew his citations of Aristotle, and the *De nuptiis* of Theophrastus.

[29] *Adv. Jov.,* II (*PL,* 23, 307-10); Courcelle, *op. cit.,* 62-3; E. Bickel, *Diatribe in Senecae philos. fragm.,* I (Leipzig, 1915), 395-420.

[30] *Vita Hilarionis,* I (*PL,* 23, 29).

[31] *Vita Pauli* (*PL,* 23, 17-28).

[32] *Vita Hil.* (*PL,* 23, 29-54).

[33] *Vita Malchi* (*PL,* 23, 53-60).

[34] Cf. O. Bardenhewer, *Gesch. d. altk. Lit.* 3 (Fri.-in B., 1912), 638-639; S. Schiweitz, *Das morgenländische Mönchtum* 3 (Mainz, 1938), 214-20.

[35] O. Bardenhewer, *op. cit.,* 639-40.

[36] Jer., *Ep. 53 (Ad. Paulin.).*

[37] Cf. Courcelle, *op. cit.,* 65-6.

[38] *Ibid.*

[39] Cf. W. Stade, *Hieronymus in proemiis* (Rost., 1925); F. Stummer, *Einführung in die Latein. Bibel* (Paderborn, 1928).

[40] Jer., *De vir. illus.* (ed. E. Richardson, Leipzig, 1896).

[41] C. Bernoulli, *Die Schriftstellerkatalog des Hier.* (Fri.-in B., 1895); St. von Sychowski, *Hieronymus als Litterarhistoriker* (Münster, 1894); A. Feder, *Studien z. Schriftstellerkatalog des hl. Hier.* (Leipzig, 1927).

[42] P. Courcelle, *op. cit.,* 78-111.

[43] *Ibid.,* 66-78; on Josephus, 71ff.

[44] E. Luebeck, *Hieronymus quos noverit scriptores . . .* (Leipzig, 1872).

[45] Ruf., *Apol.,* II, 7 (*PL,* 21, 588).

[46] Cf. notes 17 and 19.

[47] *Comm. in Gal.,* II, prol. (*PL,* 26, 353).

[48] *Ibid.,* III, prol. (399).

[49] Jer., *Apol.,* I, 30 (*PL,* 23, 422).

[50] *Quaest. Hebr. in Gen.* (*PL,* 23, 935-1010). Cf. Courcelle, *op. cit.,* 67, n. 3; F. Cavallera, "Les quaestiones in Gen. de S. Jérôme et de S. Augustin," *Misc. Agost.,* II (Rome, 1931), 360-72.

[51] *Quaest. Hebr. in Gen.,* 10, 2 (*PL,* 23, 950-1).

[52] *Lib. de Nomen. Hebr.* (*PL,* 23, 771-858).

[53] *Onomastica Sacra* (ed. f. Wutz, *Texte und Untersuchungen* ii [41]).

[54] *In Mich.,* II (*PL,* 25, 1189); Courcelle, *op. cit.,* 95-6.

[55] *Comm. in Isaiam* (*PL,* 24, 9-687); cf. 30-31.

[56] *Ibid.,* 5:13 (158-9).

[57] *Ibid.,* 17:12 (177).

[58] *Praef. in Pentat.* (*PL,* 28, 151); cf. also *Adv. Ruf.,* II, 25 (*PL,* 23, 470); *Comm. in Ezech.* 6:12 (*PL,* 25, 55).

[59] *Comm. in Ep. ad Philem.* 4ff. (*PL,* 26, 609); the passage is taken almost verbatim from Origen, cf. E. Dorsch, "Aug. und Hier. über die Wahrheit der bibl. Geschichte," *Zeit. f. kat. Theol.* 35 (1911) 641 and 646.

[60] *Comm. in Jerem.* 28: 10-11 (*PL,* 24, 855).

[61] Cf. C. Dawson, "St. Augustine and His Age," *A Monument to St. Augustine* (New York, 1930), 44-5.

[62] Cf. W. Irwin, "The Hebrews," *The Adventures of Ancient Man* (Chicago, 1946), 322-3.

[63] P. Courcelle, *op. cit.,* 63-4; J. Lataix, "Le commentaire de saint Jérôme sur Daniel," *Rev. d'hist. et de litt. relig.,* II (1897), 164-173.

[64] *Comm. in Dan.,* praef. (*PL,* 25, 494).

[65] *Ibid.,* 11:21 (565).

[66] *Ibid.,* 11:44-5 (573-4).

[67] *Ibid.,* (574); cf. *Comm. in Jerem.* 19:10-11 (*PL,* 24, 801-2).

[68] *Comm. in Isaiam* 24:17 (*PL,* 24, 258-86).

[69] *Comm. in Dan.* 3:40 (*PL,* 25, 504): "Sicut enim in principio nihil Romano imperio fortius et durius fuit, ita in fine rerum nihil imbecillius; quando et in bellis civilibus, et adversum diversas nationes, aliarum gen-

tium indegimus auxilio . . .”; cf. *ibid.,* 7:8; (551).

[70] *Comm. in Is.* 11:6ff. (*PL,* 24, 148); *Ibid.,* 5:23-25 (*PL,* 24, 187-8).

[71] *Ibid.,* 60:10ff. (593).

[72] *Chronici canones,* 332.

Harald Hagendahl (essay date 1958)

SOURCE: “Jerome’s Attitude: Principles and Practice” in *Latin Fathers and the Classics: A Study on the Apologists, Jerome, and Other Christian Writers,* Elanders Boktryckeri Aktiebolag, 1958, pp. 309-28.

[*In the following excerpt, Hagendahl discusses Jerome’s ambivalent attitude toward his predecessors, concluding that he struggled with an apparent conflict between his Christian asceticism and the cultural legacy of pagan literature.*]

. . . Jerome’s attitude towards the cultural legacy left by the ancients cannot be defined in a plain and unequivocal formula. It is inconsequent, inconsistent, reflecting opposite tendencies, fluctuating like the currents of the tide.

On the one hand it shows the same negative rigorousness which, since Paul, had distinguished the old church, and which found a sonorous expression in Tertullian:[1] *Quid ergo Athenis et Hierosolymis? quid Academiae et ecclesiae? quid haereticis et Christianis?* This renunciation is echoed in Jerome’s equally famous antithesis: *Quid facit cum psalterio Horatius? cum evangeliis Maro? cum apostolo Cicero?*[2] It recurs more than thirty years later in this form: *Quid Aristoteli et Paulo? Quid Platoni et Petro?*[3]

On the other hand Jerome is an exponent of a new current, distinguished by a less prejudiced recognition of pagan thought and literature. It emerged in the Greek world at the end of the second century and had its centre in the Christian school at Alexandria, whose leaders, Clement and Origen, strove to assimilate and utilize the essence of Greek philosophy.[4] It found another expression in the apologists, above all in Minucius Felix and Lactantius, when they tried to win over people of education. After being officially recognized, the church could not maintain her cultural isolation. In proportion as she aimed at universality, she had to make room for culture and create a literature that was on a par with secular literature. That is what came about in the century after Constantine.

However, this process of assimilation had its limits and was not accepted without difficulty. Jerome’s case is not unique. The inconsistency of his attitude recurs in almost every educated Christian writer. It proceeded from the feeling that classical culture and Christianity were fundamentally incompatible. In Jerome this feeling is reflected more distinctly than in anybody else, in the words he seemed to hear in the dream: *Ciceronianus es, non Christianus;* Cicero, the protagonist of Latin humanism, is opposed to Christ.[5] The conflict between the two worlds of thought gave birth, in Jerome’s soul, to a dissonance which he never resolved. As a Christian he felt obliged to condemn pagan literature, but he could not cease admiring—and reading—what he condemned.

Christianity triumphed over the pagan religions, but it had to yield to the pagan school-system, the last stronghold of classical culture. In the first four centuries the Christians did not dream of creating Christian schools; the pagan educational system, to which they were once, at best, indifferent, became in course of time indispensable to them.[6] The pagan schools of grammar and rhetoric exercised upon them an influence that can hardly be overrated. They affected, as Homes Dudden put it, “not merely the literary style of those who were bred in them, but also their feeling and habit of thought.”[7]

Jerome is perhaps the best example of this influence. No other Christian writer, former teachers like Lactantius and Augustine not excepted, has so much to say about school education. Again and again he recalls his schooldays, first in Stridon, then in Rome.[8]

In the grammar school, where he studied under the distinguished grammarian Donatus, he acquired the intimate knowledge of the Latin classics which we have endeavored to track and laid the foundations for his masterly use of the Latin language. He often discusses questions of grammatical correctness and scoffs at the shortcomings of his adversaries in this respect.[9]

Rhetoric attracted Jerome still more than grammar. The established curriculum of rhetoric, as it was taught in the schools for centuries, developed his versatile genius and gave him an intellectual training and a stylistic skill which are already conspicuous in his earliest writings. He often refers to the instructions of the rhetors[10] and dialecticians.[11] Above all he was influenced by the school declamations, *controversiae,* where the pupils had to act alternately as prosecutor and as defendant in fictitious legal cases far remote from real life. As an old man he still dreamed that he was standing before the *rhetor,*[12] he recurs now and then to his school declamations[13] and quotes many sentences from *controversiae,* both extant ones and lost ones.[14]

Jerome’s principles and practice in the matter of style are a counterpart to his attitude towards classical literature and may therefore claim our attention.

The first writings are distinguished by a redundant style which smells of the rhetorical school. A typical example is the letter to Heliodorus, *Epist.* **14,** of which Jerome, nearly twenty years later, judged as follows (*Epist.* **52,** 1, 1): *In illo opere pro aetate tunc lusimus et calentibus adhuc rhetorum studiis atque doctrinis quaedam scholastico flore depinximus.* In the same letter, one of the most refined in his correspondence, he disclaims all pretentions to oratory: *Ne a me quaeras pueriles declamationes, sententiarum flosculos, verborum lenocinia et per fines capitum singulorum acuta quaedam breviterque conclusa, quae plausus et clamores excitent audientium* (Chap. 4, 1). There is every reason not to take such utterances too literally; according to literary etiquette modesty was required of an author when talking of himself.[16] *In hoc libello nulla erit rhetorici pompa sermonis,* says Jerome in a letter to Eustochium which from a stylistic point of view is one of the most extravagant things he ever wrote. In the pamphlet against Helvidius he begins by saying: *Non campum rhetorici desideramus eloquii,* but he gives the lie to this in practice and finally concedes: *Rhetoricati sumus et in morem declamatorum paululum lusimus.* The examples could easily be multiplied.

However, in Jerome and other Christian writers, there is another ground for the breach between theory and practice in the matter of style.[19] Christianity was founded by fishermen,[20] the Scriptures were translated in vulgar Latin,[21] simplicity was imposed by tradition.[22] In Jerome's opinion simplicity was required above all in sermons; he disapproved of preachers who indulged in rhetoric and provoked applause.[23] He also disclaims oratory in the commentaries: *In Amos* lib. III praef. pp. 309-310 *In explanatione sanctarum scripturarum non verba composita et oratoriis floribus adornata, sed eruditio et simplicitas quaeritur veritatis.*[24] His interest was centred in exegetics, he wrote for those who were concerned with exegesis, not for persons of literary taste.[25]

In spite of this he by no means despises oratory in the commentaries.[26] *Tribuatque nobis Dominus,* he writes in the commentary on Ezekiel (16, 13 p. 157), *ut divinum sensum accipere mereamur atque sapientiam et id quod mente concipimus eloquii venustate proferre.* He bestowed care upon the style even in translations, as he confesses about his rendering of Theophilus' *epistula paschalis* (*Epist.* **98**);[27] it is so elaborated that it could serve as a basis for an analysis of Jerome's own style. But, of course, he is at his best in the letters and the polemical writings, where he gives free rein both to his personal feelings and to his rhetorical skill. As a letter-writer he can be compared only with Cicero—it suffices for his glory. By nature and education he was a controversialist, inferior to none in satirical verve and subtlety, alas also in recklessness. His polemical tone is low, to say the least.[28] In this he adopted the bad habits of Roman lawyers, as he de-

picts them.[29] He took advantage of his superiority in rhetorical training and ridiculed without mercy the deficiencies of his adversaries. On the other hand he does not forget to praise the style of his friends. If he praises the beauty of secular literature—and nobody has done it more unreservedly—[30] he is no less eager to emphasize the merits of Christian writers; it is enough to call to mind his efforts to glorify their oratory in *De viris illustribus.*[31] In short, he lives as a writer in the atmosphere of the rhetorical school.[32]

In judging his style we must take into consideration some important circumstances. Mostly he did not write in his own hand, but dictated to stenographers. He excuses himself (*Epist.* **74,** 6, 2), *si scatens oratio solito cursu non fluat. Non enim eodem lepore dictamus, quo scribimus, quia in altero saepe stilum vertimus, "iterum quae digna legi sunt scripturi", in altero, quidquid in buccam venerit, celeri sermone dictamus.*[33] He often complains of being compelled to dictate in great haste and of not having time to correct or even to read through what he has dictated.[34] He emphasizes himself the difference *inter subitam dictandi audaciam et elucubratam scribendi diligentiam*[35]. The analyser of his style will go wrong if he does not keep this in view.[36]

It does no credit to classical scholarship that we are still in want of up-to-date monographs on Jerome's style. Latin prose has stylists of a richer individuality and a greater artistic perfection, but no one since Cicero can compete with the easy fluency of Jerome's style. His register is wide, he possesses all modes and tempos, from plain instruction and discussion to sharp polemics, from edification and consolation to jokes and humour, from insinuation and irony to sentiment and pathos. Rufinus, who knew him better than anyone else, called him *rhetor noster,*[37] and with that he hit the mark. Jerome, as I have said before, is "an antique rhetor with all the merits and faults, mental and literary, which rhetorical training implies: the brilliancy and fluency of style, the power of invention, the subtlety of mind, the ready wit and recklessness of a thorough controversialist, the tendency to superficial ostentation and self-conceited overbearingness".[38]

Among his teachers Jerome mentions after the *grammatici* and *rhetores* also the *philosophi,* but in reality his interest in philosophy was as slight as his knowledge of it was superficial. In this respect he was a true Roman. The numerous references to Greek philosophers are, as we have pointed out several times, nothing but boasts of a learning he did not possess; they are due to Latin intermediaries, as he himself had to admit, above all to Cicero. His attitude towards the philosophers is mostly unfavourable or hostile, partly on the ground that the heretics rely on them.[42] He is far from the broad-mindedness of Lactantius, who held that every single part of the truth is to be found in the philosophers, although none of them attained it in its entirety. Only one passage, *In Dan.* 1, 2 (PL 25, 518),[44] forms an exception; it is so remarkable that I almost feel tempted to suppose that Jerome took it over from one of the Greek Fathers whom he followed in this commentary. Elsewhere, if by chance he approves or makes use of philosophers and their ideas, he does so with a view to practical utility, as he says in a letter to Damasus (*Epist.* 21, 13, 6): *Atqui et nos hoc facere solemus, quando philosophos legimus, quando in manus nostras libri veniunt sapientiae saecularis: si quid in eis utile repperimus, ad nostrum dogma convertimus, si quid vero superfluum, de idolis, de amore, de cura saecularium rerum, haec radimus.*

Thus the *artes liberales* in Jerome's opinion are useful or necessary. They are enumerated in *Adv. Pelag.* I. 21 (above p. 264) and in *Epist.* 53, 6, I: *Taceo de grammaticis, rhetoribus, philosophis, geometricis, dialecticis, musicis, astrologis, medicis, quorum scientia mortalibus vel utilissima est.* He distinguishes between *veritas quae non habet pietatem* and *scientia pietatis.*[45] He admires the immense *œuvre* of polyhistors such as Varro and Didymus and opposes it to the materialism of his time (*Epist.* 33, 1, 2): *Nos Epimenidis dormire somnum et studium, quod illi posuerunt in eruditione saecularium litterarum, in congregandis opibus ponere.* Albeit his learning has turned out to be less extensive than his writings could give to understand, he was no doubt the most learned of all Latin Fathers, being called *philosophus, rhetor, grammaticus, dialecticus, Hebraeus, Graecus, Latinus, trilinguis* (*Adv. Rufin.* III. 6). He was a hard worker, and he spoke from personal experience when he said: *Litterae marsupium non sequuntur. Sudoris comites sunt et laboris, sociae ieiuniorum, non saturitatis, continentiae, non luxuriae* (ib. I. 17).

We have looked at several aspects of Jerome's attitude towards secular culture and can now approach our main problem: his attitude towards Latin literature.

From the very outset I have placed the tale of his dream (*Epist.* 22, 30) in the foreground, and I have explained how I read this document, which, agreeable to its importance, has become a bone of contention among scholars.[46] The difference of opinion is partly owing to the fact that it is decked in so much rhetoric that some scholars fail to see anything but rhetoric in it.[47] I think this is to underrate matters. Nor can I see that the parallels pointed out by de Labriolle[48] in pagan and Christian writings make against the authenticity of the dream; they only attest—if attestation is needed—that the belief in dreams was common in antiquity. As I take it, two points are decisive. First: in A.D. 400, when Rufinus charged him with perjury because of the oaths he had taken in the dream, Jerome did not deny having had it;[49] he only declined to be bound for life by a promise given in a dream. Second: without any external provocation, Jerome in the commentary on Galatians

calls Paula and Eustochium to testify that for more than fifteen years neither Cicero nor Virgil nor any pagan writer whatsoever has come into his hands (*In Gal.* lib. III praef. pp. 485-486, see above p. 120). This is an evident allusion to the dream related in the letter to the same Eustochium (*Epist.* 22).

For these reasons I take the dream seriously: it is a specimen of Jerome's state of mind, most interesting from a psychological point of view.

Before going farther we have to clear up another point. The account of the dream is inserted in the context in the following way. Jerome warns the virgin not to indulge in a taste for literature or mince her words. Then, rather abruptly, he quotes Paul's antithesis: *Quae enim communicatio luci ad tenebras? qui consensus Christo et Belial?* (2 Cor. 6, 14-15) and subjoins an antithesis of his own: *Quid facit cum psalterio Horatius?*, etc. It would be preposterous to presume that he is here addressing himself only to Eustochium or to the Christian virgins. His words have a wider bearing, they aim at all Christians, including himself. *Simul bibere non debemus calicem Christi et calicem daemoniorum.* Secular literature is incompatible with Christianity; it is the *calix daemoniorum.*[50]) In order to confirm this view he then relates what he experienced in his dream.

The dream dates, as is generally accepted, from the early years of Jerome's first stay in the East (about 374), and the account of it was written in 384 during his last stay in Rome. One year before, he had unfolded his views concerning the problem in question in a letter to Damasus (*Epist.* 21, 13, 4 sqq., quoted pp. 109). Expounding the parable of the prodigal son he takes the husks, *siliquae,* to be secular literature[52] which, in spite of its formal beauty, is devoid of *saturitas veritatis* and only leaves an empty sound. It can be used only if treated like the captive woman in Deut. 21, 10-13. Even with this restriction, however, Jerome is in doubt because of Paul's warnings against idolatry (1 Cor. 8, 9-11):[53] *Nonne tibi videtur sub aliis verbis dicere, ne legas philosophos, oratores, poetas, ne in eorum lectione requiescas?*

Psychologically this attitude is easy to understand. It is that of primitive Christianity; it is an integral part of the same tendency to isolation which gave rise to monasticism. The early letters bear witness to Jerome's ecstatic turn of mind during his first stay in the East. Hence the pangs of conscience reflected in the agony of the dream. The writings dating from his last stay in Rome are distinguished by a rigorousness and ascetic zeal which are a prelude to his final retirement from the world, and which also account in full for his severe principles as to secular literature.

And his practice? If we are to believe Jerome, he did not read pagan authors for more than fifteen years. Is this true?

In the first period his memory of what he learned at school is still fresh. The earliest letters, overflowing with sentiment, are enriched by reminiscences of secular authors of whom some (Turpilius, Lucilius and Florus) leave no traces in his later writings (see p. 102). On the other hand literal quotations do not appear in writings intended for the public (with one exception)[54] or in the letters written in Rome, and the reminiscences are neither particularly frequent nor conspicuous. Thus I conclude that Jerome, at least towards the end of this period, put his principles into practice.

In the second period matters are different. Whole lines from poetry, not allowed before in writings for the public (except in **Vita Pauli**), appear not infrequently in the great commentaries, viz.

In Gal.: Virgil 1 line, Terence 1, *quidam de neotericis* 2.

In Eph.: Virgil 6, Horace 2.

In Eccles: Virgil 10, Horace 3.

In Nah.: Virgil 2.

In Hab.: Virgil 2.

In Mich.: Terence 5, Horace 1.

Every reader of my Chap. 3 (pp. 115-141) can be sure that quotations of less than one line and paraphrases of lines are far more numerous. There is no doubt that Jerome has changed his attitude in practice. We must ask, then: Does he really quote from memory, as he says in the same passage where he denies having read the classics during the last fifteen years:[55] *Et si quid forte inde, dum loquimur, obrepit, quasi antiqui per nebulam somnii recordamur?*

There is a great deal to be said against this. When Jerome wrote the first commentaries, his school-days, according to Cavallera's chronology, were at least twenty years back in the past. And would his memory of secular authors read at school still have been so fresh—in spite of his learning Greek and Hebrew, in spite of the manifold new interests and the literary activity that filled the many years between? There is very little likelihood of its being possible; I think psychologists will agree on this point. Now, special circumstances, too, call for our attention.

1. The prefaces to **Quaest. hebr. in gen.** and **In Mich.** lib. II (quoted in full pp. 130 sqq. and 137 sq.) are composed, like a mosaic, of pieces put together both from the Bible and from many secular authors. The latter contains literal quotations from three of Terence's prologues, those to *Andria, Eunuchus* and *Adelphoe,* besides other borrowings from the prologue to *Andria.* It stands to reason that Jerome looked up these passages when he, like Terence, had to answer malevolent criticism.

2. Is it mere chance, I have asked before (p. 128), that three of the four quotations from Horace occurring in **In Eccles.** belong to the first book of the *Epistles,* and, more expressly, to the first two epistles?

3. The only imitation of Seneca's tragedies that has been pointed out hitherto is to be found in this period (see p. 118).

4. If poetical lines, because of their metrical form, easily imprint themselves on our mind, it is just the contrary with prose. It therefore gives cause for reflection that a passage in Cicero's *Pro Marcello* (Ch. 10, see p. 134) is quoted word for word in **In Hab.** 2,9 p. 617, and that the following paragraph likewise is quoted literally in a much later commentary (**In Ezech.** lib. III praef. p. 80). It is out of the question that Jerome could have retained in his memory the very wording of those passages for about 20 and 45 years respectively. Considering the other cases mentioned here I do not doubt that he had Cicero's speech before him when he wrote.[56]

5. Not until this period did Jerome take a real interest in Cicero's philosophical works (see pp. 291 sq., 331, 377).

6. The same can be said in the case of Sallust. Nearly half of the quotations from him are to be found in the writings of this period; above all some prefaces are conspicuous for such adornment (see p. 294).

Whether or not Jerome kept the oaths taken in the dream, is a bone of contention among scholars. Among those who believe his word, Eiswirth has recently taken matters to an extreme: he denies that Jerome ever read secular classics after the dream, either during the period in question or subsequently.[57] Most scholars take up a sceptical attitude. This is to-day the *communis opinio,* as Eiswirth concedes (p. 13), quoting Rostagni's verdict: "Il solenne giuramento— si sa—non fu mantenuto."[58] Only there are differences of opinion as to the date of Jerome's resuming his reading of the classics. According to Geffcken[59] and Kunst,[60]) he did so a short time after the dream, according to Grütz-macher,[61] and Cavallera[62] he kept his promise for a long time. Pease is more precise: "In the light, then", he says, "of Jerome's statements and practice it is likely that the vision had some effect for fifteen years or so, but after that he regarded it as in no way binding."

I for my part agree in the main with Pease's opinion. Considering the arguments, both general and special, which I have brought forward, I think it is out of the question that Jerome at the time of the first commentaries quoted from memory. I conclude that at this time there was a change in his attitude in two respects: he began both to read and to quote the secular authors. Facts have a greater weight than words.

The discrepancy between Jerome's words and actions appears distinctly in other passages of the commentary on Galatians. He declines to quote Varro and states the reason for it as follows: *Nobis propositum est incircumcisos homines non introducere in templum Dei* (*In Gal.* lib. II praef. pp. 425-426, see above p. 120). But in the same book he quotes *illa sententia nobilis apud Romanos poetae* (Ter. *Andr.* 68. In the preface to the third book he discusses principles of style in a way so contradictory that Eiswirth admits having the impression that there were two souls in his breast.[63]) This is the heart of the matter. Asceticism and culture were the two poles in Jerome's life. As has been said before (p. 92), "he never succeeded in getting over the internal conflict or in reaching a stable equilibrium".

Why did he change his attitude? I think we can answer this question by considering his situation. When he burst into literary activity, he had for many years been silent before the public. His tongue was corroded by rust, as he says;[64] he had ruined his style, *omnem sermonis elegantiam et Latini eloquii venustatem,* by learning Hebrew, by desisting from reading the classics, by the necessity of dictating instead of writing.[65] "I know what I have lost in the use of my language".[66] No wonder if renewed acquaintance with the classics suggested itself to him as a remedy. Later he suspected Rufinus of being a reader of Cicero: *Aut ego fallor aut tu Ciceronem occulte lectitas* (*Adv. Rufin.* I. 30; see above p. 174); only so, he says ironically, could he account for the richness of his style *(tanta verborum copia, sententiarum lumen, translationum varietas).* Jerome speaks from personal experience. At the time of Galatians his own case was the same.

The radical change of procedure is undisguised in the pamphlet against Iovinianus (A.D. 393) with which the third period begins. The introductory chapter (quoted pp. 143 sqq.) could as well have been written by a lettered pagan, some other chapters are entirely filled with pagan topics, others are a mosaic put together from Christian and pagan elements and quotations. And, finally, Jerome declares openly that he will allege *exempla saecularis quoque litteraturae, ad quam et ipse* (sc. Iovinianus) *provocat* (I. 4) and mentions as his sources Aristotle, Plutarch and Seneca (I. 49); moreover, a long quotation is passed off under the name of Theophrastus (I. 47). It is quite another matter that we cannot take it for granted that he really read and used precisely those authors, except Seneca (and

perhaps Plutarch); there is every probability that he got his knowledge of Aristotle and Theophrastus through Porphyrius, the Neo-Platonic philosopher and enemy of Christianity, whom he plagiarizes unblushingly in II. 6-14, of course without mentioning him.[67]

This reticence as to his real source is as misleading as the boastful reference to authors known only through intermediaries. Both procedures are well-known from other writings of the ten years 393-402. The long borrowings from Cicero's *Cato maior* in **Epist. 52** (pp. 192 sq.) and from Quintilian in **Epist. 107** (pp. 197 sqq.) are unacknowledged, and so are also the two quotations of Plin. *Epist.* II. 3, 8-9 in **Epist. 53.** Nobody who knows anything about literary technique can doubt that Jerome, when writing, had those authors before him.

On the other hand, nobody will believe that he was familiar, as he says in **Epist. 60,** with Crantors, Plato's, Diogenes', Clitomachus', Carneades' and Posidonius' consolatory writings; the chances are that his knowledge of them was due to Cicero, whose *Consolatio* is hinted at in passing. As to his habit of scattering about in his writings the names of Greek philosophers, he was bound to admit, in reply to Rufinus' mockery, that he derived his knowledge of them from Cicero, Brutus and Seneca.

There is a distinct increase in Cicero's influence in this period; in fact, everything goes to show that it was not until then that Jerome took a real interest in Cicero's philosophical writings. The quotations from Virgil, too, increase considerably and reach their height in the last commentaries of the fourth period. It is also a matter of importance that authors who have left no traces in earlier writings make their appearance: Pliny the Younger is quoted only in letters dating from A.D. 395 and 398, Lucanus for the first time in a letter written in 394-395 and then not until the years 408-414. As to Terence, his influence seems to undulate; it suggests that Jerome again and again resumed his reading of the *comicus.*

Now, what we must infer from our analysis of Jerome's writings, is in perfect harmony with facts of which Rufinus gives us a glimpse (*Apol. adv. Hier.* II. 8). Firstly, in Rufinus' convent on the Mount of Olives, his monks copied most of Cicero's dialogues on behalf of Jerome, and Rufinus often had the copies in his hands and corrected them, because Jerome paid a higher price for them than for other writings. Secondly, Rufinus himself got from Jerome a codex containing *unus dialogus Ciceronis et idem ipse Graecus Platonis.* Thirdly, a few years before A.D. 400 Jerome in his convent in Bethlehem performed the duties of a teacher of a grammar school *(partes grammaticas exsecutus sit)* and explained Virgil, the comedians, the lyrics and the historians to boys *(Maronem suum comicosque ac lyricos et historicos auctores traditis sibi ad discendum Dei timorem puerulis exponebat).* It is true, we have only Rufinus' word for these data, but, as Jerome does not answer the indictment in his pamphlet against Rufinus, we can take it for granted that they are true.

The alteration of Jerome's attitude, which we have endeavoured to follow step by step, is reflected in *Epist.* **70** (written in 397). Against reproaches for quoting secular literature Jerome advances in his defence that Moses, the prophets, Solomon and Paul did the same. In comparison with Greek apologists, who answered the enemies of Christianity, Jerome, he says, will be found to be *indoctissimus.* A long succession of Greek Fathers is passed in review whose works are so filled with pagan philosophy that it is impossible to know, *quid in illis primum admirari debeas, eruditionem saeculi an scientiam scripturarum.* The same is true of Latin ecclesiastical writers.

Nowhere else has Jerome taken such a firm stand in defence of secular learning. There is the greatest distance conceivable between this attitude and that proclaimed fourteen years before in the letter to Damasus (*Epist.* **21**), and it is thrown into strong relief by the different use made of Deut. 21, 10-13 about the captive woman getting married to an Israelite. At the same time, however, we get new evidence of Jerome's inconsistency. For he repeats substantially the statement made in the preface to Galatians: *Invenies nos . . . imperitissimos et post tanti temporis otium vix quasi per somnium, quod pueri didicimus, recordari* (*Epist.* **70**, 3, 2).

He falls back upon the same line of defence in *Adv. Rufin.* I. 30: *Dixi me saeculares litteras deinceps non lecturum: de futuro sponsio est, non praeteritae memoriae abolitio. "Et quomodo", inquies, "tenes, quod tanto tempore non relegis?"* The answer is characteristic of Jerome's polemical method. First, he says, he will allege *aliquid de veteribus libris* and quotes a Virgilian line: *'Adeo in teneris consuescere multum'* (*Georg.* II. 272). Then he begins to talk of his childhood—*Quis nostrum non meminit infantiae suae?*—of the first years at school and of the declamations before the rhetor. The short tale is coloured by reminiscences of Cicero (*Tusc.* III. 31), Horace (*Epist.* II. 1, 70 sq.; ib. I. 2, 69 sq.) and Lucretius (cf. VI. 1074 sqq.). After mentioning his study of dialectics (with a borrowing from Cicero, *Tusc.* I. 14) he proclaims solemnly: *Iurare possum me postquam egressus de schola sum, haec numquam omnino legisse.* An inattentive reader can easily be deceived by this oath; in reality, it refers only to dialectics. Lastly he makes a counter-attack and supposes Rufinus to be a reader of Cicero because of his much boasted style.

"This would be my answer", he continues, "if I had made a promise when awake. Now, by an unprec-edented shamelessness, he expostulates with me on a dream! Listen to the prophets: dreams are not to be trusted". *Non tibi sufficiunt quae de vigilante confingis, nisi et somnia crimineris.*

Nobody, I think, will be swayed by such quibbling which only shows to what a state of embarrassment Jerome was brought by the indictment. He denies being bound by a dream; so far his practice is in harmony with his words. But when he gives us to understand that he still quotes from memory, he makes too great a call upon our credulity.

In the fourth period there is nothing new to be seen in his attitude besides the fact that Cicero's and Virgil's influence increases and reaches its maximum.

Writings dating from about the same time often differ considerably as to the use made of secular learning and literature. Generally speaking, the more the style is elaborated, the more frequent are the non-Christian elements, and vice versa. The one extreme is represented by the artless sermons which, with only a few exceptions, are devoid of classical elements, the other by the polemical pamphlets, the necrologies, the didactic and moralizing letters where frequent quotations of the classics, above all of Virgil, serve to enhance and adorn the style. This suggests also that the kind of literature to which a writing belongs plays an important part. Jerome likewise pays regard to the degree of education of those to whom he writes or dedicates a work, as we have seen in the case of Paulinus of Nola (pp. 185 sqq.) and of Pammachius (p. 224). But we are warned not to overstress this point by recalling the difference in classical quotations between *In Isaiam* and *In Ezechielem* both of which are dedicated to Eustochium.

The inconsistency of Jerome's attitude easily conveys the impression that he yielded to strong prejudices in the Christian world which he did not dare to brave, and so far we could be, and in some measure also are, entitled to talk of hypocrisy. But we do not do Jerome justice, I think, by laying too much stress upon this point of view. In his case, matters lie deeper. His inconsistency reflects the inner conflict of his soul. He was a Christian ascetic and felt strongly the incompatibility of this ideal and the humanism of pagan antiquity. But he was also a rhetor brought up in the atmosphere of the old cultural legacy. He felt attracted and repelled—at the same time. For a time the one feeling prevailed over the other, but he never reached a stable equilibrium. As a Christian he felt bound to reject pagan literature. But he did not cease admiring it and reading it—apart from a short interruption caused by the dream. To this reading he owes more than his incomparable style. If any Latin Father can be called a humanist, it is certainly Jerome.

Notes

[1] *Praescr. haer.* 7.

[2] *Epist.* 22, 29, 7.

[3] *Adv. Pelag.* I. 14.

[4] Cf. Gerard L. Ellspermann, *The Attitude of the Early Christian Latin Writers toward Pagan Literature and Learning* (*The Catholic University of America Patristic Studies,* LXXXI, Washington 1949), pp. 9 sqq.

[5] A. D. Leeman, *Hieronymus' droom. De betekenis van Cicero voor Christendom en humanisme* (Leiden 1952), p. 3: "De zielestrijd in deze mens (sc. Hieronymus), waarin Cicero optreedt als de tegenspeler van Christus, kunnen wij zien als een paroxysme in de strijd tussen twee werelden, twee geesteshoudingen, die van de tijd der kerkvaders tot in onze dagen heeft voorgeduurd". Why and how Cicero played this part, is the subject of this excellent paper (an inaugural lecture at the University of Amsterdam).—Cf. also P. Antin *Essaisur saint Jérôme* (Paris, 1951), p. 55: "Dans la grande alternative, qui est proposée à Jérôme, cicéronien ou chrétien, Cicéron représente toute la littérature profane, tout l'humanisme gréco-romain".

[6] Cf. Henri-Irénée Marrou, *Histoire de l'éducation dans l'éducation dans l'antiquité* (2e éd. Paris 1950), chap. IX, pp. 416 sqq; Ellspermann, pp. 1 sqq.

[7] T. Homes Dudden, *The Life and Times of St. Ambrose* (Oxford 1935), I, p. 8.

[8] E. g. Praef. Iob (PL 28, 1141) = *Adv. Rufin.* II. 29 *In Latino paene ab ipsis incunabulis inter grammaticos et rhetores et philosophos detriti sumus.*—On Jerome's education I refer to Grützmacher, I, pp. 111-129; Cavallera, I, pp. 5-17.

[9] Cf. about Helvidius *Virg. Mar. 1 Hominem rusticanum et vix primis quoque imbutum litteris;* ib. 16 *Praetermitto vitia sermonis quibus omnis liber tuus scatet;* about Iovinianus *Adv. Iovin.* I. 1 *Verum scriptorum tanta barbaries est et tantis vitiis spurcissimus sermo confusus, ut . . .* (see above p. 143; cf. also *Adv. Pelag.* prol. 2 p. 695 *Iovinianus . . . tam elinguis et sic sermonis putidi, ut magis misericordia dignus fuerit quam invidia*); about Vigilantius *Adv. Vigil. 4 Est quidem imperitus et verbis et scientia et sermone inconditus.* Above all he criticizes Rufinus (see p. 174) and advises him to put himself to school again. . . .

[10] E. g. about the *genera dicendi: Epist.* 49, 13, 1 (see above p. 158) *Adv. Rufin.* I. 15 *Docebo senex quod puer didici, multa esse genera dictionum;* about the panegyric: *Epist.* 60, 8, 1 *Praecepta sunt rhetorum, ut maiores eius qui laudandus est et eorum altius gesta*

repetantur sicque ad ipsum per gradus sermo perveniat.

[11] E. g. *Epist.* 50, 1, 2 sq. . . .

[12] *Adv. Rufin.* I. 30 *Nunc cano et recalvo capite saepe mihi videor in somnis comatulus et sumpta toga ante rhetorem controversiolam declamare. Cumque experrectus fuero, gratulor me dicendi periculo liberatum.*

[13] *Adv. Ioh.* 2 (PL 23, 372) *Putes eum non expositionem fidei sed figuratam controversiam scribere. Quod iste nunc appetit, olim in scholis didicimus. Nostra adversum nos dimicat armatura. Adv. Pelag.* I. 23 *In ipsis controversiis in quibus quondam pueri lusimus . . . .*

[14] Quotations from Seneca rhetor: see p. 297, from Pseudo-Quintilian's *Declamationes maiores:* pp. 296 sq., from anonymous *controversiae: In Mich.* 6, 5-7 p. 517, etc. . . .

[16] I refer to my book *La correspondance de Ruricius* (*Göteborgs Högskolas Årsskrift,* LVIII, Göteborg 1952), pp. 93 sqq. . . .

[19] Cf. E. Norden, *Die antike Kunstprosa,* II, p. 529: "In der Theorie haben sie (die christlichen Autoren) von den ältesten Zeiten bis tief in das Mittelalter hinein fast ausnahmslos den Standpunkt vertreten, dass man ganz schlicht schreiben müsse, in der Praxis haben sie das gerade Gegenteil befolgt".

[20] This had been a commonplace since Origen (cf. Norden, op. cit., II, p. 516 n. 1). Sulpicius Severus had luck with his antithesis: *Meminerint* (sc. lectores) *salutem saeculo non ab oratoribus . . . sed a pisca-toribus praedicatam* (*Mart.* praef. 3 sq.).

[21] Jerome's attitude, as usual, is inconsistent. Compare e. g. *Epist.* 22, 30, 2 *Si quando . . . prophetam legere coepissem, sermo horrebat incultus* and *Epist.* 53, 10, 1 *Nolo offendaris in scripturis sanctis simplicitate et quasi vilitate verborum, quae vel vitio interpretum vel de industria sic prolatae sunt, ut rusticam contionem facilius instruerent.*

[22] *Tract. de ps.* 78 (*Anecdota Maredsolana,* III: 2 p. 67, 14: *Ego vero simpliciter rusticana simplicitate et ecclesiastica ita tibi respondebo: ita enim apostoli responderunt, sic sunt locuti, non verbis rhetoricis et diabolicis.*

[23] *In Eccles.* p. 467 *Quemcumque in ecclesia videris declamatorem et cum quodam lenocinio ac venustate verborum excitare plausus, risus excutere, audientes in affectus laetitiae concitare, scito signum esse insipientiae tam eius qui loquitur quam eorum qui audiunt. Epist.* 52, 8, 1 *Dicente te in ecclesia non clamor populi, sed gemitus suscitetur . . . Nolo te*

declamatorem esse et rabulum garrulumque . . . In Ezech. 33, 23 sqq. p. 404. *Tales sunt usque hodie multi in ecclesiis qui aiunt: 'Venite audiamus illum et illum, mira eloquentia praedicationis suae verba volventem', plaususque commovent et vociferantur et iactant manus.* Ib. 34, 1s sqq. p. 412.—Jerome's own sermons (*Anecdota Maredsolana*, III: 2-3) are so accommodated to the simplicity of the brethren that the style is all but unrecognizable as his.

24 Cf. further *In Sophon.* 3, 14 sqq. p. 730 *Haec scio molesta esse lectori, qui si animadverterit non me controversias et declamationes scribere nec in locis exsultare communibus sed commentarios et commentarios prophetarum, reprehendet potius sicubi rhetorum more ludere voluero quam arguet in tantis obscuritatibus ut dignum est immorantem. In Os.* 2, 16-17 p. 25 *Neque enim Hebraeum prophetam edisserens oratoriis debeo declamatiunculis ludere et in narrationibus atque epilogis Asiatico more cantare.* Ib. 10, 13 p. 118 *Neque enim rhetorum more sententias repetimus, verba construimus et audientes vel legentes in laudes nostras declamationibus suscitamus, sed quae obscura sunt, maxime alienae linguae hominibus explanare nitimur. In Ezech.* lib. V praef. p. 164 *In quo* (sc. quinto volumine) *nihil ex arte rhetorica, nihil ex compositione reperies et venustate verborum.*

25 *In Is.* lib. VIII praef. p. 328 *Certe nos studiosis scribimus et sanctam scripturam scire cupientibus, nec fastidiosis et ad singula nauseantibus.*

26 "Encore qu'il vise dans ses commentaires à un style dépouillé, simple et claire", says Dom P. Antin (op. cit., p. 158), "il ne peut s'empêcher parfois de parler en rhéteur habile et magnifique".

27 *Epist.* 97, 3, 1 *In qua laborasse me fateor, ut verborum elegantiam pari interpretationis venustate servarem . . . et eloquentiae eius fluenta non perderem.*

28 Cf. pp. 111, 143, 166, 173. Cavallera (I: 1, p. 12) cites de Tillemont's judgment: "Quiconque l'a eu pour adversaire a presque toujours été le dernier des hommes".

29 *In Gal.* 2, 11-13 p. 408 (PL 26, 365) *Aliquoties cum adolescentulus Romae controversias declamarem et ad vera certamina fictis me litibus exercerem, currebam ad tribunalia iudicum et disertissimos oratorum tanta inter se videbam acerbitate contendere, ut omissis saepe negotiis in proprias contumelias verterentur et ioculari se invicem dente morderent.*

30 *In Ionam* 3, 6 sq. p. 420 (PL 25, 1198) *Quem non inebriavit eloquentia saecularis? Cuius non animos compositione verborum et disertitudinis suae fulgore perstrinxit?* Even though he rejects the *carmina poetarum, saecularis sapientia, rhetoricorum pompa verborum* as being *daemonum cibus* (*Epist.* 21, 13, 4), he cannot hold back his admiration: *Haec sua omnes suavitate delectant et, dum aures versibus dulci modulatione currentibus capiunt, animam quoque penetrant et pectoris interna devinciunt. . . .*

32 A few passages referring to school education may be quoted. *Epist.* 60, 5, 1 *Quid agimus, anima? quo nos vertimus? quid primum adsumimus? quid tacemus? Exciderunt tibi praecepta rhetorum et occupata luctu, oppressa lacrimis, praepedita singultibus dicendi ordinem non tenes! Ubi illud ab infantia studium litterarum . . . ?* Ib. 69, 6, 1 *Reddamus, quod paulo ante promisimus, et de schola rhetorum aquarum laudes et baptismi praedicemus.* Ib. 117, 12, 1 *Haec ad brevem lucubratiunculam celeri sermone dictavi . . . quasi ad scholasticam materiam me exercens . . . simulque ut ostenderem obtrectatoribus meis, quod et ego possim quicquid venerit in buccam dicere* (cf. *Adv. Vigil.* 3 p. 389). *Adv. Rufin.* I. 1 *Videtis nos intelligere prudentiam eius et praedicationis diasyrticae strophis in scholis saepe lusisse?*

33 Cf. *In Abd.* 20-21 *Neque enim ea lenitate* (to write laevitate?) *et compositione verborum dictamus ut scribimus. Epist.* 21, 42 *Saepe causatus sum excoli non posse sermonem, nisi quem propria manus limaverit. Itaque ignosce dolentibus oculis, id est ignosce dictanti.*

34 *In Ezech.* lib. VII praef. pp. 239-240 *Ista quae notariorum stilo cudimus et ad quae emendanda spatium vix habemus. In Zach.* lib. II praef. pp. 825-826. *Quem* (sc. librum) *tanta celeritate dictamus, ut paene non sit emendandi spatium.* Ib. lib. III praef. pp. 881-882 *Urget me frater Sisinnius incompta et impolita transmittere, ut non dicam emendandi sed ne relegendi quidem habeam facultatem . . . et quicquid sensu concipimus, composito non licet ornare sermone. In Is.* lib. V praef. pp. 169-170 *Dictamus haec, non scribimus, currente notariorum manu currit oratio.* Ib. lib. XIII praef. p. 534 *Hanc praefationem tumultuario sermone dictavi, ut quae habentur in schedulis describantur et plena emendatio lectoris iudicio reservetur.*

35 *In Matth.* prol. p. 5-6.

36 I refer to my remarks in *Gnomon* XV (1939), 88 sq. about two dissertations on Jerome's prose rhythm: P. C. Knook, *De overgang van metrisch tot rythmisch proza bij Cyprianus en Hieronymus* (thesis, Amsterdam 1932) and Sister Margaret Clare Herron, *A Study of the Clausulae in the Writings of St. Jerome* (The Catholic University of America Patristic Studies LI, thesis, Washington 1937).

37 *Apol. adv. Hier.* I. 10 (PL 21, 548).

[38] P. 93. . . .

[42] Cf. Arthur Stanley Pease, *Transactions and Proceedings of the American Philogical Association,* L, (1919), 161 sq.; Ellspermann, pp. 155 sq.—Tertullian's verdict (*Adv. Hermog.* 8): *Philosophi, patriarchae hereticorum,* is quoted with approval in *Epist.* 133, 2, 1. . . .

[44] In Dan. 1, 2 *Si enim cunctos philosophorum revolvas libros, necesse est ut in eis reperias aliquam partem vasorum Dei, ut apud Platonem fabricatorem mundi Deum, ut apud Zenonem, Stoicorum principem, inferos et immortales animas et unum bonum, honestatem.*

[45] *In Tit.* 1, 2 sqq. (PL 26, 593) *Est plane veritas quae non habet pietatem, si quis grammaticam artem noverit vel dialecticam, ut rationem recte loquendi habeat et inter falsa et vera diiudicet. Geometria quoque et arithmetica et musica habent in sua scientia veritatem, sed non est scientia illa pietatis.*

[46] For a survey of their opinions see Rudolf Eiswirth, *Hieronymus' Stellung zur Literatur und Kunst* (*Klassisch-Philologische Studien,* herausgegeben von Hans Herter und Wolfgang Schmid. Heft 16. Wiesbaden 1955), pp. 10 sqq.

[47] The extreme is represented by *A. Schöne,* who calls Jerome's relation "eines der ärgerlichsten Musterstücke verlogener Rhetorik, mühsam ausgesonnener Begeisterung und unechter Frömmigkeit" (*Die Weltchronik des Eusebius in ihrer Bearbeitung durch Hieronymus,* Berlin, 1900, p. 240). E. Bickel, "Das asketische Ideal bei Ambrosius, Hieronymus und Augustin", *Neue Jahrbücher für das klassische Alterium, Geschichte und deutsche Literatur,* XIX (1916), p. 456, agrees with Schöne.

[48] Pierre de Labriolle, "Le songe de St Jérôme", *Miscellanea Geronimiana* (Roma 1920), pp. 227-235.

[49] Cavallera (I: 2, p. 77) calls special attention to this fact: "Les passages où il s'en occupe dans la controverse avec Rufin . . . confirment expressément la réalité du songe. Jéróme ne pense pas à la nier".

[50] In the preceding letter (*Epist.* 21, 13,4) it is called *daemonum cibus.* . . .

[52] This line of exegesis goes back to Origen and is followed by both Ambrose, Jerome and Augustine; owing to their influence it was transmitted to the Middle Ages, where it played an important rôle; see Bernhard Blumenkranz' interesting paper "*Siliquae porcorum* (cf. Luc, XV, 16). L'exégèse médiévale et les sciences profanes", *Mélanges d'histoire du moyen âge dédiés à la mémoire de Louis Halphen* (Paris, 1951), pp. 11-17.

[53] It may be noticed that the same passage is hinted at in *Epist.* 22, 29, 7.

[54] Except in two letters to Marcella . . . .

[55] *In Gal.* lib. III praef. pp. 485-486.

[56] Cf. above p. 239.

[57] P. 18 "Als Gesamtergebnis lässt sich feststellen, dass ernstlich kein Beweis vorliegt, dass Hieronymus nach seinem Traumgelöbnis bis zu den Pauluskommentaren die Klassiker sich neu vorgenommen, wenn er sie auch von Zeit zu Zeit zitiert, um seinen Stil zu heben". Pp. 28 sq. "So scheint es mir im ganzen nicht möglich, aus den von Kunst angeführten oder sonst bekannten Beispielen zwingend zu beweisen, dass Hieronymus sein Traumversprechen gebrochen . . . ; ja nicht einmal, dass er die Klassiker wieder gelesen habe . . . Allerdings zitiert er die Klassiker in späteren Abschnitten seines Lebens wieder häufiger als unmittelbar nach dem Traum. Auch sind die Zitate bisweilen umfangreicher. Doch is nirgends mehr als sein gutes Gedächtnis zur Erklärung notwendig". Eiswirth, here as elsewhere, makes too great a demand upon a scholar's credulity: hundreds of passages quoted word for word over more than fifty years without any refreshing of the memory! Psychologists could teach him something about the capacity and function of memory. Eiswirth is preceded by Lübeck who says (p. 9): "Probabile est quae postea ex 'gentilibus' scriptoribus affert ea memoriae magis quam iteratae lectioni deberi".

[58] A. Rostagni, *Storia della Letteratura Latina,* II (Torino, 1952), p. 664.

[59] J. Geffcken, "Antike Kulturkämpfe", *Neue Jahrbücher für das klassische Altertum, Geschichte und deutsche Literatur,* XXIX (1912), p. 606 n. 1: "Hieronymus hat sich jedoch ziemlich schnell von seiner geistigen Beklemmung erholt".

[60] Op. cit., p. 176 "Hoc quidem promisso stare nequivit ac perbrevi vetus studium et consuetudo diuturna revixerunt".

[61] Op. cit., I, p. 154 "Längere Zeit hat er dieses Gelübde auch gehalten".

[62] Op. cit., I: 1, p. 31 "Il est incontestable toutefois qu'au moment même et de longues années encore, l'impression persista profonde et se traduisit par le renoncement absolu à toute lecture profane n'ayant pour but que le divertissement".

[63] Op. cit., p. 15 "Lässt man den Prolog so auf sich wirken, dann hat man den Eindruck, dass Hieronymus zwei Seelen in seiner Brust hat", etc.

[64] *Vita Malchi* 1 p. 41 *Ego qui diu tacui . . . prius exerceri cupio in parvo opere et veluti quandam rubiginem linguae abstergere.*

[65] *In Gal.* lib. III praef. pp. 485-486.

[66] Ib.

[67] I refer to Bickel's *Diatribe in Senecae philosophi fragmenta* and to my account in Chap. 4, pp. 150 sqq. Eiswirth mentions Bickel's book once (p. 23: "Bickel hat ja glänzend nachgewiesen, dass er in adv. Iovinian u. a. auch Seneca benutzt hat", etc.), but he has not been much influenced by this research, the most penetrating that exists into Jerome's method of using sources. Nor does he pay regard to *Adv. Iovin.*, where pagan topics and quotations take up a greater deal of space than in any other work of Jerome's. . . .

David S. Wiesen (essay date 1964)

SOURCE: "O Tempora! O Mores!" in *St. Jerome as a Satirist: A Study in Christian Latin Thought and Letters,* Cornell University Press, 1964, pp. 20-64.

[*In the following excerpt, Wiesen discusses Jerome's writings as commentaries on the state of his contemporaries. According to Wiesen, "St. Jerome's sense of the decline of civilization and his disgust with the vices of 'the world' form an important theme in all categories of his writings, from the letters written in the desert of Chalcis when he was a young man to his late exegetical and homiletic works."*]

It is a commonplace for satirists to castigate the age in which they live, to compare contemporary society unfavorably with the past, and to declare that the vices which they lampoon are peculiar to their own time. In his first satire Juvenal expatiates on the question, *Et quando uberior vitiorum copia?*[1] The satirist goes as far as to say in his thirteenth satire:

Nona aetas agitur peioraque saecula ferri
temporibus, quorum sceleri non invenit ipsa
nomen et a nullo posuit natura metallo.[2]

Persius expresses his weariness with the empty life of his day in a line which Jerome twice quotes:

O curas hominum, o quantum est in rebus inane![3]

Seneca contrasts the decadent luxury of his own age with the manly simplicity of Scipio's time. At the beginning of his satiric description of Roman bathing habits he tells us, *Magna ergo me voluptas subiit contemplantem mores Scipionis et nostros.*[4] Ammianus Marcellinus too takes the time of Scipio as the high point of human morality as he contrasts the swollen

hypocrisy of Roman social life in his own day.[5] Ammianus suggests that the vices of the nobility, which he describes in great detail, are peculiar to his own age.[6] Of course, the contrast between the evils of a modern age and the purity of a time long past was also popular as a *locus communis* in the schools of declamation throughout the imperial period.[7]

The same deprecation of the age in which he lived and the same unfavorable view of its morality in contrast to the past are found in St. Jerome's writings. The attitude of a fourth-century Christian moralist to contemporary society was of necessity somewhat ambiguous. On the one hand there was considerable reason for optimism. The swift progress made by the forces of Christianity in the latter part of the fourth century was unmistakable. Writing about the year 400, St. Jerome declares, probably with some exaggeration, "The gilded Capitoline is filthy, all the temples of Rome are covered with soot and cobwebs . . . and a flood of people runs past the half-ruined shrines to the tombs of the martyrs."[8] About the same time Jerome addressed a letter to two Goths, Sunnia and Fretela, who had asked him for guidance through the textual difficulties of the Psalms. Jerome begins his letter with some highly optimistic remarks on the condition of society:

> Dudum callosa tenendo capulo manus, et digiti tractandis sagittis aptiores, ad stilum calamumque mollescunt; et bellicosa pectora vertuntur in mansuetudinem christianam. Nunc et Esaiae vaticinium cernimus opere completum: "Concident gladios suos in aratra, et lanceas suas in falces; et non adsumet gens contra gentem gladium, et non discent ultra pugnare."[9]

In spite of the obvious attempt at flattery, these words do at least show that Jerome's view of society and morals was sometimes favorable and approving. Yet such expressions of optimism are rare. Jerome saw more clearly than most of his contemporaries that he lived in the twilight of Greco-Roman civilization and that night could not be long delayed. In his commentary on Daniel, he clearly states that the military weakness of the Empire revealed that the end of Roman hegemony had arrived.[10] In his sixtieth letter Jerome recounts the tragic history of the emperors from Constantius to the usurper Eugenius and, after describing the chaos caused by the barbarian invasions, adds: *Romanus orbis ruit et tamen cervix nostra erecta non flectitur.*[11] Thirteen years later, in 409, learning that Alaric and his Gothic host were approaching the walls of Rome, Jerome was filled with just and gloomy apprehension. *O lugenda res publica,* he exclaims, as he describes in detail the lands of the Empire lost to the barbarians. Then, citing Lucan, Jerome declares: *Potentiam Romanae urbis ardens poeta describens ait: quid satis est, si Roma parum est? Quod nos alio mutemus elogio: quid salvum est, si Roma perit?*[12]

We see then that in spite of several expressions of optimism on the improvement of society effected by the advance of Christianity, St. Jerome was thrown into deep gloom by the political events of his day. Yet his real dissatisfaction with the world in which he lived was not the result of political affairs but sprang rather from his disapproval of the moral state of society. Jerome could not fail to observe that Christianity's external victories had not wrought any significant reform of social mores. Indeed, he directly attributes the distracted state of the Empire to the wickedness of the age. In his description of the barbarian incursions he exclaims, "Through our sins are the barbarians strong, through our vices is the Roman army defeated."[13] Let us now follow chronologically, through each category of Jerome's writings, his satiric expression of disgust with the condition of his age.

Letters

Many of the letters written during Jerome's second sojourn in Rome (382-385) contain satiric references to the faults of contemporary society. In his thirty-third letter Jerome draws up catalogues of the enormous scholarly output of Varro and of Origen the Adamantine.[14] These catalogues reveal, says Jerome, that we in our own day are sleeping the sleep of Epimenides and that the labor expended by Varro and Origen on literature we use in gathering riches.[15] To be sure we too have learned men in our day:

> Sciuntque pisces in quo gurgite nati sint, quae concha in quo litore creverit. De turdorum salivis non ambigimus. Paxamus et Apicius semper in manibus; oculi ad hereditates, sensus ad patinas, et si quis de philosophis, vel de Christianis qui vere philosophi sunt, trito pallio et sordida tunica lectioni vacaverit, quasi vesanus exploditur.[16]

In this passage Jerome suggests that excessive interest in food was a vice peculiar to his own age. And yet gluttony had always been grist to the satirist's mill. Lucilius, Varro, Horace, Persius, Petronius, and Juvenal had ridiculed the Roman passion for delicacies of the table.[17] Among later writers Tertullian comments satirically on the refined voracity of the Romans, and Ammianus Marcellinus describes the host at a banquet calling for scales to weigh the fish, fowl, and dor-mice.[18] In satirizing the corruption of Rome, Ammianus mentions only by *praeteritio* the "abyss of dinner-table luxury and the varying ways of arousing pleasure," since the full exposition of these topics would be excessively long.[19] Subsequently in a tone very much like that of Jerome, Ammianus ridicules supposedly educated contemporaries for their greater interest in food than in books: "And if in the circle of the learned the name of an ancient author is dropped, they think it is a foreign name for a fish or a canape."[20]

Thus in attacking the gluttony of his age Jerome is working well within the satiric tradition. Even the diction of his remarks shows the influence of pagan satire. We may compare Jerome's words, *de turdorum salivis non ambigimus,* with Persius' expression, *turdarum nosse salivas.*[21] Moreover, the sense of the ridicule of gluttony cited above has a close parallel in Juvenal:

> Nulli maior fuit usus edendi
> tempestate mea: Circeis nata forent an
> Lucrinum ad saxum Rutupinove edita fundo
> ostrea callebat primo deprendere morsu,
> et semel aspecti litus dicebat echini.[22]

Furthermore in mentioning Apicius, Jerome recalls a standard pagan prototype of gluttony. Juvenal uses Apicius as a symbol of voracity twice and Martial three times.[23]

Jerome touches briefly in this passage upon another fault which he considers characteristic of his age, the longing for legacies. So conspicuous is legacy hunting in the picture of society drawn by the classical satirists that one might perhaps suspect that Jerome, in his desire to attack his age, hits upon a failing which was no longer common but which he had learned of from his reading.[24] Yet the testimony of Ammianus Marcellinus shows that legacy hunting was still a widespread practice in the Roman society of the fourth century.[25] The edict of the emperor Valentinian in 370 which prohibited legacy hunting among ecclesiastics shows how common this fault was among the clergy.[26] Indeed, St. Jerome himself has been accused of legacy hunting as a result of his numerous invitations to wealthy Romans to join him in Bethlehem.[27]

Jerome concludes his letter by comparing the men of contemporary Rome to Aristippus and Epicurus, that is, lovers of luxury and sloth.[28] This theme of the worldliness and sensuality of Babylon, as Jerome calls Rome, is ubiquitous in his letters of the years 382-385.[29] Writing to the wealthy and noble Marcella in 384, Jerome describes Rome as "[a city] of pomp, of lewdness, of pleasures, a city in which to be humble is to be wretched."[30] The Christian poet Prudentius, a contemporary of St. Jerome, agrees with him. He envisages *Luxuria,* who *pervigilem ructabat marcida cenam,* arising on the western bounds of the world.[31] This has been interpreted to mean that Rome is regarded as the original home of sensuality.[32]

The luxury and materialism of the city stifle the life of the spirit, says Jerome. In his forty-third letter he again contrasts the learned diligence of the great Origen with the typical scholar of his own day. If the latter reads for as much as two hours, he yawns, rubs his face with his hand, tries to restrain his desire for food, and after so much intellectual labor returns to worldly occupations.[33] This brief caricature is but the beginning of an attack on the life of Babylon. Gluttony is briefly touched upon: *Praetermitto prandia, quibus onerata mens premitur,* says Jerome. Social life, he claims, consists of an endless round of meaningless visits dominated by malicious gossip: *Deinceps itur in verba . . . vita aliena describitur et mordentes invicem consumimur ab invicem.*[34] In this sentence the master of the biting insult inveighs against the art at which he was so adept. He then touches lightly upon the luxuriousness of clothing and passes to a satiric picture of the businessman:

> Ubicumque conpendium est, velocior pes, citus sermo, auris adtentior; si damnum, ut saepe in re familiari accidere solet, fuerit nuntiatum, vultus maerore deprimitur. Laetamur ad nummum, obolo contristamur.[35]

Jerome proceeds to compare the changing countenance of a businessman with the masks of an actor who plays now Hercules, now Venus. In his careful construction of this passage, Jerome is trying to achieve the greatest possible vividness. He chooses three details to highlight, *pes, sermo,* and *auris,* using these as the subjects of brief successive clauses. With these three quick strokes he immediately draws the sarcastic picture of greedy profit seekers. The asyndeton of the three clauses and the omission of the verbs also aim at swiftness.[36] Satiric contrast is achieved by chiasmus: *Laetamur ad nummum, obolo contristamur.*

Jerome concludes with a general statement of disgust with the worldliness of Rome: *Habeat sibi Roma suos tumultus, harena saeviat, circus insaniat, theatra luxurient et, quia de nostris dicendum est, matronarum cotidie visitetur senatus.*[37] The passage demonstrates that Jerome did not hesitate to castigate faults of which he himself was guilty. In speaking of *nostri* who visit *matronarum senatus,* he is presumably referring to those clergymen who were closely attached to noble patronesses, a type of ecclesiastic whom Jerome bitterly satirizes as foppish and hypocritical in his twenty-second letter.[38] Yet it must be remembered that Jerome's entire life at Rome revolved around aristocratic and pious ladies such as Marcella, her mother Albina, her companion Asella, and, of course, the famous Paula, who was to be the closest friend and support of Jerome's later life. It is just such a *matronarum senatus* which Jerome in this letter dismisses as one of the most unpleasant aspects of the worldly life of Babylon. The remark seems to be in particularly poor taste in a letter addressed to the very Marcella who was the center of Jerome's social circle.

Jerome's tone of disgust with the tumult of Rome, its arena, circus, and theater closely resembles in spirit those passages of Horace and Juvenal in which the satirists reject the inconvenience and confusion of Rome in favor of the peace of the countryside.[39] The resemblance is heightened when Jerome juxtaposes to his caustic portrayal of Rome an idyllic description of country life with its cheap and simple diet, its leaves and flowers, and its chirping birds.

> Quam primum licet quasi quendam portum secreta ruris intremus. Ibi cibarius panis et holus nostris manibus inrigatum, lac, deliciae rusticanae, viles quidem sed innocentes cibos praebeant. . . . Si aestas est, secretum arboris umbra praebebit; si autumnus ipsa aeris temperies et strata subter folia locum quietis ostendit. Vere ager floribus depingitur, et inter querulas aves psalmi dulcius decantabuntur.[40]

Yet this description decidedly lacks the odor of reality. It appears to be rather a rhetorical exercise in drawing the traditional contrast between the city and country life. We know from Quintilian that the question *Rusticane vita an urbana potior?* was a standard rhetorical thesis.[41] Surely when a monk who is an ascetic zealot and a secretary to the pope suggests to a noble Roman widow, *secreta ruris intremus,* the invitation cannot be seriously meant.

And yet even if the invitation was not meant to be accepted literally, it reflected Jerome's profound and passionate desire for escape from the endless troubles and grief which he had brought upon himself during his stay in Rome. His longing praise of country life is contained in one of the last letters that he wrote before his final departure from the city.[42] The death of Jerome's powerful patron, Pope Damasus, on December 11, 384, removed the great dam which had long held back a sea of enmity.[43] Jerome's letters reveal his increasingly difficult position. His attacks on the luxury of the city had not been well received. "We who refuse to wear silken garments," complains Jerome, "to get drunk, to part our lips in raucous laughter are called gloomy monks. If our tunic is not gleaming white we are pointed out at the street corner and called 'imposter and Greek.'"[44] Jerome concludes this letter with a brief but penetrating sketch of his accusers: *Cavillentur vafriora licet, et pingui aqualiculo farsos circumferant homines.*[45] In these words of ridicule the influence of pagan satire is clearly visible. Persius uses the word *aqualiculus,* which literally signifies "the maw of a pig," to mean "belly." Jerome's phrase *pinguis aqualiculus* is taken from Persius 1. 57:

> Pinguis aqualiculus protenso sesquipede extet.[46]

Thus Jerome relies upon the Stoic satirist to supply the most striking phrase in his description of the profligate enemies of Christian asceticism.

Jerome's thirty-ninth letter, the *epitaphium* of Blesilla, clearly reveals how much hostility his ascetic propaganda had aroused. Blesilla, the young daughter of the noble Paula, had been converted to the ascetic life by

Jerome. When she died suddenly, her death was attributed to the ascetic rigors imposed upon her by Jerome. At her funeral the hostility of the mob broke forth, as the people murmured, "How long before this detestable class of monks will be driven from the city, crushed with stones, tossed into the waves?"[47] And yet Jerome's propaganda for reform was only partially responsible for the enmity of the city of Rome toward him. In his parting letter to Rome **(No. 45),** he catalogues the charges brought against him, "I am infamous, I am tricky and slippery, I am a liar and deceive with satanic art."[48] It is absolutely clear from this letter that it was Jerome's ambitious and bitter personality which drove him from Rome, the city which, he claimed, had once considered him worthy of the papacy itself.[49] In this letter, written at the very moment of his departure, Jerome delivers himself of some Parthian shots against the sensuality of the city. Addressing Rome in general he says:

> Tibi placet lavare cotidie, alius has munditias sordes putat; tu attagenam ructuas et de comeso acipensere gloriaris, ego faba ventrem inpleo; te delectant cachinnantium greges, Paulam Malaniumque plangentium; tu aliena desideras, illae contemnunt sua; te delibuta melle vina delectant, illae potant aquam frigidam suaviorem; tu te perdere aestimas quidquid in praesenti non hauseris, comederis, devoraris. . . . Bono tuo crassus sis, me macies delectat et pallor; tu tales miseros arbitraris, nos te miseriorem putamus: Par pari refertur sententia; invicem nobis videmur insani.[50]

In the month of August, 385, when the Etesian winds were blowing, St. Jerome set sail from Rome, never to return.[51] At Cyprus he was joined by Paula and her daughter Eustochium, who had rejected the pleas of their relatives and with great courage and religious fervor abandoned forever the evil life of Babylon. In company with these ladies Jerome made an extensive tour of the Holy Land and Egypt, piously visiting a large number of biblical sites.[52] Finally in the summer of 386 they settled in Bethlehem with the intention of building two cloisters, one for men under Jerome's direction and a convent for women to be headed by Paula.

Some years after his settlement in the East, Jerome dispatched to Marcella an invitation to join him in Bethlehem.[53] This letter purports to have been written by Paula and Eustochium, but it is generally agreed that it came from the hand of Jerome.[54] In this document Jerome's old hatred for the evils of decadent Rome again blazes forth. The quiet piety of Bethlehem is contrasted to the luxury of the city:

> Procul luxuria, procul voluptas. . . . Ubi sunt latae porticus? ubi aurata laquearia? ubi domus miserorum poenis et damnatorum labore vestitae? ubi ad instar

palatii opibus privatorum extructae basilicae, ut vile corpusculum hominis pretiosius inambulet et, quasi mundo quicquam possit esse ornatius, tecta sua magis velit aspicere quam caelum?[55]

This attack on the Roman passion for grandiose buildings recalls a traditional moralistic theme. Seneca attacked luxury in building, using *laquearia* as a symbol of wanton magnificence.[56] Juvenal satirized the Roman love of *latas porticus*.[57] One might suspect that Jerome's denunciation of building is more a rhetorical commonplace which belongs by tradition in a castigation of urban vices than an honest expression of moral outrage. Indeed, elsewhere in his writings we can see how his denunciation of the passion for building was guided more by tradition than by present reality. As early as 376 Jerome had written from the desert of Chalcis a letter in which he contrasted the piously ascetic life of the desert with Roman luxury. Addressing Heliodorus, a friend of his school days, he says, *Et tu amplas porticus et ingentia spatia metaris?*[58] Since Jerome certainly knew that his friend was a monk and hence in no position at all to construct magnificent porticoes, we must assume that he was speaking in a traditional and rhetorical manner. This opinion is strengthened when it is discovered that Jerome's words contain a reminiscence of Horace's praise of old-time frugality (*Carmen* ii. 15. 15):

> Nulla decempedis
> metata privatis opacam
> porticus excipiebat Arcton.

We have in fact striking confirmation from Jerome himself of the derivative nature of his critique of city life in the letter to Heliodorus. About twenty years after that letter, he wrote to Heliodorus' nephew Nepotianus, admitting:

> Dum essem adulescens, immo paene puer, et primos impetus lascivientis aetatis heremi duritia refrenarem, scripsi ad avunculum tuum sanctum Heliodorum exhor-tatoriam epistulam plenam lacrimis querimoniisque, et quae deserti sodalis monstraret affectum. Sed in illo opere pro aetate tunc lusimus, et calentibus adhuc rhetorum studiis atque doctrinis, quaedam scolastico flore depinximus.[59]

This admission should give us serious pause. If Jerome can describe his censure of urban luxury as rhetorical play, it is probable that other aspects of his satire were heavily influenced by inherited declamatory moralism. We will have to face this problem frequently in the course of this study.

Although Jerome's denunciation of the passion for building is influenced by traditional pagan moralism, his remarks do in fact represent a theme found in other Christian writers of his time [such as John Chrysostom]. . . . We find, then, that the emphasis in pagan moralism on simplicity and frugality is continued in Christianity. It is precisely this continuity of ethical commonplaces which permits St. Jerome to borrow repeatedly from those representatives of pagan moralism with whom he was so well acquainted, the satiric poets.

John Chrysostom confines his attack on the luxury of building to private edifices. It is curious to see how Jerome's repudiation of luxury in building extends even to churches. We find the ardent champion of Christian orthodoxy attacking the magnificent churches built *ad instar palatii opibus privatorum.*[61] Jerome is fond of contrasting the outward splendor of the contemporary Church with certain inner weaknesses. In his letter of exhortation on the ascetic life addressed to Nepotianus, Jerome writes: *Multi aedificant parietes et columnas ecclesiae subtrahunt; marmora nitent, auro splendent lacunaria, gemmis altare distinguitur et ministrorum Christi nulla electio est.*[62] In another letter of exhortation, to Paulinus of Nola, Jerome asks: *Quae utilitas parietes fulgere gemmis, et Christum in paupere fame mori?*[63] Again, in his letter to the nun Demetrias, Jerome satirizes mildly the builders of luxurious churches:

> Alii aedificent ecclesias, vestiant parietes marmorum crustis, columnarum moles advehant, earumque deaurent capita pretiosum ornatum non sentientia, ebore argentoque valvas et gemmis aurea vel aurata distinguant altaria—non reprehendo, non abnuo.[64]

Jerome's mocking purpose is shown in his use of the highly ironic phrase *capita pretiosum ornatum non sentientia.* Grützmacher, who has in general a very low opinion of Jerome's character and motives, suggests that he had "persönliche Absichten" in his advice to Demetrias. Jerome preferred that Demetrias send money to his own monastery, which at the time of this letter (A.D. 414) was in serious financial difficulty, rather than spend it on showy basilicas.[65] But Grützmacher's opinion cannot be maintained in view of Jerome's frequently expressed scorn for glorious churches.[66]

Even after he took up permanent settlement in the East, Jerome did not cease to lampoon the failings of his age in general and of the city of Rome in particular. In his invitation to Marcella to join him in the East **(Letter 46)**, Jerome, after comparing Rome to *mulier purpurata Babylonis,* proceeds to the following satiric description:

> Sed ipsa ambitio, potentia, magnitudo urbis, videri et videre, salutari et salutare, laudare et detrahere, audire vel proloqui et tantam frequentiam hominum saltim invitum pati, a proposito monachorum et quiete aliena sunt. Aut enim videmus ad nos veni-

entes et silentium perdimus, aut non videmus et superbiae arguimur. Interdumque, ut visitantibus reddamus vicem, ad superbas fores pergimus et inter linguas rodentium ministrorum postes ingredimur auratos.[67]

This unpleasant description again illustrates a remarkable aspect of Jerome's moralizing: his readiness to attack faults of which he too was guilty. We have already seen this tendency at work in **Letters 43** and **44.** In the present list of the objectionable aspects of Roman social life Jerome includes backbiting and the *linguas rodentium ministrorum,* although he specifically claims for himself the right *laudare et carpere* and was well aware that his own evil tongue was a major cause of his enforced retirement from Rome.[68]

Jerome's tendency to see only the faults of others is exemplified by another letter written in the early years of his settlement in Bethlehem. We have seen that in his forty-third epistle, written while he was still in Rome, Jerome had charged that the age in which he lived was unlettered and unscholarly. His removal to Bethlehem had not changed this view at all. Writing to Paulinus of Nola, Jerome again attacks the ignorance of the day. "Today how many men, imagining that they understand literature, hold in their hands a sealed book which they cannot open, unless He shall unlock it 'who has the key of David, who opens and no man closes, who closes and no man opens.'"[69] The idealization of an age long past, so common in satire, is implied by the contrast with "today." Jerome then calls upon Horace to reinforce his strictures:

> Quod medicorum est,
> promittunt medici, tractant fabrilia fabri.

Sola scripturarum ars est, quam sibi omnes passim vindicent:

> Scribimus indocti doctique poemata passim.

> Hanc garrula anus, hanc delirus senex, hanc soloescista verbosus, hanc universi praesumunt, lacerant, docent, antequam discant.[70]

A mocking description of these pseudo scholars is then given:

> Alii adducto supercilio grandia verba trutinantes inter mulierculas de sacris litteris philosophantur, alii discunt—pro pudor!—a feminis quod viros doceant, et, ne parum hoc sit, quadam facilitate verborum, immo audacia disserunt aliis quod ipsi non intellegunt.[71]

This portrayal is highly effective, with its detail of the haughtily raised eyebrow of the pompous and ignorant weigher of words. The passage again illustrates

Jerome's habit of satirizing faults of which he himself was guilty. What had been his major occupation during his years in Rome if not *inter mulierculas de sacris litteris philosophari?* He himself admits that at Rome, "a great crowd of maidens frequently surrounded me; to some I explained the divine books, according to my ability."[72] Jerome was well aware that his relationships with women were the source of considerable scandal.[73] His attack in the letter to Paulinus of Nola on those who explain scripture to women reveals the inconsistency in his moralizing which led Eiswirth to declare that, "Hieronymus war ein sehr sensibiler Charakter, der stark von der Augenblickstimmung abhängig war."[74] In his wish to convert Paulinus of Nola to the life of perfect asceticism Jerome shoots his arrows broadcast at the vices of the age, meanwhile quite unaware that he is hitting some of the faults of which contemporaries thought him guilty.

A much more important and puzzling example of Jerome's inconsistency is discovered when his **Letters 46** and **53** are compared with **Letter 58.** In his invitation to Marcella **(Letter 46)** Jerome had strongly contrasted the debauchery of Rome with the quiet piety of Bethlehem. In **Letter 53** Jerome invites Paulinus to come to Bethlehem in order, like Paul, to sit at the feet of Gamaliel and be armed with spiritual weapons. But suddenly and unexpectedly we find Jerome in another letter **(58)** urging Paulinus by no means to voyage to the East if he wishes to maintain the ascetic life: Jerusalem had suddenly become the old painted woman of Babylon, as Jerome launches into a satiric attack on the Holy City:

> Si crucis et resurrectionis loca non essent in urbe celeberrima, in qua curia, in qua ala militum, in qua scorta, mimi, scurrae et omnia sunt quae solent esse in ceteris urbibus, vel si monachorum solummodo turbis frequentaretur, expetendum revera huiusce modi cunctis monachis esset habitaculum; nunc vero summae stultitiae est renuntiare saeculo, dimittere patriam, urbes deserere, monachum profiteri, et inter maiores populus peregre vivere quam eras victurus in patria. De toto huc orbe concurritur; plena est civitas universi generis hominibus, et tanta utriusque sexus constipatio, ut quod alibi ex parte fugiebas hic totum sustinere cogaris.[75]

The puzzlement aroused among modern scholars by this sudden attack on the life of Jerusalem and its environs and the withdrawal of the invitation to Paulinus was largely the result of a chronological difficulty: which letter was earlier, the invitation in **Letter 53** or its withdrawal in **Letter 58**? In the manuscripts **Letter 58** is placed before **53,** but Vallarsi reversed the order because of the phrase *in principio amicitiarum* in **Letter 53. 1.** On the basis of this reversed order Grützmacher built the theory that Jerome withdrew the invitation when he realized that the strong-minded Paulinus would never be subject to his own direction. Furthermore,

Jerome feared, claims Grützmacher, that Paulinus might take sides against him in the incipient quarrel with Bishop John of Jerusalem.[76] More recent scholarly opinion, however, has restored the original order of the letters, placing the letter now numbered **58** before **53.**[77] Grützmacher's theory, so unfavorable to Jerome's character, is no longer tenable if this order of the two letters is accepted, for now the satiric attack on Jerusalem precedes rather than follows the invitation to Paulinus. The solution to this chronological problem significantly affects our view of Jerome's attacks on the age. Grützmacher's theory implies that Jerome wrote his satiric description of the busy life of Jerusalem solely for personal reasons: to prevent the arrival in the East of a distinguished and strong-minded cleric who might question his own authority. But Cavallera seems right in maintaining that Jerome's invitation to Paulinus is only comprehensible if it was made after an exchange of letters had drawn the two men closer together and after Jerome had become concerned for Paulinus' spiritual well-being.[78] On this theory the unfavorable picture of Jerusalem would have been painted in Jerome's first letter to Paulinus and thus would have been the free expression of his wrath at the moral delinquencies of the Holy City. It is then reasonable to conclude that Jerome was truly shocked, at Jerusalem as at Rome, by the contrast between an ideal of Christian behavior and the reality of a society nominally Christian but still tainted by many vestiges of pagan immorality. We may then say that, like the satiric pictures of pagan society found in earlier Latin Fathers, Jerome's satire arose from his moral indignation and from his consequent desire to reveal before society the vices which to his mind implied the failure of a Christian ideal.

As the years passed and Jerome's memories of Rome faded, his anger and indignation at that city appear to have cooled. In 397 he wrote a letter to the aristocratic, wealthy Roman senator Pammachius. In this document the former satiric attacks on Rome have been transformed into a paean to the Eternal City as the capital of Christian asceticism. Jerome's satire now refers only to the past. The present merits unqualified praise. *Tunc rari sapientes, potentes, nobiles christiani, nunc multi monachi sapientes, potentes, nobiles.*[79] With this sentiment we may compare **Letter 33. 3**, a passage written about twelve years earlier: *At e contrario nostra saecula habent homines eruditos, sciuntque pisces in quo gurgite nati sint.* In his later epistle Jerome proceeds to praise the disappearance of luxury from the city:

> Ardentes gemmae, quibus ante collum et facies ornabatur, egentium ventres saturant; vestes sericae et aurum in fila lentescens in mollia lanarum vestimenta mutata sunt, quibus repellatur frigus, non quibus nudetur ambitio; deliciarum quondam supellectilem virtus insumit.[81]

Only twelve years earlier Jerome had spoken of *vestes sericae, nitentes gemmae, picta facies, auri ambitio* as characteristic elements in the life of the city.[82] Now, however, he applies his satire only to failings already corrected. *Fores quae prius salutantium turbas vomebant nunc a miseris obsidentur.*[83] Jerome's earlier views on Roman social life may be compared: *Sed ipsa ambitio, potentia, magnitudo urbis, videre et videri, salutari et salutare . . . a proposito monachorum et quiete aliena sunt.*[84]

To what cause may Jerome's reversal of opinion on Rome be attributed? It is difficult to suppose that Jerome suddenly began to think of Rome as the holiest city on earth. A consideration of the nature of the letter in which his new opinion is contained may be helpful. The immensely wealthy senator Pammachius, to whom the letter in question was addressed, had been married to Paulina, the second daughter of Jerome's companion Paula.[85] Upon Paulina's death in 398, Jerome addressed to Pammachius an *epitaphium,* which is the letter under consideration. The *epitaphium,* however, occupies only the beginning of the letter, which quickly becomes a highly exaggerated panegyric of Pammachius. At his wife's death Pammachius had adopted the ascetic life and had dared to enter the senate house in the duncolored garb of a monk.[86] Jerome was well aware how meaningful was the adherence of a rich and noble senator to the cause of asceticism. The enemies of the monastic movement had been mounting strong attacks.[87] Jerome had already been forced to reply in his polemical tracts **Adversus Helvidium** and **Adversus Iovinianum.** Moreover, the Origenist controversy was currently raging hotly. In both these quarrels Pammachius was a powerful ally in Rome. By flattering Pammachius through excessive praise of the improvements his conversion to asceticism had wrought in the moral life of Rome, Jerome hoped to make him even more favorable to the monastic cause. Hence the glowing portrayal of Rome, for in the description of the city's transformation, Pammachius is glorified as *magnus in magnis, primus in primis, monacho monachorum.*[88] The artificiality of the letter is revealed by the turgid rhetoric of its diction: *Nobis post dormitionem somnumque Paulinae Pammachium monachum ecclesia peperit postumum,* declares Jorome.[89] This artificiality reaches its height in Jerome's description of a mute mendicant: *Alius elinguis et mutus, et ne hoc quidem habens unde roget, magis rogat quia rogare non potest.*[90]

Jerome's picture of a Rome transformed, a picture in which satire is used to contrast a decadent past with an improved present cannot be accepted as the true expression of an optimistic view of the morals of the day. The passage of time had probably softened the old anger, and the desire to flatter Pammachius had dictated Jerome's praise of the new Rome. Yet in the very same letter the indignation of earlier years flares up

briefly once again. Inconsistently Jerome turns to satirize the profligacy of the city:

> Ubi videris fumare patinas et Phasides aves lentis vaporibus discoqui, ubi argenti pondus, ferventes mannos, comatulos pueros, pretiosas vestes, picta tapetia, ubi ditior est largitore cui largiendum est, pars sacrilegii est rem pauperum dare non pauperibus.[91]

Jerome's return here to his more usual view of the moral state of Rome strongly supports the theory that he had ulterior motives in praising the city to Pammachius. Again he emphasizes gluttony and luxury, delivering a slap *en passant* at the wealth of certain worldly clergymen who might be the unworthy recipients of Pammachius' bounty. Jerome's mockery of *comptos pueros* recalls Juvenal's disdain for dandified slave boys (*Sat.* II. 149-151) and his preference for servants who have:

> tonsi rectique capilli
> atque hodie tantum propter convivia pexi.

His mention above of pheasants *(Phasides aves)* recalls Juvenal's use of *Scythicae volucres,* the same bird under another name, as a symbol of overrefined eating habits.[92] Jerome again uses these traditional "birds of Phasis" as a symbol of gluttony in one of his later letters, and pheasants also appear in one of John Chrysostom's attacks on luxury of the table. . . .

Jerome now proceeds, with a monk's scorn for the ways of the world, to characterize the eating habits of laymen: *Saecularis homo in quadragesima ventris ingluviem decoquit, et in coclearum morem suo victitans suco, futuris dapibus ac saginae aqualiculum parat.*[94] In these few words Jerome demonstrates his use of ridiculing description as a means of ascetic propaganda. His aim is plainly to arouse the disgust of the reader for the behavior of the *saecularis homo.* Thus his choice of the word *ingluvies,* which is literally the maw of an animal, to mean gluttony. The word *ingluvies* is used in the same scornful way by Horace:

> Hunc si percontreris, avi cur atque parentis
> praeclaram ingrata stringat malus *ingluvie*
> rem.[95]

Furthermore, Jerome in this passage again uses *aqualiculus,* as did Persius, with a strongly pejorative meaning, in satiric reference to gluttony.[96] This description is meant, then, to be a brief but effective exposé of the sensuality of the worldly life.

Jerome's later letters reveal deepening despair over the state of the world. This despair was in part the result of the catastrophic political events of the first decade of the fifth century. Although a recluse and ascetic,

Jerome could hardly avoid a feeling of profound shock and grief at the terrible incursions of the barbarians into the western part of the Empire. *Aruerant vetustate lacrimae,* he exclaims.[97] In such times one can hardly hope for more than merely to stay alive: "But in view of the miseries of the time and the savagery of the swords everywhere raging, he is rich enough who is not in need of bread, he is excessively powerful, who is not compelled to be a slave."[98] Yet the tragic events of those days did not quiet Jerome's enthusiasm for moral reform. On the contrary, they but strengthened his appeal for the rejection of worldly evils. The world collapses about us, *et solliciti sumus, quid manducemus aut quid bibamus?*[99] In spite of his old hatred of Rome, the news of the city's capture by Alaric in 410 filled him with gloom. In meditating on this dark event, Jerome turns to a consideration of the worldly vices which he had always associated with the fallen city:

> Pro nefas, orbis terrarum ruit et in nobis peccata non corruunt. Urbs inclita et Romani imperii caput uno hausta est incendio. Nulla regio, quae non exules eius habeat. In cineres et favillas sacrae quondam ecclesiae conciderunt et tamen studemus avaritiae. Vivimus quasi altera die morituri et aedificamus quasi semper in hoc victuri saeculo. Auro parietes, auro laquearia, auro fulgent capita columnarum et nudus atque esuriens ante fores nostras in paupere Christus moritur.[100]

The satirist's censure of his society gains new significance when that society is in very fact proved to be in a state of total collapse.

In reviewing now the passages of St. Jerome's letters in which he condemns the age in which he lived, one can see the special qualities which fitted him for his satiric role: the power keenly to observe the minute details of human behavior, the ability so to describe these details that their absurd elements are much exaggerated, and a certain lack of sympathy for human failings. It is a much more difficult task to try to evaluate the motives for his satire. The powerful influence of Jerome's rhetorical education which is so apparent in many passages suggests that his satire is at times based more on traditional ethical commonplaces than on his own immediate observations. Thus when he addresses to a simple monk a warning against building a luxurious home, the complete inappropriateness of the exhortation in its context makes it plain that Jerome is drawing on a traditional moralizing theme dear to the heart of satirists.[101] In contrasting in a letter to Marcella the hatefulness of the city and the pleasantness of the simple country life, he recalls, without much reference to reality, a theme on which the sixth satire of Horace's second book and the third and eleventh satires of Juvenal are built.[102] Yet there is no necessary conflict between a fully sincere disapproval of the faults of one's age and a somewhat artificial method of castigating those faults. Jerome's ardent championship of the nascent monastic movement indicates how strongly he sensed the gap between an ideal of Christian life and the reality of human behavior. Much of his mockery of social mores arose directly from his mission as an ascetic propagandist. We can perceive this in Jerome's own explanation of his attacks on gluttony: "Not because God . . . is delighted by the rumbling of our intestines and the emptiness of our belly, but because chastity cannot otherwise be safe."[103] In St. Jerome's writings one can see how the indignation of a Christian ascetic at the failings of society was strengthened by a scholar's knowledge of the traditional modes of moralistic exhortation.

Furthermore, the element of personal animus in Jerome's attack on his age must be considered. Jerome could never forgive Rome for having been the scene of the defeat of his personal ambitions. Certainly it is hard to believe that if Jerome had received in Rome the recognition he thought he deserved as a scholar and monk he would have said to Rome, after lampooning the city's immorality: *Invicem nobis videmur insani.*[104] Yet one might go too far, with Grützmacher, in finding "persönliche Absichten" in much of Jerome's satire. For Jerome, the success of moral reform was indistinguishable from his own success as a moral reformer. His personal zeal for the lofty cause of asceticism would justify in Jerome's mind his artful and apparently selfish use of social satire in his letter to Pammachius. In Jerome's writings, hatred of luxury and immorality becomes a profoundly personal statement of his own hopes and ambitions. Our task now is to see whether these views of Jerome's satire are strengthened or modified by his remarks on the state of the world in his nonepistolary writings.

Historical Works

We include under the heading "Historical Works" the three biographies of the monks Paul, Hilarion, and Malchus, in spite of Gibbon's remark that, "the only defect in these pleasing compositions is the want of truth and common sense."[105] The earliest of these, the **Life of Paul,** is attributed by Cavallera to the time of Jerome's sojourn at Antioch after his return from the ascetic rigors of the Syrian desert.[106] The sudden change from the harsh habits of self-denial practiced by a desert hermit to the luxurious and decadent society of Antioch, so vividly described by St. John Chrysostom, must have heightened for Jerome the contrast between the aims of a Christianized society and its accomplishments. At the end of his description of the saintly and ascetic life of Paul, Jerome draws a satiric contrast between this ideally Christian life and the wantonness he could see around himself:

> Libet in fine opusculi eos interrogare, qui sua patrimonia ignorant, qui domos marmoribus vestiunt,

qui uno filo villarum insuunt pretia; huic seni nudo quid umquam defuit? Vos gemma bibitis, ille naturae concavis manibus satisfecit. Vos in tunicis aurum texitis, ille ne vilissimi quidem indumentum habuit mancipii vestri. Sed e contrario illi pauperculo paradisus patet, vos auratos gehenna suscipiet. Ille vestem Christi, nudus licet, tamen servavit; vos vestiti sericis, indumentum Christi perdidistis. Paulus vilissimo pulvere coopertus iacet resurrecturus in gloriam: vos operosa saxis sepulcra premunt cum vestris opibus arsuros. Parcite, quaeso, vos, parcite saltem divitiis quas amatis. Cur et mortuos vestros auratis obvolvitis vestibus? Cur ambitio inter luctus lacrymasque non cessat? An cadavera divitum nisi in serico putrescere nesciunt?[107]

This description of luxury is not entirely original. The phrase *gemma bibitis* comes from Vergil's satiric denunciation of urban luxury at the end of the second book of the *Georgics*.[108] The scornful reference to necklaces as "estates and country houses sewn on one thread" is derived from a writer who spiritually was closely akin to Jerome. Tertullian, in an attack on luxury, says of necklaces, *Uno lino decies sestertium inseritur.*[109] Jerome's scorn and distaste are even more ardent than Tertullian's. Later in the passage, however, Jerome is clothing in Christian garb a traditional piece of pagan moralism when, turning to the silk-clad men who do not even know how much money they have, who dress their homes in marble and drink from jeweled cups, he says that in spite of their sculptured tombs they are doomed to burn in hell, wealth and all. We may compare Horace, *Carmen* ii. 14. 5-12:

Non, si trecenis, quotquot eunt dies,
　amice, places illacrimabilem
Plutona tauris, qui ter amplum
　Geryonen Tityonque tristi

compescit unda, scilicet omnibus,
quicumque terrae munere vescimur,
　enaviganda, sive reges
　sive inopes erimus coloni.

Jerome's reference to burning in hell adds a superficially Christian color to his invective against luxury. Nonetheless, the traditional spirit of this passage is plain. Jerome's remarks are in fact a Christian version of the attacks on luxury found in Stoic literature and epecially in Seneca.[110]

The *Life of Malchus* belongs to a later period of Jerome's life, the early years of his settlement in Bethlehem.[111] His view of society had scarcely improved in the years which separated the biography of Paul from that of Malchus. On the contrary, his opinions had grown far more critical in that he came to see the level of human civilization in general as having sunk to a new low. The Church too had shared in this decline. A separate chapter will be devoted to Jerome's

bitter remarks on the corrupt state of the Church. Here, however, a passage must be pointed out in which the deterioration of the Church appears to be mentioned as part of the larger decline of human society as a whole. In his introduction to the *Life of Malchus,* Jerome declares that he is planning to write a complete history of the Church,

ab adventu Salvatoris usque ad nostram aetatem, id est, ab apostolis usque ad nostri temporis faecem, quomodo et per quos Christi ecclesia nata sit, et adulta, persecutionibus creverit, et martyriis coronata sit; et postquam ad Christianos principes venerit, potentia quidem et divitiis maior, sed virtutibus minor facta sit.[112]

The reference to *faecem nostri temporis* implies that society has been steadily declining until the bottom has been reached in Jerome's own day.[113] We have seen above that such a view is common to moralists and especially to satiric moralists. But as a Christian critic of his times Jerome sees the Church as having taken part in this decline. The sentence in which the stages of the Church's deterioration are expressed bears a remarkable similarity to a passage in which Gibbon outlines the early history of Christianity: "The indissoluble connexion of civil and ecclesiastical affairs has compelled and encouraged me to relate the progress, the persecutions, the establishment, the divisions, the final triumph, and the gradual corruption of Christianity."[114] Since the chapter of Gibbon in which the sentence is found is replete with references to Jerome's works in general and to the *Life of Malchus* in particular, it is possible that Gibbon was recalling here the passage in which Jerome described the decline of Christianity.[115] It would be indeed ironic if the great critic of Christianity were borrowing the words of the most ardent champion of orthodoxy to sketch the Church's gradual corruption.

Polemical Works

The works written by Jerome expressly to crush his personal enemies and those of the Church are, as might be expected, filled with the bitterest kind of satiric references to individual persons. They are not, however, entirely devoid of caustic remarks on larger and more general themes, the vices of society as a whole.

One of Jerome's most acid polemical works is his pamphlet against Jovinianus. This "Urprotestant" held, among other heterodox opinions, the view that fasting was no more holy than moderate eating *cum actione gratiarum*. This opinion gave Jerome the opportunity to describe and lampoon gluttony in two highly colored passages:

Propter brevem gulae voluptatem, terrae lustrantur et maria; et ut mulsum vinum pretiosusque cibus

Painting of St. Jerome in his study, by Vittore Carpaccio (c.1460-1525).

fauces nostras transeat, totius vitae opera desu-
damus.[116]

The again:

Cum variis nidoribus fumant patinae, ad esum sui,
expleta esurie, quasi captivos trahunt. Unde et morbi
ex saturitate nimia concitantur; multique impatien-
tiam gulae vomitu remediantur; et quod turpiter
ingesserunt, turpius egerunt. . . . Noli timere ne, si
carnes non comederis, aucupes, et venatores frustra
artificia didicerint.[117]

Suddenly Jerome appears to realize the kinship between his theme and the ridicule on sensuality in
pagan satire, for into this specifically Christian
attack on an enemy of fasting, he introduces
Horace:

Irridet Horatius appetitum ciborum, qui consumpti
reliquerunt poenitentiam:

Sperne voluptates, nocet empta dolore

voluptas.

Et cum in amoenissimo agro in morsum voluptu-
osorum hominum se crassum pinguemque describeret, lusit his versibus:

Me pinguem et nitidum, bene curata cute,
    vises,
cum ridere voles, Epicuri de grege porcum.[118]

Jerome then returns to a more specifically Christian
tone, as in a vivid passage he warns those who eat
even simple foods to avoid excess:

Nothing so overwhelms the mind as a full and boiling
belly which turns every which way and releases itself
with a blast in belching and breaking wind. What
kind of fasting is it . . . when we are swollen with
yesterday's banquets and our throat becomes merely
a waiting room for the latrine? And while we wish
to acquire a reputation for prolonged abstinence, we
eat so much that the next night will hardly see it
digested. Accordingly, this ought not be called fasting
so much as drunkenness and stin-king indigestion.[119]

This detailed description of the effects of overeating reveals Jerome as an extremely vigorous and effective ridiculer of human behavior, but as one who did not always bother to adhere to the highest standards of taste.

Turning now to a much later controversial work, the **Dialogus contra Pelagianos,** in which an orthodox Catholic and a follower of the Pelagian heresy discuss the problem of free will, we find Jerome satirizing a defect which was characteristic of a Christian society and for which there was no pagan counterpart—hypocrisy in the giving of alms. Nevertheless the orthodox interlocutor is probably quoting classical satire when he addresses the heretic and declares that the Gospel injunction to love one's enemies is hard to fulfill: *Forsitan in vestro coetu invenitur, apud nos rara avis est.*[120] The orthodox speaker then draws a brief picture of brotherly love as he has seen it:

> Ad largiendum frustum panis et binos nummulos praeco conducitur, et extendentes manum, huc illucque circumspicimus, quae si nullus viderit, contractior fit. Esto, unus de mille inveniatur, qui ista non faciat.[121]

Here again we see Jerome using satire to expose the failure of a Christian ideal. One characteristic feature of satiric diction which occurs often in Jerome's passages of ridicule is the use of scornful diminutives (e.g. *nummulos*), a device favored also by Juvenal.[122]

Exegetical Works

In studying St. Jerome's contributions to biblical exegesis, the most voluminous category of his writings, one must deal with works of a highly derivative nature, for Jerome is largely dependent on the long traditions of Jewish and Christian exegesis and especially on the works of Origen and the Alexandrian school.[123] Nonetheless, these writings are extremely rich sources for comments on the contemporary world, for time and time again we find Jerome applying the moral strictures of the Old Testament to his own day and embroidering these strictures in a highly picturesque manner.

The earliest of Jerome's commentaries, that on Ecclesiastes, is full of satiric descriptions of the gatherers of worldly wealth. Thus, expounding Ecclesiastes 2:24, *Non est bonum bomini, nisi quod comedat, et bibat, . . .* he writes: *Quid enim boni est, aut quale Dei munus, vel suis opibus inhiare, et quasi fugientem praecerpere voluptatem, vel alienum laborem in proprias delicias vertere?*[124] With the vivid image *opibus inhiare* we may compare *opibus incubare,* used by Jerome elsewhere in this commentary.[125] With both these images may be compared Horace's

> congestis undique saccis
> indormis inhians.[126]

It is possible, though of course uncertain, that Jerome had Horace's first satire in mind when he used these two images, for elsewhere in this commentary he makes clear and abundant use of Horace's ridicule of worldly pursuits.[127]

The words of the Preacher, "a time to cast away stones, and a time to gather stones," rouse Jerome to an attack on the worldly passion for building:

> Alii congregent lapides ad aedificia construenda, alii quae exstructa sunt destruant, secundum illud Horatianum:
>
> Diruit, aedificat, mutat quadrata rotundis.
> Aestuat et vitae disconvenit ordine toto.[128]

Jerome here takes up a theme often discussed in his letters, using the words of a pagan satirist to support the Old Testament moralist.

We find exactly the same procedure when Ecclesiastes speaks against the lovers of gold.[130] Jerome calls upon Horace to support the strictures:

> Flacci quoque super hoc concordante sententia, qui ait:
>
> Semper avarus eget. . . .
>
> Quanto enim maior fuerit substantia, tanto plures ministros habebit, qui opes devorent congregatas. Ille autem videat tantum quod habet, et plus quam unius hominis cibum capere non possit.[131]

The last sentence may be an oblique reference to Horace's

> Non tuus hoc capiet venter plus ac meus.[132]

Jerome's description of a typical rich man in this commentary is pure satire:

> Dives vero distentus dapibus, et cogitationibus in diversa laceratus, dormire non [valet], redundante crapula, et incocto cibo in stomachi angustiis aestuante.[133]

In contrast to the corruption and degeneracy here portrayed, Jerome pictures the ascetic ideal of a poor man walking the straight and narrow path which leads to eternal life.[134]

After commenting on Ecclesiastes, Jerome turned his attention to the New Testament, expounding Paul's letters to Philemon, the Galatians, Titus, and the

Ephesians. The first three of these works are virtually devoid of satiric remarks on the contemporary world, except for some caustic descriptions of clerical hypocrisy, a discussion of which may be deferred until we turn to Jerome's satire on the decline of the Church.[135] However, in expounding the Epistle to the Ephesians, Jerome delivers a curious attack on various forms of secular activity:

> Nonne vobis videtur in vanitate sensus et obscuritate mentis ingredi, qui diebus ac noctibus in dialectica arte torquetur: qui physicus perscrutator oculos trans coelum levat, et ultra profundum terrarum et abyssi quoddam inane demergit, qui iambum struit, qui tantam metrorum silvam in suo studiosus corde distinguit et congerit; et (ut in alteram partem transeam) qui divitias per fas et nefas quaerit. Qui adulatur regibus, haereditates captat alienas, et opes congregat, quas in momento cui sit relicturus, ignorat?[136]

Jerome's disapproval of *dialectica ars* is not surprising, for he frequently expresses dislike of subtle argumentation, connecting it with the treachery of heretics.[137] More puzzling is the attack on physical scientists and on poets. In view of the age in which Jerome lived, an age which could never be justly criticized for excessive love of science or poetry, these words of strong disapproval seem highly artificial. Yet Jerome does display a theoretical dislike of scientific speculation by twice quoting sympathetically the line of Aristophanes in which the poet mocks the physical speculations of Socrates. . . .

Since Jerome's attack on intellectual endeavor is accompanied by deprecatory remarks on the gathering of wealth and on legacy hunting, the words of disapproval should probably be considered to reflect a monkish rejection of all forms of worldly activity, including intellectual labor. This same attitude is reflected in other passages in this commentary where Jerome rails against those "who dispute about physical things, claim they can count the sands of the shore and the drops in the ocean, who, drunk with thoughts of this world, vomit, go mad, and fall headlong."[139] It is of course highly incongruous for St. Jerome to express such violent disapproval of worldly knowledge, since, as we have seen, he elsewhere (**Letters 33, 43,** and **53**) points to the lack of interest in secular learning as an indication of the degeneracy of the age. Jerome was never able to reconcile in his own mind his love of worldly knowledge and his feeling that such knowledge was fundamentally unchristian.

After his exposition of the Pauline Epistles, Jerome returned to the Old Testament and began his series of commentaries on the twelve minor Hebrew prophets. In interpreting Micah, he mentions in passing the lovers of *villas istius saeculi,* a phrase in which the image of a large and noble home is significantly used to rep-

resent worldliness.[140] Then in his commentary on Zephaniah, Jerome delivers a brief but effective attack on effeminacy, an onslaught which in the bitterness of its ridicule recalls Juvenal's second satire: *Peribit qui in femineo languore mollitus comam nutrit, vellit pilos, cutem polit, et ad speculum comitur, quae proprie passio et insania feminarum est.*[141] We have no indication that Jerome is here referring to a particular individual. Apparently the words are aimed at a widespread vice of the age.

The commentary on Zechariah belongs to a later period of Jerome's life, the opening years of the fifth century.[142] Taking his cue from the words of the prophet, *Quis enim despexit dies parvos?* Jerome lampoons the worldly splendor of the rich: *Cum viderimus potentes saeculi fulgere auro, purpura, gemmis rutilare, circumdari exercitu, dicamus in nobis: quis, putas, despicit dies parvos?*[143] The satiric element in this passage lies in two words, *rutilare* and *exercitu.* These are the two brush strokes which transform a simple drawing into a caricature of arrogant pomp. Jerome achieves his aim of exposure and ridicule by a subtle use of two exaggerated descriptive details.

In the commentary on Amos, too, Jerome lashes out at the rich and powerful. Explicating Amos 6:1, "Woe to them that are at ease in Zion," he says:

> Isti sunt capita populorum, qui confidunt in divitiis, et opulenti sunt in Sion. . . . Et ingrediuntur pompatice domum Israel, ut tumorem animi corpus ostendat, et pomparum ferculis similes esse videantur.[144]

This passage reveals Jerome as a mosaic artist setting into his works highly colored extracts from pagan literature. The satiric description of a haughty manner of walking borrows from Cicero's warning: *Cavendum autem est, ne . . . tarditatibus utamur in ingressu mollioribus, ut pomparum ferculis similes esse videamur.*[145] Jerome the *Ciceronianus* cannot repress a reminiscence of his beloved author even in a commentary on an Old Testament prophet. Evidently the phrase *pomparum ferculis similes* struck Jerome as an apt portrayal of arrogance, for he uses the expression on several occasions.[146]

The detailed commentaries on the three major prophets, Isaiah, Jeremiah, and Ezekiel, were composed by Jerome toward the close of his life. They belong to the years 408-416. The earliest of them, that on Isaiah, contains several bitter references to the faults of the age. It is an age of ignorance in which men's ears are scornful of the products of hard intellectual labor but are delighted by showy eloquence. We become nauseated by the effort required for the understanding of Sacred Scripture.[147] This theme recalls Jerome's attacks on the ignorance of his age in his letters written from Rome.[148] Furthermore, claims Jerome, it is an age in which the rich are flattered but the poor despised, in which the rich taste all the sensual delights of luxurious banquets in houses whose ceilings are gilded, whose walls are clothed in crusts of marble and are agleam with cut ivory, while the poor, without the meanest shelter, freeze to death.[149] This attack on current society is elicited by Isaiah's apocalyptic vision of the destruction of the earthly city. It clearly demonstrates Jerome's use of biblical exhortations as the starting point for his expression of anger at the elements in contemporary society which he considered corrupt and unchristian.

Two of Jerome's attacks on the vices of society in the commentary on Isaiah show the influence of Horace. The first example is obvious and certain: Isaiah's attack on avarice recalls the remark of Horace, *Semper avarus eget.*[150] The second instance is less definite. Jerome describes the dissatisfaction of men with their place in life:

> Saepe videmus in saeculo quosdam de alio proposito transire ad aliud. Verbi gratia, ut qui militiam male experti sunt, transeunt ad negotiationem. Rursumque causidicos bellatorum arma corripere. Mutant industriam, ut mutent infelicitatem.[151]

The sentiment of this passage is highly reminiscent of the opening lines of the first satire of Horace's first book, in which the longing of businessmen, soldiers, and lawyers to change their role in life is described. Although there is no verbal similarity between Jerome and Horace, it is possible that Jerome is here drawing upon the pagan satirist or at least upon the same moralistic material which Horace used in composing Satire I. 1.

The commentary on Ezekiel belongs to the years 410-412 and is strongly marked by the tragic political events of those years. The fate of the Roman nobility in Alaric's capture of the city is reflected in the remark that the rich, whose lives were passed amid silk, gems, and the weight of gold and silver, end their days as beggars.[152] Those who belched with their fullness, who did not even know the extent of their wealth, are now in need of food, clothing, and shelter.[153] In spite of the formerly dissipated lives of such people, Jerome gazes upon their fate with tears and groans. And yet he must admit that their spirits have been but little softened by their chastening. On the contrary, they seek gold even in their captivity. Some of the rich have gone so far as to pretend by their vile clothing that they are poor, though they "lie upon the wealth of Croesus."[154] In spite of Jerome's brief attempt to be sympathetic to the plight of the rich, his more usual attitude returns as he attacks their hyprocrisy and secret avarice. Indeed, his view of the rich is only partially and temporarily governed by the actuality of their sad fate at the time he is writing, for sometimes his words recall an earlier period of dissipation before the disastrous events of the Gothic invasion. Thus he suggests that the rich do not dress to keep out the cold but rather choose garments *quae tenuitate sui, corpora nuda demonstrent.*[155]

Conclusion

St. Jerome's sense of the decline of civilization and his disgust with the vices of "the world" form an important theme in all categories of his writings, from the letters written in the desert of Chalcis when he was a young man to his late exegetical and homiletic works. Every opportunity offered by a biblical text to mount an attack upon contemporary failings is immediately seized upon, with the result that these invectives sometimes appear as leitmotivs automatically recalled whenever the context of a passage suggests worldly sin. Jerome can rarely mention the contemporary world without adding a portrayal of silken garments, gluttonous banquets, and marble-encrusted buildings. In Jerome's mind the disastrous political events of the day are the result of the decline of morals.

To be sure, disdain for the contemporary world and its standards is an attitude to be expected in the writings of an ascetic enthusiast such as Jerome. Moreover, it should be considered neither surprising nor coincidental that the manner in which Jerome expresses his disdain closely resembles in thought and diction passages in such pagan writers as Horace, Persius, Seneca, and Juvenal. All these writers were influenced to a greater or lesser extent by Stoicism, and between the ethics of the Stoa and those of ascetic Christianity were many points of contact.[156] Jerome himself refers to *Stoici, qui nostro dogmati in plerisque concordant.*[157] Certainly the Stoic doctrine that virtue is the only source of happiness led to a repudiation of commonly accepted standards of behavior. There is a powerful note of asceticism in later Stoicism.[158] Zeller compares the Stoic sense of the depth and extent of human depravity as expressed, for instance, by Seneca to the attitude of the early Christian theologians.[159] The forged correspondence between Seneca and St. Paul implies that the early Christians sensed in Seneca a kindred spirit. St. Jerome includes Seneca in his catalogue of illustrious Christians.[160] But Jerome's realization of the similarity of his own moral outlook to that of certain pagan writers extended beyond an appreciation of Seneca alone. As a scholar whose mind was deeply imbued with pagan Latin letters, Jerome seized upon those passages in pagan writers in which contemporary standards were lampooned and in which he found abumbrated his feelings toward his own society. The richest source of such passages were the satiric poets.

However, in addition to Jerome's ascetic outlook on the world and his acquaintance with pagan Latin letters, the element of personal animus should not be overlooked in investigating the hostilities of this harsh and bitter man. Jerome had had his worldly ambitions, the complete failure of which filled him with bitterness toward the society that had refused to recognize his claims and that had driven him into the comparative retirement of his Bethlehem monastery.

Yet it is too simple to see in Jerome's attacks on society merely the propaganda of a leader of the monastic movement or the petulant anger of a disappointed recluse. The ideals which lay behind his satiric attacks were higher. We find them expressed in a passage in his commentary on Jonah: "It is difficult for powerful men and noble men and rich men, and much more difficult for eloquent men, to believe in God. For their mind is blinded by riches and wealth and luxury, so that, surrounded by vices, they cannot see the virtue and simplicity of Holy Scripture."[161] Again, in the commentary on Ezekiel: "Pride, satiety of food, abundance of possessions, leisure and pleasure are the sins of Sodom and on account of them forgetfulness of God follows, that forgetfulness which imagines that present goods will last forever and that the necessities of life will never be needed."[162] Jerome's feeling that contemporary morals had reached a new depth of debasement was, then, the same sense of the failure of Christianity to reform society completely which kindled the growth of the monastic movement in the latter part of the fourth century. To be sure, the highest ideal of the ascetic was complete indifference to the affairs of the world: *Nos quoque eos, qui ad saeculi mala et bona vel contristantur vel exultant, mulieres appellemus, molli et effeminato animo.*[163] But St. Jerome, unable by nature to achieve this ideal, returns again and again *ad saeculi mala.* His caustic personality and his keen and penetrating powers of observation precluded his merely denouncing the social evils which he perceived. Rather he portrays them with an exactness and an amplitude whose obvious aim is to lampoon and ridicule. Even in his monk's cell at Bethlehem his mind ranged over the faults and failings of the Worldly City, and he could truthfully say in a passage in which his devotion to Christian scholarship and to the ascetic life is strikingly blended with his concern for the fate of the world: *Totum me huic trado studio, et quasi in quadam specula constitutus, mundi huius turbines atque naufragia, non absque gemitu et dolore contemplor.*[164]

Notes

[1] *Sat.* 1. 87.

[2] *Sat.* 13. 28-30. In line 28 *nona* is Clausen's reading. Others read *nunc* with the *P* manuscript. For the sentiment, cf. *Sat.* 6. 1-20 and 11. 56-161.

[3] Persius 1. 1. This line probably comes from Lucilius.

See Marx, I, 9. For St. Jerome's use of the line, see *Anecdot. Mared.,* III, 2, 130, and III, 3, 83.

[4] *Epist.* 86. 4. Cf. *Quaest. nat.* i. xvii. 8 for a similar idealization of Scipio's age.

[5] Amm. Marc. xiv. 6. 11. Note the characteristic *at nunc* with which both Seneca and Ammianus introduce their satiric description of present decadence. Cf. Juvenal 11. 120: *At nunc divitibus cenandi nulla voluptas.* Also Juvenal 14. 189: *Haec illi veteres praecepta minoribus, at nunc. . . .*

[6] Amm. Marc. xxviii. 4. 17.

[7] For the *locus communis de saeculo,* see J. de Decker, *Juvenalis declamans* (Ghent, 1913), 22-38.

[8] Letter 107. 1. For date, Cavallera, II, 47. Cf. Prudentius, *Peristephanon,* II, 509-529.

[9] Letter 106. 1. On the identity of Sunnia and Fretela see J. Zeiler, "St. Jérôme et les Goths," in *Miscellanea Geronimiana* (Rome, 1920), 123-130. He accepts the identification of the two with the editors of the Latin-Gothic Bible, the *Codex Brixianus.* He also identifies Fretela with a Gothic bishop of Thracian Heraclea of that name, but Cavallera (I, 292, n. 1) demurs. De Bruyne believes the circumstances of the letter to be completely fictitious, *Zeitschr. für neutest. Wiss.,* XXVIII (1929), 1-13.

[10] *PL* 25, 504A. See J.-R. Palanque, "St. Jerome and the Barbarians," in *A Monument to St. Jerome* (New York, 1952), 173-199. Also, E. Demougeot, "St. Jérôme les Oracles Sibyllins et Stilicho," *Rev. des Et. Anciennes,* LIV (1952), 83-92, who gives an account of other contemporary predictions of the end of the Roman Empire.

[11] Letter 60. 16. H. Levy has demonstrated that this passage was influenced by Claudian's *In Rufinum:* see "Claudian's *In Rufinum* and an Epistle of St. Jerome," *Am. Journ. Philol.,* LXIX (1948), 62-68.

[12] Letter 123. 15 and 16. Cf. Lucan v. 274. Jerome's reaction to the capture of Rome is expressed in Letter 127. 12. For St. Augustine's first reaction, see his sermon *De urbis excidio,* ii. 3 (*PL* 40, 718): *Horrenda nobis nuntiata sunt; strages facta, incendia, rapinae, interfectiones, excruciationes hominum. Verum est, multa audivimus, omnia gemuimus, saepe flevimus, vix consolati sumus; non abnuo, non nego multa nos audisse, multa in illa urbe esse commissa.* For a summary of contemporary views on the collapse of the Roman world, see H. Daniel-Rops, *The Church in the Dark Ages,* tr. by A. Butler (London, 1959), 76-79.

[13] Letter 60. 17.

[14] So called after Didymus Chalcenterus, of whom Origen is the Christian equivalent. Jerome says of him, *Tanto in sanctarum scriptuarum commentariis sudore laboravit, ut iuste adamantis nomen acceperit* (Letter 33. 4).

[15] It is noteworthy that Jerome here (Letter 33. 1) chides his contemporaries for their lack of interest in *secular* letters, since throughout his biblical commentaries he constantly derides heretics and pagans for their devotion to *saecularis sapientia* (see below, Chapter V). This incongruity is of singular importance in Jerome's life and career. Jerome again lampoons the ignorance of his age in Letter 43. 2.

[16] Letter 33. 3. The date is probably 385. See Cavallera, II, 26. There are very similar passages in Letter 27. 1 and 52. 6. See also S. Dill, *Roman Society in the Last Century of the Western Empire* (London, 1899), 130-131.

[17] Lucilius iv, 167; viii, 308-318; ix, 327-329; xiii, 140, in Marx's edition. Varro had treated the subject in his Menippean satire . . . (Schanz-Hosius I⁴, 558); Horace in *Sat.* ii. 2 and 4. For a list of satiric passages on gluttony (many of them similar to Jerome's attack) in Seneca and Juvenal, see Carl Schneider, *Juvenal und Seneca* (Würzburg, 1930), 27-28. For the Greek background of this topic, see G. Fiske, *Lucilius and Horace* (Madison, 1920), 398-405.

[18] Tertullian *De Pallio* v. 6; Amm. Marc. xxviii. 4. 13.

[19] Amm. Marc. xiv. 6. 16.

[20] *Ibid.*, xxx. 4. 17.

[21] Persius 6. 24.

[22] Juvenal 4. 139-143. Cf. *Sat.* 14. 8-10, Juvenal's description of the education of a youthful glutton who:

"Boletum condire et eodem iure natantis
mergere ficedulas didicit nebulone parente
et cana monstrante gula. . . . "

[23] Juvenal 4. 23 and II. 1; Martial ii. 69. 3; ii. 89. 5; iii. 2. 1. On Paxamus, see Morel in Pauly-Wissowa-Kroll, 36³, 2436.

[24] Horace *Sat.* ii. 5 is devoted to legacy hunting. Also Juvenal 1. 37-44; 5. 137-145; 12. 93-130. See in addition, Horace *Epist.* i. 1. 78-79, Cicero *Paradoxa Stoic.* 5. 2. 39, Seneca *De ben.* vi. 38 and *Ad Marc.* 19. 2.

[25] Amm. Marc. xxviii. 4. 22.

[26] See *Codex Theodosianus* 16. 2. 20, and *Novels of Valentinian,* III. 21. 3.

[27] Grützmacher, II, 223.

[28] Letter 33. 6.

[29] For Rome as Babylon, see Letter 45. 6. Cf. *Praefat. trans. libri Didymi de Spiritu Sancto, PL* 23, 107A: *Cum in Babylone versarer: et purpuratae meretricis essem colonus.*

[30] Letter 24. 5.

[31] *Psychomachia,* 310-343.

[32] By T. R. Glover, *Life and Letters in the Fourth Century* (Cambridge, 1901), 264.

[33] Letter 43. 2. Cf. Letter 33.

[34] Letter 43. 2.

[35] *Ibid.*

[36] Asyndeton as a device for creating vividness is common in Juvenal. See I. G. Scott, *The Grand Style in the Satires of Juvenal,* in "Smith College Classical Studies" (Northampton, 1927), 26; also William S. Anderson, "Juvenal and Quintilian," *Yale Classical Studies,* XVII (1961), 84. For asyndeton in Jerome, see J. N. Hritzu, *The Style of the Letters of St. Jerome (Cath. U. of Am. Patristic Studies,* LX), 48.

[37] Letter 43. 3.

[38] Letter 22. 16 and 28. It seems not previously to have been noticed that the expression *matronarum senatus* is probably derived from Porphyry's lost work on chastity in which he made bitter remarks on women and marriage. In his commentary on Isaiah, *PL* 24, 67C, Jerome says that Porphyry had spoken of *mulieres* and *matronae* as a *senatus.* E. Bickel has brilliantly succeeded in reconstructing Porphyry's work on chastity and has shown that Jerome was thoroughly acquainted with it and used it in writing *Adversus Iovinianum.* See Bickel's *Diatribe in Senecae Philosophi fragmenta* (Leipzig, 1915), 195-204. Since the phrase *matronarum senatus* does not seem to be derived from any of Porphyry's extant works (Luebeck did not attribute it to any known work), it is probable that it was derived from this work, in which Porphyry made bitter references to women.

[39] Horace *Sat.* ii. 6. 17-58, and Juvenal *Sat.* 3 and 11. 183-208. Cf. Jerome Letter 125. 8: *Mihi oppidum carcer est, et solitudo paradisus. Quid desideramus urbium frequentiam, qui de singularitate censemur?*

[40] Letter 43. 3. Cf. the praise of country life as an aid to asceticism in *Adv. Iovin., PL* 23, 311C-312A.

[41] Quintilian ii. 4. 24.

[42] Chronology in Cavallera, II, 26.

[43] On the relationship between Jerome and Damasus see esp. A. Penna, *S. Girolamo* (Rome and Turin, 1949), 64-74, and E. Caspar, *Geschichte des Papstums* (Tübingen, 1930), I, 246-256. Jerome claims to have been the Pope's mouthpiece, Letter 45. 3. The extremely unfavorable opinion of Damasus found in Amm. Marc. xxvii. 3. 12. and in the *Libellus precum* (*PL* 13, 81-112, and *CSEL,* XXXV, ed. O. Guenther) is reflected nowhere in Jerome's writings.

[44] Letter 38. 5. The sentiment is repeated in Letter 54. 5.

[45] Letter 38. 5.

[46] Cf. Letter 107. 10. There are open references to this line of Persius in *Adv. Iovin.* 329C and *Comm. in Jer., PL* 24, 794C; *CSEL,* LIX, 164. Conington in his edition of Persius refers to the scholiast's comments on this line and to Isidore of Seville *Orig.* xi. 1. 136. for the original meaning of *aqualiculus.* Conington suggests that Persius was the first to apply the word to the human paunch.

[47] Letter 39. 3.

[48] Letter 45. 2.

[49] Letter 45. 3. It is not known whether Jerome had any reasonable grounds for this claim. See E. Caspar, *Geschichte des Papstums,* I, 257.

[50] Letter 45. 5.

[51] *Contra Ruf.* iii. 22 (*PL* 23, 494C).

[52] This whole tour is described in detail in Letter 108.

[53] Letter 46. Although Jerome's relations with Rome were broken for about seven years after his departure, the favorable view of the spiritual life of the Holy Land expressed in this letter suggests that it was written not too long after Jerome's settlement there. See Cavallera, II, 43; the year 392 is a probable date.

[54] Cavallera, I, 165.

[55] Letter 46. 10 and 11.

[56] *Ep.* 90. 42. *Laquearia* are used with the same moral significance in *Ep.* 90. 15.

[57] *Sat.* 7. 178. Cf. *Sat.* 4. 6 and 14. 85-95.

[58] Letter 14. 6.

[59] Letter 52. 1, dated 394. With Jerome's use here of the word *lusimus* may be compared Horace's references to his writing of satire as *ludere* and *illudere* (*Sat.* i. 10. 37 and i. 4. 39). . . .

[61] Letter 46. 11.

[62] Letter 52. 10. Jerome is referring here, of course, to the corruption of the clergy.

[63] Letter 58. 7.

[64] Letter 130. 14. Cf. *Comm. in Zach., PL* 25, 1467B, where the language describing the outward luxury of churches is very similar but where the tone is much less disapproving, since there Jerome is trying to use these outward signs as proof of the progress of Christianity. On the "marble crusts" mentioned by Jerome cf. Ulpian's legal principle that when a building is sold, *Quae tabulae pictae pro tectorio includuntur itemque crustae marmoreae aedium sunt.* See *Digest* 19, 1, 17, 3; *Corpus iuris civilis,* I (Berlin, 1954), 280.

[65] Grützmacher, III, 256. The letter is attributed to the year 414 by N. Pronberger, *Beiträge zur Chronologie der Briefe des hl. Hieronymus* (Amberg, 1913), 95.

[66] It is possible that the disapproval of ornate churches expressed in the spurious Letter 148. 19 influenced its erroneous attribution to Jerome. Vallarsi (*PL* 22, 1204, Note D) attributed the letter to Sulpicius Severus. As a leader of the monastic movement, Sulpicius, like Jerome, would probably have felt the ascetic's dislike of elaborate churches. For Jerome's attitude toward the plastic arts in general, see Eiswirth, *Hieronymus' Stellung,* 53-72.

[67] Letter 46. 12.

[68] Jerome insists (Letter 24. 1), *Nemo reprehendat quod in epistulis aliquos aut laudamus aut carpimus, cum et in arguendis malis sit correptio ceterorum et in optimis praedicandis bonorum ad virtutem studia concitentur.* Jerome well knew the effect his satire was creating. Writing to Marcella, he says, *Scio te cum ista legeris rugare frontem, et libertatem rursum seminarium timere rixarum, ac meum, si fieri potest, os digito velle comprimere, ne audeam dicere quae alii facere non erubescunt* (Letter 27. 2).

[69] Letter 53. 3; Revelation 3:7.

[70] Letter 53. 7. The quotation is from Horace, *Epist.* ii. 1. 115-117. P. Courcelle believes that these barbs are directed specifically against Vigilantius. See his "Paulin de Nole et Saint Jérôme," in *Revue des Etudes Latines,* XXV (1947), 263, n. 4.

[71] Letter 53. 7. Cf. Persius 3. 82, from which Jerome

has borrowed some descriptive details.

[72] Letter 45. 2.

[73] Letter 45. 3.

[74] Eiswirth, *Hieronymus' Stellung,* 43.

[75] Letter 58. 4. Apparently Paulinus took Jerome's portrayal of Jerusalem seriously. In his Letter XXXI. 3 (*CSEL,* XXIX, 270), Paulinus repeats part of Jerome's description. See the work of Courcelle cited above (n. 70), p. 254, n. 1. Jerome's inconsistency is clearly revealed when Letter 58, in which Jerusalem is described as another Rome, is compared with Letter 127. 8, where Rome is hailed as a new Jerusalem.

[76] Grützmacher, II, 228.

[77] Cavallera, II, 89; Labourt's edition of the Letters, III, 235; Eiswirth, *Hieronymus' Stellung,* 73-96. Courcelle's brilliant reconstruction of Paulinus' letters to Jerome requires Letter 58 to precede Letter 53. See above, n. 70.

[78] Cavallera, II, 90. Even if Cavallera's reasonable view is accepted, the truth of the following remark of Grützmacher cannot be denied: "Dem vielgewandten Hieronymus ist es natürlich ebenso gut möglich, für die Wallfahrt nach Jerusalem, wenn er sie wünscht, wie gegen eine solche, wenn er sie nicht wünscht, eine Fülle von Argumenten beizurbringen" (II, 228).

[79] Letter 66. 4. . . .

[81] Letter 66. 5.

[82] Letter 45. 3.

[83] Letter 66. 5. This passage may recall Vergil *Georgics* ii. 461-462.

[84] Letter 46. 12.

[85] On this important aristocrat, who played a considerable role in many of the religious controversies of the later fourth century, see W. Ensslin in Pauly-Wissowa-Kroll, 36[2], 296-298.

[86] Letter 66. 6.

[87] On the opposition to monasticism see Fliche and Martin, *Histoire de l'Eglise* (Paris, 1950), III, 358-364.

[88] Letter 66. 4.

[89] *Ibid.*

[90] Letter 66. 5.

[91] Letter 66. 8.

[92] Juvenal 11. 139. Petronius too uses the birds of Phasis in his satiric references to gluttony, *Satyricon* 119, lines 36-37. . . .

[94] Letter 107. 10.

[95] *Sat.* i. 2. 8. Cf. Tertullian *De ieiunio* i. 1 for a similar use of *ingluvies.*

[96] Persius 1. 57. Cf. Letter 38. 5 and *Adv. Iovin., PL* 23, 329C.

[97] Letter 123. 16.

[98] Letter 125. 20.

[99] Letter 123. 14.

[100] Letter 128. 5. Cf. Letter 23. 15. Cf. also Tertullian *Apologeticum* xxxix. 14: *De nobis scilicet Diogenis dictum est: "Megarenses obsonant quasi crastina die morituri, aedificant vero quasi numquam morituri"* (*CSEL,* LXIX, 94).

[101] Letter 14. 6.

[102] Letter 43. 3.

[103] Letter 22. 11.

[104] Letter 45. 5.

[105] *Decline and Fall,* ch. xxxvii, n. 17 (Bury's ed., IV, 66). It might be objected that Jerome was well aware that he was not writing history in composing these lives. This is probably true. But since the standard histories of literature class the hagiographical writings as historical works, it has been thought wise to accept this classification. See Schanz-Hosius 4[1], 435; Bardenhewer, 3, 637; Altaner, *Patrologie,* 361. Cf. also De Labriolle, II, 507. For a perceptive treatment of these biographies, which were meant to be primarily works of edification, see H. Delehaye, *Les Légendes Hagiographiques* (3d ed.; Brussels, 1927).

[106] Cavallera, II, 16-17.

[107] *PL* 23, 28A-30A. Cf. *Comm. in Matt., PL* 26, 223C: *Ex simplici sepultura Domini, ambitio divitum condemnatur, qui ne in tumulis quidem possunt carere divitiis.*

[108] *Georgics* ii, 506. The phrase *gemma bibere* is also used in Letter 30. 13. This phrase is also found in Ambrose's satiric denunciation of female luxury: *Illa tibi inponet sumptuum necessitatem, ut gemma bibat, in ostro dormiat, in argentea sponda recumbat.* . . .

De Nabuthae, 5, 25-26. Quoted by Weston, 80.

[109] *De cultu feminarum* I, 9; *CSEL,* LXX, 70. The interpretation of *uno filo villarum insuunt pretia* here given follows Vallarsi's note on the passage. For *pretia* Vallarsi prints *praedia,* which cannot be correct.

[110] E.g., *Naturales quaestiones* i. *praef.* 8: *Non potest [animus] ante contemnere porticus et lacunaria ebore fulgentia et tonsiles silvas et sderivata in domos flumina quam totum circumit mundum et, terrarum orbem superne despiciens.* . . . Cf. *ibid.,* i. xvii and iii. xviii.

[111] Cavallera, II, 27.

[112] *PL* 23, 55A-B.

[113] It is possible that *faecem nostri temporis* refers only to the condition of the Church. It is much more probable however that Jerome here is speaking of the decline of civilization in general, for he expresses this pessimistic view of the world elsewhere. Cf. *Comm. in Eccles., PL* 23, 1090B: *Nunc vero pro saeculorum quotidie in peius labentium vitio.*

[114] *Decline and Fall,* IV, 62.

[115] For references to the *Vita Malchi,* see Gibbon, ch. xxxvii, n. 17 and 34.

[116] *PL* 23, 311A.

[117] *PL* 23, 313B and 315A.

[118] *PL* 23, 315B; Horace *Epist.* i. 2. 55, and i. 4. 15. On Porphyry's influence, see Luebeck, 70.

[119] *PL* 23, 315C.

[120] *PL* 23, 572A-B. It is impossible to determine whether the expression *rara avis* here refers to Persius 1. 46, Juvenal 6. 165, or to the general body of proverbial expressions about *aves* of which other examples are given by A. Otto, *Die Sprichwörter der Römer* (Leipzig, 1890), 51-52. Luebeck, 195, n. 4, attributes the phrase, without giving any authority, to Persius.

[121] *PL* 23, 572A-B. Cf. *Anecdot. Mared.,* III, 2, 256. (*CC* 88, 278): *Invenias aliquos de Christianis ideo dare elemosinam, ut laudentur a populo. Si quando pauper rogat, huc illucque circumspiciunt; et nisi testem viderint, pecuniam non dant. Si solus fuerit, manus contractior est, non dat libenter.*

[122] E.g. 1. 11 *pelliculae;* 1. 40 *unciolam;* 7. 119 *petasunculus;* 13. 40 *virguncula.* On Jerome's use of diminutives, see H. Goelzer, *Etude Lexicographique et Grammaticale de la Latinité de Saint Jérôme* (Paris, 1884), 121-130.

[123] See esp. A. Penna, *Principi e caratere dell' esegesi di S. Girolamo* (Rome, 1950), and L. N. Hartmann, "St. Jerome as an Exegete," in *A Monument to St. Jerome,* ed. F. X. Murphy (New York, 1952), 37-81.

[124] *PL* 23, 1085C; *CC* 72, 272.

[125] *PL* 23, 1100B. Also *Comm. in Jer., PL* 24 742D; *Comm. in Ezech., PL* 25, 290B and 316C.

[126] *Sat.* i. 1. 70-71.

[127] *Sat.* i. 10. 72 is quoted immediately above *opibus inhiare, PL* 23, 1085A. The image of brooding upon wealth may be a reminiscence of Vergil *Aeneid* vi. 610:

"aut qui divitiis soli incubuere repertis."

Cf. *Georgics* ii, 463 and 507 and see also Sulpicius Severus' attack on the clergy: *inhiant possessionibus . . . auro incubant* (*Chron.* i. 23).

[128] *PL* 23, 1088C. Horace *Epist.* i. 1. 99-100. The reversed order in which Jerome cites these lines suggests that he was quoting from memory. . . .

[130] *Eccles.* 5: 10.

[131] *PL* 23, 1109A-B; Horace *Epist.* i. 1. 56. The remarks on the *ministri* who devour the gathered wealth are reminiscent of Horace *Sat.* i. 1. 77-78:

"Formidare malos fures, incendia, servos,
ne te compilent fugientes, hoc iuvat?"

For the thought cf. Juvenal 14. 303-331.

[132] *Sat.* i. 1. 46.

[133] *PL* 23, 1109B-C. *CC* 72, 295.

[134] *PL* 23, 1113B. *CC* 72, 299.

[135] *PL* 23, 452B-C. Below, Chapter IV.

[136] *PL* 26, 536D-537A.

[137] E.g. *PL* 25, 863D, 927A, 1025A, and 1044B. . . .

[139] *PL* 26, 552B; cf. 561B.

[140] *PL* 25, 1167B.

[141] *PL* 25, 1350C.

[142] Cavallera, II, 51-52.

[143] *PL* 25, 1444C.

[144] *PL* 25, 1058A.

[145] *De off.* i. 36. 131.

[146] Cf. Letter 3. 6 and 125. 16.

[147] *PL* 24, 22A and 289D.

[148] Cf. Letters 33. 3; 43. 2; and 53. 5.

[149] *PL* 24, 293A-B.

[150] *PL* 24, 49A; Horace *Epist.* i. 2. 56.

[151] *PL* 24, 288A. The same sense of the weary uselessness of earthly activity is found in Jerome's exposition of the text *Anni nostri sicut aranea meditabuntur.* The psalmist, says Jerome, *nihil pulchrius potuit dicere quam ut humanam vitam et omnem sollicitudinem nostram studiaque describeret, quibus huc illucque discurrimus et opes praeparamus, divitias quaerimus, aedificamus domos, liberos procreamus; et videte cui rei comparantur. Anni nostri sicut aranea meditabuntur* (*Anecdot. Mared.,* II, 3. 65; *CC* 78, 418).

[152] *PL* 25, 71D.

[153] *PL* 25, 175B and 199B.

[154] *PL* 25, 231C-D.

[155] *PL* 24, 432C. Cf. Letter 127. 3.

[156] On the influence of Stoicism on Roman Satire see Duff, *Roman Satire,* 116; for Horace and the Stoa, 78 and 80-81; for Juvenal, 162. Also De Decker, *Juvenalis declamans,* 19-20, and R. Schütze, *Juvenalis ethicus* (Greifswald, 1905). G. Highest, "The Philosophy of Juvenal," *TAPA,* LXXX (1949), 254-270, sees Juvenal as an Epicurean late in life.

[157] *Comm. in Isa.,* XI, 6-9 (*PL* 24, 151B).

[158] See E. Hatch, *The Influence of Greek Ideas on Christianity* (Hibbert Lectures, 1888; reprinted, New York, 1957).

[159] E. Zeller, *Outlines of the History of Greek Philosophy,* tr. by L. R. Palmer (13th ed.; London, 1955), 221.

[160] *De vir. ill.* XII (*PL* 23, 662A).

[161] *PL* 25, 1143C. We may contrast the Stoic position as phrased by Seneca: *Hanc praecedentem causam divitiae habent: inflant animos, superbiam pariunt, invidiam contrahunt, et usque eo mentem alienant, ut fama pecuniae nos etiam nocitura delectet* (*Epist.* 87. 31). Cf. Matt. 19:23.

[162] *PL* 25, 155A.

[163] *PL* 25, 83A.

[164] *PL* 24, 195B.

FURTHER READING

Biography

Cutts, Edward L. *Saint Jerome.* London: Society for promoting Christian Knowledge, n.d., XXXp.

   Brief biography of Jerome's life.

Kelly, J. N. D. *Jerome: His Life, Writings, and Controversies.* New York: Harper & Row, 1975, 353p.

   Thorough biography of Jerome's life, with specific attention to his writings.

Sigüenza, José de. *The Life of Saint Jerome, the Great Doctor of the Church,* translated by Mariana Monteiro. London: Sands, 1907, 668p.

   Translation of the extensive spiritual biography of 1595 by Father José de Sigüenza, a monk in the Order of Saint Jerome and one of the first Castilian classical writers.

Criticism

Adams, Jeremy Duquesnay. *The "Populus" of Augustine and Jerome.* New Haven: Yale University Press, 1971, 278p.

   Explores the use of the word 'populus' in the Vulgate *Bible* and in the writings of Augustine and Jerome in order to explore the opinions of patristic and early medieval thinkers regarding humankind and its subgroups.

Erasmus. *Collected Works of Erasmus,* Vol. 61: *Patristic Scholarship; the Edition of St. Jerome,* edited and translated by James F. Brady and John C. Olin. Toronto: University of Toronto Press, 1992, 293p.

   Contains Erasmus' *Life of Jerome* as well as se-lections from Jerome's letters with Erasmus's commentaries. An excerpt from the "Dedicatory Letter to Erasmus's Edition of St. Jerome" appears in the above entry.

Hritzu, John Nicholas. *The Style of the Letters of St. Jerome.* Washington, D.C.: Catholic University of America Press, 1939, 121p.

   Identifies and catalogues the stylistic devices used in the *Letters* and the extent to which they reveal the influence of sophistic rhetoricians.

Hughes, L. *The Christian Church in the Epistles of St. Jerome.* London: Society for Promoting Christian Knowledge, 1923, 116p.

Examines Jerome's letters in an attempt to clarify his opinions regarding the clergy, the scriptures, the ascetic and monastic movement, Rome, heresies, and the progress and practice of the Church. Hughes's "Conclusion" is contained in the above entry.

Kelly, M. Jamesetta. *Life and Times as Revealed in the Writings of St. Jerome Exclusive of His Letters.* Washington, D.C.: Catholic University of America Press, 1944, 173p.

Dissects Jerome's writings in order to illuminate the economic and professional, social, public, and religious contexts in which he wrote.

Levy, Harry L. "Claudian's *In Rufinum* and an Epistle of St. Jerome." *American Journal of Philology* LXIX (1948): 62-68.

Argues, in agreement with T. Birt's *Claudii Claudiani Carmina,* that Claudian influenced Jerome's sixtieth epistle, in which he laments the fall of Rome to the barbarians.

Meiss, Millard. "Scholarship and Penitence in the Early Renaissance: The Image of St. Jerome," in *The Painter's Choice: Problems in the Interpretation of Renaissance Art,* pp. 189-202. New York: Harper & Row, 1976.

Surveys the ways in which Jerome was represented in early Renaissance painting. Meiss claims that Jerome is portrayed in two very different ways–as ecclesiastical scholar in his study and as a self-bloodied penitent in the wilderness–and concludes that these "symbolized perfectly the diverse values of the Renaissance humanists."

Murphy, Francis X., ed. *A Monument to Saint Jerome: Essays on Some Aspects of His Life, Works and Influence.* New York: Sheed & Ward, 1952, 295p.

Collection of biographical, historical, and critical essays on Jerome and his work.

O'Connell, John P. *The Eschatology of Saint Jerome.* Mundelein, Ill.: Seminarii Sanctae Mariae Ad Lacum, 1948, 199p.

Explores Jerome's doctrines regarding death and the afterlife.

Oldfather, William Abbott, ed. *Studies in the Text Tradition of St. Jerome's "Vitae Patrum."* Urbana, Ill.: University of Illinois Press, 1943, 566p.

Extensively outlines the manuscript transmission of Jerome's three *Vitae*–in the Latin original, in Greek, and in versions derived from the Greek.

Olin, John C. "Erasmus and Saint Jerome: The Close Bond and Its Significance." *Erasmus of Rotterdam Yearbook* 7 (1987): 33-53.

Examines the importance of Jerome in the work of Erasmus, particularly his attempts "to reform theology by returning it to its scriptural and patristic sources."

Pease, Arthur Stanley. "Notes on St. Jerome's Tractates on the *Psalms.*" *Journal of Biblical Literature* XXVI, Pt. 2 (1907): 107-31.

Examines the structure of Jerome's three studies of the *Psalms* in an attempt to show the *Breviarium in Psalmos* to be part of a lost work by Jerome.

Semple, W. H. "St. Jerome as a Biblical Translator." *Bulletin of the John Rylands Library* XLVIII (1965-66): 227-43.

Studies the Latin prefaces of Jerome's translation of the *Old Testament* in an effort to elucidate his critical method and explore his replies to Augustine's criticisms.

Wiesen, David S. *St. Jerome as a Satirist: A Study in Christian Latin Thought and Letters.* Ithaca, N.Y.: Cornell University Press, 1964, 290p.

Positions Jerome in the satiric tradition through his writings on politics, culture, and religion.

Táin Bó Cualnge

c. Seventh Century

Irish prose epic.

INTRODUCTION

Often called the "Iliad of Ireland," the *Táin Bó Cúalnge (Cattle-Raid of Cualnge)* is considered the national epic of ancient Ireland. The longest heroic tale of the Ulster cycle, perhaps the oldest existing literature of any people north of the Alps, the *Táin* has an oral tradition that may date back to the second century B.C. The tale provides unique insight into the cultural and religious mores of a pre-Christian Ireland, and is now valued as much for its historical significance as its literary merit.

Plot and Major Characters

The *Tain* begins one night at the palace of Cruachan in Connacht, where Queen Medb, the wife of Conchobar, king of Ulster, disagrees with her consort Ailill about which of them has the greater possessions. To settle the dispute, they send messengers to assemble their cattle holdings, which are then found to be equal, except for a bull owned by Ailill called Finnbennach, "the white-horned," which is unmatched in Medb's herd. Medb's herald, macRoth, informs her that, in Cualnge, the land of Medb's former husband, a landowner named Darè macFiachna owns a bull named Donn Cualnge, "the Brown Bull of Cualnge," which is superior to Finnbennach. Medb sends her messengers to ask to borrow the bull, to which Darè agrees. However, during the course of the festivities, an intoxicated messenger speaks against him and Daré's offer is withdrawn.

Enraged, Medb organizes an army composed of Connachtmen, allies from throughout Ireland, and Ulster chieftains who had been exiled by King Con-chobar of Ulster. Chief among these men is Fergus, who, in order to win the widow Ness, had abdicated the throne to her son Conchobar for one year, only to have his attempts later to regain his kingship thwarted by the youth. Fergus now leads the company–including the King, Queen, and the Princess Finnabair–toward Cualnge. During this time, the Ulsterman are debilitated by *cess,* or "pains," due to an ancient curse on them. As a result, the seventeen-year-old Cú Chulainn, who has in his charge Murthemne, near Cualnge, and who, along with his father, Sualtaim, is exempt from the curse, becomes responsible for defending Cualnge against the invaders.

Cú Chulainn, whose heroic deeds are recounted by the Ulster exiles, deflects the army's advance; he allows the Connacht host to continue only on the condition that every day they send one of their finest warriors to meet him in single combat, and that when Cú Chulainn has defeated him, the army will halt until the next morning. In each of these contests, Cú Chulainn defeats the dispatched warrior, so finally an impatient Medb ignores the laws of chivalry and orders the army into Ulster, where they overrun the province–even to the walls of Emain Macha, the home of Conchobar–and take the Brown Bull. Conchobar then summons the Ulster noblemen, who drive Medb's army out of Ulster and back to Connacht. During this time, the Brown Bull cries out so loudly that Finnbennach bursts his stall in Cruachan and meets the Brown Bull in battle; after a long struggle, the Brown Bull scatters Finnbennach over all Ireland, then returns to Ulster, where he, still in a rage, dashes his head against a rock and dies.

Major Themes

Written in a mixture of prose and verse, the *Táin* is traditionally considered an epic or heroic saga; its main theme is commonly said to be the celebration of the courage, martial artistry, and chivalry of Cú Chulainn, to whom the bulk of the *Táin* is devoted. But recent historical and exegetical work on the *Táin* has led many recent critics to a different view. According to them, the mixture of pagan oral tradition and the Christian attitudes of the tale's redactors results in thematic ironies: for example, Cú Chulainn, a character who may originally have been a symbol of ancient Irish heroism, becomes in the written version a figure who satirically emobodies warrior values. Joan N. Radner has claimed the the Ulster cycle itself depicts the "tragic breakdown" of the societal virtues upon which ancient Irish society is based: "behind the immense vitality, humor and imagination of the Ulster stories is a picture of society moving to dysfunction and self-destruction." The lack of extended descriptions of large-scale battles, the bloodlessness of the final confrontations, and Cú Chulainn's exclamation on hearing the clamor of the Connachtmen's final charge–*conscar bara bith,* "anger destroys the world"–contribute to the popular view that the *Tain* is a pagan story interlaced with Christian pacifism.

Textual History

The *Táin* survives in several manuscripts–ranging in

date from the twelfth to the nineteenth century–most of which were produced much later than its first written appearance, but all of which are descended from versions dating to the seventh century. Of the surviving manuscripts of the *Táin,* three serve as the primary source materials. The *Lebor na hUidre* (LU)–"The Book of the Dun Cow"–dates from about 1100; this manuscript is the conflation of two ninth-century versions, with some late additions, and is incomplete. A different manuscript, called the *Yellow Book of Lecan* (YBL), from the late fourteenth century, also is missing the tale's beginning, but does not include some of the later additions made to the LU, thus providing a *Táin* thought to be more faithful to the poem's original written version. Finally, the *Book of Leinster* (LL), dated before 1160, provides a longer and more complete version, but is more modern in style and language, indicating that the manuscript was an attempt to flesh out the much earlier narrative. A version of the *Táin* preserved in the YBL, evidenced by the archaic language forms it preserves, dates back to the seventh century; this is consistent with the tradition that ascribes the compilation of the *Táin* to a bard named Senchan Torpeist. According to many philologists, the YBL continued to be copied down, but in slightly different forms as the language developed. Different accounts of some of the episodes eventually appeared, however, which generated a new redaction, which is represented in LL; many of these episodes appear in an earlier form in LU. So, while YBL was composed later than both LU and LL, it is thought to contain a version of the *Táin* truest to the seventh-century original.

Critical Reception

Along with James Macpherson's *Ossian,* the *Táin* considerably influenced the narrative styles and historical opinions of the nineteenth century; but, when literary fashions changed, interest in the saga waned. While it continued to hold a central place in the literary identity of Ireland–serving as the source for five of W. B. Yeats's plays, for example–only recently has critical interest outside of Ireland began to steadily increase, as interest in the *Táin* as an early Gaelic permutation of the epic has grown. Many scholars have suggested that the *Tain* depicts a country attempting to delineate its emerging national culture; comparisons between other national epics–such as Homer's *Iliad* and Virgil's *Aeneid*–have become more widely accepted. As both a self-contained literary achievement and a historical document revealing the Ireland of both the pre-Christian era and the *Táin*'s Christian redactors, the epic has captured the attention of many critics. Joseph Dunn has called the *Táin* "one of the most precious monuments of the world's literature, both because of the poetic worth it evidences at an early stage of civiliza-

tion, and for the light it throws on the life of the people among whom it originated and that of their ancestors centuries earlier."

PRINCIPAL ENGLISH TRANSLATIONS

The Cattle-Raid of Cualnge [translated by L. Winifred Faraday] 1904

The Táin [translated by Mary A. Hutton] 1907

An Ancient Irish Epic Tale Táin Bó Cúalnge [translated by Joseph Dunn] 1914

Táin Bó Cúalnge from the Book of Leinster [translated by Cecile O'Rahilly] 1967

The Tain [translated by Thomas Kinsella] 1970

CRITICISM

Joseph Dunn (essay date 1914)

SOURCE: A preface to *The Ancient Irish Epic Tale "Táin Bó Cúalnge,"* translated by Joseph Dunn, David Nutt, 1914, pp. xi-xxxi.

[*In the following excerpt, Dunn explores the cattle-raid plot and speculates about the historical genesis of the* Táin.]

The Gaelic Literature of Ireland is vast in extent and rich in quality. The inedited manuscript materials, if published, would occupy several hundred large volumes. Of this mass only a small portion has as yet been explored by scholars. Nevertheless three saga-cycles stand out from the rest, distinguished for their compass, age and literary worth, those, namely, of the gods, of the demigod Cuchulain, and of Finn son of Cumhall. The Cuchulain cycle, also called the Ulster cycle—from the home of its hero in the North of Ireland—forms the core of this great mass of epic material. It is also known as the cycle of Conchobar, the king round whom the Ulster warriors mustered, and, finally, it has been called the Red Branch Cycle from the name of the banqueting hall at Emain Macha in Ulster.

Only a few of the hundred or more tales which once belonged to this cycle have survived. There are some dozen in particular, technically known as *Remscéla* or "Foretales," because they lead up to and explain the great **Táin,** the **Táin Bó Cúalnge, "The Cualnge Cattle-raid,"** the Iliad of Ireland, as it has been called, the queen of Irish epic tales, and the wildest and most fascinating saga-tale, not only of the entire Celtic world, but even of all western Europe.

The mediaeval Irish scholars catalogued their native literature under several heads, probably as an aid to the memory of the professional poets or story-tellers whose stock-in-trade it was, and to one of these divisions they gave the name *Táinte,* plural of *Táin.* By this term, which is most often followed by the genitive plural *bó,* "cows," they meant "a driving," or "a reaving," or even "a drove" or "herd" of cattle. It is only by extension of meaning that this title is applied to the **Táin Bó Cúalnge,** the most famous representative of the class, for it is not, strictly speaking, with the driving of cattle that it deals but with that of the Brown Bull of Cualnge. But, since to carry off the bull implies the carrying off of the herd of which he was the head, and as the "Brown" is always represented as accompanied by his fifty heifers, there were sufficient grounds for putting the Brown Bull Quest in the class of Cow-spoils.

The prominence accorded to this class of stories in the early literature of Ireland is not to be wondered at when the economic situation of the country and the stage of civilization of which they are the faithful mirror is borne in mind.[1] Since all wars are waged for gain, and since among the Irish, who are still very much a nation of cattle raisers, cattle was the chief article of wealth and measure of value,[2] so marauding expeditions from one district into another for cattle must have been of frequent occurrence, just as among the North American Indians tribal wars used to be waged for the acquisition of horses. That this had been a common practice among their kinsmen on the Continent also we learn from Caesar's account of the Germans (and Celts?) who, he says, practised warfare not only for a means of subsistence but also for exercising their warriors. How long-lived the custom has been amongst the Gaelic Celts, as an occupation or as a pastime, is evident not only from the plundering incursions or "creaghs"[3] as they are called in the Highlands and described by Scott in *Waverley* and *The Fair Maid of Perth,* but also from the "cattle-drives" which have been resorted to in our own day in Ireland, though these latter had a different motive than plunder. As has been observed by Sir Henry Sumner Maine, Lord Macaulay was mistaken in ascribing this custom to "some native vice of Irish character," for, as every student of ancient Ireland may perceive, it is rather to be regarded as "a survival, an ancient and inveterate habit" of the race.

One of these many Cattle-preys was the **Táin Bó Cúalnge,**[4] which, there can be little doubt, had behind it no mere myth but some kernel of actual fact. Its historical basis is that a Connacht chieftain and his lady went to war with Ulster about a drove of cattle. The importance of a racial struggle between the north-east province and the remaining four grand provinces of Ireland cannot be ascribed to it. There is, it is true, strong evidence to show that two chief centres, political, if not cultural and national, existed at the time of the **Táin** in Ireland, Cruachan Ai, near the present Rathcroghan in Connacht, and Emain Macha, the Navan Fort, two miles west of Armagh in Ulster, and it is with the friendly or hostile relations of these two that the Ultonian cycle of tales deals. Ulster, or, more precisely, the eastern portion of the Province, was the scene of all the Cattle-raids, and there is a degree of truth in the couplet,—

> Leinster for breeding, And Ulster for reaving;
> Munster for reading, And Connacht for
>   thieving.

But there are no indications of a racial clash or war of tribes. With the exception of the Oghamic writings inscribed on the pillar-stones by Cuchulain, which seem to require interpretation to the men of Connacht by Ulstermen, the description of the warriors mustered by the Connacht warrior queen and those gathered round King Conchobar of Ulster accord quite closely.

The **Táin Bó Cúalnge** is the work not of any one man but of a corporation of artists known as *filid.* The author of the **Táin** in its present state, whoever he may have been, was a strong partisan of Ulster and never misses an opportunity of flattering the pride of her chieftains. Later a kind of reaction against the pre-eminence given to Ulster and the glorification of its hero sets in, and a group of stories arises in which the war takes a different end and Cuchulain is shown to disadvantage, finally to fall at the hands of a Munster champion. It is to this southern province that the saga-cycle which followed the Cuchulain at an interval of two hundred years belongs, namely, the Fenian saga,—the saga of Finn son of Cumhall, which still flourishes among the Gaelic speakers of Ireland and Scotland, while the Cuchulain stories have almost died out among them. The mingling of the two sagas is the work of the eighteenth-century Scots Lowlander, James Macpherson.

The **Táin Bó Cúalnge** is one of the most precious monuments of the world's literature, both because of the poetic worth it evidences at an early stage of civilization, and for the light it throws on the life of the people among whom it originated and that of their ancestors centuries earlier. It is not less valuable and curious because it shows us the earlier stages of an epic—an epic in the making—which it does better perhaps than any other work in literature. Ireland had at hand all the materials for a great national epic, a wealth of saga-material replete with interesting episodes, picturesque and dramatic incidents and strongly defined personages, yet she never found her Homer, a gifted poet to embrace her entire literary wealth, to piece the disjointed fragments together, smooth the

[55]

Page from a facsimile manuscript of the Táin *published in Dublin in 1870.*

asperities and hand down to posterity the finished epic of the Celtic world, superior, perhaps, to the Iliad or the Odyssey. What has come down to us is "a sort of patchwork epic," as Prescott called the Ballads of the Cid, a popular epopee in all its native roughness, wild phantasy and extravagance of deed and description as it developed during successive generations. It resembles the frame of some huge ship left unfinished by the builders on the beach and covered with shells and drift from the sea of Celtic tradition. From the historical standpoint, however, and as a picture of the old barbaric Celtic culture, and as a pure expression of elemental passion, it is of more importance to have the genuine tradition as it developed amongst the people, unvarnished by poetic art and uninfluenced by the example of older and alien societies.

According to the Chronicles of Ireland, as formulated in the Annals of Tigernach,[5] who died in 1088, King Conchobar of Ulster began to reign in the year 30 B.C., and he is said to have died of grief at the news that Christ had been crucified. His reign therefore lasted about sixty years. Cuchulain died in the year 39 A.D. in the twenty-seventh year of his age, as we learn from the following entry: "The death of Cuchulain, the bravest hero of the Irish, by Lugaid son of Three Hounds, king of Munster, and by Erc, king of Tara, son of Carbre Niafer, and by the three sons of Calatin of Connacht. Seven years was his age when he assumed arms, seventeen was his age when he followed the Driving of the Kine of Cualnge, but twenty-seven years was his age when he died."[6]

A very different account is given in the manuscript known as H. 3. 17, Trinity College, Dublin, quoted by O'Curry in his *Manuscript Materials,* page 508. The passage concludes with the statement: "So that the year of the **Táin** was the fifty-ninth year of Cuchulain's age, from the night of his birth to the night of his death." The record first quoted, however, is partly corroborated by the following passage which I translate from the Book of Ballymote, facsimilé edition, page 13, col. a, lines 9-21: "In the fourteenth year of the reign of Conairè (killed in 40 B.C.) and of Conchobar, the Blessed Virgin was born. At that time Cuchulain had completed thirteen years; and in the fourth year after the birth of Máry, the expedition of the Kine of Cualnge took place . . . that is, in the eighteenth year of the reign of Conairè. Cuchulain had completed his seventeenth year at that time. That is, it was in the thirty-second year of the reign of Octavius Augustus that the same expedition took place. Eight years after the **Táin Bó Cúalnge,** Christ was born, and Mary had completed twelve years then, and that was in the fortieth year of the reign of Octavius Augustus; and in the twenty-sixth year of the reign of Conairè and Conchobar, and in the second year after the birth of Christ, Cuchulain died. And twenty-

seven years was Cuchulain's age at that time."

These apparent synchronisms, of course, may only rest upon the imagination of the Christian annalists of Ireland, who hoped to exalt their ancient rulers and heroes by bringing them into relation with and even making them participate in the events of the life of the Saviour. But in placing the date of the expedition of the **Táin** at about the beginning of the Christian era, Irish tradition is undoubtedly correct, as appears from the character of the civilization depicted in the Ulster tales, which corresponds in a remarkable degree with what authors of antiquity have recorded of the Celts and with the character of the age which archaeologists call "la Tène," or "Late Celtic," which terminates at the beginning of the first century of our era. Oral tradition was perhaps occupied for five hundred years working over and developing the story of the **Táin,** and by the close of the fifth century the saga to which it belonged was substantially the one we have now. The text of the tale must have been completed by the first half of the seventh century, and, as we shall see, its oldest extant version, the Book of the Dun, dates from about the year 1100.

But, whatever may be the precise dates of these events, which we are not in a position to determine more accurately, the composition of the **Táin Bó Cúalnge** antedates by a considerable margin the epic tales of the Anglo-Saxons, the Scandinavians, the Franks and the Germans. It is the oldest epic tale of western Europe, and it and the cycle of tales to which it belongs form "the oldest existing literature of any of the peoples to the north of the Alps."[7] The deeds it recounts belong to the heroic age of Ireland three hundred years before the introduction of Christianity into the island, and its spirit never ceased to remain markedly pagan. The mythology that permeates it is one of the most primitive manifestations of the personification of the natural forces which the Celts worshipped. Its historical background, social organization, chivalry, mood and thought and its heroic ideal are to a large extent, and with perhaps some pre-Aryan survivals, not only those of the insular Celts of two thousand years ago, but also of the important and wide-spread Celtic race with whom Caesar fought and who in an earlier period had sacked Rome and made themselves feared even in Greece and Asia Minor.

Notes

[1] "L'histoire entière de l'Irlande est une énigme si on n'a pas sans cesse à l'esprit ce fait primordial que le climat humide de l'île est tout à fait contraire à la culture des céréales, mais en revanche éminemment favorable à l'élevage du bétail, surtout de la race bovine, car le climat est encore trop humide pour l'espèce ovine." F. Lot, in *La Grande Encyclopédie,* XX, 956.

[2] As it is to this day in some parts of Ireland, and as for example a female slave was sometimes appraised at three head of cattle among the ancient Gaels.

[3] In fact the Clan Mackay was known as the Clan of the creaghs, and their perpetuation was enjoined on the rising generation from the cradle. See *The Old Highlands,* vol. III., p. 338, Glasgow.

[4] Pronounced approximately *Thawin' b Hūln'ya. . . .*

[5] *Revue Celtique,* 1895, tome xvi. pp. 405-406; *Rerum Hibernicarum Scriptores,* ii. 14.

[6] *Mois Conchulaind fortissimi herois Scottorum la Lugaid mac trí con, i. ri Muman, agus la Ercc, i. ri Temrach, mac Coirpri Niad fir, agus la trí maccu Calattin de Chonnachtaib; vii. mbliadna a áes intan rogab gaisced. xvii. mbliadna dano a aes intan mbói indegaid Tána Bó Cúalnge. xxvii. bliadna immorro a aes intan atbath. Revue Celtique,* tome xvi. page 407.

[7] Ridgeway.

Charles Bowen (essay date 1975)

SOURCE: "Great-Bladdered Medb; Mythology and Invention in the *Táin Bó Cuailnge,*" *Éire-Ireland,* Vol. 10, No. 4, 1975, pp. 14-34.

[*In this essay, Bowen examines the interaction of "mythology and invention" in the character of Queen Medb, claiming that "she has become a queen who, in spite of being human and fallible, is never quite free of her former divinity."*]

"Probably the greatest achievement of the *Táin* and the Ulster Cycle," says Thomas Kinsella in the preface to his recent translation, "is the series of women, some in full scale and some in miniature, on whose strong and diverse personalities the action continually turns. . . . It may be as goddess-figures, ultimately, that these women have their power; it is certainly they, under all the violence, who remain most real in the memory."[1] Queen Medb is often said to be a goddess, or a goddess-figure; probably no one who reads Irish literature will find the notion unfamiliar. But having made the assertion, what in fact have we said? The modern reader who attempts to understand the *Táin Bó Cuailnge* in the light of it is left somewhat at a loss. Medb is not presented there as a goddess, but as a human queen. To what extent is this headstrong, savage, powerful, wrongheaded woman, who by her wilfulness turns all established values upside down and causes a slaughter unprecedented in Irish memory, behaving as a divinity rather than a human being? The *Táin,* after all, is not a book of mythology, but an epic. The pious scholars who handed it down certainly did not do so in the

belief that they were saving for posterity the primordial shenanigans of pagan gods and goddesses. Is that what they *were* doing, in spite of themselves?

Obviously such questions cannot be answered unequivocally. The storytellers and redactors who gave the *Táin* its present written form, or forms, in the 8th or 9th century, were influenced by the traditions of the past, many of them in origin mythological, and they were also capable of making their own contributions.[2] Queen Medb, as we encounter her in the *Táin,* presents an opportunity to examine the interaction of these elements—mythology and invention—in the formation of her literary character, and to observe the continuing power, some four or five centuries after its official demise, of the pagan mythological tradition in Ireland.

Of course that tradition did not expire as soon as Patrick set his foot on an Irish beach, but it must have begun to come apart at that time. The unconverted Irish, like other Indo-European peoples, had been the possessors of a great body of traditional learning, which in its higher manifestations was entrusted to the care of a professional learned class. It included what we would distinguish as law, medicine, astronomy, tribal history, genealogy, gnomic and antiquarian wisdom of all kinds. The list does not contain literature as a separate item, because all of these things were literature, and literature was all of these things. The same is true of religion: in the form of myth it permeated the entire tradition. To a certain extent we distort the truth when we speak of this traditional learning as if it were composed of separate fields—medicine, history and so on—for it certainly did not look that way to the ancient Irish. Celtic culture was not departmental, but interdisciplinary.

The conversion of Ireland was neither complete nor instantaneous, to be sure, and one way the old myths might have survived is in the minds of those who were stubborn holdouts, or half-converts at best. But a much more important reason for its survival is to be found in the way myth was diffused throughout every other department of knowledge. The orderly functioning of tribal society, which of course continued into the Christian period, would have been impossible if the tradition on which it was founded had been rejected *in toto.* Add to this the inherent conservatism of the Irish temperament, never willing to lay a scrap of old knowledge aside unless forced to do so, and it becomes obvious that a great deal of the old learning was bound to survive in one way or another.

Nevertheless, it could not have survived unchanged in its original form. The learned class who were its custodians may not have been among the most eager new catechumens, but the Christian religion made rapid progress among the tribal and provincial kings, on whom they depended for support, and inevitably an accommodation had to be made. The ancient functions of these learned experts were essential to the working of Irish society—James Carney has remarked that the society could no more have done without them than a modern state could abolish its civil service[3]—and they had to go on exercising many of these functions. But of course they could no longer be priests—that is, druids—and anything that was specifically religious in their learning had to be suppressed. Moreover, during the first century or so of Christian impact, about 450 to 550, the Irish language was going through such drastic changes that oral-formulaic poetry—the medium in which one assumes the learned class preserved its lore—must have become virtually impossible to practice according to the established conventions.[4] In combination with the gradual conversion of the learned class, this change must have knocked much of the mythological tradition loose from its moorings in the ancient oral culture.

During the centuries that intervened between Patrick's time and the period in which the surviving versions of the *Táin* took shape—the 8th and 9th centuries—the two intellectual traditions were integrated. The monasteries, far from being centers of opposition to the old learning, became the places where it was enshrined in books, that is, all of it that could be preserved. Unfortunately, no first-hand evidence has come down to us from this transitional period, so that it is impossible to observe the process of integration directly. But it seems to have taken place in a fairly thoroughgoing way. Even though the oral storytelling tradition continued to flourish, and presumably remained capable for some centuries longer of providing tidbits of material that had not previously been written down, nothing that was unabashedly pagan and incompatible with the new dispensation seems to have been in general circulation. On occasion the scribes may have felt nervous about recording details that seemed to them extravagant, as their interpolated comments and marginal notes attest,[5] but in general the evidence suggests that the marriage of the traditions had been consummated by the 9th century, the point at which our literary evidence really begins.

The means by which the lore of the native intellectual tradition had been preserved, in spite of its religious discreditation, was primarily the technique of euhemerization. In essence this is the conversion of myth into pseudo-history and gods into heroes. In order to reconcile their reluctance as Christians to write about forbidden subjects with their reluctance as Irishmen to discard even a jot or a tittle of their own cultural tradition, the early generations of *literati* found it necessary to transform ancestor-deities into mere ancestors, albeit prodigious ones. The pagan gods, who collectively were known as the Tuatha Dé Danann ('Peoples of the Goddess Danu') became a tribe of tall, good-looking humans with unusual skill in magic.

Anything that conflicted directly with Christian doctrine or Biblical history had to be abandoned: for instance, the Irish have left us no pre-Christian account of the Creation. All the traditions that could be salvaged, however, were eventually organized into a canonical body of pseudo-historical doctrine. This purported to chronicle every notable event in Ireland since its first settlement, immediately before the Flood, and to trace the ancestry of every native population-group all the way back to Adam.[6] Every saga and cycle was assigned a place in the scheme, so that the events it related, no matter how little they might accord with literary realism or even common sense, could be regarded as historical "fact," and thus legitimate matter for preservation. The fall of Dind Ríg was as much a part of history as the fall of Jericho or Troy, and Cú Roi mac Daire as real a king as Saul or Theseus. And since the characters in the sagas were real human beings, there could be nothing unchristian about recording their adventures.

Even though a great bulk of ancient material had been preserved, however, it had not come down in homogeneous form, but in multiple and fragmentary transmissions over a long period of time. A redactor in the 9th century or later, attempting to put in writing a tale or even a brief episode, might have at his disposal, or at least in his memory, several manuscript versions, some incomplete and none in agreement, besides other different versions he had heard recited, and possibly still others suggested to his mind by common sense. Even if he wanted nothing more than to transmit the story unaltered, he could hardly avoid manipulating the material in order to achieve this end. In attempting to bring order and clarity out of the jumble he had inherited, he would have to risk doing violence to tradition. Even a careful scribe would need great good fortune to avoid such violence, and not all scribes were careful. We can be almost certain that some such damage has been done to the substratum of myth that underlies the *Táin.*

Nevertheless, damage or no, the substratum is there. Not only is it possible that the story itself has its basis in one or more ancient mythic narratives, but several of the characters, among whom Medb is certainly to be included, have independent standing as figures of mythology, being mentioned in numerous traditions outside the *Táin.* It is necessary here to set aside the question of what we might call the mythic "deep structure" of the *Táin,* and to pursue Medb's independent associations instead, to see what light they can shed on the character that has been created for her as the rambunctious queen of Connacht.

The most widespread and persistent traditions about Medb are clustered around the myth of the king's *hieros gamos* or 'sacral marriage.' It was believed that every tribal and provincial king had to unite with a goddess in a symbolic wedding in order to inaugurate and confirm his kingship. According to Irish belief, there was a distinct goddess for each kingship, who would of course be known by different names in different places, but the goddess's function in the myth, and the inaugural ritual connected with it, is always the same. This is quite in keeping with the nature of Celtic religion, whose deities, in the words of Proinsias Mac Cana, "appear under an endlessly varied nomenclature, while remaining essentially unchanged in terms of function."[7] Thus, it is possible for us to learn something about what the goddess Medb was like from stories whose heroines have different names, once we have established her connection with the myth, and it is easy to establish that connection; a number of scholars have done so.[8] Queen Medb of Connacht, for instance, is said to have had a succession of husbands, each of whom, like Ailill, was king of Connacht by virtue of his marriage to her. Needless to say, such an arrangement bears no relation to the means by which eligibility for kingship was established in real life. Another Medb, who was given the epithet *Lethderg* ('Red-side' or 'Half-red'), but on the mythic level is obviously the same figure, was married to a number of successive kings of Tara. The Book of Leinster says, "Great indeed was the strength and power of that Medb over the men of Ireland, for it was she would not allow a king in Tara without his having herself as wife."[9] In other words, it was the ritual union, here treated as historical, with the goddess Medb that validated the kingships of Connacht and Tara.

In what may be regarded as the early stage of this myth, the goddess represents the earth in general and the tribal territory in particular. Her role is both sexual and maternal; she can appropriately be considered a goddess of fertility. The king is chosen as a flawless representative of this tribe and united to her in a ritual marriage ceremony at his inauguration feast. The name for such a feast was *banais rígi* ('wedding-feast of kingship'); sometimes it was simply called *feis*. This word—which is also the basis of the compound *banais,* that is, *ban* 'woman' + *feis*—ultimately means 'spending the night, sleeping together, sexual intercourse.' After the wedding, if the king proves to be worthy and the marriage valid, the earth will be fertile and everything from crops to livestock to the human birthrate will flourish. Unworthy behavior on his part can bring all these blessings to an end, as many stories attest.

The king's role in this stage of the myth, which might be called the fertility-myth, is almost as symbolic as the goddess's; his office is clearly conceived as more religious than political. But times change. Whether there was ever a purely non-political king in real Irish life, or whether the myth represented a religious ideal that had long since vanished from the actual world, there is no question that the business of kingship at some stage moved away from ritual and into *realpolitik.* Royal

power became something to be fought and lusted for. This development seems to have given rise to a new interpretation of the myth, a second stage which grew up alongside the old one, and which will be called the sovereignty-myth to distinguish it from the fertility-myth of the earlier stage. Now the goddess, the king's divine consort, came to be seen as symbolizing not so much the land and its bounty as the idea of sovereignty itself: the mysterious blessing of destiny that conferred power on the man who was chosen to receive it. Since the Irish had no law of primogeniture, a number of men were theoretically eligible to succeed to a given kingship. The question of who would do so and how was naturally surrounded by a high degree of anxiety and developed a potent mystique, which found expression in the myth of the goddess's choice.

The best-known story that reflects this sovereignty-myth concerns the sons of Eochaid Mugmedon.[10] Camping out in the woods, they are all very thirsty, but the only well they can find is guarded by an ugly hag, who refuses each of them a drink unless he will kiss her. Only one accepts: he is Niall, who will become ancestor to the powerful Uí-Néill. As soon as he embraces her, the hag becomes a beautiful young woman and identifies herself as the sovereignty of Ireland, which will belong to him and his descendants thenceforward. Clearly, the goddess's role is still a sexual one, but the interest is now focused on her choice of a partner and on the test which confirms and manifests that choice, rather than the subsequent wedding and the fecundity it brings into being.

The sovereignty-myth continued to exert its force on the Irish imagination through the centuries. There is a direct line from the goddess in the myth to that personification of Ireland we find in the *aisling* poems Egan O'Rahilly and others wrote during the Penal times, where she appears as a young woman in need of the right lord and master to wed her—a role the poets unfortunately assigned to the Stuarts.[11] For the purposes of this discussion, however, it is important only to emphasize the connection between the sovereignty-myth and the tradition that the kingship of Connacht or Tara depended on marriage to one Medb or another.

The gift of a drink seems to be important in all tales of the sovereignty-myth type: usually the woman offers not water, as she does to Níall, but wine, mead, or ale. An etymological connection has been made by medieval as well as modern scholars between the words *flaith* ('sovereign' or 'sovereignty') and *laith* ('beer'). Apparently the drinking of some symbolic intoxicant functioned to confirm the kingship in a manner parallel with the ritual marriage. Rudolf Thurneysen has speculated, plausibly enough, that a ritual drinking-bout was part of the inauguration ceremony.[12] It is obviously significant for our inquiry that the name Medb, formed from the same Indo-European root that gives the word 'mead' in many languages, including English, can mean either 'the drunken one' or 'she who intoxicates.'

Drunkenness, at least in this context, would not have been seen as degenerate behavior, but as a kind of ecstatic state in which a human was lifted out of himself and might hope to achieve contact with the divine. One of the most characteristic traits of Celtic culture is the importance it placed on the state of frenzy or ecstasy, which could be cultivated not only in drunkenness, but also in the mad fury to which Celtic warriors worked themselves up when they went into battle. Some evidence also suggests that sexual ecstasy was associated with these other two kinds, and had a similar significance—might, in fact, have been regarded as a manifestation of the same kind of supernatural force.[13] Thus, the king's ritual drunkenness at the inaugural feast might be interpreted as an image of the sacred orgasm in which he was united with the goddess.

As a beneficent mother who could confer the blessings necessary to communal life, or as the alluring nymph whose love-test brought success and royal power to those who passed it, the goddess was obviously a positive and attractive force, but it is important to understand that she had a negative aspect also. She could confer and bless, but she could, if she chose, withhold and curse as well. In both the fertility and the sovereignty-myths, the candidate's worthiness is a matter for some concern: if he is unworthy, there may be serious consequences for him or for the whole community. Therefore, the goddess was also associated with evil and danger. This dualistic conception is reflected in the story of Níall, where the old woman at the well appears loathesome, at least to those whose qualities do not fit them for kingship. All the brothers refuse her the kiss she asks for except Níall, who offers not only to kiss her, but to lie with her as well. We should not judge him either callous or perverse for this: the point is that he alone is gifted with insight into her true nature, an imporant sign of his worthiness. After the ugly hag has become a lovely nymph, she explains the change allegorically: kingship, she says, is often achieved through hardship and strife, but it is sweet once possessed. This pat little moral has a rationalizing sound to it, and has probably been added to the myth at a relatively late stage. More likely the goddess was originally regarded as good and evil, desirable and abhorrent, protective and destructive, at the same time.

In a story similar to that of Níall and the hag at the well, it is possible to see the goddess's vicious side a little more fully. This story concerns Macha Mongruad, not represented as a goddess, but certainly playing a goddess's role.[14] Macha is a claimant for the kingship of Ulster who, having received no justice from those who are supposed to share the royal power with her, successfully asserts her claim in arms, and defeats all her rivals. Among these are the five sons of Dithorba, whom she pursues into the wilds of Connacht, disguising herself as a leper. In this repellent guise she joins the five brothers at their campfire. Apparently her dual aspect is not hidden from them any more than the hag's was hidden from Níall, although here it is presumably a matter of her tactics rather than their perceptiveness. At any rate, once dinner is over, the brothers say, "Beautiful is the hag's eye! Let us lie with her." Taking them into the woods one at a time, Mancha overpowers each one in turn, and takes them all back to Ulster as her prisoners, where they are enslaved.

It is important to emphasize the dualism in the conception of this goddess, the simultaneous goodness and evil she was paradoxically able to represent. Perhaps only in that way can we attempt to understand how she could have been regarded—as she indisputably was— not only as the goddess of fertility and sovereignty, but also as the goddess of war. With our assumptions based on the compartmentalized Classical pantheon, which in this respect has little in common with Celtic religion, we find this association difficult to comprehend, but its existence cannot be doubted. Both Anne Ross and Marie-Louise Sjoestedt-Jonval, the scholars who have worked most intensively on Celtic goddess-types, have observed and commented on it. Sjoestedt says, "The series of mothers merges into that of goddesses of slaughter so that one cannot establish a clear opposition between them."[15]

The war-goddess expresses none of the joy in combat we might expect to find among a warlike people; she is an object of fear and loathing even to those who are blessed with her help. Cú Chulainn, for example, sometimes receives favors from the war-goddess, but when he encounters her directly, their relations are usually hostile. It is typical that, when she takes part in a battle, she does so only by magically demoralizing one side or the other, and it would be fair to say that she represents terror and carnage more than any other aspects of warfare. The Irish tradition tends to conceive her as a trio: the Mór-rígain, whose name probably means 'Great Queen,' the Badb, or 'Crow,' and the Nemain, 'Frenzy' or 'Panic.' The latter two seem to be mainly personifications of the most terrifying aspects of battle. Usually when they appear in the *Táin,* for instance, it is more or less as figures of speech. The Mór-rígain, however, manifests a little more personality. In the *Táin* she carries on a minor feud with Cú Chulainn while he is still single-handedly holding off Medb's army. In general, throughout the *Táin,* the Mór-rígain seems delighted by the slaughter; although she occasionally gives help or advice to either side, she seems more interested in insuring that a battle will take place than in which side will win it.

If we attempt to see this forbidding divinity as an extension of the goddess's negative aspect, a kind of fiercely logical carrying of the dualism to its natural extreme, we will possibly be on the right track, although the mental territory we enter here is so barren of familiar landmarks that it is hard to speak with much assurance. At any rate, the war goddess, like the others, has a strongly sexual aspect, and this tends to reinforce the association. It may also be worthwhile to point once again to the association of different forms of ecstasy, such as intoxication, sexual ardor, and warlike fury. If all three were in fact seen as variant manifestations of the same supernatural force, that may help explain how the pagan Celts were able to maintain such apparently incompatible conceptions of the same divine power.

One episode shows all of these opposing elements in rather close association, and is worth examining for the detail it can add to the complex pattern of fertility, sovereignty, and war affinities. It occurs in the tale called *The Second Battle of Mag Tured,* which contains a number of traditions about warfare among the gods, distorted, fragmented, and disguised as history. Shortly before the climactic battle, a sexual encounter takes place between the Dagda (the 'Good God') and the Mórrígain. The time is Samain, the Celtic New Year:

> Now the Dagda had an appointed meeting with a woman . . . about the Samain of the battle, in Glenn Edinn. The river Unnius of Connacht roars to the south of it. He saw the woman in the Unnius . . . washing, with one of her two feet . . . to the south of the water, and the other . . . to the north. . . . The Dagda conversed with her, and they made a union. "The Bed of the Couple" is the name of that place since then. The Mór-rígain is the woman that is mentioned here.[16]

Now, the Dagda is a god who certainly fits the type of the father-and-chieftain divinity. If he mates with a goddess at the time of year when important festivals were held, including such inaugural rites as that of Tara, it is certainly safe to see this encounter as a divine analogue of the sacral marriage between king and goddess.[17] But, on the other hand, is it necessary to accept the word of the text that the goddess in question is the war-goddess? After all, *The Second Battle of Mag Tured* is a confused text. Could not the identification here, which sounds like an editorial aside, be mistaken? It might be reasonable to think so, if not for the passage that follows:

> Then she told the Dagda that the Fomorians would land at Magh Scetne, and that he should summon Ireland's men of art [magicians] to meet her at the Ford of Unnius, and that she would go into Scetne to destroy Indech . . . [king] of the Fomorians, and would take from him the blood of his heart and the kidneys of his valor. Now she gave two handfuls of that blood to the armies that were waiting at the Ford of Unnius.

Obviously, then, she is the Mór-rígain, or at least the war-goddess, for these actions are hardly appropriate to a goddess exclusively concerned with fertility. Altogether, then, this passage provides impressive evidence that the goddesses of fertility/sovereignty and war played overlapping roles.

It is significant that the encounter between the Dagda and the Mór-rígain begins, and may even be consummated, with the goddess astride a river. Here is what Anne Ross has to say about the symbolism of rivers for the Celtic peoples:

> Springs, wells and rivers are of first and enduring importance as a focal point of Celtic cult practice and ritual. Rivers are important in themselves, being associated in Celtic tradition with fertility and with deities, such as the divine mothers and the sacred bulls, concerned with this fundamental aspect of life. . . . The Celtic mother-goddesses who frequently also function in the role of war-goddesses . . . have a widespread association with water. This is due, no doubt, to their own obvious connection with fertility which, in the popular mind, could be likened to the life-giving powers of water which could be witnessed by man himself. So we find, for example, the powerful river Marne taking its name from that of the Gaulish *Matrona,* 'Divine Mother.' No doubt there was at one time a cult legend in circulation associating the Mother with the river, which became the physical personification of the goddess, mirroring her own supernatural forces— strength, the powers of destruction, fertility.[18]

It is worth recalling at this point that river-names in Celtic languages were invariably feminine, and that where tradition has assigned eponyms, they are always women. The position of the Mór-rígain in the glen, straddling a river with one foot on each bank, suggests that the river is to be envisioned as emanating from between her legs. There should be nothing startling about such a notion. Springs and wells are, after all, primary female symbols. The locus of fertility, in a female divinity, would obviously be the womb. Seen in this context, the source of the river is the point at which the fluid of life issues from the body of the earth-mother.

To carry the analogy a bit farther, we might ask whether Ross's idea that the river "became the physical personification of the goddess, mirroring her own supernatural forces," is capable of further extension. If the river is the fluid of life, emanating from the goddess's body, what might be its specific referent? A number of possibilities suggests themselves. For one, there is the amniotic fluid that fills the womb during pregnancy: the "water of life" *par excellence,* in which the body of a new human being mysteriously takes shape. The ancient Gauls, perhaps by analogy with this process, invested the waters of springs and sources with curative powers.[19]

If we should seek an analogue for the goddess's malevolent and destructive powers, we might consider the menstrual blood, an object of fearful taboo in many cultures, where it has often been regarded as especially dangerous and destructive to men. One might look back to the two handfuls of blood given by the Mór-rígain to the magicians she was helping. In the narrator's mind they were certainly taken from the enemy leader's heart, but it is tempting to wonder if they might not originally have consisted of her own menstrual blood, envisioned as a destructive charm against enemy warriors.

Whatever the value of these speculations, there is one more symbol of the goddess's sexual power that is sufficient in itself to account for the Mór-rígain's symbolic posture over the river Unnius: that is her urine. Support for this assertion can be found in yet another text, a remarkably primitive story that survives among the lesser fragments of the Ulster cycle, *The Death of Derbforgaill*:

> One day at the end of winter there was deep snow. The men made a great pillar of the snow. The women went up on the pillar. This was what they thought of: "Let us urinate on the pillar to see whose urine will go deepest into it. The woman who penetrates it completely is the best lover among us." However, their urine did not go through. Derbforgaill was called by them. It was not to her liking because she was not wanton. Nevertheless, she went onto the pillar. It went through from her to the ground.

> "If the men knew this, now, no woman would be loved in comparison with this one. Let her eyes be taken out of her head, and her two ears, and her hair. She won't be well-desired after that."

So the women mutilate Derbforgaill. According to the other manuscript, they tear off "her nose and her hair and the flesh of her buttocks." She very shortly dies, after having refused to open the door to her husband, Lugaid, and Cú Chulainn takes vengeance on the nameless women, killing them all.[20]

There are several remarkable features to this frank and gruesome little tale. The women's contest takes place on top of a phallic symbol erected by the men; in winning the contest Derbforgaill equals the measure of this monument, and perhaps she can even be said to demolish it symbolically in the process. What is most important for our purpose, however, is the sentence where the meaning of the contest is explained, and here we have some choice in both the text and the translation. The women say, referring to the one who will demonstrate the most impressive capacity, either *"as ferr congaib úan"* or *"as ferr ergaire uainn,"* that

is, depending on the manuscript, either her *congaib* or her *ergaire* is the best among us. *Ergaire* usually means 'the act of checking or hindering,' though in some expressions it can mean 'being a match or an equal for' something. However, it occurs with an apparent sexual connotation in a passage describing Fergus mac Roig in his more virile aspect: "Seven fists [i.e. 42 inches] the length of his penis. His scrotum the size of a bushel basket. Seven women to curb him [*dia ergaire*] unless Flidais should come," Flidais being one of his usual consorts.[21] The editor of this passage, Whitley Stokes, marks *ergaire* and queries in a footnote, "in *sensu obscaeno?*" It seems clear that the meaning *is* sexual. If it were simply a matter of physical restraint, one would expect seven men rather than seven women, and in addition there is the testimony of the context. So presumably the statement "her *ergaire* is best" means "her matching or checking (in the obscene sense) is best."

Now, the other word, *congaib,* which Carl Marstrander translates 'to keep' and Rudolf Thurneysen 'to satisfy (enclose) a man'[22] must be related to the verb *con-gaib* 'contains, maintains, keeps,' as both translations imply. But the context calls for the verbal noun rather than a finite form of the verb, and the verbal noun of *con-gaib* is not *congaib* but *congbal*. On the other hand, there is a noun *conga(i)b*, which is more loosely related to the same verb; it means 'gathering or host,' but also 'equipment.' In the latter sense it has been used with a sexual meaning. The R.I.A. Dictionary cites a reference to emasculation in the Yellow Book of Lecan: *"robhean a chongaib ferda as"*—'lopped off his manly equipment.' The dictionary cautiously places our sentence next to this one, and whether or not caution is necessary, the meaning must be something like, "she has the best (sexual) equipment of all." Thus, both readings establish that bladder capacity is synonymous with sexual performance.

The episode thus establishes beyond doubt that there is a relationship between copious urination and sexuality, but it does more than that: it refers specifically to a physical measure of sexual power. Just as the phallic myth depends on the notion that a man's potency is reflected by the size of his genitals, the corresponding female myth, as we see it here, measures a woman's sexual power by the capacity of her "inner space," with the bladder undoubtedly serving as an analogue for the vagina and uterus. All of this, perhaps, makes the relevance of river and urine symbolism to the figure of the fertility-sovereignty-war goddess a little clearer.

To return to Medb as a literary character in the *Táin,* scholars have shown that much of her behavior can be accounted for by reference to her divine background. Tomás Ó Máille and Rudolf Thurneysen, half a century ago, pointed out the connection between the fertility-sovereignty myth and Medb's promiscuity.[23] They were responding to an article Heinrich Zimmer had written in 1911, in which he cited Medb as evidence that sexual life in ancient Ireland had come sadly short of the moral standards of his own day. If Medb boasts that she "never had one man without another waiting in his shadow," argued Ó Máille and Thurneysen, if she continually offers "the friendship of her thighs" to whomever she wants to influence, if she conducts an affair with Fergus so flagrantly that even Ailill's celebrated complaisance is strained, she is only living up to the spirit of the myths that lie beneath her character. Her hapless daughter Finnabair is also promised to many, although the promise is never fulfilled. She is so passive a pawn of her mother that it seems best to regard her as nothing more than an extension of Medb herself, a mere variant on the promise of friendly thighs. In the *Táin,* such promises are usually made while the prospect is being plied with strong drink, and even this has been traced back to the sovereignty-myth and the symbolic beverage given to the chosen candidate.[24] Although this line of argument is basically sound, it is worth keeping in mind that some of these actions may be natural enough in the circumstances of the plot: we may not need a myth to explain why Medb would find it practical to get a man drunk, or offer him her daughter's hand or her own thighs, in order to persuade him to risk challenging Cú Chulainn to single combat.

Medb's affair with Fergus, on the other hand, does not seem quite necessary to the plot. It is not an unnatural development, given her promiscuous character, but as we have been seeing, that character is to a certain extent the consequence of her mythological background. Fergus, too, has a background, and it reveals him to be a fertility-god just as surely as Medb is a fertility-goddess. The passage quoted above, on his virile dimensions, lends support to this thesis; it is also worth reflecting that his name means something like 'Manly Force, son of Great Stallion.' Under the circumstances, then, their romance may have been foredoomed by mythological influences regardless of the requirements of the story.

These examples of mythological influence on the characterization of Medb come, it might be said, from outside the *Táin,* inasmuch as they are based on the memory of a mythic prototype that is in a way independent of the story-pattern exemplified in the *Táin* itself. We may seek for further examples of the same kind. Thus, it may seem obvious that, in commanding an army, Medb is manifesting the character of a war-goddess. Anne Ross certainly makes this assumption; she speaks of Medb as a lone exception to the rule that war-goddesses do not take up arms but operate instead through magical means.[25] But the exceptional nature of Medb's case is even more striking than that. Apart from the mythological battle of Mag Tured, we seldom find this goddess identifying herself with either side in a battle. As we have already seen, she gives the impression of being delighted only by the prospect of carnage, and indifferent to the interests of the combatants. It is hard to imagine her supporting one side, let alone commanding it. Medb's attitude in the *Táin,* of course, is far removed from such impartial malignance, and for that reason, the mythic prototype of the war-goddess should probably receive no credit for determining her characterization.

Obviously, then, there is more to Medb than we can account for by looking to her supernatural prototype. The whole cattle-raid is begun by her ambition to surpass her husband, and sustained by her ruthless drive to succeed in the project without regard to what may be prudent or just. At first glance it might seem to be a logical development of the sovereignty-myth that the woman who represents sovereignty should become a human queen lusting to extend her power. No doubt it *is* the myth that has caused Medb to be remembered as a true sovereign, rather than a passive royal consort, as queens were in real life. But ambition on her part does not belong to the myth; it is quite unnecessary. The female has sovereignty entirely in her keeping; in fact, she *is* sovereignty. There is no suggestion that, in mating with the mortal king and giving him a draft of her powerful ale, she is taking a subordinate role. Kings come and go; she remains. The goddess has no reason to envy her beneficiaries. Therefore, it is not enough to point to the sovereignty-myth as the explanation for Medb's ambitious drive. We must also give some credit to the plot of the *Táin,* where as instigator and commander of the great cattle-raid she is committed to a ruthless and self-centered role. The question of the origin of the plot—whether it derives from ancient mythic story-patterns or from the pseudo-historical speculations of the early Christian period—is too large to take up here. It is safe to say, however, that evidence can be found to support the hypothesis of a mythic origin for the cattle-raid, whether or not it is conclusive.[26] Here, of course, we would have an "internal" mythological influence, as distinct from the "external" ones considered above.

The 8th- and 9th-century redactors found Medb's role already defined by the story, and they proceeded to interpret it in the light of their robust antifeminism and their conservative notion of a properly-ordered cosmos. T. F. O'Rahilly observed that, with the transition from goddess to masterful woman, Medb's character degenerated sadly.[27] Her sexual behavior was less tolerable in a mortal than it had been in a goddess, and perhaps led some of the saga writers to conclusions like Heinrich Zimmer's. But above and beyond that, it was quite foreign to Irish tradition for a woman to exercise kingship: there was no equivalent concept of queenship. The idea of a woman commanding royal authority and organizing a great military expedition would have outraged the patriarchist prejudices of the redactors, laymen no less than clerics, and Medb could hardly appear otherwise to them than as a wilful woman of dangerously subversive tendencies. Once the narrative had acquired its basic outline, certainly prior to the 8th century, the men who worked and reworked it operated not as free and autonomous authors, but as scholarly redactors, trying to bring out and clarify the shape of the story as they perceived it in what had been handed down to them. They could invent incidents and speeches, but they would have done so in order to realize the implications of the story as they understood these to be given; it is unlikely that they would have attempted to alter its fundamental shape in a consciously original way. It would thus be fair to say that all their invention was a form of interpretation, and that invention had no greater role to play in creating Medb's character. With each retelling, as the mythic substratum became ever more dim in the collective memory, the subversiveness of the headstrong queen would tend to stand out more and more sharply, and the arrangement of speech and incident would assert this interpretation with greater and greater clarity. Medb would tend to become ever more high-handed and imperious, ever less respectful of the sanctity of treaties, truces, and other gentlemen's agreements.[28]

Of course this process was invisible to the storytellers and redactors who were collectively responsible for it. For them the story was fixed and given, a fact no longer of literature but of history. They thought of Queen Medb not as a goddess, nor as a fascinating literary creation, but as a larger-than-life ancestress; when they looked on her their disapproval was real, but it was mingled with awe. It is hard to keep your lips pursed when your jaw keeps dropping. If the redactors' undoubted antifeminism had controlled their responses to the extent Frank O'Connor implies,[29] we would probably have gotten a much less powerful and impressive Queen Medb in the *Táin*—perhaps a pouting Maureen O'Hara spoiling for a thwacking from John Wayne—and surely not the giantess we have instead. A lingering consciousness of Medb's divinity was always there, somewhere in the back of the writers' consciousness, and it produced an odd but powerful tension in the narrative. Perhaps nothing in the *Táin* illustrates it better than the scene at the end of the last battle:

> Medb had set up a shelter of shields to guard the rear of the men of Ireland. She had sent off the Brown Bull of Cuailnge by a roundabout road. . . .
>
> Then Medb got her gush of blood.
>
> 'Fergus,' she said, 'take over the shelter of shields . . . until I relieve myself.'
>
> 'By god,' Fergus said, 'you have picked a bad time for this.'

'I can't help it,' Medb said. 'I'll die if I can't do it.'

> So Fergus took over the shelter of shields . . . and Medb relieved herself. It dug three great channels, each big enough to take a household. The place is called Fual Medba, Medb's Foul Place, ever since. Cú Chulainn found her like this, but he held his hand. He wouldn't strike her from behind.[30]

Obviously more than one thing is going on here. The storyteller's purpose is to place Medb in a helpless and ridiculous position, where she will be not simply humiliated, but humiliated specifically as a woman, when Cú Chulainn catches her. The effect of the scene, however, is much more complex and ambivalent than this simple purpose would lead us to expect.

The natural process referred to, by the way, is not quite certain. The phrase translated 'gush of blood' by Kinsella and 'issue of blood' by Cecile O'Rahilly means literally 'urine of blood.' In the rest of the passage, however, a phrase meaning 'to pass urine' is used three times, and the name of the place afterwards means not 'Medb's Foul Place' but 'Medb's Urine.' Kinsella, who gives the correct meaning in his notes, is merely trying to resolve the ambiguity in favor of menstruation for editorial reasons. Neither menstruation nor urination, therefore, can be discarded as a possibility. Either would have seemed appropriately ignominious to the narrator, whose point of view is entirely in harmony with the sentiment expressed by Fergus at the end of the earliest surviving version, the one from the 9th century: "We followed the rump of a misguiding woman . . . it is the usual thing for a herd led by a mare to be strayed and destroyed."

The scene above, however, is found only in the 12th-century version, although it may be based on something earlier.[31] But whether or not it goes very far back in the textual tradition of the *Táin,* the lurking symbolism in the scene suggests strongly that it must be based on something very old. And this ancient symbolism pulls the narrative in a direction the writer presumably did not intend. The last thing he would want Medb to do, if his intention has been represented correctly, is demonstrate her strength. But the power inherent in the symbolism will not be denied. Whether it is urine or menstrual blood, Medb produces it in such quantities that she creates a new landmark. The same thing happens in a derivative story called *Táin Bó Flidaise II,* which may be based on a lost version of the *Táin.* Caught at a difficult moment during a retreat, Medb urinates so prodigiously that, in the words of one manuscript,

> neither root nor underbrush nor stick of wood was left, down to the gravel of the earth, but it was stripped bare, and the mighty stones remained afterward. And neither root nor growth nor grass, in its

pure, lovely ripeness, was left in that place forever after, so that Leacán ('Stony Place') and Mún Medhbhi ('Medb's Urine') is the name of that place since then.[32]

Both versions of the story contain these little onomastic tags to explain the place-name, and they may perhaps point to an origin in the *dindshenchas* tradition. Bits of genuine myth have sometimes been preserved in these place-name legends, and it is worth noting that goddesses, who are more often identified with a particular locality than gods, play a proportionally large role in them. But whatever its origin, the story has maintained its integrity to the extent that the writer is unable to adapt it fully to his purpose. Even in the midst of a disorderly and humiliating retreat, Medb manages to give a demonstration of the power—the supernatural, female power—that once made her feared and honored. Mythology retains its power over the tradition, and here it has fought invention to a standstill. Will anyone deny that the scene is greater, not less, for the conflict?

A woman whose desire to possess a treasure is so strong that she willingly sacrifices a huge army for it, whose reluctance to share glory is so powerful that she casually proposes to slaughter the best of her allies, whose determination to achieve her purpose is so intense that she bribes, threatens, and seduces one man after another into a single combat she knows he will not survive, and occasionally mocks these victims to her husband as they go; a goddess who can bring the earth to life or make it barren, who can delude some men into destruction and make kings of others, who can intoxicate her followers with superhuman exhilaration on one occasion and emasculating terror on another—Medb is a powerful mixture. From a goddess who is never quite one thing without also being its opposite, she has become a queen who, in spite of being human and fallible, is never quite free of her former divinity. It is no wonder she had such power over the imagination of the medieval storytellers who shaped the **Táin Bó Cuailnge,** or that we who read their words can feel that power today.

Notes

[1] In a slightly different version, this paper was presented to the 1975 Conference of the American Committee for Irish Studies. *The Táin* (London: Oxford University Press, 1970), pp. xiv-xv.

[2] For a concise discussion of the history of the *Táin* and the question of its origin, see Cecile O'Rahilly, *Táin Bó Cuailnge from the Book of Leinster* (Dublin: Dublin Institute for Advanced Studies, 1967), Introduction.

[3] *The Irish Bardic Poet* (Dublin: Dolmen Press, 1967), p. 8.

[4] According to Albert Lord, *The Singer of Tales,* Cambridge, Mass.: Harvard University Press, 1960), the practice of oral poetry requires the use of a conventional vocabulary of formulae, each of which is designed to express a given idea in a given metrical form. These formulae are language-specific, since their utility depends on a particular arrangement of accented and unaccented syllables. Such linguistic changes as syncope and loss of final syllables would have thrown the entire system into confusion. For a discussion of the changes in Irish during the century in question, see Kenneth Jackson, *Language and History in Early Britain* (Edinburgh: Edinburgh University Press, 1953), ch. 4.

[5] See, for instance, the famous notes at the end of the *Táin* in the Book of Leinster: Kinsella, p. 283; O'Rahilly, pp. 136, 272.

[6] The central documents of this body of doctrine are the *Lebor Gabála,* or 'Book of Invasions,' ed. and tr. R. A. S. Macalister, 5 vols. (Dublin: Irish Texts Society, 1938-1955), and the genealogies mainly collected in Michael A. O'Brien, *Corpus Genealogiarum Hiberniae* (Dublin: Dublin Institute for Advanced Studies, 1962), vol. I (all published). But virtually the entire corpus of Irish saga conforms at least superficially to the same plan, with due allowance made for its numerous inconsistencies.

[7] "Conservation and Innovation in Early Irish Literature," *Études Celtiques,* vol. 13, fasc. 1 (1972), 115.

[8] See Tomás Ó Máille, "Medb Chruachna," *Zeitschrift für Celtische Philologie (ZCP),* 17 (1927), 129-46; Rudolf Thurneysen, "Zu Göttin Medb," *ZCP,* 18 (1929), 108-10; (1933), 352-53; Josef Weisweiler, *Heimat und Herrschaft* (Halle: Max Niemeyer, 1943), ch. 6, especially pp. 91-93, 113-14; Jan de Vries, *Keltische Religion* (Stuttgart; Kohlhammer, 1961), pp. 129-31; Anne Ross, *Pagan Celtic Britain* (London: Routledge & Kegan Paul, 1967), pp. 223-25, 360.

[9] Ó Máille, pp. 137-38.

[10] "The Death of Crimthann, Son of Fidach, and the Adventures of the Sons of Eochaid Muigmedon," ed. and tr. Whitley Stokes, *Revue Celtique (RC),* 24 (1903), 190-203.

[11] The subject is covered most thoroughly by Weisweiler, chs. 3, 4, 6.

[12] *ZCP* 18 (1927), 110.

[13] Cf. de Vries, p. 138, although he appears to attribute

the association in the passage he is discussing to confusion. See also Marie-Louise Sjoestedt-Jonval's discussion of the Celtic concept of the hero in *Gods and Heroes of the Celts,* tr. Myles Dillon (London: Methuen, 1949), pp. 57-59.

[14] Edward Gwynn, ed. and tr., *The Metrical Dindshenchas,* Royal Irish Academy Todd Lecture Series, vol. 11 (Dublin: Royal Irish Academy, 1924), IV, 124-31, 308-11; Whitley Stokes, ed. and tr., "The Rennes Dindshenchas," *RC,* 16 (1895), 279-83.

[15] *Gods and Heroes,* p. 93. See also ch. 3, and Ross, ch. 5. De Vries is less explicit, but does place *Kriegsgöttinen* under the heading *Die Göttinen der Fruchtbarkeit* (sect. D, ch. III, pt. 3).

[16] From Whitley Stokes' ed. and tr. in *RC,* 12 (1891), 82-85. I have altered the translation superficially.

[17] See Sjoestedt, pp. 40-41.

[18] *Pagan Celtic Britain,* p. 20.

[19] See, for instance, Emile Thevenot, *Divinités et sanctuaires de la Gaule* (Paris: Fayard, 1968), chs. 5, 9.

[20] Carl Marstrander, ed. and tr., *Ériu,* 5 (1911), 201-18. My translation differs from his at several points.

[21] *Ériu,* 4 (1910), 26-27.

[22] Thurneysen, *Irische Helden- und Königsage* (Halle: Max Niemeyer, 1921), p. 428; *"einen Mann . . . befriedigen (umfangen)."*

[23] See note 8 above.

[24] *Weisueiler,* p. 113.

[25] *Pagan Celtic Britain,* p. 223.

[26] A fascinating argument is made by Erica Mumford in her unpublished dissertation, *Medb and the Goddess of the Near East,* Diss. Harvard 1973. Other speculations may be found in Duncan Norton-Taylor, *The Celts* (New York: Time-Life Books, 1974), pp. 77-82.

[27] "On the Origin of the Names *Érainn* and *Ériu,*" *Ériu,* 14 (1943), 15-16.

[28] Cecile O'Rahilly, p. liii, has listed a number of changes made between the earlier and later written versions that appear to illustrate this process at work.

[29] See *The Backward Look: A Survey of Irish Literature* (London: Macmillan, 1967), p. 32.

[30] Kinsella, p. 250. Cf. Cecile O'Rahilly, pp. 133, 269-70.

[31] See Cecile O'Rahilly's notes on the Pillow-Talk episode, pp. 273-74.

[32] Royal Irish Academy MS. B. IV, 1 fol. 147 (144)ᵛ. My translation, made from a photographic facsimile of the MS in Houghton Library, Harvard University.

Cecile Crovatt Gay Gray (essay date 1979)

SOURCE: "The Irish Epic," "The Epic Hero," and "Tragedy in the Epic" in *The "Táin Bó Cuailnge" and the Epic Tradition,* Ph.D. dissertation, University of Dallas, 1979, pp. 14-157.

[*In the following excerpt, Gray enumerates the different narrative and structural elements, as well as character types, present in the* Táin *and compares the poem with other epic poems, including the* Iliad, *the* Odyssey, Beowulf, *the* Chanson de Roland, *and the* Mabinogion.]

The Irish Epic

The **Táin Bó Cuailnge** suffers from obscurity outside the country in which it originated. If it is known at all, it is generally perceived only as a source for some of W. B. Yeats's works, a notion which intensifies the suspicion with which it is regarded. For although Yeats may be, as T. S. Eliot proclaimed him, the greatest modern lyric poet to write in English, he was known to dabble in strange matters, even to be deceived by charlatans; and his enthusiasm for the Irish heroic materials is perceived as somewhat bizarre. In fact, the **Táin** is no stranger or more esoteric than the *Iliad;* and it is certainly far less so than the *Odyssey,* in which one-eyed giants and monsters of every sort may appear just beyond the crest of each approaching wave. The comparison between the Irish prose narrative and these Classical epics may at first seem surprising. To determine whether or not there is any justification for including the **Táin** in this most august literary company, an inquiry into its form and action must be undertaken.

Although the scholars who deal with them do not see the stories of the Ulster cycle as partaking of the strange, religio-mythic nature of the Welsh *Mabinogion,* some readers, like W. P. Ker, feel that they do.[1] Others call them sagas, presumably because they are written in mixed prose and verse rather than entirely in verse, looking at first glance more like the Old Icelandic sagas or the *Prose Edda* than they do like the epics of Greece. Even the translator Cecile O'Rahilly calls them sagas.[2] However, the Old Man who speaks to the audience at the beginning of Yeats's play *The Death of Cuchulain* calls the Irish heroic tales "the old epics."[3] Here again, some critics would agree with this classification, while others would deny that it applies.

Oral narratives are diverse in form, and it is impossible to isolate any one tale and label it as being of only this type or that. And yet certain broad categories can be defined which tell something about the works which embody them. All lengthy oral narratives come out of and are sophisticated and elaborate reworkings of the homely folk-tale, which is often observable just below the more polished surface of the mythological or magical story, the saga and the epic. But that is not necessarily to favor one form above the rest, since each performed a different function in the society from which it arose.

The first of these narrative types with which come have equated the **Táin Bó Cuailnge** is the mythological, magical story. Because of certain clearly supernatural elements of the Ulster Cycle, a group of prose narratives including the **Táin** about the kings and warriors of Ulster, some would equate this narrative with what Gwyn Jones describes as "the kind of folktale which its most recent and distinguished classifiers call tales of magic, and I without originality call wondertale."[4] Jones places the Welsh *Culhwch and Olwen* within this category, although he makes abundantly clear that just as wondertale finds its way into the epic *Beowulf, Culhwch and Olwen,* a wondertale, is in part heroic and epical. Perhaps a better example of wondertale might be the Welsh *Mabinogion,* which H. Munro and N. Kershaw Chadwick say cannot "fairly be regarded as heroic."[5] By "heroic" is generally meant an action which is within the realm of human ability although beyond the compass of most mortals, an act which is defined by superb human prowess rather than by a resort to the use of magic. Great feats of sorcery and shamanism glitter through the pages of the *Mabinogion:* Arawn, the king of the Underworld, exchanges forms with Pwyll, the central character of the First Branch of the Mabinogi, and sleeps unsuspected beside his wife for a year; in the Second Branch, "Branwen Daughter of Lyr," Bendigeidfran gives the King of Ireland Matholwch "a cauldron, and the virtue of the cauldron is this: a man of thine slain to-day, cast him into the cauldron, and by to-morrow he will be as well as he was at the best, save that he will not have power of speech"[6] and in the Fourth Branch, Gwydion "made by magic twelve stallions and twelve greyhounds, each of them black but whitebreasted, and twelve collars and twelve leashes upon them. . . . "[7] In these incidents the feats are more exciting and more memorable than the characters who performed them. And these are only a few examples of the enchantments which dominate the *Mabinogion.*

Nothing of this nature happens within the **Táin** proper; the hero Cúchulainn may slay an incredible number of men in one day, look more hideous in his battle-fury than any other warrior, and wield a weapon greater than any other, but he does these things by virtue of his extraordinary physical power, and not through casting spells. He does cast a spell at one point in order to convince Lóch, one of Medb's warriors, that he is bearded and therefore old enough to fight.[8] However, his victory over Lóch is brought about by his magnificent human strength. But within the Ulster Cycle there are supernatural feats as bizarre as anything in the Welsh tales. The story of "The Sick-bed of Cú Chúlainn" recounts an episode in which the hero is enchanted and as a vision. In it two fairy women flog him; and Fann, the wife of the sea god Manannan mac Lir, is offered to him in exchange for his military services. His charioteer goes into the fairy world and describes its wonders to Cúchulainn, and the warrior undertakes and wins the battle. The tale ends with his abandonment by the fairy woman, and his re-entry into his normal state after his king's "people of skill" have "chanted wizard and fairy spells against him" and given him and his wife a "drink of forgetfulness," and after the sea god has shaken "his cloak between Cú Chúlainn and Fann so that they might never meet again throughout eternity."[9] Some of the Ulster stories even more closely related to the **Táin** are likewise wondrous in nature, like "The Quarrel of the Two Pig-keepers and how the Bulls were Begotten." This tale tells of the origins of the two bulls, Finnbennach, whose desertion of Mebb's herd has left her less wealthy than her husband, and Donn Cuailnge, the Brown Bull of Cuailnge, which she goes cattle-raiding to obtain. The tale runs thus: two pig-keepers of the *síd,* or fairy-folk, are dismissed from their jobs after each tries to prove that his power is equal to that of the other through casting spells on the other's swine. They take the form of quarrelling birds, then successively water creatures, stags, warriors, phantoms, dragons and maggots, which are drunk from water by two cows who bear the two famous bulls. The metamorphoses of these shape-changers are not unlike those of Gwydion and Gilfaethwy in the Welsh "Math Son of Mathonwy." The Welsh characters are punished for raping Goewin by being placed under spells that make them take the forms of several different sorts of wild beasts, one type each year; they must couple and bring forth the young of each kind.

The **Táin** proper, however, contains no such comparable magic deed. Even Ferdia, whom some have identified as a sort of supernatural or mythological figure because of his unassailable horny skin, is discovered by Kuno Meyer to be wearing a tunic made of horn. The usual translation, Meyer says, is the culprit in causing this misunderstanding. It is not that his flesh cannot be hacked, but that "'There will not be found a hero's hand to hack warrior's flesh like that of Fer Diad. . . . '"[10]

Some dauntless critics like Eileen M. Bolton nevertheless see the **Táin**—and indeed the whole Ulster Cycle—

as mythology in disguise, a sort of theogony for those who can understand its symbols. This perspective arises from the paucity of description of the deities in the **Táin** in contrast to the greater amount of discussion of the gods in other epics. To conclude that the Celts were not particularly religious is offensive to some scholars, who rather ingeniously assert that the priests who wrote down the old heroic stories were actually recording mythology—but euhemerizing it so that they would be able to save fine stories without preserving pagan beliefs. But as the Chadwicks point out in *The Growth of Literature,* this search for deities beneath the flesh of heroes has hardly been limited to Celtic studies. Their argument against the acceptance of such theories is especially important:

> It was formerly an accepted article of faith and is still apparently believed by many scholars that Sigurdr (Siegfried) and Brynhildr themselves were products of fiction, though not fiction in the ordinary (modern) sense of the word. They were believed to have originated in personifications of light, who meet with their doom in conflict with the powers of darkness. . . . A similar origin has been claimed for the stories of Achilles, CúChulainn, and other heroes, though in the case of the former we believe that it is now generally abandoned, at least in this country. *All these claims in our opinion spring from a fundamental misconception of the nature of heroic poetry and saga.* The characters on whose behalf they are made are essentially and primarily heroic; but the claims are based on secondary works composed in later times in a more or less non-heroic milieu.[11] [Italics mine]

W. P. Ker agrees that the notion of "dress[ing] up ideas or sentiments to play the part of characters" is not applicable to an heroic literature, which "will keep its hold upon common matters. . . . "[12] Gerald Murphy generally concurs with this point of view, although he does not make his case as strongly. About the lack of mythology displayed in the Irish stories he reminds the reader that there are mythological tales—the group of stories known as the Mythological Cycle—but he is not concerned about their limited revelations. This problem he shrugs off by saying that these tales "throw no more light on ancient Celtic religion than the Roman versions of Greek myths, unaided by Greek religious monuments, would throw on ancient Greek religion," a fact which does not mean that the Romans or the Greeks were necessarily lacking in highly developed beliefs and rituals; this absence of mythology should not reflect poorly upon the ancient Irish, either.[13] James Carney is unwilling to assert too strongly that the heroes could not possibly be euhemerized gods, but he is also unwilling to make any really strong claim in favor of the theory. Only in the case of Medb is he willing to accept this hypothesis, since there was known to be a goddess by that name who by symbolic marriage conferred kingship on the rulers of Tara.[14]

Although it may now be unfashionable to see Achilleus as a god of light, mythological studies of the Irish materials seem to be the vogue. Bolton has written about the **Táin** in the *Anglo-Welsh Review* in two articles which provide an astronomical mythology of Cúchulainn "the sun-hero"[15] and of his struggles. Her articles are ingenious and well-argued, but they seem to lose the heroic milieu in their flights to the stars. A more plausible argument is made by Charles Bowen in his "Great-Bladdered Medb: Mythology and Invention in the **Táin Bó Cuailnge**." He always keeps Queen Medb of Connacht in the fore, realizing that it is she with whom the reader must deal, while he investigates her mythic ancestry in order better to comprehend the epic queen. He never loses touch with the physical, humorous, scatological side of her characterization, the excesses of which are often boisterously funny, as he is willing to admit. The Chadwicks see the fantastic exploits of the hero Cúchulainn, too, as "intended as much to amuse as to impress"[16]; this opinion, of course, undercuts any notion of his god-likeness.

It is with the Irish Mythological Cycle, rather than with the heroic Ulster Cycle which contains the epic, that the Welsh stories may best be compared. The parallels between these two groups of tales have been pointed out by numerous scholars. Murphy says that "the Irish mythological tales remind one of the Welsh *Mabinogion.* . . ."[17] And Alwyn Rees compares the Tuatha De Danann who dominate this cycle with the Children of Don who appear in their Welsh counterpart. He also points out correspondences of names in the two narratives and some "broad similarities between some of the stories on either side," while he denies any relationship between the Ulster Cycle and the *Mabinogion.*[18] The gods which the mythologists seek in the Ulster Cycle appear, Murphy says, in the account of the Battle of Moytura in this Mythological Cycle; and the comparisons that he draws in describing the appearance of the Irish pantheon apply to the Greek and Teutonic stories as well as the Welsh accounts. "Its theme, a battle in which the Tuatha De Donann defeat the Formoiri, is reminiscent of Greek traditions concerning the defeat inflicted on Cronus and his Titans by Zeus and the Olympian gods, or of Scandinavian traditions concerning wars between Aesir and Vanir."[19] For example, Snorri Sturlson's *Prose Edda,* in which Gylfi is informed about the doings of the gods, is closer to the Mythological tales than to the story of the cattle-raiding queen and the hero who defends Ulster's Brown Bull.

Another test which may be applied to an oral narrative, in order to determine whether or not the wondertale is a dominant element in it, is to examine how far it veers toward romance. The Welsh wondertales' offspring are the Arthurian romances, and there must therefore be something of the romance in them for them to bring it forth. The Finn Cycle, another group of Irish narratives, contains the story of Diarmuid and Grainne which, Jan de Vries says, "reminds us of the Welsh story of Tristan," but "one may . . . wonder if there is any question here of a love that might be called 'romantic'." That even such an apparently romantic story might not be romantic he suggests by calling to mind the "Ulster story of Deirdre [which] can give us an idea of the true nature of such a love. In the Irish stories this love is indeed no romanticism, but a tragic reality."[20] Raymond Cormier compares Cúchulainn himself to Yvain, concluding that the Irish hero is absolutely not a "romantic lover. He is more akin to Achilles, to Beowulf, even to Roland, whereas Yvain's near cognates are Erec, Lancelot, Perceval, Gauvain and others."[21] And he makes this comparison in light of that most nearly romantic of Cúchulainn's adventures, "The Wasting-Sickness of Cú Chúlainn."

Certain essential characteristics of the wondertale, then, do not appear in the *Táin Bó Cuailnge.* The fantastic and mythological elements of this sort of narrative are not to be found in the heroic *Táin,* which describes an essentially human reality. Character is all-important to the *Táin;* in fact, both its shape and texture grow out of the characters of Cúchulainn, Medb and Ailill and a few others. And though a few of the elements of romance can be found within the Ulster Cycle, they are at best subsidiary to the stories' heroic milieu. Like the *Prose Edda,* however, the *Táin*'s form is a mixture of verse and prose, and the prose tales which make up the *Mabinogion* bear more resemblance to the *Táin* than to the heroic poetry of other peoples when they appear on the printed page; for as well as being written mostly in prose, the verses which are scattered throughout the Irish narrative are stanzaic and varied rather than conforming to a single standard heroic line.

A look at the *Táin* in juxtaposition with the Icelandic sagas seems to disclose a more likely analogy for it. The form—the mixture of verses with prose—is the same in both, and both are definitely heroic. Murphy provides a concise definition for heroic literature. He says that it is "aristocratic in outlook":

> As virtues it recognizes loyalty, prowess, and fulfilment of one's word. . . . It idealizes its heroes, yet remains fundamentally realistic: those heroes are made of flesh and blood; their success or failure depends more on character and action than on accident or magic, though fate and the gods may be regarded as inscrutable and yet necessary factors in life. . . . Description of the ceremony of court life, of the interior of palaces, and of the ornament of clothes and weapons, is universal in heroic literature.[22]

Scholars as sage as the Chadwicks consistently refer to the *Táin Bó Cuailnge* as a saga, presumably making this judgment mostly on the basis of form. De Vries says:

Irish "heroic epic" can hardly be discussed without a glance at the Icelandic *saga.* Both are, in regard to their form, so remarkably similar that the thought at once arises that there must be a close kinship, perhaps even a close connexion. For both are prose stories in which stanzas have been inserted, which have the character partly of lyrics, partly of dialogues. In both cases the almost obvious view that the prose stories have been dissolved from an older poetic form, the remnants of which are still scattered throughout the story, can be considered to be correct.[23]

But these similarities do not imply a close relationship between the two types of narrative, because, as de Vries notes, the poetry that is mixed with the prose serves entirely different functions within the two forms. (And he goes on to point out that when the poetry is excluded from the comparison, "the similarity of the Irish and Icelandic prose story is really not very great."[24]) The difference is that the verses serve an ornamental function in the Irish tales, whereas the stanzas in at least the older Icelandic sagas are scaldic[25] in nature, and rather than decorating the prose they confirm that what it presents is true.[26] The Chadwicks classify two types of poems in the *Táin:* those "dealing with situation or emotion, and consisting wholly or mainly of speeches,"[27] as well as "many which are of an informative (antiquarian) character, consisting largely of catalogues."[28]

And if the two narrative forms, the Icelandic and the Irish, are apparently similar but in reality quite different, the tales which they contain are quite obviously constructed in a dissimilar manner. The *Táin Bó Cuailnge* concerns a single event: the cattle raid and its outcome; the Icelandic sagas record the actions of several generations. A single folk tale could well comprise the *Táin*'s basis, although it is embellished by other subsidiary tales. But, as Jones indicates, "the nature of the saga," on the contrary, "is to proceed by means of linked sections in a chronological and genealogical way, so that no one folk tale could underlie it in its entirety."[29] For instance, in the *Laxdaela Saga,*[30] the action begins with the settling of Iceland, followed by a brief account of several generations of a particular family in the Laxdale River valley. The main story begins with the birth of Olaf the Peacock, the bastard son of one of the family members, to a captive Irish princess. The story continues with Olaf's son Kjartan, who becomes involved in a blood feud with his cousin over a woman. Both are murdered, and after many more deaths the feud peters out and the story ends. There are, obviously, many incidents in this saga; and they are organically and chronologically bound tightly together in a way that the Ulster Cycle's tales are not. Each of the tales in the Irish group could stand on its own, although of course it would lack some of its richness if extricated from the Cycle.

The Icelandic sagas are family chronicles interested in preserving the history of the clans who settle in Iceland; the *Táin* is concerned with the doings of two kings and their heroes, all of whom live simultaneously and have the advantage of a tradition which has long existed on the island where they live. The purpose of the Icelandic sagas is to structure such a tradition; de Vries says that "every family is proud of the row of its acestors who have established and enhanced the prestige and the power of the family."[31] The *Táin* records the heroic deeds of two kingdoms rather than those of a single family and its enemies. There are, of course, genealogies in the *Táin Bó Cuailnge,* but they are only indirectly concerned with the action, whereas they inform it intrisically in the Icelandic sagas.

In matters of love, the Icelandic and the Irish narratives appear to be more similar. If the Irish love stories are far more tragic than romantic, the Icelandic sagas reveal a love that is even more so. In *Njal's Saga,* to take just one example, there is a story in which Gunnar marries Hallgerd against all advice, and out of petty revenge she costs him his life. And if the Irish stories are non-romantic, this relationship is anti-romantic. The involvement between Gunnar and Hallgerd begins only after he has gone to the Althing in the ornate clothing that reflects a courtly attitude which is catastrophic in this society.

Such motifs point to one of the greatest differences between the Irish and the Icelandic narratives. The Icelandic sagas provide something of a code for aristocratic behavior, by showing men's triumphs as well as their downfalls. The Irish tales of the Ulster Cycle provide no fine example of kingship or of aristocratic behavior; Conchobor, Medb and Ailill are seriously flawed and at times despicable, and scenes of the doings of the court, such as "Bricriu's Feast," reveal little that one might label as "manners." What the *Táin* shows, instead, is Cúchulainn, the ultimate hero, who can only be admired, not emulated, and who is so thoroughly isolated an individual that his errors are not even particularly useful warnings for others. There is no intention here of suggesting that the Icelanders who are presented in the sagas are ordinary mortals, although they certainly live in a far more mundane sphere than the Irish heroes; they are "great figures of a great past."[32] Scholes and Kellogg say:

> Lionel Trilling has said that all characters in fiction, even Priam and Achilles, exist by reason of their observed manners. This may be so, but Achilles is not presented in a context of manners to the same extent that Gunnar and Njal are. . . . It would make no sense to say that Achilles was well- or ill-bred, or that he was prosperous. These considerations are irrelevant in his case. They would be descriptions of manners in a world in which manners are not really significant. But in the world of the saga they are significant because the saga-man

or the saga tradition requires that they be so.[33]

A code of manners, then, is more carefully drawn in the sagas.

Nevertheless, it should not be construed that the Irish narratives provide no display of deportment or of excellent conduct. As the Chadwicks point out, in his fight with the cattle-raiders from Connacht, "CúChúlainn's conduct to his opponents is uniformly chivalrous"—more so than that of the Greek hero. "He spares the life of Fraech in his first encounter, and will not attack Nad-Cranntail, who has come against him without proper weapons. He frequently declares that he will not slay charioteers, messengers, and persons unarmed."[34] But Cúchulainn's actions here are presented, like his other feats, for admiration, not for emulation, since he is the exceptional man in this matter as in others, and not the norm.

Because these two narrative forms are unlike on this level, it may be surprising that one element which appears to be closer to the magic of the wondertale than to codes of behavior is the same in the *Táin* and in one Icelandic saga. Cúchulainn's "warp-spasm"— that strange physical contortion that he undergoes in his battle-fury—has a parallel "in a story from an Icelandic saga. The Viking Egill Skallagrimsson had similar berserk fits of rage. . . . "[35] But although these two contortions may be the same on the surface, one wonders whether or not they may in reality be as different from one another as the alternating passages of verse and prose in the two narrative types. Egill's berserk fury can be retraced to the god Odin, who had only one eye and was the deity who ruled berserk heroes.[36] Cúchulainn's transformation, on the other hand, is more likely to arise from the exaggerating imagination of the Irish storyteller. Before he goes out to fight, the narrative goes,

> The . . . warp-spasm seized Cúchulainn, and him into a monstrous thing, hideous and shapeless, unheard of. His shanks and his joints, every knuckle and angle and organ from head to foot, shook like a tree in the flood or a reed in the stream. His body made a furious twist inside his skin, so that his feet and shins and knees switched to the rear and his heels and calves switched to the front. The balled sinews of his calves switched to the front of his shins, each big knot to the size of a warrior's bunched fist. On his head the temple-sinews stretched to the nape of his neck, each mighty, immense, measureless knob as big as the head of a month-old child. His face and features became a red bowl: he sucked one eye so deep into his head that a wild crane couldn't probe it onto his cheek out of the depths of his skull; the other eye fell out along his cheek. His mouth wierdly distorted: his cheek peeled back from his jaws until the gullet appeared, his lungs and liver flapped in his mouth and throat, his lower jaw struck the upper a lion-

killing blow, and fiery flakes large as a ram's fleece reached his mouth from his throat. His heart boomed loud in his breast like the baying of a watch-dog at its feed or the sound of a lion among bears. (p. 150)

The description continues for another few pages. The hero's grimace is surely terrible and terrifying; the beautiful youth in his battle-fury is hideous to look upon. And that horrifying ugliness seems to be exactly the point of this fanciful description. The Chadwicks say that the "superhuman prowess attributed to heroes is . . . conventional, . . . due to . . . hero-worship in the modern sense and the tendency to exaggeration stimulated thereby,"[37] an explanation which certainly sounds plausible.

The *Táin,* then, is no more closely related to the Icelandic saga than it is to the Welsh wondertale or to any species of religious mythology. The love relationships in the Icelandic sagas do resemble those in some of the stories from the Ulster Cycle, but in form, plot and social function the two narrative types differ. And the saga may cover many years, while the *Táin Bó Cuailnge* takes place in only a few months.

But if the *Táin Bó Cuailnge* is neither wondertale, mythic story nor saga, what is it? Many scholars have called it an epic. Thomas Kinsella, with more or less nonchalance, calls it "the oldest vernacular epic in Western literature" (p. vi). Before identifying it as an epic, I would like to offer a brief definition of this form. First of all, an epic is a long, traditional narrative which may contain humorous elements but is nevertheless serious in intent. It is usually delivered in nonstanzaic verse. It is concerned with conflict among men which takes the form of combat. One central hero dominates the epic, and he is both a man and a cultural representative, although he is not a typical representative of his society. The epic may contain many episodes, but it centers around an isolated event—like the playing out of the "wrath of Achilles" of the homecoming of Odysseus. This central event and the hero's role in it illuminate the finest part of the spirit of the people, and the hero is usually triumphant in the end. (The Classical epic is, of course, the model for this definition, which is at odds with certain elements of *Gilgamesh* and of late Medieval epics.) The *Táin* seems generally to fit this description.

Immediately a difficulty arises because the *Táin Bó Cuailnge* is in prose; although it contains older passages in verse, these are stanzaic and have an ornamental rather than a narrative function. Only the "rhetorics" which are characterized by archaic, difficult language and appear in the oldest of the tales are nonstanzaic.[38] Of course no piece of literature fits tidily into a critical category; but this prose character must be noted as a rather obvious exception to the rule of epic form. De Vries says that for the Irish, the telling in prose was a matter of simple preference. Some scholars, he notes, have proposed that the stories might have been given prose form because their complex, peculiar, stanzaic verse forms were unsuitable for narrating epics; but he sensibly argues with this point of view by asking "whether a way out would not have been found by choosing a simpler verse-form, if a real need for poetic treatment had existed," since the Irish were skillful technicians in a variety of verse forms.[39] Another hypothesis might be suggested. The difficulty of transcribing stories from an oral to a written form before the time of the tape recorder has been noted by many scholars. If the flow of the story is slowed to a pace convenient for transcription, the teller is severely hampered in his activity. Perhaps the redactors found the story easier to put into writing if it could be told in prose, saving the original poetic form of only the most lyrical passages. But that the *Táin* has come into prose from a verse origin is not particularly important to this discussion, which seeks to deal with the narrative as it exists rather than with an analysis of its historical development. Even if its poetic beginnings are to be accorded importance, they do not make a particularly strong case for a similarity in form between the Irish narratives and the Greek epics.

The tone of many passages of the *Táin Bó Cuailnge* is likewise different from that of the classical epics. If the *Táin* is too heroic and too much of this world to make it a wondertale, and if it is too far divorced from society per se to be like the saga, it is for some too earthy, too rough-and-tumble in tone to be truly epical. The Chadwicks acknowledge this difference, and note that the modern reader is likely to be offended by the "lack of restraint" these stories show. They say that "the dignified and fastidious tone which prevails in Teutonic and Greek heroic poetry is not generally characteristic of Irish heroic saga," and often "the love of the grotesque and the fantastic and of rough horseplay throws all sense of dignity to the winds."[40]

And to compare the story of a cattle raid to that of a war fought over the most beautiful woman in the world may seem at first to be a travesty. But both Ker and de Vries indicate that tales of cattle-raids are indigenous to heroic societies, and de Vries even locates this activity in Homer: the condition for the bestowing of Neleus' daughter is that the oxen of Iphiclea be taken out of Phylace.[41] Nor is the *Táin Bó Cuailnge* the only Irish tale of a cattle raid; it is one of the most common forms of Irish heroic story.

The Irish epic may seem to lack classical propriety in its choice of subject matter, but the distance placed between the reader and the heroes is basically the same in the Homeric epic and the *Táin*. Both are dramatically presented, thoughts of the characters being revealed through dialogue, or occasionally in monologue. These speeches can be quite revealing of what the character experiences. One example is Helen's statement in the *Iliad* that

"I wish that on that day when my mother first
    bore me
the foul whirlwind of the storm had caught
    me away and swept me
to the mountain, or into the wash of the sea
    deep-thundering
where the waves would have swept me away
    before all these things had happened.
Yet since the gods had brought it about that
    these vile things must be,
I wish I had been the wife of a better man
    than this is,
one who knew modesty and all things of
    shame that men say.
But this man's heart is no steadfast thing, nor
    yet will it be so
ever hereafter; for that I think he shall take
    the consequences.
But come now, come in and rest on this chair,
    my brother,
since it is on your heart beyond all that the
    hard work has fallen
for the sake of dishonored me and the blind
    act of Alexandros,
us two, on whom Zeus set a vile destiny, so
    that hereafter
we shall be made into things of song for men
    of the future."[42]

And as Carney shows, Medb's "Humanistic observation" that "'Everyone . . . who parts here from his dear one and his friend will curse me, for it is I who have gathered this host',"[43] provides a similar insight. But sympathy for a character never reaches the point of empathy, partly because to empathize with an epic hero smacks of something hardly less than hubris on the part of the reader. The hero is a superior man at his greatest. And the reality in which he acts is far removed from the reader's. If there are cattle-raids and abductions, they are not simply that; the Donn Cuailnge is a great bull, perhaps even a supernatural one, and Helen is a superlatively beautiful and desirable queen, and the daughter of a god. The tones of the two epics are similarly lofty in keeping with their presentations of the great men whose stories they tell.

The actions of the *Táin* and the *Iliad* are surprisingly similar. In the first place, the praxis in each case arises from the protagonist. Scholes and Kellogg say that this circumstance is in the nature of epic: the "plot is inherent in the concept of the protagonist, but that concept is not realized in the narrative until this character is expressed through action."[44] In both instances, only one incident in the middle of the hero's life is spoken of: in the case of Achilleus, his anger,[45] and in that of Cúchulainn, his solitude. The first of these assertions,

that the anger of Achilleus is the subject-matter of the *Iliad,* has been made many times. The opening lines of the epic support it.

But the assumption that the **Táin Bó Cuailnge** is about the solitude of Cúchulainn is more implicit. There is no statement directly to this point in the text, but the action bears it out. Because the men of Ulster are incapacitated by their "pangs" at the beginning of the story, Cúchulainn must face the Connacht forces singlehanded. He is accompanied only by his charioteer as he meets, in single combat, one of Medb's followers each day. The final stage, and the culmination, of his solitude is his combat with his friend and foster-brother, Ferdia, whom he kills. After this episode, while he lies almost mortally wounded and outside the battle, the forces of Ulster come to his aid and the battle is won. A curious parallel between the two stories is evident; the death of the friend, at the hand of the hero or as good as at his hand, is the turning point of both actions. In the *Iliad,* Achilleus is the only hero who is not fighting for most of the battle, while in the **Táin Bó Cuailnge** Cúchulainn is the only hero who is fighting, almost until the end. And whereas in the *Iliad* the turning point, the death of Patroklos, brings Achilleus back into the battle, in the **Táin** the death of Ferdia results in Cúchulainn's removal from it. Rhys Carpenter comments upon the isolation of the Greek hero, too. He asks, "who can say whether his famous 'wrath' is cause or consequence of this isolation?"[46]

Neither of these narratives brings the hero to his death, although the deaths of the heroes must come soon thereafter to both: to Achilleus because he has killed Hektor, and to Cúchulainn because of his arming by the druid Cathbad.[47] The stories end with the heroes triumphant, the *Iliad* with the truce for the burial of the dead and the attendant funeral games, and the **Táin Bó Cuailnge** with the exit from the battle-field, in which "the Connachtmen went back to their own country, and the men of Ulster went back to Emain Macha full of their great triumph" (p. 253). In neither case, however, has the hero regained for his people what has been stolen from them. Helen is still among the Trojans, and the Donn Cuailnge is dead. The triumph in both cases has to do with something else. As Scholes and Kellogg have commented, in the *Iliad* the funeral of Hektor "represents the triumph of Achilles over his greatest antagonist, himself. It represents the final purgation of his accumulated rage. . . . The narrative has reached equilibrium."[48] The *Iliad* is concerned with Helen only secondarily. The **Táin**'s interest in the Brown Bull of Cuailnge is more in the foreground. He is captured at the beginning of the narrative, and at its end he dies. Nevertheless, Cúchulainn's victory is the culmination of the narrative.

The men of the enemy—of Troy and of Cruachan Aí— are portrayed, curiously enough, far more intimately than the heroes from Greece or from Ulster. The Greeks are seen in their tents, but the Trojans are seen in their city, even in domestic scenes with their families. The Ulstermen, likewise, are shown mostly on the field of battle. There is an episode when their daily lives are revealed, and that is in Fergus' tales of Cúchulainn's boyhood deeds. But the revelation of the Ulster court is of something that happened in the past, and it lacks the emotional intensity of Hektor's farewell to his wife. Fergus' story is an entertainment given before the campfire of the Connachtmen. Medb and Ailill are first met, however, in the intimacy of their bed, and this is the scene which opens the **Táin.** The variety of dimensions in which their enemies are shown accentuates the sense of the single dimension in which the principal heroes of the two epic, Achilleus and Cúchulainn, act.

The only parts of the *Iliad* which seem to have no parallel in the **Táin** are the invocation to the Muse and the Diomed. There is a story, however, which Kinsella includes with his translation of the **Táin** that shows something similar to the invocation: a reclaiming of the lost story of the cattle raid through supernatural means. Muirgen, the son and student of the poet Senchan, chants to the gravestone of Fergus, telling it that if it were the hero instead of a rock the **Táin** could be recovered. Fergus then appears and chants the story to him (pp. 1-2). And so before each narrative begins there is a relationship set up among the gods, the heroic action and the poetry which speaks of it. But these two stories do not deal with the casting of spells or primarily with sacred matters; the supernatural presents itself as an integral part of the tales, but the heroic matters about which the Muse sings, or which Fergus—who is no ordinary shade, but that of a hero—relates, are the heart of them.[49] The other "missing element" in the **Táin Bó Cuailnge** is the Diomed, in which a foil to the character Achilleus is established. Diomedes is a fine warrior, but only through the intervention of a god can he perform the sort of feats that Achilleus can do out of his own heroic strength. The Myrmidon hero's greatness is thereby magnified. But the price of this interruption in the narrative is that the action leaves Achilleus for so long that the fabric of the epic is loosened; the gain in characterization brings about a raveling, which may be construed as a weakening in structure. The focus of the **Táin Bó Cuailnge** is far less shifting; all the events before the entry of Cúchulainn lead directly to his emergence, and once he appear his presence directs all the action.

The **Táin** is more, then, than the "centre-piece of the Ulster Cycle" (p. xii). It is an epic which closely resembles the great Homeric epic, the *Iliad,* and the other stories of the Cycle buttress it rather than control it. They give the origins of many of the events of the epic, but they do not determine its outcome. The story of "The Pangs of Ulster" explains the incapacity of the Ulstermen at the coming of the Connacht cattle-raid-

ers, and "The Exile of the Sons of Uisliu" tells how Fergus and his men happen to be fighting against Cúchulainn instead of being by his side. Likewise the tale "How Cúchulainn was Begotten" helps to reveal the reason why he is favored by certain gods in the battle. "The Quarrel of the Two Pig-keepers and how the Bulls were Begotten" gives not only the origin of the two great bulls, but also provides a thematic parallel for the argument between Medb and Ailill and possibly even indicates the origin of their quarrel. And like the subsidiary legend of the death of Achilleus, the story of Cúchulainn's death completes a story that needed finishing but whose ending was not appropriate to the epic about the hero.

With so much similarity between the two epics one wonders whether or not the redactor who transcribed the **Táin Bó Cuailnge** might have been familiar with the *Iliad* and integrated classical motifs into the Irish tale. De Vries feels that some classical influence is possible:

> The clergy's wide knowledge of classical literature suggests that the author or the successive redactors of the Táin legend also drew on it for their motifs. . . . [The *Táin*] shows this influence in the careful drawing of the characters, in the dramatic beginning of the fighting, and especially in the description of various earlier events which—with the technique so well known from the *Odyssey*—seems to overtake the events in the course of the story. It is possible that classical influence is also shown in the strongly rhetorical dialogues, which for that matter are among the most favored stylistic devices in Irish literature.[50]

This possibility of classical influence does not sound unlikely, although it may be refuted—along with Rudolf Thurneysen's idea that the **Táin** was greatly influenced by the *Aeneid*—by Carney's objection: the **Táin** is very much a part of the entire Irish tradition of oral literature, pretty well in its entirety.[51] And even if there is classical influence, there is no reason to ascribe all the excellences of the **Táin Bó Cuailnge** to it. If the "classisized" motifs and structures of the **Táin** are integral to it and function organically within it, it is perhaps more useful critically to observe the *Iliad* and the **Táin** as analogues rather than as source and by-product.

The heroic poetry of one people is not like that of another because of "influences" on one side and imitation on the other. Rather, all heroic ages are, to some extent, alike. C. M. Bowra's study of the characteristics of such literature shows the universality of the essential ingredients of an heroic poem. All heroic poetry, he says, "is inspired by the belief that the honour which men pay to some of their fellows is owed to a real superiority . . . [which] he [the hero] must realize . . . in action." Furthermore, this hero "gives dignity to the human race by showing of what feats it is capable.

. . . "[52] The poetry itself "works in conditions determined by special conceptions of manhood and honour. It cannot exist unless men believe that human beings are in themselves sufficient objects of interest and that their chief claim is the pursuit of honour through risk."[53] Many societies, then, have produced heroic poetry when they passed through phases of history in which they held heroic attitudes.

Despite its prose form, then, the **Táin** is a part of the epic tradition. It is the story of the central event in the life of one hero, who dominates the story. The tone of the **Táin Bó Cuailnge** is heroic, though not classically restrained; but the action is of sufficient magnitude, and the characterization is of sufficient excellence and nobility to overshadow this lack of restraint. The **Táin**'s action is in many ways parallel to that of the *Iliad,* and the heroes of the two poems show many similarities. The relationship among gods, men and poetry is important to both, and both have subsidiary legends which are essential for an understanding of the two actions. The **Táin Bó Cuailnge** is far more than an exotic curiosity; it is in the mainstream of the epic tradition.

The Epic Hero

The Irish hero, Cúchulainn, like his Greek counterpart, Achilleus, is unlike any other warrior in his epic. Both are set apart from their fellows: Cúchulainn fights while all the men of Ulster lie helpless from their pangs, and Achilleus sulks in his tent while the Greeks fight and die in a raging battle. The movement of the Irish epic is, in part, the transition of Cúchulainn from a state of solitude into unity with his community. The gods who preside over the fray, as well as the men who enact it, have a relationship with the hero that is unlike that with any other man.

If the *Iliad* is on the one hand the story of the anger of Achilleus, it is on the other the manifestation of the working out of Zeus's will. The reader's interest is more on the side of Achilleus, but without the gods and their doings, there would be no *Iliad;* after all, the war was the result of a beauty contest among goddesses. To understand the role of the hero in an epic, then, one must also see him in relation to the gods, since he dwells on the middle ground between the Otherworld and day-to-day secular life. As Scholes and Kellogg say, "epic . . . stands midway between sacred myth, a story whose events take place entirely outside of the profane world of historical men and events, and secular narrative, a story whose events take place entirely within the profane world. . . . "[54] In fact, the tension between those two extremes defines the hero, for he is partially divine at its outset and has throughout a special relationship with the deities. On the other hand, his people depend upon him utterly at some point in the fray. And the hero is himself not entirely of his people; he is somehow godlike in his powers and ancestry—many of the warriors in the *Iliad* are tagged "godlike." And he is isolated from his people at some stage, suffering under the burden of his own actions.

All these distinctions regarding the epic hero, and here specifically the **Táin**'s hero, Cúchulainn, hang upon the relationship between the warriors who fight the battles and the gods who are never far away. If the course of the *Iliad* is established by the Judgement of Paris, the **Táin** unfolds—apparently quite directly—from the "bad blood between Ochall Ochne, the King of the *síd* in Connacht, and Bodb, King of the Munster *síd.*"[55] The quarrel between their two pig-keepers, who become the two bulls on whose account the Táin is fought, is resolved only at the very end of the epic, where the two senselessly destroy one another. Like the Ulster warriors, the Donn Cuailnge is the victor, but his own death after the conflict means that nothing material is gained on the one side or preserved on the other, since the Táin's prize no longer exists. What is strange about this matter is that these two *síd* pig-keepers and their kings seem to be as unable to fulfill their own destinies without the aid of men as the Greek goddesses are unable to know who is most beautiful without consulting the opinion of a mortal. The gods seem to depend upon human strength for conclusions to their dilemmas; without the **Táin** it seems that the two *síd* pig-keepers would have persisted forever in their mutual persecution. If man's weakness in comparison to the gods is that he exists in the context of time rather than that of eternity, this potential for an ending seems to be a capacity that the gods must come to man to borrow.

At one point there is a reference to Medb's promise that the two bulls will be brought together to battle it out. Diarmait comes from Conchobor to the Connacht camp in order to request that the King and Queen of that province release the plundered cattle, make retribution for the damage that they have caused and arrange the confrontation of the bulls. Maine, the queen's son, says that his mother will not agree to this arrangement (p. 163), however, and so the war must go on among the people. As in the *Iliad,* destiny seems to have arranged a situation that no combat can decide, though a longer struggle can accomplish at least that much.

This situation is clarified by the Morrígan's speech, early in the **Táin,** to the Brown Bull. She settles near him on a stone and says:

'Dark one are you restless
  do you guess they gather
to certain slaughter
  the wise raven
groans aloud
  that enemies infest
the fair fields

                    ravaging in packs
                learn I discern
                    rich plains
                softly wavelike
                    baring their necks
                greenness of grass
                    beauty of blossoms
                on the plains war
                    grinding heroic
                hosts to dust
                    cattle groans the Badb
                the raven ravenous
                    among corpses of men
                affliction and outcry
                    and war everlasting
                raging over Cuailnge
                    death of sons
                death of Kinsmen
                    death death!'

                                        (p. 98)

The bull responds to these verses by tearing a trench through the ground as he moves away, and by killing two thirds of "three and fifty boys who always played on his back" (p. 100); the message from this war-goddess awakens the malevolent powers of the bull.

The *Táin Bó Cuailnge* is not the only part of the Ulster Cycle where this need exists for the arm of a warrior to settle a conflict between immortals. Raymond Cormier points out that in "The Wasting-Sickness of Cú Chúlainn," "the kings of the Otherworld go to war but cannot win without the aid of a human (perhaps because . . . they are only feeble shadows?)"[56] In both cases the principal human involved is Cúchulainn, perhaps indicating that this greatest of Irish heroes has a special relationship to the gods. The Chadwicks say that the "want of power" on the part of the gods is a characteristic common to Greek and Irish heroic tales. "They are scarcely more than a match for great kings and heroes. The Dagda has to call Ailill to his assistance against Ethal Anbuail; and his success in the end is chiefly due to his human ally. . . ."[57]

And the gods, of course, have much to do with the battles of men. They appear at several points in the *Táin,* usually to aid the Ulstermen. After the episode in which Cúchulainn sees through Ailill's attempt to trick him with Finnabair, their daughter, and Tamun the fool, certain gods manifest themselves. After Cúchulainn has screamed his war-cry, "demons and devils and goblins of the glen and fiends of the air replied, so hideous was the call he uttered on high. Then the Nemain stirred the armies to confusion" (p. 141).[58] A few lines later Lug mac Ethnenn, who identifies himself as Cuchulainn's "father from the *síde,*" comes to heal the hero's wounds and to give him a healing sleep. After the men of Ulster arise from their pangs, the Nemain appears again, bringing "confusion

on the [Connacht] armies and a hundred of their number fell dead" (p. 223). Before the last battle begins, the Morrígan speaks terror-inspiring verses from her situation between the camps of Ulster and Connacht, which verses end, "Hail Ulster! / Woe men of Ireland! / Woe to Ulster! / Hail men of Ireland!" But she is not unprejudiced: "This last ('Woe to Ulster') she said in Connachtmen's ears only, to hide the truth from them." The text continues that the "same night Net's wives, Nemain and the Badb, called out to the men of Ireland near the field at Gairech and Irgairech, and a hundred warriors died of fright" (pp. 238-39). Apart from these appearances, these gods are mentioned several times, especially in verses. The gods, then, like the gods in the *Iliad,* exist within the same reality as the men. Especially at the time of the greatest battle in each epic the boundaries between the world and the heavens are broken down. And the supernatural parents of the most important heroes come to care for their sons.

But although the Irish gods are involved in the fray as much as their Greek counterparts are, even to the extent of choosing sides and causing deaths, there is a great deal of difference in the bardic attitude toward them. The Irish gods are aloof, unfathomable and universally awe-inspiring. They and their foibles are never the subjects of laughter. Their motives are their own; there is no attempt to show them in conversation with one another or to represent them when they are not directly involved in the action of the epic. There are, of course, stories about some of the gods which do reveal their more anthropomorphic sides, but in the *Táin* only Lug and the Morrígan are presented in human shape, and they retain their superiority to even the greatest hero. The reader of the *Táin* is influenced in his admiration of Cúchulainn because he is favored by the gods. This favor from the deities, one should remember, is actively sought by Achilleus in the *Iliad.* Cedric Whitman says that "he will have 'honor from Zeus,' by which he means he will risk all. . . ."[59] Yet in the Greek epics, where the gods may be silly or even cowardly, "Agamemnon, Diomede, Odysseus, Ajax and Achilles set the standard by which the gods are judged."[60] In the *Táin Bó Cuailnge* this basis for evaluating the behavior of the gods does not apply; the Celtic gods, at least in the epic itself, seem to be above human evaluation.

The epic hero, then, is not one of the gods; but neither is he entirely one with his people. Some scholars have suggested that he may be a character from folklore, from some favorite story, who has been introduced into an historical or semi-historical tale. This theory seeks to explain the discrepancy between the naturalistic milieu of the epic and its more fantastic elements. For example, de Vries indicates that although the Táin might have occurred, its hero is not even from Irish folklore; he is Gaulish in origin.[61] Scholes and Kellogg agree that "epic narrative . . . takes actual historical persons, places, or events, and combines them with characters derived from myth in a fictional fusion. . . . Thus, in *Beowulf,* in the *Chanson de Roland,* and in the *Nibelungenlied* we find combinations of this order, in which a more or less recognizable Hygelac, or Charlemagne, or Atilla is found side by side with a mytho-fictional Beowulf, Roland, or Siegfried. . . . "[62] One tends to agree with the Chadwicks, who feel that inferences of this nature are unjustified[63]; they seem to be especially wary of this argument's tendency to lead on to celestially mythological theorizing.[64] Rather, they feel that elements of folktales tend to be attracted to the heroes: "if the hero gains in popularity—which is perhaps due in the main to poets—he may come before very long to be credited with new exploits, which seem chiefly to be borrowed from folktales and stories of earlier heroes, presumably because this was the material most ready to hand."[65]

There is something to be said for both sides of this argument, but I believe that if one is cautious in his judgments he may be able to find a middle ground. The hero is different from his fellow warriors, and he does seem at times to be composed more of the filaments of folk tale than the flesh and blood of an historical personage. He is not an elemental deity, but neither is he as human as his comrades-in-arms, at least at the outset of the epic. Whatever the origin of his superhuman characteristics may be, they do exist. And at the same time, the character whom they adorn is far more human than a figure from a mythological tale.

The ordinary barriers between the earth and the heavens, between the world of men and the world of the gods, though, are not absolute in the epic. These narratives represent points in the lives of humans and deities in which this limit is in a state of flux. The world of man may be entirely naturalistic at one moment, and then it may at the next become a setting for the entry of a god. Zeus, in the *Iliad,* controls the situation, now allowing the gods to join in the battle, and now restraining them. The *Táin Bó Cuailnge* veils the mechanics of the movements of its gods with a fog of mystery.

Within the world of men, the hero is something of an outsider. Carpenter says that "like [Achilleus] himself, his folk the Myrmidons are a lonely race . . . , unrelated to Argives and Danaans and Achaens. . . . "[66] Scholes and Kellogg note further that in "Greece the archaeologists have succeeded in finding the golden Mycenae of Agamemnon and the sandy Pylos of Nestor, but Achilles and his Myrmidons have left no marks on the real world because they are not of it."[67] And whatever the history of his literary evolution may be, Cú-chulainn, too, is shown to be a different sort of being from the Ulstermen whose possession he defends.

Within the action of the *Táin* Cúchulainn manifests the traits of an outsider. His home is also obscure; the Chadwicks say that it is impossible to be sure where Cúchulainn's home was, and they indicate that because the *Táin* does not give this information it can be inferred that he lacked an Irish fort of his own.[68] That he is not from Conchobor's Ulster is made abundantly clear. One of the stories which Fergus relates of his boyhood deeds tells of the day on which he smashed Conall Cearnach's chariot-shaft with a stone. In reply to Conall's query as to why he did it, he replies: "'To test my hand and the straightness of my aim. . . . Now, since it is your Ulster custom not to continue a dangerous journey, go back to Emain . . .'" (p. 87). It is obvious from this statement that Ulster's customs are not Cúchulainn's. Later, when he and his charioteer are travelling through the Ulster countryside they see some deer. Cúchulainn asks, "'What are those nimble beasts there?'" (p. 90), a question that he surely would not have needed to put if he were familiar with this territory. But if he does not belong to Ulster, Medb says that his mother—who is Conchobor's, the king's, sister—does (p. 170). And at the end of the epic, Ailill and Medb make peace with Ulster *and* Cúchulainn (p. 253). His isolation begins with this distinction from his fellow warriors.

He is further differentiated from the rest of the *Táin*'s characters by evidences of his superiority to them, which are to greater or lesser degrees the accoutrements of magic or of godlikeness. First, because of an offense against the wife of the Ulsterman Crunniuc—she was forced to race two chariot horses despite the onset of her labor pains—the men of Ulster were doomed to suffer the pangs of child-birth "for five days and four nights in their times of greatest difficulty" (p. 7). Since the Ulstermen, except for the exiles in Medb's army, have been taken by these "Pangs of Ulster" when attacked by the Connachtmen, Cúchulainn has to face the enemy alone until they recover. He is aided in the battle only by Lug, the god, and by the boy troop of Ulster, until the men arrive. Fergus explains the reason that Cúchulainn is immune from this disability: "'[it] never came to our women or our youths, or anyone not from Ulster—and therefore not to Cúchulainn or his father'" (p. 81). It should be noted that the father is not named here, but whether he is Lug or Sualdam, he is not of Ulster.

Two even stranger manifestations of Cúchulainn's singularity are his supernatural horses and the hero light that shines from him in his battle-fury. In these two particulars he is seen once again to have a great deal in common with Achilleus. His horses are born under the same mysterious circumstances that attend his own birth, and the story of their coming forth is so strange and complex that perhaps it should be recounted briefly here. Conchobor and his sister Deichtine stop for the evening in a house whose mistress is in labor. She bears a son, and the same night a mare in the stable throws twin foals. In the morning, however, everything but the boy and the foals has disappeared; and the king and his sister take the boy and the horses back to Emain Macha, where Deichtine undertakes the fostering of the baby. He dies in childhood, and his foster-mother grows thirsty from making a long lament for him. When she takes a drink, she accidentally swallows a small creature which is in the cup. That night the god Lug appears to her in a dream, telling her that she is pregnant with his child, and that the foals which they took from the enchanted house are to be raised along with him. As if matters were not already complicated enough, she is given in marriage to Sualdam mac Roich. She is so ashamed of going to bed with her new husband when she is already pregnant that she vomits away the pregnancy. She at last becomes pregnant again, apparently by Sualdam, and her son is Setanta, who later is given the name Cúchulainn (pp. 22-23).

There is another story in the Ulster Cycle, "The Death of Cúchulainn," in which these horses prove their supernatural natures. The Chadwicks draw from this tale and another in their account of the horses' origins: "in *Bricriu's Feast* . . . , they come from two different lochs and have just been caught. At his [Cúchulainn's] death they flee to their lochs; but one of them returns and defends his body, and afterwards makes its way home to his wife. It lays its head on Emer's lap to let her know what has happened. . . . "[69] In this story one of them, the Gray of Macha, furthermore refuses to come to the chariot-driver for harnessing, and when its master reproaches it, it weeps tears of blood onto Cúchulainn's feet.[70] This relationship of the hero to his horse is like that of Achilleus and Xanthos, which sorrowfully prophesies its master's death.[71] This horse, too, is a part of the hero's inheritance, "which the sea-god gave his father at his wedding."[72]

Cúchulainn also has a "hero halo" or hero-light. It is described as "long and broad as a warrior's whetstone, long as a snout" (p. 153), and it is part of his "warp-spasm" that comes over him, the product of his battle-fury, before he performs his greatest heroic feats. Murphy calls the recording of this feature a "primitive Indo-European" credence "reflected in . . . the Greek *Iliad*."[73] Carpenter, too, calls attention to Achilleus' "cloud of fire [which] blazes magically about his head."[74] These manifestations may be more a matter of poetic exaggeration of the great military valor of these two heroes than a supernatural manifestation, but it is important to note that they alone among their fellow warriors have the hero light.

And if Cúchulainn and his horses, like Achilleus and his, have these super-human characteristics, the two heroes also possess special weapons and shields. Cúchulainn fights in a dazzling fashion; his battle feats include:

the apple-feat—juggling nine apples with never more than one palm; the thunder-feat; the feats of the sword-edge and the sloped shield; the feats of the javelin and rope; the body-feat; the feat of Cat and the heroic salmon-leap; the pole-throw and the leap over a poisoned stroke; the noble chariot-fighter's crouch; the *gae bolga;* the spurt of speed; the feat of the chariot-wheel thrown on high and the feat of the shield-rim; the breath-feat, with gold apples blown up into the air; the snapping mouth and the hero's scream; the stroke of precision; the stunning-shot and the cry-stroke; stepping on a lance in flight and straightening erect on its point; the sickle-chariot; and the trussing of a warrior on the points of spear. (p. 34)

What some of these feats, like the apple feat, have to do with battle is obscure; perhaps they were intended to terrify the opponent by sheer displays of virtuosity. They are not as naturalistic modes of combat as are those described in the *Iliad,* although from time to time precise and credible accounts of wounding and killing are recorded in the **Táin.** At any rate, most of the best fighters in the **Táin** know most of these feats, and Ferdia, Cúchulainn's greatest opponent, has all of these feats, in addition to many of his own invention, except the *gae bolga,* since he studied the art of war under the same tutor that taught Cúchulainn. But the *gae bolga* makes all the difference. The exact nature of this weapon is not given in the **Táin,** but it seems to be used to disembowel the opponent—at least this is its effect upon both Conla, the hero's son, and upon Ferdia. The Chadwicks suggest that it might be a "forked spear."[75] Achilleus, as Carpenter indicates, likewise has a weapon which only he can use: "When at last he goes to war he takes with him his father's mighty ashen spear, which none but he among the warriors can lift, . . ."[76] And when he finishes Hektor, it is this instrument which accomplishes his aim.

The shield of Achilleus, with its detailed representation of war and peace, and with its divine crafting, is one of the most wonderful features of the *Iliad.* Cúchulainn's shield, although far less elaborately described in the **Táin,** may possess some shadow of the greatness of the one that Achilleus had. Cúchulainn's shield likewise is impossible for any enemy to pierce, and Alwyn Rees and Brinley Rees say that its iconography suggests that it is more than natural: "Cúchulainn had five wheels on his shield, which is particularly noteworthy when we remember that Achilles' shield was made in five layers . . . [possibly] representing the cosmos. . . . "[77] The arming of the heroes, however, is directly connected with their early deaths. When Thetis agrees to get her son his immortal armor, she weeps and tells him that she will soon lose him since there is a prophecy that his death will follow closely upon Hektor's, and this armor will allow him to kill the Trojan, which would decide the war and win his fame (*Iliad,* XVIII. 95-96). Cúchulainn's armor is not immortal, but there is a prophecy made on the day that he accepts it: "if a warrior took up arms for the first time that day his name would endure in Ireland as a word signifying mighty acts, and stories about him would last forever" (p. 84). A similar prophecy is made on the day that he first steps into a chariot. Like Achilleus, he is forewarned about the doom which accompanies his arming, and he, too, is eager to accept it. He says, "'That is a fair bargain. . . . If I achieve fame I am content, though I had only one day on earth'" (p. 85).

The hero, then, with his obscure origin, his hero-light and his horses, his weapons and his shield, and in the case of Cúchulainn, his special relationship with the gods—the story of his death has it that even the Morrígan wanted to protect him from his fall in battle—lives in a reality different from that of the lesser figures who surround him. Carpenter confirms this notion in respect to Achilleus: "Whatever his ultimate origin, Achilles must derive from a different realm from the severely practical Menelaos, the garrulous old politician Nestor, or for that matter all the other leading figures of the Achaean expeditionary force."[78] The hero—Irish or Greek—can only be made one with his society through the poem which tells the story of his great feats, through which he becomes indigenous to their tribal memories. He may never be, like a character from Icelandic saga, anyone's physical ancestor, but he can become the ancestor to all the greatness in the culture which he has touched.

If, on the one hand, the hero must be integrated with his culture on one level, he must become completely a part of humanity on the other. His special relationship with the gods stems from his parentage. Cúchulainn's father, some versions of the *Táin* (including Kinsella's) have it, is the god Lug—and one remembers that Achilleus was the son of the Neriad Thetis. The case of the Myrmidon hero is not terribly unusual; in the *Iliad* many warriors—Sarpedon, Aeneas, and Eudoros, to name a few—have a god for one parent. The unusual thing is that, as Rhys Carpenter says, "*both* of Achilles' parents are superhuman, since his mother Thetis is a mermaid from the depths of the sea and his father Peleus bears the marks of a *Märchen* hero" [italics mine].[79] A *Märchen,* briefly, is a wonder-tale or motif of the fairy-tale sort, and its hero is a being typical of his milieu. Carpenter goes on at some length to demonstrate that both Peleus and his son are of the *Märchen*:

> various familiar *Märchen* motifs cluster about him [Peleus]. . In order to win his bride he clings fast to her while she . . . changes herself into lion and snake. Any son by her is predestined to become greater than his sire. . . . Peleus is the wielder of a wonderful weapon, the ashen spear which Achilles is to inherit. . . . *Märchen* heroes tend to stand out as lonely wanderers, as folk from far away or from nowhere.[80]

Cúchulainn, too has a god for a parent in most versions of the story, but he is the only character in the *Táin Bó Cuailnge* who has one. The Chadwicks indicate that "most of the royal geneologies contain the names of gods, usually Lug or Nuadu, or both."[81] In the *Táin,* however, the divine ancestry of the others is not mentioned. Some critics, like Cormier, warn the reader not to take it for granted that Lug is Cúchulainn's father, since the evidence of this relationship is not consistent.

I see no particular reason to doubt that he was sired by the god, however, since the only other option is to accept that he was actually the child of Dechtine and Sualdam. Kuno Meyer shows that the belief that Sualdam was the hero's father was a late interpolation:

> I believe that a . . . mistake is responsible for the name, if not for the creation of another well-known figure of ancient Irish story-telling, that of the human father of Cúchulainn. . . . Now by itself *mac soalte* would mean 'well-nurtured son', and that this is actually the original phrase to which the name of the father may be traced is proved. . . . [82]

Even if his father is Sualdam, though, and not Lug, the *Märchen* nature of his parenting still persists. For this Sualdam, it seems, is no average man. When the Ulster hosts arise from their pangs, and Sualdam hears that his son is lying wounded after his many single combats with Connachtmen, he sets up a cry at his son's behest to arouse the warriors to combat. Conchobor and his druids consider what he has said, but in his haste to effect an attack he falls over his shield and beheads himself. If he were only a man this beheading would put a stop to his urgings, but when the head is brought back to Sualdam's house it speaks its warning once more (pp. 218-19). This scene recalls the severed head of Bendigeidfran which directs his men in the *Mabinogion*[83]; Sualdam must surely be considered to be of the wondertale kind. Cúchulainn's chariot-driver, Laeg, also manifests *Märchen* characteristics at least once in the epic. In the scene following the healing by Lug, this charioteer "casts a protecting spell on his horses and his companion-in-arms and made them obscure to all in the camp, while everything remained clear to themselves" (p. 148).

The raising of the hero is also reminiscent of the *Märchen*. Among Carpenter's examples of the *Märchen* characteristics of Achilleus, he cites that hero's upbringing. "His [Achilles'] mother tries to make him immortal . . . [and because she is] unable to take her mortal child with her beneath the waves, she entrusts the infant to a wizard of the forest, Cheiron the centaur . . . [in whose keeping] Achilles grows to a man's strength and more than a man's prowess."[84] Cúchulainn, likewise, has his training in arms from a mysterious creature, the witch Scáthach. He goes to her on his own, and from her he learns all the arts of warfare as well as a prophecy regarding his future. And while he stays with her he apparently becomes her foster-son, for two of her other pupils, Ferbaeth and Ferdia, are bound to him as both friends and foster-brothers.

And for a long time the Irish hero seems to lead a charmed life. Although Cúchulainn has opted for long fame and few years, he does not seem to be vulnerable to wounding in ordinary combat. He is blooded four times within the *Táin*: once by the boy-troop of Ulster; once by the warrior Lóch, but only with the help of the Morrígan; by Ferbaeth; and by Ferdia. The wounding by the boy-troop happens when the hero is still a child, and before he is fostered by Scáthach or armed by his king. After this point, however, it seems that Cúchulainn can be wounded only in some extreme circumstance, one in which his existence between the world of the gods and that of man is brought into some tension. The wounding of the mature Cúchulainn is at the heart of the action.

One case of wounding which happens at the Táin itself occurs during the hero's fight with Lóch mac Mofemis, a single combat which comes between Cúchulainn's fight with Ferbaeth and his conflict with Ferdia. The episode begins with the entry of a young woman who comes to the hero offering him her treasure and her cattle, and proclaiming her love for him. She identifies herself as "King Buan's daughter," but he apparently does not recognize her as the Morrígan. He dismisses her curtly, telling her that he has no time now for a woman, despite her offer of help to him. When he continues to reject her, she threatens him. She will use her shape-changing abilities against him and will attack him in the form of an eel, a she-wolf, and a "harmless red heifer" which causes the cattle that follow her to stampede him. He replies with threats to crack her ribs, burst her eye, and shatter her leg, which injuries can be undone only by a blessing from him (pp. 132-33). The scene moves then to the Connacht camp, where Medb and Ailill are coercing Lóch to fight the young hero. Lóch says that he cannot deign to confront a child with no beard, and the hero has to make himself a beard with berry juice and by speaking into "a fistful of grass" so that everyone will be deceived that he has a beard. This conflict, then, will be a *Märchen* battle, in which the hero must fight against both a warrior and a shape-changing supernatural woman, and before which he must alter his own appearance with magic (p. 134).

The situation is from *Märchen,* but the way in which the battle takes place is purely heroic. Cúchulainn fights both Lóch and the Morrígan with his strength and his heroic fury, and not with magic. Both warriors are incited to fight by words which attack their honor. Medb taunts Lóch: "'It is a great shame on you . . . that the man who killed your brother can destroy our army, and

you still haven't gone to fight him. Surely a peppery overgrown elf like him can't resist the fiery force of a warrior like you'" (p. 134). Likewise, when Cúchulainn is in dire straits with the Morrígan coiled about his legs in the form of an eel and Lóch hacking away at him, the satirist "venom-tongued Bricriu mac Carba"— one of the Ulstermen in Medb's camp—forces him to react valiantly by saying, "'Your strength is withered up . . . if a little salmon can put you down like this, and the men of Ulster rising out of their pangs. If this is what happens when you meet a tough warrior in arms, it's a pity you took on a hero's task, with all the men of Ireland looking on'" (p. 135). The hero immediately recovers enough to crush the Morrígan's ribs as he had promised when his anger is roused after this attack on both his personal prowess and his responsibility to the Ulster forces. And so the hero eventually wins the battle at the cost of much of his heroic strength and after receiving several wounds. The episode ends with more trickery on the part of the Morrígan, who thereby gets a blessing from Cúchulainn which heals each of her wounded parts.

The healing of the hero's wounds by Lug follows soon after this combat, the injuries received through the agency of magic being likewise cured with supernatural aid. These two episodes which show most strongly the hero's supernatural connections are juxtaposed against—indeed, form an interlude among—the combats which heighten his sense of his own humanity. The conflict with Lóch, in fact, proceeds from both these sides of his personality, another reason for his vulnerability. He walks the boundary here between the supernaturalism surrounding him and within him, and the terribly powerful fact that Lóch was the pupil of the same Scáthach who had trained him, and was, like Cúchulainn, also her foster-son. There was not, apparently, also the "blood pact of friendship" (p. 203) binding these two warriors that bound Cúchulainn and Ferdia, but their common foster-mother is still a strong human tie. Cúchulainn is forced to kill Lóch with the *gae bolga,* the weapon whose use he learned from that same foster-mother, which is perhaps one of the reasons that after the battle a "great weariness fell on" him. And this tie to the man he kills, while he is totally separated from those he defends who lie in their pangs, is surely what gives rise to the verses that he speaks: "'I am almost worn out / by single contests. / I can't kill all their best / alone as I am'" (p. 136).

Cúchulainn's recent battle with Ferbaeth, also his foster-brother, and one of the three men who draw blood from him, is a more terrible experience for the hero. If this combat is untouched by supernatural adversity, it is equally lacking in supernatural aid. This fight has the extra dimension of being a struggle between two foster-brothers whose friendship was once apparently deep. Neither of the heroes goes delightedly into the combat; first their friendship must be broken. The Ulster exile, Ferbaeth, is made drunk with wine, and Finnabair, Medb's daughter, is promised to him. He complies, saying, "'I don't want all this. . . . Cúchulainn is my foster-brother and sworn to me for ever. Still, I'll meet him tomorrow and hack his head off'" (p. 129). Cúchulainn, a man who would not stoop lightly to imploring an enemy, "begged him [not to renounce their friendship and fight with him] by their foster-brotherhood and by their common foster-nurse, Scáthach" (p. 130). Ferbaeth answers that he cannot stop now, because he has promised Medb to fight him. He has, that is to say, put his honor before his friendship and the bonds of their common fostering. Once he has broken faith with his foster-brother, Cúchulainn is no longer bound to respect the tie, either. He tells Ferbaeth to "'keep your friendship, then!'" (p. 130). But a curious thing happens; this hero, who has come out of many single combats unmarked, accidentally steps on a "piece of split holly" as he furiously storms away into the glen. It pierces his foot and emerges at his knee. It is this offending piece of holly that Cúchulainn uses to put an end to Ferbaeth.

Cúchulainn talks with his friends and foster-father Fergus, the leader of the Ulster exiles, after this killing. Fergus says, "'Your comrade is fallen. . . . I wonder will you pay for his death tomorrow?'", to which Cúchulainn replies, "'Sometime I must pay'" (p. 131). Kinsella explains this exchange by citing Thurneysen's explanation that the payment may be a matter of *Wergeld* (p. 268, n. 131). But even if, on one level, the payment is a matter of blood price, on another it is something far more serious. After this breaking of the family tie, three other such incidents occur: the fight with Lóch which leaves him more badly wounded than did the holly-branch, his confrontation by his foster-father Fergus, and his climactic combat with his "own ardent and adored foster-brother" (p. 168), Ferdia. His anger with Ferbaeth sets off a long succession of events in which friendship vies with honor for supremacy in the hero's estimation, a series of conflicts in which the hero will move into his loneliest and darkest hours in the *Táin,* and as a result of which he can finally become one with his people, fully humanized and free of his *Märchen* trappings. The names of the three heroes with whom Cúchulainn has his most significant single combats suggest this metamorphosis: Ferbaeth, Fergus, and Ferdia all carry the prefix *fer,* apparently a form of *fear,* "man."

The combat with Ferdia is more complex and more moving than either the battle with Lóch and the Morrígan, or the conflict with Ferbaeth. It begins in much the same way, with Medb taunting and bribing the warrior in order to bring him to fight his foster-brother. Finnabair herself comes in to tempt him; "at the neck-opening of her shirt she offered him certain fragrant sweet apples, saying that Ferdia was her darling and her chosen beloved of the whole world" (pp.

168-69). But Medb goes further in her subterfuge this time. She does not merely taunt him, but she actually lies to him, telling him that Cúchulainn thinks little of him. This speech arouses Ferdia's anger to the point that the queen has little difficulty in sending him out to fight, even though he is first provided a "surety" of six champions whom he must face at home if he does not fight the Ulster hero. And his charioteer does his part, also, to prepare the warrior for the battle, although perhaps he does not intend what he says to have this effect, by praising Cúchulainn extravagantly, and by expressing his own fear of him. Ferdia accuses his charioteer of being false in his friendship (p. 180)—an ironic accusation, considering what he intends to do. This continued praise for his foster-brother is unlike the taunts used from time to time. Later in this conflict Laeg will use this method of enspiriting his master. But Ferdia's charioteer, if he is using the praise of the enemy in order to goad his master, is using envy as his instrument, the very emotion whose insidious power began the battle between the pig-keepers, and the argument between Medb and Ailill. At any rate, the effect of the charioteer's words is limited. Ferdia when he speaks to Cúchulainn's face, is eager for the battle. But when he is alone with his chariot-driver he says that "'I wouldn't have come looking for this fight'" (p. 178). The two warriors formally break off their friendship and taunt one another, and when Cúchulainn seems to be softening in his antagonism, Ferdia rejects the speech he makes as "cunning" (p. 186).

Cúchulainn's own attitude is much steadier in its love for Ferdia. He accepts the challenge and the breaking of the friendship, and he joins his foster-brother in an exchange of insults. And yet even in the midst of this verbal parrying, when he has just been called "a clumsy and feeble / chicken-hearted / trembling boy,'" he replies:

> 'While we stayed with Scáthach
> we went as one
> with a common courage
>   into the fight.
> My bosom friend
> and heart's blood,
> dear above all,
>   I am going to miss you'
>
> (p. 184).

He seems to understand well how Ferdia came to oppose him, and he seems to forgive him and to wish, even now, that the combat might be avoided. He recounts to Ferdia all that Medb has done to entice him into the battle, omitting only the lies which Medb told him about his attitude toward his friend. Ferdia replies that "'Our friendship is finished through foul play'" (p. 187), apparently assuming the "foul play" to be on the part of Cúchulainn, and not himself or his new sovereign. And so at this point there is little that can be done except to fight, and Cúchulainn must acquiesce to this necessity.

Before the meeting of the two heroes, however, two factors are different this time. Fergus, who has just had a battle with Cuchulainn himself, comes to warn the hero of his opponent for the next day. Cuchulainn tells his foster-father how little he wants to fight Ferdia after he has given Fergus the beautiful greeting which Kinsella unhappily supplies only in a note:

> 'If a flock of birds were to settle on the plain, I would give you one wild goose and share another; if the fish were running in the river-mouths, I would give you one and share another; with a fistful each of cress and marshwort and sea-herb, and afterward a drink of cold water out of the sand.' (p. 276, n. 174)

He has greeted Fergus in this way before, and in this second greeting omits to say that he will place "myself in your place in the ford of battle, watching while you slept" (p. 118). This speech is no doubt a stock greeting in Irish poetry, a formulaic phrase, but it is singularly appropriate at this moment in the action of the **Táin**, omission and all, since it bespeaks a generosity in friendship which Cúchulainn will show many times before the end of this battle with his dearest friend, and since it adds great poignancy to this act which is in any case an "abomination,"[85] the killing of a friend and foster-brother.

And in contrast to the rebuffing of the Morrígan's lure before the battle with Lóch, Cúchulainn is shown going out to be with his wife Emer the night before he begins the encounter with Ferdia. In the hero's decision to go to his wife before meeting Ferdia, so that he may likewise be "washed and bathed, with hair nicely plaited and freshly trimmed" (p. 175) there is a sense of the ritual importance of the battle that is about to take place. No such preparations are deemed necessary before any of his other combats. And, too, another side of love and loyalty is implied by "sweet-haired" Emer's "waiting in Cairthenn Chiana-Da-Dam . . . at Sliab Fuait" (p. 175). The implicit tenderness and concern of this meeting, which causes Cúchulainn to be late the next morning for the encounter at the ford, amplifies the sense of the breach in affection and steadfastness which must be a part of it.

As the battle itself begins, the rules of courtesy are observed; because Ferdia is first to reach the ford of battle he is given the choice of weapons for the first day's fighting. Each wounds the other badly in the fray, but despite the injuries sustained and the swearing off of the friendship, after the fighting on each of the first two days "they came up to each other and each put his arm around the other's neck and gave him three kisses. Their horses passed that night in the same paddock and their charioteers by the same fire" (p. 188). Furthermore, Cúchulainn sends healing herbs to Ferdia, who sends food and drink to Cúchulainn; until the third day there is still a tie between them, and the breaking of vows of friendship has only allowed them to act in this antagonistic way toward one another without changing their hearts. On the third day of battle, when the end is coming into sight, Ferdia admits that "Medb has ruined us" (p. 192), but at their parting on that evening they do not observe the same practices that have characterized the two previous nights. On the fourth day the battle which has moved to the ford itself ends in the death of Ferdia; this death Cúchulainn, grievously wounded himself, brings about with the *gae bolga*.

By this point the Ulster hero is unrecognizable. He is no longer the warrior who could, with a thunder-feat, kill "a hundred, then two hundred, then three hundred, then four hundred, then five hundred, where he stopped" (p. 154) in his "first full battle with the provinces of Ireland" (p. 155). After carrying his friend's body away from the water, Cúchulainn faints, and when he arises from his faint he does not even bother to move himself away from a place where he is vulnerable to attack by Ferdia's vengeful allies. Laeg, his charioteer, tries to hearten him; but he is so incapacitated by grief that he can only make a long lament for Ferdia.

His sorrowings after killing Ferdia are reminiscent of Achilleus' mourning after his decision, first not to fight and then to allow Patroklos to wear his armor and go into the battle in his place. But if possible the Irish hero's burden is even more awesome than the Myrmidon's; his friend has fallen by his own hand, and there is no Hektor on whom to vent his sorrow and rage. These must come back upon himself. And while he lies suffering, wounded physically and emotionally, there is no supernatural cure. The hero, transformed by this sorrow, suffers humanly. He can only wait for the men of Ulster to arise from their pangs and finish the war. Paolo Vivante's description of the result of Achilleus' grief at Patroklos' death also provides an acute analysis of the outcome of Cúchulainn's sorrow: "The great scene of mourning marks the irrevocable break: Achilles dying, the proudest of lives forever cut off from its divine background . . . is resigned, even eager to die. His humanization is spontaneous, intimately realized; it is not a doom imposed upon him from without."[86] Honor, a matter of immortality, has come before human love in the epic until this point, with only one exception; and after this scene friendship will become the order of the action.

There is a commonly held notion that Patroklos is more than Achilleus' friend, and that he is his alter-ego. When Patroklos wears the hero's armor into combat with Hektor, Achilleus sees himself killed, not just his friend. And because Achilleus later confronts the Trojan wearing his own captured armor, Achilleus must kill himself. What Cúchulainn faces in the person of Ferdia, too, is in some sense himself, although it is not his more ethical side as in the case of Achilleus and Patroklos. Ferdia does not have Cúchulainn's armor, but he does have his feats, which he has learned from their common foster-mother. They are more than equals in battle; they are reflections of one another. Only on the last day of the battle, after the night of separate fires for charioteers and separate paddocks for horses, do the opponents invent feats of their own. Cúchulainn comes to the ford after Ferdia and sees him do "a thousand thrilling feats on high, multiple and miraculous, that no-one had ever taught him—not his foster-mother or foster-father, nor Scáthach nor Uathach nor Aife—but drawn from him that day at the thought of Cúchulainn" (p. 193). Cúchulainn responds by performing a similar series of feats of his own invention, after which he kills Ferdia. But if he destroys some part of himself in bringing death to this friend, what he destroys is not the human side as one might expect; this side of himself is only wounded, while his immortal part is driven from him, as the waters of the river are driven from their bed.

The exception to this rule of honor before friendship is, of course, his encounter with Fergus. Fergus is Cúchulainn's foster-father, and when he comes against his foster-son he is unarmed; Ailill has stolen his sword in revenge for Fergus' amorous dealings with Medb. Like the others, he is not willing immediately to go out to fight Cúchulainn, but after he is intoxicated with the wine that they have given him, and after they implore the drunken Fergus to fight, he agrees. Out he proceeds to meet the hero, who comments to him that he must be under strong security to confront him unarmed. Fergus replies that if there were a sword in his scabbard, he "wouldn't use it on you" (p. 165). He then makes a rather amazing request—that his foster-son yield before him, thus appearing to be a coward. Cúchulainn is unwilling to do so at first, according to the Book of Leinster version: "'I am loath to do that,' said Cú Chulainn, 'to flee before one man on the Foray of Cúalnge.'"[87] Fergus, however, offers to flee from Cúchulainn at another time, and the hero falls back before him. Fergus' allies encourage him to chase the hero, which he refuses to do. This episode, in which friendship, and foster-parent and sonship are held above honor, occurs shortly before the combat with Ferdia.

And there is a sequel to this scene. In the Last Battle Cúchulainn, marked with the wounds he received in his battle with Ferdia but in his battle-fury, tells Fergus that the debt has fallen due, and that he must now retreat. Fergus makes good the debt, and the result of his yielding is the turning point of the *Táin.* After he falls back "with his troop of three thousand," the conflict goes against the army which the king and queen of Connacht have mustered. "The men of Galeoin and

the men of Munster went away as well. They left Medb and Ailill to the battle, with their seven sons and their nine troops of three thousand men" (p. 249). The sacrifice of Fergus has been the greater, since Cúchulainn is able to show his courage and skill at arms in the combat with Ferdia, whereas Fergus ends his participation on the Táin with a retreat.

These two encounters between Cúchulainn and his foster-father provide a variation upon the father-and-son combat theme found in another story from the Ulster Cycle, "The Death of Aife's One Son." In another tale Cúchulainn, under the tutelage of Scáthach, has helped his foster-mother to defeat her greatest enemy, a female warrior called Aife. Despite his prior agreement with Emer that each of them will "stay pure until they met again, unless the other died" (p. 29), he forces the defeated queen to agree to share a bed with him and to bear him a son. The result of this breaking of vows is disastrous; the son, when he has grown large enough to fit the ring which Cúchulainn left with his mother, comes to Ireland. The boy, as one might expect, causes the Ulstermen a great deal of trouble upon his arrival, as Conall Cearnach says, making "little of Ulster's honour" (p. 42). Emer warns her husband that the child is his son, but he is unmoved by her protests and says to her that "'no matter who he is . . . I must kill him for the honour of Ulster'" (p. 44). This he does using the *gae bolga.* Upon realizing what they have lost, the Ulstermen set up a lament for him. Clearly some momentous change must take place in the character who is willing to kill his own son to protect the honor of his province, before he can yield to his foster-father, who poses the same threat. This giving way before Fergus happens after the battles with Ferbaeth and Lóch; the metamorphosis which is completed only after the death of Ferdia has already begun at this point. And it is only after the death of Ferdia that the action becomes panoramic; instead of single combats, a full-scale battle is fought. Cúchulainn engages Fergus in this second conflict in the midst of the encounter, with his fellow Ulstermen fighting on either side of him on the broad plain beyond the river.

Fergus' yielding to his foster-son shows that something even more radical has occurred; when the hero of the epic is thus transformed, his transformation colors the attitude of the others as well. His presence permeates every angle of the action. Whereas he has once had supernatural affinities, he now has become supremely human, and the people of the epic's world cannot escape the influence of his own attitude.

If the *Táin Bó Cuailnge* shows how the hero is humanized, the setting of the major combats further indicates the nature of his struggles. Rivers are especially important. Most of Cuchulainn's single combats are fought at or in fords, and rivers are even capable of arising in protest against human actions. Initially, the water seems to be antithetical to Cúchulainn's military genius; when Fraech decides to attack him, just after the stories of his childhood have been told, Medb's champion decides: "'I'll attack him there in the water; he isn't good in water'" (p. 93). Fraech's analysis of the situation is imperfect, though; he dies in the conflict. Later, however, Cúchulainn's attitude seems to change. Fergus relates to the Connachtmen that the hero has chosen to take them on one by one in the ford of the Cronn River (p. 117).

The Cronn River is more than the setting for a battle, although it is that, too. If rivers form natural boundaries, the Cronn is a self-conscious one. It rises against the crossing of Medb's army, rearing "up to the tree-tops" (p. 111), and possibly it does so at Cúchulainn's command. Whether the river arises of its own volition, though, or whether it is invoked by the hero, it shows a definite animation—almost a god-like personality. The obvious corollary to this action, of course, is the rising of the river Xanthos in the *Iliad* against the bloodying of its waters. The motivation is not the same, since the Cronn actually aids the warrior, but the events themselves are similar. Just after the Cronn attacks Medb's and Ailill's army, two other rivers, the Colptha and the Gatlaig, stand up in their beds to thwart the encroaching warriors. At one other time, too, another river leaves its bed. In the battle between Cúchulainn and Ferdia, when the heroes fight so closely on the last day of the conflict that "their shield-rims and sword-hilts and spear-shafts screamed like demons and devils and goblins of the glen and fiends of the air," they "drove the river off its course and out of its bed, leaving a dry space in the middle of the ford big enough for the last royal burial-ground of a king or queen—not a drop of water on it except what the two heroes and high warriors splashed there . . ." (pp. 195-96). Although the contest may sound more than human, and although there is doubtless some exaggeration in this description, what happens with this river is natural. It lacks—or at least does not manifest—the powerful consciousness of the Cronn.

There is a possible explanation for the Cronn's strange behavior. The entire Connacht force is bearing down upon the hero and his charioteer when they reach the ford, and the hero is in an extremely poor position to hold them all back. He requests that the river "save Muirtheimne from the enemy / until the warrior's work is done / on the mountain-top of Ochaine" (p. 111). Since the river is "Nes's Cronn River" according to Ailill (p. 107)—that is, the river which bears some special relationship to Conchobor's mother Nes—it might be expected to show displeasure at the invasion of Conchobor's territory, especially by an army which includes the legions of Fergus, who once was Ulster's king, before Nes found a way, through trickery, to procure it for her son. This reasoning, however, is shaky as an explanation for the behavior of the Colptha and

the Gatlaig. In these cases one can presume only that the rivers are something like gods, determined sometimes to carry out their bordering functions.

A ford, then, is almost a conscious concession or courtesy to men, which allows them to transgress the boundary, though only by getting their feet wet from it. Kinsella comments in a note:

> A ford is frequently the place of challenge and single combat. In a practical sense it would be natural to defend a boundary, following a river, at such a crossing-place . . . ; but warriors appear also to select a ford in a more formal way, as an arena for certain kinds of combat. . . . Looking at the symbolism of the matter, and taking account of the mysterious nature of boundaries in themselves, Alwyn and Brinley Rees . . . suggest that the ford 'partakes in some measure of the nature of a divination rite' (p. 263, n. 73).

I would like to suggest an alternate explanation of this choice of "arena" which is perhaps less fanciful than that suggested in *Celtic Heritage*. If a river is a boundary, and if Cúchulainn is a character who exists between the *Märchen* or mythological world of his father and the world of the Ulstermen, perhaps the ritual of the ford is related to this humanizing process. To be human is to be mortal; the river's universal symbolism as the flow of time, the short-lived hero's greatest enemy, would seem to fit this case. When Laeg gives Cúchulainn the *gae bolga,* he floats it down the stream to him—the weapons whose victories ironically send the hero into his human and humanizing sorrow arrive by way of time's waters. And after the hero is mortalized, he moves away from the boundary, leaving it behind to join the battle which rages on the plain beyond, and to join with these men who can offer another sort of immortality—that which is found in song.

The crossing of the boundary is dramatized in the final portions of the two epics, the *Iliad* and the **Táin.** Achilleus' treatment of old Priam shows that he has undergone a radical change. The scene in which Cúchulainn spares Medb is less complex, but it likewise shows a transformation in character. He comes upon her in a helpless situation, although he "held his hand. He wouldn't strike her from behind." And to her plea for mercy he replies, "'If I killed you dead . . . it would only be right.'" The redactor explains his sparing of her by telling the reader that he is not "a killer of women" (p. 250). These two comments, though, are not sufficient explanation for his show of mercy. When others deserved it, he struck them from behind (p. 96), and he previously attempted to kill Medb and spared Aife only because she offered him a better bargain (pp. 96, 33). If anyone beside himself can be blamed for Ferdia's death, furthermore, it is Medb. Yet he spares her, and finally even makes peace with her (p. 253).

Cúchulainn, then, like Achilleus, begins his participation in the epic as an isolated figure, tinged with characteristics of a *Märchen* world. Through his responsibility for the death of a friend—and in the case of the **Táin,** a friend who is also a foster-brother—he goes through a period of intense human suffering which breaks down this isolation and lessens the difference between the hero and the other warriors. He is mortalized; Cúchulainn is wounded, and having done the deeds which bring him great glory and long life in the songs of men, he draws closer to his confrontation with the short physical existence which he has agreed to as its price. Some critics see the epic hero as therefore tragic, but for reasons which will be provided in the chapter, I do not concur with this point of view.

Tragedy in the Epic

The prevalent opinion about Achilleus is that he is a tragic hero as well as an epic one. Such an attitude arises from a number of observations about the *Iliad,* the first of which is that epic action is there dramatically presented. Rhys Carpenter even finds the structure of Attic tragedy in the *Iliad.*[88] And certainly what occurs within the epic's characters is presented as external action. W. P. Ker says that the "tragedy of Atilla. . . . , like the story of Achilles, is fit for a stage" since the "events" in both narratives are "played out in the clashing of one will against another."[89] Other critics, like Cedric Whitman, tend to read the *Iliad* as an epic which may present external events, but whose real concern is with the warriors' inner lives. He does not understand its conflict as a matter of will against will, but as a psychological self-examination by Achilleus, whose will is most of all in conflict with itself. Whitman comments that "the whole tragic paradox of Achilles centers upon this scene [in which Patroklos begs the hero to fight, then to lend him his armor], and in order to understand it, it is necessary to remember that the wrath of the hero is a search for himself which is complete only when the poem is complete."[90] James M. Redfield refutes Whitman's argument by warning that a critic's familiarity with the existential quests undertaken by many protagonists of modern literature can interfere with his ability to understand heroes like Achilleus. Whitman, he feels, discovers these encounters with the "Absolute and the Absurd" in narratives where they do not exist.[91] As well as being aware that a modern perspective can cause a certain existentialistic myopia, one should also avoid the tendency to regard Achilleus—or any other epic hero for that matter—as a pre-Hellenic Hamlet. Achilleus is indeed "complete only when the poem is complete," but his new state is not dependent upon the internal ambivalence which would bring about the tragic soul-search. Achilleus does not sit on the sidelines because he is unsure whether or not he should act; he sulks in his tent because he is determined not to fight.

Cúchulainn, likewise, is presented dramatically, and he is rendered in terms of his decisions. The epic hero, unlike the tragic hero, is active even in regard to his fate. Early death, the price of great and long-lasting fame, is his because he chooses it freely; he is no Oedipus—or Derdriu, for that matter—who has been born to a terrible doom. Both Achilleus and Cúchulainn hear and comprehend their fates long before they are accomplished, and while there is the time and the opportunity to avoid them. Their cases are not unique; Beowulf and others share this characteristic with them. Achilleus' mother and his horse warn him against going out to meet Hektor, and both Scáthach and Cathbad tell Cúchulainn what will happen if he persists in his heroic course. The fate which the Irish hero accepts, moreover, is hardly cruel; Scáthach concludes her description of his future by telling him that

> 'you will keep for thirty full years
> your sharp valour and your force
> I will not add another year
> nor tell you more of your career
> full of triumph and women's love
> what matter how short'
>
> (p. 37).

His life ends early, as foretold. Even so, he does not die as the result of some terrible deed of his own, brought about by a tragic flaw in his character. He succumbs because he has been placed in what Alwyn and Brinley Rees call "a series of ambiguous situations where heroism is of no avail."[92] Trickery and a series of conflicting taboos undo him. On the day of his death, Cúchulainn sets out for the field of battle despite a number of inauspicious signs and the pleas of his loved ones to abstain from the fighting. He is then met on the road by three crones who detain him and ask him to share their meal of hound's flesh. He must decide whether to refuse the feast and break one taboo, or else eat the meat of the creature for which he was named and therefore ignore another prohibition.[93] He partakes of the food, and suffers as a result the withering of a hand—because it brought the hound's flesh to his mouth—and the loss of power in one thigh—because he put the bones under it. Next he loses his charioteer and his horse, and is mortally wounded by his own spear, because of a ploy of his enemies' satirists. His spear, it seems, carries an injunction of its own, that it must be yielded upon demand, or it will kill its owner. The satirists make use of this double-bind by demanding the weapon. They threaten to revile him; but he kills them before they can dishonor him in any way. He does not die either humbled or humiliated, but standing on his feet, tied by his belt to a standing stone beside a loch. He meets his end with his hero-light playing about his head and his friend, Conall the Victorious, already riding out to avenge him.[94] This heroic death is entirely suitable for one who has lived such a life of valor, and nothing about it lessens his greatness.

The ***Táin Bó Cuailnge,*** of course, does not contain this story which is one of the Death Tales of the Ulster Heroes; in the final moments of the epic the hero is alive and triumphant. Whether or not his Greek counterpart fares quite as well in the end of his epic has been debated, especially because of the complexities of the hero's meeting with Priam. And if he does not die quite as beautifully as Cúchulainn, at least he is never humiliated as his enemy Hektor is. He falls, not because he is any man's inferior in single combat, but because he is found by a chance arrow. And he dies on the field of a full-scale battle, with his fellow warriors fighting all around him.

If there is nothing about Achilleus' death that smacks of a tragic fall, there is likewise nothing about him that inspires in the reader the tragic emotions of pity and fear. As an epic hero he arouses the reader's awe, as stated in the previous chapter. Even Whitman acknowledges "the triumph of the spirit amid self-destruction."[95] Maurice McNamee takes this notion further, differentiating the epic hero from both tragic and low-comic characters:

> Since the epic poem is built not upon incongruities in the actions of the main characters but upon the congruity between their action and the ideals of the culture which the epic embodies, it is neither pity nor laughter that it aims at, but admiration. . . . Precisely because it is the man of heroic stature accomplishing truly great deeds that the epic holds up for our admiration we do not identify ourselves as closely with the epic as we do with the tragic hero. There is a certain awesome distance maintained between ourselves and the epic hero, but it is not, as in comedy, a critical but an approving distance.[96]

To weigh this difference between the emotions evoked by the epic and tragic heroes, one might consider the difference between the way that he reacts to Homer's mighty Telemonian Aias and to the Ajax in Sophocles' tragedy.[97]

Pity and fear are lacking from the reader's attitude toward the epic hero because he does not "fall" as the tragic hero does. He suffers intensely, but his pain makes him human and a part of a human community, rather than isolating him from it. That is not to say, however, that the epic contains no tragedy or no tragic hero, but rather to maintain simply that neither Cúchulainn nor Achilleus plays that role. The theory put forth by Redfield's book is that Hektor is the *Iliad*'s tragic hero, and that his tragedy, juxtaposed against Achilleus' epic heroism, gives the Myrmidon "a location in the human world,"[98] since "the pathos of the poem is concentrated in the death of Hector."[99] If tragedy, then, has a place in the epic, and a function in the humanizing of the hero, it cannot be a characteristic of the great hero himself.

The foil for the *Märchen* hero cannot be other than human. He must begin his participation in the epic as a man who has, like Hektor, all the trappings of humanity—a wife, a son, a city which he loves, and a home in that city. He can never begin as a lonely outsider with supernatural parents, horses, and armor. Perhaps by the end of the epic the hero is capable of tragic action, but that would involve yet another metamorphosis than the one which made him human. Cúchulainn, for certain, never enters the tragic domain.

The world of the tragic hero has at its heart the problem of honor, and because honor is also an epic matter, the two realms are likely to become confused. Familiarity with tragedy generally precedes a reader's familiarity with epic, and as a result he may make the equation of the search for honor and the evil which it usually brings about in tragedy. In itself, though, honor is of two kinds; indeed, in the epic it is the highest form of greatness. The epic hero furthermore seeks honor with a pride that in tragedy would be a defect; but the honor is the due of his kind, and his pride in it is fully justified. McNamee rightly holds that honor for the epic hero is inevitable, that it is the "instinctive reaction to such greatness."[100] And if the hero is a cultural representative, then the glory which is accorded him illuminates the people whom he represents.

This proud stance of the epic hero, nevertheless, is the focal point for those critics who interpret the actions of the epic hero as tragical. Achilleus, for instance, is called "essentially a tragic character" because "by an excess of anger and hurt pride, [he] brings about the death of his dearest friend. . . . " But, McNamee contends, the "Greeks themselves, for whom *The Iliad* was written, would probably have reacted to his character quite differently. . . . They would . . . probably have admired him as a rather good embodiment of their notion of a hero."[101] What is excessive in the tragic hero is, contrary to the belief of some critics, appropriate in the epic hero, because his pride is a public matter. The tragic hero's pride is personal, narrow, and selfish, whereas the epic hero's pride is extended to his race and is a condition of his status and function. This difference is reflected in the fates of the Greeks who return to their homes after the conflict in Ilium. What has been a rightful seeking after honor breaks down into self-centeredness. Agamemnon is an especially good representative of this change.

Diomedes, too, provides an example of the difference between tragic excess and epic sufficiency. His fight with gods and his wounding of them would surely come under the heading of hubris if he were being represented as a tragic figure. But he is not; no righteous vengeance is taken upon him. His action reveals no flaw. Rather, it reveals his magnificence; Aphrodite looks silly beside him. Turning to the ***Táin Bó Cuailnge,*** it should be noted that Cúchulainn's temporary victory over the Morrígan in the contest with Lóch likewise reveals the hero's great power, although the comparison does not degrade the goddess. In the epic, where gods and men function in a common reality, pride which would otherwise affront them loses its irreverence. Even others than great heroes may be proud without risking excess; Fergus describes one of the minor champions of Ulster as a "flood of skill and courage, . . . a flood of hot blood, vigour, power and pride—a force to hold armies together; my own foster brother, Fergus mac Lete, King of Line, the battle-crest of the north of Ireland" (p. 230). There is certainly no condemnation of this man's pride.

But if even a direct, physical attack upon gods can be justified in the cause of epic heroism, an affront to fate apparently cannot be. The heroes of the *Iliad* and the *Táin,* Achilleus and Cúchulainn, are quick to embrace their fates; but Hektor's lapse at the end of Book VIII, in which he denies his doom, is his undoing. Even Zeus knows better than to go against destiny. To deny what the gods respect is excessive pride in the epic, and the act which originates the tragedy in the *Táin,* like the act which causes Hektor's fall in the *Iliad,* comes out of this kind of excess. This wrongful pride likewise has its root in a moral flaw; envy, in the *Táin,* brings about Medb's wrongdoing and consequent fall.

To return for the moment to the notion of the pride which is the hero's right, it should be remembered that this attitude is expressed in boasting. But the claims of their own greatness made by the likes of Achilleus or Cúchulainn or Beowulf are more than mere words. The epic hero's "self-definition," according to Redfield, "is a boast and a promise he makes to himself and to others."[102] It is a verbal expression of this race-encompassing pride, and it is unlike Hektor's blind and foolish claims that the victory may yet be Troy's. On a practical level, the hero's boast helps him to prepare himself emotionally for the battle to come, insuring that there will be no lack of great deeds owing to weakness of heart. And it also acts as a kind of "surety" against his failure; to return in disgrace after an impressive boast would surely be as important to avoid as the facing of any number of champions.

If there is pride and pride, then there are boasts and boasts. Medb's and Ailill's bickering over which of them is superior is certainly of the imperfect sort. In the first place, mere wealth is the basis for the comparison, and in the second, the argument leads on to the doing of base deeds rather than heroic ones. The "Pillow Talk" controversy is seen for what it is when it leads Medb to commit an affront to fate. When the Connacht troops begin to muster for the cattle raid, a woman in a chariot arrives on the scene. She identifies herself to Medb and Fedelm, a poetess who possesses the "Light of Foresight." The queen requests a prophecy regarding her host, and Fedelm replies, "'I see it

crimson, I see it red.'" Obstinately, Medb argues against this prophecy, which the poetess repeats several times. Her final comment to Fedelm shows that she is determined to ignore what she could hardly miss understanding as a forecast of doom: "'It doesn't matter. . . . Wrath and rage and red wounds are common when armies and large forces gather. So look once more and tell me the truth'" (p. 61).

If both the *Táin* and the *Iliad* contain tragedies, then, there is a real difference between the two epics, since the opposing queen, rather than the antagonist in battle, plays the major tragic part in the Irish work. But the two similarly undo themselves by denying fate, and both are humiliated by their enemies. Medb does not die in the course of the epic, but she is taken by Cúchulainn. At the Last Battle he comes upon her in her tent as she is performing some embarrassing bodily function[103] and captures her there. To add injury to this insult, the next event of any importance is the battle of the two bulls; because they both die, the goal of the lost contest has been negated. The bull from Ailill's herd, the one possession which made him materially "greater" than the queen, no longer exists. The pathos of the situation, though, is the terrible irony that this contest was unnecessary in the first place and not needed to prove Medb greater than her husband. Her superiority to him must be clear to everyone but herself. Charles Bowen points out that even the "robust antifeminism" of the redactors of the *Táin*[104] is insufficient to bring her down to size; they write about her with some real disapproval, but it is "mingled with awe." She is, for all their attempts to discredit her, a "giantess," not some "pouting Maureen O'Hara spoiling for a thwacking from John Wayne."[105] Her husband, on the other hand, is a cuckold and a patsy; he meekly accompanies his powerful wife on the cattle-raid which is designed to undermine his only advantage of her.[106]

Medb further demonstrates her refusal to accept the fate which Fedelm has lain before her, and shows her destructive lack of insight into her situation, when she contradicts Fergus' warning about Cúchulainn's ability to fight. She says, "'Let us not make too much of it. . . . He has only one body. He can suffer wounding'" (p. 76). And her blindness to fate, to her relationship with her husband, and to the godlikeness of her enemy are akin to her ruthlessness. The extremity of this characteristic causes Carney to describe her as "a spiritual ancestress to Lady Macbeth." Her lack of scruples is truly amazing; Carney points out as an example her willingness to murder the finest group of warriors in her entire army because if they won the war they would take all the credit for the victory, and if they were left behind they would seize all the property that was left unguarded.[107] She does not glory in carnage; she is probably not capable of that much emotion. Medb simply does not care what the outcome of her thoughtless decisions may be. When Fergus suggests to her that they might do better to disperse these gifted fighters throughout the army she replies, "'I don't mind . . . as long as they break up their present order'" (p. 67).

Medb is concerned, then, with neither the honor of her people nor the dictates of fate. She wishes to settle a personal grievance, even at the cost of her entire army. Pathetically again, the argument which she heads out to win, and the envy which drives her on, are not even her own. Unbeknown to the queen, this quarrel has originated with the two supernatural pig-keepers who are now embodied as bulls. Although she holds herself to be more powerful than fate, she is really the pawn in a contest for superiority between two gods. Yet when they die, she is left with material parity with Ailill, though the price has been most of her army, many of her sons, her only daughter, and—probably most important to her—her dignity. She has the last laugh, but hardly the best one, since the cost of it has been so great; nevertheless, it is obvious that fate has been more generous to her than it is to most of her sort.

The glory which Cúchulainn seeks is part of his responsibility; a sovereign like Medb is accountable for other matters. Unlike heroes, rulers must be concerned with preserving ordered societies. And because of her part in bringing about this conflict Medb is guilty of violating this trust. If she comes off badly as a queen, one might note that her failing is common to other rulers in heroic poetry. Conchobor, one remembers, has behaved despicably in "The Exile of the Sons of Uisliu"; in his anxiety to claim the beautiful, cursed woman Derdriu, he causes the deaths of many great warriors. His slaughter of them fails to gain his designed purpose, however, since Derdriu kills herself after he takes possession of her. Similarly, in the *Iliad*, Agamemnon is certainly no model for leadership. Even Odysseus, so grand upon the field of battle and on the homeward voyage, brings about the wrath of his people when he kills the suitors, representatives of the finest families in his country. Yet all these kings are somehow redeemed in the epics. Conchobor does nothing unworthy in the *Táin;* he goes as quickly as he can to the defense of his province. Agamemnon, Whitman says, "never meets with full disgrace." Homer, by avoiding an overt "drawing [of] the feebleness of Agamemnon" avoids pushing the *Iliad* in the direction of satire.[108] And Odysseus is certainly justified in setting his own house in order. Like Cúchulainn in the story of his death, although to a lesser degree, Odysseus has been placed in double jeopardy, since whatever he decides to do will be at least partly wrong.

The case of Medb, however, is complicated by several factors. One of these is that she bears the name of the goddess Medb, although she is herself quite human. Bowen describes the goddess Medb as the deity who confers sovereignty upon a man; through a "sacral marriage" she creates the king of a province: "It was believed that every tribal and provincial king had to unite with a goddess in a symbolic wedding in order to inaugurate and confirm his kingship."[109] He continues his argument by saying that "the goddess, the king's divine consort, came to be seen as symbolizing not so much the land and its bounty as the idea of sovereignty itself: the mysterious blessing of destiny that conferred power on the man who was chosen to receive it."[110] De Vries maintains that as a goddess, and therefore as the king's superior, Medb preserves the right and the ability to dethrone him and make some worthier man ruler if he proves to be inadequate.[111] Medb's contest with Ailill, then, takes on an additional significance. Names are meaningful in deciding what is good or evil for a character, as has been seen in the case of Cúchulainn. Medb, accordingly, may be regarded in one of two lights: she is either within her rights (as a namesake of the goddess) to test the worthiness of her husband the king, who shows himself to be disrespectful of her,[112] or she is a terrible perversion of the goddess. De Vries judges this second possibility to be the right one, saying that she has earned well the derision that she receives, by her "thirsting after love and power" rather than bequeathing them upon her chosen mate, and by her use of a "demonic power" to chain "men to herself" while seeming "to play with their fate."[113] I think, however, that it is the tension between this right and her misuse of it, between her greatness and her foolishness, that makes her a tragic figure.

The queen's methods as well as her goals are open to criticism. When she has great difficulty convincing warriors to go out singly to meet Cúchulainn, she resorts to underhanded techniques of persuasion. She threatens their honor, as in the case of Ferdia; she makes them drunk with wine, as in the case of Ferbaeth; she offers warrior after warrior marriage with her daughter; and she even offers the most recalcitrant her own sexual favors. The first three types of persuasion illustrate her nonchalance about dishonesty, while her promiscuity discloses an even more serious failing; because of her connection with the goddess whose name she shares, she is guilty of irreverence.

Medb has many foils in the *Táin,* and among them is Fergus, the leader of the Ulster exiles, who is often at loggerheads with her despite their alliance against Conchobor. Apparently, although this motive is never stated directly in the epic, he fights against Ulster as vengeance upon its king, who dishonored him by slaying men under his protection in "The Exile of the Sons of Uisliu." Nevertheless he remains a loyal friend and a generous one to Cúchulainn. Because of Fergus' impeccable handling of the trusts which this relationship involves, despite their delicacy in this war, the reader tends to sympathize with him, approving of his scorn for the ruthless queen. After the Last Battle, Medb turns to her conquered ally and says, "'We have had

shame and shambles here today, Fergus.'" He replies,
"'We have followed the rump of a misguiding woman.
. . . It is the usual thing for a herd led by a mare to
be strayed and destroyed'" (p. 251). His comment
should be closely examined. Before accepting his observation at face value as simply a piece of anti-feminism which the *Táin*'s redactors included as a good
joke, or as the final, just condemnation of a poor queen
who is also a bad example of femininity, the reader
should take note of the speaker of the sentiment.

Fergus is more honorable than Medb, but he is no
better as a leader. He has led his men into ambush
once, and on the Táin he leads them to defeat. There
is something wrong with his judgment, it would seem,
since he is neither weak like Ailill nor careless about
fate like Medb. His acceptance of destiny is illustrated
by a comment that he makes in the episode in which
he asks Cúchulainn to fall back before him. He clearly
sees the price which he must pay for this victory. He
says to Cúchulainn: "'I shall flee before you when you
shall be covered with wounds and blood and pierced
with stabs in the battle of the Táin, and when I alone
shall flee, then all the men of Ireland will flee.'"[114] If
this speech shows that he will accept his fate when it
confronts him, it also foreshadows his inability to lead
his men to victory.

If Fergus' leadership is less than excellent, his relationships with women are even worse. The malignity
of Woman harrasses him constantly, and his poverty of
leadership is tied up with this problem. In the Ulster
Cycle he is in some way the victim of three women:
Nes, his wife; Derdriu; and Queen Medb. Fergus is the
king of Ulster when he chooses Nes for his consort.
She agrees to marry him only if he will, in turn, allow
her son by Cathbad to be king for one year. Her reason
for this request, she says, is that she would like for
Conchobor's, her son's, sons to be able to claim royal
lineage. Fergus agrees, and with the apparent consent
of the people of Ulster Conchobor takes his place on
the throne for a year. When the time is up, however,
the men of Ulster feel "greatly insulted that Fergus had
given them over, like a dowry, while they were grateful to Conchobor for all he had given them." There is,
obviously, a tinge of misogyny in the mood of the
Ulstermen. "They decided, 'What Fergus sold, let it
stay sold; what Conchobor bought, let it stay bought'"
(p. 4).

Derdriu's beauty, likewise, is partially responsible for
the reprehensible slaughter that Conchobor commands
in the story of Uisliu's sons,[115] the carnage and broken
trust which cause the dishonor that sends Fergus on
the Táin. And the reader wonders whether Fergus would
have taken the job as emissary from Conchobor to the
exiles in the Derdriu tale if he had not had the beauty
of this woman, as well as the promise of the king, to
encourage him. On the cattle-raid itself, Medb often

uses her "friendly thighs" to persuade Fergus to this or
that. His comment about the "rump of a mare" has a
second, obscene meaning. The women are certainly
not blameless, and yet there must be something amiss
with Fergus himself for him to fall such easy prey to
their seduction.

They are not irresistible sirens, only calculating human
females. Cúchulainn provides a meaningful foil to this
weakness of Fergus, showing it to be just that, when
he resists the advances of the Morrígan. She not only
takes the form of a lovely young woman, but she has
all the powers of a goddess to aid her in her guile.
Perhaps Fergus' susceptibility to sexual persuasion
results from his own exaggerated masculinity. Vivian
Mercier provides the information that Fergus' name
means "virility." And he quotes a description of Fergus
from another scholar: "'He eats seven times as much
as an ordinary man, he has the strength of seven hundred men, his nose, his mouth, and his penis are seven
fingers in length, his scrotum is as big as a sack of
flour. He needs no less *[sic]* than seven women when
separated from his wife Flidais.'"[116] The grandiosity of
this description can be attributed to the Irish penchant
for hyperbole; however the fact remains that a man
with such awesome physical traits cannot easily be
faulted for the liaisons which he forms in order to vent
his great lust.

And yet the repeated dishonoring that he endures must
come from some failing of his own if it is anything
more than an instrument of anti-feminist invective on
the part of the *Táin*'s redactors. Perhaps, like
Shakespeare's Brutus, Fergus is susceptible to pleas
from others whom he wrongly judges to be as honest
as himself, with similarly terrible results. Conchobor,
as well as Nes and Medb, take advantage of this weakness, while only Cúchulainn is faithful to him. This
overabundance of trust and total lack of guile, which
contrast so strongly to Medb's dishonesty, are the frail-
ties—although they can hardly be considered to be
flaws—which allow him to make his first terrible error
in kingly judgment. All his later misfortunes seem to
begin with his gift to Conchobor's mother of a year
with her son on the throne. If his difficulties originate
in part from his trouble with women, they have another
possible cause as well. Like Medb, Fergus, although
human, is associated with the more-than-natural gift of
kingship. He is thought of in connection with the stone
at Tara (called the *Bod Fearghuis,* or "Fergus' Penis")
which, Mercier cites Dineen as saying "'was supposed
to shriek on the inauguration of the rightful monarch
of all Ireland.'"[117] If the association is more meaningful than the obvious connection between Fergus' masculinity and the phallic significance of this standing
stone, then this information can provide a clue to the
reason for the apparently unjust dishonorings which
come to such a noble man. It is entirely possible that
when he allows Nes to talk him out of his responsibil-

ity of kingship, which has a "sacral character,"[118] he commits blasphemy. He must suffer for this offense, which allows, in turn, the slaughter of Uisliu's sons to occur in Ulster. Thus this infinitely masculine, honorable king earns, not the single defeat which is Medb's, but disgrace upon disgrace.

Both the Connacht queen and the former king of Ulster have a counterpoint in Ailill. If Medb's notion of honor is a false one, and if Fergus has brought about his own dishonor and loses his chance to clear himself, Ailill responds to his own dishonoring with a laugh and a prank. He discovers that, as he has long suspected, his wife is Fergus' mistress. His servant Cuillius brings him Fergus' sword as a sign that his suspicions have been correct, and his first reaction to this news is to exchange a grin with his charioteer, telling him to keep the sword. Ailill does not take action against either of the offenders himself; he declares Medb "'justified. She does it to keep his help on the Táin'" (p. 103). This assumption is not necessarily true. As has been said, she is not justified in her seduction, and Fergus has other reasons than his fascination with Medb for remaining with the Connacht army. Besides, Fergus can hardly be particularly helpful in combat without his weapon. Ailill, however, is not as unmoved by his wife's promiscuity as he pretends to be. He calls Fergus to his tent for a game of *fidchell* after his sword is stolen. He laughs in Fergus' face, and when the Ulsterman grows angry Ailill scoffs at him as though it were Fergus who had just been dishonored.

Ailill said:

'Why so wild
    without your weapon
on the heights of a certain
    royal belly
in a certain ford
    was your will worked
or your heroism
    an empty shout
to Medb's oaths
    tribes of men
can bear witness
    sucked dry in the struggle . . .'
                  (pp. 104-105).

They continue to exchange unfriendly words and to play *fidchell,* and Ailill eventually comes up with something like a threat: "'these wise men [the pieces in the game] / I move against Fergus / let right be done / as our game goes'" (p. 106). But still he makes no actual move to avenge himself. Medb, who is watching them play, finally reprimands her husband, telling him to "'Hold a while/ your clownish words . . .'" (p. 106). The matter then remains unchanged until Ailill returns the sword to Fergus at the Last Battle. True to his commitment, and forgiving of the theft, Fergus springs

into action against the Ulster warriors, despite a sarcastic remark by Conall to the effect that he fights only "'for the sake of a whore's backside'" (p. 247). Ailill's failure, then, is perhaps an insufficient concern for his honor. It matters to him enough to incite him to allow his servant to keep Fergus' sword and leave him vulnerable when facing his enemies, even Cúchulainn; but Ailill never takes the initiative to challenge Fergus himself. The theft of the sword is admittedly a witty vengeance for cuckoldry, but it does nothing to recoup Ailill's lost honor.

The weakness of the Connacht king provides an illuminating contrast for Fergus' action in the poignant scene in the Last Battle between the exile and the king of Ulster. He has his sword raised against Conchobor, when Cormac catches his hand and reminds him that to attack Ulster's king in this manner "'would be mean and shameful, and spoil friendships. These wicked blows will cheapen your enmity and break your pacts'" (p. 248). Fergus, who is mindful of his honor, but even more concerned with his friendships, turns aside at these words and attacks three nearby hills. The commotion that his blows make summons Cúchulainn to the battle where Fergus must suffer his last defeat, failing to obtain his revenge, but still guiltless of any betrayal of his "pacts," either with Cúchulainn or with any other Ulsterman.

If Fergus' valor points up Ailill's weakness, it is still important to remember that the Connacht king has not always been a puny character. As mentioned in Chapter Two, he was once powerful enough to aid one god in his fight against another. The responsibility for Ailill's diminished state must go to Medb. She has made him the king of his province by marrying him, but she has made him the clown and weakling that he is by her own emasculating infidelity. And in so doing she has unwittingly diminished herself by turning herself into the consort of a buffoon; once again, her grasping nature has deprived her of something valuable.

There is one other tragic figure in the **Táin Bó Cuailnge.** She is Finnabair, the daughter of Ailill and Medb, who is so terribly humiliated by her realization of her own dishonesty that she literally dies of shame. Almost to the end of the conquest she aids her parents in the war by pretending to acquiesce to their bestowal of her person upon many of the warriors in the camp— once even offering her to Cúchulainn. She barely escapes this last deceit with her life, and the strategy ends in a worsening of Medb's situation. The plan has been to dress Támun, the camp fool, to look like Ailill— an appropriate man to wear this disguise—and have him promise Finnabair to the hero in exchange for his leaving their armies alone until the Last Battle. Then the two of them are to escape quickly. Cúchulainn, however, recognizes the fool and kills him, leaving both his corpse and the girl bound to two standing stones. "There was," the redactor comments, "no further truce for them with Cúchulainn after that" (p. 141). This incident is merely humorous, but the girl quickly develops into a more rounded, and more sympathetic character.

The incident which proves to be her undoing involves her being promised to a certain Rochad mac Faithemain. He is an Ulsterman, and when his pangs end he sets out to aid Cúchulainn ahead of the rest of Ulster's army. Ailill spots him as he nears his friend, and sends a horseman out to detain him with the offer of Finnabair. She is more than agreeable to this arrangement since she has been in love with him for a long time. She sleeps with him for one night; then he returns to Ulster, keeping his bargain. Several of Medb's allies hear that the girl has been given, for once and for all, to this warrior from Ulster, and they reveal to one another that she has previously been promised to them in return for their military services. These revelations of Finnabair's deceit result in chaos; seven hundred men die in the mutiny that ensues. Seemingly Finnabair has been somehow unaware of either what her parents have promised regarding her, or of what the outcome of these promises could be. In either case her ignorance is a bit hard to understand. But her reaction to the results of her dishonesty is both real and tragic; she dies of shame.

Finnabair evokes far more pity than her cold and calculating mother. De Vries contends that Medb is tragic in that "she has to send into the fight men that are particularly dear to her,"[119] both her lovers and her sons. But while such sacrifices would be heart-rending to any ordinary mortal, there is little evidence to suggest that Medb is particularly sorrowful to lose any man. Finnabair reacts far more humanly, feeling an anguish which may be, once again, hyperbolic, but which reflects an awareness of the evils of deceit, and the value of honesty which is laudable, even if it comes too late. The death of the girl also suggests that her loss of honor, as well as her misery over the deaths which she has caused, contributes to her own dying.

Tragedy, then, plays a significant part in establishing the structure of the **Táin Bó Cuailnge.** For many reasons, its hero is not tragic himself, the most important of which are that his character development is a matter of becoming human while the tragic hero must be human from the start, and that his function as a warrior does not offer the same opportunity for a tragic fall that kingship presents. An epic hero might die in battle, but such a death is appropriate for him; far more disgrace would be implied if he died in bed of a weakening disease. The kings and queen of Ulster and Connacht, simply by carrying the different responsibility of ruling, are more vulnerable to tragic errors and falls which must follow.

Finnabair is a foil for the faithful Emer, who stays with her husband the night before his conflict with Ferdia begins. The three more important tragic characters provide, by their degradation, a dark background which amplifies the triumph and splendor of the epic hero. The contrast between the goddess Medb and her flawed, human counterpart especially highlights first the godlikeness, then the triumphant humanity embodied in Cúchulainn.

The hero is caught up in someone else's tragedy. In the *Iliad* Agamemnon suffers the revenge of Apollo because he has insulted the god. He tries to make up for the losses that his payment of reparations to Apollo's priest entails by insulting Achilleus; a full-scale tragedy on Agamemnon's part is only narrowly averted. The **Táin Bó Cuailnge** begins with Medb's envy and her own consequent bad behavior. In both cases the hero is tossed into another character's situation, as well as into the gods' difficulties, as was discussed in Chapter Two. The human struggle catches him unawares, and initiates his humanizing, but his presence also transforms the essentially tragic action of the plot. As he becomes the center of the epic, the element of tragedy loses its centrality and even clarifies the nontragic nature of the epic action.

To point out the tragedies of the characters and the greatness of Cúchulainn, however, is not to deny the humor of the **Táin.** This ingredient is as essential to the reader's perception of the epic's human element as is the tragedy.

Notes

[1] He sees "Celtic epic" as standing at "one extreme" of the literary spectrum becaise of its "mythological romance and fantasy." While "the Homeric poems observe the mean," the "extremes may be found in the heroic literature of other nations; the extreme of marvellous fable in the old Irish heroic legends, for example. . . . " W. P. Ker, *Epic and Romance: Essays on Medieval Literature* (New York: Dover Publications, Inc., 1957), pp. 44, 37.

[2] Cecile O'Rahilly, *Táin Bó Cúalnge from the Book of Leinster* (Dublin: Dublin Institute for Advanced Studies, 1970), p. ix.

[3] William Butler Yeats, *The Collected Plays of W. B. Yeats* (New York: Macmillan Publishing Co., Inc., 1952), p. 438.

[4] Gwyn Jones, *Kings, Beasts and Heroes* (New York: Oxford Univ. Press, 1972), p. xviii.

[5] H. Munro Chadwick and N. Kershaw Chadwick, *The Ancient Literatures of Europe,* Vol. I of *The Growth of Literature* (Cambridge: Cambridge Univ. Press, 1932),

p. 44.

[6] Gwyn Jones and Thomas Jones, trans., *The Mabinogion,* Everyman's Library (New York: Dutton, 1974), p. 29.

[7] Jones and Jones, p. 57.

[8] Thomas Kinsella, trans., *The Táin* (Dublin: Dolmen Press, 1969), p. 134. All further references to the *Táin* will be to this edition unless otherwise indicated.

[9] Tom Peete Cross and Clark Harris Slover, eds., *Ancient Irish Tales* (New York: Barnes and Noble, Inc., 1936), pp. 197-98.

[10] Kuno Meyer, *Miscellanea Hibernica,* Univ. of Illinois Studies in Lang. and Lit., Vol. II, No. 4 (1917; rpt. New York: Johnson Reprint Corporation, 1967), pp. 12-13.

[11] Chadwick and Chadwick, pp. 234-35.

[12] Ker, pp. 8-9.

[13] Eleanor Knott and Gerald Murphy, *Early Irish Literature* (New York: Barnes and Noble, Inc., 1966), pp. 106-107.

[14] James Carney, Introd., *Early Irish Literature,* by Eleanor Knott and Gerald Murphy (New York: Barnes and Noble, Inc., 1966), p. 14.

[15] Eileen Bolton, "The Combat of Ferdiad and Cuchulain," *Anglo-Welsh Review,* 26, lvii (1976), 143.

[16] Chadwick and Chadwick, p. 213.

[17] Knott and Murphy, p. 106.

[18] Alwyn Rees and Brinley Rees, *Celtic Heritage: Ancient Tradition in Ireland and Wales* (London: Thames and Hudson, 1961), p. 69.

[19] Knott and Murphy, p. 106.

[20] Jan de Vries, *Heroic Song and Heroic Legend,* trans. B. J. Timmer (New York: Oxford Univ. Press, 1963), p. 89.

[21] Raymond Cormier, "Cú Chúlainn and Yvain: The Love Hero in Early Irish and Old French Literature," *Studies in Philology,* 72 (1975), 139.

[22] Knott and Murphy, pp. 114-15.

[23] de Vries, p. 92.

[24] de Vries, p. 93.

[25] These scaldic verses were "short fixed texts which managed to survive many generations intact until they achieved definite form in the written texts of the sagas. The verses often epitomize the high moments of a story and serve a structural as well as a thematic function. They should probably be regarded as an essential element in the oral tradition of historical prose." This definition is taken from Robert Scholes and Robert Kellogg, *The Nature of Narrative* (New York: Oxford Univ. Press, 1966), p. 46.

[26] de Vries, p. 92.

[27] Chadwick and Chadwick, p. 28.

[28] Chadwick and Chadwick, p. 54.

[29] Jones, *Kings, Beasts and Heroes,* p. xxi.

[30] Magnus Magnusson and Hermann Palsson, trans. *Laxdaela Saga* (Baltimore: Penguin Books, 1969).

[31] de Vries, p. 96.

[32] de Vries, p. 98.

[33] Scholes and Kellogg, p. 174.

[34] Chadwick and Chadwick, p. 87.

[35] de Vries, p. 84.

[36] Donald A. Mackenzie, *Teutonic Myth and Legend* (London: Gresham Publishing Company, n.d.), pp. 21-29.

[37] Chadwick and Chadwick, p. 215.

[38] Chadwick and Chadwick, p. 58.

[39] de Vries, pp. 72-73.

[40] Chadwick and Chadwick, p. 78.

[41] Ker, pp. 8-9; de Vries, pp. 74-75.

[42] Homer, *The Iliad,* trans. Richard Lattimore, Phoenix Books (Chicago: Univ. of Chicago Press, 1951), VI. 345-358. All further references to the *Iliad* will be to this translation.

[43] James Carney, *Studies in Irish Literature and History* (Dublin: Dublin Institute for Advanced Studies, 1955), p. 68.

[44] Scholes and Kellogg, p. 209.

[45] Scholes and Kellogg, p. 209.

[46] Rhys Carpenter, *Folk Tale, Fiction and Saga in the Homeric Epics* (Los Angeles: Univ. of California Press, 1962), p. 72.

[47] The import of these actions in relation to the heroes' deaths will be discussed more fully in Chapter Two.

[48] Scholes and Kellogg, p. 210.

[49] The role of the gods will be dealt with more thoroughly in Chapters Two and Three.

[50] de Vries, p. 82.

[51] Carney, *Studies,* p. 66.

[52] C. M. Bowra, *Heroic Poetry* (New York: St. Martin's Press, 1966), p. 4.

[53] Bowra, pp. 4-5.

[54] Robert Scholes and Robert Kellogg, *The Nature of Narrative* (New York: Oxford Univ. Press, 1966), p. 28.

[55] Thomas Kinsella, trans., *The Táin* (Dublin: Dolmen Press, 1969), p. 46. All future references to the *Tain* will be to this edition unless otherwise indicated.

[56] Raymond Cormier, "Cú Chúlainn and Yvain: The Love Hero in Early Irish and Old French Literature," *Studies in Philology,* 72 (1975), 125.

[57] H. Munro Chadwick and N. Kershaw Chadwick, *The Ancient Literatures of Europe,* Vol. I of *The Growth of Literature* (Cambridge: Cambridge Univ. Press, 1932), pp. 261-62.

[58] Kinsella describes "Nemain (Panic) . . . [as] one of the three goddesses of war, the others being Badb (Scald-crow), haunter of battle-fields, and Morrigan (Great Queen or Queen of Demons). Nemain and the Badb are mentioned as wives of the war-god Net" (p. 263, n. 68).

[59] Cedric Whitman, *Homer and the Heroic Tradition* (Cambridge, Mass.: Harvard Univ. Press, 1958), p. 183.

[60] W. P. Ker, *Epic and Romance: Essays on Medieval Literature* (New York: Dover Publications, Inc., 1957), p. 37.

[61] Jan de Vries, *Heroic Song and Heroic Legend,* trans. B. J. Timmer (New York: Oxford Univ. Press, 1963), pp. 84-85.

[62] Scholes and Kellogg, p. 59.

[63] Chadwick and Chadwick, p. 215.

[64] Chadwick and Chadwick, p. 236.

[65] Chadwick and Chadwick, p. 238.

[66] Rhys Carpenter, *Folk Tale, Fiction and Saga in the Homeric Epics* (Los Angeles: Univ of California Press, 1962), p. 72.

[67] Scholes and Kellogg, p. 59.

[68] Chadwick and Chadwick, p. 300.

[69] Chadwick and Chadwick, p. 74.

[70] Tom Peete Cross and Clark Harris Slover, ed., *Ancient Irish Tales* (New York: Barnes and Noble, Inc., 1936), pp. 333-34.

[71] Homer, *The Iliad,* trans. Richard Lattimore, Phoenix Books (Chicago: Univ. of Chicago Press, 1951), XIX.404-24. All further references to the *Iliad* will be to this translation.

[72] Carpenter, p. 9.

[73] Eleanor Knott and Gerald Murphy, *Early Irish Literature* (New York: Barnes and Noble, Inc., 1966), p. 117.

[74] Carpenter, p. 74.

[75] Chadwick and Chadwick, p. 73.

[76] Carpenter, p. 9.

[77] Alwyn Rees and Brinley Rees, *Celtic Heritage: Ancient Tradition in Ireland and Wales* (London: Thames and Hudson, 1961), p. 189.

[78] Carpenter, p. 73.

[79] Carpenter, p. 71.

[80] Carpenter, p. 72.

[81] Chadwick and Chadwick, pp. 206-207.

[82] Kuno Meyer, *Miscellanea Hibernica,* Univ. of Illinois Studies in Lang. and Lit., Vol. II, No. 4 (1917; rpt. New York: Johnson Reprint Corporation, 1967), p. 10.

[83] See "Branwen Daughter of Llyr," in Gwyn Jones and Thomas Jones, trans., *The Mabinogion,* Everyman's Library (New York: Dutton, 1974), pp. 25-40.

[84] Carpenter, p. 74.

[85] Cormier, p. 120.

[86] Paolo Vivante, *The Homeric Imagination: A Study of Homer's Poetic Perception of Reality* (Bloomington: Indiana Univ. Press, 1970), pp. 57-58.

[87] Cecile O'Rahilly, ed., *Táin Bó Cúalnge from the Book of Leinster* (Dublin: Dublin Institute for Advanced Studies, 1970), p. 208.

[88] Rhys Carpenter, *Folk Tale, Fiction and Saga in the Homeric Epics* (Los Angeles: Univ. of California Press, 1962), p. 79.

[89] W. P. Ker, *Epic and Romance: Essays on Medieval Literature* (New York: Dover Publications, Inc., 1957), p. 23.

[90] Cedric H. Whitman, *Homer and the Heroic Tradition* (Cambridge, Mass.: Harvard Univ. Press, 1958), p. 179.

[91] James M. Redfield, *Nature and Culture in the* Iliad: *The Tragedy of Hector* (Chicago: Univ. of Chicago Press, 1975), p. 11.

[92] Alwyn Rees and Brinley Rees, *Celtic Heritage: Ancient Tradition in Ireland and Wales* (London: Thames and Hudson, 1961), p. 333.

[93] Cúchulainn means "Hound of Culann." He was given this name, according to Fergus' story, because once, when he was a boy, he had served this man Culann as a watchdog. He had been forced to kill Culann's hound because it attacked him, but he made up its loss to its master by replacing it with himself until he could raise another puppy to defend the man's property (pp. 82-84).

[94] Tom Peete Cross and Clark Harris Slover, ed., *Ancient Irish Tales* (New York: Barnes and Noble, Inc., 1936), pp. 333-340.

[95] Whitman, p. 220.

[96] Maurice B. McNamee, *Honor and the Epic Hero: A Study of the Shifting Concept of Magnanimity in Philosophy and Epic Poetry* (New York: Holt, Rinehart and Winston, Inc., 1960), p. x.

[97] W. B. Yeats wrote five plays about Cúchulainn. They are strange, lyrical works which sometimes approach high comedy—as in the case of *The Green Helmet* and *The Only Jealousy of Emer*—and tragedy, in *At the Hawk's Well, On Baile's Strand,* and *The Death of Cuchulain.* But of all these works, not one takes its story from the *Táin* itself, though all originate, to some degree, in tales from the Ulster Cycle. Several of Yeats's critics express perplexity at the fact that he never adapted the fight with Ferdia for a tragic work. In light of the present study, I think that it would be safe to put forward the premise that he never did so because that action does not contain the tragic possibilities of the other stories, and that Yeats, perceiving this difference, bypassed the most significant event in the great Irish hero's life rather than do violence to it.

[98] James M. Redfield, *Nature and Culture in the* Iliad: *The Tragedy of Hector* (Chicago: Univ of Chicago Press, 1975), p. 28.

[99] Redfield, p. 29.

[100] McNamee, p. x.

[101] McNamee, p. 8.

[102] Redfield, p. 154.

[103] Charles Bowen notes that it is unclear exactly what she is doing, but that "neither menstruation nor urination . . . can be discarded as a possibility." Charles Bowen, "Great-Bladdered Medb: Mythology and Invention in the *Táin Bó Cuailnge*," *Eire,* 26 (1975), 32.

[104] Bowen, p. 30.

[105] Bowen, p. 31.

[106] Some scholars have speculated that the anti-feminism of Irish poetry has its origin in the transition, in Ireland, from a matriarchal to a patriarchal society. Succession, H. M. Chadwick says in *The Heroic Age* (Cambridge: Cambridge Univ. Press, 1912), was indeed reckoned through the female members of the royal family until the eighth century, "and there are said to be traces of the same type of succession in Ireland" (p. 428). In *The Growth of Literature,* furthermore, the Chadwicks point out examples of the evidence which would support a claim to matrilineal succession: "some of the leading heroes are frequently . . . called after their mothers, e.g. Conchobor (mac Nessa), Fergus (mac Roich), Ailill (mac Magach or mata), Cúchulainn (mac Dechtire)." This practice, however, does not offer certain proof of this form of succession, since "with this usage is probably to be connected the variation in the statements as to the paternity of these heroes . . ." (p. 177). Whether or not it has any anthropological basis, this form of succession exists in the *Táin:* Conchobor says to Medb that "I came and took the kingship here, in succession to my mother . . ." (p. 54). The power of Medb, and an anti-feminist attitude toward it, are certainties within the *Táin Bó Cuailnge.*

[107] James Carney, *Studies in Irish Literature and History* (Dublin: Dublin Institute for Advanced Studies, 1955), p. 69.

[108] Whitman, p. 163.

[109] Bowen, p. 18.

[110] Bowen, p. 20.

[111] Jan de Vries, *Heroic Song and Heroic Legend,* trans. B. J. Timmer (New York: Oxford Univ. Press, 1963), p. 91.

[112] Ailill says to her that "'It struck me . . . how much better off you are today than the day I married you'" (p. 52). He later claims that he "'took the kingship here'" because he had "'never heard of a province run by a woman'"—admitting that Connacht was hers before it was his, and that he became king only by marrying her.

[113] de Vries, p. 91

[114] Cecile O'Rahilly, ed., *Táin Bó Cúalnge from the Book of Leinster* (Dublin: Dublin Institute for Advanced Studies, 1970), p. 208.

[115] This story, too, has quite a strong anti-feminist element; a woman, Derdriu, is at the root of the trouble. She is another tragic heroine, doomed from before her birth to cause great destruction in Ireland, but the way that she brings it about is damning. She cannot help her great beauty, any more than Helen of Troy can, but she must be held accountable for her seduction of Noisiu. He rejects her at first because she has been promised to Conchobor, but she persists with threats and insults until he agrees to take her with him (p. 12).

[116] Vivian Mercier, *The Irish Comic Tradition* (New York: Oxford Univ. Press, 1962), p. 58.

[117] Mercier, p. 58.

[118] de Vries, p. 91.

[119] de Vries, p. 77.

Joan N. Radner (essay date 1982)

SOURCE: "'Fury Destroys the World': Historical Strategy in Ireland's Ulster Epic," *The Mankind Quarterly,* Vol. XXIII, No. 1, Fall, 1982, pp. 41-60.

[*In this essay, Radner explores why the* Táin *was so popular during the eighth century, a time when Ireland's political situation differed so markedly from that of the* Táin's *audience. She concludes that the epic represents "a complex and strategic gesture of farewell to that [pagan] era" that both glorifies the past and recognizes that its political environment was doomed to failure.*]

Like other heroic literature which has been long maintained in oral tradition before its written redaction, the Ulster sagas of early Ireland present a highly archaic picture of life, and this fact has attracted much commentary.[1] The earliest of these sagas were probably committed to writing during the eighth century A.D., at least three hundred years after Christianity came to Ireland, and yet they portray a pagan warrior culture, at an earlier stage of organization and material culture than is documented elsewhere in early Irish literature— more comparable, in fact, to the Continental Celtic tribal culture described by Classical authors before the birth of Christ than to the Irish Celtic culture so far investigated by archaeologists.[2] Professor Kenneth Jackson's famous Rede Lecture of 1964 justifiably spoke of the Ulster epic as "A Window on the Iron Age."

The Ulster stories present not only a cultural, but also a political situation that bears little resemblance to the Ireland of their redactors' era. The whole island is represented, interconnected by relationships and alliances on a scale unknown in the early historical period. One province, the large northeastern division of the Ulaid, the Ulstermen, stands out against the others, whose troops are collectively referred to simply as the "Men of Ireland." In the *Táin Bó Cúailnge* **(The Cattle-Raid of Cooley),** the central and most extensive narrative of the cycle, this enmity is sharply dramatized, as the domineering Medb and her husband Ailill, queen and king of Cruachan Aí in what is now Co. Roscommon, lead the massed armies of the Men of Ireland on an ambitious raid to steal the supernatural and gigantic bull Donn Cúailnge, The Brown One of Cúailnge, symbol and source of the power of the Ulster kingship.[3]

By the middle of the eighth century, when the Ulster stories began to be written down, and for several centuries following, the political situation in Ireland was radically different from that in the *Táin.* The Uí Néill, an ambitious dynasty in the midlands and the north whose ancestors scarcely appear in the Ulster sagas, had grown in power to become the strongest political force in Ireland, and were even making claims to an overkingship of the island symbolically based at Tara. Uí Néill expansion in the north had pushed the Ulaid eastwards beyond Lough Neagh and the River Bann, into a mere corner of the territory they dominated in the Ireland of the *Táin,* and away from Emain Macha, their legendary capital.[4]

It is fascinating, though also frustrating, to speculate about whether or not the Ulster sagas present valid historical and cultural evidence concerning prehistoric Ireland; but I am not here going to add my voice to all the opinions on this matter.[5] Instead, this essay addresses a different set of questions, one which has not yet received much attention: Why, in an era dominated by those who were insignificant in the epic cycle, was the Ulster Cycle so popular? Why was it preserved so carefully in manuscripts, and why did Ulster stories bulk so large in the repertoires of medieval Irish *filid* (court poets)?[6] How did this material have significance for its contemporary audiences, so far removed themselves from the pagan heroic culture and the political scheme of the Ulster stories?

We have some evidence that the scholars who wrote down the Ulster material made judgments and exercised choices in the process. The oldest surviving recensions of the Ulster sagas do not necessarily reflect the forms in which the tales had previously existed in oral tradition. Professor James Carney has recently drawn together the earliest Irish sources of information about the remote history of the *Táin Bó Cúailnge,* and has shown that some versions of the *Táin* prior to Recension I differed considerably from the story which reached vellum in or about the eighth century A.D.[7] Several clues indicate that there once existed a version of the *Táin* in which the raid on Ulster came not from Cruachan in the west, but rather from the south—from the direction of Kells or Tara, archaic royal sites controlled, respectively, by the ancestors of the Uí Néill (whom Carney refers to as the "Bregians," from their legendary ancestor Cobthach Cóel Breg) and of the Laigin, the Leinstermen.[8] There are allusions to such a version in the early Leinster genealogical tracts, as well as in alternate and conflicting versions of the army's itinerary within Recension I itself.[9] Such a plot makes good sense, in fact. Medb, daughter of the Bregian king Eochaid Feidlech, and herself perhaps in origin the sovereignty goddess of Tara,[10] surely belongs in the east rather than at Cruachan, and her husband Ailill is of the stock of the Gaileóin of Leinster. Their marriage and campaign against the Ulaid thus seem to represent a political union of the midlands and Leinster, a plausible threat to the power of Ulster. Professor Carney dates one of the major archaic references to this version of the *Táin,* in Luccreth moccu Chíara's poem *Conaille medb míchuru,* to the vicinity of A.D. 600, and notes that the poet referred to his material as *sen-éolas,* "old knowledge," even at that time; he suggests, therefore, that we can trace this early version of the *Táin* back to roughly a century from the pagan period, and that there may in fact be some historical basis for the events it portrays.[11]

There is of course no way of telling whether this early version of the Ulster epic represents the only, or even the major version of the Ulster material in the centuries prior to the redaction of Recension I of the *Táin.* Oral tradition could have carried many variants. The question we are investigating here—the question of the relationship between the early redactions of Ulster stories and their contemporary audiences—does not require us to go on a quest for the "original" forms of the tales; but it is important to note that there existed in early Christian Ireland, whether in writing, in oral tradition, or in both, well-known versions of the stories which differed from those that have survived in writ-

ing. The significant point is that although these versions were available, they were *rejected* by the scholars who were keeping the written records, and the Ulster epic was firmly grounded in an alternate plot represented in such tales as *Echtra Nerai* (The Otherworld Adventure of Nera), *Longes mac nUislenn* (The Exile of the Sons of Uisliu), *Fled Bricrenn* (Bricriu's Feast), and Recension I of the *Táin* itself.[12] In other words, what we see in the written Ulster stories reflects deliberate choices and, probably, revisions on the part of composers and transmitters of the tradition in the eighth century and later, and it will be useful to examine some of these choices, as we attempt to interpret the Ulster tradition and decide what it signified, particularly in political terms, to its early redactors.

It is noteworthy that the *Táin* and other early Ulster sagas do not show an overt relationship to contemporary political configurations in Ireland, and in particular, that they do not directly reflect the emergence of the Uí Néill, who by the eighth century were clearly the most powerful dynasty in Ireland—though not overkings of the whole island by a long stretch.[13] Pressing their conquests steadily against both the Laigin (Leinstermen) and the Ulaid confederation, they had since the fifth century expanded to control the midlands and the northern half of Ireland. The annals show a fairly constant struggle in the north, despite the fact that the Uí Néill had promptly established subject peoples, the Airgialla tribes, in most territories vacated by the Ulaid during the fifth century. Although the Ulaid confederation had probably been driven from the area of Emain Macha, their legendary capital, before 500 A.D. and was soon restricted to the area of the present counties Antrim, Down, and northern Louth, it was not until 851 that the Uí Néill King of Tara, Máel Sechnaill I, forced the submission of the king of the Ulaid. Ulster did not yield easily.

Thus conflict between the Uí Néill and the Ulaid was a historical fact throughout the period of the primary written development of the Ulster sagas, and it is interesting that it is not more directly reflected in them, and that there is not an obviously "Uí Néill" version, for instance, of the *Táin Bó Cúailnge.* Whether or not Professor Carney's inference be correct, that the "historical" attack that lay behind the *Táin* was from the direction of Tara, not Cruachan, there existed at least one version of the story in which this was the case; then why was such a version not developed further to show a "Bregian" triumph over the Ulaid, and thus to serve the Uí Néill's purposes? They were, after all, concerned to lay ancient claim to Tara and to an Uí Néill high-kingship at that site, which as early as the seventh century Muirchú, St. Patrick's biographer and partisan of the Uí Néill, was already calling *caput Scotorum,* "the capital of the Irish."[14] Surely such interests could have been served by a *Táin* which portrayed an alliance of the Men of Ireland, united at Tara against the Ulaid.

The most obvious response to this is that these were, of course, *Ulster* stories, and that it was not at all in the interests of the Ulaid that their epic cycle should advertise the successes of their upstart neighbors, the Uí Néill. There may also have been some minor influences on the retention of the Ulster stories. We should note Professor Carney's observation that early genealogies show some subject peoples in southern Ireland, such as the Corco Ché, claiming remote descent from the Ulaid; to such groups, he proposes, the Uí Néill "were powerful, but *parvenus,* and for them the concept 'Ulster' would connote not merely 'real aristocracy' but 'people of our blood.'"[15] It seems likely, in any case, that the Ulster stories were first redacted in Ulaid monasteries in the northeast—Bangor, Druim Snechta, Louth, and perhaps others. Thus the original decision as to the shape of the *Táin* and the other stories written prior to the Viking Age was probably an Ulaid decision. After all, such victory as there is in the *Táin* belongs to the Ulaid and to Cú Chulainn, the youthful hero who protects his province singlehanded; and the historical kings of the Dál nAraide of Ulster traced their descent to Conall Cernach, the only major character in the Ulster stories who is a direct ancestor of an important Northern royal line.

But if the original shaping of the Ulster material lay within Ulaid control, its subsequent development and preservation did not. It was the monasteries patronized by the Uí Néill in the Shannon basin, particularly Clonmacnois, that were responsible for the written maintenance of the "prime-tales" of Ulster, and it is in the great eleventh-century manuscript of Clonmacnois, Lebor na hUidre, that a great many of the early Ulster stories, including the *Táin,* have survived.[16] Uí Néill scribes had ample opportunity to modify the tales; they would even have had the sanction of tradition for adapting the already-extant alternate versions of the *Táin.* There was, as Carney and others have remarked, a "general phenomenon, a constant policy, in early Irish monastic schools, of revising early tradition for either religious or political reasons," and "these revisions could go as far as fictional creation."[17]

It would not have been out of character, indeed, for Uí Néill historians to have "recomposed" the Ulster stories, both orally and in writing. The Uí Néill were not only vigorous political innovators, but also clever propagandists and revisers of myth. There are several instances on record of their "revision" of other peoples' stories to serve their own ends. One striking example—indeed, involving the very homeland of the *Táin*—was their successful effort to link St. Patrick of Armagh to the Uí Néill claim to a high-kingship of Ireland, the kingship of Tara; this appears earliest in Muirchú's account of Patrick's contest with Lóegaire mac Néill's

druids at Tara, culminating in the saint's victorious conversion of Lóegaire.[18] And outside of the ecclesiastical sphere, we can see the Uí Néill historians at work adapting the traditions of another province, Munster, to their own ends in the stories of *Cath Maige Mucrama* and *Scéla Eógain 7 Cormaic,* which present an account of the birth, rearing, and accession to the throne of Tara of the important Uí Néill ancestor Cormac mac Airt. As Máirín O Daly has demonstrated, this story "in its original form had nothing to do with Cormac mac Airt or Tara, . . . it was a purely Munster tale which originated among the Corco Loígde and was later altered and added to by the partisans of the Connachta in order to lend support to the claim of the race of Conn [i.e. the Uí Néill] to the kingship of Tara."[19]

The essential Ulaid shape of the *Táin,* then, seems to have been retained even in the manuscripts kept by their enemies, despite those enemies' tendencies towards partisan revision. However, if we look more attentively at the Ulster tales and at their relationship to contemporary politics, we can see that they were in fact made to serve Uí Néill interests very well. True, they lack overt reference to dynastic themes: Tara is usually insignificant, as are direct prehistoric ancestors of the Uí Néill. But nevertheless the Ulster stories, as they were written and transmitted, were made to present a picture of Ireland's past that served and complemented the vision of the Uí Néill historians in various ways: through the development of themes that emphasize the dilemmas of the heroic past, offsetting its glories; through the incorporation of strategic anomalies into the plots; and through the historians' strategic and deliberate positioning of the *Táin Bó Cúailnge* and related events and personnel in their scheme of the history of Ireland. The Ulster stories in fact teach the Uí Néill lesson: the Ulaid were heroic but doomed, and the Uí Néill have legitimately inherited their power.

Thematically, the Ulster Cycle as a whole tends to present the tragic breakdown of those relationships on which early Irish society was founded: the relationships between host and guest, between kindred, between fosterbrothers, between men and women, between lords and clients and kings and overkings, between the human world and the gods. Behind the immense vitality, humor and imagination of the Ulster stories is a picture of society moving to dysfunction and self-destruction. Relationships no longer operate as they should. Communal feasts—occasions to reinforce social bonds, to establish reciprocal obligations—become in the sagas calculated occasions of strife and danger because of the duplicity of the host. In *Fled Bricrenn* (Bricriu's Feast) when the trickster Bricriu incites the Ulster heroes to compete for the Champion's Portion of meat, the resultant struggles are comic, and though a clear order of precedence in the warband is ultimately established, there is an undercurrent of ridicule; on the other hand, a similar contest in *Scéla Mucce meic Dathó* (The Story of Mac Datho's Pig) is far from lighthearted, and despite their victory it ends ultimately in a shameful situation for the Ulaid.[20] In *Mesca Ulad* (The Drunkenness of the Ulstermen) a contest in hospitality leads the Ulstermen into a feast which is the cover for a treacherous murder plot.[21]

Time and again in the Ulster tales warriors find themselves unable to function without violating sacred bonds. In *Aided Óenfhir Aífe* (The Tragic Death of Aífe's One Son) Cú Chulainn is trapped: to protect his people and his honor, he must slay his only son (and worthy successor) in single combat, but the consequence for the Ulaid is a great loss. "If only I had five years among you," says the boy, "I would slaughter the warriors of the world for you. You would rule as far as Rome."[22] In the *Táin,* Cú Chulainn is also caught between personal and public responsibilities as he defends Ulster; three times he is obligated to fight and kill men who are foster-brothers to him. The replication of this event in the tale emphasizes its significance, as does the fact that one of the combats, that with Fer Diad, and a separate existence outside of the *Táin* as an independent tragic tale.

Relations between the sexes in the Ulster tales are often disastrous. The beautiful woman Deirdriu, wrongfully claimed by Conchobor, lures away the great warrior Noísiu and his brothers and triggers a revenge by Conchobor that breaks up the Ulster warband.[23] Uncontrolled by her husband Ailill, Medb's wayward desires dominate and doom the cattle-raid; "We followed the rump of a misguiding woman," comments Fergus at the end; "It is the usual thing for a herd led by a mare to be strayed and destroyed."[24] Finnabair, daughter of Ailill and Medb, is peddled by her own mother to any warrior who can be bribed to fight Cú Chulainn. Cú Chulainn's wife, Emer, is barren, and his only son, Connla, is begotten on a foreign warrior-woman under circumstances that poison his future and, ultimately, that of his father's kin.[25]

Much of the chaos, the frustration of order and of social relations in the Ulster tales, can be immediately laid to the breakdown of royal control. Ailill is weak, and Medb is patently unfitted to lead the army or to govern. On the Ulaid side, not only has Conchobor initiated the break-up of his warband by indulging his selfish desire for Deirdriu despite a seer's warnings, but he has also caused the exile of Fergus, massive and vital Ulster warrior, by manipulating and violating the legal contracts it is his royal function to uphold.[26]

It is not only kingship that breaks down in the Ulster cycle: it is the entire sacred sphere. Men and gods are disastrously out of harmony. Sometimes this conflict seems to stem from human offenses. At the start of Medb and Ailill's cattle-raid, for instance, the men of

Ulster cannot define their province, because it is the season at which they are in the grips of a mysterious affliction, the *ces noí(n)den,* and are said to be as weak as women in childbirth; this sickness, said to derive ultimately from the betrayal of the goddess Macha by her human husband at the founding of Emain Macha, may be seen as the tangible and persistent symbol of a radical flaw in the Ulstermen.[27]

Often in the Ulster tales, however, the Otherworld seems to have turned against men out of a kind of viciousness, for its own reasons, and with a mysterious selectivity. Thus Nera in *Echtra Nerai* (Nera's Otherworld Adventure) goes into the *síd,* the dwelling of the gods, and is favored, obtaining from the gods a wife, a son, cattle, and the interpretation of a vision which enables him to save Cruachan, royal seat of Ailill and Medb, from a forthcoming attack from the *síd.*[28] But in the larger picture we see that the Otherworld has merely used Nera's mediation to further its destructive intentions. Nera's son in the *síd* is given a cow, which is later stolen by the battle-goddess Mórrígan and driven to Ulster, where it is impregnated by the great Ulster bull, the Donn Cúailnge, before returning to the Connacht *síd.* The bull-calf born of this mating issues to the Finnbennach, Ailill's great White-Horned Bull, a challenge on behalf of its father, Donn Cúailnge, and this challenge, interpreted by the cowherd to Medb, motivates her great cattle-raid—and thus, after all, causes the massacre of the warband of the Men of Ireland. The Otherworld deviously sets men against men.

The massacre of the Men of Ireland by the Ulaid, however, the final human battle in the *Táin,* is not the culmination of the *Táin;* instead, final attention is focused on the mutually destructive battle of the bulls, the symbolic resolution of the malignant disorder of the supernatural world that lies behind all these events. From their origin as supernatural herdsmen,[29] the two bulls, Finnbennach Aí and Donn Cúailnge, have represented those guarantees of wealth, fertility and power that underlie Celtic sovereignty.[30] Both bulls are described as enormous and of immense sexual potency. A long description of the Donn Cúailnge in the twelfth-century Book of Leinster version of the *Táin* makes clear his power and the nature of the protection he affords to his province:

> Here are some of the virtues of the Donn Cúailnge: He would bull fifty heifers every day. These would calve before the same hour on the following day, and those of them that did not calve would burst with the calves because they could not endure the begetting of the Donn Cúailnge. It was one of the virtues of the Donn Cúailnge that fifty youths used to play games every evening on his back. Another of his virtues was that he used to protect a hundred warriors from heat and cold in his shadow and shelter. It was one of his virtues that no spectre or

sprite or spirit of the glen dared to come into one and the same canton as he. It was one of his virtues that each evening as he came to his byre and his shed and his haggard, he used to make a musical lowing which was enough melody and delight for a man in the north and in the south and in the middle of the district of Cúailnge.[31]

Although less description is devoted to the Finnbennach than to Donn Cúailnge, we are told that "because of the Finnbennach, no male animal between the four fords of all Mag Aí . . . dared utter a sound louder than the lowing of a cow."[32]

At the end of the *Táin* the bulls meet near Cruachan, and fight all day, and then, circling round Ireland, they fight through the night, as the armies listen to the uproar in the darkness. In the morning the men see the Donn Cúailnge coming past Cruachan with the remains of Finnbennach hanging from his horns. He wanders through Ireland, and wherever he stops and lowers his head to drink, a piece of the defeated bull falls from his horns to the ground, and—Irish topography becoming the monument of this epic—the place is named from the falling portion: Finnleithe, "The White One's Shoulderblade"; Áth Lúain, "The Ford of the Loins." Finally Donn Cúailnge makes his way to Ulster, his every action changing the landscape and naming its features, and falls dead himself, at Druim Tairb, "The Ridge of the Bull."

The mutual destruction of the divine bulls seals the doom of the Ulaid and the Men of Ireland. It is not incidental that as they fight the bulls trample to death the trickster Bricriu, whose abrasive challenges and incitements have often tested and reaffirmed order among the Ulaid. With so much lost, the victory of the Ulaid is hollow indeed. There is no more real or lasting triumph here than at the funeral games of Hector. Cú Chulainn, son of the god Lug and the sister of King Conchobor, destined by his qualities as well as by his birth to act as mediator between gods and men, has failed to reconcile those forces; he has been charged with protecting his people when they have ceased to be capable, and probably even worthy, of protecting themselves; in a world gone incoherent, he has failed to maintain coherence. Donn Cúailnge and all that he symbolized is lost to Ulster. The victory of the Ulaid is temporary: admirable, but doomed.

Not only in the thematic development of the Ulster stories, but also in their political geography and genealogical relationships we can see a depiction of the past harmonious with the interests of the Uí Néill. Looking at the alliances and family relationships of the characters, one is constantly confronted with anomalies. There seems to have been a deliberate effort, in the shaping of the material, to conceal or blur genealogical or political connections, especially among the Men of

Ireland. As noted above, Medb is situated at Cruachan in Connacht, though she is the daughter of Eochaid Feidlech of Tara. Her husband Ailill is actually a Leinsterman, a member of the group called Gaileóin, and yet there is no hint of this in Recension I despite the fact that the Gaileóin are allied with the Men of Ireland. Indeed, theirs are the most competent warriors in Medb's army, and as the troops set forth on the cattle-raid, Medb herself, jealous of the Gaileóin prowess and fearful that they will reap all the expedition's glory, recklessly suggests that all the Gaileóin soldiers should be killed! There seems to be no acknowledgement, on her part or Ailill's, that the Gaileóin are his people. The lines are blurred still further by the monastic historians' attempts to trace the genealogical relationships of the characters. Conchobor himself is variously attached to pedigrees,[33] and his wives Mugain and Eithne are in the historical scheme in fact sisters to Ailill's wife Medb.

Furthermore, the lines of enmity and alliance are not very firmly drawn in the Ulster stories. Cú Chulainn has friends and fosterbrothers among the Men of Ireland. Ailill and Medb serve as cooperative arbiters in the contest among the Ulaid warriors in *Fled Bricrenn*. Donn Cúailnge and Finnbennach Aí, the bull embodiments of the sovereignty and wealth of Emain Macha and Cruachan, originate as the swineherds of the *síd* kings of Connacht and *Munster*.[34] Furthermore, Erc son of Cairpre Nia Fer of Tara, a Gaileóin, is not allied with Ailill and Medb; instead, he is Conchobor's grandson and Cú Chulainn's first cousin, and thus brings his men (the *fir Themra*, Men of Tara) to the aid of the Ulaid in the final great muster of the *Táin.*

Thus although the *Táin,* like other Indo-European epics, may well have originated as a tale of internecine dynastic warfare,[35] it seems that in the forms in which the Ulster stories were transmitted in writing the aim was not so much to emphasize particular relationships as to create a general, and rather deliberately fuzzy, sense of interrelationships across Ireland. This too can be seen as complementing the Uí Néill interests; the effect is to minimize the sense that Ireland is politically divided into fixed and competing kingships, and thus to create a "historical" basis for the Uí Néill claim that Ireland can be ruled by one overking.

Indeed, the Uí Néill historians went to considerable effort to incorporate the "prime stories" of Ulster into their own elaborate myth of Ireland's past.[36] That myth makes much use of traditional lore, including not only the Ulster sagas, but also, for the bulk of the pre-Christian period, some relics of the pagan Irish cosmogony, brewed up with lavish handfuls of the Old Testament and Latin learning into the *Lebor Gabála Erenn,* The Book of the Taking of Ireland.[37] Focusing ultimately on the succession rights to the kingship of Ireland, the Uí Néill historical scheme was essentially complete by the late eighth century, according to Professor Kelleher; it was reflected not only in the relatively late *Lebor Gabála* and the king-list appended to it, which stretched back to the "beginning" of human settlement in Ireland, but also in the annals, in genealogies, in synchronisms, and in regnal lists and other items of *senchas* (traditional historical lore).

The historians' scheme is not easy to deal with. Clearly it was the work of many men over time, and different sources reflect varying and contradictory versions of, for instance, the succession to the kingship of Tara, the regnal lengths of kings, and the dates of key events. The scheme must have been tinkered with frequently, as new situations arose or new interpretations became expedient—and, in any case, that portion of it which deals with the period prior to the late sixth century, when annalistic record-keeping begins to be contemporary in Ireland, was largely based on legendary material whose dating was entirely an act of the imagination. Despite all the confusion of detail, however, the Uí Néill Scheme of the past can easily be seen as a metaphorical base for their contemporary aspirations—and in this scheme, the heroic tales of Ulster play a crucial part.

In the annals and regnal lists, the *Táin* is said to have taken place just prior to the birth of Christ during a period referred to as the Pentarchy *(aimser na cóicedaig),* when the kingship of Ireland lay vacant, and rule in Ireland was divided among five provincial kings. There is no general agreement, and much contradiction even within single sources, as to the duration of the Pentarchy, the regnal lengths of kings during and adjacent to this period, and even the identities of the pentarchs—except that the list always includes the Ulster sagas' Conchobor and Ailill. Regardless of these confusions, the Pentarchy's significance is clear: it is actually a metaphorical time-out-of-time, a liminal period of chaos. Its major theme is defective sovereignty. It follows immediately on the death of the legendary King of Ireland Conaire Mór, which is narrated in the tale *Togail Bruidne Dá Derga* (The Destruction of Dá Derga's Hostel).[38] According to the tale, Conaire's kingship began as a model of peace and prosperity:

> Now during his reign there were great bounties, that is, seven ships arriving at Inber Colptha in every June of every year, and oak-mast up to the knees in every autumn, and plenty [of fish] in the Bush and Boyne rivers in June every year, and such abundance of peace that no man slew another in Ireland during his reign. And to everyone in Ireland his fellow's voice seemed as sweet as harpstrings. From mid-spring to mid-autumn no wind disturbed a cow's tail. His reign was neither thunderous nor stormy.

The general peace was shattered by the king's sins as sovereign, which cut him off from his supernatural protection; after a crescendo of portents of doom, Conaire was destroyed in a cataclysmic battle. According to the historical scheme, since there was no king to succeed him, Ireland was divided among the pentarchs for some years, until the kingship was restored in the person of Lugaid Ríab nDerg (or Réo Derg), a nephew of Medb's, begotten by her three brothers by triple incest with their sister Clothra. Lugaid later compounded the incest by begetting *his* son—and eventually King of Ireland also—Crimthainn Nia Nár, on his mother. As Kelleher has pointed out, this multiple incest "makes Lugaid a sort of ultimate ancestor of Dál Cuinn [the Uí Néill stock]" by concentrating the line of descent, and may indeed symbolize the historical threefold federation of the Uí Néill, Connachta, and Airgialla.[39]

Thus Lugaid metaphorically ushers in the Uí Néill era, just after the birth of Christ. And on the threshold of this era the *Táin* takes place—arranged to serve the Uí Néill historical vision very well. The *Táin*'s presentation of an Ireland interconnected, interrelated both by alliance and genealogy, complements the claim that Ireland is in fact a unit, capable of being controlled by a central high-kingship. At the same time (like *Togail Bruidne Dá Derga* and the notion of the Pentarchy) the Ulster sagas show this interdependent Ireland lacking the essential element—effective sovereignty—that would preserve its wealth and harmony; and thus Ireland's noble warriors, however admirable they are in the Ulster tales, are tragically self-destructive and ineffective. In the armies' last battle in the *Táin* Fergus's culminating rage, deflected from vengeance on Conchobor and forever memorialized in the Máela Midi, the three flat hills whose tops he shears off with his sword, calls forth that exclamation from Cú Chulainn which seems to sum up the *Táin*'s theme: *Conscar bara bith!*—"Fury destroys the world!"

The root of the destruction—men's loss of harmony with the Celtic Otherworld—is also, I would suggest, deliberately connected to the Uí Néill presentation of themselves as a Christian dynasty tested and sanctioned by Patrick. In part, of course, the Ulster sagas' portrayal of the malignant tendencies of the gods may be explained as reflecting the Christian era's jaundiced view of the pagan past (although this theme is nowhere near so explicit in the Ulster sagas as it is, for instance, in *Beowulf*). But there is also a distinct political connotation. Professor Binchy has pointed out that as early as the *Liber Angeli,* that is by the early eighth century, the head of Armagh, Patrick's foundation, "stakes a claim to hegemony over all churches throughout Ireland, a claim strikingly similar to that put forward about the same time by the head of the Uí Néill dynasties, the king of Tara, to suzerainty over the other provincial kings. This is but one of many indications that the ecclesiastical pretensions of Armagh, based on the Patrick legend, and the secular pretensions of Tara, based on the myth of the 'High Kingship,' advance hand in hand."[40] In the Ulster sagas Emain Macha—so near in name as well as in place to Ard Macha, or Armagh—is championed by the hero Cú Chulainn, whose actions in the service of his king are beyond reproach. In the synchronic scheme as well as in *Aided Con Culainn,* the tale of his death,[41] Cú Chulainn is deliberately portrayed as a forerunner of Christ. His lifespan and Christ's are coordinated, so that his death date in the annals is put one year after Christ's birth, and, as Professor Kelleher has pointed out, his lifetime—ideally 27 years—is, like Christ's, divisible by three.[42] Deliberate allusions to Cú Chulainn's likeness to Christ abound in *Aided Con Culainn,* where he dies bound upright, wounded by a spear; after his death, his spirit returns to prophesy the Christian dispensation and the conversion of Emain from war to peace. From his ghostly chariot over Emain Macha he begins

> "Emain, great Emain
>   great in lands
> in Patrick's lifetime
>   [priests] will till
> Emain's lands. . . . "[43]

Emain Macha will be absorbed, as it were, by Ard Macha. Patrick will succeed Conchobor. Indeed, the death-tale of Conchobor seems to have been composed deliberately to sanction the Christian (and Patrician) succession: Conchobor's death (placed at A.D. 33 in the annals) is caused by his passionate dismay on hearing of Christ and the Crucifixion, and he is said to have been one of the two Irishmen who believed in the Christian God before the coming of the Faith to Ireland.[44]

Thus Emain Macha and Armagh are interconnected within the Ulster saga tradition. And the historical scheme was completed by the establishment of a vital connection between Emain Macha and the Uí Néill kingship of Ireland through the figures of Cú Chulainn, Emain's hero, and Lugaid Ríab nDerg, restorer of the Tara kingship and symbolic Uí Néill ancestor. As the Ulster sagas developed under the sponsorship of the Uí Néill historians, there evolved a tradition that Lugaid was fosterson to Cú Chulainn. This is of course a significant connection in itself, but as it appears in narrative it is even more suggestive. Into the middle of the tale *Serglige Con Culainn* (The Wasting Sickness of Cú Chulainn) was interpolated a baldly doctrinal episode describing how the Pentarchy was brought to an end. An assembly took place to determine who should be the next King of Ireland, "for they did not like the hill of the lordship and rule of Ireland, i.e. Tara, to be without the government of a king, and they did not like the peoples to be without the rule of a king ordering their common life."[45] Through a divination ceremony,

the bull-feast, Lugaid is identified as the destined king; significantly, the messengers who seek him for inauguration find him in Emain Macha, at the bedside of his sick fosterfather. Cú Chulainn revives from his affliction long enough to recite to Lugaid the *Bríatharthecosc Con Culainn,* a ritual set of instructions in proper royal behavior; such gnomic texts probably formed part of Irish inaugural rituals.[46] Promising to heed the instructions, Lugaid sets forth directly for Tara, and is made king. Metaphorically, therefore, Cú Chulainn inaugurates not only the Christian era and Armagh's primacy, but also in a sense the Uí Néill high-kingship, as he passes on to its founder the wisdom that the kings of the *Táin* era have so disastrously ignored: the rules of proper royal conduct, without which "fury destroys the world."

We must conclude that even if the Ulster epic cycle began as a simple celebration of a "heroic age" (and we have no way of knowing if it did), it became at the hands of the Uí Néill scholars, in its early years of written transmission and historical interpretation, a complex and strategic gesture of farewell to that era. As in so much early epic literature—the *Iliad,* the *Mahabharata, Beowulf* spring to mind—so also in the **Táin** and its related tales the seeds of doom seem implanted in the very nature of the heroic world. I am not prepared to hazard guesses about the functions of epic traditions in other cultures; but in the case of the Irish audience and the Ulster sagas, at least, it seems that that oscillation between admiration and rejection, kin-feeling and separation, that sense of "the pastness of the past" which is the hallmark of epic, was calculated and adapted to function very specifically in the present.

Notes

[1] Jackson 1964; Dillon 1947; Dillon 1975, 70-94; Harbison 1971.

[2] Tierney 1960; Powell 1959; Filip 1977; de Paor 1964.

[3] The earliest version of the *Táin Bó Cúailnge,* Recension I, survives in four manuscripts, the oldest of which is Lebor na hUidre, or LU, dating from c. 1100 A.D. (Best and Bergin 1929); the earliest linguistic stratum in the story belongs to the eighth century (Thurneysen 1921, 99-113). Edition with translation, O'Rahilly 1976; translation, Kinsella 1970. General discussions and summaries of the Ulster Cycle: Dillon 1948; Murphy 1961; Ó Coileáin 1978.

[4] It is one of the more interesting archaisms of the Ulster Cycle that it presents Emain Macha as a living domestic and ceremonial royal site; archaeological evidence has demonstrated that the major ceremonial site at Emain Macha had been destroyed, buried and abandoned as early as the third century B.C., and there

is no evidence for continuous domestic settlement (Wailes 1982; 'Navan Fort' 1970).

[5] Jackson 1964; O'Rahilly 1964; Chadwick 1932-40; Murphy 1961; Carney 1979.

[6] Mac Cana 1980.

[7] Carney 1979.

[8] A somewhat similar hypothesis, though based on different assumptions and evidence, was made by O'Rahilly 1964, 176-83.

[9] Haley 1970.

[10] Ó Máille 1927.

[11] Carney 1971, 75; Carney 1979; poem text is printed in Meyer 1912, 306-307.

[12] *Echtra Nerai:* Meyer 1889-90; *Longes mac nUislenn:* Hull 1949; *Fled Bricrenn:* Henderson 1899, Best and Bergin 1929, 246-77.

[13] Ó Corráin 1972, 14-23; Byrne 1973.

[14] Byrne 1973, 48-105, 254-74.

[15] Carney 1971, 75.

[16] Kelleher 1971, 122-26, has demonstrated that the probable line of transmission from Ulster to the midlands lies with the ecclesiastical family that became the Maic Cuinn na mBocht, who moved from the monastery of Louth to Clonmacnois in the early ninth century; Máel Muire mac Céilechair, chief scribe of LU, was also of the family.

[17] Carney 1979.

[18] Gwynn 1913, 3-10; White 1920, 83-91.

[19] O Daly 1975, 3.

[20] Henderson 1899; Thurneysen 1935.

[21] Watson 1941; Watson 1938; Guyonvarc'h 1960-61.

[22] Van Hamel 1956, 15; translated, Kinsella 1970, 45.

[23] In *Longes mac nUislenn,* Hull 1949.

[24] Kinsella 1970, 251.

[25] *Tochmarc Emire* (The Wooing of Emer), Van Hamel 1956, 55-56.

[26] In *Longes mac nUislenn,* Hull 1949.

[27] *Ces Noínden Ulad,* Windisch 1884; transl. also by Kinsella 1970, 6-8. See Ó Broin 1963.

[28] Meyer 1889-90.

[29] Windisch 1891; most recent English translation (from the Book of Leinster version) is Kinsella 1970, 46-50.

[30] There are various indications that pagan Celtic religion involved bulls with supernatural attributes. In addition to representations of bulls on surviving Gaulish inscriptions and altars, such personal and place names on the Continent as Tarva, Tarvisium, Tarvius, Donnotaurus, and so forth (see Holder 1896-1913) are suggestive; and Pliny the Elder mentions that the druids sacrificed white bulls (*Natural History* xxx, 13).

[31] O'Rahilly 1967, 36 and 174.

[32] O'Rahilly 1967, 134 and 270.

[33] The several sources of information about this are well set forth by Kelleher 1971.

[34] *De Chophur in dá Muccida,* Windisch 1891.

[35] Melia 1972, 244-45.

[36] Kelleher 1971 thoroughly documents this incorporation; my interpretation here is built upon his evidence.

[37] Macalister 1938-56.

[38] Knott 1936; Stokes 1901-02.

[39] Kelleher 1971, 120.

[40] Binchy 1962, 61; for further discussion see Hughes 1966, 111-20.

[41] Best and O'Brien 1956, 442-57; Tymoczko 1981.

[42] Kelleher 1971, 122.

[43] Tymoczko 1981, 67.

[44] Meyer 1906, 2-21.

[45] Dillon 1953; translation of interpolated text is in Dillon 1951, 55-58.

[46] Kelly 1976, xiv.

References

Best, R. I. and Osborne Bergin, ed.

1929 Lebor na hUidre: Book of the Dun Cow. Dublin:

Royal Irish Academy.

Best, R. I. and M. A. O'Brien, ed.

1956 The Book of Leinster, vol. II. Dublin: Dublin Institute for Advanced Studies.

Binchy, Daniel A.

1962 Patrick and His Biographers: Ancient and Modern. *Studia Hibernica* 2: 7-173.

Byrne, Francis John

1973 Irish Kings and High-Kings. London: B. T. Batsford Ltd.

Carney, James

1971 Three Old Irish Accentual Poems. *Ériu* 22: 23-80.

1979 The History of Early Irish Literature: the State of Research. Plenary Address, Sixth International Congress of Celtic Studies, Galway, Ireland, 12 July 1979. In press.

Chadwick, H. Munro and N. Kershaw Chadwick

1932-40 The Growth of Literature. 3 vols. Cambridge: Cambridge University Press.

Dillon, Myles

1947 The Archaism of Irish Tradition. *PBA* 33: 245-64.

1948 Early Irish Literature. Chicago: University of Chicago Press.

1951 (transl.) The Wasting Sickness of Cú Chulainn. *Scottish Gaelic Studies* 7: 47-88.

1953 (ed.) Serglige Con Culainn. Medieval and Modern Irish Series No. 14. Dublin: Dublin Institute for Advanced Studies.

1975 Celts and Aryans: Survivals of Indo-European Speech and Society. Simla: Indian Institute of Advanced Study.

Filip, Jan

1977 Celtic Civilization and Its Heritage. 2nd rev. ed. Wellingborough, Northamptonshire: Collet's Holdings Ltd.

Guyonvarc'h, Christian-J.

1960 and 1961 (transl.) L'Ivresse des Ulates (Mesca Ulad). *Ogam* 12: 487-506; 13: 343-60.

Gwynn, John

1913 (ed.) The Book of Armagh. 3 vols. Dublin: Royal Irish Academy.

Haley, Gene C.

1970 Unpublished doctoral dissertation. Cambridge, Mass.: Department of Celtic Languages and Literature, Harvard University.

Harbison, Peter

1971 The old Irish 'chariot.' *Antiquity* 45: 171-77.

Henderson, George

1899 (ed.) Fled Bricrend, The Feast of Bricriu. London: Irish Texts Society.

Holder, Alfred

1896-1913 Alt-celtischer Sprachschatz. Band I-II. Leipzig.

Hughes, Kathleen

1966 The Church in Early Irish Society. London: Methuen & Co., Ltd.

Hull, Vernam

1949 Longes mac n-Uislenn (ed. and transl.). New York: Modern Language Association.

Jackson, Kenneth H.

1964 The Oldest Irish Tradition: A Window on the Iron Age. The Rede Lecture of 1964. Cambridge: Cambridge University Press.

Kelleher, John V.

1971 The Táin and the Annals. *Eriu* 22: 107-127.

Kelly, Fergus

1976 Audacht Morainn (ed. and transl.). Dublin: Dublin Institute for Advanced Studies.

Kinsella, Thomas

1970 The Tain (ed. and transl.). London and New York: Oxford University Press.

Knott, Eleanor

1936 Togail Bruidne Dá Derga (ed.). Medieval and Modern Irish Series No. 8. Dublin: Dublin Institute for Advanced Studies.

Macalister, R. A. S.

1938-56 Lebor Gabála Erenn. The Book of the Taking of Ireland (ed. and transl.). Parts I-V, Vols. 34,35,39,41,44. Dublin: Irish Texts Society.

Mac Cana, Proinsias

1980 The Learned Tales of Medieval Ireland. Dublin: Dublin Institute for Advanced Studies.

Melia, Daniel F.

1972 Narrative Structure in Irish Sagas. Unpublished doctoral dissertation, Department of Celtic Languages and Literature, Harvard University.

Meyer, Kuno

1889-90 The Adventures of Nera (ed. and transl.). *Revue Celtique* 10: 212-28; 11: 209-10.

1906 The Death-Tales of the Ulster Heroes (ed. and transl.). Royal Irish Academy Todd Lecture Series, Vol. 14. Dublin: Hodges, Figgis, and Co. Ltd.

1912 The Laud Genealogies and Tribal Histories (ed.). *ZCP* 8: 291-338.

Murphy, Gerard

1961 Saga and Myth in Ancient Ireland. Dublin: At the Sign of the Three Candles.

'Navan Fort'

1970 Navan Fort. *Current Archaeology* 22: 304-08.

Ó Broin, Tomás

1963 What is the 'Debility' of the Ulstermen? *Éigse* 10: 296-99.

Ó Coileáin, Seán

1978 Irish Saga Literature. In Heroic Epic and Saga, ed. Felix J. Oinas, pp. 172-92. Bloomington: Indiana University Press.

Ó Corráin, Donncha.

1972 Ireland before the Normans. Dublin: Gill and Macmillan.

O Daly, Máirín

1975 Cath Maige Mucrama (ed. and transl.). Dublin: Irish Texts Society.

O Máille, Tomás

1927 Medb Cruachna. *ZCP* 17: 129-46.

O'Rahilly, Cecile

1967 Táin Bó Cúailnge from the Book of Leinster (ed. and transl.) Dublin Institute for Advanced Studies.

1976 Táin Bó Cúailnge, Recension I (ed. and transl.). Dublin: Institute for Advanced Studies.

O'Rahilly, Thomas F.

1964 Early Irish History and Mythology. Dublin: Dublin Institute for Advanced Studies.

de Paor, Maire and Liam de Paor

1964 Early Christian Ireland. 4th rev. ed. London: Thames and Hudson.

Powell, T. G. E.

1959 The Celts. New York: Frederick A. Praeger.

Stokes, Whitley

1901-02 The Destruction of Da Derga's Hostel (ed. and transl.). *Revue Celtique* 22: 9-61, 165-215, 282-329, 390-437; 23: 88.

Thurneyson, Rudolf

1921 Die irische Helden- und Königsage bis zum siebzehnten Jahrhundert. Halle: Max Niemeyer.

1935 Scéla Mucce meic Dathó (ed.). Medieval and Modern Irish Series No. 6. Dublin: Dublin Institute for Advanced Studies.

Tierney, J. J.

1960 The Celtic Ethnography of Posidonius. Proceedings of the Royal Irish Academy 60 C 5.

Tymoczko, Maria

1981 Two Death Tales from the Ulster Cycle: The Death of Cu Roi and The Death of Cu Chulainn (transl.). Dublin: The Dolmen Press.

Van Hamel, A. G.

1956 Compert Con Culainn and other stories (ed.). Medieval and Modern Irish Series No. 3. Dublin: Dublin

Institute for Advanced Studies.

Wailes, Bernard

1982 The Irish 'Royal Sites' in History and Archaeology. *Cambridge Medieval Celtic Studies* 3: 1-29.

Watson, J. Carmichael

1938 Mesca Ulad (transl.). *Scottish Gaelic Studies* 5: 1-34.

1941 Mesca Ulad (ed.). Medieval and Modern Irish Series No. 13. Dublin: Dublin Institute for Advanced Studies.

White, Newport J. D.

1920 St. Patrick: His Writings and Life. New York: Macmillan and Co.

Windisch, Ernst

1884 Die irische Saga Noíden Ulad (ed. and transl.). K. sächs. Gesellsch. der Wissensch. zu Leipzig, *Philologisch-Hist. Klasse* 26: 336-47.

1891 De Chophur in dá Muccida (ed. and transl.). Irische Texte, ed. Whitley Stokes and Ernst Windisch, Ser. III, pp. 230-78. Leipzig: Verlag von S. Hirzel.

Patricia Kelly (essay date 1992)

SOURCE: "The *Táin* as Literature" in *Aspects of "The Táin,"* edited by J. P. Mallory, December Publications, 1992, pp. 69-102.

[*In the essay that follows, Kelly analyzes the* Táin *in the general context of early Irish storytelling in order to discern its intended meaning and audience; in doing so, Kelly provides the background necessary to assess the poem's literary value.*]

An approach to *Táin Bó Cúailnge* as literature is dependent on an understanding of early Irish saga in general. This wider perspective, however, provides neither readily applicable analytic methods nor instant solutions, for 'we are still at an early stage in the investigation of the nature of Irish saga' (Ó Cathasaigh 1986a, 123). While mediaeval Irish literature is, compared with other mediaeval European vernacular literatures, extensive, varied and remarkably early, any given text is more likely to have been treated as a source of information about mythology and (pre)history than examined for its literary properties.[1] An appreciation of this material as literature has also been hampered by the fact that many tales still stand in need of considerable linguistic analysis before literary critics have a reliable text to work on. A perhaps more fundamental obstacle to the development of orthodox literary criticism of Irish saga has been a belief in its 'otherness', its alleged irrationality or primitiveness. Murphy illustrated the critical mood of the time when he contrasted 'the maturer literatures of other countries' with Irish narrative, which offers 'something to delight [the reader] from the youth of the world, before the heart had been trained to bow before the head or the imagination to be troubled by logic and reality' (Murphy 1955, 5). In the same year this long-prevailing orthodoxy was challenged by Carney in a controversial and seminal book, *Studies in Irish Literature and History,* which presented a diametrically opposed view of these texts. For Carney, early Irish literature, while it incorporated traditional materials, was the conscious artistic product of the learned Christian milieu of the monasteries. Carney's views have been vindicated by the convincing results of a recent dramatic change of paradigm in Early Irish Studies: a fresh consideration of many of these texts shows them to be much more amenable to standard literary analysis than was heretofore realized. The results of this on-going research have greatly sharpened our understanding of the detail, structure and overall purpose of many early vernacular narratives.[2] Among the sagas which have been illuminated by scrutiny under the new paradigm are the major tales of the Mythological and King Cycles, viz *Cath Maige Tuired* (The battle of Moytura) and *Togail Bruidne Da Derga* (The destruction of Da Derga's hostel), respectively. Some of the Ulster tales have also been satisfactorily explicated along these new lines, but *Táin Bó Cúailnge,* the primary text of this cycle, remains a conspicuous Cinderella. While the *Táin* admittedly holds a unique place in early Irish literature, there is no reason to think that in theme or treatment it is qualitatively different from contemporary tales, or would resist the kind of analysis which has yielded such convincing results to date. Encouraged by these considerations, we may attempt a fresh evaluation of *Táin Bó Cúailnge.* First, however, it may be helpful to touch on some general aspects of saga texts which have come into focus in the scholarship of recent years.

Manuscripts and Mandarins

Earlier generations of scholars were apt to remark disparagingly on what they saw as flaws in mediaeval Irish narratives. Recension I of the *Táin* is a case in point, featuring as it does strata of different linguistic dates, doublets, variants, inconsistencies and interpolations, and passages so compressed as to be barely intelligible. The extant text is clearly not self-contained, as it makes allusions which require prior knowledge of the situation: for example, the purpose of the expedition from Crúachu is not revealed, and the first reference to the Donn Cúailnge calls him simply 'the bull' (*TBC I* 132).

A number of explanations of the alleged shortcomings of some manuscript versions of tales have been put forward. The most frequent was a charge of general narrative incompetence levelled against bungling copyists, who ignorantly interfered with the texts in their exemplars. A recent study (Ó Corráin 1986) of some examples of allegedly faulty narratives has challenged the traditional assumptions about the function of both the manuscripts and the texts preserved in them. Ó Corráin argues that it was not the purpose of many of the extant manuscripts to present finished products, in the form in which they were delivered to the patrons, but to assemble materials which could be used to that end. The great mediaeval codices thus resemble, not so much libraries (a frequently made comparison), as filing cabinets, in which potential components of complete texts are stored. The scholars who produced all the secular and ecclesiastical materials of early Ireland, whether in Latin or in the vernacular, far from being clumsy copyists, were 'a highly trained, highly self-aware mandarin class' (*ibid* 142).

That the eleventh-century compiler of Recension I of the **Táin** had a primarily scholarly purpose was recognized by Thurneysen (1921, 101): 'His aim is not to create an artistic whole, but to try not to omit any of the individual strands he finds.' While Thurneysen doubts (*ibid* 30 and 113) that it will ever be possible to reconstruct the original work of literature from the 'crude jumble' which is all that has survived, this paper will argue that even in this detritus it may be possible to excavate the tale 'that was once regarded as a masterpiece' (O' Connor 1967, 30).

Creative Literature or Functional Writing?

A separate but related issue is that of the functions of the texts themselves. Ó Cathasaigh (1986a, 123) warns against taking it for granted 'that the sagas represent the organisation of the narrative lore into literary form.' One important element of native narrative lore *(senchas)* was genealogy. This can be preserved in the form of 'straight' genealogical trees, of the 'A begat B and B begat C' variety. Irish tradition also encodes such data, more colourfully and memorably, in narrative. This treatment is generally only accorded major figures, such as the founders of important dynasties, whose biographies are recorded in the 'origin tales' of their royal line. The best documented case is that of Cormac mac Airt, the ancestor of the Uí Néill, the dominant royal dynasty from the seventh century to the tenth century. Native tradition assigns Cormac a *floruit* in the third or fourth century, but the tales about him linguistically date from the eighth century at the earliest. Though the plots are ostensibly about Cormac's life and reign, at a 'deeper level' they can be read as 'political scripture' (Carney 1969, 169; 1968, 155): they explain and justify Uí Néill supremacy and relations with dependent kingdoms at the time of composition. Though such

narratives may be so well-written as to have a literary quality, and appeal to a modern taste for this reason, their primary purpose is not to provide an aesthetic experience, but to convey information. This purpose can be met by a functional style, in which literary effects may be incidental. Carney (1969, 169) attributes what he sees as a certain lack of unity in many early narratives to the writers' indecision about which hat they are currently wearing, that of the sober historian or the story-teller.

Some tales, such as *Fingal Rónáin,* (How Rónán killed his son) are generally agreed to be primarily literary in intention. What then of **Táin Bó Cúailnge**? While the earliest references 'to the events of the tale occur in a genealogical context,[3] as early as the eighth century the Ulster Cycle would seem to have acquired a literary autonomy. For instance, the originally independent saga *Táin Bó Fróich* (Fróech's cattle-driving) was adapted in the eighth century to function as a foretale to the greater **Táin.** Motifs of the cycle are already parodied in two eighth-century tales, *Scéla Muicce meic Dathó* (The story of Mac Da Thó's pig), and *Fled Bricrenn* (Bricriu's feast).[4]

While Recension II of the **Táin** conforms more to modern expectations of an aesthetic creation, presenting a smooth narrative in a unified style,[5] the focus of this article will be on Recension I, which, it is hoped to show, is more than 'a mass of workshop fragments, not yet assimilated or amalgamated' (O'Rahilly 1976, xviii). Recension II will occasionally be drawn on where it supplies extra material or helps to clarify the terse account of the earlier version.

New Wine in Old Bottles

It would seem to be a general rule that early Irish sagas are sited in times long anterior to the date of composition. The events of the Ulster Cycle, and thus of the **Táin,** relate to the time of the Pentarchy (government by five provincial kings), which according to tradition preceded the era of the High-Kingship of Tara. This is fixed by (pseudo-historical) annalistic obits to around the beginning of the Christian era. Other tales, such as those of the Mythological Cycle, are of course anterior to this time, and yet others, for example the cycles of kings such as Cormac mac Airt, are located some centuries later. That narratives set in a pre-Christian past, portraying pagan gods and depicting a society some of whose practices were contrary to Christian teaching, should have been preserved for posterity by Christian monks was long considered surprising by scholars: they took the texts at their surface value as traditions of a remote past, and envisaged that these must have been transmitted orally for centuries before being captured in writing by remarkably tolerant monastic scribes. However, we have seen above that an origin legend purporting to recount events in, say, the third century

A.D., can be interpreted as validating either aspirations or a state of affairs at the time of its redaction. This device, of encoding statements about the present in terms of events of the past, is not confined to the genre of origin legends, but has been demonstrated in the other narrative cycles. The validation can be sought as far back as the time of the gods. *Cath Maige Tuired,* for example, is ostensibly a tale about the conflict between two races of gods, and until recently elicited bafflement rather than analysis. A new generation of scholars, however, working within the new paradigm, have succeeded in decoding much of the meaning of this text.[6] It deals with issues of perennial and immediate concern to its tenth-century audience, ranging from the familial (kinship, father-son relations) to the social (the role of kingship and the functions of the learned class) and political (the need for unity in the face of the Viking threat). The controlling hand of the Christian redactors can be seen not just in the exploration of the requirements of an ideally organized society, but in the characterisation of some of the *dramatis personae* in terms which recall major Old Testament figures.

This technique, of exploring contemporary issues by means of narratives set in the past, or by association with famous figures of the past, is so widely attested that one needs to ask whether it is not applied in the **Táin** also. The opposing claims of the historical and mythological interpretations of the Ulster sagas, and the ongoing debate about the influence of postulated oral predecessors on early Irish tales in general, have deflected attention from the question of the contemporary relevance of the **Táin** for the milieu in which it first received its extant form.

The present analysis will focus on this latter concern. It will proceed via an examination of specific salient episodes and characters, which it is hoped will cast light on the narrative meaning of the tale, and lead to a thematic interpretation of the **Táin** as a whole. We begin with the *macgnímrada,* the account of Cú Chulainn's boyhood deeds. This is not just possibly the best-known section of the **Táin,** but also the one which has enjoyed the closest scrutiny, revealing ramifications which may sensitize us to the potential implications of other portions of the tale.

The Boyhood Deeds of Cú Chulainn

The central and most lengthy episode in the *macgnímrada* shows Cú Chulainn taking up arms when only seven years of age, defending the borders of Ulster, killing three fearsome enemies and bringing back a prey of birds and wild animals. The young boy expresses the heroic ethos memorably when he declares that he values everlasting fame more than life: *Acht ropa airderc-sa, maith lim cenco beind acht óenlá for domun* 'Provided I be famous, I am content to be only one day on earth' (*TBC I* 640-641). Much of the action

of the **Táin** shows Cú Chulainn living out his heroic ambitions. He fulfils his early promise when he compensates for the Ulstermen's inability to defend their province, and wards off the Connacht offensive in a series of single combat encounters. A mimetic interpretation of the *macgnímrada* episode would view it as a depiction of the initiation of a young man into warrior status as a fully integrated member of his *túath* (kingdom), and Cú Chulainn's characterisation in the body of the narrative as an exemplification of the warrior ideal. But Cú Chulainn's heroic biography also has mythological resonances, and these are reflected in this section by the scene in which the triumphant returning warrior is greeted by the bare-breasted Ulster women. This has been explained as a reflex of Cú Chulainn's original role as the vigorous young male who brings about the renewal of the year in an old seasonal vegetation drama (Ó Broin 1961-63, 282 n.28).

The preceding episode is an even better indication of how densely-layered the meaning of an ostensibly straightforward narrative can be. *Aided con na cerda,* 'The death of the smith's hound', explains how the boy Sétantae acquired his adult name: forced to kill the fierce hound of Culann the smith-hospitaller in self-defence, he undertakes to substitute temporarily as a guard-dog, and accepts Cú Chulainn 'the hound of Culann' as his new name. Greene describes this as a 'simple well-told story' and signals disapproval that 'scholars have looked for deeper meanings' (1968, 103). That the story can be appreciated at the surface level of plot is undeniable, but in view of the sophistication of many early sagas, as recent scholarship has demonstrated, it seems implausible that the 'national epic' (*ibid* 98) should be an anomalous case of naiveté. And indeed it has been shown that there is more to this 'simple story' than is immediately apparent.

Given the literary convention that tales set in the distant past were primarily of relevance to the time and milieu in which they were redacted, it is clear that a knowledge of social idiom and particularly of the legal system is crucial to a deeper understanding of early Irish saga. The role of the warrior was obviously vital to that society. A number of recent studies[7] have illuminated the institution of the *fian(n),* 'an association of propertyless and predominantly young, unmarried warrior-hunters on the fringes of settled society' (McCone 1990, 163). The *Männerbund* culture of such sodalities of young men is well attested in Germanic and Greek traditions, so that here we have a trace of Ireland's pagan inheritance. The *fian*'s wild life was expressed in the wearing of wolf-skins or wolf-heads, which is reflected in the proliferation of names incorporating elements meaning 'wolf': such an element is *cú,* which signifies both the canine and lupine kind. Members of a *fian* were traditionally credited with the ability to experience ecstatic distortions. Both these features, the canine/lupine aspect and the distortion, are expressed in the warrior-hero of the *Táin:* Cú Chulainn's name marks him as a 'hound' or 'wolf', and the contortions he undergoes in his *ríastrad* are mentioned frequently. With this background knowledge, *Aided con na cerda* can be read as a predictable stage in Cú Chulainn's martial career. By killing the hound Sétantae appropriates its martial spirit. The symbolism of the episode and its wider societal implications would presumably not have been lost on an early Irish audience.

Aided con na cerda is not the only literary reflex of the warrior's initiation to be expressed in terms of a confrontation with a canine adversary. In two other tales the motif of the killing of a magnificent hound figures prominently. In the concluding scene of *Scéla Muicce Meic Dathó,* Fer Loga, a charioteer and thus an unlikely hero, wins a brief fame by killing the hound of the Leinster hospitaller which both Connacht and Ulster have sought to obtain. *Aided Cheltchair maic Uthechair* (The death of Celtchar mac Uthechair) revolves around a series of warrior/hound conflicts sparked off by Celtchar's murder of an Ulster hospitaller. In these three narratives McCone (1984a) detects a basic story pattern involving heroes, hounds and their hospitaller owners: in the 'normal' paradigm, as reflected in *Aided con na cerda,* the hero, by killing the hound, acquires his martial qualities, and in continuing his guardian functions can be seen to be exercising his martiality to the benefit of the *túath.* The unjustified killing of a hospitaller, as in *Aided Cheltchair,* leads to protracted and unresolved conflicts between warrior and hound, eventually causing the death of the luckless protagonist by the hound. *Aided Cheltchair,* then, represents an inversion of the desirable paradigm, and an appreciation of the implications of the tale requires an understanding of the underlying story pattern. In *Scéla Muicce Meic Dathó,* the story pattern is parodied, as the death of the hound is not achieved by Fer Loga through any heroic efforts or abilities, but by an ignoble act, and as a charioteer he can only cut a ludicrous figure as a would-be champion.

We see that a full aesthetic enjoyment of Irish saga on occasion calls not just for background knowledge of the society and its customs, but also an appreciation of the literary forms in which the traditional material was cast, as well as the possible permutations of these forms.

Playing variations on story patterns seems to have been part and parcel of the repertoire of narrative devices of early Irish redactors. The story patterns can be traditional or borrowed. The Deirdre story has been read as a reversal of some of the 'heroic biography' pattern (McCone and Ó Fiannachta 1992, 105-108). Carney considers *Echtrae Chonlai,* in which a man is tempted to a land without sin by an Otherworld woman proffering an apple, to be an inversion of the Biblical story of the Fall (1969, 162-165). A familiarity with the convention, and a knowledge of the basic story patterns were presumably shared by author and audience of the early period, but may require a considerable effort of explication today.

The Táin Bó Tale Type

As analysed above, the *macgnímrada* are seen to be based on at least two basic story patterns of the initiation of the young warrior. The *Táin* as a whole, however, is identified by its title as belonging to a particular class of tale. A native mediaeval classification of tales grouped them according to the first element in their titles. Thus we get, for example, *comperta* 'births', *aideda* '(violent) deaths', *tochmarca* 'wooings', *tána bó* 'cattle raids' and so forth. Thirteen *táin bó* titles (Mac Cana 1980a, 154) have survived, but there are only seven such tales extant, some in fragmentary form.

On the subject matter of this tale type Mac Cana says: 'The *tána* are the literary reflex of a social practice which was not merely Irish, but Celtic and Indo-European, and which is found elsewhere among cattle-rearing peoples . . . For the Celts the successful cattle-raid was an assertion of the integrity of the tribal community *vis-á-vis* its neighbours and a vindication of its leader's claim to primacy over his people . . . It is no mere accident, therefore, that the greatest of Irish tales, *Táin Bó Cúailnge* . . . belongs to the category of the *tána'* (*ibid* 79-80). What was at stake in *Táin Bó Cúailnge* on the political level was therefore the continued independence of the kingdom of Ulster. Such a conflict could easily provide the stuff of narrative, but surely does not exhaust the literary meaning of the tale. That something more than a normal, albeit major, cattle raid is involved is shown by the fact that the defeat of Ailill and Medb does not end the tale: the climax is not the battle between Connacht and Ulster forces, but the fight of the two bulls and their ensuing deaths. As the various encounters between Cú Chulainn and his adversaries leave an abiding mark on the landscape in the form of new place names, so too the battle of the bulls gives rise to a new onomastic inventory. The rivalry of the two bulls and the cosmogonic significance of the final scene, in which the physical landscape is recreated, is thought to reflect the original mythological nucleus of the tale. Between these two poles, the mimetic and the mythic, must lie the literary significance of the tale.

The other *táin bó* tales may give an indication of what is involved in a literary presentation of the cattle-raid. They all function as fore-tales *(remscéla)* to *Táin Bó Cúailnge,* the motivation for the raid being of no great political importance, but merely to provide food for the duration of the larger foray. None of the raids is conducted by a reigning monarch, or against such a major political opponent, and as one would expect, the protagonist is always a man. Finally, as Carney noted (1955, 62) there is often a love interest: the driving off of cattle goes hand in hand with the acquisition of a woman. I suggest that these two narrative strands are figuratively linked, via a metaphor which equates cattle with humans, and particularly women with cows.

This metaphor is memorably exploited in a famous passage from another Ulster Cycle tale, *Longes mac nUislenn* (The exile of the sons of Uisliu). The beautiful Deirdre, who is being raised in seclusion as a future consort for Conchobar, meets and is smitten by Noísiu, a handsome young warrior. Their conversation is couched in figurative language:

>—'A fine young heifer that that is going by,' he said.

>—'The heifers are bound to be fine where there are no bulls,' she answered.

>—'You have the bull of the province: the king of Ulaid,' Noísiu said.[8]

Thus the identification of cows and women in the plot of the *táin bó* genre is supported in the language by a metaphor in which terms for cattle can denote humans. In *Táin Bó Cúailnge,* of course, the roles of male and female are reversed. It is a woman who is the initiator of the raid, and her primary objective is not cattle-herds, but a particular prize bull, the Donn Cúailnge, the 'bull of the province' of Ulster, i.e. the Ulster king, Conchobar. The choice of a female protagonist therefore brings about a variation on the normal *táin bó* pattern, and the interpretation of Medb's anomalous behaviour is seen as crucial to the understanding of this tale.

Medb: Sovereignty Goddess or All-too-human?

Medb's role in the *Táin* is pivotal. She identifies herself at the outset as the chief instigator of the foray: *is mé dorinól in slúagad sa* (26) 'it is I who have mustered this hosting', and remains the driving force throughout the narrative. Her decisions are carried even against the advice of Ailill and Fergus. She has a major say in the choice of warriors sent against Cú Chulainn and the rewards they are promised. In her marriage she is the dominant partner: Ailill is a complaisant husband, virtually conniving in her cuckoldry of him with Fergus, as a means of securing Fergus's support in their expedition. It is she who quells the disturbance in the ranks caused by the attack of the war-goddess and the dire prophecy of Dubhthach (212-213). She leads a sub-expedition of her own for a fortnight to Dál Riata (1531-1534). At the end of the tale she participates actively, and initially with success, in the actual fighting (4037-4039).

While much in the presentation of Medb's character has the impact of a tour-de-force of verisimilitude, her exercise of power is unlikely to reflect the reality of early Irish society. Ó Corráin (1978, 10) comments: 'On the political level, women never inherited political power as such and never governed as independent sovereigns or rulers, though, of course, strong-minded women had a powerful influence on the political activities of their husbands. Indeed, Medb . . . is the archetypal strong woman—determined, domineering and wanton—and we need not doubt that there were many like her in real life'. Kelly (1988, 69) points out that 'the annals provide no instances of a female political or military leader. Indeed, the male imagery which surrounds the office of kingship . . . would seem to preclude even the possibility of a female ruler.' The imagery of kingship is well-attested in the literature of all periods. Its fundamental element symbolizes the land as a woman, with whom the prospective king must mate if his reign is to be legitimate. Various reflexes of this mythic female have been identified, but Medb is considered 'the outstanding figure of the territorial goddess in Irish literature' (Mac Cana 1955-56, 88). One of the ways the goddess signalled acceptance of a would-be king was to offer him a drink: this aspect is conveyed in Medb's very name, which has been explained as a derivative of the word *med* 'mead', meaning 'the intoxicating (or intoxicated) one'. Medb Lethderg of Tara who is considered to be the original sovereignty goddess, of whom her namesake, the queen of Connacht in the Ulster Cycle, is a literary reflex. Medb Chrúachna's divine aspect is only 'vestigial in Recension I of the Táin,[9] but Recension II is more explicit when it has her stipulate the qualities she demands in a husband: he should be *cen néoit, cen ét, cen omon* (*TBC II* 28) 'without meanness, without jealousy, without fear'. Absence of jealousy is necessary 'for I was never without a man in the shadow of another' (i.e. without one lover quickly succeeding another) (*TBC II* 37-9). This was once seen as a reference to the loose morals of pre-Christian Ireland, but Medb's promiscuity has been more plausibly explained (Ó Máille 1927) as a reflection of her original role as the mythic sovereignty figure, union with whom is constantly sought by candidates for the kingship.

For all that some contexts do identify Medb as a classic sovereignty figure, this aspect is certainly not to the fore in *Táin Bó Cúailnge.* O'Rahilly (1943, 15-16) notes that here 'she is no longer a goddess but a masterful woman, with the inevitable result that her character has sadly degenerated, so much so that at times she is no better than a strong-willed virago with unconcealed leanings towards a multiplicity of husbands and paramours.' I suggest that O'Rahilly's view of Medb's 'degeneracy' is shared by her literary creator, and that it is a central purpose of the *Táin* to depict her in a thoroughly unflattering light.

Medb's conduct of her expedition is shown to be severely wanting. She makes an inauspicious start when she rejects the vision of the prophetess Fedelm, whom she has asked 'How do you see the fate of the army?' Fedelm replies three times, chillingly, *'Atchíu forderg, atchíu rúad'* 'I see it bloody, I see it red'. Twice Medb disputes the veracity *(fír)* of this prediction, and finally dismisses it as of little significance *(ní báa aní sin trá)* (*TBC I* 46-65). She proposes to kill the crack regiment, the Gaileóin, lest they gain all the credit for the success of the raid, or eventually turn against the Connacht forces and defeat them. Ailill remarks laconically: *'Ní chélam as banchomairle'* 'I shall not deny that is a woman's counsel' (163). That following a woman's advice can only have negative results is a topos in many texts, and in a later scene Fergus pleads with Ailill not to heed the 'foolish counsels of a woman' *(banairle baetha)* when Medb predicts victory (2438). She airily discounts Fergus's lengthy eulogy of Cú Chulainn (382-395). When the river Cronn floods, Medb rejects the possibility of travelling upstream to its source to find a passage, but sets the troops three days and nights digging up the mountain to make a pass through it, since that will remain as a permanent insult to the Ulstermen (1007-1010). The Connacht leaders repeatedly violate the warriors' honour code *(fír fer* literally 'truth of men', usually translated 'fair play')* against Ulster warriors (*TBC I* 915, 1552, 2031, 2494), but Medb is the only one who personally recommends this course: *Brister fír fer fair* 'Let terms of fair play be broken against him' (1885). Other characters make negative comments which reveal her reputation. When she plans a 'mock peace' *(sída celci)* to lure Cú Chulainn to a meeting unarmed, his charioteer warns: *At móra glonna Medbi . . . Atágur lám ar cúl aci* 'Many are Medb's treacherous deeds . . . I fear that she has help behind the scenes' (1932). Although she fights actively, and initially with success, in the final pitched battle, in the end she is in the ignominious position of having to beg Cú Chulainn to spare her (4115).

The last scene in which Medb appears shows her viciously disparaged as a woman for aspiring to military leadership. Her admission to Fergus that their forces are routed elicits this savage riposte from him: *'Is bésad . . . do cach graig remitét láir, rotgata, rotbrata, rotfeither a móin hi tóin mná misrairleastair'* (4123-4) 'That is what usually happens . . . to a herd of horses led by a mare. Their substance is taken and carried off and guarded as they follow a woman who has misled them.' The implication is that a 'stallion' would have been a more suitable choice of leader, and Fergus's patronymic mac Roeich 'son of great horse' marks him out as an ideal candidate. The final verdict of the narrative on Medb is therefore that she has usurped

a man's function, and this is what has doomed the expedition from the start.

The positioning of this comment of Fergus's at a crucial point in the tale suggests that this aspect is of greater importance to the overall meaning of the *Táin* than has been acknowledged. Frank O'Connor noted 'the rancorous anti-feminist irony that occurs again and again through the story', and declared his conviction that 'the purpose of the original author would seem to have been to warn his readers against women, particularly women in positions of authority' (1967, 34 and 32), O'Connor's thesis is considered 'clearly extreme' by O'Leary (1987, 43-44), though even he concedes that 'distrust of women is by no means an insignificant theme' in the tale.

A further indication that Fergus's jibe may provide a clue to part of the central message of the *Táin* is that it echoes a phrase which occurs at other significant points in the narrative. The phrase is *tóin mná,* which has also been rendered less delicately as 'the rump of a woman' (Kinsella 1970, 251) or 'a woman's buttocks' (Charles-Edwards 1976, 47). The first use of the term in the tale certainly requires the literal translation. When the Morrígan in the guise of a beautiful young woman tries to distract Cú Chulainn from his task he dispatches her brusquely: *Ní ar thóin mná dano gabus-sa inso* (1855) 'it is not for a woman's body that I have come'. Conall Cernach taunts Fergus by implying a dishonourable motive for his Connacht allegiance: *'Ba ramór in bríg sin,' ar Conall Cernach, 'for túaith 7 cenél ar thóin mná drúithi'* (4068-9) 'Too great is that force which you exert against (your own) people and race, following a wanton woman as you do,' said Conall Cernach.[10] The editor's discreet rendering notwithstanding, the sexual innuendo is again clear.[11]

Conall Cernach's description of Fergus has further derogatory connotations. The phrase *tóin mná* occurs in a legal context which lists the kinds of men whose honour price is dependent on that of their wives. One of these is *fer inetet toin a mna tar crich* (Thurneysen 1931, 64) 'a man who follows his wife's buttocks across a boundary',[12] i.e. a man who marries a woman from outside the *túath*. This is a dishonourable union, as normally a woman's honour price is assessed as half that of her husband. Fergus himself acknowledges that his dalliance with Medb is ill-advised: when Ailill laughs at him on their first meeting after the adulterous scene, Fergus assigns the blame to *búaid mná misrálastar* (1071) 'a woman's triumph [which has] misdirected (me)'.[13]

The conversation between Ailill, Fergus and Medb here is unfortunately not fully intelligible, as the difficult, 'alliterative rhythmical exchanges still await a full edition,[14] but it is clearly an important scene (1065-1146), which the 'rhetorical' style is perhaps chosen to reflect. Not only have Fergus and Medb been discovered in *flagrante,* but Ailill has had Fergus's sword removed from its sheath, while he was engaged in lovemaking. This too dishonours Fergus, as another scene reveals. Cú Chulainn is admonished by his charioteer not to forget his sword when he goes to parley with Medb: *ar ní dlig láech a enecland dia mbé i n-écmaic a arm. Conid cáin midlaig no ndlig fón samail sin* 'for if a warrior is without his weapons, he has no right to his honour-price, but in that case he is entitled only to the legal due of one who does not bear arms' (1935).[15] And O'Connor (1967, 38) is surely right to suggest that the loss of the sword is also a metaphorical castration. Thus Fergus's union with the 'sovereignty goddess' leads, not to kingship, but to loss of his warrior status, and of his manhood.

Medb is therefore not just a 'heavily rationalized' (Mac Cana 1958-59, 61) reflex of the sovereignty goddess, but a negative manifestation of the figure. Granted, the classic 'straight' version of the myth of the sovereignty woman can depict her as mentally deranged or physically unattractive or deformed; but this when she is bereft of a suitable lover. The negative depiction of Medb in the *Táin* has also been interpreted in this light: 'It is of the essence of the myth that the beautiful sympathetic goddess is transformed into a harpy or a harridan whenever the cosmic plan is out of joint—as when usurpers or unworthy pretenders lay claim to her favours—and in this instance the monastic redactor has chosen to present her as a lusty and overbearing autocrat with a puppet husband' (Mac Cana 1980, 28). Medb however retains all her beauty (3205-3210), and the focus of the text is not on Ailill's failings as a spouse, though of course they are a precondition for his wife's excesses. Of Medb's two male partners, it is Fergus who comes off the worst in the *Táin;* but he is rehabilitated as an honourable figure at the end.

One realization of the goddess which might be seen to merit the 'harpy or harridan' formulation is Sín, in *Aided Muirchertaig meic Erca* (The death of Muirchertach mac Erca). Sín is 'a diabolical sovereignty woman who bewitches the Tara monarch [Muirchertach], causes him to abandon his former wife, and leads him to conflict and death' (McCone 1990, 133). Here again, however, the narrative does not put the burden of blame on Muirchertach's inadequacy as king: 'Sín leads a hitherto flawless sovereign astray out of personal malice' *(ibid).* O'Hehir (1983, 168) characterizes this tale as an 'anti-goddess story, reversing the pagan polarities' and attributes it to a 'Christian redactor bent on discrediting otherworld goddesses as queens'. *Aided Muirchertaig meic Erca* can thus be seen as an inversion of the 'normal' sovereignty goddess story pattern, and this strengthens the case for reading the *Táin* in a similar way.

There is some support therefore for the view that the characterisation of Medb as a negative paradigm of the sovereignty goddess is a serious thematic concern of *Táin Bó Cúailnge.* Its author takes the matter a step further, however.

As we have seen, Medb does not confine herself to traditionally female spheres of activity. And the narrative judges her in accordance with the traditional criteria for the male role she aspires to. This can be seen in the legal implications of a number of incidents.

As mentioned above, in the final battle Medb is reduced to asking Cú Chulainn for his protection. He complies *úair nád gonad mná* 'because he used not to kill women' (4117). Medb, however, is a would-be combatant and should maintain the warrior ethos she seeks to embody. And 'pleading for quarter' is listed by the laws among the seven things which 'reveal the falsehood of [one party in] a duel' (Kelly 1988, 212-213). That doing so amounts to an admission of cowardice is shown by a contrasting instance where a defeated adversary asks a favour of Cú Chulainn. The full import of the scene is spelled out in Recension II: the dying Lóch asks that his body be let fall in such a way as to allay any suspicion that he was killed in flight. He justifies his plea: *Ní ascid anacail nó midlachais iarraim-se fort* 'No favour of quarter do I ask nor do I make a cowardly request', and Cú Chulainn concurs: *is láechda ind ascid connaigi* 'it is a warrior's request you make' (*TBC II* 2005-2010).

The examples adduced so far which present Medb in a negative light all refer to traditionally gendered behaviour. A further incident through reference to a specifically female biological function highlights the incongruous results of Medb's invasion of male domains. In Recension II when Cú Chulainn comes upon her she is immobilised by a prodigious menstrual flow which fills three great trenches (*TBC II* 4824-33).[16] The Old Irish term for menstruation is *galar místae,* literally 'monthly sickness'. This too points up Medb's failure on the battle-field, for another sign of 'the falsehood of [one party in] a duel' is to suffer an attack of illness *(galar)* after coming onto the field of combat (Kelly 1988, 212-213).

By sparing Medb, 'because he used not to kill women' (4117), Cú Chulainn is shown to be observing the strictures of the late seventh-century law tract *Cáin Adamnáin* 'not to slay women' (Stokes and Strachan 1903, 306). But he is simultaneously withholding acknowledgement of her as a legitimate participant in the battle, on the grounds of her sex. The sphere of activity envisaged by the monastic *literati* as appropriate for women is also a biologically determined one, that of motherhood. A Middle Irish preface to *Cáin Adamnáin* draws an emotive picture of a slave-woman driven into battle with her babe on her back, and ends with a paean of motherhood: 'For a mother is a venerable treasure, a mother is a goodly treasure, the mother of saints and bishops and righteous men, an increase of the Kingdom of Heaven, a propagation on earth' (Meyer 1905, 5 4). The hagiography also emphasises maternal qualities, even in virgin saints (Davies 1983, 158). Medb's interpretation of her maternal role is more exploitative than protective: she subordinates the interests of her children to those of the expedition, and only once, in the case of her foster-child Etarcomol, does a death elicit any 'motherly' protest from her (1382). Both she and Ailill indiscriminately offer their daughter Findabair as a bribe to prevail on warriors to fight with Cú Chulainn. On one occasion Findabair is promised to seven kings concurrently (3357).

But the criteria by which Medb is judged and condemned are even wider still. This can be seen in some further incidents and their correlation with legal maxims. At the very start of the tale, as the Connacht forces set out, and before the encounter with Fedelm, Medb remarks to her charioteer:

'Cach óen scaras sund trá indiu . . . fria chóem 7 a charait, dobérat maldachtain form-sa úair is mé dorinól in slúagad sa'

'All those who part here today from comrade and friend will curse me for it is I who have mustered this hosting' (25-26).

Carney is puzzled by this 'humanistic observation', which he considers 'quite out of keeping with the spirit of conventional Irish saga' (1955, 68).[17] The purpose of the passage, I suspect, is rather to illustrate the most fundamental and far-reaching of Medb's shortcomings, and its positioning at the beginning of the tale is not insignificant. A legal tract on kingship includes the following among the characteristics of a just king: *ní fírflaith nad níamat bí bendachtnaib* 'For he whom the living do not glorify with blessings is not a true ruler' (Kelly 1976, 18 sec. 59). Thus Medb acknowledges herself not to be a 'true ruler', and the contrast is conveyed through the antonyms *maldacht* 'curse' and *bendacht* 'blessing'. The same text describes a further sign of the rightful king: *fris-tibi fírinni indecluinethar* 'he smiles on the truth when he hears it' *(ibid)*. Medb, for her part, dismisses Fedelm's prophecy twice as *Ní fír són* (51, 56) 'that is not true'. The outcome of the final battle also disqualifies her pretensions to rule, for *maidm catha* 'defeat in battle' is one of the 'seven living candles . . . which expose the falsehood of every king' (McCone 1990, 144). The animal image employed in Fergus's final jibe to her (*graig remitét láir* 4123-24) is a further pointer to the fact that ultimately it is the quality of her 'kingship' which is at issue. While martial features are expressed in canine/lupine terms, and the associations of cattle are with fecundity and

prosperity, horses have a ritual significance as symbols of kingship (McCone 1990, 112). Medb is therefore being assessed here with respect to sovereignty: she is found wanting, and it is her sex which disqualifies her. More than merely a negative paradigm of the sovereignty goddess, Medb is thus a failed embodiment of kingship itself, the supreme male role which she seeks to usurp.

The requirements for kingship are of a threefold nature, *viz* material, martial and mental, reflecting the king's role as the ideal representative of the three main functional divisions of society, the landowning class, the warriors, and the men of art (McCone 1990, 127-128). Medb's failure to measure up to the ideal in the martial sphere has been discussed above. At an earlier point in the tale, she herself seems to anticipate criticism of the other two aspects of her rule. In the 'rhetorical' exchange with Ailill and Fergus after the love-making scene she declares: *Nita cailtech esbrethach* (1097) 'I am not niggardly and given to unjust judgements'.[18] Generosity and justice exemplify the material and mental qualities of a righteous king, so that here Medb can be understood to be protesting her suitability for the role in respect of these two areas.

A Biblical Analogue

The possibility of Biblical and classical influence on early Irish literature was acknowledged long ago by Gwynn, who had observed repeated parallels between Cormac mac Airt and King Solomon of the Old Testament: 'the mediaeval authors who rehandled the native stuff were men of scholarly training, versed especially in Biblical and patristic learning; and it is as well to allow for the influence of their literary studies; their erudition and their patriotism alike tempted them to discover and underline points of resemblance between the culture and history of primitive Ireland and the elder civilizations of Rome and Palestine' (Gwynn 1903, 74). Despite this insight, the dominant scholarly paradigm of this century has focused more on the vestiges of pagan and Indo-European traditions preserved in the texts. In recent years the pendulum has swung back to an emphasis on the unitary nature of the learned classes of early Ireland. If the vernacular sagas are considered to emanate from the same intellectual environment which produced ecclesiastical texts in both Latin and Irish, Christian and classical influences on them are more readily allowed. Such influences can consist either of a Christian message conveyed by the theme, or of stylistic and narrative models drawn from the written materials current in the monastic milieu.[19]

Noting Thurneysen's suggestion (1921, 96-97) that the author of the ***Táin*** was aiming to produce an Irish *Aeneid*, O'Connor (1967, 32) perceptively recommended consideration of the Old Testament story of

Samson and Delilah (Judges 16) as a possible model for the relationship between Medb and Fergus. The parallel between Samson, characterised through his relations with women as lacking in moral fibre, and Fergus, who is portrayed as forsaking his own people *ar thóin mná,* is indeed striking. The symbolic castration of Fergus is perhaps an echo of Delilah's enfeeblement of Samson by causing his hair to be cut. In the *Táin* too there is a hair-cutting scene, but again the roles of male and female are reversed. Findabair, who is offered to Cú Chulainn in exchange for a truce, suffers a double humiliation at his hands: he cuts off her plaits and penetrates her symbolically with a pillar-stone (1602).[20] Edel (1989, 116) notes the similarity between the list of places which the Connacht army passes on its route to Cúailnge (114-130) and the 'journeys of the children of Israel' from Egypt to the plains of Moab (Numbers 33). Carney (1956, 72) remarks that the atmosphere of the early tales in general is redolent of the world of Eastern splendour.

One of the details thought to be a reminiscence of classical epic is the flooding of the rivers to impede the progress of the Connachtmen (1000, 1018, 1024, 1164); this has been compared with a passage in the *Iliad,* where the river Scamander rises up against Achilles (Thurneysen 1921, 96). The attribution to classical influence is still a point of controversy, and the Biblical parallel may be more pertinent. In the Song of Deborah, one of the two great Old Testament canticles, the river Kishon floods and sweeps away the army of the Canaanites, the occupiers of the Promised Land (Judges 5, 21).

A cluster of similarities and contrasts between the story of Deborah and the *Táin* prompts one to pursue the analogy further. Deborah, a prophetess and judge, is notable for being one of the few female figures in the Old Testament to exercise political power, and she wields it successfully. Among her achievements is that she overcomes tribal divisions to unite the Israelite tribes against their Canaanite enemies. Medb however is a failure as a political leader. She succumbs to tribal jealousies, being prepared to weaken her own army and alienate her Ulaid supporters rather than permit the crack regiment of the Gaileóin to exist. Deborah prophesies the outcome of the battle correctly, and predicts that the victory of the day will go to a woman. Medb, for her part, ignores the prophecy of Fedelm at the outset, and is herself denigrated as a woman in the end.[21]

To take Medb as an anti-Deborah implies reading the *Táin* as a whole as a further example of the pointed inversion of familiar story patterns. Medb then suffers a triple negative characterisation: as an anti-goddess, as a failed sovereign, and as the diametrical opposite of the great Biblical heroine.

Themes

In keeping with the view that *Táin Bó Cúailnge* is epic or heroic literature, the main thematic concern has been formulated as 'the celebration of the martial heroism of Cú Chulainn; of his courage and ingenuity, his mastery of the martial arts, his unswerving loyalty' (Ó Cathasaigh 1986b, 156). Certainly the greatest bulk of the tale is devoted to Cú Chulainn's exploits, and he is depicted in a wholly favourable light. This rubs off on the Ulaid, who are the victors in the contention. Some scholars however dispute the apparent corollary that the whole heroic age in general is also being celebrated. Radner (1982, 55) notes that the tale emphasises the negative effects of war, summarised in Cú Chulainn's statement on hearing the clamour of the final battle: *conscar bara bith* 'anger destroys the world' (4076). 'Thematically', she argues (1982, 47), 'the Ulster Cycle as a whole tends to present the tragic breakdown of those relationships on which early Irish society was founded: the relationships between host and guest, between kindred, between fosterbrothers, between men and women, between lords and clients and kings and overkings, between the human world and the gods. Behind the immense vitality, humor and imagination of the Ulster stories is a picture of society moving to dysfunction and self-destruction'.

Yet the blame for the breakdown of social order is not laid impartially on both sides, or on all participants. As far as 'societal' virtues such as *goire* 'filial piety' and *condalbae* 'love of kin, patriotism' are concerned, as exemplified in the behaviour of the Ulster characters, they prove resilient in the end. Fergus's kin-love *(condalbae)* causes him to sabotage the Connacht venture (216, 229), he can be prevailed upon to desist from attacking the Ulaid in the final battle (4068-73), and his ties of fostership with Cú Chulainn preclude their engaging in direct combat (2501-2518; 4103-7). The Ulaid are presented as strongly motivated by *condalbae* (3834-37) in relation to Conchobar's grandson. It is Medb who sets foster-brothers, foster-fathers and foster-sons against each other, who offers her daughter as a bribe to any likely opponent of Cú Chulainn, and who seduces Fergus into disloyalty to his kin.

The most negative point about the Ulaid is their inability to support Cú Chulainn through the winter months, and Radner makes the attractive suggestion that their mysterious sickness, the *ces nóinden,* is 'the tangible and persistent symbol of a radical flaw in the Ulstermen' (1982, 49).[22] Aitchison (1987, 110) also notes the ambiguous tone in the depiction of Ulster glory, but his conclusion that the Ulster Cycle is anti-Ulaid propaganda is informed less by the *Táin* than by other Ulster tales. In the *Táin* the Ulaid are certainly not singled out for criticism, but I would agree that wholehearted approval of war is withheld. The tale does not dwell indulgently on descriptions of the large-scale battle, and the final encounters, between Fergus on the one hand and Conall Cernach and Cú Chulainn on the other, pass off without human casualties. This I would interpret as a reflection of a general pacifist stance, which would accord well with a hypothesis of clerical authorship.

The immediate catalyst for the chaos and killing is the cattle raid itself. Though such raiding may have been 'the most typical and abiding event recorded in the annals down the centuries' and 'a commonplace, not to say routine, experience to every individual in the population' (Lucas 1989, 125), there is evidence that efforts were made by the Church to put a stop to it, or to alleviate the destruction it could entail. Killing plough oxen and stealing milch kine are said to be among the three most serious offences which Patrick proscribed (Kelly 1988, 276). The canons of Adamnán, no later than the ninth century, lay down that 'cattle seized in a raid are not to be taken by Christians whether in trade or as gifts' (Bieler 1963, 178 sect. 15). An ecclesiastical *Cáin* attributed to a sixth-century nun Dar Í enjoined 'not to kill cattle' (Stokes and Strachan 1903, 306). The annals record its promulgation four times between 810 and 826 (Lucas 1989, 189). This concern with the destructive potential of cattle-raiding is perhaps only implied in the narrative message of *Táin Bó Cúailnge,* but may have found more explicit literary reflection elsewhere in the Ulster Cycle: a passage in *Táin Bó Regamna* has been interpreted (Russell 1988, 253) as advice to Cú Chulainn to give up cattle-raiding.

As the instigator of the cattle raid, Medb is the primary culprit, who as a woman has unjustifiably arrogated power and status to herself. It is her challenge to male superiority, the bedrock of a patriarchal society, which upsets the natural balance and destabilises society. One of the thematic concerns of the tale, then, is the perennial question of the relative roles in society of men and women. More specifically, it concentrates on Medb's unseemly aspirations towards the supreme male role, that of the king. This is a theme worthy to elicit a first-class performance from a clerical author: 'The mandarin managers of the past are at their best when they engage in polysemic discourse on the nature of kingship, its possession and legitimation' (Ó Corráin 1987, 31). And such a weighty theme, and a superb narrative treatment of it, could justify the warranty of a year's protection for anyone who hears the tale (Meyer 1906, 8 sect. 62).

One could go a step further and see in the *Táin,* not just an exploration of the nature of legitimate kingship, but a comment on the literary treatments of the topic, and on the dangerous potential of the sovereignty goddess myth to privilege the female at the expense of the male. While most discussions of this myth emphasise

the endurance of the image of Ireland as woman in the literature down to the vision poetry of the eighteenth century, a recent study has drawn attention to a development in the presentation of the woman which diminishes her role. In the oldest traditions she exercises choice in conferring the kingship, but in *Baile in Scáil* 'The Phantom's Vision' she acts at the behest of her divine spouse Lug, showing that 'the locus of power has shifted from female to male' (Herbert 1992, 269). I suggest that the *Táin* is a more elaborate narrative expression of the same iconoclastic impetus. The first of the dire results Fergus predicts for the raid, which include vultures feasting on corpses, and the rampaging of werewolves, is the inflation of the power of queens: *Bíait rígnai dermara* 'Great queens will be there' (2412).

Contemporary Relevance: tempus, locus, persona et causa scribendi

The previous section was an attempt to establish the general thematic import of the *Táin.* To particularise this requires the examination of the text in its own context of dynasty, time and place. Radner's suggestion (1982, 53-57) that its purpose was to make propaganda for firm overkingship by the Uí Néill dynasty does not permit a location in a narrower time framework than the sixth to the tenth centuries. A linguistic analysis allows a more precise dating, for the main body of the prose of Recension I points to the first half of the ninth century.[23]

The most circumstantial anchoring of the *Táin* in time and place and politico-dynastic context is that of Kelleher (1971, 122-125), who suggests tentatively that Recension I is a political allegory for the struggle between traditional and reforming clergy for control of Armagh in the first quarter of the ninth century. According to this interpretation Emain Macha in the *Táin* is code for Armagh. The fight for power over Armagh had a local dimension in the dissensions between branches of the Airgialla, who had displaced the historical Ulaid from the territory around Armagh, and had long-standing claims to the prestigious ecclesiastical offices of the monastery, and a wider dimension in the rivalry between the northern and southern branches of the Uí Néill. A turning point in the struggle was the battle of Leth Cam in 827, at which the Ulaid, allied with the Airgialla sept of the Uí Chremthainn, both supporters of the reform party, were defeated by the Cenél nEógain king Niall Caille. Kelleher suggests that the *Táin* was written some years previous to this battle, by Cuanu, the reforming abbot of Louth, who identifies himself with Cú Chulainn, on whose shoulders the burden of the defence falls. Is the *Táin* then a *roman à clef?* If so, one is tempted to take the Ulster king as fictional code for his namesake Conchobar (mac Donnchadha), Clann Cholmáin rival of, and successor to, the Cenél nEógain King of Tara, Áed Oirdnide.[24]

Intriguingly, the mother of Áed Oirdnide's son Niall Caille, who succeeded Conchobar in the high-kingship, was one Medb, a Connacht woman (Dobbs 1930, 310; 1931, 225).[25] This neat solution unfortunately fails to account for the fact that the Connacht king Muirgius mac Tomaltaig (d. 815) supported Conchobar mac Donnchadha and opposed Áed Oirdnide. Perhaps Muirgius's entry onto the stage of all-Ireland politics (Byrne 1973, 251) was unwelcome to some party whose point of view is reflected in the **Táin**. It is clear that a full decoding would require detailed knowledge about 'the appallingly complex political situation that lay behind the disruptions in Armagh' from the mid-eighth to the mid-ninth century (McCone 1984b, 319). Could we see the pacifist stance discussed above as a plea from the Armagh clerics for a cessation of hostilities in this long-drawn out struggle?[26] The victory of the Ulaid in the **Táin** is at best Pyrrhic: the Donn Cúailnge is lost to both sides, and before dying it turns on and kills the *innocentes,* the non-combatant women and children, of its own tribe (*TBC II* 4115-6).

Two more of the general themes identified above may also have had a more immediate relevance in the ninth century. The diminution in the role of the sovereignty goddess in *Baile in Scáil* is present in its oldest section.[27] This stratum must have been composed during the high-kingship of Mael Sechnaill, whose reign began in 846. The trend to subtly alter the sovereignty myth so as to redress the female/male imbalance may therefore have been an on-going one at this time.

An early ninth-century drive to eradicate or curtail cattle-raiding is perhaps reflected in the fact that *Cáin Dar Í* was promulgated three times between 810 and 813, in Munster, Connacht and Uí Néill territory respectively. Thirteen years later it was re-issued in Connacht: this may point to a resurgence of the problem in the western province in the intervening period, which would have facilitated the depiction of the Connachtmen as aggressors in the **Táin.**

If even some of the above suggestions are valid, there are grounds for thinking that Recension I of the **Táin,** for all its timeless appeal, may also be satisfactorily mapped onto a specific historical background by the coordinates of *tempus, locus, persona et causa scribendi.*

Style and Structure

It is generally agreed that one of the best features of early Irish storytelling is the terse, fast-paced style, consisting of taut, almost elliptical, sentences or phrases. It is deployed to striking advantage in conversation, lending passages of direct speech a staccato-like effect. As an example I quote from the touching exchange between Cú Chulainn and his mother in the first section of the *macgnímrada* . . .

"Cú Chulainn asked his mother to let him go to join the boys.

'You shall not go,' said his mother, 'till you be escorted by some of the Ulster warriors.'

'I think it too long to wait for that,' said Cú Chulainn. 'Point out to me in what direction is Emain.'

'To the north there,' said his mother, 'and the journey is hard. Slíab Fúait lies between you and Emain.'

'I shall make an attempt at it at all events,' said Cú Chulainn" (*TBC I* 406-14).

In general, the older the text, the more economical the prose. A comparison with the Recension II version of the above scene may serve to illustrate the development in style between the ninth and twelfth centuries:

'It is too soon for you to go, my son,' said his mother, 'until there go with you a champion of the champions of Ulster or some of the attendants of Conchobar to ensure your safety and protection from the youths.' (*TBC II* 751-754). The effect is smoother, but tends to the verbose.

In another instance from Recension I, the succinctness of Medb's speech is a perfect vehicle for the stark message it conveys. She feels threatened by the superiority of the Gaileóin. Ailill tries to divine her intentions . . .

'Well then, what shall be done with them,' asked Ailill, 'since neither their staying nor their going pleases you?'

'Kill them!' said Medb (*TBC I* 160-162).

The limpid quality prevails even in descriptive passages, as in the following extended word portrait of the prophetess Fedelm, which consists largely of verb-free nominal phrases . . .

'She had yellow hair. She wore a vari-coloured cloak with a golden pin in it and a hooded tunic with red embroidery. She had shoes with golden fastenings. Her face was oval, narrow below, broad above. Her eyebrows were dark and black. Her beautiful black eyelashes cast a shadow on to the middle of her cheeks. Her lips seemed to be made of partaing. Her teeth were like a shower of pearls between her lips. She had three plaits of hair: two plaits wound around her head, the third hanging down her back, touching her calves behind. In her hand she carried a weaver's beam of white bronze, with golden inlay. There were three pupils in each of her eyes. The maiden was armed and her chariot was drawn by two black horses' (*TBC I* 30-39).

An eleventh-century addition to Recension I, which contains a description of Cú Chulainn's hair, provides a contrast and highlights the later tendency to heap up adjectives: 'Fair was the arrangement of that hair with three coils in the hollow in the nape of his neck, and like gold thread was each fine hair, loose-flowing, bright-golden, excellent, long-tressed, splendid and of beautiful colour, which fell back over his shoulder. A hundred bright crimson ringlets of flaming red-gold encircled his neck' (2342-47).

Some stretches of direct speech in the *Táin* are in a rhythmical alliterative style called *rosc(ad)* or *retoiric*. Their syntax is frequently marked, and they have therefore often been held to belong to an older linguistic stratum of the text. Corthals (1989a, 219) points out, however, that in the *Táin* such passages are fully integrated into the surrounding 'straight' prose as regards narrative content. Rather than reflecting a chronological divide, they exemplify one of the possible varieties in the 'supple stylistic continuum' (McCone 1990, 50) of early Irish writing. A lengthy stretch of *roscad* occurs in the exchange between Ailill, Fergus and Medb after the love-making scene (1069-1146). Another context which features this style is the Morrígan's prophecy to the bull (958-961). The style here is even more highly marked, through the use of metre for the words of the actual prophecy, contained in the two central lines below, which are linked by alliteration to the surrounding rhetorical prose (alliterating consonants in boldface) . . .

> ' . . . I have a secret which the Black one will find out: 'If he will (=would) eat in May (?) the very green grass of the bogland, he would be overpowered (and driven) out of his field by fire (and) contest of strong warriors.' The flowering splendour of the host seduces the Bodb' (Corthals 1989b, 56).

Another variation in style is brought about by an alternation between prose and syllabic verse. Some sections have no syllabic verse at all, e.g. the *macgnímrada,* while the eleventh century Fer Diad episode (2567-3142) features almost a half-and-half distribution between these two modes. After this episode the remaining thousand or so lines are entirely in prose, with some short passages of *roscad*.

The narrative technique also features diversity. A popular means of ringing the changes on conventional exposition is the 'watchman device'. This consists of description presented by a knowledgeable participant in the events (the 'watchman'), rather than by an omniscient narrator. The device has not found favour with the taste of modern scholars, who have dismissed instances in other texts as 'long and tedious', or 'repetitive and wearisome'. With an effort of empathy, however, it is possible to see some virtue in its employment in the *Táin.*

If it is correct to suggest that it is no concern of the tale to glorify war, the author is faced with the problem of how to create a credible battle scenario without direct description of the carnage. He conveys a sense of the strength of the defending army in the lengthy account of the approach of the Ulster warriors as viewed by the Connachtmen (3544-3870). The use of the watchman device here is far from mechanical: a reconnaissance man is sent out and returns with descriptions of individual warriors, who Fergus, their one-time comrade, is asked to identify. His answers are not stereotyped, and his personal reactions are varied. Another sophisticated use of the technique furnishes a *post hoc* and indirect account of bloody combat in 'The hard fight of Cethern' (3161-3282). The wounded Ulsterman Cethern will not suffer any physician near him, so the diagnosis of his injuries is conducted at a distance: he describes the warriors who wounded him, and here it is Cú Chulainn, all too familiar with the Connacht adversaries, who identifies them. In contrast, the account of Cú Chulainn's own participation in the final fray is a gem of understatement . . .

> 'It was midday when Cú Chulainn came to the battle. When the sun was sinking behind the trees in the wood, he overcame the last of the bands, and of the chariot there remained only a handful of the ribs of the framework and a handful of the shafts round the wheel' (4110-13).

This stunning image is expressed with all the eloquence and brevity of the most admired passages of early Irish prose, but the other narrative responses to the task of describing the battle need not therefore be denied structural validity and artistic intent.

The structure of the opening scenes of the *Táin* has evoked unanimous critical approval. Some of the best literary effects here have been analysed by Carney (1955, 67-71). In the initial portion, some eight hundred lines, from the mustering of the Connacht forces to the end of the *macgnímrada,* he detects the hand of a literary personality, 'not a mere story-teller' (*ibid* 68). The *pièce-de-résistance* is undoubtedly the 'Boyhood deeds' (398-824). After the advance of the Connachtmen has been held up by some displays of Cú Chulainn's prowess, the forward movement of the narrative is interrupted with a flashback to enable the exiled Ulstermen to recall the most striking martial feats of his precocious childhood. The build-up to this flashback is also impressive. The narrator's attention is initially directed entirely to the Connacht side. The prophecy of Fedelm soon casts an ominous shadow on their proceedings. Cú Chulainn only slowly comes into focus: he is first referred to, but not named, in the prophecy of Dubthach (194), as the army traverses the centre of the country. When they reach the east, Fergus sends him a warning. From then on, Cú Chulainn's presence is increasingly felt, until he kills four of the vanguard of the invading army and sets their heads up on spits to confront the Connachtmen when they arrive. It is at this point that Ailill and Medb inquire about their formidable opponent, and the Ulstermen each contribute their memories of his 'boyhood deeds': this sets the scene for the ultimate triumph of the Ulster defence, and reinforces the sense of foreboding which dogs the Connacht forces throughout. Such 'tricks of presentation' Carney (*ibid* 71) considers to be evidence of a wholly literary sophistication, of a quality rare even in the early texts.

The remainder of the tale has not received anything like the same accolades. Greene's judgement (1954, 32) that 'the long series of single combats becomes wearisome and the story tails off badly' is probably representative of modern scholarly opinion. For Carney (1955, 67) the decline in the quality of the narration sets in with the very first of the single combats, the interpolated 'Death of Fróech' (833-857). Admittedly 'after this point . . . there are a greater number of incidents which are merely of antiquarian interest' *(ibid),* but perhaps there are some points of significance encoded in the placenames or personal names in the single encounters which may yet be elucidated. However that may be, O'Rahilly concedes that 'the skill with which these encounters are varied in circumstance and detail is remarkable' (1967, xxiii).

Literary Impact

The earliest comprehensive assessment of the *Táin* is contained in the famous Latin *coda* to the Book of Leinster recension: 'But I who have written this story, or rather this fable, give no credence to the various incidents related in it. For some things in it are the deceptions of demons, others poetic figments; some are probable, others improbable; while still others are intended for the delectation of foolish men' (*TBC II* 4021-4025).

Modern critical comment on the value of the *Táin* as literature differs in content, but not in its negative thrust. While some individual components are universally applauded for their literary excellence, the consensus among scholars is that, judged as a whole, the *Táin* is a failure. Greene attributes the alleged lack of artistic success to the fact that 'even to the present day, the native genius has felt more at home with short stories than with long works of complicated construction' (1968, 104). As against that one could advert to recent scholarly work on two other lengthy and complex early tales, *Togail Bruidne Da Derga* and *Cath Maige Tuired,* which shows them to be not wanting in coherence and artistry.

A reliable verdict is, however, only possible if the text's aims have been correctly identified. As the present discussion has shown, there is scope for considerable work on such a basic matter as the meaning of the narrative, before the techniques of presentation can be assessed.

On the basis of the analysis presented here I would take issue with Greene's conclusion *(ibid)* that 'there is nothing in the fragmentary *Táin* we have that would allow us to suspect the existence of a planned and developed prose epic—nothing to suggest that the *Táin* was ever otherwise than jerky and episodic', and argue that even the 'hotch-potch' (*ibid* 103) of Recension I allows us more than a glimpse of a coherent whole, in which consciously chosen elements are deployed in a carefully planned order, and expressed in an appropriate form. Ultimately concerned with the theme of kingship, the tale deals with the three fundamental areas of mental, martial and material qualities and functions, and comments on their relative importance. The animal imagery and symbolism—equine, canine and bovine—reflect the tale's concerns on a metaphorical plane, and supply an artistic cohesion.[28] The narrative can be read as a series of conflicts on these three levels. Medb's exchange with Fedelm is a confrontation in the spiritual domain: her faulty judgement reveals the defect in the Connacht kingship, and portends her inevitable defeat. The main body of the narrative is devoted to physical encounters, which express the martial function. Far from tailing off badly after the series of single combats, the narrative works up to a resounding crescendo in which pacifism triumphs and the proud queen is dishonoured. The Ulstermen win the battle, but the victory is hollow: the final conflict, that of the animal forces, sees the destruction of the two bulls, the symbols of fertility and material wealth. The last scene[29] can be read as a powerful image of the futility of martial victory achieved at the expense of fecundity.

Further analysis will surely reinforce this vindication of the literary skill and artistic purpose of the author of **Táin Bó Cúailnge.**

Notes

[1] Reviews of the types of investigation to which these texts have been treated to date are found in Herbert (1988) and Ó Cathasaigh (1984).

[2] McCone (1990) exemplifies the new paradigm and contains a comprehensive bibliography.

[3] The genealogical poem *Canailla Medb míchuru* is discussed by Ó hUiginn in this volume.

[4] Mac Eoin (1983, 121) disagrees with Thurneysen's (1921, 449 and 667) eighth-century date for *Fled Bricrenn,* finding nothing in the oldest portions to warrant a date before 900.

[5] The later recension is also linguistically more accessible, and has been translated virtually in its entirety by Cecile O'Rahilly. Large chunks of Recension I, however, particularly the rhythmical dialogue passages, still await edition and translation.

[6] Cf. Gray (1980-81, 1982-83), Ó Cathasaigh (1983), McCone (1989).

[7] See McCone (1990 Chapter 9) for a thorough discussion, which incorporates his own earlier articles (1984a, 1986, 1987) and Sharpe (1979).

[8] Translation according to Gantz (1981, 260).

[9] Thurneysen (1930, 108) sees traces of Medb's divinity in the references to places named after her in Ulster territory (*TBC I* 1534-36).

[10] The prose introduction to *Conailla Medb míchuru* also says that Fergus fought against his own people *ar imtóin mná* (Meyer 1912, 305) 'for a woman's great buttocks'.

[11] Another tradition about Fergus also represents him as having dishonoured his people for a woman's body. He cedes the kingship of Ulster for a year to Conchobar in return for the sexual favours of his mother Ness. When the year is up the Ulstermen decide not to allow Fergus to regain the kingship, for 'they deemed it a great dishonour that Fergus had given them (to Ness) as a bride-price' *(hi tindscra)* (Stokes 1910, 24 §7).

[12] Translation from Charles-Edwards (1976, 47).

[13] O'Rahilly (1071) follows the translation of Binchy (1972, 35), who adopts the manuscript reading *misrairlustair:* This form is repeated in Fergus's final taunt to Medb (4124).

[14] Corthals (1989) has in some cases provided fuller translations than O' Rahilly (1976).

[15] The usual meaning of *midlach* in the sagas is 'coward, weakling'.

[16] De Paor (1923, 126-128) makes no use of this incident in her discussion of the personal contribution of the author of Recension II to the characterisation of Medb.

[17] De Paor (1923, 127) considers that the utterance 'fails altogether to illumine the character of the Connacht queen' and contrasts the corresponding LL passage with approval: 'There are many who part here today from comrades and friends,' said Medb, 'from land and territory, from father and mother, and if not all return safe and sound, it is on me their grumbles and their curses will fall. Yet none goes forth and none stays here who is any dearer to us than we ourselves' (*TBC II* 177-181).

[18] O'Rahilly (1976) translates 'destruction' here.

[19] McCone (1990) contains a wealth of evidence for Biblical and patristic parallels.

[20] There may also be an echo of the story of Salomé and John the Baptist (Matthew 14.3-12) in the scene in which Findabair is offered as a bribe to Láiríne mac Nóis to induce him to bring back the head of Cú Chulainn as a trophy (1818-1823).

[21] Note also the similarities between the calls which rouse Deborah and Barak for the battle (Judges 5, 12: 'Awake, awake, Deborah; awake, awake, utter a song; arise, Barak') and the series of exhortations 'Arise, (valiant) kings of Macha!' in the *Táin* (3905, 3918, 3930).

[22] Ó Broin (1961-63) argues that the debility is in origin a death or winter sleep which is an element of an old vegetation myth of cyclic decline and renewal.

[23] Thurneysen's dating (1921, 666) has been confirmed and refined by Manning (1985).

[24] He may also have been the father of the reform candidate for the abbacy, Artrímac Conchobair (Kelleher 1971, 124).

[25] The identification of her father with Innrechtach, King of Connacht, who died in 723, would indicate that her son Niall Caille (d. 846) was already an old man at the time of the battle of Leth Cam.

[26] The earliest 'authorial' ascription of the *Táin,* in the ninth-century *Triads,* is to a seventh-century Airgialla poet Nainíne Éces, the direct ancestor of Fethgna, abbot of Armagh from 859 to 874 (Ó Fiaich 1960-62).

[27] Murphy (1952, 150 n.1) considers the early portion to extend up to §50, which names Mael Sechnaill as King of Tara: the dates of his reign, from 846 to 862, suggest a mid-ninth century date for this stratum of the text.

[28] The Rees brothers make the only other attempt known to me to interpret the *Táin* in terms of the tripartite ideology, but in taking the bulls to symbolize the warrior function they conclude—I would say erroneously—that the tale 'appears as an example of the classic struggle between the priestly and the warrior classes, each of which tends to usurp the functions and privileges of the other' (Rees 1961, 124).

[29] I follow O'Rahilly (1967, xxxvi) in taking lines 4156-59 to be an addition of the YBL scribe or his exemplar.

References

Aitchison, N. B.

1987 'The Ulster cycle: heroic image and historical 'reality',' *Journal of Medieval History* 13 no. 2, pp. 87-116.

Bieler, L.

1963 The Irish penitentials. *Scriptores Latini Hiberniae,* Vol. 5. Dublin.

Binchy, D. A.

1972 'Varia hibernica 1. the so-called 'rthetorics' of Irish saga', in *Indo-Celtica: Gedächtnisschrift für Alf Sommerfelt,* ed. H. Pilch and J. Thurow. München, pp. 29-38.

Bowen, C.

1975 'Great-bladdered Medb; mythology and invention in the *Táin Bó Cúailnge'. Éire-Ireland* 10, pp. 14-34.

Breatnach, R. A.

1953 'The Lady and the King: a theme of Irish literature', *Studies* 42, pp. 321-36.

Byrne, F. J.

1973 *Irish Kings and High-Kings.* London.

Carney, J.

1969 'The deeper level of early Irish literature', *The Capuchin Annual,* pp. 160-171

1968 'Cath Maige Muccrime', in *Irish Sagas,* ed. Myles Dillon, Cork, pp. 148-155.

1956 'The impact of Christianity', in *Early Irish Society,* ed. M. Dillon, Dublin, pp. 66-78

1955 *Studies in Irish Literature and History.* Dublin

Charles-Edwards, T. M.

1976 'The social background to Irish Peregrinatio', *Celtica* 11, pp. 43-59.

Corthals, J.
1989a 'Zur Frage des mündlichen oder schriftlichen Ursprungs der Sagenroscada', in Tranter and Tristram, pp. 201-220.

1989b 'The retoiric in *Aided Chonchobuir', Ériu* 40, pp. 41-59.

Davies, W.

1983 'Celtic women in the early middle ages', in *Images of Women in Antiquity,* eds Averil Cameron and Amélie Kuhrt, London, pp. 145-166.

de Paor, Á.

1923 'The common authorship of some Book of Leinster texts', *Ériu* 9, pp. 118-146.

Doan, J.

1985 'Sovereignty aspects in the roles of women in medieval Irish and Welsh society', *Proceedings of the Harvard Celtic Colloquium* 5, pp. 87-102.

Dobbs, M. C.

1931 'The Ban-Shenchus', *Revue Celtique* 48, pp. 163-234.

1930 'The Ban-Shenchus', *Revue Celtique* 47, pp. 283-339.

Edel, D.

1989 'Die inselkeltische Erzähltradition zwischen Mündlichkeit und Schriftlichkeit', in Tranter and Tristram, pp. 99-124.

Gantz, J.

1981 *Early Irish Myths and Sagas.* Harmondsworth.

Gray, E. A.

1982-83 '*Cath Maige Tuired:* myth and structure (24-120)', *Éigse* 19, pp. 1-35; (pp. 84-93; 120-67) pp. 230-62.

1980-81 '*Cath Maige Tuired:* myth and structure (1-24)', *Éigse* 18, pp. 183-209.

Greene, D.

1968 '*Táin Bó Cúailnge',* in *Irish Sagas,* ed. Myles Dillon, Cork, pp. 93-104.

1954 'Early Irish literature', in *Early Irish Society,* ed. Myles Dillon, Dublin, pp. 22-35.

Gwynn, E. G.

1903 The Metrical Dindsenchas Part I. *Todd Lecture Series* Vol. VIII, Dublin.

Herbert, M.

1992 'Goddess and king: the sacred marriage in early Ireland', in *Women and Sovereignty,* ed. Louise D. Fradenburg (*Cosmos* Vol 7), Edinburgh, pp. 264-275.

1988 'The world, the text, and the critic of early Irish heroic narrative', *Text and Context,* pp. 1-9.

Kelleher, J. V.

1972 'Humor in the Ulster Saga', in *Veins of Humor,* ed. Harry Levin, Cambridge, Mass., pp. 36-57.

1971 'The *Táin* and the annals', *Ériu* 22, pp. 107-27.

Kelly, F.

1988 *A Guide to Early Irish Law.* Dublin.

1976 *Audacht Morainn.* Dublin.

Kinsella, T.

1970 *The Tain.* Oxford.

Lucas, A. T.

1989 *Cattle in Ancient Ireland.* Kilkenny.

Mac Cana, P.

1980a *The Learned Tales of Medieval Ireland* Dublin.

1980b 'Women in Irish mythology', *The Crane Bag* 4, no. 1, pp. 7-11.

1958-59 'Aspects of the theme of king and goddess in Irish literature', *Études Celtiques* 8, pp. 59-65.

1955-56 'Aspects of the theme of king and goddess in Irish literature', *Études Celtiques* 7, pp. 76-114; pp. 356-413.

Mac Eoin, G.

1983 'The dating of Middle Irish texts', *Proceedings of the British Academy* 69, 1982, pp. 109-37.

Manning, G.

1985 The verbal system of *Táin Bó úailnge*–Recension I. Unpublished M. Litt. thesis, Trinity College Dublin

McCone, K.

1990 *Pagan Past and Christian Present* Maynooth.

1989 'A tale of two ditties: poet and satirist in *Cath Maige Tuired* in *Sages, Saints and Storytellers: Celtic studies in honour of Professor James Carney,* eds Donnchadh Ó Corráin, Liam Breatnach, Kim McCone, Maynooth, pp. 122-143.

1987 'Hund, Wolf und Krieger bei den Indogermanen', *Studien zum Indogermanischen Wortschatz,* ed. Wolfgang Meid, Innsbruck, pp. 101-154.

1986 'Werewolves, *cyclopes, díberga* and *fíanna:* juvenile delinquency in early Ireland', *Cambridge Medieval Celtic Studies* 12, pp. 1-22.

1984a 'Aided Cheltchair maic Uthechair: hounds, heroes and hospitallers in early Irish myth and story', *Ériu* 35, pp. 1-30.

1984b 'Clones and her neighbours in the early period: hints from some Airgialla saints' lives', *Clogher Record* 11, pp. 305-25.

McCone, K and P. Ó Fiannachta

1992 *Scéalaíocht ár Sinsear.* Dublin.

Meyer, K.

1912 'The Laud genealogies and tribal histories' *Zeitschrift für celtische Philologie* 8, pp. 291-338.

1905 *Cáin Adamnáin. An Old-Irish treatise on the law of Adamnan.* Oxford.

Murphy, G. M.

1955 *Saga and Myth in Ancient Ireland.* Dublin.

1952 'On the dates of two sources used in Thurneysen's *Heldensage',* *Ériu* 16, pp. 145-156.

Ní Bhrolcháin, M.

1980 'Women in early Irish myths and sagas', *The Crane Bag* 4, no. 1, pp. 12-19.

Ó Broin, T.

1961-63 'What is the 'debility' of the Ulstermen?', *Éigse* 10, pp. 286-299.

Ó Cathasaigh T.

1986a 'The Rhetoric of *Fingal Rónáin',* *Celtica* 17, pp. 123-144.

1986b 'The sister's son in early Irish literature', *Peritia*

5, pp. 128-160.

1984 'Pagan survivals: the evidence of early Irish narrative', in *Irland und Europa, die Kirche im Frühmittelalter / Ireland and Europe, the Early Church,* eds Próinséas Ní Chatháin and Michael Richter, Stuttgart, pp. 291-307.

1983 '*Cath Maige Tuired* as exemplary myth', in *Folia Gadelica: essays presented to R. A. Breatnach,* eds Pádraig de Brún, Seán Ó Coileáin and Pádraig Ó Riain, Cork, pp. 1-19.

O'Connor, F.

1967 *The Backward Look.* London.

Ó Corráin, D.

1987 'Legend as critic', in The writer as witness: literature as historical evidence, *Historical Studies* 16, ed. Tom Dunne, Cork, pp. 23-38.

1986 'Historical need and literary narrative', in Proceedings of the *Seventh International Congress of Celtic Studies, Oxford 1983,* Oxford, pp. 141-158.

1978 'Women in early Irish society', in *Women in Irish Society,* eds Margaret MacCurtain and Donncha Ó Corráin, Dublin, pp. 1-13.

Ó Fiaich, T.

1960-62 'Cérbh é Ninine Éigeas?', *Seanchas Ard Mhacha* 4 ii, pp. 95-100.

O' Hehir, B.

1983 'The christian revision of *Eachtra Airt meic Cuind ocus Tochmarc Delbchaime ingine Morgain',* in *Celtic Folklore and Christianity: studies in memory of William W. Heist,* ed P. K. Ford, Santa Barbara, pp. 159-179.

O'Leary, P.

1987 'The honour of women in early Irish literature', *Ériu* 38, pp. 27-44.

Ó Máille, T.

1927 'Medb Chruachna', *Zeitschrift für celtische Philologie* 17, pp. 129-146.

O' Rahilly, C.

1976 *Táin Bó Cúailnge Recension I.* Dublin.

1967 *Táin Bó Cúalnge from the Book of Leinster.*

Dublin.

O'Rahilly, T. F.

1943 'On the origin of the names Érainn and Ériu', *Ériu* 14, pp. 7-28.

Ó Riain, P.

1990 'A misunderstood annal: a hitherto unnoticed *cáin',* *Celtica* 21, pp. 561-566.

Radner, J. N.

1982 'Fury destroys the world': historical strategy in Ireland's Ulster epic', *Mankind Quarterly* 23, pp. 41-60.

Rees A. and B.

1961 *Celtic Heritage: ancient tradition in Ireland and Wales.* London.

Russell, P.

1986 *'Varia I: Táin Bó Regamna',* *Études Celtiques* 25, pp. 247-254.

Sayers, W.

1985 'Fergus and the cosmogonic sword', *History of Religions* 25, pp. 30-56.

Sharpe, R.

1979 'Hiberno-Latin *laicus,* Irish *láech* and the devil's men', *Ériu* 30, pp. 75-92.

Stokes, W.

1910 'Tidings of Conchobar son of Ness', *Ériu* 4, pp. 18-38.

Stokes W. and J. Strachan

1903 *Thesaurus Palaeohibernicus,* Vol. II, Cambridge.

Thurneysen, R.

1931 *Irisches Recht.* Abhandlungen der Preussischen Akademie der Wissenschaften. Phil.-hist. Klasse, Nr. 2. Berlin.

1930 'Allerlei Keltisches 7. Göttin Medb?', *Zeitschrift für celtische Philologie* 18, pp. 108-10.

1921 *Die irischen Helden- und Königsage bis zum siebzehnten Jahrhundert.* Halle.

Tranter and Tristram

1989 *Early Irish literature–media and communication/ Mündlichkeit und Schriftlichkeit in der frühen irischen Literatur,* eds Stephen N. Tranter and Hildegard L. C. Tristram, Tübingen.

Tomás Ó Cathasaigh (essay date 1993)

SOURCE: "Mythology in *Táin Bó Cuailnge*" in *Studien zur "Táin Bó Cuailnge,"* edited by Hildegard L. C. Tristram, Gunter Narr, 1993, pp. 114-32.

[*In the essay that follows, Ó Cathasaigh explores the presence of Celtic and Indo-European mythological elements in the* Táin *and demonstrates how they were made meaningful for its Irish audience.*]

Táin Bó Cúailnge is a work of some complexity, and it should therefore be amenable to a wide range of critical approaches, literary, linguistic, historical and mythological. The complex character of the *Táin* is sometimes overlooked by individual critics, but it is reflected in the diversity of the criticism which has been devoted to it. While that criticism is as yet quite modest in extent, the *Táin* has been discussed, in whole or in part, separately or as part of the Ulster Cycle, from a number of viewpoints, all of them having some implications for the general theme of orality and literacy. The Ulster Cycle was considered by the Chadwicks and their disciples as a reflection of a lost Heroic Age;[1] it has also been discussed, by Ó Corráin and Aitchison, in terms of the historical circumstances in which it was given shape.[2] The mythological components in the *Táin,* and in the Cycle generally, have been considered by O'Rahilly, Sjoestedt, Rees and Rees and others.[3] James Carney held that the *Táin* was a work of literature, created in a mixed culture, and he agreed with Thurneysen that it was deliberately imitative of the classics.[4] John Kelleher argues that the *Táin* was created in response to certain historical circumstances, but he implies that its dominant figure, Cú Chulainn, was based on the model of Jesus Christ.[5]

In view of all this it will be helpful to begin our discussion of the *Táin* with the question "Cid so?"; in other words to ask ourselves "What is it?". The answer is "not dificult": *Táin Bó Cúailnge* is an epic, and it follows that its primary claim on our attention must be as a work of literature. It is useful to make this point at the outset, because there has been a tendency to discredit the literary status of early Irish narrative texts, to see them, not as works in their own right, but rather in relation to myth or history or oral tradition. This tendency can be put down to the fact that the serious study of early Irish literature has historically (and necessarily) been the domain of philologists, who have understandably fought shy of the concerns and methods of literary critics. This is usually done without explanation or apology, but one eminent philologist, Jaan Puhvel, makes the case for his own discipline by expressing undisguised disdain for literary criticism:

> Modern literary myth-critics, armed with ungainly ritualist and psychoanalytic panoplies, may indeed set to work on any ancient epic, as well as take apart to their own satisfaction a work by James Joyce or Scott Fitzgerald: they will never get any closer to the core of one than the other, because in their butcher shop all carcasses hang equal. If we are to make any headway in studying Indo-European epic as a narrative genre, philology alone will help us along.[6]

Our knowledge of early Irish literature we owe in large measure to philologists, and in the case of the *Táin* we are especially indebted to the late Cecile O'Rahilly for her remarkable editorial achievement;[7] it is therefore with no disrespect for philology that I say that it alone, as traditionally practised, will not suffice if we are to understand our texts. There is of course nothing amiss in viewing the *Táin* within a mythological or historical perspective, nor would I suggest for a moment that it is not a suitable case for consideration within the general topic of this series of colloquia. All that I am saying is that we should always bear in mind what it is that we are dealing with. If that is done, we need not, and should not, exclude any critical approach to the *Táin* which remains faithful to the transmitted texts, and which helps to illuminate them.

Commentators on the *Táin* have ignored, rather than reviled, literary criticism, but the result is that we are still very much in the dark as to how the *Táin* is constituted as a work of literature. Moreover, one of the weaknesses of much of the commentary on the *Táin* has been the reductive way in which theories have been applied to it: thus T. F. O'Rahilly, being satisfied that the Ulster tales "are wholly mythical in origin," contends that "they have not the faintest connexion with anything that could be called history, apart from the fact that traditions of warfare between the Ulaid and the Connachta have been adventitiously introduced into a few of them, and especially into the longest and best-known tale, 'Táin Bó Cualgne'."[8] Kenneth Jackson, on the other hand, states that the Ulster Cycle "belongs to the genre of literature of entertainment and contains very little that can reasonably or safely be taken for myth or ought to be interpreted as such."[9] It is in no such reductive spirit that I begin my paper with a brief consideration of the *Táin* as epic.

For a general description of epic, we may turn to M. H. Abrams, who says that "in its strict use by literary critics the term 'epic' or 'heroic poem' is applied to a work that meets at least the following criteria: it is a long narrative poem on a great and serious subject, related in an elevated style, and centred on a heroic or quasi-divine figure on whose actions depends the fate of a tribe, a nation, or the human race."[10] Setting aside the fact that it comprises a mixture of prose and verse, the *Táin* meets the criteria set out by Abrams: it is a long narrative work, related for the most part in an elevated style; its subject matter, the invasion and defence of Ulster, is great and serious; it is centred on the heroic figure of Cú Chulainn, on whose actions the fate of Ulster depends. The difference between the *Táin* and short sagas such as *Scéla Mucce Meic Da Thó* ('The Story of Mac Da Thó's Pig') is not merely, or even mainly, a matter of relative length; the difference in scale, in subject matter, and in treatment of subject matter bespeaks a difference of genre between the *Táin* and the short sagas. This is not something which we can pursue here. For our purposes it is enough that the identification of the *Táin* as an epic helps us to put its mythic content into focus, and to see how what may seem to be quite disparate mythic strands are woven into a literary work which is simple in its general outline, but remarkably complex in its detail; single-minded in the achievement of its purpose, but multifarious in the means so used.

A question of literary history arises at this point. Was the *Táin* composed in deliberate imitation of classical epic, of Homer's *Iliad* or Vergil's *Aeneid?* Or is it rather a "primary epic," a type, which, as Abrams puts it, would have been "shaped by a literary artist from historical and legendary materials which had developed in the oral traditions of his nation during a period of expansion and warfare."[11] Thurneysen detected what he claimed were reminiscenses of classical epic in the *Táin,* and he was inclined to assign these to the *Grundtext,* in which, as it seemed to Thurneysen, an Irishman had for the first time attempted to compile a single extensive narrative from the "short narratives and episodes as the storytellers were accustomed to relate them," and which would compare with classical epic.[12] Thurneysen's view has been endorsed by James Carney,[13] but Gerard Murphy and Proinsias Mac Cana have argued against it.[14] Very briefly one might say that whereas Carney holds that the *Táin* was composed in imitation of Homer, Murphy rejects this and offers two other explanations for such similarities as exist between the *Iliad* and the *Táin,* the first being "a common Indo-European tradition," the second "the natural resemblance of manners in any Heroic Age."[15] It is important to note that when Carney says that the *Táin* "consists in part of traditional material, in part of imaginative reconstruction of the remote pagan Irish past in form and terms that belong to the mixed culture of early Christian Ireland,"[16] he recognizes the presence in the *Táin* of elements derived from oral narrative. Murphy, for his part, goes some of the way to meet Carney, saying that when Carney "warns us against regarding Christian elements in Irish stories about pagan times as 'interpolation' he is on firm ground. The

pagan stories are available only in Christian versions, and the Christian element is as definitely a part of them as the Christian language in which they are told."[17] What is in question, therefore, is the role of those who gave the *Táin* written form. Neither Murphy nor Carney would support Mac Cana's remarkable assertion that "it is (. . .) very possible—indeed probable—that an oral version of the *Táin* not radically different from the first written version was already in existence during the seventh century."[18] The notion that the early writers of Irish saga were passive traditors of oral narrative is dismissed by Carney, who sees them "as literary authors rather than as scribes."[19] I agree in general with this view of Carney's, which now commands increasing consent among scholars,[20] but I have to say that, whatever may have motivated or influenced the composition of the *Táin,* it has not as yet been demonstrated that the content of the *Táin* is derived in any significant measure from classical epic. It has also become necessary, in view of what has recently been happening in Irish studies, to mention the possibility of biblical influence, but again it remains to be shown that the content of the *Táin* is significantly indebted to the Bible.[21]

The *Táin,* as Cecile O'Rahilly puts it, "tells of a foray made by Medb of Connacht into the territory of the Ulaid for the purpose of carrying off the bull Donn Cúalnge from the district of Cúalnge, present-day Cooley, Co. Louth." As O'Rahilly remarks in this context, "plundering raids, especially cattle-raids, are a characteristic feature of Irish heroic saga;"[22] we are reminded too of *Scéla Mucce Meic Da Thó* in which contention of the Connachta and the Ulaid for a gigantic pig is framed by their contention for an extraordinary hound. We cannot say whether this cattle-raid represents an ancient invasion-myth which here provides the kernel of an epic. What we can say is that the object of the quest, the Donn Cúalnge, is a creature of mythical proportions; his role in the *Táin* is complemented by that depicted or alluded to in other Irish texts; his Celtic congeners are represented in iconography and nomenclature; and he is an Irish reflex of an Indo-European male bovine, whose primary role in a myth of cosmogony by dismemberment is reflected in the *Táin* and in one of its associated *remscéla* ('prefatory tales'), *De Chophur in da Muccida.* Our knowledge of Donn Cúalnge is thus greatly extended by attending to the comparative data.

The mythological study of early Irish narrative has been conducted in two main ways, one of them being concerned with Celtic mythology, the other being the wider discipline of comparative mythology. The two are not always kept apart, but they nevertheless represent different orientations in the mythological study of Irish texts. Each of them, in its way, has light to cast on Donn Cúalnge.

In the narrower field of Celtic mythology, the texts are interpreted in conjunction with evidence from other sources for Celtic religion. An account of this kind of work is given by Anne Ross in the introduction to her *Pagan Celtic Britain,*[23] where she discusses the three kinds of evidence which are available: the evidence of archaeology, the testimony of Greek and Roman commentators, and the vernacular literatures of Ireland and Wales.

Ross points out that "the evidence for the cults is very much of an archaeological nature, but its interpretation is another matter. The material evidence is suggestive of certain patterns of belief, but an understanding of these apparent patterns cannot be based on archaeology alone;" for such an understanding we must turn to the other two varieties of evidence. As for the comments of Greek and Roman writers, these "are too insubstantial and fragmentary to do more than point the way in certain instances. Moreover, it is only too easy to misinterpret archaeological evidence, and in complex societies such as those which existed in Celtic countries during the period of Roman occupation, where classical and exotic cults became fused and confused with the more homely native equivalents, we are indeed in the middle of a quagmire." Much more abundant than the testimony of Greek and Roman commentators is the evidence of vernacular narrative, which Ross characterizes as being "on the whole more reliable than the two sources already discussed." Our assessment of the reliability of Irish narrative as a source for Celtic mythology will depend, of course, on our view of the nature and extent of the oral component in the transmitted texts. Ross's view is that "we may suppose that certain cult legends, changed in a Christian milieu into hero tales or topographical legends, may have circulated for centuries until they found written form under the sympathetic aegis of the Irish church;" indeed I would say that her work presupposes that the cult legends *must* have circulated for centuries until they "found written form." Comparison of the narrative with the other sources can be helpful in two ways: "The other sources can assist in getting the mythology contained in these early literary traditions into perspective, and the literary material can act as an invaluable yard-stick against which the conclusions the archaeological material allows us to draw can be compared and measured." The fruits of this kind of work are described with some modesty: "And when, as is not infrequently the case, the three sources can all be shown to point in the same direction, then we may feel justified in concluding that, for a little while, and in a very limited fashion, we have managed to check the constantly shifting and changing patterns of Celtic religion, and have penetrated a little below the confusing, moving surface, to discover something of the permanent core which underlies the unstable picture which normally confronts us."

What we tend to get in this way is a thematic skeleton, derived in large measure from the archaeological evidence, but fleshed out with stories from Irish, and, to a lesser extent, Welsh manuscripts. The narrative material is indeed brought into perspective, but there must be some doubt as to the validity of that perspective. The criticism of Ross's book by Liam de Paor should be borne in mind: he reminds us that the Celts were an essentially non-literate people, and says that "if we wish to study the Celts at all, we are forced to see them as a half-Hellenised or half-Romanised people—because they are shown to us in the framework of Greek or Roman ideas—or we are forced to try to understand the society and ideas of one people, such as the Gauls or Britains of pre-Roman times, through the writings (about themselves) of another people, the Irish of a thousand years later."[24] Ross's work is nevertheless valuable as a work of reference: the material which she has gathered, for example, about the bull shows the importance of this animal in Celtic iconography and nomenclature, and tends to confirm the impression which we get from the Irish literary sources that the Donn Cúalnge has its origins in a bull-cult.[25]

The second way in which the mythological content of the texts can be studied is that of comparative mythology. The work which we have been considering is of course comparative, in so far as it entails the comparison both of different kinds of evidence, and of the narrative texts of Ireland and Wales. But the study of comparative mythology differs from that of Celtic mythology in taking a wider canvas, either within a general science of comparative religion, in which typological comparisons are made, as in the work of Mircea Eliade, or a comparison of the myths and literatures of speakers of Indo-European languages, where similarities are deemed to spring from a genetic relationship among the items compared. Here we are comparing text with text; in this we are perhaps on firmer ground than when the comparison is of text with icon or other item of material culture. But it must be remembered that the reading of any given text is to some degree interpretive, and, in the case of early Irish narrative, the hypothesis is that we are dealing with mythology refracted through literature.

In the nineteenth century, comparative mythology was practised by philologists, but criticism of their theories led, by the end of the century, to what has been aptly called 'the eclipse of solar mythology'.[26] Comparative mythology had something of a second coming in Ireland in the work of T. F. O'Rahilly: he criticised John Rhŷs for having applied "'solar' methods of interpretation in all directions with incredible recklessness,"[27] but he was able, for his own part, to see a solar deity in the type of personage which he called the 'Otherworld God', and of which he names as examples, among many others, both Donn Cúalnge and Culann's Dog, who is slain and replaced by Cú Chulainn.[28] In France, in the meantime, Georges Dumézil was rehabilitating the comparative study of mythology on a foundation which combined anthropological and sociological considerations with those of philology.[29]

Two aspects of Dumézil's work are relevant to our topic. In the first place he has uncovered a number of story-patterns which can be taken to have their origins among the speakers of Proto-Indo-European. Secondly, he has discerned in numerous texts in the Indo-European languages a common ideology which he has also attributed to the speakers of the original language. We shall consider the matter of ideology somewhat later, but here I want to draw attention to an Indo-European story-pattern which Bruce Lincoln has uncovered in the *Táin*.[30] Lincoln analyses what he calls the Indo-European myth of the first sacrifice, of which independent Indian, Iranian, Germanic and Roman versions can be located, in addition to Greek, Russian, Jewish, and Chinese versions "that seem to be the result of secondary diffusion."[31] In each of the primary texts, a primordial being is killed and dismembered, and from his body the cosmos is fashioned.[32] On the basis of comparative reconstruction, Lincoln argues that the Proto-Indo-European myth is one which is characteristic of pastoralists. It tells of the creation of the world through the primordial sacrifice of a man and an ox or a bull, and it establishes a pattern for all future sacrifice and for all future creation.[33] Two major variants of the Indo-European myth are reconstructed, one Indo-Iranian and the other European.[34]

Now Lincoln sees a reflex of this myth in the confrontation of the bulls at the end of the *Táin* and in the prefatory tale *De Chophur in da Muccida*.[35] (The latter tells that the bulls originated as pig-herds, and went through a series of transformations as various creatures before they reached their final condition; there is an allusion to this story in the *Táin* itself when Dubthach prophesies: "There will come a leader of armies who will try to recover the cattle of Murthemne. Because of the companionship of the two swineherds, ravens of the battle-field will drink men's blood.")[36] Lincoln remarks:

> This Irish variant of the Proto-Indo-European myth has been much transformed. Relegated to a position as prologue and postscript to an epic tale of battle and adventure its characters and values are thoroughly subjugated to those of the epic. Its heroes become retainers and servants of epic kings, or alternatively, the bulls sought by those kings as booty. Its central act of sacrifice becomes an epic duel between those noble bulls. For all these trans-formations, it remains recognizable nonetheless and provides valuable confirmation of the authenticity of the Indo-Iranian versions of the myth on numerous points.[37]

Here, then, we have an example of myth refracted through literature. In this respect the *Táin* and its prefa-tory tale belong to the category which Jaan Puhvel has recently described as follows:

> Yet equally important is the next level of transmission, in which the sacred narrative has already been secularized, myth has been turned into saga, sacred time into heroic past, gods into heroes, and mythical action into 'historical' plot. Many genuine 'national epics' constitute repositories of tradition where the mythical underpinnings have been submerged via such literary transposition. Old Chronicles can turn out to be 'prose epics' where the probing modern mythologist can uncover otherwise lost mythical traditions. Such survival is quite apart from, or wholly incidental to, the conscious exploitative use of myth in literature, something that Western civilization has practiced since artful verbal creativity began.[38]

There are some questions here for the comparatist: for example, is it not possible to think of an Indo-European epic hero, of which Cú Chulainn is to some degree a reflex? I, for one, find it hard to credit that he is an Indo-European god who has been transformed into an Irish hero. But the general point that an epic like the *Táin* constitutes a repository of tradition is well illustrated by Lincoln's findings.

Enough has been said about the great bull which was the object of the raid; let us turn now to consider some of the other mythological components of the epic, and we may begin with a look at the *cess* or 'debility' with which the Ulstermen were afflicted; this is a necessary condition of the raid, since it renders the Ulstermen unable to defend their territory. This *cess* has been much discussed, and the most plausible interpretation of the way it is presented in the *Táin* seems to me to be that of Tomás Ó Broin, who sees it as "a death or winter sleep" of the kind represented in seasonal myth and ritual.[39] The effects of the winter sleep are overcome by the actions of Cú Chulainn; the basic idea is "the triumph of life and fecundity over death and decay."[40]

We first hear of the 'debility' of the Ulstermen before the raiders set out from Connacht. Medb encounters Fedelm, a poetess who is possessed of the power of prophecy called *imbas forosna,* and asks her to prophesy the fate of Medb's expedition. Fedelm's chilling prophecy is: "I see it blood-stained, I see it red." But Medb is nothing daunted: "'That is not true;' said Medb, 'for Conchobor lies in his debility in Emain together with the Ulstermen and all the mightiest of their warriors, and my messengers have come and brought me tidings of them'."[41] The expedition sets out "on the Monday after Samain."[42] Fergus sends a warning to the Ulstermen "who were still suffering from their debility, all except Cú Chulainn and his father Súaltaim;"[43] it was apparently they who received Fergus's warning, and it was Cú Chulainn in particular who acted upon it. The reason for Cú Chulainn's immunity is later hinted at by Fergus. He is recounting one of Cú Chulainn's Boyhood Deeds, and he says: "On another occasion, the Ulstermen were in their debility. Among us women and boys do not suffer from the debility nor does anyone outside the territory of Ulster, nor yet Cú Chulainn and his father."[44] Cecile O'Rahilly points out[45] that this particular passage seems to derive from the tale *Noínden Ulad,* which purports to explain the origin of the debility, and which explicitly states that Cú Chulainn did not suffer from the debility because he was not an Ulsterman *(ar nírbo do Ultaib dó).*[46]

There are clear indications in the *Táin* that the debility lasted for the three month from Samain (1st November) to Imbolc (1st February), which in Ireland are the three months of winter. So much is implied in Recension II,[47] while in Recension I we are told that Cú Chulainn fought single-handed "from the Monday after Samain until the Wednesday after the festival of Spring" *('ón lúan íar Samain cosin Cétáin íar n-imolg');*[48] we are also told twice that he fought for the three winter months *('trí mísa gaimrid').*[49] Ó Broin's notion that the debility is a winter sleep is obviously consistent with these indications as to its duration.

A difficulty which must be considered is the surprise expressed by Fergus at the duration of the debility in the *Táin:* "'And I find it strange', said Fergus, 'that they are so long in recovering from their debility'" *('"Ocus machdad limsa," ol Fergus, "a fot co tecatside assa cessaib".')*[50] We would expect Fergus, of all people, to know the facts of this matter. It is conceivable that this utterance of his is intended to deceive the Connachta, whom he is addressing on this occasion. We have clear evidence of the duplicitous side of his character in the passage of the *Táin* in which he takes the invading Connachta on a detour to give the Ulaid time to complete the mustering of their army.[51] The narrator tells us about this, adding for good measure that Fergus acted "out of affection for his own kin" *('ar chondalbai').*[52] When Medb challenges Fergus and suspects that he may be feeling "the pull of kinship," he denies his treachery.[53] Whatever about Fergus's intentions in relation to the Connachta, however, his expectation that the Ulaid would have time to complete the mustering of their army is scarcely compatible with their debility, and it suggests therefore that Fergus was unaware that they were in that condition. Perhaps we should simply remember that absolute consistency is not to be expected on matters of this kind. By way of illustration in the *Táin* itself, we may compare the clear implication, to which I have already alluded, that Cú Chulainn was immune to the debility because he was not an Ulsterman with the remark made by Follomon son of Conchobor when the young Cú Chulainn (then called Sétantae) came as a stranger to Emain Macha: "The boy insults us . . . Yet we know he is of the Ulstermen" *('sech rafetamár is di Ultaib*

dó').[54] In any case, even if Fergus's avowed surprise at the duration of the debility is to be taken as genuine, it may indicate a certain instability in the tradition relating to the matter, but it does not negate the clear statement in the *Táin* that on this particular occasion the Ulstermen were afflicted for three months.

Cecile O'Rahilly points out that there is also in Recension I "a suggestion that the attack of *cess* was intermittent:"

> In a long passage denoted by the scribe as *córugud aile* containing many *roscada* and obviously belonging to the oldest stratum of *TBC* we are told that Cú Chulainn goes to Conchobor to warn him of the enemy's attacks, but Conchobor tells him that the warning is useless and comes too late: *'Indiu tonánic ar tinorcuin in chétnae'* (1219-20), 'Today we have been smitten (by the cess) as before'. The H-interpolator later takes up the same point and borrows the word *tinnorcain* when he tries to explain how the Ulsterman Munremar can come to fight with Cú Roí. 'At this point the *noéden Ulad* came to an end. According as they awoke (from their *cess*) a band of them kept attacking the (enemy) host until they were once more smitten (by their *cess*)' . . . 1629-30.[55]

The remark of Conchobor's which O'Rahilly quotes would not seem to be very telling one way or the other: it could simply be a way of saying that the Ulstermen are still afflicted by the debility. As for the narrator's words as given by the H-interpolator, they certainly indicate that a temporary remission from the debility was considered possible. This is not necessarily incompatible with the notion of a winter sleep: we could say in seasonal terms that spring has seemed to come early, but that it is a false spring, and quickly yields once more to the sleep of winter.

Ó Broin has been accused of distorting the textual evidence,[56] but it is quite clear that the *cess* is presented in the *Táin* as a winter sleep. In accepting this, however, it is not necessary to follow Ó Broin in his theory that the *cess* is based on a fertility ritual.[57] The seasonal character of the debility does suggest a connection with fertility, however, and we shall see presently that the circumstances of Cú Chulainn's conception imply that he is to be a fecundating hero. The *cess* in the *Táin* is also symptomatic of the collapse of social order. As Joan Radner has said in a different context:

> Thematically, the Ulster Cycle as a whole tends to present the tragic breakdown of those relationships on which early Irish society was founded: the relationship between host and guest, between kin-dred, between fosterbrothers, between men and women, between lords and clients and kings and overkings,

between the human world and the gods.[58]

It is Cú Chulainn, in Sjoestedt's words, "their defence and their champion (. . .) at once the glory and the living rampart of his tribe"[59] who saves Ulster from final disaster, and so I turn now to a brief consideration of what has been called the Myth of the Hero, as it is represented in the Ulster Cycle, and in the *Táin* in particular.

We have seen that an epic is said to be "centred on a heroic or quasi-divine figure on whose actions depends the fate of a tribe, a nation or the human race."[60] In the *Táin,* Cú Chulainn is that figure: the work celebrates his martial heroism, his courage and ingenuity, his mastery of the martial arts, his unswerving loyalty. In short, he is an epic hero, the epic theme of the *Táin* being his single-handed defence of Ulster. When we look at his life as a whole, however, we find that it is a realisation of the heroic biographical pattern common to Indo-European and Semitic tradition.[61] This pattern is not confined to epic heroes, but in Cú Chulainn's case it is realised in martial terms that are altogether appropriate to epic.

It is characteristic of the heroic biography that the birth of the hero is anomalous, and Cú Chulainn is no exception. The early version of his conception-story[62] opens with the theme of the Waste Land: the fruits of Emain Macha are consumed to the roots by birds. The Ulidians set out in pursuit of the birds, and they are led to Bruig na Bóinne, the great necropolis at the end of the Boyne, and a site of singular importance in Irish myth. There Sétantae was born, and he was brought back to Ulster; he died, but he was conceived again. The parents of his first conception were the god Lug and his (unnamed) Otherworld consort, those of his second Lug and Dechtine, sister to the Ulster king, Conchobor. Sétantae was not born of his second conception, but was conceived for a third time, his parents now being the human Sualdam and Dechtine. (Sétantae later went on to acquire the name Cú Chulainn, in circumstances which are recounted in the *Táin.*)

The theme of the Waste Land implies the need for a fecundating hero, an element which is of course consistent with Ó Broin's interpretation of the debility of the Ulstermen as a winter sleep, from the effects of which Ulster is rescued by this vigorous young male as the vital force in nature. Cú Chulainn shares with many sacred or mythic personages the characteristic of dual paternity: he is at once the son of a god (Lug) and of a human father (Sualdam). As I have already said, anomalous birth is a predictable feature of the heroic biography. It is therefore quite unnecessary to assume that the numerous Irish examples of this phenomenon are based on the life of Christ. John Kelleher, however, has noted that Irish annalists placed the death of Cú Chulainn at 2 A.D., and, having made the unexcep-

tionable point that "the choice of that date—like 33 A.D. for the death of Conchobor—was clearly to associate these heroes with Christ,"[63] he goes on to say: "Thus the lives of Christ and Cú Chulainn overlap by one year—to which may be added that each of them has a life-span divisible by three; each has a divine father but is known as the son of a mortal father; each dies for his people, erect and pierced by a spear. By such manipulations the pre-eminence of the *Táin* was again asserted."[64] The implication is that just as the death of Cú Chulainn was dated to overlap with the life of Christ, so also the other features of his biography mentioned by Kelleher were "manipulations" whereby Cú Chulainn was associated with Christ.

This seems to me to be extremely far-fetched. Cú Chulainn's role in the *Táin* is indeed that of saviour of his people, but he is a very different kind of personage from Jesus Christ. Moreover, while he shares with Christ, and with many other heroes, the characteristic of dual paternity, he differs from them in having a triple conception, which shows a sequence from fully divine, through mixed divine and human, to fully human parentage. I have elsewhere said of this sequence that in it

> the hero recapitulates in his own life the history of man, since, if we may judge from the occurrence of deity names in their pedigrees, the Irish apparently believed themselves to be descended from the gods. Furthermore, this sequence gives us a singularly clear example of the manner in which the hero mediates between the gods and men: the second (or middle) conception, linked to the first and third by Lug and Dechtine respectively, mediates the opposition between the divine and the human. In this case at least the 'meaning' of the triplicity of the hero is inseparable from the structure of the narrative."[65]

Kim McCone, who accepts Kelieher's views on Cú Chulainn, writes as follows about the conception-story:

> Going as it does well beyond the standard requirements of heroic liminality, this genesis of the Ulster hero *par excellence* can hardly be understood except as an orthodox allegory and 'native' typology of Christ's mysterious incarnation as set forth in the New Testament.[66]

One has to say, however, that the narrative also goes well beyond what might reasonably be required of an orthodox allegory and "native" typology of Christ's incarnation. The three-fold conception of Cú Chulainn is not directly based on the story of Christ, and it must be seen rather in the light of the prevalence of triplicity of gods and heroes in Irish literature, and of the occurrence of triplicity in Celtic iconography. Perhaps this is what McCone has in mind when he speaks of "native" typology, but it can be understood as such without recourse to the hypothesis of Christian allegory. Moreover, there are good comparative grounds for holding that Cú Chulainn's triplicity is an inherited feature which is inextricably bound up with his destiny as a warrior. Cú Chulainn's warrior initiation is achieved by successful combat with the three sons of Nechta Scéne;[67] taken together, his conception and his initiatory combat exemplify the Indo-European theme which Dumézil has summed up in the formula 'The third kills the triple'.[68]

We have wandered away from the **Táin** in our treatment of Cú Chulainn as hero, but with the three sons of Nechta Scéne we have returned, not, it is true, to the three-month time frame of the great raid, but to Cú Chulainn's 'Boyhood Deeds', which are recounted to the invaders by exiled Ulstermen. There is evidence in the Book of Leinster of some disagreement as to the status of the 'Boyhood Deeds' in relation to the **Táin;** we are informed that they were classified by some people as 'prefatory tales', but that they are in fact narrated in the body of the **Táin**.[69] Daniel Melia has pointed out, however, that we have no version of the **Táin** which lacks the 'Boyhood Deeds', and he is doubtless correct in saying that they "were considered a part of the *Cattle Raid of Cooley* from the time that it was put together as an entity."[70]

The episodes which constitute Cú Chulainn's 'Boyhood Deeds' are successive stages in the development of the martial hero and of his incorporation into society. Melia has shown that many of them share the pattern of arrival, opposition, and final acceptance: Cú Chulainn enters from outside; he asserts himself against the men of Ulster; and he is accepted by the Ulstermen as a warrior (several times by Conchobar himself). Within the framework of this recurrent pattern we find a cumulative exposition of heroic themes, which have been well treated by Alwyn and Brinley Rees.[71] We can regard them as mythical in origin, but it is instructive also to consider their place in the epic.

The 'Boyhood Deeds' present Cú Chulainn as a precocious hero: "one can say that for the purpose of the larger story his precocious heroism cannot simply be stated but must be illustrated graphically."[72] The Connacht army—and the reader—are being prepared for Cú Chulainn's prodigious feats in the **Táin,** and those very feats are lent a degree of verisimilitude by the accumulation of eye-witness accounts of his youthful exploits. Within the framework of the **Táin,** then, the 'Boyhood Deeds' arouse expectations, and in a way authenticate Cú Chulainn's subsequent actions in all their extravagance. The narrative device which is used—that of the so-called 'flashback'—enables the narrator to escape from the tyranny of linearity, and to appropriate for his purpose events which lie outside the temporal frame of the

cattle raid. One of the major themes of the **Táin** is martial heroism, and the portrayal of the hero is deepened by the details of the 'Boyhood Deeds'.

Much of the ideological content of the **Táin** is centred on the heroic figure of Cú Chulainn. Proinsias Mac Cana has drawn a contrast between the king tales and those devoted to martial heroes:

> The king tales taken as a whole have a social orientation, centred as they are on the paramount institution in Irish society. By contrast, when we turn to the heroic literature *pur sang* we find by and large that each protagonist stands as an in-dividual rather than as a kind of surrogate for society. The hero *par excellence* is the hero alone.[73]

There can be no gainsaying that the martial hero *par excellence* is the martial hero alone; indeed, the best example we have is Cú Chulainn who stands alone against the invaders of Ulster. Yet in doing so he is a kind of surrogate for society, and in particular for the men of Ulster who lie stricken by their debility. But this is scarcely what Mac Cana has in mind: the social orientation of the king tales is seen in their ideological content, and this is presumably what Mac Cana thinks is lacking in the tales of martial heroism. The fact is, however, that the ideology of warfare is richly explored in the **Táin,** and in other tales of the Ulster cycle. Important work on this aspect of the material has been published by Philip O'Leary.[74] I would also mention here the way in which kinship is presented in these tales, and especially Cú Chulainn's status as a sister's son to Conchobor (and to the Ulaid as a whole).[75] There is no lack of social orientation in the Ulster cycle: what we need is further detailed analysis of the ideological content of the texts.

T. F. O'Rahilly discerned two basic myths in the Irish material, the Myth of the Birth of the Hero, and the Myth of the Rival Wooers. The latter, more prosaically known as the eternal triangle, is represented in the **Táin** by Medb, her husband Ailill, and her lover Fergus. Medb shows many of the characteristics of the goddess of sovereignty, but we see little of this in the **Táin**. It has been suggested that the three essential attributes of a king—justice, victory, and the power to give fruitfulness to the earth and health to mankind—are reflected in Medb's requirements in a husband: he must be without jealousy, without fear, without niggardliness.[76] There is also an ideological dimension in the relation-ship between Fergus and Medb, the essential notion being that, by yielding to Medb's attractions, Fergus is unmanned, and betrays his own kith and kin.

The unmanning of Fergus is expressed in terms of the taking of his own sword from its scabbard. This is done by Ailill's charioteer while Fergus and Medb are engaged in intercourse. When Fergus discovers his loss, he fashions a wooden sword as a replacement.[77] Cú Chulainn later speaks derisively of Fergus's "empty rudder."[78] Connall Cernach upbraids Fergus for assailing his own people "for the sake of a woman's buttocks."[79] These sentiments are echoed by Fergus himself when he finally speaks of the folly of following a woman's buttocks.[80] In general, this is an expression of the inappropriateness of following a woman into battle: we may compare Ailill's contemptuous dismissal of *banchomhairle* (woman's counsel).[81] More precisely, however, the sexual nature of Fergus's relationship with Medb is in contrast with Cú Chulainn's response to the advances of a beautiful young woman (who in reality is the Morrígan in disguise): he rejects them, saying that it was not for a woman's buttocks that he had undertaken his task.[82] The warrior is single-minded in pursuit of his aims, and is not to be distracted by sexual temptation. It is true that Cú Chulainn had earlier abandoned his post for an encounter with Fedelm Nóichride, but he does this in fulfillment of a pledge which he has already given, and he takes precautions to ensure that the raiders will not be able to take advantage of his absence.[83]

A further layer of meaning is encoded in the allusion by Conall Cernach, Fergus and Cú Chulainn to a woman's buttocks. Thomas Charles-Edwards has pointed out that these allusions echo the account given in the laws of the circumstances in which a freeman forfeits his legal rights: he "follows the buttocks of his wife across a boundary," and henceforth depends for his status upon the status of his wife.[84] This is obviously regarded with disdain: loyalty to kindred is an absoluted value, and it is love of kindred which saves Ulster in the *Táin*.[85] In all of this we have further evidence of the "social orientation" of the heroic literature.

It has not been possible to do more in the space at my disposal than to touch upon some aspects of the mythological component in the *Táin*. We can claim, however, that some of the personages, some of the story-patterns, and some incidental details in the *Táin* reflect the Celtic, and even the Indo-European, heritage of Ireland. To the extent that they do so, credit must be divided between the oral traditors who made them available to the epic's authors, and those authors in turn for having used them in their literary work. Out of fairness to these authors, it must be stressed that the *Táin* is no mere "respository of tradition," still less a "dessicated husk."[86] By way of illustration, we may take Cú Chulainn's role as sister's son, which I have already mentioned as part of the ideology of kinship which is presented in the *Táin*. The role of the sister's son, which is also a central concern of *Cath Maige Tuired,* is part of the

ideological framework within which the Irish accommodated the story of Christ: so much is clear from the manner in which his life and death are narrated by the eight-century Blathmac. His work "offers a clear demonstration of the presence of a set of concepts relating to the sister's son in the ideological matrix within which the poet apprehended the life of Jesus. This set of concepts is an inherited one: it is reflected in the kinship terms, in the laws, and in the literature."[87] The ideology which is expressed in the *Táin* includes inherited elements, then, which cannot be dismissed as mere baggage, retained for the purposes of a literature of entertainment. That the ideology which underlies the *Táin* was charged with meaning for Irish people in the eighth century is shown by Blathmac's recasting of the life of Christ within the framework of that ideology.

Recent scholarship has fruitfully attended to the specifically ecclesiastical elements in early Irish literature. It is important that this new emphasis should not lead to a devaluation of the material which derives from extra-ecclesiastical sources. I have remarked elsewhere that

> early Irish literature is not the detritus of a lost mythology, nor yet a new phenomenon, born, like Athena, fully grown. It is the creation of a society which had two sets of cultural institutions, one indigenous and oral in its medium, the other ecclesiastical and literate. These were sometimes hostile, sometimes amicable, but between them they contributed to the formation of a literature which combined matter drawn from the oral tradition with other elements and transmuted them into something new.[88]

Ulster's epic, **Táin Bó Cúailnge,** is one of the works of literature which was thus brought into being.

Notes

[1] H. M. Chadwick and N. K. Chadwick, *The Growth of Literature,* Vol. I (Cambridge, 1932), *passim;* Gerard Murphy, *Saga and Myth in Ancient Ireland* (Dublin, 1955), pp. 25-47, reproduced in Eleanor Knott and Gerard Murphy, *Early Irish Literature* (London, 1966), pp. 114-31; K. H. Jackson, *The Oldest Irish Tradition: A Window on the Iron Age* (Cambridge, 1964), *passim.* Criticism of the Heroic Age theory will be found in J. N. Radner, "'Fury Destroys the World'," *Mankind Quarterly,* 23 (1982), 41-60; Tomás Ó Cathasaigh, "Pagan Survivals: the Evidence of Early Irish Narrative," in: *Ireland and Europe: The Early Church,* ed. Próinséas Ní Chatháin and Michael Richter (Stuttgart, 1984), 291-307, pp. 296f.; N. B. Aitchison, "The Ulster Cycle: Heroic Image and Historical Reality," *Journal of Medieval History* 13, 87-116.

[2] Donnchadh Ó Corráin, "Irish Origin Legends and Genealogy: Recurrent Aetiologies," in: History and Heroic Tale: A Symposium, ed. Tore Nyberg and others (Odense, 1985), 51-96, p. 85; N. B. Aitchison, op.cit.

[3] T. F. O'Rahilly, *Early Irish History and Mythology* (Dublin, 1946), p. 271 and *passim;* Marie-Louise Sjoestedt, *Gods and Heroes of the Celts* (London, 1949); Alwyn Rees and Brinley Rees, *Celtic Heritage* (London, 1961), *passim.*

[4] James Carney, *Studies in Irish Literature and History* (Dublin, 1955), pp. 276ff., 321f.; *idem,* "The History of Early Irish Literature: The State of Research," in: *Proceedings of the Sixth International Congress of Celtic Studies,* ed. Gearóid Mac Eoin (Dublin, 1983), 113-130, pp. 128-30.

[5] J. V. Kelleher, "The *Táin* and the Annals," *Ériu* 22 (1971), 107-27.

[6] Jaan Puhvel, "Transposition of Myth to Saga in Indo-European Epic Narrative," in: *Antiquitates Indogermanicae,* ed. Manfred Mayrhofer and others, 175-184, p.175.

[7] She edited *The Stowe Version of Táin Bó Cuailnge* (Dublin, 1961); *Táin Bó Cúalnge from the Book of Leinster* (Dublin, 1967); *Táin Bó Cúailnge: Recension I* (Dublin, 1976). The latter is referred to hereinafter as *TBC Rec. I* and cited by line.

[8] Op. cit., p. 271.

[9] Op. cit., p. 2.

[10] M. H. Abrams, *A Glossary of Literary Terms* (3rd ed., New York 1971), p. 49.

[11] Ibid.

[12] Rudolf Thurneysen, *Die irische Helden- und Königsage bis zum 17. Jahrhundert* (Halle 1921), pp. 96 f. Thurneysen then tentatively assigned the *Grundtext* to the eighth century, but he later revised this to the middle of the seventh (*idem,* "Colmán mac Lénéni and Senchán Torpéist," *ZCP* 19, 193-209, p. 209).

[13] James Carney, *Studies,* esp. pp. 321 f.; *idem,* "History of Early Irish Literature," pp. 128-30.

[14] Gerard Murphy, review of Carney's *Studies, Éigse* 8 (1955-57), 152-64; Proinsias Mac Cana, "Conservation and Innovation in Early Celtic Literature," *EC* 13 (1972-73), 61-119, pp. 86-89. See also Patrick Sims-Williams, "Riddling Treatment of the 'Watchman Device' in *Branwen* and *Togail Bruidne Da Derga,*" *SC* 12/13, pp. 83-117.

[15] Op. cit., p. 158.

[16] Carney, *Studies,* p. 321.

[17] Op. cit. p. 162.

[18] Op. cit., p. 89.

[19] Murphy, op. cit. p. 158.

[20] See especially Kim McCone, *Pagan Past and Christian Present in Early Irish Literature* (Maynooth, 1990).

[21] For a judicious comment on the difficulty of assigning the ultimate origins of certain motifs which occur in the *Táin* to "either classical or biblical models as opposed to pagan Celtic or common Indo-European models," see William Sayers, "*'Mani maidi an nem . . . ':* Ringing Changes on a Cosmic Motif," *Ériu* 37 (1986), 99-117, pp. 114 f.

[22] C. O'Rahilly, *Táin Bó Cúalnge from the Book of Leinster,* cit., p. ix. See also Wolfgang Meid, *Die Romanze von Froech und Findabair* (Innsbruck 1970), p. 67.

[23] Anne Ross, *Pagan Celtic Britain* (London, 1967), pp. 1-3.

[24] Liam de Paor, review of Ross, *op. cit., Studia Hibernica* 10 (1970), pp. 156 f.

[25] Ross, *op. cit,* 302-308. For some further information on Donn, see Tomás Ó Cathasaigh, "The Eponym of Cnogba," *Éigse* 23 (1990), 27-38, pp. 34-35 and references there cited.

[26] Richard M. Dorson, "The Eclipse of Solar Mythology," in: *Myth: A Symposium,* ed. Thomas A. Sebeok (Bloomington, 1965), pp. 25-63.

[27] T. F. O'Rahilly, op. cit., p. 270, n. 2.

[28] Op. cit., p. 454, n. 4 (Donn Cúalnge); p. 314 (Culann's Dog). On the latter, see Tomás Ó Cathasaigh, *The Heroic Biography of Cormac mac Airt* (Dublin, 1977), pp. 14 f.; Kim McCone, "*Aided Cheltchair Maic Uthechair:* Hounds, Heroes and Hospitallers in Early Irish Myth and Story," *Ériu* 35 (1984), 1-30, pp. 8-11.

[29] See C. Scott Littleton, *The New Comparative Mythology* (Berkeley, 1966).

[30] Bruce Lincoln, *Priests, Warriors and Cattle* (Berkeley, 1981). See also William Sayers, "Fergus and the Cosmogonic Sword," *History of Religions* 25 (1985), 30-56.

[31] Lincoln, op. cit., p. 69.

[32] Ibid., p. 75.

[33] Ibid., p. 92.

[34] Details, ibid., p. 87.

[35] E. Windisch, ed., *Irische Texte* III (1891), pp. 230-247; Ulrike Roider, *De Chophur In Da Muccida* (Innsbruck, 1979).

[36] *TBC Rec. I,* lines 194 ff. (There may also be an allusion in the placename *Mag Muceda* (ibid., line 827), which is perhaps for Old Irish *Mucedae.*)

[37] Ibid., p. 92.

[38] Jaan Puhvel, *Comparative Mythology* (Baltimore, 1987), p. 2.

[39] Tomás Ó Broin, "What is the 'Debility' of the Ulstermen?," *Éigse* 10 (1961-63), 286-299, p. 288.

[40] Ibid., p. 289.

[41] *TBC Rec. I,* lines 51 f.

[42] Ibid., line 114.

[43] Ibid., line 216.

[44] Ibid., lines 524 ff.

[45] Note *ad loc.*

[46] Vernam Hull, ed., "Noínden Ulad: The Debility of the Ulidians," *Celtica* 8 (1968), 1-42, p. 29, lines 65 f.

[47] *TBC Rec. I,* note to line 51.

[48] Ibid., line 2138.

[49] Ibid., lines 3397, 3434.

[50] Ibid., lines 1283 f.

[51] Ibid., lines 227-255.

[52] Ibid., line 229.

[53] Ibid., lines 244-255.

[54] Ibid., lines 421 f.

[55] *TBC Rec. I,* note to line 51.

[56] P. L. Henry, *Saoithiúlacht na Sean-Ghaeilge* (Dublin, 1978), p. 33.

[57] See now the discussion in Edgar M. Slotkin, "*Noínden;* Its Semantic Range," in: *Celtic Language, Celtic Culture,* ed. A. T. E. Matonis and Daniel F. Melia (Van Nuys, 1990), pp. 137-150.

[58] J. N. Radner, "'Fury Destroys the World': Historical Strategy in Ireland's Ulster Epic," *Mankind Quarterly* 23 (1982), 41-60, p. 47.

[59] Sjoestedt, op. cit., p. 59.

[60] See above, fn. 10.

[61] See Ó Cathasaigh, *Heroic Biography, passim.*

[62] *Idem,* "The Concept of the Hero in Irish Mythology," in: *The Irish Mind,* ed. R. Kearney (Dublin, 1985), 79-90, pp. 81-83.

[63] Kelleher, op. cit., p. 121.

[64] Ibid., pp. 121 f.

[65] Ó Cathasaigh, op. cit., p. 82 f.

[66] McCone, *Pagan Past,* p. 199.

[67] *TBC Rec. I,* lines 608-821.

[68] Georges Dumézil, *The Destiny of the Warrior* (Chicago, 1970), pp. 15 f.

[69] R. I. Best and M. A. O'Brien, *The Book of Leinster* V (Dublin, 1967), p. 1119, lines 32905 ff.

[70] Daniel Melia, "Parallel Versions of 'The Boyhood Deeds of Cuchulainn'", *Forum for Modern Language Studies* 10 (1974), 211-226, p. 215.

[71] Op. cit., pp. 246-249.

[72] Melia, loc. cit.

[73] Proinsias Mac Cana, *Literature in Irish* (Dublin, 1980), p. 27.

[74] Philip O'Leary, "Contention at Feasts in Early Irish Literature," *Éigse* 20 (1984), pp. 115-127; idem, "Verbal Deceit in the Ulster Cycle," *Éigse* 21 (1986), pp. 16-26; idem, "*Fír Fer:* An Internalized Ethical Concept in Early Irish Literature," *Éigse* 22 (1987), pp. 1-14.

[75] See Tomás Ó Cathasaigh, "The Sister's Son in Early Irish Literature," *Peritia* 5 (1986), 128-160, pp. 150-156.

[76] See Rees and Rees, *op. cit.,* pp. 129 f.; Alwyn D. Rees, "Modern Evaluations of Celtic Narrative Tradition," in: *Proceedings of the Second International Congress of Celtic Studies* (Cardiff, 1966) 31-61, p.

53.

[77] *TBC Rec. I,* lines 1039-63.

[78] Ibid., line 1306.

[79] Ibid., lines 4068 f.

[80] Ibid., lines 4123 f.

[81] Ibid., line 183.

[82] Ibid., line 1855.

[83] Ibid., lines 222-224.

[84] T. M. Charles-Edwards, "Some Celtic Kinship Terms," *Bulletin of the Board of Celtic Studies* 24 (1970-72), 105-122, pp. 115 f., 119 f.

[85] See Ó Cathasaigh, "Sister's Son," pp. 156 f.

[86] Compare the remarks of Puhvel *(loc. cit.):* "Yet in the course of human events societies pass and religious systems change: the historical landscape gets littered with the husks of dessicated myths."

[87] Ó Cathasaigh, op. cit., p. 145.

[88] *Idem,* "Pagan Survival," p. 307.

Alan Bruford (essay date 1994)

SOURCE: "Cú Chulainn—An Ill-Made Hero?" in *Text und Zeittiefe,* edited by Hildegard L. C. Tristram, Gunter Narr, 1994, pp. 185-215.

[*In the following essay, Bruford argues that the* Táin *was originally set down in writing by a cleric who intended it for secular aristocrats. According to Bruford, the popular interpretation of Cú Chulainn reveals the tension arising from the poem's exposure to a wider public.*]

Táin Bó Cuailnge (hereinafter "the ***Táin***") is sometimes described as the national epic of ancient Ireland. In fact it is a prose epic (with a very poor epic structure) from a country which had hardly begun to think of itself as one nation. The obvious comparison with artificial national epics, such as Virgil's *Aeneid,* Macpherson's *Ossian,* or Lönnrot's *Kalevala,* may not be so inappropriate as Celtic scholars of the last generation might have thought. Indeed *Ossian* was composed using very similar materials and, I would suggest, with very similar aims to the *Táin,* and both of them were forgotten when literary fashions changed, though in their time they had considerable influence, particularly on styles of narration and attitudes to the past, whose effects lingered on.

At any rate there is no longer any need for modern scholars to study the ***Táin*** as if it were a folk epic as defined by Parry and Lord, orally improvised in sung verse on a basis of traditional themes and formulas. Whatever its basis, the ***Táin*** as we have it was composed in prose, and I think most scholars today would agree with me that it was also composed in writing. The considerable variations between the various surviving manuscript texts of the ***Táin,*** and in the style of different parts of the older texts, are quite consistent with the way in which Irish scribes up to the eighteenth century have been prepared to rewrite or add to the texts they were copying whenever they felt they could improve them. This need not be a sign of oral transmission, though oral tradition as well as copying or imitation of other texts—not necessarily Irish or secular—and a good measure of pure creative invention may all have contributed to the additions. What I have argued in the past has not been that scholars like Gerard Murphy were wrong in seeing elements of oral tradition in the make-up of mediaeval Irish tales, but that they were wrong in assuming—as I think is implied generally—that they were (a) communally created by "the folk" in some immemorial past as complete and consistent tale-types, and (b) taken down word for word from the mouths of gifted peasant narrators.[1] A quarter century's involvement in collecting folktales (and ballads) from living traditional storytellers of several culture and dialect areas, and sometimes attempting to re-tell tales orally in my own language, has given me some insight into the ways in which oral narrative may be created, transmitted and sometimes very consciously re-created, and I still feel that (a) all tales are created by someone, and mediaeval Irish tales, which name people and places constantly, unlike *Märchen* (international folktales), are likely to have been composed by members of the literary class rather than the peasantry; (b) nobody before the invention of tape-recording ever recorded an oral tale in writing in the exact words anyone else used to tell it, and an element of reconstruction, if not complete re-writing, must be expected in any early text, whether it be the *Iliad* or the ***Táin.***

What I want to suggest in this paper is that (a) the ***Táin*** was originally an artificial composition in writing by a cleric, though one with a wide knowledge of historical legends, pagan myths and indeed *Märchen* preserved by the poetic class, and deliberately designed as a work of art which could be used to gain political credit; (b) it was written originally for people like the author, added to so that it could be performed and enjoyed by secular aristocrats, and never appealed to a wider public, so that the few versions recorded from "peasants" in the past century tend to treat the overglorified central figure, Cú Chulainn, as a figure of fun rather than a noble hero. I am assuming here that the early accounts of how the ***Táin*** was written (or one might say literally "ghost-written", dictated by the spirit of the eye-witness Fergus mac Roich) have some reason based on genuine tradition for dating this in the middle of the seventh century, though what was written then need not have been much like any form of the text we have now: indeed that shows every sign of having been rewritten again and again to suit the political and literary prejudices of different periods. I am also assuming that Thurneysen's analysis of the different redactions and interpolations which go to make up its surviving written texts is basically correct, and that the sequence in which he places them may still generally be accepted, though better linguists than myself may be able to say that his datings are centuries out. The stylistic differences are obvious, though I would not be too sure that a single author could not change his style drastically for a *tour de force* equivalent to the "runs" of later mediaeval romances and modern Gaelic folktales.

Why write an epic?

Why the vernacular narrative we have in Irish as against any other language of Western Europe before 1000 A.D. is in prose I have tried to explain elsewhere[2], but to resume the argument briefly, it seems very likely that in pagan times there was alliterative, regularly stressed verse in Irish which could have been improvised in the performance of oral epics. However, the later poetic order was part of the druid caste, the pagan priesthood which was naturally suppressed by the early Christians. Those who wrote verse in praise of the aristocracy soon regained their status at the price of using syllable-counting metres with increasingly complex schemes of rhyme rather than alliteration and stress, apparently based on Latin hymns. The others, including the most learned members of the druidic order who knew the tribal histories and charter myths, clung to the few surviving pagan rulers or perhaps took to the hills with the young warriors or *fénnidi,* who in any case formed a sort of licensed robber band, not subject to the normal laws of the settled kingdoms whose borders they defended.[3] But the Church soon developed into an organisation built round large, rich monastic settlements, the nearest thing to towns early Ireland produced. Their wealth was largely based on their endowment of land from the secular aristocracy, and they had no written charters to their land: the charters were in the tribal myth, legend and history known to the learned men of the druidic order. So some of those who remembered these stories were sought out and brought back into the fold, but a generation or two had passed. They might still know the stories, but they had lost the technique of improvising them in verse, though a few lines of the old style of alliterative verse, whether fossilised by frequent repetition or reconstructed from fragments that stuck in someone's memory, do seem to have survived. In any case when the stories were first written down, they were written for the record as prose summaries with occasional pieces of archaic verse interspersed, and that gradually developed into a more artistic form of narrative, written now with an eye to reading aloud (the only way in which a book could be communicated to the mediaeval laity, most of whom would have remained illiterate even in the unusually learned society of Ireland) and *from that* passed on to generations of oral storytellers.[4]

But why was the *Táin* written—and I am sure it was literally written: it has very little resemblance to genuine oral literature—and why was the Ulster Cycle, which seems to have grown up around it, the most highly-esteemed matter for narrative in Ireland, until it was supplanted by the Fenian Cycle around the time of the first English incursions? The Fenian Cycle as we have it has the makings of a national epic, as James Macpherson realised when he changed the setting to Scotland and rewrote the only later mediaeval body of Gaelic narrative verse as turgid romantic prose. The heroes are employed by a king of Tara, or "king of Ireland" as he was by then claimed to have been, and spend much of their time on beaches all round the country fighting off invaders, mostly of a vaguely Scandinavian appearance. But the heroes of the Ulster Cycle fight other Irishmen, sometimes referred to simply as "the men of Ireland", but led by the nobles of Connacht who were in fact ancestors of the kings of Tara, under Queen Medb who is represented as daughter of a king of Tara and in another avatar is Medb Lethderg, tutelary goddess of Tara. The Ulster headquarters, Emain Macha, is a fortress (or more likely a ritual centre) from which the Ulstermen had been expelled by the kings of Tara centuries before the stories were written, and was then in an area, Airgialla, whose very name implied that it was a dependency of the kings of Tara, while the descendants of the Ulster kings huddled in a corner of their former kingdom, not daring after the battle of Moira in 637 to challenge the pre-eminence of the kings of Tara in the northern half of Ireland—indeed by the eighth century the kings of Tara were beginning to claim the high-kingship of the whole island. What sort of basis is that for a national epic?

The answer is surely that it was an epic designed to honour a particular part of Ireland, not as large an area as the whole theoretical province of Ulster, while taking care not to dishonour the kings of Tara. The time when the nucleus of the *Táin* was written, we assume, was towards the middle of the seventh century. In that case the place where it was written, most likely by an educated author who used Latin artificial epics as his model and wanted to add to the credit of his home area, must surely be the monastic city of Armagh, which used relentless pressure and the patronage of its secular overlords, the Uí Néill kings of Tara, throughout the 7th and 8th centuries until it attained the primacy of the Irish church which it has enjoyed ever since. Part of this pressure took the form of exalting its founder, St. Patrick, as the sole apostle of Ireland—a claim which has only recently begun to be questioned—and probably the most politically effective part consisted in persuading the rulers of other parts of Ireland to promulgate the "Law of Patrick"; but the land they owned, as I have said, was also important to Irish monasteries, and along with literature in praise of the founding saint it was natural to produce literature to exalt the importance of the place itself—what later Irishmen have called "the Ould Sod" or "the Holy Ground", but here in a quite restricted sense. The early Irish valued books highly—a quarrel over the mere ownership of a gospel book is supposed to have led to St. Columba leaving Ireland—and the performance of praise-poetry and other secular, orally delivered literature continued to add prestige to the households of Gaelic kings and chieftains throughout the next thousand years. The possession of a book with a finely written heroic epic, claimed to be about the history of their own region at the time of Christ, might have been as much to the credit of the monastery of Armagh in the eyes of outsiders as, say, the possession of St. Patrick's bell or staff, or some of his bones in a finely ornamented jewelled golden reliquary. The monk who undertook to write the epic could have had a good knowledge both of Latin secular works by such authors as Virgil, Lucan and Livy and of native oral tradition. He probably already had practice in manipulating the latter by mixing traditional names of kings and heroes with fragments of legend and a great deal of new invention to compile the genealogies and pseudo-historical tracts which we know now in later forms, not to mention works such as the early Lives of St. Patrick.

It has been suggested that Patrick chose to make his most important foundation *Ard Macha,* Armagh, because it was very close to Emain Macha, the traditional capital of Ulster before its conquest by the Connachta of Tara. I wonder whether the reverse is not true, and Emain became the capital in the literature because it was close to Armagh. The Irish were not city-builders, and the only settlement which was anything like a king's capital in early Christian Ireland was the Rock of Cashel, whose very name seems to be an import derived from Latin *castellum.* Other centres named in royal titles, such as Cruachu, Ailech or Tara itself, were not permanently inhabited settlements but ritual sites, in the case of Tara at least deliberately abandoned in early Christian times because of its pagan associations. Emain seems to have been such a ritual site, though we await full publication and interpretation of the excavations there; but was it the most important one in Ulster? Certainly before the Uí Néill took Tara, Emain was not the most sacred site in Ulster. There is clear evidence that at that time the Boyne was the frontier between Ulster and Leinster, and Brugh na Bóinne, the Neolithic chamber tomb at Newgrange with its neighbours on the north bank of the Boyne,

appears in later sources as the most celebrated seat of the Tuatha Dé Danann, the euhemerised pagan gods. Surely it would be the most sacred site of Ulster: indeed Tara, at one time Leinster's equivalent to the south, with just the little chamber tomb at the Mound of the Hostages, looks like a rather feeble rival. Or was the Brugh *too* sacred to be a royal inaugural site?

The title of the epic

The name **Táin Bó Cuailnge** itself, though its fame in later literature is undoubted, is a puzzle. Some cattle-raiding by the Connacht forces in the Cooley peninsula does form part of the story as we have it, but it is far from central, and could very well have been inserted just to make sense of the title. The aim of the invasion is taken by most of the later redactors of the **Táin** as being to take possession of the bull Donn Cuailnge, which could hardly be described as a *Táin Bó,* literally a raid of cows. It is accepted that cattle-raiding had more than an economic significance in early Ireland: not only did it form part of most regular warfare and the imposing of authority by over-kings on under-kings, but there is evidence that a *crech ríg* or 'royal raid' on a neighbouring tribe was a necessary part of the inauguration of any new king.[5] We would expect that *Táin Bó* in the titles of tales would be followed by the name of the raided tribe, but in fact apart from **Táin Bó Cuailnge** itself all the other titles of surviving tales of this class, and as far as we can tell all those listed for lost tales except possibly *Táin Bó Rois,* and *Táin Bó Aidne* in the Edinburgh list,[6] are formed with the names of individual persons, two of them (Dartaid and Flidais) women, who would not normally own cattle in their own right. Moreover Cuailnge (like Aidne) is not the name of a tribe or kingdom either—it is the name of a district: and what is the importance of that district? It consists now mainly of heathery hills, with a sloping coastal strip of arable land, and can hardly have been especially good cattle country; it is certainly not on any direct route from Connacht or Tara to Emain; it is beyond the part of the present County Louth in which most of the existing story is set. Its only significance seems to be bound up either with the name of the story or that of the bull Donn Cuailnge.

Of the other surviving *Tána,* the main part of *Táin Bó Fraich* seems to have nothing to do with cattle-raiding, and was probably given a title of this class just because of the prestige it carried. The others are all told, as might be expected, from the point of view of the raiders, unlike **Táin Bó Cuailnge,** where the heroes are clearly the defenders. I wonder whether the title may not have been borrowed from an already celebrated tale (of which perhaps, as the stories of the finding of the **Táin** imply, nothing but the name was remembered) and a new, epic, Ulster story written round it? I say this because there *is* a tribe, or at least a sub-tribe called Cualnge in the genealogies. They are apparently a branch of the Corcu Baiscinn in the south-west of the present County Clare: though St. Patrick is said to have baptised the great-grandfather of their eponym Cualnge, the names of his ancestors suggest he belongs to a mythological stratum.[7] The raiders who might have taken their cattle would most likely have been from a neighbouring tribe, either the Ciarraige across the Shannon to the south, or more likely the Corco M(od)ruad in the Burren, poor cattle country, to the north of them. The mythical ancestor of both these tribes is Fergus mac Roich, who by later accounts dictated the *Táin* to the poets from his grave,[8] and could well have been the hero, on the invading side, of the original story. Whether or not more than this was remembered in Co. Clare, the Ulster epic-makers would simply have needed to take the famous title (perhaps remembered for the finest or longest piece improvised by one of the last pagan epic singers) and mis-apply it to a district of Ulster, follow the tradition which made Fergus ancestor of the Érainn of Ulster as well as Munster, and turn the story round, perhaps using parts of an Ulster myth, to make him an exile invading his own country. If in the original story he was raiding southwards from the Burren, he could well have had support from the over-kings of Connacht, for until late pagan times Co. Clare was part of Connacht.[9] It is just possible, indeed, that the defender Cú Chulainn comes from this Clare background, too: several seemingly old tales connect him with the hero of the Munster Erainn, Cú Roí, and possibly the only surviving place-name incorporating his name, Léim Chon Culainn, Cú Chulainn's Leap or Loop Head, is at the extreme south-west corner of the territory of the Corcu Baiscinn.[10]

Casting the hero's role

Another strange fact about the *Táin* is that neither the king of Ulster, Conchobor, nor the central hero, Cú Chulainn, appears as an ancestor of any of the many Irish royal lines whose genealogies are recorded, and Cú Chulainn's friend and nominal foster-father Fergus, who appears in many such lines, is represented as an exile fighting on the other side. It was obviously to the advantage of the monks of Armagh to keep on the right side of their overlords, the Uí Néill, rather than supporting the claims of the Dál Fiatach, the surviving descendants of the Ulaid kings who had once ruled the whole province. Kings of that race, and of the Dál nAraidi who now sometimes claimed the overlordship of the whole province, still might occasionally be more powerful than the current Uí Néill king of Tara at times into the seventh century, but never apparently got anywhere near reconquering the territory of the Airgialla where Armagh lay. There are however considerable traces of an attempt to build a major literary cycle round the figure of Mongán mac Fiachnai, the son of Fiachnae mac Baetáin, a king of Dál nAraidi who was killed in 626 (a year after his son) and seems to have had a serious claim to be more powerful than

the king of Tara:[11] it is not unlikely that the *Táin* was created as a direct response to this propaganda exercise. Even more important to Armagh could be the fact that the Dál Fiatach's remaining territory included the actual burial-place of St. Patrick at Downpatrick, which might profit more than Armagh itself from Armagh's campaign to aggrandise the saint, unless something else was done to underline where he had established his seat. Byrne says (of the eighth century) that "the Ulaid had always accepted Armagh's primacy",[12] but they might have felt differently if their successes before and after 600 had lasted longer. Obviously, then, Armagh did not want a main hero who was an ancestor of the present rulers of the Ulaid, and preferred to treat the latter as degenerates who could claim no part in the high deeds of the Golden Age.

One puzzle which probably cannot be solved at this date is who the ancestors of the kings of Airgialla actually were. They are represented as descendants of the Three Collas, members of the Connachta line who were barred from the succession because they had committed the crime of *fingal,* kin-slaying, having killed their uncle, a legendary king of Tara and great-grandfather of Niall of the Nine Hostages. O'Rahilly suggested that they were disguised versions of three of Niall's own sons, who probably really conquered much of Ulster for the Connachta, and Byrne points out the incongruity of the account: in practice many members of early Irish and Scottish dynasties killed an uncle or a cousin and took over his throne without anyone accusing them of a crime, and the direct father-to-son inheritance of Niall's ancestors is unparalleled in the historical record. Byrne also suggests that the Airgialla (whose name simply means "hostage-givers") may actually have descended from vassal tribes who joined the invading Connachta in ejecting their Ulaid overlords.[13] The linking of their line to that of the conquerors would have been a political reward for their support, giving them prestige but with an inbuilt safeguard against their actually claiming a right to the throne of Tara. This sort of dynastic manipulation has probably been used by many cultures, though earlier historians did not pay enough attention to genealogy as a source. Unfortunately it means that we cannot tell whether heroes of the Ulster Cycle like Conchobor who seem to have left no descendants among the Ulaid may have been legendary ancestors of an Airgialla royal line, ousted from the genealogies by the Three Collas and revived by a descendant composing the *Táin.*

Fergus mac Roich poses no such problems. He is always depicted in the surviving literature as an Ulster hero, but as we have seen is an ancestor-figure for families of the Érainn, the racial group to which the Ulaid or Dál Fiatach belonged, in different parts of Ireland, especially Munster. His patronymic or more probably metronymic, 'son of the great horse' or 'mare', may underline his royal nature: it recalls the inauguration ceremony reported by Giraldus Cambrensis as a pagan survival in a remote part of Ulster, in which the king was symbolically reborn from a cauldron containing the flesh of a newly-sacrificed mare. I have suggested elsewhere[14] that Fergus provided all pagan Ulster kings with their role-model and title, so that the divine Fergus of myth and the reigning Fergus of Ulster might both appear in the same legend. The author of the original Táin, whether he was a monk, a poet or a committee, was governed by political considerations: he could not make Fergus, the ancestor of a hostile dynasty, either king of Ulster or the hero of his story. On the other hand the name was too important to be left out. He therefore drew on the myth of the divine Fergus, whose mate was a goddess one of whose names was Medb. She represented the sovereignty of Ulster, as well as the sovereignty of Connacht and its ritual centre Cruachu, and (under the title of Medb Lethderg, "the Red-sided") that of Leinster and the ritual centre that belonged to that province until the 5th century, Tara. Fergus thus becomes an Ulster exile in the camp of Medb of Connacht and a rival of her consort Ailill. That this is happening on the level of myth is clear from the way that Medb is depicted as more important than her husband: masterful women often appear in Gaelic literature and folktale, but always with a trace of the supernatural—early Irish law subordinated women so firmly to men, preventing them from inheriting property or rank or even having these things inherited through them, that it suggests a violent reaction to a previous state of affairs which had not entirely died out among the Celts of southern Britain at the time of the Roman invasion, where Boadicea and Cartimandua led armies and ruled tribes, or among their northern cousins the Picts whose kingship was still inherited in the female line at the time when the *Táin* was written. By some accounts Medb's two consorts, Ailill and Fergus, are themselves known by their mothers' names, and have the same father, Rús Ruad, who as I have pointed out,[15] bears a transposed and syncopated form of the name Ruad Ro-fhessa, one of the titles of the Dagda, the father of the Irish pantheon. Incidentally, calling the enemy queen Medb of Cruachu rather than Medb of Tara helps to make the epic more acceptable to the kings of Tara, whose special relationship with Connacht had long been less important than that with the Airgialla, while keeping what I take to be a historical background based on memories of the actual fifth-century invasion of Ulster by the Connachta.

Fergus is thus left in the enemy camp, but reluctant as he is to fight his fellow-countrymen and especially his protégé Cú Chulainn, he functions much more in his divine capacity, advising Cú Chulainn in nocturnal visits much like one of the gods in the Iliad. His replacement as king of Ulster, Conchobor, appears in no genealogy of a surviving royal line, and may be entirely a literary creation, though the fact that earlier sources give him too a metronymic and make him the son of his own

high priest Cathbad the druid suggests that he may originate from a myth, perhaps one more like a folktale such as the one that brings Cormac the Bear's Son to the throne of Tara.[16] Perhaps Conchobor's name ("hound-" or "wolf-help") implies that like Cormac he was fostered by wolves,[17] and he was originally the culture-hero of Emain as Cormac was of Tara.[18] However, the name was not uncommon among early Christian kings (not to mention being used for a stream, after which the child was called according to the later and longer version of his birth-tale, *Compert Conchobuir*). It is not impossible that it was chosen for the king of Ulster in the *Táin* simply to underline his role in the story, as the person who most benefits from the help of the "hound" Cú Chulainn. There must be some significance in the name of an Ulster kinglet killed in 698 at a battle in Fernmag, to the west of Armagh, named by the Annals of Ulster as Conchobor Machae, Conchobor of Macha, son of Mael Dúin, especially as Byrne identified him as the king of Airthir, the dynasty of the "eastern region" of Airgialla which surrounded Armagh and in the following centuries abandoned secular ambitions to concentrate on establishing a hereditary claim to the abbacy.[19] I doubt whether he was the model for the king in the *Táin,* but he may have been given his name and epithet as a future defender of an area whose local patriotism had recently been rekindled by the epic.

In any case the king himself could not be the real hero. In later Irish literature and Gaelic folk hero-tales the active protagonists are always kings' sons, and this may reflect an element in the structure of pagan Irish society, surviving against the condemnation of the Church into early Christian times, which has been made much of in recent scholarship,[20] as the basis of the Fenian Cycle and a good deal else. Well-born young men, it is suggested, spent the years between the ages of fourteen and twenty as members of a *fian,* a peer-group outside the law and outside the cultivated fields of the tribal territory, living largely by hunting in the hills and forests, training for war and acting as a mobile defence force on the frontiers. After the age of twenty they could and usually did hold land and marry, and formed part of the settled tribe under the law, of which the king was legal and symbolic head. The king symbolised the kingdom, and his health ensured its health, fertility and justice, so in the original pagan theory, he should not lead his men into battle, but at most direct the action from the rear, or invoke divine support, like Brian Ború praying in his tent at Clontarf while his sons fought. The annals show many kings taking the field in practice, and being killed there, but the theory continued to dominate in works of fiction up to the modern Gaelic folktales.

The most obvious younger hero for the *Táin* might

have been Conall Cernach, who appears in other tales as Cú Chulainn's closest rival, occasionally (as in *Scéla Muicce Meic Da Thó* or *Togail Bruidne Da Derga*) replaces him as main Ulster hero, and eventually avenges his death. He is also the eponymous ancestor of the Conailli of Muirthemne, the tribe which in early Christian times occupied most of the area in which the *Táin* is set, and that which is depicted as Cú Chulainn's own homeland. The Conailli Muirtheimne, however, seem to have had little political importance, and were only recognised as a separate small kingdom between the late seventh and eleventh centuries.[21] Conall Cernach, like Fergus, features in the genealogies of several other kingdoms, and most notably perhaps as the distant ancestor of the kings of Dál nAraidi. The Armagh abbacy may have helped the Uí Néill to divide their enemies by sometimes supporting, perhaps indeed inventing the claim of the Dál aAraidi to be the *fir-Ulaid,* the real descendants of the ancient Ulaid kings as against the Dál Fiatach, whose line of descent, as recorded by scholars from other regions, does seem rather patchy in places. A king of Dál nAraidi died in 698 in the same battle as Armagh's Conchobar Machae and apparently as his ally against rivals within Airgialla. On the other hand the Uí Néill would not want too much favour shown to Dál nAraidi, since the last two Ulster kings who were a serious threat to their primacy in the Northern half of Ireland, as recently as 637, had been of that line,[22] so Conall can be allowed some glory but certainly not the central role in the *Táin.* In fact he is given contradictory roles to play in different redactions: he is one of the exiles with Fergus in the earlier parts of the earlier (LU) text, and on the Ulster side in other parts and throughout the later (LL) text, and in both cases is rather outshone by his own ageing father.

The late James Carney deduced from an early 7th-century poem, *Conailla Medb míchuru*[23], that the young hero in the original form of the story was Fergus's own son Fíacc. The name Fíacc has various mythological connotations, most notably its association with the pool on the Boyne, Linn Féicc, where Finn mac Cumaill acquired his thumb of knowledge by tasting Fíacc's salmon *(eo Féicc);* where his predecessor as deity and *féinnid,* Fothad Canainne, was killed by a jealous husband; and where according to one early account Cú Chulainn killed Fráech.[24] The name could be related to *féic(e),* a roof-tree or summit (hence a supreme hero), but the association with the salmon of knowledge suggests a form connected with the (Middle Irish?) verb *féccid* or *fégaid,* implying the power of a seer, connected with derivations proposed for the term *éces,* poet, and the name Find.[25] Fíacc son of Fergus does not appear in the Táin, but he may be represented in other Ulster tales by Fiacha son of Fergus, who is killed protecting the heroes of *Longes mac nUislenn,* and an apparent doublet, Fiachra Caech, killed at *Bruiden Da-Chocae.*[26]

I heard with interest Garrett Olmsted's "*Conailla Medb míchuru* and the Origins of the *Táin*" at the International Celtic Congress in Paris, and have tried to follow the edition of the text he gave me. He argues that Fíacc in the poem is an early form of these last two, and that the poem mentions incidents in both these tales as well as the *Táin,* and his intention is to disprove Carney's suggestion in his Galway paper that the poem is an account of a historical 5th-century campaign between Ulster and the Leinster kings of Tara, and the principal characters are historical characters. I am not convinced that Olmsted is any better equipped than Carney to translate obscure archaic Irish alliterative verse, and he shows scant regard for the metre of the poem, but in any case I accept Carney's contention that when this poem was written the *Táin* as we know it did not exist, and the corollary that the other Ulster tales as we know them did not exist either. It may eventually be possible to interpret the poem as telling, or more likely referring to, a single coherent story which may have contributed elements to the *Táin, Longes mac nUislenn* and *Bruiden Da-Chocae,* but I think that story will be myth rather than history. It is interesting evidence that Conchobor's replacement of Fergus as king of Ulster is a central feature of the story. Whether Fíacc is a prototype for Cú Chulainn, or for his son Conlaech who dies in a later tale fighting his father, or both or neither, we may eventually discover, but not yet.

In any case the *Táin,* as an epic written at least partly to be published to secular audiences in the usual mediaeval from of reading aloud (presumably in instalments or extracts), and designed like the *Aeneid* to enhance the political as well as the cultural credit of its sponsors, may have drawn on the plots and characters of existing legends and myths, but was in no way bound to follow them. I see no reason to doubt the assumption implicit in early Irish scribal comments and headings that at least the setting and the central dramatis personae for the whole Ulster Cycle were laid down by the *Táin,* and there was nothing like the cycle we now have before it was written. Certainly the one hero who dominates the greater part of that story has no obvious background as an individual in any material outside his own cycle, and is conspicuously absent from tales such as *Togail Bruidne Da Derga,* set by the author of the surviving version at the same period, in which Cú Chulainn could not well replace the doomed central hero. In the *Táin* Cú Chulainn takes the place which might have been filled by Fergus or Fergus's son or by Conall Cernach, because they were politically undesirable candidates: his characteristics (before later interpolations like the fight with Fer Diad) are almost entirely those of a stereotyped, indeed an exaggerated version of the typical young hero: I feel he is the creation of the original author of the *Táin.* His original name Sétanta, if we accept a derivation from *sét,* path, is very suitable for a model hero, a pagan Galahad; but where did Cú Chulainn come from, and what does the second element of his name mean?

If he were a totally new invention one would expect a more obvious meaning, so I suggest that the Armagh author may have borrowed the name of a local hero, perhaps one who actually helped to defend Ulster against the early attacks of the Connachta a few years before the fall of Emain in the fifth century. In that case his name may involve a place-name, which makes more sense than any other explanation of the second element. The name of the smith whose hound he killed, replaced, and took as his name "the hound of Culann" is Caulann, not Culann, in the older texts of the *Táin* and *Compert Con Culainn.* This may be evidence for the antiquity of the form Cú Chaulainn, which does appear occasionally in genealogical tracts and the like[27], and may have been regularised by generations of scribes, if not modern editors, in other texts. It is no evidence for the existence of, say, a pagan smith-god called Caulann. Why he is a smith I will try to explain below, but unless there is some vastly significant connection with the word *caull,* a testicle, I doubt if the character or his name can be anything but our original author's invention. There is a word or name *culaind* or *Culuinn* in one very obscure archaic text from the Book of Ballymote, but it would probably take a year's study to interpret the three words involved,[28] unless someone has already done it. Names in Cú were common enough in seventh-century Ireland, and one historical Leinsterman of the period actually seems to have borne the name Cú Cholainn, with an O: his son Cairpre was killed in the aftermath of a battle involving the Uí Cheinnselaig in 709 according to the *Annals of Ulster.* The word involved can hardly be *colainn,* body, whose genitive is *colna:* might it be an early borrowing of the hero's name from the new best-seller, which his mother fancied—or rather, since I have argued that uncommon names at this period probably usually began as nicknames given during *fénnidecht,*[29] which other boys gave him in admiration, or possibly mockery? It seems unlikely that the real name, at least from this obscure Leinster nobleman, was the source of the literary one.

Culann could however be a variant, perhaps in a local dialect, of *cuilenn,* "holly-tree"—this is the only meaning we know for sure, though the compound *cuilennbocc,* a he-goat, is difficult to explain by this. The reference to dangerous forest creatures called *na Coin cuilind (sic!)* in *Echtra Airt meic Cuind*[30] may be just a later author having fun with our hero's name. Names beginning with Cú often follow it with a place-name—there are examples such as Cú Ulad, Cú Macha, and even Cú Chuailnge in the annals and genealogies which might have been more obvious choices for our hero—and Cuil(l)enn (like some other names of "noble trees", *(airigh fedha)*) is common

as a place-name, and several instances are recorded in the neighbourhood where the *Táin* is set. The best-known today is Slieve Gullion (Sliab gCuilinn) in Co. Armagh, perhaps too far north to be relevant, though it is a landmark on the present border, and is mentioned in the *Táin* as a refuge of the bull Donn Cuailnge. Another Slieve Gullion is west of Crossakeel, the village west of Kells identified as the Iraird Cuilenn where the Connacht forces found the first trace of Cú Chulainn in the *Táin.* More relevant to the central scenes of the story are references to a place called Cuilend in Muirthemne, probably the Cuillenn Cinn Dúin where Cú Chulainn killed a hundred men, and a river of the same name in the territory of the Conailli on which it may have stood—perhaps the Cully Water north of Dundalk. The most interesting name to me, however, is (Ochtar) Colland in Druimne Breg, the hilly area of Co. Louth north of the Boyne: this is presumably the village now called Collon, west of Monasterboice. A later reference to a Cuillend, a grange of Mellifont Abbey, is no doubt the same place, and a form Culann or Caulann would come somewhere between these two. The place is only a few miles up the River Mattock from the probable site of Ath Gabla, where Cú Chulainn first holds up the invaders and the Ulster exiles tell of his boyhood deeds.[31] Until someone comes up with a more convincing explanation, I suggest that "Cú Chulainn" may simply mean the Hound of Collon.

The too perfect hero

For modern readers perhaps translating the place-name and calling the hero "Hound of Hollywood" might not be so far from the mark. Cú Chulainn in the *Táin* and most of the other early Ulster tales is too good to be true, a perfect and invincible hero. Throughout the earlier part of the *Táin* he simply displays his skill in martial arts by killing people without getting a scratch himself, or behaves like a modern sniper firing unexpected shots into the Connacht camp. The only relief is in the Ulster exiles' accounts of his boyhood deeds, which derive directly from conventional accounts of the young hero and show little individual character. John Kelleher and Kim McCone have drawn attention to some ways in which the life of Cú Chulainn (as described in the tales of his birth and death and as dated in the annals), as well as that of Conchobar, is not only linked to Christ's incarnation but made to parallel it.[32] If a perfect secular hero was being created by a monastic author using the Saviour himself as his model, but with victories in place of miracles, it is no wonder that he seems too good to be true, a forerunner of the comic book "Super-hero" who eliminates the would-be destroyers of his community. Like Superman he has superhuman strength and endurance, like Batman he also has special skills, which the Early

Modern text *Tóruigheacht Gruaidhe Griansholus* makes fun of by turning them into special equipment that his charioteer has to lug around,[33] on the basis of the one which from the first involves a secret weapon, the *gae bolga*. In addition he is a beardless youth of seventeen (in the middle of the years of *fénnidecht* which extended between the ages of fourteen and twenty),[34] so he has an element of Peter Pan as well. All this adds up to a figure who may very easily seem ridiculous to a modern reader, though it is difficult to know how it would impress Irishmen hearing it recited in the seventh or eleventh century. (It is arguable that an element of burlesque and self-mockery is built into the story from the first, and may have been as traditional in seventh-century Ulster as it is in twentieth-century Connemara folktales, where the hero dons his battledress of slippery eelskin or india-rubber, and sallies out to slay hundreds or wrestle a single giant as appropriate. The freedom to exaggerate for effect has always been taken for granted in Irish literature, and does not imply that stories containing such exaggeration should not be taken seriously. It merely implies acknowledgement of the fact that a story, whether it is meant as history, instructive parable or pure entertainment, need not obey the same rules as real life.) ·

The unique hero

Apart from bombastic set pieces like the *Seisrech bresligi,* where Cú Chulainn drives in his chariot at top speed round the entire enemy host mowing them down in a circle six deep, and the series of lists which explain half the place-names of the present County Louth as derived from men he killed, the most unbelievable piece of exaggeration in the *Táin* is the claim that he held off the enemy (or at least conducted a punishing guerilla campaign against their basically successful cattle-raid) single-handed for three months. The period, from (the week after) Hallowe'en *(Samain)* to (the week after) Candlemas *(Imbolc),* has a fairly obvious mythical significance and no doubt derives from the myth which must have been one source for the *Táin.* The reason why the author used this claim is clearly to exalt the status of his hero. But he surely cannot just have invented the affliction which kept any of the other Ulster warriors from joining him, from nothing but his own imagination, proclaimed his hero free from it, and expected to be believed. This "debility of the Ultonians" has two names, each used several times throughout the *Táin, ces* or *noínden.* The second apparently means a period of nine days (though the same word can be used in some sense like "hosting" or "affray"), while early versions of the story of Macha's curse, which is given as an origin-legend for the first name, explain it as half that time, five days and four nights or four days and five nights.[35] If the true form is one that seemingly first appears

in rather later texts, *ces noíden,* "weakness of travail"—a cliché that may have been borrowed from the Old Testament—the period of three months seems no more appropriate, though the fact that it ends around *Imbolc,* the feast of Brigid, patroness of childbirth, could be more to the point.

It may help to consider why Cú Chulainn should be free from the curse. One simple explanation would be his divine parentage, but this will not do: he shares the exemption with his nominal father or mortal stepfather Sualdam, as Fergus plainly states in introducing an episode of the boyhood deeds, but giving no reason. Women and outsiders, and according to the Macha story children, are also exempt, so it can hardly be meant to describe a natural epidemic (though this could explain the discrepancy in duration: it might run its course in nine days for one person, but effectively tie up the whole population for three months, except for a few who like Cú Chulainn and his father lived near the frontier and escaped the infection.) It is also not clear what brings it on: Macha's curse apparently is to take effect when it will do most damage, surely meaning when Ulster is under attack, but at the beginning of the *Táin* Medb has evidently sent spies to make sure that the Ulstermen are already suffering from it before she ever sets out, while the episode in the boyhood deeds involves a surprise raid also apparently taking advantage of an existing *noínden.* It is possible that it is conceived in the *Táin* as an annual event starting at *Samain,* a sacred season when spirits were about and an enforced truce for a few days—but not three months—might be expected; it could even be a rationalisation of a fairly normal understanding that the winter months were not suitable for campaigning. But why is Cú Chulainn exempt? The Macha story (redaction 1) baldly states that Cú Chulainn was not an Ulsterman, and this has been accepted by later writers up to Thomas Kinsella, whose excellent translation of the *Táin* adds it to Fergus's statement.[36] But Thurneysen's interpretation of this as meaning that he is an *Elfensohn,* son of Lug, contradicts the inclusion of Sualdam, as we have seen. Cú Chulainn's mother Dechtire is Conchobar's sister[37] and unquestionably belongs to Ulster; his mortal father is called a son of Roich, like Fergus, in the earlier version of his birth-tale, and should be just as much an Ulsterman (but clearly Fergus and his fellow-exiles have become outsiders and are now free of the *ces.*) Sualdam's more frequent patronymic suggests that he may be a son of the seemingly supernatural owner of the house where Cú Chulainn is begotten in the other redaction of the birth-tale,[38] so the *Elfensohn* interpretation may apply after all; but he is given no patronymic in the first redaction of the *Táin* as far as I know.

My feeling is that this motif has been deduced from

an element of the myths used to construct the *Táin,* but used quite ruthlessly to ensure that Cú Chulainn alone defends Ulster for the three months. The myth I am reconstructing would have been acceptable to anthropologists a century ago, and in fact the theory of sacral kingship on which it depends now seems to be less ridiculed than it was thirty years ago. I suggest that it is the narrative account of the arrival of Fergus, who as I have proposed elsewhere is the divine paradigm and also a title for every early king of Ulster,[39] to claim the kingship from the preceding Fergus. He is therefore accompanied by the goddess of sovereignty, who may be called either Medb or Macha, and is certainly able to impose her curse on the Ulstermen at least for the nine days of the installation festival (which may have involved the killing, even the eating of the previous king, or some ritual which symbolised these.) The curse, however, applies only to adult men, with wives and land: the youthful *fénnidi* arrive at the frontier to hold off the invaders. At this point in the ritual I would expect a brief mock battle after which the *fénnidi* are convinced that the new Fergus has a legitimate claim and welcome him in: how the myth would reflect this I am not sure, but in any case this is all the original author of the *Táin* needed, and he used legend or his own imagination to supply further details of the battle.

He also changed the myth to suit his own purposes, by making Medb's Connacht army include men from other parts of Ireland (which may also come from recent historical legends), and to make the combat more uneven and his hero more glorious, he erased all but one member of the Ulster *fian*. Cú Chulainn, as one might say of a schoolboy, has no friends of his own age: the *macrad* which comes to help after he is wounded and a little ahead of the adult army is the under-fourteen age group, and all the other heroes who are summoned shortly afterwards are adults and hold lands from which they are summoned. Cú Chulainn is not "Cuchulainn of Muirtheimhne" as Lady Gregory put it, but a landless *fénnid,* outside the law (and the disadvantages which go with the law, such as the *ces*): he is also the only one, the paradigm of *fénnidecht* as Fergus is of kingship, and the whole institution is conspicuously absent from the Ulster Cycle, perhaps because the Church manifestly disapproved of it.

There is one possible alternative explanation for Cú Chulainn's uniqueness in this situation. In some cases, it has been suggested, sacred kings might avoid death at the end of a given period by providing a surrogate, sometimes a youth or child, who reigned for a while and was then sacrificed as "the king" in place of the real king, who was spared to resume his throne for a second term of office.[40] This has been put forward as the origin of more recent customs involving "kings for a day", "Lords of Misrule" and similar role reversals, often associated with midwinter festivals such as the

Saturnalia or Twelfth Night. Cú Chulainn might represent such a surrogate, keeping Fergus out of his kingship for the full three months of the winter quarter, until his return with the lengthening days of spring. In addition to doubts as to the evidence for the surrogate system, however, I have misgivings about the roles involved here: Cú Chulainn is obviously the warrior rather than the reigning king, and I prefer to see him as a *fénnid* with his personal achievement exaggerated by the first writer of the *Táin.*

Myths and folktales as sources

Of course, any reconstruction of the mythic element in the *Táin* must be speculative. It is tempting, for instance, to suggest that Donn Cuailnge, the bull which Medb wants to carry off, is a metaphor for the king whom Fergus wants to kill and replace, the 'bull of the province' as Derdriu actually describes Conchobor to Noísiu in *Longes mac nUislenn*. In the article cited above I suggested that Fergus might be equated with Finn, or even the Connacht bull Finnbennach, and opposed to the dying god or ancestor deity Donn; and I drew attention to the magical significance of the one eye (one arm, one leg) given up in exchange for wisdom by the children of Calatín who are destined to cause Cú Chulainn's death, and other Irish heroes, as it is by Odin in Norse mythology.[41] Though Cú Chulainn mainly represents the valorous hero rather than the wise hero like Finn, one consistent element of his famous, fearsome distortion *(ríastrad)* before a crucial battle is that one eye shrinks to almost nothing while the other is distended: I suggest that the significance of this is connected with the one lost eye as a sign of magic power, and may be borrowed from Fergus's son Féic or Fiachra *Caech* (the One-Eyed). However, that is as far as I am prepared to go now in looking for mythical elements in the *Táin.* What matters is that it should be recognised that memories of some such pagan myth were available to the original author; so almost certainly were historical legends based on the fifth-century campaigns between Ulaid and Connachta; so were materials comparable to modern international folktales, which I want to consider next. All these forms of oral tradition contributed elements of narrative plot and the character of a hero to the politically motivated epic which I believe an Armagh monk deliberately set out to compose in writing.

The folktale elements do not necessarily come from the peasantry. As Kenneth Jackson put it in introducing similar elements in the *Mabinogion,*[42] "the popular tale is a kind of general common denominator of narrative—I do not say 'lowest common denominator'—whose nature has been dictated by its essentially oral and universal character, but which was formerly as much at home in the baronial hall as in the cottage of the serf." They could as well be called myths, since many of the ancient Greek myths are similar stories, but I have preferred to restrict that term to narrative closely linked to religious belief and practice, which may have been told to reinforce such belief. The episode in the boyhood deeds where Cú Chulainn wakes up one night to find the Ulstermen losing a battle against Eogan mac Durthacht (elsewhere represented as an Ulster under-king and ally) and goes to help them, is strongly reminiscent of an anecdote often told in twentieth-century Ireland about a man who after confessing in a strange house that he has no story to tell, goes to bed there and dreams that he wakes in the night to be forced, for instance, to carry a corpse for a stranger. In the morning his host remarks that now he has a story to tell.[43] Cú Chulainn, less easily intimidated, kills the man (or demon) who throws half a corpse on to him and another who is cooking a wild boar in the woods, and feeds the boar to Conchobor. The point of the story is not Cú Chulainn's ability to kill men, lift the king out of a pit or carry the latter's wounded son on his back, so much as his lack of fear among corpses and demons in pitch darkness on the battlefield: Conchobor asks why he has come there in search of horror, which is reminiscent of the title of a more international *Märchen,* AT 326, "The Youth Who Wanted to Learn What Fear Is." It is likely enough that horror stories of this sort were already circulating orally in early Ireland, and could be easily adapted by the author of the **Táin.**

The most important use of a folktale in the **Táin,** I think, is also in the childhood deeds. It has not to my knowledge been recognised before because the ancient and very widespread hero-tale which opens the "Tales of Magic" section of the Aarne-Thompson index, AT 300, is labelled as "The Dragon-Slayer", but recent Irish and Scottish Gaelic versions often replace the dragon with a giant, or a series of three gaints, each with extra heads, on three successive days. Still more frequent are versions where, as a prelude to the main fight with dragon or giant(s) to save a princess, the hero's first task is to herd cattle which tend to stary on to land claimed by giants and be lost to them, along with the herdsman's life; so he has to fight three successive giants here, and finally their still more terrible mother. Sometimes the hero takes weapons from them, or is given them to spare their lives (which of course he does not.)[44] At any rate it seems to me that this could have been the model for Cú Chulainn's first feat of arms, when he tricks Conall Cernach into handing over the watch on the frontier—cattle-herding obviously is beneath him—and promptly leaves it, to fight against the three sons of Nechtan Scéne who have killed many Ulstermen. Their more terrible mother is only heard crying out after Cú Chulainn has killed them, using a word *(faíd)* which could suggest lamentation as much as threats of vengeance: but in any case the author had decided that Cú Chulainn would never wittingly harm a woman, so he could not meet

her. (It may be pointed out that in this he differs from most other Gaelic heroes, who frequently battle with supernatural hags—Cú Chulainn is attacked by the Morrígan and fights back, but only when she is in animal form, and he does not kill Medb when he has the chance. This doubtless reflects a feeling among the Irish clergy that the traditional involvement of women in warfare should be stopped, well before the *Cáin Adamnáin* which forbade killing women and children was promulgated in 697.) Another folktale motif is suggested by the charioteer's advice—this character too being a typical folktale helper, who knows everything and can warn the hero—that the first of the three sons of Nechtan, Foill, should be killed with the first blow or he will never be killed. It is a regular trick of dying giants to ask for a second blow, which brings them back to life.

Much that comes before is also typical of this tale-type, notably the taking of arms, where he breaks all the shields and spears he is offered until he gets the king's own set (except that in the folktales this usually happens with a sword.) The taking of arms on an auspicious day overheard from Cathbad the druid, however, is a re-working of the folktale to suit an aristocratic setting. This does not mean that the folktale was a peasant version: in fact it probably began with something like the birth-tale *Compert Con Culainn*. Version I of this has preserved a detail which clashes with the account in the *Táin,* and has therefore been erased by the interpolator in LU and replaced with a text from Version II. Other manuscripts leave it: *"Gabsi Caulann cerd. Ba sí a aite."* "Caulann the smith took him. She was his foster-father."[45] *Cerd* means a metalworker or other craftsman, and also his craft: in the latter sense it is feminine, in the former normally treated as masculine in surviving texts—the feminine pronoun may reflect an archaic usage, but it could also reflect a typical folktale introduction in which an unmarried smith found the abandoned baby and brought it up himself as both mother and father. Obviously this would make a tougher, more masculine, less ordinary hero, though the class-conscious author of the **Táin** turned the fosterage—during which according to the *Compert* the boy killed the dog while playing *(oc cluichiu)* and took his place and name—into a mere visit.[46] The smith himself can then obviously provide his foster-son with weapons.[47] The best-known literary example of the smith as foster-father or at least tutor is in the Norse *Völsunga Saga* and the much older *Reginsmál,* but the treacherous smith Regin there hardly fits into our story, though he does invite comparison with written and oral versions of the childhood of Finn.[48]

The reception of the epic and the hero

Most of this paper has concentrated on the creation of the *Ur-**Táin,*** as it might be called, as a conscious literary work composed in written form,[49] but using materials from oral tradition, including survivals of pagan myth, folktale and local historical legends. This was added to, as jewels might be added to a reliquary, by generations of later authors who in most cases wrote more enjoyable prose than the original, and produced exuberant set-piece descriptions and lists which must have sounded magnificent when read aloud, though they did little to improve the patchy and incoherent structure of the epic as a whole. They also added the rest of the Ulster Cycle, which includes many more attractive tales than the *Táin,* though shorter, the best of them apparently constructed largely by using well-known international themes from oral tradition—birth of the hero, training of the hero, contest between rival heroes, otherworld visit, battle between father and son, death of the hero—and slotting in the hero of the *Táin,* Cú Chulainn, who is often more vulnerable and likeable in these situations. But hero and epic were apparently adopted as centrepieces for a "Matter of Ireland" at the time when the first Irish manuscripts of secular narrative prose were being compiled, and have been accepted as such by modern scholars, less on their merits, I think, than because of a "hard sell" from Armagh, which I contend manufactured them and had one of the leading monastic *scriptoria* of early Ireland ready to circulate copies as soon as they were written. Every publisher knows that good publicity can make a best-seller of anything, and on a smaller scale this could apply even to seventh and eighth-century Ireland.

But how did the public react? It is well-known that the Fenian cycle, with its much clearer-cut distinction between the right side and the wrong side—the opponents are normally malevolent supernaturals or invading foreigners, not almost-as-good warriors from another province—and its companionable group of young *fénnidi* with different skills and characters, rather than one super-hero, was more favoured than the Ulster Cycle by authors, scribes and presumably audiences from the Middle Irish period onwards, and soon drove it into second place and by the end of the Middle Ages into third place in public esteem, behind "Romantic" tales of overseas adventure. So Cú Chulainn becomes a not-quite-assimilated Fenian in Scottish Gaelic oral tradition, and passes into Macpherson's Ossian in that guise; so *fianaíocht* is the modern Irish term for *all* hero-tales. In 15th-century and later manuscripts a few copies of the *Táin* still appear, but they are less popular than the tale of Cú Chulainn's death and his training in arms, much less popular than the Ulster tale *Oidheadh Chloinne Uisneach* which does not include Cú Chulainn,[50] and soon swamped by Fenian and Romantic tales.

Occasionally Early Modern Irish romances, surviving in the MSS of scribes from the 17th to early 18th century South-East Ulster school, use heroes from the Ulster Cycle, no doubt through local loyalty. In the

only one where Cú Chulainn is the main hero, *Tóruigheacht Gruaidhe Griansholus,* the author, as noted above, while "evidently well versed in the Cúchulainn saga",[51] treats the hero's accurately listed feats as weapons that can be bundled up and taken aboard ship, and makes the hero himself boast and bluster comically and behave with exaggerated chivalry, more like an Irish Don Quixote than his laconic prototype. Nevertheless the plot of the story is close enough to folktale for it to have been adopted in Donegal oral tradition. The story is not likely to be much older than its surviving MS, 1679. The title of one of the five tales published as *Sgéalta Rómánsuíochta* gives a typical lineup for later members of the series: *Eachtra Chonaill Cheithearnaigh* [sic!] *agus an Fhir Dia, Lughaidh Mhac Nós, Bhricín, agus Chú Chuilín go hOileán an Ár a rígheachta Rígh Innse Toirc.*[52] Bricín is the form which the Ulster trouble-maker Bricriu's name usually takes in folktales, but he seems to be just another hero here, and he and Fer Diad from Connacht and Lugaid mac Nois from Munster, both friends of Cú Chulainn though on the enemy side in the *Táin,* are all sent without comment as defenders of Ulster in the same boat on an overseas quest. In *Eachtra na gCuradh* Bricín is not in the line-up, but a much longer adventure begins with the other four accompanied by Fergus, Cú Roí (Munster), Ailill Finn (Connacht) and Deirdre's future lover "Náos mhac Uisneach" sailing away in search of glory together. Its companion *Coimheasgar na gCuradh* centres on Cú Roí, Ailill Finn and Conall Cernach and leaves out Cú Chulainn because he was a mere infant at the time. The others and two more of the *Sgéalta Rómánsuíochta* include him as *primus inter pares* at most, perhaps the best fighter among the group but not usually the leader, who tends to be Conall.[53] The pattern is thus much closer to that of Fenian romances: pre-eminent heroes were not popular with the readers.

Finally, the oral tradition. Those Ulster tales which have been recorded as folktales in Scotland and Ireland in the past century correspond fairly closely in popularity and form to those found in seventeenth-century or later manuscripts, which we know continued to be read aloud in Munster farm kitchens until the last century, and were probably similarly used in other Gaelic-speaking areas until after 1700.[54] Of the tales about Cú Chulainn, the most popular is certainly the story of how he got his name, collected in Scotland as well as all four provinces of Ireland, where it may well come from Keating's *Foras Feasa ar Éirinn:* I leave it to Caoimhín Mac Giolla Léith to comment on the influence which this compendium of legend and history had in Ireland.

Three different selections of episodes from the hero's life seem to have been the standard "Cú Chulainn story" in different regions: Connemara around Cárna, Co. Donegal around Ranafast, and the Hebrides in the Uists and Benbecula.[55] All include the naming, but in

Connemara this is the only episode from the **Táin** itself: the others are a version of the Macha story from Keating; Cú Chulainn's training in arms *(Oileamhain Con Culainn)* and the sequel in which he unknowingly kills the son he begot then *(Oidheadh Chonlaoich)*—both of these are also in the Donegal compendium, and less regularly in the Hebridean one; and at the end the deflating folk anecdote *Cú na hAdhairce* which we shall consider shortly. The Donegal compendium begins with a simplified but recognisable version of the hero's birth-tale, follows the naming with what may be a version of another boyhood deed from the **Táin,** the killing of three giants like the sons of Nechtan Scéne, and ends with his death-tale. (While this is reasonably heroic, other Donegal combinations include versions of *Tóruigheacht Gruaidhe Griansholus* where the hero is satirised with even more gusto than in the written romance—after a defeat he pulls out his heart through his wounds to see how small it is, or he lies down in a huff to sulk himself to death.) The Hebridean compendium is the only one which regularly includes episodes from the main body of the **Táin,** beginning with the opening of the LL recension—the pillow-talk and Medb's first unsuccessful attempt to buy the bull Donn Cuailnge, in which one version conflates Medb's envoy Mac Roth and Fergus mac Roich into "Fearchar Mac Ro". This is usually followed by a reasonably accurate telling, in spirit at least, of Cú Chulainn's fight with his friend (or brother) Fer Diad mac Damáin ("Fear Fada Diag mac Daimhein" to Angus MacLellan). But while several versions end with an equally good version of Cú Chulainn's heroic death tale and even its sequel of Conall Cernach's vengeance *(Deargruathar Chonaill Chearnaigh),* they may also include one or both of two much less heroic folktales about the hero, also known in Argyll and Connemara.

One of these is told only in Scotland of Cú Chulainn and a giant opponent, usually Garbh mac Stairn, whom he kills in a late mediaeval ballad well known in Scotland. The oldest known text of the story, I believe, noted as a free-verse supplement to the ballad by Dr. Irvine in 1801, actually substitutes Fionn for Cú Chulainn in both ballad and story,[56] and the story is now widely known in Ireland with Fionn as hero and a rival "giant", occasionally named as Cú Chulainn, as his victim. The point of the story, surely, is that the hero is small—as the youthful Cú Chulainn is often felt to be in oral tradition at least—but strong: he lies in a cradle pretending to be his own baby and bites the visitor's finger off, so that the latter is convinced that if the baby is so strong the father must be more so. There may be other tricks like making the giant break his teeth on an oatcake with the iron girdle (griddle) baked inside it, or asking him to turn the whole house round to keep the wind out of the door as Cú Chulainn would—very much in the tradition of international "stupid ogre" Märchen (AT 1000 ff.) This is nothing like the dauntless hero of the **Táin:** nor is the sequel.

Irvine's version goes on to an episode where a bull is torn in half, and this is usual in Scottish Cú Chulainn stories as the anti-climax of the **Táin:** Garbh has been sent for the Donn Cuailnge (interpreted as "Donn-Ghuailfhionn", the brown white-shouldered one),[57] and he and Cú Chulainn tear it, or in some versions another bull which Cú Chulainn pretends is it, in half.

There may follow the tale which in Connemara may be the end of Cú Chulainn's biography or an anecdote on its own, though Scottish versions precede it with at least the naming incident.[58] Cú Chulainn sees an enormous giant driving a huge bull (ox, bullock) and helps him, usually, to kill, cook and eat it. An even larger giant comes in pursuit of the bull, which he claims was stolen from him; the two giants fight, and Cú Chulainn tries to help the one he first met, but is flung off like a fly and lands inside the dead bull's horn. The sequel in at least one Scottish version and all the Irish ones is that he brings his broken sword to a blacksmith to be mended. The smith will only mend it if he is told a story (of how the sword was broken), but Cú Chulainn will not tell it if a woman is present. One hides in the smithy to hear the tale, and when Cú Chulainn tells how he was stuck in the horn, she shouts out: "So now you are called the Hound of the Horn *(Cú na hAdhairce)*!" This seemingly pointless gibe seems difficult to explain without recourse to irrelevant ideas about horns and cuckoldry, but it is tempting to think that we have a recrudescence in oral tradition of something like the mythic basis of the story—two great supernatural heroes (both called Fergus?) fighting for the kingdom, symbolised by a bull which is eaten at the inaugural feast—and the little interpolated hero thrown away like a midge. There could be an echo of the folktale source in the smith mending the sword, as Regin re-forged Sigurd's father's sword: the breaking of the taboo against a woman hearing the story leads straight on to Cú Chulainn's death in Carmichael's South Uist text. In any case, my point is made: Cú Chulainn was created too perfect to be credible, and he has not lasted well, ending up as an object of ridicule, a dwarf among giants, in oral tradition.

Notes

[1] This statement of my own position is partly a reaction to finding myself cited as a diehard defender of written as against oral origins in J. F. Nagy's article, "In Defence of Rómán-saíocht", *Ériu,* 38 (1987) 9-26. In fact, though I felt I had given sufficient evidence in my *Gaelic Folk-Tales and Mediaeval Romances* (Dublin, 1969) to show that most of the stories considered there were composed by the persons who first wrote them down, I believed when I wrote it that Old Irish "sagas" were essentially oral in origin, though composed by members of the poetic class rather than "peasants"—the fact that *aithech,* a rent-payer, has come to mean an ogre in Modern Irish folktales is proof enough of

that. After twenty years of collecting and editing folktales, asking myself where the Gaelic prose tradition could come from, and reading some convincing arguments from "non-nativist" scholars like Kim McCone and Liam Breatnach, I have changed my mind about this.

On scribal practice, I had written: "Considering the general archaism of the tradition . . . it may be fair to infer that many of the liberties taken were of a kind which might have been sanctioned at an earlier period. Seventeenth- and eighteenth-century scribes show no compunction about improving on their exemplars: the differences are far greater than can be explained by textual misreadings or mishearings" (*op. cit.,* p. 48.) Cf. Edgar M. Slotkin, "Mediaeval Irish Scribes and Fixed Texts", *Éigse* 17 (1978-9) 437-50, p. 450: "Given the attitude of scribes towards their work, we can think of each one of their productions as a kind of multiform of their original . . . we may treat such a manuscript as if it were a somewhat specialized separate performance." Slotkin is the only scholar working in the early Irish field who to my knowledge has paid sufficient attention to scribal practice, though he is still mainly searching for evidence of oral style.

² Alan Bruford, "Song and Recitation in Early Ireland", *Celtica,* 21 (1990) 61-74, pp. 72-4.

³ Kim McCone, *Pagan Past and Christian Present in Early Irish Literature* (Maynooth, 1990) Ch. 9, "Druids and outlaws", pp.203-32, sums up most of the arguments for the historicity of the institution.

⁴ A recent parallel to this process can be seen in the Lowland Scottish travellers (tinkers), who, though some are still illiterate and nearly all were in the last century, have nevertheless amassed a vast repertoire of narrative, much of it based on recognisable sources such as Hans Andersen and Nathaniel Hawthorne's *Wonder Book,* and probably many unidentifiable Victorian magazine stories, because a literate few and probably visiting do-gooders read aloud to them. See Alan Bruford, "Legends Long Since Localised or Tales Still Travelling?", *Scottish Studies,* 24 (1980) 43-62, pp. 47-9.

⁵ Francis John Byrne, *Irish Kings and High-Kings* (London, 1973), p. 46; Proinsias Mac Cana, *The Learned Tales of Mediaeval Ireland* (Dublin, 1980), pp. 79-80, citing an article by Pádraig Ó Riain in *Éigse* 15 (1973-4) 24 ff.

⁶ Mac Cana, *op. cit.,* p. 64. Rudolf Thurneysen, *Die irische Helden- und Königsage bis zum siebzehnten Jahrhundert* (Halle (Saale), 1921), pp. 535-6, suggests that *Táin Bó Rois* is another name for *Aided Chonchobuir,* which involves a Connacht raid on the Fir Rois in the south of Ulster. I apologise for the use of "tribe" to render *tuath,* a petty kingdom, which is rather misleading, but conventional and difficult to avoid.

⁷ M. A. O'Brien, *Corpus Genealogiarum Hiberniae* (Dublin, 1962), pp. 382-3. The orthographic difference between Cualnge and Cuailnge is of no significance.

⁸ Thurneysen, *Heldensage,* pp. 251-67.

⁹ Byrne, *Kings,* pp. 76, 169, 180, 239, 241 (the last two references suggest that the Munster conquest may not have been complete until the mid-seventh century, in the reign of Guaire Aidne, the Connacht king for whom most of the accounts referred to in note 8 say the *Táin* was "recovered").

¹⁰ Cf. Bruford, *Gaelic Folk-Tales,* p. 98. The recent onomastic legend seems to be English, and the original name may be simply Léim Chon: the identification of the dog who made the leap as Cú Chulainn could be the work of some antiquary in the past two or three centuries. "Loop" is apparently a dialect form of "leap", cf. Scots "loup".

¹¹ Byrne, *Kings,* p. 112: see also Nagy, *op. cit.*

¹² Byrne, *Kings,* p. 117.

¹³ *Ibid.,* pp. 72-4; T. F. O'Rahilly, *Early Irish History and Mythology* (Dublin, 1946), pp. 222-32.

¹⁴ Alan Bruford, "The Twins of Macha", *Cosmos,* 5 (1989) 125-41, pp. 133, 136.

¹⁵ *Ibid.,* p. 132.

¹⁶ Tomás Ó Cathasaigh, *The Heroic Biography of Cormac mac Airt* (Dublin, 1977), pp. 81-3; see further note 18 below.

¹⁷ *Ibid.,* pp. 33-8.

¹⁸ I have argued in an as yet unpublished paper read at the Ninth International Congress of Celtic Studies in Paris, July 1991, "Some implications of Early Irish and Scottish names and epithets", that Cormac's name reveals him to be specifically the culture-hero of Tara when it belonged to Leinster, and he and his bear father must have been incorporated in the genealogy of the Connachta after they had conquered Tara, to strengthen their hold on it.

¹⁹ Byrne, *Kings,* pp. 117, 125.

²⁰ Cf. note 3, and Joseph Falaky Nagy, *The Wisdom of the Outlaw* (Berkeley and Los Angeles, 1985).

²¹ Byrne, *Kings,* pp. 90, 118, 125.

[22] *Ibid.,* pp. 111-14.

[23] James Carney, "Three Old Irish Accentual Poems", *Ériu* 22 (1971) 1-80, pp. 78-80; *id.,* "Early Irish Literature: the State of Research", in *Proceedings of the Sixth International Congress of Celtic Studies,* ed. Gearóid Mac Eoin (Dublin, 1983) 113-30, pp. 122-5.

[24] Cf. Nagy, *Outlaw,* p. 155; Kuno Meyer, *Fianaigecht,* RIA Todd Lecture Series 16 (Dublin, 1910), pp. 9-10; Thurneysen, *Heldensage,* p. 140, n.3.

[25] Royal Irish Academy, *(Contributions to a) Dictionary of the Irish Language* (Dublin, 1913-76), *s.v. éices, féc(c)id, fégaid, féic;* cf. Nagy, *Outlaw,* pp. 22, 236 on *Finn,* and also Byrne, *Kings,* pp. 141-2 on Fiachu ba hAiccid. However, Holger Pedersen, *Vergleichende Grammatik der keltischen Sprachen,* (Göttingen, 1909-13), 2, pp. 489-90, insists that verbal forms in *fécc-* are Middle Irish, not from **fo-in-ci,* and the different origin he suggests for *fégaid* can hardly explain an archaic *Fíacc.*

[26] Cf. Thurneysen, *Heldensage,* pp. 326, 593.

[27] *Ibid.,* p. 270 (the earlier redaction of *Compert Con Culainn*); O'Brien, *Corpus,* pp. 284-5. *Ibid.,* p. 154 refers to a family among the Conailli or Dál nAraide *(i Cruithniu)* called Corco Caullain, descended from Caulnia, one of the twins whom Lebarcham the woman satirist (!) bore to Cú Chulainn: this could be a sighting of the original local hero concealed in a later note in the Book of Leinster genealogies. Their version of the hero's own genealogy *(ibid.,* p. 285) through Sualtam son of Dubthach to Cermat son of the Dagda (and on to Míl Espáin!) is also interesting in giving a completely different "divine" ancestry from that through Lug.

[28] *Mulan Culuinn (mo lan culaind) cumlachta:* differently transcribed in RIA *Dictionary, s.v. cuimlecht* and *culaind.*

[29] Bruford, "Implications" (see note 12 above).

[30] Ed. Osborn Bergin, *Ériu* 3 (1907) 149-73, pp. 166, 168.

[31] Cf. Edmund Hogan, *Onomasticon Goedelicum* (Dublin, 1910), *s.v.* Ath Gabla, Colland, Cuilend, Cuillend. The possibility of a Co. Clare origin remains, but Máirtín Ó Briain noted with interest the proximity of Collon to Monasterboice, "cradle of Lebor na hUidre" and Knowth, seat of an Uí Néill dynasty whose last king of Tara, Congalach Cnogba son of Máel Mithing, killed nearby in 956, seems to have been a notable patron of literature, including perhaps the *Táin* as we know it.

[32] McCone, *Pagan Past,* pp. 197-8, citing J. V. Kelleher, "The Táin and the annals", *Ériu* 22 (1971) 107-27, pp. 112, 121-2.

[33] Cecile O'Rahilly, ed., *Tóruigheacht Gruaidhe Griansholus,* Irish Texts Soc. vol. 24 (London, 1924), pp. 20-31 and *passim.*

[34] McCone, *Pagan Past,* pp. 203-5.

[35] Cf. RIA *Dictionary s.v. noínden* (1) and (2); Thurneysen, *Heldensage,* pp. 97-8, 361-3.

[36] Thurneysen, *Heldensage,* p. 363; Thomas Kinsella (transl.), *The Tain* (Oxford, 1970), p. 81: " . . . This affliction," Fergus said, "never came to our women or our youths, or anyone not from Ulster—and therefore not to Cúchulainn or his father."

[37] Or his daughter, according to the oldest text of his birth-tale (Thurneysen, *Heldensage,* p. 268; A. G. Van Hamel, ed., *Compert Con Culainn and other stories,* Mediaeval and Modern Irish Series 3 (Dublin, 1933), p. 3). This makes better sense than the later version which makes both her and Conall Cernach's mother Finnchóem into Conchobor's sisters, if Conchobor's mother died giving birth to him as some texts seem to say (Thurneysen, *Heldensage,* p. 276), but it makes the generation gap between him and Cú Chulainn ridiculously large.

[38] Cf. Thurneysen, *Heldensage,* pp. 271-3: the man of the house is Becfholtach ("Little Wealth"), and Sualdam (perhaps from *suaill-dáim,* "Insignificant Retinue", *ibid,* p. 91) in the LL *Táin* and Rawl. B.502 genealogical tracts (O'Brien, *Corpus,* p. 285) is son of Becaltach (son of Móraltach). Some of these texts show the change of Sualdam to the later form Sualtach, and assonance at this point may be more important than meaning; but the earlier forms suggest that Cú Chulainn was at one point presented as the typical folktale hero, son of a poor nobleman if not a woodcutter or a widow.

[39] Cf. note 7 above.

[40] Cf. Robert Graves, *The Greek Myths* (Harmondsworth, 1955), 1, pp. 18-19.

[41] Bruford, "Twins of Macha", pp. 138-9; 134-6.

[42] Kenneth H. Jackson, *The International Popular Tale and Early Welsh Tradition* (Cardiff, 1961), p. 6.

[43] Cf. Seán Ó Súilleabháin and Reidar Th. Christiansen, *The Types of the Irish Folktale,* FF Communications No. 188 (Helsinki, 1963) p. 343, type 2412B; Sean O'Sullivan, *Folktales of Ireland* (Chicago/London 1966), pp. 182-4, is an accessible example. For another comparison to this episode of the *Táin,* cf. Wil-

liam Sayers, "*Airdrech, Sirite* and other Early Irish battlefield spirits", *Éigse,* 25 (1991) 45-55.

[44] Cf. Reidar Th. Christiansen, *Studies in Irish and Scandinavian Folktales* (Copenhagen, 1959), pp. 64-7, though this makes as much of the variations as of what I would consider the basic pattern.

[45] Van Hamel, *op. cit,,* p. 6 and n. 10: after noting masculine forms in two other MSS, the editor says simply "But *cerd* is fem. in O. Ir." But cf. RIA *Dictionary, s.v. cerd.*

[46] In Recension II, after a passage in which various heroes promise their own gifts to the child much in the manner of fairy godmothers in *Sleeping Beauty* and other *contes des fées,* Conchobor hands him over, apparently at birth, to his other sister Finnchóem and her husband Amorgein. Thurneysen, *Heldensage,* p. 273, n. 1, suggests that this is because Cú Chulainn generally appears as their son Conall Cernach's foster-brother, though Fergus seems to be his foster-father in the *Táin.* But Cú Chulainn addresses Conall as "*a phopa*" in the boyhood deeds, the same form he uses to Fergus and Conchobor there—is this merely a polite form of address to elders (in which case Conall must be considered more like a father than an older brother, or is this exaggerated respect?) or does it imply some form of joint fosterage?

[47] *Cerd* is sometimes used (e.g. in *Cath Maige Tuired,* see T. F. O'Rahilly, *op. cit.,* p. 14) specifically for a bronze-smith as against a blacksmith *(goba),* who would be more likely to make swords or spear-heads, and provide him with magical protection, like Cormac mac Airt's grandfather, the *druígoba* Olc Aiche (cf. Ó Cathasaigh, *Cormac,* pp. 48-51). But if the original author supplied the name he may have been more concerned with alliteration than such incidents which he dropped from the story. Christiansen, *op. cit.,* p. 78, n. 3, describes the weapon-breaking sequence as "well-known both from romance and from folktales".

[48] Cf. Alan Bruford, "Oral and Literary Fenian Tales", in *The Heroic Process,* edd. Bo Almqvist, Séamas Ó Catháin & Pádraig Ó hEalaí (Dun Laoghaire, 1987) 25-56, pp. 44-7.

[49] Later versions of the story of the *Táin*'s discovery certainly depict the epic as having been written down from Fergus's dictation (Thurneysen, *Heldensagé,* pp. 254, 267) but by Thurneysen's summary it seems that his (1) and (2) versions do not specify writing.

[50] Cf. Cecile O'Rahilly, *op. cit.,* p. xxi.

[51] *Ibid.,* p. xix.

[52] Máire Ní Mhuirgheasa & Séamus Ó Ceithearnaigh, edd., *Sgéalta Rómánsuíochta,* Leabhair ó Láimhsgríbhnibh 16 (Baile Átha Cliath, 1952), p. 123.

[53] *Ibid.* pp. 1-62 (*Tóruigheacht na hEilite le Cú Chuilinn agus Oillioll Fionn,* where the latter has most of the adventures); pp. 63-122 (*Tóruigheacht Eileann Sgiamhach*) and pp. 123-183 (*Eachtra Chonaill Cheithearnaigh:* in both of these Conall is the leader of an overseas adventure including Cú Chulainn); in pp. 184-240 (*Eachtra Foirbe mac Chonchubhair mhic Neasa Rígh Uladh*) Conall takes part in an early episode and Cú Chulainn merely turns up with Conall and Conchobor at the end. *Eachtra na gCuradh* and *Coimheasgar na gCuradh,* both edited by Meadhbh Ní Chléirigh, were also published in the series Leabhair ó Láimhsgríbhnibh, 1 (Baile Átha Cliath 1951) and 6 (Baile Átha Cliath 1952).

[54] Bruford, *Folk-tales and Romances,* Chapters 6 and 8.

[55] *Ibid.,* pp. 93-6, 256-7. Though I said then (p. 95) "In Scotland one cannot speak of an oecotype", I feel now that while Uist versions differ more than Connemara ones, it is possible to see a fairly consistent oral compilation behind them, taking into account a long version from Benbecula in Alexander Carmichael's MSS, quite close to Carmichael's H1 from South Uist, which D. A. MacDonald and I found in 1979, and the fact that A3, which J. F. Campbell noted in Mull, was from William Robertson, a North Uist man who had settled in Tobermory.

[56] *Ibid.,* p. 104, n. 2; Ó Súilleabháin & Christiansen, *Types,* pp. 218-9, under AT 1149; J. F. Campbell, *Leabhar na Féinne* (London, 1872), pp. 6-8.

[57] I owe this identification and clearer spelling of the traditional cattle-name *Guailfhionn* (usually transcribed *Guailleann,* cf. the better-known *Druimeann*) to my colleague D. A. MacDonald, who remembers hearing it in North Uist in the 1930s.

[58] Ó Súilleabháin & Christiansen, *Types,* under AT 1376A*: a version is translated in O'Sullivan, *Folktales,* pp. 74-9. Published Scottish versions in J. F. Campbell, *Popular Tales of the West Highlands,* 2nd ed., 3, pp. 194-7 (from John Dewar, Arrochar: without smith's wife); A. A. Carmichael, "*Toirioc na Taine*" (from Eachann MacIosaig, Iochdar, S. Uist) in *Transactions of the Gaelic Society of Inverness,* 2 (1873) 25-39, pp. 36-7.

FURTHER READING

Bibliography

Corthals, Johan. "Zitierte Literatur." In *Táin Bó Regamna:*

Eine Vorerzählung zur Táin Bó Cuailnge. In *Studien zur Táin Bó Cuailnge,* pp. 7-10. Verlag: Der Österreichischen Akademie der Wissenschaften, 1987.

Bibliography of published versions of the *Tain* and secondary sources in Irish, German, French, and English.

Tristram, Hildegard L. C. "Auswahlbibliographie zur *Táin Bó Cuailnge.*" In *Studien zur Táin Bó Cuailnge,* edited by Hildegard L. C. Tristram, pp. 245-62. Tübingen: Gunter Narr Verlag, 1993.

Bibliography of secondary sources in German, Italian, French, and English.

Criticism

Berger, Pamela. "Many-Shaped: Art, Archaeology, and the *Táin.*" *Éire-Ireland* 17 (1982): 6-18.

Relates the language of the *Táin,* which preserves the language of the La Tène Celts, to surviving artifacts of the period. By associating the literature and art of the period, Berger attempts to "partially recover and probe the mentality of the Iron Age Celts."

Butler, Mary Eugene. *Epic Evidences in the Irish Heroic Saga, "Táin Bó Cualnge."* M.A. Thesis, University of Notre Dame, 1941, 89p.

Discusses the use of epic conventions in the *Táin.*

Mac Mathúna, Liam. "The Topographical Components of the Place-Names in *Táin Bó Cúailnge* and Other Selected Early Irish Texts." In *Studien zur Táin Bó Cuailnge,* edited by Hildegard L. C. Tristram, pp. 100-13. Tübingen: Gunter Narr Verlag, 1993.

Analyzes the topographical significance of place-names in the *Táin* "with a view to determining their semantic and other relationships to the topographical vocabulary of the text in general."

Mallory, J. P. "The World of Cú Chulainn: The Archaeology of the *Táin Bo Cúailnge.*" In *Aspects of "The Táin,"* edited by J. P. Mallory, pp. 103-59. Belfast: December Publications, 1992.

Discusses the historical and social world of the *Táin* with reference to archeological artifacts of the period.

McHugh, Máire. "The Sheaf and the Hound: A Comparative Analysis of the Mythic Structure of *Beoweulf* and *Táin Bó Cúalnge*" in *La Narrazione: Temi e Tecniche dal Medioevo ai Nostri Giorni,* pp. 9-43. Abano Terme: Piovan Editore, 1987.

Explores the similarities and differences betweeen the *Táin* and *Beowulf,* concluding that, despite their radically different narrative strtuctures, the two epics express similar cosmologies.

Ó Cathasaigh, Tomás. "The Concept of the Hero in Irish Mythology." In *The Irish Mind: Exploring Intellectual Traditions,* edited by Richard Kearney, pp. 79-90. Dublin:

Wolfhound Press, 1985.

Explores the ideological underpinnings of early Irish mythology, especially the role of the hero in writings such as the *Tain.*

O'Connor, Mary. "Sex, Lies and Sovereignty: Nuala Ní Dhomhnaill's Re-Vision of *The Táin.*" *Working Papers in Irish Studies* 91, Nos. 2-4 (1992): 1-10.

Interprets the "Atáin" poems of Nuala Ní Dhomhnaill's *Féar Suaithinseach* as feminist revisions of the *Táin* stories.

O'Daly, Máirín. "The Verbal System of the LL. Táin." *Ériu* 14 (1946): 31-139.

Catalogues the verbal system of the *Táin,* including textual locations.

Olmsted, Garrett S. *The Gundestrup Cauldron.* Brussels: Latomus Revue D'Etudes Latines, 1979, 306p.

Studies the style, iconography, and narrative conventions of the illustrations on the Gundestrup cauldron, considering the myth portrayed to be a prototype of the later *Táin.*

O'Rahilly, Cecile. "Introduction." In *The Stowe Version of Táin Bó Cuailnge,* edited by Cecile O'Rahilly, pp. vii-lxi. Dublin: Dublin Institute for Advanced Studies, 1961.

Surveys the relationship of the Stowe version of the *Tain* to the LL version and recensions.

————. "Introduction." In *Táin Bó Cúailnge from the Book of Leinster,* edited by Cecile O'Rahilly, pp. ix-iv. Dublin: Dublin Institute for Advanced Studies, 1967.

Surveys the sources of the LL version of the *Tain,* including its different recensions.

Simms, Katharine. "Propaganda Use of the *Táin* in the Later Middle Ages." *Celtica* 15 (1983): 142-49.

Chronicles the O'Néill family's attempts to bolster their political ambitions by associating themselves with characters in the *Táin.*

Swartz, Dorothy Dilts. *Stylistic Parallels between the Middle Irish Epic "Táin Bó Cúalnge" in the Book of Leinster and Twelfth-Century Neo-classical Rhetoric, with an Excursus upon the Personality of the Redactor.* Ph.D. Thesis, Harvard University, 1983, 310p.

Uses linguistic evidence to argue that the *Táin* was compiled in the twelfth century.

Tristram, Hildegard L. C. "Aspects of Tradition and Innovation in the *Táin Bó Cuailnge*" in *Papers on Language and Mediaeval Studies Presented to Alfred Schopf,* edited by Richard Matthews and Joachim Schmole-Rostosky, pp. 19-38. Frankfurt am Main: Verlag Peter lang, 1988.

Argues that Recension I of the *Táin* is the product of the late tenth or early eleventh centuries, when isolated episodes were incorporated into an integrated whole. Contrary to some critics' opinions, Tristram states that she does "not believe that the *Táin* existed in any cohenrent narrative form prior ro the Middle Irish period."

Torah

c. Fourth Century B. C.

(Also known as the Pentateuch, the Five Books of Moses, *Hummash, Mikra,* and *Law.*) Hebrew history.

INTRODUCTION

One of the most important religious documents in the Western world, the *Torah* is composed of the first five books of the Hebrew *Bible–Genesis, Exodus, Leviticus, Numbers,* and *Deuteronomy.* The books contain an account of the events from the creation of the world to the death of Moses, and within that narrative is outlined the covenant between God and the Hebrew people and the laws they must adhere to in order to fulfill this relationship. Although historiographers disagree about the tenability of Mosaic authorship, the *Torah* forms the basis of the Jewish religion both as a historical account of Hebraic origins and as a written account of divinely-legislated morality.

Plot and Major Characters

The narrative of the *Torah* begins with an account of God's creation of heaven and earth, the introduction of sin into the world, the beginning of civilization, and the growth of the world's population. Adam is created upon the earth and permitted access to everything, with the exception of the tree of knowledge of good and evil. The animals on the earth do not provide him with suitable companionship, so God creates for him a woman named Eve. But the Devil in the form of a snake persuades Eve, and through her Adam, to eat the fruit of this tree, and they are driven from Eden. Eve later bears Cain and Abel; Cain kills his brother, and the initial evil spreads throughout the growing society. As civilization spreads, sin grows, until God creates a flood that destroys the human race, except the family of Noah, whose descendants repopulate the earth.

In the tenth generation after Noah, God tells Abram (later Abraham) to emigrate from Babylonia to Canaan with the promise that he will found a great nation. Abraham and his wife, Sarah, bear a son, Isaac, in their old age; God tests Abraham by ordering Isaac's sacrifice, but allows Isaac to live when Abraham is found willing to obey. Isaac and his wife, Rebekah, later bear Esau and Jacob, the latter of whom secures Abraham's birthright and blessing. One of Jacob's sons, Joseph, arouses the jealousy of his brothers, who plot to kill him. However, Joseph survives and is carried to Egypt as a slave, where he rises to the highest position in the service of the Pharoah. Compelled by famine, Joseph's siblings eventually move to Egypt, where they are reconciled with Joseph and grow into a powerful tribe. The succeeding Pharoah attempts to exterminate them by ordering the massacre of Hebrew infants, but one baby, named Moses, survives and is brought up in the Pharoah's palace as an Egyptian.

Moses later witnesses an Egyptian beating a Hebrew worker and kills the Egyptian, burying the body. When word of the homicide spreads, Moses flees to Midian, where he marries Zipporah, daughter of a priest. While guarding sheep, Moses is visited by YHWH (Yahweh, or I Am Who I Am), God of the Hebrews, who instructs him to lead his oppressed people out of bondage. With his brother Aaron, Moses succeeds in freeing them, but only after YHWH visits several plagues upon the Egyptians, culminating in the death of their firstborn children. The Hebrews head into the wilderness and are pursued by the Egyptian army; the Red Sea parts to let the Hebrews cross, but the Egyptians are destroyed by the closing waters.

The Israelites eventually travel to Sinai, where Moses receives a revelation from YHWH; first, the ten commandments are delivered to the people, then a collection of further laws are communicated to Moses. During Moses's absence, however, the Israelites begin to doubt YHWH and to worship an idol. God punishes them for this betrayal by allowing only their children to enter into the promised land; the adults will all die in the wilderness. The Israelites are unsuccessful in invading Canaan, so they proceed to Moab, east of Jordan. Preparations are made to enter the land on the west bank, but before they enter, Moses reminds his people of their covenant with God and instructs them in laws they must follow in their new land. Moses dies at the age of 120 and is succeeded by Joshua.

Major Themes

The first group of books in the Old Testament is called *Tōrāh* ("law") because it contains nearly the entire Jewish legal system. The unifying subject of the books is God's promise to Abraham–that he shall be the beginning of a great nation blessed by God (*Genesis* 12:1-3)–and the covenant based upon it, so that the *Torah* is primarily constituted by two related themes: tracing the historical formation of the Israelites as the people of God, and the legislative restrictions that are to provide them with the means to fulfilling this special relationship. The first task is covered from the beginning of the world to the Hebrew Patriarchs in *Genesis,* and in the organization of Israel and its settlement in Canaan described in the other four books. Legal material comprises more than one-third of the narrative and is to some extent covered in all of the books, most notably in *Leviticus,* which consists entirely of laws. Outlined in the *Torah,* this way of living dictated by the covenant between God and the people of Israel forms the basis of Jewish morality.

Textual History

According to traditional Judaism, God gave the *Torah* to Moses during the revelation on Mount Sinai. Early proponents of this view, such as Philo of Alexandria, Josephus, and the Babylonian *Talmud,* as well as modern critics, cite thematic and stylistic continuities as well as portions of the Old and New Testaments that refer to the Pentateuch as the Five Books of Moses to defend the assumption of Mosaic authorship of all but the final account of Moses's death. During the Reformation, however, some scholars began to voice doubts about Mosaic authorship, including Isaac ben Jasos, Ibn Ezra, Martin Luther, and Andreus Masius, because they found it difficult to reconcile some passages with the hypothesis that there was a single author. Despite these views, the belief in Mosaic authorship was generally maintained, despite later thinkers such as Benedict de Spinoza, who contended that the books attained their present form under Ezra, and others, most notably Richard Simon in his *A Critical History of the Old Testament* (1678), who argued that a group of Hebrew historiographers composed the books, which were collected by Ezra.

Modern critics generally have adopted, with revisions, the stance of Jean Astruc, who was the first to maintain that Moses drew on earlier historical sources from which he compiled the Pentateuch; according to Astruc, two principal sources–the Elohistic and the Yahwistic (or Jehovistic)–and several minor sources were incorporated into *Genesis,* in whole or in part, by Moses, who wrote the other four books. Later theorists expanded on Astruc's hypothesis, calling attention to different linguistic styles and word-uses to support the opinion of multiple authors. Although some scholars have even claimed that the books are composed of an agglomeration of numerous fragments with no inherent connection, a more modest position has gained prominence, according to which the Pentateuch is composed of at least four documents that originally existed independently, either in oral or written form: E (Elohistic document), characterized by its use of the divine name "Elohim"; J (Jehovistic document), characterized by its use of the divine name "Jehovah"; D (Deuteronomic Code), comprising the bulk of *Deuteronomy*; and P (Priestly Narrative), combining history and law. Although the chronology of the compilation of these four sources is still being debated, it is generally agreed among those who now deny Mosaic authorship that J

and E were first combined by a redactor. The unified work JE, after circulating for some time, was further enlarged by redactors who added D and P.

Critical Reception

The *Torah* is considered the word of God by millions of people; its description of the Hebrew people's divine covenant with God forms the basis of Judaism and, more generally, all subsequent revelations of the *Bible,* including the teachings of Jesus Christ. Some critics claim that denying Mosaic authorship tends to undermine the historical basis of biblical religion, that the stories were probably transmitted orally for centuries, from generation to generation, and were subject to all the dangers of such transmission. But others insist that whether they were divine commandments communicated through Moses or the product of a number of writers from Moses to Ezra, the legislative principles of the *Torah* reflect the convictions of a nation's experience over thousands of years and embody a unique understanding of the relationship between God and human beings, providing us with a text rich in religious, moral, and literary value.

PRINCIPAL ENGLISH TRANSLATIONS

The Pentateuch and Haftorahs: Hebrew Text, English Translation and Commentary. 5 vols. [translated by J. H. Hertz] 1929

The Torah: A Modern Commentary [translated by W. Gunther Plaut and Bernard J. Bamberger] 1981

The Torah: The Five Books of Moses [translated by the Jewish Publication Society] 1981

The Five Books of Moses: Genesis, Exodus, Leviticus, Numbers, Deuteronomy [translated by Everett Fox] 1995

CRITICISM

William H. Green (essay date 1892)

SOURCE: "Pentateuchal Analysis" in *Moses and His Recent Critics,* edited by Talbot W. Chambers, Funk & Wagnalls Company, 1892, pp. 101-37.

[*In the following essay, Green focuses on the first eleven chapters of* Exodus *to claim, contrary to many other critics, that there is no convincing evidence for the hypothesis that the* Pentateuch *was composed by several authors who combined and enlarged three or four distinct treatises.*]

In the limited space allowed in these essays it is impossible to undertake the full discussion of the critical division of the **Pentateuch** in all its length and breadth, to which such a multitude of volumes has been devoted, and upon which so many learned dissertations have been written. A treatment of this subject in general terms would be of no practical benefit. Critical partition is professedly based on the minute examination of paragraphs, words and phrases, and cannot be met by generalities, but only by a similarly minute investigation, in which the arguments adduced in its favour can be rebutted in detail and the opposing considerations, which show it to be unreasonable or impracticable, can likewise be exhibited. Such an investigation must from the nature of the case be tedious, and task the patience of the reader. But it is inevitable, if effective work is to be done, or any intelligent comprehension of the subject is to be gained; for the region in which the discussion moves is the minutiæ of diction, style, conception and the connection of paragraphs and sentences, which are only redeemed from their apparently petty character by the momentous consequences deduced from them or dependent on them. The work of the critic is the cross-examination of witnesses, which busies itself with trivial circumstances aside from the leading features of the testimony. But it is precisely by its coherence in these minor and incidental matters, or by the lack of it, that its credibility and value on the whole are to be tested. We do not object to the searching character of this critical investigation. Our only demand is that it should be fairly and honestly conducted.

The Pentateuch, which to ordinary readers seems to be one continuous production, resolves itself upon close examination, we are told, into three or four treatises or documents giving every indication of distinct authorship, which must in the first instance have existed separately, but have been subsequently woven together. These are technically denoted by the symbols E (Elohist), J (Jahvist), D (Deuteronomist), P (Priestly Narrator). J and E were first combined by a Redactor (Rj), and the united work JE, after circulating for some time, was further enlarged by other Redactors, Rd and Rp, who added Deuteronomy and the Priestly Document. And thus by successive steps the work reached its present compass.

An obvious remark at the outset is that the existence of these documents and redactors is purely a matter of critical discovery. There is no evidence of their existence and no pretence of any apart from the critical tests which have determined the analysis. All tradition and all historical testimony as to the origin of the Pentateuch are against them. The burden of proof lies wholly upon the critics. And this proof should be clear and convincing in proportion to the gravity and the revolutionary character of the consequences which it is proposed to base upon it.

It is further obvious that the composite character of the **Pentateuch,** supposing this were established, would not justify the critics in attributing a different sense to the documents in their original form from that which the passages extracted from them are capable of having in their present connection, or in assuming a conflict between them which does not exist as they now stand. The critics have no right upon their own principles to impeach needlessly and arbitrarily the integrity and capacity of the Redactors. The Redactors by the hypothesis had the documents before them separate and complete, with every opportunity to ascertain their true meaning; and it ought not to be assumed without clear proof that this has been obscured or falsified. Modern critics, who possess only the commingled and dislocated fragments that have been preserved to us, are far more likely to be mistaken. If new meanings may be imposed upon paragraphs or sentences incompatible with their present context; if variance may be created by expunging explanatory or harmonizing clauses; if discrepancy may be inferred from a silence which is itself produced by first removing the very statements that are desiderated from the connection; if what are narrated as distinct events may be converted into irreconcileable accounts of the same transaction, the most closely connected composition can be rent asunder into discordant fragments. Such methods are subversive of all just interpretation. The operator imposes his own ideas upon the text before him and draws conclusions which have no warrant but in the flights of his own fancy.

It should also be observed that the insertions, omissions and modifications attributed to the Redactors are merely ingenious methods of evading or explaining away phenomena at variance with the proper requirements of the hypothesis. Wherever it is assumed that the Redactor has altered the characteristic words or phrases of his sources, has modified their language or ideas or inserted expressions and views of his own, the meaning simply is that the facts do not correspond with the hypothesis. The proof relied upon to establish the existence of these otherwise unknown documents is that they are uniformly characterized by a certain diction, style and mode of thought. But inasmuch as they are not always so characterized, they must have been changed by the Redactors. This is building the hypothesis upon the hypothesis and supporting assumption by assumption. It is plain that every alleged interference of the Redactors weakens by so much the evidence on which the hypothesis itself reposes.

Another evasive expedient which naturally creates distrust in critical processes as they are at present conducted, is the minute subdivision to which the Redactors are at times assumed to have resorted in piecing together their sources. It might with a show of reason be claimed that a judgment can be formed of the authorship of considerable paragraphs and sections from their diction and style. But that individual sentences and clauses can be referred with any certainty to their proper authors, or that a sensible compiler would have constructed his paragraphs like a piece of mosaic from bits and scraps culled alternately from different documents, or that any semblance of continuity could be given to paragraphs so framed, it is not easy to suppose. This simply amounts to a confession that the phenomena cannot be brought into harmony with the hypothesis by any less violent procedure. What the critics reckon to be criteria of distinct writers are found closely conjoined in sections which have every appearance of proceeding from the same pen, but which under the requirements of the hypothesis must be torn to shreds.

The present discussion will be limited to the first eleven chapters of Exodus, which together with chapters 12, 13, whose unity has been sufficiently treated elsewhere,[1] cover the entire abode of the children of Israel in Egypt. This is a portion quite long enough to test the hypothesis, and to exhibit its principles and methods, while it is as much as can be brought under review in the space at our command. And it is besides especially suited to our purpose; for the assumption of preexisting documents in Genesis does not stand in such obvious conflict with Mosaic authorship as the extension of this hypothesis into the books that follow.

The section proposed for consideration may be divided into two parts: 1. Chapter 1-7:7, the oppression of Israel in Egypt and the preparation of Moses to be a deliverer; 2. 7:8-11:10, the plagues by which Pharaoh's obstinacy was broken and Israel released. In the first part the critics assign to P 1:1-7, 13, 14 (except some words in verses 7, 14, and perhaps verse 6), 2:23*b*-25, 6:2-7:7.

It is alleged that chapter 3 and 6:2ff. are parallel accounts of the same transaction. Everything is duplicated. God twice reveals to Moses his name Jehovah (3:13-15, 6:2, 3), and twice announces to him his purpose to deliver Israel and bring them to Canaan by his instrumentality (3:7-10, 6:6-8, 11), and upon Moses' pleading unfitness Aaron is twice associated with him (4:10-16, 6:30-7:2). The critical hypothesis, it is said, is here explicitly justified. These accounts must be from two different writers, 6:2ff. from P, and chapter 3 from E. This being in the intent of each writer according to the critics the first communication of the name Jehovah, neither of them could have employed this name in the antecedent portion of his narrative. All preceding passages that contain the name Jehovah, must accordingly be by a third writer, J, who had a different view of its origin. A firm basis, it is contended, is thus laid for tracing the record to three distinct sources.

But this is foisting a meaning upon these passages which they plainly will not bear. It is inconsistent, 1. with the repeated occurrence of the name Jehovah in the antecedent history, showing that the author of the **Pentateuch** in its present form, whether Moses, or if the critics please, the three Redactors (Rj, Rd and Rp), did not so understand them. 2. With chapter 3 itself. If the author meant that the name Jehovah was first revealed in 3:14, 15 and systematically abstained for that reason from using it before, he could not use it as he does in verses 2, 4, 7. The critics confess this and expunge Jehovah from these verses as an insertion by R, thus reconstructing the text in accordance with their hypothesis. And how could a name previously unheard of assure the children of Israel that Moses had really been commissioned by the God of their fathers (3:13, 15)? 3. With the real meaning of 6:2ff., which is not that Abraham, Isaac and Jacob had never heard the word Jehovah, but that they had had no such experience of what the name involved as was now to be granted to their descendants. God is known by his name Jehovah not by the utterance of the word but by an experience of what it denotes. It is so uniformly throughout the Scriptures, *e.g.,* Isa. 52:6. Jer. 9:24, 16:21, Ezek. 39:6, 7. God's not being known by the patriarchs by his name Jehovah is in evident contrast with the repeated declarations that Israel (6:7, 10:2), the Egyptians (7:5, 14:4, 18), and Pharaoh (7:17, 8:10, 22, 9:14, 29, comp. 5:2), should know that he was Jehovah.

The support which the critics would draw for their hypothesis from Ex. iii. and vi.:2, etc., thus collapses entirely. As these passages do not declare the occasion of the first employment of the name Jehovah, there is no propriety in regarding them as distinct versions of the same event, and thus tracing them to separate writers; nor in holding that they present a different view of the origin of the name Jehovah from those sections of Genesis which employ it from the earliest periods, and are in consequence referred to a third writer.

That chapter iii. and chapter vi. relate different events is as plain as the history can make it. One took place at Horeb, the other in Egypt. They occurred at different times and at distinct stages in God's revelation to Moses; one when Moses was first commissioned, the other after he had, in pursuance of his commission, made a demand upon Pharaoh on the people's behalf which only resulted in increasing their burdens. That under these circumstances the Lord should renew his former assurances to Moses with increased emphasis, that the people should lose the faith (6:9) which they had before (4:31), that Moses, who had distrusted his own qualifications at the beginning (4:10), should now be hopeless of success with Pharaoh (6:12), and that Aaron, who had been appointed to help him with the people (4:16), should now be made his assistant before the king (7:1, 2), is perfectly natural and suggests no suspicion that the story is repeating itself.

The narrative assigned to P is halting at every point from the want of those connecting or explanatory parts which have been sundered from it. The critics violate their own maxim that repetitions give evidence of distinct writers by confessing that the enumeration of Jacob's family (Ex. 1:1-5) can only be an abridgment by P of his own fuller statement Gen. 46:8-27; and their multiplication (Ex. 1:7) had already been stated by him in almost identical terms (Gen. 47:27). From this he leaps quite unaccountably to their oppression by the Egyptians (verses 13, 14), who had so hospitably received them. This needs for its explanation the omitted verses 8-12, in which moreover "more and mightier" . . . (verse 9) is a plain verbal allusion to "multiplied and waxed exceeding mighty" . . . (verse 7), as is also "multiply" (verses 10, 12), "multiplied and waxed very mighty" (verse 20). In fact verse 7 supplies the keynote of all that follows in the chapter, binding the whole indissolubly together. Verse 9 severed from it is quite unexplained in a writer who had spoken of the descent of Jacob's family into Egypt, but had said nothing of the great increase of his descendants. Verse 6, "And Joseph died," etc., plainly prepares the way for verse 8, the "new king which knew not Joseph." The "mortar and brick" (verse 14) both allude to the building of treasure cities (verse 11), and to the brickmaking of 5:7, etc., which is associated with "burdens" (5:4, 5), as in 1:11, 14. These obvious references by one writer to paragraphs assigned to another are evaded by various feats of critical surgery which have no justification but the necessity created by the hypothesis.

From the account of Egyptian oppression (1:13, 14) whose meagre baldness is due to its having been rent from its proper place in the series of inflictions of growing severity (verses 11-22), P springs at once to 2:23*b*-25 with its mention of a covenant with Isaac, although none such is recorded except by J (Gen. 26:2-5, 24); and thence to 6:2, etc., where God suddenly speaks to Moses and shortly after (verse 13), to Moses and Aaron, as if they were well-known personages, though there had been no previous mention of their existence. This incongruity, created by the removal of the very account (chapter 2, etc.,) here presupposed, gives rise to new critical assumptions. Kuenen fancies that P had spoken before of Moses and Aaron in some passage which has not been preserved. Kayser gets rid of the allusion to Aaron by referring 6:13-30 to the Redactor. Dillmann declines to do this, but with a like view of finding the first mention of Aaron in 7:1 he transposes 6:30-7:5 before 6:13 and places 7:6 immediately after it. Wellhausen undertakes to supply the missing mention of Moses and Aaron by the conjecture that the account of their ancestry (6:16ff.) may originally have preceded 6:2, though the record of Aaron's wife and children (verse 23, etc.) is in his judgment inappropriate and a later addition. But the appositeness of the entire genealogy, every clause of

which is in analogy with those previously given, appears from the fact that it not only introduces Aaron and Moses, who are just entering upon the momentous task assigned them, but likewise Korah, Nadab, Abihu, Eleazar, Ithamar and Phinehas, who are to figure in the subsequent history. Nöldeke confesses the suitableness of the table in general, but stumbles at the sons of Reuben and Simeon (verses 14, 15) as here uncalled for, and in his opinion an interpolation. Jülicher very properly replies that an interpolator would not have stopped with inserting these two names only, when there was equal reason for adding all the rest of Jacob's sons. In fact there is a suitableness in verses 14, 15 standing where they do to indicate Levi's place as the third in age in his father's family. Jülicher proposes to relieve the suddenness of the mention of Moses in 6:2 by transposing before it the entire genealogy with 6:13 as its title, which will thus connect directly with 2:25; although this would place "Jehovah" in 6:13 prior to what he considers the first revelation of this name in 6:2, 3. But after all this self-imposed trouble and these fruitless conjectures of the critics, it is difficult to see why the reasons, be what they may, which led the imaginary Redactor to give to this whole passage its present position, may not have been equally influential with the original writer. This busy tinkering betokens merely a weak spot, which needs in some way to be covered up.

It is urged that 6:2ff. would connect well with 2:23-25, to which its language contains manifest allusions—"heard the groaning," "children of Israel," "remembered my covenant," "bondage," "Abraham, Isaac and Jacob." But each of these passages connects perfectly with its present context. And while there is an obvious and designed relationship between them, they need not on that account have been contiguous. On the other hand, it is perfectly plain that 2:23-25 is bound in the closest manner to the immediately following chapter, which must have proceeded from the same pen, and cannot possibly have been from a different writer and independently conceived, as the critics would have us suppose. God's appearance to Moses (chapter 3) and the message which he gives him flow directly from 2:23-25, which shapes the expressions used, *e. g.,* the motive drawn from God's relation to Abraham, Isaac and Jacob (3:6, 15), God saw, heard and knew (3:7), (precisely as 2:24, 25 where A. V. "looked upon" is in Heb. "saw," and "had respect unto" is in Heb. "knew"), the cry (. . . 2:23 . . .) of the children of Israel came unto God (3:7, 9).

In 6:6-8 the criteria of the different writers are sadly mixed; "bondage," "stretched out arm," "judgments," which belong to P are combined with "burdens," "rid," "bring into the land," and God's swearing to give the land, of which lifting the hand is the significant gesture, elsewhere attributed to J or E. Among the phrases counted as P's are "of uncircumcised lips" (6:12, 30),

which occurs nowhere else, and can therefore be no criterion of style; groaning (2:24, 6:5), and nowhere else in the **Pentateuch**; "Pharaoh king of Egypt" (6:11, 13, 27, 29), which is also found (Gen. 41:46) in JE; God remembering (6:5), but also (Gen. 30:22, Ex. 32:13) in JE; "wonders" (7:3), but also (4:21) in JE; "armies" or hosts (6:26, 7:4), but also (Gen. 21:22, 32, 26:26) in JE; and though it does not chance to be applied to Israel, other expressions are used suggesting the same conception; "judgments" (6:6, 7:4), and but twice elsewhere in the **Pentateuch**; "bring forth my people, the children of Israel" (7:4), as 3:10 E.

But the most striking words and phrases of this passage are drawn from Gen. 17:1, 7, 8, which it reproduces almost completely, "appeared to Abraham," "God Almighty," "establish my covenant," "give the land of Canaan," "land of their pilgrimage," "I will be to you a God." And in almost every instance in which these same expressions are found elsewhere, they are directly and obviously traceable to this one source. They cannot properly be urged, therefore, as characteristics of style. They simply show familiarity with the passage upon which they are all alike based. The critics nevertheless use them as criteria; and every passage that contains them is for that reason, wherever it is at all practicable, assigned to P. And yet "God Almighty" is confessedly found in J (Gen. 43:14), and "Almighty" in Gen. 49:25. The phrase "establish a covenant" suggests its perpetuity. It is accordingly used only of God's covenants and chiefly of those with Noah and Abraham, when prominence was to be given to the idea of their permanence. The alternate phrase attributed to J, "make (Heb. *cut*) a covenant," is equally applicable to those of men, and is used of a divine covenant only when the thought is directed to its ratification, especially if that was solemnized, as in Gen. 15:18, Ex. 24:8, by sacrificial rites. Comp. Ps. 50:5. "Land of Canaan," according to Kayser, occurs in JE no less than fifteen times in the book of Genesis. "Pilgrimage" (or wherein he was a stranger) is found six times in Genesis, and is in every instance referred to P. "I will be to you a God" is here associated with a phrase, "I will take you to me for a people," which occurs nowhere else in P.

The result so far as concerns the passages assigned to P is this: The critics sunder a few verses from their present connection in which they fit perfectly well, and omitting the intervening sections, they claim that these verses were originally continuous. But the omissions leave gaps unfilled and confuse events shown to be distinct by recorded differences of place and circumstances, needlessly assuming discrepancies which are wholly created by these critical processes, and imputing incapacity or fraud to the Redactor or the author of the book in its present form. And that the characteristic diction which is the principal plea urged for this critical dissection is not such as to warrant it, appears from the occasional intermingling of the criteria of different documents, from the fact that some of the alleged criteria are of so rare occurrence as to be no evidence of style; that others exhibit conformity to sundry other paragraphs simply because all are alike drawn from one fundamental passage; and others still are not peculiar to P, but found in what is ascribed to J or E as well.

After removing P's share of 1:1-7:7, the critics are not a little perplexed in their attempt to parcel the remainder between J and E.[2] Kayser thinks it impossible to disentangle the two accounts without breaking the connection. Kuenen confesses that "here we cannot separate two distinct documents and assign its share to each with confidence. The most we can hope for is to determine whether it is E or J that lies at the basis of the narrative; and sometimes even this is doubtful." Wellhausen gives to J 1:8-10 because of its resemblance to Gen. 11:6,7, thus depriving the oppression 1:11, 12 in E of its motive; also verses 20*b*, 22, making this barbarous edict the very first expedient instead of a desperate resort after all other attempts had failed, and sundering it from E's account of Moses' infancy (2: 1-10), which presupposes it throughout. Dillmann, Schrader and Jülicher avoid these incongruities by excluding J from chapter 1 altogether.

That Moses' parents are spoken of indefinitely in 2:1 while the line of his descent is accurately traced in 6:10 is no proof of diversity of authors, one of whom had more exact information than the other. The precise statement was purposely reserved for the supreme crisis in Moses' life, and the new period in Israel's history thus opened as the most fitting place for his genealogy in accordance with the plan of the **Pentateuch.** Wellhausen is alone in the attempt, which after all he confesses to be impracticable, to sunder 2:1-10 into two inconsistent stories, one of which knows nothing of an older sister of Moses, nor of his mother being engaged as nurse.

Schrader fancies an inconsistency in the motive for Moses' flight (verse 14 and verse 15), and so assigns 2:1-14 to E and verses 15-23*a* to J. Dillmann admits that no such inconsistency exists, but retains the same division, thus connecting verses 11-14 with verses 1-10, to which verse 11 evidently alludes. Wellhausen, on the other hand, connects them with verses 15-23*a*, and verse 15 is unintelligible without them. In fact both are right; verses 11-14 link the whole chapter together, being alike firmly bound to what precedes and to what follows; and so Julicher confesses, who refers 2:1-22 to E, as the allusions in 18:3, 4 E to 2:15, 22 further require. But in giving verse 23*a* to J, he severs it from verse 15, to which it manifestly alludes.

While attributing the story of Moses' birth and infancy to E and his residence in Midian to J, the critics nevertheless confess that J and E must alike have recorded both. E must have had a section similar to that which is imputed to J, and J must have had one similar to that of E. So that after the narrative has been sundered in twain, it is straightway necessary to assume that each part originally had just such a complement as has been severed from it.

In chapters 3-5 it is once more assumed that J and E had parallel accounts which have been interwoven in the most intricate manner. Dillmann derives chapters 3 and 5 from E, though with modifications from R in almost every verse. Wellhausen derives chapter 5 and 3:1-9, 16-20 from J and Julicher also from J nearly the whole of chapter 5 together with 3:7, 8, 16-22. Dillmann assigns 3:1 to J in distinction from 2:18 E, because the Reuel of the latter is in the former called Jethro. These verses are alike attributed to J by Wellhausen and to E by Jülicher, on the assumption that the name Reuel was a subsequent addition, and in the opinion of Wellhausen Jethro likewise. But this interchange of names warrants no critical conclusions whatever, the simple explanation being that Reuel is his proper name, and Jethro, as Clericus long since observed, his official designation; so that there is no more mystery in the case than in the substitution of "Pharaoh" for "king of Egypt" (1:18, 19).

Wellhausen admits that 3:1-4:17 creates the impression of "a piece from one casting." The critics, however, insist that there is an incongruity implying diversity of authorship between 4:19 (J) Moses' return to Egypt by immediate divine direction and verse 18 (E), his previous resolution to go with Jethro's permission. In verses 20a, 24-26 (J) he takes his family with him evidently intending to remain, whereas verse 18 (E) merely contemplates his going alone on a brief visit and chapter 18 (E) his wife and children remained with Jethro, where verse 2b, "after he had sent her back," is regarded as a harmonizing interpolation by R. In 4:17, 20b (E) "this rod" and "the signs" (with the article in Heb.) seem in their present connection to refer to verses 1-9 (J); but the rod was there used in only one sign, and then not as an instrument but as the object wrought upon. The conclusion is thence drawn that the allusion is not to verses 1-9, but to some narrative now lost in which a miraculous rod was given to Moses with directions regarding the signs to be wrought by it. Again the signs in verses 1-9 were to be exhibited before the people (verses 1, 5), while verse 21 (E) speaks of "wonders before Pharaoh," and of his return to Egypt as yet future, whereas in verse 20a (J) he had already returned.

Chapter 4:10-12, recording Moses' reluctance and God's promise to be with his mouth, is assigned to J. With this Wellhausen and Jülicher regard the appointment of Aaron to be his spokesman as incompatible; they therefore eject verses 13-16 as a later addition, notwithstanding the identical phrases, "O, my Lord"

(verses 10, 13) and the coincidences in verses 12, 15. Consistency then obliges them to trace verses 27, 28 to Rj, and to attribute to the same source the insertion of Aaron's name in verses 29-31 (J,) so as to make it appear that in J's original account it was Moses who spake to the people and performed the signs. Dillmann sets all this aside by pointing out that verses 13-16 do not annul but confirm verse 12. God promises to be with Moses' mouth as well as with Aaron's, and Aaron is associated with Moses, not substituted for him. There is consequently no discrepancy and no need of assuming an interpolation, whether of these verses or of verses 27, 28, or an unauthorized insertion of Aaron's name. But as Dillmann imputes 3:18 to E (contrary to Wellh. and Jül.), and thence infers that E speaks of the elders and J of Aaron, verses 29-31 are sliced accordingly. Parts of verses 29, 31 are assigned to E, viz., "he gathered all the elders of the children of Israel; . . . and they heard that Jehovah had visited the children of Israel and that he had looked upon their affliction;" and the remainder to J. From all which it appears how easy it is for a critic to manipulate or sunder the text in accordance with a preconceived theory, be that what it may.

The discrepancies alleged in this chapter are so manifestly of the critics' own making that it seems a needless waste of words to refute them. After Moses had been commissioned to deliver Israel, 3:1-4:17, he obtained Jethro's permission to return to Egypt, ver. 18. Whereupon the Lord confirms his resolution by the encouraging information of the death of those who sought his life, ver. 19. This had been before communicated to the reader, 2; 23a, but Moses did not know it until now. The explanatory remark 18:2b showing the consistency of the narrative is rejected by the critics as an interpolation, without the slightest authority and contrary to all reason, for the mere sake of creating a contradiction where none exists. The rod, 4:17, as is plain from 7:15, is that of 4:2-4, and the signs are those—whether heretofore described or not—which were to be wrought by its instrumentality, in the presence both of the people and of Pharaoh. The preliminary statement that Moses returned to the land of Egypt is made at the outset, ver. 20, before detailing the occurrences on the way, just as the comprehensive statement is made, 7:6, that Moses and Aaron did, as the Lord commanded them, prior to the detailed narrative which extends through this and the subsequent chapters.

The section 7:8-11:10 is acknowledged to show a regular progression in the severity and effectiveness of the plagues described until they reach their awful climax in the death of the first-born and the deliverance of Israel. It is nevertheless affirmed that it yields to critical analysis, and that by following suggestions furnished by the preceding chapters it can be separated into three constituents. P makes Aaron the prophet of

Moses, 7:1, insists on letting the children of Israel go unconditionally, 6:11, 7:2, and declares that Jehovah will lead forth his people in spite of Pharaoh's continued refusal, 7:5. J and E make Moses the speaker before the king, 4:22; he only asks permission to hold a feast in the wilderness, 5:1, 3, and Pharaoh shall himself drive the people out of his land, 6:1. According to E. 4:17, but not J, the miracles were to be wrought by Moses with his rod.

Guided by these criteria the critics resolve the plagues as follows.[3] In P Aaron with his rod works the miracles. These are conceived of not as plagues inflicted on the Egyptians so much as exhibitions of power, with which the sorcerers vie with partial success at first but to their final discomfiture. P uses a fixed form with regularly recurring phrases, "Jehovah spake unto Moses, Say unto Aaron Stretch out thy rod, etc., that there may be, etc. And they did so. And Aaron stretched out his rod, etc., and there was, etc. And the magician's did so with their enchantments, etc. And Pharaoh's heart was hardened, and he hearkened not unto them, as Jehovah had said."

In J Moses goes to Pharaoh and demands that he should let the people go to serve Jehovah, and threatens him, in case of refusal, with a particular plague mostly at a fixed time. This is inflicted by Jehovah without any human instrumentality. Thereupon the king commonly summons Moses and Aaron—the latter being simply the companion of Moses—and asks their intercession, promising to let the people go. Moses consents to intercede, mostly designating an interval beforehand, and at the appointed time the plague is removed. In some of the plagues a distinction is expressly made between Israel and Egypt.

In E, which is much more fragmentary than the others, the miracles are wrought by the rod of Moses, and after particular plagues Pharaoh makes greater and greater concessions.

Upon this scheme no one of the narrators has recorded all the plagues. P only four, J six, E four or five. All these unite upon one (blood); two on four (P and J frogs; J and E flies, hail, locusts). Of the four remaining, two (lice, boils) are peculiar to P, one (murrain) to J, and one (darkness) to E. Whence it is inferred that these different traditions agreed that certain extraordinary events preceded and facilitated the exodus; but they were not agreed as to what these events were. The gravity of the conclusion makes it important that we should examine with some care the basis upon which it rests.

It requires but a moment's inspection to see that the alleged diversities, which are made the criteria of the different writers, and are urged in justification of the proposed severance, do not exist. Thus the alleged

superior prominence of Aaron in P is groundless. Precisely the same function is assigned to him 4:14-16 (J) as in 7:2 (P). According to 4:30 (J) "Aaron spake the words which the Lord had spoken to Moses and did the signs"—the very criterion by which the critics propose to distinguish P. So in 5:1 (E) Moses and Aaron go in and speak to Pharaoh. Here, as in other passages assigned to JE where the two brothers are combined, the critics summarily eject "Aaron" from the text for no reason but to adapt it better to their hypothesis. Moses was directed, 3:18 (E), to take the elders with him to the king. This is no warrant, however, for substituting the elders for Aaron in 5:1, confirmed as the latter is by verses 4. 20. It simply shows that the writer was not painfully precise in stating everything in so many words which could be readily enough inferred from what he had said previously. Moreover Aaron did not work all the miracles which the critics ascribe to P. Not to speak of the plague of the firstborn (12:12) which was inflicted by Jehovah without human agency, the boils were produced not by Aaron's rod, but by Moses sprinkling ashes toward heaven (9:8, 10); so that by the confession of the critics the miracles recorded by the same writer need not all be wrought by an absolutely uniform method. It is purely arbitrary, therefore, on their own principles, to refer 9:22, 23, 10:12, 13, 21, 22 to a different writer from 7:19, 8:5, 6, 16, 17, where the expressions are identical even to the remarkable interchange of "hand" and "rod," only the actor is Moses instead of Aaron. In 11:10 P ascribes the miracles to the agency of Moses as well as Aaron.

Besides, if the letter of 7:2, 3 be pressed, no mention is there made of Aaron as concerned in working miracles. God says that He will himself multiply his signs and wonders (the very feature attributed to J), while Aaron is simply to speak to Pharaoh. Express mention is made (10:3, 8) (J) of Aaron as joined with Moses in speaking to Pharaoh, which, coupled with the fact that the king was in the habit of summoning both the brothers to an interview, makes it probable that whenever Moses is said to have spoken to Pharaoh the meaning is that he did so through the medium of Aaron. But however this may be, if we accept the division made by the critics, P never represents either Moses or Aaron as uttering a word to Pharaoh. A series of miracles is wrought with no other object apparently than to see whether Aaron can outdo Pharaoh's jugglers. It is repeated time after time that Pharaoh's heart was hardened, and he hearkened not unto them. But what they had said or to what Pharaoh refused to listen does not appear. Jülicher makes himself merry over P's description, which he likens to a tournament with its successive feats at arms, and in which no regard is had to time or place. Moses and Aaron remain in the presence of the king from beginning to end, whether in the palace or the open air is not said, only once running into a neighboring house for some ashes, the miracles crowding one upon another in quick succession till all are ended. He seems quite unconscious that his ridicule really falls upon the absurd division which the critics have made of a narrative that is perspicuous and well ordered throughout.

The alleged difference in the demand made upon Pharaoh in P and in J and E is also without foundation, as is evident from what has just been said. P records no demand whatever upon Pharaoh in even a single instance. That the king's unreasonable obstinacy might be set in the strongest light, no more is ever asked of him than to let Israel go for three days in the wilderness to sacrifice to Jehovah. This is stated fully in the first interview (5:1, 3), but commonly in the briefer form "let my people go, that they may serve me" (8:1). Every such application to Pharaoh is without exception referred either to J or E, and an attempt made to establish a difference in their phraseology—as though J said "serve" and E "sacrifice," or "hold a feast"—which can only be carried through by assuming that wherever the wrong word is used it has been altered by R. As no passage is allowed to P in which Moses and Aaron address the king on this subject there is no material for comparison. The reason why the limited form of the request is nowhere found in P is simply because every paragraph or clause in which it is expressed or implied is for that reason declared not to belong to him. To be sure, Moses and Aaron are directed in P to speak to Pharaoh to let Israel go out of his land (6:11, 7:2, comp. 11:10), but the form of expression is precisely parallel to 7:14 J. And that it was the divine intention from the outset to effect Israel's absolute release is as plain from what is attributed to J and E (3:8, 10, 19, 20), as from anything contained in P.

And that Pharaoh, constrained by God's strong hand, should drive Israel out of his land (6:1, JE) is not inconsistent with P's declaration (7:4) that Pharaoh should refuse to hearken, and that the Lord would bring forth Israel out of Egypt by great judgments. JE gives the solution 3:19, 20. The design of the judgments was to break Pharaoh's obstinacy and compel his stout heart to yield. And P nowhere affirms that at the critical moment of Israel's departure they had failed to accomplish this end.

The basis on which the critics professedly rest their analysis thus fails them at every point.

The space devoted to different plagues varies considerably; and it has been urged that this indicates the composite character of the narrative. But this argument is of no avail for the critics, for the disparity continues after they have made their partition. Murrain (J) and darkness (E) have in all but seven verses each; while after E and R have each had their share Dillmann still reserves fifteen verses for J in the account of the hail, and thirteen in that of the locusts. It is further observ-

able that the attendant circumstances and the dealings with Pharaoh are assigned to JE, while P is limited to the bare record of the plague itself. This is an unwarranted sundering of what belongs together, and is only properly intelligible in connection.

Scarcely any account is made of diction in dividing this section; and, as it would appear, with good reason, for what is urged is meagre enough. P uses the term "wonders" (7:3, 9, 11:9, 10), but so does E (4:21); and "pool" (7:19), which occurs but twice besides in the whole **Pentateuch.** P says "hearken to," J "hearken to the voice of." "Magicians," though in Genesis used by E, is here ascribed to P. Three words are employed to denote the hardening of Pharaoh's heart, which vary slightly in signification, . . . hard or obdurate, . . . stout or obstinate, . . . heavy, hard to move or stubborn. These are used in both intransitive and transitive forms, and the latter with the Lord of Pharaoh himself as subjects. Strenuous endeavours have been made to parcel these in some distinctive way among the different writers; but with all the liberties that the critics have allowed themselves, they have not been very successful as yet.

In 8:15 J's phrase "hardened his heart" and P's "hearkened not unto them" occur together; and instead of drawing the natural conclusion that one writer used both phrases the critics split the sentence and divide it between J and P. Two different words for "hardening" occur after the plague of hail (9:34, 35), one transitive attributing it to Pharaoh's own agency, the other intransitive. Instead of admitting that the same writer has here used both words, the critics isolate the second verse from its context and seek for it some other connection. The same thing is done with 10:20, where the wrong word occurs for the theory. The theory rules, and the text is remodelled to correspond. . . .

If two of these supposititious writers employ the same word to express this idea, and one of them uses two distinct words for the purpose, why is it not quite as easy to suppose that the same writer has, for the sake of varying the expression of a thought so frequently repeated, employed all three of the terms? The theory neither explains nor simplifies the matter, and is not worth the pains that are taken to carry it consistently through.

P has a different word for "serpent" (7:9, 10, 12) from that of J (4:3). The critics find here two versions of the same story, which J locates in the desert and P at the court of Pharaoh. In Dillmann's opinion the latter is the original form of the incident, while Jülicher is equally confident that the former is its proper place. They are both right; each occurrence was appropriate to the occasion on which it is related. And it is not unlikely that the new application of the miracle suggested the altered term, so that the ordinary word for serpent was replaced by one less usual, which may possibly have had special appositeness to Egypt, or to the arts of serpent charmers. Enough is not known of the usage of the word to verify this conjecture; but it is more plausible surely than the critical assumption that it is an unmeaning characteristic of style.

According to Knobel and Schrader, P's account of the first plague, the change of water to blood, is found in 7:19-22. But if that be so, one of the discrepancies insisted on between P and JE ceases to exist. It is said that P represents all the water in the land of Egypt as turned to blood, while JE limits this to the water of the river. But while verse 19 speaks of streams and rivers and ponds and pools and even the water in vessels of wood and stone as converted into blood, verse 20 lays stress only upon the water of the river, and verse 21 speaks of the fish dying in the river and the impossibility of drinking the water of the river. Noldeke and Kayser, therefore, assign these last two verses which occur in the midst of P's statement to JE, with the exception of the first clause of verse 20, "And Moses and Aaron did so as the LORD commanded." Dillmann and Wellhausen do the same, only they except in addition the last clause of verse 21, "And there was blood throughout all the land of Egypt."

The last named critics further undertake to separate J from E. They call attention to the sudden change of speaker in verse 17. In the first clause "I" means Jehovah; in the second clause with no formal indication that another is speaking, "I" as evidently means Moses. This is regarded as indicating a confusion in the text arising from the blending of two accounts. Verses 14 to 17, as far as the words "Behold, I," or "I will smite," belong to J, who attributes the plagues to the immediate agency of God. The remainder of verse 17 and perhaps verse 18 belong to E, who always employs the instrumentality of Moses' rod. E's account recommences verse 20 with the words, "And he (the pronoun is by the critics referred to Moses) lifted up the rod," etc., and continues in verse 21 as far as "water of the river," and finally embraces verses 23, 24. Then verse 25, which speaks of Jehovah smiting the river, is the conclusion of J's account. This partition by Dillmann, from which Wellhausen's varies slightly, is exceedingly ingenious, and accommodated with marvellous skill to the phenomena of these verses. The close verbal correspondence between verses 17*b*, 18 and 20*b*, 21*a*, the correspondence again between verse 19 and 8:5, and the divergence between verses 19 and 20, seem at first sight to recommend it.

But a moment's reflection is sufficient to show that it cannot be correct. 1. The message to Pharaoh (verses 14-18), the direction to Aaron to execute what had been announced to Pharaoh (verse 19), and his doing as he was directed (verse 20), belong together, and are necessary to complete one another. They cannot be

assigned to different writers without making each part a disconnected fragment. According to the critics' division J gives no account of the infliction of the plague; and E's portion begins in the middle of a sentence, with no intimation who is speaking or to whom the words are addressed. 2. The verbal correspondence already remarked upon is no argument for the divisive hypothesis, for it is at once explained if all is from the same writer. The double application of the pronoun "I" in verse 17 obviously arises from the fact that the words are those of Moses (verse 16), who passes from direct citation of the language of Jehovah, to speaking in his own person, as the prophets and other messengers of the Most High so often do. The assumption that it is due to the Redactor's confusing separate sentences imputes a degree of carelessness or stupidity to him that is quite inconceivable. The mention of the rod, so far from being out of place or requiring the assumption of a different writer, is just what verse 15 prepares us to expect. Moses is there told to take in his hand the rod which was turned to a serpent, in order of course to use it in working the miracle. This is particularly perplexing to the critics, for it completely annuls their distinction of J and E. It is in a context belonging to J. It refers explicitly to 4:2, 3, also belonging to J, and of which E knows nothing. And yet it implies a use of the rod characteristic of E and foreign to J. They can only get rid of it, as they rid themselves of everything inconsistent with their hypothesis, by expunging it from the text as an insertion by R.

There is no inconsistency in Moses speaking of smiting the waters, when in fact they were smitten by Aaron at his bidding. Moses simply acts through the instrumentality of Aaron. Nor is there any want of agreement between the command "Take thy rod and stretch out thine hand upon the waters" and the consequent action, "he lifted up the rod and smote the waters." Stretching out the rod and smiting with the rod are similarly combined (8:16, 17), only there both terms are inserted in each clause, while here the two clauses supplement each other. That the action cannot be severed from the preceding command and assigned to a different writer is further apparent because in that case there would be no detailed statement as in the parallel instances (8:6, 17) of Aaron's doing as he was directed. Nor is there any discrepancy in all the waters of Egypt becoming blood, whereas Moses had simply spoken to Pharaoh of the water of the river. This was singled out as the most conspicuous and important; and so again in recording the fulfillment, which yet proceeds to add that there was blood throughout all the land of Egypt. And the suggestion that the Lord's smiting the river involves a different conception from its waters being changed to blood when smitten by divine direction refutes itself.

The plague of blood thus refuses to yield to the analysis of the critics. They reduce a connected and well arranged narrative to mutilated fragments upon pleas which will not bear examination. With others of the plagues they are less successful still; notably so with those of the hail and locusts. In fact they confess themselves that the analysis cannot be carried through: and the marvellous medley which they make is apparent from the manner in which they riddle the text into bits in their attempt to disentangle J and E.

One plea for the critical partition of the plagues remains to be briefly considered. It is that while there is an evident plan and progress in them in various respects, this is intermittent instead of being continuous throughout. It is commonly conceded that there is a consistent advance in severity from first to last. But the magicians only appear in the 1st, 2nd, 3rd and 6th. The effect on the king is noted in the 2nd, 4th, 7th, 8th and 9th. The 1st, 2nd and 4th, and especially the 7th and 8th, are related in a diffuse and circumstantial manner, while in other cases the record is briefer and more scanty.

But the complaint arises wholly from the failure to observe the scheme of the whole. The nine plagues preceding the tenth and last are arranged in three series of three each. In the first two members of each series the plague is preannounced to Pharaoh, the first beginning each time with the same identical phrase (7:15, 8:20, 9:13); so the second more briefly (8:1, 9:1, 10:1); in the third no preannouncement is made (8:16, 9:8, 10:20). In the first three the magicians use their enchantments, failing in the third, after which they make no further attempt, and are only mentioned once again in the plague inflicted upon persons, where their discomfiture is completed by their suffering from boils like the rest. From the first member of the second series onward a distinction is made between Egypt and Goshen, where the children of Israel dwelt. In the first series and again in the second the king sent once for Moses and Aaron to intercede for him in that particular plague which he found personally most distressing; in the last series the unparalleled character of each is specially remarked, and the king sent for Moses and Aaron at each successive plague with increasing urgency. The first series is regularly brought on by Aaron with his rod, the third by Moses with his rod; in the second no rod is mentioned. Other particulars might be noted; but these are sufficient to show that there is a regular scheme consistently carried out from first to last, such as cannot be accounted for by the promiscuous blending of different independent accounts.

The critics can say plausible things in defence of their hypothesis, and they show surprising adroitness in handling it. But it seems to me that it is clogged with insuperable difficulties which should prevent its acceptance by thoughtful and considerate minds who are not captivated by brilliant novelties, and who are not

willing to surrender the truth of the sacred history and the firm basis on which it rests, until some good reason can be given for so doing.

Notes

[1] The Hebrew Feasts, ch. iii. and iv.

[2] WELLHAUSEN.

J. 1:6, 8-10, 20*b*, 22; 2:11-23*a*; 3:1-9, 16-20; 4:1-12, [13-16], 18, 20a, 24-26, 27-31; 5:1-6:1.

E. 1:11, 12, 15-20*a*, 21; 2:1-10; 3:10-15, 21, 22; 4:17, 19, 20*b*, 21-23.

Modified by R. 3:4, 6, 9, 21, 22; 4:17, 27-30.

DILLMANN.

J. 2:15-23*a*; 4:1-16, 19, 20*a* [22,23 transposed from elsewhere], 24-29*a*, 30, 31*a, c*.

E. Chapter 3 (verses 2*, 4*, 7*, 8*, 17*, 22*); 4:17, 18, 20*b*, 21, 29*b*, 31*b*; chapter 5 (verses 1*, 2*, 4*, 5*, 6*, 9*, 10*, 11*b**, 13*, 14*, 15*, 19*, 20*, 21*-23*.

The verses marked with an asterisk have been modified by the Redactor.

JULICHER.

J. 2:23*a*; 4:19, 20*a*, 24-26; 3:7, 8, 16-22; 4:1-12, 29, 30*b*, 31; 5:3, 4, 6-21, 22, 23; 6:1.

E. 1:8-12, 15-22; 2:1-21; 3:1-6, 9-14; 4:17, 18, 20*b*; 5:1, 2, 5.

R. 1:20; 2:22, 25; 3:15; 4:13-16, 21-23, 27, 28, 30*a*,

[3] WELLHAUSEN.

P. 7:8-13, (1) 7:19, 20*a*, 21*c*, 22, 23 (2) 8:5-7, 15*b*, (3) 8:16-19 (6) 9:8-12, 11:9, 10.

J. (1) 7:14-18, (2) 7:25, 8:1-4, 8-15*a*, (4) 8:20-32, (5) 9:1-7, (7) 9:13-21, 22*-25*, 26-34, (8) 10:1*-11, 13*b*, 14*b*, 15*-19, (9) 10:28, 29, 11:4-8.

E. (1) 7:17*b*, 20*b*, 21*a, b*, 24, (7) 9:22*-24*, 35, (8) 10:12, 13*a*, 14*a*, 15*, 20, (9) 10:21-27, 11:1-3.

DILLMANN

P. 7:8-13, (1) 7:19, 20*a*, 21*b*, 22, (2) 8:5-7, 15*b*, (3) 8:16-19, (6) 9:8-12, 11:9, 10.

J. (1) 7:14-17*a*, 25, (2) 8:1-4, 8-15*a*, (4) 8:20*b*-22, 23*b*, 24, 28*b*, 29*a*, 30-32, (5) 9:1-7, (7) 9:13, 17-21, 23*b*,

24*b*, 25*a*, 26-30, 33, 34, (8) 10:1-7, 13*bc*, 14*b*, 15*a*, 16-19, (9) 10:28, 29, 11:4-8.

E. (1) 7:15*, 17*b*, 18, 20*b*, 21*a*, 23, 24 (4) 8:20*a*, 23*a*, 25-28*a*, 29*b*, (7) 9:13*, 22, 23*a*, 24*a*, 25*b*, 31, 32, 35 (8) 10:8-12, 13*a*, 14*a*, 15*bc*, 20 (9) 10:21-27, 11:1-3.

R. 9:14-16.

JULICHER.

P. 7:8-13, (1) 7:19, 20*a*, 21*b*, 22, (2) 8:5-7, 15*b*, (3) 8:16-19, (6) 9:8-12, 11:9, 10.

J. (1) 7:14-17*a*, (15*b**, 17*), 23, 25*b* (2) 8:1-4, 8*-14 (12*) (4) 8:20-32 (22*b**, 23*, 25*, 26*, 27*), (5) 9:1-7, (7) 9:13, 17, 18, 23*b*, 24*, 25*, 26, 27*, 28*, 29*, 31-33*, 34*, (8) 10:1*a*, 3*-6*a*, 13*bc*, 14*b*, 15*ac*, 16*-19, 11:4-8.

E. (1) 7:17*b*, 18, 20*b*, 21, 24, 25*a*, (7) 9:22, 23*a*, 24*, 28*. 30, 35*a*, (8) 10:7, 8-13*a*, 14*a*, 15*b*, (9) 10:21-29, 11:1-3.

R. 9:14-16, 19-21, 29*b*, 30, 35*b*, 10:1*b*, 2, 6*b*.

The figures enclosed in parentheses represent the different plagues in their order. (1) blood, (2) frogs, (3) lice, (4) flies, (5) murrain, (6) boils, (7) hail, (8) locusts, (9) darkness.

Alexa Suelzer (essay date 1964)

SOURCE: "Themes of the Pentateuchal Narratives" in *The Pentateuch: A Study in Salvation History,* Herder and Herder, 1964, pp. 22-100.

[*In this essay, Suelzer examines the themes that structure what he takes to be an essentially unified* Torah.]

Introduction

The partition of the **Pentateuch** into the individual books of Moses was a practical measure undertaken to render the massive work more manageable and intelligible. The essential unity of the work as a whole however was not impaired, for no matter what additions and redactions the **Pentateuch** underwent it ever retained a basic constant in the light of which disparate traditions were eliminated, adapted or transformed. That normative was the Hebrews' vital experience of Yahweh effecting his will for all men and for Israel in particular; hence the traditions chosen by the sacred writers for preservation in the **Pentateuch** are all aspects of the dominant thesis: Yahweh's salvific deeds and Israel's response. Some scattered traditions reflect isolated elements of the theme; others, like facets having similar angles of reflection, converge their light on a

particular phase, reinforcing and clarifying a single aspect of the leitmotif. No single treatment can hope to display all the facets of the **Pentateuch;** therefore in our selection of materials we will follow the sacred writers and stress the themes they hold paramount in Israel's account of her salvation history.

What are the salient motifs in the salvation history? The Pentateuchal materials are grouped around major traditions which include theologized reflections about Yahweh in his relation to Israel: Yahweh, creator of the world, effected his plan for man's salvation by calling apart the patriarchs and promising them land and posterity. Later he rescued the children of the patriarchs from Egyptian slavery, guided them through hardships in the desert, climaxed his deeds by a personal alliance at Sinai and at last brought his people to the land he had pledged to their fathers. The motifs here so tersely recapitulated developed from slender beginnings; in the process of growth they absorbed and reshaped the most diverse materials until the basic themes blossomed into a work of gigantic theological proportions. The exact process of this growth is one of the key problems in Pentateuchal studies.

Strictly speaking the primitive history (Gn 1-11) is an introduction to the salvation history, not one of its themes. In this study however it is treated with the other motifs because it provides a background—the theological realities and the Semitic world—against which the salvation drama unfolds with added depth and clarity. The drama begins with the choice of Abraham and the promise of land[1] and progeny to him and his descendants. The stories of the fathers bring out the sovereignty of the divine will; with equal freedom Yahweh employs or rejects human instruments and for the most part accomplishes his designs by what seem to be the ordinary ways of Providence. But in the Exodus Yahweh's action is of a different sort altogether; here he is a God of obvious power: "Or did any god venture to go and take a nation for himself from the midst of another nation, by testings, by signs and wonders, by war, with his strong hand and outstretched arm, and by great terrors, all of which the Lord, your God, did for you in Egypt before your very eyes?" (Dt 4:34). The vivid memory of delivery from bondage was the germinal cell from which grew Israel's fuller realization of Yahweh as pre-eminently her God.

In return for the divine goodness which had wrought her deliverance from Egypt Israel showed surly ingratitude. The stories of the desert wandering with their alternate themes of divine solicitude and human caviling sharpen the contrast between the largesse of Yahweh and the niggardly response of Israel to her God. Yet at Sinai—his will to save unchanged by his children's ingratitude—Yahweh concluded a covenant with Israel, thus binding himself irrevocably to his people. The covenant will be treated more fully in the discussion of Hebrew law; for the present it will suffice to place the Sinai revelation in its proper context and to relate it to the other themes of salvation history.

The traditions included in the themes are far more than cherished memories of the past. They bear the revelation of the Lord and, although rooted in the temporal order, they have validity for all generations and present to Israel of every age a renewed challenge of total response to the divine election. The sacred writers generally develop a given theme within defined limits of a book, e.g. the promises to the patriarchs in Gn 12-50. Within a particular theme however numerous isolated traditions may occur, e.g. Gn 14; these have been omitted or referred to only in passing in order to strengthen the impact of the theme in question. Where a key motif treated in one section is enhanced by echoes elsewhere in the **Pentateuch** (e.g. Dt's frequent mention of the promises made to the patriarchs), these references have been incorporated into the treatment of the main theme.

The primitive history

The primitive history of Gn 1-11 stands at the head of the **Pentateuch** as a background for the greatly expanded traditions of the patriarchs, the Exodus and Sinai, in which are recapitulated Yahweh's merciful designs. As the traditions of salvation history burgeoned, the sacred writers felt the need to trace the antecedents of Israel's election by describing Yahweh's relation to the world from its creation until the time of Abraham. Living as she did in an atmosphere permeated by myths about cosmic and human origins Israel at an early age must have formed her own cosmogony relating the creation of the world to Yahweh. However, creation accounts in written form appear only late in Israel's history. Apparently long theological reflection was required to correlate the traditions of origins with her prime interest: the portrayal of Yahweh's action in history. Properly speaking there is no Hebrew doctrine of creation, for nowhere is creation treated for itself; the creation account is only an introduction to the saving plan initiated by the call of Abraham. Creation was seen as an historical event opening the course of human existence, a fact stressed in the careful chronology of the Priestly writer.

It may seem that Gn 1-11 has already received its due meed of attention in dogmatic and apologetic writings. The chapters of the primitive history have played a vital part in the development and exposition of such doctrines as creation, grace, original justice, concupiscence and original sin. Catholic apologetes, furthermore, must consider the relation of the biblical recital of human origins to modern scientific theories. The day has passed when apologetes can be flustered by supposed conflicts between the Bible and biological evolution; but there is still a legitimate need to examine contemporary hypotheses of cosmic and human origins in the light of Church teaching, which is based in part on the biblical accounts. Our present concern however is not with such a use of biblical materials. It frequently happens that when the Bible is used for doctrinal, moral or apologetic content inherent in a later stage of revelation the sacred accounts are not permitted to yield their true and complete message; they are not considered in and for themselves but only in relation to some other interest or concern. Our study, untrammeled by direct dogmatic or apologetic preoccupations, will let the narratives relate for themselves the significance the events described in Gn 1-11 held for the sacred writer—and hence for Israel as a whole.

Creation

The different cycles of tradition present in the **Pentateuch** are immediately obvious in the double creation accounts: the Priestly narrative of Gn 1:1-2,4a and the Yahwist version of 2:4b-25. The Priestly writer conceives creation as development from chaos to cosmos; he emphasizes the intial *tōhûāwsbōhû*, the formlessness and utter lack of distinction; and in an orderly framework of seven days he describes the constitution and adornment of the world in which man appears as the climax. The first words of Gn seem to be a summary of the story to follow: the visible world owes its origin to God. Although creation out of nothing is not explicit in the Priestly narrative it might be implied. It is also true that the verb *bara'* is reserved for the divine activity, and no reference to the material used ever accompanies it. For the Yahwist, creation is progress from the desert to the sown: "There was not yet any field shrub on the earth nor had the plants of the field sprung up, for the Lord God had sent no rain on the earth and there was no man to till the soil" (2:5). From the very beginning of the Yahwist report man is the center of attention and the process of creation is complete only when "the Lord God took the man and placed him in the garden of Eden to till it and to keep it" (2:15).

Both writers emphasize that the world and all it contains are the work of Yahweh; but the Priestly writer stresses Yahweh's effortless and transcendent creation by a mere word ("God said, 'Let there be light,' and there was light" [Gn 1:3]). Even where the Priestly writer uses the phrase "God made," as in Gn 1:16, it is preceded by the divine creative word, as if to say that all things were effected by the power of his word. The Yahwist on the contrary conceives Yahweh as a potter fashioning man from clay and then breathing into his nostrils the breath of life (2:7). The sole reference to the creation of woman in the Priestly narrative is the brief text: "Male and female he created them" (1:27). The Yahwist however regards the creation of woman as the definite climax of his story in ch 2. He views woman as the equal of man because she is of the same nature and is given by Yahweh to be man's helpmate, not his chattel. If the report in Gn 2:7 of the creation of Adam is not a literal description of how the first man came to be, it would also seem that the account of the creation of Eve is not to be taken literally, but rather as an analogy illustrating the writer's thoughts on the nature of woman and her relation to man.

Gn 1-2 contains some elements common to ancient pagan mythologies and these common elements raise the question: what is the relationship between creation myths of the ancient Near East and the story of creation in Gn? Critics of an earlier time dismissed the biblical narratives as Hebrew modifications of older creation myths; nowadays the question cannot be answered so simply. Since certain parallels to Gn are found in *Enuma elish,* a dramatic recital of the struggle between cosmic order and chaos, a brief summary of the Akkadian epic will reveal points of resemblance and contrast. In the strife among the gods (begotten by the primordial Apsu and Tiamat, fresh and salt waters respectively) Marduk cuts in two the defeated Tiamat and uses her body to form the heavens and the earth. Then the victorious Marduk discloses his plan:

> Blood I will mass and cause bones to be.
> I will establish a savage, "man" shall be his
>   name.
> Verily, savage-man I will create.
> He will be charged with the service of the
>   gods
> That they might be at ease
>
> (6:5-8).

The god Kingu who had incited Tiamat to rebellion is selected:

> They bound him, holding him before Ea.
> They imposed on him his guilt and severed
>   his blood (vessels).
> Out of his blood they fashioned mankind.
> He imposed the service and let free the gods
>
> (6:31-34).

The *Enuma elish* obviously has rough parallels with the Gn creation account; doubtless Tiamat is related etymologically to the abyss *(tᵉhôm)* of Gn 1:2 and the formation of man from the blood of a god recognizes godlike characteristics in man, characteristics which Gn attributes to his being made in the image and likeness of God. The tenor of the biblical narrative is so distinctive however and the method and purpose of the creation it describes so different that a real dependence of Gn on Babylonian mythology is inconceivable. The gross polytheism of the *Enuma elish* and its atmosphere of struggle between hostile forces are totally absent from Gn, where Yahweh as sole creator accomplishes his works effortlessly by omnipotent decrees.[2] No suggestion of creation from nothing is found in the pagan

myths because the "creation" is always achieved with pre-existent materials—the body of Tiamat or the blood of Kingu. In contrast to the idea that man was created for the service of the gods both the Yahwist and Priestly traditions portray Adam as the object of Yahweh's personal concern. He is surrounded with every good, blessed and made fruitful; by his dominion over the earth he is even permitted to share the divine creativity.

It is clear then that the resemblance of Gn 1-2 to older creation myths is limited chiefly to conceptualization. Although the sacred writer was inspired he did not necessarily receive his materials by revelation. In fact revelation, either primitive or direct, should be excluded as the source of the creation story. (This exclusion does not however extend to the role of revelation in the formation of the story.) As he fashioned his story of the primeval world the author may have employed literary forms well known to his audience, just as a modern author writes in the familiar genre of the novel or play to convey his thought. In using ancient literary forms the biblical writer deliberately freed them from their mythological dimensions and concepts. Thus the Priestly writer's casual description of the sun and moon as two great lights and his stress upon their limited function (Gn 1:14-19) are possibly a polemic directed against the worship of these luminaries as depicted in the mythic materials. The Priestly description is more subtle but perhaps no less effective than Dt's direct prohibition: "And when you look up to the heavens and behold the sun or moon or any star among the heavenly hosts, do not be led astray into adoring them or serving them" (Dt 4:19). Again, the organization of old materials into a seven-day framework lifts the story from the realm of myth into the temporal order and presents creation as a definite historic act.

This appeal to resemblances in literary form is not intended to oversimplify the relation between Gn and myth, for, as the Biblical Commission noted in its reply to Cardinal Suhard, the question of genres in the primeval history is obscure and complex; "one can, therefore, neither deny nor affirm their historicity without unduly attributing to them the canons of a literary style within which it is impossible to classify them."[3] It is evident however that the creation accounts are not meant as a literal description of events as they actually transpired but as analogies which the sacred writer used to express the burden of his thought: Yahweh alone created all that exists, arranged it in a suitable order and climaxed his work by the creation of man and woman in his own image.

Temptation and fall

One theological concern of the Priestly writer is to demonstrate that all of Yahweh's creation is good; seven times he repeats the refrain "God saw that it was good."

Given the transcendent perfection of Yahweh the creator it is unthinkable that his works can be anything but perfect. Nevertheless the world has degenerated from its pristine goodness. Having described cosmic and human origins in his introduction to salvation history the sacred author must now explain how deterioration in man and in the world came about. Why must man painfully wrest a living from the earth he was meant to dominate; why does a woman bear her children in travail and sorrow; why do death and decay await man at the end? Where does sin come from? In answering these questions the Yahwist rejects the notion that a primal principle of evil exists in the world. Evil is an intrusion; originally it had no place in the goodness of Yahweh's creation. Here too the story of how sin, suffering and death entered the world need not be a literal report of what actually happened. Sin and its consequences are the burden of the message; the vehicle of the message could well be familiar genres appealing to the imagination as well as to the mind.

The Yahwist conceives all suffering and death as the result of man's disobedience to Yahweh's decree not to eat the fruit of the tree of knowledge of good and evil (Gn 2:17). Gn 2:9 also speaks of the tree of life, which is not mentioned again until 3:22. The two trees perhaps represent a double tradition in the Yahwist narrative. (The dirge over the king of Tyre in Ez 28:11-19 is based on still another tradition of the paradise story, one in which there is no mention of woman.) The temptation and fall are recorded with great psychological insight. The serpent offers a casual opening gambit: "Did God say, 'You shall not eat of any tree of the garden?'" (3:1). The woman exaggerates the divine prohibition; the serpent pursues the issue until "the woman saw that the tree was good for food, pleasing to the eyes, and desirable for the knowledge it would give. She took of its fruit and ate it, and also gave some to her husband and he ate" (3:6-7).

Although an exact determination of their sin is impossible the context of the story gives some clues to its nature. The serpent assures Eve that eating from the forbidden tree will bring knowledge, not death: "You will be like God, knowing good and evil" (Gn 3:5). Then after the fall Yahweh says: "Indeed! the man has become like one of us, knowing good and evil" (3:22). What does it mean, to know good and evil? The Hebrew idiom used in 3:5 and 3:22 can be interpreted as totality of knowledge. The context suggests another meaning: by disobedience Adam and Eve tried to attain familiarity with mysteries beyond their human status; they set themselves as arbiters of the moral order, thus usurping Yahweh's prerogatives. Thomas Aquinas notes that man sinned by coveting the likeness of God as regards good and evil, so that with his own native powers he might decide good and evil for himself (*S th*, II, II, 163, a. 1). Neither of these interpretations however sheds light on the nature of the transgression.

A third connotation identifies knowledge of good and evil with some kind of sexual experience. Certainly normal intercourse between the sexes cannot be meant, although some scholars have so interpreted the texts.[4] The tenor of the narrative of the creation of Adam and Eve indicates that the union of the sexes is planned and blessed by Yahweh (see Gn 1:27ff; 2:21ff). Nevertheless, in the face of the excesses of Canaanite fertility cults with their exaltation of the female principle, the sacred writer could have conceived the primal sin as a perversion of lawful sexual activity. The relation between vv 5 and 7 in ch 3 strengthens the possibility of this interpretation. The serpent's promise: "Your eyes will be opened, and you will be like God" is echoed and expanded in v 7: "Then the eyes of both were opened, and they realized that they were naked" (see also 3:11). At first glance an interpretation of the sin as a sexual offense may seem improbable because the knowledge acquired is supposed to make Adam and Eve like God, who in Hebrew thought is never associated with sexual activity. The difficulty disappears with the realization that fertility cults had as one of their objectives communion with divinity. Further the serpent was used as a sexual symbol in the ancient Near East, and it is possible that the author of the biblical narratives was so employing it. The identity of the serpent is never fully clarified; he represents man's enemy, also Yahweh's foe, but he remains a creature nonetheless.

The aftermath of the transgression is portrayed with equal psychological accuracy. Adam gives Yahweh the faltering explanation: "The woman you placed at my side gave me fruit from the tree and I ate" (Gn 3:12); then Eve in turn excuses herself: "The serpent deceived me and I ate" (3:13). Punishment is inevitable; yet before he decrees it Yahweh addresses a curse to the serpent:

> Because you have done this, cursed are you among all animals, and among all the beasts of the field; on your belly you shall crawl, dust shall you eat, all the days of your life. I will put enmity between you and the woman, between your seed and her seed; he shall crush your head, and you shall lie in wait for his heel (3:14-15).

The phrase "you and the woman" applies literally to the serpent and Eve; "her seed" is the descendants of Adam and Eve. The seed of the serpent is less easily determined; it is probably a literary expression of resistance to God by all created forces of evil. The picture in v 15b ("He shall crush [*šûf*] your head and you shall lie in wait for [*šûf*] his heel") is one of perpetual struggle between the seed of Eve and that of the serpent. Within the context of the Yahwist's sin-deliverance theme however the words indicate more than a continuing, indecisive conflict and one can assume ultimate victory for mankind. In addition Gn 3:14-15 is from first to last a curse addressed to the serpent; this fact also permits an interpretation of final defeat for the tempter of mankind.[5]

The punishments meted out by Yahweh touch Adam and Eve in the activities most proper to them. Man's easy dominion over the earth is now at an end; henceforth he will eat its fruit only in sweat and toil. As for woman not only will pain and distress accompany her childbearing, but her longing for man will serve to increase the humiliation of her subjection to him. For man and woman alike the term of life's labors is a return to the dust from which they were drawn. Once the sanctions have been declared there is no return for Adam and Eve to their former relationship with Yahweh; the irreversibility of their new status is stressed vividly in their expulsion from the garden: "He drove out the man; and at the east of the garden of Eden he placed the Cherubim, and the flaming sword, which turned every way, to guard the way to the tree of life" (Gn 3:24).

Certainly it is legitimate and even necessary to analyze the paradise story for a greater knowledge of the author's intent; but little is gained by an attempt to delineate details meticulously. Particulars like the location of the garden of Eden or the identity of the four rivers of paradise (Gn 2:10-14) are uncertain, for these are only accessories of the author's portrayal of how life's disorders stem from the original transgression of the first man and woman.

The progress of sin

Once introduced into the world sin with its consequences advances steadily, and the documentation of the relentless encroachment of evil on Yahweh's creation fills the remaining chapters of the primitive history; thus the progressive human deterioration can be called the principal theme of chs 4-11. The first instance is the murder of Abel, a story which raises almost as many questions as it answers. Is this tribal or personal history? Why was Cain's sacrifice rejected and how did he know that God did not favor him? What was the mark given Cain and what purpose did it serve? Originally the story may have been a tribal history, for Cain was popularly regarded as the eponymous ancestor of the Kenites, people with the same ancestry as Israel but outside the covenant. Furthermore, since the story supposes a rather advanced agricultural civilization and a formal cult, it is not likely that sons of the first man and woman figured in the original version. The story may echo the conflict between two types of civilization—pastoral and agricultural. A similar motif may be the foundation of the struggles between Jacob and Esau in Gn 25-28.

As Yahweh once questioned Adam and his wife so now he addresses Cain: "What have you done? The voice of your brother's blood cries to me from the ground" (Gn 4:10). Punishment follows swiftly: "When you till the soil, it shall not give its fruit to you; a fugitive and a wanderer shall you be on the earth" (4:12). The token which Yahweh placed on Cain is sometimes regarded as a sign of disgrace; from the context however it appears to be a protective mark, perhaps against blood vengeance exacted for fratricide.

Cosmic degeneration is further illustrated in the puzzling narrative of marriages between the sons of God and the daughters of men (Gn 6:1-4). Attempts to render the account more specific by identifying the sons and daughters have not been very successful. At most it is arbitrary to identify the sons of God with the Sethites and the daughters of men with the Kenites. Undoubtedly the sacred writer used mythological stories about the marriage of titans to human women to exemplify the ruthless advance of wickedness throughout the world.

Rebellion, violence, bloodshed—such is the record of mankind from Adam to Noe. As a summary judgment on preceding events and as a prelude to the ensuing story of the Flood the Yahwist reports the Lord's decision: "I will wipe from the earth man whom I have created—man and beast, crawling creature and bird of the air as well—for I regret that I made them" (Gn 6:7).[6] The Flood narrative is interwoven from Yahwist and Priestly traditions, each preserved almost intact with little attempt to suppress discrepancies which arose from the combination of traditions; for example the number of animals in Gn 7:2-3 differs from the number in 6:19-20. The cataclysm described by the Priestly writer is greater in every way; it covers the entire earth and lasts more than a year. Human corruption and Yahweh's judgment on it occupy all the Priestly writer's attention and he is oblivious to the details the Yahwist lingers over. The Priestly author devotes a single brusque verse to reporting the bird sent from the ark (8:7); the Yahwist speaks of several birds and dwells upon the event for seven verses (8:6, 8-12). On occasion however the author of the Priestly account is very detailed; he records the exact measurements of the ark and calculates times and seasons with great care. Behind these minutiae is his conviction of Yahweh's personal activity, which he tries to portray with due theological objectivity.

Modern discoveries of ancient literary materials offer evidence that the story of the Flood in the Bible is but one among many legends of catastrophic inundations. The narrative most resembling the biblical traditions appears in the so-called Flood Tablet (11) of the *Epic of Gilgamesh,* an Akkadian work composed around 2000. The epic was discovered in the library of Ashurbanipal (seventh century) in 1853. Besides the texts in Akkadian other fragmentary recensions testify to the popularity of the work. First published in 1873 when rationalist criticism of the Bible was approaching its zenith, the Babylonian flood story was hailed as the direct model of the biblical narrative; a discrediting of the historicity of the account in Gn soon followed. Specific parallels do exist, but one cannot speak of literary dependence. The stories in both the biblical and the Babylonian texts are based on the same heritage, i.e. memories of one or more severe floods, floods made even more catastrophic by popular tradition. This complex of flood traditions may have been brought from Mesopotamia by the ancestors of the Hebrews, but the biblical story nonetheless has a totally different orientation; it is the vehicle of a religious and moral message quite foreign to the Babylonian version.

A summary of the story in *Gilgamesh* will highlight the chief resemblances and contrasts to the biblical account. A council of the gods decides to destroy the city of Shurrupak. The god Ea warns Utnapishtim, instructing him to build a ship and to take aboard his family and kin as well as the seed of all living things. During the storm and the ensuing flood the frightened gods "cowered like dogs crouched against the outer wall" (11:115). On the seventh day the tempest ceases and the boat comes to rest on Mount Nisir. After another seven days Utnapishtim sends out a dove and then a swallow, both of which return to him; next he sends a raven, which "eats, circles, caws, and turns not round" (11:154). Leaving his boat Utnapishtim offers sacrifice to the gods, who smelled the savor and "crowded like flies about the sacrifice" (11:161). Utna-pishtim and his wife are admitted to the assembly of the gods and given a home at the mouth of the rivers.

The biblical Flood story is distinguished from the Babylonian accounts in its presentation of the all-holy Yahweh's righteous judgment on the moral transgressions of his creatures: "The end of all creatures of flesh is in my mind; the earth is full of violence because of them. I will destroy them with the earth" (Gn 6:13). *Gilgamesh* does not mention any moral causes of the disaster; indeed the action of the gods may be arbitrary and capricious. If Utnapishtim escapes it is not because of his justice but simply because Ea chooses to save him. Like the creation narrative of Gn the biblical story of the Flood may borrow the trappings of myth, but the soul and substance of the biblical accounts owe nothing to mythological concepts.

When Noe returns to dry land his act of sacrifice brings the favor of Yahweh to himself and to all men: "I will never again curse the ground on account of man, for the inclination of man's heart is evil from his youth; I will never again destroy every living creature, as I have done" (Gn 8:21). In this soliloquy Yahweh's reason for sparing man (the evil inclinations of man's heart) is the same as that which prompted his decision to punish man in Gn 6:5ff. The Priestly writer tells of no sacrifice (for in his traditions cultic sacrifice arose in Mosaic times), but he significantly records the blessing given at the new beginning of the world. This benediction, a deliberate evocation of the blessing bestowed upon the first man (see 1:28-29), reinstates mankind to the divine favor with the promises of fertility and a certain dominion over the earth. Not content with blessing Noe Yahweh also makes an alliance with him—the first of the covenants treated by the Priestly writer (9:8-17). The passage is a theological construct enabling the writer to dwell upon his concept of the relation between Yahweh and his people. As a pledge that he will never again destroy all flesh by a flood Yahweh retires his bow of war, placing it in the sky as a perpetual reminder to Noe and his descendants.

The genealogies

At four points in the primitive history genealogies have been inserted: Gn 4:17ff; 5:1ff; 10:1ff; and 11:10ff. The first two sketch the decendants of Adam as far as Noe; the others the descendants of Noe until Abraham. The Yahwist table in 4:17ff lists the progeny of Adam through Cain but it evinces much greater interest in reporting the progress of civilization than it does in recording genealogical data. The Kenite genealogy is certainly different from the story of Cain and Abel in ch 4, in which Cain is described as a vagabond, not the builder of a city. The genealogy evidently is unaware of the Flood, for it names the sons of Lamech as ancestors of shepherds, musicians and artisans. The parallel Priestly account (5:1ff) follows a strict chronological pattern in tracing Adam's line through Seth: "When Seth was one hundred and five years old, he became the father of Enos. Seth lived eight hundred and seven years after the birth of Enos, and had other sons and daughters. The whole lifetime of Seth was nine hundred and twelve years; then he died" (5:6-8). The key to the Priestly writer's use of numbers is still unknown; thus all attempts to set up an actual historical chronology according to his lists have been futile. The esoteric use of numbers is characteristic of the Semites, as evidenced in the fantastic numbers of the Babylonian King Lists. Similar chronological precision characterizes the Semite genealogy in 11:10ff.

It is sometimes assumed that the Priestly writer's interest in genealogies is merely a pedantic preoccupation with records. Quite the contrary: his concerns are doctrinal or theological and his tables are an effort to arrange the ages of the world and of man theologically. Just as his chronological framework for the creation narrative placed the events he described within the temporal order, so his careful genealogical records deliberately emphasize Yahweh as the Lord of history who deals with his people in definite and irrevocable temporal actions. Even the precision of the chronology, artificial though it may be, is theologically pertinent. The ancients from Adam to Noe have a life span of seven hundred to one thousand years; from Noe to Abraham, two hundred to six hundred years; the patriarchs, one hundred to two hundred years. The Priestly writer does not explain the diminution, but in view of his remarks in Gn 6:11-13 ("The earth was corrupt in the sight of God, and it was filled with violence") the decreasing life span can be considered a subtle commentary on the loss of human vigor as corruption becomes rampant.

The broadened scene of the Table of Nations (Gn 10:1ff) illustrates the fulfillment of Yahweh's blessing of Noe: "Be fruitful and multiply, and fill the earth" (9:1). Here the Priestly writer has organized nations and peoples as descendants of the three sons of Noe: Sem, Ham and Japheth. Ethnic and linguistic relationships do not dictate the grouping, nor are there genuine political ties between the members of a division. Geographic and historical associations seem to explain the alignment; thus the descendants of Japheth compose the northern Peoples of the Sea; Ham's descendants are the men of the southern countries (to which Canaan is joined for historical reasons); and the progeny of Sem are the eastern peoples closely associated with the Hebrews.

It is noteworthy that Israel is not mentioned in the Table of Nations, her derivation from Arphachsad being developed only in Gn 11:10ff. From this fact it is evident that the writer is not concerned to exalt Israel or to contrast her with nations outside the covenant, but rather to testify that the total historical situation (of which Israel forms only a small part) is the creation of Yahweh. The author's ultimate concern of course is to pursue the line of Sem through Arphachsad to Abraham, and he does so in 11:10-32. But if he is thus to narrow his field to a single line why does he elaborate the Table of Nations? His procedure shows that the Priestly writer was aware of the mystery of divine election and wanted to make it theologically vivid by contrasting Israel with the other people who were equally the creation of Yahweh, but who were not the object of special predilection.

The conclusion of primitive history

The recital of man's irreversible deterioration reaches its terminus in the story of the Tower of Babel, which concludes the prehistory. The narrative speaks of two distinct constructions: the building of a city and of a lofty tower or ziggurat. The reference to Babel at the conclusion of the story suggests that the tower—like the 270-foot ziggurat of Etemenanki dedicated to Marduk, protector of Babylon—was a shrine to a heathen deity. The writer does not specify the nature of man's offense. That the building involved rebellion against Yahweh is not stated directly, but the Hebrew connotation of the word "Babel" indicates that such defection is implied. Pride is likewise implicit in the

builders' exhortaton: "Let us make a name for ourselves lest we be scattered all over the earth" (Gn 11:4), as well as in Yahweh's decision to curb their presumptuous aspirations: "This is the beginning of what they will do. Hereafter they will not be restrained from anything which they determine to do" (11:6).

Interrupting the work in progress Yahweh confused *(balal)* the builders' speech and scattered them over the earth. Two etiologies, perhaps the original point of the earlier traditions, are thus still retained: the origin of various languages and a popular etymology of Babel, which actually means gate of God. The etiologies however are only incidental to the dominant interest: the portrayal of man's arrogant attempt to usurp divine prerogatives. The bold anthropomorphism of Yahweh's concern over the tower and his investigation of the work are not reminiscent of a mythic struggle between titans and the gods; in fact there is no extant extrabiblical parallel to this story. The picture furnishes an ironic contrast between puny human efforts and the calm, majestic action of Yahweh. Men lay their solicitous plans: "Let us make bricks and bake them. . . . Let us build. . . . Let us make a name . . . ;" but Yahweh with a single decision brings all their plans to nought: "Let us go down, and there confuse their language" (Gn 11:3-7).

The gloomy scene of mankind confounded at the Tower of Babel closes the primitive history. The dismal conclusion departs from the pattern in the preceding accounts whereby sin made ever more devastating progress in the world which God had created good. Adam's initial deviation from the divine will incurred dire sanctions but the harsh situation was mitigated by Yahweh's fatherly solicitude: "The Lord God made garments of skin for Adam and his wife and clothed them" (Gn 3:21). Likewise the Lord punished the murderer Cain, yet at the same time afforded him a protective mark as he wandered restless through the earth (4:15). Then after the Flood Yahweh renewed the blessing first bestowed upon Adam: "Be fruitful and multiply, and fill the earth" (9:1).

Despite so many fresh starts men repeated the wretched pattern of rebellion and violence until finally the Lord confused their speech and scattered them over the earth (Gn 11:7-8). The story marks a point of no return in man's relations to God. Cut off from the Lord, men find themselves separated from their brethren as well. On this note the story ends; no compassionate utterance of the Lord, no promise of rescue intrudes a vestige of hope. The sacred writer has completed his account of man's progressive perversion and he is at the end also of his assurances that the Lord, despite man's wickess, has not cast off his creatures utterly. The dry statements of the genealogy which follows (11:10-32) underline the bleakness of affairs for which no happy denouement seems possible.

The patriarchal history

Precisely at this point, the nadir of man's relations to God, the salvation history introduces a new approach of God to man in the choice of Abraham as the father of a chosen people. Like a seed the salvific plan lies hidden within the catalogue of Sem's descendants: "There was the father of Abram, Nahor, and Aran" (Gn 11:27); but who could suspect that this laconic report is prelude to the grandeur to be unfolded in the promises?

The rise of Israel as a people rests historically on the union of her tribes in the worship of Yahweh, a fact upon which all later Hebrew history is built. Paradoxically however our understanding of how Israel evolved into an historical reality is based on pretribal traditions whose contents, though admittedly of decisive importance, presuppose the subsequent history of Israel. The primitive cultic credo of Dt 26:5ff summarizes one of these traditions: "My father was a wandering Aramean who went down to Egypt with a small household and lived there as an alien. But there he became a nation great, strong and numerous." Other similar traditions, expanded and unified, compose the patriarchal history of Gn. In their earliest forms these traditions were oral, localized reminiscences of family forebears or etiologies of names and customs which were amalgamated after a protracted process of modification that cannot now be traced in detail. In their definitive version in the **Pentateuch** the patriarchal adventures have been incorporated into a broad theme recording how Israel's ancestors under divine guidance migrated from northwest Mesopotamia, entered the land of Canaan and there lived as resident strangers while awaiting the possession of the land promised them by divine favor. The memory she preserved of her beginnings testifies that the Lord of the world marked Israel as the vehicle through which all peoples of the earth would be blessed.

That this testimony exists is itself an historical fact and hence part of the history of Israel. But the degree to which the traditions witnessed by the testimony can be used to reconstruct historical events is debatable. True, the historicity of the patriarchal accounts is not a direct concern of the critic in his task of showing how the traditions were linked to Israel's consciousness of her relation to Yahweh; nonetheless the biblicist must inevitably come to grips with the problem of the relationship between history as presented in the patriarchal narratives and the religion in whose service the traditions are employed. This encounter is necessary because the reconstruction of the history and faith of early Israel affects the interpretation of later Israelite history and of the Old Testament as a whole.

The first problem concerning the historicity of the patriarchal traditions stems from the lack of contemporary records of the period. Working on the principle that ancient narratives are primarily sources for the period in which they were written, not for the times they report, many proponents of the documentary theory refused to acknowledge the historical worth of traditions referring to remote ages. Reinforced by the theory of evolutionary religious development their view quickly reduced patriarchal religion to a projection of later Yahwism; and to explain the presence of the patriarchs in the traditions they had recourse to theories more ingenious than satisfying. Critics like Wellhausen failed to realize that the writing of a tradition marks the end of an era, not the beginning. Although the dates assigned to a document may be accurate they give no clue to the age of the traditions described in the document.

As we have already noted, archeological discoveries have altered the harsh view prevalent in the last century, and thousands of texts contemporaneous with the period of Israel's beginnings have supplied a frame of reference for the historical evaluation of biblical traditions. In no instance has the new evidence submitted "proof" of a single event in the patriarchal stories; yet by furnishing many parallels and by corroboration of countless details it has shown that the narratives must be taken seriously as an exact portrait of institutions and customs in the patriarchal period, and hence that they reflect a valid memory of the past.[7] Despite the presumption of authenticity thus attached to the patriarchal traditions not all scholars concede that the biblical narratives are reliable sources of history. Martin Noth, possibly the most influential of these critics, agrees that the Pentateuch as a coalescence of sacred traditions does contain historical information, but he denies that the Books of Moses can be accepted as a coherent historical narrative. Just how far the **Pentateuch** can be taken as a source for Israelite history is a problem to be solved only by an examination of each separate unit of tradition, i.e. by a construction of a history of the traditions. Noth values the contribution made by extrabiblical remains to Israel's history, and he does not completely dismiss the worth of archeological discoveries; but he insists that their witness is after all indirect and therefore incapable of establishing the historical accuracy of the narratives. His negative evaluation of the historical elements in Israelite traditions leaves unanswered the question of Israel's origin and offers no adequate explanation of her faith.

Gerhard von Rad shares Noth's views to some extent but his work is distinguished by decidedly theological interests. Whereas Noth stresses the impossibility of determining historical content von Rad emphasizes the irrelevancy of such determination. An historical kernel is found, to be sure, in many of the stories but the genuine historical concern is always Yahweh's dealings with his people. Accordingly, says von Rad, the faith of the Hebrews must be explained in terms of what Israel thought of her relation to Yahweh, not by the results of modern studies on Israel's actual bearing to her neighbors or by historical facts.

While agreeing with Noth that history properly so called is not available in the Pentateuchal records, critics like William F. Albright and John Bright are more sanguine in their appraisal of the patriarchal narratives as dependable sources for Israelite history. If the writing of Israelite history is not be be completely nihilistic, they assert, one must examine the traditions against the world of their day, and in this light draw whatever conclusions the evidence allows. In the reconstruction of Hebrew history the distinction between the empiric methodology of Albright and the tradition-history of Noth is becoming ever more acute.[8]

The promises

One of the earliest and most perduring of the traditions comprising the heritage of Israel is that of the promises made to the patriarchs. Events at Babel indicated that the relationship between Yahweh and his creatures was at an end; must man now continue to live severed from the Lord? The onset of salvation history with the call of Abraham answers the question:

> Leave your country, your kinsfolk, and your
>   father's house,
> for the land which I will show you;
> I will make a great nation of you.
> I will bless you and make your name great,
> so that you shall be a blessing.
> I will bless them that bless you,
> and curse them that curse you.
> In you shall all the nations of the earth be
>   blessed
>
> (Gn 12:1-3).

The command of leaving home and family is attached to two promises: a new land and a great posterity. Today numerous progeny is still regarded as a great blessing, a special mark of divine favor among peoples of the East; and to nomads and seminomads sown land with its abundance of food and its stable life is an inestimable good. The double theme of land and children here introduced for the first time echoes again and again throughout the pages of Gn. Although individual traditions emphasize now the one, now the other aspect the two ideas are rarely separated in passages which directly report the conference of the divine pledges. In only two instances is the promise of posterity given apart from the promise of the land in Gn: the promise of a child to Sara (18:10) and the promise of descendants to Isaac (26:24). Seven times the assurances of Gn 12:1-3 are repeated to Abraham: 12:7; 13:14-17; 15:5-7, 18; 17:4-8; 18:10; and 22:17-18. The promises are renewed for Isaac in 26:2-5 and again in 26:24. At various times Jacob also receives a reitera-

tion of Yahweh's intent to give him land and posterity: 28:13-15; 35:9-12; and 46:3-4. Besides these direct reports of the bestowal and renewal of the promises there are frequent indirect references to one or both of them: 24:7; 28:3-4; 32:13; 48:4; and 50:24.

The promise as covenant

In calling Abraham, Yahweh seemingly narrowed the field of his redemptive operations. The blessing of Noe carried an injunction to multiply and fill the earth (Gn 9:1); the promise to Abraham particularizes the blessing: it is Abraham's progeny which will become a great nation. "In you shall all the nations of the earth be blessed" admits of several interpretations. A possible translation is: "May you be blessed as Abraham was," a grammatically more exact rendering than the usual translation which appears in the Septuagint and which has been canonized by use in Acts 3:25 and Gal 3:8. So considered the benediction pronounced on Abraham will pass into proverb as the epitome of all a nation can hope for and his blessing will be a model for every benediction they invoke upon themselves. But besides having this reflexive meaning the verb can also be construed passively; hence it is through Abraham that all nations will participate in the divine blessings; through Abraham as mediator Yahweh's plan of salvation will be effected throughout the world. The first of the promises is somewhat vague: the territory pledged to Abraham is referred to only as "the land which I will show you." Moreover, except for the notation "Now Sarai was barren" in the genealogy (Gn 11:30), no hint is given of the difficulties which will impede the fulfillment of the promise of progeny.

The most solemn enunciations of the promises occur in Gn 15 and 17 where Yahweh binds himself by covenant to their fulfillment. In the account of Gn 12:1ff Abraham's response to God's pronouncements was evident only in the obedience he rendered, but in ch 15 his more immediate reactions are noted. As it now stands the chapter is a skillful blend of two traditions, roughly delineated by the sections 1-6 (E) and 7-18 (J). The promises of vv 1-6 center in the progeny, those of vv 7-18, the land. When the puzzled Abraham remonstrates: "To me you have given no descendants; the slave born in my house will be my heir," Yahweh reassures him: "He shall not be your heir; your heir shall be one of your own flesh" (15:3-4). Again Abraham queries: "O Lord God, how am I to know that I shall possess it [the land]?" (15:8). Yahweh replies with directions for the covenantal ceremonies described in vv 9-11 and 17. The rites of cutting the victims in two and of the transporting of the smoking oven and fiery torch through the lane between the halves are very mysterious, although they may be cultic actions familiar to the hearers. Aside from his preparation of the victims Abraham is passive: "As the sun was setting, Abram fell into a deep sleep; and terror came upon him, a great darkness" (15:12). Nor is the relation of Yahweh to the phenomenon elaborated. In any event the gist of the narrative conveys Yahweh's solemn commitment to his pledge: "To your posterity I will give this land" (15:18).

The Priestly writer also has an account of a covenant with Abraham, an account vastly different however from the more primitive narrative of ch 15. The characteristic promises are imbedded in a heavy, verbose, theological passage which pays scant attention to the patriarch's reactions except to note that "Abram fell prostrate" (Gn 17:3). The repetitions throughout Yahweh's speech indicate that several Priestly traditions have been joined; the total effect is somewhat ponderous and makes of Abraham a mere lay figure against which to arrange theological considerations. Heretofore Yahweh had exacted nothing from Abraham beyond faith and obedience to the command to leave his home, but in the covenant of ch 17 he imposed the obligation of circumcision for the patriarch and his descendants. The fully developed legislative details on the ceremony of circumcision suggest a late period for this passage. Although circumcision was no doubt practiced in early times it was not a distinctively Israelite custom nor was it legislated in the principal biblical corpora. The Priestly writer himself does not refer to it outside Gn 17 except in Ex 12:44 and Lv 12:3. Other references to circumcision do not speak of it as a rite imposed by divine command. Only after the Exile did circumcision become the distinctive sign of allegiance to Yahweh and the covenant. To gain authority and prestige for the postexilic observance the Priestly writer in ch 17 sought to establish circumcision as a primitive obligation imposed by Yahweh as a token of the covenant.

The usual terminology for covenant making, *karat berît*, to cut a covenant, is not employed by the Priestly writer; he uses instead *qum berît*, to establish a covenant (17:7) or *natan berît*, to give a covenant (17:2). The deliberate change of vocabulary is significant. The ordinary term was used in covenants initiated by the free will of both participants; Yahweh's covenant however involves no exchange between equals. Rather it is a gratuitous bestowal of divine favor quite beyond the power of man to achieve for himself. If the covenant exists at all it is only because Yahweh has chosen to establish it, not because man has entered into negotiations for it.

Obstacles to the promise

Once he is aware of the divine will in his regard Abraham sets out to fulfill it. Considering the close ties between tribal members the command to leave country and kinsfolk is no small thing. So intent is the sacred writer upon the promises however that he shows no interest in the patriarch's migration from Haran to Canaan. Suddenly Abraham appears in Sichem (Gn 12:6), where the promise of land is further specified by Yahweh's declaration: "To your descendants I will give this land" (12:7). But even as Abraham pitches his tent near Bethel and thinks, perhaps, that he is at journey's end there comes the first indication that the twofold pledge will not be readily attained. Because of famine Abraham is forced to move south to Egypt; there he jeopardizes the future mother of the promised child by pretending Sara is his sister and letting her be taken into the royal harem. Since marriage was not basically monogamous a man could have intercourse with women of his own household, such as slaves or prisoners. Adultery strictly so called however was always severely punished; hence if Abraham was known as the husband of Sara he would in all probability have been killed before Sara was taken by Pharao. Yahweh will not permit Abraham's careless and cowardly behavior to void his promise; rather "the Lord struck Pharao and his household with great plagues because of Sarai, Abram's wife" (12:17). Pharao had acted in good faith, yet he was punished. The statement reflects the biblical theory which judges primarily on the basis of the act itself and pays little heed to the agent's conscious intention or state of soul. On discovering the true situation Pharao rebuked Abraham and summarily dismissed him.

Twice the same motif of threat to the child of promise recurs: once involving Abraham and Sara at Gerara (Gn 20:1-18 [E]) and a second time concerning Isaac and Rebecca at Gerara (26:6-11 [J]). The facts in both these accounts closely resemble those of Gn 12:10-16, but there are differences in tone and emphasis between the three versions. The story of Isaac and Rebecca is the simplest and perhaps the earliest of the three; subsequently the narrative was developed, given a new setting and assigned different characters. As the Elohist handles the story (20:1-18) the dominant motif of threat to the mother of the promised child has been glossed over by preoccupation with the question of guilt. The writer is at pains to justify Abimelech (20:4-6) and to exonerate Abraham by noting that Sara is really his half sister. (Marriage with a half sister was permitted according to 2 Sm 13:13. The later legislation of Lv 18:9, 11 and Dt 27:22 forbade it.) The vindication of Abimelech is readily appreciated but the defense of Abraham creates a certain tension: why should the man who regards God's promise so cheaply be made intercessor for the innocent king? (Gn 20:7, 17). The incident may reflect a later tradition of Abraham as intercessor (see also 19:29); at the same time it underscores that Yahweh is beholden to no one and bestows his favors where he will. The Yahwist on the contrary prunes away all superfluous details, even those in which the reader, at least the modern reader, is vitally interested. What leads Pharao, for instance, to connect the plagues with the presence of Sara in his harem? The reader also looks, but vainly, for some moral reflection on the disagreeable situation. The events are simply allowed to speak for themselves.

Yahweh's power has protected Abraham's wife, but to what avail? Sara is barren. Abraham's lament: "I am childless. . . . To me you have given no descendants" (Gn 15:2-3) continues the ever-present theme: how is the promise of posterity to be kept? Sara herself took a hand in promoting the divine plan by human contrivance (ch 16). Following a custom evidenced in the Nuzu tablets she bade Abraham: "Go in to my maid; perhaps I shall get children through her" (16:2). Abraham's feelings in the matter are not revealed. Did he too think to advance God's designs by human means? When the slave maid Agar conceived by Abraham she viewed her mistress with contempt and thus gave Sara the legal right to humiliate her. (The Code of Hammurabi has a similar provision.) The humiliation imposed by Sara caused the pregnant Agar to flee southward to the desert; there an angel of the Lord appeared to her, assured her a great posterity and bade her return to Sara (16:9-10).

The controversial figure of the angel of the Lord, *mal'akh YHWH,* is here introduced for the first time. In its most probable derivation *mal'akh* signifies messenger, though translated through the Greek as angel. The actions and words of the messenger frequently suggest however that the *mal'akh YHWH* is to be identified with the Lord himself. In the present story for example vv 7, 9 and 10 specify that the *mal'akh YHWH* spoke to Agar; yet in v 13 (which is the point of the narrative etiologically considered) Agar "named the Lord, who spoke to her: 'You are the God of vision;' for she said, 'Have I really seen God and remained alive after my vision?'" The same discrepancy occurs in the variant of the Agar story, Gn 21:17-18. Similar use of the term is found throughout the patriarchal history: 22:11 (the sacrifice of Isaac); 31:11-13 (Jacob recounting his labors for Laban); and 48:16 (Jacob's blessing of Joseph's sons). The phrase is also employed elsewhere in the **Pentateuch,** especially in Ex and Nm. The same puzzling ambivalence between Yahweh and his angel is also found in Gn 18 and 32:22-31, although in these places the particular phrase *mal'akh YHWH* is not used.

Such consistent dichotomy must be deliberate. One explanation is that the angel is an addition to primitive traditions in which Yahweh himself was the agent; the insertion of the messenger was the result of theological reflection which, through reverence for the divine transcendence, blurred the immediacy of man's relation to God by intruding a mediating figure who still spoke the direct words of Yahweh. Other critics hold that the messenger was the original figure in these passages. By analyses of texts and comparisons with usage in Babylonian and Egyptian literature they would prove that Yahwism, having reduced the original role of the messenger or vizier of God, inserted the direct action of Yahweh into passages where the messengers appear.

The Elohist version of the Agar story places the event after the birth of Ishmael and Isaac. This presentation of the double tradition as two separate occurrences, one before and one after the birth of Ishmael, has created chronological difficulties since the stories were inserted into the Priestly traditions without any consistent effort to harmonize them. According to Gn 16:16 and 21:5 Ishmael must have been nearly seventeen years old at the time of the second expulsion. The discord was not lost upon the ancient scribes, who evidently manipulated the text (e.g. v 14) to tone down the jarring effect.

The two accounts display marked differences in spirit and emphasis. The Yahwist does not seek to enlist the reader's sympathy in any particular direction. He carefully avoids revealing his own views and furnishes no clue to Abraham's feelings beyond the simple statement: "Abram listened to Sarai. . . . 'The maid is in your power; do to her what seems good to you'" (Gn 16:3-6). Agar's adventure in the desert is related with such paucity of detail that one is scarcely aware of her suffering. How different the Elohist narrative is. Sympathy for Agar is first aroused by Sara's petty complaints about her (21:9-10). That sympathy is increased as the details of the expulsion unfold: the wandering, the thirst, the mother's pain at the prospect of the child's death (21:14-16). Abraham's feelings are also spelled out: "The matter was very distressing to Abraham on account of his son" (21:12); and the writer carefully excuses him from any blame in the heartless action. It may also be noted that the Yahwist stresses the etiology of Beer-lahai-roi (16:13-14); whereas the Elohist only mentions the well with no reference to its name.

Both stories however stress Ishmael's future as the father of a mighty nation; far from minimizing the pledges given Abraham for the child of promise, the blessings accorded Ishmael are a foil to the still more lavish gifts reserved for Isaac. The angel depicts Ishmael as a fitting ancestor for the proud Bedouin: "He shall be a wild ass of a man, his hand against everyone, and everyone's hand against him; he shall dwell apart, opposing all his kinsmen" (Gn 16:12). This description may have formed part of an early tradition about the Ishmaelites; later it was added to the more fully developed Abraham cycle. Legends about Ishmael's later life are preserved in 21:21 and 25:9, 12-18.

The tribal history and the etiology in the Agar narrative should not obscure the central point: Yahweh's plans do not require human prudence and ingenuity for their advancement, nor do human estimations of what is right and fitting sway the Lord in his unhampered distribution of divine favors. The Priestly writer reinforces the element of gratuity as he relates how Abraham implores Yahweh: "Oh, that Ishmael may live in your favor!" (Gn 17:18), to which the Lord answers: "No, but Sara your wife will bear you a son, and you shall call him Isaac. I will establish my covenant with him as a perpetual covenant for his descendants after him" (17:19). And again: "As for Ishmael, I have heard you. I will bless him, . . . but my covenant I will establish with Isaac" (17:20). The promises do not preclude divine favors to other nations—the Ishmaelites too are the object of blessing—but the promises Yahweh has reserved for the people peculiarly his own.

Advance of the promise

Clearly it is not through Ishmael that Yahweh will make of Abraham a great nation. But the manifestation of the divine will in Ishmael's regard makes no positive contribution to the accomplishment of the promise, for Sara is now both barren and old; how can a child come from her? The Yahwist answers by posing a query: "Is anything too wonderful for the Lord?" (Gn 18:14). Heretofore the promises had spoken in general terms of descendants and posterity, or in poetic fashion of progeny like the stars of heaven or the sands of the sea shore. Now Yahweh moves to the concrete fulfillment of the promise in terms of a particular child, Abraham's son to be born of Sara within a year. While visiting the patriarch and his wife, Yahweh makes the astounding announcement: "I will surely return to you at this time next year . . . and Sara your wife shall have a son" (18:10). How Abraham received this statement is not recorded but the realistic Sara, listening inside the tent door, greeted the announcement with laughter. Her mirth was soon stifled by the visitor's uncanny question: "Why did Sara laugh? . . . Is anything too wonderful for the Lord?" (18:13-14). With keen insight the narrator describes Sara's confusion: "But Sara denied it, saying, 'I did not laugh'; for she was afraid" (18:15). The scene closes with Yahweh's firm and categoric utterance: "You did laugh" (18:15).

Finally, after long years marked by gracious renewal of the promises, by careless disregard of Yahweh's pledges or by faltering efforts to achieve them by human expedients, the birth of the child is announced in very simple terms: "The Lord looked after Sara as he had said; the Lord did to Sara as he had promised" (Gn 21:1-2). All the anxious hopes of Gn 12-21 come to their fulfillment in the birth of Isaac.[9] The arrival of the child however is not simply a happy ending to the isolated recital of trials and tests imposed on Abraham; it is an event which carries the salvation history forward into a new phase directed to the achievement of Yahweh's more comprehensive designs. The birth of Isaac is a stage, not the final goal of Yahweh's plan.

Accordingly it is no surprise that soon the inscrutable ways of Yahweh are again operative in a manner which

seems to threaten the very gifts he had bestowed: Abraham is commanded to travel to the district of Moria (traditionally regarded as the site of the city of Jerusalem) and there sacrifice his beloved son, all the dearer because he was so long awaited (Gn 22). What greater renunciation can be asked of a father than the death of his son? But the command to sacrifice the promised child also imposes an excruciating test on Abraham's faith in the Lord through whose favor Isaac had been given. The patriarch had not importuned Yahweh for his gifts; the promises were not so much objects of Abraham's desires as free pledges from the Lord. Quite unexpectedly the words had burst upon his startled ear: "I will make a great nation of you" (12:2). And Abraham had believed. All the more shocking then is Yahweh's seeming determination to bring to ruin what he had proposed so gratuitously. Before his birth Isaac had been the object of divine predilection and solicitude. Will Yahweh now make void his promise? The Elohist lingers over the aspects calculated to bring out the heart-rending nature of the demand: "Take your only son Isaac whom you love and go into the district of Moria, and there offer him as a holocaust on the hill which I shall point out to you" (22:2). Abraham's inner emotions are depicted with marked restraint but the graphic particulars of his actions provide an appropriate background for his somber thoughts which, though unexpressed, pulse through the scene. The structure of vv 7 and 8 is particularly effective, with the slow question and answer set to the rhythm of the travelers' footsteps as they inexorably approach the moment of sacrifice.

Although the sacrifice of Isaac may have been a cultic saga justifying the substitution of animal for human sacrifice, such a concept is quite foreign to the narrative as it is preserved in the **Pentateuch.** The material was in constant flux up to the time of its final redaction and is therefore open to many meanings. The etiological emphasis of the earlier traditions was lost as other elements assumed greater importance, so that the name Yahweh-yireh (the Lord sees or the Lord provides) is a minor note, not being the name of a prominent cultic center. The structure of the pericope tones down the horror of child sacrifice and by concentrating on Abraham's actions points to the test of his obedience as the essence of the story. Earlier his trust and faith had been tried by delay in the fulfillment of the promise; at Moria his faith was scrutinized even more searchingly as Yahweh, in seeming contradiction to all previous assurances, demanded the sacrifice of Isaac. To crown Abraham's obedience Yahweh repeats and expands the promises: like the stars of heaven will his progeny be and his descendants will possess the gates of their enemies (Gn 22:17). When the promises were first revealed, and before Abraham could prove his obedience, Yahweh had declared: "In you shall all nations of the earth be blessed" (12:3). Now that the patriarch has passed through the fire of obedience this assurance resounds more significantly: "In your descendants all the nations of the earth shall be blessed, because you have obeyed me" (22:18).

The promise of the land

Posterity and land of his own—these are Abraham's portion from the Lord. The traditions of Gn 12-22 are so centered in future offspring however that the promise of land remains in the background. Indirectly the subject was broached early in the cycle by a story contrasting the behavior of Abraham and Lot as they prepared to separate from one another (Gn 13).[10] Availing himself of Abraham's magnanimity Lot took the fertile, well-watered section of the land, "like the Lord's garden, or like Egypt" (13:10); nonetheless Abraham's is the better portion, for he let Yahweh choose for him. Lot's territory lay on the left, Abraham's on the right. Such a designation was an immediate clue to the Hebrew listener, who proverbially regarded the right as the favorable side and the left as the unlucky one. The writer inserts an additional subtle reminder of the disastrous consequences of Lot's supposedly felicitous choice: "Now the men of Sodom were wicked, and sinned exceedingly against the Lord" (13:13). Abraham's generosity and trust bring a renewal of the promise, this time elaborated and dramatically expressed: "Raise your eyes, and from where you are now look to the north and the south and the east and the west. All the land which you see I will give to you and your posterity forever" (13:14-15).

Failure to attain permanent possession of the territory apportioned to him posed no less a trial to Abraham's faith than did obstacles to the birth of the promised child. Despite years of residence in Canaan no portion of the land was his own; always he had dwelt as a *ger*, a resident stranger. Was he to die without entering into the possession assured him by Yahweh? The Priestly writer answers this question by relating Abraham's purchase of burial ground for his beloved Sara (Gn 23). Why should the writer who is generally satisfied to condense and abbreviate narrative sections here expatiate on Abraham's purchase of the field of Machphela? The reason is that the purchase, even though a mere business transaction, actually marks the initial step in the acquisition of the promised land and hence has a vital connection with the faith of Abraham—and of Israel. At first Abraham bargains only for the cave at the end of the field, but he ends by purchasing the entire piece of land. The Priestly narrator does not indicate the significance of the transaction; nonetheless his emphasis upon the transfer of the land and its location leaves no doubt that the full import of the deed is clear to him:

> Thus Ephron's field in Machphela, facing Mamre, that is, the field, the cave and all the trees in the entire field, became the property of Abraham in the presence of all the Hethites, his fellow citizens. After this Abraham buried his wife Sara in the cave of the field at Machphela, facing Mamre, that is Hebron, in the land of Chanaan. Thus the field with its cave passed from the Hethites to Abraham for use as a burial ground (Gn 23: 17-20).

We have already noted that there is close correspondence between customs described in the patriarchal narratives and those known from extrabiblical sources. Abraham's purchase of Machphela is a case in point, for a Hittite law imposes feudal dues upon the man in whose name an entire piece of property is held. The provision clarifies Abraham's insistence on buying the cave alone and the Hittites' insistence on selling him the whole field. The intimate knowledge of the subtleties of Hittite law and custom, which fell into disuse about 1200, attests the antiquity of the tradition behind the story.[11]

Machphela was not the resting place for Sara alone; when Abraham was gathered to his kinsmen he was laid beside his wife (Gn 25:10). Isaac too, although he lived as a stranger in Canaan, was buried in Machphela, the one portion of land he possessed. Jacob's final request of Joseph is for burial with his fathers "in the cave which is in the field of Ephron, the Hethite, the cave in the field of Machphela, facing Mamre in the land of Chanaan" (49:29-30). Thus in Machphela the patriarchs owned some small part of the promised land and at least in death they entered into their possession.[12]

The promise in the life of Isaac

After the climactic birth and sacrifice of Isaac the biblical narrative levels off to a more leisurely, less dramatic phase as it records the advance of the promises in the lives of Isaac and Jacob. How tenaciously Abraham clung to the assurance that Canaan would belong to his descendants is evident in the plans he makes for Isaac's marriage. Although desirous that his son should marry one of his own kindred Abraham insists that Isaac must not return to the former home in northwest Mesopotamia: Aram Naharaim, the land of the two rivers. Solemnly he admonishes his servant:

> Never take my son back there. The Lord, the God of heaven, who took me from my father's house, from the land of my kindred, who spoke to me and swore to me, 'I will give this land to your descendants,' will send his angel ahead of you and you will obtain a wife for my son there. If the woman does not wish to follow you, you will be released from this oath; but do not take my son back there (Gn 24:6-8).

The chronicle of the servant's efforts at matchmaking shows a texture different from that of the preceding narratives; it is more unified in structure and more secular in tone. Eliezer's discharge of his commission is related in a manner perhaps too repetitive for modern tastes, for example in Gn 24:34-49 when all the events of 24:1-23 are leisurely reviewed in the message to Laban and his family. Such treatment needs no justification other than the literary tastes of the writer and his readers; in addition a savoring of the details helps illustrate how Yahweh has providentially brought the mission to a successful completion, as both Eliezer and Laban point out (vv 27, 48, 50).

Once the marriage has been arranged and Rebecca has consented to accompany Eliezer back to Canaan the continuation of Abraham's line seems assured. The story then moves along brusquely with a minimum of detail: "So the servant took Rebecca and departed. . . . The servant told Isaac all that he had done. Isaac led Rebecca into the tent and took her to wife" (Gn 24:61, 66-67). A disconcerting genealogy has been inserted at this point—disconcerting because the recital of Abraham's children by another wife, Cetura, detracts from the uniqueness of the promised child and weakens the theme of promise and fulfillment. The list cannot be explained by the Priestly writer's penchant for genealogies since Gn 25:1-6 is usually attributed to the Yahwist.

The contrasts between the patriarchs raise the question: what was the original relationship of the patriarchs to one another? Gn 12-50 describes Abraham, Isaac and Jacob as father, son and grandson, but perhaps this relationship is a supplement to primitive traditions. It is generally agreed that the narratives grew from local legends of family ancestors; the localization of the Abraham-Isaac stories in southern Palestine and those of Jacob in central Palestine and the land east of the Jordan tends to verify this assumption. Quite possibly then the persons described as father, son and grandson originally had no connection with one another. As stories from one region began to circulate in other sections there was an inevitable revision of details and reassignment of roles. Certain aspects of the traditions were dropped; still others were developed or duplicated; and some figures emerged at the expense of other characters. In contrast to Abraham and Jacob, the patriarch Isaac is a shadowy figure; indeed whatever color glows in his life is reflected through Abraham or Jacob. Although on two different occasions Yahweh renews the original pledges (Gn 26:2-5 and 23-25) the absence of conflict and opposition lessens interest in the promises. A passing reference to the barrenness of Rebecca (25:21) does revive the problem of how the promise is to be fulfilled, but the difficulty immediately fades away when Rebecca conceives in answer to Isaac's prayer. And since Rebecca's danger in the royal harem at Gerara (26:6-11) occurs after the birth of Esau and Jacob, the incident creates no problem for the attainment of the promise and hence rouses less

concern than it did in the other versions. Not until the conflict between Esau and Jacob, first over the birthright and then over the blessing, does the subject of the promise come alive once again and suggest fresh problems.

The promise in the life of Jacob

In the Jacob chronicle the sacred writer stresses yet another aspect of the relation between the divine promises and human activity: can Yahweh's plans evolve despite man's machinations; can Yahweh incorporate into his designs faulty—that is, guilty—human acts? When Sara tried to secure offspring for Abraham through Agar (Gn 16:1 ff) Yahweh rejected her help, but his action on this occasion does not tell the whole story. On the one hand Yahweh can dispense with human activity in achieving his goal (thesis of the Abraham cycle); on the other he may, if he so chooses, utilize man's help, turning to his own ends even human malice (thesis of the Jacob cycle).

To develop his topic the sacred writer has made use of popular traditions for his own purposes. Recollections of a wily, calculating ancestor were a source of delight to the clever man's descendants, the more so if the persons outwitted were themselves forebears of the descendants' enemies. Thus Esau through additions to the primitive traditions is portrayed in contemptuous terms as the father of the hated Edomites. He is described as red *(admôni)* and hairy *(sē'ār)*—references to the location of Edom *('edôm)* in the south *(sē'îr)*. The play on words is repeated in Gn 25:30. Early versions of the story possibly played up the opposition between hunting and pastoral life. Esau is shown as a nomadic hunter, "a man of the open country;" Jacob is "a settled man who stayed among the tents" (25:27). While retaining their robust secular character the adventures of the nimble-witted Jacob were diverted to support the premise that Yahweh can write straight with crooked lines. So subtly is the point made that it can be easily missed by the reader, distracted by his effort to justify what is at best questionable behavior on the part of Jacob, Rebecca, et al.

Born grasping his brother's heel, even at birth Jacob merited his name of supplanter (Gn 25:23-26). Later he took advantage of Esau's carelessness and greed to get for himself the elder's birthright (25:29-34). These events are preludes to his calculated usurpation of the firstborn's blessing, whereby the promises were diverted to Jacob (Gn 27). The multiplicity of details builds up suspense until the moment when Isaac, convinced that Esau was standing before him, imparted his final benediction. To the Hebrews a blessing was an ontological reality having an existence in some way independent of the one conferring it; once given it could not be revoked.[13] Knowing this, Esau cried out in anguish "He took my birthright *(bekōrâh)* and now he has taken my blessing *(berākâh)"* (27:36). Now Isaac has exhausted his blessing with the bestowal of fertility and dominion upon Jacob: "God give you dew from heaven, and fruitfulness of the earth, abundance of grain and wine. Let nations serve you, peoples bow down to you. Be master of your brothers; may your mother's sons bow down to you" (27:28-29). Moved by Esau's pleading Isaac can only repeat to him a formula which, despite its external resemblance to the blessing accorded Jacob, stresses that the full force of the paternal benediction has been expended on the younger son: "Without the fruitfulness of the earth shall your dwelling be; without the dew of heaven above" (27:39).

The trickery of Rebecca and her son has constantly scandalized exegetes. Augustine was not the last to worry about the guilt of the bearer of the promise; his uneasy decision that the deceit of Jacob and Rebecca constituted "non mendacium, sed mysterium" has been echoed in subsequent efforts to palliate their action. Surely there is a mystery but it is not the lie; the true mystery is the inscrutable ways of the Lord, who directs even the wickedness of his creatures to his own ends. Jacob, not Esau, was to be the beneficiary of the divine promises first made to Abraham: such was Yahweh's decree. All things are in his hands and so completely is he master of the situation that he can accomplish his designs even through the perverted ways of men.

Jacob is now the man of the promise; to him accordingly the pledges are renewed. Since Esau bore a grudge—not unnaturally—because of the stolen blessing, Jacob fled to his uncle Laban in Aram Naharaim. Resting one night enroute Jacob was granted a dream and a theophany (Gn 28:10-22), perhaps two distinct experiences, which the narrator combined with indifferent success. Yahweh revealed himself as "the God of Abraham your father, and the God of Isaac" (28:13) and in language reminiscent of the promises to Abraham renewed the guarantee that a numerous posterity would own the land on which Jacob lay.

The initial manifestation of the Lord's favor is followed by Jacob's twenty-year sojourn in Aram Naharaim, during which time little is heard of the promises. The battle of wits between the shrewd patriarch and his grasping father-in-law, the rivalry between Rachel and Lia, the growth of Jacob's family—all these are secular both in subject and in treatment. The relation of the material to the theme of the promise appears nebulous until one remembers that these are the family traditions of the Israelite tribes among whom the patriarchal promises were so abundantly fulfilled. An appreciative audience never tired of hearing the family sagas of how Jacob the supplanter was tricked into marrying the wrong girl (Gn 29:16-30); how he retaliated and became rich at Laban's expense (30:25-43); finally how he fled from Laban back to Canaan

(Gn 31). In the account of Jacob's sons and their names, listeners could indulge their love of ingenious etymologies. (Preoccupation with names is a common Semitic characteristic. Etiologies occur about sixty times in Gn, Ex and Nm, chiefly in the Yawhist source. The Priestly writer rarely uses them and they are not even found in Lv and Dt. Some of the etiologies are entirely profane; some are cultic; others are theologized inventions which formerly had nothing to do with the salvation history.) Occasionally, it is true, there are reminders that it is Yahweh who guides and prospers the bearer of the promise (30:28; 31:7); and later portions of the cycle— the flight from Laban, the meeting with Esau and the return to Canaan—are more directly linked with Yahweh's protection of the man to whom he has tendered the promise. For the most part however the thread of salvation history is in some measure eclipsed by the profane spirit of the narrative.

Despite the blessings of prosperity and progeny Jacob is eager to return to the land promised him in the Bethel theophany. Several motives underlie his decision to go back; the most significant is Yahweh's command: "Rise now, leave this land, and return to the land of your kin" (Gn 31:13). Having obtained the consent of Rachel and Lia, Jacob sets out with his household for Canaan, once more outwitting his father-in-law. Laban's pursuit, his blustering accusations and his futile search for the household gods[14] paint a humorous picture of a clever man who has met his match. But there is more than amusement in the scene; Yahweh's protective power shines through the episode, especially when he warns Laban to do Jacob no harm (31:24). Jacob too, in defending his conduct, pays homage to the favors of the Lord: "If the God of my father, the God of Abraham, and the God whom Isaac fears had not favored me, even now you would have sent me away empty-handed" (31:42). Wisely Laban declines to contest the divine will; he concludes a covenant with Jacob and returns home.

As Jacob advances toward Canaan he makes characteristically shrewd preparations for his encounter with Esau. Between the initial embassy (Gn 32:4-21) and the actual meeting (Gn 33) Jacob had an uncanny experience: "Someone [*'iš*] wrestled with him until dawn" (32:25). The motifs of struggle with a divinity and of a wrestling which must cease at dawn have parallels in ancient myths and demonic tales; here they have been strangely incorporated into a story of Jacob's contending with Yahweh, climaxed by a blessing and the change of his name to Israel, "because you have contended with God and men, and have triumphed" (32:30). It is difficult to harmonize all the elements of the narrative. The assailant is obviously the more powerful (he cripples Jacob by touching his thigh); yet he pleads with Jacob to release him. In his reply Jacob recognizes the superiority of his adversary: "I will not let you go till you bless me" (32:27). The divine nature of the visitation is further witnessed by the name: "Jacob named the place Phanuel, saying, 'I have seen a heavenly being ['*elohim*] face to face, yet my life has been spared'" (32:31). At best the passage is mysterious and there is little prospect of working out all its irregularities; nevertheless the essential points of blessing and change of name are clear.

In the other patriarchal narratives Yahweh's manifestations to Abraham, Isaac and Jacob were accompanied by reiterated pledges of land and posterity; such renewal of the promises is totally lacking in the story of Jacob's wrestling. The blessing and the change of the patriarch's name however are equivalent to assurances of Yahweh's favor, and subsequently they are associated with the Priestly version of the promises in Gn 35:9-15—albeit a pale reflection of the enigmatic encounter at Phanuel. When Jacob first left Canaan, Yahweh had renewed the promises and assured him of personal protection (see 28:10-22); now as Jacob returns to the land apportioned to him Yahweh again meets him and by the mysterious action at Phanuel changes the worldly-wise, crafty patriarch and raises him to new dignity—"strong against God."

Jacob's arrival in Canaan, the goal of his journey and the goal of the promise, is reported succinctly: "Jacob came safely to the city of Sichem, in the land of Chanaan. . . . For the price of one hundred pieces of money he bought the plot of ground on which he had pitched his tent, from the sons of Hemor, the father of Sichem" (Gn 33:18-19). The casual mention of Sichem betrays little hint of the prominent role this cultic center may have played in the development of the patriarchal cycles, since this sanctuary was the center of the later Israelite amphictyony.

The life of Jacob as an old man naturally did not include adventures like those of his youth. The figure of Jacob fades into the background of the Joseph story; he has little active part in Gn 37-50; but he shows traces of his old spirit in Gn 48:14-20 when he manipulates the blessings of Ephraim and Manasses. After the story of Dina (Gn 34) there are no broadly developed narratives to serve as a conclusion to the Jacob saga, only a few sparse traditions like the pilgrimage from Sichem to Bethel (Gn 35:1-8). The preparations for the pilgrimage include cultic observances more characteristic of later Yahwism than of the patriarchal religion: "Do away with the strange gods you have among you, purify yourselves, and change your garments."

Passages like the above referring to patriarchal worship raise the question: what precisely was the religion of the patriarchs? There is no doubt that the final redaction of the **Pentateuch** identifies the God of Abraham, Isaac and Jacob with Yahweh, who operates throughout the whole course of Hebrew history. So much is clear. It is less certain however that the Pentateuchal picture represents the actual historical situation:

> Patriarchal religion is incorporated into the integrated theological pattern of Genesis-Kings. This pattern is viewed as being rooted in history, and patriarchal religion is presented in Genesis as the historical record of Yahweh's earliest dealings with the ancestors of Israel. The dilemma confronts us: is this identification factual, or is it due to later theological rewriting of the earlier documents?[15]

The attempt to resolve the dilemma usually begins with a consideration of the divine epithets appearing in the patriarchal history: the generic term '*el* or '*elōhim*, thought by some to be a proper name; '*el šadday*, God the Almighty, the favorite term of the Priestly writer, '*el 'elyôn*, the Most High God; '*el 'olam*, Everlasting God; and the proper name *YHWH*, Lord. The origin and meaning of these titles, as well as their relation to pre-Israelite gods, is currently the subject of extensive investigation.

The complex problem of patriarchal religion is sometimes reduced to the query: were the patriarchs polytheists or monotheists? The biblical evidence does not yield a univocal answer. According to Jos 24:2 Abraham's immediate ancestors were polytheists: "In times past your fathers down to Thare dwelt beyond the river . . . and served other gods." The household gods mentioned in Gn 31:19 show that Laban has many gods, but this fact tells nothing about the religion of Jacob. The covenant between Jacob and Laban seems to indicate Jacob's monotheism: "The God of Abraham and the gods of Nahor judge between us" (Gn 31:53). Since '*elohim* is used for both "God" and "gods" however the passage gives no clear statement of monotheism or of polytheism. Jacob's word: "Do away with the strange gods you have among you" (Gn 35:2) again shows that those persons surrounding Jacob were polytheists, but it tells nothing about Jacob himself.

That there was growth in the revelation and knowledge of God among the Israelites is a tenet of the Priestly writer (see Ex 6:2-3). The Yahwist however assumes that Yahweh was known and worshipped from earliest times (see Gn 4:26b).

The story of Joseph

In tone and structure the Joseph story (Gn 37-50) is a forceful contrast to the cycles which precede it. The theme of the promise so conspicuous in the lives of Abraham, Isaac and Jacob is scarcely touched on; consequently the relation of Joseph's history to salvation history is not immediately clear. Like the Jacob saga the story of Joseph displays Yahweh's subtle conversion of evil into good. Moreover the narrative as a whole documents the divine action which protects the children of the promise—Joseph and his brothers—in every vicissitude. The long biblical narrative develops without apparent divine intervention and without any advance in Yahweh's revelation; yet each stage of the composition reinforces the central theme of divine Providence epitomized in Joseph's pronouncement: "You intended evil against me, but God intended it for good, to do as he has done today, namely to save the lives of many people" (50:20; see also 45:5-8).

If the story lacks the promises which are the leitmotif of the patriarchal narratives up to this point, how does the composition advance the salvation history? By explaining how Joseph's family came to Egypt the history of Joseph bridges the gap between the themes of the patriarchal promises and the Exodus from Egypt. The saga is more than a literary synthesis however; it is salvation history, for the silent guidance of the Lord is one of his saving deeds no less than are his more vivid interventions in history. Joseph's dying words orientate the narrative to both patriarchal promises and to the Exodus: "I am about to die, but God will certainly come to you and lead you up from this land to the land which he promised on oath to Abraham, Isaac, and Jacob" (Gn 50:24; see also 46:3-4). As the cultic formula in Dt 26:5 notes, memories of a sojourn in Egypt were among the earliest traditions of Israel: "My father was a wandering Aramean who went down to Egypt with a small household and lived there as an alien." The event so briefly noted in the credo was later elaborated, perhaps within the house of Joseph, as a panegyric for a tribal ancestor. Moreover the shadow of Jacob hovers in the background as a constant reminder of the theme of the promises. Thus for example the vision at Bersabee (46:1-4) is a deliberate tie-in with the earlier theophanies at Bethel and Phanuel; the blessing the ancient patriarch pronounces on Joseph and his sons (48:15-16, 19-20) suggests the terms of the promises; and the so-called blessings of Jacob (49:1-27) anticipate the days when settlement in the promised land is a reality. These texts which link the story to salvation history are generally acknowledged to be for the most part later additions to the traditions.

The literary structure of the Joseph saga

In addition to its contribution to the main theme of salvation history the story of Joseph commands attention on artistic grounds. Showing no interest in etiology or in separate traditions tied to persons and places, the narrative is a carefully plotted unit resembling a novella. Accurate psychological perception, both in character delineation and in motivation, gives an appeal not found in the other patriarchal stories. The brothers' hatred for Joseph (Gn 37:5-11), their deferential behavior in the presence of the polished Egyptian official (42:6-17) and the gradual revelation of their change of heart (44:18ff) are credible and con-

vincing. Moreover the judicious use of motifs enhances the unity of the work as a whole. Joseph's pretentious dreams for example motivate his brothers' hatred and prepare for the later dream interpretations which bring Joseph into favor with Pharao (Gn 40-41). Then the motif disappears, only to be evoked once again at the conclusion of the story when "his brothers came to him in person and prostrated themselves before him, saying 'We are your slasves'" (50:18).

The story of Joseph is obviously related by a non-Egyptian for non-Egyptians, but no less obvious is the fact that those who formed the traditions used Egyptian materials and techniques. The opinion long prevailed that the Egyptianisms in the narrative are a superficial coloration, dependent on shallow and confused knowledge of life in the Nile delta and that, in fact, much of what is related about Joseph is pure fiction. Recent studies have shown however that the story has roots in a deep and comprehensive knowledge of Egyptian life and may perhaps go back to Moses himself. On the other hand the literary technique and the artistry of Gn 37-50 cause the composition of these chapters to be associated with the story of Davidic succession (2 Sm 6-3 Kgs 2) in the early days of kingship.[16] The emphasis of the Davidic-Solomonic age upon humanism led in court circles to the creation of a wisdom literature geared to the education and training of young court officials. The figure of Joseph could be that of an ideal courtier exemplifying in word and act the pattern of conduct extolled in wisdom writing. The history of Joseph, like other wisdom literature, is singularly free from theological pronouncements; only at the very end does Joseph tell of the divine plan which has been operative all the while: "You intended evil against me, but God intended it for good" (Gn 50:20). This sentiment is in the best tradition of wisdom writing, which is fond of showing the contrast between human and divine modes of action:

> In his mind a man plans his course,
> But the Lord directs his steps.
>
> . . . . .
>
> Many are the plans in a man's heart,
> But it is the decision of the Lord that endures
> (Pv 16: 9; 19:21).

Only among a people supremely convinced that Yahweh acts in the temporal order could the patriarchal narratives grow to the proportions shown in Gn 12-50. The primitive core of the conviction is doubtless founded on the real activity of the Lord in the Exodus and at Sinai. If deliverance from Egypt and the subsequent convenant with Yahweh occurred in time and marked an advance toward divinely appointed ends, then the period before these events must likewise be orientated to future goals. Hence the era before the Exodus and

Sinai is not sheer empty time but a period of initial revelation of divine goals, a time of gradual progress toward their attainment. Progeny and land were the two great promises given in the first disclosure of Yahweh's plan. In the patriarchal history the traditions dwell principally on the first of these promises, i.e. how the childless Abraham, despite obstacles of every kind, secured a numerous posterity flourishing in the land of Egypt. The fullfillment of the first promise is itself a pledge that Yahweh will be no less faithful in accomplishing the second; but its attainment must be in Yahweh's time and in his own way. ·

Themes of the Exodus

The narrative of the divine action in favor of the patriarchs constitutes a prelude to the tradition which Israel perpetually maintained as the most glorious example of Yahweh's work in her behalf: deliverance from Egypt and guidance to the promised land. The tremendous impact of the Exodus tradition on the religion and history of Israel is undeniable; it is the first of Yahweh's mighty deeds, the cell from which all Israelite theology developed. To this work of the Lord Israel attributed her whole existence and her exceptional place in the circle of nations. Memories of rescue from "that iron foundry, Egypt" (Dt 4:20) recur constantly within the traditions of the Pentateuch and beyond it. Wherever Yahweh's powerful acts are recalled, whether in the narratives or in the legislative sections, there the Exodus is brought first to mind, frequently by the hymnic epithet "Yahweh, your God, who brought you out of the land of Egypt," as in Ex 20:2. The narratives in the Deuteronomic histories usually recall deliverance from Egypt as a sign of Yahweh's continued help in the present and future: "For we have heard how the Lord dried up the waters of the Red Sea before you when you came out of Egypt" (Jos 2:10). Sometimes they invoke the Exodus as a motive for gratitude and obedience, as in 1 Sm 10:18. In the prophetic admonitions it is Yahweh himself who reminds the people how they were rescued: "I brought you up from the land of Egypt, from the place of slavery I released you" (Mi 6:4); and "When Israel was a child I loved him, out of Egypt I called my son" (Os 11:1). In the psalms the escape from Egypt is frequently proposed as a motive for praise (see Pss 78:12ff; 135:8-9). The motif of miraculous delivery from slavery continues to exert its influence in Christian times; it figures prominently in the typology of the Fathers and in the prayer life of the Church. A favorite theme of patristic typology is the correlation of events of the Exodus with the rites of Christian initiation.

Israelite cult evoked the Exodus theme by deliberately aligning the primitive Passover feast with deliverance from Egypt. Three times Dt gives this orientation:

> Observe the month of Abib by keeping the Passover of the Lord, your God, since it was in the month of

Abib that he brought you by night out of Egypt. . . . For seven days you shall eat with it only unleavened bread, the bread of affliction, that you may remember as long as you live the day of your departure from the land of Egypt; for in frightened haste you left the land of Egypt. . . . In the evening at sunset, on the anniversary of your departure from Egypt, you shall sacrifice the Passover (16:1, 3, 6).

Exodus and Passover are similarly associated in the festal legislation of Ex 12:23 and 34:18. (Lv 23:43 however links the Exodus with the Feast of Tabernacles.) The parenesis woven into the social legislation also recalls the hard days in Egypt as a motive for kindly treatment of slaves and resident strangers: "For remember that you too were once slaves in the land of Egypt, and the Lord, your God, ransomed you" (Dt 15:15); and "So you too must befriend the alien, for you were once aliens yourselves in the land of Egypt" (10:19).

Among the earliest texts commemorating deliverance from Egypt are the so-called cultic credos of Dt 6 and 26, both of which associate the Exodus with the tradition of acquisition of the land:

> We were once slaves of Pharao in Egypt, but the Lord brought us out of Egypt with his strong hand and wrought before our eyes signs and wonders, great and dire, against Egypt and against Pharao and his whole house. He brought us from there to lead us into the land he promised on oath to our fathers, and to give it to us (6: 21-23).

> My father was a wandering Aramean who went down to Egypt with a small household and lived there as an alien. But there he became a nation great, strong and numerous. When the Egyptians maltreated and oppressed us, imposing hard labor upon us, we cried to the Lord, the God of our fathers, and he heard our cry and saw our affliction, our toil and our oppression. He brought us out of Egypt with his strong hand and outstretched arm, with terrifying power, with signs and wonders; and bringing us into this country, he gave us this land flowing with milk and honey (26: 5-9).

Although Deuteronomic phraseology permeates the two passages the rhythmic and alliterative pattern indicates their great age. If the credos circulated orally for a long period of time before being written down (and this seems to be the case), their use would assume a rendition of salvation history which became quasi-canonical at a very early age. The stylized structure of the cultic confessions does not permit elaboration of the Exodus events, but the salient features of Egyptian oppression and divine rescue appear even in these abbreviated accounts.

Themes of oppression and deliverance

The basic facts mentioned succinctly in the cultic credos are rounded out in Ex 1-15, where separate traditions have been combined to display many aspects of Yahweh's activity in favor of Israel. So strong is the conviction that the Lord had marvelously rescued his people, so forcefully does the theme of deliverance pervade the Old Testament writings that it is necessary to posit an extraordinary historical event occasioning the conviction. The event itself however remains veiled. The persons involved, the date, the circumstances—these are matters which cannot at present be accurately determined. 3 Kgs 6:1 places the Exodus four hundred and eighty years before the fourth year of Solomon's reign, i.e. about 1438. There are reasons to question this date: the artificiality of the chronology (twelve generations reckoned at forty years each) and the archeological evidence unfavorable to so early a date.

The consensus of modern critics is that the Pharao of the oppression was Seti I (1302-1290) and that the long-lived Rameses II (1290-1224) was the Pharao of the Exodus. Some scholars however identify Rameses II as the Pharao of the oppression and his successor, Merneptah (1224-1214), as the Pharao of the Exodus. Although critics generally agree that the oppression and the Exodus fall within the nineteenth dynasty, probably between 1302 and 1214, others hold that a double exodus occurred, the first about 1400 and the second about 1250. In any event the tradition of deliverance became the property of all Israel, but this does not mean that all the tribes took part in the historical Exodus. One can only say that the people of the Exodus were elements from which the tribes of united Israel were subsequently formed.

The cultic credos refer briefly to the hard lot of the Hebrews in Egypt: "We were once slaves of Pharao in Egypt" (Dt 6:21); and "the Egyptians maltreated and oppressed us, imposing hard labor upon us" (26:6). With greater detail Ex 1 elaborates the theme of persecution by a description of successively more oppressive measures which the Pharao "who knew nothing of Joseph" employed against the Hebrews: forced labor, enslavement, inhuman killing of newborn males. In the enumeration of miseries separate traditions have been combined into larger units without our modern attention to proportion and emphasis; the story of the death of the newborn Hebrew males for instance has retained the names of the midwives, Sephra and Phua, but does not identify the Pharao (Ex 1:15).

Harried and bereft, the Israelites had no happy prospects either for themselves or for their posterity. At this point Moses appears. Although he dominates four books of the **Pentateuch** there is little that can be said about him with certainty. All traditions are unanimous however in according him the preeminent role as organizer of his people, as legislator and as the founder of Yahwism.[17] Born during the oppression, Moses was providentially saved and reared, according to a non-

Pentateuchal tradition, "in all the wisdom of the Egyptians" (Acts 7:22). Forced to flee Egypt (Ex 2:11-16) he took refuge in Madian in southern Arabia, south of Edom and east of the Gulf of Aqaba. Moses' relation to the Madianites (or more precisely to one of their tribes, the Kenites; see Jgs 4:11) has assumed new importance upon the adoption by some scholars of the Kenite theory of Yahwism. Since it was in Madian that Yahweh first appeared to Moses it has been suggested that Yahweh was the local god of the Kenites and that Moses adopted the worship of the place. Proponents of the hypothesis find additional support in Ex 18; Moses' father-in-law, the Kenite priest Jethro, offers sacrifice in Moses' presence and states: "Blessed be the Lord . . . who has rescued his people from the hands of Pharao and the Egyptians. Now I know that the Lord is a deity great beyond any other" (18:10-11).

In Madian Yahweh revealed himself and laid upon Moses the task of leading the Israelites out of Egypt. The portentous commission, so pregnant with vital consequences for all Hebrew history, is enhanced by the episode of the burning bush. From the midst of the fire Yahweh identified himself as "the God of your father, . . . the God of Abraham, the God of Isaac, the God of Jacob" (Ex 3:6). This Kenite theory of Yahwism (a favorite thesis with H. H. Rowley) has not found general acceptance.

As always in the salvation history Yahweh takes the initiative and commissions Moses to deliver the Hebrews. And, as always, human weakness is unable to take Yahweh at his word. Moses protests: "Who am I . . . ?" (Ex 3:11); "But suppose . . ." (4:1); "If you please, . . ." (4:13). But the divine will brooks no opposition. A second tradition of Moses' appointment is preserved in the Priestly writing of 6:2-7:13. The repetition of substantially the same account indicates the great significance Israel attached to this event (especially as regards the revelation of the divine name), but the retention of the second narrative is occasioned by another reason. By inserting the events of 6:2-7:13 after the similar JE narrative of 3:1ff and after the story of Moses' first encounter with Pharao (5:1ff), the redactor has presented the Priestly version of Moses' appointment as a confirmation of the original commission and as a summons to continued negotiations with Pharao.

The commission of Moses also gives the Priestly writer the opportunity to recount the revelation of the name "Yahweh." According to Yahwist traditions this divine name was known almost from the beginning; the conclusion of the Kenite genealogy reads: "At that time men began to call upon the name of the Lord" (Gn 4:26b; see also 13:4, where Abraham calls upon the name of the Lord). It is in keeping with the universalist theology of the Yahwist that he should trace the worship of Yahweh to the origins of the world. The Elohist

tradition on the other hand indicates that the name was not known until Moses' question brought its disclosure (Ex 3:13-14). What the Elohist implies the Priestly author makes explicit: "God also said to Moses, 'I am the Lord. As God the Almighty I appeared to Abraham, Isaac, and Jacob, but my name, Lord, I did not make known to them'" (Ex 6:2-3). The Priestly writer is here emphasizing the special character of Hebrew religion by linking revelation of the divine name with the events which led to the constitution of Yahwism.

The etymology of the word "Yahweh" has not been resolved to universal satisfaction; even if it could be, the etymology arrived at by modern philology would not necessarily be that of the sacred writer. A widely accepted view is that the name is a third-person form from the root *HYH* (earlier *HWY* and *HWH*) meaning to fall, to become or to come into existence; thus the form *yahweh* means "he causes to be what comes into existence." Originally the name may have had a longer litanic phrasing, such as *Yahweh s āb'ôt*—"he who creates the hosts of Israel."

Yahweh revealed to Moses his name: "*'Ehyeh 'ašer 'ehyeh*"—"I am who I am." Then he said: "This is what you shall tell the Israelites: 'I AM sent me to you'" (Ex 3:14). This translation has led to the interpretation common among Catholic philosophers and theologians that the proper name of God is Being. It is highly improbable however that the Semitic writer entertained such abstractions as being-as-such or aseity. The interpretation is based moreover on the Septuagint's mistranslation of the Hebrew form, which was doubtless a causative.

Some critics contend that Yahweh's answer is equivalent to a refusal to tell his name.[18] Among the ancients knowledge of a person's name was supposed to give power over the person. Moses' question then is not prompted by ignorance of the divine title but by a desire to know its essential meaning. Yahweh's answer indicates that God is not to be comprehended by the creature. Such a reading is justified by adducing biblical parallels in which the reduplication of the verb shows nuances of indetermination as in 1 Sm 23:13. Yahweh answers Moses: "I am who I am," i.e. "I will not tell you who I am."

But the meaning of the divine name cannot be based on etymology and syntax alone. The context must also be considered, and the context suggests that God is really telling his name, not refusing to disclose it. Since the Priestly writer is very insistent that the divine name was revealed only at the time of Moses the true meaning of the name seems peculiarly associated with the events of the Exodus, and perhaps with the Sinai covenant which followed. Even the Yahwist, who assumes the name was known from earliest times, links to the Sinai covenant a special proclamation of God's name:

"He [Yahweh] answered, 'I will make all my beauty pass before you, and in your presence I will pronounce my name, "Lord;" I who show favors to whom I will, I who grant mercy to whom I will'" (Ex 33:19); and again: "Having come down in a cloud, the Lord stood with him there, and proclaimed his name, 'Lord'" (34:5). In the final analysis however it seems impossible at present to determine the exact significance of the divine name for the Mosaic age. Given the context of Exodus and Sinai, the name refers to God as dynamically present to his people for the accomplishment of their salvation.

The contest with Pharao

The pace of the narrative accelerates as it depicts the struggle between Yahweh and Pharao, who repeatedly refuses permission for a festal celebration in the desert and imposes still heavier burdens upon the Hebrews (Ex 5:6-13). The royal obduracy is answered by the wondrous signs Yahweh had promised in chs 3, 4 and 7. The plague stories are secondary traditions developed and unified to translate into concrete terms Israel's realization of Yahweh as her champion against the forces that would enslave and crush her. The stories of the plagues in Ex 7:14-11:10 are mainly from the Yahwist and Priestly traditions, with occasional additions from the Elohist. The Priestly tradition emphasizes, as might be expected, the part of Aaron in the performance of the wonders; with his staff he produces the first three plagues and in each case confounds the magicians. The staff of Moses is also important (see 4:1-5, 17:15-17; 9:23; 10:13). The Elohist, though, stresses the hand of Moses in the accomplishment of the marvels (see 9:22; 10:12, 21; 14:21).

Each encounter between Moses and Pharao brings to nought the occult devices of the royal magicians, until finally the latter admit "the finger of God," thus vindicating the power at work in Moses and Aaron (8:14-15). The suspense of the narrative mounts as the king himself shows signs of weakening. The Israelites may leave if they pray for him (8:24); only the men may leave (10:11); the children may leave but the flocks and herds must remain (10:24). In a sense however each of the plague stories ends in an impasse; despite successive, undeniable manifestations of Yahweh's supreme mastery Pharao obstinately refuses to let the Hebrews depart—and then the whole situation is repeated in the account of the next plague. The motif of Pharao's obstinacy, referred to more than a dozen times in the plague narratives, further exemplifies Yahweh's sovereign control: "But the Lord made Pharao obstinate, and he would not listen to them" (9:12; see also 7:3; 10:1; 11:10). A creature's obduracy cannot shatter the divine plans, for Pharao no less than Moses is an instrument of Yahweh, and the power of the Lord is only magnified by all that men can do to thwart it.

The unified plague stories were put at the service of the Passover narrative, which is their climax; and the entire complex—plagues and Passover—was consciously employed to illustrate the salvific power which found supreme expression in the Exodus. It appears that the plagues are natural phenomena to be expected in Egypt; yet the disasters are certainly not described as natural phenomena but as prodigious deeds of Yahweh working through his servants Moses and Aaron. The stories may be rooted in folklore, but in a folklore utilized to extol Yahweh's free disposition of man and natural forces, to answer Pharao's insolent query: "Who is the Lord, that I should heed his plea to let Israel go?" (Ex 5:2).

Modern philosophy of nature does not recognize the divine action in ordinary physical events. Plagues, whether they are called natural phenomena or even extraordinary natural phenomena, do not belong in the realm of the marvelous. Among the Hebrews however the consciousness of Yahweh's activity in the universe was so keen that even natural phenomena were esteemed wonderful and mysterious: every work of the Lord is marvelous. This Hebrew concept is admirably shown in the happenings of the Exodus; what is remarkable about the plagues is not so much the phenomena themselves as the fact that Yahweh used these events to accomplish the rescue of his people. And although the modern critic must try to ascertain what natural forces were at work in the biblical stories of the plagues, the attempt to reduce the afflictions to a series of specific, integrated events has not as yet been successful.

As the affliction touching the Egyptians most cruelly the death of the firstborn properly climaxes the series of punishments sent against Pharao and his people. The life setting and attendant circumstances are unknown; the terse account of the fulfilled threat simply reports: "At midnight the Lord slew every firstborn in the land of Egypt, from the firstborn of Pharao on the throne to the firstborn of the prisoner in the dungeon, as well as the firstborn of the animals" (Ex 12:29). The killing of the firstborn impressed itself deeply upon Hebrew thought: first, because of its natural significance as the climax of the plagues; second, because of its association with the Feast of Passover, the meaning of which was greatly modified by the new orientation.

According to Ex 12-21 the Passover was probably a feast celebrated by the Hebrews while they were still in Egypt, although its precise significance is not known. The feast may have been one kept by nomads before moving to new grounds. In this case it would logically be associated by the Hebrews with their final break with Egypt, and the Passover sacrifice would be directed against the evil powers represented by Egypt. The account of these evils might naturally include the plagues. The Priestly writer links the old nomadic shepherd feast with the escape from Egypt and decrees its celebration as a perpetual ordinance: "When your children ask you: 'What does this rite of yours mean?' you shall reply, 'This is the Passover sacrifice of the Lord, who passed over the house of the Israelites in Egypt; when he struck down the Egyptians, he spared our houses'" (Ex 12:27). The ritual directions likewise connect the Passover with the Feast of Unleavened Bread, perhaps originally a separate celebration. The sacred writer attributes the origin of this feast to the commemoration of the hasty departure from Egypt when the Hebrews carried only unleavened bread with them (see 12:34, 39).

The Exodus proper

The event of the Exodus itself is difficult to follow not only because details are lacking but also because conflicting traditions have been retained. The manner of the Hebrews' departure is reported in different ways. The principal tradition affirms that Pharao granted permission to leave after the death of his first-born son, but traces of another tradition suggest that the departure was unknown to him: "When it was reported to the king of Egypt that the people had fled, Pharao and his servants changed their minds about them" (Ex 14:5). The story of the despoliation of the Egyptians (3:21-22; 11:2-3; 12:33-36) is not easily reconciled with the main tradition. That the Egyptians should urge the Hebrews to leave is understandable; that they should be well disposed and grant them silver, gold and clothing is less readily comprehensible. In addition the chronological relationship between the events is very obscure. The Passover ritual following the threat of the tenth plague implies that the three happenings—death of the firstborn, Passover and escape from Egypt—transpired in a single night (see 12:11, 31, 50-51); but variant traditions have been kept. In Ex 12:21-23 the Hebrews are told not to depart until morning; according to 12:30ff their flight evidently took place during the night. The Passover directions (12:1ff) indicate that the people are prepared for the flight which follows but other passages show that their departure was unexpected (see 12:33-36, 39).

What route the Israelites followed when they made good their escape is likewise not certain. Rameses, a city in the eastern part of the Nile delta, is named as their point of departure (Ex 12:37), and the tradition specifies that the people were not led "by way of the Philistines' land," i.e. directly along the shores of the Mediterranean, but rather "toward the Red Sea by way of the desert road" (13:17, 18). Despite these and other indications (Nm 33) their exact itinerary is not known, although new identifications of place names are continually being made. Finally there is no way of ascertaining the number of Israelites taking part in the Exodus. Ex 12:37 says 600,000 men but this total is far too high. A group of this size would imply a total population of nearly three million. The departure of such a horde—plus flocks and herds—is an utter impossibility. Moreover the country through which they marched could not conceivably sustain them. It is useless to conjecture what the original figure may have been.

The stirring display of Yahweh's protection during the plagues leads up to the supreme feat of the Exodus: the passage of the Hebrews through the Red Sea, more correctly translated as Reed Sea *(yâm sûf)*. Very probably it is the Papyrus Sea or Marsh Sea located in the northeastern Nile delta, a southern extension of the present Menzahleh Lake in the Mediterranean. The entire region is near the modern Suez Canal. Here again the actual event is obscure because two variant traditions have been preserved. One tradition relates how Moses is told to take his staff and with outstretched hand to split the sea in two (Ex 14:16); another recounts how the Lord swept the sea with a strong east wind and transformed it into dry land (14:21). The fate of the Egyptians is variously described. Yahweh with a glance throws their forces into panic and clogs the chariot wheels so that they could not easily drive (14:24-25). In a variant tradition Yahweh commands Moses: "Stretch our your hand over the sea, that the water may flow back upon the Egyptians, upon their chariots, and their charioteers" (14:26). And in v 27 it is related that "the Egyptians were fleeing head on toward the sea, when the Lord hurled them into its midst." The divine protection is also described in parallel traditions. The Elohist version tells that the angel of Yahweh, who had been leading the camp of Israel, moved to the rear (14:19a). In the Yahwist tradition the divine presence is represented by a column of cloud coming between the Egyptians and the Israelites (14:19b-20). These discrepancies do not touch the main issue since the historical facts of the situation are not of supreme moment. What matters—and this could not be uttered with greater clarity—is that "the Lord saved Israel on that day from the power of the Egyptians" (14:30), a fact which Israel recognized in Miriam's chant: "Sing to the Lord, for he is gloriously triumphant; horse and chariot he has cast into the sea" (15:21b).

The wandering in the desert

The theme of desert wandering connects the motifs of the Exodus with those of the conquest of the promised land. At one time the stories composing the history of the desert sojourn were undoubtedly independent narratives with a life setting now beyond recovery. In some cases the stories are quite old, although they assumed their position in the sacred traditions only at a later date. The wonder wrought at the Red Sea was a striking augury of Yahweh's solicitude for his people all the days of their wandering, days when he carried Israel "as a man carries his child" (Dt 1:31). He furnished them water (Ex 15:22ff; 17:1ff); he sent manna for their food (16:4-36; Nm 11:6-9); and he conde-

scended to their desire for meat by giving them quail (Ex 16:12-13; Nm 11:31-34). Dt gives equally impressive evidence of the divine protection: "The clothing did not fall from you in tatters, nor did your feet swell these forty years" (Dt 8:4; see also 29:5). During the early days in the desert Yahweh helped the Israelites defeat the Amalecites, Bedouin marauders of Sinai and southern Palestine (Ex 17:8-16), and throughout their wanderings he continued to support them in battle (Ex 21). Not content with satisfying their physical needs and with defeating their foes Yahweh preceded the Israelites in a pillar of cloud by day and a column of fire by night (Ex 13:21-22; Dt 1:33). A variant tradition recalls how the angel of the Lord was sent as a guide (Ex 14:19; Nm 20:16).

And what was the response of the Hebrews? The absorbing recital of the plagues and the negotiations between Moses and Pharao left scant opportunity for noting the reaction of the Hebrews. At the start of Moses' mission it was stated: "The people believed, and when they had heard that the Lord was concerned about them and had seen their affliction, they bowed down in worship" (Ex 4:31). Even in Egypt however some among them opposed Moses, for when they saw the Egyptians in pursuit they bitterly reminded him: "Why did you bring us out of Egypt? Did we not tell you this in Egypt when we said, 'Leave us alone. Let us serve the Egyptians'" (14:11-12). Later, awed by the exercise of divine power against Egypt at the Red Sea, "they feared the Lord and believed in him and in his servant Moses" (14:31). But scarcely were they out of Egypt when they began that steady stream of complaints which brand their years in the desert both before and after Sinai. Salvation history records not only Yahweh's deeds but also the interplay of human and divine activity—Yahweh's offer of grace and man's response. The murmurings in the desert document Israel's ungrateful response to all that Yahweh had effected in her behalf. Perhaps the stories are not a part of the original traditions of salvation history. But the narratives of the murmurings are so deeply imbedded in the traditions that they may be regarded as a very early theological concept of the mystery of proffered salvation and its rejection.

Thus after only three days' journey from the Red Sea the Hebrews grumbled because of the bitter waters of Mara (Ex 15:22-25). Again at Raphidim they quarreled with Moses: "Why did you ever make us leave Egypt? Was it just to have us die here of thirst with our children and our livestock?" (17:3; see also Nm 20:4). In both cases Yahweh listens to Moses' appeal and grants water to the maundering Israelites. The contrast between human petulance and divine condescension, between man's selfishness and Yahweh's generosity effectively reveals the utter gratuity of salvation. Doubtless these stories were at one time popular etiologies of the place name Mara (bitter), Massa (testing) and

Meriba (quarrel); one need not think that the narratives pretend to catalogue actual day-to-day events of the desert sojourn. Rather they have been amalgamated with the other traditions in order to point up the relation between Yahweh and his people more vividly and completely. Another etiological tale provides the foundation of Nm 11:1-3. When the people complained, "the fire of the Lord burned among them and consumed the outskirts of the camp. . . . Hence that place was called Thabera, because there the fire of the Lord burned among them."

Once more, longing for the hearty fare of Egypt, the Hebrews received the Lord's promise: "I will now rain down bread from heaven for you" (Ex 16:4). The story of the manna has been elaborated beyond the theme of murmuring but there is little doubt that its original core belongs to the narratives of the Israelite complaints. The meticulous directions concerning the manna, e.g. Moses' instructions to place an urn of manna in front of the Commandments (Ex 16:32-34), are a result of later reworking. The Deuteronomist sees a new lesson in the manna: "He therefore let you be afflicted with hunger, and then fed you with manna, a food unknown to you and your fathers, in order to show you that not by bread alone does man live, but by every word that comes forth from the mouth of the Lord" (Dt 8:3). Ex 16 mentions briefly the quail sent by the Lord (vv 8, 12, 13); a more forceful story in Nm 11 tells that this meat-food was given them after the complaint: "Would that we had meat for food" (Nm 11:18). Their greed brought swift punishment: "While the meat was still between their teeth, before it could be consumed, the Lord's wrath flared up against the people, and he struck them with a very great plague. So that place was named Cibroth-Hatthaava, because it was there that the greedy people were buried" (Nm 11:33-34).

Later these rebellious murmurings brought equally strict sanctions from Yahweh. After the death of Aaron the complaints of the Israelites were punished by the stings of saraph serpents. (The serpent pericope seems a latecomer to the traditions of desert murmuring. As 4 Kgs 18:4 indicates, its point of origin was very likely the bronze serpent idol which until the time of Hesekia was honored as a cultic symbol dating from the time of Moses. The story may have arisen to legitimatize the popular cult.) Only when the Israelites acknowledged their guilt and begged Moses' intercession did the Lord remove the affliction. Again, struck with fear at the scouts' report of a land defended by fierce inhabitants in fortified towns, the people reviled Moses, who nonetheless interceded for them (Nm 14:1-38; Dt 1:26-40). The Lord answered:

> I pardon them as you have asked. Yet, by my life and the Lord's glory that fills the whole earth, of all the men who have seen my glory and the signs I have worked in Egypt and in the desert, and who nevertheless have put me to the test ten times already and have failed to heed my voice, not one shall see the land which I promised on oath to their fathers (Nm 14: 20-22).

Most frequently the murmurings are directed against Moses (or Moses and Aaron) as Yahweh's representative, and usually there is nothing personal in the Israelites' charges. In two stories however the complaints are obviously dictated by personal resentment. The murmurings of Miriam and Aaron (Nm 12:1-15) are based on rancor over Moses' marriage to a Chusite woman and on jealousy of the favors Moses had received from Yahweh.

Later Core, Dathan and Abiram rebel against Moses' domination (Nm 16 and 17). The pericopes include two distinct rebellions: the religious uprising of Core (Nm 16:1-11, 16-24; Nm 17) and the revolt of the Rubenites Dathan and Abiram (Nm 16:13-15, 25-34; Dt 11:6). A desire to extol the Aaronite priesthood was probably one reason for the development of the Core narrative.

Even the conduct of Moses was not free from reproach. At Cades when they struck the rock to secure water for the Hebrews, Moses and Aaron incurred Yahweh's displeasure because they failed to manifest his sanctity to Israel (Nm 20:2ff). As a punishment they were not allowed to enter the land of promise. Ultimately it remains mysterious why the performance of the brothers on this occasion should prompt Yahweh to forbid them entry into Palestine.

Grumbling and murmuring led the Israelites to overt rebellion against the Lord in the worship of the golden calf (Ex 32) and in the sacrifices made to Baal Phogor (Nm 25). The ingratitude and stubborn resistance which characterized their response to divine favors earned for them Yahweh's epithet "stiff-necked people" (Ex 32:9; Dt 9:13). Although the memory of rebellious Israel in the desert is not lost for later writers (see Os 9:10; 11:1-2), it is interesting to note how this period is idealized in the prophetic books. Jeremia recalls: "I remember the devotion of your youth, how you loved me as a bride, following me in the desert in a land unsown" (2:2); and Osee looks for a return of that blissful time: "So I will allure her; I will lead her into the desert and speak to her heart. . . . She shall respond there as in the days of her youth, when she came up from the land of Egypt" (2:16-17b). Israel by the time of the prophets had repeatedly spurned the divine overtures and had accumulated a sorry record of failures. Yahweh's lasting covenant guaranteed opportunity for a fresh start and a zealous response in each and every age; yet the prophets thought nostalgically of the pristine desert milieu as the ideal circumstance for worthy response to the invitation of the Lord.

The Sinai theme

Conscious of election by Yahweh, Israel recognized herself as his special possession, dearer to him than all other peoples of the earth. That election—present germinally in the promises to the patriarchs and singularly indicated by the Exodus with its subsequent protection in the desert—Yahweh ratified at Sinai by a covenant not with a single individual (as he had made with Noe and Abraham), but with all Israel. By the terms of the alliance Yahweh became in a special manner the God of the Israelites and they became his people. In the persons of her ancestors Israel for many generations had realized Yahweh's predilection and had responded to it; never before Sinai however were the full implications of both election and response brought home to her so forcibly. Like the Exodus materials the Sinai tradition has its roots in history, but the Pentateuchal records yield no meticulous reports of events in orderly sequence. Although it is impossible to correlate the variant traditions satisfactorily the central message is strong and clear: at Sinai Yahweh revealed himself to Israel, inaugurated a unique covenantal relationship with his people and, by disclosing his moral will, provided the means to guarantee continued life within the covenant's bonds. Since the covenantal nature of the relationship between Yahweh and Israel will be discussed later it will here suffice to examine the Sinai theophany in general and to show its role in the formation of Israel's concept of salvation history.

The tradition of divine revelation at Sinai is vital to Yahwism. Not community of blood, or of land or of government but alliance with the Lord united the "crowd of mixed ancestry" (Ex 12:38) which fled Egypt. The course of early Israelite history, in which the sense of religious solidarity is bound up with the Sinai tradition, shows that the covenantal union established on the mountain of God is an original element in all sources, and it testifies to the factual character of the divine revelation. The evidence of later Yahwism also witnesses the primacy of the covenantal theme: the prophets reproach Israel for her great sin—betrayal of her election, rejection of the gifts and leadership of Yahweh. Surprisingly enough however the Sinai tradition long maintained its independence of other Pentateuchal traditions. The ancient cultic credos of Dt 6 and 26 pass immediately from the Exodus to entrance into the promised land, with no mention of the divine encounter at Sinai. The omission is the more striking because Dt 6:21ff purports to explain the meaning of the ordinances, statutes and decrees enjoined by the Lord—legislation bestowed at the time the covenant was initiated. Outside the **Pentateuch** the association of Sinai with other elements of salvation history became popular only in postexilic days; Ps 106 and the prayer of Nehemia (Neh 9:6ff) contain the first instances of the Sinai material joined to the other traditions of salvation history.

The dearth of references to the covenant in early texts and the relatively late association of the Sinai material to companion themes have occasioned the opinion that the Sinai tradition arose much later than the primitive traditions of the Exodus and the conquest of the promised land. Following Wellhausen many critics viewed the Sinai pericope as an interruption of the events at Cades, the account of which is broken off at the end of Ex 18 and resumed in Nm 10-14. Whatever Israel received in the way of law, according to Wellhausen, she received at Mara: "It was here that the Lord, in making rules and regulations for them, put them to the test" (Ex 15:25b). Therefore the critics regarded the ancient significance of Sinai as independent of any covenant or imposition of law. The late incorporation of so important a concept as the Sinai covenant into the Pentateuchal traditions does pose a problem, but to argue that because the Sinai tradition is absent from the earliest texts it therefore did not exist is to reconstruct the history and religion of Israel by literary criticism exclusively. After all, the only legitimate and safe starting point for an examination of Israel's relation to Yahweh is the evidence of the Old Testament taken as a whole: the worship of Yahweh was based on the covenantal agreement the Lord himself had established for Israel at Sinai. And the force and influence of the Sinai tradition are such that the theme must be accounted an independent primitive tradition in Israel.

Why the traditions of the covenant circulated independently and were not united with other themes in the preliterary stages of the **Pentateuch** is difficult to ascertain.[19] Perhaps it was because the revelation at Sinai was unique among Yahweh's saving acts. Israel's experience at Sinai differed from all her previous experiences of Yahweh because it was an encounter binding her to his declared moral will. To a degree therefore it is understandable why the events of Sinai would not readily be combined with other recollections of Yahweh's mighty deeds; the very uniqueness of the revelation kept it a thing apart. Sinai is primarily an encounter with Yahweh; therefore its traditions are kept separate from the cultic commemoration of Yahweh's salvific acts.

The Pentateuchal traditions of Sinai

The experiences of Israel at Sinai are recorded in Ex 19-24 (with supplementary matter in Ex 32-34) and, more briefly, in Dt 4:9-15; 5:1-5. Of the accounts in Ex almost four chapters are devoted to law (the Decalogue, Ex 20:2-17; and the Code of the Covenant, Ex 20:22-23:19), leaving a scant sixty verses to report the divine meeting so crucial to Yahwism. Because different traditions have been juxtaposed in these verses it is almost impossible to determine the sequence of events. Critics hold that both the Yahwist and the Elohist are represented in the Sinai narrative but there is little agreement on the sections to be assigned to each. Moreover some portions of the narrative, such as Ex 19:3-9 and 23:20-33, are almost certainly later additions. While the Israelites camped in the desert near the mountain of God[20] Yahweh bade Moses prepare the people for a theophany on the third day; all were to sanctify themselves and carefully avoid the sacred mountain as forbidden territory (see Ex 19:12-13). Then "on the morning of the third day there were peals of thunder and lightning, and a heavy cloud over the mountain, and a very loud trumpet blast. . . . The smoke rose from it as though from a furnace, and the whole mountain trembled violently" (Ex 19:16, 18b). Dt further states that the mountain was ablaze with fire (4:11; 5:23-26).

The phenomena accompanying the theophany are those of a storm and a violent volcanic eruption. The unusual combination has caused some critics to seek earnestly for geographic and climatic conditions which will account for the phenomena in their least details; they forget that the essential note of the theophany is the divine activity manifested in physical phenomena, which the sacred writer may have constructed so as best to convey the principal idea. Because a storm was linked with the event through which Israel was initiated into the covenant so vital to her religion, the storm theophany became the chief model for the depiction of subsequent divine manifestations—e.g. in the psalms.

The traditions vary in reporting what, if anything, the people saw in addition to the signs and wonders accompanying Yahweh's revelation. Ex 19:11 notes: "On the third day the Lord will come down on Mount Sinai before the eyes of all the people" (see also Ex 19:17); and Dt 5:4 recalls: "The Lord spoke to you face to face on the mountain from the midst of the fire." But in other passages the Hebrews only hear the words addressed by Yahweh to Moses or to themselves: "Then the Lord spoke to you from the midst of the fire. You heard the sound of the words, but saw no form; there was only a voice" (Dt 4:12; also Ex 19:19). Throughout the narrative Moses mediates between Yahweh and the people. Moses alone is permitted to approach God upon the holy mountain (see Ex 19:12ff; 24:2). Through him Yahweh gave directions to the people: "Thus shall you speak to the Israelites. . . . " (Ex 20:22); and through Moses the people respond to Yahweh: "We will do everything that the Lord has told us" (Ex 24:3).

The awesome phenomena occurring on Mount Sinai are but accouterments to the essence of the theophany: the revelation of Yahweh's will to establish a personal alliance with Israel. Unfortunately the texts provide scanty information on the exact nature of the covenant revealed by Yahweh. The stress upon law in Ex 19-24 by reason of the insertion of the Decalogue and the Code of the Covenant into the Sinai context suggests that the chief element in the Sinai encounter is the disclosure of divine moral law for Israel. At times the covenant (*bᵉrît*) is even equated with law: "And he wrote on the tablets the words of the covenant, the Ten Commandments" (Ex 34:28; see also Dt 4:13). Elsewhere however there are indications that the covenantal agreement is distinct from the commands which accompany it: "This is the blood of the covenant which the Lord has made with you in accordance with all these words of his" (Ex 24:8; see also 34:27).

The traditions of covenant ratification appear in Ex 24:2-11. According to one tradition—vv 1-2, 9-11—Moses and the seventy elders ascended the holy mountain and there, after seeing the God of Israel, partook of a sacred meal. Although ratification is not mentioned in the verses it could be that the sacred banquet, by symbolizing community of life and interests among the participants, was regarded as a seal of the relationship established. There is no question of Yahweh participating in the meal. But the banquet in his presence is nevertheless a symbol of the communion established with Yahweh through the covenant. The second tradition (vv 3-8) tells of solemn sacrifices at the foot of Mount Sinai in confirmation of the people's promise to heed all that the Lord had told them. In this pericope the ceremony of ratification is quite clear. After sprinkling blood upon the altar Moses read the Israelites the Book of the Covenant. Then he sprinkled blood upon the people, saying: "This is the blood of the covenant which the Lord has made with you in accordance with all these words of his" (Ex 24:8). Christ's explicit reference to these ceremonies at Sinai shows the continuing centrality of the covenant in Christianity. On the eve of his passion, which was to inaugurate a new dispensation, Jesus instituted the sacrament of his body and blood with the words: "This is my blood of the new covenant, which is being shed for many" (Mk 14:24).

The Sinai block proper (Ex 19-24) is supplemented by chs 32-34, which contain additional pericopes loosely related to the core of Yahweh's revelation on Sinai. Israel's worship of the golden calf is the center of interest in these chapters. More than once did Israel turn from Yahweh and spurn his covenant. In the episode of the golden calf the sacred writer has recapitulated this continual series of rejections. A supplement to the Sinai tradition, the story of the golden calf is doubtless a polemic against the calf worship introduced by Jeroboam I in Dan and Bethel (3 Kgs 12:28b). Discrepancies and a certain unevenness indicate that the tradition suffered many accretions. From the proclamation: "Tomorrow is a feast of the Lord" it would appear that the calf was not intended as an idol but as a throne for the invisible Yahweh. The association of the bull with Semitic fertility cults however made the use of this figure dangerous to Yahwism. Linked chronologically to the events of Sinai the story heightens Israel's wickedness in spurning the God who had so recently admitted her to special favors. The narrative serves still another purpose. Moses' breaking of the stone tablets in wrath over his people's conduct necessitated a second conference of commandments by Yahweh. Thus the redactor had an opportunity to utilize the Ritual Decalogue (Ex 34:14-26), which could not be fitted in the traditions of Ex 19-24.

According to Ex 19:1 the Hebrews arrived at the Sinai desert three months after their departure from Egypt. Here they remained after the great theophany until "the second year, on the twentieth day of the second month" (Nm 10:11), when they moved on into the desert of Pharan toward the plains of Moab. Preliminary successes over Sehon, Arad, Og and the Madianites (Nm 21 and 31) are portents of the successful conquest of the promised land. Nevertheless the spirit of revolt among the people occasioned a severe sentence from the Lord:

> Forty days you spent in scouting the land; forty years shall you suffer for your crimes: one year for each day. Thus you will realize what it means to oppose me. I, the Lord, have sworn to do this to all this wicked community that conspired against me: here in the desert they shall die to the last man (Nm 14:34-35).

Since the conquest of Palestine did not actually follow upon the immediate conclusion of the Exodus the traditions had to explain the delay in the fulfillment of the promise. The murmurings in the desert and during the delay in entering Canaan were regarded as cause and effect. (Dt 7:22 deals with the problem by noting: "He will dislodge these nations before you little by little. You cannot exterminate them all at once, lest the wild beasts become too numerous for you.") Consequently the Israelites are delayed forty years in the plains of Moab until the time decreed by Yahweh for their passage across the Jordan. In this land east of the river the exhortations of Dt have their setting. On the eve of entering into possession of their heritage the people hear a résumé of the deeds of the Lord—deeds which should prompt their grateful response:

> Your ancestors went down to Egypt seventy strong, and now the Lord, your God, has made you as numerous as the stars of the sky (Dt. 10:22).

> For love of your fathers he chose their descendants and personally led you out of Egypt by his great power, driving out of your way nations greater and mightier than you, so as to bring you in and to make their land your heritage, as it is today (Dt 4:37-38).

> The Lord, our God, made a covenant with us at Horeb; not with our fathers did he make this covenant, but with us, all of us who are alive here today (Dt 5:2-3).

The divine mercies elaborated in the **Pentateuch** prompt loving compliance with the divine will. However, no matter how impressive the deeds of Yahweh are, Israel remains free to reject the claim they make on her. The choice is her own:

> I call heaven and earth today to witness against you: I have set before you life and death, the blessing and the curse. Choose life, then, that you and your descendants may live, by loving the Lord, your God, heeding his voice, and holding fast to him. For that will mean life for you, a long life for you to live on the land which the Lord swore he would give to your fathers Abraham, Isaac, and Jacob (Dt 30:19-20).

Notes

[1] The tradition of conquest of the land is sometimes treated as a separate theme, especially by those critics who work with the Hexateuch, since this division includes Jos, in which the promise of the land is fulfilled. For our present purposes the tradition of the promised land will be treated with the promise made to the patriarchs.

[2] Elsewhere in the Bible however there are faint allusions to a struggle between Yahweh and the forces of chaos:

> You rule over the surging of the sea;
> you still the swelling of its waves.
> You have crushed Rahab with a mortal blow;
> with your strong arm you have scattered your
> enemies
>
> (Ps 89:10-11).

See also Is 51:9; Jb 7:12; 9:13; 25:12; Ps 104:7-9. These texts imply a continuing creativity and a continuous act of divine omnipotence holding in check the forces of chaos.

[3] AAS 40 (1948) 47 and RSS, ed Conrad Louis (7th ed, St. Meinrad, Ind. 1962) 152. Re Gn 1-3 read the decree of the Biblical Commission on the historical character of Gn 1-3 (AAS 1 [1909] 567-69 and RSS, 122-24) in the light of the reply made to Cardinal Suhard, ibid, 150-53.

[4] Joseph Coppens, "L'interpretation sexuelle du péché du Paradis," ETL 24 (1948) 395-439, endeavors to show that the western Fathers generally regard the transgression of Adam and Eve as sexual, some of them even holding that their sin was the normal use of sex.

Robert Gordis, "The Knowledge of Good and Evil in the Old Testament and in the Qumran Scrolls," JBL 76 (1957) 123-38, asserts that sexual consciousness is the only meaning of knowledge of good and evil which fits all the biblical passages where the term occurs.

[5] Although the same verb is used in both members of v 15b, some critics seek to substantiate a judgment of final victory for man by the relative positions of the man and the serpent: standing above the serpent, man is able to deal a mortal blow on the head, whereas the serpent can only attack his adversary on the heel. Given the physical structure of both man and the serpent however it is difficult to see how any other position is possible. Other critics offer a syntactic justification for their judgment by translating the connective in a concessive sense: "He will attack your head, while you will be able only to snap at his heel."

The messianic import of this *Protoevangelium* need not concern us here. The application of the text "He shall crush your head, etc." to Mary is a time-honored interpretation which found its way into the Vulgate text, where a feminine subject pronoun, *ipsa,* was substituted for the masculine form.

[6] R. A. F. MacKenzie, "The Divine Soliloquies," CBQ 17 (1955) 277-86, points out that Yahweh's soliloquies—his thinking aloud how he will deal with man—form a kind of literary genre of their own. See also Gn 2:18; 3:22; 6:3; 8:21ff; 11:6ff; and 18:17-19.

[7] There is an ample bibliography of extrabiblical parallels to usages found in the patriarchal narratives: Roger O'Callaghan, "Historical Parallels to Patriarchal Social Customs," CBQ 6 (1944) 391-405; H. H. Rowley, *From Joseph to Joshua: Biblical Traditions in the Light of Archaeology* (London 1950); ibid, "Recent Discoveries and the Patriarchal Age," BJRylL 32 (1949-50) 44-79; and Roland de Vaux, *Ancient Israel: Its Life and Institutions,* tr John McHugh (New York 1961).

[8] Von Rad's attitude to history is well illustrated in his *Old Testament Theology: The Theology of Israel's Historical Traditions,* vol I, tr D. M. G. Stalker (New York 1962). Noth's methodology is best exemplified in *The History of Israel,* tr P. R. Ackroyd (rev ed, New York 1960); and *Überlieferungsgeschichte des Pentateuch* (Struttgart 1948). For a different approach see John Bright, *A History of Israel* (Philadelphia 1959).

For criticism of Noth, et al see John Bright, *Early Israel in Recent History Writing* (Studies in Biblical Theology 19; London 1956); and G. Ernest Wright, "Archaeology and Old Testament Studies," JBL 77 (1958) 39-55; ibid, "History and the Patriarchs," ExpT 71 (1959-60) 292-96; and von Rad's reply to Wright, ExpT 72 (1960-61) 213-16.

[9] Sara explains Isaac's name in two ways: "God has given me cause for laughter, and whoever hears of it will laugh (*śahaq)* with me" (Gn 21:6). The notion of laughter associated with Isaac occurs in all three traditions. The Yahwist narrative of the prophecy of Isaac's birth makes much of Sara's laughter on that occasion; see 18:12-15. The word *śahaq* is used in the Elohist's description of Isaac playing with Ishmael (21:9) and again in the Yahwist account of Isaac fondling Rebecca (26:8). The word also occurs in the Priestly tradition. When Abraham heard the promise of his son's birth he fell prostrate and laughed (17:17). Besides the popular etymology which derives the name of Isaac from *śahaq,* there is obviously some further association which remains unknown.

[10] Wherever Lot appears he serves as a foil for the more imposing figure of his uncle. Abraham's superiority to his nephew is evident in ch 14; the patriarch frees Lot from the harassment of the four kings. Lot's proposal to give his daughters to the Sodomites (Gn 19:6-9) is one more example of his ineffectiveness. He is not a bad man—he even evokes sympathy at times—but his fearful and temporizing actions contrast unfavorably with those of Abraham. Completely ineffectual against the Sodomites, unable to impress his intended sons-in-law (19:14), he hesitates in the dread moment of God's judgment upon Sodom and has to be led from the doomed city (19:16).

[11] Manfred Lehmann, "Abraham's Purchase of Machphela and Hittite Law," BASOR 129 (1953) 15-18.

[12] The importance of the basic tradition concerning the promise of land can scarcely be exaggerated. The patriarchal history is organically related to it and the originally independent themes of the primitive history and Sinai have been correlated with it. The promised land is *the* great theme of Dt, where it is mentioned an average of about three times in each chapter, except in the legislative core of chs 12-26. The motif of possession of the land is part of the larger theme of inheritance throughout the Bible; see F. Dreyfus, "La thème de l'heritage dans l'Ancien Testament," RScPhTh 42 (1958) 3-49.

[13] Johannes Pedersen, *Israel: Its Life and Culture* tr Mrs. Auslaug Møller and Annie Fausbøll (2 vol, London 1926 and 1940) II, 182-212, has perhaps the best treatment of the Hebrew blessing. The frequent mention of eating to gain strength for the act of blessing (see Gn 27:4, 10, 31) stresses the idea that benediction is much more than an expression of pious wishes; it is a "creation" of the one who blesses and as such it engages all his vital forces.

[14] Stealing the wooden household god—*t^erāfîm*—was perhaps more than a spiteful trick on Laban, for the Nuzu tablets reveal that possession of the household gods gave title to the family property.

If Rachel told the truth about her condition (Gn 31:35) then the idols would be defiled by one in her state of impurity (see Lv 15:19)—a neat satire against gods of wood and stone.

[15] John J. Dougherty, "The Origins of Hebrew Religion: A Study in Method," CBQ 17 (1955) 258.

[16] Gerhard von Rad, "Josephsgeschichte and ältere Chokma," *Gesammelte Studien zum Alten Testament* (Munich 1958) 272-73. This book is scheduled to appear in English in early 1965 under the title *Collected Old Testament Studies;* see bibliography.

[17] The classic documentary theory which ruled against Mosaic authorship inevitably led to the rejection of Moses as he appears in the Pentateuch. With no disinterested contemporary reports to guide them, critics employing exclusively literary criticism could only conclude the impossibility of knowing the historical Moses. Recent scholars have returned to a more moderate position; they generally agree that to deny the historical reality of the person of Moses is to render inexplicable the course of Israel's history, her devotion to the law and her fidelity to Yahwism. Having denied the historicity of Moses as he appears in the Pentateuch, critics have been compelled to acknowledge him as an historical figure on the basis of the judgment of subsequent history.

[18] A. M. Dubarle, "La signification du nom de Iahweh," RScPhTh 35 (1951) 3-21.

[19] See von Rad's explanation of a cultic origin for the Sinai tradition, "Das formgeschichtliche Problem des Hexateuch," *Gesammelte Studien,* 20-27. For criticism of von Rad see Artur Weiser, *Introduction to the Old Testament,* tr from 4th ed by Dorothea Brandon (London 1961) 83-99; and W. Beyerlin, *Herkunft und Geschichte der ältesten Sinaitradition* (Tübingen 1961).

[20] The sacred mountain (called Sinai by the Yahwist and Priestly writers, Horeb by the Elohist and Deuteronomist) is commonly located in the south of the Sinai peninsula. On the evidence of Ex 3 and Ex 18 however some scholars place it in the land of Madian, i.e. southwestern Arabia. The mention of Horeb in the theophany to Moses (Ex 3:1ff) may be an addition, and it is possible that Ex 18 (which does not actually name the mountain) may be misplaced in the narrative. To locate the mountain in Arabia intensifies the difficulty of reconstructing the itinerary of the Exodus.

Abbreviations

AAS: *Acta Apostolicae Sedis*

AASO: *Annual of the American Schools of Oriental Research*

AER: *The American Ecclesiastical Review*

ANET: *Ancient Near Eastern Texts Relating to the Old Testament,* ed James B. Pritchard

ASS: *Acta Sanctae Sedis*

BA: *The Biblical Archaeologist*

BASOR: *Bulletin of the American Schools of Oriental Research*

Bib: *Biblica*

BJRylL: *Bulletin of the John Rylands Library*

BZAW: *Beihefte zur Wissenschaft für die alttestamentliche Wissenschaft*

CBQ: *The Catholic Biblical Quarterly*

CSEL: *Corpus scriptorum ecclesiasticorum latinorum*

DAFC: *Dictionnaire apologetique de la foi catholique*

DowR: *The Downside Review*

ETL: *Ephemerides Theologicae Lovanienses*

ExpT: *The Expository Times*

HAT: *Handkommentar zum Alten Testament* (Göttingen)

HSAT: *Die Heilige Schrift des Alten Testaments* (Bonn)

HUCA: *Hebrew Union College Annual*

Interpr: *Interpretation*

IsrEJ: *The Israel Exploration Journal*

JBL: *The Journal of Biblical Literature*

JBR: *The Journal of Bible and Religion*

JNES: *The Journal of Near Eastern Studies*

JR: *The Journal of Religion*

JSemS: *The Journal of Semitic Studies*

LXX: Septuagint

MT: Masoretic text

NRT: *Nouvelle revue théologique*

PL: *Patrologia latina, Migne*

RB: *Revue biblique*

RGG³ : *Die Religion in Geschichte und Gegenwart,* 3d ed

RScPhTh: *Revue des sciences philosophiques et théologiques*

RSS: *Rome and the Study of Scripture,* ed Conrad Louis

S: Samaritan Pentateuch

Scr: *Scripture*

SZ: *Stimmen der Zeit*

TS: *Theological Studies*

VD: *Verbum Domini*

VDBS: *Dictionnaire de la Bible: Supplément* (Vigouroux)

VT: *Vetus Testamentum*

VTS: *Vetus Testamentum: Supplementum*

ZAW: *Zeitschrift für die alttestamentliche Wissenschaft*

Norman C. Habel (essay date 1971)

SOURCE: "Interpreting Literary Sources: The Yahwist and the Promise" in *Literary Criticism of the Old Testament,* Fortress Press, 1971, pp. 43-64.

[*In the following essay, Habel dissects the literary structure and style of the Yahwist in order to recognize the writer's characteristic way of interpreting Israel's past.*]

As a literary artist the Yahwist[1] has been compared to Homer and as a theologian to St. Paul. These accolades may be true but they may also prove a smoke screen for the beginning student of the **Pentateuch.** He wants to see the evidence for a Yahwist source beyond the texts of Genesis 2-9. We could, of course, follow the lead of most introductions to the source hypothesis of the **Pentateuch** and list all proposed Yahwist style and theology. Such a method is comfortable. It adopts the findings of some great scholar and assumes that the evidence for identifying the Yahwist writer throughout, the **Pentateuch** is the same or similar to that provided in the preceding analysis of Genesis 1-9. The critical reader, however, will want to test these assumptions. He will want to know what kind of data, criteria, or evidence play a role in the identification and understanding of the Yahwist in the patriarchal, exodus, and wilderness traditions.

It is obvious that we will not have opportunity here to discuss each proposed Yahwist passage. Nor will we have a chance to treat many passages where the separation of Yahwist and Elohist sources is problematical. We shall therefore choose typical and normative materials to illustrate the literary character of the Yahwist subsequent to Genesis 2-9. In so doing we hope that convincing connections with the Yahwist texts of Genesis 2-9 will become apparent and the governing characteristics of the Yahwist's total literary work will be revealed. At the same time we do not want the bold outline of the Yahwist which follows to obscure the fact that many contours of the Yahwist literary source have become blurred in the course of textual redaction and transmission.

The Yahwist at work: a classic passage

Genesis 18 provides a profitable example of Yahwist literary formulation. In this chapter we can discern many of those features which are normative and typical of his literary artistry. A brief analysis of the chapter points up the following structural outline.

18:1-15 The Theophany at Mamre a. The Meal (1-8) b. The Annunciation (9-15)	(A) A patriarchal tradition story with editorial marks.
18:16-21 The Decisions of Yahweh a. Moving to Sodom (16) b. Soliloquy One (17-19) c. Soliloquy Two (21-21)	(B) A transition text with programmatic Yahwist passages
18:22-23 The Dialogue over Sodom a. Introduction (22) b. The Dialogue (23-32) c. Conclusion (33)	(C) A patriarchal tradition of heroic intercession

The three kinds of literary material suggested by the above outline provide suitable general categories for studying much of the Yahwist's literary work. To the first category belongs that mass of patriarchal traditions which have been preserved and formulated by the Yahwist in concise and classic story form. In this connection scholars have praised the grace, simplicity, economy of words, rapid movement of events, the suggestion of a setting with but limited detail, the building of suspense and the ability to involve the reader in the drama of an episode, as features typical of this master storyteller. Much of this honor may be due to ancient bards and elders of Israel who retold these incidents in the community circle. Be that as it may, many of these traditions have been preserved, reformulated, introduced, and combined by someone into a literary whole. Marks of one literary artist, identified here as the Yahwist, reappear within the text and context of these classic stories.

What are the grounds for that assertion? Let us consider first the literary features of Genesis 18:1-15. Legends about men entertaining divine beings or the annunciation of special births by heavenly figures can be found elsewhere in ancient literature. But few compare with this one in irony, simplicity, and beauty. Three men appear before Abraham in the heat of the day. The very hour of their appearance suggests something unusual about the adventure. Mystery shrouds the entire scene. The men are not identified to Abraham and their purpose is not revealed until after the meal. Abraham must first play the hospitality game. The account of that game is a masterpiece of humor and style. Each action is reported with extreme brevity and each statement is an ironic understatement. Abraham depicts himself as the supremely unworthy host. Typical Yahwist expressions which highlight that feature in the speeches of Abraham include, "your *servant*," "if I have found *grace*," "a *little* water," and "a *morsel* of bread."

By contrast, the actions of Abraham betray his intense efforts to please his guests with a massive display of hospitality. It is the heat of the day and yet every move of Abraham denotes great exertion. He "*runs* to meet" his unexpected, unidentified guests. "He *bows* to the earth" and "*washes* their feet." He "*hastens* to the tent" and orders cakes to be "made ready *quickly*." He "*runs* to the field," "*takes* a calf," and has his servant "*hasten* to prepare it." After this frenzy of activity on behalf of his alien guests he steps aside in silence as they conclude their veritable banquet of veal, curds, milk, and fresh cakes.

After the meal, the first remark of the satisfied guests has the potential to shock even the most congenial host in the ancient Near East. They bluntly ask for Abraham's wife. The gasping listener is quickly assured that their purpose in coming is honorable if indeed ridiculous. What man would be interested in Sarah, that laughing old woman eavesdropping from within the goatskin tent? Then suddenly the mood switches. The hospitality game is followed by a divine joke. The guests announce a miracle. Barren old Sarah is to have a baby boy by the following Spring. That was too much too soon for Sarah. She laughs her head off and reveals her unfaith. In so doing she establishes the character and name of her future son as Isaac, the Joke, the Laughing One. He is to be the miracle child whose coming was announced by the passing strangers at the banquet in the heat of the day.

How does the Yahwist betray his hand? Apart from the subtleties and word colors of the story already mentioned and specific expressions such as "find grace in your eyes," we can recognize an editorial framework. The story as such relates the advent of three men to Abraham's tent. Their names are unknown to Abraham. In his editorial preface, however, the Yahwist inter-

prets the story of their coming as a theophany. He explains that God "appeared" to Abraham (v. 1). The Yahwist, moreover, identifies that God as "Yahweh," the God of Israel. Likewise in verse 13 he identifies the previously anonymous spokesman of the three as Yahweh. In short, we see signs of an author retelling and interpreting this ancient patriarchal tradition in terms of his faith in "Yahweh's" guidance of patriarchal history. This observation is supported by the connected segment of material in Genesis 18:16-21. To this text we shall turn our attention below.

Many other patriarchal stories are preserved by the Yahwist with minimal editorial change. Typical examples include the jeopardizing of Abraham's beautiful wife (Gen. 12:10-20), the destruction of Sodom (Gen. 19:1-28), the discovery of Rebekah and the betrothal of Isaac (Gen. 24:1-67), and the blessing of Isaac (Gen. 27:1-45).[2]

The second major literary unit of Genesis 18 consists of verses 16-21. This unit, in turn, has three relatively independent sections (v. 16, vv. 17-19, and vv. 20-21). The first of these (v. 16) is a unifying passage designed to link the preceding theophany episode with the following record of Abraham's intercession for Sodom. The same function is served by verse 22. These two verses introduce the Sodom setting and the opportunity for Abraham to confront Yahweh with an alternate solution. Verses 20-21 go a step further and provide the divine rationale for the forthcoming destruction of Sodom. This rationale is given in the form of a divine soliloquy and corresponds to the divine musings in passages such as Genesis 6:7; 8:21-22; or 11:6-7. In typical Yahwist style Yahweh is the speaker and the reader is the listener. Yahweh is heard speaking to himself about the latest problem that has arisen on earth. As on other occasions Yahweh is portrayed in blatantly human terms. He has to check out the situation at Sodom to determine its seriousness. Then he will "know." As at the tower of Babel, Yahweh sighs, "Let me go down and take a look. . . . " It is in these soliloquies and similar passages where we find the Yahwist giving an explicit interpretation of Yahweh's role and character as he directs the course of history. They offer Yahweh's rationale for his own action. These texts, as in Genesis 18, are usually supplementary to the story line of the context but are given to interpret, introduce, or reflect upon the episode involved. Among the list of these rationale passages we should mention Genesis 2:18; 3:22; 6:5-8; 8:21-22; 11:6-7; 18:20-21.

The divine soliloquy of Genesis 18:17-19 is equally important. Its significance lies in its programmatic character. Yahweh's words' are not a command to Abraham concerning a specific situation in the life of the patriarch. His divine self-deliberation is not part of the story line of the episodes that precede or follow. Rather these words interpret what Yahweh was "up to" in the total life of Abraham. They give the divine program for the destiny of the patriarchs. Through this soliloquy the writer interprets what Yahweh was doing. Precisely because this is a programmatic passage we meet a set of loaded terms that reflect the theological perspective of the Yahwist. Verse 17 expressly asserts that Yahweh has a plan for the seed of Abraham. The nature of his destiny is summarized in the great Yahwist expressions clustered together in verse 18: "a great and mighty nation," "by him they will be blessed," "all nations of the earth."

Variations of these thematic expressions occur in other programmatic passages, but not with sufficient consistency to argue for a second literary hand in these texts. These programmatic texts provide the basis for our study of how the Yahwist develops his interpretation of the patriarchal promise. All of these passages have Yahweh speaking to himself or to a hero. Usually they are cast in the form of a promise. The passages involved include a sequence relating to the future of Abraham (Gen. 12:1-3; 13:14-17; 15:4-5; 18:17-19; 26:2-5; 28:13-15) and a similar sequence pertaining to the promised land (Gen. 12:7; 15:18-21; Exod. 3:7-8, 16-17). Many of the thematic terms from these programmatic passages appear as earmarks of Yahwist interpretation in other contexts as well. As examples we might cite Genesis 24:7; 27:27-29; 30:27; Numbers 22:6 and 24:9.

The third major literary unit of Genesis 18 is the dialogue over Sodom (vv. 22-33). Dialogues are not unusual in themselves, but when we meet God and man locked in this kind of bold verbal duel we sense something special. In the **Pentateuch** that kind of encounter reflects the mood and message of the Yahwist. Apart from the Yahwist connection in verses 16-21, the dialogue is introduced with Yahweh standing before Abraham in a typical human stance of subservience. (The RSV at this point preserves the later version of the text according to which Abraham stands before Yahweh). The dialogue itself enables Abraham to be the hero, the mighty mediator. He makes a valiant effort to save despicable Sodom. He appeals for justice to Yahweh, "the judge of all the earth." Ultimately his demand is dependent on more than justice. Only on the basis of mercy could Yahweh spare that city and on that score Abraham, Jacob, and Moses appeal for deliverance again and again. They are portrayed as the great heroes of the promise. The language of this dialogue reflects that kind of bold epic encounter. "Far be it from you," cried Abraham. Or in a modern translation he cries, "How dare you? Surely the Judge of all the earth will do the decent thing" (v. 25). Abraham cajoles God down from fifty to ten potential redeemers within the city. But the city apparently has no righteous inhabitants. As in the story of the flood they all deserve to die. Lot alone finds grace.

Similar dialogues appear throughout the Yahwist materials of the **Pentateuch.** In most cases we feel the same direct fearless encounter with the deity. There is something epic and mighty in the way these men of God grapple with their Lord. They are giants of prayer and intercession. Their God is so accessible he almost seems vulnerable.

The need for the promise

Our analysis of Genesis 18 was more than an exercise in literary skill. Here we saw the Yahwist at work as an interpreter in one segment of Genesis. Literary cirticism is also concerned with tracing the hand of this interpreter wherever he may be found. In so doing we can discover one way in which the ancient traditions of Israel were understood by its spokesmen. How does the Yahwist treat his traditions? What fresh insights into Israel's past are gained by tracing his interpretations through the **Pentateuch?** What do we unveil if we follow the trail of his programmatic passages and comments from Abraham to Moses? The outline of the Yahwist source which follows does not claim to cover all of the major themes or techniques of its author. We shall focus upon the motifs of programmatic texts such as Genesis 18:17-19 treated above. This means that the promises to the patriarchs will be at the core of our investigation. We shall discuss their function in the literary plan of the Yahwist. Thus we shall highlight their importance for a rich understanding of this literary strand in the **Pentateuch.** We hope thereby to illustrate further how the results of literary criticism aid the student of the Pentateuch.

Genesis 12:1-3 stands at the head of the patriarchal history and sets the agenda for the program of salvation.[3] In the wording of the Yahwist, Yahweh outlines a plan of blessing for the patriarchs, their seed, and their neighbors. The governing thematic terms are italicized in the following translation.

> Now *Yahweh* said to Abram:
> "Go from your country and your kindred
> and from your father's house
> to the *land* that I will show you.
> And I will *make you a great nation*
> and I will *bless you,*
> and I will *make your name great*
> so that you will be *a blessing.*
> And I will *bless* those who bless you;
> and those whom you curse I will *curse.*
> *By you all families of the ground*
> *will be blessed.*"

This plan of blessing begins with the patriarchs. It is absent from the primeval history. In fact the term "blessing" plays no important role in the Yahwist texts of Genesis 2-11. He views the primeval era as the age of man under the curse. With Genesis 12:1-3 a new way of blessing is opened for one family and its contacts. Genesis 2-11 shows the need for that new plan of salvation. His unique portrait of the background and need for these promises commences with Genesis 2, which is programmatic for the Yahwist's understanding of man.

The Yahwist begins by establishing an intimate bond between Yahweh and man *('adam)* on the one hand, and between man and the ground *('adamah)* on the other. Yahweh molds man and gives him life. Man is animated dust and Yahweh is his personal master (Gen. 2:4b-7). Man's tie with the earth is also expressed in his character as a farmer. Before his advent there was no man *('adam)* to till the ground *('adamah)*. After his creation Yahweh plants a garden for man to till and keep. Yahweh, in turn, cares for man and experiments with various forms of life to find a suitable companion for man. Like man, all the animals are formed from the ground. A special creative act was required, however, to produce a partner fitting for man (Gen. 2:8-25). The symbol of Yahweh's authority is found in the form of a tree called the tree of the knowledge of good and evil. Thus the stage is set for the progress of primeval history.

The Yahwist narratives in Genesis 3-11 follow a general pattern of sin, judgment, and grace or sin, punishment, and forgiveness. This pattern is evident in the Adam, Cain, Noah, and Babel stories. In each case sin disturbs the balance between Yahweh, man, and the ground. The first humans rebel by eating from the forbidden tree. The crime of Cain is murder in the first degree. At the time of the flood, evil is rampant in the hearts and lives of all men. The tower of Babel episode portrays man challenging Yahweh in heaven above. In these accounts the Yahwist portrays man as a powerful rebel. He has surging evil drives that must be controlled by one means or another. From the beginning man chose a course in opposition to Yahweh and in conflict with his fellowman. Adam and Cain are characteristic of all men.

In his preface to the flood story the Yahwist defines the nature of man (Gen. 6:5-8). His heart is so corrupt that all of his ideas are evil. This utter perversity of man is the basis for Yahweh's decision to exterminate all men. Because man is apparently trapped in this condition Yahweh discards annihilation as a future solution (Gen. 8:21). Yahweh's answer to the uprising of mankind at Babel was dispersion by confusion of languages. Here again the abnormal potential of evil man is emphasized. "Nothing that they propose to do will now be impossible for them" (Gen. 11:6). A similar limitation of human control is reflected in the soliloquy of Genesis 3:22 where Yahweh decides to expel man from the garden because "he has become like the gods, knowing good and evil." According to the Yahwist, man has the drive to conquer the heavens and

partake of the divine. That urge must be kept within bounds. "Hence," says Yahweh, "my spirit will not abide in man *forever,* for he is flesh" (Gen. 6:3). There must be a limit to man's life span. As Yahweh faces man's growing potential for evil he sets new limits to his capacity. The patriarchs are men of like character. They are heirs of these primeval rebels and in need of divine deliverance. Accordingly the Yahwist portrays the patriarchs in their full human colors.

The judgment phase of the Yahwist pattern of primeval history is regularly defined in terms of the curse. After the fall, the snake is cursed by Yahweh and destined to eat dust (Gen. 3:14). The ground *('adamah)* is cursed because of man *('adam)*. In the sweat of his brow he must till that ground until he returns to the dust from which he came (Gen. 3:17-19). Thus the eternal link between man and the ground is reaffirmed. The curse expresses the alienation of man from that ground. The curse is evoked by man but the ground suffers as a result. Cain too is "cursed from the ground" when Yahweh hears the blood of Abel crying from that ground (Gen. 4:10-11). This enmity persists between Cain and the ground. It will never yield to Cain's hand (Gen. 4:12).

With the flood story Yahweh's judgment reaches extreme proportions. He plans a universal curse. Man is to be exterminated "from the face of the ground" (Gen. 6:7; 7:23). For Noah's son Canaan the curse meant a history of abject slavery. "Cursed be Canaan, a slave of slaves he shall be to his brothers" (Gen. 9:25). Dispersion is the course of action taken at Babel; man is scattered abroad "across the face of all the earth" (Gen. 11:8-9). Like Cain he is forced to wander and his powers are curtailed. Hence, at the brink of the patriarchal age we find man spread over the accursed ground. Man has failed to achieve a great name for himself (Gen. 11:4). The future of man under the curse is a vast question mark.

Punishment by Yahweh is normally followed by expressions of his grace and forgiveness. The very survival of Adam is evidence of divine forbearance. Yahweh did not execute his threat of capital punishment. There is life for man despite the curse. Adam names his wife Eve because she is "the mother of all living" (Gen. 3:20). Further, Yahweh fashions clothing for the first couple. This act symbolizes the divine acceptance of man regardless of his sin and disgrace (Gen. 3:21). Cain, too, is given a sign of Yahweh's grace. The mark he receives assures him of protection while wandering through the earth (Gen. 4:13-16). Even this murderer is not put to death. Despite his deed, he confronts Yahweh with a blunt protest, "I cannot stand this punishment." This bold appeal of Cain wins mercy. He is protected even though he deserves death. In this he becomes a hero. The Yahwist includes many such heroes. They are men under the curse whose audacity gains them Yahweh's goodwill. Man is not impotent before the curse. He can scream to Yahweh for a revised plan of action.

It is typical of the Yahwist that Yahweh can and will change his mind. The decision of Yahweh to annihilate man means that his "experiment" with mankind has apparently failed. "He changed his mind about making man" (Gen. 6:7). That decision, in turn, is reversed by divine grace. "Noah found grace in the eyes of Yahweh" (Gen. 6:8). The decision, however, is not a fickle change of mind. He "grieved" over the condition of man before the flood (Gen. 8:6) and he rejoiced with Noah after the flood (Gen. 8:21). The welfare of man demands that Yahweh never again "curse the ground because of man" nor disrupt the cycles of nature (Gen. 8:21-22). Man can only survive if Yahweh operates on the grounds of free and forthright grace.

The sudden dispersion of mankind after the Babel episode leaves the world inhabited by a mass of frustrated rebels who have thwarted Yahweh's kindness at every turn. But with the advent of Abraham we hear the good news of a fresh program of redemptive action announced by Yahweh himself (Gen. 12:1-3). The sweeping array of promises wrapped in a concise message to Abraham offer Yahweh's personal dramatic answer to the looming question about God's goodwill to all men scattered across the "face of the ground." Now "all families of that ground will be blessed through Abraham," whispers Yahweh (Gen. 12:1-3). By Abraham the curse which was rampant over the ground during primeval times will be reversed and a bold new plan of blessing set in motion. As we trace this bundle of promises through the **Pentateuch** we shall be demonstrating a concern for more than literary style. Terminological features will inevitably be involved in the analytical process and certain identifying features will continue to be underscored, but thematic and programmatic characteristics will also be given due attention. For the theological perspective and groundwork uncovered in our study of Genesis 2-11 must now be related to the major centralizing motif of the promise to Abraham. Can that motif be isolated as a literary thread of the Yahwist? Does it persist as a governing theme in the midst of a vast panorama of old stories that seem to capture the interest of the reader on their own terms? Can a literary analysis discern those features of the record which reveal the Yahwist as an interpreter as well as a brilliant storyteller?

The patriarchs and the promise

Genesis 12:1-3 appears to be both the structural climax to the fourfold cycle of sin, judgment, and grace developed in the primeval history and also the *magna carta* for the fresh plan of redemption extended to the patriarchs. In the chapters which follow Genesis 12:1-3 the

Yahwist is especially interested in how these promises fare at the hands of doubting and devious men like the patriarchs. Hence the Yahwist's selection of patriarchal narratives seems to be related to the fate of the promise given to Abraham in Genesis 12:1-3 and subsequently reiterated in various forms. The patriarchal stories illustrate the numerous obstacles that stood in the way of accepting the promise and the extreme lengths to which Yahweh went in order to fulfill the promise. Interpretive comment and promise formulation within the narrative accounts indicate how the Yahwist links his stories and relates them to the governing motif of his work. The central unifying elements of the programmatic passages are drawn together in the text of Genesis 12:1-3. These themes can be summarized under four heads: seed, land, greatness, and mediation of blessing.

Seed: those chosen descendants who heard and transmitted the promises through the era of doubtful beginnings to the day of expansion and nationhood.

Land: that territory of Canaan and beyond which Yahweh bound himself by covenant to give to Abra-ham's seed as their inheritance.

Greatness: the destiny of Abraham's sons to achieve a great name and nationhood, despite the repeated possibility of their annihilation.

Mediators of Blessing: the privilege and responsibility of Abraham's seed to mediate the blessing of life to neighboring nations.

The bundle of promises in Genesis 12:1-3 is also a direct call for Abraham to express his faith in Yahweh by leaving his homeland and wandering off to some unknown corner of the earth. This initial outburst of faith is immediately tested when Abraham discovers that the promised land is really controlled by Israel's ancient enemy. Indeed, comments the Yahwist, "the Canaanites were then in the land" (Gen. 12:6). As we will come to expect in Yahwist contexts, the pertinent promise is repeated when its potential fulfillment has been challenged. "To your seed I will give *this land*" cries Yahweh. Canaan is not for the Canaanites, but for Abraham's progeny.

Time and again the promise stands in jeopardy. The sequence of narratives which the Yahwist selects for Genesis accentuates this precarious pose of Yahweh's good news to the patriarchs. For hardly has the promise been announced and confirmed upon arrival in Canaan when Abraham's land and seed are both in danger of becoming lost dreams. A famine arises in Canaan and Abraham runs to the nearest prosperous civilization for aid (Gen. 12:10-20). His lack of trust is further exhibited when he thinks of his own neck and allows Sarah to become Pharaoh's wife. Only by drastic divine intervention is Abraham rescued and his wife restored unharmed. Curse rather than blessing is mediated to the Egyptians as plagues fall on Pharaoh's household and foreshadow greater plagues to come.

Despite his spectacular deliverance from Egypt, Abraham must live with Canaanites and with a brother (Lot) who grabs the choicest regions of the land (Gen. 13:1-18). This situation prompts the Yahwist to add a postlude addressed to Abraham that heightens the previous promises of territory and progeny:

> All the *land* which you see I will give *to you* and to *your seed* forever. I will make *your seed* as *the dust* of the earth, so that if one can count the dust of the earth, *your seed* also can be counted (Gen. 13:14-16).

Abraham's need for a son is the focal point for several episodes selected by the Yahwist interpreter. Abraham doubts whether any natural course of procreation will provide him with an heir. He therefore tries to guarantee progeny by proposing that he follow the ancient Near Eastern custom of adopting a slave as one's heir (Gen. 15:1-6). Yahweh immediately rejects this scheme of Abraham and counters with a clear repetition of the promise that a son from Abraham's own loins will be his heir. The closing comment of the Yahwist at this point expresses succinctly his whole theological attitude to the patriarchal promise and its function in the life of those men. "Abraham believed in Yahweh and Yahweh counted that faith to him as righteousness" (Gen. 15:6). His living faith in the face of unbelievable odds establishes a true relationship with Yahweh. No cultic or sacrificial act was necessary to gain public recognition as a righteous man before God.[4] Faith in Yahweh and his promise was the crucial ingredient that bound Abraham to his God. This dilemma of faith continues to be posed by the Yahwist as generation after generation confront Yahweh and his good news.

Even the doubts of Abraham persist. "O Yahweh God, how am I to know that I shall possess it (the land)," he retorts (Gen. 15:8). Yahweh's complete commitment to his promise of the new land is publicized by an ancient covenant rite (Gen. 15:7-21). Here only do we find the Yahwist linking the patriarchal promise to an explicit covenant. He reports that, "Yahweh cut a covenant with Abraham saying, 'To your seed I will give this land, from the river of Egypt to the great river, the river Euphrates'" (Gen. 15:18). The extent of this projected empire suggests the greatness of the Davidic domain.[5] Those who were flushed by the sudden advent of power, greatness, fame, and international influence under David and Solomon certainly needed to hear the message that all their might was an undeserved gift and all their blessings due to Yahweh's patient guidance of his promised plan. Neither Israel nor their patriarchal forefathers had done anything along the way to earn that kind of goodness and glory.

The machinations of Abraham lead him to devise another means of obtaining progeny by begetting children through his concubine Hagar (Gen. 16:1b-2, 4-14). His scheme backfires, however, when Sarah forces the woman and her child out into the wilderness. Ironically Hagar is protected and given the divine blessing because of her association with Abraham. Thus Abraham unwittingly mediates blessing to the Ishmaelites, the descendants of Hagar's son Ishmael. Barren and disbelieving Sarah remains the final great obstacle to any possible fulfillment of Yahweh's promise for seed from Abraham's loins. She laughs with disdain at the announcement of her forthcoming pregnancy. The prediction of the three mysterious messengers from the desert is no more than a joke to her (Gen. 18:1-15). As analyzed earlier, this narrative is followed by a programmatic passage outlining Yahweh's intentions for Abraham. Once again the reason for the promised miraculous birth is the ultimate goal of greatness and mediated blessing which Yahweh plans to effect through the seed of Abraham. The soliloquy of Yahweh makes this conclusion clear:

> Then *Yahweh* said, "Shall I hide from Abraham what I am about to do, seeing that Abraham shall become *a great and mighty nation,* and that *by him all nations of the earth shall be blessed?* For I have *chosen* (known) him, that he may charge his children and his household after him to keep the way of Yahweh by doing righteousness and justice; so that Yahweh may bring to Abraham what he has promised him" (Gen. 18:17-19).

The following heroic dialogue between Yahweh and Abraham suggests a further explication of Abraham's role as a mediator of blessing. He attempts to salvage Sodom by a direct appeal to Yahweh (Gen. 18:22-33). The account of the destruction of Sodom is somewhat similar to the flood narratives (Gen. 19:1-38), for this account functions as an illustration of the continuing evil of man in need of Abraham's blessing and the ultimate judgment that descends when evil reaches unbearable proportions. The cry had reached heaven and Yahweh was moved to action (Gen. 18:20). As in the Noah tradition, the household of Lot survives the holocaust by the grace of God. His family, too, believes they are the last surviving people on the earth.

Into that evil world the promised son is born. Yahweh overcomes all the obstacles set by Abraham or his household and visits Sarah with a miracle (Gen. 21:1-2). "Who would have said to Abraham that Sarah would suckle children?" she cries (Gen. 21:6-7). With this dramatic beginning the promise is finally on the road to fulfillment. This seed is not a part of the natural order of things implanted in man at the beginning (as in Gen. 1:28). Isaac represents a new line that arises in the face of old, impotent, and doubting parents. The child is a gift of grace, a seed of hope, and a sign of the promise. Such is the perspective of the Yahwist program of salvation through promise. The Yahwist expansion of the story of the attempted sacrifice of Isaac underscores this governing viewpoint (Gen. 22:15-18).[6]

As the Yahwist interprets the course of patriarchal history, the line of Isaac has to be kept intact and kept pure. Isaac is not to select a wife "from the daughters of the Canaanites" among whom Abraham dwelt (Gen. 23:3). The story of the courtship of Rebekah illustrates this motif and highlights several others (Gen. 24:1-67). Foremost among these is the theme of greatness for Abraham and his progeny. Abraham has been blessed and his servant is certain that the God of Abraham will prosper his way. The extent of Abraham's might is related by the servant to the household of Laban:

> I am Abraham's servant. Yahweh has greatly *blessed* my master, and *he has become great;* he has given him flocks and herds, silver and gold, menservants and maidservants, camels and asses (Gen. 24:34-35).

Wealth is the first expression of that greatness. A second element is enunciated by the relatives who bless Rebekah with the words, "Our sister, be the mother of thousands and tens of thousands, and may your seed possess the gate of those who hate them" (Gen. 24:60).

The greatness of Abraham is surpassed by the wealth of Isaac. His prosperity is achieved at the hands of the Philistines despite his own folly in surrendering his wife to Abimelech (Gen. 26:1-33). This achievement of Isaac at Philistine expense anticipates the later role played by David. The blessing of Isaac is described in Yahwist terms:

> Isaac sowed in the land and reaped in the same year a hundredfold. Yahweh *blessed him* and the man *became great*. And *he became even greater* until he *became very great*. He had possessions of flocks and herds and a large household so that the Philistines envied him (Gen. 26:12-14).

This account of the jeopardizing of Rebekah and the subsequent prosperity of Isaac is preceded by a lengthy introduction in Genesis 26:2-5. These verses are not integral to the story itself but provide the Yahwist's continuity between the promise to Abraham and the first of his seed. The past promise to Abraham is now defined as an oath that must be kept by Yahweh. The consistent dimensions of the promise are reflected in the recurring terminology:

> Sojourn in this land of which I shall tell you. I will be with you and bless you; for *to you* and *to your*

seed I will give all these lands, and I will fulfill *the oath* which I swore to Abraham your father. I will multiply *your seed* as *the stars* of heaven, and I will give to *your seed* all these lands. And *by your seed all nations of the earth shall bless themselves* (Gen. 26:3-4).

The promise to Abraham is viewed as normative for his descendants. They gain salvation because of the oath sworn to Abraham and are blessed "for my servant Abraham's sake" (Gen. 26:24).

The oath to Abraham is threatened by the antics of Jacob. The Yahwist exposes Jacob as a scoundrel who usurps the blessing and takes advantage of its power. Like his father Isaac, Jacob is a miracle child born from a barren mother (Gen. 25:21-26). Through Yahweh's special answer the promise of seed is preserved. Jacob's character, however, is hardly appropriate for Yahweh's chosen line. He tricks Esau into gaining birthright privileges from his brother (Gen. 25:27-34), and he schemes with his mother to obtain the filial blessing of Isaac (Gen. 27:1-45). That blessing turns out to be a poetic version of the patriarchal promise of greatness that suggests the might of David's empire:

> May God give you the dew of heaven and of the fatness of the earth, and plenty of grain and wine. Let *peoples* serve you and *nations* bow down to you. Be lord over your brothers and may your mother's sons bow down to you. *Cursed be every one who curses you and blessed be every one who blesses you* (Gen. 27:28-29).

The stolen blessing from Isaac is confirmed by the promise of blessing from Yahweh himself (Gen 28:13-16). This passage is the Yahwist's programmatic text introducing the life of Jacob. The promise is connected with his journey away from the promised land, just as the initial promise to Abraham was linked to his trip from Mesopotamia and the opening promise to Isaac was tied to his journey into Philistine regions. In this promise to Jacob, great progeny and the mediating of blessing are closely related to the immediate assurance of inheriting the land. The continuity between this promise and its predecessors is reflected in Yahweh's self-identification as the God of both Abraham and Isaac. The dispersion of Jacob's seed in all directions is designed to provide blessing for all nations of the earth. This promise naturally recalls the expansion of the Davidic empire and suggests the divine reversal of Yahweh's earlier curse on all peoples when he scattered them in all directions (Gen. 11:109). This promise given to Jacob is worded as follows:

> I am Yahweh, the God of Abraham your father and the God of Isaac; the land on which you lie I will give *to you and to your seed;* and *your seed* shall

be like *the dust* of the earth, and you shall spread abroad to the west and to the east and to the north and to the south; and *by you and your seed shall all families of the ground be blessed.* Behold I am with you and will keep you wherever you go, and will bring you back to this ground, for I will not leave you until I have done that of which I have spoken to you (Gen. 28:13-15).

The narrative cycle relating to Jacob and Laban seems to include at least two different traditions (Gen. 29-31). The editorial hand of the Yahwist, however, is clearly evident. Not only does Jacob gain a large family, but he is blessed at every turn. He cannot help prospering (Gen. 30:30). More significantly, this blessing is mediated to Laban. "I have learned by divination," states Laban, "that Yahweh has *blessed me because of you*" (Gen. 30:27). And Jacob confesses that, "If the God of my father, the God of Abraham and the Fear of Isaac, had not been on my side, surely now you would have sent me away empty-handed" (Gen. 31:42).

The narratives about Jacob's return from Haran and his confrontation with Esau are again interpreted in the light of the promise. Jacob's prayer for help is worded in terms of Yahwist theology. Jacob admits he was blessed by the undeserved grace of Yahweh and recognizes his two companies as the result of divine goodness. His demand for future deliverance, however, is not based on any vow of loyalty, any oath of allegiance to God's law, any commitment of homage, but upon Yahweh's past promise of numerous seed. To Yahweh's face he cries, "*You yourself said,* 'I will do you good, and make your seed as the sand of the sea, which cannot be numbered for multitude'" (Gen. 32:12). That promise is the ground of Jacob's violent appeal. His is a heroic demand matched only by his nocturnal struggle for a special blessing (Gen. 32:24-32). The greatness of Jacob lies in these bold encounters with Yahweh from whom he wins protection, blessing, and a new name. His name Israel expresses that greatness, "for," says the angel of the night, "you have striven with God and men and have prevailed" (Gen. 32:28).

The cycle of stories related to Joseph and the descent of Jacob's household into Egypt highlights the mediating of blessing to Egypt in the face of apparent disaster for Israel (Gen. 39-47). Immediately upon arrival in Egypt the Yahwist declares that "Yahweh blessed the Egyptian's house for Joseph's sake; the blessing of Yahweh was upon all he had, in house and field" (Gen. 39:5). Even in prison Joseph continues in favor with both Yahweh and his prison keeper. His activity in prison is prospered by Yahweh himself. Nothing could stop the power of his blessing. His good fortune and political power are divine schemes to rescue his own family from starvation. Once in Egypt the household of Jacob again prospers until the Egyptians cry, "Behold the people of Israel are too many and too power-

ful for us" (Exod. 1:9). The Yahwist concludes the development of the patriarchal blessing motif in Genesis by incorporating Jacob's blessings for each of his twelve sons (Gen. 49:1-28). In this sequence the promise of ultimate political greatness and national might is given to Judah. He is to inherit the scepter and the obedience of the peoples (Gen. 49:8-12). In this blessing it seems that the Yahwist is deliberately linking the promise to the patriarchs with a later fulfillment under the Davidic monarchy. Through David the tribe of Judah gained "the scepter" of kingship and became a nation capable of ruling other peoples. With poetic beauty this final patriarchal promise reads:

> The scepter shall not depart from Judah,
> nor the ruler's staff from between his feet,
> until he comes to whom it belongs;
> and to him shall the obedience of the peoples
>   be
>
> (Gen. 49:10).

Moses and the promise

The patriarchal promise motif does not die with the patriarchs. Granted it does not appear with the same frequency or with the same full complement of terminological identification marks as in Genesis, but the basic promise theme remains a driving impulse for motivating Yahweh's actions. Many new colors and concepts now arise in the Yahwist portraits of Israel's history, but at crucial scenes in the life of Moses' people the promise reappears as the word of deliverance or the salutary basis for appeal. A demonstration of how this governing motif operates in the Mosaic period is attempted here as we quickly trace several normative Yahwist catchwords and concepts through Exodus and Numbers.

Throughout the Mosaic era we find deliverance evoked by heroic pleas of intercession, public cries of agony, or direct prayers of mediation. The endless scream of Israel under Egyptian bondage is the first great appeal that moves Yahweh to keep his promise (Exod. 3:7-8). As on past occasions the Yahwist describes Yahweh "coming down" to get personally involved in the human struggle (cf. Gen. 11:7). His goal is to deliver Israel from Egypt and return his people to their land, the land of the Canaanites. In the words of the Yahwist, the Lord is acclaimed as "Yahweh, the God of your fathers, the God of Abraham, of Isaac and of Jacob" (Exod. 3:16). Yahweh is identified by virtue of his association with the heroes of the promise, and he renews that ancient promise of land to his oppressed people in slavery (Exod. 3:16-17). In this connection Moses becomes the peculiar symbol of Yahweh's mercy and the mediator of his promised program. "They will not *believe* me," objects Moses (Exod. 4:1). Like their forefathers the Israelites are not ready to "believe" without the assurance of signs and wonders (Exod.

4:1-31). At the crossing of the Red Sea the Israelites finally come to trust Yahweh and his representative. Only then do they "see the great work which Yahweh did against the Egyptians," and "*believe* in Yahweh and in his servant Moses" (Exod. 14:31).

The obstacles to fulfilling Yahweh's promises experienced by the patriarchs are dwarfed by the catastrophe of Israel's slavery. Deliverance called for drastic measures. And while the Yahwist includes the many plagues imposed upon Egypt to effect deliverance, he still sees opportunitites for mediating forgiveness and blessing even to the oppressor. "Forgive my sin, I pray you, only this once, and entreat Yahweh your God only to remove this death from me," pleads Pharaoh to Moses and Aaron (Exod. 10:17). After the Passover Pharaoh grants permission for Israel to worship for three days in the wilderness. At this time he is heard to summon Moses, "Go serve Yahweh your God, as you have said. Take your flocks and your herds, as you have said, and be gone, *and bless me also*" (Exod. 12:29-32). Pharaoh, too, seems to want the blessing available through the line of Abraham. Thus it is that Israel leaves Egypt, having "*found grace* in the eyes of the Egyptians," and having expanded to a "mixed multitude" (Exod. 12:33-39).

Throughout the wilderness travels Moses is portrayed as the mediator of life for the sons of Israel. Through direct communication with Yahweh he can avert doom for his own people just as he could revoke the curses upon Egypt. Like the patriarchs before him, his word can evoke unequivocal divine grace because of the promise. When the Israelites murmur over conditions at Marah and Rephidim, Moses intercedes on their behalf and Yahweh provides a convenient solution to the problem (Exod. 15:22b-25a; 17:1-7). Moses not only represents the people before Yahweh, however, but he also mediates Yahweh's will to the people. The fate of Israel depends on believing Moses, the mediator. The great theophany of Yahweh at Sinai (Exod. 19:9-25) is therefore designed to arouse trust in Yahweh and in Moses his spokesman:

> And Yahweh said unto Moses, "Lo, I am coming to you in a thick cloud, that the people may hear when I speak *with you,* and may also *believe you forever* (Exod. 19:9).

According to the Yahwist, Moses and Joshua ascend the mountain to receive the two tables of stone (Exod. 24:12-15a). Before descending they are confronted by Yahweh with an ultimatum for disaster. The golden calf built by God's people at the foot of the mountain is viewed by God as an enormity comparable to the evil of Sodom. It means death for Abraham's family line and a chance for Moses to inherit the promised blessings of progeny and great nationhood. It means an end to the old plan and the beginning of a new. It means starting another experiment, this time with Moses as the projected great nation:

> Now therefore let me alone that my wrath may burn hot against them; but *you I will make a great nation* (Exod. 32:10).

Moses' response to the tirade and decision of Yahweh reflects the themes and theology of the Yahwist's work evident in the patriarchal stories. The grace of Yahweh is won by the bold word of a hero. The ground is Yahweh's own promise, for on that basis he can change his mind about the annihilation of his people. The classic protest of Moses recalls explicitly the oath to Abraham, Isaac, and Jacob. The promise is indeed Israel's means of survival.

> Moses *entreated Yahweh* his God and said, "O Yahweh, why does your wrath burn hot against your people, whom you have brought forth from the land of Egypt with great power and with a mighty hand? Why should the Egyptians say, '*With evil intent* he brought them forth to slay them in the mountains and consume them *from the face of the ground?*' Turn from your fierce wrath and *change your mind concerning this evil* against your people. Remember *Abraham, Isaac and Israel* your servants to whom *you swore* by your self and said to them, 'I will multiply *your seed* as *the stars* of heaven and all *this land* that I have promised I will give to your seed, and they shall inherit it forever.'"
>
> *So Yahweh changed his mind* concerning *the evil* he planned to do to his people (Exod. 32:11-14).

A series of crisis situations arise after this dramatic act of deliverance at Sinai that reflect a similar pattern of salvation by intercession typical of Yahwist thinking.[7] These crises culminate in Israel's cowardice before the giants of Canaan. Once again Yahweh chides his people for disbelief, and threatens to reorganize the program of promise around Moses by making him a great nation. Israel is not to inherit the promised land.

> And Yahweh said to Moses, "How long will this people despise me? and how long will they not *believe in me,* in spite of all the signs I have wrought among them? I will strike them with pestilence and disinherit them, and I *will make of you a nation greater and mightier* than they" (Num. 14:11-12).

Moses thereupon takes up the cudgels for his people and bluntly confronts Yahweh with the situation. As Moses sees it, to disinherit Israel means that Yahweh will lose face in the sight of the other nations. Blessing cannot be mediated by annihilating the agents of blessing. Hence, Moses pleads for forgiveness and power from Yahweh commensurable with his past promises: "Let the power of Yahweh be as great as you have promised" (Num. 14:17). He asks for forgiveness on the ground that Yahweh has forgiven previously (Num. 14:13-19). The response of Yahweh is a modified expression of grace (Num. 14:20-25). As in previous instances the rebellion of man reaches a point where judgment is necessary. All but one of that generation of Abraham's seed would die before the land sworn to the fathers would be conquered and possessed. Caleb alone, like others before him, has a different spirit and finds grace in the eyes of Yahweh. The final great act of saving intercession by Moses is found in Numbers 21:4-9 where Yahweh instructs Moses to set up a bronze snake as a symbol of life to which all would turn in faith for healing.

Many of the Yahwist motifs are drawn together in the final series of texts dealing with Balaam. Moses' intercessions had rescued Israel time and again. Balaam's prayer now threatened to overthrow her. The Yahwist introduces Balaam as a professional expert in the art of cursing and blessing. He is summoned precisely because Israel had become a mighty nation and his curse is requested to counter the fulfilled blessing of Yahweh. "Come now curse this people for me," asks Balak, "since they are too mighty for me . . . I know that he whom you bless is blessed, and he whom you curse is cursed" (Num. 22:6). This wording recalls the promise of blessing and curse given to Abraham in Genesis 12:2-3. Balaam, however, is prevented from bringing a genuine curse upon Israel and ends up repeating an oracle of victory, prosperity, and blessing (Num. 24:3-9). This oracle reaffirms the past promises of Yahweh to the patriarchs and concludes with a recollection of Genesis 12:2:

> Blessed is every one who blesses you
> and cursed is every one who curses you
>   (Num. 24:9).

A subsequent oracle focuses upon the conquest of all the neighboring nations of Israel at the hand of the "star of Jacob." This figure is probably to be identified as the house of David through whom the promise of a great Israelite nation is fulfilled in the mind of the Yahwist writer (Num. 24:15-24).

Whether the Yahwist text ends at this point is not clear. The Balaam oracles, however, do provide a fitting finale to the Yahwist portrait of the plan for the patriarchal promise. Israel has become a nation too powerful for Moab to handle (Num. 22:6). The promised land awaits Israel's invasion. A glorious and prosperous kingdom is envisioned for God's people (Num. 24:6-7). A plan of conquest through the "star of Jacob" is spelled out by Balaam (Num. 24:15-24). He also delineates the same program of mediated blessing or cursing to any who acknowledge or reject Israel respectively. All of this is by the grace of Yahweh. If Israel has any doubt about that truth they need only recall one other incident that happened at Baal Peor (Num.

25:1-5). For at the very last minute, with a land in their grasp and Yahweh's promises all but completely fulfilled, the Israelites again revert to disbelief. They worship Baal and indulge in the fertility orgies of the local shrine.

When the greatness of the Davidic empire was finally achieved, Israel was forced to admit that she did not deserve the land or the fulfilled promises. To the bitter end, the history of the promise is a history of sheer grace in the eyes of the Yahwist. With literary finesse, beauty, and polish that message is conveyed through colorful narrative form. And with strategically placed references to the governing promise motif, the Yahwist work illustrates a provocative ancient mode of interpreting Israel's past traditions. The forcefulness of these insights, we contend, can only be fully appreciated when the techniques of literary criticism employed above are rigidly applied.

Notes

[1] The writer of the Yahwist literary source is usually designated the Yahwist as though he were a clearly identifiable individual. For the sake of convenience we have preserved this traditional designation. See P. Ellis, *The Yahwist* (Notre Dame, Ind.: Fides Publishers, 1968) for a recent analysis of Yahwist style and theology. This book provides a complete text of the Yahwist.

[2] See also Genesis 38:1-30; Exodus 2:1-10; 2:11-22; Numbers 12:1-16 and 24:4-59.

[3] Perhaps the best treatment of the promise texts of the Yahwist is that of Hans Walter Wolff, "The Kerygma of the Yahwist," *Interpretation* 20 (1966): 131-58.

[4] Note especially G. von Rad, "Faith Reckoned as Righteousness," in *The Problem of the Hexateuch and Other Essays* (New York: McGraw-Hill, 1966) for a complete discussion of this text.

[5] R. Clements in *Abraham and David* (London: SCM Press, 1967) has isolated royal terminology in Genesis 15 and thereby introduced additional evidence for linking the chapter with the Davidic era. We should also make it clear that there is considerable difference of opinion among critics on the extent of the Yahwist material in this chapter. A variety of factors in the transmission of the traditions has no doubt led to a blurring of the original literary source contours.

[6] The story of Isaac's near sacrifice is usually assigned to the Elohist, although this is far from certain. In any case the appendix to the story in Genesis 22:15-18 bears the marks of a Yahwist reinterpretation.

[7] See Numbers 11:1-3; 12:1-16; 11:7-15 (especially v. 15); 11:16-19 and 11:31-35.

Richard Elliott Friedman (essay date 1981)

SOURCE: "Sacred History and Theology: The Redaction of *Torah*" in *The Creation of Sacred Literature: Composition and Redaction of the Biblical Text,* edited by Richard Elliott Friedman, University of California Press, 1981, pp. 25-34.

[*In this essay, Friedman claims that the Priestly redaction of the* Torah—*the combination of the Priestly source with the Elohist-Jahvist document—significantly shaped the* Pentateuch*'s conception of God and the portrayal of the* magnalia Die.]

One of the significant consequences of the enterprise of source criticism is the demonstration that the **Torah** (and ultimately the Hebrew Bible), more than perhaps any other book, is the product of a community—it is quintessentially a national work of literature, not the creation of a particular man or woman in a particular historical moment, but the offspring of a continuing, developing culture.

A more troubling consequence of the source-critical enterprise is the difficulty it engenders when one returns from it to the reading and studying of the whole. Thus is born redaction criticism, the study of the final literary product which we call **Torah** with the sophistication of one who knows something of the complex literary history of the text. The focus now is upon the literary figure who assembled the received texts into a single work. The combinatory design which this redactor conceived did more than house the received texts. It gave birth to new narrative syntheses.

Martin Noth wrote that, precisely because the Priestly source (P) depended upon the JE sources (or because both depended upon a common *Grundlage*), the combination of P and JE did not result in any major new element, historical or theological, in the unified work.[1] I believe, however, that we may perceive several significant metamorphoses in the conception of God and in the portrayal of the *magnalia Dei* which result from the design of the Priestly tradent who was responsible for the redaction of the work.[2]

The juxtaposition of the J and Priestly Creation accounts, first, precipitated a narrative synthesis with exegetical possibilities which neither of the original documents possessed independently. The humans who reach to the Tree of Knowledge of Good and Evil are different from all other creatures in that they bear the stamp of the *imago Dei*. Without pursuing the precise meaning of *selem* and *demût,* one can say at minimum that humans are portrayed as embodying some divine element—and this element is critical to the events of Eden. Insofar as beings who share some quality with Yhwh are nonetheless treated by him as his subordinates, his communication with them being initially and

nearly exclusively commands, the stage is set for their disobedience even before the introduction of the serpent as catalyst. When Mark Twain queried, "If the Lord didn't want humans to be rebellious then why did he create them in his image?" he was at his theologically ironic best. Depicted as creating humans in his own image and then setting under prohibition the fruit whose very attraction is to endow one with a divine power, Yhwh is thus portrayed as himself creating the terms of that tension which results in human disobedience. Themselves possessing some godly quality, the humans are attracted precisely by the serpent's claim that if they eat from the tree they will be like God(s). This tension, however, is neither the work of the author of J nor the work of the Priestly author. It is purely a by-product of the combination of the two at the hand of the tradent. P does not portray a primal human rebellion; J does not portray the creation of humans in the image of God. The combination of these two re-cast the interpretive range of the motive of the humans' actions in Eden. In the final product we call **Torah,** one cannot separate the creation *in imago Dei* from the natures of the humans who disobey the divine instruction. Interestingly, Noth referred to this identification of the humans who are created in the divine image with the humans who rebel, but he concluded only that the combined text thus accurately reflects a condition of humankind, while he held nonetheless that this effect of combination of texts still constitutes no new narrative or theological component of the whole.[3] In response, I would insist that the effect of the combination of these originally alternative texts was profound—in this case refocusing the perspective of the first chapters of the biblical narrative. Indeed, insofar as the struggle between Yhwh and the human community persists as an obvious and dominant theme in biblical narrative, the Genesis 1-3 account of the archetype of that struggle sets a fundamental *Leitmotif* of those narratives. From this perspective, it is difficult to overestimate the impact of the tradent who produced in Genesis 1-3 a narrative which is quite literally more than the sum of its components.

One may observe a broader metamorphosis in the portrayal of Yhwh in the unified Priestly work when one compares certain features of the JE and Priestly theologies. It is regularly noted in theological studies of the Hebrew Bible that one finds in P a more cosmic perspective of Yhwh than in the other sources.[4] Specifically, one observes, first, that the Sabbath is fixed in the orders of Creation in P, while it is not in J, and functions as commemorative of historical national events in D. Second, the Priestly Creation account depicts the construction of the entire universe, describing a "cosmic bubble" of sky over earth with water above and below, while the J Creation focuses exclusively on the earth and the birth of plant and animal life thereon, with Yhwh personally moving about among his creatures. Interestingly, the Priestly narrative begins: "When God began to create *the heavens and the earth*" (Gen 1:1), while J begins, "In the day that Yhwh God made *earth and heaven*" (2:4b). The reversed order, as it happens, is appropriate to the respective points of view, as E. A. Speiser has observed.[5] Again in the Flood account, P portrays a cosmic crisis in which the habitable bubble is threatened; the fountains of the deep are divided, thus causing the waters to flow up from below; and the windows of heaven are divided, thus causing the waters to flow down from above. The J version meanwhile merely reports rain. P, further, adds the Noahic covenant to those of JE tradition (the Abrahamic and Israelite covenants), thus setting the latter covenants, which bind Yhwh to a particular community of humans, into a larger framework of a covenant with all flesh. In all of these instances the Priestly writer portrays Yhwh in conceptually broader terms than those of the JE portrayal. The Priestly compositions consistently desist from the angelic and blatantly anthropomorphic portrayals which are widespread in JE tradition. In the Priestly portrayal of history there is never an appearance of an angel. There is never a portrayal of Yhwh so anthropomorphic as the JE portrayals of Yhwh's walking in the Garden, standing on a rock in the wilderness, wrestling with Jacob, making Adam's and Eve's loincloths, and closing Noah's ark. There is never a talking animal. There is never a dream narrative. It is no oversimplification to characterize P as a more clearly cosmic portrayal of the deity, and JE as a more personal conception. But, again, the merging of the two portrayals in the unified work of the Priestly tradent yielded a new formula, i.e., a synthesis in which the cosmic and the personal aspects of God stood in a balance unlike that of either of the component compositions. It is this theological synthesis, in which Yhwh appears as both universal and personal, as both the Creator and "the God of your father," that has seeded Jewish and Christian conceptions of God for millennia. Yet it was neither the conception of JE nor of P—but, rather, something new, a product of the union of the two at the hand of the Priestly tradent.

A second synthetic theological formulation was born in the unified Priestly work with regard to the portrayal of the mercy of Yhwh. The centrality of the mercy of Yhwh to JE tradition is manifest in the divine formula revealed to Moses on Sinai in Exod 34:6f. Yhwh is "merciful and gracious, long-forbearing and abundant in *hesed*. . . . " It is upon this formula that Moses bases his appeal that Yhwh rescind his condemnation of the nation following the spy incident in Num 14:13-20. The appeal is successful, as is Moses' prior appeal following a similar condemnation in the golden calf incident (Exod 32:11-14). Israel's God, in JE portrayal, is a deity who can be "grieved to his heart" by the actions of his humans (Gen 6:6). The well-known compassion of Yhwh, which is responsible for innumerable reprieves for Israel's continual violations

of covenant in JE and Deuteronomistic literature—and which pervades the Psalms and Prophetic literature—is, however, almost entirely unknown in P. The fundamental vocabulary of the category of mercy, formalized in the divine formula of Exodus 34, is completely missing in the Priestly compositions. All forms of the root *rhm* are missing, as are all forms of *hnn*.[6] There is not a single reference to the *hesed* of Yhwh.[7] The regular biblical term for repentance, *šwb*, never appears in P, as Jacob Milgrom has observed.[8] Not only is the terminology of divine mercy absent in P, but the portrayal of it as a phenomenon in narrative is exceedingly rare as well. Notably, Moses' appeal for mercy in the matter of the spies in JE is simply eliminated in the Priestly version of that episode. In P, instead of Yhwh's sentence being made more lenient as a result of the arguments of Moses, the sentence is simply pronounced and carried out. The similar appeal of Moses in the matter of the golden calf in JE of course has no counterpart in P—the latter, being the product of the Aaronid priesthood, eliminated the story of the golden calf, in which the eponymous ancestor of the Aaronids figured centrally as culpable in the incident.

This reduced concern with mercy, grace, *hesed,* and repentance in P is itself a valuable datum for exegesis, and for dating as well.[9] My present concern, however, is specifically to note the effect of the combination of the differing compositions. Quite simply, the uniting of the JE and Priestly texts within the single Priestly work resulted in a new theological formula of justice and mercy which corresponded neither to that of JE nor to that of P. The proportional ratio of these qualities to one another within the character of Yhwh in the Priestly work bore no resemblance to that of either of its components. The portrayal of Yhwh in the united **Torah** therefore depicts the deity as embodying a quality of compassion which the Priestly writer(s) never intended to emphasize so, while it develops the reverse constituent of the divine character far beyond the original portrayal thereof in JE texts. A new view of the tension between the divine traits of mercy and justice was thus born in the design of the Priestly tradent.

The enterprise of the Priestly tradent thus resulted in a **Torah** whose theology was neither independent of its sources nor a simple composite of them. We have seen three examples of the impact of this literary process upon the component texts which have significant theological implications. The question is whether this phenomenon of narrative metamorphosis through combination is the chance result of the mechanical combination of the sources, of interest now primarily to a sociologist or cultural anthropologist as reflecting layers of a culture—or can we pursue the intention of the redactor and uncover and identify a theological consciousness.

Initial study of the text would lead one to believe that the tradent's redactional decisions in combining and arranging his sources were motivated primarily by mechanical considerations. In the narrative of the Flood, for example, each of the two accounts which we have, J and P, when separated from one another, constitutes a complete, flowing account of the Flood event. The Priestly tradent's method clearly was to segment the two versions and to place the thematically corresponding blocks adjacent to one another: e.g., entrance into the ark, initiation of the deluge, expiration of living creatures, recession of water, dispatching of birds, etc. The redactional design here does not seem to be theologically motivated, but, rather, the product of a literary mechanical decision. The same goes for the Red Sea narrative, in which at least the P and J accounts (though not the E) are each independently complete, flowing stories and are combined in a brilliant synthesis in which the differing versions are united in an incomparably unified continuous narrative. Here, especially, the redactional genius seems to be mechanical rather than theological or ideological. The episode of the spies in the Book of Numbers reflects the same *modus operandi:* two accounts, each a complete, fluent story, segmented and combined with adjacent juxtaposition of thematically corresponding blocks. In each of these three cases—the Flood, the Sea, the spies—the natural mechanics of the process of redaction are sufficient to explain the combinatory constructions before us.

A variation of this technique is segmentation and distribution. The Priestly version of the Abraham/Lot sequence of events, for example, is an abbreviated account (merely four verses long; Gen 12:5; 13:6, 11b, 12a; 19:29). When separated from the JE materials (12:4, 6-20; 13:1-11a, 12b-18; 18:1-33; 19:1-38) these four verses flow comfortably as a unit, a summary version of the longer JE narrative. The redactor, patently, has segmented this unit and distributed the pieces over eight chapters of Genesis in thematically appropriate junctures. The result of this segmentation and distribution design was that the redactor was able to retain this Priestly material without contradicting the narrative sequence of events in the JE texts. The same redactional process seems to have been in operation in the handling of the Jacob/Esau materials and of the accounts of the migration and settlement of the Israelites in Egypt. In each of these cases we have a short Priestly narrative, complete or nearly so in itself, segmented and distributed through a larger body of narrative material at thematically satisfactory junctures.[10] In all three cases, again, the design before us is an editorial mechanism, demonstrably a response to the mechanical requirements of this redactor's unique enterprise.

If we focus upon smaller pericopes in a more specific way, the case becomes even clearer. In the account of

the Patriarchal migration from Mesopotamia, for example, we have both a Priestly and a J account of the event. The Priestly account portrays the migration in two stages: namely, Terah brings the family from Ur to Haran; Abram brings the family from Haran to Canaan. The J material contains only the command of God to Abram to leave his birthplace, followed by the report that Abram did as God had commanded him. (P: Gen 11:31, 12:4b, 5; J: 12:1-a) The tradent who received these two texts did not choose to set the P text before the J, nor the J before the P, nor to eliminate one or the other. He rather chose to combine them by having the J narrative intersect the two stages of the Priestly record. Thus in our **Torah** we read that Terah brings the family to Haran, then Yhwh commands Abram *lēk lekā,* then Abram brings the family to Canaan. This arrangement is mechanically mandated. The Priestly account of the Terah-led migration (with Terah "taking" the family) had to precede the J divine command to Abram to migrate. The J divine command to Abram to migrate had to precede the Priestly account of the Abram-led migration (with Abram "taking" the family). One may object that the present arrangement still has a structural problem in that as it now stands Abram is being told (12:1) to leave his birthplace *(mwldtk),* but his birthplace is back in Ur, and he is already in Haran! Indeed, Rashi, Ibn Ezra, and Ramban raise this very question and propose the most complex models of migration to reconcile the facts. Such a problem, however, is a constant, for if the tradent had chosen to set the J narrative wholly before that of P, the problem of "Leave your birthplace" would have been solved, but a problem of "Leave your father's house *(mbyt 'byk)*" would then be born, because Abram's being taken by Terah would then look even clumsier than we observed earlier.[11] To have set the J version wholly after that of P would be less credible still, for then Abram would already have left home prior to the divine command to *lēk lekā* . In short, the redactional design of our united text is based on factors of the mechanics of the literary construction.

The redaction of the Abrahamic covenant traditions likewise reflects decisions grounded in the mechanics of literary combination. In this case the redactor placed the J version (Genesis 15) before that of P (Genesis 17) and separated the two by placing the J and P accounts of Hagar and the birth of Ishmael between them. The arrangement reflects the requirements of the received texts. In the J tradition, the Abrahamic covenant precedes the birth of Ishmael; and the wording of the J text holds the redactor to maintaining the integrity of this tradition, for in the text Abraham remarks that he is childless *(hōlēk 'arîrî;* 15:2). Priestly tradition, however, specifically develops the notion that Ishmael is already born prior to the inception of the hereditary covenant, but God rejects Abraham's appeal for Ishmael as covenantal heir and announces the forthcoming birth of Isaac (17:18f). Thus this text, too, holds the redactor to its integrity. The result: the Torah as we have it.

The account of the divine acquaintance and commission to Moses is a third example of this redactional activity. The J charge to Moses, set at the burning bush, includes the divine assurance that when Moses goes to the people in Egypt they will listen to him (Exod 3:18). Exodus 4 then concludes with the notation that the people do listen (4:31). In the Priestly version of the commission (which does not identify the place in which it occurs) Yhwh sends Moses to the people with the announcement of imminent rescue, and the text specifically notes: "But they did *not* listen . . ." (6:9). The Priestly tradent, thus confronted with a contradictive doublet, introduced the Priestly text of the charge to Moses following the J account of Moses' *second* meeting with the leaders of the people. In the tradent's design, as it now stands, God charges Moses in Midian, Moses goes to the people in Egypt and announces the coming liberation, the people listen, Moses' first exchange with Pharaoh results in increased burdens upon the people, the leaders of the people express their anger to Moses—then, following this second, unsatisfactory encounter with the people, comes the Priestly text: God charges Moses to go to the people with an announcement of liberation, and the people do not listen.

Through these several cases, the method of the redactor begins to be apparent, as follows: he apparently tried to retain as much of the received material as possible, this balanced against the editorial considerations of producing a narrative which, *for him,* had sufficient unity and sense. He was not bound to any one fixed design, but rather he might place two complete narratives side by side, or intersect one with the other, or relocate one or the other, or use segmentation and thematic combination or distribution. Finally, he united the whole within two editorial frameworks, themselves derived from received texts, as Frank Cross has described.[12] Cross identified the first of these as the *'ēlleh tôledōt* series of headings, a genealogical framework derived from a "*tôledōt* Book," which provided a continuity for the collected narrative materials in the book of Genesis. The second such framework was the "Wilderness Stations" series of headings, an itinerary framework derived from the Numbers 33 list of Israel's movements during the forty years' wilderness journey, which provided a continuity for the narrative and legal materials from Exodus 12 through the arrival of Israel at the Plains of Moab in the Book of Numbers.

In all of the material which I have noted here, mechanical considerations are a sufficient explanation of the redactional design. In several of the cases, mechanical considerations are a necessary explanation. Still we must be hesitant to pronounce the redactor's task to be wholly grounded in editorial mechanics.

Where this is a sufficient explanation, we must be open to the possibility of theological or ideological redactional motives which are no less sufficient explanations. And even in those cases in which mechanical considerations are so patent as to compel us to acknowledge their determinism of the redactor's decisions in these pericopes, this is not to say that the redactor was an unthinking creature who was not sensitive to the literary implications—theological or others—of his designs. I therefore seek evidence of the presence of a theological consciousness on the part of the Priestly tradent who redacted the **Torah.**

One narrative in particular points to the existence of such a theological consciousness, namely, the plagues narrative of the Book of Exodus. Brevard Childs, Moshe Greenberg, and Ziony Zevit have observed that in the plagues traditions J and P do not stand in tension but are bound together to form a richer narrative.[13] The plagues traditions of Exodus form one of the most complex constructions of Priestly and JE composition in the **Torah.** Separated from one another, neither JE nor the Priestly material flows comfortably. As Cross has pointed out, it is hardly possible to picture the present shape of the section as the basically mechanical juxtaposition of corresponding blocks of two narratives by a redactor.[14] Upon examination one finds that this construction is a special design of the tradent who produced the unified Priestly work. In the plagues narrative one may uncover an editorial framework which, like the *tôledōt* and Stations frameworks which respectively precede and follow it, gives shape to the materials which it encloses, thus accounting for what is otherwise a thirteen-chapter gap between the two structures which Cross identified. Just as the *tôledōt* and Stations frameworks are based on received texts which the tradent had at his disposal, so the framework of the plagues section is derivative from a received text, namely, the Priestly account of Moses and Pharaoh. In this account, Yhwh informs Moses prior to the latter's first meeting with Pharaoh that "I shall harden Pharaoh's heart . . . and he will not listen to you" (Exod 7:3f). The realization of this prediction is then noted several times in the account of Moses and Pharaoh which follows. Using the verbs *qšh* and *hzq* for "to harden," this is the Priestly alternative to the JE account, which regularly uses the verb *kābēd* for the hardening of Pharoah's heart. The latter is consistent with a regular play upon the term *k b d* in the JE account. Moses is . . . (literally, "hard of tongue and hard of mouth"), while Pharaoh is . . . ("hard of heart"). After his first meeting with Moses, Pharaoh declares, . . . ("let the work be hard"; 5:9). Moses predicts . . . ("hard pestilence"; 9:3). There falls . . . ("hard hail"; 9:24).

The difference between the JE and Priestly portrayals of the hardening of Pharaoh's heart, though, is more than one of terminology. The JE account is a confrontation in which the personality of Pharaoh, his strengths and his weaknesses, figures integrally in the dynamic. Pharaoh is a thinking, arguing, *deciding* character. It is Pharaoh himself who makes his heart hard. Pharaoh several times agrees to liberate the people if only the current plague will cease, but upon seeing respite hardens his heart. He bargains with Moses several times over the terms of the liberation. The focus is upon his (Pharaoh's) decision. At the burning bush, God informs Moses: "I know that the king of Egypt will not *permit* you to go . . ." (Exod 3:19), claiming only precognition of Pharaoh's will, not divine determination. Moses continually speaks to Pharaoh in a manner which suggests volition on the king's part: "How long will you refuse . . . ?" (7:27; 8:17; 9:2, 17f.; 10:3f.); and God himself says to Moses: "The heart of Pharaoh is hard, he refuses to send forth the people" (7:14), suggesting only *knowledge* of the condition of Pharaoh's will, not control. Only once does the text associate the power of God with the hardening of Pharaoh's heart. In Exod 10:1, after five plagues have already occurred in the JE narrative, Yhwh tells Moses: "*I* have hardened his heart. . . . " So anomalous is this statement compared to all that which precedes it and follows it in the JE plagues account that it is widely held among scholars that this verse and the one following must be a secondary insertion. Even if we do not call for a gloss here, though, we must at minimum see this passage as a surprising turn from the rest of the text, never developed further by the author, albeit perhaps intentionally.

The Priestly story of the plagues, however, carries this notion to divine control of Pharaoh's will full-blown. As we have already observed, in the Priestly version God informs Moses at the outset that *he* will harden Pharaoh's heart. In P, further, Pharaoh has no dialogue; he makes no promises of liberation and no reversals. Whereas in JE it is apparently the respite from plagues itself that makes Pharaoh harden his heart, no such action appears in P, where the development is rather a fast crescendo: in the plagues of blood and frogs the Egyptian magicians duplicate the wonders; in the plague of lice the magicians fail to duplicate it, and they say, "it is the finger of God"; in the plague of boils, the magicians are themselves afflicted. But the developing divine victory, from which no respite is mentioned, does not turn Pharaoh's thinking around, because Yhwh has predetermined to *harden Pharaoh's heart.*

Examination of each of the appearances of this notation clarifies for us the redactional design which the Priestly tradent constructed to house these materials.

The episode of Aaron's rod becoming a snake (P) concludes with the prediction-fulfilling Priestly notation, "And the heart of Pharaoh was hard *(wyhzq),* and he did not listen to them, as Yhwh had said" (7:13). The description of the blood plague (P and JE combined) concludes identically (7:22). The description of the plague of frogs (P and JE combined) ends with the JE notation that Pharoah hardened *(hkbd)* his heart (8:11), but attached to this JE statement is the Priestly remainder: " . . . and he did not listen to them, as Yhwh had said." The plagues of lice and boils (both wholly P) conclude with the full Priestly statement (8:15; 9:12). The plagues of flies and pestilence (both wholly JE) each conclude with the full JE statement: "And Pharaoh hardened *(wkybd)* his heart, and he did not send forth the people" (8:28; 9:7). Thus the plague accounts which are wholly P conclude with the P notation, those which are wholly JE conclude with the JE notation, and those which are combined conclude with the P notation or with a combined notation. This unsurprising picture changes, however, in the remaining plagues. The plague of hail is entirely a JE composition, yet it concludes with a mixed notation in which the Priestly elements predominate, thus: "And the heart of Pharaoh was hard *(wyhzq),* and he did not send forth the children of Israel, as Yhwh had said" (9:35). A Priestly statement has somehow come to summarize a JE pericope.[15] The lengthy narrative which follows, climaxing in the plague of locusts, likewise is wholly JE, but concludes: "And Yhwh hardened *(wyhzq)* the heart of Pharaoh, and he did not send forth the people" (10:20). The account of the plague of darkness follows; it, too, is entirely a JE composition, yet it concludes similarly to the two preceding accounts (10:27). There follows a JE portrayal of the last dialogue of Moses and Pharaoh, at the end of which stands a Priestly conclusion to the entire sequence of Moses/Pharaoh encounters, thus:

> And Moses and Aaron performed all these wonders before Pharaoh, and Yhwh hardened *(wyhzq)* the heart of Pharaoh, and he did not send forth the children of Israel from his land. (11:10)

The presence of Priestly conclusions upon JE narratives, fulfilling the prediction which is made in a Priestly introduction, and arriving finally at a Priestly summation, indicates that we have in the Exodus account of Moses and Pharaoh portions of two received texts, one P and one JE, which have been combined by the Priestly tradent in a framework which he modeled upon the P version. A final indicator that this is the case is the presence of the Priestly formulation of the hardening-of-the-heart phrase in the midst of the account of God's initial instructions to Moses (4:21b). The context is somewhat awkward as it stands (4:21-23) and apparently reflects the tradent's unifying work. Indeed, the specific combination of phrases in this verse (4:21b) viz., that God will harden *(hzq)* Pharaoh's heart and that Pharaoh will not send forth the people, otherwise occurs only in the four passages which we last observed.

The effect of this redactional design was to cause the Priestly notion of divine control of the chain of events to dominate the entire combined narrative. With the Priestly predictions that God would harden Pharaoh's heart now located at the beginning of the narrative, not only did the subsequent *Priestly* notations of this hardening portray fulfillment of this divine intention; now the *JE* expressions of hardening fell into this rubric as well. Every JE notation that Pharaoh hardened his heart now appeared to be the fulfillment of the original prediction, with the invisible power of Yhwh controlling Pharaoh's action. The JE picture of a confrontation between Pharaoh and the power of God in which the divine might proves victorious was now a part of a larger scheme in which the deity controls both sides of the dynamic, both Moses' challenge and Pharaoh's response.

Nothing of the redactional design which we have observed in the plagues narrative is critical to the mechanics of the combination of the texts. If we remove the references to God's hardening of Pharaoh's heart which I have identified as redactional additions, the narrative still flows continuously and sensibly. In this case the Priestly tradent has conceived a literary structure based on considerations other than purely mechanical demands. He has not been governed by the character of the received texts to the extent that he was in the case of the Flood texts or the Abrahamic covenant texts. He has, rather, increased his share of the literary partnership between himself and the authors of his received texts. He has favored and developed a particular theological notion, he has imposed it upon the whole, and thus he has produced a united narrative which, like the united creation accounts, is more than the sum of its components. Even as God controls both sides of the confrontation, owing to the Priestly text and the derivative framework, it is still the thinking, struggling Pharaoh of the JE texts who is thus controlled. The combined portrayal thus magnifies the power of the God of Israel, who now exercises supreme determinism over a more worthy opponent. And this picture is not the chance by-product of mechanical editing. The nature of the design rather points to a theological consciousness on the part of the designer.

Thus, in addition to the retention of received materials and the fashioning of unified, sensible constructions, another factor enters the formula of the tradent's *modus operandi,* namely, the tradent's own theological sensitivities.

In any given pericope, these factors may stand in different balance. The theological considerations may play a significant part in the tradent's conception of the redactional design, or mechanical considerations may be determinative. Our task now is to analyze each narrative, independently and in context of the whole, to weigh with more particularity the balance of factors which motivated the tradent's design in each case: what did he perceive to be contradiction? Which contradictions were to him tolerable, and which did he perceive to require resolution? Ultimately, what was the nature and the extent of the Priestly tradent's contribution to the creation of the **Torah**? Even these early researches point to the likelihood that his contribution was no less significant and no less creative than that of the authors who, knowingly or not, bequeathed their work into his care.

Notes

[1] "Partly in consequence of a common harking back to a fully developed oral narrative tradition, and partly in consequence of mutual literary dependence, the course of history was narrated so much the same in all the sources that even their combination with one another could change nothing essential in this regard." Noth, *A History of Pentateuchal Traditions* (Englewood Cliffs, New Jersey, 1972), 250; German edition, *Überliefe-rungsgeschichte des Pentateuch* (1948).

[2] I use the term *tradent* to denote one who is both editor and writer, one whose handling of received texts involves both arrangement and elaboration. I have elsewhere described his task and identified the texts which are to be ascribed to him: R. E. Friedman, *The Exile and Biblical Narrative* (Harvard Semitic Monographs 22, Chico, Calif., 1981). Following F. M. Cross, I identify him as Priestly and refer to his final product (which includes at least the Tetrateuch, and possibly Deuteronomy as well) as the Priestly work.

[3] Noth, *History,* 251.

[4] E.g., Gerhard von Rad, *Old Testament Theology,* 1 (New York, 1962), 148f. (German edition, *Theologie des Alten Testaments,* 1957); E. A. Speiser, *Genesis: The Anchor Bible* (Garden City, New York, 1964), xxvff.

[5] Speiser, *Genesis,* 18f.

[6] The second element of the threefold Priestly blessing, Num 6:25, is the lone possible exception to the absence of the root *hnn,* but this passage may be Exilic, i.e., the addition of the tradent himself, and in any event is almost certainly the insertion of an actual formal cultic ceremony, not narrative composition.

[7] The mention of *hesed* in the Decalogue is common to the Exodus 20 and Deuteronomy 5 versions and is clearly related to the Exodus 34 formula. It is therefore not original to P.

[8] *Cult and Conscience* (Leiden, 1976), 121ff.

[9] If P were Exilic, the absence of any reference to repentance or to divine mercy would be strange indeed.

[10] The Priestly Jacob/Esau account: Gen 26:34f.; 27:46; 281-9. The Priestly migration account: Gen 37:1; 41:45b, 46a; 46:6, 7; 47:27b.

[11] The objection is questionable in any event since the term *mwldtk* has a broader range of meaning than merely "birthplace." See, e.g., Esth 2:10, and S. Talmon's treatment in "The Textual Study of the Bible—A New Outlook," in F. M. Cross and S. Talmon, eds., *Qumran and the History of the Biblical Text* (Cambridge, Massachusetts, 1975), 360.

[12] *Canaanite Myth and Hebrew Epic* (Cambridge, Massachusetts, 1973). 301-317.

[13] Childs, *The Book of Exodus* (Philadelphia, 1974), 155; Zevit, "The Priestly Redaction and Interpretation of the Plague Narrative in Exodus," *JQR* 66 (1976), 199; Greenberg, "The Redaction of the Plague Narrative in Exodus," *Near Eastern Studies in Honor of William Foxwell Albright,* ed., H. Goedicke (Baltimore, 1971), 243-252.

[14] Cross, *Canaanite Myth,* 318.

[15] The distinction between *hzq* and *kbd* is consistently confirmed in the LXX. Note also the doublet of the hardening of Pharaoh's heart in 9:34 *(kbd)* and again in 9:35 *(hzq). Hzq lb,* further, continues as a key term in P through the Sea episode, Exod 14:4, 8 (cf. v 5, JE), 17.

Bernard J. Bamberger (essay date 1981)

SOURCE: "The *Torah* and the Jewish People" in *The "Torah:" A Modern Commentary,* Union of American Hebrew Congregations, 1981, pp. xxix-xxxvi.

[*In the following excerpt, Bamberger explores the role of the* Torah *in forming the Jewish community.*]

The **Torah** was always the possession of all Israel. It was addressed to the entire people, who were to learn its contents and teach them diligently to their children. A number of biblical passages, in particular Psalms 19 and 119, testify to the love which the **Torah** evoked and the widespread concern of the people with its teachings.

The Book of Nehemiah (chs. 8-10) reports a public reading of the **Torah** in Jerusalem, probably in the year 444 B.C.E. This reading was conducted by Ezra the Scribe, with the aid of assistants who were to make sure that all those present heard and understood what was read to them. A few days later, the entire people entered into a solemn undertaking to obey the **Torah;** and this agreement was ratified in writing by the leaders. From the traditional standpoint, this incident was a reaffirmation of the covenant at Sinai. But many modern scholars explain the event as marking the completion of the written **Torah** in substantially its present form and its adoption as the official "constitution" of the Jewish community.

The **Torah** and the Synagogue

We do not know exactly where, how, or when the synagogue came into existence; it must have been some time between 500 and 200 B.C.E. From the start, one of the principal activities of the synagogue was the public reading and exposition of the **Torah.** A portion was read every Sabbath. But there were farmers who lived in scattered communities, too far from a synagogue to travel to it on the Sabbath. That they might not be deprived of hearing the sacred word, a **Torah** passage was read in the synagogues each Monday and Thursday—the market days when the country-folk came to town to sell their produce. This custom survives to the present in the traditional synagogues.

The reading of the **Torah** portion in Hebrew was often followed by a translation, in Greek or Aramaic, for the benefit of those who did not understand the original. It is out of such translation or paraphrase, in all probability, that the sermon arose. This explains why the sermon was normally based on the **Torah** reading of the week.

From an early date, the instruction of children was associated with the synagogue. The effectiveness of its educational program, for young and old, was fully recognized by the enemies of Judaism. When the Syrian King Antiochus IV wished to break down Jewish solidarity and hasten the assimilation of Jews into Hellenistic society, he not only forbade the practice of Jewish ritual but also prohibited the reading and teaching of the **Torah,** on pain of death. But the decrees could not be enforced.

Similarly, the Roman Emperor Hadrian, after he finally put down the Jewish revolt in 135 C.E., proscribed all those who persisted in teaching the **Torah.** It was then that the aged Rabbi Akiba defied the edict and suffered death by torture. The **Torah,** he declared in a famous parable, is Israel's natural element, as water is the natural element of the fish. In water the fish is exposed to many dangers, but out of water it is sure to perish at once (Berachot 61b).

The Oral **Torah**

Thus far we have used the word **Torah** with reference to the Five Books. But some kind of commentary was always needed. A sacred text, and especially one containing laws and commandments, must be interpreted and applied to the concrete situations of life. Those who proposed to make the **Torah** the rule of their life found many provisions which required more exact definition. The **Torah,** for example, forbids work on Sabbath; but what precisely constitutes work, and what activities are permissible? Again, the **Torah** speaks of divorce (Deut. 24:1 ff.) but does not make clear the grounds for divorce. And on many important subjects—the method of contracting a marriage, real estate law, the prayers in the synagogue, to name a few—the written **Torah** gives no guidance at all.

Such problems generated the concept of the oral **Torah,** in part explanation and elaboration of the written **Torah,** in part supplement to the latter. This oral **Torah** was not created consciously to meet the need of a certain time. Much of it was no doubt derived from established legal precedents and from popular custom and tradition. Once, however, the process of applying the law to new situations was undertaken in earnest, the material grew rapidly.

For a long time this was literally oral **Torah;** it was deemed improper to put down in writing what Moses had not written down at God's command. Only much later was it found necessary to compile this material in the Mishnah and other works of talmudic literature. But it was generally agreed that the entire body of oral **Torah** was also given to Moses at Sinai. It was to learn this vast corpus of teaching that Moses remained on the mountain forty days and nights.

The teachers of the oral **Torah** were chiefly laymen (that is, nonpriests) who are known to us as the Pharisees. From about the year 100 C.E. on, accredited teachers bore the title of rabbi. These teachers were opposed by a conservative party, made up mostly of priests, known as the Sadducees. They denied the validity of oral tradition and regarded the written text alone as authoritative. They interpreted the commandments in a strict literalist fashion. Perhaps it was this opposition which led the Pharisees to devise the method of midrash, in order to find some support in Scripture for their oral teachings. The Midrash uses a free, creative, and—let us admit—often far-fetched method of biblical interpretation. In expounding legal passages—what the Rabbis called halachah—the teachers were subject to some rules and restrictions in the use of midrash. But it was applied with virtually unlimited freedom to nonlegal materials, to the ethical, theological, and folkloristic subject matter known as aggadah or haggadah. Many beautiful examples of midrash are to be found in this commentary, especially in the sections headed "Gleanings." (It should be noted that the word "midrash" is used in three ways: to apply to a method in general, to a single instance of the method, and to literary works in which the method is employed.)

For most Jews, the written **Torah** was understood in accordance with the interpretation of the oral **Torah,** just as in modern law a written statute means what the courts interpret it to mean. The commandment "eye for eye, tooth for tooth" (Exod. 21:24) meant that one who injures another must pay money damages to his victim. "You shall not boil a kid in its mother's milk" (Exod. 23:19) was taken to prohibit the cooking or eating of any kind of meat with milk or milk products. Similarly, people did not always differentiate between biblical stories and their aggadic elaborations.

Though the growth of the oral **Torah,** later written down in the Talmud, obscured the plain sense of Scripture in many instances, it was a force for progress which enriched Judaism. Beginning in the eighth century C.E., a countertrend appeared in Persia and spread widely. The rebels against talmudic Judaism were called Karaites (Scripturalists). Returning to the Sadducean position, they proposed to live strictly by the simple word of the written **Torah.** But this program was not easy to carry out. The Karaites disputed bitterly among themselves as to the proper interpretation of many commandments. Moreover, many rabbinic modifications of scriptural law were both reasonable and humane, and to reject them meant turning the clock back—always a futile undertaking.

Christian and Moslem Views

The Christian apostle Paul, himself a Jew by birth, proposed in his writings a new view of the **Torah.** Its innumerable commandments, he held, constitute an overwhelming burden; no one can ever fulfill them properly. The "Law," in fact, was given by God to make us conscious of our sinfulness, that we may despair of attaining salvation by our own strivings. Now, Paul taught, salvation is available through faith in the crucified and risen Jesus; the "Law" has served its purpose, and, for Christian believers, it is abrogated (Romans 7:8; Galatians 2:15-3:14). This view has profoundly influenced Christian thought, though the churches rarely adopted Paul's teaching in its radical form and usually asserted the validity of the ethical laws of the **Pentateuch** (cf. Matthew 5:17-20; 19:18 f.).

In contrast to, and perhaps in reply to, the Pauline doctrine, Jewish teachers insisted on the continuing authority of the **Torah** and on its beneficent character. "The Holy One, blessed be He, desired to confer merit on Israel; that is why He gave them a voluminous **Torah** and many commandments" (Mishnah Makkot, end). Failure to obey the **Torah** fully does not result in damnation; rather it calls for repentance (return) and a fresh start.

Christian teachers through the centuries found in the **Torah**—and indeed the entire Hebrew Bible—many passages which they interpreted as prophecies of the career and the messianic (or divine) character of Jesus of Nazareth. In the past, Jewish spokesmen had to devote much time and effort to refuting these christological interpretations; today they have been discarded by competent Christian scholars.

Centuries later, Mohammed, founder of the third monotheistic religion, was to call the Jews "the people of the Book" because their religion was founded on Scripture. He did not know the book at first hand, or even in translation, for he never learned to read, but in his contacts with Jews and Christians he acquired a sketchy knowledge of biblical narratives with their aggadic embellishments. To these stories he occasionally alludes in the Koran (some selections will be found in the Gleanings). The Koran, which records the revelations received by the prophet, holds a position in Islam similar to that of the **Torah** in Judaism. It is supplemented by a tradition analogous to the oral Torah.[1]

The Middle Ages

In its wanderings, Judaism encountered many new constellations of ideas. Sometimes these novelties were rejected by Jewish thinkers; but often they were accepted as compatible with Judaism. In such cases an effort was made to show that these ideas were already suggested in Scripture.

The first examplar using this method was Philo of Alexandria, who lived at the beginning of the Christian era. A devout Jew, Philo was deeply influenced by Plato and the Stoics; and so he was led to "discover" the ideas of the philosophers in the text of the **Torah.** For Philo, the biblical word veiled deeper meanings and had to be explained allegorically. (For instance, Sarah symbolizes divine wisdom, her handmaid Hagar typifies secular learning.) The Jewish philosophers of the Middle Ages also employed allegorical interpretations, though with more restraint. They used this method to deal with Bible passages which appeared to contradict reason or morality, especially those describing God in human terms. Such authors as Saadia, Maimonides, and Ibn Ezra frequently found sophisticated philosophic concepts in the biblical text.

Still more extreme were the methods of the mystics. "We possess an authentic tradition," wrote Rabbi Moses ben Nachman, "that the entire **Torah** consists of the names of God, in that the words may be redivided to yield a different sense, consisting of the names." In general, the Kabalists found cryptic meanings in the words and letters of Scripture, without any reference to the meaning of the text as a coherent whole. The Zohar, the chief work of the Kabalah, is a vast mystical midrash on the **Torah;** and many Kabalists, and later on Chasidim, wrote their mystical treatises in the form of commentaries on the **Pentateuch.**

Ultimately the view emerged that there are four ways to expound the **Torah,** each valid in its own area: the rabbinic midrash, the philosophical implication *(remez),* and the mystical arcanum *(sod),* in addition to the plain meaning *(peshat).*[2]

In the Middle Ages, in fact, Jews recovered an awareness of the literal meaning of Scripture. This trend away from midrash to a simpler exegesis may have been stimulated by the Karaite revolt. The first great exponent of the *peshat* was Rav Saadia Gaon, the outstanding critic of Karaism. He was followed by a distinguished school of grammarians and commentators in Moslem Spain, who developed a genuinely scientific approach to the Hebrew language and to textual studies. These scholars wrote chiefly in Arabic; their findings were made accessible to the Hebrew reading public by Abraham ibn Ezra, who hailed from northern (Christian) Spain, and the Provençal Hebraists Joseph and David Kimchi.

Meanwhile another school of biblical scholars appeared independently in northern France; they were more traditionalist, less systematic and philosophic than the Spaniards, but they displayed a keen sense for niceties of language and for the spirit of the Bible. The outstanding production of this school is the **Torah** commentary of Rashi (Rabbi Solomon Itzchaki of Troyes), the most popular commentary ever written in Hebrew. Its popularity was due both to the clarity of Rashi's style and to the fact that he combined the exposition of the plain sense with a judicious selection of attractive *midrashim,* legal and nonlegal. His successors, however, concentrated more and more on the *peshat.*

The last of the great medieval expositors, Moses ben Nachman, despite his mystical tendencies, also offered original and independent comments on the plain sense. He and his predecessors had no difficulty with the fact that their simple exegesis sometimes contradicted biblical interpretations given in talmudic literature. In nonlegal matters there was no problem, since the aggadists gave many diverse explanations of the same verse. On halachic matters, these writers accepted the talmudic expositions for practical legal purposes but noted that, according to the rules of grammar, a given verse might be understood differently.

These medieval exegetes (and others we have not mentioned) made a permanently valuable contribution to the understanding of the biblical text. Though many other Hebrew commentaries on the **Torah** were written between the fourteenth and nineteenth centuries, they added little that was new. Only in the last two hundred years have new resources been available to broaden our understanding of Scripture; at the same time, new problems have arisen for the modern Bible reader.

*The **Torah** Scroll*

From an early date in the Christian era, manuscripts, including Hebrew manuscripts, were written in the form of books, consisting of a number of pages fastened together along one edge. We have many manuscripts of the Hebrew Bible of this sort; they are usually provided with vowel signs and with the punctuation indicating both sentence structure and the traditional chant. It is on such vocalized manuscripts that our printed Hebrew Bibles are based.

For ceremonial use in the synagogue, however, Jews have continued to employ **Torah** manuscripts in the more ancient scroll form. Each scroll is made up of numerous sheets of parchment, stitched together to make a continuous document, which is attached at either end to a wooden roller. The public reading of the **Torah,** to this day, is from such a scroll *(Sefer Torah),* containing only the consonantal text, without vowel points or punctuation, written on parchment with a vivid black ink. Tradition prescribes many details concerning the Sefer **Torah**—the beginning and end of paragraphs, the arrangement of certain poetic passages in broken instead of solid lines, the care of the scroll, the correction of mistakes, even the spiritual preparation of the scribe.

A synagogue usually possesses several scrolls. In ancient times they were kept in a chest (Hebrew *tevah* or *aron*), which was placed by the wall of the synagogue on the side nearest Jerusalem. In many early synagogues this "ark" stood in a niche, before which, in some cases, a curtain was hung. In modern synagogues the ark is usually a built-in recess, with a shelf for the scrolls; it is closed either by a curtain or by ornamental doors of wood or metal.

The removal of the scroll from the ark to the pulpit for reading and its return to the ark after the reading constitute a ceremony of considerable pomp, including the singing of processional melodies and demonstrations of respect and affection on the part of the congregants. When the ark is opened, and especially when the Sefer **Torah** is carried in procession, everyone stands.

The reverence and love evoked by the scroll is expressed in its outward adornments. Oriental Jews generally keep the scroll in a hinged metal or wooden case, often handsomely painted or carved, from which the ends of the rollers project. The scroll remains in the case while it is open on the reading desk, and it may be rolled to a new passage without removing it from this receptacle. When it is closed, the upper rollers are often adorned with artistic metal finials (called *rimonim,* "pomegranates"). In most European and American congregations, however, the scroll, after being fastened with a band of some woven material, is covered with a robe of silk or velvet, through which the

top rollers protrude. It may be decorated with a silver (or other metal) breastplate *(tas)* as well as with *rimonim.* Sometimes a single crown covers both wooden uprights. Eastern and Western Jews alike use a pointer *(yad,* literally, "hand"), most often of silver, with which the reader keeps his place in the scroll.

Some congregations, chiefly Sephardic, attach a silk or other woven strip to the outside of the parchment, which is rolled with the scroll to provide additional protection.

The Public Reading

It is customary to read from the scroll during every Sabbath and festival morning service, as well as on Monday and Thursday mornings. At the Saturday afternoon service *(minchah),* part of the following week's portion is read. There is no **Torah** reading on holy day afternoons, with the exception of the Day of Atonement and certain other fast days.

In the early centuries of the Christian era, the Jews of Palestine completed the reading of the entire **Torah** once in three years. We know, for the most part, how the text was divided into sections for this purpose; but scholars disagree as to when the triennial cycle began and ended—i.e., at what time in year 1 of the cycle the first chapter of Genesis was read.

Babylonian congregations, however, read through the entire **Torah** each year, and their custom ultimately became standard. It was the Babylonian Jews who created the festival of Simchat **Torah,** rejoicing over the **Torah.** On this day, all the scrolls of the congregation are carried around the synagogue in joyous procession; the closing chapter of Deuteronomy is read from one *sefer,* and then the first chapter of Genesis is read from another.

For the annual cycle, the **Torah** is divided into fifty-four sections, called *sidrot.* They are read consecutively, starting with the Sabbath following Simchat **Torah.** To complete the reading in a year, two sections must be read on certain Sabbaths, except when a leap year adds an additional month. Each *sidrah* is known by its first (or first distinctive) Hebrew word. For each holiday, a suitable selection is designated, apart from the weekly series. On holidays and certain special Sabbaths, an additional passage is read from a second scroll.

Each *sidrah* is divided into seven subsections. It is customary to "call up" seven worshipers to take part in reading the several subsections. (The number of participants varies on holidays, weekdays, etc.) Originally each person called up was expected to read a passage with the correct chant, and to recite the benedictions before and after the reading. Those who were insufficiently familiar with the text recited the benedictions and someone else read the portion for them. This was embarrassing to the unlearned; so it became customary long ago to assign the reading to one qualified person (the *ba-al keriah*), and those "called up," no matter how learned, recited only the benedictions.

In many traditional congregations, the lengthy period of the **Torah** reading became a disorderly part of the service. Those who had the honor of participating were expected to make contributions, which were duly acknowledged in the prayer *(Mi Sheberach)* recited on behalf of the donor or the donor's dear ones. Others present might also have recited special prayers of thanks or petition. On important holidays, moreover, the honors were sold at auction before the **Torah** service was conducted.

In reaction against such practices, Reform synagogues abolished the entire system of honors and limited participation to the ministry and to the congregational officers on the pulpit. More recently, some temples have reintroduced participation from the membership, but eliminating the old abuses. In order to shorten the weekly reading, some of the early Reformers proposed a return to the triennial cycle; but the suggestion met with little favor. So Reform congregations follow the annual cycle, but instead they usually read only one subsection of each *sidrah*. The passage is most often read without the chant; and the reader frequently translates it into the vernacular after reading it, or even sentence by sentence.

In the interest of relevance and inspiration, Reform made a number of changes in the readings for the holy days. Recently, a few congregations have made changes also in the weekly reading, omitting *sidrot* which seem to have no message for our time (the opening sections of Leviticus, for example) and substituting selections from other parts of the **Torah.**

The Torah and the Modern Jew

The last three centuries have seen a great upheaval in the religious thinking of Western man, in general, and of the Jew, in particular. The development of natural science has undermined belief in the supernatural and miraculous and, thus, brought into question the authority of all sacred scriptures. Further, the champions of religion could no longer follow the method of Philo, who read into the **Torah** the ideas of Plato, or of Maimonides, who understood the same texts in terms of Aristotelian thought. We cannot claim to discover the findings of Darwin or Einstein in the **Torah,** for modern methods of Bible study preclude such an approach. Philological analysis and historical criticism make it impossible to "explain away" errors of fact and, to us, unacceptable theological apprehensions and moral injunctions. All of these must be understood in

their own context and their own time. Furthermore, the rediscovery of the rich culture and literature of the ancient Near East revealed many similarities between biblical and non-Israelite writings, and even some cases in which the biblical authors borrowed from their pagan neighbors.

These new methods and discoveries have added enormously to our understanding of the biblical world. But they raise basic and difficult questions. Can the informed Jew of today regard the **Torah** as the world of God? And, if so, to what extent and in what sense? . . .

Notes

[1] The Arabs regard themselves as descendants of Ishmael, Abraham's oldest son. Some of the Moslem teachers accused the Jews of misinterpreting (or even falsifying) the biblical text in order to give preference to their ancestor Isaac. Similar charges, that Jews have tampered with the Hebrew text of the Bible, were made by some early Christian teachers.

[2] A similar doctrine of the fourfold sense of Scripture was held by Christians.

Douglas A. Knight (essay date 1985)

SOURCE: "The *Pentateuch*" in *The Hebrew Bible and Its Modern Interpreters,* edited by Douglas A. Knight and Gene M. Tucker, Fortress Press, 1985, pp. 263-96.

[*In the essay that follows, Knight examines the literary structure and intentions of the author(s) of the* Torah *through a critical survey of Pentateuchal scholarship.*]

It would be difficult to overestimate the role that the **Pentateuch** has played in the course of biblical scholarship. In all likelihood, these first five books have been subjected to scrutiny more than any other single block of the Bible, with the sole possible exception of the Gospels. It is significant that the **Pentateuch** has generally served as the staging ground for many if not most of the critical questions and methods that later spread to other areas of the biblical literature. Consider the following examples: Eight centuries ago Ibn Ezra wrote a commentary on the **Pentateuch** in which he delicately asked whether Moses could in fact have written all parts of the books normally attributed to him; subsequently, of course, such questioning of traditional authorship has extended to all parts of the **Pentateuch** as well as to, for example, Davidic composition of the psalms, Solomonic responsibility for wisdom literature, the origin of the prophetic writings, the authorship of the Gospels, the writer of various Pauline letters, to say nothing of the source of many of Jesus' sayings. Second, even before source criticism the idea that oral and written traditions might have been transmitted from generation to generation was proposed in the sixteenth and seventeenth centuries in the Hexateuchal studies of such scholars as John Calvin, Martin Chemnitz, Andreas Masius, Blaise Pascal, Baruch Spinoza, and Richard Simon; again, this notion has become common fare throughout the range of biblical studies, with the special twentieth-century perception that such traditions would not have been handed down passively but would have actually developed in the course of their transmission. Third, source criticism, as is well known, was first proposed for Genesis in the eighteenth century, initially by Henning Bernhard Witter in 1711 and then by Jean Astruc in 1753; now it is commonplace for scholars to inquire about the unitary or composite character of biblical passages and the authorship, date, and provenance of any sources we may discover. Fourth, the method of Religionsgeschichte seems, as can best be determined, to have emerged from a circle of friends that included Albert Eichhorn, Wilhelm Wrede, Hermann Gunkel, Wilhelm Bousset, Hugo Gressmann, and Ernst Troeltsch, but Gunkel's landmark study of 1895, *Schöpfung und Chaos,* was one of the very first full attempts to study a portion of biblical literature from this perspective. Fifth, form criticism of biblical literature originated with Gunkel's commentary on Genesis in 1901; it is now inconceivable to conduct critical exegesis without attention to form, genre, Sitz im Leben, and intention. In all of these cases—and many more could be added to them—the **Pentateuch** was the literary material that first invited closer study and presented in the process other problems demanding attention. The majority of biblical criticism holds itself in debt to these five books of the **Torah**.

However, the vital importance of the **Pentateuch** extends beyond its role in the development of critical methods, for it has long been used as the primary key to understanding Israel's history, society, religion, and morality. These are all addressed matter-of-factly in these ancient writings. The creation of the world, the origin of the people, the institution of religion, the ordering of family and social life—all are recounted in narratives, genealogies, laws, and speeches. But they were not presented simply out of antiquarian interest, as if merely to record what occurred in earliest times. Rather, this literature seems to be designed to lay out the program for Israel's life in later periods: settlement, monarchy, exile, and reconstruction. This is evident quite explicitly in the Mosaic sermons in Deuteronomy, but it cannot be mistaken elsewhere as well—from the relationship with neighboring peoples implied in eponymous ancestral stories, to the details for the temple building, to the cultic and moral ordinances for a settled agricultural and urban life. Of course, historical criticism has argued persuasively that most of these details stem not from the pre-settlement period as they purport to do, but instead are projected from later centuries back into the ancestral and Mosaic

times. Thus the Pentateuch, which ends with the death of Moses (generally thought to have occurred in the thirteenth century B.C.E.), serves actually as a major source for our reconstruction of the cultural and religious life of the people from that point all the way down to the fifth century. This itself could scarcely be accomplished were it not for the division of the literature into documentary sources that could then be dated to successive periods. Such use of the **Pentateuch** in historiography is nowhere more evident than in the work of Julius Wellhausen (especially 1878).

Given these two factors—that the **Pentateuch** has so often served as the subject matter for innovative criticism throughout the history of biblical scholarship and that this literature is of crucial importance for our study of Israel's cultural history—it is all the more disconcerting to observe that uncertainties and disputes at very fundamental points are prevalent in current Pentateuchal studies. Not long ago it seemed that real clarity had been achieved, but the state of affairs has now turned. These general problems of method and interpretation deserve attention at this point before we focus on more specific parts of Pentateuchal research.

I. A Synthesis and Its Dissolution

It would be fair to say that Gerhard von Rad and Martin Noth have offered the most significant comprehensive work on the **Pentateuch** in modern biblical scholarship. Wellhausen's decisive contributions, in comparison, were limited primarily to source criticism (1876-77), in which he amassed the findings of his predecessors and ordered them cogently into the Grafian sequence of JEDP, a structure that in general has held now for a century—no small achievement. However, Wellhausen's work on the **Pentateuch** included little more than drawing—very extensively, to be sure—on its postulated documents for his reconstruction of the history of Israel and its religion. He produced no commentaries, theologies, or further critical studies of the whole. Gunkel did write a nonpareil commentary on one of its books, Genesis, but his seminal form-critical work on this literature was left to be applied by others to the rest of the **Pentateuch.** He also presented no indepth analysis of the whole. In contrast, both von Rad and Noth devoted themselves massively and repeatedly to the **Pentateuch.** For von Rad, the comprehensive proposal came in 1938 in his *Form-Critical Problem of the Hexateuch.* He added to this numerous other studies including commentaries on Genesis (1953) and Deuteronomy (1964) and a major section in his *Old Testament Theology* (1st ed. in 1957). Similarly, Noth offered his general study in the form of an even more detailed, intensive analysis, *A History of Pentateuchal Traditions,* first published in 1948 and several times reprinted and translated. Beyond this seminal study Noth wrote commentaries on Exodus (1959), Numbers (1966), and Leviticus (1962), but these were not as closely related to his 1948 monograph as was his 1950 *History of Israel,* in which he demonstrated how this history should be understood in the light of his reconstructed development of the Pentateuchal traditions.

Between the two of them, von Rad and Noth managed to put together a critical synthesis that has informed nearly two generations of students and scholars. For all of the critical responses that they have received from the very beginning—and there have always been dissenting voices—their combined view of the origins of the **Pentateuch** long survived as the ruling hypothesis about how the **Pentateuch** came to be. What is especially important in this regard is the hermeneutical assumption: that the meaning(s) or intentions which a given text had at its origin and during its subsequent development are relevant for our understanding of the text in its present form. Thus most subsequent commentaries on the books of the Torah have been overwhelmingly concerned with focusing exegetically on this period of formation rather than on the longer postbiblical period in which the church and the synagogue interpreted these texts, often quite differently. So the critical framework that von Rad and Noth provided has had an impact not only in the area of literary history but also in exegetical interpretation and in historiography.

Before saying more about this hypothesis and its subsequent demise, one might well ask whether it is even proper to consider the separate work of von Rad and of Noth as indeed parts of a common synthesis. To be sure, the two did not explicitly collaborate on any specific project, an important exception being the development of the influential series, Biblischer Kommentar. Furthermore, von Rad's primary interest in theological questions was noticeably at variance with Noth's preoccupation with historical matters. However, the two critics themselves viewed their work as complementary to each other. On the second page of his 1948 volume Noth referred favorably to von Rad's earlier study of the "confessions/creeds" which gave a very early order to the series of themes that were essential for the faith of the Israelite tribes, confessions that were recited repeatedly in the early cult (also 1948:48). What Noth then attempted to do beyond this was to determine the nature and origin of these individual themes and to show how they were gradually filled out with innumerable other independent traditions. Von Rad, for his part, emphasized in later editions of his *Form-Critical Problem of the Hexateuch* that he wished it to be read in conjunction with Noth's volume. The various differences between the two seem to pale in comparison with the central preoccupation of both: to move the discussion beyond the then prevalent "stalemate" and "boredom" in Pentateuchal work (as von Rad [1938:1] described it at the time) and, in Noth's words, "to understand, in a manner that is historically responsible and proper, the essential content and important concerns of the **Pentateuch**—which, from its manifold beginnings, variously rooted in cultic situations, to the final stages in the process of its emergence, claims recognition as a great document of faith" (1948:3f.; Eng. tr. 3). Above all, in this the concern—again as Noth three times emphasized it (1948:4, 161, v)—is more to raise the proper questions than to offer definitive solutions.

The main features in this von Rad/Noth synthesis can be described as follows, without attempting to note all of the differences between the two. For both von Rad and Noth the **Pentateuch** as we have it is decidedly an "Endstadium," the final stage in a long process of development. Their primary task was not to engage in a literary-critical analysis of its smaller elements, but instead to try to recover this history of growth. They pictured this consistently as a living process, often oral; the operative category for it is "Vergegenwärtigung," understood in both senses of reinterpretation and actualization—a legitimatizing process in which one generation receives the traditions from the past and then has the opportunity to reaffirm them, adjusting them as they find appropriate, before passing them to the next generation. These traditions thus have to do with matters of vital importance to the Israelites' faith, society, and self-understanding. As a rule, the **Pentateuch** is based on innumerable traditions that were at first largely independent of one another. Only in the course of time did they become fused together, a process that von Rad and Noth sought to unlock. Noth concentrated much more on the precompositional stage; von Rad, on the compositional period. Noth identified five central themes that served as crystallization points for much that is in the **Pentateuch:** Promise to the Patriarchs, Guidance out of Egypt, Guidance in the Wilderness, Revelation at Sinai, and Guidance into the Arable Land. Each of these may well rest on some kernel of historical fact involving one or another group, but in no instance did all of Israel experience any one of these. Von Rad dealt also with these five themes, although he linked the exodus and conquest into one complex (hence also his insistence on a Hexateuch) and stressed especially the independence of the Sinai tradition from the others.

Perhaps the main difference between the two scholars, however, lies in how they viewed the merger of these themes. Noth set it in the period prior to the Yahwist, whereas von Rad attributed this decisive change to the compositional work of the Yahwist himself. For Noth, during the settlement period the Israelite tribes became aligned in the form of an amphictyony, with a central cult and several institutional functions in common (1930). It was in this cultic context that the themes merged together and that much of the remaining traditions were introduced into the whole. Von Rad postulated that the faith of Israel in this premonarchic period would have been expressed in a creedal form (the best example is in Deut 26:5b-9) and that such confessional statements would have provided the outline for the later composition. But he attributed to the Yahwist this innovation of creating a linear narrative based on the exodus-wilderness-conquest complex, through the "Einbau" (inclusion) of the Sinai tradition, the "Ausbau" (extension) of the ancestral traditions, and the "Vorbau" (addition at the beginning) of the primeval history. However, neither one considered this merger of the themes to be accidental or arbitrary, even though they tended to give different reasons for it: Noth, the development of the amphictyonic community; von Rad, the theological intentionality of the Yahwist. They agreed on seeing this early period as the formative stage of the faith as well as of the traditions, and wherever possible they tried to attribute these processes to specific groups, cultic celebrations, and geographical locations. They also shared a heuristic dichotomy between tradition and history, that is, between Israel's picture of her history and the historical-critical reconstruction of what actually happened. This discrepancy was not a problem for either of them: von Rad tied the kerygmatic, heilsgeschichtlich theology to Israel's traditional interpretation of her past, and Noth used these traditions themselves as indicators not of presettlement history but of the beliefs and ideas of the settled tribes. And finally, these two scholars were fully persuaded that this early formative period was so important that it must necessarily be penetrated if the structure and contents of the present **Pentateuch,** both as a whole and in its details, are to be understood properly. Small wonder, then, that von Rad in his commentary on Genesis gave explicit exegetical preference to the Yahwistic and Elohistic levels of the text—even though he clearly admitted that "the question of whether the preacher and teacher are also tied to this hermeneutical point of departure is another question entirely" (1953:31; Eng. tr. 1961:40). While both von Rad and Noth maintained a critical interest in the later Pentateuchal stages as well, for them the early period carried special significance.

A historical hypothesis can be considered valid only if it manages to explain all the evidence better than any other hypothesis can. Seen in this light, it is no wonder that the von Rad/Noth synthesis had the degree of success it has enjoyed since the 1940s. No other rival hypothesis concerning the growth of the **Pentateuch** has been so comprehensively and cogently developed nor so widely accepted during this period. However, so many specific features of this proposal have gradually fallen victim to attack that the cohesion of the whole has steadily eroded. Some of the most serious criticisms should be mentioned before we move on to the primary dilemma facing Pentateuchal studies today.

(1) One of the key items of the synthesis is von Rad's suggestion that there were creedal statements in the pre-Yahwistic period that set the central themes in order and thereby served as the outline according to which the **Pentateuch** was arranged. The antiquity of these creeds has now been effectively repudiated by Brevard Childs (1967), Wolfgang Richter (1967), J. Philip Hyatt, Leonhard Rost, and others. The confessions cited by von Rad contain too many Deuteronomistic elements to be dated any earlier than probably the seventh century. They are, therefore, in the nature more of theological summaries or systematic recapitulations at the end of the developmental process than of ancient faith statements that from an early point onward affected this process itself.

(2) Related to this, the antiquity of covenantal theology itself has been persuasively discounted by Lothar Perlitt. Both von Rad and Noth had, like Albrecht Alt before them, envisioned a covenant-renewal festival at Shechem when the Sinai theme would have been reactualized, and they regarded this as probably the oldest extensive tradition preserved in the Hebrew Bible. But Perlitt has undercut this thoroughly now by tracing the theological concept of covenant no earlier than the seventh century. Of course, this also affects the hypotheses advanced by George Mendenhall and others.

(3) Because the "creeds" were unanimous in omitting the Sinai revelation from their concatenation of the heilsgeschichtlich events, von Rad and Noth both concluded that this theme was wholly independent of the others. This has been roundly challenged by A. S. van der Woude, Walter Beyerlin, and others on the grounds of literary and theological affinities or by positing a covenant/treaty model, the latter of course a questionable point.

(4) The formative period of the Pentateuchal traditions reputedly occurred during the stage of oral transmission, with several folkloristic characteristics indicating this. John Van Seters (1975), however, has disputed that one can comfortably determine such orality from the written literature.

(5) Like Gunkel and Alt before them, von Rad and especially Noth considered many of the cultic, geographical, and popular narratives to be etiologically based. John Bright, Brevard Childs (1963), and Burke O. Long have cautioned, however, against prematurely discounting the authenticity of such traditions, for the etiological elements could in many cases be secondary redactional additions.

(6) Although most literary critics before him had normally maintained that the sources J and E were independent of each other, Noth made the interesting suggestion that preceding these two was a G source, a "Grundlage," comprising already in the amphictyonic period the elements common to both J and E (1948:40-

44; Eng. tr. 38-41). This proposal has not been convincing to such scholars as Hannelis Schulte in her study of the Joseph story or Van Seters in his work on the Abraham narrative; they attribute such common materials rather to author-editors who succeeded one another and made use of their predecessor's work, in other words through a series of literary dependency and redaction.

(7) By elevating the five themes to a position of supremacy in the early formation of the **Pentateuch,** von Rad and Noth unwittingly reduced all else to secondary or even less importance. Stated differently, the scheme was allowed sometimes to control the data, rather than vice versa. Thus for Noth especially, the traditions that serve merely to fill out the themes or in some way to connect them together include much of the Isaac and Jacob stories, the Joseph narrative, genealogies, itineraries, the plagues account, much of the wilderness tradition, the story of the Midianites in Exodus 18, the golden calf apostasy and covenant renewal in Exodus 32 and 34, and several other traditions as well. However, the element that has produced the most contrary response from scholars is the role assigned to the figure of Moses. According to Noth, the main reliable historical information we have about Moses is the tradition of his marriage to a foreign woman and the tradition about his grave. Just as Moses plays a negligible role outside the **Pentateuch** in the Hebrew Bible, so also he is not indispensable to any of the five themes—but belongs instead to the narrative elaboration as a linking element among several of the themes (1948:172-91; Eng. tr. 156-75). Noth's thesis regarding Moses has met with a storm of protest—not all of which, however, is argued as carefully or researched as thoroughly as is Noth's initial proposal.

(8) For both Noth and von Rad, the primary Sitz im Leben for the pre-Yahwistic developments was the amphictyony in its cultic, political, and military functions. As suggestive as this amphictyonic model seemed to be after Noth first elaborated it in 1930, it has not proved itself resilient to such attacks as those of Harry Orlinsky and Georg Fohrer (1966). Noth had maintained that it was through the amphictyony that the traditions attained their all-Israel orientation, so this matter needs to be reconsidered now also. Add to this the massive sociological proposal by Norman Gottwald and others: that Israel came into existence not through migration into the land but through a peasant uprising against the exploitative Canaanite overlords. What remains for the critic is a welter of hypotheses but no firm consensus regarding institutional, social, or cultic structures that could have aided the growth of the Pentateuchal traditions. For that matter, there seems now to be as little agreement on the emergence of Israel and the origin of Yahwism as there ever has been, although additional material data now coming to

light should assist on this question (see the discussion in the chapter by J. M. Miller in this volume).

(9) Von Rad's division between scientific history and the theological interpretation of history has come under fire from several sides. Franz Hesse called it "double-tracking" and insisted that the actual course of Israel's history, not simply Israel's interpretation of it, must be the vital arena of God's activity. In line with this, others have attempted—often through an illegitimate use of archaeological finds—to confirm the historical veracity of Pentateuchal events, customs, and other evidences. Thomas Thompson and John Van Seters, in separate monographs, have firmly refuted any such efforts at isolating elements in the ancestral narratives that might point unequivocally to the second millennium B.C.E. Although this would seem to make tradition and history even more distinct from each other than von Rad and Noth maintained, one must admit that the issue is far from settled in many scholars' eyes.

(10) The idea of Heilsgeschichte, on the other hand, seems to have gone the way of the Biblical Theology movement (Childs, 1970: Barr: 65ff.). It is too selective in highlighting only major historical junctures as occasions where God acts, as if the regular cultic interaction between God and humans is of much less importance. Second, it becomes too readily a theology of deliverance rather than a theology of justice with moral claims on humanity. Third, it is too facilely turned into a type of kerygmatic theology, in which one attempts to reduce the complexity of the literature and history to a primary kerygma. For example, Hans Walter Wolff (see the articles reprinted in Brueggemann and Wolff) finds the kerygmatic message of the Yahwist in the charge to Israel to be a blessing to the world; for the Elohist, the kerygma is the call to "fear God"; and for the Deuteronomist it is the call to repentance and return. There is little willingness among scholars anymore to bypass the varied nature of the literature in order to arrive at such simple reductions.

(11) At the level of the literary sources there has also occurred a serious departure from the Wellhausen/von Rad/Noth schema. Most notably, the Yahwistic source has come under heavy fire. John Van Seters has been insistent on dating this source closer to the exile, and Hans Heinrich Schmid wanted to consider it in terms of a much longer redactional period than the traditional dating in the tenth century would allow. Rolf Rendtorff (1977), in a very thorough criticism, even accused von Rad of departing from the normal source-critical model in arguing so strongly that the Yahwist was a theologian, rather than a literary document. The E material was also seen by Van Seters and others as more of a redactional level than a separate source. There continues to be considerably divided opinion on whether and how much the Deuteronomists laid their hands on

the **Pentateuch.** And finally, several critics remain unconvinced by Noth's provocative proposal (1948:7-19) that P was a separate source document that became the framework into which J and E were incorporated to make the final **Pentateuch.** Frank Cross, among others, maintained that it is much more likely that P was not a separate source but rather represented the final redaction of the JE material. Further complicating the discussion is the argument by several Jerusalem scholars that P is in fact a document of the preexilic period.

(12) To conclude this list we can simply point to the general lack of unanimity on where the **Pentateuch** ends. That is, in terms of literary history does the book of Deuteronomy belong more with Genesis-Numbers or with Joshua-Kings, the so-called Deuteronomistic History? This question is tied as well to the problem of where the conquest tradition belongs. On these points von Rad and Noth themselves disagreed. While von Rad spoke of a Hexateuch that ended with the conquest narrative, Noth preferred the notion of a **Pentateuch**—although with the bulk of Deuteronomy excluded he virtually operated with a Tetrateuch (as did Engnell more explicitly). A similar divergence on such a major point as this continues to the present.

Reference has been made here only to rather general points of contention. It hardly needs to be said that many of von Rad's and Noth's interpretations of specific literary units have also faced substantial and telling criticism. The important point for us is that Pentateuchal studies is hardly in a favorable position at the present point. The synthesis that explained so much about the formative history and meaning of the literature has met with such formidable opposition at individual points that only with multiple reservations can one defend it any longer. Heuristically, it still continues to prompt productive debate—not the least with regard to the determination of the right questions to ask of the text. However, there is no other grand plan, at the present, which promises to take the place of this influential proposal.

II. History of the Pentateuchal Literature

Pentateuchal research has largely followed Gunkel's lead (1906) in reconstructing a history of the literature ("Literaturgeschichte") from the earliest origins on down to the last stages. There has been, in comparison, remarkably little synchronic study of pericopes; examples of the exceptions are R. Polzin and D. Patte. Somewhat more attention has been focused on stylistics, for example, with regard to Hebrew narrative art (see the volume edited in 1975 by R. Culley, as well as other studies). Yet most scholars, like von Rad and Noth, have sought instead to clarify the ways in which the literature came into existence. What specifically comes under scrutiny in any study may be as short as a portion of a verse or as long as an entire book. Simi-

larly, attention can shift variously from oral tradition to genre to documentary source to redaction. There would be few scholars who would not understand their individual analyses to be contributions to the larger program of reconstructing the development of the literature along its full course of growth. There can be both theological and historical motivations for this enterprise, as we noted above to be the case also for von Rad and Noth.

Preliterary Tradition

In the section above we have described in some detail the work of von Rad and Noth and various points of critical reaction to it. It was in regard to the preliterary stage of the development of traditions that these two scholars made some of their most important contributions, not the least in their basic insistence that this period holds vital information for the proper understanding of the text. Most researchers of the **Pentateuch** have tended to agree with this, even if opinions vary on many specific points. A detailed study of traditiohistorical work since its inception is available in Knight, 1975; therefore, our comments here can be limited to a few general aspects of it in Pentateuchal studies.

Especially notable is the increased attention given to oral tradition. Literary materials could not only be remembered but also could actually be created at the oral stage. A tradition could thereby emerge as an expression of anything that was important to the ongoing life of the community. Scholarship has often envisioned an oral stage for almost every one of the various Pentateuchal literary forms: narrative, laws, songs, and even lists; there has also been a similar inquiry for most other literary sections of the Hebrew Bible, particularly the prophetic and psalmic literature. Although such research dates back to Gunkel and his predecessors, Scandinavians such as H. S. Nyberg, I. Engnell, and S. Mowinckel have been especially strong proponents of it in the past forty years—and with a distinctive direction. In several studies they have argued that very much of the Hebrew Bible originated as "oral literature," in part in cultic contexts and in part in other institutional or everyday situations. In contrast to Mowinckel, Nyberg and Engnell maintained that the oral process had a type of "Schmelzofen" effect, causing the tradition leading up to a given text to become so fused within itself that any layers of meaning stemming from various periods could not be distinguished from one another. For Engnell, the methodological implication of this was that scholars must virtually abandon source criticism in favor of tradition history, which is not oriented toward a "book-view" or an *"interpretatio europeica moderna"* of this ancient Hebrew literature. With respect to the **Pentateuch,** he adjusted the standard sigla to phrases (e.g., the "P-work" or the "D-group") or set them in double quotation marks ("J," "E," "P"). There was not actually a

Pentateuch but a Tetrateuch (without "D"), and "P" was not a documentary source but the last transmitter and editor of it. Following a debate with Mowinckel over critical method, Engnell seemed to modify his position somewhat about the extent of oral tradition in the Hebrew Bible, but he continued to argue stridently against attempts to stratify the tradition into primary and secondary elements. The influence of Nyberg and Engnell on such matters has steadily decreased over the years among other Scandinavian scholars, while researchers elsewhere have tended to consider it an idiosyncratic turn in scholarship. (For a full discussion of this traditio-historical work, see Knight, 1975:217-399; specifically also Engnell; Nyberg, 1947, 1972.)

However, the emphasis on oral means of transmission and oral devices in the literature has not been lost. Most scholars now recognize that a strict dichotomy between oral and written tradition is probably inappropriate, that both could have continued alongside each other and contributed to each other, that the oral probably preceded the written during the growth of the tradition but that oral interpretation could have continued long after a written text became fixed (note, e.g., the oral law in early Judaism) and that long compositions or cycles of traditions, if not actually created in written form, must have been committed early to writing rather than been retained solely as oral literature. Very often it is difficult or impossible to determine whether a given composition existed first in oral or written form; Noth (1948:41; Eng. tr. 39) acknowledged this for the Pentateuchal "Grundlage," his postulated source for the common elements in J and E. As indicated above concerning the dissolution of the von Rad/Noth synthesis, J. Van Seters (especially 131-48) has even questioned whether oral tradition can be identified on the basis of our present written texts except at a few isolated points where folkloristic criteria point clearly to preliterary genres. Most scholars tend to attribute a greater role to the oral prehistory of the biblical text than this (see, e.g., the various articles in Culley, 1976), with some recognition also of its theological implications (R. Lapointe).

As will be seen in the sections below on source and redaction criticism, F. Winnett, J. Van Seters, H. H. Schmid, R. Rendtorff, and others have sought to shift the emphasis from tradition history to a history of successive literary developments, which would then be studied by redaction criticism. Rendtorff's work (1977) is especially important at this point. Briefly stated, the traditio-historical problem of the **Pentateuch** in his view does not concern itself with the smaller, independent traditions that arose and circulated at the very earliest period in Israel's history (Gunkel's project), nor does it have to do with the compilation of the bulk of the epic tradition by the Yahwist (von Rad's contribution). Rather, he observed that what has been neglected is the stage in between when the independent, often dis-

parate traditions became gathered together into "larger units," prior to the time when these various units were in turn structured together to make our present **Pentateuch.** He surveyed the numerous such units identifiable in the **Pentateuch,** but he spent the bulk of his analysis in an attempt to reconstruct this traditio-historical stage for the ancestral traditions. Here, for example, he dealt with such units as the Abraham cycle, the Isaac traditions, the Jacob traditions, and the Joseph story. In attempting to determine how and why the various traditions came together to form each of these originally separate units, Rendtorff focused especially on literary and thematic elements (such as the types of promise to the ancestors) rather than on geographic, social/political, or cultic circumstances (such as Noth elevated as criteria). This study of literary and thematic elements holding the units together constitutes in fact one of the primary contributions of this book, although Rendtorff failed to relate them adequately to the other factors just mentioned and thereby did not create a plausible setting for these traditio-historical developments. After thus executing his brief analysis of the formation of these larger units, Rendtorff turned to a criticism of recent Pentateuchal research and then to the implications of his study. His basic thesis in this regard was that there were no continuous "sources" in the sense of comprehensive drafts of Pentateuchal materials, such as scholars for a century have seen in J and P. He based this thesis in part on the lack of consensus among scholars about the precise extent and characteristics of J and P, in part on the lack of solid evidence for these source documents in the **Pentateuch** or even in the preexilic prophetic literature, in part on the lack of continuity among the larger units, and furthermore in part on the simple fact that with the multitude of these larger units in the **Pentateuch** the sources J and P are no longer really necessary. At most they might represent editorial reworkings of the materials. Rendtorff concluded in fact that only at the level of the Deuteronomistic redaction did any editor have the comprehensive **Pentateuch** on which to work. Having thus called into serious question the standard results of source criticism, the book concluded with some further observations about how important the origin of the several larger units is for the overall understanding of the **Pentateuch** and its development.

Rendtorff's critique is suggestive, especially for the attention which he drew to the "larger units" in the **Pentateuch,** but substantially more analyses of texts and units are needed if his thesis is to be established. In the face of his work and that of the others who prefer to think of the Pentateuchal growth as mainly a literary process of successive redactions, one still cannot lose the sense that more can be said about the developmental process than just this. Very much of the Pentateuchal research in recent decades has focused on the larger cycles of similar materials or on the five

themes of Noth, with results that are admittedly hypothetical but nonetheless often plausible (for a brief
overview of such studies see, among others, R. Smend,
1978:96-100). To the extent that these forays into the
uncharted terrains of preliterary (as well as literary)
traditions provide us with reasonable insights, they will
continue to be pursued.

Literary Development

Of all the stages in the history of the Pentateuchal
literature, the documentary sources have enjoyed the
longest and most thorough scrutiny. Indeed, source
criticism, which attempts to identify the literary sources
that may have served as the basis for the final text, was
the first of the historical-critical exegetical methods to
develop after the seventeenth-century onset of modern
biblical criticism. The eighteenth and nineteenth centuries saw this work produce a succession of different
proposals: the older documentary hypothesis, the fragment hypothesis, the supplementary hypothesis, and
finally the new documentary hypothesis. It is the latter
that has continued to have an impact up to the present,
above all because of Julius Wellhausen's cogent presentation of the literary evidence (1876-77) and the
relation of these sources to the history of Israel, especially to the history of its religion (1878; for an appraisal of Wellhausen's significance, see the volume
edited by D. Knight, 1982). Following the suggestion
of Eduard Reuss and Karl Heinrich Graf, Wellhausen
envisioned four primary sources set in the following
order: J (ca. 850 B.C.E.), E (ca. 700), D (ca. 623), and
P (500-450). In the following decades and still to the
present this delineation has for most scholars continued to represent the base point of Pentateuchal criticism. Modifications were offered up through the 1930s
in primarily two different areas: proposing alternate
dates for the sources or subdividing the various sources
into multiple strands. However, these were generally
intended by the source critics to be little more than
adjustments to the established scheme. (For detailed
discussions of source criticism during that period, see
especially Houtman; Kraus.) It is significant, however,
that most of the early source critics assumed that to
identify the literary sources was sufficient for explaining the origins of the **Pentateuch.**

Yet by the 1940s there was a different mood afoot.
With attention being turned increasingly to other stages
in the history of the Pentateuchal literature—especially
to the genres and the traditions—scholars began to
sense, as Gunkel had earlier proposed, that much, if
not most, of the creative activity had already occurred
well before the sources were written. Most critics tended
to consider the problem of source delineation to be
basically resolved, and they presupposed this
Wellhausenian structure for the work which they preferred to conduct. Already in his landmark study of
1938 Gerhard von Rad noted that source criticism had

come to a halt—and in the eyes of some had even gone
too far. Both in this area and in the study of the smaller
units he observed a "Stillstand" and a
"Forschungsmüdigkeit" which had regrettably taken
hold, especially among younger scholars (1938:1). A
mere decade later, however, Martin Noth referred to
"the continuing lively debate over the literary-critical
analysis of the **Pentateuch**" (1948:5; Eng. tr. 6). These
divergent evaluations are due to several elements. Noth
engaged in more explicit source criticism than did von
Rad and offered several novel proposals. Noth tended
to relate such source investigation to the history of the
literature, whereas for von Rad the theological aspects
were more important, especially as these related to the
final compositions. Noth could also, of course, look
back on a decade of increased attack on source criticism from several sides, especially from Scandinavian
scholars (see Knight, 1975). Finally, von Rad's own
contributions to the relationship between the theolo-
gizing Yahwist and the final state of the **Pentateuch/**
Hexateuch reopened questions about the significance
of the sources. Actually, the years following 1938 would
confirm von Rad's comment only for the specific matter
of source division, that is, the assigning of texts to one
continuous source document or another. Even Noth
(1948:4-44) and most commentators since that time
have tended to follow the division elaborated by
Wellhausen. Nonetheless, the debate has hardly been
stagnant if one considers the fundamental questions
that have been and still are raised, issues that have to
do with the whole literary development of the
Pentateuch from initial written sources on down to
final redactions.

The Yahwistic Literature (J)

The liveliness of this discussion can be seen immediately with the source that has traditionally been set as
the first: J. Although there is some divergence among
scholars on questions of composition, the greatest variance of views—and thereby the most unsettled questions of vital significance for the understanding of J—
is to be found on matters of origin and intention.

The literary composition of J, which embraces the largest single narrative block in the **Pentateuch,** has long
been suspect of "Mehrschichtigkeit." Earlier generations of scholars have at times fragmented J into multiple strata. This source-critical tendency has been
largely abandoned, except at one specific point.
O. Eissfeldt divided J into two sources—the older
termed the Lay source (L) and dated ca. 950-850 B.C.E.
and the younger simply called J and assigned anywhere
between 900 and 721. He first gave graphic portrayal
of these sources in his *Hexateuch-Synopse* (1922, repr.
1962) and continued to argue this division in his influential *Introduction*. Notably, these sources were traced
beyond the **Pentateuch** into the books of Joshua and
Judges. Just as significant, Eissfeldt maintained that

the two sources stemmed from opposing circles: L from groups committed to the nomadic ideal and to the unity of Israel despite its division into two kingdoms after 922; and, in direct contrast, J from circles enthusiastically interested in agricultural life and in the national political power and cult. Georg Fohrer's modification of this division (1969:173-79) consisted especially in renaming L with N (= Nomadic source) and setting it not before but after J as a conservative reaction against J's satisfaction with the arable land ("Kulturlandbegeisterung"). Previously, C. A. Simpson (1948), one of the other main proponents of a divided J source during the period since 1945, assigned his J1 source to the southern tribes and considered that the J2 source had then, in the period around 900 B.C.E., used and revised J1 in the light of additional traditions from the Joseph tribes. Later, around 700 B.C.E., E reworked all the material in a thoroughgoing manner in the light of other northern interests. Simpson furthermore posited a complex subsequent redactional history of these sources. Eissfeldt, Simpson, and Fohrer have not found wide support for their proposals, which to many appear to be rather artificial and improbable divisions of J. By far the dominant inclination has been to account traditio-historically or redaction-critically for any materials in J that seem to deviate from its usual character.

On this point of its character, one can find descriptions of J—with greater or lesser detail but with little substantial deviation from each other—in any number of introductory volumes on the Hebrew Bible. R. Smend (1967:27-87), Peter F. Ellis (225-95), and others have reproduced the text in translation, joining all parts together into a flowing narrative. Henri Cazelles (771-91) provided an overview with source-critical notes about the materials that are assigned to J; commentators, of course, usually do the same for their respective books. A list of Hebrew words and forms that are distinctive to J can be found in Simpson (403-9), and Ellis (113-46) described some of the primary literary techniques used by the Yahwist; Aage Bentzen (2: 45-51) discussed both sets of criteria with reference to the problem of distinguishing between J and E. With few exceptions (especially U. Cassuto and I. Engnell), scholars have tended not to contest these matters to any degree approaching their disputes over how the data are to be interpreted.

The problem of date looms largest—and consequently the questions of audience, place, and intention are necessarily attached to it as well. Few scholars would deny that some or even most of the J material may extend back in time to the premonarchic period of settlement. Noth argued forcefully that "the actual formation of Pentateuchal tradition is to be placed essentially in the period of prestate tribal life" (1948:248; Eng. tr. 229), and for him this included not only the source "G" but also many other narratives that were subsequently used in J, E, and P to fill out the traditional materials in

each. Furthermore, it is often maintained by scholars that these pre-J and pre-E traditions were not necessarily still in the form of disparate small units when they were incorporated into J or E, for there could well have existed cycles or collections—for example, stories about the ancestors, early laws, descriptions of the wanderings of the people—in oral or written form before the extensive written sources later emerged. Thus the question of the origin of the various *contents* of a given source tends to be held separate from the question of when the *whole* was constituted as a documentary source.

The most common date assigned to the origin of J is the period of the early monarchy. Von Rad associated it with a "Solomonic humanism" (1962:68-69; Eng. tr. 55), a period of enlightenment under Solomon marked by political security, a nationalistic spirit, building programs, new interest in culture and the arts, and an appreciation of human existence. "What else is the Jahwist's wonderful work but one great attempt to make Israel's past relevant to the spirit of a new age by reviewing and, above all, spiritualizing it?" (1962:69; Eng. tr. 55). Even though von Rad's notion of a "Solomonic Enlightenment" may be somewhat excessive (see, e.g., the critique by J. Crenshaw [16-20]), the vast majority of interpreters have followed him in dating J somewhere between the mid tenth and the late ninth century (see, e.g., the seven observations supporting a Solomonic date in H. P. Müller [52]). This Yahwistic history is thereby associated with the succession narrative and other literary productions of this monarchy, all seen as examples of Israel's initial efforts in historiography (von Rad, 1944; Hölscher; Schulte). Not only did J first emerge as a written source in this period; but also it is seen to represent "Hoftheologie," and its author is considered a "court theologian" (Richter, 1966; Brueggemann, 1968)—although how officially sanctioned is unclear. W. von Soden proposed Nathan or his disciple as the author of J or substantial parts of it, with a certain prophetic-type critique of Solomon to be found in Genesis 3 and 11 (cf. also M.-L. Henry). Adherents to this early dating of J vary in assigning it to the reign of David, Solomon, or Rehoboam, but they quite uniformly agree to its southern provenance. J was thus a collection of old narratives that were gathered together at that point in order to celebrate the new monarchy by recounting God's beneficent dealings in Israel's earlier past history. H. W. Wolff (1964) identified Gen 12:1-3 as the key indicator of J's theological kerygma: YHWH's promise of blessing to Abraham, which was becoming fulfilled in J's period when the early monarchy was established and secured (see also L. Schmidt).

A very different conception of J has emerged in recent years, a view that challenges directly the position held by those scholars who trace their critical heritage back to Noth, von Rad, and Wellhausen. In 1964 Frederick

V. Winnett delivered his Presidential Address to the Society of Biblical Literature, which was published in 1965 under the provocative, if not iconoclastic, title "Re-examining the Foundations." The "foundations" he examined were those represented in the foregoing description of the J source. In a word, Winnett disputed the idea of two parallel strands, J and E, running through the book of Genesis, and in its place he proposed a succession of "official revisions," extensive supplementations by later hands. The emphasis on "official" is important because it is improbable that various scribes along the way would have been permitted to "tamper" with the narrative, introducing glosses and interpolations without the sanction of the basically conservative religious body for whom this narrative was so important (1965:12). Winnett posited an early J document, probably cultic in origin, which was composed of Abraham and Jacob stories linked together sequentially. The first official revision was E's work of supplementing—not altering—this J source still in the preexilic period. However, the book of Genesis owes its present form to the major revision done by the author whom Winnett called "Late J" and dated in the postexilic period. This Late J composed the primeval history on the basis of diverse sources ("mainly oral but possibly some written" [1965:18]), incorporated the Abraham-Jacob narrative as revised by E, and drew on the E story of Joseph, recasting it to give Judah a more prominent role. The impetus for this work by the Late J, whose outlook was notably universalistic and monotheistic, was the fall of Jerusalem in 587 B.C.E. There was a later official revision of Late J's Genesis by P about 400 B.C.E. The major achievement by P, however, was the creation of the **Pentateuch**: prefixing Genesis to the Mosaic tradition in the books of Exodus and Numbers (the latter two books were also significantly revised by P) and detaching the book of Deuteronomy from the Deuteronomistic History in order to append it to the Mosaic tradition. This means, then, that the book of Genesis is later than Exodus and Numbers, and thus that the promises of land in Genesis do not presuppose a JE narrative extending as far as the story of the conquest and settlement of Canaan. In an earlier study (1949) Winnett had also disputed the theory of parallel J and E strands in Exodus and Numbers, so his study challenged the regnant documentary hypothesis not merely for Genesis but for the entire **Pentateuch** as well.

Winnett's proposal has not won the day among Pentateuchal scholars, but it has had a strong impact on several researchers, particularly some of his own students. These, together with other scholars who have independently reached similar conclusions, have pressed the critical questions to the point where they must be faced directly. To some extent P. Volz and W. Rudolph anticipated part of the argument already in 1933 when they maintained that only J could be considered an authentic "source" and that E was not an independent

narrative strand but rather a later redactor and supplementer. S. Sandmel, only four years before Winnett's article, defined the developmental growth of the **Pentateuch** as a process of midrashic augmentation, that is, one in which subsequent redactors would have been loath to alter their received text in any way other than to add new materials to it—thus a "process of neutralizing by addition" (120). N. Wagner questioned whether one could legitimately assume that what we identify as J or E in Genesis is the same J or E found in Exodus, or even whether there is a common origin for all J (or E) materials in the various parts of the book of Genesis itself.

Three other lengthy studies, from independent contexts yet all within three years of each other, have heightened the issue. J. Van Seters, in a 1975 publication dedicated to his teacher, Winnett, limited his attention to the Abrahamic tradition in Genesis. Methodologically, as we have mentioned above, Van Seters disputed the claims of tradition historians who have attempted to retrace the development of these materials in the realm of oral tradition. Like T. L. Thompson, furthermore, Van Seters found nothing that could reliably be dated in the second millennium B.C.E.; the question of Abraham's historicity is thereby left wholly unanswerable. His literary analysis produced a picture very similar to Winnett's. There was a pre-Yahwistic first stage comprised of only the stories of Abraham in Egypt (Gen 12:10-20), Hagar's flight (16:1-12), and Isaac's birth (18:1a, 10-14; 21:2, 6-7). This was followed by a pre-Yahwistic supplement ("E"), the story of Abraham and Abimelech (20:1-17; 21:25-26, 28-31a). The Yahwist, working in the exilic period and addressing the despair of the exilic community, drew on these sources, added new materials of his own, and thus composed the whole Abrahamic cycle. Later, the Priestly writer added some genealogical and chronological details as well as the episodes found in Genesis 17 and 23. Finally, Genesis 14 was inserted, bringing the literary development to a close. Van Seters thus followed—although without managing to prove them to the satisfaction of most subsequent researchers—Winnett's basic tenets: a series of successive supplements of the previous written tradition; doubt about the existence of E as a separate Pentateuchal source; an exilic or postexilic date for the Yahwist, who was primarily responsible for the composition; and P as a later supplementary revision.

The next monographic study came from the pen of Hans Heinrich Schmid (1976), who acknowledged early in his discussion the contributions of Winnett and Van Seters to the current upheaval in Pentateuchal research. Schmid's analysis focused on J materials in several blocks of literature beyond Genesis: the call of Moses, the Egyptian plagues, the Reed Sea crossing, the wilderness wanderings, the Sinai pericope, as well as the promises to the ancestors. His conclusion coincided with that of Winnett and Van Seters in that he did not find it tenable to date the Yahwist's comprehensive theological redaction and interpretation in the Solomonic period. However, more so than did the other two, Schmid based his argument on evidence about preexilic prophecy and the Deuteronomic-Deuteronomistic tradition. For him, the Yahwist presupposed the preexilic prophets at numerous points, a clear indication of a late date. Significantly, Schmid advocated that the "so-called Yahwist" should not be seen as an individual collector, author, or theologian; rather, the "Yahwist" was a "Redaktions- und Interpretationsprozess" (1967:167) which took place during approximately the same time frame as that of the Deuteronomic-Deuteronomistic group and shared some viewpoints with it. This would conform well to the thesis of L. Perlitt that a full "covenantal theology" was a product of this Deuteronomic-Deuteronomistic movement, for such a theology is also reflected in some of the J pieces of the **Pentateuch.**

Work by a third scholar has further extended the dilemma. R. Rendtorff's 1977 monograph was discussed above concerning general matters of tradition history. His thesis about the Yahwist was advanced in 1975 and reissued in English translation in 1977 together with brief responses by Van Seters, Schmid, and R. N. Whybray. Rendtorff accused von Rad of turning a literary problem into a theological issue insofar as he considered the Yahwist as a theologian rather than a literary source. This fundamentally changed the type of question being asked of the text, for the emphasis was drawn away from the literary characteristics of the sources. It also led to an interest in determining the role that this Yahwist had in theologically shaping the **Pentateuch.** Rendtorff, in contrast, understood the Yahwist neither as a personality nor as a comprehensive theological editing of the materials. Even more clearly in 1977 (e.g., 112) he maintained that the Yahwistic work could hardly be understood in the sense of the usual documentary hypothesis, that is, as an extensive narrative running through the **Pentateuch.** At most J, like P, might represent editorial reworkings of the materials. Only at the level of the Deuteronomistic redaction did an editor have the whole **Pentateuch** to work on.

The state of research on J is currently in a rather perplexing condition. The majority of scholars quite clearly adhere more to the views of Wellhausen and von Rad, with the earlier date and ideological intention quite in keeping with the early monarchy. However, the critiques by those described above have shaken confidence in the usual hypothesis. Even if the Yahwist does not emerge as an exilic or postexilic source, it will henceforth be much more difficult to disregard the suggestion that there was redactional activity in the Yahwistic vein over the course of several centuries down to and probably including the exilic period.

There has been significantly less fundamental critique of the other three documents—E, D, and P—during the past three decades in comparison with what the J source has had to endure. Some of the substantial questions about these three have already been described above, especially the issue of whether they were comprehensive sources or, rather, supplementary revisions over the long redactional history of the **Pentateuch.** We will consequently restrict our comments to only a few other distinctive points about each.

The Elohistic Literature (E)

The Elohistic source received a substantial challenge in the 1930s by P. Volz and W. Rudolph, first by both together in a volume on Genesis and then later by Rudolph in a study of Exodus through Joshua. They argued that E could not have existed as an independent narrative with substantial scope, as the traditional form of the documentary hypothesis claimed. Instead, E represented a redactional stage in which additions were made to the Yahwistic source document. Volz (Volz and Rudolph: 135-42) even went on to posit that P was also not an independent narrative source but a redactional level, although Rudolph (1938:253-55) differed with him on this point. The problem regarding E, of course, is its fragmentary character, a point that virtually every writer on the subject makes at the very outset. On the whole, there is less significant disagreement among scholars on the identification and interpretation of E texts, however, than there is on the question of origin.

Noth (1948:36-44, 247ff.; Eng. tr. 33-41, 228ff.) upheld the documentary hypothesis despite the argument of Volz and Rudolph. For him, E constituted a whole narrative parallel to J on which a redactor drew in order to augment J, which served as the literary basis. E must have been much more extensive, but it was primarily the special materials that were taken from it to be added to J. Originally J and E existed independently, although they were both based on the older source G, which contained mainly those traditions that they both had in common. Noth even considered E, taken as a whole, to have been closer to G than was J. Other studies, for example, A. W. Jenks and K. Jaroš as well as most commentaries, have followed this view of E as a narrative source with its own distinctive provenance (usually the north), theological intention (e.g., for Wolff [1969] it is "the fear of God" and the opposition to syncretism), and literary style.

The dissenting position follows closely that of Volz and Rudolph and has been mentioned above in the discussion of J. According to Winnett, Van Seters, and others, E is not a separate source but a redactional supplementation of the old Yahwistic narrative, the latter being indeed sparse at many points. H.-C. Schmitt even carried this argument further in his recent study of the Joseph narrative. Without considering E to be a documentary source, Schmitt proposed that E was a redactor, yet even more than this insofar as E brought together the narrative blocks that had been distinct until then—the ancestral tradition, the Joseph story, and at least the Moses story in Exodus 1-3—thereby producing a new and continuous historical composition. This thesis is suggestive, but like others it serves primarily to emphasize the open questions that still exist about the E materials.

The Deuteronomic Literature (D)

The D source may seem to pose fewer problems because of its supposed confinement to the book of Deuteronomy, thus not being present throughout the whole **Pentateuch** to the same extent as the other primary sources. This, however, would be to mask the real difficulties that have continued to confront researchers: Is there an older core to the present book of Deuteronomy, and what can be known about its origin? How does this core relate to its literary context? Furthermore, is there a close connection between it and redactional strata outside the book of Deuteronomy?

It has long been held that Deuteronomy 12-26 constituted an "Urdeuteronomium," a core of laws to which the remaining chapters subsequently were added. The roots of this legal corpus normally have been found in the northern kingdom prior to its fall in 722 B.C.E. R. P. Merendino attempted to identify the parts of this old Deuteronomic law through a careful analysis of both form and content, and he concluded that there were several smaller, originally independent series of laws (cultic laws, apodictic laws, abomination laws, marriage laws, humanitarian laws) that were brought together to form this core. G. Seitz focused in his study mainly on the Deuteronomic redaction of these earlier materials, finding especially an emphasis on humanitarian aspects, apostasy, and cultic unity at this level. Although it has often enough been thought that many of the laws themselves date back to very early times and have some affinity to the Book of the Covenant in Exodus 21-23, P. C. Craigie has revived the traditional dating of the whole book to an even earlier period. Arguing on the basis of the covenantal form and significance of the book, he found "it not unreasonable to assume that the book comes from the time of Moses or shortly thereafter" (28). Few would concur with Craigie on this point about the book, although it is clear that there were pre-Deuteronomic laws in the collection. More form-critical and comparative legal study is necessary before we can hope to understand better the relation of such early laws to the first Deuteronomic corpus. As Seitz, Merendino, A. D. H. Mayes, and others have sensed, the proper approach to this is to attempt to determine what the Deuteronomic redactor added to the received legal sources.

Since W. M. L. de Wette in the early nineteenth century it has been common to identify Deuteronomy, or only the Deuteronomic core (chaps. 12-26), with the "book of the law" that was discovered in the Jerusalem temple during Josiah's reign, as recounted in 2 Kings 22-23. As much support as this thesis has found in recent decades, substantial questions have also been raised. Mayes (85-103) presented these in his full review of the issue and concluded that the story in 2 Kings 22-23 was introduced later by the Deuteronomist and that there was thus no immediate relation between Josiah and the Deuteronomic corpus of laws. S. Mittmann, in his study of Deut 1:1-6:3, furthermore concluded that the law preached in Deuteronomy did not exist apart from the historical introduction in these opening chapters. This is quite in contrast to the opinion introduced by M. Noth (1943) that Deuteronomy 1-3(4) was written by the exilic Deuteronomist not so much as a part of the book of Deuteronomy but as an introduction to the whole Deuteronomistic History. However these matters are viewed, one can hardly escape the conclusion that the book of Deuteronomy experienced a rather long and complex series of redactions, perhaps even in the sense of a supplementary hypothesis, until its present form was reached.

The authorship of Deuteronomy, without its latest redactions, has proved difficult to resolve. Von Rad (1947) advocated that the "country Levites," who were in allegiance with the reform-minded "people of the land," were responsible for it, while Mayes attributed it to Levites with priestly prerogatives who were attached to the Jerusalem temple. E. W. Nicholson argued that prophets of the north stood behind it, whereas M. Weinfeld proposed scribes of the Jerusalem court because of the connections that he identified between Deuteronomy and wisdom. Several scholars have maintained that the form of the book of Deuteronomy had some connection with a covenantal form—whether because of a covenant-making or covenant-renewing festival (von Rad, 1938:30-37; Eng. tr. 33-40) or through a covenant formulary based on the form of international treaties (K. Baltzer and others). As with other matters, such questions will likely need different answers depending on the redactional level under consideration.

The Priestly Literature (P)

Issues similar to those facing J, E, and D have confronted the P source in recent decades—with not totally dissimilar results. First, the dating of P has been set in widely divergent periods. J. G. Vink assigned it to the Persian period; most others have dated it in the exilic or post-exilic age. Quite differently, Y. Kaufmann (174-211) considered it pre-exilic, in fact pre-Deuteronomic, before the idea of cultic centralization began to rise under Hezekiah. This early dating has also received some support from A. Hurvitz on the basis of a linguistic comparison of P with Ezekiel, Ezra-Nehemiah, Chronicles, and the Mishnah; he concluded that P idioms and terminology do not presuppose the exilic or postexilic period as do the others. Yet to whichever period P as a whole is dated, the problem of its sources remains pertinent. There has been a consensus that JE existed before P and that P could not have been unacquainted with such a significant historical narrative. Beyond that, one has looked for such other sources as a "Toledoth-Book" (Noth, 1948:9ff.; Eng. tr. 10ff.; modifying the earlier view of von Rad, 1934), certain narrative blocks, and various legal collections (e.g., Leviticus 1-7; 11-15; and 17-26, the "Holiness Code"; see Rendtorff, 1954; Koch; Reventlow; and Kilian). In virtually all such cases P would have edited the received materials before inserting them into the P history, some stylistic aspects of which process are depicted well by S. E. McEvenue.

The essential critical problem, although not original to this recent period of research, parallels that of the other documents: What, precisely is P—a source or a redaction? Noth (1948:7-19, 228ff.; Eng. tr. 8-19, 228ff.) was unequivocal in identifying P as an intact narrative independent of other sources, and he then posited that this P served as the literary basis into which JE was woven. P was normative for the final **Pentateuch**, beginning at Genesis 1 and ending at Deuteronomy 34. Thus for Noth it was not simply an editorial process of combining JE and P together but rather of fitting JE into P. Quite a different view has been proposed by F. M. Cross (293-325). Noting the absence of numerous important Pentateuchal traditions, the presence of various framing devices, the occurrence of archaizing language, and other evidences, Cross argued that P could only be considered a redactional stage and not an independent narrative document. The basis was JE, which the Priestly tradent edited and supplemented with Priestly lore during the latter period of the exile, the purpose being to revive the Sinaitic covenant and to aid the restoration of Israel. Rendtorff (1977:112-42) maintained just as strongly that P was not a continuous narrative but rather a redactional level, comprised especially of chronological and some theological texts that were made to link the previous traditions together. Winnett and Van Seters have taken similar positions, as we have seen above. Also regarding P we find, therefore, a situation in which careful studies and bold argumentation have combined to unsettle old positions in favor of a more redaction-critical view of the development of the **Pentateuch.**

The **Pentateuch** as a Whole

Much more scholarly attention has been devoted—as might well be expected given the predominant critical methods—to the meaning and history of parts of the **Pentateuch** than to the nature of the **Pentateuch** as a whole. Nonetheless, the latter has been a matter of

concern with respect especially to three questions: extent, literary basis, and intention.

We have already indicated that von Rad and Noth themselves disagreed on where the **Pentateuch** as a literary unity actually ends. The problem involves both the book of Deuteronomy and the conquest tradition. In his 1943 publication Noth tied Deuteronomy as well as the conquest narrative in Joshua to the Deuteronomistic History, which runs through the books of Kings; and thereby he was left with essentially a Tetrateuch plus some P materials at the end of Deuteronomy. Von Rad, for his part, considered the conquest narrative to be the natural conclusion to the creedal affirmation that begins with the promises to the ancestors, including the promise of the land. Scholars have had difficulty in moving the discussion beyond this difference of opinion, even if the word "Pentateuch" is much more frequently used than either "Tetrateuch" or "Hexateuch." Mowinckel (1964b; 1964a) found in the book of Joshua some traces of both J and P concerning a conquest of the land, but above all a Deuteronomistic redaction which made such fragments into a full history of the conquest by "all-Israel." For him, then, there was never a Tetrateuch nor a Hexateuch in the sense of an independent historical work—but only a **Pentateuch** with the D laws incorporated and the J and P conquest materials included in the Deuteronomistic History (1964b:77). However, the more difficult problem has been associated with the book of Deuteronomy. Ever since Noth's 1943 study scholars have been inclined to see in Deuteronomy the ideological basis for the following Deuteronomistic History, and in some cases (e.g., W. Fuss) also to identify a Deuteronomistic redactional layer in the earlier books of the **Pentateuch.** In all of this, however, it is extremely difficult to move beyond the ancient tradition of a canonical corpus of five books, that is, with Deuteronomy connected with what precedes it more than with what follows it.

On what literary basis was the **Pentateuch** formed? For Noth (1948:7-19; Eng. tr. 8-19), P was an extensive narrative work and served as the literary framework into which JE was incorporated; however, this was not simply a matter of adding JE to P but rather a process in which P drew on JE to enrich its own narrative. The opposing position of Winnett, Van Seters, Cross, Schmid, and Rendtorff has been detailed above: that P was not a distinct source but rather a redactional layer, a reworking of JE. This point is far from resolution at present, and it will scarcely be adjudicated until more work has been done on the nature of redactional activity itself, the various postulated redactional layers have been compared, and the distinctively P materials (both narrative and laws) have been further examined for internal and stylistic coherence.

Not unrelated to these issues is the question of the **Pentateuch**'s intention or purpose. Noth (1948:267-

71; Eng. tr. 248-51) assigned it no greater significance traditio-historically than merely the literary adding together of all of the source materials, even if later synagogue and church have seen in this whole a theological unity that it originally did not have. For Noth, there was such similarity among the separate documentary sources in their narration of the course of Israel's history that their amalgamation did not affect this theological affirmation. Quite a different approach to this question of the meaning of the final compilation of the **Pentateuch** has more recently emerged, however. J. A. Sanders, J. Blenkinsopp, and B. S. Childs (1979) have all called attention to the role that the formation of the **Pentateuch** as authoritative or "canonical" literature played for the community. This process, especially in the postexilic period, involved a corporate search for meaning as well as a need to regularize the people's relation to their God. All three of these scholars as well as S. Tengström, R. Rendtorff (1977), and D. J. A. Clines assigned a key role to the theme of promise, especially as articulated to the ancestors. Here and also in the establishment of the law, the Pentateuch constituted a compelling message that helped to shape and preserve the people as much as the people had molded and retained the literature. This reciprocal relationship between community and text, together with the many other suggestive proposals reviewed above, will continue to command further inquiry in future Pentateuchal research.

Bibliography

Baltzer, Klaus

1964 *Das Bundesformular.* WMANT 4. 2d ed. Neukirchen-Vluyn: Neukirchener Verlag. English trans., 1971.

Barr, James

1966 *Old and New in Interpretation: A Study of the Two Testaments.* London: SCM.

Bentzen, Aage

1952 *Introduction to the Old Testament.* 2 vols. 2d ed. Copenhagen: G. E. C. Gad.

Beyerlin, Walter

1961 *Herkunft und Geschichte der ältesten Sinaitraditionen.* Tübingen: J. C. B. Mohr (Paul Siebeck). English trans., 1965.

Blenkinsopp, Joseph

1977 *Prophecy and Canon: A Contribution to the Study of Jewish Origins.* Notre Dame, IN: University of Notre Dame Press.

Bright, John

1956 *Early Israel in Recent History Writing: A Study in Method.* SBT 19. London: SCM.

Brueggemann, Walter

1968 "David and His Theologian." *CBQ* 30: 156-81.

Brueggemann, Walter, and Hans Walter Wolff

1975 *The Vitality of Old Testament Traditions.* Atlanta: John Knox.

Cassuto, U.

1961 *The Documentary Hypothesis and the Composition of the Pentateuch.* Jerusalem: Magnes. Hebrew original, 1941.

Cazelles, Henri

1966 "Pentateuque: IV, Le nouveau 'status quaestionis.'" *DBSup* 7. 736-858.

Childs, Brevard S.

1963 "A Study of the Formula 'Until this Day.'" *JBL* 82: 279-92.

1967 "Deuteronomic Formulae of the Exodus Traditions." Pp. 30-39 in *Hebräische Wortforschung: Festschrift zum 80. Geburtstag von Walter Baumgartner.* VTSup 16. Leiden: E. J. Brill.

1970 *Biblical Theology in Crisis.* Philadelphia: Westminster.

1979 *Introduction to the Old Testament as Scripture.* Philadelphia: Fortress.

Clements, Ronald E.

1979 "Pentateuchal Problems." Pp. 96-124 in *Tradition and Interpretation: Essays by Members of the Society for Old Testament Study.* Ed. George W. Anderson. Oxford: Clarendon.

Clines, David J. A.

1978 *The Theme of the Pentateuch.* JSOTSup 10. Sheffield: Department of Biblical Studies, University of Sheffield.

Craigie, Peter C.

1976 *The Book of Deuteronomy.* NICOT. Grand Rapids: Eerdmans.

Crenshaw, James L.

1976 "Prolegomenon." Pp. 1-60 in *Studies in Ancient Israelite Wisdom*. New York: Ktav.

Cross, Frank M.

1973 *Canaanite Myth and Hebrew Epic: Essays in the History of the Religion of Israel*. Cambridge, MA: Harvard University Press.

Culley, Robert C., ed.

1975 *Classical Hebrew Narrative. Semeia* 3. Missoula, MT: Scholars Press.

1976 *Oral Tradition and Old Testament Studies. Semeia* 5. Missoula, MT: Scholars Press.

Eissfeldt, Otto

1922 *Hexateuch-Synopse: Die Erzählung der fünf Bücher Mose und des Buches Josua mit dem Anfange des Richterbuches*. Leipzig: J. C. Hinrichs. Reprinted, Darmstadt: Wissenschaftliche Buchgesellschaft, 1962.

1964 *Einleitung in das Alte Testament: Entstehungsgeschichte des Alten Testaments*. 3d ed. Tübingen: J. C. B. Mohr (Paul Siebeck). 1st ed., 1934. English trans., 1965.

Ellis, Peter F.

1968 *The Yahwist: The Bible's First Theologian* Collegeville, MN: Liturgical Press.

Engnell, Ivan

1945 *Gamla Testamentet: En traditionshistorisk inledning*, I. Stockholm: Svenska Kyrkans Diakonistyrelses Bokförlag.

Fohrer, Georg

1966 "Altes Testament—'Amphictyonie' und 'Bund'?" *TLZ* 91: cols. 801-16, 893-904. Rev. and reprinted pp. 84-119 in *Studien zur alttestamentlichen Theologie und Geschichte (1949-1966)*. BZAW 115. Berlin: Walter de Gruyter, 1969.

1969 *Einleitung in das Alte Testament*. 11th ed. Heidelberg: Quelle & Meyer. English trans., 1968.

Fuss, Werner

1972 *Die deuteronomistische Pentateuchredaktion in Exodus 3-17*. BZAW 126. Berlin: Walter de Gruyter.

Gottwald, Norman K.

1979 *The Tribes of Yahweh: A Sociology of the Religion of Liberated Israel 1250-1050 B.C.E.* Maryknoll, NY: Orbis Books.

Gunkel, Hermann

1895 *Schöpfung und Chaos in Urzeit und Endzeit: Eine religionsgeschichtliche Untersuchung über Gen 1 und Ap Joh 12*, mit Beiträgen von Heinrich Zimmern. Göttingen: Vandenhoeck & Ruprecht.

1901 *Genesis, übersetzt und erklärt*. Göttingen: Vandenhoeck & Ruprecht. 7th ed., 1966.

1906 "Die israelitische Literatur." *Die Kultur der Gegenwart* 1/7: 51-102. 2d ed., 1925. Reprinted separately, Darmstadt: Wissenschaftliche Buchgesellschaft, 1963.

Henry, Marie-Louise

1960 *Jahwist und Priesterschrift: Zwei Glaubenszeugnisse des Alten Testaments*. Arbeiten zur Theologie, 3. Stuttgart: Calwer.

Hesse, Franz

1958 "Die Erforschung der Geschichte Israels als theologische Aufgabe." *KD* 4: 1-19.

Hölscher, Gustav

1952 *Geschichtsschreibung in Israel: Untersuchungen zum Jahvisten und Elohisten*. Skrifter utgivna av Kungl. Humanistika Vetenskapssamfundet i Lund, 50. Lund: Gleerup.

Houtman, C.

1980 *Inleiding in de Pentateuch: Een beschrijving van de geschiedenis van het onderzoek naar het ontstaan en de compositie van de eerste vijf boeken van het Oude Testament met een terugblik en een evaluatie*. Kampen: J. H. Kok.

Hurvitz, Avi

1974 "The Evidence of Language in Dating the Priestly Code: A Linguistic Study in Technical Idioms and Terminology." *RB* 81: 25-46.

Hyatt, J. Philip

1970 "Were There an Ancient Historical Credo in Israel and an Independent Sinai Tradition?" Pp. 152-70 in *Translating and Understanding the Old Testament: Essays in Honor of Herbert Gordon May*. Ed. H. T. Frank and W. L. Reed. Nashville and New York:

Abingdon.

Jaroš, Karl

1974 *Die Stellung des Elohisten zur kanaanäischen Religion.* OBO 4. Göttingen: Vandenhoeck & Ruprecht.

Jenks, Alan W.

1977 *The Elohist and North Israelite Traditions.* SBLMS 22. Missoula, MT: Scholars Press.

Kaufmann, Yehezkel

1960 *The Religion of Israel: From its Beginnings to the Babylonian Exile.* Trans. and abridged by Moshe Greenberg. New York: Schocken Books. Hebrew original, 1938-56.

Kilian, Rudolf

1963 *Literarkritische und formgeschichtliche Untersuchung des Heiligkeitsgesetzes.* BBB 19. Bonn: Peter Hanstein.

Knight, Douglas A.

1975 *Rediscovering the Traditions of Israel.* Rev. ed. SBLDS 9. Missoula, MT: Scholars Press.

Knight, Douglas A., ed.

1982 *Julius Wellhausen and His* Prolegomena to the History of Israel. *Semeia* 25. Chico, CA: Scholars Press.

Koch, Klaus

1959 *Die Priesterschrift von Exodus 25 bis Leviticus 16: Eine überlieferungsgeschichtliche und literarkritische Untersuchung.* FRLANT 71. Göttingen: Vandenhoeck & Ruprecht.

Kraus, Hans-Joachim

1969 *Geschichte der historisch-kritischen Erforschung des Alten Testaments.* 2d ed. Neukirchen-Vluyn: Neukirchener Verlag.

Lapointe, Roger

1977 "Tradition and Language: The Import of Oral Expression." Pp. 125-42 in *Tradition and Theology in the Old Testament,* ed. D. A. Knight. Philadelphia: Fortress; London: S.P.C.K.

Long, Burke O.

1968 *The Problem of Etiological Narrative in the Old Testament.* BZAW 108. Berlin: A. Töpelmann.

McEvenue, Sean E.

1971 *The Narrative Style of the Priestly Writer.* AnBib 50. Rome: Biblical Institute Press.

Mayes, A. D. H.

1979 *Deuteronomy.* NCB. London: Oliphants.

Mendenhall, George E.

1955 *Law and Covenant in Israel and the Ancient Near East.* Pittsburgh: Biblical Colloquium.

Merendino, Rosario Pius

1969 *Das deuteronomische Gesetz: Eine literarkritische, gattungs- und überlieferungsgeschichtliche Untersuchung zu Dt 12-26.* BBB 31. Bonn: Peter Hanstein.

Mittmann, Siegfried

1975 *Deuteronomium 1,1-6,3: Literarkritisch und traditionsgeschichtliche Untersucht.* BZAW 139. Berlin and New York: Walter de Gruyter.

Mowinckel, Sigmund

1964a *Erwägungen zur Pentateuchquellenfrage.* Oslo: Universitetsforlaget.

1964b *Tetrateuch—Pentateuch—Hexateuch: Die Berichte über die Landnahme in den drei altisraelitischen Geschichtswerken.* BZAW 90. Berlin: A. Töpelmann.

Müller, Hans-Peter

1969 *Ursprünge und Strukturen alttestamentlicher Eschatologie.* BZAW 109. Berlin: A. Töpelmann.

Nicholson, E. W.

1967 *Deuteronomy and Tradition.* Philadelphia: Fortress.

Noth, Martin

1930 *Das System der zwölf Stämme Israels.* BWANT 4/1. Stuttgart: W. Kohlhammer. Reprinted, Darmstadt: Wissenschaftliche Buchgesellschaft, 1966.

1943 *Überlieferungsgeschichtliche Studien: Die sammelnden und bearbeitenden Geschichtswerke im Alten Testament.* Halle: Max Niemeyer. 3d ed., Tübingen: Max Niemeyer, 1967.

1948 *Überlieferungsgeschichte des Pentateuch.*

Stuttgart: W. Kohlhammer. 3d ed., 1966. English trans., *A History of Pentateuchal Traditions*. Trans. with an introduction by B. W. Anderson. Englewood Cliffs, NJ: Prentice-Hall, 1972. Reprinted, Chico, CA: Scholars Press, 1981.

1950 *Geschichte Israels*. Göttingen: Vandenhoeck & Ruprecht. English trans., 1958.

1959 *Das zweite Buch Mose, Exodus, übersetzt und erklärt*. ATD 5. Göttingen: Vandenhoeck & Ruprecht. 4th ed., 1968. English trans., 1962.

1962 *Das dritte Buch Mose, Leviticus, übersetzt und erklärt*. ATD 6. Göttingen: Vandenhoeck & Ruprecht. 2d. ed., 1966. English trans. 1965.

1966 *Das vierte Buch Mose, Numeri, übersetzt und erklärt*. ATD 7. Göttingen: Vandenhoeck & Ruprecht. English trans., 1968.

Nyberg, Henrik Samuel

1947 "Korah's uppror (Num. 16f.): Ett bidrag till frågan om traditionshistorisk metod." *SEÅ* 12: 230-52.

1972 "Die schwedischen Beiträge zur alttestamentlichen Forschung in deisem Jahrhundert." Pp. 1-10 in *Congress Volume: Uppsala, 1971*. VTSup 22. Leiden: E. J. Brill.

Orlinsky, Harry M.

1962 "The Tribal System of Israel and Related Groups in the Period of the Judges." *OrAnt* 1: 11-20.

Patte, Daniel, ed.

1980 *Genesis 2 and 3: Kaleidoscopic Structural Readings*. Semeia 18. Chico, CA: Scholars Press.

Perlitt, Lothar

1969 *Bundestheologie im Alten Testament*. WMANT 36. Neukirchen-Vluyn: Neukirchener Verlag.

Polzin, Robert M.

1977 *Biblical Structuralism: Method and Subjectivity in the Study of Ancient Texts*. Semeia Supplements. Philadelphia: Fortress; Missoula, MT: Scholars Press.

Rad, Gerhard von

1934 *Die Priesterschrift im Hexateuch*. BWANT 65. Stuttgart: W. Kohlhammer.

1938 *Das formgeschichtliche Problem des Hexateuch*. BWANT 78. Stuttgart: W. Kohlhammer. Reprinted, pp.

9-86 in *Gesammelte Studien zum Alten Testament*. 3d ed. Munich: Chr. Kaiser, 1965. English trans., "The Form-Critical Problem of the Hexateuch," pp. 1-78 in *The Problem of the Hexateuch and Other Essays*. Edinburgh and London: Oliver & Boyd, 1966.

1944 "Der Anfang der Geschichtsschreibung im alten Israel." *Archiv für Kulturgeschichte* 32: 1-42. Reprinted, pp. 148-88 in *Gesammelte Studien zum Alten Testament*. Munich: Chr. Kaiser. English trans., pp. 166-204 in *The Problem of the Hexateuch and Other Essays*. Edinburgh and London: Oliver & Boyd, 1966.

1947 *Deuteronomium-Studien*. FRLANT 58. Göttingen: Vandenhoeck & Ruprecht. English trans., 1953.

1953 *Das erste Buch Mose, Genesis, übersetzt und erklärt*. ATD 2-4. Göttingen: Vandenhoeck & Ruprecht. 9th ed., 1972. English trans., 1961: rev. ed., 1972.

1962 *Theologie des Alten Testaments. I: Die Theologie der geschichtlichen Überlieferungen Israels*. 4th ed. Munich: Chr. Kaiser. 1st ed., 1957. English trans., *Old Testament Theology. I: The Theology of Israel's Historical Traditions*. Trans. D. M. G. Stalker. Edinburgh and London: Oliver & Boyd, 1962.

1964 *Das fünfte Buch Mose, Deuteronomium, übersetzt und erklärt*. ATD 8. Göttingen: Vandenhoeck & Ruprecht. 2d ed., 1968. English trans., 1966.

Rendtorff, Rolf

1954 *Die Gesetze in der Priesterschrift*. FRLANT 62. Göttingen: Vandenhoeck & Ruprecht. 2d ed., 1963.

1975 "Der 'Jahwist' als Theologe? Zum Dilemma der Pentateuchkritik." Pp. 158-66 in *Congress Volume: Edinburgh, 1974*. VTSup 28. Leiden: E. J. Brill. English trans., "The 'Yahwist' as Theologian? The Dilemma of Pentateuchal Criticism." *JSOT* 3 (1977) 2-10.

1977 *Das überlieferungsgeschichtliche Problem des Pentateuch*. BZAW 147. Berlin: Walter de Gruyter.

Reventlow, H. Graf

1961 *Das Heiligkeitsgesetz formgeschichtlich untersucht*. WMANT 6. Neukirchen: Neukirchener Verlag.

Richter, Wolfgang

1966 "Urgeschichte und Hoftheologie." *BZ* 10: 96-105.

1967 "Beobachtungen zur theologischen Systembildung in der alttestamentlichen Literatur anhand des 'kleinen geschichtlichen Credo.'" Pp. 175-212 in vol. I of

Wahrheit und Verkündigung: Festschrift M. Schmaus. Ed. L. Scheffczyk. Munich/Paderborn/Vienna: Ferdinand Schoningh.

Rost, Leonhard

1965 *Das kleine Credo und andere Studien zum Alten Testament.* Heidelberg: Quelle & Meyer.

Rudolph, Wilhelm

1938 *Der "Elohist" von Exodus bis Josua.* BZAW 68. Berlin: A. Töpelmann.

Sanders, James A.

1972 *Torah and Canon.* Philadelphia: Fortress.

Sandmel, Samuel

1961 "The Haggada within Scripture." *JBL* 80: 105-22.

Schmid, Hans Heinrich

1976 *Der sogenannte Jahwist: Beobachtungen und Fragen zur Pentateuchforschung.* Zurich: Theologischer Verlag.

Schmidt, Ludwig

1977 "Überlegungen zum Jahwisten." *EvT* 37: 230-47.

Schmitt, Hans-Christoph

1980 *Die nichtpriesterliche Josephsgeschichte: Ein Beitrag zur neuesten Pentateuchkritik.* BZAW 154. Berlin and New York: Walter de Gruyter.

Schulte, Hannelis

1972 *Die Entstehung der Geschichtsschreibung im Alten Israel.* BZAW 128. Berlin and New York: Walter de Gruyter.

Seitz, Gottfried

1971 *Redaktionsgeschichtliche Studien zum Deuteronomium.* BWANT 13. Stuttgart: W. Kohlhammer.

Simpson, Cuthbert Aikman

1948 *The Early Traditions of Israel: A Critical Analysis of the Pre-deuteronomistic Narrative of the Hexateuch.* Oxford: Basil Blackwell.

Smend, Rudolf

1967 *Biblische Zeugnisse: Literatur des alten Israel.*

Frankfurt am Main: Fischer Bücherei.

1978 *Die Entstehung des Alten Testaments.* Stuttgart: W. Kohlhammer.

Soden, Wolfram von

1974 "Verschlüsselte Kritik an Salomo in der Urgeschichte des Jahwisten?" *WO* 7,2: 228-40.

Tengström, Sven

1976 *Die Hexateucherzählung: Eine literaturgeschichtliche Studie.* ConBOT 7. Lund: Gleerup.

Thompson, Thomas L.

1974 *The Historicity of the Patriarchal Narratives.* BZAW 133. Berlin: Walter de Gruyter.

Van Seters, John

1975 *Abraham in History and Tradition.* New Haven: Yale University Press.

Vink, J. G.

1969 "The Date and Origin of the Priestly Code in the Old Testament." *OTS* 11: 1-144.

Volz, Paul, and Wilhelm Rudolph

1933 *Der Elohist als Erzähler: Ein Irrweg der Pentateuchkritik?* BZAW 63. Giessen: A. Töpelmann.

Wagner, Norman E.

1967 "Pentateuchal Criticism: No Clear Future." *CJT* 13: 225-32.

Weinfeld, Moshe

1972 *Deuteronomy and the Deuteronomic School.* Oxford: Oxford University Press.

Wellhausen, Julius

1876-77 "Die Composition des Hexateuchs." *JDT* 21: 392-450, 531-602; 22: 407-79. Reprinted, pp. 1-208 in *Die Composition des Hexateuchs und der historischen Bücher des Alten Testaments.* 3d ed. Berlin: Georg Reimer, 1899.

1878 *Geschichte Israels. In zwei Bänden. Erster Band.* Berlin: G. Reimer. 2d ed., *Prolegomena zur Geschichte Israels.* Berlin: G. Reimer, 1883. English trans., *Prolegomena to the History of Israel.* With Preface by W. Robertson Smith. Edinburgh: Adam & Charles Black, 1885. Reprinted, New York: Meridian Books,

1957.

Winnett, Frederick V.

1949 *The Mosaic Tradition.* Toronto: University of Toronto Press.

1965 "Re-examining the Foundations." *JBL* 84: 1-19.

Wolff, Hans Walter

1964 "Das Kerygma des Jahwisten." *EvT* 24: 73-98. Reprinted, pp. 345-73 in *Gesammelte Studien zum Alten Testament.* Munich: Chr. Kaiser, 1964. English trans., pp. 41-66 in Brueggemann and Wolff.

1969 "Zur Thematik der elohistischen Fragmente im Pentateuch." *EvT* 29: 59-72. Reprinted, pp. 402-17 in *Gesammelte Studien zum Alten Testament.* 2d ed. Munich: Chr. Kaiser, 1975. English trans., pp. 67-82 in Brueggemann and Wolff.

Woude, Adam Simon van der

1960 *Uittocht en Sinai.* Nijkerk: C. F. Callenbach.

Abbreviations

AASF	Annales academiae scientarium fennicae
AB	Anchor Bible
ACOR	American Center for Oriental Research
AfO	*Archiv für Orientforschung*
AJA	*American Journal of Archaeology*
AnBib	Analecta biblica
ANET	*Ancient Near Eastern Texts,* ed. J. B. Pritchard
AnOr	Analecta orientalia
AOAT	Alter Orient und Altes Testament
AOATS	Alter Orient und Altes Testament, Sonderreihe
AOS	American Oriental Series
ARM	*Archives royale de Mari*
AS	Assyriological Studies
ASOR	American Schools of Oriental Research
ASTI	*Annual of the Swedish Theological Institute*
ATAbh	Alttestamentliche Abhandlungen
ATANT	Abhandlungen zur Theologie des Alten und Neuen Testaments
ATD	Das Alte Testament deutsch
ATDan	Acta theologica danica
ATR	*Anglican Theological Review*
BA	*Biblical Archaeologist*
BARev	*Biblical Archaeology Review*
BASOR	*Bulletin of the American Schools of Oriental Research*

BBB	Bonner biblische Beiträge
BCSR	*Bulletin of the Council on the Study of Religion*
BDB	F. Brown, S. R. Driver, and C. A. Briggs, *A Hebrew and English Lexicon of the Old Testament*
BETL	Bibliotheca ephemeridum theologicarum lovaniensium
BEvT	Beiträge zur evagelischen Theologie
BHS	*Biblia hebraica stuttgartensia*
Bib	*Biblica*
BibB	Biblische Beiträge
BibLeb	*Bibel und Leben*
BibOr	Biblica et orientalia
BibS(N)	Biblische Studien (Neukirchen-Vluyn)
BJRL	*Bulletin of the John Rylands University Library of Manchester*
BKAT	*Biblischer Kommentar: Altes Testament*
BO	*Bibliotheca orientalis*
BR	*Biblical Research*
BSac	*Bibliotheca Sacra*
BT	*The Bible Translator*
BWANT	Beiträge zur Wissenschaft vom Alten und Neuen Testament
BZ	*Biblische Zeitschrift*
BZAW	Beihefte zur *ZAW*
CAT	Commentaire de l'Ancien Testament
CBC	Cambridge Bible Commentary
CBQ	*Catholic Biblical Quarterly*
ConBOT	Coniectanea biblica, Old Testament
CRAIBL	*Comptes rendus de l'académie des inscriptions et belles-lettres*
CRB	Cahiers de la *RB*
CTM	*Concordia Theological Monthly*
DBSup	*Supplément au Dictionnaire de la Bible*
EB	Echter Bibel
EdF	Erträge der Forschung
EKL	*Evangelisches Kirchenlexikon*
EncJud	*Encyclopedia Judaica*
EstBib	*Estudios bíblicos*
ETL	*Ephemerides theologicae lovanienses*
EvT	*Evangelische Theologie*
ExpTim	*Expository Times*
FRLANT	Forschungen zur Religion und Literatur des Alten und Neuen Testaments
HAT	Handbuch zum Alten Testament
HDR	Harvard Semitic Monographs
HO	*Handbuch der Orientalistik*
HSM	Harvard Semitic Monographs
HTR	*Harvard Theological Review*
HUCA	*Hebrew Union College Annual*
HUCM	Monographs of the Hebrew Union College
IB	*The Interpreter's Bible*
ICC	International Critical Commentary
IDB	*Interpreter's Dictionary of the Bible*
IDBSup	Supplementary volume to IDB

IEJ	*Israel Exploration Journal*
Int	*Interpretation*
IOSCS	International Organization for Septuagint and Cognate Studies
ITQ	*Irish Theological Quarterly*
JAAR	*Journal ofthe American Academy of Religion*
JANESCU	*Journal of the Ancient Near Eastern Society of Columbia University*
JAOS	*Journal of the American Oriental Society*
JBL	*Journal of Biblical Literature*
JBR	*Journal of Bible and Religion*
JCS	*Journal of Cuneiform Studies*
JDT	*Jahrbuch für deutsche Theologie*
JEA	*Journal of Egyptian Archaeology*
JNES	*Journal of Near Eastern Studies*
JPOS	*Journal of the Palestine Oriental Society*
JQR	*Jewish Quarterly Review*
JR	*Journal of Religion*
JSOT	*Journal for the Study of the Old Testament*
JSOTSup	JSOT, Supplement
JSS	*Journal of Semitic Studies*
JTC	*Journal for Theology and the Church*
JTS	*Journal of Theological Studies*
KAT	Kommentar zum Alten Testament
KD	*Kerygma und Dogma*
Kl. Schr.	*Kleine Schriften*
LUA	Lunds universitets arsskrift
MDOG	Mitteilungen der deutschen Orient-Gesellschaft
MGWJ	*Monatsschrift für Geschichte und Wissenschaft des Judentums*
MIO	*Mitteilungen des Instituts für Orientforschung*
MRS	Mission de Ras Shamra
NCB	New Century Bible
NICOT	New International Commentary on the Old Testament
OBO	Orbis biblicus et orientalis
Or	*Orientalia*
OrAnt	*Oriens antiquus*
OTL	Old Testament Library
OTS	*Oudtestamentische Studiën*
OTWSA	*Die Ou Testamentiese Werkgemeenskap in Suid-Afrika*
PEQ	*Palestine Exploration Quarterly*
PRU	*Le Palais Royal d'Ugarit*
PTMS	Pittsburgh Theological Monograph Series
RA	*Revue d'assyriologie et d'archéologie orientale*
RAI	Rencontre Assyriologique Internationale
RB	*Revue biblique*
RGG	*Die Religion in Geschichte und Gegenwart,* ed. K. Galling
RHA	*Revue hittite et asianique*
RHPR	*Revue d'histoire et de philosophie religieuses*
RLA	*Reallexikon der Assyriologie*
RoB	*Religion och Bibel*
RSO	*Rivisti degli studi orientali*
RTP	*Revue de théologie et de philosophie*
SANT	Studien zum Alten und Neuen Testament
SB	Sources bibliques
SBFLA	*Studii biblici franciscani liber annuus*
SBLDS	Society of Biblical Literature Dissertation Series
SBLMS	Society of Biblical Literature Monograph Series
SBLSBS	Society of Biblical Literature Sources for Biblical Study
SBS	Stuttgarter Bibelstudien
SBT	Studies in Biblical Theology
SEA	*Svensk exegetisk arsbok*
Sem	*Semitica*
SHVL	Skrifter utgivna av Kungl. Humanistiska Vetenskapssamfundet i Lund
SJLA	Studies in Judaism in late Antiquity
SJT	*Scottish Journal of Theology*
SNTSMS	Society for New Testament Studies Monograph Series
SNVAO	Skrifter utgitt av Det Norske Videnskaps-Akademi i Oslo
SOTSMS	Society for Old Testament Studies Monograph Series
SPAW	Sitzungsberichte der preussischen Akademie der Wissenschaften
SQAW	Schriften und Quellen der alten Welt
SR	*Studies in Religion/Sciences religieuses*
SSN	Studia semitica neerlandica
ST	*Studia theologica*
SUNT	Studien zur Umwelt des Neuen Testaments
TBü	Theologische Bücherei
TD	*Theology Digest*
TLZ	*Theologische Literaturzeitung*
TRE	*Theologische Real-enzyklopädie*
TRu	*Theologische Rundschau*
TSK	*Theologische Studien und Kritiken*
TToday	*Theology Today*
TTZ	*Trierer theologische Zeitschrift*
TynBul	*Tyndale Bulletin*
TZ	*Theologische Zeitschrift*
UF	*Ugarit-Forschungen*
USQR	*Union Seminary Quarterly Review*
VD	*Verbum Domini*
VF	*Verkündifung und Forschung*
VT	*Vetus Testamentum*
VTSup	Vetus Testamentum, Supplements
WMANT	Wissenschaftliche Monographien zum Alten und Neuen Testament

WO	Die Welt des Orients
WTJ	Westminster Theological Journal
WZKM	Wiener Zeitschrift für de Kunde des Morgenlandes
ZA	Zeitschrift für Assyriologie
ZAW	Zeitschrift für die alttestamenliche Wissenschaft
ZDPV	Zeitschrift des deutschen Palästina-Vereins
ZTK	Zeitschrift für Theologie und Kirche

Wilson G. Baroody and William F. Gentrup (essay date 1993)

SOURCE: "*Exodus, Leviticus, Numbers,* and *Deuteronomy*" in *A Complete Literary Guide to the "Bible,"* edited by Leland Ryken and Tremper Longman III, Zondervan Publishing House, 1993, pp. 121-36.

[*In the essay that follows, Baroody and Gentrup examine the literary structure of* Exodus, Leviticus, Numbers, *and* Deuteronomy *in order to establish the complex interrelationship between their narrative elements and the presentation of* Torah *as law.*]

The life of Moses, from his birth and early years in the opening of Exodus to his death and legacy at the close of Deuteronomy, provides the narrative frame for most of the **Pentateuch.** As distinguished from Genesis, which encompasses a human history of at least four thousand years, these four monumental books, after the first two chapters of Exodus, span a period of only forty years, from Moses' calling at age 80 until his death at age 120.

A marvelous collection of narrative and law is concentrated within this time frame. Nothing short of an epiclike birth and odyssey of a nation, achieved by the divine agency of spectacular miracles, is recounted here. Its whole legal and religious constitution is also included, a narrative strategy that is roughly equivalent to setting a country's legislative and theological principles within the biography of its founder. Through its fascinating combination of story and statute, these books, anticipating Horace, teach and delight simultaneously. The events of Moses' life and the emergence of Israel into nationhood are presented as a series of encounters and dialogues with God, whose main plan, through personal revelation in the form of miracles and laws, is to restore his people to the divine image and companionship of creation (Gen. 1:26-27; 3:8-9).

Literary critics with a background in Western literature tend to view these books, especially Exodus, as an epic (at least epiclike) and to compare them to the *Iliad,* the *Odyssey,* the *Aeneid,* and *Paradise Lost.* Richard Moulton, whose *Literary Study of the Bible* in its 1895 and 1899 editions can justly be regarded as the first major modern work emphasizing purely literary analysis of the Bible, is associated with this view. Its most persuasive advocate is Leland Ryken, who detects in Exodus the epic conventions of a journey and founding of a nation, supernatural intervention and machinery, a central national hero, a basis in history, the values and experiences of an entire society, and what he calls "type scenes" and "high style" (*Words* 127-35; see also *Literature*). As an epic hero Moses best parallels Virgil's Aeneas: both figures require divine persuasion to obey their calling to found a nation, both continually receive divine direction, and both perform religious worship. The most recent tendency, however, has been to follow Robert Alter's *Art of Biblical Narrative* (1981) in considering narrative without comparison to classical epic (see also Sternberg).

Both the Romans and the Hebrews were also known for their fully developed legal systems. A major difference, however, is that the national epic of the Romans is wholly narrative; its laws must be found in separate official documents, whereas the story of the founding of the Hebrew nation is replete with law, so much so that the traditional understanding of the **Pentateuch** as books of instruction (i.e., **Torah**) neglected its narrative features. It is the significant contribution of modern critics to have called attention to the literary quality of Hebrew narrative, which, nevertheless, some have regarded as primarily a framework for the presentation of law.

Narrative and Law

The books of Exodus, Numbers, Leviticus, and Deuteronomy certainly do constitute a marvelous unity of narrative and legislative genres, a fusion expressing indirectly the biblical axiom that principles and actions are inseparable. Earlier combinations occur in the creation and patriarchal accounts in Genesis, but the pattern is particularly developed in these latter four books, in which the juridical often predominates.

Literary critics of biblical and Jewish literature, such as Edward Greenstein (84) and Barry Holtz ("Midrash" 178-79), have increasingly recognized the interrelationship between these seemingly distinct genres. The point is perhaps more easily understood when Torah or law is translated "instruction" or "teaching." Joel Rosenburg describes how narrative is frequently "a didactic prop for the laws" and how laws often appear as "events" in the narrative (65). David Damrosch considers this mixture in the **Pentateuch** "the most important generic innovation of its age" (*Narrative Covenant* 35-37). This hybrid genre sometimes adds poetry (e.g., Ex. 15; Deut. 32) and prophecy (e.g., Ex. 34:11-17; Lev. 26:32-46; Deut. 18:15). Other scholars focus on distinct genres. Leland Ryken identifies Exodus 1-20 and 32-34, Numbers 10-14 and 20-24, and Deuteronomy 10 and 34 as the "main narrative sections" (*Words* 130). Leonard Thompson recognizes the acknowledged law codes as Exodus 20-23, 25-31, and 34:10-27, all of Leviticus, and Deuteronomy 12-26 (154).

Exodus

Reflecting this broader pattern in the four books, there are two main parts to Exodus: the primary narrative (chs. 1-19) describing Moses' early life and calling, the ten plagues and subsequent liberation from Egyptian bondage, and the journey to Mount Sinai; and the legal material pertaining to the giving of the Ten Commandments and to tabernacle worship (chs. 20-40). Each part contains insertions of the other genre, mixing storytelling and lawgiving. J. P. Fokkelman outlines the major alternations of these (56-58).

The combination of the tenth plague and Passover is a clear example. The narrative first announces the certain deaths of the firstborn of humans and livestock (ch. 11), except of those who observe the elaborate instructions of Passover. YHWH's people must take an unblemished lamb one-year old and roast and eat it with unleavened bread and bitter herbs. On this first occasion, they must apply the lamb's blood to the doorposts and lintels of their dwellings and consume the meal after clothing and preparing themselves for immediate departure from Egypt. These and other details are to be observed in perpetuity (12:1-28).

The rest of the account shifts back to narrating the terrible fulfillment of the plague on the Egyptians and the Israelites' flight from the land (12:29-42) but returns briefly at the end to proscriptions against the participation of uncircumcised "foreigners" or "strangers" in the Passover. This is a logical digression, since for the first time in at least eighty years Israel was liberated from slavery to the uncircumcised. Laws for consecrating the firstborn follow, inserted here rather than being included with subsequent ones because the tenth plague was based on the value of the firstborn (13:1-2, 11-16). After the Passover account, the Exodus begins, signaled by a return to narrative. The pursuing Egyptians destroyed at the Red Sea, the miracle supplies of manna and water, the war with Amalek, the appointment of judges on Jethro's advice, and the arrival at Sinai are then recounted (chs. 16-19).

The second part of Exodus focuses on legal instructions, beginning when the Lord dispenses the Ten Commandments (20:1-20) and the "Book of the Covenant" (20:21-23:33), a series of laws that clarifies the Decalogue and begins and ends with prescriptions about worship that anticipate those related to the building and equipping of the tabernacle (25-31, 35-40). Within these passages there are also alternations between narrative and legislative material. Just as the primarily narrative first half of Exodus had been interrupted by

the lengthy legislative Passover section, so, conversely, the primarily legal second half is relieved by the story of the idolatry of the golden calf (chs. 32-34).

The episode dovetails well with the material that precedes and follows it, namely, the instructions for proper tabernacle worship (chs. 25-31) and their later repetition in the construction narrative (chs. 35-40). The topic of true worship unifies each segment. Although the Hebrews have been liberated from Egypt and have experienced other miracles, they readily seek to worship another god. While Moses is on Mount Sinai receiving the instructions for the tabernacle, the people revolt and command Aaron, "Make us gods." Ironically, the gold and silver used for the image, part of the spoils taken from the Egyptians, were intended for the furnishing of the tabernacle (36:2-7). The jewelry specified, earrings, symbolizes the people's failure to use their ears properly in hearing YHWH's words as they promised (19:7-8).

In contrast to the detailed account of the tabernacle, Aaron makes the calf very quickly—in less than a sentence: "I cast it [the gold] into the fire, and there came out this calf" (Josipovici's translation, 97). (Aaron's passive posture and self-defensive tone, Gabriel Josipovici observes, recalls that of Adam blaming his fall on Eve [97].) The figure of the idol recalls the cattle that had such a prominent role in the conflict with Pharaoh, who refused to let the Israelites leave Egypt to sacrifice properly to YHWH (Ex. 3:18; 5:3-17; 8:8-29) and anticipates the calf idol of Jeroboam (1 Kings 12:25-33).

Although the account of the fashioning of the false image is terse, "the narrative lovingly lingers on every detail of the making of the Tabernacle" (Josipovici 96-97; see also his whole treatment of the subject, 90-107). The earlier call in Egypt to proper worship is consummated at the close of Exodus when the tabernacle has been built and the Lord's presence inhabits it. The account represents the lengthiest use of repeated description in the Pentateuch or any book of the Bible, rivaled only by the related one of the temple of Solomon, first commanded to David (2 Sam. 7; 17:1-15; 28:11-29; 1 Chron. 21:28-22:19) and later constructed by Solomon (1 Kings 5-8; 2 Chron. 2-7).

The description of the tabernacle moves from the interior to the exterior. First described is the Holy of Holies with its ark, tablets of the Ten Commandments, cherubim, and mercy seat; then the features of the Holy Place, the table of shewbread, lampstand, and altar of incense; and finally the outer court with its bronze altar. When repeating all this information in the actual construction, the account switches to a narrative format (chs. 35-40). Thus, the repeated third-person perspective: "he [or, 'they'] did . . . as the Lord had commanded Moses." This second version has an exterior-to-interior organization. The building of the whole tabernacle is described first, then its smaller units, such as the inner sanctuary. This is, of course, the reverse of the original instructions, a pattern of repetition that results in a chiastic structure for chapters 20-40, the description of Holy of Holies-exterior courts-exterior courts-Holy of Holies.

By ending with the construction of the tabernacle, the book of Exodus concludes precisely in contrast to its beginning. Whereas in Egypt the Israelites were enslaved, with no opportunity to worship their God, now they are free and able to serve him. The penultimate words of the book fittingly encapsulate what has been the goal of all the building effort: "So Moses finished the work. Then a cloud covered the tent, and the glory of the LORD filled the tabernacle" (40:33-34).

Later readers have commonly associated the tabernacle of Exodus with creation, the ark of Noah, and Solomon's stone temple. The links are ancient; they are assumed at least as early as Philo and Josephus (Josipovici 95, 99-102). The New Testament book of Hebrews also features the tabernacle and portrays Jesus as fulfilling the sacrifice and priesthood systems of the **Pentateuch.**

Leviticus and Numbers

While Exodus decrees the structure of the tabernacle and outfits the priesthood that functions there, Leviticus records YHWH's commands about the sacrificial system (chs. 1-7) and the ritual holiness he requires (chs. 11-17). The narrative passage between these two sets of laws unites them and serves to distinguish between true and false worship (chs. 8-10).

Here is recounted how Moses consecrates Aaron and his sons according to the divine directions of Exodus 29, after which Aaron properly offers sacrifice. Immediately, however, his two sons, Nadab and Abihu, offer the "strange fire" specifically prohibited in Exodus 30:9 and are themselves consumed by fire. Because the incident involves sacrifice, it relates to the content of the first set of laws, and because the mysterious sin of Aaron's sons reflects on their moral character, it also relates to the second set. The episode illustrates perfectly the overall role of law in the Bible. In Leviticus, Damrosch says, "the law is represented in its ideal, fully functioning from, the best model against which to assess the complicated uses and misuses of law by characters throughout Old Testament narratives" ("Leviticus" 66).

Although nearly all readers have seen this interlude as the book's only narrative, several scholars have recently examined laws that seem to share those generic features. For example, in his discussion of levitical burnt offerings, Damrosch suggests that the different kinds of sacrifices permitted, depending on economic status—bullock, lamb or goat, dove or pigeon—are "instances of narrative variety within the ritual order" ("Leviticus" 66-69). The tripart discription of each type of offering and certain repeated phrases such as "sweet savour unto the LORD" confer even a lyrical and dramatic quality to these laws.

Numbers is a narrative and a supplemental lawbook between the sacramental lawbook of Leviticus and the social lawbook of Deuteronomy. It recounts the journey of the emerging nation from Sinai to the eastern side of Jordan, where it is about to enter the Promised Land. Here the mixed form of narrative and legal material is particularly striking and elaborate. The dozen major shifts back and forth, not counting the short passages of narrative implementation within the legal sections, are almost dizzying. Jacob Milgrom (xv-xvii) identifies the major alternations between narrative (N) and law (L) as follows: 1-10:10 (L) 10:11-14:45 (N); 15 (L); 16-17 (N); 18-19 (L); 20-25 (N); 26-27:11 (L); 27:12-23 (N); 28-30 (L); 31-33:49 (N); 33:50-56; 34-36 (L). The alternating sections entail two major topics—God's continuing elaboration of his principles and, despite his meticulous care, the sustained murmuring and rebellion of his people.

YHWH's additional statutes are decreed at major stations along the way, for example, at Sinai, where Passover is again observed (1-10:10), at Kadesh (chs. 15, 18-19), and at Moab (chs. 28-30, 34-36). Sometimes a new law is introduced to meet a specific need, as with the daughters of the deceased Zelophehad to insure their family inheritance (27:1-11), a provision later repeated in the closing chapter and applied generally to other heiresses (36).

Within Numbers the main narratives tell of rebellion, recalling the ones in Exodus. Those who resist YHWH and Moses include Miriam and Aaron (ch. 12), Korah (chs. 16-17), the elder generation of Israelites who refuse to enter the land (chs. 13-14), and the new generation who, just as they are about to enter it, worship Baal-Peor (ch. 25). The most significant episode is the refusal to enter this land of "milk and honey," figs, pomegranates, and grapes so huge that two men are needed to carry one cluster (ch. 13). The report that the present inhabitants are giants next to whom "we were in our own sight as grasshoppers" causes the congregation to reject the enthusiastic belief of Caleb and Joshua that they can win the land. For this disobedience they are forbidden to enter it, and instead, ironically, their children, whom they claimed would die victims in the desert, will fulfill the national destiny.

In contrast to this dispiriting incident, successes are also recounted, such as the conquest of Sihon, king of the Amorites, and Og, king of Bashan (ch. 21), and the turning of the attempted curses of the prophet Balaam into blessings (chs. 22-24).

Deuteronomy

The fifth book of the **Pentateuch** follows the pattern of narrative and legal combination as Moses recapitulates to the new generation their salvation history (chs. 1-11) and then elaborates upon the social significance of the law (chs. 12-30). As Jacob Milgrom summarizes, "By the admixture of these two genres," Deuteronomy is "a parade example of this literary type" (xvi). After the people recite the detailed list of curses for disobedience and of blessings for obedience to YHWH (chs. 27-30), Moses commissions Joshua as his successor (ch. 31) and sings a song of celebration (ch. 32). Now 120 years old, he views the land from Mount Nebo, a land that he, like his generation, cannot enter, and then, like Jacob in Genesis, blesses each of the tribes (ch. 33). The final brief narrative records his death and eulogizes him, avowing that the people have finally learned to obey divinely appointed leadership in the case of Joshua (ch. 34).

The book does not proceed chronologically but in the reverse order of preceding material: from the wilderness journeys of Numbers back to the two presentations of the Decalogue in Exodus. This is an appropriate order for the new generation, its intended audience. Moses recalls their recent experience before charging them with the law and describing events before they were born. The structure of Deuteronomy presents itself in chiasmic relationship with the previous three books, particularly Exodus and Numbers.

Blessings and Cursings

The pattern of alternation between narrative and law throughout these four books is supplemented by a series of blessings and curses. These naturally culminate in Deuteronomy as the people are about to enter their land. Each book closes with a blessing that is dependent on right worship and the avoidance of idols and images, as Leviticus 26 makes clear. Otherwise, disastrous results are assured.

At the end of Exodus Moses blesses the nation for completing the tabernacle (39:43), and afterwards, the habitation of the Lord's glory within it furnishes a nonverbal blessing (40:34). Numbers begins with the blessing of the people by the priests (6:24-27) and concludes with the blessings of Balaam who was hired to curse Israel (chs. 22-24). The blessings of the narrative in Deuteronomy (chs. 7 and 11) include the promise that remembrance and obedience will bring about "the days of heaven upon the earth" (11:21). The most extensive blessings and curses occur after the law is restated and the nation is gathered on Mount Ebal and Mount Gerizim to repeat them responsively (chs.

27-28). After a song of Moses, longer than his celebration after crossing the Red Sea forty years before, the leader pronounces blessings on each of the tribes (chs. 32-33). These benefits are implementations of the priestly blessing commanded by YHWH himself:

> The LORD bless thee, and keep thee:
> The LORD make his face shine upon thee,
>   and be gracious unto thee:
> The LORD lift up his countenance upon thee,
>   and give thee peace.
>
>   (Num. 6:24-27)

Stylistic Arrangements of Laws

The laws on a particular subject in Exodus, Leviticus, Numbers, and Deuteronomy are rarely codified in one place but appear in at least two books, often in three, or even all four. To find all that the **Pentateuch** has to say on a subject, the various particulars and details of a legal topic must be gathered together. In other words, the commands are not fully expounded in a logically arranged legal treatise. This lack of organization produces a pattern like a weaving or a tapestry.

The format of commandments is also relevant to their interpretation. They are structured according to two basic formulas, absolute or conditional, and the former varies additionally according to a negative or positive pattern, slightly similar to the parallelism of Hebrew verse, which amplifies statements through the means of complement, development, or antithesis.

The laws or teachings begun in Exodus and concluded in Deuteronomy, then, are of two kinds, absolute or apodictic ones, usually introduced by the contrasting formulas "Thou shalt" or "Thou shalt not," and conditional or casuistic ones, expressed in a narrative form, such as "If a man [does this], then [this will happen]." The Decalogue illustrates the apodictic kind in contrasting forms, three positive and seven negative. Although most of the Ten Commandments are stated negatively, the introduction and central laws uniting commitment to God and to the human family are stated affirmatively: "I am the LORD thy God, which have brought thee out of the land of Egypt, out of the house of bondage," "Remember the sabbath day to keep it holy," and "Honor thy father and thy mother." Then follow the remaining negations: not to kill, commit adultery, steal, bear false witness, or covet.

Brief commands of this kind are often embellished by a positive/negative pattern. For example, the prescription "Judges and officers shalt thou make thee in all thy gates" is a positive command requiring judges in all cities in all of the tribes to be "just," but this is followed by two negative warnings against favoritism and bribery and then by a final reminder to be "just" (Deut. 16:18-20). Thus, the law is given four times, developed by parallel negative statements in a parallel positive frame.

Other series of laws are usually arranged to achieve variety by alternating absolute and conditional forms. Sometimes the casuistic instructions are brief, and sometimes they treat a specific topic at length. Those found in Deuteronomy 22 are good examples. Observing the usual pattern, the passage starts with the absolute type of command (two in this case), followed by two conditional ones, then a series of absolute commands, and an even longer series of conditional ones; it concludes with a terse absolute command.

More specifically, the first precept combines a negative-positive (shalt not-shalt) formulation for variety: "Thou shalt not see thy brother's ox or his sheep go astray, and hide thyself from them: thou shalt in any case bring them again to thy brother." Then a number of conditional and absolute clarifications are added, such as if the unfortunate person does not live near or is unknown, one is expected to retain the lost goods until they are claimed (vv. 1-4). This rather lengthy command is succeeded by a briefer absolute one about distinctions between male and female dress (v. 5). Two conditional situations ensue: if a bird's nest is discovered and there are young in it, the mother bird must be spared for she is needed by her youth (vv. 6-7); and when building a new house, a battlement or railing must be built for the roof so that no one can fall from it (v. 8). A series of absolute laws then condemns other mixtures, like those against which the above gendered-dress codes were based, to represent the divine insistence against any kind of compromise with pagan practice and to reemphasize the divine distinctions of creation. Thus vineyards may not be planted with mixed seed, nor plowing be done with both an ox and an ass, nor wool and linen be combined in the composition of clothes (vv. 9-12). The last is combined with the absolute command that fringes or *tefillin* be worn on the borders of the garments. This is succeeded by a series of "if" conditions about marriage and chastity, concluding with the law that if a man has sexual relations with a single woman he is required to compensate her father and must marry her for a lifelong union (vv. 13-28). And there is a final absolute statement that no man shall abuse his father's wife (v. 30).

Scholars and critics have been puzzled by the seeming lack of logical or literary unity among various topics addressed in legal sequences and have found each other's explanations unsatisfactory. Victor Hamilton summarizes the attempts by Gerhard von Rad, Moshe Weinfeld, Norman Geisler, Calum Carmichael, and S. Kaufmann, for example, at configuring some sort of inherent order in the laws (415-18). But instead of solutions based on models outside of or elsewhere in the **Pentateuch,** as some of the above critics propose, the unity of a collection of laws might well be as-

sumed. The juxtaposition of assorted commandments suggests a subtle relationship. Their miscellaneousness itself may be the unifying principle. Chapter 22 just discussed is such a passage.

An analogy to this type of organization is that of the great American poet Walt Whitman in section 15 of "Song of Myself." This section shares the structure and many of the same details as Deuteronomy 22. For example, in the first nine lines Whitman combines images of a contralto singing from the organ loft with a carpenter dressing his plank and singing with his plane, the married and the unmarried celebrating a festival dinner, the hunter of wild birds seeking his prey, deacons being ordained at an altar, spinning girls making clothes, and farmers observing their growing grain.

The subsequent lines in the section, and *Leaves of Grass* as a whole, achieve just what chapter 22 and the whole book of Deuteronomy do: they give insight into how unrelated elements may be associated. Both continually mix the obviously divine and sacred with the ordinary and common, the social hierarchy with the simplest occupations of each human being. Some of the elements in "Song of Myself" may even allude to Deuteronomy. Whitman refers to making a roof, to the one-year honeymoon, to various forms of sexual expression and, like the Bible, to the ideals of family life. Both proclaim the unity of life and the sanctity of every part and aspect of it. Walt Whitman's "I make holy whatever I touch" expresses the spirit of Deuteronomy. God's attention to the seemingly insignificant and disparate details of life sanctifies them. Together, they affirm the call of everyone and of every activity to be holy.

The commandments in Exodus, Leviticus, Numbers, and Deuteronomy develop, comment on, or expand the Decalogue. The tradition is that 248 are positive ("Thou shalt") and 365 are negative ("Thou shalt not"), thus making up 613 commandments. (Jesus reduces these 613 to two commandments in Matthew 22:37-39). Any given topic may be expressed by what "thou shalt" or what "thou shalt not" do. For example, there are 53 positive commands about sacrifices offered to God and 69 negative ones, 19 mandatory commandments about the temple and 22 prohibitions. Food, festivals, agriculture, commerce, justice, and all personal and community activity receive similar parallel treatment (Wigoder 129-39). Such a lengthy list of laws on these subjects reflects the consciousness of the holiness of all of life.

Literary Devices

Repetition is the chief literary device of the **Pentateuch,** indeed of the entire Old Testament. The series of plagues upon Egypt and the pattern of repeated deliverance from them illustrate the method. So too does the series of rebellions, judgments, and deliverances during the journey of the Hebrews to the Promised Land, a pattern repeated in the book of Judges and in the prophets until the nation goes into captivity, as recorded in 2 Kings.

Robert Browning's *The Ring and the Book* and William Faulkner's *As I Lay Dying* provide analogues for repeating episodes or parts of a story from new or different perspectives. Both authors narrate the same events in these works from the points of view of different characters. Similarly and specifically, repetition in Deuteronomy gains in perspective from retelling material after forty years of wandering and from the contrast between the people's point of view and Moses'.

Three times in his opening address of Deuteronomy Moses tells the congregation, "The LORD was angry with me for your sakes" (1:37; 3:26; 4:21) due to their behavior recounted in Exodus and Numbers. They provoked YHWH "from the day that thou didst depart out of the land of Egypt, until ye came unto this place" and "ye have been rebellious against the LORD from the day that I knew you" (9:7, 24). The suggestion is that Moses feels his punishment at being forbidden to enter the Promised Land is not primarily due to his own failure but to his frustration brought about by them. In Numbers the emphasis is clearly on Moses' own culpability, on his harsh outcry at Horeb and his disobedience in striking, instead of speaking to, the rock to bring forth water, as he had done earlier at Massah in Exodus 17.

Through the device of repetition Deuteronomy provides other fresh perspectives and details on previously recorded actions. For example, Moses interceded not only for the people when the golden calf was made but also for Aaron, with whom the Lord was "very angry" (9:20; cf. Ex. 32). We discover for the first time that Moses, not only Joshua and Caleb, had addressed the people when they rejected their destination and had encouraged them to remember their miraculous deliverance out of Egypt and their divine preservation in the wilderness when God cared for them as a father cares for a son (1:21-23). Also new is the information that while heeding the advice of his father-in-law Jethro about appointing judges, Moses himself had anticipated this need and gave careful instructions to the appointees (1:9-18). We hear more of his activities, exhortations to obedience, and warnings, especially against idolatry.

We also hear more about YHWH in Deuteronomy and are given more commentary on earlier episodes. In the conquest of Sihon, king of the Amorites, a victory often recalled in the Old Testament, we learn that Moses himself sent messengers to that ruler, whereas in the account in Numbers only Israel the nation is mentioned. Israel's role in this event, presumed to be divinely ordained, is specifically ascribed to YHWH in Deuteronomy, and the conquest is associated with the deliverance from Egypt. Sihon's resistance is like Pharaoh's. The Lord "hardened his spirit, and made his heart obstinate," and he provided victory for the Hebrews over him (Deut. 2:26-37).

Another form of repetition involves codes of law. Sometimes they are briefly interrupted or slightly changed, as in the two receptions of the Decalogue and the two accounts of the tabernacle in Exodus. The most extended case is the two parts of Deuteronomy: the first, as already discussed, restates Israel's history, while the second, giving the book its Greek name, repeats the whole law, adding new provisions on specific subjects. In most cases the repeated version involves significant modifications, elaborations, and differences in focus from the first, and these help complete the sacred history and teaching. For example, there is a new emphasis on rejoicing in, not just obeying, YHWH (12:7, 12, 18; 14:26; 16:11, 14-15; 26:11; 27:7). Another form of repetition is a summary, and Deuteronomy is able, fittingly, as the final legal book, to encapsulate the whole law in the familiar *shema:* "Hear, O Israel: The LORD our God is one LORD: and thou shalt love the LORD thy God with all thine heart, and with all thy soul, and with all thy might" (6:4-5).

The legal material in Exodus and Deuteronomy has much in common, but it is arranged differently and the contexts are different. J. A. Thompson provides a list of parallel laws for the two books (25-30). Exodus, with its proximity to the tabernacle and Leviticus, emphasizes worship; Deuteronomy emphasizes personal and social relationships.

Other literary devices are *irony* and *reversal*. The abject slavery of the Hebrews and the decree for the deaths of male newborn as Exodus opens is the complete reversal of the great favor enjoyed by Joseph and Jacob and all his family at the close of Genesis. There is, however, the irony that the future deliverer of the people will be spared and even brought up in the household of Pharaoh by the intervention of his daughter. The self-efforts of the young Moses to help his people only result in his rejection and exile for forty years.

Ironically, only when he is thoroughly convinced of his inadequacies, which he exhibits by arguing against YHWH's call, can he lead the nation to liberty. A crueler irony perhaps consists in Moses' final failure. After his great patience with the rebellious Israelites for forty years and the three times he interceded with the Lord to spare their impending annihilation, the "meekest of men" loses his temper, and he, like the adult generation, misses the Promised Land.

Despite God's special miracles on their behalf, the daily supernatural manifestations of the daytime pillar of cloud and the nighttime pillar of fire, the presence of God in the tabernacle, and the daily provision of manna, the people still grumble, complain, rebel, and apostatize. The explicit irony involved consists of the comparison made between the ten occasions when Egypt's pharaoh rejected YHWH's demands in the account of the ten plagues in Exodus and the "ten times" his own nation rejected him (Num. 14:22).

Most ironic of all is the people's rejection of the real meaning of the central events of their history: the Creation and the Exodus. The first affirms their companionship with God by being created in his image. The second, the Exodus, proclaims the freedom of his people to be true worshipers of the only true God. The persistent underlying message of these four books is that human beings are the only ordained image of divinity. By rejecting the original "image and likeness" in themselves, human beings are doomed to seek in various forms of idolatry and false worship an image of God.

There are also, however, affirmative ironies and reversals. Thus, in Numbers 22-24 Balaam tries three times to curse Israel but instead blesses them. There is even a comic element to the story in the prophet's failure to perceive an angel blocking his path whom his donkey can see. Finally, God reminds his people, as in Deuteronomy, that they do not enter the Land of Promise because of their greatness or righteousness. They are indeed the least of peoples, selected to show God's glory, and have been most unfaithful, but the Lord loves them and wishes to fulfill his promises to their fathers (7:7-8; 9:4-8).

Themes

As Martin Buber and Abraham Heschel have observed, the major goals of the whole Old Testament are *the celebration of the human race and the realization of intimacy between God and humankind.* Even those who emphasize that the **Pentateuch**'s primary concern is to reveal God's greatness, not man's, recognize that salvation is the "characteristic activity" of God (Cole 28). God wishes his people to enjoy him and to be his friends and stewards of creation. In Genesis the companionship theme is developed through individuals and families in the figures of Adam and Eve, Abraham, Isaac, and Jacob. In the next four pentateuchal books this concept is expanded to a whole nation.

YHWH's chief means of establishing this intimacy between himself and his people is the institution of laws and a system of worship. His deliverance of Israel from slavery (Ex. 1-15), the provision for his physical presence (chs. 25-40), his sustaining them (Numbers), and the declaration of his principles (Leviticus and Deuteronomy) exemplify this divine desire for rela-

tionship. Such intimacy requires, most of all, holiness. Through the law, *every detail of life is sacramentalized.* As YHWH states in Exodus 31:3 and over and over again in Leviticus, he intends to "make holy" this representative people. Victor Hamilton appropriately observes that even "Leviticus describes a holiness that applies to everyone," not just to priests, "a holiness within the reach of all, out of the reach of none" (245-46).

The main way God's people can show their loyalty and reciprocal desire for intimacy with him is through *the avoidance of idolatry.* One of the first commands of the Decalogue, spoken in YHWH's own voice (just as he spoke to Adam and Eve in the Garden) is "I am the Lord thy God, which have brought thee out of the land of Egypt, out of the house of bondage. Thou shalt have no other gods before me" and "Thou shalt not make thee any graven image or any likeness of anything . . ." (Ex. 20:2, 4).

So intense is the condemnation of idolatry that it engages much of Moses' later commentary on the first dispensation of the commandments (Deut. 5-9). To worship other gods will result in destruction "from off the face of the earth" (6:14-15) instead of the promised blessings, which include the absence of "all sickness" (7:12-16). False images must be destroyed by fire and no vestige retained, not even the silver or gold on them: "for it is an abomination to the Lord thy God" (7:25). Even if a prophet, family member, "or thy friend who is as thine own soul" suggests worshiping a false god, that person must be executed (ch. 13). Moses says of such worshipers that "they sacrificed unto devils, not to God" (32:17). (Milton's view of the false gods in *Paradise Lost,* books 1 and 2 especially, derives from passages such as this.) Prohibition of idolatry is just as strong a thematic interest in later biblical books.

Anticipating the New Testament's two greatest commandments, worshiping and obeying God must be concurrent with *love and care for others,* which may be summarized thus: "Thou shalt love thy neighbor as thyself: I am the Lord" (Lev. 19:17). This is the theme of the second half of the Decalogue, of some concluding commandments of Exodus and Leviticus, and especially of the second half of Deuteronomy.

Loving God is inseparable from loving others, which the numerous provisions for the poor, the widow, and the orphan affirm, as do the many allusions designating others as "brother" or "neighbor." The order to rescue and return any lost or endangered possession of another (22:1-4), the requirement to leave some of any harvest behind for those in need (24:19-22), the right to satisfy one's hunger in any field or vineyard but not to take more food than is needed (23:24-25), and the command not to embarrass by repossession (24:10-11) illustrate the biblical responsibility for others' welfare and reputation treated in these books. As Nahum Sarna observes, there is also a strong emphasis on caring for the stranger, usually accompanied by the statement "Remember you were once strangers in Egypt" (4-5). Because of these provisions, Thomas Henry Huxley, the champion of agnosticism, claimed that the code of Deuteronomy transcends the most humane considerations of modern law.

Conclusion

The mass of Scripture that comprises Exodus through Deuteronomy is traditionally read either for its legal content (Torah) or for its remarkable narratives, rarely both together. Later retellings of the Passover and the Exodus, for instance, testify to their inherent narrative appeal and historical applicability; in Dante's letter to his patron comparing the allegory of *The Divine Comedy* to an allegorical interpretation of the exodus from Egypt, in the American slave song "Go Down, Moses," and in the film *The Ten Commandments,* for example. On the other hand, the long tradition of Jewish commentary on the legal portions of these books testifies to their importance distinct from the narrative content. The literary approach taken here has attempted to give due attention to both genres and to consider their interrelationship. A literary approach to these books combines the traditionally Jewish focus on the law and the traditionally Christian concentration on the narrative parts that the New Testament especially allegorizes. A literary approach takes account of all that is there.

What is found in Exodus through Deuteronomy is a sophisticated patterning of both narrative and legal sections, which often serve each other as "breaks" or shifts. A mixing of genres seems to be the norm, unlike the neoclassical disdain for it. The combinations often follow either a chiastic or an A-B-A pattern, that is, a narrative passage relieved by a legal one and succeeded by another narrative text, or vice versa. Another organizational device operating in the arrangement of laws could be designated *discordia concors,* a harmony in disunity. The miscellaneous variety of these ordinances embraces all of human experience and calls all of it to the life of holiness. Every detail of life is sacramentalized.

It is these two elements of Exodus, Leviticus, Numbers, and Deuteronomy—the legal component, which addresses humanity's need for righteousness, and the narrative one, which describes the miraculous saving acts of God that give proof to the covenant on which that righteousness is founded—that together reveal YHWH's plan in these books to restore his people to the divine image and companionship purposed in creation.

Works Cited

Alter, Robert. *The Art of Biblical Narrative.* New York: Basic Books, 1981.

Alter, Robert, and Frank Kermode, eds. *The Literary Guide to the Bible.* Cambridge, Mass.: Harvard UP, 1987.

Buber, Martin. *I and Thou.* New York: Scribner, 1958.

Cole, R. Alan. *Exodus.* London: Inter-Varsity, 1973.

Damrosch, David. *The Narrative Covenant.* San Francisco: Harper & Row, 1987.

———. "Leviticus." *Literary Guide to the Bible.* Ed. R. Alter and F. Kermode. 66-77.

Fokkelman, J. P. "Exodus." *Literary Guide to the Bible.* Ed. R. Alter and F. Kermode. 56-65.

Greenstein, Edward L. "Biblical Law." *Back to the Sources.* Ed. B. W. Holtz. 83-103.

Hamilton, Victor P. *Handbook of the Pentateuch.* Grand Rapids: Baker, 1982.

Heschel, Abraham. *The Prophets.* 2 vols. New York: Harper & Row, 1962.

Holtz, Barry W., ed. *Back to the Sources: Reading the Classic Jewish Texts.* New York: Summit, 1984.

———. "Midrash." *Back to the Sources.* Ed. B. W. Holtz. 177-211.

Huxley, Thomas Henry. *Science and the Hebrew Tradition.* 1893. Rpt. New York: Appleton, 1913.

Josipovici, Gabriel. *The Book of God: A Response to the Bible.* New Haven: Yale UP, 1988.

Milgrom, Jacob. *Numbers.* Philadelphia: Jewish Publication Society, 1990.

Moulton, Richard G. *The Literary Study of the Bible.* Boston: Heath, 1899.

Rosenberg, Joel. "Biblical Narrative." *Back to the Sources.* Ed. B. W. Holtz. 31-81.

Ryken, Leland. *The Literature of the Bible.* Grand Rapids: Zondervan, 1974.

———. *Words of Delight.* Grand Rapids: Baker, 1987.

Sarna, Nahum. *Exploring Exodus.* New York: Shocken, 1986.

Sternberg, Meir. *The Poetics of Biblical Narrative.* Bloomington: Indiana UP, 1985.

Thompson, J. A. *Deuteronomy.* London: Inter-Varsity,

1974.

Thompson, Leonard. *Introducing Biblical Literature: A More Fantastic Country.* Englewood Cliffs, N.J.: Prentice Hall, 1975.

Whitman, Walt. *Leaves of Grass.* Philadelphia: David McKay, 1891-1892.

Wigoder, Geoffrey, ed. *Encyclopedic Dictionary of Judaica.* Jerusalem: Keter, 1974.

Tamara Cohn Eskenazi (essay date 1995)

SOURCE: "*Torah* as Narrative and Narrative as *Torah*" in *Old Testament Interpretation: Past, Present, and Future; Essays in Honor of Gene M. Tucker*, edited by James Luther Mays, David L. Petersen, and Kent Harold Richards, Abingdon Press, 1995, pp. 13-30.

[*In this essay, Eskenazi surveys the literary approaches to the* Torah *that have recently emerged in an effort to understand how they provide for a fuller religious and historical appreciation of the text.*]

> *When, in time to come, your children ask you, "What mean the decrees, laws, and rules that YHWH our God has enjoined upon you?" you shall say to your children, "We were slaves to Pharaoh in Egypt and YHWH freed us. . . . " (Deut 6:20, TANAKH)*

Poised ready to possess the promised land, Israel on the plains of Moab receives, again, the command to tell the story of its past: "We were slaves. . . . " The meaning of the "decrees, laws, and rules of YHWH" is disclosed through the *story,* the telling and re-telling of which is both remembering and re-membering.

> When all Israel comes to see the face of YHWH your God in the place where [God] will choose, you will read this **Torah**. . . . Gather the people, the men and the women and the little ones and the stranger within your gate, in order that they will hear and learn . . . and their children who did not know will hear and will learn. . . . (Deut 31:11-13)

The **Torah** is meaningful memory written explicitly for a purpose: to engage and teach a community (and each member within it) how to live in relation to God. The story is not a dispassionate report of what happened, merely told to satisfy curiosity. It seeks to promulgate a public memory of a shared past and define a common future. And the medium it uses, narrative, is inseparable from the messages it seeks to convey.

What, then, are the critical, responsible, effective ways to understand the **Torah**? Must one stand outside and gaze at it objectively or may one enter its universe as a participant? What skills must one have to analyze narrative, especially this one? And what does it mean "to understand" such a text? One of the major developments in biblical studies in the last twenty-five years is the emergence of responses to these questions in which literary, rather than historical, criteria predominate.

The Hebrew word Torah means "teaching" (note the singular). It refers in its narrower sense to the first books of the Bible, known also as the **Pentateuch** or the **Five Books of Moses** (Genesis, Exodus, Leviticus, Numbers, and Deuteronomy). The translation of Torah as "Law" (as in "the Law and the Prophets") obscures the narrative nature of the **Torah.** Calling this collection Torah imposes a unity and designates a category. The term "Torah" has been used for the **Pentateuch** from around the fifth century BCE. The familiar story it relates spans events from the creation of the world to the formation of a people by God and Moses. It concludes just before the divine promises to ancestors are fulfilled, with Israel hearing Moses' "last will and testament" before entering the land.

For reasons no longer discernible, ancient Israel preserved its formal sacred traditions in prose narrative, in sharp contrast to the poetry that dominates the surviving ancient Near Eastern texts. Of course not all the material in the **Torah** is prose narrative; the **Torah** incorporates laws, songs, genealogies, and lists. But these are carefully embedded in narrative and receive their meaning from the narrative context. Why narrative? Was it a polemic against the epic Mesopotamian and Canaanite literature? Was it because narrative constitutes a specific form of communication best suited for forming and informing the kind of persons and community the **Torah** seeks to create or perpetuate? Literary critics conclude that the answer to both questions is yes.

Prose narratives or stories have distinct features that set them apart from other types of literature such as poems, proverbs, or philosophical treatises, all of which are equally familiar modes for transmitting traditions, sacred or otherwise. To use stories is to organize meaningful reality in a certain way: narratives endow structure, characters (i.e., particular persons), and time with significance. They also make certain modes of knowing possible, while bracketing other modes.

The choice of narrative is anything but irrelevant or haphazard. Yet for roughly two centuries, biblical narrative has been eclipsed in scholarly circles, although not outside such circles, by historical considerations. The emergence of literary approaches to the Bible thus signals a major shift. In what follows I review some newer methods, theories, and practices of literary approaches to the **Torah** that have mushroomed. To illustrate how they assist in interpretation, I show the variety of readings of Genesis 1-3 that result when the different literary lenses focus the analysis.

Torah as Narrative

Although the **Torah** is undeniably a composite of sources, reflecting different periods and concerns, it is also a coherent composition in which these sources were combined expressly to convey meanings. Literary critics therefore begin with the text in its final form as a unity whose meanings can be discerned by attention to its literary features. Put simply, literary criticism analyzes *what* is said by looking at *how* it is said.

Biblical narrative, like all narrative, depends on certain necessary conventions. A story is told from at least one point of view by an implicit narrator (to be differentiated from an actual narrator or author), often to an implicit reader (again, to be differentiated from a real reader). Characters and plot develop through time in narrative. The specific arrangement of these components conveys the particular intention(s) of the text, and therefore must be examined skillfully.

There are, in addition, techniques and emphases distinct to biblical narrative. For example, the biblical narrator is typically anonymous. Later Jewish and Christian traditions assigned authorship to Moses whereas historical critics have suggested Ezra the scribe as possible author. The **Torah** does not make either claim. The identity of the reporter is not disclosed in the text. The narrator is also omniscient, reporting events that exceed ordinary human knowledge, such as the thoughts of God. Furthermore, this narrator often withholds explicit value judgments and leaves readers to reconstruct evaluations. While some messages are boldly proclaimed ("You shall have no other gods. . . . ") others are subtle. Is Abraham lauded or criticized for pretending that Sarah is his wife (Genesis 12 and 20)? To uncover the possible answers encoded in the tale one must give close attention to the clues in the text, clues like shifts between first person reports by Abraham and those of the anonymous narrator. One must cultivate awareness of conventions such as type scenes and composite artistry that serve to communicate intention.

Repetition plays an inordinately important role in biblical narrative. Robert Alter observes that the repetition of keywords, motifs, themes, or type scenes is the most misunderstood aspect of biblical narrative. Far from being a mere relic from the past, repetition of words and events creates a network of meanings that demands acute attention. The leading keyword, often in several permutations, guides the attentive reader through the maze of complex ideas and narrative tensions.

The Joseph story illustrates how overlooking keywords lead scholars astray. Alter shows that repetition integrates the otherwise puzzling story of Judah and Tamar in Genesis 38. He shows how this story's keywords, themes, and motifs intimately link with the rest of the Joseph narrative and with the larger purposes of Genesis as a whole.

The leading word *nkr*, "recognize," plays a pivotal role. The word first appears when the brothers use clothing to deceive by presenting Joseph's bloodied tunic to Jacob: " . . . *Recognize* this please. Is this your son's tunic?" (Gen 37:32). Recognizing, Jacob reaches the wrong conclusions: "He *recognized* it and said. . . . " (Gen 37:33).

In the very next chapter clothing will deceive once again. Tamar uses clothing to disguise herself in order to get her father-in-law Judah to impregnate her. She uses clothing also as clues to compel recognition: "*Recognize* please to whom these belong . . ." she says, sending him items he had left in her possession when he lay with her. "And Judah *recognized* and said 'She is more right than I am!'" (Gen 38:25-26). The climax of this story comes when the brothers appear before Joseph. The text is buzzing with repetition: "And Joseph saw his brothers and *recognized* them and made himself *unrecognizable* [meaning also "a stranger"] to them" (Gen 42:7) and again, to emphasize the centrality of the issue, "And Joseph *recognized* his brothers and they did not *recognize* him" (Gen 42:10).

The delicate and vital task of "recognizing" not only shapes the story of Joseph, but also that of Judah and Tamar. It also constitutes a moral imperative to readers: the importance of cultivating knowledge. Biblical art is not simply about aesthetics; and literary sensibilities are not simply a luxury. On the contrary, the Bible displays "a complete interfusion of literary art with theological, moral, or historiographical vision, the fullest perception of the latter dependent of the fullest grasp of the former" (Alter, 19).

The relationship between the two creation stories in Genesis 1-3 illustrates the different approaches of the historical and the literary critic. The first creation story (Gen 1:1-2:4a) depicts symmetries and harmony: "God splits off the realm of the earth from the realm of the heaven. . . . Darkness and light, night and day, evening and morning, water and sky, . . . each moment of creation is conceived as a balancing of opposites. . . . " (Alter, 142-3). The second (Gen 2:4b-3:24) is more interested "in the complicated and difficult facts of human life in civilization" (145). But the accounts are not merely different; they also appear contradictory, most notably in their account of the creation of humanity. The first story states simply: "Male and female he created them" (Gen 1:27). The second story "on the other hand, imagines woman as a kind of divine afterthought, made to fill a need of man, and made, be-sides, out of one of man's spare parts" (141).

Source critics resolve the tension by designating different sources. They identify the first account as a Priestly source (P) and 2:4*b*-3:24 as the Yahwist (J). For the literary critic this explanation is insufficient. It fails to address the important question about the meaning of the final form. Why did someone choose to leave these contradictory accounts side by side without modifying them? What does this juxtaposition accomplish? A literary response explores what the text expresses through this arrangement of sources. One such conclusion is that the text creates a bifocal vision. It allows one to see a cosmic scale of events alongside a more human scale. Such a bifocal vision also coerces readers away from a single, monolithic perspective into a plurality and establishes a degree of indeterminacy. Like a postcubist painting that superimposes two perspectives in a single frame, it keeps in tension two realities that cannot be expressed linearly: there are paradoxical dimensions of man and woman. Complexity abounds with regard to God as both magisterially remote (Genesis 1) and intimately engaged with creation (Genesis 2). The story incorporates diverse perspectives by a montage. Monotheism is always caught in the need to make sense of the intersection of two incompatibles—the relative and the absolute, "human imperfection and divine perfection, the brawling chaos of historical experience and God's promise to fulfill a design in history" (154). The contradiction, therefore, is not accidental but an example of composite artistry expressing the paradoxical nature of the human experience within a divinely ordered universe.

Literary approaches to the Bible display a variety of positions concerning the role of history in interpreting biblical narrative. Some altogether dislodge narrative from historical context. Others, like Alter, and even more forcefully Meir Sternberg, underscore the need for historical sensibilities in interpretation. Sternberg, in fact, defends the historiographic character of biblical narrative. He reminds readers that "history-writing is not a record of fact—what 'really' happened—but a discourse that claims to be a record of fact" (Sternberg, 25). The Bible represents a new mode of historiography, emerging to convey certain distinctive messages that could not be conveyed by other available forms.

The role of author and the location of meaning also constitute a bone of contention in literary analysis of the Bible. While many biblical scholars avoid invoking an author, Alter and Sternberg refer to an author whose intentions are embedded in the carefully crafted narrative. The competent reader must discover these intentions. Sternberg also claims that in the Bible "foolproof composition" leads the "competent reader" on a journey from "truth to the whole truth," a view that provoked heated debates in which every one of these quoted expressions has been vociferously challenged.

By "foolproof composition" (unfortunately an inflammatory term), Sternberg asserts something more modest than at first appears. He means that biblical narrative is so constructed as to lead readers to definitively prescribed conclusions. Competent readers who respond to the clues—to what is in the text and what is deliberately omitted—will typically reach a consensus about meanings. The better the reader, the fuller the "truth" discovered.

Sternberg does not deny indeterminacy and ambiguity. On the contrary, they are in the text and they are plentiful. They are not subjective. The author put them there. For example, in the story of Joseph we cannot easily fathom Joseph's motivation in tormenting his brothers. Such inability is not accidental. It is deliberately controlled by the narrative, which is replete with explicit emotions, but leaves out the most important one. All of this serves specific ends. The biblical author has definite notions of truth and seeks to lead readers to them, sometimes explicitly and oftentimes by compelling one to tease out truths. Truth can be nuanced, ambiguous, or conflicted. What is the truth about Joseph's motives? Is he punishing, testing, teaching, or fulfilling dreams? The text deliberately keeps us in suspense because all four are at work (Sternberg, 285-308). Indeterminacy here is the product of foolproof composition. The untrained reader might only grasp a partial truth, such as the fact that Joseph teaches his brothers about true repentance by giving them a chance to relive scenes from their past and undo their original criminal behavior. The more sophisticated might discover two or more, such as the correspondence between the suffering that Joseph inflicts on his brothers and those they had inflicted on him. All these readings are on a continuum. They are facets of the "whole truth" of this particular story. Sternberg adamantly rejects the notion that the Bible is elitist literature that gives one set of messages to the initiated "insiders," and a substantially different one to the "outsiders."

For Sternberg, Genesis 1-3, among other things, expresses with knowledge this unique concern of biblical narrative. Other ancient Near Eastern traditions dangle immortality before humanity as the lure for a quest. Gilgamesh journeys to find the elixir that will keep him from dying. In the Bible, however, knowledge takes this role. Trees and other features of the garden of Eden story recur in other mythologies, but the tree of knowledge is unique to the Bible. Medium and message coincide. Knowledge is not merely one of the subjects of biblical narratives. Nor is it merely an important quest that fundamentally defines humanity (hence the tree of knowledge). Knowledge also constitutes the very reason for the specific narrative form.

The **Torah** casts reality as narrative and presents knowledge as a process that unfolds in time (rather than a set of rules or wisdom sayings).

Many contributions of literary analyses such as Alter's and Sternberg's have antecedents in scholarly circles going back to the turn of the century, and even in rabbinic traditions when one casts a wider net. Gunkel, Buber, Muilenburg, and this century's great commentaries on the **Torah** incorporate many of such readings and anticipate much of this work. Profound, new literary insights often echo Cassuto and Jacob commentaries on Genesis and Exodus; von Rad and Westermann on Genesis; Childs and Greenberg on Exodus; and Plaut on the **Torah** as a whole. Three important elements, however, differentiate the current literary approaches to biblical narrative. First, attention is given to theoretical underpinnings. Second, a unique synthesis reshapes earlier interpretive insights and practices into more self-conscious strategies of reading and speaking about biblical narrative (see also Bar Efrat, Fokkelman, and Robertson). Third, this widespread systematic literary analysis of biblical narrative in a modern idiom consolidates the inquiry and makes possible a new and urgent level of discussion.

Literary approaches also serve to reconnect in new ways the scholarly concerns with the wider culture. It helps nonspecialists reclaim the Bible as a communal, comprehensible text. Because the interpretation's starting point is the text's final form the novice can begin interpreting and go much further.

The emergence of feminist criticism of the Hebrew Bible offers an important example of the merging of literary issues and wider cultural concerns. Contemporary feminist criticism was launched in biblical studies as an effort to "depatriarchalize" biblical narrative. In her pioneering work, Trible claimed that important biblical texts have been distorted by patriarchal misreadings and need to be reclaimed for their egalitarian, liberating vision of womanhood and God.

Trible's approach is literary, which she initially defined as rhetorical criticism. She offers "close readings" of texts, focusing on surface meanings. Genesis 1-3 plays the crucial role in Trible's depatriarchalizing project. As a literary critic, Trible uses rhetorical analysis of narrative from a feminist perspective, paying attention to the structure of the story, characterization, word play, translation issues, and, above all, the relation between the sexes that the text inscribes.

She begins by drawing attention to the more complex meaning of the key term *'ādām,* misleadingly translated as man.

> Ambiguity characterizes the meaning of *'ādām* in Genesis 2-3. On the one hand, man is the first

creature formed (2:7). . . . On the other hand, *'ādām* is a generic term for humankind. In commanding *'ādām* not to eat of the tree of the knowledge of good and evil, the Deity is speaking to both the man and the woman (2:16-17). Until differentiation of female and male (2:21-23), *'ādām* is basically androgynous: one creature incorporating two sexes. (35)

Man and woman as gendered creatures come into being only after surgery (Gen 2:21-24). As Trible notes, only now do the distinctive words man . . . and woman . . . appear. "Before this episode the Yahwist has used only the generic term *'ādām.* No exclusively male reference has appeared. . . . Male does not precede woman as female but happens concurrently with her" (37).

The so-called Fall, according to Trible, offers an astonishing portrait of a thoughtful woman and a thoughtless man. The woman takes up the theological problem posed by the serpent's question. She weighs the evidence and acts on the basis of three compelling reasons: the forbidden fruit is nutritious, attractive, and a source of wisdom. "If the woman be intelligent, sensitive and ingenious, the man is passive, brutish and inept. These character portrayals are truly extraordinary in a culture dominated by men. I stress their contrast not to promote female chauvinism but to undercut patriarchal interpretations alien to the text" (40).

Feminist biblical criticism and Trible herself have come a long way from this initial, optimistic position to a more complicated range of assessments. Like other critical approaches to the Bible, feminist criticism ramified into multiple modes of analysis, theories, methods, and practices. Feminist studies typically combine with other critical perspectives (e.g., feminist-literary criticism to be distinguished, say, from feminist-historical criticism).

What unifies feminist approaches is the common concern with the relationship between gender and power. Feminists debate, however, whether feminism can merely investigate gender issues descriptively or must, prescriptively, advocate certain positions—either deliberately or inevitably—namely gender equality or the liberation of women.

The relation of biblical narrative to history often looms large in many feminists' analyses. Feminists concentrate on five related tasks: (1) retrieving images and voices of women in the Bible; (2) analyzing these representations of women and absence of women; (3) reconstructing lives of women; (4) analyzing the Hebrew Bible as a patriarchal construct; and (5) developing responses to these findings.

The role of reader takes a different form in feminist circles from the one emphasized by Alter's and Sternberg's approach. Since reading as a woman differs from reading as a man (men find themselves included, women excluded), feminist critics begin with a "hermeneutic of suspicion." They do not merely analyze underlying ideologies and tensions, but question them as well. They also pay attention to what is not there, especially the female presence. Feminist critics who position themselves within the biblical traditions of Judaism and Christianity have devised several different strategies for coping with androcentric, patriarchal, or sexist texts sanctioned by their communities as authoritative.

Some look for perspectives within the Bible to counteract those inimical to women. Yes, admittedly women are displaced in the text. Moses prepares the people to encounter God at Sinai by addressing only men, saying "Do not go near a woman" (Exodus 19). But this negative address can be contrasted and balanced by stories where women are prominent in Israel's other formative event, the Exodus itself. Women of different classes and ethnicity (the midwives Shiphra and Puah, Moses' mother and sister, and the daughter of Pharaoh) initiate nonviolent civil disobedience that saves baby boys, including Moses (Exodus 2) and makes the Exodus possible. They also have the final word: "And Miriam the prophetess, Aaron's sister, took a timbrel in her hand, and all the women went out after her, dancing with timbrels. And Miriam responded to them: 'Sing to YHWH. . . .'" (Exod 15:20-21).

While some feminist critics reread texts in ways that revalorize women by claiming that this reading represents the narrative's point of view, others take issue with the narrative's perspective by reading *against* the grain. Some critics acknowledge the patriarchy in the text but separate the text's meanings from the historically contingent (as a product of its own time and place) and seek enduring messages in other portions of the Bible. Critics often relocate authority, shifting it from the early community responsible for the Bible (and subject to the conventions of its time) to the contemporary community of interpreters.

The question of where meanings reside is central to a number of new literary theories, but it takes on special urgency in feminist approaches. Feminists wrestle with the contradictions between biblical representations of women and archaeological information that reflects more participatory roles for women in culture (religious or secular). They often engage not only in the recovery of women, text, and tradition but also in an analysis of ancient and modern patriarchy with an eye towards change.

As a result, narratives in the **Torah** receive varied interpretation in feminist circles. Take again the story of Judah and Tamar (Genesis 38) where Tamar deliberately breaks a cultural taboo in order to coerce Judah to do his duty. Is this a story of a woman subverting patriarchal conventions or of transgression in the *service* of patriarchy? What is the force of Judah's conclusions about Tamar's breach of the tradition, "She is more right than I am!" (Gen 38:26)? Is Tamar's labor meant to encourage women to risk everything in order to produce male children or a mandate for women to refuse to be written out of history and take whatever measures are necessary to ensure their place? What about Miriam? Should feminists focus on her glorious role in the Exodus or in the stories that follow? What could be done with the narrative that shows how, when she stands up for equal public power, and not for maternal roles (Numbers 12), both God and the text silence her? How to process the fact that she is buried unceremoniously a few chapters later (Num 20:1), and Moses only recalls the sister who had saved his life by setting her as a warning (Deut 24:9)?

Feminist readings of biblical narratives and those of the **Torah** in particular, remain varied and provocative. No consensus is in view. Genesis 1-3 plays a prominent role in debates about biblical narrative and feminist perspectives.

Alter, for example, notes the linguistic correspondence between the two Hebrew words: "remembered" . . . and "male" . . . .[1] The male is the one who remembers, whose memory is enshrined in the book. In patriarchy, "the only memory is the male memory, because the only members are male members" (Alter, 45). But the memory is not monolithic and within it are seeds that can flower into more inclusive models of self and others. Alter holds the two stories of the creation together, refusing to let either dominate. The first story (P source) depicts gendered humanity created as two varieties of a single species. "The creation precedes not by polarization but by differentiation within wholeness." Male and female, the two varieties of *'ādām,* "embody diversity within similarity" (46). The second story (J source) is the birth of patriarchy, a process of opposition and partialization. "Adam in this story is a male individual and bears a curious resemblance to the motherless asocial resident of the state of nature posited by liberal political theory" (46). Woman has no independent being. Her very definition (woman . . .) is derivative from man . . . in Gen 2:23. Together they are the human and his woman (Gen 2:25). Genesis 2 is best understood as the creation of patriarchy, depicting "the patriarchs' inner experience—loneliness, and a sense of mutilation—and its attempt to recover the banished other through fusion. . . . An Eden founded upon a fantasy of obliterating the other is bound to be unstable" (46).

Pardes, however, refuses to disconnect Genesis 3 from the larger story of Genesis 1-11. To end with chapter 3 is to highlight the so-called Fall and distort the story. But Eve does not fade from view with her naming or with the expulsion. On the contrary, Pardes argues,

Eve makes an impressive comeback: in the unfolding story she is not subjugated by either the man or by the narrative. She speaks more than the man, before and after the expulsion from the garden. In fact, only the woman speaks after that point (Gen 4:1 and 4:25). The names she chooses for her children claim a close connection with God. She defines motherhood as a partnership with God and boasts of her generative power in naming her son (Gen 4:1). "Through her naming of Cain, Eve rewrites Genesis 2 as a subversive comment on Adam's displacement of the generative power of the female body" (Pardes, 48). In her final appearance Eve, not the man who has been and will remain silent, comments on the tragic murder of Abel: " . . . she bore a son, and called his name Seth . . . , for 'God had appointed . . . me another seed instead of Abel, whom Cain slew'" (4:25).

Bal recasts the questions. Reading Genesis 1-3, Bal accomplishes several different things, one of which will occupy us here. Bal offers a complementary perspective to Trible's (even if at times she contests Trible's views), seconding Trible's conclusions that the text depicts woman positively. She does not claim that this reading is the correct one but only one among several possible options. Bal wants to understand why sexist readings have dominated cultures from antiquity to the present when the positive readings of renditions of women in the text are as defensible.

She approaches the Bible as neither a feminist resource nor a sexist manifesto but as an influential text with cultural repercussions. In *Lethal Love* she demonstrates the relative arbitrariness of all readings, including sexist readings, by examining their emergence in biblical narrative. Her purpose is not to cancel "dominant readings" but to expose their relative position. She also examines the unacknowledged influence of popular culture upon scholarship.

Narrative as Torah

With the work of Bal we are already well within a second major development in recent biblical studies, one that can be organized loosely under the heading "Narrative as Torah." Since biblical narrative is Torah, that is a teaching, what does it teach by virtue of being narrative and how does it teach? Torah aims to persuade. Narrative as Torah seeks to impart teachings powerful enough to affect an entire people. What does that entail? Here the overarching question, "Where does meaning reside?" is refocused to examine some broader issues about language and culture as reflected and reproduced in biblical narrative. The overlap among many of these angles of visions, and their intimate connections to the approaches mentioned above, is inevitable and often salutary.

Bal herself deliberately uses several different sets of theories and practices in analysis of biblical narrative.

With many postmodern critics she claims that the text is not an object to be interpreted but a subject who speaks to us. Interpretation is equally dependent on a reader's response. Her work, deliberately, stands at the intersection of several major tributaries of current biblical research on narrative. The critical task, not just the feminist task, is to account for the permanent interaction between social and individual processes.

Because all interpretations and critical analyses come from within several interdependent systems, unmasking presuppositions is necessary. The goal is neither to debunk theories or interpretations nor to plead for some Archimedean or purist stance. It is a necessary exercise for realizing the inevitable relativity of all interpretation, and therefore the relative status of any interpretive claims to authority.

Undergirding the critical perspectives that Bal and other postmodern critics represent is the recognition that biblical narrative presupposes a writer, a reader, a text, and a world. In recent decades scholars have reflected in new ways on how these elements intersect in the production of meaning(s). Although these approaches baffle the uninitiated with their technical, inbred vocabulary, they constitute a significant development in biblical studies in the ways they problematize the questions of meaning. They jar interpreters out of the naive assumption that what we mean by meaning is self-evident.

Structuralism locates meanings of narrative not in the vocabulary, plot, or characters of the text, but in its deep structures. Structuralists bracket individual features in favor of the linguistic, symbolic, or cultural codes embodied in the narrative through universal principles of communication. Genesis 1-3, for example, is replete with bipolar oppositions that must be held together, heaven/earth, night/day, man/woman, good/evil, death/life, and mortality/immortality. Structuralists chart the movements between these oppositions and analyze the transformations that follow.

Deconstruction (among other things) is the skeptic's challenge to structuralism and to any claims that meanings are stable entities. Meanings are not contained *in* any of the identifiable or identified elements in the text, but discerned in the perpetual processes of differentiation from what they are and what they are not. Therefore meanings are fluid and contextual, indeterminate in nature. It is an error to construe deconstruction as a nihilist denial of meaning. What it rejects is privileged claims on behalf of some essential meanings that persist through time in language or words. According to deconstruction, the futile quest for authoritative, original meaning or permanent meaning is a misapprehension of what meaning is and how it operates.

From a deconstructionist perspective, Genesis 1-3 exemplifies the ways meaning and identity emerge through a process of differentiation. The sea and the earth, for example, are not entities as much as differentiations. This is even clearer in the development of humans: first we find differentiation from earth to create the first human, *'ādām*. Then follows yet another differentiation in which first woman . . . and then man . . . are further distinguished, culminating in the case of woman with the name. The meaning of man or woman in these chapters is contextual and relative. They derive their identity through their differences and separation.

Speech-acts theory asks not what narrative *means* but what it *does*. Words create events. They do not merely lie inert on a flat surface; they shape history (not merely reflect history) and must be understood within the historical context they have modified. The **Torah** in the sense of the teachings embodied in the **Pentateuch** is not merely descriptive but also prescriptive. It intends consequence: "So that your children will learn . . ." (Deut 31:13). For speech-acts theory, Genesis 1 is the paradigm example of the creative power of speech. However, this approach also seeks to understand the more ordinary ways in which the mutuality between language and world takes place *in* biblical narrative and *through* biblical narrative.

Historical considerations of a different sort emerge in a variety of investigative models that examine ideological aspects of biblical narrative. Although Sternberg identifies the ideological nature of the Hebrew Bible, he retains a narrow definition of the ideology. The social-philosophical work by Foucault, Jameson, and Eagleton illuminate texts as cultural products, serving a particular class, and exerting real socio-economic power on the world rather than a private intellectual experience of a reader. Materialist and new historicist investigations approaches to the Bible are among those that develop this line of investigation. Narratives are not only religiously "loaded" but economically charged. Decoding these dynamics is part of responsible interpretation. The reader may resist rather than assent to the forces embedded in the text. In biblical studies Gottwald stands out as pioneer in this line of interpretation.

Genesis 2-3, for example, takes on different meanings when we contemplate the prominence of food in this text and examine the repercussions. The root meaning "eat" occurs fourteen times in nineteen verses (Gen 3:1, 2, 3, 5, 6 [3 times], 11, 12, 13, 14, 17, 18, 19)! Food is linked with knowledge and domination. Genesis 2-3 focuses on means of production, splits them along gender lines, and subordinates one (woman and her procreation of children) to the other (man and his production of food). One asks: who benefits from these constructions of reality? What class produced these narratives? Who was to read them and why? How does this story function in society? What social and economic powers does it serve? What positions can a

responsible reader take vis-à-vis such a text, whether as a member of biblical religions or not? Like feminist analysis of gender issues, these analyses explore issues of class, race, and other overlooked ideologies in the text. The overarching assumption is that there are no texts or readers without ideologies. The question is always *what* they are, not *whether* they exist.

These perspectives, and others related to them, seek to discern or create commonly accessible responses to questions such as: Are meanings located in texts? If so how? What does it mean to interpret? Is meaning something stable, embodied in the words themselves or in the network of their specific or universal relations? Are the important relations on the surface or below it? And if it is in both, is there contiguity or tension between the two? What social forces and powers influence the creation and use of this text? How can we understand the world(s) of the text? How can it help us understand our world(s)? Given the significance that the **Torah** has been granted in religious and other cultural arenas, discussions about the very nature of meaning and its location remain consequential even when inconclusive.

Narrative theology, like speech-acts theory, attends to the impact of speech on the "real world" beyond the text. It focuses on the specific theological consequence of stories and on the ways this prescriptive literature functions. Like Alter's literary approach, narrative theology takes narrativity as a significant starting point but asks different questions. How are stories true? What does it mean really "to hear" a biblical story? What distinctive relations are there between stories and persons in communities? Narrative theology does not ask whether Genesis 1-3 is true as an event that happened but what does it mean to be true to the story. This account is a living tradition that shapes communities and the individuals within them. Selves and communities are consolidated by stories. Biblical stories contributed to the means and mode of this consolidation in particular ways. Biblical stories, especially the **Torah,** seek to compel moral and practical assent not merely convey information.

Canonical approaches attend to the meanings of the Hebrew Bible as Scripture, i.e., as accepted (and in the case of the **Torah** also self-proclaimed), authoritative, and sacred teachings. Imputed sanctity is not just another ingredient superficially added after everything else has been done. It is a transformative category for the purpose of interpretation and must be investigated as such. Even before Alter's literary approach, canonical criticism insisted on examining the text in its final form. Before narrative theology, it also argued for the unique role of the biblical text in communities. Childs's canonical approach is especially decisive for the **Torah.** In contrast to the two approaches just mentioned, it puts historical criticism at the service of interpreting the final form of the text in the context of communities for whom the text is authoritative. Childs's layered exploration in his Exodus commentary exemplifies the depth and breadth of such possibilities. It also differs from other approaches listed above in originating uniquely in biblical studies.[2]

Torah as Torah

In theory and practice, the **Torah** has been the centerpiece of Jewish life for over two millennia and the subject of its most intensive analytic explorations. For Jews who lived mostly in exile, as a minority among host nations, the text became homeland. It was the most deeply and persistently probed reality. Because Hebrew remained the language of study and prayer, not merely the language of the subject matter (Torah), rabbinic interpretations accrued a vast treasury of insights especially attentive to linguistic nuances. The Jewish exegetical tradition came to influence scholarly readings once the similarities between rabbinic interpretive practices and certain contemporary approaches were noted. Buber helped bridge the rabbinic approaches to the Bible and the scholarly world in earlier decades. Indirectly Alter serves a similar role. A new synthesis is developing through the work of scholars grounded in contemporary biblical scholarship and also deeply immersed in Jewish exegetical practices.

Intertextuality, philology, polyvalent meanings, indeterminacy, and word play are some rabbinic hallmarks that overlap with recent approaches to biblical narrative. The rabbis revelled in multiplicity of meanings and the playfulness of the text long before these were discovered by modern critics. They said the **Torah** has seventy faces. And the revelation at Sinai had 600,000 different meanings, as many as the persons who heard it. In the Medieval period the term *Pardes*—a loan word and cognate of the English paradise—came to encapsulate exegesis. The four letters that form the Hebrew word, P, R, D, and S respectively designated levels or meanings: plain *(peshat),* allusive *(remez),* deep *(derash),* and secret *(sod).* Every text must be plumbed for these levels. An appropriate, multilevel reading is a paradise. It is not that the **Torah** guides you to paradise; it is paradise. You enter and inhabit it through the gates of exegesis.

Magonet's reading of Genesis 2-3 exemplifies such a synthesis.[3] The title of his essay, "Leaving the Garden: Did They Fall or Were They Pushed?" already hints at the conclusion and plants a measure of indeterminacy. It also reflects the sense of play that characterizes this most serious, holy task of rabbinic exegesis.

Magonet notes the different narrative structures implicit in Jewish and Christian readings. In the Hebrew Bible, the unit goes uninterrupted from Gen 2:4 to 3:21. In the Hebrew version, then, the story pauses at

"And YHWH made skin clothings for Adam and his woman and dressed them." The encounter in the garden thus ends with divine compassion and practical provisions. "It is only the Christian chapter divisions, presumably because of the later importance attached to the story of the Fall, that make the artificial division at the beginning of chapter 3, thus isolating the episode of the snake" (113).

Magonet explores the pun on "naked" . . . in Gen 2:25 and "cunning" . . . in Gen 3:1. What does "naked" mean? He concludes that sexual connotations are at most secondary because the philological study of the verb in other contexts shows that the term means "helpless" or "vulnerable." Elsewhere it describes captives dragged to war (Isa 20:2-4), a fugitive soldier (Amos 2:16), or a helpless baby (Eccl 5:14). As for sin, it only enters the picture with the story of Cain (115-18). The story of the garden is thus the story of God as an overprotective parent who tries to keep the children from the pain of knowledge but nevertheless gives them the impetus to explore. "So did they fall, or were they pushed? And is the 'Fall' the cataclysm that some theologies see it as—or is it a first, necessary step towards emancipation of humanity?" (115). Magonet concludes with the earlier rabbis that eating of the fruit and the expulsion from the garden "gave the 'children' in Eden the chance to grow up. God cut the strings of the puppets and let them walk erect upon the earth" (121-22).

Like the title of Magonet's book, which gently and humorously points a finger at God, (who else could have pushed them?), so too the conclusion challenges God even as it affirms. In this reading, as in other Jewish arguments with God, loving and wrestling flow together.

Future Directions

With newer approaches to Torah as narrative firmly established alongside historical ones, the most urgent task for the decades ahead is implementing, rigorously, the basic insights of such approaches. A vast number of excellent literary analyses of narratives in the **Torah** have been published, but the book of the **Torah** as a unified story remains largely unexamined. Scholars looking at trees have overlooked the forest. Since the parts and the whole are invariably interdependent, atomistic analyses lose anchorage as long as the **Torah** has not been studied as an integrated narrative. One can only point to Clines's *The Theme of the Pentateuch,* which uses literary analysis to understand the ways the promises to ancestors function in the multiple levels throughout the entire **Torah** and to Mann's *The Book of the Torah,* which uses Alter's literary approach to read the **Torah** as an integrated story. Plaut's *The Torah,* although it does not do so in a systematic fashion, nevertheless attempts to connect the parts with the whole. One still looks for studies that investigate in light of the new questions just how the five books of the **Torah** interact as "chapters" of the **Torah.** The literary significance of weaving poetry and laws into narrative still requires careful attention. Point of view studies are yet to appear. Polzin's pioneering analysis on the tension between the voice of Moses and those of the narrators in Deuteronomy[4] needs to extend to the **Torah** as a whole in order to understand how Moses is portrayed and what the undercurrents communicate. The development of characters such as God, Moses, Israel, or less prominent ones, in relation to plot, still awaits close scrutiny.

The dialogue between literary and historical issues needs to be revived in light of changing presuppositions and questions. Alter rightly claims that the Bible reflects "a complete interfusion of literary art with theological, moral, or historiographical vision, the fullest perception of the latter dependent of the fullest grasp of the former" (Alter, 19). It remains a future task to translate this assertion into studies of the **Torah.** At this stage literary critics largely pay lip service to traditional or postmodern historical questions and do not engage their findings. They wrestle more directly with theological issues, but shy away from exploring the moral implications of **Torah** narratives. Here contributions from other fields can assist the biblical scholar. Nussbaum's study of literature and the moral point of view[5] opens new perspectives for understanding how great literature shapes readers' morality by *complicating* their sympathies. Her insights shed light on the sympathetic treatment of Esau and other marginalized figures, and presses one to reformulate notions of morality. Pursuing these new directions demands greater collaboration among approaches and among critics. Like Israel at the end of the **Torah,** biblical scholars at the end of the millennium have heard the promises, have witnessed their potential, and have accepted obligations. Fulfillment belongs to the future.

Notes

[1] "A Question of Boundaries: Toward a Jewish Feminist Theology of Self and Others," in *Tikkun* 3/6 (May/June) 1991 43-46 and 87.

[2] See B. S. Childs, *The Book of Exodus: A Critical, Theological Commentary,* OTL (Philadelphia: Westminster, 1974), and *Introduction to the Old Testament as Scripture* (Westminster, 1979).

[3] Jonathan Magonet, *A Rabbi's Bible* (London: SCM, 1991) esp. 111-22.

[4] Robert Polzin, *Moses and the Deuteronomist: A Literary Study of the Deuteronomic History* (New York: Seabury, 1990) esp. 1-72.

[5] See Martha C. Nussbaum, *Love's Knowledge: Essays on Philosophy and Literature* (New York and Oxford: Oxford University Press, 1990) esp. 230-44 and 335-64.

Selected Bibliography

Alter, Robert. *The Art of Biblical Narrative.* New York: Basic Books, 1981.

Bal, Mieke. *Lethal Love: Feminist Literary Readings of Biblical Love Stories.* Bloomington: Indiana University Press, 1987.

Bar-Efrat, Shimon. *Narrative Art in the Bible.* JSOTSup. 70. Sheffield: Almond, 1989 (orig. in Hebrew, 1979).

Buber, Martin. *Moses: The Revelation and the Covenant.* Atlantic Highlands, N.J.: Humanities Press International, 1988 (origin. 1946).

Clines, David J. A. *The Theme of the Pentateuch.* JSOTSup. 10. Sheffield: JSOT, 1978.

Fokkelman, Jan P. *Literary Art in Genesis: Specimens of Stylistic and Structural Analysis. JSOT.* Sheffield: JSOT, 1991. (origin. 1975).

Leibowitz, Nehamah. *Studies in Genesis,* 4th rev. ed. Translated by Aryeh Newman. Jerusalem: World Zionist Organization, Department of Torah Education and Culture in the Diaspora, 1981.

———. *Studies in Exodus.* Translated by Aryeh Newman. Jerusalem: World Zionist Organization, Department of Torah Education and Culture in the Diaspora, 1981.

———. *Studies in Leviticus.* Translated by Aryeh Newman. Jerusalem: World Zionist Organization, Department of Torah Education and Culture in the Diaspora, 1980.

———. *Studies in Numbers,* rev. ed. Translated by Aryeh Newman. Jerusalem: World Zionist Organization, Department of Torah Education and Culture in the Diaspora, 1981.

———. *Studies in Deuteronomy.* Translated by Aryeh Newman. Jerusalem: World Zionist Organization, Department of Torah Education and Culture in the Diaspora, 1981.

Mann, Thomas W. *The Book of the Torah: The Narrative Integrity of the Pentateuch.* Atlanta: John Knox, 1988.

Pardes, Ilana. *Countertraditions in the Bible: A Femi-*

nist Approach. Cambridge, Mass. and London: Harvard University Press, 1992.

Plaut, Gunther, Bernard J. Bamberger, William W. Hallo. *The Torah: A Commentary*. New York: Union of American Hebrew Congregations, 1981.

Sternberg, Meir. *The Poetics of Biblical Narrative: Ideological Literature and the Drama of Ideological Reading*. Bloomington: Indiana University Press, 1985.

Trible, Phyllis. *God and the Rhetoric of Sexuality*. OBT. Philadelphia: Fortress, 1978.

Abbreviations

Abbreviations of Commonly used Periodicals, Reference Words, and Serials (with additions to the SBL abbreviation list noted with an asterisk)

AB	Anchor Bible
ABD	*Anchor Bible Dictionary**
ARBL	Anchor Bible Reference Library*
ANET	J. B. Pritchard (ed.), *Ancient Near Eastern Texts*
AOAT	Alter Orient and Altes Testament
ATD	Das Alte Testament Deutsch
ATDan	Acta theologica danica
BAR	*Biblical Archaeologist Reader*
Bib	*Biblica*
BibRev	*Bible Review*
BZAW	Beihefte zu ZAW
CBQ	*Catholic Biblical Quarterly*
CBQMS	Catholic Biblical Quarterly Monograph Series
DJD	Discoveries in the Judean Desert
FOTL	The Forms of Old Testament Literature
FRLANT	Forschungen zur Religion und Literatur des Alten und Neuen Testaments
HAR	Hebrew Annual Review
HBC	J. L. Mays, et al. (eds.), *Harper's Bible Commentary*
HKAT	Handkommentar zum Alten Testament
HSM	Harvard Semitic Monographs
HTR	*Harvard Theological Review*
HUCA	Hebrew Union College Annual
IBC	Inerpretation: A Bible Commentary for Teaching and Preaching
IDB	George Buttrick (ed.), *Interpreter's Dictionary of the Bible*
IEJ	*Israel Exploration Journal*
JAAR	*Journal of the American Academy of Religion*
JBL	*Journal of Biblical Literature*
JSOT	*Journal for the Study of the Old Testament*
JSOTSup	Journal for the Study of the Old Testament--Supplement Series

NCB	New Century Bible
ORO	Orbis biblicus et orientalis
OBT	Overtures to Biblical Theology
OTL	Old Testament Library
RB	*Revue biblique*
SBLDS	SBL Dissertation Series
SBLMS	SBL Monograph Series
SBLSP	SBL Seminar Papers
SBLSS SeL	Semeia Series
SBT	Studies in Biblical Theology
SHANE	Studies in the History of the Ancient Near East*
SJOT	*Scandinavian Journal of Theology**
SSN	Studia semitica neerlandica
SUNT	Studien zur Umwelt des Neuen Testaments
TUMSR	Trinity University Monograph Series in Religion*
VT	*Vetus Tesamentum*
VTSup	Vetus Tesamentum, Supplements
WBC	Word Biblical Commentary
WMANT	Wissenschaftliche Monographien zum Alten und Neuen Testament
ZA	*Zeitschrift für Assyriologie*
ZAW	*Zeitschrift für die alttestamentliche Wissenschaft*

Abbreviations of Books Cited Often in this Work

Blenkinsopp,	*Pentateuch* Blenkinsopp, Joseph. *The Pentateuch: An Introduction to the First Five books of the Bible*, ARBL. New York: Doubleday, 1992.
Childs,	*Introduction* Childs, Brevard. *Introduction to the Old Testament as Scripture*. Philadelphia: Fortress, 1979.
Clines,	*Theme* Clines, David J. A. *The Theme of the Pentateuch*, JSOTSup 10. Sheffield: JSOT, 1978.
Cross,	*Canaanite Myth* Cross, Frank More. *Canaanite Myth and Hebrew Epic: Essays in the History of the Religion of Israel*. Cambridge: Harvard University Press, 1973.
Hayes, ed.,	*Form Criticism* Hayes, John. *Old Testament Form Criticism*, TUMSR 2. San Antonio: Trinity University Press, 1974.
Knight/Tucker, eds.,	*Hebrew Bible* Knight, Douglas, and Gene Tucker, ed. *The Hebrew Bible and Its Modern Interpreters*. Chico, CA: Scholars Press, 1985.
Mann,	*Torah* Mann, Thomas W. *The Book of the Torah; The Narrative Integrity of the Pentateuch*. Atlanta: John Knox Press, 1988.
Polzin,	*Moses* Polzin, Robert. *Moses and the Deuteronimist: A Literary Study of the Deuteronomic History,Part I: Deute-*

Polzin,   *ronomy, Joshua, Judges.* New York: Seabury, 1980.

Samuel Polzin, Robert. Samuel and the Deuteronimist: A Literary Study of the Deuteronomic History, Part II: 1 Samuel. San Francisco: Harper & Row, 1989.

David L. Petersen (essay date 1995)

SOURCE: "The Formation of the *Pentateuch*" in *Old Testament Interpretation: Past, Present, and Future: Essays in Honor of Gene M. Tucker,* edited by James Luther Mays, David L. Petersen, and Kent Harold Richards, Abingdon Press, 1995, pp. 31-45.

[In this essay, Petersen examines the compositional history of the Pentateuch *and its effect on interpreting the literary and historical unity of the text.]*

The title of this essay betrays one way of thinking about the **Pentateuch,** namely, a concern with its history, how it came to exist. To be sure, not all scholars today are interested in this issue. Some would prefer to talk about the literary configuration of the **Pentateuch,** its theme, canonical shape, or theological purport. In fact, the move away from questions about compositional history mark one major development in Pentateuchal studies during the twentieth century. Nonetheless, concern about Pentateuchal origins continues to generate important contributions to the field and regularly appears as a prime topic of interest for firsttime students of the Hebrew Bible. Moreover, theories about the formation of the **Pentateuch** serve as watermarks for the critical study of biblical literature.

In this essay, I will first address several introductory issues, followed by comments about theories concerning the formation of the **Pentateuch.** Then, after brief remarks concerning the literary and canonical approaches, I will take a specific case, the flood account, and examine it from the perspective of the current discussion as well as point to one potential mode for future research.

Introductory Issues

The first portion of this essay addresses four important introductory issues: (1) diversity in source-critical theories about the formation of the **Pentateuch;** (2) the impact of diverse methods on understanding the formation of the **Pentateuch;** (3) the problem of Deuteronomy as a part of the **Pentateuch;** and (4) ambiguity in the meaning of "literary."

First, when one reads general introductions to Hebrew Bible studies, one receives the impression that there is one general hypothesis, namely the source-critical

theory, that scholars have used to explain the origins of the **Pentateuch** (or the Tetrateuch—Genesis through Numbers, or the Hexateuch—Genesis through Joshua). Such a judgment, however, does us a disservice to the extent that it masks the complexity of earlier discussions about these origins.

By the end of the nineteenth century, scholars in Europe had advanced three basic models for the formation of the **Pentateuch.** The source-critical model was only one of these, though its general contours are now the most widely known. Franz Delitzsch acted as a powerful spokesman for the notion that the **Pentateuch** is made up essentially of three narrative sources (P=Priestly; E=Elohistic; J=Yahwistic) and one embellished legal collection (D=Deuteronomy). A redactor or editor, spliced these documents together, resulting in the composition Genesis through Deuteronomy. Though Julius Wellhausen's name is routinely associated with this notion, Wellhausen was not responsible for identifying the four constituent documents. He inherited the idea of multiple sources from a long line of studies devoted to the **Pentateuch.** Wellhausen rang a change on the earlier theories by arguing that the relative age of the sources was different than had been supposed, namely, that P, instead of being the earliest, was the latest one, hence the well-known sequence, JEDP (one earlier theory had it PEJD). The source-critical answer to the question about how the **Pentateuch** was formed achieved such prominence and consensus that the **Pentateuch** could be divided, verse by verse, into these four sources (see, conveniently, the Appendix to Noth's *A History of Pentateuchal Traditions* and more recently, Campbell and O'Brien's *Sources of the Pentateuch*).

This source-critical hypothesis not only allowed the **Pentateuch** to be divided into three narrative strands (D is not really a narrative); it also involved theories about their respective relationships. Most scholars of this persuasion thought that there were at least three independent versions of Israel's early history. One version had it that J represented a version rooted in the Southern Kingdom, E a version native to northern soil, and P a document that, while not geographically distinctive, focused on a particular topic, the ritual implications of God's relation to Israel. All three arose somewhat independently, at least in their written versions, and were synthesized either by P or by a later redactor in the postexilic era.

However, two other models competed with the aforementioned source-critical or documentary one. The so-called fragmentary theory admitted that the **Pentateuch** was indeed made up of resources. But rather than extended narratives, Alexander Geddes, among others (e.g., Vater and De Wette), maintained that the ingredients were smaller, e.g., a few laws or a set of stories about one person. Documents or sources may have eventuated, but in the formative period much smaller literary units existed than those Delitzsch thought extended across several biblical books. By contrast, Geddes thought there were two primary series, characterized by the presence of the two different divine names, but these were redactional collections, not unified sources. They held nothing of the thematic or literary consistency claimed for a J or P by source critics.

A third model—the supplementary approach—attempted to combine the most compelling features of the two aforementioned ones, i.e., the notions of both source and fragment. Since there is a story line in the **Pentateuch,** some have thought that it should be attributed to a basic source, rather than to the final editor, which is the case with the fragment hypothesis. To this basic source, additions of various sorts—stories, genealogies, legal materials—have been added over time. Ewald, for example, argued early in his career that E was the basic source and had been supplemented by J material. Others, like Bleek, maintained that J was primary and had been supplemented by E. Unlike the source-critical hypothesis, however, the supplementary theory does not necessarily ascribe coherence to the various so-called E entries into the J document. If the criteria for identifying a source include coherence and significant scope, the supplementary theory allows for only one source, everything else is smaller-scale addition.

In sum, by the end of the nineteenth century, there were a number of models, each of which included the assumption that the **Pentateuch** resulted from a complicated history of literary developments. And though the models are conceptually distinct, each allowed the claim that the **Pentateuch** resulted from the integration of diverse texts and/or traditions. As we will see, all three models have their advocates in the late twentieth century.

Second, the pursuit of other methods, i.e., form criticism and tradition history, has created a challenge to the most common model, the source-critical hypothesis. Major turns may be associated with the names of Gunkel, Noth, and Rendtorff. One hallmark of the source-critical hypothesis was the notion of a long story narrated in several distinct literary traditions. Not only was there a narrative involving the family of Terah in Genesis, this story continued with the group known as Israel, in Egypt with Moses, and in the wilderness, with the people poised to return to the Promised Land. Moreover, the story had its beginnings in the so-called primeval period, in which the generational sequence involved all humans. The tale was virtually epic in scale. It moved from considering all people, to a family and its geographic movements and exile to the beginnings of a people, who migrated with difficulty from Egypt and stood, looking at the Promised Land from the plains of Moab.

Gunkel's investigations of Genesis narrowed the focus from that large narrative down to the individual stories, each of which appeared to have its own literary integrity. The stories within the story received pride of place. These sagas (also termed "legends") themselves possessed the hallmarks of narrative, e.g., Gen 32:22-32, and, hence, could be studied as such. And since some of these stories could apparently occur in one or another context, e.g., Gen 12:10-20-20:1-18, the larger story line no longer seemed so important. The more scholars devoted attention to these smaller scenes, the less they attended to the longer sources. Still, most scenes were regularly deemed to have the characteristics of J (e.g., Gen 18:1-16), E (e.g., Gen 20:1-18) or P (e.g., Gen 17:1-14). Hence, even though form-critical work had focused on individual sagas, there was, initially, no perceived tension between that perspective and earlier source-critical work. Form criticism was typically understood to focus on the oral stage of Israel's literature whereas source criticism was treating a later, written form. Gunkel continued to use source-critical language, but for him the sources were more accretions of sagas rather than a carefully worked out narrative structure.

One should observe that the very model for understanding early Israelite literature had shifted. Whereas Wellhausen et al., had spoken about literary documents and written sources, Gunkel attended to the preliterary, predocumentary stages of Israelite literature. Though Wellhausen agreed that oral material lay behind the great sources, he maintained "this, however, is not the place to attempt a history of the development of Israelite legend" (296). Gunkel provided that place.

Martin Noth attempted to explain the process by means of which the small sagas emerged in larger literary compositions. Building on Gunkel's own judgments, Noth argued that the shorter narratives ("traditions") were combined around certain individuals and at discrete locations, e.g., Jacob at Shechem as opposed to Jacob in the Trans-Jordan. At a later stage, these localized traditions, which could include several narratives, coalesced around several "themes," e.g., "promise to the patriarchs," that make up the **Pentateuch** (Noth identified five such themes).

As had Gunkel before him, Noth, too, attempted to accommodate a source-critical approach to his so-called traditio-historical method. He continued to speak of J, E, and P. Noth understood P, the latest significant literary activity to be an editorial context into which the earlier J/E material was placed. However, behind J/E, Noth postulated a basic source ("G"—*Grundlage*) that presented the earliest form of the Israelite story extending across the **Pentateuch.** Noth offered this analysis at the outset of his *A History of Pentateuchal Traditions* and returned to it at the end, but the relation between the rest of the volume and this homage to earlier source-critical work was never entirely clear.

More impressive than the literary coherence of Israel's narrative was Noth's identification of a number of diverse collections of traditions within the **Pentateuch.**[1] The narratives in Genesis 12-37 seemed fundamentally different from those involving the wilderness, which in turn are different from those involving Sinai. In addition, Noth maintained that the narratives about each patriarch were originally unrelated, in large part because the individuals were geographically isolated. Some redactor had created their genealogical relationships as a late artifice. And the more one focused on those "themes" or even smaller collections (e.g., Jacob at Shechem), the more one is pulled away from studying the story line of an entire Pentateuchal source. Von Rad and Noth had intended to speak about the midrange stage in the evolution of Israelite literature. If the short sagas came first, and if the **Pentateuch** came last, then medium length collections, themselves of various levels of complexity (e.g., Jacob is made up of Jacob/Laban and Jacob/Esau), were a logical step. But how do the classical sources fit with form critically or traditio-historically defined literary units? For von Rad, the answer was more clear than it was for Noth.

To be sure, each of the methods treats a different entity and on a different scale, form criticism—the individual saga, tradition history—a collection such as that about Abraham and Sarah, and source criticism—the literary unit that extends throughout four books. And yet, if the genesis of the literature occurs in a manner like that proposed by Noth, the sources are really no longer sources. They are the results of a long process of literary formation, and far less the result of conscious redaction like the one von Rad proposed for J. In sum, one could say that both form criticism and tradition history challenge implicitly the claims of source criticism. With Noth one focuses on discrete "themes" or collections, not on consistent literary narratives that extend across the first four books of the Hebrew Bible.

What was implicit in Noth's work, R. Rendtorff made explicit. Rendtorff reviewed the aforementioned studies and sensed that Noth had posed a fundamental challenge to the classical source-critical hypothesis. If the literature began with the short sagas, which were later collected in smaller entities, and if these entities developed into even larger units (Noth's "themes"), Rendtorff wanted to know whether the sorts of continuities argued in the source-critical hypothesis were common to these larger units. Hence, he analyzed one of the mid-size complexes, the patriarchal stories, and, as well, assessed the nature of the connections between such complexes.[2] On the basis of that research, Rendtorff maintained that these "larger units" are remarkably independent and betray different histories of

development as well as diverse theological perspectives. Only with the priestly tradition or redactor may one identify an integration of several (but not all of the) literary components that make up the **Pentateuch.** Rather than a narrative, "P" comprises a set of chronological notices (e.g., Gen 16:16; 17:24) and "theological passages" (e.g., Gen 17; 35:9-13). Rendtorff maintained, however, that P did not provide the overarching redaction that, in effect, created the **Pentateuch.** Rather, he discerned a number of texts that highlight the promise of land (e.g., Gen 22:16; 26:3; 50:24; Exod 13; 33:1-3*a;* Num 11:11-15), texts that Rendtorff attributes to some form of D. This D material occurs in every major unit in the **Pentateuch** except the primeval history. Still, Rendtorff and others have called the very notion of a Pentateuchal source fundamentally into question. The challenge is rooted in the methods at work, here form criticism followed by tradition history.

Third, the mention of D raises questions both about that source and the book of Deuteronomy itself. The book of Deuteronomy concludes the **Pentateuch.** And yet, its place in the **Pentateuch** as well as in discussions about the formation of the **Pentateuch** remain problematic. Since Deuteronomy ends with Israel outside the land, some scholars maintain that the first literary entity of the Hebrew is not the **Pentateuch,** but is rather the Hexateuch, namely, a body of literature ending with Joshua in which Israel enters the land. Only in this way are the promises made to the mothers and fathers of Israel about entering and possessing land brought to fruition. However, others have observed that Israel stands in roughly the same location at both the end of Numbers and Deuteronomy, viz., in the plains of Moab. When one takes seriously the **Pentateuch** in its final form, Israel is positioned outside the land (one might say in exile). Moreover, such an emphasis on life outside the Promised Land allows one to speak of a Tetrateuch that would have the same position on the fulfillment of promises concerning land as does the **Pentateuch.** The notion of a Tetrateuch with its own literary and theological integrity complements Noth's conception of a deuteronomistic history, of which Deuteronomy is the prologue. Hence, with the model either of the Hexateuch or the Tetrateuch, it is possible to maintain that Deuteronomy has a remarkably ambiguous role as the final literary component of the **Pentateuch.** According to such a reading, the **Pentateuch** may be understood as a late literary and theological construct, with Deuteronomy more integral to the deuteronomistic history than it is to the **Pentateuch** itself.

And there is a related question: To what extent is D, whether nuanced as deuteronomic or deuteronomistic (see the essay by D. Knight on this distinction), material present in Genesis-Numbers? If D is not present in the Tetrateuch, then the book of Deuteronomy looks even more unrelated to the initial portion of the Hebrew Bible. But if, on the other hand, D appears in Genesis through Numbers, then the **Pentateuch** would appear to have greater coherence.

Not surprisingly, scholars differ in their judgments about the measure of D in the Tetrateuch. It would probably be best to conduct such a discussion on a book by book, or major section by major section inventory. For example, there have been stronger arguments made on behalf of D in Exodus (e.g., Exod 13:3-16) than there have on behalf of D in Genesis. Noth apparently discerned nothing in Genesis that might reasonably be attributed to D. Others, e.g., Rendtorff, have identified D in all four Tetrateuchal books. Moreover, Rendtorff has identified critical instances in which linkages between the Tetrateuch and the deuteronomistic history occur when D material occurs in the Tetrateuch, e.g., Exod 1:6, 8 and Judg 2:8, 10. Blum has argued on behalf of an even more important D presence. For him, the first literary unit that crosses the boundaries of biblical books is a product of D (Blum's so-designated KD, D-Komposition), which reaches from the patriarchal literature to the narratives locating Israel in the desert (even for Blum, there is some evidence for an earlier and longer narrative, something akin to Noth's *Grundlage*). Since Blum and, more recently, Blenkinsopp have argued on behalf of D (or D-related) material throughout the Tetrateuch (e.g., Exodus 19-24), one might claim that there is a trend toward identifying greater and greater deuteronomistic redactional activity in the Tetrateuch, though the evidence for such D material in Genesis is less than assured (Blenkinsopp argues that Genesis 15 includes D-like material).[3]

To conclude this discussion about the place of D in the **Pentateuch,** one should raise a more formal question, which is relevant to literature beyond that normally ascribed to D: How are we to explain the place of legal material in the **Pentateuch** or Tetrateuch? Apart from the laws in Deuteronomy itself, there are legal collections in Exodus, Numbers, and Leviticus, the book of the Covenant (Exod 20:22-23:33), law of the Nazirite (Num 6:1-21), and Holiness Code (Leviticus 17-26), respectively. There has been a strong tendency to view these materials both to be the result of supplements and to be, themselves, supplemental additions to the more original narratives. And yet, if the speeches of Moses provide an intense soliloquy near the end of the **Pentateuch,** their purport must not be underestimated. Alternatively, some have appealed to the principle of literary symmetry and maintained that the prescriptions of Leviticus occupy the pivotal position in the **Pentateuch.** The key issue requiring further analysis, however, is the role that the laws play—whether in Exodus, Leviticus, or Deuteronomy—in their narrative setting.

Fourth, the previous pages presume a refined set of critical vocabulary, e.g., D and Dtr. Yet one term remains almost systematically ambiguous. During the twentieth century, the adjective "literary," when used in pentateuchal studies, has born a variety of meanings, a situation that bedevils those reading studies of the **Pentateuch** written in various decades. Earlier, scholars used the term literary criticism as simply another way of describing source criticism. This happened primarily because German scholars had used the term *Literarkritik* to label the source-critical endeavor (*Quellenforschung* and *Urkundenhypothese* were also part of the German vocabulary). And, after all, the primary criteria for identifying the hypothetical sources were literary, variations in vocabulary, literary style, et al.

As is well known now, however, a sea of change in biblical scholarship occurred during the final third of the twentieth century. Scholars began exploring biblical texts using the analytical tools of literary studies, i.e., by attending to issues like imagery, theme, characterization, plot development, and the like. This exercise, too, was deemed literary criticism. But it was often fundamentally uninterested in questions of literary formation. Hence, the phrase literary criticism, when applied to the **Pentateuch,** may mean quite different things, an ambiguity that regularly perplexes newcomers to biblical studies.

Theories About the Formation of the Pentateuch

Many writers commenting recently on Pentateuchal studies have described the field as in crisis, in part because there have been such diverse proposals concerning the formation of that literature. To be sure, disagreements do run rife. But I would maintain that the current discussion about the **Pentateuch**'s origins corresponds in considerable measure to earlier differing hypotheses. Whereas earlier vigorous disagreements often cut on religious lines (i.e., so-called liberal versus conservative positions), the dividing lines are now less religious and more methodological. One might, therefore, claim that there is no more of a crisis in pentateuchal studies than there ever has been.

One may review a number of recent, influential works in Pentateuchal studies and maintain that the three major alternatives within the critical paradigm are still before us. First, though sometimes deemed dated, most scholars adjudge that some form of the source-critical hypothesis still serves well to explain certain features of the **Pentateuch,** i.e., that there are at least two originally independent literary traditions of significant scale that have been combined in the Tetrateuch. In much of the current discussion, the debate has centered around whether P is truly a source or is simply a supplement. The former option has been advocated vigorously by, among others, Steck and Westermann.[4] So, even though the presence of E is ambiguous, the **Pentateuch** results from at least JDP.

The supplementary hypothesis probably has more adherents than might appear to be the case. Although such classifications are risky, it would appear that both Blenkinsopp's and Van Seters's work belongs in this vein. Van Seters has argued that the J source runs throughout the **Pentateuch.** Unlike the standard source-critical hypothesis, Van Seters deems the Yahwist to be a late, i.e., exilic, composition using earlier sources, and designed to function as a prologue to the deuteronomistic history. Since Van Seters denies the existence of E, his model is something like DJP (though D stands outside the Tetrateuch). Van Seters analysis results from a combination of explicit concern for form, "history writing," and more implicit (and traditional) source criticism. Blenkinsopp, too, uses fairly traditional source-critical perspectives, but, in his case, in dialogue with literary (new literary) observations. And, Blenkinsopp claims that P is primary, with J as a supplement.

Though presented in more programmatic than definitive fashion, Cross has articulated this position with considerable force. Cross maintains the primacy of a so-called poetic epic tradition, which evolved in two different prose forms; J in the south and E in Israel. In the Tetrateuch, at least, there is no evidence of D. And P, rather than an independent prose tradition, was a supplement or redaction to the J/N narrative. P structured the earlier material by introducing a system of convenants, formulaic references to generations . . . , e.g., Gen 5:1; 6:9, and station formulae (Exod 16:1). However, Cross identifies few if any P narratives (the cave of Macpelah episode, Genesis 23, is the primary exception). In sum, Cross, too, advances a perspective that may be viewed as consistent with the supplementary approach.

Rendtorff's analysis is, in my judgment, consistent with those whose work has been identified with the fragment approach. As had scholars in the nineteenth century, Rendtorff denied that any sources extended throughout Genesis, much less the Tetrateuch. Rather, as sketched above, Rendtorff argued on behalf of originally distinct collections of tradition that were placed into a story line only at a fairly late stage.

Literary and Canonical Approaches to the Pentateuch

Discussions about the form, if not formation, of the **Pentateuch** are, however, proceeding along other tracks as well, in part because some scholars have adopted a postcritical paradigm. And to this extent, contemporary scholarly discussions of the **Pentateuch** are indeed more complicated than they were at the end of the nineteenth century. As noted earlier, some scholars are interested in understanding the literary structures, themes, et al., and often uninterested in questions about the formation of the text. A similar ploy, though sometimes a more theologically motivated one, involves an interest in exploring the canonical shape of books or larger entities, such as the **Pentateuch.** Though quite different in their conceptual positions, those pursuing either a literary or a canonical approach may, in principle, be uninterested in pursuing questions about the origins of a text.

Both literary and canonical methods have achieved important results. As for the former, David Clines has argued that it is possible to speak about a primary theme at work throughout the **Pentateuch.** He provides the following definition:

> The theme of the **Pentateuch** is the partial fulfillment—which implies also the partial non-fulfillment—of the promise to or blessing of the patriarchs. The promise or blessing is both the divine initiative in a world where human initiatives always lead to disaster, and a re-affirmation of the primal divine intentions of man. The promise has three elements: posterity, divine-human relationship, and land.[5]

Such a judgment depends upon a carefully wrought definition of theme, which derives from the world of literary criticism. Moreover, such a judgment reflects in no consequential way considerations about the historical background of the literature in question or questions about the development of that literature. Instead, the reader treats the **Pentateuch** in its final form, without attending to genetic questions.

The latter mode, what has been termed by some as canonical criticism, also focuses on a given, the first five books of the Hebrew Bible. However, it is a given not simply as literature but because religious communities deemed it to be a Pentateuch, a controlling portion of the canon. For Childs, there is a "canonical shape" and shaping. Not only is there a conscious five-fold division, with the interior three books distinct from the surrounding frame, but also the very shape of the canonical story leaves Israel outside the land, a situation that emphasizes the prominence of Torah rather than territory.

> For the biblical editors, the first five books constituted the grounds of Israel's life under God and provided a critical norm of how the Mosaic tradition was to be understood by the covenant people.[6]

As the vocabulary of that sentence demonstrates, Childs is fully open to the notion of various authors and editors, i.e., the question of the **Pentateuch**'s formation. Moreover, his canonical perspective is informed by the notion of editors shaping material. However, the canonical form presents testimony apart from reconstructions of the **Pentateuch**'s formation.

There has been a tendency among some recent literary critics to pursue purely literary issues and then use their conclusions to address the problems of literary formation a la the source-critical hypothesis, without engaging the hypothesis directly. For example, it is not unusual to find an individual arguing that a biblical author is using the artifice of tension—different vocabulary and different literary style—to create a narrative, whereas such evidence would have been used by the source critic to maintain the presence of diverse traditions or sources. Similarly, evidence of a complicated plot or literary structure is often deemed as evidence for a sole author, rather than multiple traditions.[7] Such judgments may, on occasion, seem interesting, and yet rarely do they have the force necessary to offer an alternative to the various source-critical hypotheses.

The Flood Narrative

There are a number of parade examples for the classical form of the source-critical hypothesis. One that regularly appears in textbooks and introductory lectures is the flood story, Gen 6:5-9:17. During much of the twentieth century, most commentators agreed not only that these chapters could be allocated either to the J or P source, but they also held J to be the earlier version, which had later been supplemented by the P material (whether as independent source or redactional addition). The consensus was strong enough that the two versions were printed up separately in a standard volume such as von Rad's *Genesis*.

In thinking about these texts, it may prove useful to review the aforementioned recent proposals about the formation of the **Pentateuch** by articulating their respective positions, when evident, on the flood narrative. Blenkinsopp and Van Seters both argue that the flood story contains J and P material. Van Seters attributes the primary narrative to J and deems P to constitute a number of additions, chronology and the like, but P offers no different narrative elements. Blenkinsopp posits a diametrically opposed notion, namely, that P provides the primary story line and that J constitutes a series of additions, most notably the bird-sending scene. Here, two scholars, both working with source-critical perspectives, develop positions that stand in stark contrast. Cross appears similar to Van Seters, namely, maintaining the primacy of J and the supplementary character of P. Finally, Rendtorff, who would not admit a J source extending beyond the primeval history, does identify "two different literary strata" in the flood narrative.[8] However, he offers no explicit judgments about the primacy of one over the other, nor does he allow the status of either one as an independent narrative. Instead, he is inclined to speak of a narrative that has been supplemented. Especially

interesting here is the prominence of "supplementary" vocabulary in most of these positions.

Few scholars who work on the flood narrative dispute the multiple voices in that material, i.e., the sorts of arguments adduced in typical source-critical discussions. However, at the moment, there are at least three unresolved questions: (1) Are both traditions narratives, or is one only a supplement, i.e., not a full narrative? (2) Is it possible to determine which version is basic or primary? and (3) Is either tradition connected to or a part of a tradition outside the primeval history?

The third question lies beyond the scope of this essay. However, the first two questions, which are of fundamental importance to an assessment of the flood narratives' origins, may be addressed here. And in so doing, I offer one suggestion about the manner in which future study of these narratives (and more generally the **Pentateuch**) might proceed. Specifically, it would seem appropriate to use literary critical perspectives to address some of the issues that have arisen in the source-critical discussion.

The first question requires us to identify what we mean by a narrative. A narrative is more than a chronicle or annal. A chronicle may report events in a sequence, but it is not a narrative per se. A chronicle or annal does not present the literary dynamics typically associated with a story. Some literary critics speak of narrative structure that presents three primary components: an initial platform, followed by a complication and then a resolution. Others speak of rising and then falling action. Still others refer to the beginning, middle, and end of a narrative. All this language constitutes different ways to conceptualize what we mean by plot.

The notion of plot is of pivotal importance in addressing the first aforementioned question. If a body of textual material that has been attributed to one of the classic sources does not possess plot structure, then one might assume it to have the character of a supplement, and not that of a basic story.

If one reviews the flood texts attributed to J and P, it should, in theory, be possible to determine if either one or both embodies a plot.[9] Without making the exercise too arcane, one might ask specifically: does each of the accounts present a beginning, middle, and end? To address this question, we must make a tentative judgment about where the respective flood stories begin. The answer for P seems clear: with Gen 6:9. And most readers working from a source-critical perspective would point to Gen 6:5 for the J material. Yet, there is something peculiar about this beginning of the J flood account. Genesis 6:5-8 are a prologue to the story like that preserved in the Atrahasis epic, namely, that a deity wanted to destroy humankind. In that epic, the deity (Enlil) attempted drought and disease before turning to a flood. Genesis 6:5-8 does not refer specifically to a flood, only that God will "blot out humanity." And then J, in Gen 7:1, jumps to orders according to which Noah is to load and enter the ark. A major early portion of the flood story (as told in Atrahasis, Gilgamesh, and P) is not present in J, namely, the specific decision by the deity to effect a flood and the interaction with a human that results in the creation of an ark.

From this perspective alone, one might begin to argue that J presents only a partial narrative, a skeleton for the flood story as we know it elsewhere. It is important to note the methodological move, namely, to utilize a literary-critical category, narrative structure, to address a source-critical problem. In so doing, one is able to achieve leverage of a new sort on the topic of the literature's formation. In this case, the P version of the flood appears to present a more complete beginning of the narrative. J appears fragmentary when compared with the more complete narrative structure of P. Moreover, J seems to supplement that P narrative, for example, by introducing more detail regarding the bird-sending scene. But in no way does J present major new narrative moments. Such a judgment suggests that P has provided the basic narrative and that J works as a supplement to it. And these are the sorts of judgments that classical source criticism entailed, but could not readily resolve.

Such blending of critical perspectives should prove useful in addressing some of the basic questions vexing those interested in the formation of the **Pentateuch.** And, more generally, it may be possible for critical and postcritical perspectives to engage in fruitful dialogue, rather than to stand in an either isolated or antagonistic posture.

Directions for Future Research

This overview of theories about the formation of the **Pentateuch** suggests that the basic positions adumbrated by earlier scholars will continue to reappear. Theories articulated in the nineteenth century have achieved prominence in the twentieth century as well. Hence, one should expect to see the source, fragment, and supplementary theories in various forms. Vigorous debate between the various critical positions will continue. And, in the postcritical vein, some scholars with special interest in literary matters will be inattentive to questions about the **Pentateuch**'s formation. Others will utilize newer literary perspectives to argue that the **Pentateuch** was not so much formed—out of diverse traditions and at different times—but was created by a primary author. What one may hope for is a crossover, namely, that some scholars with expertise in literary matters will broach the question of the **Pentateuch**'s formation and will be conversant with the vigorous contemporary discussion about Pentateuchal formation.

In that way, new perspectives might be brought to bear upon a nodal problem in Hebrew Bible studies.

Scholars will also struggle with even broader questions: Is the **Pentateuch** a meaningful entity in its own right? What is the primary early Israelite story—is it presented in Genesis through Numbers, Genesis through Deuteronomy, or Genesis through Joshua? If the first, then the covenant at Sinai, particularly as understood from a ritual perspective, seems primary. If the second, then the promulgation of Mosaic Torah has been highlighted. And if the third, then accession of the land is the primary point of resolution.

These various judgments are essentially literary. However, the issues they raise will broaden to include social-world problems. For example, it will be necessary to ask: In what social environment would any of these literary works have been important? Some scholars maintain that the **Pentateuch** was elicited by the religious and social needs of Persian period Judah, particularly as that community was encouraged to codify its own "native" religious traditions by the Achaemenid empire. How would this community view the **Pentateuch**'s story of Israel outside the land? These topics are best suited to the social-world approach, a fact that emphasizes the need both for methodological clarity and the complementary use of various perspectives in the future.

Notes

[1] At this point in the argument, Noth depended decisively on von Rad's articulation of the various literary moments that make up the Pentateuch. And von Rad, even more than Noth, honored the source-critical perspective. For von Rad, the Yahwist was *the* author of the Pentateuch—both as writer and as redactor.

[2] For Rendtorff, important "larger units" in the Pentateuch are: the primeval story, the patriarchal story, Exodus 1-15 (Moses and Exodus), Exodus 19-24 (Sinai), Exodus 16-18 and Numbers 11-20 (wilderness), and occupation of the land.

[3] There is, of course, a related issue, namely, even if the Tetrateuch were deemed not to contain D material, it may have been composed to serve as a prologue to the deuteronomistic history.

[4] For example, O. Steck, "Aufbauprobleme in der Priesterschrift," *Ernte, was man sät: Festschrift für Klaus Koch zu seinem 65 Geburtstag,* ed. D. Daniels et al. (Neukirchen-Vluyn: Neukirchener, 1991) 28-308; C. Westermann, *Genesis 1-11* (Minneapolis: Augsburg, 1984), 588-600.

[5] D. Clines, *The Theme of the Pentateuch,* JSOTSup 10 (Sheffield: JSOT, 1978) 29.

[6] B. Childs, *Introduction to the Old Testament as Scripture* (Philadelphia: Fortress, 1979), 131-32.

[7] In that regard it is interesting to compare two articles that appeared in 1978: B. Anderson, "From Analysis to Synthesis: The Interpretation of Genesis 1-11," *JBL* 97 (1978), 23-39; G. Wenham, "The Coherence of the Flood Narrative," *VT*28 (1978) 336-48. The respective authors made a very similar argument about literary structure and yet diverged on the issue of literary formation.

[8] R. Rendtorff, *The Old Testament: An Introduction* (Philadelphia: Fortress, 1986) 133.

[9] Much in the analysis depends upon the specific divisions of the textual material. It is instructive to compare von Rad's divisions with those of Van Seters.

Selected Bibliography

Blenkinsopp, J. *The Pentateuch: An Introduction to the First Five Books of the Bible.* ABRL. New York: Doubleday, 1992.

Blum, E. *Studien zur Komposition des Pentateuch.* BZAW 189. Berlin: Walter de Gruyter, 1990.

Campbell, A., and M. O'Brien. *Sources of the Pentateuch: Texts, Introductions, Annotations.* Minneapolis: Augsburg, 1993.

Clines, D. *The Theme of the Pentateuch.* JSOTSup 10. Sheffield: JSOT 1978.

Cross, F. "The Priestly Work." In *Canaanite Myth and Hebrew Epic.* Cambridge, Mass.: Harvard University Press, 1973, 293-325.

de Pury, A. *Le Pentateuque en question: Les origines et la composition des cinq premiers livres de la Bible à la lumière des recherches récentes.* Le Monde de la Bible. Geneva: Labor et Fides, 1989.

Gunkel, H. *The Legends of Genesis: The Biblical Saga and History.* New York: Schocken, 1964.

Noth, M. *A History of Pentateuchal Traditions.* Englewood Cliffs, NJ: Prentice-Hall, 1972.

Rendtorff, R. *The Problem of the Process of Transmission in the Pentateuch.* JSOTSup 89. Sheffield: JSOT 1990.

Seters, J. Van. *Prologue to History: The Yahwist as Historian in Genesis.* Louisville: Westminster/John Knox, 1992.

von Rad, G. "The Form-Critical Problem of the Hexateuch." In *The Problem of the Hexateuch and Other Essays.* New York: McGraw-Hill, 1966, 1-78.

Wellhausen, J. *Prolegomenon to the History of Ancient Israel.* New York: Meridian, 1957.

Whybray, R. *The Making of the Pentateuch: A Methodological Study.* JSOTSup 53. Sheffield: JSOT 1987.

Mordechai Breuer (essay date 1996)

SOURCE: "The Study of *Bible* and the Primacy of the Fear of Heaven: Compatibility or Contradiction?" in *Modern Scholarship in the Study of "Torah": Contributions and Limitations,* edited by Shalom Carmy, Jason Aronson Inc., 1996, pp. 159-80.

[*In this essay, Breuer asserts that the* Torah *was directly written by God and that its different styles reflect different qualities of God.*]

The topic assigned to me implies a possible contradiction between the study of Bible and *yirat shamayim* (fear of heaven). The God-fearing student of the Bible must confront this presumed contradiction and seek to resolve it. Failing to do so, his wisdom will take precedence over his piety; even worse: as the result of psychological conflict, the scholar in him will undermine his piety and as one who is God-fearing he will reject his scholarship.

To address the alleged contradiction we must first define the concepts involved, the study of Bible, on the one hand, and *yirat shamayim* on the other hand. Then we shall see whether a real conflict exists and if it has a resolution. "Study of Bible," in our context, does not refer to the type of Bible study familiar to the Jewish people from the day the **Torah** was given. It is inconceivable that such Bible study could detract from one's *yirat shamayim*. To the contrary: not only is **Torah** study valuable because it leads to moral and religious action, but a strong grounding in all the areas of Jewish study, Bible, Mishnah, Jewish Law and Midrash, is essential to sustain the fear of God. The kind of study under scrutiny is that which has appeared in recent centuries, beginning with Jean Astruc, maintaining that the **Torah** is composed of distinct documents, each written in its own style, whose contents are in conflict. This paper will deal exclusively with the implications of this method of studying the **Torah,** by which I mean the Five Books of Moses (the **Humash**).

This hypothesis led to a new method of studying the Bible, known as "critical study of the Bible." This science, developed mainly by gentile scholars, achieved impressive results. The critics persuasively described the nature of the documents that, in their opinion, make up the **Torah.** Holding that the authorship of these documents by one person, as natural authorship is understood, is impossible, whether in Moses' generation or in any other, they inferred that several authors, differing among themselves in world outlook and literary style, wrote the **Torah.**

As we shall see below, when we look at the critical analysis of Genesis chapters 1 and 2, the author, called J, is distinguished by a sensitive, poetic soul. Another, dubbed P, was a man of law and order, of scientific mind-set, whose writing, exact and concise, lacks feeling and poetic flourish. The critics also characterized the other primary writers of the **Torah,** naming them E and D. These authors inhabit different spiritual worlds and different times and places. J came first, living in Judah at the height of the monarchy. Shortly afterward came E, who resided in Ephraim. Subsequent to and close to in spirit to E came D, who lived at the time of the prophet Jeremiah. P, the final writer, who had the most profound influence on the Jewish religion, lived either during the period preceding the destruction of the first temple or during the subsequent exile. Hundreds of years separate the first and last authors of the Bible. Yet these writers did not create their texts alone; they summarized and refined ancient traditions that reached them either through oral transmission or as written documents.

The transformation and development that made these sources into the **Torah** is often apparent between the lines. The editors exercised exquisite craftsmanship on centuries of tradition. The final stage of the **Torah's** composition is due to the redactor, R, who made an integrated text of these documents, which until then were distinct literary creations. When the redactor transcribed earlier documents without addition or subtraction, the strata are easily identified. When, however, he combined material from two or three documents, additions and deletions were necessary to avoid contradiction or repetition. Often the editor's patchwork does not disguise the gap between the original documents and the redactor's version.

The power of these inferences, based on solid argument and internally consistent premises, will not be denied by intellectually honest persons. One cannot deny the evidence before one's eyes. As committed believers, we cannot ignore what human reason points to with confidence; we cannot pretend that falsehood is truth. Therefore we cannot regard God's **Torah** as the unified composition of *one human author* in *one generation.* Willy-nilly, the **Torah** contains several documents, which, viewed as *natural products of human culture,* must have been written by different people over the course of many generations before their final redaction. It is the implications for *yirat shamayim* of the study of the **Torah** based on this method that we must investigate. But this requires that we define what is meant by *yirat shamayim.*

The accepted meaning of *yirat shamayim* is fear of sin. One who fears God is diligent in obeying His commandments, as meticulous in fulfilling the "lighter as the more grave," rigorously adhering to all that the halakhic literature determines as law. He wholeheartedly believes this law to be God's word, that God is concerned with the "four cubits of *halakhah,*" that defiance of God's will is inconceivable. This is what Jews mean by *yirat shamayim.* This definition engenders no conflict between the study of Bible and *yirat shamayim,* provided that the person who accepts the tenets of Bible Criticism truly fears God and scrupulously executes the obligations of Jewish law, dreading sin and joyful in the performance of the *mitzvot.* We might draw an analogy from Rav Kook's comments regarding the debate over the date of the composition of the Mishnah:

> The sanctity of the basic measures of the **Torah** is the same, whether these units were transmitted to Moses at Sinai or decrees of a court of law, because it is the nation's acceptance that is significant, and it is due to their commitment that we fulfill in purity even matters that are only decrees of later generations, such as the decrees of R. Gershom. Likewise there should be no difference in our wholehearted loyalty to the oral law, whether it was completed earlier or later. (*Iggerot HaRe'iyah* I 194)

These comments about the Oral Law might be applied to the written **Torah.** We can imagine an individual who holds that it makes no difference to our attitude toward the sanctity of the written **Torah** whether Moses wrote the **Torah** or whether an editor at the time of Ezra compiled the text. The essential point, in the view of such an individual, is the commitment of the nation to accept as binding the words of the **Torah** in its present form. What obligates us is our tradition; our ancestors and sages declare that God commands us to follow the teachings of the Sages even when there is no clear source for this in the written **Torah.** And just as the Jewish people have always fulfilled the Sages' teachings, the individual we are considering is prepared to accept the demands of the **Torah** even though, for him, its authority is based on the Sages' affirmation.

From the perspective of this individual, there is no possible conflict between critical study and *yirat shamayim:* at worst, he will continue to observe the entire **Torah** faithfully based on the authority of the Sages. The **Torah's** power to obligate us is undiminished; it derives from God, who commanded us to abide by the Sages' decrees. This is enough to provide *yirat shamayim.* Just as the God-fearer would never mock the law of the *Shulhan Arukh,* the Jewish Code of Law, even when it encodes later decrees, just as, for example, he eschews leavened bread that had been owned by a Jew during the Passover as carefully as he avoids bread on Passover itself, just as he joyfully celebrates the second festival day of the Diaspora as he fulfilled the obligations on the previous day—so he will treat with sanctity the **Torah** whose origin, in his opinion, derives from a post-Mosaic redactor.

The previous discussion is not merely hypothetical. Quite a few scholars, and their students, identify with the findings of biblical scholarship, yet faithfully and reverently observe the full scope of *halakhah,* meaning that they adopt halakhic minutiae as determined by recognized rabbinic authority, even as they harbor no doubt about the late authorship of the **Torah.** This is because they see the acceptance by the Jewish people as the essential factor and they are committed to obeying the word of God, the *halakhah,* as transmitted by tradition.

If this position is true, then the contradiction implied by the title is nonexistent. But I do not accept it. The problem is not that of faithful observance, but rather of belief. And for this reason I cannot claim that the difficulties regarding critical study of Bible can be removed in this way.

II

The Liberal Solution

Belief is certainly no less important for Judaism than the network of laws and commandments. The framework of faith specifically includes belief in *Torah min ha-shamayim,* "the divinity of the **Torah.**" At first glance it seems that this belief is compromised, if not totally destroyed, by the critical study of Bible. It is *this* contradiction between the scientific study of Bible and the belief in a heavenly **Torah** that must be addressed. For this purpose we must define the character of this belief. The observant scholars we are discussing might try to solve the problem by giving the divinity of **Torah** a relatively flexible, liberal, rationalistic interpretation. Divinity would then mean that the **Torah** derives from prophetic inspiration rather than human intellect. The author was not transcribing his own thoughts but acting as a "man of God," who saw divine images and heard God's speech. This **Torah,** we declare, is divine because a person who experienced the divine inscribed the heavenly directives.

This view does not, indeed cannot, assert that Moses alone wrote the **Torah,** as a human author composes a book. For even a prophet writing under divine inspiration retains his personality and style. The style of his prophecy manifests the depths of his soul; he hears God's word, but absorbs according to the nature of his soul. Nothing is revealed to him by God that his nature is incapable of comprehending. Moreover, when a prophet formulates what he heard and saw in his prophetic experience, he speaks in his own language, lim-

ited by his personality. Therefore Hosea could not have heard what was spoken to Isaiah, and Zephaniah would not utter the words of Jeremiah; it is inconceivable that Ezekiel's prophecy would have been transmitted to Amos or that Micah would speak Zephaniah's words. By this logic Moses could not have composed all the documents included in the **Torah** since, as suggested above, their content and style indicate different authors at different times. If Moses is the author of the **Torah,** as we normally think of an author, it is all the more difficult to believe that he would contradict himself so frequently, as the documents appear to do. To view Moses himself as the editor of the **Torah** borders on absurdity: having composed conflicting accounts, he then, on this scheme, labored strenuously to disguise the discrepancies. Biblical scholarship has argued convincingly, according to the view we are discussing, that no individual person, neither Moses nor any other prophet, could have composed the **Torah.** Yet, according to that approach, this in no way affects Jewish faith.

That is because the view we are discussing accepts *Torah min ha-shamayim* as a belief that the **Torah** was transmitted through prophecy, not that Moses was *the* unique prophet who received the **Torah** from heaven. If Moses is to be viewed as the "author" of the **Torah,** in the conventional sense of the term, he should have written "And God spoke to me saying," like other prophets who wrote their own prophecies. The view we are now discussing would argue that only one passage in the Oral Law explicitly asserts that "Moses wrote his book" (*Bava Batra* 14b), and that it is nowhere stated that one who denies Moses' composition of the **Torah** loses his share in the next world as is the case with one who denies the divinity of the **Torah** (*Sanhedrin* 90a). Many of the greatest scholars in the medieval and early modern periods deviated, on occasion, from a rabbinic dictum, when it flew in the face of the text's simple meaning.[1] Using their example as precedent, one might take the liberty of disregarding the view expressed in *Bava Batra,* insofar as a reading of the biblical text does not support the view that Moses wrote the **Torah** in the manner of a conventional human composition.[2]

The position we are discussing concedes that the **Torah** comprises several documents, written by different prophets in various eras. The documents are *min ha-shamayim,* because they are the words of the living God. There is an infinite gap between God, the source of the **Torah,** whose heavenly abode transcends space and time, and man, the recipient of prophecy, created from earth, who lives within the confines of space and time. The human intellect is limited; man cannot grasp or utter contradictory ideas. God is not bound by this constraint. Hence the one God reveals Himself in the world by exhibiting manifold traits and contradictory actions—like an old man seated at rest and a young man at war—with the attribute of justice and the attribute of mercy.[3] The unity of God is disclosed through the encompassing of opposing aspects and actions. The one God who embraces justice and mercy can communicate seemingly contradictory prophecies, corresponding to these aspects of divinity.

The prophecies given to individual prophets at different times thus reveal paradoxical elements. One prophet, oriented to justice and whose generation is particularly suited to hear the providential perspective of justice, received and transcribed the prophecy of judgment. Another, oriented to mercy and whose generation is particularly suited to hear of a world guided by mercy, will receive and transcribe the prophecy characterized by kindness. The diversity of these two prophecies reflects different authorship; yet both emanate from one source and from one shepherd. The view we are examining treats the composition of the **Torah** like the handing down of prophecy just described. The editor of the **Torah** had before him the various sources. But the **Torah** is not limited, as would be the prophecy of the individual prophet, to the perspectives of law *(din)* or mercy *(rahamim);* rather the **Torah** expresses the quality of harmony *(tiferet),* combining law and mercy. By God's instruction, the editor inscribed the **Torah,** and this quality of *tiferet* governs the **Torah** as a whole. We shall have more to say about this further in this discussion. Now, however, we are still occupied with the liberal approach.

Except for its significant omission of the specific role of *Moses,* an issue to which we will return, the ideas already outlined avoid any conflict between the modern study of Bible and *yirat shamayim.* The scholars identify the documents that comprise the **Torah** and try to explain the centuries of development behind them, prior to the coming of the prophet who consolidated the sources. The religious student, for his part, recognizes the hand of God in combining the various aspects of His revelation.

So far we have described the discoveries of *Biblical Criticism,* not the beliefs of *biblical critics.* Our adoption of the discoveries of biblical scholarship does not, by any means, imply assent to the beliefs of the scholars. We must know that an iron curtain separates, not faith and scholarship, but many men of scholarship and men of faith. While the scholars view the **Torah** as a grand literary creation, composed by human beings, we believe that the **Torah** is from heaven. This is not a debate between faith and science but rather a confrontation of faith and heresy. Science can only investigate what reason apprehends. The human intellect cannot comprehend God and is therefore unable to certify prophecy. Scholarly study of the **Torah** postulates the biblical text as the product of human agency, and as the product of human activity the **Torah** must reflect multiple sources. But this presupposition of the

scientific approach, which enables the human mind to proceed, is not subject to confirmation or refutation. Scholars cannot prove that the **Torah** is a human product, because that is the assumption that underlies the entire enterprise. At the same time it would be impossible to demonstrate that the **Torah** is divine, based on the assumptions of scholarship, because that belief contradicts the axioms with which the proof must be consistent; in any event, it would be an attempt to demonstrate something beyond the capacity of human reason. Whether the **Torah** is a human or divine creation cannot be decided by scientific reason, which has no authority over the domain that transcends reason. Where the intellect falls short faith responds confidently. Faith knows with certainty "the foundation of wisdom, to know that there is a first cause" (Rambam *Hilkhot Yesodei ha-Torah* 1:1) and it is a basic religious truth that God reveals Himself to man. An honest scholar acknowledges that this judgment is beyond his competence as a man of science.

In fact, scholars frequently reiterate their conviction that the **Torah** is a merely human composition, in no way different from other literary creations. But this claim already abandons the realm of science and enters that of faith. With this pronouncement they become spokesmen for a "faith," and its content is heretical. We who believe wholeheartedly in the divinity of the **Torah** must oppose them. But the debate about that which lies beyond science cannot be judged from within science. Only a heavenly voice acknowledged by all can resolve this conflict authoritatively.

Before addressing the role of Moses, let us summarize our conclusions so far. The position we are now describing is prepared to accept without reservation the views of scholarship so long as the scholars have not ventured beyond the limits of scientific method, which include the demarcation of the various documents in the **Torah,** the development that preceded them, and the editorial process that followed. Only when scholars deviate from the scientific framework and introduce heretical beliefs about the **Torah**'s human composition must we reject their assertions and hold fast to our tradition. This traditional belief suffuses our personal lives. The **Torah** we study day and night is not a **Torah** propounded by human authors, but a divine **Torah** received by prophets who inscribed a vision revealed to them by God.

III

The Traditional Alternative

Everything we have articulated up to this point is compatible with the liberal definition of *Torah min ha-shamayim,* which ignores the specific role of Moses in transmitting the **Torah**. In reality, however, this definition of **Torah** *min ha-shamayim* does not prevail in

Jewish thought. From antiquity, our Sages have never considered equating the Five Books of Moses with other prophecy. They regarded the equation, not as proper faith, but as utter heresy. The status of Moses is inherently different from that of all other prophets. The latter saw God in a vision, through a glass darkly; they heard His voice as a riddle that required clarification and interpretation. When they subsequently transmitted God's message to the people, when they wrote it down, they could not convey literally what they had seen and heard. Instead each adopted his own style and language. Moses was different. The loyal servant in God's house, to whom God spoke as one converses with a companion; he perceived God through a clear glass, as it were, and heard His message expressed precisely. Therefore Moses wrote the words of the **Torah** as God spoke them, without injecting his own. Thus the **Torah** of Moses was literally *min ha-shamayim;* the Lawgiver summoned His prophet to the heavens themselves. "Like an author dictating a book to his scribe," God dictated the **Torah** to His prophet from beginning to end.

Just as the content and style of the **Torah** are independent of Moses' personality, so too they transcend his particular time. The book of Jeremiah, for example, could only have been written during or after the life of Jeremiah, since it includes his spoken words, which could not have preceded him. Because the **Torah,** however, is not the words of a prophet but those of God who transcends time, the sages could speak of the **Torah** preexisting the world, "black fire upon white fire." By dating the **Torah** before the creation of time, the sages figuratively depicted the **Torah**'s immediate relationship to God Himself, He who is an all-consuming fire. A thousand generations before the world's creation, when God and His name were still one, and no prophet existed to share in its composition, the **Torah** already existed. Thus God's direct creation of the **Torah** is like that of heaven and earth, on the first day of the world, when even the angels did not exist.

This midrash alludes to a specific analogy between the process of creation and the order of writing. Creation proceeds from the absolute free will of the divine, not subject to the law of natural development of the cosmos. The same applies to God's writing of the **Torah,** which derives from God's free will, not subject to the rules of literary development. God spoke, "And it was so" defines both creation of the world and creation of the **Torah.** The sages taught that the **Torah** preexists the world, like the architect's blueprint that precedes the building. The **Torah** is the blueprint because it incorporates the divine attributes employed in the creation as well.[4]

This definition of belief in the unique divinity of *Torat Mosheh* is the only one recognized by the Jewish people, adopted by all sages. Whoever views the **Torah** as an ordinary prophetic work denies its unique status. In the previous section we examined the *possibility* of interpreting the meaning of **Torah** *min ha-shamayim* liberally, insofar as this option is attractive to some scholars. It is impossible, however, to maintain this possibility as an account of the way this doctrine was understood throughout the generations of Jewish belief. Traditional belief means God's revelation of the **Torah** through Moses. Only Moses, the worthy scribe to whom God committed the task of writing every section, verse, and letter of the **Torah** from His very "lips." Other prophets did not attain this level: "No prophet arose in Israel like Moses, whom God recognized face to face" (Deuteronomy 34:11).

Let us revert to the statement in *Bava Batra* about the authors of the biblical books. As we saw, the Talmud ascribes the **Torah** and the book of Joshua to Moses and Joshua respectively. As we also saw, there were *Rishonim,* like Abravanel, who held that Joshua did not author his book. Analogous arguments of at least equal strength could have been deployed against Mosaic authorship, and although the commentators were duly aware of them, no one would have dared to propose such a conclusion. The reason for this difference is clear from the previous discussion. Whether the book of Joshua was written by Joshua or, as Abravanel thought, by Samuel, does not affect principles of faith; it is merely an historical query about prophetic authorship. Since Abravanel held that the simple meaning of the biblical text conclusively shows that *Joshua* was not written by the man Joshua, he did not adopt the rabbinic view. The role of Moses in writing the **Torah,** by contrast, engages fundamental issues of faith; **Torah** *min ha-shamayim* depends on Moses writing it. Had Abravanel concluded that Moses did not write the **Torah** he would ipso facto have dissented from the doctrine that the **Torah** is from heaven. Such a heretical notion could never have entered his mind.

Abravanel's distinction between the **Torah** and the book of Joshua is not a random imposition of dogma, but goes together with our entire conception of the **Torah.** Why shouldn't the arguments for post-Joshua authorship apply to the **Torah** as well? Many verses in the **Torah** are indeed incompatible with Moses' particular historical and personal situatedness. Hence Moses, *viewed as a flesh and blood author,* could not have written such a **Torah.** But this point is totally unremarkable: our Sages did not teach that Moses wrote the **Torah** in the same way that other prophets wrote their books. Since Moses inscribed the words of God, no conventional argument about authorship can undermine his role. God is beyond space and time, His writing is not subject to natural limitation; hence conventional scientific debate cannot determine the nature of the Authorship.

IV

The Point of Divergence

Let us review the salient positions of Biblical Criticism, as applied to the **Torah.** First, there is the thesis that the **Torah** contains discrete documents integrated by an editor whose work is evident throughout the **Torah.** We too must acknowledge these arguments because we too assert that God's **Torah,** in its plain sense, speaks "the language of human beings." When read by the rules that govern human speech, the **Torah** is consonant with the scholarly evaluation of the text.

In addition, the scholars assert that the **Torah** is a human composition, similar to other literary works. This view, as we have noted, pre-supposes itself. A human author is limited by his specific time and place, unable to grasp the conflicting aspects in one idea, unable to employ strategies of authorial multiplicity, unable to dispense with generations of development. If the **Torah** is a human document, the conclusion is inescapable that it was composed piecemeal in the manner that the critics imagine. Thus, the religious believer can reject the assumption about the source of the text without denying the literary analysis the scholars have proposed.

This is the position that we have staked out. God, who is beyond the limitations of time and space, prepared the **Torah,** declaring in one utterance what man can comprehend only as a combination of differing sources. Before the world was created, God redacted one document characterized by justice and one characterized by mercy, and synthesized them with the quality of harmony. After a thousand generations this **Torah,** "black fire on white fire," descended to earth. Moses, the faithful shepherd, was summoned to the upper realm, and brought it down to the terrestrial sphere.

Earlier we mentioned the relationship between the creation of the world and the **Torah.** This parallel is also relevant to the relationship between faith and science. Faith informs us that the world came into being in six days; science claims convincingly that the world was slowly formed over millions of years. Yet here it is commonly recognized that the conflict is imaginary. The scientific evidence assumes that the world coalesced spontaneously. But this very supposition, if it is not self-evident, is unprovable. For this reason men of faith can set this assumption aside and declare that God's free act created the world and that this untrammeled freedom is perfectly consistent with His creation of the world in six days through divine utterance. It is because of a division of domains of this sort that intelligent people today are rarely troubled by conflict between faith and the natural sciences.

Inexplicably, the truce between faith and science has not penetrated the discipline of biblical scholarship.

Instead the emphasis is put on the contradiction between faith and science. Unable to withstand the contradiction, most men of faith consciously avoid biblical scholarship in order to safeguard their traditional belief. Few faithful Jews are prepared to risk their souls in order to resolve the tension. The truth is, however, that this conflict is illusory, the product of unsophisticated thinking. It arises because both men of faith and scientists have strayed from their disciplines and entered foreign areas. The scholars believe they have indisputably proven that Moses did not write the **Torah,** oblivious to the fact that this entire argument depends on their heretical assumptions. The believers, on the other hand, wearing the mantle of the "scientist," attack the scientific arguments of their interlocutors, instead of opposing their heretical presuppositions.

How did this situation come about? Why do so many believing Jews see a conflict in the area of Bible study? Possibly the historical context of the discussion is responsible, as much of early Biblical Criticism was nurtured in an ambience of antipathy to Judaism. But it seems that a more significant reason for this situation is confusion about the meaning of *Torah min ha-shamayim.* It is likely that many believing Jews have difficulty with *Torah min ha-shamayim* in its traditional connotation. Consciously or unconsciously they equate *Torah min ha-shamayim* with the divine origin of the other prophetic works, written by the prophet himself, in his own language, based on his transcendental experience. They naively think that their belief in the divinity of the **Torah** is intact and that the Mishnah's stricture against one who denies the **Torah's** divine origin does not refer to them. They also know well that the Sages throughout history wholeheartedly affirmed that Moses wrote the entire **Torah,** and that this belief is so fundamental to Judaism that one who rejects it undermines the entire **Torah.** Yet they fail to recognize that the traditional position regarding Mosaic composition of the **Torah** is a corollary of the *primary belief* that God created the **Torah.** As a result of this misstep, they are content to treat the **Torah** as Moses' composition, like other prophetic books. But we have claimed that the scholars are right: Moses, as a human individual, could not have composed the **Torah,** and this is precisely what the *unique* status of Moses is all about. Unfortunately, these believers hold tightly to Jewish faith as they understand it, combining belief in Mosaic authorship with a failure to recognize the unique role of Moses. Consequently, they must wage war against science, attempting to refute scientifically all that scholars and scholarship have proven. The battle is lost from the start. The naïve believer is at a distinct disadvantage because the fight is neither between faith and heresy nor between faith and science, but rather between faith and ignorance, speaking in the name of a mistaken conception of faith. Science gets the better of ignorance, undermining their imagined faith.

Even among people who do not tend to obliterate the distinction between **Torah** and the Prophets, another factor is at work. They reject the position proposed in this chapter because they view it as impossible that the one God who created the **Torah** could possibly produce apparently inconsistent documents. In effect they are applying what is true of secular literature to the holy. A secular author who contradicts himself testifies to thoughtlessness and a lack of intellectual and spiritual integrity. The **Torah,** they argue, must be unified and uniform without contradictions and internal "flaws," like God Himself.

This position is correct in its definition of *Torah min ha-shamayim* but seriously mistaken about the content of *Torah min ha-shamayim*. It displays a kinship with the pagan attitude that moves from an awareness of the manifold nature of Divine actions to the assertion of divine multiplicity. God declared at Mount Sinai: "I am the Lord your God. I-in Egypt, I-at the Sea, I-at Sinai, I am past and I am future, I am for this world and I am for the next." For Jewish faith God's unity in the world is made manifest when He reveals His many aspects in what appear to be conflicting actions. This conception of God underlies the unity of the **Torah.** It is the pagan mentality that infers from contradictory aspects of God's activity, reflected in the multiple literary aspects of the **Torah,** the existence of multiple deities, and, correspondingly, multiple authors of the **Torah.** This wrongheaded approach leads one to think that conflicting documents in the **Torah** are irreconcilable with a unified **Torah** from God. Hence the strained denial that the discrepancies exist, and the compulsion to adduce scientific refutations of dubious cogency. Hence the attempt to persuade themselves and us that all biblical scholars, including the great minds among them, are deluded and deluding, motivated by wickedness, folly, or hatred of Jews.

The principle emerging from all of this is that there is no real tension between faith and science so long as the conception of faith is free of distortion. One who adopts the inferior (liberal) concept of *Torah min ha-shamayim* as no different from the other prophetic books is in danger of concluding that the **Torah** was not written by Moses at all. He is distinguished from the outright heretic only by his belief in the divinity of the **Torah,** as he understands it. The heretical scholars deem the **Torah**'s writers and editors mere mortals, while the believer who adopts the liberal concept of *Torah min ha-shamayim* maintains that the **Torah,** like other prophetic works, was written and edited by men of God based on revelation.

In contrast to this, the superior (traditional) concept of *Torah min ha-shamayim* implies necessarily that only Moses could be its author. He accepts the results of the critical method, insofar as God's **Torah** was written in the language of human beings. The scholarly arguments, which rely on linguistic principles of human communication, are significant for him too, and require neither refutation nor opposition. But he rejects every word of what the scholars maintain with respect to the writing and editing of the **Torah,** because he is committed to God's authorship, and regards as heresy the view that the **Torah** is man-made.

Let us contrast the three views we have discussed. The secular scholarly position views the **Torah** as a collection of documents, written by J, E, P, and D, edited by R. The liberal religious view accepts this hypothesis, but ascribes the documents to authentic prophets of God. The traditional belief, which we advocate, holds that the **Torah** is directly authored by God. Since we acknowledge the phenomena uncovered by the scholars, this means that God provided J, E, P, D, and R the editorial layers. Our belief differs inherently from the first two, because those approaches see the **Torah** as the work of man. If, however, we consider, not the question of authorship but the nature of **Torah** study, the essential distinction is between the first view and the latter two. According to the first perspective the **Torah** presents a merely human understanding; according to both of the "religious" views the **Torah** manifests the supreme divine intellect. The scholar who adopts the first position studies **Torah** with the measure of detachment appropriate to other literary study. The believer, by contrast, learns **Torah** with holy trepidation and reverence, in the awareness that he is studying the word of God. This reverence is possible even if one believes that the **Torah** was formulated by prophets who heard God's word rather than by God himself; either way it is the divine word. In fact, Jews cultivate this sense of awe toward all the biblical books: no one would think of distinguishing between the **Torah,** on the one hand, and the book of Isaiah for example, on the other hand. The Jew studies both with the same degree of assiduity, respect, and dignity due to the word of God.

V

Example: Genesis, Chapters 1 and 2

We have alluded to the many contradictions between passages in the **Torah.** For earlier generations these contradictions attracted exegetical attention, as each exegete strove to resolve the difficulties. The Documentary Hypothesis altered the situation. The contradictions now serve as markers for the various documents: questions of exegetical conflict now become questions about the accounts of different authors. The scholar aims to diagnose the personal and historical factors responsible for the conflicting versions of the documents.

Let us take one example: the well-known discrepancy between the first two chapters of the **Torah.** According to the scholarly consensus, P wrote the first chapter. P looked at the world like a natural scientist. Therefore the order of creation follows the natural development of species: vegetation and animate beings precede man. The fundamental purpose of nature, in this account, is to preserve the created species. Hence one would not imagine man being created alone. God created him male and female; for only thus is his existence perpetuated. No doubt, the scholar concludes, this account bespeaks a late date, for it presupposes a highly developed consciousness of natural law.

The second chapter expresses a totally different perspective. J, its author, is a sensitive poetic soul who saw the world through the eyes of a poet. His world cannot be portrayed as alienated, governed by the mechanical forces of nature; its only goal, survival. Self-preservation in the biological sense is not enough; a spiritual end must be imported, a meaning beyond brute existence, one that radiates nobility, beauty, and love. Only man endows the world with meaning and only through him can a purpose be conceived. For this reason God formed him first. Vegetation and animal life are recounted afterwards: their significance is tied to their human meaning. Man, in this account, had to precede woman. Only thus could man experience the pain of being alone. When woman is subsequently created he rejoices over her like a groom over a bride. With the gifts of joy and love, the creation process is complete. This description, the critic might claim, befits the nation's early stages: a world full of song and imagination, consciousness of the mechanical nature still undeveloped.

The critic links the portrayals in the two documents to the distinct personal and historical backgrounds of their authors. The editor's achievement was to accept both portrayals and combine them into one book, thus embracing the truth that both express. Indeed the **Torah** articulates complementary aspects of the created world. In the wild forests, for example, vegetation sprouts without man's help; in settled regions grass grows only after man tills the earth. From one perspective God created male and female together to perpetuate the species. From another, He created the two sexes separately so that woman's creation would mark the entry of happiness, joy, and love into a lonely world. The critic does not believe that these respective interpretations were intended by the authors of the two documents. Each document presents the monochromatic outlook of its author. Only the editor, by distilling the partial truth in each version, uncovered the broad perspective which permitted him to embrace several true texts within one **Torah.** When traditional rabbinic commentaries reconcile the conflicting views, they are explaining the *peshat* of the redactor's final product.

When we, who believe in the divinity of the **Torah,** adopt the critical division of sources, we do not assign the contradictory portrayals of creation in the **Torah** to different human authors and redactors. Instead, we refer the distinctions to the different qualities of God. In chapter 1, God is identified with the quality of justice implied in the name *Elohim,* and creates a world governed by law. In chapter 2, the quality of mercy, associated with the Tetragrammaton, engenders a world of mercy. The internal differences between these worlds include discrepancies in the order of creation (vegetation, living things, and man), and in the way man and woman were created. The believer knows that God contains all variation within Himself as surely as His rainbow contains the spectrum of colors. He encompasses justice and mercy; He can therefore juxtapose conflicting accounts reflecting these conflicting qualities. The critics claim that J preceded P chronologically, in line with their presuppositions. We would say instead that, within human culture, the spiritual conception of the world precedes perception in terms of natural order. The Creator, who is beyond time and space, not subject to the laws of historical development, presents these two conflicting perspectives simultaneously.

God formed the world neither according to pure justice or pure mercy, but rather justice tempered by mercy and mercy limited by justice. The two qualities were not expressed in their pure form, but were synthesized. This offers a partial expression of the qualities of justice and mercy, but a complete realization of a creation manifesting both of these qualities. Man, who is unable to comprehend polar opposites, perceives contradiction. The divine narrative, however, integrates both versions and their philosophical perspectives. This integration takes place by means of the "redaction," which reflects the attribute of *tiferet,* "harmony." Neither source is to be read literally, as presenting one-dimensional aspects of justice or mercy. They should be understood, rather, in the light of the received text where the Almighty interwove these two aspects.

Unlike the secular scholar, for whom each document represents no more than the subjective perspective of a human author, the religious individual knows that each document expresses a partial truth, a divine truth, an articulation of His holy attributes. Each creation story, taken in itself, reveals how a world created exclusively according to one of these characteristics would have appeared. The textual components of the **Torah,** like the **Torah** as a whole, are true. Israel was commanded to love truth and peace (i.e., the reconciliation of opposites) which derive from the God of Israel whose seal is truth and whose name is peace. Thus the study of Bible by the religious individual fortifies the bond between the Holy One, Israel, and the Holy **Torah.**

VI

Torah Lishmah and Intellectual Integrity

We have seen that the believer and the scientist differ most, not in their recognition of phenomena, but in their evaluation of the phenomena. This is eminently true of their respective attitudes toward the study of **Torah.** The scientist relates to the **Torah** as he does to all literary works. Having examined its content, and applied to it the critical method, he will accept it or reject it. The **Torah,** for him, does not speak in the name of a higher authority, compelling his submission. This is especially the case when it comes to the **Torah**'s legal portions. The scholar will find some laws pleasing and progressive, others unseemly and inane. This attitude implies a lack of reverence even for *mitzvot* he chooses to fulfill. He adopts these laws not because of the **Torah**'s normative demands but as the outcome of subjective attraction. Hence he never fulfills God's will but his own.

The believer, by contrast, does not subject the laws to his critical review: he declares, from the outset, *naaseh ve-nishma,* "we will follow and then understand"— whether he finds them attractive or not. He does not merely *study* **Torah** but *learns* from it. When he opens the **Torah** he enters the house of God, he brings himself before God for guidance.

Acceptance of the **Torah**'s supreme authority does not, to be sure, relieve the believer from religious struggle. No individual can deny the truth in his heart, and God does not expect His children to suppress their inner sense of ethics and justice in the face of what is written in the **Torah.** Therefore the religious individual is allowed, and in fact is obligated, to wage the **Torah**'s battle *within* the world of **Torah** itself. You ought not encourage falsity in your heart by negating your own truth as falsehood. God chastised Job's friends for their false justification of God. The tormented struggle between the heart's truth and what is written in the **Torah** is often a most difficult one. Yet the believer will never consider the secular student's judgment that some laws are acceptable and others are not. When he finds himself unreceptive to the **Torah**'s truth he will put its words "on his heart," faithfully awaiting the hour when his closed heart will open and embrace the **Torah**'s words. There is no way to know when this miraculous event will occur. Yet one may assume from the outset that it will never be demanded of him to abandon the truth of the heart. Eventually it will become clear that there never was a real contradiction between that truth and the **Torah**'s. It was only his insufficient readiness for the **Torah**'s truth that engendered the apparent conflict. His certainty in the triumph of truth supports him during the struggle of the conflict.

VII

The "Intention" of the Author

Our theological conception of ***Torah*** *min ha-shamayim,* distinguishing between the **Torah** given to Moses and the words of the prophet sent by God, has practical

halakhic ramifications: no man or prophet has the authority to abrogate anything God has written in his **Torah.** Moreover this conception of ***Torah*** *min ha-shamayim* affects the study and interpretation of the **Torah.** This point requires an elaboration of our position on literary interpretation in general.

It used to be taken for granted that literary criticism meant understanding the author's intention. To ignore the author's meaning was to impose the critic's own meaning on the text. According to this approach the ideal commentator is the author himself. But the author is often an unreliable guide to his own work: the intentions informing the work may have been forgotten or unconscious, their imprint apparent though he fails to recognize it. Thus the critic, who can read between the lines and determine the author's conscious and subconscious intentions, becomes the superior authority. The critic can locate internal contradictions that the author missed, since these are due to conflicting attitudes the author has not acknowledged. Nowadays literary criticism is not preoccupied with the author's intention. Once the literary work has left his hands it occupies its own place, defining a world of its own. It is our possession to interpret as we understand it.

Taken without qualification, this approach would make literary study an exercise in anarchy, without rules or standards. One could comment as freely as he pleases, so long as the interpretation maintained some connection to the text. It would be impossible to discriminate between correct and incorrect interpretations; the only criterion would be plausibility to the reader. Any literary work could thus be approached with all the interpretive methods used to analyze the **Torah:** *peshat, derash, remez* and *sod, atbash* and *gematriya.* This is illegitimate. I would maintain that a literary critic's primary responsibility is to the author's conscious or unconscious intention, explicit or implicit in the work. The critic has every right to broach various ideas that emerge from the text, whether directly or indirectly. He may assert that these are implications of the work, although the author never intended them, and that the author's failure to say what the critic is saying is due to the limitations of his time and environment. Such an interpretation would artfully and effectively explicate the literary work without claiming to provide an accurate account of the writer's intention.

What I have proposed regarding a secular literary work surely applies to sacred scripture as well. The student of Bible must first understand what the writer intended to convey. The obligation to study **Torah** requires more than this. It includes the text's implications for future generations, especially its relevance for the reader's situation. Although the writer did not intend this specific meaning of the text it exists nonetheless. The **Torah** is "deeper than the sea," its possible ramifications are unlimited, and those who search will always uncover new features. Every idea found in the **Torah** engenders others, whether directly or indirectly. The full range of interpretations, derivations, and derivations of derivations pertaining to the **Torah** is pregnant with truth.

But this general principle regarding authorial intention does not apply to the **Torah** in the same manner that it pertains to other biblical books. The student of the prophets (and the same would go for the **Torah** according to the liberal understanding of *Torah min ha-shamayim* that we reject) can readily distinguish between the author's intention and the implicit intentions of the text. The prophet is rooted in a specific time and place. Hence his interpretation of his own prophecy is affected by his context and capabilities. Later readers may adduce new ideas from his prophecy, which were hidden from the prophet because their time had not yet come. This cannot be the case with respect to the **Torah.** The Author's intention is not limited by the time of the writing since the Author—God—transcends time and His writing preceded creation. Nonetheless, we may suggest that when God transmitted the **Torah,** He directed it to a specific generation, that of the Exodus and the desert, that would receive it, and to later generations that would study the text.

This last point is pertinent to the scientific study of the Bible. When the biblical critics match a particular passage to the time period that suits its style of writing and content they have identified the generation that the passage addresses at the primary literary and historical level. Genesis, chapter 1, for example, may directly address those whose understanding of the world is suited to that version; that group would constitute the primary audience. There is, of course, a secondary audience, to whom the **Torah** is also transmitted. Although, when speaking of God as the Author, a distinction between the writer's intention and that which is written is inconceivable, one must distinguish between two different authorial intentions, one to the primary audience and one to other readers, the secondary audience.

The first level of intention in **Torah** corresponds to the author's intention in the other books. This includes what is normally understood by the primary recipient generation. The second level of intention in the **Torah** parallels the implicit levels of the text in other prophetic works. What comprises the deeper meaning of other biblical texts is part of the Author's intended meaning in the divine **Torah.** Both levels become available to later students, though the primary audience may penetrate only the first level.

Thus the significant distinctions between the various definitions of **Torah** *min ha-shamayim,* which are central to our theological judgment about the compatibility of source division and Jewish piety, bear impli-

cations for the practice of **Torah** study as well. If one believes that the **Torah** was written by man, albeit with prophetic inspiration, his sense of the relationship between his understanding and the author's intention must be tenuous. The matter is entirely different for one who believes he studies *God's* **Torah.** This individual will attempt to seek undiscovered nuances in the **Torah**'s meaning that will excite his heart and satiate his soul. Yet he will be confident that these novel interpretations are included in the **Torah**'s design. He will bless God who has taught him **Torah,** who commanded him to immerse himself in the study of **Torah,** and who has made His words pleasant, generously endowing him with wisdom to understand the content of His creation.

Notes

[1] See, for example, Rashbam's introduction to the Torah; Ibn Ezra's introduction to the Torah; Abravanel's introduction to the Prophets; Or haHayyim's introduction to the Torah *inter alia.*

[2] This principle can also be applied to historical assertions that conflict with the text's plain meaning. Of the talmudic discussion (*Rosh Hashanah* 3b) that assumes "Cyrus is Darius is Artaxerxes," Rabbi Zerahia Ba'al ha-Maor observes that the biblical text plainly regards Cyrus, Darius, and Artaxerxes as three different people. This approach has also been applied to the talmudic passage immediately following the statement "Moses wrote his book." The Talmud in *Bava Batra* goes on to say that "Joshua wrote his book," and Abravanel (in his general introduction to early prophets) infers, from several verses in Joshua, that Joshua could not have authored his book. Similarly the author of *Shaagat Aryeh* posits, in opposition to the implication of another part of the talmudic statement in *Bava Batra,* that Ezra the scribe did not write the book of Chronicles himself but compiled documents of previous authors: he edited the book but did not write it. (See my article "The Documentary Theory of the *Shaagat Aryeh,*" *Megadim* 2 [Fall 5747 (1986)]: 9-22.) Using such reasoning, the scholars we are discussing might propose that Moses only wrote the part of "his book" that the Torah explicitly attributes to him (Deuteronomy 31:9). The rest of the Torah, however, could derive from other men of God, living at other times. These documents, redacted by a prophet who added and subtracted according to God's will, form one book, one *torah,* in which there is not one letter belonging to the human intellect, being wholly *Torah min ha-shamayim,* from the first word to the last.

[3] See Maimonides *Hilkhot Yesodei ha-Torah* 1:9.

[4] The two blessings before the *Shema* reinforce this association of Torah and creation. The first praises God as "creator of light and darkness," while the second

thanks Him for teaching us the Torah's commandments and laws. These blessings parallel the two halves of Psalm 19, which first recount God's glory and then extol the Torah. The same duality is found in the Sabbath prayers: the evening prayer celebates the Sabbath of creation; the morning prayer refers to the Sabbath of the Torah-giving. The blessing after *Shema,* Psalm 19, and the afternoon Sabbath prayer culminate with the world's redemption. The purpose of the creation and the subject of the entire Torah is nothing less than God's redemption of history.

Frank Crüsemann (essay date 1996)

SOURCE: "The Pentateuch as *Torah*: The Way as Part of the Goal" in *The "Torah": Theology and Social History of Old Testament Law,* translated by Allan W. Mahnke, Fortress Press, 1996, pp. 329-67.

[*In the following essay, Crüsemann explores the social and political context in which the* Pentateuch *was produced in an effort to understand the development of the Judeo-Christian* Torah. *According to him, the* Pentateuch *unifies the strictures of a monotheistic religion with regulations of justice set against the background of Persian law.*]

> There came a voice of revelation saying,
> *"These and those are words of the living God."*
>
> *Babylonian Talmud, Erubin* 13b[1]

The Pentateuch as a Product of the Persian Period

Literary Presuppositions and Conceptual Self-Designation

The historical juxtaposition of the legal corpora in the **Pentateuch** are parts of one law of Moses. Codes criticizing previous laws, which they sought to replace, were combined with those laws into a single entity. The sequence of laws became a cooperation, and contradiction became cooperation. The path to the goal became part of the goal, in fact it basically became the goal, for little that was substantially new was added.

Frequently, portrayals of Israelite legal history ignore this, culminating with strata the authors believed to be latest.[2] It was, however, only by means of this step that Torah was developed, which then became the basis of the entirety of later Jewish legal history. It is only when we understand this process that we appreciate the text, which is the only starting point for a reconstruction of the history that precedes it.

Nevertheless, the process by which the **Pentateuch** as a whole was developed was apparently subordinate to other laws, which were in effect when the earlier legal

texts came into existence. They all adopted and expanded the contents and important decisions of their predecessors, incorporating and editing more or less clearly identifiable documents. As in other legal corpora, however, the conception is, by and large, consistent, and its solution lay within the historical challenge presented. For the moment, however, repetitions and contradictions of the most egregious kind remain unresolved. That sort of thing seems almost a compositional principle of the **Pentateuch.**

In what follows we will investigate the historical circumstances, theological conception and legal meaning of this process and its consequences. As an introduction, here are the most important literary presuppositions on which this examination is based:

It is critical that we distinguish the overall form of the **Pentateuch** and its final redaction(s) from the priestly writings, which would contradict theories suggesting that we regard the development of the main priestly document (followed by a few less significant redactions) as the critical formative step for canonical Torah.[3] The following reasons are especially important:

s—However we want to deal with the literary structure and scope of priestly writings (or of a priestly document), they do not include Deuteronomy. Why this great corpus was included, and in some way integrated into the priestly writings, is beyond the purview of this discussion. The juxtaposition of the two legal corpora, most significant in scope and influence, makes up the actual inner tension and thus also something of the "essence" of the **Pentateuch.** Its shape developed as they were brought together.

—On the other hand, the **Pentateuch** presumes that the books of Moses were separate from the Book of Joshua and the books associated with Joshua: Judges, Samuel and Kings. Some "finger prints," however, lead from the **Pentateuch** at least to Josh 24, which suggests earlier correlations.[4] Furthermore, we probably cannot deny the presence of part of the priestly texts or priestly redaction in Joshua.[5] It is, however, only the separation of the Book of Joshua that makes the **Pentateuch** an independent authority, the book of Torah.[6]

What is certainly true for Deuteronomy is also probably true for the Book of the Covenant and the Decalogue. For our purposes we need not deal with whether the priestly stratum incorporated and reshaped earlier narrative texts, and which these were. It is extremely unlikely that it presumed a comprehensive Sinai pericope including a theophany and the concluding of a covenant.[7] Because of the priestly conception Sinai became the central place of the proclamation of God's will. The markedly deuteronomistic construction of the Sinai pericope in Ex 19-24 incorporated the pre-priestly legal corpora. As a whole, however, it represented a post-priestly textual area that approximates or is part of the final redaction.

Thus the final form of the **Pentateuch** deals especially with a new way of combining older materials. Apart from the narratives, new legal materials amplifying the already extant corpora are only found in the Book of Numbers. Surprisingly, there were additional laws having a post-priestly character, which were given on the way through the desert. The innovations in content resemble what the previously described new codification had intended, but on another level.[8] We will not reconstruct the literary growth either here or for the non-priestly Sinai pericope, the problems are well-known. It is clear, however, that we must reckon on a longer coexistence of priestly and deuteronomistic strata (or their corresponding groups).

Let us begin with the question of the designation and therefore the self-understanding of this creation.[9] Thus far I have used the term "Torah" to describe the overall structure. To what degree is this justified? The question gets us directly into the old debate, whether the **Pentateuch,** as a whole, is narrative or law. There are great differences of opinion on this question, especially between Christianity and Judaism.[10] There are about equal amounts of both, weighed quantitatively,[11] and since neither term was used at that time, perhaps such an alternative is already misleading for our effort to comprehend how the **Pentateuch** understands itself. *Tora* means something different than history or law. Did, however, "the" or "a" concept of Torah, already present from the start, become the name of the whole once it had come into existence? For this there are more aspects to note.

As nearly as I can tell, there is only clear evidence for the use of the term Torah to describe the **Pentateuch** as a whole, including narrative portions, from the second century BCE. Thus, in Job 30:12 the narrative of Gen 34 is regarded as part of the "law." The law is introduced as the first part of the canon in the prolog to Jesus Sirach. For the period before this, including the late strata of the Old Testament itself, including the evidence in the books of Chronicles, Ezra and Nehemiah,[12] O. Eissfeldt's statement applies: "We cannot tell for sure whether this comprehensive use of this term already appears in the Old Testament, since the places under consideration can all be understood in such a way as to include only the legal parts (Ezr 10:3; 2 Chr 30:16; Neh 8:3; 2 Kg 14:6)."[13] The same is true of related expressions, such as "Book of Moses."

Against the background of earlier interpretations and especially the use as a technical term for priestly in-

struction, *tora* as we know became the most important concept for Deuteronomy and the will of God formulated in it (Deut 4:8, 44, etc.).[14] Of course, in many places this "book of Torah" contained references to history (especially the exodus) which appear in the context of the founding of many laws. Torah is later the most important concept for the law of Ezra, where we are unable to tell what shape it had.[15] Were we to ask whether the word *tōrā* might also designate narrative complexes, two texts might bear on the question, both originating in deuteronomic/deuteronomistic theology.

One text is Ps 78. In verse 1 the poet, employing wisdom language, describes what is to follow as "my Torah" . . . . This includes, from verse 12, a generous historical narrative. Israel's history is an important part of wisdom instruction. Interestingly, the same thing is true of YHWH's Torah, mentioned in verses 5 and 10. "Witness and instruction" . . . , which God instituted in Israel (verse 5), are supposed to be handed down from fathers to sons (verses 5f.) with the intent that they would put their trust *(késel)* in God. Thus, the remembrance of historical acts . . . and keeping the commandments . . . are parallel (verse 7). In verse 10, the combination "covenant" . . . and *"tōrā"* parallels verse 11 "deeds and marvels." If the narrative beginning in verse 12 (in which, as in nearly all historical summaries, the giving of the law is omitted) is understood as a concretization and demonstration of what was said in verses 5 and 10, the proclaiming of Torah will include history. Thus narrative and Torah should not be separated.[16]

Obviously, *tōrā* became a designation for history in Deut 1:5, "Beyond the Jordan in the land of Moab, Moses undertook to expound this law as follows." By means of the last word . . . , the speech starting at verse 6 is designated as the beginning of Torah. Therefore, the first three chapters of Deuteronomy, a historical review, are clearly a part of Torah itself. This applies to the present text, independent of how we might explain its current state, or whether or not we regard it as a late emendation,[17] as most do, and independent of the meaning of the verb *(b'r).*[18]

From the evidence, we cannot tell for sure whether the word *tora* was the chief concept of the **Pentateuch** from the beginning, or whether the designation of the earlier Deuteronomy, the deuteronomistic, was expanded to the narrative portions, and only later became the name for the whole thing. The word *tōrā* clearly can designate the narrative portions and, what is even more important, there is no other term for the self-understanding of this gigantic work.[19] In summary, the evidence suggests that the redaction and canonization of the **Pentateuch** may have taken place without a name and a label for the whole concept, but it is improbable.

The Temporal and Historical Framework

When did the **Pentateuch** as we have it come into being? Of course, we must presume long literary processes. Such procedures have already been accepted regarding the growth within the priestly texts, and they are also probable for the juxtaposition of priestly and deuteronomistic strata.[20] We are talking about the time when the great legal texts (Book of the Covenant, Deuteronomy, and the priestly writings) were brought together in a single document. Furthermore, this is the time at which the literary productive work on the **Pentateuch** came to an end. On the basis of the sources the two questions are inseparable.

The **Pentateuch** must have come into existence between the exile and the beginning of the hellenistic period—in other words, during the Persian period. This *terminus post quem* can be determined with certainty. In general scholars agree that such a work could not have existed during the exilic period. There are clear historical references, especially in the execration chapters of Deuteronomy and the priestly Holiness Code.[21] It is unanimously agreed that the deuteronomistic history was developed at that time, in which Deuteronomy formed a literary unity with Joshua through 2 Kings.[22] Even the priestly writings in their present form originated in the postexilic period.[23]

The end of productive literary work is much harder to fix and it is highly disputed. We can no longer refer to the separation from the Samaritans (who regarded only the **Pentateuch** as canonical scripture), which for a long time was regarded as important.[24] Of course, there was the building of the Samaritan temple on Mount Gerizim at the beginning of the hellenistic period,[25] but that still did not mean a definitive separation from Judaism.

The separation occurred at the time of the destruction of the temple by John Hyrcanus 129-128 BCE.[26] In spite of the long, common textual history and other arguments,[27] the question remains, whether it is likely, in view of the cultic schism that came about because of the construction of their own temple, that a canonical book would be adopted, which was developed after the split. It would be easier to imagine additional common textual history and other forms of mutual influence than the later adoption of a document originating after the separation.[28]

Other aspects, however, are more important. Today it is assumed that the Greek translation of the **Pentateuch** was made in the middle of the third century BCE.[29] Thus, in any case, it agrees with Pseudo-Aristeas. Such a translation, however, presupposes the conclusion and canonic validity.[30] This is supported by the fact that there is no evidence of hellenism or the disputes that came about with it in the **Pentateuch**.[31] All of this

suggests that it is quite likely the **Pentateuch** was completed at the beginning of the hellenistic period, that is, the last third of the fourth century. It may have been the wide-ranging changes in the geopolitical situation, with its unforeseen consequences for Judea and Judaism as a whole that—at latest—brought the redactional work to an end.

The Law of Ezra and the Authorization of the Kingdom

Rabbinical tradition regarded Ezra as a second Moses,[32] and since the beginnings of historical-critical research with Spinoza,[33] the relation of **Pentateuch** and the law of Ezra has been a key question for the development of Torah. We will now try to work out, in spite of gross unclarities, what can be regarded as reliable material about the historical Ezra.

For a long time scholars have been deeply divided over everything about Ezra.[34] Beginning with his dates, there is practically nothing over which there is consensus. The only available reference speaks of the seventh year of the reign of Artaxerxes (Ezr 7:7f.), nevertheless, this is neither clear nor uncontroverted.[35] If we associate this reference with Artaxerxes II, we arrive at the year 458, and if the third king of this name is intended, 398 BCE is the date. The important connection to the person and work of Nehemiah (who came to Jerusalem in 445 BCE) is questionable.[36] It is especially doubtful whether Ezr 7-10 or Neh 8-10 represent reliable sources. Furthermore, since it has been demonstrated that the order of the present form of the books of Ezra and Nehemiah is by no means secondary or accidental, but in every respect they have been consciously shaped, especially theologically,[37] the theory of a pre-chronistic[38] Ezra source is even less likely.[39]

As with Meyer and Schaeder, we are still concerned with evaluating the Aramaic letter of Artaxerxes in Ezr 7:11-26.[40] According to the letter Ezra was assigned by the king to go with a group of exiles to Jerusalem, and there "to make inquiries about Judah and Jerusalem according to the law of your God, which is in your hand" (verse 14). In addition to being given a significant contribution from the court and the diaspora to the temple, they are granted the right to demand support from the state tax system in the trans-Euphrates satrapy (verses 21ff.); temple employees are declared free of taxes (verse 24). The important statements (in addition to verse 14) are in verses 25f.:

> *Ezr 7:25 "And you, Ezra, according to the God-given wisdom you possess, appoint magistrates and judges who may judge all the people in the province Beyond the River who know the laws of your God; and you shall teach those who do not know them. 26 All who will not obey the law of your God and of the king, let judgment be strictly executed on them, whether for death or for banishment or for imprisonment.*[41]

Is there a genuine Persian decree which underlies the entire Ezra story,[42] or is this decree an invention of the chronicler?[43] There really is not much unity in the text[44] and it is clearly written from a Jewish perspective.[45] The subordination of the entire satrapy of Trans-Euphrates[46] to the law of Israel is neither historically probable nor does the narrative, as it follows the decree, rely on its existence. The theory that Ezra or the Jewish people themselves wrote the document, having it approved at a later time,[47] is hardly tenable. All in all, arguments against genuineness seem to prevail today, but certainty is hard to achieve.

Of course, there are important references suggesting the text presumes historical reality and it aspires to the origin of that reality. That said, even critics who would regard the letter as a product of judaistic invention, the work, e.g. of someone like the chronicler, must simultaneously acknowledge that it asserts a kernel of historical reality.[48] Thus, on the one hand, Kaiser says, "We must acknowledge that we have an edifying story in the Book of Ezra,"[49] regarding which, "We are better off avoiding a historical evaluation of this text."[50] On the other hand, the same author says: "We might now regard the historical value of the Ezra narrative as more or less believable, and as a result, regard Ezra to be the man who brought the **Pentateuch** from Babylon to Jerusalem . . . but we must assume that the **Pentateuch,** *at latest at the turn of the 5th/4th centuries,* was essentially *complete,* and in the course of the next century achieved its unequalled place of honor. This is the only way the origin of the Ezra narrative is comprehensible."[51] Even an unhistorical aetiology can describe what is real!

Gunneweg is of a similar opinion in his commentary of the Book of Ezra. After thorough testing of the arguments, he too comes to the opinion that Ezr 7:12-26 does not represent an original document of the Persian government, but rather "a Jewish text and a component of the chronicler's narrative." Nevertheless, according to Gunneweg, we should not doubt the core of the material is historical. "Historically—that is, in the sense of the harsh reality— . . . the legal position of the postexilic Jewish community was centered in Judah and Jerusalem but also outside the narrower homeland. It was characteristic that the Persians recognized traditional law, but they also declared it to be legally binding."[52]

The conception of the decree of Artaxerxes, which at first seems purely theological, "proves to be an aetiology of the autonomous Jewish community around the temple and synagogue based in law and synagogal jurisdiction.[53] Thus, it can also be said: "If the chronicler associates Persian recognition of Torah with the person of Ezra, it may indeed be that Ezra was involved in this area."[54]

While skeptical about the Artaxerxes decree, we must accept the important statement in Ezr 7:25, which equates the laws of God and of the Persian king as both legally applicable and juridically binding. There was a policy of the Persian empire, known today from a whole series of examples, which sanctioned local law through the empire, recognizing it as binding.[55] The best known example of these is the collecting and codifying of Egyptian law which remained in effect under Darius I.[56] Another important example is what is fixed in the trilingual stele from the Letoön at Xanthos, bearing resolutions of the congregation of Xanthos affecting the cult of Carian gods.[57] After studying the relevant texts, P. Frei categorized "the process of recognition of local norms by authorities of the empire "as state authorization."[58]

The same thing is also largely true for Israel: Israelite law, thus the traditional law of the God of Israel, simultaneously became the law of the Persian empire for Jews: according to Ezr 7:25, for all who live in the satrapy of Syria.[59] This situation, wherein the Persian government recognized the existing written law, is presumed to have been the case on the basis of what we know about the features of Persian policy, according to all of the Old Testament sources and especially according to the further history of the hellenistic period.[60] The Ezra story with the edict of Artaxerxes at its center is the aetiology of this policy. Historical particulars are not especially enlightening but it is historically probable that this event was connected with a person named Ezra.

The main question remains: how did a law, coming into force in this way, relate to the **Pentateuch**? Scholars have investigated every conceivable possibility to identify the law of Ezra. It may, e.g. have been the **Pentateuch,** the priestly writings, the Holiness Code or even Deuteronomy.[61] Convincing support for a particular answer is, however, hard to find.

It is, of course, expressly said that this is a new law, but in principle the inhabitants already knew the contents (Ezr 7:25). The nature of empire authorization makes this seem plausible. Furthermore, the chroniclers were probably already thinking of the **Pentateuch,**[62] but were writing at a much later time. If we cannot identify the law of Ezra according to the evidence we have, we ought not to speculate.

Is there a correlation of the law of Ezra with the **Pentateuch**? This is especially disputed by Rendtorff.[63] He refers to fundamental differences between the law in Ezr 7, designated with a Persian loan word *(dāt),* and what is called *tōrā* in Neh 8, saying that these must be kept separate. In Ezr 7 we are concerned with a law that "has a purely legal meaning."[64] On the other hand, Neh 8 describes Ezra's activity entirely as reading Torah in worship.[65] He was "the first of whom it could be said that he studied and taught *tora*."[66]

Both activities were brought together in later redactional processes, especially in Ezr 7:6. Rendtorff is surely correct to note that Ezr 7:12ff. and Neh 8 present different perspectives, different languages, and probably also different literary documents, which were brought together at a later time. Nevertheless, even for Rendtorff they are bracketed together in the picture presented for example in Ezr 7:6, if I understand correctly.[67]

Still, the exposition of the word *dāt* is not entirely convincing.[68] To be sure, *dāt* is probably really "not a specific designation for Jewish religion or Jewish 'law'."[69] We would not argue, however, that it becomes a designation even for those in important places. If we read in Esth 3:8 regarding Israel, "their laws . . . are different from those of every other people, and they do not keep the king's laws . . . ," *d t hem* can only refer to the law of Israel, in other words *tora,* which raises questions about the meaning of the law of God and the law of the king in Ezr 7. In Dan 6:6 the "law of God" . . . can only refer to Torah. What Aramaic word would be a better equivalent to *tōrā* than *dāt?* The only other candidate might be *dī n.*[70] In later legal language *d t* as well as *d n* is used in aramaic phrases like "the law of Moses and Israel" in marriage contracts.[71] Thus, there is nothing to dispute the idea that *dāt* in Ezr 7:12ff. can also refer to Torah.

Analogous situations of authorization by the Persian empire are not limited to legal procedures in the narrow sense. Clearly, at least cultic (thus religious) questions are a part of this. No matter what we want to call the law of Ezra, since it deals with older, already traditional Israelite law (this is one of the few points over which there is no controversy), it *could not* have involved legal matters only. Already in the Book of the Covenant alongside legal requirements in the strictest sense there are cultic, religious, theological and ethical demands together with their justification. This is true for later Israelite law books up through the **Pentateuch.** To posit a legal document, similar to ancient Near Eastern law books, underlying the law of Ezra would contradict the entire history of Israelite law. It is in the decree of Artaxerxes of Ezra 7, in the midst of dealing with the Jerusalem temple and cult, that we find a subject dealing with the contents of *dāt.*

Thus it follows that we are unable to conclude even the shape of the law of Ezra, the date of Ezra's investiture or his activity from the sources. How ever this law might have looked, how much it was like the finished **Pentateuch;** it was out of this law that what we know as the **Pentateuch** developed somewhere near the end of the Persian period. This and already its pre-

forms, as the law of the God of Israel, were simultaneously established as law by the Persian king. "What was in legal substance . . . the law of God, was in legal form the law of the state."[72]

In my opinion, we can come to irrefutable conclusions regarding our understanding of Torah without giving fundamentally unsupportable answers to the many controverted questions about Ezra and his law. From this understanding we can draw conclusions for the following interpretation of the **Pentateuch** as a whole.

The Pentateuch in the Social-Political Field: Supporting Groups and Tendencies

In what follows we will attempt to grasp the social context in which the **Pentateuch** achieved its final form. Indeed, on the basis of our limited knowledge of the historical context, it is a question of dealing with the elementary observations and reflections made about the social-political role and function of the **Pentateuch** during the Persian period, which ought to supplement what has been said about Moses and his significance.[73] Methodologically, we will connect the final form of the **Pentateuch** with the most important, clearly discernible political and social powers. Unlike the issue of historical sequence, we have a clearly reliable source: the memoir of Nehemiah. In Neh 1:1-7:5aba, 12*, 13* (over which scholars are almost entirely in agreement), we have an authentic report of Nehemiah.[74] Certainly, the text reproduces only a brief glimpse from the end of the second third of the fifth century, and this from a subjective point of view.[75] Nevertheless, we can see the basic historical pattern, it had not altered dramatically before the change to hellenism.

Those in Debt and the Priests: The Social Coalition

According to Nehemiah's memoir and other contemporary sources, e.g. the Book of Malachi, there were two observable, fundamental conflicts within the population of the small province of Judah, which was a subunit of the Trans-Euphrates satrapy.[76] The one was the common, ancient antagonism, already so important during the preexilic period) between the indebted small farmers and their richer creditors. In Neh 5 the opposition came to a head, because of the compulsory construction of the wall.[77] Nehemiah was able to enact an initially "one-off" remission of debts. It is clear that special circumstances like the political necessity to complete the work on the wall, the pressure of the population and their strike, as well as his influence as the Persian governor . . . permitted him to prompt the aristocrats to take such a step.

On the other hand, there were the very different interests of the laity, especially the less consequential, agricultural population, and the cult personnel consisting of priests and Levites in the Jerusalem temple. Their material support, which relied especially upon the offering of the tithe, was always in danger (Neh 3:10ff.; Mal 3:8). This was also true for permanent support for the entire temple cult. The lack of wood for the permanent sacrificial fire (Lev 6:12) indicates the obvious difficulties (Neh 10:35; 13:31). The extremely poor province with its enormous economic problems stood at the limits of survival.

In view of these two basic conflicts, the **Pentateuch** and its laws have a very clear purpose. There were the large number of priestly laws imposing the regular tithe on priests and laity (Num 18), which also obligate the offering of firstfruits (firstborn, etc.) for all Israelites. On the other hand there were the social laws in the Book of the Covenant and Deuteronomy, such as the prohibition against charging interest (Ex 22:24; Deut 23:20; cf Lev 25:36ff.); regular remission of debts (Deut 15:1ff.); manumission of slaves (Ex 21:2ff.; Deut 15:12ff.); slave asylum (Deut 23:16f.); and general protection for the weak in society. It was especially the connection of older, preexilic laws with the priestly, which enabled a clear connection to the social nexus in the province of Judah during the Persian period. It was not just the priestly laws that dominated during this period, as was presumed to be the case for a long time after Wellhausen. The significance of the coexistence of differing traditions is recognizable right here.

One document clearly underscores this trend: the agreement in Neh 10 to observe a series of actually important laws from Torah. According to the covenant, the people entered a written obligation agreeing to observe the following ten requirements:

1. No mixed marriages (v. 31);

2. Sabbath (v. 32a);

4. The offering of a third of a shekel, as a yearly temple tax for the bread of the Presence, as well as for regular public sacrifice, including sin offering . . . for the people (vv. 33-34);

5. The regular contribution of wood for the temple (v. 35);

6. Firstfruits (v. 36);

7. Firstborn (v. 37);

8. A regular contribution of dough, fruit, wine and oil (v. 38a);

9. Tithe (vv. 38b-40);

10. Regular care for the temple (v. 40b).

This is the earliest extant document of a detailed expli-

cation of Torah. There is much to suggest that it originates from a time when the text of the **Pentateuch** was not yet in its final canonic form. Thus, the requirement of a regular temple tax in the form of a third of a shekel is only attested here. On the other hand, in Ex 30:11ff.; 38:25f. reference is made to a half shekel tax, and the later Jewish temple tax supports it on this mention of an, initially "one-off", levy.[78] General considerations argue that the higher offering represents the later version.[79] Scholars are divided whether Neh 10 is a pre-Chronicler document, of about the time of Nehemiah[80] or not.[81] Since the text has clear connections to the problems of the Nehemiah memoir, especially Neh 13, but other themes also appear,[82] it is frequently regarded as a later document.[83] Reference to a remission of debt in the seventh year (10:32b) is only connected to Neh 5, but rather than being unique, this is to be a regular payment. The solemn form of the written personal obligation, which parallels the "we" style of the text, is especially noteworthy (10:1, 13).[84] This is noteworthy because it is not just the authority of God but also that of the Persian king behind the law. Does this, as Gunneweg suggests,[85] reflect the transition to the hellenistic period? Still, all questions of dating can and should remain open.

Quite apart from how old we regard this text as being, it is the oldest outside the **Pentateuch** to identify divine law as a *combination* of all the great law texts. The incorporation of important priestly texts such as the law of the tithe in Num 18 and the priestly conception of offering (sin offering) is incontrovertible. The obligation to guarantee remission of debts in the seventh year, as we find it in Neh 10:32b, clearly contradicts the ideas of Lev 25 and adopts Deut 15:1ff. The renunciation of profit from harvest, also occurring in that year, is not found in Deut 15, coming, as shown by the term "renounce, hand over" . . . , not from Lev 25:1-7, but from Ex 23:11, the Book of the Covenant. In the Ezra-Nehemiah period, the much disputed question of mixed marriage, which verse 30 places at the head of the provisions, is an activation, necessitated by the exile, of Ex 34:16, Deut 7:3;[86] and in this radicality it has no basis in the priestly texts.[87] The Book of the Covenant, Deuteronomy and the priestly law, all three great law codes form the basis of Neh 10; the legal aspect of the entire **Pentateuch** is fully present.

At the same time, Neh 10 is powerful evidence for the beginning of the interpretation of law. Clines's demonstration of this is impressive.[88] The way in which biblical texts are taken up and used parallels the basic principles of later rabbinic interpretation. Thus, in part, the actual legal norm is replaced by the procedure of its practice, e.g. when the demand for a permanent sacrificial fire (Lev 6:5) is made possible by the obligation to supply wood, which is regulated in detail. Or, when the tithe offering (Neh 13:10ff., Mal 3:8), which is frequently not observed, is secured by the process in which those who are profiting (the Levites) receive the tithe under the supervision of a priest (verses 38bf.). This is what the Mishnah tractate Abot calls a "fence around Torah" (Abot 1.1),[89] and is connected with the men of the great assembly (thus the time after Ezra).

Neh 10 attests what is also apparent in other places: with the development of the **Pentateuch** there came a need for its interpretation. Which laws should apply and how the different formulations fit together, all of this requires continuing interpretation in and through practice. The fact that the **Pentateuch** contains differing corpora that have not been adjusted makes interpretation more than usually necessary.

The gathering of laws from completely different levels of social concern and the way they have been arranged, already by Nehemiah himself, especially in Neh 10, permits us to come to solid conclusions regarding the authorities behind the development, at least in its use in the province of Judah. Combining the interests of the free farmers with those of the cult personnel is very important.[90] The great emphasis upon the subject of debt in all comparable ancient societies gives the enforcement of Deut 15:1ff. a weight, which generally balances the scales from the perspective of the participants for the many cultic offerings.[91] This "coalition" is clearly distinguished from other contemporary social groups in Judea, e.g. the aristocratic-wisdom and eschatological-prophetic groups. Socially as well as literally, they clearly stand alongside Torah.[92] Simultaneously, it is precisely these two great theological groups or schools that stand out from among the material interests investigated here, which with a variety of other reasons underlie the overall composition of the **Pentateuch**.[93] On a new level, the new arrangement of (deuteronomic) social law and (priestly) cultic law in the **Pentateuch** doubled the basic principle of Torah, which was established in the Book of the Covenant, and which, if in a different way, shaped all of the pre-canonic legal corpora.

Judea and the Diaspora: The Unity of the Nation

Israel's existence was scattered since, at the very latest, the beginning of the Babylonian exile. Even the postexilic reestablishment of the temple cult and the development of a separate province of Judea did not lead to a self-contained association of settlements.[94] A basic document of Judaism, recognized as the law of the Persian empire, would also be required to secure the relationship of Judah with the rest of the diaspora. The **Pentateuch** succeeded as being canonically valid only because it fulfilled this function. Its basic structure responds to this assignment precisely. By adopting and developing the relevant foundational material secured by the priestly writings,[95] especially in the stories of the patriarchs, they sketched a picture of life with the God of Israel. This was immediately relevant

and applicable for the diaspora. We must, of course, make a distinction between the eastern and the Egyptian diaspora.

Historically, the influence of the eastern diaspora[96] during the Persian period was tremendous. It is, in fact, difficult to overstate its importance. The figures who gave decisive stimulus to the reshaping came from here. At first it was Sheshbazzar and Zerubbabel and then Ezra and Nehemiah. They came directly from the king and their actions were obviously very closely coordinated with the king's intentions. We may surmise that the law of Ezra, or the **Pentateuch,** was shaped and edited there. Nevertheless, lacking the necessary sources, we must allow this question to remain completely unresolved. In any case, before Ezra's mission, his law, as it is emphasized in Ezr 7:25, was well-known to those for whom it mattered: those for whom the law gained new significance because of his mission.

Business documents give us rather a good picture[97] of day-to-day life in the eastern diaspora, but we know next to nothing about their religious life.[98]

We should not, however, conceive of this life in analogy to later diaspora Judaism, e.g. of the Roman period. None of the elements is here yet, because they only begin to develop at this time. This applies above all to the synagogue,[99] which we may not yet presume to exist. It was probably pharisaism, with its new interpretation of Torah independent of the cult site, that penetrated the everyday life of the laity with its Torah commandments. Apart from basic priestly regulations for any diaspora[100]—circumcision, passover, sabbath, endogamy as well as the prohibition against blood— there is no evidence of a religious life.

The stories of the patriarchs do offer us an extremely graphic portrayal of life in the interaction between the eastern diaspora and Judea. This is also true for the final form of Genesis, quite independent of questions regarding the age of relevant passages or the literary-redactional processes. The patriarchs had their homeland in Babylon proper. Abraham left Ur-Kasdim (Gen 11:28, 31) and went by stages to Palestine. There are repeated references to connections to his place of origin, especially through marriages.[101]

It was from that homeland, according to Gen 24, that Isaac received a wife, and it was there that Jacob fled from Esau, gaining his wives and wealth from Laban. Quite in contrast to Egypt, there were no conflicts with rulers. If there were problems, they were with relatives, as e.g. between Jacob and Laban. To be sure, Abraham was supposed to leave Mesopotamia and go to the Promised Land in order to be blessed there (Gen 12:1-3), and this probably also applied to all of his descendants. Other relatives, however, remained behind and established the foundations for the wealth of the nation.

If the center of the empire was in the east, during the Persian period Egypt was a country that was frequently shaken by insurrection (especially 486-484, 460-454, 405 BCE) since the conquest of Cambyses (525 BCE), until it finally became independent again (401 BCE). Finally, it was conquered again in 342 BCE.[102] This history must have played a significant role for Egypt's neighbor, the province of Judah,[103] but it also must have affected the fate of the Jewish diaspora in Egypt. Unfortunately, we know little about it.[104] Actually, we only have the documents about the Jewish military colony in Elephantine to shed light on the events here.[105] There are some things, such as the fact that apparently there were gods (including Anat) venerated alongside the God of Israel in the temple there, that correspond to the historically uncertain reports of the beginning (especially Jer 44) of the diaspora there.

The portrait that the **Pentateuch** paints of Egypt and its relationships with Israel is marked by deep ambivalence. On one hand it is a country where a person can especially find escape from hunger. This was already true of Abraham (Gen 12:16ff.), and it is illustrated by the events around Joseph and his brothers. There is an abrupt change from one pharaoh to the next (Ex 1:8), and the picture is affected by the exodus tradition. When dealing with the eastern powers, who were more important and more powerful at the time of the final redaction, there is no parallel to the idea that all the powers of God must be mobilized to defeat Egypt's pharaoh and his forces (Ex 5-14). If prophetic language and concepts played a part in this in addition to ancient tradition, it is important that Egypt, which is here attacked and from whom Israel escapes, was a dangerous and aggressive power for the Persian king.[106]

Persian Rule: The Difference it made for Prophecy

As the texts tell us, both Ezra and Nehemiah came with a direct, personal assignment from the Persian king. The relative autonomy of the province of Judah, which was completed during the time of their activity,[107] was part of Persian policy. Shortly after the Megabyzus insurrection,[108] the period of activity of Nehemiah and Ezra,[109] is closely connected with the great Persian interest in the pacification of this region of the empire. The tolerance that was guaranteed ended where Persian interests were affected—that is, in what concerned the support of authority and payment of the required taxes.[110] For that reason we may assume that there was nothing in the legal documents recognized by the empire's authorization that could contradict these interests.

Already in the Aramaic chronicle of the Book of Ezra there was warning about the revival of old Israelite and especially Jerusalem traditions of independence (Ezr 4:12f.; 15:19f.). Danger threatened Nehemiah's work, when he was libeled about wanting to set up an independent monarchy (Neh 6:6, cf already 2:19). Interestingly, prophets also played a role in this. They are alleged to have been bought by Nehemiah in order to proclaim him king (6:7). Thus, we are probably to understand Nehemiah's difficulties with the prophetess Noadiah and other prophets as being behind this (6:14).

The correlation of monarchy and prophecy suggests messianic proclamation. The prophecy of this period known to us is generally dominated by eschatological and early apocalyptic ideas. The end of all foreign domination is a continuing theme in all of this. Beginning with what Haggai has to say about Zerubbabel, it is clear that we are also dealing concretely with freedom from Persian domination. It was no more than of secondary importance for the Persians whether the report concerned an annihilating judgement (e.g. Isa 63:3ff.; Joel 3-4), or a peaceful pilgrimage by the people to Zion to bring their wealth there (Isa 60) or instruction to be received (Isa 2:2ff./Mi 4:1ff.).

Against such a background, we can hardly over-estimate the importance of the description of Moses at the end of the **Pentateuch** (Deut 34). Contrary to deuteronomic prophetic law with its promise of a constant flow of prophets like Moses (Deut 18:15ff.), Moses is here elevated above all other prophets, which is critical for an understanding of the whole work. "Never since has there arisen a prophet in Israel like Moses, whom the Lord knew face to face. He was unequaled for all the signs and wonders . . ." (Deut 34:10f.). Moses and his **Torah** supersede all other prophecy in a fundamental way.[111]

If we choose to reject the **Pentateuch** on this basis and are aware of the great role of eschatology and early apocalytic at this time, the enormous work must be regarded as extremely unprophetic and unescha-tological, even anti-eschatological. This characterization in no way implies that it did not adopt prophetic traditions and continue the functions. This is not only clear for the early traditions, but also for many narrative contexts and formulations.[112]

In any case, the question is still whether this origin gives the text something like prophetic features,[113] or whether—more likely—the opposite is the case.[114] If prophetic characteristics are adopted in the plague narratives when pharaoh was hardened, it does not tell us whether and how such things worked prophetically at the time of the final redaction.[115] In any case, it never achieved the critical power of contemporary prophecy. This was significantly affected by eschatological-pre-apocalyptic expectation, according to which Israel's domination by foreign powers was to be brought to an end. We cannot, however, find such expectation anywhere in the **Pentateuch.** To be sure, we find great promises made repeatedly to the patriarchs, but they are restricted to a limited area. Alongside these there are a very few places in which very broad exegesis might produce an eschatological sense. In some of these, like the protoevangelium (Gen 3:15) or the Shiloh statement of Gen 49:10f., such an interpretation contradicts the clear sense of the text.

There are probably only two places in all the many chapters that speak of a divinely instituted, world-wide shift in power, the fourth song of Balaam and the conclusion of the song of Moses. Both passages are rather unclear and their exegesis is controverted. We cannot tell about whom is Num 24:24 speaking, or who is meant by the ships from Kittim.[116] It might be a cryptic reference to Alexander the Great and the end of the Persian empire. In Deut 32:43 there are significant textual differences between LXX and MT, so that it is nearly impossible to determine the original text with certainty.[117] Apart from these two marginal places, there is nothing that might be interpreted as endangering the power of Persia.

The Neighboring Provinces: The Open Promise

Nehemiah, and perhaps also Ezra,[118] functioned as governors . . . of the province of Judah, which was a separate part of the satrapy and independent of Samaria.[119] Judah[120] is a small area; there is only a distance (north-south) of about 50 km between Beth-Zur and Bethel. We can tell quite clearly from Nehemiah that at all costs the neighboring regions wanted to prevent the construct of the wall (Neh 2:19f.; 3:33ff. among others), which the Aramaic chronicle had already recognized (Ezr 4:8ff.). The disagreements went as far as verging on military conflicts (Neh 4:1ff., especially verse 10).

We only need to look at a map of the province of Judah, together with the neighboring regions of Samaria, Ashdod, Idumea, Moab and Ammon,[121] comparing them with the places and areas promised to the patriarchs in order to discover an essential message of the **Pentateuch** at the time in which it received its final form. It was first called the Promised Land in Gen 12, in conjunction with the journey of Abraham. He came first to Shechem, where he received the promise, "To your offspring I will give this land," and built an altar there (Gen 12:6f.). Then he camped between Bethel and Ai where he built an altar, and finally he went into the Negev (verses 8f.). From here the story continues through all the many promise texts up to the climax in Deut 34. Before Moses' death, God showed the whole land to him from Mount Nebo, and there is a precise description: "the whole land: Gilead as far as Dan, all of Naphtali, the land of Ephraim and Manasseh, all of the land of Judah as far as the Western Sea, the Negev and the plain—that is, the valley of Jericho, the city of

palm trees—as far as Zoar" (34:1-3). All of it "is the land of which I swore to Abraham, Isaac and Jacob, saying, 'I will give it to your descendants'" (verse 4).

Moses was not permitted to enter the land, and the Jews of the Persian period possessed only a small fraction of it. From the long list of places in Deut 34, this is Judah, but not to the sea, and the district of Jericho. Everything else that has been promised and sworn lies in hostile neighboring provinces. The important places of the promises and patriarchal traditions, like Beersheba, Hebron, Mamre, Shechem, Mahanaim and others lie outside. Bethel and Ai were disputed border localities.[122] This means that only a portion of the promises have been fulfilled, and they would have to wait for the rest. So, as the conflicts between the provinces of the region under Persian rule were apparently possible, it was also possible in this way to sustain a claim to the great districts of the neighboring provinces as having been promised by their God.

They must, however, remain promises. The same thing was not true for the conquest of the land through Joshua's military campaigns and the consequent division among the tribes of Israel. Torah ends in Deut 34 with the death of Moses and the renewal of the promise. Scholars have found or theorized literary threads in many places connecting the **Pentateuch** with the Book of Joshua or even beyond. There is even the theory of an original Hexateuch, there are theories of connections between Deuteronomy and the deuteronomic history, and other ideas abound.

The much discussed question, why the **Pentateuch,** as an independent authority, was separated from all of the other documents with which it (or parts of it) might correlate, belongs among the literary problems that cannot be resolved by literary-historical methods alone. The key to the understanding lies in the validity of the **Pentateuch** as Israel's Torah, the legitimation experienced as the law of the Persian empire. There is no way that a report of the conquest of the most powerful of the neighboring provinces by force and their apportionment to Israel could find a place among legal documents valid in this way. That only applies to the traditions of the Books of Samuel, which aim toward an independent nation-state. It was only in another time, and then with a little less pomp, that this early document could, together with the later prophets, become part of the canon.[123]

Composition Components and their Theology

A Persian Legal Principle as Background

The following attempt to examine the inner theological sense of the **Pentateuch** composition must be limited to a very few, exceptionally remarkable and important characteristics. It is not just its size and complexity that make the study of its historical sense so difficult in every case. Some of its structural characteristics do not permit us to anticipate a clear result, rather they cause it to appear incomplete. This includes the juxtaposition of narrative and law,[124] but also probably the peculiarity of combining together several, different, older, contradictory laws. In legal-historical terms this is quite remarkable. It probably also made a significant contribution to the potency of Torah, that it constantly withdrew fresh material from itself.

A certain need to have a single law, a single document as the divine law of their own God must have continued to exist from the beginning of the process of the empire's authorization of their law. This would be a law to which all Israel would submit, and it would be valid as the law of the king. A juxtaposition of different, mutually contradictory laws would diverge from the intent. Why, then, were Israel's various older legal codes not adjusted? In principle it would have been easy to arrange them as a single, consistent picture of the will of God as we find it in the tradition. That is precisely what any exegesis must achieve from the outset. Correspondingly, this is to be observed in any of the older legal documents, in the priestly documents and into the postexilic period. Each of them, if our literary analysis is correct, have incorporated older material—previous collections of legislation—creating a relatively homogenous, new entity. Why was this not handled in this way? Instead of this approach, why was an additive principle selected, which led to so many repetitions and so many obvious contradictions?

It is not a sufficient explanation to fall back on the inviolable dignity of the older texts. It is even a question of how and why, in the relatively short period since the exile and the development of the priestly writings, attitudes toward their own tradition had so completely changed. Why was the wording of these texts still regarded as more or less sacrosanct, so that something that is obviously no longer practicable could not be deleted but something new could or had to be placed alongside of it?

There is an Old Testament parallel for the idea of the unalterability of written law, and I suggest that we attempt to use it by way of explanation. In Esth 8, Esther asked the king to revoke the written decree he had previously sent, decreeing the extermination of the Jews in all the provinces (verse 5). The king, who had meanwhile changed his mind, answered: "You may write as you please with regard to the Jews, in the name of the king, and seal it with the king's ring.[125] Still an edict written in the name of the king and sealed with the king's ring cannot be made retroactive" (8:8). The new edict has the purpose of preventing what the old decree had commanded. Practically speaking, it cancelled the results of the first decree by enabling the Jews to defend themselves and take revenge (verse 11).

Such a complicated route is necessary because, as it says in verse 8, "an edict written in the name of the king and sealed with the king's ring cannot be revoked." New law can be placed alongside older law without formally canceling the first, even when the second contradicts the first.

Scholars are divided over whether there was really a Persian legal principle at work here.[126] There is, in any case, no further direct evidence for such a custom.[127] Still, as the Book of Esther shows, Israel thought this was a Persian legal principle. This too is a fact, even if it does not correspond to historical reality. Nevertheless, there are a few other places that regard the written laws of the Medes and the Persians as permanently valid (Esth 1:19; Dan 6:9, 13, 16). Taken on their own, these formulations only mean that the decrees currently in force were permanently valid. In conjunction with Esth 8:8 they could also be understood in the sense of applying to the decree under discussion.

For Frei, the applicability of the decrees well into the future was closely connected with the fact that the instructions were written.[128] Once something is written, it becomes permanent. He mentions the fact that the process of authorization of the Trilingue of Letoon was written and thus its character as "document" and its validity are connected.[129] Frei even suggests that we might be able to see the origin of the authorization of the empire in this practice.[130] When certain norms (of local institutions, for example) are transferred to the authority of the empire, and this authority writes them down, they receive permanent legal applicability.

Can we, should we see a correlation between this principle of Persian law and the characteristics of Torah?[131] When Ezra or others before or after him in the Persian empire refer back to their own ancient, written law to gain the authorization of the empire, it is likely and perhaps inevitable that they regard their own tradition—thus YHWH's action—as analogous to that of the king. What was presented in ancient written law in Israel and happened in the name of God, was permanently established and could not be revoked. Because it was written, it had permanent validity. Things that were different, even contradictory, must be placed alongside without making compensatory adjustment. Israel transferred to scribes and legal authorities responsibility for decisions regarding needs for adjustment in the substance and decisions regarding actual proceedings.

There is something fundamental to the biblical canon that developed with this process, whose inner logic cannot be derived from the legal history of Israel. There is a kind of "tolerance" produced by this juxtaposition and interplay of texts, which, as parts of one canonic document, contradict each other directly in significant points. God's will is not a more or less closed system, nor is it a principle for the integration of many truths into a single entity. It comprises things mutually exclusive. This does not just apply to the present, but is also true for the things that have come from various times and eras. The canon, which came into existence with Torah, functioned throughout the various periods as an enduring foundation, because it helped to illuminate and explain widely differing situations and demands. This characteristic, however, is closely connected with and corresponds to the inner structure of the canonical text. It is this feature of the **Pentateuch** composition that really contributes something new to the previous corpora. Its power is, of course, only apparent as we view the overall history of reception. We can only deal with drawing attention to a few features of Torah here.

"Do not let God speak to us" (Ex 20:19): The Role of the Decalogue

The Decalogue (Ex 20; Deut 5) plays a role in the composition of the **Pentateuch** that cannot be overemphasized. As the introduction to the central Sinai law in Ex 20 it rises above the rest of the laws because it alone was given as God's direct word to the nation. The mediating role of Moses only comes about because of the fearful reaction of the people who were unable to bear God speaking to them directly (20:19). The function of Ex 20 as literary connection becomes very clear in the way that, unlike its parallel (Deut 5), it establishes the foundation of the sabbath commandment (Ex 20:11) in Gen 2:1-3, therefore the beginning of the enormous work. On the other hand, the Decalogue and its proclamation is repeated in Deut 5, thus representing one of the means by which Deuteronomy is connected to the very different Tetrateuch. The tradition-historical position of the Decalogue is in accord with this literary-reference function. As a whole, it is quite close to Deuteronomy and its theology, but the version in Ex 20 clearly shows signs of priestly amplification and redaction. The unity of the Sinai pericope, which is composed of differing materials, is achieved through its shape.

This special position of the Decalogue in the compositional unity of Old Testament law must be examined.[132] Of course, it only came about in its current form in the later phases of the redaction. Ex 20 had the more self-contained Deut 5 as its immediate model.[133] What does the elevated status of the text over against the rest of Torah mean?

Theologically, this question deals with nothing less than the position of the Decalogue in Christian theology, its ethics and especially its catechesis. The Decalogue has played a very special role, beyond that of the rest of Torah, since the days of the early church.[134] It has been regarded as a summary of the divine will that transcends time, as the essence of natural law and biblical ethics. While only a few of the remaining contents of the rest of Torah have been adopted and applied to

Christianity in an incidental and eclectic manner, the Decalogue is regarded differently. Jewish exegesis and tradition has been critical of this special role, and have sought to prevent this appropriation.[135] Closer inspection quickly shows that the contents of Torah do not support such a special position for the Decalogue. It cannot be regarded as a kind of summary, or the essence of Torah, nor was it ever intended to be such. Too many central themes are absent entirely and, as the history of interpretation shows, when interpreted into the Decalogue, they have rather little power.[136]

When we examine the meaning, role and function of the "elevated" Decalogue in the canonic shape of the **Pentateuch** and the Sinai pericope, we are asking whether this traditionally special role can be legitimized. Can or should it be regarded in some way, as the sum and summary of God's will, to dominate the rest of Torah? Is the disregard of Torah in Christian ethics and tradition in some way justified?

After various other attempts, Norbert Lohfink most recently has worked out the canonical special role.[137] He did it in a new way, after convincingly rejecting older attempts, e.g. that of Claus Westermann.[138] Westermann believed that there is a basic difference between commandment and law, which was valid up into the Pauline theology of law, and he supported this in Hebrew legal terminology as well as the age and provenance of the traditions in accord with the assessment of Albrecht Alt. In view of the textual evidence as well as recent scholarly discussion, none of this is tenable. Lohfink emphasizes that the Decalogue is divine speech in no way different from the rest of Torah, consequently it may not be extracted from Torah.

About this special position of the Decalogue, Westermann and Christian theology in general are largely in agreement.[139] It comes, according to Lofink, solely from the function that the canonic text ascribes to this text. To the degree that the portrayals in Deut 5 as well as Ex 20 permit us to recognize a "difference" in the basic significance between the Decalogue and the rest of Torah, which is quite pertinent for the entire Old Testament, and behind which we cannot go.[140] The Decalogue receives a higher position in the canonical composition with respect to the rest of the law, which is only supposed to be interpreted as an unfolding of what had been established in the Decalogue.[141] It somehow anticipates the rest of the will of God[142] and would have a "key position" for interpretation.[143] Lohfink thinks that already in Deut 5 there is a conception of parts of the law hidden in this formal elevation of the Decalogue above the rest of Torah.[144] This, of course, involves the "historical relativity of all other legal traditions in Israel."[145] The distinction between temporally conditioned or changing norms and those that are permanent and unalterable is critical. For the redactors, the elevation of the

Decalogue was part of the "distinction developed in the Old Testament between what changes and what endures in the will of God."[146] The immutable heart, the Decalogue, was placed before, and thus ultimately above, the remaining alterable law.

The traditional matrix of Christian Torah reception—that is, the special position of the Decalogue—is newly established here. The following critique is not intended to attack what Lohfink has done. It does not detract from the ever present need to be concrete, which the individual laws demonstrate, but which simultaneously renders them subject to changing conditions, nor does it intend to make the Decalogue the sum of all the laws. It is neither intended to remove the authority of the Decalogue as God's word to Moses, nor to withhold from it the Pauline criticism of the law. Nevertheless, of course, with all of these refinements, the essential, traditional role of the Decalogue as an expression of moral and natural law, which transcends time, is newly established. Exegetically, this happens in a remarkable way. The critical notion, which the special position of the Decalogue illustrates—its ability to transcend the bounds of time, meaning that it is not subject to historical and societal change—is not supported anywhere by exegesis of contents. On the contrary, quite astonishingly, it appears as an unproven presupposition by Lohfink.[147] Even the notion that special position of the Decalogue is a "theory" dealing "somehow" with their contents is not supported exegetically.

In both places (Ex 20 and Deut 5), the statements of the biblical text itself lead in an entirely different direction. The difference between the Decalogue and everything that follows lies completely and exclusively in the fact that it is *direct speech by God*. The difference is in the mode not the content. It is never indicated that what is said in this way is special or different from the rest of Torah. As we know, for each of the commandments in the Decalogue, there are more or less precise parallels in the other parts of Torah. Of course, the formulations included in the Decalogue are much more general, covering many more possible offenses,[148] but none of this has anything to do with timelessness.

We cannot dispute that the introduction of a collection of laws states something especially important for the document. This is shown by the introductions to all of the biblical collections of laws, but it is illustrated especially well by the Decalogue itself. Nevertheless, this should not cause us to think that this introduction of a speech is able to summarize everything else, or that it is more important, or that everything else is just an unfolding. The redactors nowhere assume that the very concrete individual collections of laws—the Book of the Covenant, Deuteronomy and the priestly law—are temporally bound in their concreteness and their detail, thus the will of God formulated in them might change

with the circumstances, or be lost altogether. Ultimately, is this idea not a product of modern historical consciousness? It is precisely the process of the integration of entirely different, older laws, with very different regulations, into a single Torah that permits us to recognize something completely different. The remaining history of Jewish law accomplishes the same thing. Practically speaking, of course, new situations could render old laws partially or entirely unusable; this is particularly true of the kingship law, legislation regarding sacrifice, and many social laws. Nevertheless, the will of God formulated in them endures and is never rendered historically relative. On the other hand, it hardly needs to be mentioned that for modern historical consciousness, naturally even the Decalogue is included in the mutability of all things human.

Of course, Ex 20, like Deut 5, says something very different about the special position of the Decalogue than Lohfink wants, and we will discuss this next. It is not something in the contents that gives it a special position, but only the mode of direct speech by God. What we have here is a problem in communication. The break from direct speech by God, desired by the people after this introduction, is the aetiology for the position of Moses as mediator for the transmission of all other commands.

Now, of course, there is attestation elsewhere for a critique of Mosaic authority. In Num 12:2 Miriam and Aaron ask, "Has YHWH spoken only through Moses? Has he not spoken through us also?" (Cf also Num 16f.) In Ex 20/Deut 5, however, we are not dealing with this kind of questioning of Moses' authority. There is no alternative to him, and furthermore, Deut 5 presents the whole as a recapitulation, formulated in Moses' own words. Thus, we find here no questioning of Moses' authority.

In order to begin to grasp the significance of this break, we assume that Deut 5 is a model for Ex 20. "Because it is in Deut 5, **Pentateuch** redaction must also have introduced it at a later time into the Sinai pericope of the Book of Exodus"—I am in agreement with Lohfink's observation.[149] Literary combination of Tetrateuch and Deuteronomy was only possible in this way. We should remember the following:[150]

—Deut 5 involves a new version of the tablet tradition of Ex 34, wherein the deuteronomically influenced Decalogue is inserted in place of the cultic text Ex 34:11ff.

—This was probably already a reaction to the inclusion of Ex 32-34 in the priestly writing, and

—Thus deuteronomic law is likewise connected to Sinai, the place that is becoming increasingly important as the place of the giving of the law (Deut 5:31).

In short, amplifying older deuteronomic law with Deut 5 and the Decalogue cited there, had the function, above all, of connecting the law proclaimed in Moab with the new place of the giving of the law. What was first intended to contrast with the priestly conception, verified itself and increased in significance with the development of the canonical **Pentateuch.** If Ex 20 is modelled after the example of Deut 5, and at the same time is an expression of what deuteronomic and priestly strata have in common, then it is here that we can begin to understand the significance of the special position of the Decalogue.

God's revelation on Sinai begins with the concentrated, striking formulation of the Decalogue. It is an introduction, but it should not at all be taken as the summary of all that follows. Because the people could not endure the voice of God, Moses was made a mediator. All other laws were handed down from God to Moses, and only later were they shared with the people. In importance they were all equal, no one ranked above the other. The priestly document is presented as God's word to Moses on the mountain. Stereotypically, the laws are introduced with variations of the sentence, "YHWH spoke to Moses: Say to the Israelites . . ." The carrying out of the commands themselves, together with their consequences are only described in a few places.[151] Conversely, deuteronomic law was transmitted orally to the people in Moab before Jericho. We never learn where and how this happened; we only have the summary phrase in Deut 5:31. Like the Book of the Covenant, both come from the two-party conversation of God and Moses. Deuteronomy is thus not a "second law," and the priestly document is unable to claim superiority because of its origin on Sinai.

Herein lies the special achievement of the Decalogue; more precisely, the interruption of the transmission of the law, which was desired by the people, and the introduction of Moses as mediator: In this way we have the theological and substantive equality of all of the laws that taken together form the **Pentateuch.** I am in complete agreement with Lohfink's observation, that with the Decalogue and its position, there was achieved "a historical relativity of all other legal traditions in Israel,"[152] but I would understand it differently. The Decalogue does not claim a higher rank than the other laws, nor is this suggested anywhere. Everything is God's word and enduring will. Because, however, everything else was transmitted only to Moses, the distinctions between the laws become relative. It makes no difference whether the laws were given on Sinai through God's words or on Moab through Moses.

Exegetically, the special position currently granted to the Decalogue in Christian ethics must be regarded as misleading. Neither the exegesis of the Decalogue nor that of the other laws, nor of the difference in the way they were transmitted, is able to support this position.

According to the canonical text of the Old Testament, the Decalogue is not the will of God in any sense that is not also true of the rest of Torah. It is neither the summary, nor the timeless principles of Torah. The many attempts to gain a single comprehensive will of God from the Decalogue alone result in problematic abbreviation of that will, and they are connected with the serious aberrations in church history and Christian policy. The difference from the rest of Torah lies exclusively in the mode of transmission, and the significance of this is revealed in the history of the composition. The Decalogue, or more precisely, the change in the manner of transmission that occurs after it, functions as a rectifier for the various corpora, which are present in the canonic Sinai pericope or Deuteronomy. They are all equally God's Word. Aggressive attempts to lift the Decalogue out of everything else, making it alone the basis for Christian ethics, have cut Christianity off from Israel's Torah. They are exegetically untenable and theologically, they ought not be continued.

"All the congregation are holy" (Num 16:3): The Open Conflict

For eyes schooled in two hundred years of **Pentateuch** criticism, nearly every passage of this gigantic work dissolves into a variety of disparate material, strata and blocks. Still, many generations of perceptive Bible readers hardly notice most of the alleged contradictions and tensions. When viewed in a "scholarly" fashion, many of these fissures resemble the hair-line cracks in old pictures, and we can't see the picture for the cracks. Many, perhaps even most passages are formed out of completely different traditions and texts into amazingly concise (certainly not accidental or awkward), rational entities.

On the whole, this also applies to the Sinai pericope and the texts anchored within it. The text as we have it represents itself as being completely logical and expressive, if we take it seriously as literature and theology. Even the obvious contradictions between the legal corpora were no great problem for the history of interpretation that began with canonization. Many of them were settled by the practice of adding rival provisions, as the tithe laws show.[153]

Against this background, the cases become all the more important in which not only is no attempt made to balance the problematic redactions, but where the contradictions are frequently allowed to remain with harsh obviousness. In this respect probably the most important subject area may be the one where we find the most insurmountable contradictions between the two theological camps which together shaped the **Pentateuch.** This is the disagreement over the holiness of the people (or the privilege of the priesthood). There is no consensus here or, more precisely, the consensus consists of not trying to conceal contradictions.

To work our way through this conflict, it is probably best to begin with the priestly narrative of Num 16, which is entirely wrapped up in this question. The text takes material which is clearly older, giving indication of multiple stratification (even intra-priestly).[154] Nevertheless, it is not only possible, but it is methodologically and substantively appropriate to read it as having been intended to be a single entity.[155] The chapter begins with Korah, Dathan, Abiram and 250 élite representatives of the people bringing serious charges against Moses and Aaron: "You have gone too far! All the congregation are holy, every one of them, and YHWH is among them. So why then do you exalt yourselves above the assembly of YHWH?" (verse 3).

The ensuing extremely complex narrative permits us to see different claims (or charges) raised among the various groups, and they are also concluded differently. There are Dathan and Abiram who basically challenge Moses' rule. Raising serious charges, they declare that they will not follow him (verses 12-14). They were swallowed by the earth (verses 31-34). Korah, who appears as a leader of a group of Levites, was swallowed up with them. His charges involved the priestly position that had been allotted to them (especially verses 8-11). They appear to question the difference between priests and Levites, which was so important for priestly theology. Finally, there are the 250 lay people designated as the élite leaders of the people (verse 2). Because the whole congregation is holy, they demand that the privileges reserved for Moses and Aaron (thus the priesthood) be revoked. As a punishment, they were killed by a fire that came out of the sanctuary (verse 35). The priestly answer to this mutiny was an ordeal which Moses initiated (verses 5, 7, 16-18). God used the incense offering reserved for the priests but offered by a person not authorized to show whom he regarded to be holy.

For the priestly narrator this was obviously an evil common to a variety of groups, but one with a common root. It lay in the claim of the ringleaders in verse 3, at the beginning of the story. The holiness of the entire congregation obviates any need for Moses and Aaron's special status. God's nearness to all Israelites—"YHWH is among them" (verse 3)—ought not to be connected with the privileges and groups to special holiness. For the priestly authors the claims of the Levites to the priesthood and of the laity to holiness are essentially identical. Basically, this raises questions about the concept of graduated holiness running throughout the entire priestly work. As necessary and salutary as this priestly status is to the special closeness of God, according to verses 20ff., it was only the prayer of those who were privileged for the whole people that saved them from destruction. The narrative that follows in Num 17 expressly underscores the role of the élite yet again.

What is behind this attack, the destruction of which Num 16 describes so impressively, is precisely the understanding of holiness that Deuteronomy and the texts around the narrative demonstrate. Scholars have seen this quite clearly.[156] The rebels' complaint in Num 16:3 parallels what is said with very similar language in Deut 7:6 and 14:2 (see also Ex 19:7). Of course, for the priestly text the whole people was made holy by the exodus and therefore could be in the presence of God.[157] This was expressly stated again in Num 15:40, immediately before the conflict in Num 16.[158] There are suggestions of important statements, especially those we find in the Holiness Code, "You shall be holy for I YHWH your God am holy" (see Lev 19:2 among others).

The holiness of the people is not in dispute, only its consequences. According to the priestly understanding, the holiness of the people does not exclude the special holiness of the Levites and priests but presumes that it is a possibility. Only because Aaron and his priestly descendants as Israel's representatives are aware of the special problems of close proximity to God, can they exist as God's holy people. The atonement rites are the greatest example of this.

Deuteronomy, however, expressly makes Levites and priests equal in 18:6ff. It grants full priestly rights to each Levite, clearly guaranteeing to them fewer material shares in sacrifices and tithes, and it subordinates them to the people and their representatives. Correspondingly, they are only responsible for a marginal share of the judicial process. In contrast to priestly hierarchical thinking, the holiness of the people is realized with rather democratic institutions.

Num 16, part of the priestly writings not included in Deuteronomy, is a sharp rebuke of deuteronomic thinking and theology. It is a part of a broad "debate about Israel's identity as YHWH people and the tangible conflicts of interest woven into it,"[159] which existed between priestly and deuteronomic, but also priestly and Levitical groups. While Deuteronomy is part of the same Torah, to which also Num 16 and the basic priestly texts belong—where the structures defended here are unfolded (Num 3 and 18 among others)—here we find clearly antithetical concepts coming together to form a single entity.

We find the same contrast in the narrative passages of the Sinai pericope. We only need recall that there is little in the texts themselves, especially in the heavily deuteronomically influenced texts of Ex 19 and 24, where there are contradictions and repeated breaks of the narrative thread, to help understand the sense of these breaks.[160] What is important is the question of what actually holds these texts together, not unraveling them into various literary threads, which has been notoriously unsuccessful here. Along with this, we have the problem of priestly privilege or the right of access to the presence of God, not the only, but certainly an especially clear and open conflict.

The promise in Ex 19:3ff. is placed before the entire Sinai narrative as we have it.[161] It is a preliminary sign, an advance explanation of what follows.[162] As we find in God's first words to Moses from the mountain, God brought the people to himself (verse 4). If they heed his voice and keep the covenant, they will be his possession (. . . , verse 5) and will become a kingdom of priests . . . , and a holy people (. . . , verse 6). The closeness to God achieved through the exodus is demonstrated by the holiness and priestly status of the whole nation.[163] This is certainly a deuteronomistic text,[164] and the deuteronomistic reception of the priestly concept of holiness is of special importance. If the concept of holiness became a key legal term in the priestly writings, with which the legal tradition could be reshaped in the situation of the exile,[165] this fundamental idea could be used deuteronomistically here and be placed at the head of all the Sinai laws as an indication for interpretation.

Along with the reception, the formulation contains a critique of the priestly conception. The nation becomes a "priestly kingdom" (. . . , verse 6). The expression is aimed at a political community or a state[166] consisting of priests. We find a related notion from the postexilic period in Isa 61:6. The expression is apparently intended to mean that all Israelites will become priests or will exercize priestly function. There is some question about the existence of degrees within the divine-human relationship in Israel, with the kind of basic legal consequence that the priestly texts seem to recognize. The fact that they serve as an introduction to the events at Sinai shows the importance attaching to this question. The material dealt with in Ex 19:6 is taken up again in Ex 24, this time in a narrative form: the ritual which the young men of the people perform as a covenant ceremony corresponds to the priestly consecration (Ex 29:20; Lev 8:24, 30). The people, as a whole, are consecrated as priests, and actual priests do not take part.[167]

The same basic questions—to what degree are the people as a whole permitted to draw near to God, and whether (if so, which) mediators exist (or ought to exist)—run through the stories in Ex 19 and 24. According to Ex 19:10, the people are to prepare for God's arrival on the mountain by acts of ritual cleansing. Verses 12, 13a make that concrete: boundaries are established for the people. The mountain, sanctified by the presence of God, in many respects corresponds to a sanctuary with God present. It may not be touched, under penalty of death (verse 13a). This, however, is hardly an absolute boundary, because verse 13b tells us exactly the opposite: "When the trumpet sounds a long blast, they may go up the mountain."

How close the people may come to God is clearly an unresolved issue. When God descends upon the mountain, amid all of the signs appropriate to a theophany (verse 20), the people are warned to step back (verse 21). There would be mortal danger for anyone looking upon God. Even the priests, whose duties bring them in close proximity to God, are only able to do so because of the ritual purification which they have received (verse 22). On the other hand, according to verse 24 priests are specifically excluded from this nearness to God; only Moses and Aaron are allowed to come.

This conflict is carried on in chapter 24. In verse 1 there is a command to Moses, Aaron, Nadab and Abihu as well as the seventy elders to go up the mountain. One group was to represent the priests and the other stood for the entire nation. They are then to pray from a distance (verse 1b), only Moses was permitted to come closer. The representatives, like the people themselves, were to observe the distance (verse 2). After the convenant ceremony is described in verses 3-8 (in which the priests do not play a role, and in which there is a kind of priestly consecration for the people), they all (Moses, Aaron, Nadab, Abihu and also the seventy elders) go up the mountain. They see the God of Israel and they eat a meal in the immediate presence of God.

Such an overt juxtaposition of directly contradictory material is found almost nowhere else. Here, if anywhere, we need literary criticism, but it has not given us a convincing explanation. We are unable to isolate clear strata, nor do we have an explanation why no redactional attempts have made to explain what is happening here. The evidence suggests an intentional commemoration of a disagreement between two completely different conceptions.

Nothing here is smoothed over, because apparently there was nothing to smooth over. A compromise would be inconceivable. This feature may be especially important for an appropriate understanding of the development as well as the theological significance of the **Pentateuch.** There are so many things in common between groups or schools at the time of development as we see them on the one hand in prophetic-eschatological circles, and on the other in wisdom-aristocratic groups,[168] that even such significant differences did not force them apart.

A holy text containing such an obvious, profound contradiction may be affected by that contradiction in a special way. Ever since, communities who connect themselves to the heart of the canon developed here have lived with similar contradictions and continue to do so: Sadducees and Pharisees, the Eastern and Western churches, Protestantism and Catholicism—and perhaps all others. The same larger context establishes the common priesthood of all the faithful and the dignity of the priesthood. We will allow the question whether other parts of the canon have altered this (especially the prophets) to remain unresolved here.

"And thereafter, throughout your generations" (Num 15:23): Instructions for the Journey into the Future

After staying at Sinai for almost two years, Israel left in order to go to the Promised Land (Num 10:11ff.). At Sinai they heard the Decalogue and turned away in fear. It was there that Moses received the Book of the Covenant, and Israel pledged itself to it. It was at Sinai that they received instructions for the construction of the shrine, and it was built. The priests were consecrated and the cult begun. The calf was made at Sinai, and ultimately God's promise was renewed. Israel received the stone tablets, and it was there that Moses heard the remainder of the laws, which were only announced to the people at the end of the journey through the desert. As the final version of Torah has it, Israel received all of its law from this mountain.

Nevertheless, when the people left, they fell into deep conflicts rather quickly (Num 11-14). Very shortly they hear the direct, unmediated words of God, "YHWH spoke to Moses and said: Speak to the Israelites and say to them . . ." (Num 15:1f.). A stream of laws followed as if Israel were still at Sinai. After Korah's rebellion and the consequent crushing of that activity and his followers (chapter 16f.), God spoke to Aaron (chapter 18) and then to Moses and Aaron together with commandments for the people (chapter 19). This is continued, especially, in the last part of the Book of Numbers. There, the daughters of Zelophehad request the right to inherit from their father and receive it upon instruction from God (chapter 27). It is here that we find the most comprehensive cultic calendar in the Old Testament (chapter 28f.), the rules for making vows (chapter 30), regulations for the establishment of places of asylum (chapter 35), and finally, once again, the right of women to inherit (chapter 36). These are laws like those received on Sinai, but they are given on the way through the desert. Nowhere is it indicated, as it is in Deut 5, that these actually came from Sinai.[169]

Scholars agree that these texts are among the latest passages in the **Pentateuch**[170]—this is essential for their understanding—outside of the actual priestly writings.[171] The content as well as the language of many of these texts are alien to priestly thinking. Thus, Num 18 gives the most important material foundation for the entire cult personnel with the instructions for the tithe to support Levites and priests.

Other texts are also clear continuations or amplifications of the priestly system; for example, the provisions for making sacrifice in Num 15 extend the otherwise unknown drink offering or they supplement parts of the law of sin offering. Num 19, with the instruc-

tions for the production of a special water of purification from the ashes of the red heifer, belong here.

Still, there are also clear tensions with the priestly text. It is especially important that these laws are hard to combine with basic priestly concepts. The priestly document contains a variety of laws situated *before* Sinai, and thus gives a priestly-theological foundation for the situation in the diaspora.[172] This, however, does not mean that it becomes a kind of appendage within the Book of Numbers.

This is especially shown by the fact that the institution for which the priestly writings expressly provides, plays no part in the transmission of the law. In establishing the atonement device . . . in the holy of holies they created a place of which it is said—the very first time it is mentioned: "There I will meet with you, and from above the mercy seat, from between the two cherubim that are on the ark of the covenant, I will deliver to you all my commands for the Israelites" (Ex 25:22). Shortly before they left Sinai, this was repeated (Num 7:89). The presence of God among his people, which is given when the splendor of God . . . enters the holy of holies, becomes a kind of moveable Sinai.

According to Lev 1:1, God speaks the entire sacrificial law from this tent (compare Ex 40:34-38).[173] This, however, never takes place in Num 10-36. Of course, we find important priestly traditions in which the "splendor" appears and God acts from the shrine all over in this section. There are, e.g. Num 14:10; 16:19; 17:7 as well as 20:6. Always the decisive resolution of the conflict portrayed is achieved by the intervention of God who is present in the tent shrine.[174]

Nowhere, however, do we have the pronouncement of laws from this place. They do not dovetail the priestly conception with the critical question of the source and authority of the additional laws. The sample narratives (Num 15:32ff.; 27:1ff.; 36:1ff.) are not accidental, but are connected with wide-ranging questions about the difference between "Moses," Aaron and other cultic representatives.[175]

We are dealing here with texts that together shaped the final redaction(s). Some are similar to priestly writings, but closer examination shows them to have features which are probably also typical of deuteronomism. The final texts, from Num 25:1 on, are in any case explicitly situated in that place about which Moses addressed the deuteronomic law in Moab across from Jericho (especially Num 35:1). They are already influenced by the combining of Tetrateuch and Deuteronomy, as well as the separation of the **Pentateuch** from Joshua.

In order to understand the sense of these post-Sinai laws, we should begin by taking a look at the overall composition of Num 10-36.[176] Immediately after their departure, Israel was enmeshed in conflicts that had mortal consequences. In Num 11 we find the desire for meat and for a return to slavery in Egypt, in Num 12 the insurrection of Miriam and even Aaron against Moses, and finally in Num 13f. the questioning of the purpose of the entire journey through the desert, in the spy narrative. These end with the divine decree that no one of the old Sinai generation would live to see the promised land (14:28ff.).

It is only immediately after the announcement of this generation break in Num 15 that we have the first block of post-Sinai laws. The next big turning point gives the second census of the nation in Num 26. At the end of this we have the statement that the generation of the first census in Num 1 is no longer alive (26:64f.). In other words, we have an entirely new generation. At the center of this generation we have the question of the right of women to inherit. It is certainly significant that this subject is again taken up in the last chapter (Num 36), which deals with the new generation and its wandering in the desert.

The context permits us to see the theological intent. These texts are not about the orientation of the subjects of the commandments to the record of the exodus—as in the variety of deuteronomic traditions of the various places where the law was given.[177] Rather, the question addressed is how God's new instructions ought to be heeded under changed circumstances among entirely new generations.

The conclusion of the revelatory event at Sinai cannot be the end of God's revelation. Israel received new instructions on its journey between Sinai and the promised land when they needed them. In content, these were extrapolations, realizations, supplements and amplifications of subjects and questions that had already been regulated in the revelation at Sinai—such as sacrifice, sabbath, priests, purity, festivals, places of asylum.

However, it also deals with subjects which had not appeared before, e.g. manner of dress (15:37ff.), vows (30) and the basic subject of inheritance, and thus the legal position of women (27, 36). Especially the illustrative narratives, which begin at Sinai (Lev 24:10ff.; Num 9:6ff.) and continue in the desert (Num 15:32ff., and chapters 27 and 36), show to what degree we have the necessary reaction to problems that have newly arisen and were not already treated in Sinai Torah. The renewed treatment of the theme of Num 27 in chapter 36 shows how in the course of events problems continue to develop and continually require new legal regulation.

Fixing God's will in written form, in the shape of a book, requires amendment by means of continuously innovative, divine speech; it ought not lead to rigidity. The canon and the living voice belong together. The history of the development of the canon shows[178] step by step how the two condition and supplement each other. At the very center, in Deuteronomy, there was the establishment of the central court as well as a prophet like Moses; both speak permanently with the authority of Moses, and both institutions are of great importance: the sanhedrin invoked the one, and the other ultimately produced the second part of the canon—the prophets. In the priestly writings the place from which God will speak in the future establishes itself in the center of the sanctuary, around which everything else revolved. The final redaction, with its revelations of the law on the journey through the desert, in the midst of mortal dangers both from within and without, created another model.

At only one place is there an opening into the world of the narrator and the reader. In Num 15:22f., as part of the introduction to the expanded sin offering law, we are told that God speaks through Moses "from the day YHWH gave the commandment and thereafter throughout your generations" (verse 23b). Linguistically, it is not clear whether this sentence is connected with the divine declaration[179]—God speaks through Moses throughout all generations—or rather with Israel's offenses.[180] The latter sense, however, in which we are at least able to listen along—in the same way that later rabbinic interpretation does—corresponds precisely with what complements the written Sinai revela-tion as a conception of an oral Torah . . . .[181]

It also understands itself as having come from Sinai and Moses. This concept is expressed quite clearly in the Talmudic legend, according to which Moses himself entered the school of Rabbi Akiba and sat in the eighth row—and was unable to understand anything. Even that was a "halakha of Moses from Sinai" (bMenahot 29b). This concept of a continuing revelation that is and remains fundamentally connected with Sinai, is probably already based in the reports of new commandments on the march through the desert as described in Numbers.

The written principle and the living voice belong inseparably together. They are part of the development of the first part of the canon and a part of the tension contained in it. The one informs the other. Alongside Torah comes the prophetic canon and the expectation of an eschatological revelation of Torah.[182] Without this living voice there would be a danger of rigidity. What the Christian church generally does in connection with the foundation of the biblical canon is no less problematic. It has forgotten the indispensable base—Israel's Torah—in favor of the new revelation. The problems with which we live are not least a result of this process, which has distorted God's living voice; God's Word remains tied to his Torah.

The Unity of God and the Unity of Torah: A Starting Point for a Christian Reception of Torah

As we said at the outset,[183] Christian theology has also made a distinction between what is still valid and what no longer applies. Both historical distance, and the attendant changed historical reality alike compel such activity. This practice is also employed by the most orthodox Judaism. It always requires a creative hermeneutic and disavows any blind fundamentalism. Theologically such a separation seems unavoidable in a very basic sense: Christians are not supposed to become Jews. Nevertheless, what is the heart and center of Torah eliminates all such divisions, whether between the Decalogue and the rest of the law, between the first commandment and that of circumcision, between ritual and moral law, between the traditions of social justice and patriarchal animosity toward women.

Here at the end of our discussion of the genesis of Torah, we can describe more precisely what both entail. We can summarize many observations with the thesis that the steps toward the development of Torah are an inseparable part of the way in which Israel formulated the unity of God ever more clearly. We need remind ourselves of only a few points.

At the beginning of the history of written law in Israel, somewhere in the ninth century BCE, there were probably two documents. The one (Ex 34:11f.) formulated regulations for a strict veneration of the one God in the context of an iron age, agricultural world. The other (Ex 21f.) is a collection of laws in the ancient Near Eastern tradition in which important societal conflicts of the era were given regulations intended to introduce justice (that is, compensation). The coming together of these two legal documents with principles for the protection of the economically as well as legally most vulnerable in society in the Book of the Covenant, can be called the actual birth of Torah structure. Thus, a part of exclusive veneration is law together with the justice that is a part of that law.

Deuteronomic law expanded the purview significantly. Above all, it now included wide-ranging political and other public institutions, the family as well as the treatment of animals and the rest of the environment. In scope all area of life were thus included in God's instructions. Still, out of experiences during the exile, the priestly writings expanded the purview once again. They had to move beyond the foundations of previous law-functioning cult, ownership of land, effective freedom. Independent of all social presuppositions, Israel was here subordinated to the divine command in the overall area of creation. We see the change in the fact that first position is given to the creation of the world instead of an altar law. Furthermore, the inclusion of guilt and forgiveness means that an entirely new area of experience has been added. The entire composition of Torah ultimately binds all of these steps together into a single document.

What was achieved in this history, sketched in a cursory manner here, is nothing less than a process in which the entire reality of a period, all areas of human life and experience are exposed to the light of Israel's God. The path from exclusive veneration to something resembling basic monotheism could only be traversed if all of the realities saturated and dominated by the many deities of polytheism were disclosed in a new way. The unity of God had to achieve a new form by a reworking of all of reality together with a redefinition of that reality. Otherwise there would only have been isolated (e.g. prophetic) initiatives. On the basis of experiences with the God of Israel, those areas must be included in which previously only other gods acted. The genesis of Torah, with its stepwise inclusion of new areas of reality, illustrates this process. Torah became the medium in the process, which the unity of God and the variety of areas of experience and reality were brought together. For that reason the identity of the biblical God is dependent upon the connection with his Torah.

All of this can only mean that—quite apart from the historical distance—Torah alone can be the foundation of a biblically oriented Christian ethic. It is, however, formulated for Israel, not for all of humanity. The one will of the only God has Israel as an inseparable human partner. It is not possible to remove Israel from Torah, nor can we replace Israel with Christianity. The dilemma contained in that statement can only be resolved by a Christian reception of Torah which enters into Torah as formulated for Israel, not for the Church. Thus it makes the unity of God, Torah and Israel as its foundation from which all concrete interpretation proceeds. Historical foundations ought to be prepared for this kind of reception; it is much more than an exegetical task.

In conclusion, the starting point for such a hermeneutic, is formulated nowhere more clearly than Deut 4:5-8.[184] A reception of Torah that does not divide its unity, and does not seek to replace Israel will always be amazed that we are told about "the peoples" (*'amm m*) here (verse 6). There are two reasons for this surprise: the uniqueness of God's nearness to Israel (verse 7) and even the content of Torah itself: in other words, that which this book is supposed to be talking about in verse 8: "What other great nation has statutes and ordinances as just as this entire law that I am setting before you today?"

Abbreviations

. . . AfO: Archiv für Orientforschung

AGJu: Arbeiten zur Geschichte des antiken Judentums

und des Urchristentums (Leiden, Cologne) . . .

AJBA: Australian Journal of Biblical Archaeology . . .

ANRW: Aufstieg und Niedergang der römischen Welt (Berlin 1972)

Ant: Josephus, Antiquities of the Jews

AOAT: Altorientalische Textes zum AT . . .

ATD: Das Alte Testament Deutsch (Göttingen) . . .

BA: Biblical Archaeologist . . .

BBB: Bonner Biblische Beiträge . . .

BEThL: Bibliotheca Ephemeridum Theologicarum Lovaniensium

BEvTh: Beiträge zur evangelische Theologie . . .

BK: Bibel und Kirche

BN: Biblische Notizen . . .

BZ NF: Biblische Zeitschrift (New Series)

BZAW: Beihefte zur Zeitschrift für die Alttestamentliche Wissenschaft . . .

CBQ: Catholic Biblical Quarterly . . .

CThM: Concordia Theological Monthly

DBAT: Dielhemier Blätter zum Alten Testament . . .

EThL: Ephemerides Theologicae Lovanienses . . .

EvTh: Evangelische Theologie . . .

FS: Festschrift

GAT: Grundrisse zum Alten . . .

HAT: Handbuch zum Alten Testament, Tübingen . . .

HSAT: Die Heilige Schrift des AT (Kautzsch)

HSM: Harvard Semitic Monographs

HThR: Harvard Theological Review

HUCA: Hebrew Union College Annual . . .

JBL: Journal of Biblical Literature . . .

jBer: Jerusalem Talmud, tractate Berakot

JBTh: Jahrbuch für biblische Theologie . . .

JQR: Jewish Quarterly Review . . .

JSOT: Journal of the Society for Old Testament Studies

JSOTS: Journal of the Society for Old Testament Studies (Supplement)

JSS: Journal of Semitic Studies

JThS NS: Journal of Theological Studies (New Style) . . .

KAT: Kommentar zum Alten Testament (Leipzig, Gutersloh) . . .

KEH: Kurzgefasstes exegetisch es Handbuch zum Alten Testament (Leipzig)

KHC: Kurzer Hand-Commentar zum Alten Testament (Freiburg i Br, Leipzig, Tübingen)

KT: Kleine Texte für theologische und philosophische Vorlesungen . . .

MThSt: Münchener Theologische Studien . . .

NEB: New English Bible

NF: New series . . .

NTA: Neutestamentliche Abhandlungen / New Testament Abstracts

OBO: Orbis Biblicus et Orientalis . . .

OTS: Oudtestamentische Studien . . .

PhB: Spinoza . . .

QD: Quaestiones disputatae . . .

RThPh: Revue de Théologie et de Philosophie . . .

S: supplement

SBAB: Sitzungsberichte der Deutschen Akademie der Wissenschaften zu Berlin . . .

SBLMS Society of Biblical Literature Monograph Series . . .

SDGSTh: Studien zur Drgmengeschichte und Systematischen Theologie . . .

SJLA: Studies in Judaism in Late Antiquity

SKG.G: Schriften der Konigsberger Gelehrten Gesellschaft

SNVAO: Skritter utgitt Det Norske Videnskaps-Akademie (Oslo) . . .

St Th: Studia Theologica . . .

StEv: Studia Evangelica . . .

StUNT: Studien zum Umwelt des Neuen Testament . . .

tKet: Tosefta, tractate Ketubot

THAT: Theologisches Handbuch zum Alten Testament

ThB: Theologische Blatter . . .

TRE: Theologische Revue . . .

VT: Vetus Testamentum

VT.S: Supplements to Vetus Testamentum . . .

WMANT: Wissenschaftliche Monographien zum Alten und Neuen Testament . . .

ZAW: Zeitschrift für die alttestamentliche Wissenschaft . . .

ZNW: Zeitschrift für die neutestamentliche Wissenschaft . . .

ZThK: Zeitschrift für Theologie und Kirche

Notes

[1] See also jBer 1.7.3b.72-74. We are dealing with the conflict between the schools of Hillel and Shammai. Both interpretations are God's Word. Nevertheless, the halakha, i.e. the teaching to be followed, will be decided in accordance with Hillel's word. For the phenomenon of the voice of revelation *(bat qol)*, see Kuhn, *Offenbarungsstimme.*

[2] See e.g. Noth, *Gesetze;* Boecker, *Recht:* Patrick, *Law;* Martin-Achard, *Loi.* It is not atypical that Noth does not base his understanding of the law as "an absolute authority of the late period" in the Pentateuch, in which all of the texts and theological values exist which Noth emphasizes. Instead, he employs a rather vague authority.

[3] Thus Blum, *Pentateuch* 361. This affects his entire assessment. See also, e.g. Lohfink, *Priesterschrift,* who suggests that the investigation of the self-understanding of the Pentateuch is the same as for P.

[4] See e.g. the correlation of Gen 33:19; 50:25f.; Ex 13:19; Josh 24:32ff. There are also connections between Gen 35:1ff. and Josh 24, among others. See Blum, *Vätergeschichte* 40f.; ibid., *Pentateuch* 363.

[5] Against the generally accepted opinion of Noth, *Studien* 182ff. (see already Wellhausen, *Prolegomena* 356f.), most recently especially Lohfink, *Priesterschrift* 222ff. (especially note 30) and Blum, *Pentateuch* 224ff. emphatically referred to the correlations. See also Mowinckel, *Tetrateuch;* Peterson, *Priestly Material;* Blenkinsopp, *Structure;* Cortese, *Joshua* 13-21 among others. For an overview of the research, see Auld, *Joshua.*

[6] See Freedman, *Formation of the Canon.*

[7] See above pp. 46ff.

[8] See below pp. 351ff., especially pp. 358ff.

[9] For what follows, see Crüsemann, *Pentateuch als Tora.*

[10] See Lohfink, *Priesterschrift* 213, cf de Pury/Römer, *Pentateuque* 67ff., Amsler, *Les Documents* 235ff.; for the overall problem, see also Cazelles, *Pentateuque.*

[11] If we count the chapters (a very approximate assessment!), there are about 97 that are generally narrative and 90 chapters of laws. The decision is really arbitrary especially in Numbers (see Num 1-3 and the like).

[12] See below p. 334.

[13] Eissfeldt, *Einleitung* 206.

[14] For the term, see Liedke/Peters, article on *tora* and see above pp. 1f.

[15] See above pp. 105f., and below pp. 337ff.

[16] See Kraus, *Psalms* II 127f.

[17] Thus Noth, *Studien* 28 note 1; Mittmann, *Deuteronomium* 13ff.; Preuss, *Deuteronomium* 84.

[18] Mittmann, *Deuteronomium* 14f. would, on the basis of Deut 27:8, Hab 2:2, confer the meaning "to write, reduce to writing" on the verb *b'r;* nevertheless, see also Amsler, *Loi orale* 52 note 4; Perlitt, *Deuteronomium* 22f.

[19] For *dat* see below pp. 337ff.

[20] See above pp. 47ff., 280f., and below pp. 349ff. and elsewhere.

[21] E.g. Deut 28:36, 68; Lev 26:33ff., 41ff.

[22] For the discussions, see Kaiser, *Einleitung* 172ff.

[23] See above pp. 282ff.

[24] See especially, Purvis, *Samaritan Pentateuch;* Coggins, *Samaritans.*

[25] See Kippenberg, *Garizim* 48ff.; Mor, *Samaritan History* 5ff.

[26] See Kippenberg, *Garizim* 87ff.; Mor, *Samaritan History* 16.

[27] Especially Purvis, *Samaritan Pentateuch* 98ff.; see also Tov, *Proto-Samaritan Texts* 398f.

[28] With due caution, see also Tov, *Proto-Samaritan Texts* 3948f.

[29] See Jellicoe, *Septuagint* 55; Brock, article on Bible translations 163; Hanhart, *Septuagintforschung* 4f.; ibid., *Bedeutung* 67; Dorival, *Septante* 56ff.; Tov, *Bibelübersetzungen* 134f.

[30] See, e.g. Hanhart, *Bedeutung* 71ff.

[31] For a possible exception in Num 24:24, see below pp. 347f.

[32] See Kraft, *"Ezra" Materials;* for the rabbinical picture, see Munk, *Esra* as well as above pp. 105f.

[33] Spinoza, *Traktat* 149ff. and elsewhere; for this, see Kraus, *Geschichte* 61ff.

[34] There is an overview of the history of the research and the positions in Lebram, *Esragestalt;* there is a brief outline of the problems in Williamson, *Ezra.* See Widengren, *Persian Period;* Donner, *Geschichte* II 416ff.; Meier, *Zwischen den Testamenten;* Stern, *Persian Empire* for the period of the restoration; see also Koch, *Ezra;* Cross, *Reconstruction.* For the methodological problems raised by the sources, see Ackroyd, *Problems.* He draws an analogy from chess: "the movements of a limited number of pieces, themselves restricted as to mobility, are not unlike the moving to and fro the pieces in the Achameid period for Judah. But checkmate eludes us" (54).

[35] See the overview in Kellermann, *Esradatierung.* Methodologically, all attempts to improve the number in Ezr 7:7 by emendation are fundamentally questionable; see Emerton, *Did Ezra Go* 1ff.; Williamson, *Ezra* 56. Gunneweg, *Esra* 126ff., e.g. regards the number as a purely theological construct and thus historically useless.

[36] See the overview of the discussion of the relationship of both in Yamauchi, *Reverse Order;* Clines, *Ezra*

15ff. Doubt regarding the traditional dating of Nehemiah in Saley, *Date.*

[37] Thus especially Gunneweg, *Interpretation;* ibid., *Esra* 28ff.; Eskenazi, *Age of Prose;* ibid., *Structure;* see also the discussion between Eskenazi, *Ezra-Nehemia* and Clines, *Force of the Text.*

[38] We need not attempt to resolve here the much discussed question, whether Ezr/Neh were conceived with 1/2 Chr as a single literary work, or as two different authorities (Japhet, *Common Authorship;* Williamson, *Israel;* Thronveit, *Linguistic Analysis;* Talshir, *Reinvestigation;* Ackroyd, *Concept of Unity* among others). Of course we are dealing with chronicles by closely connected author (groups), but there are clear differences (most recently see especially Talmon, *Esra-Nehemia*).

[39] See already the earlier critiques of Torrey, *Ezra Studies;* Hölscher, *Esra und Nehemia;* see especially Kapelrud, *Question of Authorship;* see also Noth, *Studien* 145ff., Smitten, *Esra.* The thesis of a prechronist Ezra source (e.g. Ahlemann, *Esra-Quelle;* Mowinckel, *Studien III;* Rudolph, *Esra und Nehemia* XXIV; most recently—with care—Williamson, *Esra-Nehemiah* XXVIIIff., as well as Deniels, *Composition*) is difficult to support.

[40] Lebram, *Esragestalt* 117, with reference to Meyer, *Entstehung* and Schaeder, *Esra,* both of whom assess the genuineness of the Aramean document.

[41] Translation in conjunction with Gunneweg, *Esra* 128.

[42] Thus Meyer, *Entstehung* 60ff.; Noth, *Studien* 145ff.; Galling, *Bagoas* 165ff.; Cazelles, *Mission;* Kellermann, *Nehemia* 60ff.; Smitten, *Esra* 11ff.; Clines, *Ezra* 102ff.; Williamson, *Ezra/Nehemiah* 98ff.; Donner, *Geschichte* II 426ff.; Blenkinsopp, *Ezra* 146f. There are only allusions to the questions: which parts are genuine or where was emendation done?

[43] See most recently Gunneweg, *Esra* 129ff.; Lebram, *Esragestalt* 117ff.; Becker, *Esra/Nehemia* 43ff.

[44] See especially the other addresses in verses 21-24. Here as elsewhere scholars presume literary work.

[45] Especially Gunneweg, *Esra* 129ff.; Lebram, *Esragestalt* 117ff.

[46] For this great fifth satrapy, see e.g. Donner, *Geschichte* II 297ff.; Dandamaev/Lukonin, *Ancient Iran* 948ff.; and especially Rainey, *Satrapy.*

[47] Already Meyer, *Entstehung* 65.

[48] Lebram, especially, represents an exception. He re-

gards the entire Ezra stratum of the books of Ezra and Nehemiah to be the product of the period after 180 BCE (*Esragestalt* 126ff.). It is a "critique of a radical group, faithful to the law, against the temple theocracy of the Hasmoneans" (131); behind it is "the pharisee's demand to recognize the law of Moses as the constitution of Jerusalem" (132). The historical Ezra is perhaps, according to Neh 12:1, 13 and Ezr 4 a figure of the exilic period. A late dating of this kind for clearly chronistic texts is improbable; the usual placement between 400 and 200 might be hard to dispute. Lebram supports his position exclusively on the fact that in Jesus Sirach, in contrast to Nehemiah (49:13), is passed over in silence, presuming that such a figure was unknown. The remarkable situation can be explained in other ways—e.g. that Jesus Sirach was interested in construction (thus Begg, *Non-mention;* see also, e.g. Höffken, *Warum schweigt*).

[49] Kaiser, *Einleitung* 181.

[50] Kaiser, 181f.; The statement is made in relation to the lists in the Book of Ezra.

[51] Kaiser, 407 where the arguments of pp. 179-183 are summarized.

[52] Gunneweg, *Esra* 140.

[53] Gunneweg, *Esra* 139.

[54] Gunneweg, *Esra* 141.

[55] See especially Frei, *Zentralgewalt.* For the so-called Persian policy of tolerance and the great religious and legal variety there, see e.g. Donner, *Geschichte* II 392ff.; Dandamaev/Lukonin, *Ancient Iran* 116ff.; Briant, *Pouvoir central* 3ff.; ibid., *Polytheismes.* Koch, *Weltordnung,* has attempted to describe the religio-historic background for this openness.

[56] Spiegelberg, *Chronik;* for this, see Reich, *Codification;* Dandamaev/Lukonin, *Ancient Iran* 125.

[57] Metzger, among others, *Fouilles de Xanthos;* see Frei, *Zentralgewalt* 12ff.

[58] Frei, *Zentralgewalt* 13. See Kippenberg, *Erlösungsreligionen* 181f., who would rather speak of "sanctioning by the empire."

[59] See Blum, *Pentateuch* 345ff.

[60] See especially Kippenberg, *Erlösungsreligionen* 183ff.

[61] See the overview in Kellermann, *Esragesetz.* Presuming an early dating of Ezra, before Nehemiah, he comes to the conclusion that this was Deuteronomy

(381ff.); he furthermore thinks that the document could have contained exclusively the legal texts. This thesis has now been adopted by Kippenberg, *Erlösungsreligionen* 127ff. This raises the significant question how the entire Pentateuch might have come out of this. That would presuppose a great change in the relationships.

[62] See below, pp. 341ff.

[63] Houtman, *Ezra* also contests any correlation between the law of Ezra and the Pentateuch because a few laws in Ezra/Nehemiah have no parallel in the Pentateuch. For a critique, see Williamson, *Ezra* 93, who points out the exegetical methods which underlie the the variants. For the central text, see below, Neh 10; see below 395ff.

[64] Rendtorff, *Esra* 183, where the arguments of 169-173 are summarized.

[65] See also Wahl, *Grundelemente.*

[66] Rendtorff, *Esra* 183.

[67] Rendtorff, *Esra* 183.

[68] For the following critique, see also Williamson, *Ezra* 92f.; Kratz, *Translatio Imperii* 228ff.

[69] Rendtorff, *Esra* 168.

[70] The usual word in Targum *royetaa* (see Jastrow, *Dictionary* 34) is only attested much later.

[71] For *dat* see tKet 4.9; see Beyer, *Die aramäischen Texte* 325; for *din* see the marriage contract from Wadi Murabba'at, *Beyer* 309.

[72] Gunneweg, *Esra* 138. For this first step in the development of the canon, see also Kratz, *Translatio Imperii* 233ff.; Steck, *Kanon* 236ff.; ibid., *Abschluss der Prophetie* 13ff.

[73] See above pp. 102ff.

[74] See especially Kellermann, *Nehemia,* who considers 1:1-7:5abá: 12:27aá, 31f., 37-40; 13:4, 5aá, 6a, 7abá, 6a, 7abá, 8-10bá, 11-21, 22b, 23a, 24a, 25-31 part of the original Nehemiah document (in summary, p. 55f.). The further discussion has been based upon this, frequently only criticizing in details, see e.g. Williamson, *Ezra/Nehemiah* XXIVff.; Blenkinsopp, *Ezra* 46 among others; see also Kaiser, *Einleitung* 182 note 15 (with a "fine analysis" that is methodologically hardly tenable). Gunneweg also speaks of an "incontrovertible, authentic, draft by Nehemiah" (*Nehemia* 176), the basic elements of which can no longer be ascertained in detail (178f.) because of chronistic redaction. In view of this

discussion, the general thesis that the document goes back to the chronicler and is in no place authentic (Becker, *Esra/Nehemia* 8), is hardly tenable.

[75] This is emphasized by Clines, *Nehemiah Memoir.* "Nehemiah is a liar" (125).

[76] For the borders and the history, see below pp. 348f.

[77] See especially Kippenberg, *Religion und Klassenbildung* 55f.

[78] See Liver, *Ransom;* for the later Jewish practice, see e.g. also Safria, *Wallfahrt* 70f. and elsewhere.

[79] Thus Blenkinsopp, *Ezra/Nehemiah* 76; Rudolph, *Esra* 178; considers a possible change in the system of measurement Williamson. *Ezra/Nehemiah* 325f. (with Clines, *Nehemiah* 10) theorizes a dependency upon the exodus passages.

[80] Thus e.g. Bertholet, *Esra* 76; Rudolph, *Esra* 172ff.; Galling, *Chronik* 242; Jepsen, *Neh 10* 98ff. (see also 100ff.) who allows the question whether this is a literary fiction or a document of post-Nehemiah origin, to remain open.

[81] Thus e.g. Hölscher, *Esra* 545; Gunneweg, *Nehemiah* 131ff., 135ff.

[82] Indeed six themes are attested in Neh 13 (tithe 13:10ff., temple care 13:11, sabbath 13:15ff., marriage 13:23, wood 13:31, firstfruits 13:31), regarding forgiveness of debts it is comparable to Neh 5. The temple tax firstborn and priestly offering are entirely absent.

[83] See the thoughts of Kellermann, *Nehemia* 39ff., however, see also Williamson, *Ezra/Nehemiah* 330f.

[84] The long list of names interrupts the complete sentence verses 1, 30b and for that reason has been regarded as an insertion (with many others, Williamson, *Ezra* 27). The question of its origin (e.g. Jepsen, *Nehemia* 10) can remain entirely unresolved here.

[85] Gunneweg, *Nehemia* 131f.

[86] See above pp. 128ff.

[87] See above pp. 296f.

[88] Clines, *Nehemiah* 10.

[89] See Zeitlin, *Halaka* 17; Patte, *Early Jewish Hermeneutics* 107ff.

[90] Blum, *Pentateuch* 359 criticizes my earlier (*Perserzeit* 214f.) descriptions "compromise" and "coalition." The former may be confusing (even though the priestly tradition did not, as Blum suggests, require forgiveness of debts and manumission of slaves to the same degree as the deuteronomic tradition) since it does not cover the process of extensive addition. He is further correct that Neh 5 does not present "*direct* evidence" for a coalition of priests and free farmers (thus also Schmitt, *Plagenerzählung* 200f., especially note 28). Historically, *how* they cooperated remains unclear. Even Nehemiah's memoir only gives us a vague impression of the milieu. Since, however, the interests of other groups recognizable at this time, especially the aristocracy, did not have an opportunity, it is probably still justified, perhaps even necessary, to speak of something like a social coalition.

[91] See how especially Kippenberg, *Erlösungsreligionen,* stakes his reconstruction of religious history on activities around the problem of indebtedness.

[92] See Crüsemann, *Perserzeit* 218ff.

[93] See above pp. 47f. and below pp. 356ff.

[94] We need only make reference here to the conflict of returnees and old-Judeans, which especially at the beginning, overlapped the fundamental social conflicts. It had a decisive affect on the history of the province. See Schulz, *Political Tensions.*

[95] See above pp. 290ff. Since there was not much that was fundamentally new to the conception of the overall composition in the priestly writings, the following description can be rather brief.

[96] See Bickermann, *Captivity,* for the problem of the diaspora during the Persian period, see Coggins, *Origins.*

[97] See especially Zadok, *Jews in Babylonia;* ibid., *Some Jews* among others; in addition to Wallis, *Sozial Situation;* Coogan, *Life in the Diaspora;* in general also Eph'al, *Western Minorities.*

[98] With Eph'al, *Western Minorities* 88.

[99] The description in Neh 8 has features of the later synagogue service, see especially Rendtorff, *Esra* 178ff.; see also Wahl, *Grundelemente.* For the development of the synagogue, see Levine, *Formative Years.* Further, Hruby, *Synagogue;* Safrai, *Synagogue;* Gutmann, *Origins* (as well as other contributions in this volume); Griffiths, *Egypt.*

[100] See above pp. 290ff.

[101] For what follows, see Diebner/Schult, *Ehen der Erzväter.* The conclusions regarding the age of the text are not convincing. For an articulated analysis, see Blum, *Vätergeschichte.*

[102] See Dandamaev, *Political History* (see pp. 351ff. for a chronological overview); see especially Salmon, *Les Relations;* Ray, *Egypt.*

[103] See e.g. Kaiser, *Zwischen den Fronten.*

[104] See Porten, *Jews in Egypt.*

[105] See e.g. Porten, *Archives.*

[106] When Schmitt, *Plagenerzählung* correctly finds prophetic traditions at work in these texts then we must note in these contexts what prophecy means in the Pentateuch in order to be able to make a proper evaluation. See below, p. 347.

[107] A whole series of new, pertinent sources has been revealed (among others: seals, coins, etc.), since Alt, *Rolle Samarias* advanced the thesis that it was only through the mission of Nehemiah that Judah achieved the rank of independent province. Previously, it had been part of Samaria. Of course, the question, at what date did the independent province come into existence, cannot be answered with complete surety even today. Nevertheless, the comprehensive and intensive discussions of all the questions connected with this in Williamson, *Governors* have made it extremely likely that already Sheshbazzar and Zerubbabel (who both have the same title as Nehemiah—*peha*) were presiding over an independent province.

[108] See Dandamaev, *Political History* 244ff.; see also, e.g. Ackroyd, *Jewish Community* 154.

[109] See e.g. Margalith, *Political Role* for an early dating. There would have been a correlation with the renewed political independence around 401 BCE for a late dating of Ezra at 398 BCE.

[110] See e.g. Donner, *Geschichte* II 393f. For the Persian tax system, see especially Tuplin, *Administration* 137ff.

[111] With Blenkinsopp, *Prophecy and Canon* 80ff. It is too indiscriminating to say that the Pentateuch redactors were entirely positive toward prophecy as Schmitt, *Plagenerzählung* 200 note 24 suggests (see also Blum, *Pentateuch* 88, 359). The ranking of Moses above all other prophets is clearly a criticism of other prophets. A "complementary" relation of law and prophecy, as Schmitt formulates in conjunction with Perlitt, *Mose* 591f. is, of course, possible. That would mean, however, that the Pentateuch itself is not prophetic, nor would it subordinate itself to any prophecy; the history of the canon supports this.

[112] See e.g. W. H. Schmidt, *Nachwirkungen;* Smend, *Ende;* H.-C. Schmitt, *Redaktion* and others.

[113] This is apparently the opinion of Schmitt, *Plagenerzählung* 199f. in his critique of my thesis *(Perserzeit).* He finds a "cooperation of prophetic groups in the development of the Pentateuch" (201). Nevertheless, neither the reception of prophetic traditions, which is undisputed, nor the reference to the "imposing opus of the prophetic books" originated at this time (201) disputes the fact that the decisive feature of contemporary prophecy as well as of the prophetic redactors, that is to say, a thoroughly eschatological outlook, is absent from the Pentateuch. We do not find hope for an earth-shaking action of God, but rather the contemporary practice of Torah together with the political space necessary to follow it, which shapes figures like Ezra and Nehemiah and the central figures of the Pentateuch. At the time of the development this was a contrast (and it still was for the Sadducees, for example). It is true that it was not an absolute, but rather a complementary opposite. In the history of canon Torah remained dominant. For the relationship, see for example also W. H. Schmidt, *Pentateuch und Prophetie.* Regarding Plöger's critique *(Theokratie* 129ff. for the dialog Schmitt, *Plagenerzählung* 202), there are clearly at least three groups in postexilic Judaism (the evidence hardly justifies the idea of "mediating forms"—against Schmitt 202 note 35). Many confusions in the discussion go back to attempts to reduce them to two groups.

[114] For the ambivalent role of the Egyptians in this context, see above p. 345.

[115] Against Schmitt, *Plagenerzählung.* Only this can resolve the issue, not, however, the tradition-historical provenance of language, motives, etc.

[116] The interpretation of these statements extend from the sea people (Vetter, *Seherspruch* 55f.) to the Seleucids (Noth, *Numbers* 169).

[117] See e.g. Bogaert, *Trois Rédactions;* Luyten, *Overtones.*

[118] Thus e.g. Margalith, *Political Role.*

[119] For the question of the period in which this independency began, see above note 107.

[120] For the question of the province of Judah, see Stern, *Province;* McEvenue, *Political Structure;* see also Betlyon, *Provincial Government.*

[121] See e.g. Alt, *Judas Nachbarn,* and now especially Lemaire, *Population et Territoires* (map, p. 74).

[122] Welten, *Geschichte* 123ff., especially 128.

[123] For the prophetic canon, see Steck, *Kanon;* ibid., *Abschluss der Prophetie.*

[124] See, for example, Nasuti, *Identity*.

[125] The word *ki* probably retains its basic, deictic meaning in a concessive sense. See Meyer, *Hebräische Grammatik III* 104f.

[126] See most recently, e.g. Dandamaev / Lukonin, *Institutions* 117, where such a principle is called "primitive law" for Persia. Unfortunately, there is no evidence. For Old Testament evidence, see Dandamaev / Lukonin, *Institutions* 118.

[127] The occasional reference (e.g. Porteous, *Daniel* 72f.) to Diodorus Siculus XVII 30 does not fit. There we have the irrevocability of the preceding murder (see Frei, *Zentralgewalt* 36 note 64).

[128] Frei, *Zentralgewalt* 23ff.

[129] We read in line 19 of the inscription, "This law has he written" *(dth dk ktb)*, which refers to the decree of the people of Xanthos (line 6); see Dupont-Sommer in Metzger, *Xanthos* VI 136f. Unfortunately, what follows, which is critical for an exact understanding, is faulty. We should probably interpret the text, which is nearly impossible to understand *(mhssn)* as Dupont-Sommer does . . . . Frei, in conjunction with a suggestion by Dupont-Sommer, interprets the text, "so that people take note" (*Zentralgewalt* 24f., especially note 73), so that legal validity is specially dependent upon the written nature of the law.

[130] Frei, *Zentralgewalt* 25.

[131] See, with a different accent, Bardke, *Esther* 368 note 3, who compares this "horror of rigid and irrevocable human law" with the presumed parallel qualities of Jewish law.

[132] For the Decalogue itself, see Crüsemann, *Dekalog*. Everything suggests that the Decalogue belongs in or near Deuteronomy, thus it is already dependent upon the critical Torah structures which developed with the Book of the Covenant. Its contribution to Old Testament legal history, along with its function in the law, lies more in its precision, clarity and ability to teach, rather than in its contents as such. It would be different if it belonged *before* the Book of the Covenant. Even Lohfink, *Unterschied* 77ff., who thinks that it might possibly be quite old, must agree that there are no discernible reasons for this. If Vincent, *Dekalogforschung* would place the norms formulated within the Decalogue before the crises of the eighth century, where they appear in prophecy (and the Book of the Covenant), then precisely that is improbable. The explication and formulation require reasons, and we find late, mature phrasing of these norms in the Decalogue.

[133] Since the studies of Perlitt, *Bundestheologie* 77ff.,

Hossfeld, *Dekalog;* Nicholson, *Decalogue;* this is no longer in dispute; see now also Lohfink, *Unterschied* 76f. Nothing, however, is decided regarding the relationship of the versions of the texts themselves; see most recently Graupner, *Dekalogfassungen;* Hossfeld, *Dekalogfassungen;* Lohfink, *Unterschied* 75. It remains unresolved here.

[134] See Borgeault, *Décalogue;* Rothlisberger, *Kirche am Sinai*.

[135] Most recently, Stemberger, *Dekalog* 99ff.; also Vermes, *Decalogue;* Vokes, *Ten Commandments;* Schreiner, *Dekalog*.

[136] See Crüsemann, *Dekalog* 3ff.

[137] Lohfink, *Unterschied*.

[138] Lohfink, *Unterschied* 65-74.

[139] Thus at the end of Lohfink, *Unterschied* 89.

[140] Lohfink, *Unterschied* 80ff.

[141] Lohfink, *Unterschied* 80.

[142] Lohfink, *Unterschied* 84.

[143] Lohfink, *Unterschied* 64.

[144] Lohfink, *Unterschied* 80.

[145] Lohfink, *Unterschied* 81.

[146] Lohfink, *Unterschied* 89.

[147] Lohfink, *Unterschied* 81.

[148] See especially Schmidt, *Erwägungen*.

[149] Lohfink, *Unterschied* 76; see above note 133.

[150] See above pp. 46ff., 55ff.

[151] Thus, the instructions in Ex 25ff. are carried out in 35ff. Aaron is consecrated as a priest, etc. but especially the commands from Lev 11 on are the words of God alone, except that they are transmitted to the people.

[152] Lohfink, *Unterschied* 81.

[153] See above p. 222.

[154] There is only inconsequential disagreement among scholars that the Dathan-Abiram episode in verses 12-15, 25-34 represents a pre-priestly text (wherein glosses, etc. are not considered here), see e.g. Noth, *Pentateuch*

32; ibid., *Numeri* 108; Fritz, *Wüste* 24ff.; Coats, *Rebellion* 158ff.; Ahuis, *Authorität* (who otherwise works with a broad deuteronomic stratum), most recently Schart, *Konflikt* 220; see even Milgrom, *Rebellion* 135f. This older core finds itself imbedded in a P center, which however is not generally regarded as a part of the P base stratum (Noth, *Pentateuch* 19 note 59; as well as–unsupported–e.g. Elliger, *Sinn* 175; Lohfin, *Priesterschrift* 222f. note 29; Schart, *Konflikt,* 137 note 1). Nevertheless, the model sketched of the priestly wilderness narrative by Westermann, *Herrlichkeit Gottes* 128ff. fits Num 16 exactly (see Blum, *Pentateuch* 267). Blum, *Pentateuch* 265f. shows that even the priestly stratum in this chapter is not unified, but represents many claims.

[155] See Magonet, *Korah Rebellion,* as well as Blum, *Pentateuch* 263ff.

[156] See already Bentzen, *Priesterschaft* 281., as well as especially, Weinfeld, *Deuteronomy* 228ff.; Friedman, *Exile* 69; Kraus, *Heiliges Volk* 41f.; Blum, *Pentateuch* 270f., 334f.

[157] See above pp. 301ff.

[158] Blum, *Pentateuch* 335 note 5 refers to this.

[159] Blum, *Pentateuch* 335.

[160] See above pp. 28ff.

[161] For the position in context, see Blum, *Pentateuch* 47ff. as well as Rendtorff, *Text in seiner Endgestalt.*

[162] See Dozeman, *Spatial Form.*

[163] From the wide-ranging discussion about the meaning of the terms used, see Dillmann, *Exodus* 214; Scott, *Kingdom;* Martin-Achard, *Israël;* Coppens, *Royaume;* Schüssler-Fiorenza, *Priester* 131ff. Blum, *Pentateuch* 51 note 22 correctly criticizes the variety of interpretations which make the sense less concrete, but more metaphoric and generalized, most recently, e.g. Fuhs, *Heiliges Volk* 158; Mosis, *Aufbau.*

[164] See Perlitt, *Bundestheologie* 167ff.

[165] See above pp. 306ff.

[166] *mamléket* means monarchy, government, to be sure, as an institution (Sybold, article on *melek* 941).

[167] Thus convincingly, Ruprecht, *Exodus* 24 167; cf Blum, *Pentateuch* 51f.

[168] See Crüsemann, *Perserzeit.*

[169] For the rabbinic interpretation, see Bamberger, *Torah after Sinai.*

[170] See Noth, *Studien* 190ff. with an outline of the results 217; ibid., Numbers. Finally, especially Schart, *Konflikt* 55ff. places this text outside the composition he calls the "final text" of Num 10-21.

[171] This applies in each case for the researchers who attempt to work out a base document (e.g. Elliger, *Sinn* 174f.; Lohfink, *Priesterschrift* 222ff. and elsewhere).

[172] See above pp. 290ff.

[173] For the—also syntactical—correlation, see Rendtorff, *Leviticus* 22f.

[174] See Westermann, *Herrlichkeit Gottes* 128ff.; also Rendtorff, *Offenbarungsvorstellungen* 48.

[175] See above pp. 102ff.

[176] For what follows, see Olson, *Death of the Old* especially 83ff., 165ff.

[177] See above pp. 38ff.

[178] Crüsemann, *Vaterland.*

[179] Thus especially Brin, *Numbers XV* citing Sifre sect. 111 as well as Rashi; see also Toeg, *Halachic Midrash.*

[180] Olson, *Death of the Old Man* 168 note 13. He rejects Brin's thesis, referring to the syntactical structure and its parallels in 1 Sam 18:9; Ez 39:22. He himself; however, points out the emphasis in the five-fold repetition of "throughout your (coming) generations" . . . in verses 14, 15, 21, 23, 38. Furthermore, the case of the person gathering wood on the sabbath we are dealing with the sample "application of a law to a new situation which requires a divine judgment" (172). The accent that Olson himself places upon the individual laws scattered throughout the composition of the Book of Numbers, corresponds exactly with that of the rabbinic tradition of understanding 15:23.

[181] Cf Schäfer, *Dogma.*

[182] Isa 42:1ff., 2:1ff. and others. See Davies, *Torah;* Jervell, *Tora;* Schäfer, *Torah.*

[183] See above p. 4.

[184] See Braulik, *Weisheit, Gottesnähe und Gesetz;* besides Levenson, *Theologies of Commandment* 25ff.

Bibliography

. . . Ackroyd, P. R., *Chronicles—Ezra—Nehemia: The Concept of Unity,* ZAW.S 100, 1988, 189-201 . . .

———, "Problems in the Handling of Biblical and Related Sources in the Achaemenid Period," in: A. Kuhrt/H. Sancisi-Weerdenburg (ed.), *Achaemenid History* III. *Method and Theory,* Leiden 1988, 33-54 . . .

Ahlemann, F., "Zur Esraquelle," ZAW 59, 1942/43, 77-98

Ahuis, F., *Autorität im Umbruch. Ein formgeschicht-licher Beitrag zur Klärung der literar-ischen Schichtung und der zeitgeschichtlichen Bezüge von Num 16 und 17. Mit einem Ausblick auf die Diskussion um die Ämter der Kirche,* CThM 13, 1983 . . .

Alt, A., "Die Rolle Samarias bei der Entstehung des Judentums" (1934), in: ibid., *Kleine Schriften* II,³ 1964, 316-337 . . .

———, "Judas Nachbarn zur Zeit Nehemias" (1931), in: ibid., *Kleine Schriften* II,³ 1964, 338-345 . . .

Amsler, S., "Les documents de la loi et la formation du Pentateuque," in: A. de Pury (ed.), *Le Pentateuque en Question,* Genf² 1991, 235-257

———, "Loi oracle et loi écrite dans le Deutéronome," in: N. Lohfink (ed.), *Das Deuteronomium,* BEThL LXVIII, Leuven 1985, 51-54 . . .

Auld, A. G., *Joshua, Moses and the Land. Tetrateuch—Pentateuch—Hexateuch in a Generation since 1938,* Edinburgh 1980 . . .

Bamberger, B. J., "Revelations of Torah after Sinai," HUCA 14, 1941, 97-113 . . .

Bardtke, H., *Das Buch Esther,* KAT XVII,5, Gütersloh 1963 . . .

Becker, J., *Esra/Nehemia,* NEB Liefg. 25, Würzburg 1990 . . .

Begg, C., "Ben Sirach's Non-mention of Ezra," BN 42, 1988, 14-18 . . .

Bentzen, A., "Priesterschaft und Laien in der jüdischen Geschichte des 5. Jahrhunderts," AfO 6, 1930/31, 280-286 . . .

Bertholet, A., *Die Bücher Esra und Nehemia,* KHC XIX, 1902 . . .

Betlyon, J. W., "The Provincial Government of Persian Period Judea and the Yehud Coins," JBL 105, 1986, 633-642 . . .

Beyer, K., *Die aramäischen Texte vom Toten Meer,* Göttingen 1984 . . .

Bickerman, E. J., "The Babylonian Captivity," in: *The Cambridge History of Judaism,* vol. I. *Introduction; The Persian Period,* Cambridge 1984, 342-357 . . .

Blenkinsopp, J., *Ezra—Nehemia. A Commentary,* London 1989

———, *Prophecy and Canon. A Contribution to the Study of Jewish Origin,* Notre Dame/Ind. 1977

———, "The Structure of P," CBQ 38, 1976, 275-292 . . .

Blum, E., *Die Komposition der Vätergeschichte,* WMANT 57, 1984 . . .

———, "Studien zur Komposition des Pentateuch," BZAW 189, 1990 . . .

Boecker, H. J., *Recht und Gesetz im Alten Testament und im Alten Orient,* Neukirchen-Vluyn² 1984 . . .

Bogaert, P.-M., "Les trois Rédactions conservées et la forme originale de l'envoi du Cantique de Moïse (Dt 32,43)," in: N. Lohfink (ed.), *Das Deuteronomium,* BEThL 68, 1985, 329-340 . . .

Braulik, G., "Weisheit, Gottesnähe und Gesetz. Zum Kerygma von Deuteronomium 4,5-8," in: *Studien zum Pentateuch,* FS W. Kornfeld, Wien 1977, 165-195 = idem., *Studien zur Theologie des Deuteronomiums,* SBAB 2, 1988, 53-93 . . .

Briant, P., "Polythéismes et empire unitaire. (Remarques sur la politique religieuse des Achéménides)," in: *Les grandes figures religieuses. Fonctionnement, pratique et symbolique dans l'Antiquité,* Centre de Recherches d'Histoire Ancienne 68, Paris 1986, 425-438

———, "Pouvoir central et polycentrisme culturel dans l'empire Achéménide. Quelques réflections et suggestions," in: H. Sancisi-Weerdenburg (ed.), *Achaemenid History I, Sources, Structures and Synthesis,* Leiden 1987, 1-31 . . .

Brin, G., "Numbers XV 22-23 and the Question of the Composition of the Pentateuch," VT 30, 1980, 351-354

Brock, S. P., "Bibelübersetzungen I,2. Die Über-setzungen des Alten Testaments im Griechischen," TRE VI, 1980, 163-172 . . .

Cazelles, H., "La mission d'Esdras," VT 4, 1954, 113-140

———, "Le Pentateuque comme Torah," in: idem., *Autour de L'Exode* (Études), Paris 1987, 9-52 . . .

Clines, D. J. A., *Ezra, Nehemia, Esther,* New Century Bible Commentary, Grand Rapids 1984 . . .

———, "The Force of the Text. A Response to Tamara C. Eskenazi's 'Ezra-Nehemia: From Text to Actuality'," in: J. C. Exum (ed.), *Signs and Wonders. Biblical Texts in Literary Focus,* Atlanta 1989, 199-215

———, "The Nehemiah Memoir: The Perils of Autobiography," in: *What Does Eve Do to Help? and Other Readerly Questions to the Old Testament,* JSOT.S 94, 1990, 124-164

Coats, G. W., *Rebellion in the Wilderness. The Murmuring Motif in the Wilderness Traditions of the Old Testament,* Nashville/New York 1968 . . .

Coggins, R. J., *Samaritans and Jews. The Origin of Samaritanism Reconsidered,* Atlanta 1975 . . .

———, "The origins of the Jewish diaspora," in: R. E. Clements (ed.), *The World of Ancient Israel. Sociological, Anthropological and Political Perspectives,* Cambridge 1989, 163-181 . . .

Coogan, M. D., "Life in the Diaspora. Jews at Nippur in the Fifth Century B.C.," BA 37, 1974, 6-12 . . .

Coppens, J., "Exode XIX6: Un royaume ou une royauté des prêtres?" EThL 53, 1977, 185f. . . .

Cortese, E., *Josua 13-21. Ein priesterschriftlicher Abschnitt im deuteronomistischen Geschichtswerk,* OBO 94, 1990 . . .

Cross, F. M., "A Reconstruction of the Judaean Restoration," JBL 94, 1975, 4-18 . . .

Crüsemann, F., *Bewahrung der Freiheit. Das Thema des Dekalogs in sozialgeschichtlicher Perspektive,* KT 78, 1983

———, "Das 'portative Vaterland'. Struktur und Genese des alttestament-lichen Kanons," in: A. u. J. Assmann (ed.), *Kanon und Zensur. Archäologie der literarischen Kommunikation* II, München 1987, 63-79 . . .

———, "Der Pentateuch als Tora. Prolegomena zur Interpretation seiner Endgestalt," EvTh 49, 1989, 250-267 . . .

———, "Israel in der Perserzeit. Eine Skizze in Auseinandersetzung mit Max Weber," in: W. Schluchter (ed.,) *Max Webers Sicht des antiken Christentums. Interpretation und Kritik,* 548, 1985, 205-232 . . .

Dandamaev, M. A., *A Political History of the Achaemenid Empire,* Engl. transl. Leiden 1989 . . .

Dandamaev, M. A./Lukonin, V. G., *The Culture and Social Institutions of Ancient Iran,* Cambridge 1989

Daniels, D. R., "The Composition of the Ezra-Nehemiah Narrative," in: *Ernten, was man sät,* FS K. Koch, ed. D. R. Daniels et al., Neukirchen 1991, 311-328 . . .

Davies, W. D., *Torah in the Messianic Age and/or the Age to Come,* Philadelphia 1952 . . .

Diebner, B. J./Schult, H., "Die Ehen der Erzväter," DBAT 8, 1975, 2-10 . . .

Dillmann, A., *Die Bücher Exodus und Leviticus* (ed. V. Ryssel), KEH 12, Leipzig³ 1897 . . .

Donner, H., *Geschichte des Volkes Israel und seiner Nachbarn in Grundzügen,* GAT 4, 2 vols., 1984 and 1986 . . .

Dorival, G., "Les origines de la Septante: la traduction en grec des cinq livres de la Torah," in: idem./M. Harl/ O. Munnich, *La Bible grecque des Septante,* Paris 1988, 39-82 . . .

Dozeman, T., "Spatial Form in Exod. 19: 1-8a and the Larger Sinai Narrative," Semeia 46, 1989, 87-101 . . .

Eissfeldt, O., *Einleitung in das Alte Testament,* Tübingen³ 1964 . . .

Elliger, K., "Sinn und Ursprung der priesterlichen Geschichtserzählung," ZThK 49, 1952, 121-143 = idem., *Kleine Schriften zum Alten Testament,* ThB 32, 1966, 174-198 . . .

Emerton, J. A., "Did Ezra Go to Jerusalem 428 B.C.?" JThS NS 17, 1966, 1-19 . . .

Eph 'al, I, "The Western Minorities in Babylonia in the 6th-5th Centuries B.C., Maintenance and Cohesion," *Orientalia* 47, 1978, 74-90 . . .

Eskenazi, T. C., "Ezra-Nehemia: From Text to Actuality," in: J. C. Exum (ed.), *Signs and Wonders. Biblical Texts and Literary Focus,* Atlanta 1989, 165-197

———, *In an Age of Prose. A Literary Approach to Ezra-Nehemia,* SBLMS 36, 1988

———, "The Structure of Ezra-Nehemiah and the Integrity of the Book," JBL 107, 1988, 641-656 . . .

Freedman, D. N., "The Formation of the Canon of the Old Testament. The Selection and the Identification of the Torah as the Supreme Authority of the Postexilic Community," in: E. B. Firmage et al., *Religion and Law. Biblical-Judaic and Islamic Perspectives,* Winona

Lake 1990, 315-331 . . .

Frei, P., "Zentralgewalt und Lokalautonomie im Achä-
menidenreich," in: idem./K. Koch, *Reichsidee und
Reichsorganisation im Perserreich,* OBO 55, 1984, 7-
43 . . .

Friedman, R. E., *The Exile and Biblical Narrative. The
Formation of the Deuteronomistic and Priestly Works,*
HSM 22, 1981 . . .

Fritz, V., *Israel in der Wüste. Traditionsgeschichtliche
Untersuchung der Wüstenüberlieferung des Jahwisten,*
MThSt 7, 1970 . . .

Fuhs, H. F., "Heiliges Volk Gottes," in: J. Schreiner
(ed.), *Unterwegs zur Kirche. Alttestamentliche
Konzeptionen,* QD 110, 1987, 143-167 . . .

Galling, K., "Bagoas und Esra," in: idem., *Studien zur
Geschichte Israels im persischen Zeitalter,* Tübingen
1964, 149-184 . . .

———. *Die Bücher der Chronik, Esra, Nehemia,* ATD
12, 1954 . . .

Graupner, A., "Zum Verhältnis der beiden
Dekalogfassungen Ex 20 und Dtn 5. Ein Gespräch mit
Frank-Lothar Hossfeld," ZAW 99, 1987, 308-329 . . .

Griffiths, J. G., "Egypt and the Rise of the Synagogue,"
JThS N.S. 38, 1987, 1-15 . . .

Gunneweg, A. H. J., *Esra,* KAT XIX1, 1985 . . .

———, "Zur Interpretation der Bücher Esra-Nehemia.
Zugleich ein Beitrag zur Methode der Exegese," in:
Congress Volume, Vienna 1980, VT.S 32, 1981, 146-
161 . . .

Gutmann, J., "The Origin of the Synagogue, The Cur-
rent State of Research," in: idem. (ed.), *The Synagogue.
Studies in Origins, Archaeology and Architecture,* New
York 1975, 72-76 . . .

Hanhart, R., *Die Bedeutung der Septuaginta für die
Definition des 'Hellenistischen Judentums',* VT.S 40,
1988, 67-80

———, "Zum gegenwärtigen Stand der Septuagint-
aforschung," in: *De Septuaginta,* FS J. W. Wevers. ed.
A. Pietersma/C. Cox, Missisauga, Ont. 1984, 3-18
. . .

Höffken, P., "Warum schweigt Jesus sirach über Esra?"
ZAW 87, 1975, 184-202 . . .

Hölscher, G., *Die Bücher Esra und Nehemia,* HSAT
II,[4] 1923, 491-562 . . .

Hossfeld, F.-L., *Der Dekalog. Seine späten Fassungen,
die originale Komposition und seine Vorstufen,* OBO
45, 1982 . . .

———, "Zum synoptischen Vergleich der Dekalog-
fassungen. Eine Fortführung des begonnenen
Gesprächs," in: idem (ed.), *Vom Sinai zum Horeb,* FS
E. Zenger, Würzburg 1989, 73-117 . . .

Houtman, C., "Ezra and the Law, in: Remembering all
the Way . . . ," OTS XXI, 1981, 91-115

Hruby, K., *Die Synagoge. Geschichtliche Entwicklung
einer Institution,* Zürich 1971 . . .

Japhet, S., "The Supposed Common Authorship of
Chronicles and Ezra-Nehemia Investigated Anew," VT
18, 1968, 330-371

Jastrow, M., *A Dictionary of the Targumim, the Talmud Babli and Yerushalmi, and the Midrashic Literature,* New York 1950

Jellicoe, S., *The Septuagint and Modern Study,* Oxford
1968 . . .

Jepsen, A., "Nehemia 10," ZAW 66, 1954, 87-106
. . .

Jervell, J., "Die offenbarte und die verborgene Tora.
Zur Vorstellung über die neue Tora im Rabbinismus,"
StTh 25, 1971, 90-108 . . .

Kaiser, O., *Einleitung in das Alte Testament,* Gütersloh[5]
1984

———, "Zwischen den Fronten. Palästina in den
Auseinandersetzungen zwischen dem Perserreich und
Ägypten in der ersten Hälfte des 4. Jahrhunderts"
(1972), = in: idem., *Von der Gegenwartsbedeutung des
Alten Testaments. Gesammelte Studien,* ed. V. Fritz et
al., Göttingen 1984, 189-198 . . .

Kapelrud, A. S., *The Question of Authorship in the
Ezra- Narrative. A Lexical Investigation,* SNVAO.HF
1944/1, 1944 . . .

Kellermann, U., "Erwägungen zum Esragesetz," ZAW
80, 1968, 373-385

———, "Erwägungen zum Problem der Esradatierung,"
ZAW 80, 1968, 55-87

———, *Nehemia. Quellen, Überlieferung und
Geschichte,* BZAW 102, 1967 . . .

Kippenberg, H. G., *Die vorderasiatischen Erlösungsreligionen in ihrem Zusammenhang mit der antiken
Stadtherrschaft, Heidelberger Max-Weber-Vorlesungen*

1988, 917, 1991

———, *Garizim und Synagoge,* RVV 30, 1971

———, *Religion und Klassenbildung im antiken Judäa. Eine religionssoziologische Studie zum Verhältnis von Tradition und gesellschaftlicher Entwicklung,* StUNT 14,[2] 1982 . . .

Koch, K., "Ezra and the Origin of Judaism," JSS 19, 1974, 173-197 . . .

Koch, K., "Weltordnung und Reichsidee im alten Iran," in: P. Frei/idem., *Reichsidee und Reichsorganisation im Perserreich,* OBO 55, 1984, 45-116 . . .

Kraft, R. A., "'Ezra' Materials in Judaism and Christianity," in: ANRW II, 19/1, 1979, 119-136

Kratz, R. G., *Translatio imperii. Untersuchungen zu den aramäischen Danielerzählungen und ihrem theologiegeschichtlichen Umfeld,* WMANT 63, 1991 . . .

Kraus, H.-J., "Das heiliges Volk," in: *Freude am Evangelium.* FS A. de Quervain, München 1966, 50-61 = idem., *Biblisch-theologische Aufsätze,* Neukirchen 1972, 37-49 . . .

———, *Geschichte der historisch-kritischen Erforschung des Alten Testaments,* Neukirchen[4] 1988

———, *Psalms,* trans. Hilton C. Oswald. 2 vols. Minneapolis: Augsburg 1987 . . .

Lebram, J. C. H., "Die Traditionsgeschichte der Esragestalt und die Frage nach dem historischen Esra," in: H. Sancisi-Weerdenburg (ed.), *Achae-menid History* I. *Sources, Structures and Synthesis,* Leiden 1987, 103-138 . . .

Lemaire, A., "Populations et territoires de la Palestine à l'époque perse," *Transeuphratene* 3, 1990, 31-74 . . .

Levenson, J. D., "The Theologies of Commandment in Biblical Israel," HThR 73, 1980, 17-33 . . .

Levine, L. J., "The Second Temple Synagogue: The Formative Years," in: *The Synagogue in Late Antiquity,* ed. idem., Philadelphia 1987, 7-31 . . .

Liedke, G./Petersen, C., Art.; *Tora,* THAT II, 1976, 1032-1043 . . .

Lohfink, N., "Die Priesterschrift und die Geschichte," in: *Congress Volume Göttingen 1977,* VT.S 29, 1978, 169-225 = idem., *Studien zum Pentateuch,* SBAB 4, 1988, 213-254 . . .

———, "Kennt das Alte Testament einen Unterschied von 'Gebot' und 'Gesetz'? Zur bibeltheologischen Einstufung des Dekalogs," JBTh 4, 1989, 63-89 . . .

Luyten, J., "Primeval and Eschatological Overtones in the Song of Mose (Dt 32,1-43)," in: N. Lohfink (ed.), *Das Deuteronomium,* BEThL LXVIII, 1985, 341-347 . . .

Magonet, J., "The Korah Rebellion," JSOT 24, 1982, 3-25 . . .

Margalith, O., "The Political Role of Ezra as Persian Governor," ZAW 98, 1986, 110-112 . . .

Martin-Achard, R., "Israël, peuple sacerdotal," VC 18, 1964, 11-28 = idem., *Permanence de l'Ancien Testament.* Recherches d'Exégèse et de Theologie, Cahiers de la RThPh 11, 1984, 129-146 . . .

McEvenue, S. E., "The Political Structure in Judah from Cyrus to Nehemiah," CBQ 43, 1981, 353-364 . . .

Metzger, H. et al., *Feuilles de Xanthos. Tome VI. La stèle trilingue du Létôon,* Paris 1979

Meyer, E., *Die Entstehung des Judentums,* Halle 1896, reprint Hildesheim 1987 . . .

Meyer, R., *Hebräische Grammatik,* I-IV, 3rd ed. Berlin 1966-72 . . .

Milgrom, J., "Korah's rebellion: A Study in Redaction," in: *De la Tôrah au Messie,* Mélanges H. Cazelles, ed. M. Carrez et al., Paris 1981, 135-146 . . .

Mittmann, S., *Deuteronomium 1-63 literarkritisch und traditions-geschichtlich untersucht,* BZAW 139, 1975 . . .

Mor, M., "I. Samaritan History. 1. The Persian, Hellenistic and Hasmonaean Period," in: A. D. Crown (ed.), *The Samaritans,* Tübingen 1989, 1-18 . . .

Mosis, R., "Ex 19,5b.6a: Syntaktischer Aufbau und lexikalische Semantik," BZ NF 22, 1978, 1-25 . . .

Mowinckel, S., *Studien zu dem Buche Ezra-Nehemia, III. Die Esrageschichte und das Gesetz Moses,* SNVAO HF, NS 7, 1965

———, *Tetrateuch-Pentateuch-Hexateuch,* BZAW 90, 1964 . . .

Munk, M., "Esra Hasofer nach Talmud und Midrasch," JJLG 21, 1930, 129-198 (reprint 1975) . . .

Nasuti, H., "Identity, Identification, and Imitation: The

Narrative Hermeneutics of Biblical Law," *Journal of Law and Religion* 4, 1986, 9-23 . . .

Nicholson, E. W., "The Decalogue as the Direct Address of God," VT 27, 1977, 422-433 . . .

Noth, M., *Das vierte Buch Mose. Numeri*, ATD 7, 1966

————, Die Gesetze im Pentateuch, SKG.G 17,2, 1940 = idem. Gesammelte . . .

————, *Studien zum Alten Testament*, ThB 6, ²1960, 9-141 . . .

Olson, D. T., *The Death of the Old and the Birth of the New: The Framework of the Book of Numbers and the Pentateuch*, Brown Judaic Studies 71, 1985 . . .

Patrick, D., *Old Testament Law*, Atlanta 1985

Patte, D., *Early Jewish Hermeneutics in Palestine*, Missoula 1975 . . .

Perlitt, L., *Bundestheologie im Alten Testament*, WMANT 36, 1969 . . .

————, *Deuteronomium*, BK 5, 1990/91 . . .

————, "Mose als Prophet," EvTh 31, 1971, 588-608 . . .

Petersen, J. E., "Priestly Material in Joshua 13-22, A Return to the Hexateuch?," *Hebrew Annual Review* 4, 1980, 131-146 . . .

Plöger, J. G., *Literarkritische, formgeschichtliche und stilkritische Untersuchungen zum Deuteronomium*, BBB 26, 1967 . . .

Porten, B., *Archives from Elephantine. The Life of an Ancient Jewish Military Colony*, Berkeley 1968

————, "The Jews in Egypt," in: *The Cambridge History of Judaism. I. Introduction; The Persian Period*, Cambridge 1984, 372-400

Porteous, N. W., *Das Buch Daniel*, ATD 23, ²²1968 . . .

Purvis, J. D., *The Samaritan Pentateuch and the Origin of the Samaritan Sect*, HSM 2, 1968 . . .

Pury, A. de/Römer, Th., "Le Pentateuque en Question: Position du Problème et brève Histoire de la Recherche," in: A. de Pury (ed.), *Le Pentateuque en Question*, Geneva² 1991, 9-80 . . .

Rainey, A. F., "The Satrapy 'Beyond the River'," AJBA

1, 1969, 51-79

Ray, J. D., Egypt: "Dependence and Independence (425-343 B.C.)," in: H. Sancisi-Weerdenburg (ed.), *Achaemenid History I, Sources, Structures and Synthesis*, Leiden 1987, 79-95

Reich, N. I., "The Codification of the Egyptian Laws by Darius and the origin of the 'Demotic Chronicle'," in: *Mizraim* I, 1933, 178-185 . . .

Rendtorff, R., "Der Text in seiner Endgestalt. Überlegungen zu Exodus 19," in: *Ernten, was man sät*, FS K. Koch, ed. D. R. Daniels et al., Neukirchen 1991, 459-470 . . .

————, "Die Offenbarungsvorstellungen im Alten Israel," in: W. Pannenberg (ed.), *Offenbarung als Geschichte*, KuD Beih.1, 1961, 21-44 = idem., *Gesammelte Studien zum Alten Testament*, ThB 57, 1975, 39-59

————, "Esra und das 'Gesetz'," ZAW 96, 1984, 165-184

————, *Leviticus*, BK III Liefg.1/2, 1985/90 . . .

Röthlisberger, H., *Kirche am Sinai. Die Zehn Gebote der christlichen Unterweisung*, SDGSTh 19, 1965 . . .

Rudolph, W., *Esra und Nehemia, samt 3. Esra*, HAT I/20, 1949 . . .

Ruprecht, E., "Exodus 24,9-11 als Beispiel lebendiger Erzähltradition aus der Zeit des babylonischen Exils," in: *Werden und Wirken des Alten Testaments*. FS C. Westermann, ed. R. Albertz et al., Göttingen and Neukirchen 1980, 138-173 . . .

Safrai, S., "Der Versöhnungstag in Tempel und Synagoge," in: H. Heinz et al., (ed.), *Versöhnung in der jüdischen und christlichen Liturgie*, QD 124, 1990, 32-55

————, *Die Wallfahrt im Zeitalter des zweiten Tempels*, Forschungen zum jüdisch-christlichen Dialog 3, Neukirchen 1981 . . .

Safrai, S., "The Synagogue," in: idem.,/M. Stern (eds.), *The Jewish People in the First Century*, vol. II, Assen 1976, 908-944

Saley, R. J., "The Date of Nehemiah Reconsidered," in: G. A. Tuttle (ed.), *Biblical and Near Eastern Studies*, FS La Sor, Grand Rapids 1978, 151-165

Salmon, P., "Les relations entre la Perse et l'Égypte de VIe au IVe siècle av. J.-C.," in: *The Land of Israel: Cross-Roads of Civilizations*, ed. E. Lipinski, Orientalia

Lovaniensa Analecta 19, 1985, 147-168 . . .

Schaeder, H. H., *Esra der Schreiber,* BHTh 5, 1930

Schäfer, P., "Das 'Dogma' von der mündlichen Tora im rabbinischen Judentum," in: idem., *Studien zu Geschichte und Theologie des rabbinischen Judentums,* AGJu 15, 1978, 153-97

————, "Die Torah der messianischen Zeit," ZNW 65,1974, 27-42 = idem., *Studien zur Geschichte und Theologie des rabbinischen Judentums,* AGJu 15, 1978, 198-213 . . .

Schart, A., *Mose und Israel im Konflikt. Eine redaktionsgeschichtliche Studie zu den Wüstenerzählungen,* OBO 98, 1990 . . .

Schmidt, W. H., "Nachwirkungen prophetischer Botschaft in der Priesterschrift," in: *Mélanges bibliques et orientaux,* FS M. M. Delcor, ed. A. Caquot et al., AOAT 215, 1985, 369-377 . . .

————, "Pentateuch und Prophetie. Eine Skizze zu Verschiedenartigkeit und Einheit alttestamentlicher Theologie," in: *Prophet und Prophetenbuch,* FS O. Kaiser, BZAW 185, 1989, 181-195

————, "Überlieferungsgeschichtliche Erwägungen zur Komposition des Dekalogs," VT.S 22, 1972, 201-220 . . .

Schmitt, H.-C., Elisa. "Redaktion des Pentateuch im Geiste der Prophetie," VT 32, 1982, 170-189

————, "Tradition der Prophetenbücher in den Schichten der Plagenerzählung Ex 7,1-11,10," in: *Prophet und Prophetenbuch,* FS O. Kaiser, BZAW 185, 1989, 196-216 . . .

Schreiner, S., "Der Dekalog in der jüdischen Tradition und im Koran," *Kairos* NF 23, 1981, 17-30

Schultz, C., "The Political Tensions Reflected in Ezra-Nehemiah," in: C. D. Evans et al., (ed.), *Scripture in Context. Essays on the Comparative Method,* Pittsburgh Theol. Monogr. Ser. 34, 1980, 221-244 . . .

Schüssler Fiorenza, E., *Priester für Gott. Studien zum Herrschafts- und Priestermotiv in der Apokalypse,* NTA 7, 1972 . . .

Scott, R. B. Y., "A Kingdom of Priests (Exodus xix 6)," OTS 8, 1950, 213-219 . . .

Smend, R., "'Das Ende ist gekommen.' Ein Amoswort in der Priesterschrift" (1981), in: idem., *Die Mitte des Alten Testaments. Gesammelte Studien I,* BEvTh 99, 1986, 154-159 . . .

Smitten, W. Th. in der, *Esra. Quelle, Überlieferung und Geschichte,* Assen 1973 . . .

Spiegelberg, W., *Die sogenannte demotische Chronik des Pap. 215 der Bibliothèque Nationale zu Paris,* Leipzig 1914 . . .

Spinoza, B., *Theologisch-politischer Traktat,* ed. G. Gawlick, PhB 93, 1976 . . .

Steck, O. H., *Der Abschluss der Prophetie im Alten Testaments. Ein Versuch zur Frage der Vorgeschichte des Kanon,* Biblisch theologische Studien 17, Neukirchen 1991

————, "Der Kanon des hebräischen Alten Testaments. Historische Materialien für eine ökumenische Perspektive," in: *Vernunft des Glaubens,* FS W. Pannenberg, Göttingen 1988, 231-252 . . .

Stemberger, G., "Der Dekalog im frühen Judentum, in: 'Gesetz' als Thema Biblischer Theologie," JBTh 4, 1989, 91-103 . . .

Stern, E., "The Persian Empire and the political and social history of Palestine in the Persian Period," in: *The Cambridge History of Judaism I. Introduction; The Persian Period,* Cambridge 1984, 70-87

————, "The Province of Yehud, the Vision and Reality," *The Jerusalem Cathedra* 1, 1981, 9-21 . . .

Talmon, Sh., "Esra-Nehemia, Historiographie oder Theologie?," in *Ernten, was man sat,* FS K. Koch, ed. D. R. Daniels et. al., Neukirchen 1991, 329-356. . . .

Talshir, D., "A Reinvestigation of the Linguistic Relationship Between Chronicles and Ezra-Nehemia," VT 38, 1988, 165-193. . . .

Throntveit, M.A., "Linguistic Analysis and the Question of Authorship in Chronicles, Ezra and Nehemiah," VT 32, 1982, 201-216. . . .

Toeg, A., "A Halakhic Midrash in Num XV 22-31," *Tabriz* 1973 / 74, 1-20 (hebr.) . . . .

Torrey, C. C., *Ezra Studies* (1910), New York², 1970P

Tov, E. "Die griechisen Bibeluebersetzungen," ANRW II, 20 / 1, 1987, 121-189

————. "Proto-Samaritan Texts and the Samaritan Pentateuch," in: A. D. Crown (ed.), *The Samaritans,* Tubingen 1989, 397-412. . .

Tuplin, Ch. "The Administration of the Achaemenid Empire," in: I. Carradice, (ed.), *Coinage and Administration in the Athenian and the Persian Empires,*

British Archaeological Reports, Intern. Series 343, Oxford 1987, 109-166. . .

Wahl, O., "Grundelement eines festlichen Wortgottedienstes nach Neh 8, 1-12," in *Die Freude an Gott–unsere Kraft,* FS O. B. Knoch, Stuttgart 1991, 47-59 . . .

Wallis, G. "Die soziale Situation der Juden in Babylon zur Archamenidenzeit auf Grund von funfzig ausgewahlten babylonischen Urkunden," manuscript Diss. Berlin 1952 . . .

Weinfeld, M., *Deuteronomy and the Deuteronomic School,* Oxford 1972 . . .

Wellhausen, J., *Prolegomena zur Geschichte Israels* (1878), Berlin⁶ 1927

Welten, P., *Geschichte und Geschichtsdarstellung in den Chronikbüchern,* WMANT 42, 1973 . . .

Westermann, C., "Die Herrlichkeit Gottes in der Priesterschrift," in: *Wort—Gebot—Glaube,* FS W. Eichrodt, Zürich 1971, 227-249 = idem., *Forschung am Alten Testament.* Gesammelte Studien II, ThB 55, 1974, 115-137 . . .

Yamauchi, E. M., "The Reverse Order of Ezra/ Nehemiah Reconsidered," *Themelios* 5, 1980, 7-18 . . .

Zadok, R., "Some Jews in Babylonian Documents," JQR 74, 1983/4, 294-297

———, *The Jews in Babylonia during the Chaldean and Achaemenian Periods according to the Babylonian Sources.* Studies in the History of the Jewish People and the Land of Israel, Monogr. Ser. III, Haifa 1979 . . .

Zeitlin, S., "The Halaka. Introduction to Tannaitic Jurisprudence," JQR 39, 1948/49, 1-40

FURTHER READING

Baker, D. W. "Diversity and Unity in the Literary Structure of *Genesis*." In *Essays on the Patriarchal Narratives,* edited by A. R. Millard and D. J. Wiseman, pp. 197-215. Winona Lake, Ind.: Eisenbrauns, 1980.
Studies the internal divisions of the Hebrew text of *Genesis* and comments on their implications.

Bissell, Edwin Cone. *The Pentateuch: Its Origin and Structure.* New York: Charles Scribner's Sons, 1910, 484 p.
Discusses the history of critical approaches to the authorship of the Pentateuch.

Blenkinsopp, Joseph. *The Pentateuch: An Introduction to the First Five Books of the "Bible."* New York: Doubleday, 1992, 273p.
Explores the story and structure of the Pentateuchal narrative.

Brenner, Athalya, ed. *A Feminist Companion to "Exodus" and to Deuteronomy.* Sheffield: Sheffield Academic Press, 1994, 269p.
Collection of feminist criticism on the characterization of women and female sexuality in the Torah.

Campbell, Antony F., and Mark A. O'Brien. *Sources of the Pentateuch: Texts, Introductions, Annotations.* Minneapolis: Fortress Press, 1993, 266p.
Presents a "source-critical model" of the Pentateuch, dissecting its different parts–the Priestly document, the Yahwist narrative, the Elohist texts, and nonsource texts–and the composite version.

Clines, David J. A. *The Theme of the Pentateuch.* Sheffield: JSOT Press, 1978, 152p.
Claims that, despite the disunity of the Pentateuch's origin, the work has a unified theme revolving around God's promise to humankind.

Cohn-Sherbok, Dan. "The *Torah*." In *The Hebrew "Bible,"* pp. 11-44. London: Cassell, 1996.
Outlines and describes the plots of the five books of the *Torah,* with specific citations for each event.

De Pinto, Basil. "The *Torah* and the *Psalms*." *Journal of Biblical Literature,* Vol. LXXXVI, Part II (June, 1967): 154-74.
Compares the relationship between God and man that is portrayed in the *Torah* with its lyrical expression in the *Psalms.*

Driver, S. R. "The Hexateuch." In his *An Introduction to the Literature of the Old Testament,* pp. 1-159. New York: Charles Scribner's Sons, 1900.
Outlines each of the books of the Hexateuch, examining stylistic differences in order to determine the authorship of its parts.

Eiselen, Frederick Carl. *The Books of the Pentateuch: Their Origin, Contents, and Significance.* New York: Methodist Book Concern, 1916, 351p.
Introduction to the historical study of the Pentateuch, with extended discussions of the authorship and chronological order of the documents.

Hammer, Reuven. *The Classic Midrash: Tannaitic Commentaries on the "Bible."* New York: Paulist Press, 1995, 528p.
Detailed commentary on *Exodus* through *Deuteronomy,* along with new translations of the passages

analyzed. The book is divided into two sections: scriptural interpretation and interpretation of legal portions.

Hertz, J. H., ed. *The Pentateuch and Haftorahs: Hebrew Text, English Translation and Commentary.* 5 vols. Oxford: Oxford University Press, 1929.

Presents an English translation of the *Torah* on pages facing the Hebrew, along with extensive commentary and illustrative maps.

Konvitz, Milton R. "The Confluence of *Torah* and Constitution." In his *"Torah" and Constitution: Essays in American Jewish Thought,* pp. 3-16. Syracuse: Syracuse University Press, 1998.

Compares the moral principles underlying the United States Constitution with those in the oral and written *Torah*.

Mackintosh, C. H. *Genesis to Deuteronomy: Notes on the Pentateuch.* Neptune, N.J.: Loizeaux Brothers, 1972, 928 p.

Chronicles the events of the Pentateuch and analyzes their religious and moral import.

Mann, Thomas W. *The Book of the Torah: The Narrative Integrity of the Pentateuch.* Atlanta: John Knox Press, 1988, 180p.

Surveys the narrative structure of the Pentateuch in an effort to delineate its literary cohesiveness.

Noth, Martin. "The Laws in the Pentateuch: Their Assumptions and Meaning." In *The Laws in the Pentateuch and Other Studies,* pp. 1-107. Edinburgh: Oliver & Boyd, 1966.

Discusses the religious, historical, and political importance of law in the *Torah*.

———. *A History of Pentateuchal Traditions,* translated by Bernhard W. Anderson. Englewood Cliffs, N.J.: Prentice-Hall, 1972, 296p.

Historical investigation in which Noth traces "the history of Pentateuchal traditions from their earliest formulations in the preliterary period down to the time of their composition in successive literary stages which finally resulted in the whole Pentateuch as we have received it."

———. "The 'Priestly Writing' and the Redaction of the Pentateuch." In *The Chronicler's History,* translated by H. G. M. Williamson, pp. 107-47. Sheffield: Sheffield Academic Press, 1987.

Attempts to delineate the priestly writing that was inserted into the Pentateuch.

Plaut, W. Gunther, and Bernard J. Bamberger. *The Torah: A Modern Commentary.* New York: Union of American Hebrew Congregations, 1981, 1787p.

Contains the Hebrew text of the *Torah* alongside an

English translation, with running commentary by Plaut and Bamberger. The book also contains a bibliography that includes recommended Bible translations, commentaries, and secondary works in English, among other materials. Bamberger's introductory article "The *Torah* and the Jewish People" appears in the above entry.

Preminger, Alex, and Edward L. Greenstein, eds. *The Hebrew Bible in Literary Criticism.* New York: Ungar, 1986, 619p.

Excerpts short passages of literary criticism on the Hebrew *Bible* by various writers.

Rabin, Chaim. "Discourse Analysis and the Dating of *Deuteronomy.*" In *Interpreting the Hebrew ""Bible": Essays in Honour of E. I. J. Rosenthal,* edited by J. A. Emerton and Stefan C. Reif, pp. 171-77. Cambridge: Cambridge University Press, 1982.

Examines the language and rhetorical style of *Deuteronomy* in an attempt to establish a likely date of its composition.

Sailhamer, John H. *The Pentateuch as Narrative.* Grand Rapids, Mich.: Zondervan Publishing House, 1992, 522p.

Traces the narrative strategy of the Pentateuch– considered as a unified, written document– in an effort to show the interrelation of seemingly disparate episodes.

———. "Genesis." In *A Complete Literary Guide to the "Bible,"* edited by Leland Ryken and Tremper Longman III, pp. 108-20. Grand Rapids: Zondervan Publishing House, 1993.

Articulates the literary themes of *Genesis* in terms of their realistic treatment of the world and humanity.

Sarna, Nahum M. "The Anticipatory Use of Information as a Literary Feature of the *Genesis* Narratives." In *The Creation of Sacred Literature: Composition and Redaction of the Biblical Text,* edited by Richard Elliott Friedman, pp. 76-82. Berkeley: University of California Press, 1981.

Contends that one of the literary methods used to unify *Genesis* is "the sudden introduction into a text of certain information which is extraneous to the immediate context but which is later seen to be crucial to the understanding of a subsequent episode or theme."

———. "Genesis": The Traditional Hebrew Text with New JPS Translation. Philadelphia: Jewish Publication Society, 1989, 414p.

Contains the Hebrew text of *Genesis* alongside an English translation, with extensive running commentary by Sarna.

Simpson, D. C. *Pentateuchal Criticism.* London: Oxford University Press, 1924, 211p.

Surveys the evidence regarding the separate sources

that served as the basis of the *Torah*. Simpson
considers the importance of the Torah's composition
to Hebrew history and comes to the conclusion that
the gradual historical genesis of the *Torah* corresponds
with the development of Israel in preparation for the
coming of the Messiah.

Whybray, R. N. *The Making of the Pentateuch: A Methodological Study.* Sheffield: JSOT Press, 1987, 263 p.
      Interprets the narrative structure of the *Torah* in terms
      of its literary form and, alternatively, as a document
      grounded in a preliterary, oral tradition.

Zerin, Edward. *The Birth of the "Torah."* New York:
Appleton-Century-Crofts, 1962, 274p.
      Draws on archeological findings to elucidate the
      historical conditions in which the *Torah* was written.

CLASSICAL AND MEDIEVAL LITERATURE CRITICISM

INDEXES

Literary Criticism Series
Cumulative Author Index

Literary Criticism Series
Cumulative Topic Index

CMLC Cumulative Nationality Index

CMLC Cumulative Title Index

CMLC Cumulative Critic Index

How to Use This Index

The main references

Calvino, Italo
    1923–1985 .... CLC **5, 8, 11, 22, 33, 39,**
                                73; SSC 3

list all author entries in the following Gale Literary Criticism series:

BLC = *Black Literature Criticism*
CLC = *Contemporary Literary Criticism*
CLR = *Children's Literature Review*
CMLC = *Classical and Medieval Literature Criticism*
DA = *DISCovering Authors*
DAB = *DISCovering Authors: British*
DAC = *DISCovering Authors: Canadian*
DAM = *DISCovering Authors: Modules*
        DRAM: *Dramatists Module*; *MST*: *Most-Studied Authors Module*;
        MULT: *Multicultural Authors Module*; *NOV*: *Novelists Module*;
        POET: *Poets Module*; *POP*: *Popular Fiction and Genre Authors Module*
DC = *Drama Criticism*
HLC = *Hispanic Literature Criticism*
LC = *Literature Criticism from 1400 to 1800*
NCLC = *Nineteenth-Century Literature Criticism*
PC = *Poetry Criticism*
SSC = *Short Story Criticism*
TCLC = *Twentieth-Century Literary Criticism*
WLC = *World Literature Criticism, 1500 to the Present*

The cross-references

See also CANR 23; CA 85-88;
    obituary CA116

list all author entries in the following Gale biographical and literary sources:

AAYA = *Authors & Artists for Young Adults*
AITN = *Authors in the News*
BEST = *Bestsellers*
BW = *Black Writers*
CA = *Contemporary Authors*
CAAS = *Contemporary Authors Autobiography Series*
CABS = *Contemporary Authors Bibliographical Series*
CANR = *Contemporary Authors New Revision Series*
CAP = *Contemporary Authors Permanent Series*
CDALB = *Concise Dictionary of American Literary Biography*
CDBLB = *Concise Dictionary of British Literary Biography*
DLB = *Dictionary of Literary Biography*
DLBD = *Dictionary of Literary Biography Documentary Series*
DLBY = *Dictionary of Literary Biography Yearbook*
HW = *Hispanic Writers*
JRDA = *Junior DISCovering Authors*
MAICYA = *Major Authors and Illustrators for Children and Young Adults*
MTCW = *Major 20th-Century Writers*
NNAL = *Native North American Literature*
SAAS = *Something about the Author Autobiography Series*
SATA = *Something about the Author*
YABC = *Yesterday's Authors of Books for Children*

Literary Criticism Series
Cumulative Author Index

Abasiyanik, Sait Faik 1906-1954
See Sait Faik
See also CA 123

Abbey, Edward 1927-1989 **CLC 36, 59**
See also CA 45-48; 128; CANR 2, 41

Abbott, Lee K(ittredge) 1947- **CLC 48**
See also CA 124; CANR 51; DLB 130

Abe, Kobo 1924-1993**CLC 8, 22, 53, 81; DAM NOV**
See also CA 65-68; 140; CANR 24, 60; DLB 182; MTCW 1

Abelard, Peter c. 1079-c. 1142 **CMLC 11**
See also DLB 115

Abell, Kjeld 1901-1961 **CLC 15**
See also CA 111

Abish, Walter 1931- **CLC 22**
See also CA 101; CANR 37; DLB 130

Abrahams, Peter (Henry) 1919- **CLC 4**
See also BW 1; CA 57-60; CANR 26; DLB 117; MTCW 1

Abrams, M(eyer) H(oward) 1912- **CLC 24**
See also CA 57-60; CANR 13, 33; DLB 67

Abse, Dannie 1923- **CLC 7, 29; DAB; DAM POET**
See also CA 53-56; CAAS 1; CANR 4, 46; DLB 27

Achebe, (Albert) Chinua(lumogu) 1930-**C L C 1, 3, 5, 7, 11, 26, 51, 75; BLC 1; DA; DAB; DAC; DAM MST, MULT, NOV; WLC**
See also AAYA 15; BW 2; CA 1-4R; CANR 6, 26, 47; CLR 20; DLB 117; MAICYA; MTCW 1; SATA 40; SATA-Brief 38

Acker, Kathy 1948-1997 **CLC 45, 111**
See also CA 117; 122; 162; CANR 55

Ackroyd, Peter 1949- **CLC 34, 52**
See also CA 123; 127; CANR 51; DLB 155; INT 127

Acorn, Milton 1923- **CLC 15; DAC**
See also CA 103; DLB 53; INT 103

Adamov, Arthur 1908-1970 **CLC 4, 25; DAM DRAM**
See also CA 17-18; 25-28R; CAP 2; MTCW 1

Adams, Alice (Boyd) 1926-**CLC 6, 13, 46; SSC 24**
See also CA 81-84; CANR 26, 53; DLBY 86; INT CANR-26; MTCW 1

Adams, Andy 1859-1935 **TCLC 56**
See also YABC 1

Adams, Brooks 1848-1927 **TCLC 80**
See also CA 123; DLB 47

Adams, Douglas (Noel) 1952- **CLC 27, 60; DAM POP**
See also AAYA 4; BEST 89:3; CA 106; CANR 34, 64; DLBY 83; JRDA

Adams, Francis 1862-1893 **NCLC 33**

Adams, Henry (Brooks) 1838-1918 **TCLC 4, 52; DA; DAB; DAC; DAM MST**
See also CA 104; 133; DLB 12, 47, 189

Adams, Richard (George) 1920-**CLC 4, 5, 18; DAM NOV**
See also AAYA 16; AITN 1, 2; CA 49-52; CANR 3, 35; CLR 20; JRDA; MAICYA;

MTCW 1; SATA 7, 69

Adamson, Joy(-Friederike Victoria) 1910-1980 **CLC 17**
See also CA 69-72; 93-96; CANR 22; MTCW 1; SATA 11; SATA-Obit 22

Adcock, Fleur 1934- **CLC 41**
See also CA 25-28R; CAAS 23; CANR 11, 34, 69; DLB 40

Addams, Charles (Samuel) 1912-1988**CLC 30**
See also CA 61-64; 126; CANR 12

Addams, Jane 1860-1945 **TCLC 76**

Addison, Joseph 1672-1719 **LC 18**
See also CDBLB 1660-1789; DLB 101

Adler, Alfred (F.) 1870-1937 **TCLC 61**
See also CA 119; 159

Adler, C(arole) S(chwerdtfeger) 1932-**CLC 35**
See also AAYA 4; CA 89-92; CANR 19, 40; JRDA; MAICYA; SAAS 15; SATA 26, 63, 102

Adler, Renata 1938- **CLC 8, 31**
See also CA 49-52; CANR 5, 22, 52; MTCW 1

Ady, Endre 1877-1919 **TCLC 11**
See also CA 107

A.E. 1867-1935 **TCLC 3, 10**
See also Russell, George William

Aeschylus 525B.C.-456B.C. **CMLC 11; DA; DAB; DAC; DAM DRAM, MST; DC 8; WLCS**
See also DLB 176

Aesop 620(?)B.C.-564(?)B.C. **CMLC 24**
See also CLR 14; MAICYA; SATA 64

Affable Hawk
See MacCarthy, Sir(Charles Otto) Desmond

Africa, Ben
See Bosman, Herman Charles

Afton, Effie
See Harper, Frances Ellen Watkins

Agapida, Fray Antonio
See Irving, Washington

Agee, James (Rufus) 1909-1955 **TCLC 1, 19; DAM NOV**
See also AITN 1; CA 108; 148; CDALB 1941-1968; DLB 2, 26, 152

Aghill, Gordon
See Silverberg, Robert

Agnon, S(hmuel) Y(osef Halevi) 1888-1970 **CLC 4, 8, 14; SSC 30**
See also CA 17-18; 25-28R; CANR 60; CAP 2; MTCW 1

Agrippa von Nettesheim, Henry Cornelius 1486-1535 **LC 27**

Aherne, Owen
See Cassill, R(onald) V(erlin)

Ai 1947- **CLC 4, 14, 69**
See also CA 85-88; CAAS 13; CANR 70; DLB 120

Aickman, Robert (Fordyce) 1914-1981 **C L C 57**
See also CA 5-8R; CANR 3, 72

Aiken, Conrad (Potter) 1889-1973**CLC 1, 3, 5, 10, 52; DAM NOV, POET; SSC 9**
See also CA 5-8R; 45-48; CANR 4, 60; CDALB

1929-1941; DLB 9, 45, 102; MTCW 1; SATA 3, 30

Aiken, Joan (Delano) 1924- **CLC 35**
See also AAYA 1, 25; CA 9-12R; CANR 4, 23, 34, 64; CLR 1, 19; DLB 161; JRDA; MAICYA; MTCW 1; SAAS 1; SATA 2, 30, 73

Ainsworth, William Harrison 1805-1882 **NCLC 13**
See also DLB 21; SATA 24

Aitmatov, Chingiz (Torekulovich) 1928-**C L C 71**
See also CA 103; CANR 38; MTCW 1; SATA 56

Akers, Floyd
See Baum, L(yman) Frank

Akhmadulina, Bella Akhatovna 1937- **C L C 53; DAM POET**
See also CA 65-68

Akhmatova, Anna 1888-1966**CLC 11, 25, 64; DAM POET; PC 2**
See also CA 19-20; 25-28R; CANR 35; CAP 1; MTCW 1

Aksakov, Sergei Timofeyvich 1791-1859 **NCLC 2**
See also DLB 198

Aksenov, Vassily
See Aksyonov, Vassily (Pavlovich)

Akst, Daniel 1956- **CLC 109**
See also CA 161

Aksyonov, Vassily (Pavlovich) 1932-**CLC 22, 37, 101**
See also CA 53-56; CANR 12, 48

Akutagawa, Ryunosuke 1892-1927 **TCLC 16**
See also CA 117; 154

Alain 1868-1951 **TCLC 41**
See also CA 163

Alain-Fournier **TCLC 6**
See also Fournier, Henri Alban
See also DLB 65

Alarcon, Pedro Antonio de 1833-1891**NCLC 1**

Alas (y Urena), Leopoldo (Enrique Garcia) 1852-1901 **TCLC 29**
See also CA 113; 131; HW

Albee, Edward (Franklin III) 1928-**CLC 1, 2, 3, 5, 9, 11, 13, 25, 53, 86, 113; DA; DAB; DAC; DAM DRAM, MST; WLC**
See also AITN 1; CA 5-8R; CABS 3; CANR 8, 54; CDALB 1941-1968; DLB 7; INT CANR-8; MTCW 1

Alberti, Rafael 1902- **CLC 7**
See also CA 85-88; DLB 108

Albert the Great 1200(?)-1280 **CMLC 16**
See also DLB 115

Alcala-Galiano, Juan Valera y
See Valera y Alcala-Galiano, Juan

Alcott, Amos Bronson 1799-1888 **NCLC 1**
See also DLB 1

Alcott, Louisa May 1832-1888 **NCLC 6, 58; DA; DAB; DAC; DAM MST, NOV; SSC 27; WLC**
See also AAYA 20; CDALB 1865-1917; CLR

1, 38; DLB 1, 42, 79; DLBD 14; JRDA; MAICYA; SATA 100; YABC 1

Aldanov, M. A.
See Aldanov, Mark (Alexandrovich)

Aldanov, Mark (Alexandrovich) 1886(?)-1957 **TCLC 23**
See also CA 118

Aldington, Richard 1892-1962 **CLC 49**
See also CA 85-88; CANR 45; DLB 20, 36, 100, 149

Aldiss, Brian W(ilson) 1925- **CLC 5, 14, 40; DAM NOV**
See also CA 5-8R; CAAS 2; CANR 5, 28, 64; DLB 14; MTCW 1; SATA 34

Alegria, Claribel 1924-**CLC 75; DAM MULT**
See also CA 131; CAAS 15; CANR 66; DLB 145; HW

Alegria, Fernando 1918- **CLC 57**
See also CA 9-12R; CANR 5, 32, 72; HW

Aleichem, Sholom **TCLC 1, 35**
See also Rabinovitch, Sholem

Aleixandre, Vicente 1898-1984 **CLC 9, 36; DAM POET; PC 15**
See also CA 85-88; 114; CANR 26; DLB 108; HW; MTCW 1

Alepoudelis, Odysseus
See Elytis, Odysseus

Aleshkovsky, Joseph 1929-
See Aleshkovsky, Yuz
See also CA 121; 128

Aleshkovsky, Yuz **CLC 44**
See also Aleshkovsky, Joseph

Alexander, Lloyd (Chudley) 1924- **CLC 35**
See also AAYA 1, 27; CA 1-4R; CANR 1, 24, 38, 55; CLR 1, 5, 48; DLB 52; JRDA; MAICYA; MTCW 1; SAAS 19; SATA 3, 49, 81

Alexander, Samuel 1859-1938 **TCLC 77**

Alexie, Sherman (Joseph, Jr.) 1966- **CLC 96; DAM MULT**
See also CA 138; CANR 65; DLB 175; NNAL

Alfau, Felipe 1902- **CLC 66**
See also CA 137

Alger, Horatio, Jr. 1832-1899 **NCLC 8**
See also DLB 42; SATA 16

Algren, Nelson 1909-1981 **CLC 4, 10, 33**
See also CA 13-16R; 103; CANR 20, 61; CDALB 1941-1968; DLB 9; DLBY 81, 82; MTCW 1

Ali, Ahmed 1910- **CLC 69**
See also CA 25-28R; CANR 15, 34

Alighieri, Dante
See Dante

Allan, John B.
See Westlake, Donald E(dwin)

Allan, Sidney
See Hartmann, Sadakichi

Allan, Sydney
See Hartmann, Sadakichi

Allen, Edward 1948- **CLC 59**

Allen, Paula Gunn 1939- **CLC 84; DAM MULT**
See also CA 112; 143; CANR 63; DLB 175; NNAL

Allen, Roland
See Ayckbourn, Alan

Allen, Sarah A.
See Hopkins, Pauline Elizabeth

Allen, Sidney H.
See Hartmann, Sadakichi

Allen, Woody 1935- **CLC 16, 52; DAM POP**
See also AAYA 10; CA 33-36R; CANR 27, 38, 63; DLB 44; MTCW 1

Allende, Isabel 1942- **CLC 39, 57, 97; DAM MULT, NOV; HLC; WLCS**
See also AAYA 18; CA 125; 130; CANR 51; DLB 145; HW; INT 130; MTCW 1

Alleyn, Ellen
See Rossetti, Christina (Georgina)

Allingham, Margery (Louise) 1904-1966**CLC 19**
See also CA 5-8R; 25-28R; CANR 4, 58; DLB 77; MTCW 1

Allingham, William 1824-1889 **NCLC 25**
See also DLB 35

Allison, Dorothy E. 1949- **CLC 78**
See also CA 140; CANR 66

Allston, Washington 1779-1843 **NCLC 2**
See also DLB 1

Almedingen, E. M. **CLC 12**
See also Almedingen, Martha Edith von
See also SATA 3

Almedingen, Martha Edith von 1898-1971
See Almedingen, E. M.
See also CA 1-4R; CANR 1

Almodovar, Pedro 1949(?)- **CLC 114**
See also CA 133; CANR 72

Almqvist, Carl Jonas Love 1793-1866 **NCLC 42**

Alonso, Damaso 1898-1990 **CLC 14**
See also CA 110; 131; 130; CANR 72; DLB 108; HW

Alov
See Gogol, Nikolai (Vasilyevich)

Alta 1942- **CLC 19**
See also CA 57-60

Alter, Robert B(ernard) 1935- **CLC 34**
See also CA 49-52; CANR 1, 47

Alther, Lisa 1944- **CLC 7, 41**
See also CA 65-68; CAAS 30; CANR 12, 30, 51; MTCW 1

Althusser, L.
See Althusser, Louis

Althusser, Louis 1918-1990 **CLC 106**
See also CA 131; 132

Altman, Robert 1925- **CLC 16**
See also CA 73-76; CANR 43

Alvarez, A(lfred) 1929- **CLC 5, 13**
See also CA 1-4R; CANR 3, 33, 63; DLB 14, 40

Alvarez, Alejandro Rodriguez 1903-1965
See Casona, Alejandro
See also CA 131; 93-96; HW

Alvarez, Julia 1950- **CLC 93**
See also AAYA 25; CA 147; CANR 69

Alvaro, Corrado 1896-1956 **TCLC 60**
See also CA 163

Amado, Jorge 1912- **CLC 13, 40, 106; DAM MULT, NOV; HLC**
See also CA 77-80; CANR 35; DLB 113; MTCW 1

Ambler, Eric 1909- **CLC 4, 6, 9**
See also CA 9-12R; CANR 7, 38; DLB 77; MTCW 1

Amichai, Yehuda 1924- **CLC 9, 22, 57**
See also CA 85-88; CANR 46, 60; MTCW 1

Amichai, Yehudah
See Amichai, Yehuda

Amiel, Henri Frederic 1821-1881 **NCLC 4**

Amis, Kingsley (William) 1922-1995**CLC 1, 2, 3, 5, 8, 13, 40, 44; DA; DAB; DAC; DAM MST, NOV**
See also AITN 2; CA 9-12R; 150; CANR 8, 28, 54; CDBLB 1945-1960; DLB 15, 27, 100, 139; DLBY 96; INT CANR-8; MTCW 1

Amis, Martin (Louis) 1949- **CLC 4, 9, 38, 62,**

101
See also BEST 90:3; CA 65-68; CANR 8, 27, 54; DLB 14, 194; INT CANR-27

Ammons, A(rchie) R(andolph) 1926-**CLC 2, 3, 5, 8, 9, 25, 57, 108; DAM POET; PC 16**
See also AITN 1; CA 9-12R; CANR 6, 36, 51; DLB 5, 165; MTCW 1

Amo, Tauraatua i
See Adams, Henry (Brooks)

Anand, Mulk Raj 1905- **CLC 23, 93; DAM NOV**
See also CA 65-68; CANR 32, 64; MTCW 1

Anatol
See Schnitzler, Arthur

Anaximander c. 610B.C.-c. 546B.C.**CMLC 22**

Anaya, Rudolfo A(lfonso) 1937- **CLC 23; DAM MULT, NOV; HLC**
See also AAYA 20; CA 45-48; CAAS 4; CANR 1, 32, 51; DLB 82; HW 1; MTCW 1

Andersen, Hans Christian 1805-1875**NCLC 7; DA; DAB; DAC; DAM MST, POP; SSC 6; WLC**
See also CLR 6; MAICYA; SATA 100; YABC 1

Anderson, C. Farley
See Mencken, H(enry) L(ouis); Nathan, George Jean

Anderson, Jessica (Margaret) Queale 1916- **CLC 37**
See also CA 9-12R; CANR 4, 62

Anderson, Jon (Victor) 1940- **CLC 9; DAM POET**
See also CA 25-28R; CANR 20

Anderson, Lindsay (Gordon) 1923-1994**CLC 20**
See also CA 125; 128; 146

Anderson, Maxwell 1888-1959**TCLC 2; DAM DRAM**
See also CA 105; 152; DLB 7

Anderson, Poul (William) 1926- **CLC 15**
See also AAYA 5; CA 1-4R; CAAS 2; CANR 2, 15, 34, 64; DLB 8; INT CANR-15; MTCW 1; SATA 90; SATA-Brief 39

Anderson, Robert (Woodruff) 1917-**CLC 23; DAM DRAM**
See also AITN 1; CA 21-24R; CANR 32; DLB 7

Anderson, Sherwood 1876-1941 **TCLC 1, 10, 24; DA; DAB; DAC; DAM MST, NOV; SSC 1; WLC**
See also CA 104; 121; CANR 61; CDALB 1917-1929; DLB 4, 9, 86; DLBD 1; MTCW 1

Andier, Pierre
See Desnos, Robert

Andouard
See Giraudoux, (Hippolyte) Jean

Andrade, Carlos Drummond de **CLC 18**
See also Drummond de Andrade, Carlos

Andrade, Mario de 1893-1945 **TCLC 43**

Andreae, Johann V(alentin) 1586-1654**LC 32**
See also DLB 164

Andreas-Salome, Lou 1861-1937 **TCLC 56**
See also DLB 66

Andress, Lesley
See Sanders, Lawrence

Andrewes, Lancelot 1555-1626 **LC 5**
See also DLB 151, 172

Andrews, Cicily Fairfield
See West, Rebecca

Andrews, Elton V.
See Pohl, Frederik

Andreyev, Leonid (Nikolaevich) 1871-1919

Behan, Brendan 1923-1964 **CLC 1, 8, 11, 15, 79; DAM DRAM**
See also CA 73-76; CANR 33; CDBLB 1945-1960; DLB 13; MTCW 1

Behn, Aphra 1640(?)-1689**LC 1, 30; DA; DAB; DAC; DAM DRAM, MST, NOV, POET; DC 4; PC 13; WLC**
See also DLB 39, 80, 131

Behrman, S(amuel) N(athaniel) 1893-1973 **CLC 40**
See also CA 13-16; 45-48; CAP 1; DLB 7, 44

Belasco, David 1853-1931 **TCLC 3**
See also CA 104; 168; DLB 7

Belcheva, Elisaveta 1893- **CLC 10**
See also Bagryana, Elisaveta

Beldone, Phil "Cheech"
See Ellison, Harlan (Jay)

Beleno
See Azuela, Mariano

Belinski, Vissarion Grigoryevich 1811-1848 **NCLC 5**
See also DLB 198

Belitt, Ben 1911- **CLC 22**
See also CA 13-16R; CAAS 4; CANR 7; DLB 5

Bell, Gertrude (Margaret Lowthian) 1868-1926 **TCLC 67**
See also CA 167; DLB 174

Bell, J. Freeman
See Zangwill, Israel

Bell, James Madison 1826-1902 **TCLC 43; BLC 1; DAM MULT**
See also BW 1; CA 122; 124; DLB 50

Bell, Madison Smartt 1957- **CLC 41, 102**
See also CA 111; CANR 28, 54

Bell, Marvin (Hartley) 1937-**CLC 8, 31; DAM POET**
See also CA 21-24R; CAAS 14; CANR 59; DLB 5; MTCW 1

Bell, W. L. D.
See Mencken, H(enry) L(ouis)

Bellamy, Atwood C.
See Mencken, H(enry) L(ouis)

Bellamy, Edward 1850-1898 **NCLC 4**
See also DLB 12

Bellin, Edward J.
See Kuttner, Henry

Belloc, (Joseph) Hilaire (Pierre Sebastien Rene Swanton) 1870-1953 **TCLC 7, 18; DAM POET; PC 24**
See also CA 106; 152; DLB 19, 100, 141, 174; YABC 1

Belloc, Joseph Peter Rene Hilaire
See Belloc, (Joseph) Hilaire (Pierre Sebastien Rene Swanton)

Belloc, Joseph Pierre Hilaire
See Belloc, (Joseph) Hilaire (Pierre Sebastien Rene Swanton)

Belloc, M. A.
See Lowndes, Marie Adelaide (Belloc)

Bellow, Saul 1915-**CLC 1, 2, 3, 6, 8, 10, 13, 15, 25, 33, 34, 63, 79; DA; DAB; DAC; DAM MST, NOV, POP; SSC 14; WLC**
See also AITN 2; BEST 89:3; CA 5-8R; CABS 1; CANR 29, 53; CDALB 1941-1968; DLB 2, 28; DLBD 3; DLBY 82; MTCW 1

Belser, Reimond Karel Maria de 1929-
See Ruyslinck, Ward
See also CA 152

Bely, Andrey **TCLC 7; PC 11**
See also Bugayev, Boris Nikolayevich

Belyi, Andrei
See Bugayev, Boris Nikolayevich

Benary, Margot
See Benary-Isbert, Margot

Benary-Isbert, Margot 1889-1979 **CLC 12**
See also CA 5-8R; 89-92; CANR 4, 72; CLR 12; MAICYA; SATA 2; SATA-Obit 21

Benavente (y Martinez), Jacinto 1866-1954 **TCLC 3; DAM DRAM, MULT**
See also CA 106; 131; HW; MTCW 1

Benchley, Peter (Bradford) 1940- **CLC 4, 8; DAM NOV, POP**
See also AAYA 14; AITN 2; CA 17-20R; CANR 12, 35, 66; MTCW 1; SATA 3, 89

Benchley, Robert (Charles) 1889-1945**TCLC 1, 55**
See also CA 105; 153; DLB 11

Benda, Julien 1867-1956 **TCLC 60**
See also CA 120; 154

Benedict, Ruth (Fulton) 1887-1948 **TCLC 60**
See also CA 158

Benedict, Saint c. 480-c. 547 **CMLC 29**

Benedikt, Michael 1935- **CLC 4, 14**
See also CA 13-16R; CANR 7; DLB 5

Benet, Juan 1927- **CLC 28**
See also CA 143

Benet, Stephen Vincent 1898-1943 **TCLC 7; DAM POET; SSC 10**
See also CA 104; 152; DLB 4, 48, 102; DLBY 97; YABC 1

Benet, William Rose 1886-1950 **TCLC 28; DAM POET**
See also CA 118; 152; DLB 45

Benford, Gregory (Albert) 1941- **CLC 52**
See also CA 69-72; CAAS 27; CANR 12, 24, 49; DLBY 82

Bengtsson, Frans (Gunnar) 1894-1954**TCLC 48**

Benjamin, David
See Slavitt, David R(ytman)

Benjamin, Lois
See Gould, Lois

Benjamin, Walter 1892-1940 **TCLC 39**
See also CA 164

Benn, Gottfried 1886-1956 **TCLC 3**
See also CA 106; 153; DLB 56

Bennett, Alan 1934-**CLC 45, 77; DAB; DAM MST**
See also CA 103; CANR 35, 55; MTCW 1

Bennett, (Enoch) Arnold 1867-1931 **TCLC 5, 20**
See also CA 106; 155; CDBLB 1890-1914; DLB 10, 34, 98, 135

Bennett, Elizabeth
See Mitchell, Margaret (Munnerlyn)

Bennett, George Harold 1930-
See Bennett, Hal
See also BW 1; CA 97-100

Bennett, Hal **CLC 5**
See also Bennett, George Harold
See also DLB 33

Bennett, Jay 1912- **CLC 35**
See also AAYA 10; CA 69-72; CANR 11, 42; JRDA; SAAS 4; SATA 41, 87; SATA-Brief 27

Bennett, Louise (Simone) 1919-**CLC 28; BLC 1; DAM MULT**
See also BW 2; CA 151; DLB 117

Benson, E(dward) F(rederic) 1867-1940 **TCLC 27**
See also CA 114; 157; DLB 135, 153

Benson, Jackson J. 1930- **CLC 34**
See also CA 25-28R; DLB 111

Benson, Sally 1900-1972 **CLC 17**
See also CA 19-20; 37-40R; CAP 1; SATA 1, 35; SATA-Obit 27

Benson, Stella 1892-1933 **TCLC 17**
See also CA 117; 155; DLB 36, 162

Bentham, Jeremy 1748-1832 **NCLC 38**
See also DLB 107, 158

Bentley, E(dmund) C(lerihew) 1875-1956 **TCLC 12**
See also CA 108; DLB 70

Bentley, Eric (Russell) 1916- **CLC 24**
See also CA 5-8R; CANR 6, 67; INT CANR-6

Beranger, Pierre Jean de 1780-1857**NCLC 34**

Berdyaev, Nicolas
See Berdyaev, Nikolai (Aleksandrovich)

Berdyaev, Nikolai (Aleksandrovich) 1874-1948 **TCLC 67**
See also CA 120; 157

Berdyayev, Nikolai (Aleksandrovich)
See Berdyaev, Nikolai (Aleksandrovich)

Berendt, John (Lawrence) 1939- **CLC 86**
See also CA 146

Beresford, J(ohn) D(avys) 1873-1947 **TCLC 81**
See also CA 112; 155; DLB 162, 178, 197

Bergelson, David 1884-1952 **TCLC 81**

Berger, Colonel
See Malraux, (Georges-)Andre

Berger, John (Peter) 1926- **CLC 2, 19**
See also CA 81-84; CANR 51; DLB 14

Berger, Melvin H. 1927- **CLC 12**
See also CA 5-8R; CANR 4; CLR 32; SAAS 2; SATA 5, 88

Berger, Thomas (Louis) 1924-**CLC 3, 5, 8, 11, 18, 38; DAM NOV**
See also CA 1-4R; CANR 5, 28, 51; DLB 2; DLBY 80; INT CANR-28; MTCW 1

Bergman, (Ernst) Ingmar 1918- **CLC 16, 72**
See also CA 81-84; CANR 33, 70

Bergson, Henri(-Louis) 1859-1941 **TCLC 32**
See also CA 164

Bergstein, Eleanor 1938- **CLC 4**
See also CA 53-56; CANR 5

Berkoff, Steven 1937- **CLC 56**
See also CA 104; CANR 72

Bermant, Chaim (Icyk) 1929- **CLC 40**
See also CA 57-60; CANR 6, 31, 57

Bern, Victoria
See Fisher, M(ary) F(rances) K(ennedy)

Bernanos, (Paul Louis) Georges 1888-1948 **TCLC 3**
See also CA 104; 130; DLB 72

Bernard, April 1956- **CLC 59**
See also CA 131

Berne, Victoria
See Fisher, M(ary) F(rances) K(ennedy)

Bernhard, Thomas 1931-1989 **CLC 3, 32, 61**
See also CA 85-88; 127; CANR 32, 57; DLB 85, 124; MTCW 1

Bernhardt, Sarah (Henriette Rosine) 1844-1923 **TCLC 75**
See also CA 157

Berriault, Gina 1926- **CLC 54, 109; SSC 30**
See also CA 116; 129; CANR 66; DLB 130

Berrigan, Daniel 1921- **CLC 4**
See also CA 33-36R; CAAS 1; CANR 11, 43; DLB 5

Berrigan, Edmund Joseph Michael, Jr. 1934-1983
See Berrigan, Ted
See also CA 61-64; 110; CANR 14

Berrigan, Ted **CLC 37**
See also Berrigan, Edmund Joseph Michael, Jr.
See also DLB 5, 169

Berry, Charles Edward Anderson 1931-

See Berry, Chuck
See also CA 115
Berry, Chuck   **CLC 17**
See also Berry, Charles Edward Anderson
Berry, Jonas
See Ashbery, John (Lawrence)
Berry, Wendell (Erdman) 1934- **CLC 4, 6, 8, 27, 46; DAM POET**
See also AITN 1; CA 73-76; CANR 50; DLB 5, 6
Berryman, John 1914-1972**CLC 1, 2, 3, 4, 6, 8, 10, 13, 25, 62; DAM POET**
See also CA 13-16; 33-36R; CABS 2; CANR 35; CAP 1; CDALB 1941-1968; DLB 48; MTCW 1
Bertolucci, Bernardo 1940-   **CLC 16**
See also CA 106
Berton, Pierre (Francis Demarigny) 1920- **CLC 104**
See also CA 1-4R; CANR 2, 56; DLB 68; SATA 99
Bertrand, Aloysius 1807-1841   **NCLC 31**
Bertran de Born c. 1140-1215   **CMLC 5**
Beruni, al 973-1048(?)   **CMLC 28**
Besant, Annie (Wood) 1847-1933   **TCLC 9**
See also CA 105
Bessie, Alvah 1904-1985   **CLC 23**
See also CA 5-8R; 116; CANR 2; DLB 26
Bethlen, T. D.
See Silverberg, Robert
Beti, Mongo   **CLC 27; BLC 1; DAM MULT**
See also Biyidi, Alexandre
Betjeman, John 1906-1984 **CLC 2, 6, 10, 34, 43; DAB; DAM MST, POET**
See also CA 9-12R; 112; CANR 33, 56; CDBLB 1945-1960; DLB 20; DLBY 84; MTCW 1
Bettelheim, Bruno 1903-1990   **CLC 79**
See also CA 81-84; 131; CANR 23, 61; MTCW 1
Betti, Ugo 1892-1953   **TCLC 5**
See also CA 104; 155
Betts, Doris (Waugh) 1932-   **CLC 3, 6, 28**
See also CA 13-16R; CANR 9, 66; DLBY 82; INT CANR-9
Bevan, Alistair
See Roberts, Keith (John Kingston)
Bey, Pilaff
See Douglas, (George) Norman
Bialik, Chaim Nachman 1873-1934 **TCLC 25**
Bickerstaff, Isaac
See Swift, Jonathan
Bidart, Frank 1939-   **CLC 33**
See also CA 140
Bienek, Horst 1930-   **CLC 7, 11**
See also CA 73-76; DLB 75
Bierce, Ambrose (Gwinett) 1842-1914(?) **TCLC 1, 7, 44; DA; DAC; DAM MST; SSC 9; WLC**
See also CA 104; 139; CDALB 1865-1917; DLB 11, 12, 23, 71, 74, 186
Biggers, Earl Derr 1884-1933   **TCLC 65**
See also CA 108; 153
Billings, Josh
See Shaw, Henry Wheeler
Billington, (Lady) Rachel (Mary) 1942- **C L C 43**
See also AITN 2; CA 33-36R; CANR 44
Binyon, T(imothy) J(ohn) 1936-   **CLC 34**
See also CA 111; CANR 28
Bioy Casares, Adolfo 1914-1984**CLC 4, 8, 13, 88; DAM MULT; HLC; SSC 17**
See also CA 29-32R; CANR 19, 43, 66; DLB 113; HW; MTCW 1

Bird, Cordwainer
See Ellison, Harlan (Jay)
Bird, Robert Montgomery 1806-1854**NCLC 1**
See also DLB 202
Birney, (Alfred) Earle 1904-1995**CLC 1, 4, 6, 11; DAC; DAM MST, POET**
See also CA 1-4R; CANR 5, 20; DLB 88; MTCW 1
Bishop, Elizabeth 1911-1979 **CLC 1, 4, 9, 13, 15, 32; DA; DAC; DAM MST, POET; PC 3**
See also CA 5-8R; 89-92; CABS 2; CANR 26, 61; CDALB 1968-1988; DLB 5, 169; MTCW 1; SATA-Obit 24
Bishop, John 1935-   **CLC 10**
See also CA 105
Bissett, Bill 1939-   **CLC 18; PC 14**
See also CA 69-72; CAAS 19; CANR 15; DLB 53; MTCW 1
Bitov, Andrei (Georgievich) 1937-   **CLC 57**
See also CA 142
Biyidi, Alexandre 1932-
See Beti, Mongo
See also BW 1; CA 114; 124; MTCW 1
Bjarme, Brynjolf
See Ibsen, Henrik (Johan)
Bjoernson, Bjoernstjerne (Martinius) 1832-1910   **TCLC 7, 37**
See also CA 104
Black, Robert
See Holdstock, Robert P.
Blackburn, Paul 1926-1971   **CLC 9, 43**
See also CA 81-84; 33-36R; CANR 34; DLB 16; DLBY 81
Black Elk 1863-1950 **TCLC 33; DAM MULT**
See also CA 144; NNAL
Black Hobart
See Sanders, (James) Ed(ward)
Blacklin, Malcolm
See Chambers, Aidan
Blackmore, R(ichard) D(oddridge) 1825-1900 **TCLC 27**
See also CA 120; DLB 18
Blackmur, R(ichard) P(almer) 1904-1965 **CLC 2, 24**
See also CA 11-12; 25-28R; CANR 71; CAP 1; DLB 63
Black Tarantula
See Acker, Kathy
Blackwood, Algernon (Henry) 1869-1951 **TCLC 5**
See also CA 105; 150; DLB 153, 156, 178
Blackwood, Caroline 1931-1996**CLC 6, 9, 100**
See also CA 85-88; 151; CANR 32, 61, 65; DLB 14; MTCW 1
Blade, Alexander
See Hamilton, Edmond; Silverberg, Robert
Blaga, Lucian 1895-1961   **CLC 75**
See also CA 157
Blair, Eric (Arthur) 1903-1950
See Orwell, George
See also CA 104; 132; DA; DAB; DAC; DAM MST, NOV; MTCW 1; SATA 29
Blais, Marie-Claire 1939-**CLC 2, 4, 6, 13, 22; DAC; DAM MST**
See also CA 21-24R; CAAS 4; CANR 38; DLB 53; MTCW 1
Blaise, Clark 1940-   **CLC 29**
See also AITN 2; CA 53-56; CAAS 3; CANR 5, 66; DLB 53
Blake, Fairley
See De Voto, Bernard (Augustine)
Blake, Nicholas

See Day Lewis, C(ecil)
See also DLB 77
Blake, William 1757-1827 **NCLC 13, 37, 57; DA; DAB; DAC; DAM MST, POET; PC 12; WLC**
See also CDBLB 1789-1832; CLR 52; DLB 93, 163; MAICYA; SATA 30
Blasco Ibanez, Vicente 1867-1928 **TCLC 12; DAM NOV**
See also CA 110; 131; HW; MTCW 1
Blatty, William Peter 1928-**CLC 2; DAM POP**
See also CA 5-8R; CANR 9
Bleeck, Oliver
See Thomas, Ross (Elmore)
Blessing, Lee 1949-   **CLC 54**
Blish, James (Benjamin) 1921-1975 **CLC 14**
See also CA 1-4R; 57-60; CANR 3; DLB 8; MTCW 1; SATA 66
Bliss, Reginald
See Wells, H(erbert) G(eorge)
Blixen, Karen (Christentze Dinesen) 1885-1962
See Dinesen, Isak
See also CA 25-28; CANR 22, 50; CAP 2; MTCW 1; SATA 44
Bloch, Robert (Albert) 1917-1994   **CLC 33**
See also CA 5-8R; 146; CAAS 20; CANR 5; DLB 44; INT CANR-5; SATA 12; SATA-Obit 82
Blok, Alexander (Alexandrovich) 1880-1921 **TCLC 5; PC 21**
See also CA 104
Blom, Jan
See Breytenbach, Breyten
Bloom, Harold 1930-   **CLC 24, 103**
See also CA 13-16R; CANR 39; DLB 67
Bloomfield, Aurelius
See Bourne, Randolph S(illiman)
Blount, Roy (Alton), Jr. 1941-   **CLC 38**
See also CA 53-56; CANR 10, 28, 61; INT CANR-28; MTCW 1
Bloy, Leon 1846-1917   **TCLC 22**
See also CA 121; DLB 123
Blume, Judy (Sussman) 1938- **CLC 12, 30; DAM NOV, POP**
See also AAYA 3, 26; CA 29-32R; CANR 13, 37, 66; CLR 2, 15; DLB 52; JRDA; MAICYA; MTCW 1; SATA 2, 31, 79
Blunden, Edmund (Charles) 1896-1974 **C L C 2, 56**
See also CA 17-18; 45-48; CANR 54; CAP 2; DLB 20, 100, 155; MTCW 1
Bly, Robert (Elwood) 1926-**CLC 1, 2, 5, 10, 15, 38; DAM POET**
See also CA 5-8R; CANR 41; DLB 5; MTCW 1
Boas, Franz 1858-1942   **TCLC 56**
See also CA 115
Bobette
See Simenon, Georges (Jacques Christian)
Boccaccio, Giovanni 1313-1375 **CMLC 13; SSC 10**
Bochco, Steven 1943-   **CLC 35**
See also AAYA 11; CA 124; 138
Bodel, Jean 1167(?)-1210   **CMLC 28**
Bodenheim, Maxwell 1892-1954   **TCLC 44**
See also CA 110; DLB 9, 45
Bodker, Cecil 1927-   **CLC 21**
See also CA 73-76; CANR 13, 44; CLR 23; MAICYA; SATA 14
Boell, Heinrich (Theodor) 1917-1985 **CLC 2, 3, 6, 9, 11, 15, 27, 32, 72; DA; DAB; DAC; DAM MST, NOV; SSC 23; WLC**
See also CA 21-24R; 116; CANR 24; DLB 69;

TCLC 1, 6, 13, 35; DA; DAB; DAC; DAM DRAM, MST; DC 3; WLC
See also CA 104; 133; CANR 62; DLB 56, 124; MTCW 1

Brecht, Eugen Berthold Friedrich
See Brecht, (Eugen) Bertolt (Friedrich)

Bremer, Fredrika 1801-1865 **NCLC 11**

Brennan, Christopher John 1870-1932 **TCLC 17**
See also CA 117

Brennan, Maeve 1917-1993 **CLC 5**
See also CA 81-84; CANR 72

Brent, Linda
See Jacobs, Harriet A(nn)

Brentano, Clemens (Maria) 1778-1842 **NCLC 1**
See also DLB 90

Brent of Bin Bin
See Franklin, (Stella Maria Sarah) Miles (Lampe)

Brenton, Howard 1942- **CLC 31**
See also CA 69-72; CANR 33, 67; DLB 13; MTCW 1

Breslin, James 1930-1996
See Breslin, Jimmy
See also CA 73-76; CANR 31; DAM NOV; MTCW 1

Breslin, Jimmy **CLC 4, 43**
See also Breslin, James
See also AITN 1; DLB 185

Bresson, Robert 1901- **CLC 16**
See also CA 110; CANR 49

Breton, Andre 1896-1966 **CLC 2, 9, 15, 54; PC 15**
See also CA 19-20; 25-28R; CANR 40, 60; CAP 2; DLB 65; MTCW 1

Breytenbach, Breyten 1939(?)- **CLC 23, 37; DAM POET**
See also CA 113; 129; CANR 61

Bridgers, Sue Ellen 1942- **CLC 26**
See also AAYA 8; CA 65-68; CANR 11, 36; CLR 18; DLB 52; JRDA; MAICYA; SAAS 1; SATA 22, 90

Bridges, Robert (Seymour) 1844-1930 **TCLC 1; DAM POET**
See also CA 104; 152; CDBLB 1890-1914; DLB 19, 98

Bridie, James **TCLC 3**
See also Mavor, Osborne Henry
See also DLB 10

Brin, David 1950- **CLC 34**
See also AAYA 21; CA 102; CANR 24, 70; INT CANR-24; SATA 65

Brink, Andre (Philippus) 1935- **CLC 18, 36, 106**
See also CA 104; CANR 39, 62; INT 103; MTCW 1

Brinsmead, H(esba) F(ay) 1922- **CLC 21**
See also CA 21-24R; CANR 10; CLR 47; MAICYA; SAAS 5; SATA 18, 78

Brittain, Vera (Mary) 1893(?)-1970 **CLC 23**
See also CA 13-16; 25-28R; CANR 58; CAP 1; DLB 191; MTCW 1

Broch, Hermann 1886-1951 **TCLC 20**
See also CA 117; DLB 85, 124

Brock, Rose
See Hansen, Joseph

Brodkey, Harold (Roy) 1930-1996 **CLC 56**
See also CA 111; 151; CANR 71; DLB 130

Brodskii, Iosif
See Brodsky, Joseph

Brodsky, Iosif Alexandrovich 1940-1996
See Brodsky, Joseph

See also AITN 1; CA 41-44R; 151; CANR 37; DAM POET; MTCW 1

Brodsky, Joseph 1940-1996 **CLC 4, 6, 13, 36, 100; PC 9**
See also Brodskii, Iosif; Brodsky, Iosif Alexandrovich

Brodsky, Michael (Mark) 1948- **CLC 19**
See also CA 102; CANR 18, 41, 58

Bromell, Henry 1947- **CLC 5**
See also CA 53-56; CANR 9

Bromfield, Louis (Brucker) 1896-1956 **TCLC 11**
See also CA 107; 155; DLB 4, 9, 86

Broner, E(sther) M(asserman) 1930- **CLC 19**
See also CA 17-20R; CANR 8, 25, 72; DLB 28

Bronk, William 1918- **CLC 10**
See also CA 89-92; CANR 23; DLB 165

Bronstein, Lev Davidovich
See Trotsky, Leon

Bronte, Anne 1820-1849 **NCLC 71**
See also DLB 21, 199

Bronte, Charlotte 1816-1855 **NCLC 3, 8, 33, 58; DA; DAB; DAC; DAM MST, NOV; WLC**
See also AAYA 17; CDBLB 1832-1890; DLB 21, 159, 199

Bronte, Emily (Jane) 1818-1848 **NCLC 16, 35; DA; DAB; DAC; DAM MST, NOV, POET; PC 8; WLC**
See also AAYA 17; CDBLB 1832-1890; DLB 21, 32, 199

Brooke, Frances 1724-1789 **LC 6**
See also DLB 39, 99

Brooke, Henry 1703(?)-1783 **LC 1**
See also DLB 39

Brooke, Rupert (Chawner) 1887-1915 **TCLC 2, 7; DA; DAB; DAC; DAM MST, POET; PC 24; WLC**
See also CA 104; 132; CANR 61; CDBLB 1914-1945; DLB 19; MTCW 1

Brooke-Haven, P.
See Wodehouse, P(elham) G(renville)

Brooke-Rose, Christine 1926(?)- **CLC 40**
See also CA 13-16R; CANR 58; DLB 14

Brookner, Anita 1928- **CLC 32, 34, 51; DAB; DAM POP**
See also CA 114; 120; CANR 37, 56; DLB 194; DLBY 87; MTCW 1

Brooks, Cleanth 1906-1994 **CLC 24, 86, 110**
See also CA 17-20R; 145; CANR 33, 35; DLB 63; DLBY 94; INT CANR-35; MTCW 1

Brooks, George
See Baum, L(yman) Frank

Brooks, Gwendolyn 1917- **CLC 1, 2, 4, 5, 15, 49; BLC 1; DA; DAC; DAM MST, MULT, POET; PC 7; WLC**
See also AAYA 20; AITN 1; BW 2; CA 1-4R; CANR 1, 27, 52; CDALB 1941-1968; CLR 27; DLB 5, 76, 165; MTCW 1; SATA 6

Brooks, Mel **CLC 12**
See also Kaminsky, Melvin
See also AAYA 13; DLB 26

Brooks, Peter 1938- **CLC 34**
See also CA 45-48; CANR 1

Brooks, Van Wyck 1886-1963 **CLC 29**
See also CA 1-4R; CANR 6; DLB 45, 63, 103

Brophy, Brigid (Antonia) 1929-1995 **CLC 6, 11, 29, 105**
See also CA 5-8R; 149; CAAS 4; CANR 25, 53; DLB 14; MTCW 1

Brosman, Catharine Savage 1934- **CLC 9**
See also CA 61-64; CANR 21, 46

Brother Antoninus

See Everson, William (Oliver)

The Brothers Quay
See Quay, Stephen; Quay, Timothy

Broughton, T(homas) Alan 1936- **CLC 19**
See also CA 45-48; CANR 2, 23, 48

Broumas, Olga 1949- **CLC 10, 73**
See also CA 85-88; CANR 20, 69

Brown, Alan 1950- **CLC 99**
See also CA 156

Brown, Charles Brockden 1771-1810 **NCLC 22**
See also CDALB 1640-1865; DLB 37, 59, 73

Brown, Christy 1932-1981 **CLC 63**
See also CA 105; 104; CANR 72; DLB 14

Brown, Claude 1937- **CLC 30; BLC 1; DAM MULT**
See also AAYA 7; BW 1; CA 73-76

Brown, Dee (Alexander) 1908- **CLC 18, 47; DAM POP**
See also CA 13-16R; CAAS 6; CANR 11, 45, 60; DLBY 80; MTCW 1; SATA 5

Brown, George
See Wertmueller, Lina

Brown, George Douglas 1869-1902 **TCLC 28**
See also CA 162

Brown, George Mackay 1921-1996 **CLC 5, 48, 100**
See also CA 21-24R; 151; CAAS 6; CANR 12, 37, 67; DLB 14, 27, 139; MTCW 1; SATA 35

Brown, (William) Larry 1951- **CLC 73**
See also CA 130; 134; INT 133

Brown, Moses
See Barrett, William (Christopher)

Brown, Rita Mae 1944- **CLC 18, 43, 79; DAM NOV, POP**
See also CA 45-48; CANR 2, 11, 35, 62; INT CANR-11; MTCW 1

Brown, Roderick (Langmere) Haig-
See Haig-Brown, Roderick (Langmere)

Brown, Rosellen 1939- **CLC 32**
See also CA 77-80; CAAS 10; CANR 14, 44

Brown, Sterling Allen 1901-1989 **CLC 1, 23, 59; BLC 1; DAM MULT, POET**
See also BW 1; CA 85-88; 127; CANR 26; DLB 48, 51, 63; MTCW 1

Brown, Will
See Ainsworth, William Harrison

Brown, William Wells 1813-1884 **NCLC 2; BLC 1; DAM MULT; DC 1**
See also DLB 3, 50

Browne, (Clyde) Jackson 1948(?)- **CLC 21**
See also CA 120

Browning, Elizabeth Barrett 1806-1861 **NCLC 1, 16, 61, 66; DA; DAB; DAC; DAM MST, POET; PC 6; WLC**
See also CDBLB 1832-1890; DLB 32, 199

Browning, Robert 1812-1889 **NCLC 19; DA; DAB; DAC; DAM MST, POET; PC 2; WLCS**
See also CDBLB 1832-1890; DLB 32, 163; YABC 1

Browning, Tod 1882-1962 **CLC 16**
See also CA 141; 117

Brownson, Orestes Augustus 1803-1876 **NCLC 50**
See also DLB 1, 59, 73

Bruccoli, Matthew J(oseph) 1931- **CLC 34**
See also CA 9-12R; CANR 7; DLB 103

Bruce, Lenny **CLC 21**
See also Schneider, Leonard Alfred

Bruin, John
See Brutus, Dennis

Brulard, Henri
See Stendhal
Brulls, Christian
See Simenon, Georges (Jacques Christian)
Brunner, John (Kilian Houston) 1934-1995
CLC 8, 10; DAM POP
See also CA 1-4R; 149; CAAS 8; CANR 2, 37;
MTCW 1
Bruno, Giordano 1548-1600 LC 27
Brutus, Dennis 1924- CLC 43; BLC 1; DAM
MULT, POET; PC 24
See also BW 2; CA 49-52; CAAS 14; CANR 2,
27, 42; DLB 117
Bryan, C(ourtlandt) D(ixon) B(arnes) 1936-
CLC 29
See also CA 73-76; CANR 13, 68; DLB 185;
INT CANR-13
Bryan, Michael
See Moore, Brian
Bryant, William Cullen 1794-1878 NCLC 6,
46; DA; DAB; DAC; DAM MST, POET;
PC 20
See also CDALB 1640-1865; DLB 3, 43, 59,
189
Bryusov, Valery Yakovlevich 1873-1924
TCLC 10
See also CA 107; 155
Buchan, John 1875-1940 TCLC 41; DAB;
DAM POP
See also CA 108; 145; DLB 34, 70, 156; YABC
2
Buchanan, George 1506-1582 LC 4
See also DLB 152
Buchheim, Lothar-Guenther 1918- CLC 6
See also CA 85-88
Buchner, (Karl) Georg 1813-1837 NCLC 26
Buchwald, Art(hur) 1925- CLC 33
See also AITN 1; CA 5-8R; CANR 21, 67;
MTCW 1; SATA 10
Buck, Pearl S(ydenstricker) 1892-1973CLC 7,
11, 18; DA; DAB; DAC; DAM MST, NOV
See also AITN 1; CA 1-4R; 41-44R; CANR 1,
34; DLB 9, 102; MTCW 1; SATA 1, 25
Buckler, Ernest 1908-1984 CLC 13; DAC;
DAM MST
See also CA 11-12; 114; CAP 1; DLB 68; SATA
47
Buckley, Vincent (Thomas) 1925-1988CLC 57
See also CA 101
Buckley, William F(rank), Jr. 1925-CLC 7, 18,
37; DAM POP
See also AITN 1; CA 1-4R; CANR 1, 24, 53;
DLB 137; DLBY 80; INT CANR-24; MTCW
1
Buechner, (Carl) Frederick 1926-CLC 2, 4, 6,
9; DAM NOV
See also CA 13-16R; CANR 11, 39, 64; DLBY
80; INT CANR-11; MTCW 1
Buell, John (Edward) 1927- CLC 10
See also CA 1-4R; CANR 71; DLB 53
Buero Vallejo, Antonio 1916- CLC 15, 46
See also CA 106; CANR 24, 49; HW; MTCW
1
Bufalino, Gesualdo 1920(?)- CLC 74
See also DLB 196
Bugayev, Boris Nikolayevich 1880-1934
TCLC 7; PC 11
See also Bely, Andrey
See also CA 104; 165
Bukowski, Charles 1920-1994CLC 2, 5, 9, 41,
82, 108; DAM NOV, POET; PC 18
See also CA 17-20R; 144; CANR 40, 62; DLB
5, 130, 169; MTCW 1

Bulgakov, Mikhail (Afanas'evich) 1891-1940
TCLC 2, 16; DAM DRAM, NOV; SSC 18
See also CA 105; 152
Bulgya, Alexander Alexandrovich 1901-1956
TCLC 53
See also Fadeyev, Alexander
See also CA 117
Bullins, Ed 1935- CLC 1, 5, 7; BLC 1; DAM
DRAM, MULT; DC 6
See also BW 2; CA 49-52; CAAS 16; CANR
24, 46; DLB 7, 38; MTCW 1
Bulwer-Lytton, Edward (George Earle Lytton)
1803-1873 NCLC 1, 45
See also DLB 21
Bunin, Ivan Alexeyevich 1870-1953 TCLC 6;
SSC 5
See also CA 104
Bunting, Basil 1900-1985 CLC 10, 39, 47;
DAM POET
See also CA 53-56; 115; CANR 7; DLB 20
Bunuel, Luis 1900-1983 CLC 16, 80; DAM
MULT; HLC
See also CA 101; 110; CANR 32; HW
Bunyan, John 1628-1688 LC 4; DA; DAB;
DAC; DAM MST; WLC
See also CDBLB 1660-1789; DLB 39
Burckhardt, Jacob (Christoph) 1818-1897
NCLC 49
Burford, Eleanor
See Hibbert, Eleanor Alice Burford
Burgess, AnthonyCLC 1, 2, 4, 5, 8, 10, 13, 15,
22, 40, 62, 81, 94; DAB
See also Wilson, John (Anthony) Burgess
See also AAYA 25; AITN 1; CDBLB 1960 to
Present; DLB 14, 194
Burke, Edmund 1729(?)-1797 LC 7, 36; DA;
DAB; DAC; DAM MST; WLC
See also DLB 104
Burke, Kenneth (Duva) 1897-1993CLC 2, 24
See also CA 5-8R; 143; CANR 39; DLB 45,
63; MTCW 1
Burke, Leda
See Garnett, David
Burke, Ralph
See Silverberg, Robert
Burke, Thomas 1886-1945 TCLC 63
See also CA 113; 155; DLB 197
Burney, Fanny 1752-1840 NCLC 12, 54
See also DLB 39
Burns, Robert 1759-1796 PC 6
See also CDBLB 1789-1832; DA; DAB; DAC;
DAM MST, POET; DLB 109; WLC
Burns, Tex
See L'Amour, Louis (Dearborn)
Burnshaw, Stanley 1906- CLC 3, 13, 44
See also CA 9-12R; DLB 48; DLBY 97
Burr, Anne 1937- CLC 6
See also CA 25-28R
Burroughs, Edgar Rice 1875-1950 TCLC 2,
32; DAM NOV
See also AAYA 11; CA 104; 132; DLB 8;
MTCW 1; SATA 41
Burroughs, William S(eward) 1914-1997CLC
1, 2, 5, 15, 22, 42, 75, 109; DA; DAB; DAC;
DAM MST, NOV, POP; WLC
See also AITN 2; CA 9-12R; 160; CANR 20,
52; DLB 2, 8, 16, 152; DLBY 81, 97; MTCW
1
Burton, Richard F. 1821-1890 NCLC 42
See also DLB 55, 184
Busch, Frederick 1941- CLC 7, 10, 18, 47
See also CA 33-36R; CAAS 1; CANR 45; DLB
6

Bush, Ronald 1946- CLC 34
See also CA 136
Bustos, F(rancisco)
See Borges, Jorge Luis
Bustos Domecq, H(onorio)
See Bioy Casares, Adolfo; Borges, Jorge Luis
Butler, Octavia E(stelle) 1947-CLC 38; BLCS;
DAM MULT, POP
See also AAYA 18; BW 2; CA 73-76; CANR
12, 24, 38; DLB 33; MTCW 1; SATA 84
Butler, Robert Olen (Jr.) 1945-CLC 81; DAM
POP
See also CA 112; CANR 66; DLB 173; INT 112
Butler, Samuel 1612-1680 LC 16, 43
See also DLB 101, 126
Butler, Samuel 1835-1902 TCLC 1, 33; DA;
DAB; DAC; DAM MST, NOV; WLC
See also CA 143; CDBLB 1890-1914; DLB 18,
57, 174
Butler, Walter C.
See Faust, Frederick (Schiller)
Butor, Michel (Marie Francois) 1926-CLC 1,
3, 8, 11, 15
See also CA 9-12R; CANR 33, 66; DLB 83;
MTCW 1
Butts, Mary 1892(?)-1937 TCLC 77
See also CA 148
Buzo, Alexander (John) 1944- CLC 61
See also CA 97-100; CANR 17, 39, 69
Buzzati, Dino 1906-1972 CLC 36
See also CA 160; 33-36R; DLB 177
Byars, Betsy (Cromer) 1928- CLC 35
See also AAYA 19; CA 33-36R; CANR 18, 36,
57; CLR 1, 16; DLB 52; INT CANR-18;
JRDA; MAICYA; MTCW 1; SAAS 1; SATA
4, 46, 80
Byatt, A(ntonia) S(usan Drabble) 1936- C L C
19, 65; DAM NOV, POP
See also CA 13-16R; CANR 13, 33, 50; DLB
14, 194; MTCW 1
Byrne, David 1952- CLC 26
See also CA 127
Byrne, John Keyes 1926-
See Leonard, Hugh
See also CA 102; INT 102
Byron, George Gordon (Noel) 1788-1824
NCLC 2, 12; DA; DAB; DAC; DAM MST,
POET; PC 16; WLC
See also CDBLB 1789-1832; DLB 96, 110
Byron, Robert 1905-1941 TCLC 67
See also CA 160; DLB 195
C. 3. 3.
See Wilde, Oscar (Fingal O'Flahertie Wills)
Caballero, Fernan 1796-1877 NCLC 10
Cabell, Branch
See Cabell, James Branch
Cabell, James Branch 1879-1958 TCLC 6
See also CA 105; 152; DLB 9, 78
Cable, George Washington 1844-1925 T C L C
4; SSC 4
See also CA 104; 155; DLB 12, 74; DLBD 13
Cabral de Melo Neto, Joao 1920- CLC 76;
DAM MULT
See also CA 151
Cabrera Infante, G(uillermo) 1929-CLC 5, 25,
45; DAM MULT; HLC
See also CA 85-88; CANR 29, 65; DLB 113;
HW; MTCW 1
Cade, Toni
See Bambara, Toni Cade
Cadmus and Harmonia
See Buchan, John
Caedmon fl. 658-680 CMLC 7

See also DLB 146

Caeiro, Alberto
See Pessoa, Fernando (Antonio Nogueira)

Cage, John (Milton, Jr.) 1912-1992 **CLC 41**
See also CA 13-16R; CANR 9; DLB 193; INT CANR-9

Cahan, Abraham 1860-1951 **TCLC 71**
See also CA 108; 154; DLB 9, 25, 28

Cain, G.
See Cabrera Infante, G(uillermo)

Cain, Guillermo
See Cabrera Infante, G(uillermo)

Cain, James M(allahan) 1892-1977 **CLC 3, 11, 28**
See also AITN 1; CA 17-20R; 73-76; CANR 8, 34, 61; MTCW 1

Caine, Mark
See Raphael, Frederic (Michael)

Calasso, Roberto 1941- **CLC 81**
See also CA 143

Calderon de la Barca, Pedro 1600-1681 **L C 23; DC 3**

Caldwell, Erskine (Preston) 1903-1987 **CLC 1, 8, 14, 50, 60; DAM NOV; SSC 19**
See also AITN 1; CA 1-4R; 121; CAAS 1; CANR 2, 33; DLB 9, 86; MTCW 1

Caldwell, (Janet Miriam) Taylor (Holland) 1900-1985 **CLC 2, 28, 39; DAM NOV, POP**
See also CA 5-8R; 116; CANR 5; DLBD 17

Calhoun, John Caldwell 1782-1850 **NCLC 15**
See also DLB 3

Calisher, Hortense 1911- **CLC 2, 4, 8, 38; DAM NOV; SSC 15**
See also CA 1-4R; CANR 1, 22, 67; DLB 2; INT CANR-22; MTCW 1

Callaghan, Morley Edward 1903-1990 **CLC 3, 14, 41, 65; DAC; DAM MST**
See also CA 9-12R; 132; CANR 33; DLB 68; MTCW 1

Callimachus c. 305B.C.-c. 240B.C. **CMLC 18**
See also DLB 176

Calvin, John 1509-1564 **LC 37**

Calvino, Italo 1923-1985 **CLC 5, 8, 11, 22, 33, 39, 73; DAM NOV; SSC 3**
See also CA 85-88; 116; CANR 23, 61; DLB 196; MTCW 1

Cameron, Carey 1952- **CLC 59**
See also CA 135

Cameron, Peter 1959- **CLC 44**
See also CA 125; CANR 50

Campana, Dino 1885-1932 **TCLC 20**
See also CA 117; DLB 114

Campanella, Tommaso 1568-1639 **LC 32**

Campbell, John W(ood, Jr.) 1910-1971 **C L C 32**
See also CA 21-22; 29-32R; CANR 34; CAP 2; DLB 8; MTCW 1

Campbell, Joseph 1904-1987 **CLC 69**
See also AAYA 3; BEST 89:2; CA 1-4R; 124; CANR 3, 28, 61; MTCW 1

Campbell, Maria 1940- **CLC 85; DAC**
See also CA 102; CANR 54; NNAL

Campbell, (John) Ramsey 1946- **CLC 42; SSC 19**
See also CA 57-60; CANR 7; INT CANR-7

Campbell, (Ignatius) Roy (Dunnachie) 1901-1957 **TCLC 5**
See also CA 104; 155; DLB 20

Campbell, Thomas 1777-1844 **NCLC 19**
See also DLB 93; 144

Campbell, Wilfred **TCLC 9**
See also Campbell, William

Campbell, William 1858(?)-1918

See Campbell, Wilfred
See also CA 106; DLB 92

Campion, Jane **CLC 95**
See also CA 138

Campos, Alvaro de
See Pessoa, Fernando (Antonio Nogueira)

Camus, Albert 1913-1960 **CLC 1, 2, 4, 9, 11, 14, 32, 63, 69; DA; DAB; DAC; DAM DRAM, MST, NOV; DC 2; SSC 9; WLC**
See also CA 89-92; DLB 72; MTCW 1

Canby, Vincent 1924- **CLC 13**
See also CA 81-84

Cancale
See Desnos, Robert

Canetti, Elias 1905-1994 **CLC 3, 14, 25, 75, 86**
See also CA 21-24R; 146; CANR 23, 61; DLB 85, 124; MTCW 1

Canin, Ethan 1960- **CLC 55**
See also CA 131; 135

Cannon, Curt
See Hunter, Evan

Cao, Lan 1961- **CLC 109**
See also CA 165

Cape, Judith
See Page, P(atricia) K(athleen)

Capek, Karel 1890-1938 **TCLC 6, 37; DA; DAB; DAC; DAM DRAM, MST, NOV; DC 1; WLC**
See also CA 104; 140

Capote, Truman 1924-1984 **CLC 1, 3, 8, 13, 19, 34, 38, 58; DA; DAB; DAC; DAM MST, NOV, POP; SSC 2; WLC**
See also CA 5-8R; 113; CANR 18, 62; CDALB 1941-1968; DLB 2, 185; DLBY 80, 84; MTCW 1; SATA 91

Capra, Frank 1897-1991 **CLC 16**
See also CA 61-64; 135

Caputo, Philip 1941- **CLC 32**
See also CA 73-76; CANR 40

Caragiale, Ion Luca 1852-1912 **TCLC 76**
See also CA 157

Card, Orson Scott 1951- **CLC 44, 47, 50; DAM POP**
See also AAYA 11; CA 102; CANR 27, 47; INT CANR-27; MTCW 1; SATA 83

Cardenal, Ernesto 1925- **CLC 31; DAM MULT, POET; HLC; PC 22**
See also CA 49-52; CANR 2, 32, 66; HW; MTCW 1

Cardozo, Benjamin N(athan) 1870-1938 **TCLC 65**
See also CA 117; 164

Carducci, Giosue (Alessandro Giuseppe) 1835-1907 **TCLC 32**
See also CA 163

Carew, Thomas 1595(?)-1640 **LC 13**
See also DLB 126

Carey, Ernestine Gilbreth 1908- **CLC 17**
See also CA 5-8R; CANR 71; SATA 2

Carey, Peter 1943- **CLC 40, 55, 96**
See also CA 123; 127; CANR 53; INT 127; MTCW 1; SATA 94

Carleton, William 1794-1869 **NCLC 3**
See also DLB 159

Carlisle, Henry (Coffin) 1926- **CLC 33**
See also CA 13-16R; CANR 15

Carlsen, Chris
See Holdstock, Robert P.

Carlson, Ron(ald F.) 1947- **CLC 54**
See also CA 105; CANR 27

Carlyle, Thomas 1795-1881 **NCLC 70; DA; DAB; DAC; DAM MST**
See also CDBLB 1789-1832; DLB 55; 144

Carman, (William) Bliss 1861-1929 **TCLC 7; DAC**
See also CA 104; 152; DLB 92

Carnegie, Dale 1888-1955 **TCLC 53**

Carossa, Hans 1878-1956 **TCLC 48**
See also DLB 66

Carpenter, Don(ald Richard) 1931-1995 **C L C 41**
See also CA 45-48; 149; CANR 1, 71

Carpentier (y Valmont), Alejo 1904-1980 **CLC 8, 11, 38, 110; DAM MULT; HLC**
See also CA 65-68; 97-100; CANR 11, 70; DLB 113; HW

Carr, Caleb 1955(?)- **CLC 86**
See also CA 147

Carr, Emily 1871-1945 **TCLC 32**
See also CA 159; DLB 68

Carr, John Dickson 1906-1977 **CLC 3**
See also Fairbairn, Roger
See also CA 49-52; 69-72; CANR 3, 33, 60; MTCW 1

Carr, Philippa
See Hibbert, Eleanor Alice Burford

Carr, Virginia Spencer 1929- **CLC 34**
See also CA 61-64; DLB 111

Carrere, Emmanuel 1957- **CLC 89**

Carrier, Roch 1937- **CLC 13, 78; DAC; DAM MST**
See also CA 130; CANR 61; DLB 53

Carroll, James P. 1943(?)- **CLC 38**
See also CA 81-84

Carroll, Jim 1951- **CLC 35**
See also AAYA 17; CA 45-48; CANR 42

Carroll, Lewis **NCLC 2, 53; PC 18; WLC**
See also Dodgson, Charles Lutwidge
See also CDBLB 1832-1890; CLR 2, 18; DLB 18, 163, 178; JRDA

Carroll, Paul Vincent 1900-1968 **CLC 10**
See also CA 9-12R; 25-28R; DLB 10

Carruth, Hayden 1921- **CLC 4, 7, 10, 18, 84; PC 10**
See also CA 9-12R; CANR 4, 38, 59; DLB 5, 165; INT CANR-4; MTCW 1; SATA 47

Carson, Rachel Louise 1907-1964 **CLC 71; DAM POP**
See also CA 77-80; CANR 35; MTCW 1; SATA 23

Carter, Angela (Olive) 1940-1992 **CLC 5, 41, 76; SSC 13**
See also CA 53-56; 136; CANR 12, 36, 61; DLB 14; MTCW 1; SATA 66; SATA-Obit 70

Carter, Nick
See Smith, Martin Cruz

Carver, Raymond 1938-1988 **CLC 22, 36, 53, 55; DAM NOV; SSC 8**
See also CA 33-36R; 126; CANR 17, 34, 61; DLB 130; DLBY 84, 88; MTCW 1

Cary, Elizabeth, Lady Falkland 1585-1639 **LC 30**

Cary, (Arthur) Joyce (Lunel) 1888-1957 **TCLC 1, 29**
See also CA 104; 164; CDBLB 1914-1945; DLB 15, 100

Casanova de Seingalt, Giovanni Jacopo 1725-1798 **LC 13**

Casares, Adolfo Bioy
See Bioy Casares, Adolfo

Casely-Hayford, J(oseph) E(phraim) 1866-1930 **TCLC 24; BLC 1; DAM MULT**
See also BW 2; CA 123; 152

Casey, John (Dudley) 1939- **CLC 59**
See also BEST 90:2; CA 69-72; CANR 23

Casey, Michael 1947- **CLC 2**

82; INT CANR-5; MTCW 1

Cheever, Susan 1943- **CLC 18, 48**
See also CA 103; CANR 27, 51; DLBY 82; INT
CANR-27

Chekhonte, Antosha
See Chekhov, Anton (Pavlovich)

Chekhov, Anton (Pavlovich) 1860-1904**TCLC
3, 10, 31, 55; DA; DAB; DAC; DAM
DRAM, MST; DC 9; SSC 2, 28; WLC**
See also CA 104; 124; SATA 90

Chernyshevsky, Nikolay Gavrilovich 1828-1889
NCLC 1

Cherry, Carolyn Janice 1942-
See Cherryh, C. J.
See also CA 65-68; CANR 10

Cherryh, C. J. **CLC 35**
See also Cherry, Carolyn Janice
See also AAYA 24; DLBY 80; SATA 93

Chesnutt, Charles W(addell) 1858-1932
TCLC 5, 39; BLC 1; DAM MULT; SSC 7
See also BW 1; CA 106; 125; DLB 12, 50, 78;
MTCW 1

Chester, Alfred 1929(?)-1971 **CLC 49**
See also CA 33-36R; DLB 130

Chesterton, G(ilbert) K(eith) 1874-1936
TCLC 1, 6, 64; DAM NOV, POET; SSC 1
See also CA 104; 132; CDBLB 1914-1945;
DLB 10, 19, 34, 70, 98, 149, 178; MTCW 1;
SATA 27

Chiang, Pin-chin 1904-1986
See Ding Ling
See also CA 118

Ch'ien Chung-shu 1910- **CLC 22**
See also CA 130; MTCW 1

Child, L. Maria
See Child, Lydia Maria

Child, Lydia Maria 1802-1880 **NCLC 6**
See also DLB 1, 74; SATA 67

Child, Mrs.
See Child, Lydia Maria

Child, Philip 1898-1978 **CLC 19, 68**
See also CA 13-14; CAP 1; SATA 47

Childers, (Robert) Erskine 1870-1922 **TCLC
65**
See also CA 113; 153; DLB 70

Childress, Alice 1920-1994**CLC 12, 15, 86, 96;
BLC 1; DAM DRAM, MULT, NOV; DC 4**
See also AAYA 8; BW 2; CA 45-48; 146; CANR
3, 27, 50; CLR 14; DLB 7, 38; JRDA;
MAICYA; MTCW 1; SATA 7, 48, 81

Chin, Frank (Chew, Jr.) 1940- **DC 7**
See also CA 33-36R; CANR 71; DAM MULT

Chislett, (Margaret) Anne 1943- **CLC 34**
See also CA 151

Chitty, Thomas Willes 1926- **CLC 11**
See also Hinde, Thomas
See also CA 5-8R

Chivers, Thomas Holley 1809-1858 **NCLC 49**
See also DLB 3

Chomette, Rene Lucien 1898-1981
See Clair, Rene
See also CA 103

Chopin, Kate **TCLC 5, 14; DA; DAB; SSC 8;
WLCS**
See also Chopin, Katherine
See also CDALB 1865-1917; DLB 12, 78

Chopin, Katherine 1851-1904
See Chopin, Kate
See also CA 104; 122; DAC; DAM MST, NOV

Chretien de Troyes c. 12th cent. - **CMLC 10**

Christie
See Ichikawa, Kon

Christie, Agatha (Mary Clarissa) 1890-1976

**CLC 1, 6, 8, 12, 39, 48, 110; DAB; DAC;
DAM NOV**
See also AAYA 9; AITN 1, 2; CA 17-20R; 61-
64; CANR 10, 37; CDBLB 1914-1945; DLB
13, 77; MTCW 1; SATA 36

Christie, (Ann) Philippa
See Pearce, Philippa
See also CA 5-8R; CANR 4

Christine de Pizan 1365(?)-1431(?) **LC 9**

Chubb, Elmer
See Masters, Edgar Lee

Chulkov, Mikhail Dmitrievich 1743-1792**LC 2**
See also DLB 150

Churchill, Caryl 1938- **CLC 31, 55; DC 5**
See also CA 102; CANR 22, 46; DLB 13;
MTCW 1

Churchill, Charles 1731-1764 **LC 3**
See also DLB 109

Chute, Carolyn 1947- **CLC 39**
See also CA 123

Ciardi, John (Anthony) 1916-1986 **CLC 10,
40, 44; DAM POET**
See also CA 5-8R; 118; CAAS 2; CANR 5, 33;
CLR 19; DLB 5; DLBY 86; INT CANR-5;
MAICYA; MTCW 1; SAAS 26; SATA 1, 65;
SATA-Obit 46

Cicero, Marcus Tullius 106B.C.-43B.C.
CMLC 3

Cimino, Michael 1943- **CLC 16**
See also CA 105

Cioran, E(mil) M. 1911-1995 **CLC 64**
See also CA 25-28R; 149

Cisneros, Sandra 1954-**CLC 69; DAM MULT;
HLC; SSC 32**
See also AAYA 9; CA 131; CANR 64; DLB 122,
152; HW

Cixous, Helene 1937- **CLC 92**
See also CA 126; CANR 55; DLB 83; MTCW
1

Clair, Rene **CLC 20**
See also Chomette, Rene Lucien

Clampitt, Amy 1920-1994 **CLC 32; PC 19**
See also CA 110; 146; CANR 29; DLB 105

Clancy, Thomas L., Jr. 1947-
See Clancy, Tom
See also CA 125; 131; CANR 62; INT 131;
MTCW 1

Clancy, Tom **CLC 45, 112; DAM NOV, POP**
See also Clancy, Thomas L., Jr.
See also AAYA 9; BEST 89:1, 90:1

Clare, John 1793-1864 **NCLC 9; DAB; DAM
POET; PC 23**
See also DLB 55, 96

Clarin
See Alas (y Urena), Leopoldo (Enrique Garcia)

Clark, Al C.
See Goines, Donald

Clark, (Robert) Brian 1932- **CLC 29**
See also CA 41-44R; CANR 67

Clark, Curt
See Westlake, Donald E(dwin)

Clark, Eleanor 1913-1996 **CLC 5, 19**
See also CA 9-12R; 151; CANR 41; DLB 6

Clark, J. P.
See Clark, John Pepper
See also DLB 117

Clark, John Pepper 1935- **CLC 38; BLC 1;
DAM DRAM, MULT; DC 5**
See also Clark, J. P.
See also BW 1; CA 65-68; CANR 16, 72

Clark, M. R.
See Clark, Mavis Thorpe

Clark, Mavis Thorpe 1909- **CLC 12**

See also CA 57-60; CANR 8, 37; CLR 30;
MAICYA; SAAS 5; SATA 8, 74

Clark, Walter Van Tilburg 1909-1971**CLC 28**
See also CA 9-12R; 33-36R; CANR 63; DLB
9; SATA 8

Clark Bekederemo, J(ohnson) P(epper)
See Clark, John Pepper

Clarke, Arthur C(harles) 1917-**CLC 1, 4, 13,
18, 35; DAM POP; SSC 3**
See also AAYA 4; CA 1-4R; CANR 2, 28, 55;
JRDA; MAICYA; MTCW 1; SATA 13, 70

Clarke, Austin 1896-1974 **CLC 6, 9; DAM
POET**
See also CA 29-32; 49-52; CAP 2; DLB 10, 20

Clarke, Austin C(hesterfield) 1934-**CLC 8, 53;
BLC 1; DAC; DAM MULT**
See also BW 1; CA 25-28R; CAAS 16; CANR
14, 32, 68; DLB 53, 125

Clarke, Gillian 1937- **CLC 61**
See also CA 106; DLB 40

Clarke, Marcus (Andrew Hislop) 1846-1881
NCLC 19

Clarke, Shirley 1925- **CLC 16**

Clash, The
See Headon, (Nicky) Topper; Jones, Mick;
Simonon, Paul; Strummer, Joe

Claudel, Paul (Louis Charles Marie) 1868-1955
TCLC 2, 10
See also CA 104; 165; DLB 192

Clavell, James (duMaresq) 1925-1994**CLC 6,
25, 87; DAM NOV, POP**
See also CA 25-28R; 146; CANR 26, 48;
MTCW 1

Cleaver, (Leroy) Eldridge 1935-1998**CLC 30;
BLC 1; DAM MULT**
See also BW 1; CA 21-24R; 167; CANR 16

Cleese, John (Marwood) 1939- **CLC 21**
See also Monty Python
See also CA 112; 116; CANR 35; MTCW 1

Cleishbotham, Jebediah
See Scott, Walter

Cleland, John 1710-1789 **LC 2**
See also DLB 39

Clemens, Samuel Langhorne 1835-1910
See Twain, Mark
See also CA 104; 135; CDALB 1865-1917; DA;
DAB; DAM MST, NOV; DLB 11, 12,
23, 64, 74, 186, 189; JRDA; MAICYA; SATA
100; YABC 2

Cleophil
See Congreve, William

Clerihew, E.
See Bentley, E(dmund) C(lerihew)

Clerk, N. W.
See Lewis, C(live) S(taples)

Cliff, Jimmy **CLC 21**
See also Chambers, James

Clifton, (Thelma) Lucille 1936- **CLC 19, 66;
BLC 1; DAM MULT, POET; PC 17**
See also BW 2; CA 49-52; CANR 2, 24, 42;
CLR 5; DLB 5, 41; MAICYA; MTCW 1;
SATA 20, 69

Clinton, Dirk
See Silverberg, Robert

Clough, Arthur Hugh 1819-1861 **NCLC 27**
See also DLB 32

Clutha, Janet Paterson Frame 1924-
See Frame, Janet
See also CA 1-4R; CANR 2, 36; MTCW 1

Clyne, Terence
See Blatty, William Peter

Cobalt, Martin
See Mayne, William (James Carter)

de Gourmont, Remy(-Marie-Charles)
See Gourmont, Remy (-Marie-Charles) de
de Hartog, Jan 1914- **CLC 19**
See also CA 1-4R; CANR 1
de Hostos, E. M.
See Hostos (y Bonilla), Eugenio Maria de
de Hostos, Eugenio M.
See Hostos (y Bonilla), Eugenio Maria de
Deighton, Len **CLC 4, 7, 22, 46**
See also Deighton, Leonard Cyril
See also AAYA 6; BEST 89:2; CDBLB 1960 to
Present; DLB 87
Deighton, Leonard Cyril 1929-
See Deighton, Len
See also CA 9-12R; CANR 19, 33, 68; DAM
NOV, POP; MTCW 1
Dekker, Thomas 1572(?)-1632 **LC 22; DAM
DRAM**
See also CDBLB Before 1660; DLB 62, 172
Delafield, E. M. 1890-1943 **TCLC 61**
See also Dashwood, Edmee Elizabeth Monica
de la Pasture
See also DLB 34
de la Mare, Walter (John) 1873-1956**TCLC 4,
53; DAB; DAC; DAM MST, POET; SSC
14; WLC**
See also CA 163; CDBLB 1914-1945; CLR 23;
DLB 162; SATA 16
Delaney, Franey
See O'Hara, John (Henry)
Delaney, Shelagh 1939-**CLC 29; DAM DRAM**
See also CA 17-20R; CANR 30, 67; CDBLB
1960 to Present; DLB 13; MTCW 1
Delany, Mary (Granville Pendarves) 1700-1788
LC 12
Delany, Samuel R(ay, Jr.) 1942-**CLC 8, 14, 38;
BLC 1; DAM MULT**
See also AAYA 24; BW 2; CA 81-84; CANR
27, 43; DLB 8, 33; MTCW 1
De La Ramee, (Marie) Louise 1839-1908
See Ouida
See also SATA 20
de la Roche, Mazo 1879-1961 **CLC 14**
See also CA 85-88; CANR 30; DLB 68; SATA
64
De La Salle, Innocent
See Hartmann, Sadakichi
Delbanco, Nicholas (Franklin) 1942- **CLC 6,
13**
See also CA 17-20R; CAAS 2; CANR 29, 55;
DLB 6
del Castillo, Michel 1933- **CLC 38**
See also CA 109
Deledda, Grazia (Cosima) 1875(?)-1936
TCLC 23
See also CA 123
Delibes, Miguel **CLC 8, 18**
See also Delibes Setien, Miguel
Delibes Setien, Miguel 1920-
See Delibes, Miguel
See also CA 45-48; CANR 1, 32; HW; MTCW
1
DeLillo, Don 1936- **CLC 8, 10, 13, 27, 39, 54,
76; DAM NOV, POP**
See also BEST 89:1; CA 81-84; CANR 21; DLB
6, 173; MTCW 1
de Lisser, H. G.
See De Lisser, H(erbert) G(eorge)
See also DLB 117
De Lisser, H(erbert) G(eorge) 1878-1944
TCLC 12
See also de Lisser, H. G.
See also BW 2; CA 109; 152

Deloney, Thomas (?)-1600 **LC 41**
See also DLB 167
Deloria, Vine (Victor), Jr. 1933- **CLC 21;
DAM MULT**
See also CA 53-56; CANR 5, 20, 48; DLB 175;
MTCW 1; NNAL; SATA 21
Del Vecchio, John M(ichael) 1947- **CLC 29**
See also CA 110; DLBD 9
de Man, Paul (Adolph Michel) 1919-1983
CLC 55
See also CA 128; 111; CANR 61; DLB 67;
MTCW 1
De Marinis, Rick 1934- **CLC 54**
See also CA 57-60; CAAS 24; CANR 9, 25, 50
Dembry, R. Emmet
See Murfree, Mary Noailles
Demby, William 1922-**CLC 53; BLC 1; DAM
MULT**
See also BW 1; CA 81-84; DLB 33
de Menton, Francisco
See Chin, Frank (Chew, Jr.)
Demijohn, Thom
See Disch, Thomas M(ichael)
de Montherlant, Henry (Milon)
See Montherlant, Henry (Milon) de
Demosthenes 384B.C.-322B.C. **CMLC 13**
See also DLB 176
de Natale, Francine
See Malzberg, Barry N(athaniel)
Denby, Edwin (Orr) 1903-1983 **CLC 48**
See also CA 138; 110
Denis, Julio
See Cortazar, Julio
Denmark, Harrison
See Zelazny, Roger (Joseph)
Dennis, John 1658-1734 **LC 11**
See also DLB 101
Dennis, Nigel (Forbes) 1912-1989 **CLC 8**
See also CA 25-28R; 129; DLB 13, 15; MTCW
1
Dent, Lester 1904(?)-1959 **TCLC 72**
See also CA 112; 161
De Palma, Brian (Russell) 1940- **CLC 20**
See also CA 109
De Quincey, Thomas 1785-1859 **NCLC 4**
See also CDBLB 1789-1832; DLB 110; 144
Deren, Eleanora 1908(?)-1961
See Deren, Maya
See also CA 111
Deren, Maya 1917-1961 **CLC 16, 102**
See also Deren, Eleanora
Derleth, August (William) 1909-1971**CLC 31**
See also CA 1-4R; 29-32R; CANR 4; DLB 9;
DLBD 17; SATA 5
Der Nister 1884-1950 **TCLC 56**
de Routisie, Albert
See Aragon, Louis
Derrida, Jacques 1930- **CLC 24, 87**
See also CA 124; 127
Derry Down Derry
See Lear, Edward
Dersonnes, Jacques
See Simenon, Georges (Jacques Christian)
Desai, Anita 1937-**CLC 19, 37, 97; DAB; DAM
NOV**
See also CA 81-84; CANR 33, 53; MTCW 1;
SATA 63
de Saint-Luc, Jean
See Glassco, John
de Saint Roman, Arnaud
See Aragon, Louis
Descartes, Rene 1596-1650 **LC 20, 35**
De Sica, Vittorio 1901(?)-1974 **CLC 20**

See also CA 117
Desnos, Robert 1900-1945 **TCLC 22**
See also CA 121; 151
Destouches, Louis-Ferdinand 1894-1961**C L C
9, 15**
See also Celine, Louis-Ferdinand
See also CA 85-88; CANR 28; MTCW 1
de Tolignac, Gaston
See Griffith, D(avid Lewelyn) W(ark)
Deutsch, Babette 1895-1982 **CLC 18**
See also CA 1-4R; 108; CANR 4; DLB 45;
SATA 1; SATA-Obit 33
Devenant, William 1606-1649 **LC 13**
Devkota, Laxmiprasad 1909-1959 **TCLC 23**
See also CA 123
De Voto, Bernard (Augustine) 1897-1955
TCLC 29
See also CA 113; 160; DLB 9
De Vries, Peter 1910-1993 **CLC 1, 2, 3, 7, 10,
28, 46; DAM NOV**
See also CA 17-20R; 142; CANR 41; DLB 6;
DLBY 82; MTCW 1
Dexter, John
See Bradley, Marion Zimmer
Dexter, Martin
See Faust, Frederick (Schiller)
Dexter, Pete 1943- **CLC 34, 55; DAM POP**
See also BEST 89:2; CA 127; 131; INT 131;
MTCW 1
Diamano, Silmang
See Senghor, Leopold Sedar
Diamond, Neil 1941- **CLC 30**
See also CA 108
Diaz del Castillo, Bernal 1496-1584 **LC 31**
di Bassetto, Corno
See Shaw, George Bernard
Dick, Philip K(indred) 1928-1982**CLC 10, 30,
72; DAM NOV, POP**
See also AAYA 24; CA 49-52; 106; CANR 2,
16; DLB 8; MTCW 1
Dickens, Charles (John Huffam) 1812-1870
**NCLC 3, 8, 18, 26, 37, 50; DA; DAB; DAC;
DAM MST, NOV; SSC 17; WLC**
See also AAYA 23; CDBLB 1832-1890; DLB
21, 55, 70, 159, 166; JRDA; MAICYA; SATA
15
Dickey, James (Lafayette) 1923-1997 **CLC 1,
2, 4, 7, 10, 15, 47, 109; DAM NOV, POET,
POP**
See also AITN 1, 2; CA 9-12R; 156; CABS 2;
CANR 10, 48, 61; CDALB 1968-1988; DLB
5, 193; DLBD 7; DLBY 82, 93, 96, 97; INT
CANR-10; MTCW 1
Dickey, William 1928-1994 **CLC 3, 28**
See also CA 9-12R; 145; CANR 24; DLB 5
Dickinson, Charles 1951- **CLC 49**
See also CA 128
Dickinson, Emily (Elizabeth) 1830-1886
**NCLC 21; DA; DAB; DAC; DAM MST,
POET; PC 1; WLC**
See also AAYA 22; CDALB 1865-1917; DLB
1; SATA 29
Dickinson, Peter (Malcolm) 1927-**CLC 12, 35**
See also AAYA 9; CA 41-44R; CANR 31, 58;
CLR 29; DLB 87, 161; JRDA; MAICYA;
SATA 5, 62, 95
Dickson, Carr
See Carr, John Dickson
Dickson, Carter
See Carr, John Dickson
Diderot, Denis 1713-1784 **LC 26**
Didion, Joan 1934-**CLC 1, 3, 8, 14, 32; DAM
NOV**

DLB 9, 12, 102, 137; DLBD 1; MTCW 1

Drexler, Rosalyn 1926-　　　　**CLC 2, 6**
See also CA 81-84; CANR 68

Dreyer, Carl Theodor 1889-1968　　**CLC 16**
See also CA 116

Drieu la Rochelle, Pierre(-Eugene) 1893-1945
　TCLC 21
See also CA 117; DLB 72

Drinkwater, John 1882-1937　　　**TCLC 57**
See also CA 109; 149; DLB 10, 19, 149

Drop Shot
See Cable, George Washington

Droste-Hulshoff, Annette Freiin von 1797-1848
　NCLC 3
See also DLB 133

Drummond, Walter
See Silverberg, Robert

Drummond, William Henry 1854-1907**TCLC
25**
See also CA 160; DLB 92

Drummond de Andrade, Carlos 1902-1987
　CLC 18
See also Andrade, Carlos Drummond de
See also CA 132; 123

Drury, Allen (Stuart) 1918-　　　**CLC 37**
See also CA 57-60; CANR 18, 52; INT CANR-18

Dryden, John 1631-1700**LC 3, 21; DA; DAB;
DAC; DAM DRAM, MST, POET; DC 3;
WLC**
See also CDBLB 1660-1789; DLB 80, 101, 131

Duberman, Martin (Bauml) 1930-　**CLC 8**
See also CA 1-4R; CANR 2, 63

Dubie, Norman (Evans) 1945-　　**CLC 36**
See also CA 69-72; CANR 12; DLB 120

Du Bois, W(illiam) E(dward) B(urghardt) 1868-
1963　**CLC 1, 2, 13, 64, 96; BLC 1; DA;
DAC; DAM MST, MULT, NOV; WLC**
See also BW 1; CA 85-88; CANR 34; CDALB
1865-1917; DLB 47, 50, 91; MTCW 1; SATA
42

Dubus, Andre 1936-　**CLC 13, 36, 97; SSC 15**
See also CA 21-24R; CANR 17; DLB 130; INT
CANR-17

Duca Minimo
See D'Annunzio, Gabriele

Ducharme, Rejean 1941-　　　　**CLC 74**
See also CA 165; DLB 60

Duclos, Charles Pinot 1704-1772　　**LC 1**

Dudek, Louis 1918-　　　　**CLC 11, 19**
See also CA 45-48; CAAS 14; CANR 1; DLB
88

Duerrenmatt, Friedrich 1921-1990 **CLC 1, 4,
8, 11, 15, 43, 102; DAM DRAM**
See also CA 17-20R; CANR 33; DLB 69, 124;
MTCW 1

Duffy, Bruce (?)-　　　　　　　**CLC 50**

Duffy, Maureen 1933-　　　　　**CLC 37**
See also CA 25-28R; CANR 33, 68; DLB 14;
MTCW 1

Dugan, Alan 1923-　　　　　　**CLC 2, 6**
See also CA 81-84; DLB 5

du Gard, Roger Martin
See Martin du Gard, Roger

Duhamel, Georges 1884-1966　　　**CLC 8**
See also CA 81-84; 25-28R; CANR 35; DLB
65; MTCW 1

Dujardin, Edouard (Emile Louis) 1861-1949
　TCLC 13
See also CA 109; DLB 123

Dulles, John Foster 1888-1959　　**TCLC 72**
See also CA 115; 149

Dumas, Alexandre (pere)

See Dumas, Alexandre (Davy de la Pailleterie)

Dumas, Alexandre (Davy de la Pailleterie)
1802-1870　**NCLC 11; DA; DAB; DAC;
DAM MST, NOV; WLC**
See also DLB 119, 192; SATA 18

Dumas, Alexandre (fils) 1824-1895**NCLC 71;
DC 1**
See also AAYA 22; DLB 192

Dumas, Claudine
See Malzberg, Barry N(athaniel)

Dumas, Henry L. 1934-1968　　　**CLC 6, 62**
See also BW 1; CA 85-88; DLB 41

du Maurier, Daphne 1907-1989**CLC 6, 11, 59;
DAB; DAC; DAM MST, POP; SSC 18**
See also CA 5-8R; 128; CANR 6, 55; DLB 191;
MTCW 1; SATA 27; SATA-Obit 60

Dunbar, Paul Laurence 1872-1906　**TCLC 2,
12; BLC 1; DA; DAC; DAM MST, MULT,
POET; PC 5; SSC 8; WLC**
See also BW 1; CA 104; 124; CDALB 1865-
1917; DLB 50, 54, 78; SATA 34

Dunbar, William 1460(?)-1530(?)　　**LC 20**
See also DLB 132, 146

Duncan, Dora Angela
See Duncan, Isadora

Duncan, Isadora 1877(?)-1927　　**TCLC 68**
See also CA 118; 149

Duncan, Lois 1934-　　　　　　**CLC 26**
See also AAYA 4; CA 1-4R; CANR 2, 23, 36;
CLR 29; JRDA; MAICYA; SAAS 2; SATA
1, 36, 75

Duncan, Robert (Edward) 1919-1988 **CLC 1,
2, 4, 7, 15, 41, 55; DAM POET; PC 2**
See also CA 9-12R; 124; CANR 28, 62; DLB
5, 16, 193; MTCW 1

Duncan, Sara Jeannette 1861-1922 **TCLC 60**
See also CA 157; DLB 92

Dunlap, William 1766-1839　　　　**NCLC 2**
See also DLB 30, 37, 59

Dunn, Douglas (Eaglesham) 1942- **CLC 6, 40**
See also CA 45-48; CANR 2, 33; DLB 40;
MTCW 1

Dunn, Katherine (Karen) 1945-　　**CLC 71**
See also CA 33-36R; CANR 72

Dunn, Stephen 1939-　　　　　　**CLC 36**
See also CA 33-36R; CANR 12, 48, 53; DLB
105

Dunne, Finley Peter 1867-1936　　**TCLC 28**
See also CA 108; DLB 11, 23

Dunne, John Gregory 1932-　　　**CLC 28**
See also CA 25-28R; CANR 14, 50; DLBY 80

Dunsany, Edward John Moreton Drax Plunkett
1878-1957
See Dunsany, Lord
See also CA 104; 148; DLB 10

Dunsany, Lord　　　　　　　　**TCLC 2, 59**
See also Dunsany, Edward John Moreton Drax
Plunkett
See also DLB 77, 153, 156

du Perry, Jean
See Simenon, Georges (Jacques Christian)

Durang, Christopher (Ferdinand) 1949-**CLC
27, 38**
See also CA 105; CANR 50

Duras, Marguerite 1914-1996**CLC 3, 6, 11, 20,
34, 40, 68, 100**
See also CA 25-28R; 151; CANR 50; DLB 83;
MTCW 1

Durban, (Rosa) Pam 1947-　　　　**CLC 39**
See also CA 123

Durcan, Paul 1944-**CLC 43, 70; DAM POET**
See also CA 134

Durkheim, Emile 1858-1917　　　**TCLC 55**

Durrell, Lawrence (George) 1912-1990 **C L C
1, 4, 6, 8, 13, 27, 41; DAM NOV**
See also CA 9-12R; 132; CANR 40; CDBLB
1945-1960; DLB 15, 27; DLBY 90; MTCW
1

Durrenmatt, Friedrich
See Duerrenmatt, Friedrich

Dutt, Toru 1856-1877　　　　　　**NCLC 29**

Dwight, Timothy 1752-1817　　　**NCLC 13**
See also DLB 37

Dworkin, Andrea 1946-　　　　　**CLC 43**
See also CA 77-80; CAAS 21; CANR 16, 39;
INT CANR-16; MTCW 1

Dwyer, Deanna
See Koontz, Dean R(ay)

Dwyer, K. R.
See Koontz, Dean R(ay)

Dwyer, Thomas A. 1923-　　　　**CLC 114**
See also CA 115

Dye, Richard
See De Voto, Bernard (Augustine)

Dylan, Bob 1941-　　　**CLC 3, 4, 6, 12, 77**
See also CA 41-44R; DLB 16

Eagleton, Terence (Francis) 1943-
See Eagleton, Terry
See also CA 57-60; CANR 7, 23, 68; MTCW 1

Eagleton, Terry　　　　　　　　　**CLC 63**
See also Eagleton, Terence (Francis)

Early, Jack
See Scoppettone, Sandra

East, Michael
See West, Morris L(anglo)

Eastaway, Edward
See Thomas, (Philip) Edward

Eastlake, William (Derry) 1917-1997 **CLC 8**
See also CA 5-8R; 158; CAAS 1; CANR 5, 63;
DLB 6; INT CANR-5

Eastman, Charles A(lexander) 1858-1939
　TCLC 55; DAM MULT
See also DLB 175; NNAL; YABC 1

Eberhart, Richard (Ghormley) 1904- **CLC 3,
11, 19, 56; DAM POET**
See also CA 1-4R; CANR 2; CDALB 1941-
1968; DLB 48; MTCW 1

Eberstadt, Fernanda 1960-　　　　**CLC 39**
See also CA 136; CANR 69

Echegaray (y Eizaguirre), Jose (Maria Waldo)
1832-1916　　　　　　　　　　**TCLC 4**
See also CA 104; CANR 32; HW; MTCW 1

Echeverria, (Jose) Esteban (Antonino) 1805-
1851　　　　　　　　　　　　**NCLC 18**

Echo
See Proust, (Valentin-Louis-George-Eugene-)
Marcel

Eckert, Allan W. 1931-　　　　　**CLC 17**
See also AAYA 18; CA 13-16R; CANR 14, 45;
INT CANR-14; SAAS 21; SATA 29, 91;
SATA-Brief 27

Eckhart, Meister 1260(?)-1328(?)　　**CMLC 9**
See also DLB 115

Eckmar, F. R.
See de Hartog, Jan

Eco, Umberto 1932-**CLC 28, 60; DAM NOV,
POP**
See also BEST 90:1; CA 77-80; CANR 12, 33,
55; DLB 196; MTCW 1

Eddison, E(ric) R(ucker) 1882-1945**TCLC 15**
See also CA 109; 156

Eddy, Mary (Morse) Baker 1821-1910**T C L C
71**
See also CA 113

Edel, (Joseph) Leon 1907-1997　　**CLC 29, 34**
See also CA 1-4R; 161; CANR 1, 22; DLB 103;

INT CANR-22

Eden, Emily 1797-1869   **NCLC 10**

Edgar, David 1948-   **CLC 42; DAM DRAM**
See also CA 57-60; CANR 12, 61; DLB 13;
MTCW 1

Edgerton, Clyde (Carlyle) 1944-   **CLC 39**
See also AAYA 17; CA 118; 134; CANR 64;
INT 134

Edgeworth, Maria 1768-1849   **NCLC 1, 51**
See also DLB 116, 159, 163; SATA 21

Edmonds, Paul
See Kuttner, Henry

Edmonds, Walter D(umaux) 1903-1998 **C L C
35**
See also CA 5-8R; CANR 2; DLB 9; MAICYA;
SAAS 4; SATA 1, 27; SATA-Obit 99

Edmondson, Wallace
See Ellison, Harlan (Jay)

Edson, Russell   **CLC 13**
See also CA 33-36R

Edwards, Bronwen Elizabeth
See Rose, Wendy

Edwards, G(erald) B(asil) 1899-1976**CLC 25**
See also CA 110

Edwards, Gus 1939-   **CLC 43**
See also CA 108; INT 108

Edwards, Jonathan 1703-1758   **LC 7; DA;
DAC; DAM MST**
See also DLB 24

Efron, Marina Ivanovna Tsvetaeva
See Tsvetaeva (Efron), Marina (Ivanovna)

Ehle, John (Marsden, Jr.) 1925-   **CLC 27**
See also CA 9-12R

Ehrenbourg, Ilya (Grigoryevich)
See Ehrenburg, Ilya (Grigoryevich)

Ehrenburg, Ilya (Grigoryevich) 1891-1967
CLC 18, 34, 62
See also CA 102; 25-28R

Ehrenburg, Ilyo (Grigoryevich)
See Ehrenburg, Ilya (Grigoryevich)

Ehrenreich, Barbara 1941-   **CLC 110**
See also BEST 90:4; CA 73-76; CANR 16, 37,
62; MTCW 1

Eich, Guenter 1907-1972   **CLC 15**
See also CA 111; 93-96; DLB 69, 124

Eichendorff, Joseph Freiherr von 1788-1857
NCLC 8
See also DLB 90

Eigner, Larry   **CLC 9**
See also Eigner, Laurence (Joel)
See also CAAS 23; DLB 5

Eigner, Laurence (Joel) 1927-1996
See Eigner, Larry
See also CA 9-12R; 151; CANR 6; DLB 193

Einstein, Albert 1879-1955   **TCLC 65**
See also CA 121; 133; MTCW 1

Eiseley, Loren Corey 1907-1977   **CLC 7**
See also AAYA 5; CA 1-4R; 73-76; CANR 6;
DLBD 17

Eisenstadt, Jill 1963-   **CLC 50**
See also CA 140

Eisenstein, Sergei (Mikhailovich) 1898-1948
TCLC 57
See also CA 114; 149

Eisner, Simon
See Kornbluth, C(yril) M.

Ekeloef, (Bengt) Gunnar 1907-1968 **CLC 27;
DAM POET; PC 23**
See also CA 123; 25-28R

Ekelof, (Bengt) Gunnar
See Ekeloef, (Bengt) Gunnar

Ekelund, Vilhelm 1880-1949   **TCLC 75**

Ekwensi, C. O. D.

See Ekwensi, Cyprian (Odiatu Duaka)

Ekwensi, Cyprian (Odiatu Duaka) 1921-**C L C
4; BLC 1; DAM MULT**
See also BW 2; CA 29-32R; CANR 18, 42; DLB
117; MTCW 1; SATA 66

Elaine   **TCLC 18**
See also Leverson, Ada

El Crummo
See Crumb, R(obert)

Elder, Lonne III 1931-1996   **DC 8**
See also BLC 1; BW 1; CA 81-84; 152; CANR
25; DAM MULT; DLB 7, 38, 44

Elia
See Lamb, Charles

Eliade, Mircea 1907-1986   **CLC 19**
See also CA 65-68; 119; CANR 30, 62; MTCW
1

Eliot, A. D.
See Jewett, (Theodora) Sarah Orne

Eliot, Alice
See Jewett, (Theodora) Sarah Orne

Eliot, Dan
See Silverberg, Robert

Eliot, George 1819-1880 **NCLC 4, 13, 23, 41,
49; DA; DAB; DAC; DAM MST, NOV; PC
20; WLC**
See also CDBLB 1832-1890; DLB 21, 35, 55

Eliot, John 1604-1690   **LC 5**
See also DLB 24

Eliot, T(homas) S(tearns) 1888-1965**CLC 1, 2,
3, 6, 9, 10, 13, 15, 24, 34, 41, 55, 57, 113;
DA; DAB; DAC; DAM DRAM, MST,
POET; PC 5; WLC**
See also CA 5-8R; 25-28R; CANR 41; CDALB
1929-1941; DLB 7, 10, 45, 63; DLBY 88;
MTCW 1

Elizabeth 1866-1941   **TCLC 41**

Elkin, Stanley L(awrence) 1930-1995 **CLC 4,
6, 9, 14, 27, 51, 91; DAM NOV, POP; SSC
12**
See also CA 9-12R; 148; CANR 8, 46; DLB 2,
28; DLBY 80; INT CANR-8; MTCW 1

Elledge, Scott   **CLC 34**

Elliot, Don
See Silverberg, Robert

Elliott, Don
See Silverberg, Robert

Elliott, George P(aul) 1918-1980   **CLC 2**
See also CA 1-4R; 97-100; CANR 2

Elliott, Janice 1931-   **CLC 47**
See also CA 13-16R; CANR 8, 29; DLB 14

Elliott, Sumner Locke 1917-1991   **CLC 38**
See also CA 5-8R; 134; CANR 2, 21

Elliott, William
See Bradbury, Ray (Douglas)

Ellis, A. E.   **CLC 7**

Ellis, Alice Thomas   **CLC 40**
See also Haycraft, Anna
See also DLB 194

Ellis, Bret Easton 1964-   **CLC 39, 71; DAM
POP**
See also AAYA 2; CA 118; 123; CANR 51; INT
123

Ellis, (Henry) Havelock 1859-1939 **TCLC 14**
See also CA 109; DLB 190

Ellis, Landon
See Ellison, Harlan (Jay)

Ellis, Trey 1962-   **CLC 55**
See also CA 146

Ellison, Harlan (Jay) 1934-   **CLC 1, 13, 42;
DAM POP; SSC 14**
See also CA 5-8R; CANR 5, 46; DLB 8; INT
CANR-5; MTCW 1

Ellison, Ralph (Waldo) 1914-1994 **CLC 1, 3,
11, 54, 86, 114; BLC 1; DA; DAB; DAC;
DAM MST, MULT, NOV; SSC 26; WLC**
See also AAYA 19; BW 1; CA 9-12R; 145;
CANR 24, 53; CDALB 1941-1968; DLB 2,
76; DLBY 94; MTCW 1

Ellmann, Lucy (Elizabeth) 1956-   **CLC 61**
See also CA 128

Ellmann, Richard (David) 1918-1987**CLC 50**
See also BEST 89:2; CA 1-4R; 122; CANR 2,
28, 61; DLB 103; DLBY 87; MTCW 1

Elman, Richard (Martin) 1934-1997 **CLC 19**
See also CA 17-20R; 163; CAAS 3; CANR 47

Elron
See Hubbard, L(afayette) Ron(ald)

Eluard, Paul   **TCLC 7, 41**
See also Grindel, Eugene

Elyot, Sir Thomas 1490(?)-1546   **LC 11**

Elytis, Odysseus 1911-1996 **CLC 15, 49, 100;
DAM POET; PC 21**
See also CA 102; 151; MTCW 1

Emecheta, (Florence Onye) Buchi 1944-**C L C
14, 48; BLC 2; DAM MULT**
See also BW 2; CA 81-84; CANR 27; DLB 117;
MTCW 1; SATA 66

Emerson, Mary Moody 1774-1863 **NCLC 66**

Emerson, Ralph Waldo 1803-1882 **NCLC 1,
38; DA; DAB; DAC; DAM MST, POET;
PC 18; WLC**
See also CDALB 1640-1865; DLB 1, 59, 73

Eminescu, Mihail 1850-1889   **NCLC 33**

Empson, William 1906-1984**CLC 3, 8, 19, 33,
34**
See also CA 17-20R; 112; CANR 31, 61; DLB
20; MTCW 1

Enchi, Fumiko (Ueda) 1905-1986   **CLC 31**
See also CA 129; 121

Ende, Michael (Andreas Helmuth) 1929-1995
CLC 31
See also CA 118; 124; 149; CANR 36; CLR
14; DLB 75; MAICYA; SATA 61; SATA-
Brief 42; SATA-Obit 86

Endo, Shusaku 1923-1996 **CLC 7, 14, 19, 54,
99; DAM NOV**
See also CA 29-32R; 153; CANR 21, 54; DLB
182; MTCW 1

Engel, Marian 1933-1985   **CLC 36**
See also CA 25-28R; CANR 12; DLB 53; INT
CANR-12

Engelhardt, Frederick
See Hubbard, L(afayette) Ron(ald)

Enright, D(ennis) J(oseph) 1920-**CLC 4, 8, 31**
See also CA 1-4R; CANR 1, 42; DLB 27; SATA
25

Enzensberger, Hans Magnus 1929-   **CLC 43**
See also CA 116; 119

Ephron, Nora 1941-   **CLC 17, 31**
See also AITN 2; CA 65-68; CANR 12, 39

Epicurus 341B.C.-270B.C.   **CMLC 21**
See also DLB 176

Epsilon
See Betjeman, John

Epstein, Daniel Mark 1948-   **CLC 7**
See also CA 49-52; CANR 2, 53

Epstein, Jacob 1956-   **CLC 19**
See also CA 114

Epstein, Joseph 1937-   **CLC 39**
See also CA 112; 119; CANR 50, 65

Epstein, Leslie 1938-   **CLC 27**
See also CA 73-76; CAAS 12; CANR 23, 69

Equiano, Olaudah 1745(?)-1797 **LC 16; BLC
2; DAM MULT**
See also DLB 37, 50

ER   **TCLC 33**
See also CA 160; DLB 85
Erasmus, Desiderius 1469(?)-1536   **LC 16**
Erdman, Paul E(mil) 1932-   **CLC 25**
See also AITN 1; CA 61-64; CANR 13, 43
Erdrich, Louise 1954-   **CLC 39, 54; DAM MULT, NOV, POP**
See also AAYA 10; BEST 89:1; CA 114; CANR 41, 62; DLB 152, 175; MTCW 1; NNAL; SATA 94
Erenburg, Ilya (Grigoryevich)
See Ehrenburg, Ilya (Grigoryevich)
Erickson, Stephen Michael 1950-
See Erickson, Steve
See also CA 129
Erickson, Steve 1950-   **CLC 64**
See also Erickson, Stephen Michael
See also CANR 60, 68
Ericson, Walter
See Fast, Howard (Melvin)
Eriksson, Buntel
See Bergman, (Ernst) Ingmar
Ernaux, Annie 1940-   **CLC 88**
See also CA 147
Erskine, John 1879-1951   **TCLC 84**
See also CA 112; 159; DLB 9, 102
Eschenbach, Wolfram von
See Wolfram von Eschenbach
Eseki, Bruno
See Mphahlele, Ezekiel
Esenin, Sergei (Alexandrovich) 1895-1925   **TCLC 4**
See also CA 104
Eshleman, Clayton 1935-   **CLC 7**
See also CA 33-36R; CAAS 6; DLB 5
Espriella, Don Manuel Alvarez
See Southey, Robert
Espriu, Salvador 1913-1985   **CLC 9**
See also CA 154; 115; DLB 134
Espronceda, Jose de 1808-1842   **NCLC 39**
Esse, James
See Stephens, James
Esterbrook, Tom
See Hubbard, L(afayette) Ron(ald)
Estleman, Loren D. 1952- **CLC 48; DAM NOV, POP**
See also AAYA 27; CA 85-88; CANR 27; INT CANR-27; MTCW 1
Euclid 306B.C.-283B.C.   **CMLC 25**
Eugenides, Jeffrey 1960(?)-   **CLC 81**
See also CA 144
Euripides c. 485B.C.-406B.C. **CMLC 23; DA; DAB; DAC; DAM DRAM, MST; DC 4; WLCS**
See also DLB 176
Eutropius c. 320-387   **CMLC 30**
Evan, Evin
See Faust, Frederick (Schiller)
Evans, Caradoc 1878-1945   **TCLC 85**
Evans, Evan
See Faust, Frederick (Schiller)
Evans, Marian
See Eliot, George
Evans, Mary Ann
See Eliot, George
Evarts, Esther
See Benson, Sally
Everett, Percival L. 1956-   **CLC 57**
See also BW 2; CA 129
Everson, R(onald) G(ilmour) 1903- **CLC 27**
See also CA 17-20R; DLB 88
Everson, William (Oliver) 1912-1994 **CLC 1, 5, 14**

See also CA 9-12R; 145; CANR 20; DLB 5, 16; MTCW 1
Evtushenko, Evgenii Aleksandrovich
See Yevtushenko, Yevgeny (Alexandrovich)
Ewart, Gavin (Buchanan) 1916-1995 **CLC 13, 46**
See also CA 89-92; 150; CANR 17, 46; DLB 40; MTCW 1
Ewers, Hanns Heinz 1871-1943   **TCLC 12**
See also CA 109; 149
Ewing, Frederick R.
See Sturgeon, Theodore (Hamilton)
Exley, Frederick (Earl) 1929-1992 **CLC 6, 11**
See also AITN 2; CA 81-84; 138; DLB 143; DLBY 81
Eynhardt, Guillermo
See Quiroga, Horacio (Sylvestre)
Ezekiel, Nissim 1924-   **CLC 61**
See also CA 61-64
Ezekiel, Tish O'Dowd 1943-   **CLC 34**
See also CA 129
Fadeyev, A.
See Bulgya, Alexander Alexandrovich
Fadeyev, Alexander   **TCLC 53**
See also Bulgya, Alexander Alexandrovich
Fagen, Donald 1948-   **CLC 26**
Fainzilberg, Ilya Arnoldovich 1897-1937
See Ilf, Ilya
See also CA 120; 165
Fair, Ronald L. 1932-   **CLC 18**
See also BW 1; CA 69-72; CANR 25; DLB 33
Fairbairn, Roger
See Carr, John Dickson
Fairbairns, Zoe (Ann) 1948-   **CLC 32**
See also CA 103; CANR 21
Falco, Gian
See Papini, Giovanni
Falconer, James
See Kirkup, James
Falconer, Kenneth
See Kornbluth, C(yril) M.
Falkland, Samuel
See Heijermans, Herman
Fallaci, Oriana 1930-   **CLC 11, 110**
See also CA 77-80; CANR 15, 58; MTCW 1
Faludy, George 1913-   **CLC 42**
See also CA 21-24R
Faludy, Gyoergy
See Faludy, George
Fanon, Frantz 1925-1961   **CLC 74; BLC 2; DAM MULT**
See also BW 1; CA 116; 89-92
Fanshawe, Ann 1625-1680   **LC 11**
Fante, John (Thomas) 1911-1983   **CLC 60**
See also CA 69-72; 109; CANR 23; DLB 130; DLBY 83
Farah, Nuruddin 1945- **CLC 53; BLC 2; DAM MULT**
See also BW 2; CA 106; DLB 125
Fargue, Leon-Paul 1876(?)-1947   **TCLC 11**
See also CA 109
Farigoule, Louis
See Romains, Jules
Farina, Richard 1936(?)-1966   **CLC 9**
See also CA 81-84; 25-28R
Farley, Walter (Lorimer) 1915-1989 **CLC 17**
See also CA 17-20R; CANR 8, 29; DLB 22; JRDA; MAICYA; SATA 2, 43
Farmer, Philip Jose 1918-   **CLC 1, 19**
See also CA 1-4R; CANR 4, 35; DLB 8; MTCW 1; SATA 93
Farquhar, George 1677-1707   **LC 21; DAM DRAM**

See also DLB 84
Farrell, J(ames) G(ordon) 1935-1979 **CLC 6**
See also CA 73-76; 89-92; CANR 36; DLB 14; MTCW 1
Farrell, James T(homas) 1904-1979 **CLC 1, 4, 8, 11, 66; SSC 28**
See also CA 5-8R; 89-92; CANR 9, 61; DLB 4, 9, 86; DLBD 2; MTCW 1
Farren, Richard J.
See Betjeman, John
Farren, Richard M.
See Betjeman, John
Fassbinder, Rainer Werner 1946-1982 **CLC 20**
See also CA 93-96; 106; CANR 31
Fast, Howard (Melvin) 1914- **CLC 23; DAM NOV**
See also AAYA 16; CA 1-4R; CAAS 18; CANR 1, 33, 54; DLB 9; INT CANR-33; SATA 7
Faulcon, Robert
See Holdstock, Robert P.
Faulkner, William (Cuthbert) 1897-1962 **CLC 1, 3, 6, 8, 9, 11, 14, 18, 28, 52, 68; DA; DAB; DAC; DAM MST, NOV; SSC 1; WLC**
See also AAYA 7; CA 81-84; CANR 33; CDALB 1929-1941; DLB 9, 11, 44, 102; DLBD 2; DLBY 86, 97; MTCW 1
Fauset, Jessie Redmon 1884(?)-1961 **CLC 19, 54; BLC 2; DAM MULT**
See also BW 1; CA 109; DLB 51
Faust, Frederick (Schiller) 1892-1944(?) **TCLC 49; DAM POP**
See also CA 108; 152
Faust, Irvin 1924-   **CLC 8**
See also CA 33-36R; CANR 28, 67; DLB 2, 28; DLBY 80
Fawkes, Guy
See Benchley, Robert (Charles)
Fearing, Kenneth (Flexner) 1902-1961   **CLC 51**
See also CA 93-96; CANR 59; DLB 9
Fecamps, Elise
See Creasey, John
Federman, Raymond 1928-   **CLC 6, 47**
See also CA 17-20R; CAAS 8; CANR 10, 43; DLBY 80
Federspiel, J(uerg) F. 1931-   **CLC 42**
See also CA 146
Feiffer, Jules (Ralph) 1929-   **CLC 2, 8, 64; DAM DRAM**
See also AAYA 3; CA 17-20R; CANR 30, 59; DLB 7, 44; INT CANR-30; MTCW 1; SATA 8, 61
Feige, Hermann Albert Otto Maximilian
See Traven, B.
Feinberg, David B. 1956-1994   **CLC 59**
See also CA 135; 147
Feinstein, Elaine 1930-   **CLC 36**
See also CA 69-72; CAAS 1; CANR 31, 68; DLB 14, 40; MTCW 1
Feldman, Irving (Mordecai) 1928-   **CLC 7**
See also CA 1-4R; CANR 1; DLB 169
Felix-Tchicaya, Gerald
See Tchicaya, Gerald Felix
Fellini, Federico 1920-1993   **CLC 16, 85**
See also CA 65-68; 143; CANR 33
Felsen, Henry Gregor 1916-   **CLC 17**
See also CA 1-4R; CANR 1; SAAS 2; SATA 1
Fenno, Jack
See Calisher, Hortense
Fenton, James Martin 1949-   **CLC 32**
See also CA 102; DLB 40
Ferber, Edna 1887-1968   **CLC 18, 93**
See also AITN 1; CA 5-8R; 25-28R; CANR 68;

DLB 9, 28, 86; MTCW 1; SATA 7
Ferguson, Helen
    See Kavan, Anna
Ferguson, Samuel 1810-1886   **NCLC 33**
    See also DLB 32
Fergusson, Robert 1750-1774   **LC 29**
    See also DLB 109
Ferling, Lawrence
    See Ferlinghetti, Lawrence (Monsanto)
Ferlinghetti, Lawrence (Monsanto) 1919(?)-
    CLC 2, 6, 10, 27, 111; DAM POET; PC 1
    See also CA 5-8R; CANR 3, 41; CDALB 1941-
    1968; DLB 5, 16; MTCW 1
Fernandez, Vicente Garcia Huidobro
    See Huidobro Fernandez, Vicente Garcia
Ferrer, Gabriel (Francisco Victor) Miro
    See Miro (Ferrer), Gabriel (Francisco Victor)
Ferrier, Susan (Edmonstone) 1782-1854
    NCLC 8
    See also DLB 116
Ferrigno, Robert 1948(?)-   **CLC 65**
    See also CA 140
Ferron, Jacques 1921-1985   **CLC 94; DAC**
    See also CA 117; 129; DLB 60
Feuchtwanger, Lion 1884-1958   **TCLC 3**
    See also CA 104; DLB 66
Feuillet, Octave 1821-1890   **NCLC 45**
    See also DLB 192
Feydeau, Georges (Leon Jules Marie) 1862-
    1921   **TCLC 22; DAM DRAM**
    See also CA 113; 152; DLB 192
Fichte, Johann Gottlieb 1762-1814 **NCLC 62**
    See also DLB 90
Ficino, Marsilio 1433-1499   **LC 12**
Fiedeler, Hans
    See Doeblin, Alfred
Fiedler, Leslie A(aron) 1917- **CLC 4, 13, 24**
    See also CA 9-12R; CANR 7, 63; DLB 28, 67;
    MTCW 1
Field, Andrew 1938-   **CLC 44**
    See also CA 97-100; CANR 25
Field, Eugene 1850-1895   **NCLC 3**
    See also DLB 23, 42, 140; DLBD 13; MAICYA;
    SATA 16
Field, Gans T.
    See Wellman, Manly Wade
Field, Michael 1915-1971   **TCLC 43**
    See also CA 29-32R
Field, Peter
    See Hobson, Laura Z(ametkin)
Fielding, Henry 1707-1754 **LC 1; DA; DAB;**
    DAC; DAM DRAM, MST, NOV; WLC
    See also CDBLB 1660-1789; DLB 39, 84, 101
Fielding, Sarah 1710-1768   **LC 1, 44**
    See also DLB 39
Fields, W. C. 1880-1946   **TCLC 80**
    See also DLB 44
Fierstein, Harvey (Forbes) 1954-   **CLC 33;**
    DAM DRAM, POP
    See also CA 123; 129
Figes, Eva 1932-   **CLC 31**
    See also CA 53-56; CANR 4, 44; DLB 14
Finch, Anne 1661-1720   **LC 3; PC 21**
    See also DLB 95
Finch, Robert (Duer Claydon) 1900- **CLC 18**
    See also CA 57-60; CANR 9, 24, 49; DLB 88
Findley, Timothy 1930- **CLC 27, 102; DAC;**
    DAM MST
    See also CA 25-28R; CANR 12, 42, 69; DLB
    53
Fink, William
    See Mencken, H(enry) L(ouis)
Firbank, Louis 1942-

See Reed, Lou
    See also CA 117
Firbank, (Arthur Annesley) Ronald 1886-1926
    TCLC 1
    See also CA 104; DLB 36
Fisher, M(ary) F(rances) K(ennedy) 1908-1992
    CLC 76, 87
    See also CA 77-80; 138; CANR 44
Fisher, Roy 1930-   **CLC 25**
    See also CA 81-84; CAAS 10; CANR 16; DLB
    40
Fisher, Rudolph 1897-1934**TCLC 11; BLC 2;**
    DAM MULT; SSC 25
    See also BW 1; CA 107; 124; DLB 51, 102
Fisher, Vardis (Alvero) 1895-1968   **CLC 7**
    See also CA 5-8R; 25-28R; CANR 68; DLB 9
Fiske, Tarleton
    See Bloch, Robert (Albert)
Fitch, Clarke
    See Sinclair, Upton (Beall)
Fitch, John IV
    See Cormier, Robert (Edmund)
Fitzgerald, Captain Hugh
    See Baum, L(yman) Frank
FitzGerald, Edward 1809-1883   **NCLC 9**
    See also DLB 32
Fitzgerald, F(rancis) Scott (Key) 1896-1940
    TCLC 1, 6, 14, 28, 55; DA; DAB; DAC;
    DAM MST, NOV; SSC 6, 31; WLC
    See also AAYA 24; AITN 1; CA 110; 123;
    CDALB 1917-1929; DLB 4, 9, 86; DLBD 1,
    15, 16; DLBY 81, 96; MTCW 1
Fitzgerald, Penelope 1916-   **CLC 19, 51, 61**
    See also CA 85-88; CAAS 10; CANR 56; DLB
    14, 194
Fitzgerald, Robert (Stuart) 1910-1985**CLC 39**
    See also CA 1-4R; 114; CANR 1; DLBY 80
FitzGerald, Robert D(avid) 1902-1987**CLC 19**
    See also CA 17-20R
Fitzgerald, Zelda (Sayre) 1900-1948**TCLC 52**
    See also CA 117; 126; DLBY 84
Flanagan, Thomas (James Bonner) 1923-
    CLC 25, 52
    See also CA 108; CANR 55; DLBY 80; INT
    108; MTCW 1
Flaubert, Gustave 1821-1880**NCLC 2, 10, 19,**
    62, 66; DA; DAB; DAC; DAM MST, NOV;
    SSC 11; WLC
    See also DLB 119
Flecker, Herman Elroy
    See Flecker, (Herman) James Elroy
Flecker, (Herman) James Elroy 1884-1915
    TCLC 43
    See also CA 109; 150; DLB 10, 19
Fleming, Ian (Lancaster) 1908-1964 **CLC 3,**
    30; DAM POP
    See also AAYA 26; CA 5-8R; CANR 59;
    CDBLB 1945-1960; DLB 87, 201; MTCW
    1; SATA 9
Fleming, Thomas (James) 1927-   **CLC 37**
    See also CA 5-8R; CANR 10; INT CANR-10;
    SATA 8
Fletcher, John 1579-1625   **LC 33; DC 6**
    See also CDBLB Before 1660; DLB 58
Fletcher, John Gould 1886-1950   **TCLC 35**
    See also CA 107; 167; DLB 4, 45
Fleur, Paul
    See Pohl, Frederik
Flooglebuckle, Al
    See Spiegelman, Art
Flying Officer X
    See Bates, H(erbert) E(rnest)
Fo, Dario 1926- **CLC 32, 109; DAM DRAM**

See also CA 116; 128; CANR 68; DLBY 97;
    MTCW 1
Fogarty, Jonathan Titulescu Esq.
    See Farrell, James T(homas)
Folke, Will
    See Bloch, Robert (Albert)
Follett, Ken(neth Martin) 1949-   **CLC 18;**
    DAM NOV, POP
    See also AAYA 6; BEST 89:4; CA 81-84; CANR
    13, 33, 54; DLB 87; DLBY 81; INT CANR-
    33; MTCW 1
Fontane, Theodor 1819-1898   **NCLC 26**
    See also DLB 129
Foote, Horton 1916-**CLC 51, 91; DAM DRAM**
    See also CA 73-76; CANR 34, 51; DLB 26; INT
    CANR-34
Foote, Shelby 1916-**CLC 75; DAM NOV, POP**
    See also CA 5-8R; CANR 3, 45; DLB 2, 17
Forbes, Esther 1891-1967   **CLC 12**
    See also AAYA 17; CA 13-14; 25-28R; CAP 1;
    CLR 27; DLB 22; JRDA; MAICYA; SATA
    2, 100
Forche, Carolyn (Louise) 1950- **CLC 25, 83,**
    86; DAM POET; PC 10
    See also CA 109; 117; CANR 50; DLB 5, 193;
    INT 117
Ford, Elbur
    See Hibbert, Eleanor Alice Burford
Ford, Ford Madox 1873-1939**TCLC 1, 15, 39,**
    57; DAM NOV
    See also CA 104; 132; CDBLB 1914-1945;
    DLB 162; MTCW 1
Ford, Henry 1863-1947   **TCLC 73**
    See also CA 115; 148
Ford, John 1586-(?)   **DC 8**
    See also CDBLB Before 1660; DAM DRAM;
    DLB 58
Ford, John 1895-1973   **CLC 16**
    See also CA 45-48
Ford, Richard 1944-   **CLC 46, 99**
    See also CA 69-72; CANR 11, 47
Ford, Webster
    See Masters, Edgar Lee
Foreman, Richard 1937-   **CLC 50**
    See also CA 65-68; CANR 32, 63
Forester, C(ecil) S(cott) 1899-1966 **CLC 35**
    See also CA 73-76; 25-28R; DLB 191; SATA
    13
Forez
    See Mauriac, Francois (Charles)
Forman, James Douglas 1932-   **CLC 21**
    See also AAYA 17; CA 9-12R; CANR 4, 19,
    42; JRDA; MAICYA; SATA 8, 70
Fornes, Maria Irene 1930-   **CLC 39, 61**
    See also CA 25-28R; CANR 28; DLB 7; HW;
    INT CANR-28; MTCW 1
Forrest, Leon (Richard) 1937-1997 **CLC 4;**
    BLCS
    See also BW 2; CA 89-92; 162; CAAS 7; CANR
    25, 52; DLB 33
Forster, E(dward) M(organ) 1879-1970 **C L C**
    1, 2, 3, 4, 9, 10, 13, 15, 22, 45, 77; DA; DAB;
    DAC; DAM MST, NOV; SSC 27; WLC
    See also AAYA 2; CA 13-14; 25-28R; CANR
    45; CAP 1; CDBLB 1914-1945; DLB 34, 98,
    162, 178, 195; DLBD 10; MTCW 1; SATA
    57
Forster, John 1812-1876   **NCLC 11**
    See also DLB 144, 184
Forsyth, Frederick 1938-**CLC 2, 5, 36; DAM**
    NOV, POP
    See also BEST 89:4; CA 85-88; CANR 38, 62;
    DLB 87; MTCW 1

See also AAYA 18; AITN 1; BW 2; CA 9-12R;
CANR 6, 24, 42; CDALB 1968-1988; DLB
2, 33, 152; DLBY 80; MTCW 1; SATA 86
Gaitskill, Mary 1954-   **CLC 69**
See also CA 128; CANR 61
Galdos, Benito Perez
See Perez Galdos, Benito
Gale, Zona 1874-1938**TCLC 7; DAM DRAM**
See also CA 105; 153; DLB 9, 78
Galeano, Eduardo (Hughes) 1940-   **CLC 72**
See also CA 29-32R; CANR 13, 32; HW
Galiano, Juan Valera y Alcala
See Valera y Alcala-Galiano, Juan
Galilei, Galileo 1546-1642   **LC 45**
Gallagher, Tess 1943-   **CLC 18, 63; DAM
POET; PC 9**
See also CA 106; DLB 120
Gallant, Mavis 1922-   **CLC 7, 18, 38; DAC;
DAM MST; SSC 5**
See also CA 69-72; CANR 29, 69; DLB 53;
MTCW 1
Gallant, Roy A(rthur) 1924-   **CLC 17**
See also CA 5-8R; CANR 4, 29, 54; CLR 30;
MAICYA; SATA 4, 68
Gallico, Paul (William) 1897-1976   **CLC 2**
See also AITN 1; CA 5-8R; 69-72; CANR 23;
DLB 9, 171; MAICYA; SATA 13
Gallo, Max Louis 1932-   **CLC 95**
See also CA 85-88
Gallois, Lucien
See Desnos, Robert
Gallup, Ralph
See Whitemore, Hugh (John)
Galsworthy, John 1867-1933**TCLC 1, 45; DA;
DAB; DAC; DAM DRAM, MST, NOV;
SSC 22; WLC 2**
See also CA 104; 141; CDBLB 1890-1914;
DLB 10, 34, 98, 162; DLBD 16
Galt, John 1779-1839   **NCLC 1**
See also DLB 99, 116, 159
Galvin, James 1951-   **CLC 38**
See also CA 108; CANR 26
Gamboa, Federico 1864-1939   **TCLC 36**
See also CA 167
Gandhi, M. K.
See Gandhi, Mohandas Karamchand
Gandhi, Mahatma
See Gandhi, Mohandas Karamchand
Gandhi, Mohandas Karamchand 1869-1948
TCLC 59; DAM MULT
See also CA 121; 132; MTCW 1
Gann, Ernest Kellogg 1910-1991   **CLC 23**
See also AITN 1; CA 1-4R; 136; CANR 1
Garcia, Cristina 1958-   **CLC 76**
See also CA 141
Garcia Lorca, Federico 1898-1936**TCLC 1, 7,
49; DA; DAB; DAC; DAM DRAM, MST,
MULT, POET; DC 2; HLC; PC 3; WLC**
See also CA 104; 131; DLB 108; HW; MTCW
1
Garcia Marquez, Gabriel (Jose) 1928-**CLC 2,
3, 8, 10, 15, 27, 47, 55, 68; DA; DAB; DAC;
DAM MST, MULT, NOV, POP; HLC; SSC
8; WLC**
See also AAYA 3; BEST 89:1, 90:4; CA 33-
36R; CANR 10, 28, 50; DLB 113; HW;
MTCW 1
Gard, Janice
See Latham, Jean Lee
Gard, Roger Martin du
See Martin du Gard, Roger
Gardam, Jane 1928-   **CLC 43**
See also CA 49-52; CANR 2, 18, 33, 54; CLR

12; DLB 14, 161; MAICYA; MTCW 1;
SAAS 9; SATA 39, 76; SATA-Brief 28
Gardner, Herb(ert) 1934-   **CLC 44**
See also CA 149
Gardner, John (Champlin), Jr. 1933-1982
**CLC 2, 3, 5, 7, 8, 10, 18, 28, 34; DAM NOV,
POP; SSC 7**
See also AITN 1; CA 65-68; 107; CANR 33;
DLB 2; DLBY 82; MTCW 1; SATA 40;
SATA-Obit 31
Gardner, John (Edmund) 1926-**CLC 30; DAM
POP**
See also CA 103; CANR 15, 69; MTCW 1
Gardner, Miriam
See Bradley, Marion Zimmer
Gardner, Noel
See Kuttner, Henry
Gardons, S. S.
See Snodgrass, W(illiam) D(e Witt)
Garfield, Leon 1921-1996   **CLC 12**
See also AAYA 8; CA 17-20R; 152; CANR 38,
41; CLR 21; DLB 161; JRDA; MAICYA;
SATA 1, 32, 76; SATA-Obit 90
Garland, (Hannibal) Hamlin 1860-1940
TCLC 3; SSC 18
See also CA 104; DLB 12, 71, 78, 186
Garneau, (Hector de) Saint-Denys 1912-1943
TCLC 13
See also CA 111; DLB 88
Garner, Alan 1934-**CLC 17; DAB; DAM POP**
See also AAYA 18; CA 73-76; CANR 15, 64;
CLR 20; DLB 161; MAICYA; MTCW 1;
SATA 18, 69
Garner, Hugh 1913-1979   **CLC 13**
See also CA 69-72; CANR 31; DLB 68
Garnett, David 1892-1981   **CLC 3**
See also CA 5-8R; 103; CANR 17; DLB 34
Garos, Stephanie
See Katz, Steve
Garrett, George (Palmer) 1929-**CLC 3, 11, 51;
SSC 30**
See also CA 1-4R; CAAS 5; CANR 1, 42, 67;
DLB 2, 5, 130, 152; DLBY 83
Garrick, David 1717-1779   **LC 15; DAM
DRAM**
See also DLB 84
Garrigue, Jean 1914-1972   **CLC 2, 8**
See also CA 5-8R; 37-40R; CANR 20
Garrison, Frederick
See Sinclair, Upton (Beall)
Garth, Will
See Hamilton, Edmond; Kuttner, Henry
Garvey, Marcus (Moziah, Jr.) 1887-1940
TCLC 41; BLC 2; DAM MULT
See also BW 1; CA 120; 124
Gary, Romain   **CLC 25**
See also Kacew, Romain
See also DLB 83
Gascar, Pierre   **CLC 11**
See also Fournier, Pierre
Gascoyne, David (Emery) 1916-   **CLC 45**
See also CA 65-68; CANR 10, 28, 54; DLB 20;
MTCW 1
Gaskell, Elizabeth Cleghorn 1810-1865**NCLC
70; DAB; DAM MST; SSC 25**
See also CDBLB 1832-1890; DLB 21, 144, 159
Gass, William H(oward) 1924-**CLC 1, 2, 8, 11,
15, 39; SSC 12**
See also CA 17-20R; CANR 30, 71; DLB 2;
MTCW 1
Gasset, Jose Ortega y
See Ortega y Gasset, Jose
Gates, Henry Louis, Jr. 1950-**CLC 65; BLCS;**

DAM MULT
See also BW 2; CA 109; CANR 25, 53; DLB
67
Gautier, Theophile 1811-1872   **NCLC 1, 59;
DAM POET; PC 18; SSC 20**
See also DLB 119
Gawsworth, John
See Bates, H(erbert) E(rnest)
Gay, Oliver
See Gogarty, Oliver St. John
Gaye, Marvin (Penze) 1939-1984   **CLC 26**
See also CA 112
Gebler, Carlo (Ernest) 1954-   **CLC 39**
See also CA 119; 133
Gee, Maggie (Mary) 1948-   **CLC 57**
See also CA 130
Gee, Maurice (Gough) 1931-   **CLC 29**
See also CA 97-100; CANR 67; SATA 46, 101
Gelbart, Larry (Simon) 1923-   **CLC 21, 61**
See also CA 73-76; CANR 45
Gelber, Jack 1932-   **CLC 1, 6, 14, 79**
See also CA 1-4R; CANR 2; DLB 7
Gellhorn, Martha (Ellis) 1908-1998 **CLC 14,
60**
See also CA 77-80; 164; CANR 44; DLBY 82
Genet, Jean 1910-1986**CLC 1, 2, 5, 10, 14, 44,
46; DAM DRAM**
See also CA 13-16R; CANR 18; DLB 72;
DLBY 86; MTCW 1
Gent, Peter 1942-   **CLC 29**
See also AITN 1; CA 89-92; DLBY 82
Gentlewoman in New England, A
See Bradstreet, Anne
Gentlewoman in Those Parts, A
See Bradstreet, Anne
George, Jean Craighead 1919-   **CLC 35**
See also AAYA 8; CA 5-8R; CANR 25; CLR 1;
DLB 52; JRDA; MAICYA; SATA 2, 68
George, Stefan (Anton) 1868-1933**TCLC 2, 14**
See also CA 104
Georges, Georges Martin
See Simenon, Georges (Jacques Christian)
Gerhardi, William Alexander
See Gerhardie, William Alexander
Gerhardie, William Alexander 1895-1977
CLC 5
See also CA 25-28R; 73-76; CANR 18; DLB
36
Gerstler, Amy 1956-   **CLC 70**
See also CA 146
Gertler, T.   **CLC 34**
See also CA 116; 121; INT 121
Ghalib   **NCLC 39**
See also Ghalib, Hsadullah Khan
Ghalib, Hsadullah Khan 1797-1869
See Ghalib
See also DAM POET
Ghelderode, Michel de 1898-1962**CLC 6, 11;
DAM DRAM**
See also CA 85-88; CANR 40
Ghiselin, Brewster 1903-   **CLC 23**
See also CA 13-16R; CAAS 10; CANR 13
Ghose, Aurabinda 1872-1950   **TCLC 63**
See also CA 163
Ghose, Zulfikar 1935-   **CLC 42**
See also CA 65-68; CANR 67
Ghosh, Amitav 1956-   **CLC 44**
See also CA 147
Giacosa, Giuseppe 1847-1906   **TCLC 7**
See also CA 104
Gibb, Lee
See Waterhouse, Keith (Spencer)
Gibbon, Lewis Grassic   **TCLC 4**

See also Mitchell, James Leslie

Gibbons, Kaye 1960- **CLC 50, 88; DAM POP**
See also CA 151

Gibran, Kahlil 1883-1931 **TCLC 1, 9; DAM POET, POP; PC 9**
See also CA 104; 150

Gibran, Khalil
See Gibran, Kahlil

Gibson, William 1914- **CLC 23; DA; DAB; DAC; DAM DRAM, MST**
See also CA 9-12R; CANR 9, 42; DLB 7; SATA 66

Gibson, William (Ford) 1948- **CLC 39, 63; DAM POP**
See also AAYA 12; CA 126; 133; CANR 52

Gide, Andre (Paul Guillaume) 1869-1951 **TCLC 5, 12, 36; DA; DAB; DAC; DAM MST, NOV; SSC 13; WLC**
See also CA 104; 124; DLB 65; MTCW 1

Gifford, Barry (Colby) 1946- **CLC 34**
See also CA 65-68; CANR 9, 30, 40

Gilbert, Frank
See De Voto, Bernard (Augustine)

Gilbert, W(illiam) S(chwenck) 1836-1911 **TCLC 3; DAM DRAM, POET**
See also CA 104; SATA 36

Gilbreth, Frank B., Jr. 1911- **CLC 17**
See also CA 9-12R; SATA 2

Gilchrist, Ellen 1935- **CLC 34, 48; DAM POP; SSC 14**
See also CA 113; 116; CANR 41, 61; DLB 130; MTCW 1

Giles, Molly 1942- **CLC 39**
See also CA 126

Gill, Eric 1882-1940 **TCLC 85**

Gill, Patrick
See Creasey, John

Gilliam, Terry (Vance) 1940- **CLC 21**
See also Monty Python
See also AAYA 19; CA 108; 113; CANR 35; INT 113

Gillian, Jerry
See Gilliam, Terry (Vance)

Gilliatt, Penelope (Ann Douglass) 1932-1993 **CLC 2, 10, 13, 53**
See also AITN 2; CA 13-16R; 141; CANR 49; DLB 14

Gilman, Charlotte (Anna) Perkins (Stetson) 1860-1935 **TCLC 9, 37; SSC 13**
See also CA 106; 150

Gilmour, David 1949- **CLC 35**
See also CA 138, 147

Gilpin, William 1724-1804 **NCLC 30**

Gilray, J. D.
See Mencken, H(enry) L(ouis)

Gilroy, Frank D(aniel) 1925- **CLC 2**
See also CA 81-84; CANR 32, 64; DLB 7

Gilstrap, John 1957(?)- **CLC 99**
See also CA 160

Ginsberg, Allen 1926-1997 **CLC 1, 2, 3, 4, 6, 13, 36, 69, 109; DA; DAB; DAC; DAM MST, POET; PC 4; WLC 3**
See also AITN 1; CA 1-4R; 157; CANR 2, 41, 63; CDALB 1941-1968; DLB 5, 16, 169; MTCW 1

Ginzburg, Natalia 1916-1991 **CLC 5, 11, 54, 70**
See also CA 85-88; 135; CANR 33; DLB 177; MTCW 1

Giono, Jean 1895-1970 **CLC 4, 11**
See also CA 45-48; 29-32R; CANR 2, 35; DLB 72; MTCW 1

Giovanni, Nikki 1943- **CLC 2, 4, 19, 64; BLC 2; DA; DAB; DAC; DAM MST, MULT, POET; PC 19; WLCS**
See also AAYA 22; AITN 1; BW 2; CA 29-32R; CAAS 6; CANR 18, 41, 60; CLR 6; DLB 5, 41; INT CANR-18; MAICYA; MTCW 1; SATA 24

Giovene, Andrea 1904- **CLC 7**
See also CA 85-88

Gippius, Zinaida (Nikolayevna) 1869-1945
See Hippius, Zinaida
See also CA 106

Giraudoux, (Hippolyte) Jean 1882-1944 **TCLC 2, 7; DAM DRAM**
See also CA 104; DLB 65

Gironella, Jose Maria 1917- **CLC 11**
See also CA 101

Gissing, George (Robert) 1857-1903 **TCLC 3, 24, 47**
See also CA 105; 167; DLB 18, 135, 184

Giurlani, Aldo
See Palazzeschi, Aldo

Gladkov, Fyodor (Vasilyevich) 1883-1958 **TCLC 27**

Glanville, Brian (Lester) 1931- **CLC 6**
See also CA 5-8R; CAAS 9; CANR 3, 70; DLB 15, 139; SATA 42

Glasgow, Ellen (Anderson Gholson) 1873-1945 **TCLC 2, 7**
See also CA 104; 164; DLB 9, 12

Glaspell, Susan 1882(?)-1948 **TCLC 55**
See also CA 110; 154; DLB 7, 9, 78; YABC 2

Glassco, John 1909-1981 **CLC 9**
See also CA 13-16R; 102; CANR 15; DLB 68

Glasscock, Amnesia
See Steinbeck, John (Ernst)

Glasser, Ronald J. 1940(?)- **CLC 37**

Glassman, Joyce
See Johnson, Joyce

Glendinning, Victoria 1937- **CLC 50**
See also CA 120; 127; CANR 59; DLB 155

Glissant, Edouard 1928- **CLC 10, 68; DAM MULT**
See also CA 153

Gloag, Julian 1930- **CLC 40**
See also AITN 1; CA 65-68; CANR 10, 70

Glowacki, Aleksander
See Prus, Boleslaw

Gluck, Louise (Elisabeth) 1943- **CLC 7, 22, 44, 81; DAM POET; PC 16**
See also CA 33-36R; CANR 40, 69; DLB 5

Glyn, Elinor 1864-1943 **TCLC 72**
See also DLB 153

Gobineau, Joseph Arthur (Comte) de 1816-1882 **NCLC 17**
See also DLB 123

Godard, Jean-Luc 1930- **CLC 20**
See also CA 93-96

Godden, (Margaret) Rumer 1907- **CLC 53**
See also AAYA 6; CA 5-8R; CANR 4, 27, 36, 55; CLR 20; DLB 161; MAICYA; SAAS 12; SATA 3, 36

Godoy Alcayaga, Lucila 1889-1957
See Mistral, Gabriela
See also BW 2; CA 104; 131; DAM MULT; HW; MTCW 1

Godwin, Gail (Kathleen) 1937- **CLC 5, 8, 22, 31, 69; DAM POP**
See also CA 29-32R; CANR 15, 43, 69; DLB 6; INT CANR-15; MTCW 1

Godwin, William 1756-1836 **NCLC 14**
See also CDBLB 1789-1832; DLB 39, 104, 142, 158, 163

Goebbels, Josef
See Goebbels, (Paul) Joseph

Goebbels, (Paul) Joseph 1897-1945 **TCLC 68**
See also CA 115; 148

Goebbels, Joseph Paul
See Goebbels, (Paul) Joseph

Goethe, Johann Wolfgang von 1749-1832 **NCLC 4, 22, 34; DA; DAB; DAC; DAM DRAM, MST, POET; PC 5; WLC 3**
See also DLB 94

Gogarty, Oliver St. John 1878-1957 **TCLC 15**
See also CA 109; 150; DLB 15, 19

Gogol, Nikolai (Vasilyevich) 1809-1852 **NCLC 5, 15, 31; DA; DAB; DAC; DAM DRAM, MST; DC 1; SSC 4, 29; WLC**
See also DLB 198

Goines, Donald 1937(?)-1974 **CLC 80; BLC 2; DAM MULT, POP**
See also AITN 1; BW 1; CA 124; 114; DLB 33

Gold, Herbert 1924- **CLC 4, 7, 14, 42**
See also CA 9-12R; CANR 17, 45; DLB 2; DLBY 81

Goldbarth, Albert 1948- **CLC 5, 38**
See also CA 53-56; CANR 6, 40; DLB 120

Goldberg, Anatol 1910-1982 **CLC 34**
See also CA 131; 117

Goldemberg, Isaac 1945- **CLC 52**
See also CA 69-72; CAAS 12; CANR 11, 32; HW

Golding, William (Gerald) 1911-1993 **CLC 1, 2, 3, 8, 10, 17, 27, 58, 81; DA; DAB; DAC; DAM MST, NOV; WLC**
See also AAYA 5; CA 5-8R; 141; CANR 13, 33, 54; CDBLB 1945-1960; DLB 15, 100; MTCW 1

Goldman, Emma 1869-1940 **TCLC 13**
See also CA 110; 150

Goldman, Francisco 1954- **CLC 76**
See also CA 162

Goldman, William (W.) 1931- **CLC 1, 48**
See also CA 9-12R; CANR 29, 69; DLB 44

Goldmann, Lucien 1913-1970 **CLC 24**
See also CA 25-28; CAP 2

Goldoni, Carlo 1707-1793 **LC 4; DAM DRAM**

Goldsberry, Steven 1949- **CLC 34**
See also CA 131

Goldsmith, Oliver 1728-1774 **LC 2; DA; DAB; DAC; DAM DRAM, MST, NOV, POET; DC 8; WLC**
See also CDBLB 1660-1789; DLB 39, 89, 104, 109, 142; SATA 26

Goldsmith, Peter
See Priestley, J(ohn) B(oynton)

Gombrowicz, Witold 1904-1969 **CLC 4, 7, 11, 49; DAM DRAM**
See also CA 19-20; 25-28R; CAP 2

Gomez de la Serna, Ramon 1888-1963 **CLC 9**
See also CA 153; 116; HW

Goncharov, Ivan Alexandrovich 1812-1891 **NCLC 1, 63**

Goncourt, Edmond (Louis Antoine Huot) de 1822-1896 **NCLC 7**
See also DLB 123

Goncourt, Jules (Alfred Huot) de 1830-1870 **NCLC 7**
See also DLB 123

Gontier, Fernande 19(?)- **CLC 50**

Gonzalez Martinez, Enrique 1871-1952 **TCLC 72**
See also CA 166; HW

Goodman, Paul 1911-1972 **CLC 1, 2, 4, 7**
See also CA 19-20; 37-40R; CANR 34; CAP 2; DLB 130; MTCW 1

Gordimer, Nadine 1923- **CLC 3, 5, 7, 10, 18, 33, 51, 70; DA; DAB; DAC; DAM MST, NOV;**

See also CA 104; 132; DLB 9; MTCW 1

Grieg, (Johan) Nordahl (Brun) 1902-1943
TCLC 10
See also CA 107

Grieve, C(hristopher) M(urray) 1892-1978
CLC 11, 19; DAM POET
See also MacDiarmid, Hugh; Pteleon
See also CA 5-8R; 85-88; CANR 33; MTCW 1

Griffin, Gerald 1803-1840   **NCLC 7**
See also DLB 159

Griffin, John Howard 1920-1980   **CLC 68**
See also AITN 1; CA 1-4R; 101; CANR 2

Griffin, Peter 1942-   **CLC 39**
See also CA 136

Griffith, D(avid Lewelyn) W(ark) 1875(?)-1948
TCLC 68
See also CA 119; 150

Griffith, Lawrence
See Griffith, D(avid Lewelyn) W(ark)

Griffiths, Trevor 1935-   **CLC 13, 52**
See also CA 97-100; CANR 45; DLB 13

Griggs, Sutton Elbert 1872-1930(?)**TCLC 77**
See also CA 123; DLB 50

Grigson, Geoffrey (Edward Harvey) 1905-1985
CLC 7, 39
See also CA 25-28R; 118; CANR 20, 33; DLB
27; MTCW 1

Grillparzer, Franz 1791-1872   **NCLC 1**
See also DLB 133

Grimble, Reverend Charles James
See Eliot, T(homas) S(tearns)

Grimke, Charlotte L(ottie) Forten 1837(?)-1914
See Forten, Charlotte L.
See also BW 1; CA 117; 124; DAM MULT,
POET

Grimm, Jacob Ludwig Karl 1785-1863**NCLC 3**
See also DLB 90; MAICYA; SATA 22

Grimm, Wilhelm Karl 1786-1859   **NCLC 3**
See also DLB 90; MAICYA; SATA 22

Grimmelshausen, Johann Jakob Christoffel von
1621-1676   **LC 6**
See also DLB 168

Grindel, Eugene 1895-1952
See Eluard, Paul
See also CA 104

Grisham, John 1955-   **CLC 84; DAM POP**
See also AAYA 14; CA 138; CANR 47, 69

Grossman, David 1954-   **CLC 67**
See also CA 138

Grossman, Vasily (Semenovich) 1905-1964
CLC 41
See also CA 124; 130; MTCW 1

Grove, Frederick Philip   **TCLC 4**
See also Greve, Felix Paul (Berthold Friedrich)
See also DLB 92

Grubb
See Crumb, R(obert)

Grumbach, Doris (Isaac) 1918-**CLC 13, 22, 64**
See also CA 5-8R; CAAS 2; CANR 9, 42, 70;
INT CANR-9

Grundtvig, Nicolai Frederik Severin 1783-1872
NCLC 1

Grunge
See Crumb, R(obert)

Grunwald, Lisa 1959-   **CLC 44**
See also CA 120

Guare, John 1938- **CLC 8, 14, 29, 67; DAM
DRAM**
See also CA 73-76; CANR 21, 69; DLB 7;
MTCW 1

Gudjonsson, Halldor Kiljan 1902-1998
See Laxness, Halldor

See also CA 103; 164

Guenter, Erich
See Eich, Guenter

Guest, Barbara 1920-   **CLC 34**
See also CA 25-28R; CANR 11, 44; DLB 5,
193

Guest, Judith (Ann) 1936- **CLC 8, 30; DAM
NOV, POP**
See also AAYA 7; CA 77-80; CANR 15; INT
CANR-15; MTCW 1

Guevara, Che   **CLC 87; HLC**
See also Guevara (Serna), Ernesto

Guevara (Serna), Ernesto 1928-1967
See Guevara, Che
See also CA 127; 111; CANR 56; DAM MULT;
HW

Guild, Nicholas M. 1944-   **CLC 33**
See also CA 93-96

Guillemin, Jacques
See Sartre, Jean-Paul

Guillen, Jorge 1893-1984   **CLC 11; DAM
MULT, POET**
See also CA 89-92; 112; DLB 108; HW

Guillen, Nicolas (Cristobal) 1902-1989 **C L C
48, 79; BLC 2; DAM MST, MULT, POET;
HLC; PC 23**
See also BW 2; CA 116; 125; 129; HW

Guillevic, (Eugene) 1907-   **CLC 33**
See also CA 93-96

Guillois
See Desnos, Robert

Guillois, Valentin
See Desnos, Robert

Guiney, Louise Imogen 1861-1920 **TCLC 41**
See also CA 160; DLB 54

Guiraldes, Ricardo (Guillermo) 1886-1927
TCLC 39
See also CA 131; HW; MTCW 1

Gumilev, Nikolai (Stepanovich) 1886-1921
TCLC 60
See also CA 165

Gunesekera, Romesh 1954-   **CLC 91**
See also CA 159

Gunn, Bill   **CLC 5**
See also Gunn, William Harrison
See also DLB 38

Gunn, Thom(son William) 1929-**CLC 3, 6, 18,
32, 81; DAM POET**
See also CA 17-20R; CANR 9, 33; CDBLB
1960 to Present; DLB 27; INT CANR-33;
MTCW 1

Gunn, William Harrison 1934(?)-1989
See Gunn, Bill
See also AITN 1; BW 1; CA 13-16R; 128;
CANR 12, 25

Gunnars, Kristjana 1948-   **CLC 69**
See also CA 113; DLB 60

Gurdjieff, G(eorgei) I(vanovich) 1877(?)-1949
TCLC 71
See also CA 157

Gurganus, Allan 1947- **CLC 70; DAM POP**
See also BEST 90:1; CA 135

Gurney, A(lbert) R(amsdell), Jr. 1930- **C L C
32, 50, 54; DAM DRAM**
See also CA 77-80; CANR 32, 64

Gurney, Ivor (Bertie) 1890-1937   **TCLC 33**
See also CA 167

Gurney, Peter
See Gurney, A(lbert) R(amsdell), Jr.

Guro, Elena 1877-1913   **TCLC 56**

Gustafson, James M(oody) 1925-   **CLC 100**
See also CA 25-28R; CANR 37

Gustafson, Ralph (Barker) 1909-   **CLC 36**

See also CA 21-24R; CANR 8, 45; DLB 88

Gut, Gom
See Simenon, Georges (Jacques Christian)

Guterson, David 1956-   **CLC 91**
See also CA 132

Guthrie, A(lfred) B(ertram), Jr. 1901-1991
CLC 23
See also CA 57-60; 134; CANR 24; DLB 6;
SATA 62; SATA-Obit 67

Guthrie, Isobel
See Grieve, C(hristopher) M(urray)

Guthrie, Woodrow Wilson 1912-1967
See Guthrie, Woody
See also CA 113; 93-96

Guthrie, Woody   **CLC 35**
See also Guthrie, Woodrow Wilson

Guy, Rosa (Cuthbert) 1928-   **CLC 26**
See also AAYA 4; BW 2; CA 17-20R; CANR
14, 34; CLR 13; DLB 33; JRDA; MAICYA;
SATA 14, 62

Gwendolyn
See Bennett, (Enoch) Arnold

H. D.   **CLC 3, 8, 14, 31, 34, 73; PC 5**
See also Doolittle, Hilda

H. de V.
See Buchan, John

Haavikko, Paavo Juhani 1931-   **CLC 18, 34**
See also CA 106

Habbema, Koos
See Heijermans, Herman

Habermas, Juergen 1929-   **CLC 104**
See also CA 109

Habermas, Jurgen
See Habermas, Juergen

Hacker, Marilyn 1942- **CLC 5, 9, 23, 72, 91;
DAM POET**
See also CA 77-80; CANR 68; DLB 120

Haeckel, Ernst Heinrich (Philipp August) 1834-
1919   **TCLC 83**
See also CA 157

Haggard, H(enry) Rider 1856-1925 **TCLC 11**
See also CA 108; 148; DLB 70, 156, 174, 178;
SATA 16

Hagiosy, L.
See Larbaud, Valery (Nicolas)

Hagiwara Sakutaro 1886-1942 **TCLC 60; PC
18**

Haig, Fenil
See Ford, Ford Madox

Haig-Brown, Roderick (Langmere) 1908-1976
CLC 21
See also CA 5-8R; 69-72; CANR 4, 38; CLR
31; DLB 88; MAICYA; SATA 12

Hailey, Arthur 1920-**CLC 5; DAM NOV, POP**
See also AITN 2; BEST 90:3; CA 1-4R; CANR
2, 36; DLB 88; DLBY 82; MTCW 1

Hailey, Elizabeth Forsythe 1938-   **CLC 40**
See also CA 93-96; CAAS 1; CANR 15, 48;
INT CANR-15

Haines, John (Meade) 1924-   **CLC 58**
See also CA 17-20R; CANR 13, 34; DLB 5

Hakluyt, Richard 1552-1616   **LC 31**

Haldeman, Joe (William) 1943-   **CLC 61**
See also CA 53-56; CAAS 25; CANR 6, 70,
72; DLB 8; INT CANR-6

Haley, Alex(ander Murray Palmer) 1921-1992
**CLC 8, 12, 76; BLC 2; DA; DAB; DAC;
DAM MST, MULT, POP**
See also AAYA 26; BW 2; CA 77-80; 136;
CANR 61; DLB 38; MTCW 1

Haliburton, Thomas Chandler 1796-1865
NCLC 15
See also DLB 11, 99

Hatteras, Owen   **TCLC 18**
See also Mencken, H(enry) L(ouis); Nathan, George Jean

Hauptmann, Gerhart (Johann Robert) 1862-1946   **TCLC 4; DAM DRAM**
See also CA 104; 153; DLB 66, 118

Havel, Vaclav 1936-   **CLC 25, 58, 65; DAM DRAM; DC 6**
See also CA 104; CANR 36, 63; MTCW 1

Haviaras, Stratis   **CLC 33**
See also Chaviaras, Strates

Hawes, Stephen 1475(?)-1523(?)   **LC 17**
See also DLB 132

Hawkes, John (Clendennin Burne, Jr.) 1925-1998   **CLC 1, 2, 3, 4, 7, 9, 14, 15, 27, 49**
See also CA 1-4R; 167; CANR 2, 47, 64; DLB 2, 7; DLBY 80; MTCW 1

Hawking, S. W.
See Hawking, Stephen W(illiam)

Hawking, Stephen W(illiam) 1942-   **CLC 63, 105**
See also AAYA 13; BEST 89:1; CA 126; 129; CANR 48

Hawkins, Anthony Hope
See Hope, Anthony

Hawthorne, Julian 1846-1934   **TCLC 25**
See also CA 165

Hawthorne, Nathaniel 1804-1864   **NCLC 39; DA; DAB; DAC; DAM MST, NOV; SSC 3, 29; WLC**
See also AAYA 18; CDALB 1640-1865; DLB 1, 74; YABC 2

Haxton, Josephine Ayres 1921-
See Douglas, Ellen
See also CA 115; CANR 41

Hayaseca y Eizaguirre, Jorge
See Echegaray (y Eizaguirre), Jose (Maria Waldo)

Hayashi, Fumiko 1904-1951   **TCLC 27**
See also CA 161; DLB 180

Haycraft, Anna
See Ellis, Alice Thomas
See also CA 122

Hayden, Robert E(arl) 1913-1980   **CLC 5, 9, 14, 37; BLC 2; DA; DAC; DAM MST, MULT, POET; PC 6**
See also BW 1; CA 69-72; 97-100; CABS 2; CANR 24; CDALB 1941-1968; DLB 5, 76; MTCW 1; SATA 19; SATA-Obit 26

Hayford, J(oseph) E(phraim) Casely
See Casely-Hayford, J(oseph) E(phraim)

Hayman, Ronald 1932-   **CLC 44**
See also CA 25-28R; CANR 18, 50; DLB 155

Haywood, Eliza 1693(?)-1756   **LC 44**
See also DLB 39

Haywood, Eliza (Fowler) 1693(?)-1756   **LC 1, 44**

Hazlitt, William 1778-1830   **NCLC 29**
See also DLB 110, 158

Hazzard, Shirley 1931-   **CLC 18**
See also CA 9-12R; CANR 4, 70; DLBY 82; MTCW 1

Head, Bessie 1937-1986   **CLC 25, 67; BLC 2; DAM MULT**
See also BW 2; CA 29-32R; 119; CANR 25; DLB 117; MTCW 1

Headon, (Nicky) Topper 1956(?)-   **CLC 30**

Heaney, Seamus (Justin) 1939-   **CLC 5, 7, 14, 25, 37, 74, 91; DAB; DAM POET; PC 18; WLCS**
See also CA 85-88; CANR 25, 48; CDBLB 1960 to Present; DLB 40; DLBY 95; MTCW 1

Hearn, (Patricio) Lafcadio (Tessima Carlos) 1850-1904   **TCLC 9**
See also CA 105; 166; DLB 12, 78

Hearne, Vicki 1946-   **CLC 56**
See also CA 139

Hearon, Shelby 1931-   **CLC 63**
See also AITN 2; CA 25-28R; CANR 18, 48

Heat-Moon, William Least   **CLC 29**
See also Trogdon, William (Lewis)
See also AAYA 9

Hebbel, Friedrich 1813-1863   **NCLC 43; DAM DRAM**
See also DLB 129

Hebert, Anne 1916-   **CLC 4, 13, 29; DAC; DAM MST, POET**
See also CA 85-88; CANR 69; DLB 68; MTCW 1

Hecht, Anthony (Evan) 1923-   **CLC 8, 13, 19; DAM POET**
See also CA 9-12R; CANR 6; DLB 5, 169

Hecht, Ben 1894-1964   **CLC 8**
See also CA 85-88; DLB 7, 9, 25, 26, 28, 86

Hedayat, Sadeq 1903-1951   **TCLC 21**
See also CA 120

Hegel, Georg Wilhelm Friedrich 1770-1831   **NCLC 46**
See also DLB 90

Heidegger, Martin 1889-1976   **CLC 24**
See also CA 81-84; 65-68; CANR 34; MTCW 1

Heidenstam, (Carl Gustaf) Verner von 1859-1940   **TCLC 5**
See also CA 104

Heifner, Jack 1946-   **CLC 11**
See also CA 105; CANR 47

Heijermans, Herman 1864-1924   **TCLC 24**
See also CA 123

Heilbrun, Carolyn G(old) 1926-   **CLC 25**
See also CA 45-48; CANR 1, 28, 58

Heine, Heinrich 1797-1856   **NCLC 4, 54**
See also DLB 90

Heinemann, Larry (Curtiss) 1944-   **CLC 50**
See also CA 110; CAAS 21; CANR 31; DLBD 9; INT CANR-31

Heiney, Donald (William) 1921-1993
See Harris, MacDonald
See also CA 1-4R; 142; CANR 3, 58

Heinlein, Robert A(nson) 1907-1988   **CLC 1, 3, 8, 14, 26, 55; DAM POP**
See also AAYA 17; CA 1-4R; 125; CANR 1, 20, 53; DLB 8; JRDA; MAICYA; MTCW 1; SATA 9, 69; SATA-Obit 56

Helforth, John
See Doolittle, Hilda

Hellenhofferu, Vojtech Kapristian z
See Hasek, Jaroslav (Matej Frantisek)

Heller, Joseph 1923-   **CLC 1, 3, 5, 8, 11, 36, 63; DA; DAB; DAC; DAM MST, NOV, POP; WLC**
See also AAYA 24; AITN 1; CA 5-8R; CABS 1; CANR 8, 42, 66; DLB 2, 28; DLBY 80; INT CANR-8; MTCW 1

Hellman, Lillian (Florence) 1906-1984   **CLC 2, 4, 8, 14, 18, 34, 44, 52; DAM DRAM; DC 1**
See also AITN 1, 2; CA 13-16R; 112; CANR 33; DLB 7; DLBY 84; MTCW 1

Helprin, Mark 1947-   **CLC 7, 10, 22, 32; DAM NOV, POP**
See also CA 81-84; CANR 47, 64; DLBY 85; MTCW 1

Helvetius, Claude-Adrien 1715-1771   **LC 26**

Helyar, Jane Penelope Josephine 1933-
See Poole, Josephine

See also CA 21-24R; CANR 10, 26; SATA 82

Hemans, Felicia 1793-1835   **NCLC 71**
See also DLB 96

Hemingway, Ernest (Miller) 1899-1961   **CLC 1, 3, 6, 8, 10, 13, 19, 30, 34, 39, 41, 44, 50, 61, 80; DA; DAB; DAC; DAM MST, NOV; SSC 1, 25; WLC**
See also AAYA 19; CA 77-80; CANR 34; CDALB 1917-1929; DLB 4, 9, 102; DLBD 1, 15, 16; DLBY 81, 87, 96; MTCW 1

Hempel, Amy 1951-   **CLC 39**
See also CA 118; 137; CANR 70

Henderson, F. C.
See Mencken, H(enry) L(ouis)

Henderson, Sylvia
See Ashton-Warner, Sylvia (Constance)

Henderson, Zenna (Chlarson) 1917-1983   **SSC 29**
See also CA 1-4R; 133; CANR 1; DLB 8; SATA 5

Henley, Beth   **CLC 23; DC 6**
See also Henley, Elizabeth Becker
See also CABS 3; DLBY 86

Henley, Elizabeth Becker 1952-
See Henley, Beth
See also CA 107; CANR 32; DAM DRAM, MST; MTCW 1

Henley, William Ernest 1849-1903   **TCLC 8**
See also CA 105; DLB 19

Hennissart, Martha
See Lathen, Emma
See also CA 85-88; CANR 64

Henry, O.   **TCLC 1, 19; SSC 5; WLC**
See also Porter, William Sydney

Henry, Patrick 1736-1799   **LC 25**

Henryson, Robert 1430(?)-1506(?)   **LC 20**
See also DLB 146

Henry VIII 1491-1547   **LC 10**

Henschke, Alfred
See Klabund

Hentoff, Nat(han Irving) 1925-   **CLC 26**
See also AAYA 4; CA 1-4R; CAAS 6; CANR 5, 25; CLR 1, 52; INT CANR-25; JRDA; MAICYA; SATA 42, 69; SATA-Brief 27

Heppenstall, (John) Rayner 1911-1981   **CLC 10**
See also CA 1-4R; 103; CANR 29

Heraclitus c. 540B.C.-c. 450B.C.   **CMLC 22**
See also DLB 176

Herbert, Frank (Patrick) 1920-1986   **CLC 12, 23, 35, 44, 85; DAM POP**
See also AAYA 21; CA 53-56; 118; CANR 5, 43; DLB 8; INT CANR-5; MTCW 1; SATA 9, 37; SATA-Obit 47

Herbert, George 1593-1633   **LC 24; DAB; DAM POET; PC 4**
See also CDBLB Before 1660; DLB 126

Herbert, Zbigniew 1924-   **CLC 9, 43; DAM POET**
See also CA 89-92; CANR 36; MTCW 1

Herbst, Josephine (Frey) 1897-1969   **CLC 34**
See also CA 5-8R; 25-28R; DLB 9

Hergesheimer, Joseph 1880-1954   **TCLC 11**
See also CA 109; DLB 102, 9

Herlihy, James Leo 1927-1993   **CLC 6**
See also CA 1-4R; 143; CANR 2

Hermogenes fl. c. 175-   **CMLC 6**

Hernandez, Jose 1834-1886   **NCLC 17**

Herodotus c. 484B.C.-429B.C.   **CMLC 17**
See also DLB 176

Herrick, Robert 1591-1674   **LC 13; DA; DAB; DAC; DAM MST, POP; PC 9**
See also DLB 126

See also CA 1-4R; CANR 1, 52; DLB 5; SATA
13

Hollander, Paul
See Silverberg, Robert
Holleran, Andrew 1943(?)-　　　　**CLC 38**
See also CA 144
Hollinghurst, Alan 1954-　　　　**CLC 55, 91**
See also CA 114
Hollis, Jim
See Summers, Hollis (Spurgeon, Jr.)
Holly, Buddy 1936-1959　　　　**TCLC 65**
Holmes, Gordon
See Shiel, M(atthew) P(hipps)
Holmes, John
See Souster, (Holmes) Raymond
Holmes, John Clellon 1926-1988　　　**CLC 56**
See also CA 9-12R; 125; CANR 4; DLB 16
Holmes, Oliver Wendell, Jr. 1841-1935 **TCLC
77**
See also CA 114
Holmes, Oliver Wendell 1809-1894 **NCLC 14**
See also CDALB 1640-1865; DLB 1, 189;
SATA 34
Holmes, Raymond
See Souster, (Holmes) Raymond
Holt, Victoria
See Hibbert, Eleanor Alice Burford
Holub, Miroslav 1923-　　　　　**CLC 4**
See also CA 21-24R; CANR 10
Homer c. 8th cent. B.C.-　　**CMLC 1, 16; DA;
DAB; DAC; DAM MST, POET; PC 23;
WLCS**
See also DLB 176
Hongo, Garrett Kaoru 1951-　　　**PC 23**
See also CA 133; CAAS 22; DLB 120
Honig, Edwin 1919-　　　　　**CLC 33**
See also CA 5-8R; CAAS 8; CANR 4, 45; DLB
5
Hood, Hugh (John Blagdon) 1928- **CLC 15, 28**
See also CA 49-52; CAAS 17; CANR 1, 33;
DLB 53
Hood, Thomas 1799-1845　　　　**NCLC 16**
See also DLB 96
Hooker, (Peter) Jeremy 1941-　　　**CLC 43**
See also CA 77-80; CANR 22; DLB 40
hooks, bell　　　　　　　**CLC 94; BLCS**
See also Watkins, Gloria
Hope, A(lec) D(erwent) 1907-　　**CLC 3, 51**
See also CA 21-24R; CANR 33; MTCW 1
Hope, Anthony 1863-1933　　　　**TCLC 83**
See also CA 157; DLB 153, 156
Hope, Brian
See Creasey, John
Hope, Christopher (David Tully) 1944- **CLC
52**
See also CA 106; CANR 47; SATA 62
Hopkins, Gerard Manley 1844-1889　**NCLC
17; DA; DAB; DAC; DAM MST, POET;
PC 15; WLC**
See also CDBLB 1890-1914; DLB 35, 57
Hopkins, John (Richard) 1931-　　　**CLC 4**
See also CA 85-88
Hopkins, Pauline Elizabeth 1859-1930 **TCLC
28; BLC 2; DAM MULT**
See also BW 2; CA 141; DLB 50
Hopkinson, Francis 1737-1791　　　**LC 25**
See also DLB 31
Hopley-Woolrich, Cornell George 1903-1968
See Woolrich, Cornell
See also CA 13-14; CANR 58; CAP 1
Horatio
See Proust, (Valentin-Louis-George-Eugene-)
Marcel

Horgan, Paul (George Vincent O'Shaughnessy)
1903-1995　　**CLC 9, 53; DAM NOV**
See also CA 13-16R; 147; CANR 9, 35; DLB
102; DLBY 85; INT CANR-9; MTCW 1;
SATA 13; SATA-Obit 84
Horn, Peter
See Kuttner, Henry
Hornem, Horace Esq.
See Byron, George Gordon (Noel)
**Horney, Karen (Clementine Theodore
Danielsen)** 1885-1952　　　**TCLC 71**
See also CA 114; 165
Hornung, E(rnest) W(illiam) 1866-1921
TCLC 59
See also CA 108; 160; DLB 70
Horovitz, Israel (Arthur) 1939- **CLC 56; DAM
DRAM**
See also CA 33-36R; CANR 46, 59; DLB 7
Horvath, Odon von
See Horvath, Oedoen von
See also DLB 85, 124
Horvath, Oedoen von 1901-1938　　**TCLC 45**
See also Horvath, Odon von
See also CA 118
Horwitz, Julius 1920-1986　　　　**CLC 14**
See also CA 9-12R; 119; CANR 12
Hospital, Janette Turner 1942-　　　**CLC 42**
See also CA 108; CANR 48
Hostos, E. M. de
See Hostos (y Bonilla), Eugenio Maria de
Hostos, Eugenio M. de
See Hostos (y Bonilla), Eugenio Maria de
Hostos, Eugenio Maria
See Hostos (y Bonilla), Eugenio Maria de
Hostos (y Bonilla), Eugenio Maria de 1839-1903
TCLC 24
See also CA 123; 131; HW
Houdini
See Lovecraft, H(oward) P(hillips)
Hougan, Carolyn 1943-　　　　　**CLC 34**
See also CA 139
Household, Geoffrey (Edward West) 1900-1988
CLC 11
See also CA 77-80; 126; CANR 58; DLB 87;
SATA 14; SATA-Obit 59
Housman, A(lfred) E(dward) 1859-1936
**TCLC 1, 10; DA; DAB; DAC; DAM MST,
POET; PC 2; WLCS**
See also CA 104; 125; DLB 19; MTCW 1
Housman, Laurence 1865-1959　　　**TCLC 7**
See also CA 106; 155; DLB 10; SATA 25
Howard, Elizabeth Jane 1923-　　　**CLC 7, 29**
See also CA 5-8R; CANR 8, 62
Howard, Maureen 1930-　　　**CLC 5, 14, 46**
See also CA 53-56; CANR 31; DLBY 83; INT
CANR-31; MTCW 1
Howard, Richard 1929-　　　**CLC 7, 10, 47**
See also AITN 1; CA 85-88; CANR 25; DLB 5;
INT CANR-25
Howard, Robert E(rvin) 1906-1936　**TCLC 8**
See also CA 105; 157
Howard, Warren F.
See Pohl, Frederik
Howe, Fanny (Quincy) 1940-　　　　**CLC 47**
See also CA 117; CAAS 27; CANR 70; SATA-
Brief 52
Howe, Irving 1920-1993　　　　　**CLC 85**
See also CA 9-12R; 141; CANR 21, 50; DLB
67; MTCW 1
Howe, Julia Ward 1819-1910　　　**TCLC 21**
See also CA 117; DLB 1, 189
Howe, Susan 1937-　　　　　　**CLC 72**
See also CA 160; DLB 120

Howe, Tina 1937-　　　　　　**CLC 48**
See also CA 109
Howell, James 1594(?)-1666　　　**LC 13**
See also DLB 151
Howells, W. D.
See Howells, William Dean
Howells, William D.
See Howells, William Dean
Howells, William Dean 1837-1920 **TCLC 7, 17,
41**
See also CA 104; 134; CDALB 1865-1917;
DLB 12, 64, 74, 79, 189
Howes, Barbara 1914-1996　　　　**CLC 15**
See also CA 9-12R; 151; CAAS 3; CANR 53;
SATA 5
Hrabal, Bohumil 1914-1997　　　**CLC 13, 67**
See also CA 106; 156; CAAS 12; CANR 57
Hroswitha of Gandersheim c. 935-c. 1002
CMLC 29
See also DLB 148
Hsun, Lu
See Lu Hsun
Hubbard, L(afayette) Ron(ald) 1911-1986
CLC 43; DAM POP
See also CA 77-80; 118; CANR 52
Huch, Ricarda (Octavia) 1864-1947 **TCLC 13**
See also CA 111; DLB 66
Huddle, David 1942-　　　　　**CLC 49**
See also CA 57-60; CAAS 20; DLB 130
Hudson, Jeffrey
See Crichton, (John) Michael
Hudson, W(illiam) H(enry) 1841-1922 **TCLC
29**
See also CA 115; DLB 98, 153, 174; SATA 35
Hueffer, Ford Madox
See Ford, Ford Madox
Hughart, Barry 1934-　　　　　**CLC 39**
See also CA 137
Hughes, Colin
See Creasey, John
Hughes, David (John) 1930-　　　**CLC 48**
See also CA 116; 129; DLB 14
Hughes, Edward James
See Hughes, Ted
See also DAM MST, POET
Hughes, (James) Langston 1902-1967 **CLC 1,
5, 10, 15, 35, 44, 108; BLC 2; DA; DAB;
DAC; DAM DRAM, MST, MULT, POET;
DC 3; PC 1; SSC 6; WLC**
See also AAYA 12; BW 1; CA 1-4R; 25-28R;
CANR 1, 34; CDALB 1929-1941; CLR 17;
DLB 4, 7, 48, 51, 86; JRDA; MAICYA;
MTCW 1; SATA 4, 33
Hughes, Richard (Arthur Warren) 1900-1976
CLC 1, 11; DAM NOV
See also CA 5-8R; 65-68; CANR 4; DLB 15,
161; MTCW 1; SATA 8; SATA-Obit 25
Hughes, Ted 1930- **CLC 2, 4, 9, 14, 37; DAB;
DAC; PC 7**
See also Hughes, Edward James
See also CA 1-4R; CANR 1, 33, 66; CLR 3;
DLB 40, 161; MAICYA; MTCW 1; SATA
49; SATA-Brief 27
Hugo, Richard F(ranklin) 1923-1982 **CLC 6,
18, 32; DAM POET**
See also CA 49-52; 108; CANR 3; DLB 5
Hugo, Victor (Marie) 1802-1885 **NCLC 3, 10,
21; DA; DAB; DAC; DAM DRAM, MST,
NOV, POET; PC 17; WLC**
See also DLB 119, 192; SATA 47
Huidobro, Vicente
See Huidobro Fernandez, Vicente Garcia
Huidobro Fernandez, Vicente Garcia 1893-

1948   **TCLC 31**
See also CA 131; HW
Hulme, Keri 1947-   **CLC 39**
See also CA 125; CANR 69; INT 125
Hulme, T(homas) E(rnest) 1883-1917 **TCLC 21**
See also CA 117; DLB 19
Hume, David 1711-1776   **LC 7**
See also DLB 104
Humphrey, William 1924-1997   **CLC 45**
See also CA 77-80; 160; CANR 68; DLB 6
Humphreys, Emyr Owen 1919-   **CLC 47**
See also CA 5-8R; CANR 3, 24; DLB 15
Humphreys, Josephine 1945-   **CLC 34, 57**
See also CA 121; 127; INT 127
Huneker, James Gibbons 1857-1921**TCLC 65**
See also DLB 71
Hungerford, Pixie
See Brinsmead, H(esba) F(ay)
Hunt, E(verette) Howard, (Jr.) 1918- **CLC 3**
See also AITN 1; CA 45-48; CANR 2, 47
Hunt, Kyle
See Creasey, John
Hunt, (James Henry) Leigh 1784-1859**NCLC 70; DAM POET**
See also DLB 96, 110, 144
Hunt, (James Henry) Leigh 1784-1859**NCLC 1; DAM POET**
Hunt, Marsha 1946-   **CLC 70**
See also BW 2; CA 143
Hunt, Violet 1866(?)-1942   **TCLC 53**
See also DLB 162, 197
Hunter, E. Waldo
See Sturgeon, Theodore (Hamilton)
Hunter, Evan 1926- **CLC 11, 31; DAM POP**
See also CA 5-8R; CANR 5, 38, 62; DLBY 82;
INT CANR-5; MTCW 1; SATA 25
Hunter, Kristin (Eggleston) 1931-   **CLC 35**
See also AITN 1; BW 1; CA 13-16R; CANR
13; CLR 3; DLB 33; INT CANR-13;
MAICYA; SAAS 10; SATA 12
Hunter, Mollie 1922-   **CLC 21**
See also McIlwraith, Maureen Mollie Hunter
See also AAYA 13; CANR 37; CLR 25; DLB
161; JRDA; MAICYA; SAAS 7; SATA 54
Hunter, Robert (?)-1734   **LC 7**
Hurston, Zora Neale 1903-1960**CLC 7, 30, 61;
BLC 2; DA; DAC; DAM MST, MULT,
NOV; SSC 4; WLCS**
See also AAYA 15; BW 1; CA 85-88; CANR
61; DLB 51, 86; MTCW 1
Huston, John (Marcellus) 1906-1987 **CLC 20**
See also CA 73-76; 123; CANR 34; DLB 26
Hustvedt, Siri 1955-   **CLC 76**
See also CA 137
Hutten, Ulrich von 1488-1523   **LC 16**
See also DLB 179
Huxley, Aldous (Leonard) 1894-1963 **CLC 1,
3, 4, 5, 8, 11, 18, 35, 79; DA; DAB; DAC;
DAM MST, NOV; WLC**
See also AAYA 11; CA 85-88; CANR 44;
CDBLB 1914-1945; DLB 36, 100, 162, 195;
MTCW 1; SATA 63
Huxley, T(homas) H(enry) 1825-1895 **NCLC 67**
See also DLB 57
Huysmans, Joris-Karl 1848-1907**TCLC 7, 69**
See also CA 104; 165; DLB 123
Hwang, David Henry 1957- **CLC 55; DAM
DRAM; DC 4**
See also CA 127; 132; INT 132
Hyde, Anthony 1946-   **CLC 42**
See also CA 136

Hyde, Margaret O(ldroyd) 1917-   **CLC 21**
See also CA 1-4R; CANR 1, 36; CLR 23; JRDA;
MAICYA; SAAS 8; SATA 1, 42, 76
Hynes, James 1956(?)-   **CLC 65**
See also CA 164
Ian, Janis 1951-   **CLC 21**
See also CA 105
Ibanez, Vicente Blasco
See Blasco Ibanez, Vicente
Ibarguengoitia, Jorge 1928-1983   **CLC 37**
See also CA 124; 113; HW
Ibsen, Henrik (Johan) 1828-1906 **TCLC 2, 8,
16, 37, 52; DA; DAB; DAC; DAM DRAM,
MST; DC 2; WLC**
See also CA 104; 141
Ibuse, Masuji 1898-1993   **CLC 22**
See also CA 127; 141; DLB 180
Ichikawa, Kon 1915-   **CLC 20**
See also CA 121
Idle, Eric 1943-   **CLC 21**
See also Monty Python
See also CA 116; CANR 35
Ignatow, David 1914-1997   **CLC 4, 7, 14, 40**
See also CA 9-12R; 162; CAAS 3; CANR 31,
57; DLB 5
Ihimaera, Witi 1944-   **CLC 46**
See also CA 77-80
Ilf, Ilya   **TCLC 21**
See also Fainzilberg, Ilya Arnoldovich
Illyes, Gyula 1902-1983   **PC 16**
See also CA 114; 109
Immermann, Karl (Lebrecht) 1796-1840
NCLC 4, 49
See also DLB 133
Inchbald, Elizabeth 1753-1821   **NCLC 62**
See also DLB 39, 89
Inclan, Ramon (Maria) del Valle
See Valle-Inclan, Ramon (Maria) del
Infante, G(uillermo) Cabrera
See Cabrera Infante, G(uillermo)
Ingalls, Rachel (Holmes) 1940-   **CLC 42**
See also CA 123; 127
Ingamells, Reginald Charles
See Ingamells, Rex
Ingamells, Rex 1913-1955   **TCLC 35**
See also CA 167
Inge, William (Motter) 1913-1973 **CLC 1, 8,
19; DAM DRAM**
See also CA 9-12R; CDALB 1941-1968; DLB
7; MTCW 1
Ingelow, Jean 1820-1897   **NCLC 39**
See also DLB 35, 163; SATA 33
Ingram, Willis J.
See Harris, Mark
Innaurato, Albert (F.) 1948(?)-   **CLC 21, 60**
See also CA 115; 122; INT 122
Innes, Michael
See Stewart, J(ohn) I(nnes) M(ackintosh)
Innis, Harold Adams 1894-1952   **TCLC 77**
See also DLB 88
Ionesco, Eugene 1909-1994**CLC 1, 4, 6, 9, 11,
15, 41, 86; DA; DAB; DAC; DAM DRAM,
MST; WLC**
See also CA 9-12R; 144; CANR 55; MTCW 1;
SATA 7; SATA-Obit 79
Iqbal, Muhammad 1873-1938   **TCLC 28**
Ireland, Patrick
See O'Doherty, Brian
Iron, Ralph
See Schreiner, Olive (Emilie Albertina)
Irving, John (Winslow) 1942-**CLC 13, 23, 38,
112; DAM NOV, POP**
See also AAYA 8; BEST 89:3; CA 25-28R;

CANR 28; DLB 6; DLBY 82; MTCW 1
Irving, Washington 1783-1859 **NCLC 2, 19;
DA; DAB; DAM MST; SSC 2; WLC**
See also CDALB 1640-1865; DLB 3, 11, 30,
59, 73, 74, 186; YABC 2
Irwin, P. K.
See Page, P(atricia) K(athleen)
Isaacs, Jorge Ricardo 1837-1895   **NCLC 70**
Isaacs, Susan 1943-   **CLC 32; DAM POP**
See also BEST 89:1; CA 89-92; CANR 20, 41,
65; INT CANR-20; MTCW 1
Isherwood, Christopher (William Bradshaw)
1904-1986   **CLC 1, 9, 11, 14, 44; DAM
DRAM, NOV**
See also CA 13-16R; 117; CANR 35; DLB 15,
195; DLBY 86; MTCW 1
Ishiguro, Kazuo 1954- **CLC 27, 56, 59, 110;
DAM NOV**
See also BEST 90:2; CA 120; CANR 49; DLB
194; MTCW 1
Ishikawa, Hakuhin
See Ishikawa, Takuboku
Ishikawa, Takuboku 1886(?)-1912 **TCLC 15;
DAM POET; PC 10**
See also CA 113; 153
Iskander, Fazil 1929-   **CLC 47**
See also CA 102
Isler, Alan (David) 1934-   **CLC 91**
See also CA 156
Ivan IV 1530-1584   **LC 17**
Ivanov, Vyacheslav Ivanovich 1866-1949
TCLC 33
See also CA 122
Ivask, Ivar Vidrik 1927-1992   **CLC 14**
See also CA 37-40R; 139; CANR 24
Ives, Morgan
See Bradley, Marion Zimmer
J. R. S.
See Gogarty, Oliver St. John
Jabran, Kahlil
See Gibran, Kahlil
Jabran, Khalil
See Gibran, Kahlil
Jackson, Daniel
See Wingrove, David (John)
Jackson, Jesse 1908-1983   **CLC 12**
See also BW 1; CA 25-28R; 109; CANR 27;
CLR 28; MAICYA; SATA 2, 29; SATA-Obit
48
Jackson, Laura (Riding) 1901-1991
See Riding, Laura
See also CA 65-68; 135; CANR 28; DLB 48
Jackson, Sam
See Trumbo, Dalton
Jackson, Sara
See Wingrove, David (John)
Jackson, Shirley 1919-1965 **CLC 11, 60, 87;
DA; DAC; DAM MST; SSC 9; WLC**
See also AAYA 9; CA 1-4R; 25-28R; CANR 4,
52; CDALB 1941-1968; DLB 6; SATA 2
Jacob, (Cyprien-)Max 1876-1944   **TCLC 6**
See also CA 104
Jacobs, Harriet A(nn) 1813(?)-1897**NCLC 67**
Jacobs, Jim 1942-   **CLC 12**
See also CA 97-100; INT 97-100
Jacobs, W(illiam) W(ymark) 1863-1943
TCLC 22
See also CA 121; 167; DLB 135
Jacobsen, Jens Peter 1847-1885   **NCLC 34**
Jacobsen, Josephine 1908-   **CLC 48, 102**
See also CA 33-36R; CAAS 18; CANR 23, 48
Jacobson, Dan 1929-   **CLC 4, 14**
See also CA 1-4R; CANR 2, 25, 66; DLB 14;

MTCW 1

Jacqueline
See Carpentier (y Valmont), Alejo
Jagger, Mick 1944-   **CLC 17**
Jahiz, Al- c. 776-869   **CMLC 25**
Jahiz, al- c. 780-c. 869   **CMLC 25**
Jakes, John (William) 1932- **CLC 29; DAM NOV, POP**
See also BEST 89:4; CA 57-60; CANR 10, 43, 66; DLBY 83; INT CANR-10; MTCW 1; SATA 62
James, Andrew
See Kirkup, James
James, C(yril) L(ionel) R(obert) 1901-1989 **CLC 33; BLCS**
See also BW 2; CA 117; 125; 128; CANR 62; DLB 125; MTCW 1
James, Daniel (Lewis) 1911-1988
See Santiago, Danny
See also CA 125
James, Dynely
See Mayne, William (James Carter)
James, Henry Sr. 1811-1882   **NCLC 53**
James, Henry 1843-1916 **TCLC 2, 11, 24, 40, 47, 64; DA; DAB; DAC; DAM MST, NOV; SSC 8, 32; WLC**
See also CA 104; 132; CDALB 1865-1917; DLB 12, 71, 74, 189; DLBD 13; MTCW 1
James, M. R.
See James, Montague (Rhodes)
See also DLB 156
James, Montague (Rhodes) 1862-1936 **TCLC 6; SSC 16**
See also CA 104; DLB 201
James, P. D. 1920-   **CLC 18, 46**
See also White, Phyllis Dorothy James
See also BEST 90:2; CDBLB 1960 to Present; DLB 87; DLBD 17
James, Philip
See Moorcock, Michael (John)
James, William 1842-1910   **TCLC 15, 32**
See also CA 109
James I 1394-1437   **LC 20**
Jameson, Anna 1794-1860   **NCLC 43**
See also DLB 99, 166
Jami, Nur al-Din 'Abd al-Rahman 1414-1492 **LC 9**
Jammes, Francis 1868-1938   **TCLC 75**
Jandl, Ernst 1925-   **CLC 34**
Janowitz, Tama 1957-   **CLC 43; DAM POP**
See also CA 106; CANR 52
Japrisot, Sebastien 1931-   **CLC 90**
Jarrell, Randall 1914-1965 **CLC 1, 2, 6, 9, 13, 49; DAM POET**
See also CA 5-8R; 25-28R; CABS 2; CANR 6, 34; CDALB 1941-1968; CLR 6; DLB 48, 52; MAICYA; MTCW 1; SATA 7
Jarry, Alfred 1873-1907 **TCLC 2, 14; DAM DRAM; SSC 20**
See also CA 104; 153; DLB 192
Jarvis, E. K.
See Bloch, Robert (Albert); Ellison, Harlan (Jay); Silverberg, Robert
Jeake, Samuel, Jr.
See Aiken, Conrad (Potter)
Jean Paul 1763-1825   **NCLC 7**
Jefferies, (John) Richard 1848-1887 **NCLC 47**
See also DLB 98, 141; SATA 16
Jeffers, (John) Robinson 1887-1962 **CLC 2, 3, 11, 15, 54; DA; DAC; DAM MST, POET; PC 17; WLC**
See also CA 85-88; CANR 35; CDALB 1917-1929; DLB 45; MTCW 1

Jefferson, Janet
See Mencken, H(enry) L(ouis)
Jefferson, Thomas 1743-1826   **NCLC 11**
See also CDALB 1640-1865; DLB 31
Jeffrey, Francis 1773-1850   **NCLC 33**
See also DLB 107
Jelakowitch, Ivan
See Heijermans, Herman
Jellicoe, (Patricia) Ann 1927-   **CLC 27**
See also CA 85-88; DLB 13
Jen, Gish   **CLC 70**
See also Jen, Lillian
Jen, Lillian 1956(?)-
See Jen, Gish
See also CA 135
Jenkins, (John) Robin 1912-   **CLC 52**
See also CA 1-4R; CANR 1; DLB 14
Jennings, Elizabeth (Joan) 1926- **CLC 5, 14**
See also CA 61-64; CAAS 5; CANR 8, 39, 66; DLB 27; MTCW 1; SATA 66
Jennings, Waylon 1937-   **CLC 21**
Jensen, Johannes V. 1873-1950   **TCLC 41**
Jensen, Laura (Linnea) 1948-   **CLC 37**
See also CA 103
Jerome, Jerome K(lapka) 1859-1927 **TCLC 23**
See also CA 119; DLB 10, 34, 135
Jerome, Saint 346(?)-419(?)   **CMLC 30**
Jerrold, Douglas William 1803-1857 **NCLC 2**
See also DLB 158, 159
Jewett, (Theodora) Sarah Orne 1849-1909 **TCLC 1, 22; SSC 6**
See also CA 108; 127; CANR 71; DLB 12, 74; SATA 15
Jewsbury, Geraldine (Endsor) 1812-1880 **NCLC 22**
See also DLB 21
Jhabvala, Ruth Prawer 1927- **CLC 4, 8, 29, 94; DAB; DAM NOV**
See also CA 1-4R; CANR 2, 29, 51; DLB 139, 194; INT CANR-29; MTCW 1
Jibran, Kahlil
See Gibran, Kahlil
Jibran, Khalil
See Gibran, Kahlil
Jiles, Paulette 1943-   **CLC 13, 58**
See also CA 101; CANR 70
Jimenez (Mantecon), Juan Ramon 1881-1958 **TCLC 4; DAM MULT, POET; HLC; PC 7**
See also CA 104; 131; DLB 134; HW; MTCW 1
Jimenez, Ramon
See Jimenez (Mantecon), Juan Ramon
Jimenez Mantecon, Juan
See Jimenez (Mantecon), Juan Ramon
Jin, Ha 1956-   **CLC 109**
See also CA 152
Joel, Billy   **CLC 26**
See also Joel, William Martin
Joel, William Martin 1949-
See Joel, Billy
See also CA 108
John, Saint 7th cent. -   **CMLC 27**
John of the Cross, St. 1542-1591   **LC 18**
Johnson, B(ryan) S(tanley William) 1933-1973 **CLC 6, 9**
See also CA 9-12R; 53-56; CANR 9; DLB 14, 40
Johnson, Benj. F. of Boo
See Riley, James Whitcomb
Johnson, Benjamin F. of Boo
See Riley, James Whitcomb
Johnson, Charles (Richard) 1948- **CLC 7, 51,**

65; **BLC 2; DAM MULT**
See also BW 2; CA 116; CAAS 18; CANR 42, 66; DLB 33
Johnson, Denis 1949-   **CLC 52**
See also CA 117; 121; CANR 71; DLB 120
Johnson, Diane 1934-   **CLC 5, 13, 48**
See also CA 41-44R; CANR 17, 40, 62; DLBY 80; INT CANR-17; MTCW 1
Johnson, Eyvind (Olof Verner) 1900-1976 **CLC 14**
See also CA 73-76; 69-72; CANR 34
Johnson, J. R.
See James, C(yril) L(ionel) R(obert)
Johnson, James Weldon 1871-1938 **TCLC 3, 19; BLC 2; DAM MULT, POET; PC 24**
See also BW 1; CA 104; 125; CDALB 1917-1929; CLR 32; DLB 51; MTCW 1; SATA 31
Johnson, Joyce 1935-   **CLC 58**
See also CA 125; 129
Johnson, Lionel (Pigot) 1867-1902 **TCLC 19**
See also CA 117; DLB 19
Johnson, Mel
See Malzberg, Barry N(athaniel)
Johnson, Pamela Hansford 1912-1981 **CLC 1, 7, 27**
See also CA 1-4R; 104; CANR 2, 28; DLB 15; MTCW 1
Johnson, Robert 1911(?)-1938   **TCLC 69**
Johnson, Samuel 1709-1784 **LC 15; DA; DAB; DAC; DAM MST; WLC**
See also CDBLB 1660-1789; DLB 39, 95, 104, 142
Johnson, Uwe 1934-1984 **CLC 5, 10, 15, 40**
See also CA 1-4R; 112; CANR 1, 39; DLB 75; MTCW 1
Johnston, George (Benson) 1913-   **CLC 51**
See also CA 1-4R; CANR 5, 20; DLB 88
Johnston, Jennifer 1930-   **CLC 7**
See also CA 85-88; DLB 14
Jolley, (Monica) Elizabeth 1923- **CLC 46; SSC 19**
See also CA 127; CAAS 13; CANR 59
Jones, Arthur Llewellyn 1863-1947
See Machen, Arthur
See also CA 104
Jones, D(ouglas) G(ordon) 1929-   **CLC 10**
See also CA 29-32R; CANR 13; DLB 53
Jones, David (Michael) 1895-1974 **CLC 2, 4, 7, 13, 42**
See also CA 9-12R; 53-56; CANR 28; CDBLB 1945-1960; DLB 20, 100; MTCW 1
Jones, David Robert 1947-
See Bowie, David
See also CA 103
Jones, Diana Wynne 1934-   **CLC 26**
See also AAYA 12; CA 49-52; CANR 4, 26, 56; CLR 23; DLB 161; JRDA; MAICYA; SAAS 7; SATA 9, 70
Jones, Edward P. 1950-   **CLC 76**
See also BW 2; CA 142
Jones, Gayl 1949- **CLC 6, 9; BLC 2; DAM MULT**
See also BW 2; CA 77-80; CANR 27, 66; DLB 33; MTCW 1
Jones, James 1921-1977   **CLC 1, 3, 10, 39**
See also AITN 1, 2; CA 1-4R; 69-72; CANR 6; DLB 2, 143; DLBD 17; MTCW 1
Jones, John J.
See Lovecraft, H(oward) P(hillips)
Jones, LeRoi   **CLC 1, 2, 3, 5, 10, 14**
See also Baraka, Amiri
Jones, Louis B.   **CLC 65**
See also CA 141

Jones, Madison (Percy, Jr.) 1925-   **CLC 4**
  See also CA 13-16R; CAAS 11; CANR 7, 54;
  DLB 152

Jones, Mervyn 1922-   **CLC 10, 52**
  See also CA 45-48; CAAS 5; CANR 1; MTCW
  1

Jones, Mick 1956(?)-   **CLC 30**
Jones, Nettie (Pearl) 1941-   **CLC 34**
  See also BW 2; CA 137; CAAS 20

Jones, Preston 1936-1979   **CLC 10**
  See also CA 73-76; 89-92; DLB 7

Jones, Robert F(rancis) 1934-   **CLC 7**
  See also CA 49-52; CANR 2, 61

Jones, Rod 1953-   **CLC 50**
  See also CA 128

Jones, Terence Graham Parry 1942- **CLC 21**
  See also Jones, Terry; Monty Python
  See also CA 112; 116; CANR 35; INT 116

Jones, Terry
  See Jones, Terence Graham Parry
  See also SATA 67; SATA-Brief 51

Jones, Thom 1945(?)-   **CLC 81**
  See also CA 157

Jong, Erica 1942-   **CLC 4, 6, 8, 18, 83; DAM**
  NOV, POP
  See also AITN 1; BEST 90:2; CA 73-76; CANR
  26, 52; DLB 2, 5, 28, 152; INT CANR-26;
  MTCW 1

Jonson, Ben(jamin) 1572(?)-1637   **LC 6, 33;**
  DA; DAB; DAC; DAM DRAM, MST,
  POET; DC 4; PC 17; WLC
  See also CDBLB Before 1660; DLB 62, 121

Jordan, June 1936- **CLC 5, 11, 23, 114; BLCS;**
  DAM MULT, POET
  See also AAYA 2; BW 2; CA 33-36R; CANR
  25, 70; CLR 10; DLB 38; MAICYA; MTCW
  1; SATA 4

Jordan, Neil (Patrick) 1950-   **CLC 110**
  See also CA 124; 130; CANR 54; INT 130

Jordan, Pat(rick M.) 1941-   **CLC 37**
  See also CA 33-36R

Jorgensen, Ivar
  See Ellison, Harlan (Jay)

Jorgenson, Ivar
  See Silverberg, Robert

Josephus, Flavius c. 37-100   **CMLC 13**

Josipovici, Gabriel 1940-   **CLC 6, 43**
  See also CA 37-40R; CAAS 8; CANR 47; DLB
  14

Joubert, Joseph 1754-1824   **NCLC 9**

Jouve, Pierre Jean 1887-1976   **CLC 47**
  See also CA 65-68

Jovine, Francesco 1902-1950   **TCLC 79**

Joyce, James (Augustine Aloysius) 1882-1941
  TCLC 3, 8, 16, 35, 52; DA; DAB; DAC;
  DAM MST, NOV, POET; PC 22; SSC 3,
  26; WLC
  See also CA 104; 126; CDBLB 1914-1945;
  DLB 10, 19, 36, 162; MTCW 1

Jozsef, Attila 1905-1937   **TCLC 22**
  See also CA 116

Juana Ines de la Cruz 1651(?)-1695 **LC 5; PC**
  24

Judd, Cyril
  See Kornbluth, C(yril) M.; Pohl, Frederik

Julian of Norwich 1342(?)-1416(?)   **LC 6**
  See also DLB 146

Junger, Sebastian 1962-   **CLC 109**
  See also CA 165

Juniper, Alex
  See Hospital, Janette Turner

Junius
  See Luxemburg, Rosa

Just, Ward (Swift) 1935-   **CLC 4, 27**
  See also CA 25-28R; CANR 32; INT CANR-
  32

Justice, Donald (Rodney) 1925-   **CLC 6, 19,**
  102; DAM POET
  See also CA 5-8R; CANR 26, 54; DLBY 83;
  INT CANR-26

Juvenal   **CMLC 8**
  See also Juvenalis, Decimus Junius

Juvenalis, Decimus Junius 55(?)-c. 127(?)
  See Juvenal

Juvenis
  See Bourne, Randolph S(illiman)

Kacew, Romain 1914-1980
  See Gary, Romain
  See also CA 108; 102

Kadare, Ismail 1936-   **CLC 52**
  See also CA 161

Kadohata, Cynthia   **CLC 59**
  See also CA 140

Kafka, Franz 1883-1924 **TCLC 2, 6, 13, 29, 47,**
  53; DA; DAB; DAC; DAM MST, NOV;
  SSC 5, 29; WLC
  See also CA 105; 126; DLB 81; MTCW 1

Kahanovitsch, Pinkhes
  See Der Nister

Kahn, Roger 1927-   **CLC 30**
  See also CA 25-28R; CANR 44, 69; DLB 171;
  SATA 37

Kain, Saul
  See Sassoon, Siegfried (Lorraine)

Kaiser, Georg 1878-1945   **TCLC 9**
  See also CA 106; DLB 124

Kaletski, Alexander 1946-   **CLC 39**
  See also CA 118; 143

Kalidasa fl. c. 400-   **CMLC 9; PC 22**

Kallman, Chester (Simon) 1921-1975 **CLC 2**
  See also CA 45-48; 53-56; CANR 3

Kaminsky, Melvin 1926-
  See Brooks, Mel
  See also CA 65-68; CANR 16

Kaminsky, Stuart M(elvin) 1934-   **CLC 59**
  See also CA 73-76; CANR 29, 53

Kane, Francis
  See Robbins, Harold

Kane, Paul
  See Simon, Paul (Frederick)

Kane, Wilson
  See Bloch, Robert (Albert)

Kanin, Garson 1912-   **CLC 22**
  See also AITN 1; CA 5-8R; CANR 7; DLB 7

Kaniuk, Yoram 1930-   **CLC 19**
  See also CA 134

Kant, Immanuel 1724-1804   **NCLC 27, 67**
  See also DLB 94

Kantor, MacKinlay 1904-1977   **CLC 7**
  See also CA 61-64; 73-76; CANR 60, 63; DLB
  9, 102

Kaplan, David Michael 1946-   **CLC 50**

Kaplan, James 1951-   **CLC 59**
  See also CA 135

Karageorge, Michael
  See Anderson, Poul (William)

Karamzin, Nikolai Mikhailovich 1766-1826
  NCLC 3
  See also DLB 150

Karapanou, Margarita 1946-   **CLC 13**
  See also CA 101

Karinthy, Frigyes 1887-1938   **TCLC 47**

Karl, Frederick R(obert) 1927-   **CLC 34**
  See also CA 5-8R; CANR 3, 44

Kastel, Warren
  See Silverberg, Robert

Kataev, Evgeny Petrovich 1903-1942
  See Petrov, Evgeny
  See also CA 120

Kataphusin
  See Ruskin, John

Katz, Steve 1935-   **CLC 47**
  See also CA 25-28R; CAAS 14, 64; CANR 12;
  DLBY 83

Kauffman, Janet 1945-   **CLC 42**
  See also CA 117; CANR 43; DLBY 86

Kaufman, Bob (Garnell) 1925-1986 **CLC 49**
  See also BW 1; CA 41-44R; 118; CANR 22;
  DLB 16, 41

Kaufman, George S. 1889-1961 **CLC 38; DAM**
  DRAM
  See also CA 108; 93-96; DLB 7; INT 108

Kaufman, Sue   **CLC 3, 8**
  See also Barondess, Sue K(aufman)

Kavafis, Konstantinos Petrou 1863-1933
  See Cavafy, C(onstantine) P(eter)
  See also CA 104

Kavan, Anna 1901-1968   **CLC 5, 13, 82**
  See also CA 5-8R; CANR 6, 57; MTCW 1

Kavanagh, Dan
  See Barnes, Julian (Patrick)

Kavanagh, Patrick (Joseph) 1904-1967 **C L C**
  22
  See also CA 123; 25-28R; DLB 15, 20; MTCW
  1

Kawabata, Yasunari 1899-1972 **CLC 2, 5, 9,**
  18, 107; DAM MULT; SSC 17
  See also CA 93-96; 33-36R; DLB 180

Kaye, M(ary) M(argaret) 1909-   **CLC 28**
  See also CA 89-92; CANR 24, 60; MTCW 1;
  SATA 62

Kaye, Mollie
  See Kaye, M(ary) M(argaret)

Kaye-Smith, Sheila 1887-1956   **TCLC 20**
  See also CA 118; DLB 36

Kaymor, Patrice Maguilene
  See Senghor, Leopold Sedar

Kazan, Elia 1909-   **CLC 6, 16, 63**
  See also CA 21-24R; CANR 32

Kazantzakis, Nikos 1883(?)-1957 **TCLC 2, 5,**
  33
  See also CA 105; 132; MTCW 1

Kazin, Alfred 1915-   **CLC 34, 38**
  See also CA 1-4R; CAAS 7; CANR 1, 45; DLB
  67

Keane, Mary Nesta (Skrine) 1904-1996
  See Keane, Molly
  See also CA 108; 114; 151

Keane, Molly   **CLC 31**
  See also Keane, Mary Nesta (Skrine)
  See also INT 114

Keates, Jonathan 1946(?)-   **CLC 34**
  See also CA 163

Keaton, Buster 1895-1966   **CLC 20**

Keats, John 1795-1821 **NCLC 8; DA; DAB;**
  DAC; DAM MST, POET; PC 1; WLC
  See also CDBLB 1789-1832; DLB 96, 110

Keene, Donald 1922-   **CLC 34**
  See also CA 1-4R; CANR 5

Keillor, Garrison   **CLC 40**
  See also Keillor, Gary (Edward)
  See also AAYA 2; BEST 89:3; DLBY 87; SATA
  58

Keillor, Gary (Edward) 1942-
  See Keillor, Garrison
  See also CA 111; 117; CANR 36, 59; DAM
  POP; MTCW 1

Keith, Michael
  See Hubbard, L(afayette) Ron(ald)

Keller, Gottfried 1819-1890 **NCLC 2; SSC 26**
See also DLB 129

Keller, Nora Okja **CLC 109**

Kellerman, Jonathan 1949- **CLC 44; DAM POP**
See also BEST 90:1; CA 106; CANR 29, 51; INT CANR-29

Kelley, William Melvin 1937- **CLC 22**
See also BW 1; CA 77-80; CANR 27; DLB 33

Kellogg, Marjorie 1922- **CLC 2**
See also CA 81-84

Kellow, Kathleen
See Hibbert, Eleanor Alice Burford

Kelly, M(ilton) T(erry) 1947- **CLC 55**
See also CA 97-100; CAAS 22; CANR 19, 43

Kelman, James 1946- **CLC 58, 86**
See also CA 148; DLB 194

Kemal, Yashar 1923- **CLC 14, 29**
See also CA 89-92; CANR 44

Kemble, Fanny 1809-1893 **NCLC 18**
See also DLB 32

Kemelman, Harry 1908-1996 **CLC 2**
See also AITN 1; CA 9-12R; 155; CANR 6, 71; DLB 28

Kempe, Margery 1373(?)-1440(?) **LC 6**
See also DLB 146

Kempis, Thomas a 1380-1471 **LC 11**

Kendall, Henry 1839-1882 **NCLC 12**

Keneally, Thomas (Michael) 1935- **CLC 5, 8, 10, 14, 19, 27, 43; DAM NOV**
See also CA 85-88; CANR 10, 50; MTCW 1

Kennedy, Adrienne (Lita) 1931-**CLC 66; BLC 2; DAM MULT; DC 5**
See also BW 2; CA 103; CAAS 20; CABS 3; CANR 26, 53; DLB 38

Kennedy, John Pendleton 1795-1870**NCLC 2**
See also DLB 3

Kennedy, Joseph Charles 1929-
See Kennedy, X. J.
See also CA 1-4R; CANR 4, 30, 40; SATA 14, 86

Kennedy, William 1928- **CLC 6, 28, 34, 53; DAM NOV**
See also AAYA 1; CA 85-88; CANR 14, 31; DLB 143; DLBY 85; INT CANR-31; MTCW 1; SATA 57

Kennedy, X. J. **CLC 8, 42**
See also Kennedy, Joseph Charles
See also CAAS 9; CLR 27; DLB 5; SAAS 22

Kenny, Maurice (Francis) 1929- **CLC 87; DAM MULT**
See also CA 144; CAAS 22; DLB 175; NNAL

Kent, Kelvin
See Kuttner, Henry

Kenton, Maxwell
See Southern, Terry

Kenyon, Robert O.
See Kuttner, Henry

Kepler, Johannes 1571-1630 **LC 45**

Kerouac, Jack **CLC 1, 2, 3, 5, 14, 29, 61**
See also Kerouac, Jean-Louis Lebris de
See also AAYA 25; CDALB 1941-1968; DLB 2, 16; DLBD 3; DLBY 95

Kerouac, Jean-Louis Lebris de 1922-1969
See Kerouac, Jack
See also AITN 1; CA 5-8R; 25-28R; CANR 26, 54; DA; DAB; DAC; DAM MST, NOV, POET, POP; MTCW 1; WLC

Kerr, Jean 1923- **CLC 22**
See also CA 5-8R; CANR 7; INT CANR-7

Kerr, M. E. **CLC 12, 35**
See also Meaker, Marijane (Agnes)
See also AAYA 2, 23; CLR 29; SAAS 1

Kerr, Robert **CLC 55**

Kerrigan, (Thomas) Anthony 1918- **CLC 4, 6**
See also CA 49-52; CAAS 11; CANR 4

Kerry, Lois
See Duncan, Lois

Kesey, Ken (Elton) 1935- **CLC 1, 3, 6, 11, 46, 64; DA; DAB; DAC; DAM MST, NOV, POP; WLC**
See also AAYA 25; CA 1-4R; CANR 22, 38, 66; CDALB 1968-1988; DLB 2, 16; MTCW 1; SATA 66

Kesselring, Joseph (Otto) 1902-1967**CLC 45; DAM DRAM, MST**
See also CA 150

Kessler, Jascha (Frederick) 1929- **CLC 4**
See also CA 17-20R; CANR 8, 48

Kettelkamp, Larry (Dale) 1933- **CLC 12**
See also CA 29-32R; CANR 16; SAAS 3; SATA 2

Key, Ellen 1849-1926 **TCLC 65**

Keyber, Conny
See Fielding, Henry

Keyes, Daniel 1927-**CLC 80; DA; DAC; DAM MST, NOV**
See also AAYA 23; CA 17-20R; CANR 10, 26, 54; SATA 37

Keynes, John Maynard 1883-1946 **TCLC 64**
See also CA 114; 162, 163; DLBD 10

Khanshendel, Chiron
See Rose, Wendy

Khayyam, Omar 1048-1131 **CMLC 11; DAM POET; PC 8**

Kherdian, David 1931- **CLC 6, 9**
See also CA 21-24R; CAAS 2; CANR 39; CLR 24; JRDA; MAICYA; SATA 16, 74

Khlebnikov, Velimir **TCLC 20**
See also Khlebnikov, Viktor Vladimirovich

Khlebnikov, Viktor Vladimirovich 1885-1922
See Khlebnikov, Velimir
See also CA 117

Khodasevich, Vladislav (Felitsianovich) 1886-1939 **TCLC 15**
See also CA 115

Kielland, Alexander Lange 1849-1906 **TCLC 5**
See also CA 104

Kiely, Benedict 1919- **CLC 23, 43**
See also CA 1-4R; CANR 2; DLB 15

Kienzle, William X(avier) 1928- **CLC 25; DAM POP**
See also CA 93-96; CAAS 1; CANR 9, 31, 59; INT CANR-31; MTCW 1

Kierkegaard, Soren 1813-1855 **NCLC 34**

Killens, John Oliver 1916-1987 **CLC 10**
See also BW 2; CA 77-80; 123; CAAS 2; CANR 26; DLB 33

Killigrew, Anne 1660-1685 **LC 4**
See also DLB 131

Kim
See Simenon, Georges (Jacques Christian)

Kincaid, Jamaica 1949- **CLC 43, 68; BLC 2; DAM MULT, NOV**
See also AAYA 13; BW 2; CA 125; CANR 47, 59; DLB 157

King, Francis (Henry) 1923-**CLC 8, 53; DAM NOV**
See also CA 1-4R; CANR 1, 33; DLB 15, 139; MTCW 1

King, Kennedy
See Brown, George Douglas

King, Martin Luther, Jr. 1929-1968 **CLC 83; BLC 2; DA; DAB; DAC; DAM MST, MULT; WLCS**
See also BW 2; CA 25-28; CANR 27, 44; CAP 2; MTCW 1; SATA 14

King, Stephen (Edwin) 1947-**CLC 12, 26, 37, 61, 113; DAM NOV, POP; SSC 17**
See also AAYA 1, 17; BEST 90:1; CA 61-64; CANR 1, 30, 52; DLB 143; DLBY 80; JRDA; MTCW 1; SATA 9, 55

King, Steve
See King, Stephen (Edwin)

King, Thomas 1943- **CLC 89; DAC; DAM MULT**
See also CA 144; DLB 175; NNAL; SATA 96

Kingman, Lee **CLC 17**
See also Natti, (Mary) Lee
See also SAAS 3; SATA 1, 67

Kingsley, Charles 1819-1875 **NCLC 35**
See also DLB 21, 32, 163, 190; YABC 2

Kingsley, Sidney 1906-1995 **CLC 44**
See also CA 85-88; 147; DLB 7

Kingsolver, Barbara 1955-**CLC 55, 81; DAM POP**
See also AAYA 15; CA 129; 134; CANR 60; INT 134

Kingston, Maxine (Ting Ting) Hong 1940-**CLC 12, 19, 58; DAM MULT, NOV; WLCS**
See also AAYA 8; CA 69-72; CANR 13, 38; DLB 173; DLBY 80; INT CANR-13; MTCW 1; SATA 53

Kinnell, Galway 1927- **CLC 1, 2, 3, 5, 13, 29**
See also CA 9-12R; CANR 10, 34, 66; DLB 5; DLBY 87; INT CANR-34; MTCW 1

Kinsella, Thomas 1928- **CLC 4, 19**
See also CA 17-20R; CANR 15; DLB 27; MTCW 1

Kinsella, W(illiam) P(atrick) 1935- **CLC 27, 43; DAC; DAM NOV, POP**
See also AAYA 7; CA 97-100; CAAS 7; CANR 21, 35, 66; INT CANR-21; MTCW 1

Kipling, (Joseph) Rudyard 1865-1936 **TCLC 8, 17; DA; DAB; DAC; DAM MST, POET; PC 3; SSC 5; WLC**
See also CA 105; 120; CANR 33; CDBLB 1890-1914; CLR 39; DLB 19, 34, 141, 156; MAICYA; MTCW 1; SATA 100; YABC 2

Kirkup, James 1918- **CLC 1**
See also CA 1-4R; CAAS 4; CANR 2; DLB 27; SATA 12

Kirkwood, James 1930(?)-1989 **CLC 9**
See also AITN 2; CA 1-4R; 128; CANR 6, 40

Kirshner, Sidney
See Kingsley, Sidney

Kis, Danilo 1935-1989 **CLC 57**
See also CA 109; 118; 129; CANR 61; DLB 181; MTCW 1

Kivi, Aleksis 1834-1872 **NCLC 30**

Kizer, Carolyn (Ashley) 1925-**CLC 15, 39, 80; DAM POET**
See also CA 65-68; CAAS 5; CANR 24, 70; DLB 5, 169

Klabund 1890-1928 **TCLC 44**
See also CA 162; DLB 66

Klappert, Peter 1942- **CLC 57**
See also CA 33-36R; DLB 5

Klein, A(braham) M(oses) 1909-1972**CLC 19; DAB; DAC; DAM MST**
See also CA 101; 37-40R; DLB 68

Klein, Norma 1938-1989 **CLC 30**
See also AAYA 2; CA 41-44R; 128; CANR 15, 37; CLR 2, 19; INT CANR-15; JRDA; MAICYA; SAAS 1; SATA 7, 57

Klein, T(heodore) E(ibon) D(onald) 1947- **CLC 34**

See also CA 119; CANR 44

Kleist, Heinrich von 1777-1811 **NCLC 2, 37; DAM DRAM; SSC 22**
See also DLB 90

Klima, Ivan 1931-   **CLC 56; DAM NOV**
See also CA 25-28R; CANR 17, 50

Klimentov, Andrei Platonovich 1899-1951
See Platonov, Andrei
See also CA 108

Klinger, Friedrich Maximilian von 1752-1831 **NCLC 1**
See also DLB 94

Klingsor the Magician
See Hartmann, Sadakichi

Klopstock, Friedrich Gottlieb 1724-1803 **NCLC 11**
See also DLB 97

Knapp, Caroline 1959-   **CLC 99**
See also CA 154

Knebel, Fletcher 1911-1993   **CLC 14**
See also AITN 1; CA 1-4R; 140; CAAS 3; CANR 1, 36; SATA 36; SATA-Obit 75

Knickerbocker, Diedrich
See Irving, Washington

Knight, Etheridge 1931-1991 **CLC 40; BLC 2; DAM POET; PC 14**
See also BW 1; CA 21-24R; 133; CANR 23; DLB 41

Knight, Sarah Kemble 1666-1727   **LC 7**
See also DLB 24, 200

Knister, Raymond 1899-1932   **TCLC 56**
See also DLB 68

Knowles, John 1926- **CLC 1, 4, 10, 26; DA; DAC; DAM MST, NOV**
See also AAYA 10; CA 17-20R; CANR 40; CDALB 1968-1988; DLB 6; MTCW 1; SATA 8, 89

Knox, Calvin M.
See Silverberg, Robert

Knox, John c. 1505-1572   **LC 37**
See also DLB 132

Knye, Cassandra
See Disch, Thomas M(ichael)

Koch, C(hristopher) J(ohn) 1932-   **CLC 42**
See also CA 127

Koch, Christopher
See Koch, C(hristopher) J(ohn)

Koch, Kenneth 1925-   **CLC 5, 8, 44; DAM POET**
See also CA 1-4R; CANR 6, 36, 57; DLB 5; INT CANR-36; SATA 65

Kochanowski, Jan 1530-1584   **LC 10**

Kock, Charles Paul de 1794-1871 **NCLC 16**

Koda Shigeyuki 1867-1947
See Rohan, Koda
See also CA 121

Koestler, Arthur 1905-1983 **CLC 1, 3, 6, 8, 15, 33**
See also CA 1-4R; 109; CANR 1, 33; CDBLB 1945-1960; DLBY 83; MTCW 1

Kogawa, Joy Nozomi 1935-   **CLC 78; DAC; DAM MST, MULT**
See also CA 101; CANR 19, 62; SATA 99

Kohout, Pavel 1928-   **CLC 13**
See also CA 45-48; CANR 3

Koizumi, Yakumo
See Hearn, (Patricio) Lafcadio (Tessima Carlos)

Kolmar, Gertrud 1894-1943   **TCLC 40**
See also CA 167

Komunyakaa, Yusef 1947- **CLC 86, 94; BLCS**
See also CA 147; DLB 120

Konrad, George
See Konrad, Gyoergy

Konrad, Gyoergy 1933-   **CLC 4, 10, 73**
See also CA 85-88

Konwicki, Tadeusz 1926-   **CLC 8, 28, 54**
See also CA 101; CAAS 9; CANR 39, 59; MTCW 1

Koontz, Dean R(ay) 1945-   **CLC 78; DAM NOV, POP**
See also AAYA 9; BEST 89:3, 90:2; CA 108; CANR 19, 36, 52; MTCW 1; SATA 92

Kopernik, Mikolaj
See Copernicus, Nicolaus

Kopit, Arthur (Lee) 1937- **CLC 1, 18, 33; DAM DRAM**
See also AITN 1; CA 81-84; CABS 3; DLB 7; MTCW 1

Kops, Bernard 1926-   **CLC 4**
See also CA 5-8R; DLB 13

Kornbluth, C(yril) M. 1923-1958   **TCLC 8**
See also CA 105; 160; DLB 8

Korolenko, V. G.
See Korolenko, Vladimir Galaktionovich

Korolenko, Vladimir
See Korolenko, Vladimir Galaktionovich

Korolenko, Vladimir G.
See Korolenko, Vladimir Galaktionovich

Korolenko, Vladimir Galaktionovich 1853-1921   **TCLC 22**
See also CA 121

Korzybski, Alfred (Habdank Skarbek) 1879-1950   **TCLC 61**
See also CA 123; 160

Kosinski, Jerzy (Nikodem) 1933-1991 **CLC 1, 2, 3, 6, 10, 15, 53, 70; DAM NOV**
See also CA 17-20R; 134; CANR 9, 46; DLB 2; DLBY 82; MTCW 1

Kostelanetz, Richard (Cory) 1940-   **CLC 28**
See also CA 13-16R; CAAS 8; CANR 38

Kostrowitzki, Wilhelm Apollinaris de 1880-1918
See Apollinaire, Guillaume
See also CA 104

Kotlowitz, Robert 1924-   **CLC 4**
See also CA 33-36R; CANR 36

Kotzebue, August (Friedrich Ferdinand) von 1761-1819   **NCLC 25**
See also DLB 94

Kotzwinkle, William 1938-   **CLC 5, 14, 35**
See also CA 45-48; CANR 3, 44; CLR 6; DLB 173; MAICYA; SATA 24, 70

Kowna, Stancy
See Szymborska, Wislawa

Kozol, Jonathan 1936-   **CLC 17**
See also CA 61-64; CANR 16, 45

Kozoll, Michael 1940(?)-   **CLC 35**

Kramer, Kathryn 19(?)-   **CLC 34**

Kramer, Larry 1935- **CLC 42; DAM POP; DC 8**
See also CA 124; 126; CANR 60

Krasicki, Ignacy 1735-1801   **NCLC 8**

Krasinski, Zygmunt 1812-1859   **NCLC 4**

Kraus, Karl 1874-1936   **TCLC 5**
See also CA 104; DLB 118

Kreve (Mickevicius), Vincas 1882-1954 **TCLC 27**

Kristeva, Julia 1941-   **CLC 77**
See also CA 154

Kristofferson, Kris 1936-   **CLC 26**
See also CA 104

Krizanc, John 1956-   **CLC 57**

Krleza, Miroslav 1893-1981   **CLC 8, 114**
See also CA 97-100; 105; CANR 50; DLB 147

Kroetsch, Robert 1927- **CLC 5, 23, 57; DAC; DAM POET**

See also CA 17-20R; CANR 8, 38; DLB 53; MTCW 1

Kroetz, Franz
See Kroetz, Franz Xaver

Kroetz, Franz Xaver 1946-   **CLC 41**
See also CA 130

Kroker, Arthur (W.) 1945-   **CLC 77**
See also CA 161

Kropotkin, Peter (Aleksieevich) 1842-1921 **TCLC 36**
See also CA 119

Krotkov, Yuri 1917-   **CLC 19**
See also CA 102

Krumb
See Crumb, R(obert)

Krumgold, Joseph (Quincy) 1908-1980 **C L C 12**
See also CA 9-12R; 101; CANR 7; MAICYA; SATA 1, 48; SATA-Obit 23

Krumwitz
See Crumb, R(obert)

Krutch, Joseph Wood 1893-1970   **CLC 24**
See also CA 1-4R; 25-28R; CANR 4; DLB 63

Krutzch, Gus
See Eliot, T(homas) S(tearns)

Krylov, Ivan Andreevich 1768(?)-1844 **N C L C 1**
See also DLB 150

Kubin, Alfred (Leopold Isidor) 1877-1959 **TCLC 23**
See also CA 112; 149; DLB 81

Kubrick, Stanley 1928-   **CLC 16**
See also CA 81-84; CANR 33; DLB 26

Kumin, Maxine (Winokur) 1925- **CLC 5, 13, 28; DAM POET; PC 15**
See also AITN 2; CA 1-4R; CAAS 8; CANR 1, 21, 69; DLB 5; MTCW 1; SATA 12

Kundera, Milan 1929- **CLC 4, 9, 19, 32, 68; DAM NOV; SSC 24**
See also AAYA 2; CA 85-88; CANR 19, 52; MTCW 1

Kunene, Mazisi (Raymond) 1930-   **CLC 85**
See also BW 1; CA 125; DLB 117

Kunitz, Stanley (Jasspon) 1905- **CLC 6, 11, 14; PC 19**
See also CA 41-44R; CANR 26, 57; DLB 48; INT CANR-26; MTCW 1

Kunze, Reiner 1933-   **CLC 10**
See also CA 93-96; DLB 75

Kuprin, Aleksandr Ivanovich 1870-1938 **TCLC 5**
See also CA 104

Kureishi, Hanif 1954(?)-   **CLC 64**
See also CA 139; DLB 194

Kurosawa, Akira 1910- **CLC 16; DAM MULT**
See also AAYA 11; CA 101; CANR 46

Kushner, Tony 1957(?)- **CLC 81; DAM DRAM**
See also CA 144

Kuttner, Henry 1915-1958   **TCLC 10**
See also Vance, Jack
See also CA 107; 157; DLB 8

Kuzma, Greg 1944-   **CLC 7**
See also CA 33-36R; CANR 70

Kuzmin, Mikhail 1872(?)-1936   **TCLC 40**

Kyd, Thomas 1558-1594 **LC 22; DAM DRAM; DC 3**
See also DLB 62

Kyprianos, Iossif
See Samarakis, Antonis

La Bruyere, Jean de 1645-1696   **LC 17**

Lacan, Jacques (Marie Emile) 1901-1981 **CLC 75**
See also CA 121; 104

Laclos, Pierre Ambroise Francois Choderlos de
1741-1803   **NCLC 4**
Lacolere, Francois
See Aragon, Louis
La Colere, Francois
See Aragon, Louis
La Deshabilleuse
See Simenon, Georges (Jacques Christian)
Lady Gregory
See Gregory, Isabella Augusta (Persse)
Lady of Quality, A
See Bagnold, Enid
La Fayette, Marie (Madelaine Pioche de la
Vergne Comtes 1634-1693   LC 2
Lafayette, Rene
See Hubbard, L(afayette) Ron(ald)
Laforgue, Jules 1860-1887**NCLC 5, 53; PC 14;**
SSC 20
Lagerkvist, Paer (Fabian) 1891-1974 **CLC 7,**
10, 13, 54; DAM DRAM, NOV
See also Lagerkvist, Par
See also CA 85-88; 49-52; MTCW 1
Lagerkvist, Par   **SSC 12**
See also Lagerkvist, Paer (Fabian)
Lagerloef, Selma (Ottiliana Lovisa) 1858-1940
TCLC 4, 36
See also Lagerlof, Selma (Ottiliana Lovisa)
See also CA 108; SATA 15
Lagerlof, Selma (Ottiliana Lovisa)
See Lagerloef, Selma (Ottiliana Lovisa)
See also CLR 7; SATA 15
La Guma, (Justin) Alex(ander) 1925-1985
CLC 19; BLCS; DAM NOV
See also BW 1; CA 49-52; 118; CANR 25; DLB
117; MTCW 1
Laidlaw, A. K.
See Grieve, C(hristopher) M(urray)
Lainez, Manuel Mujica
See Mujica Lainez, Manuel
See also HW
Laing, R(onald) D(avid) 1927-1989 **CLC 95**
See also CA 107; 129; CANR 34; MTCW 1
Lamartine, Alphonse (Marie Louis Prat) de
1790-1869**NCLC 11; DAM POET; PC 16**
Lamb, Charles 1775-1834   **NCLC 10; DA;**
DAB; DAC; DAM MST; WLC
See also CDBLB 1789-1832; DLB 93, 107, 163;
SATA 17
Lamb, Lady Caroline 1785-1828   **NCLC 38**
See also DLB 116
Lamming, George (William) 1927- **CLC 2, 4,**
66; BLC 2; DAM MULT
See also BW 2; CA 85-88; CANR 26; DLB 125;
MTCW 1
L'Amour, Louis (Dearborn) 1908-1988 **C L C**
25, 55; DAM NOV, POP
See also AAYA 16; AITN 2; BEST 89:2; CA 1-
4R; 125; CANR 3, 25, 40; DLBY 80; MTCW
1
Lampedusa, Giuseppe (Tomasi) di 1896-1957
TCLC 13
See also Tomasi di Lampedusa, Giuseppe
See also CA 164; DLB 177
Lampman, Archibald 1861-1899   **NCLC 25**
See also DLB 92
Lancaster, Bruce 1896-1963   **CLC 36**
See also CA 9-10; CANR 70; CAP 1; SATA 9
Lanchester, John   **CLC 99**
Landau, Mark Alexandrovich
See Aldanov, Mark (Alexandrovich)
Landau-Aldanov, Mark Alexandrovich
See Aldanov, Mark (Alexandrovich)
Landis, Jerry

See Simon, Paul (Frederick)
Landis, John 1950-   **CLC 26**
See also CA 112; 122
Landolfi, Tommaso 1908-1979   **CLC 11, 49**
See also CA 127; 117; DLB 177
Landon, Letitia Elizabeth 1802-1838 **N C L C**
15
See also DLB 96
Landor, Walter Savage 1775-1864 **NCLC 14**
See also DLB 93, 107
Landwirth, Heinz 1927-
See Lind, Jakov
See also CA 9-12R; CANR 7
Lane, Patrick 1939-   **CLC 25; DAM POET**
See also CA 97-100; CANR 54; DLB 53; INT
97-100
Lang, Andrew 1844-1912   **TCLC 16**
See also CA 114; 137; DLB 98, 141, 184;
MAICYA; SATA 16
Lang, Fritz 1890-1976   **CLC 20, 103**
See also CA 77-80; 69-72; CANR 30
Lange, John
See Crichton, (John) Michael
Langer, Elinor 1939-   **CLC 34**
See also CA 121
Langland, William 1330(?)-1400(?)   **LC 19;**
DA; DAB; DAC; DAM MST, POET
See also DLB 146
Langstaff, Launcelot
See Irving, Washington
Lanier, Sidney 1842-1881   **NCLC 6; DAM**
POET
See also DLB 64; DLBD 13; MAICYA; SATA
18
Lanyer, Aemilia 1569-1645   **LC 10, 30**
See also DLB 121
Lao-Tzu
See Lao Tzu
Lao Tzu fl. 6th cent. B.C.-   **CMLC 7**
Lapine, James (Elliot) 1949-   **CLC 39**
See also CA 123; 130; CANR 54; INT 130
Larbaud, Valery (Nicolas) 1881-1957**TCLC 9**
See also CA 106; 152
Lardner, Ring
See Lardner, Ring(gold) W(ilmer)
Lardner, Ring W., Jr.
See Lardner, Ring(gold) W(ilmer)
Lardner, Ring(gold) W(ilmer) 1885-1933
TCLC 2, 14; SSC 32
See also CA 104; 131; CDALB 1917-1929;
DLB 11, 25, 86; DLBD 16; MTCW 1
Laredo, Betty
See Codrescu, Andrei
Larkin, Maia
See Wojciechowska, Maia (Teresa)
Larkin, Philip (Arthur) 1922-1985**CLC 3, 5, 8,**
9, 13, 18, 33, 39, 64; DAB; DAM MST,
POET; PC 21
See also CA 5-8R; 117; CANR 24, 62; CDBLB
1960 to Present; DLB 27; MTCW 1
Larra (y Sanchez de Castro), Mariano Jose de
1809-1837   **NCLC 17**
Larsen, Eric 1941-   **CLC 55**
See also CA 132
Larsen, Nella 1891-1964   **CLC 37; BLC 2;**
DAM MULT
See also BW 1; CA 125; DLB 51
Larson, Charles R(aymond) 1938-   **CLC 31**
See also CA 53-56; CANR 4
Larson, Jonathan 1961-1996   **CLC 99**
See also CA 156
Las Casas, Bartolome de 1474-1566   **LC 31**
Lasch, Christopher 1932-1994   **CLC 102**

See also CA 73-76; 144; CANR 25; MTCW 1
Lasker-Schueler, Else 1869-1945   **TCLC 57**
See also DLB 66, 124
Laski, Harold 1893-1950   **TCLC 79**
Latham, Jean Lee 1902-1995   **CLC 12**
See also AITN 1; CA 5-8R; CANR 7; CLR 50;
MAICYA; SATA 2, 68
Latham, Mavis
See Clark, Mavis Thorpe
Lathen, Emma   **CLC 2**
See also Hennissart, Martha; Latsis, Mary J(ane)
Lathrop, Francis
See Leiber, Fritz (Reuter, Jr.)
Latsis, Mary J(ane) 1927(?)-1997
See Lathen, Emma
See also CA 85-88; 162
Lattimore, Richmond (Alexander) 1906-1984
CLC 3
See also CA 1-4R; 112; CANR 1
Laughlin, James 1914-1997   **CLC 49**
See also CA 21-24R; 162; CAAS 22; CANR 9,
47; DLB 48; DLBY 96, 97
Laurence, (Jean) Margaret (Wemyss) 1926-
1987   **CLC 3, 6, 13, 50, 62; DAC; DAM**
MST; SSC 7
See also CA 5-8R; 121; CANR 33; DLB 53;
MTCW 1; SATA-Obit 50
Laurent, Antoine 1952-   **CLC 50**
Lauscher, Hermann
See Hesse, Hermann
Lautreamont, Comte de 1846-1870**NCLC 12;**
SSC 14
Laverty, Donald
See Blish, James (Benjamin)
Lavin, Mary 1912-1996**CLC 4, 18, 99; SSC 4**
See also CA 9-12R; 151; CANR 33; DLB 15;
MTCW 1
Lavond, Paul Dennis
See Kornbluth, C(yril) M.; Pohl, Frederik
Lawler, Raymond Evenor 1922-   **CLC 58**
See also CA 103
Lawrence, D(avid) H(erbert Richards) 1885-
1930**TCLC 2, 9, 16, 33, 48, 61; DA; DAB;**
DAC; DAM MST, NOV, POET; SSC 4, 19;
WLC
See also CA 104; 121; CDBLB 1914-1945;
DLB 10, 19, 36, 98, 162, 195; MTCW 1
Lawrence, T(homas) E(dward) 1888-1935
TCLC 18
See also Dale, Colin
See also CA 115; 167; DLB 195
Lawrence of Arabia
See Lawrence, T(homas) E(dward)
Lawson, Henry (Archibald Hertzberg) 1867-
1922   **TCLC 27; SSC 18**
See also CA 120
Lawton, Dennis
See Faust, Frederick (Schiller)
Laxness, Halldor   **CLC 25**
See also Gudjonsson, Halldor Kiljan
Layamon fl. c. 1200-   **CMLC 10**
See also DLB 146
Laye, Camara 1928-1980 **CLC 4, 38; BLC 2;**
DAM MULT
See also BW 1; CA 85-88; 97-100; CANR 25;
MTCW 1
Layton, Irving (Peter) 1912-**CLC 2, 15; DAC;**
DAM MST, POET
See also CA 1-4R; CANR 2, 33, 43, 66; DLB
88; MTCW 1
Lazarus, Emma 1849-1887   **NCLC 8**
Lazarus, Felix
See Cable, George Washington

TCLC 10; BLC 2; SSC 24
See also CA 107; 153
Machen, Arthur   **TCLC 4; SSC 20**
See also Jones, Arthur Llewellyn
See also DLB 36, 156, 178
Machiavelli, Niccolo 1469-1527**LC 8, 36; DA;
DAB; DAC; DAM MST; WLCS**
MacInnes, Colin 1914-1976   **CLC 4, 23**
See also CA 69-72; 65-68; CANR 21; DLB 14;
MTCW 1
MacInnes, Helen (Clark) 1907-1985 **CLC 27,
39; DAM POP**
See also CA 1-4R; 117; CANR 1, 28, 58; DLB
87; MTCW 1; SATA 22; SATA-Obit 44
Mackay, Mary 1855-1924
See Corelli, Marie
See also CA 118
Mackenzie, Compton (Edward Montague)
1883-1972   **CLC 18**
See also CA 21-22; 37-40R; CAP 2; DLB 34,
100
Mackenzie, Henry 1745-1831   **NCLC 41**
See also DLB 39
Mackintosh, Elizabeth 1896(?)-1952
See Tey, Josephine
See also CA 110
MacLaren, James
See Grieve, C(hristopher) M(urray)
Mac Laverty, Bernard 1942-   **CLC 31**
See also CA 116; 118; CANR 43; INT 118
MacLean, Alistair (Stuart) 1922(?)-1987**C L C
3, 13, 50, 63; DAM POP**
See also CA 57-60; 121; CANR 28, 61; MTCW
1; SATA 23; SATA-Obit 50
Maclean, Norman (Fitzroy) 1902-1990 **C L C
78; DAM POP; SSC 13**
See also CA 102; 132; CANR 49
MacLeish, Archibald 1892-1982**CLC 3, 8, 14,
68; DAM POET**
See also CA 9-12R; 106; CANR 33, 63; DLB
4, 7, 45; DLBY 82; MTCW 1
MacLennan, (John) Hugh 1907-1990 **CLC 2,
14, 92; DAC; DAM MST**
See also CA 5-8R; 142; CANR 33; DLB 68;
MTCW 1
MacLeod, Alistair 1936-**CLC 56; DAC; DAM
MST**
See also CA 123; DLB 60
Macleod, Fiona
See Sharp, William
MacNeice, (Frederick) Louis 1907-1963 **C L C
1, 4, 10, 53; DAB; DAM POET**
See also CA 85-88; CANR 61; DLB 10, 20;
MTCW 1
MacNeill, Dand
See Fraser, George MacDonald
Macpherson, James 1736-1796   **LC 29**
See also Ossian
See also DLB 109
Macpherson, (Jean) Jay 1931-   **CLC 14**
See also CA 5-8R; DLB 53
MacShane, Frank 1927-   **CLC 39**
See also CA 9-12R; CANR 3, 33; DLB 111
Macumber, Mari
See Sandoz, Mari(e Susette)
Madach, Imre 1823-1864   **NCLC 19**
Madden, (Jerry) David 1933-   **CLC 5, 15**
See also CA 1-4R; CAAS 3; CANR 4, 45; DLB
6; MTCW 1
Maddern, Al(an)
See Ellison, Harlan (Jay)
Madhubuti, Haki R. 1942-**CLC 6, 73; BLC 2;
DAM MULT, POET; PC 5**

See also Lee, Don L.
See also BW 2; CA 73-76; CANR 24, 51; DLB
5, 41; DLBD 8
Maepenn, Hugh
See Kuttner, Henry
Maepenn, K. H.
See Kuttner, Henry
Maeterlinck, Maurice 1862-1949   **TCLC 3;
DAM DRAM**
See also CA 104; 136; DLB 192; SATA 66
Maginn, William 1794-1842   **NCLC 8**
See also DLB 110, 159
Mahapatra, Jayanta 1928-   **CLC 33; DAM
MULT**
See also CA 73-76; CAAS 9; CANR 15, 33, 66
Mahfouz, Naguib (Abdel Aziz Al-Sabilgi)
1911(?)-
See Mahfuz, Najib
See also BEST 89:2; CA 128; CANR 55; DAM
NOV; MTCW 1
Mahfuz, Najib   **CLC 52, 55**
See also Mahfouz, Naguib (Abdel Aziz Al-
Sabilgi)
See also DLBY 88
Mahon, Derek 1941-   **CLC 27**
See also CA 113; 128; DLB 40
Mailer, Norman 1923-**CLC 1, 2, 3, 4, 5, 8, 11,
14, 28, 39, 74, 111; DA; DAB; DAC; DAM
MST, NOV, POP**
See also AITN 2; CA 9-12R; CABS 1; CANR
28; CDALB 1968-1988; DLB 2, 16, 28, 185;
DLBD 3; DLBY 80, 83; MTCW 1
Maillet, Antonine 1929-   **CLC 54; DAC**
See also CA 115; 120; CANR 46; DLB 60; INT
120
Mais, Roger 1905-1955   **TCLC 8**
See also BW 1; CA 105; 124; DLB 125; MTCW
1
Maistre, Joseph de 1753-1821   **NCLC 37**
Maitland, Frederic 1850-1906   **TCLC 65**
Maitland, Sara (Louise) 1950-   **CLC 49**
See also CA 69-72; CANR 13, 59
Major, Clarence 1936-**CLC 3, 19, 48; BLC 2;
DAM MULT**
See also BW 2; CA 21-24R; CAAS 6; CANR
13, 25, 53; DLB 33
Major, Kevin (Gerald) 1949-   **CLC 26; DAC**
See also AAYA 16; CA 97-100; CANR 21, 38;
CLR 11; DLB 60; INT CANR-21; JRDA;
MAICYA; SATA 32, 82
Maki, James
See Ozu, Yasujiro
Malabaila, Damiano
See Levi, Primo
Malamud, Bernard 1914-1986**CLC 1, 2, 3, 5,
8, 9, 11, 18, 27, 44, 78, 85; DA; DAB; DAC;
DAM MST, NOV, POP; SSC 15; WLC**
See also AAYA 16; CA 5-8R; 118; CABS 1;
CANR 28, 62; CDALB 1941-1968; DLB 2,
28, 152; DLBY 80, 86; MTCW 1
Malan, Herman
See Bosman, Herman Charles; Bosman, Herman
Charles
Malaparte, Curzio 1898-1957   **TCLC 52**
Malcolm, Dan
See Silverberg, Robert
Malcolm X   **CLC 82; BLC 2; WLCS**
See also Little, Malcolm
Malherbe, Francois de 1555-1628   **LC 5**
Mallarme, Stephane 1842-1898 **NCLC 4, 41;
DAM POET; PC 4**
Mallet-Joris, Francoise 1930-   **CLC 11**
See also CA 65-68; CANR 17; DLB 83

Malley, Ern
See McAuley, James Phillip
Mallowan, Agatha Christie
See Christie, Agatha (Mary Clarissa)
Maloff, Saul 1922-   **CLC 5**
See also CA 33-36R
Malone, Louis
See MacNeice, (Frederick) Louis
Malone, Michael (Christopher) 1942-**CLC 43**
See also CA 77-80; CANR 14, 32, 57
Malory, (Sir) Thomas 1410(?)-1471(?)**LC 11;
DA; DAB; DAC; DAM MST; WLCS**
See also CDBLB Before 1660; DLB 146; SATA
59; SATA-Brief 33
Malouf, (George Joseph) David 1934-**CLC 28,
86**
See also CA 124; CANR 50
Malraux, (Georges-)Andre 1901-1976**CLC 1,
4, 9, 13, 15, 57; DAM NOV**
See also CA 21-22; 69-72; CANR 34, 58; CAP
2; DLB 72; MTCW 1
Malzberg, Barry N(athaniel) 1939-   **CLC 7**
See also CA 61-64; CAAS 4; CANR 16; DLB 8
Mamet, David (Alan) 1947-**CLC 9, 15, 34, 46,
91; DAM DRAM; DC 4**
See also AAYA 3; CA 81-84; CABS 3; CANR
15, 41, 67, 72; DLB 7; MTCW 1
Mamoulian, Rouben (Zachary) 1897-1987
CLC 16
See also CA 25-28R; 124
Mandelstam, Osip (Emilievich) 1891(?)-1938(?)
TCLC 2, 6; PC 14
See also CA 104; 150
Mander, (Mary) Jane 1877-1949   **TCLC 31**
See also CA 162
Mandeville, John fl. 1350-   **CMLC 19**
See also DLB 146
Mandiargues, Andre Pieyre de   **CLC 41**
See also Pieyre de Mandiargues, Andre
See also DLB 83
Mandrake, Ethel Belle
See Thurman, Wallace (Henry)
Mangan, James Clarence 1803-1849**NCLC 27**
Maniere, J.-E.
See Giraudoux, (Hippolyte) Jean
Mankiewicz, Herman (Jacob) 1897-1953
TCLC 85
See also CA 120; DLB 26
Manley, (Mary) Delariviere 1672(?)-1724 **L C
1**
See also DLB 39, 80
Mann, Abel
See Creasey, John
Mann, Emily 1952-   **DC 7**
See also CA 130; CANR 55
Mann, (Luiz) Heinrich 1871-1950   **TCLC 9**
See also CA 106; 164; DLB 66
Mann, (Paul) Thomas 1875-1955 **TCLC 2, 8,
14, 21, 35, 44, 60; DA; DAB; DAC; DAM
MST, NOV; SSC 5; WLC**
See also CA 104; 128; DLB 66; MTCW 1
Mannheim, Karl 1893-1947   **TCLC 65**
Manning, David
See Faust, Frederick (Schiller)
Manning, Frederic 1887(?)-1935   **TCLC 25**
See also CA 124
Manning, Olivia 1915-1980   **CLC 5, 19**
See also CA 5-8R; 101; CANR 29; MTCW 1
Mano, D. Keith 1942-   **CLC 2, 10**
See also CA 25-28R; CAAS 6; CANR 26, 57;
DLB 6
Mansfield, KatherineTCLC 2, 8, 39; DAB; SSC
9, 23; WLC**

See also Beauchamp, Kathleen Mansfield
See also DLB 162
Manso, Peter 1940-   **CLC 39**
See also CA 29-32R; CANR 44
Mantecon, Juan Jimenez
See Jimenez (Mantecon), Juan Ramon
Manton, Peter
See Creasey, John
Man Without a Spleen, A
See Chekhov, Anton (Pavlovich)
Manzoni, Alessandro 1785-1873   **NCLC 29**
Mapu, Abraham (ben Jekutiel) 1808-1867
NCLC 18
Mara, Sally
See Queneau, Raymond
Marat, Jean Paul 1743-1793   **LC 10**
Marcel, Gabriel Honore 1889-1973   **CLC 15**
See also CA 102; 45-48; MTCW 1
Marchbanks, Samuel
See Davies, (William) Robertson
Marchi, Giacomo
See Bassani, Giorgio
Margulies, Donald   **CLC 76**
Marie de France c. 12th cent. -   **CMLC 8; PC
22**
Marie de l'Incarnation 1599-1672   **LC 10**
Marier, Captain Victor
See Griffith, D(avid Lewelyn) W(ark)
Mariner, Scott
See Pohl, Frederik
Marinetti, Filippo Tommaso 1876-1944**TCLC
10**
See also CA 107; DLB 114
Marivaux, Pierre Carlet de Chamblain de 1688-
1763   **LC 4; DC 7**
Markandaya, Kamala   **CLC 8, 38**
See also Taylor, Kamala (Purnaiya)
Markfield, Wallace 1926-   **CLC 8**
See also CA 69-72; CAAS 3; DLB 2, 28
Markham, Edwin 1852-1940   **TCLC 47**
See also CA 160; DLB 54, 186
Markham, Robert
See Amis, Kingsley (William)
Marks, J
See Highwater, Jamake (Mamake)
Marks-Highwater, J
See Highwater, Jamake (Mamake)
Markson, David M(errill) 1927-   **CLC 67**
See also CA 49-52; CANR 1
Marley, Bob   **CLC 17**
See also Marley, Robert Nesta
Marley, Robert Nesta 1945-1981
See Marley, Bob
See also CA 107; 103
Marlowe, Christopher 1564-1593**LC 22; DA;
DAB; DAC; DAM DRAM, MST; DC 1;
WLC**
See also CDBLB Before 1660; DLB 62
Marlowe, Stephen 1928-
See Queen, Ellery
See also CA 13-16R; CANR 6, 55
Marmontel, Jean-Francois 1723-1799   **LC 2**
Marquand, John P(hillips) 1893-1960**CLC 2,
10**
See also CA 85-88; DLB 9, 102
Marques, Rene 1919-1979   **CLC 96; DAM
MULT; HLC**
See also CA 97-100; 85-88; DLB 113; HW
Marquez, Gabriel (Jose) Garcia
See Garcia Marquez, Gabriel (Jose)
Marquis, Don(ald Robert Perry) 1878-1937
TCLC 7
See also CA 104; 166; DLB 11, 25

Marric, J. J.
See Creasey, John
Marryat, Frederick 1792-1848   **NCLC 3**
See also DLB 21, 163
Marsden, James
See Creasey, John
Marsh, (Edith) Ngaio 1899-1982 **CLC 7, 53;
DAM POP**
See also CA 9-12R; CANR 6, 58; DLB 77;
MTCW 1
Marshall, Garry 1934-   **CLC 17**
See also AAYA 3; CA 111; SATA 60
Marshall, Paule 1929- **CLC 27, 72; BLC 3;
DAM MULT; SSC 3**
See also BW 2; CA 77-80; CANR 25; DLB 157;
MTCW 1
Marshallik
See Zangwill, Israel
Marsten, Richard
See Hunter, Evan
Marston, John 1576-1634**LC 33; DAM DRAM**
See also DLB 58, 172
Martha, Henry
See Harris, Mark
Marti, Jose 1853-1895**NCLC 63; DAM MULT;
HLC**
Martial c. 40-c. 104   **PC 10**
Martin, Ken
See Hubbard, L(afayette) Ron(ald)
Martin, Richard
See Creasey, John
Martin, Steve 1945-   **CLC 30**
See also CA 97-100; CANR 30; MTCW 1
Martin, Valerie 1948-   **CLC 89**
See also BEST 90:2; CA 85-88; CANR 49
Martin, Violet Florence 1862-1915   **TCLC 51**
Martin, Webber
See Silverberg, Robert
Martindale, Patrick Victor
See White, Patrick (Victor Martindale)
Martin du Gard, Roger 1881-1958   **TCLC 24**
See also CA 118; DLB 65
Martineau, Harriet 1802-1876   **NCLC 26**
See also DLB 21, 55, 159, 163, 166, 190; YABC
2
Martines, Julia
See O'Faolain, Julia
Martinez, Enrique Gonzalez
See Gonzalez Martinez, Enrique
Martinez, Jacinto Benavente y
See Benavente (y Martinez), Jacinto
Martinez Ruiz, Jose 1873-1967
See Azorin; Ruiz, Jose Martinez
See also CA 93-96; HW
Martinez Sierra, Gregorio 1881-1947**TCLC 6**
See also CA 115
Martinez Sierra, Maria (de la O'LeJarraga)
1874-1974   **TCLC 6**
See also CA 115
Martinsen, Martin
See Follett, Ken(neth Martin)
Martinson, Harry (Edmund) 1904-1978 **C L C
14**
See also CA 77-80; CANR 34
Marut, Ret
See Traven, B.
Marut, Robert
See Traven, B.
Marvell, Andrew 1621-1678   **LC 4, 43; DA;
DAB; DAC; DAM MST, POET; PC 10;
WLC**
See also CDBLB 1660-1789; DLB 131
Marx, Karl (Heinrich) 1818-1883   **NCLC 17**

See also DLB 129
Masaoka Shiki   **TCLC 18**
See also Masaoka Tsunenori
Masaoka Tsunenori 1867-1902
See Masaoka Shiki
See also CA 117
Masefield, John (Edward) 1878-1967**CLC 11,
47; DAM POET**
See also CA 19-20; 25-28R; CANR 33; CAP 2;
CDBLB 1890-1914; DLB 10, 19, 153, 160;
MTCW 1; SATA 19
Maso, Carole 19(?)-   **CLC 44**
Mason, Bobbie Ann 1940-**CLC 28, 43, 82; SSC
4**
See also AAYA 5; CA 53-56; CANR 11, 31,
58; DLB 173; DLBY 87; INT CANR-31;
MTCW 1
Mason, Ernst
See Pohl, Frederik
Mason, Lee W.
See Malzberg, Barry N(athaniel)
Mason, Nick 1945-   **CLC 35**
Mason, Tally
See Derleth, August (William)
Mass, William
See Gibson, William
Master Lao
See Lao Tzu
Masters, Edgar Lee 1868-1950   **TCLC 2, 25;
DA; DAC; DAM MST, POET; PC 1;
WLCS**
See also CA 104; 133; CDALB 1865-1917;
DLB 54; MTCW 1
Masters, Hilary 1928-   **CLC 48**
See also CA 25-28R; CANR 13, 47
Mastrosimone, William 19(?)-   **CLC 36**
Mathe, Albert
See Camus, Albert
Mather, Cotton 1663-1728   **LC 38**
See also CDALB 1640-1865; DLB 24, 30, 140
Mather, Increase 1639-1723   **LC 38**
See also DLB 24
Matheson, Richard Burton 1926-   **CLC 37**
See also CA 97-100; DLB 8, 44; INT 97-100
Mathews, Harry 1930-   **CLC 6, 52**
See also CA 21-24R; CAAS 6; CANR 18, 40
Mathews, John Joseph 1894-1979   **CLC 84;
DAM MULT**
See also CA 19-20; 142; CANR 45; CAP 2;
DLB 175; NNAL
Mathias, Roland (Glyn) 1915-   **CLC 45**
See also CA 97-100; CANR 19, 41; DLB 27
Matsuo Basho 1644-1694   **PC 3**
See also DAM POET
Mattheson, Rodney
See Creasey, John
Matthews, Greg 1949-   **CLC 45**
See also CA 135
Matthews, William (Procter, III) 1942-1997
CLC 40
See also CA 29-32R; 162; CAAS 18; CANR
12, 57; DLB 5
Matthias, John (Edward) 1941-   **CLC 9**
See also CA 33-36R; CANR 56
Matthiessen, Peter 1927-**CLC 5, 7, 11, 32, 64;
DAM NOV**
See also AAYA 6; BEST 90:4; CA 9-12R;
CANR 21, 50; DLB 6, 173; MTCW 1; SATA
27
Maturin, Charles Robert 1780(?)-1824**NCLC
6**
See also DLB 178
Matute (Ausejo), Ana Maria 1925-   **CLC 11**

DAM DRAM
See also AITN 1; CA 53-56; CANR 5; DLB 7;
INT CANR-5

Medvedev, P. N.
See Bakhtin, Mikhail Mikhailovich

Meged, Aharon
See Megged, Aharon

Meged, Aron
See Megged, Aharon

Megged, Aharon 1920-   **CLC 9**
See also CA 49-52; CAAS 13; CANR 1

Mehta, Ved (Parkash) 1934-   **CLC 37**
See also CA 1-4R; CANR 2, 23, 69; MTCW 1

Melanter
See Blackmore, R(ichard) D(oddridge)

Melies, Georges 1861-1938   **TCLC 81**

Melikow, Loris
See Hofmannsthal, Hugo von

Melmoth, Sebastian
See Wilde, Oscar (Fingal O'Flahertie Wills)

Meltzer, Milton 1915-   **CLC 26**
See also AAYA 8; CA 13-16R; CANR 38; CLR
13; DLB 61; JRDA; MAICYA; SAAS 1;
SATA 1, 50, 80

Melville, Herman 1819-1891 **NCLC 3, 12, 29,
45, 49; DA; DAB; DAC; DAM MST, NOV;
SSC 1, 17; WLC**
See also AAYA 25; CDALB 1640-1865; DLB
3, 74; SATA 59

Menander c. 342B.C.-c. 292B.C.   **CMLC 9;
DAM DRAM; DC 3**
See also DLB 176

Mencken, H(enry) L(ouis) 1880-1956 **T C L C
13**
See also CA 105; 125; CDALB 1917-1929;
DLB 11, 29, 63, 137; MTCW 1

Mendelsohn, Jane 1965(?)-   **CLC 99**
See also CA 154

Mercer, David 1928-1980 **CLC 5; DAM DRAM**
See also CA 9-12R; 102; CANR 23; DLB 13;
MTCW 1

Merchant, Paul
See Ellison, Harlan (Jay)

Meredith, George 1828-1909   **TCLC 17, 43;
DAM POET**
See also CA 117; 153; CDBLB 1832-1890;
DLB 18, 35, 57, 159

Meredith, William (Morris) 1919- **CLC 4, 13,
22, 55; DAM POET**
See also CA 9-12R; CAAS 14; CANR 6, 40;
DLB 5

Merezhkovsky, Dmitry Sergeyevich 1865-1941
TCLC 29

Merimee, Prosper 1803-1870 **NCLC 6, 65; SSC
7**
See also DLB 119, 192

Merkin, Daphne 1954-   **CLC 44**
See also CA 123

Merlin, Arthur
See Blish, James (Benjamin)

Merrill, James (Ingram) 1926-1995 **CLC 2, 3,
6, 8, 13, 18, 34, 91; DAM POET**
See also CA 13-16R; 147; CANR 10, 49, 63;
DLB 5, 165; DLBY 85; INT CANR-10;
MTCW 1

Merriman, Alex
See Silverberg, Robert

Merriman, Brian 1747-1805   **NCLC 70**

Merritt, E. B.
See Waddington, Miriam

Merton, Thomas 1915-1968 **CLC 1, 3, 11, 34,
83; PC 10**
See also CA 5-8R; 25-28R; CANR 22, 53; DLB

48; DLBY 81; MTCW 1

Merwin, W(illiam) S(tanley) 1927- **CLC 1, 2,
3, 5, 8, 13, 18, 45, 88; DAM POET**
See also CA 13-16R; CANR 15, 51; DLB 5,
169; INT CANR-15; MTCW 1

Metcalf, John 1938-   **CLC 37**
See also CA 113; DLB 60

Metcalf, Suzanne
See Baum, L(yman) Frank

Mew, Charlotte (Mary) 1870-1928   **TCLC 8**
See also CA 105; DLB 19, 135

Mewshaw, Michael 1943-   **CLC 9**
See also CA 53-56; CANR 7, 47; DLBY 80

Meyer, June
See Jordan, June

Meyer, Lynn
See Slavitt, David R(ytman)

Meyer-Meyrink, Gustav 1868-1932
See Meyrink, Gustav
See also CA 117

Meyers, Jeffrey 1939-   **CLC 39**
See also CA 73-76; CANR 54; DLB 111

Meynell, Alice (Christina Gertrude Thompson)
1847-1922   **TCLC 6**
See also CA 104; DLB 19, 98

Meyrink, Gustav   **TCLC 21**
See also Meyer-Meyrink, Gustav
See also DLB 81

Michaels, Leonard 1933- **CLC 6, 25; SSC 16**
See also CA 61-64; CANR 21, 62; DLB 130;
MTCW 1

Michaux, Henri 1899-1984   **CLC 8, 19**
See also CA 85-88; 114

Micheaux, Oscar 1884-1951   **TCLC 76**
See also DLB 50

Michelangelo 1475-1564   **LC 12**

Michelet, Jules 1798-1874   **NCLC 31**

Michener, James A(lbert) 1907(?)-1997 **C L C
1, 5, 11, 29, 60, 109; DAM NOV, POP**
See also AAYA 27; AITN 1; BEST 90:1; CA 5-
8R; 161; CANR 21, 45, 68; DLB 6; MTCW
1

Mickiewicz, Adam 1798-1855   **NCLC 3**

Middleton, Christopher 1926-   **CLC 13**
See also CA 13-16R; CANR 29, 54; DLB 40

Middleton, Richard (Barham) 1882-1911
TCLC 56
See also DLB 156

Middleton, Stanley 1919-   **CLC 7, 38**
See also CA 25-28R; CAAS 23; CANR 21, 46;
DLB 14

Middleton, Thomas 1580-1627 **LC 33; DAM
DRAM, MST; DC 5**
See also DLB 58

Migueis, Jose Rodrigues 1901-   **CLC 10**

Mikszath, Kalman 1847-1910   **TCLC 31**

Miles, Jack   **CLC 100**

Miles, Josephine (Louise) 1911-1985 **CLC 1, 2,
14, 34, 39; DAM POET**
See also CA 1-4R; 116; CANR 2, 55; DLB 48

Militant
See Sandburg, Carl (August)

Mill, John Stuart 1806-1873   **NCLC 11, 58**
See also CDBLB 1832-1890; DLB 55, 190

Millar, Kenneth 1915-1983   **CLC 14; DAM
POP**
See also Macdonald, Ross
See also CA 9-12R; 110; CANR 16, 63; DLB
2; DLBD 6; DLBY 83; MTCW 1

Millay, E. Vincent
See Millay, Edna St. Vincent

Millay, Edna St. Vincent 1892-1950 **TCLC 4,
49; DA; DAB; DAC; DAM MST, POET;**

PC 6; WLCS
See also CA 104; 130; CDALB 1917-1929;
DLB 45; MTCW 1

Miller, Arthur 1915- **CLC 1, 2, 6, 10, 15, 26, 47,
78; DA; DAB; DAC; DAM DRAM, MST;
DC 1; WLC**
See also AAYA 15; AITN 1; CA 1-4R; CABS
3; CANR 2, 30, 54; CDALB 1941-1968;
DLB 7; MTCW 1

Miller, Henry (Valentine) 1891-1980 **CLC 1, 2,
4, 9, 14, 43, 84; DA; DAB; DAC; DAM
MST, NOV; WLC**
See also CA 9-12R; 97-100; CANR 33, 64;
CDALB 1929-1941; DLB 4, 9; DLBY 80;
MTCW 1

Miller, Jason 1939(?)-   **CLC 2**
See also AITN 1; CA 73-76; DLB 7

Miller, Sue 1943-   **CLC 44; DAM POP**
See also BEST 90:3; CA 139; CANR 59; DLB
143

Miller, Walter M(ichael, Jr.) 1923- **CLC 4, 30**
See also CA 85-88; DLB 8

Millett, Kate 1934-   **CLC 67**
See also AITN 1; CA 73-76; CANR 32, 53;
MTCW 1

Millhauser, Steven (Lewis) 1943- **CLC 21, 54,
109**
See also CA 110; 111; CANR 63; DLB 2; INT
111

Millin, Sarah Gertrude 1889-1968   **CLC 49**
See also CA 102; 93-96

Milne, A(lan) A(lexander) 1882-1956 **TCLC 6;
DAB; DAC; DAM MST**
See also CA 104; 133; CLR 1, 26; DLB 10, 77,
100, 160; MAICYA; MTCW 1; SATA 100;
YABC 1

Milner, Ron(ald) 1938- **CLC 56; BLC 3; DAM
MULT**
See also AITN 1; BW 1; CA 73-76; CANR 24;
DLB 38; MTCW 1

Milnes, Richard Monckton 1809-1885 **N C L C
61**
See also DLB 32, 184

Milosz, Czeslaw 1911- **CLC 5, 11, 22, 31, 56,
82; DAM MST, POET; PC 8; WLCS**
See also CA 81-84; CANR 23, 51; MTCW 1

Milton, John 1608-1674 **LC 9, 43; DA; DAB;
DAC; DAM MST, POET; PC 19; WLC**
See also CDBLB 1660-1789; DLB 131, 151

Min, Anchee 1957-   **CLC 86**
See also CA 146

Minehaha, Cornelius
See Wedekind, (Benjamin) Frank(lin)

Miner, Valerie 1947-   **CLC 40**
See also CA 97-100; CANR 59

Minimo, Duca
See D'Annunzio, Gabriele

Minot, Susan 1956-   **CLC 44**
See also CA 134

Minus, Ed 1938-   **CLC 39**

Miranda, Javier
See Bioy Casares, Adolfo

Mirbeau, Octave 1848-1917   **TCLC 55**
See also DLB 123, 192

Miro (Ferrer), Gabriel (Francisco Victor) 1879-
1930   **TCLC 5**
See also CA 104

Mishima, Yukio 1925-1970 **CLC 2, 4, 6, 9, 27;
DC 1; SSC 4**
See also Hiraoka, Kimitake
See also DLB 182

Mistral, Frederic 1830-1914   **TCLC 51**
See also CA 122

Mistral, Gabriela   **TCLC 2; HLC**
   See also Godoy Alcayaga, Lucila
Mistry, Rohinton 1952-   **CLC 71; DAC**
   See also CA 141
Mitchell, Clyde
   See Ellison, Harlan (Jay); Silverberg, Robert
Mitchell, James Leslie 1901-1935
   See Gibbon, Lewis Grassic
   See also CA 104; DLB 15
Mitchell, Joni 1943-   **CLC 12**
   See also CA 112
Mitchell, Joseph (Quincy) 1908-1996 **CLC 98**
   See also CA 77-80; 152; CANR 69; DLB 185;
   DLBY 96
Mitchell, Margaret (Munnerlyn) 1900-1949
   TCLC 11; DAM NOV, POP
   See also AAYA 23; CA 109; 125; CANR 55;
   DLB 9; MTCW 1
Mitchell, Peggy
   See Mitchell, Margaret (Munnerlyn)
Mitchell, S(ilas) Weir 1829-1914   **TCLC 36**
   See also CA 165; DLB 202
Mitchell, W(illiam) O(rmond) 1914-1998**CLC
   25; DAC; DAM MST**
   See also CA 77-80; 165; CANR 15, 43; DLB
   88
Mitchell, William 1879-1936   **TCLC 81**
Mitford, Mary Russell 1787-1855   **NCLC 4**
   See also DLB 110, 116
Mitford, Nancy 1904-1973   **CLC 44**
   See also CA 9-12R; DLB 191
Miyamoto, Yuriko 1899-1951   **TCLC 37**
   See also DLB 180
Miyazawa, Kenji 1896-1933   **TCLC 76**
   See also CA 157
Mizoguchi, Kenji 1898-1956   **TCLC 72**
   See also CA 167
Mo, Timothy (Peter) 1950(?)-   **CLC 46**
   See also CA 117; DLB 194; MTCW 1
Modarressi, Taghi (M.) 1931-   **CLC 44**
   See also CA 121; 134; INT 134
Modiano, Patrick (Jean) 1945-   **CLC 18**
   See also CA 85-88; CANR 17, 40; DLB 83
Moerck, Paal
   See Roelvaag, O(le) E(dvart)
Mofolo, Thomas (Mokopu) 1875(?)-1948
   TCLC 22; BLC 3; DAM MULT
   See also CA 121; 153
Mohr, Nicholasa 1938-**CLC 12; DAM MULT;
   HLC**
   See also AAYA 8; CA 49-52; CANR 1, 32, 64;
   CLR 22; DLB 145; HW; JRDA; SAAS 8;
   SATA 8, 97
Mojtabai, A(nn) G(race) 1938- **CLC 5, 9, 15,
   29**
   See also CA 85-88
Moliere 1622-1673 **LC 28; DA; DAB; DAC;
   DAM DRAM, MST; WLC**
Molin, Charles
   See Mayne, William (James Carter)
Molnar, Ferenc 1878-1952 **TCLC 20; DAM
   DRAM**
   See also CA 109; 153
Momaday, N(avarre) Scott 1934- **CLC 2, 19,
   85, 95; DA; DAB; DAC; DAM MST,
   MULT, NOV, POP; WLCS**
   See also AAYA 11; CA 25-28R; CANR 14, 34,
   68; DLB 143, 175; INT CANR-14; MTCW
   1; NNAL; SATA 48; SATA-Brief 30
Monette, Paul 1945-1995   **CLC 82**
   See also CA 139; 147
Monroe, Harriet 1860-1936   **TCLC 12**
   See also CA 109; DLB 54, 91

Monroe, Lyle
   See Heinlein, Robert A(nson)
Montagu, Elizabeth 1720-1800   **NCLC 7**
Montagu, Mary (Pierrepont) Wortley 1689-
   1762   **LC 9; PC 16**
   See also DLB 95, 101
Montagu, W. H.
   See Coleridge, Samuel Taylor
Montague, John (Patrick) 1929- CLC 13, 46
   See also CA 9-12R; CANR 9, 69; DLB 40;
   MTCW 1
Montaigne, Michel (Eyquem) de 1533-1592
   LC 8; DA; DAB; DAC; DAM MST; WLC
Montale, Eugenio 1896-1981**CLC 7, 9, 18; PC
   13**
   See also CA 17-20R; 104; CANR 30; DLB 114;
   MTCW 1
Montesquieu, Charles-Louis de Secondat 1689-
   1755   **LC 7**
Montgomery, (Robert) Bruce 1921-1978
   See Crispin, Edmund
   See also CA 104
Montgomery, L(ucy) M(aud) 1874-1942
   TCLC 51; DAC; DAM MST
   See also AAYA 12; CA 108; 137; CLR 8; DLB
   92; DLBD 14; JRDA; MAICYA; SATA 100;
   YABC 1
Montgomery, Marion H., Jr. 1925-   **CLC 7**
   See also AITN 1; CA 1-4R; CANR 3, 48; DLB
   6
Montgomery, Max
   See Davenport, Guy (Mattison, Jr.)
Montherlant, Henry (Milon) de 1896-1972
   CLC 8, 19; DAM DRAM
   See also CA 85-88; 37-40R; DLB 72; MTCW
   1
Monty Python
   See Chapman, Graham; Cleese, John
   (Marwood); Gilliam, Terry (Vance); Idle,
   Eric; Jones, Terence Graham Parry; Palin,
   Michael (Edward)
   See also AAYA 7
Moodie, Susanna (Strickland) 1803-1885
   NCLC 14
   See also DLB 99
Mooney, Edward 1951-
   See Mooney, Ted
   See also CA 130
Mooney, Ted   **CLC 25**
   See also Mooney, Edward
Moorcock, Michael (John) 1939-**CLC 5, 27, 58**
   See also AAYA 26; CA 45-48; CAAS 5; CANR
   2, 17, 38, 64; DLB 14; MTCW 1; SATA 93
Moore, Brian 1921- CLC 1, 3, 5, 7, 8, 19, 32,
   90; DAB; DAC; DAM MST
   See also CA 1-4R; CANR 1, 25, 42, 63; MTCW
   1
Moore, Edward
   See Muir, Edwin
Moore, George Augustus 1852-1933**TCLC 7;
   SSC 19**
   See also CA 104; DLB 10, 18, 57, 135
Moore, Lorrie   **CLC 39, 45, 68**
   See also Moore, Marie Lorena
Moore, Marianne (Craig) 1887-1972**CLC 1, 2,
   4, 8, 10, 13, 19, 47; DA; DAB; DAC; DAM
   MST, POET; PC 4; WLCS**
   See also CA 1-4R; 33-36R; CANR 3, 61;
   CDALB 1929-1941; DLB 45; DLBD 7;
   MTCW 1; SATA 20
Moore, Marie Lorena 1957-
   See Moore, Lorrie
   See also CA 116; CANR 39

Moore, Thomas 1779-1852   **NCLC 6**
   See also DLB 96, 144
Morand, Paul 1888-1976   **CLC 41; SSC 22**
   See also CA 69-72; DLB 65
Morante, Elsa 1918-1985   **CLC 8, 47**
   See also CA 85-88; 117; CANR 35; DLB 177;
   MTCW 1
Moravia, Alberto 1907-1990**CLC 2, 7, 11, 27,
   46; SSC 26**
   See also Pincherle, Alberto
   See also DLB 177
More, Hannah 1745-1833   **NCLC 27**
   See also DLB 107, 109, 116, 158
More, Henry 1614-1687   **LC 9**
   See also DLB 126
More, Sir Thomas 1478-1535   **LC 10, 32**
Moreas, Jean   **TCLC 18**
   See also Papadiamantopoulos, Johannes
Morgan, Berry 1919-   **CLC 6**
   See also CA 49-52; DLB 6
Morgan, Claire
   See Highsmith, (Mary) Patricia
Morgan, Edwin (George) 1920-   **CLC 31**
   See also CA 5-8R; CANR 3, 43; DLB 27
Morgan, (George) Frederick 1922-   **CLC 23**
   See also CA 17-20R; CANR 21
Morgan, Harriet
   See Mencken, H(enry) L(ouis)
Morgan, Jane
   See Cooper, James Fenimore
Morgan, Janet 1945-   **CLC 39**
   See also CA 65-68
Morgan, Lady 1776(?)-1859   **NCLC 29**
   See also DLB 116, 158
Morgan, Robin (Evonne) 1941-   **CLC 2**
   See also CA 69-72; CANR 29, 68; MTCW 1;
   SATA 80
Morgan, Scott
   See Kuttner, Henry
Morgan, Seth 1949(?)-1990   **CLC 65**
   See also CA 132
Morgenstern, Christian 1871-1914   **TCLC 8**
   See also CA 105
Morgenstern, S.
   See Goldman, William (W.)
Moricz, Zsigmond 1879-1942   **TCLC 33**
   See also CA 165
Morike, Eduard (Friedrich) 1804-1875**NCLC
   10**
   See also DLB 133
Moritz, Karl Philipp 1756-1793   **LC 2**
   See also DLB 94
Morland, Peter Henry
   See Faust, Frederick (Schiller)
Morren, Theophil
   See Hofmannsthal, Hugo von
Morris, Bill 1952-   **CLC 76**
Morris, Julian
   See West, Morris L(anglo)
Morris, Steveland Judkins 1950(?)-
   See Wonder, Stevie
   See also CA 111
Morris, William 1834-1896   **NCLC 4**
   See also CDBLB 1832-1890; DLB 18, 35, 57,
   156, 178, 184
Morris, Wright 1910-1998**CLC 1, 3, 7, 18, 37**
   See also CA 9-12R; 167; CANR 21; DLB 2;
   DLBY 81; MTCW 1
Morrison, Arthur 1863-1945   **TCLC 72**
   See also CA 120; 157; DLB 70, 135, 197
Morrison, Chloe Anthony Wofford
   See Morrison, Toni
Morrison, James Douglas 1943-1971

See Morrison, Jim
See also CA 73-76; CANR 40
Morrison, Jim CLC 17
See also Morrison, James Douglas
Morrison, Toni 1931-CLC **4, 10, 22, 55, 81, 87;**
BLC 3; DA; DAB; DAC; DAM MST,
MULT, NOV, POP
See also AAYA 1, 22; BW 2; CA 29-32R;
CANR 27, 42, 67; CDALB 1968-1988; DLB
6, 33, 143; DLBY 81; MTCW 1; SATA 57
Morrison, Van 1945- CLC 21
See also CA 116; 168
Morrissy, Mary 1958- CLC 99
Mortimer, John (Clifford) 1923- CLC **28, 43;**
DAM DRAM, POP
See also CA 13-16R; CANR 21, 69; CDBLB
1960 to Present; DLB 13; INT CANR-21;
MTCW 1
Mortimer, Penelope (Ruth) 1918- CLC 5
See also CA 57-60; CANR 45
Morton, Anthony
See Creasey, John
Mosca, Gaetano 1858-1941 TCLC 75
Mosher, Howard Frank 1943- CLC 62
See also CA 139; CANR 65
Mosley, Nicholas 1923- CLC **43, 70**
See also CA 69-72; CANR 41, 60; DLB 14
Mosley, Walter 1952- CLC **97; BLCS; DAM**
MULT, POP
See also AAYA 17; BW 2; CA 142; CANR 57
Moss, Howard 1922-1987 CLC **7, 14, 45, 50;**
DAM POET
See also CA 1-4R; 123; CANR 1, 44; DLB 5
Mossgiel, Rab
See Burns, Robert
Motion, Andrew (Peter) 1952- CLC 47
See also CA 146; DLB 40
Motley, Willard (Francis) 1909-1965 CLC 18
See also BW 1; CA 117; 106; DLB 76, 143
Motoori, Norinaga 1730-1801 NCLC 45
Mott, Michael (Charles Alston) 1930-CLC **15,**
34
See also CA 5-8R; CAAS 7; CANR 7, 29
Mountain Wolf Woman 1884-1960 CLC 92
See also CA 144; NNAL
Moure, Erin 1955- CLC 88
See also CA 113; DLB 60
Mowat, Farley (McGill) 1921-CLC **26; DAC;**
DAM MST
See also AAYA 1; CA 1-4R; CANR 4, 24, 42,
68; CLR 20; DLB 68; INT CANAR-24;
JRDA; MAICYA; MTCW 1; SATA 3, 55
Moyers, Bill 1934- CLC 74
See also AITN 2; CA 61-64; CANR 31, 52
Mphahlele, Es'kia
See Mphahlele, Ezekiel
See also DLB 125
Mphahlele, Ezekiel 1919-1983 CLC **25; BLC**
3; DAM MULT
See also Mphahlele, Es'kia
See also BW 2; CA 81-84; CANR 26
Mqhayi, S(amuel) E(dward) K(rune Loliwe)
1875-1945TCLC **25; BLC 3; DAM MULT**
See also CA 153
Mrozek, Slawomir 1930- CLC **3, 13**
See also CA 13-16R; CAAS 10; CANR 29;
MTCW 1
Mrs. Belloc-Lowndes
See Lowndes, Marie Adelaide (Belloc)
Mtwa, Percy (?)- CLC 47
Mueller, Lisel 1924- CLC **13, 51**
See also CA 93-96; DLB 105
Muir, Edwin 1887-1959 TCLC 2

See also CA 104; DLB 20, 100, 191
Muir, John 1838-1914 TCLC 28
See also CA 165; DLB 186
Mujica Lainez, Manuel 1910-1984 CLC 31
See also Lainez, Manuel Mujica
See also CA 81-84; 112; CANR 32; HW
Mukherjee, Bharati 1940-CLC **53; DAM NOV**
See also BEST 89:2; CA 107; CANR 45, 72;
DLB 60; MTCW 1
Muldoon, Paul 1951-CLC **32, 72; DAM POET**
See also CA 113; 129; CANR 52; DLB 40; INT
129
Mulisch, Harry 1927- CLC 42
See also CA 9-12R; CANR 6, 26, 56
Mull, Martin 1943- CLC 17
See also CA 105
Mulock, Dinah Maria
See Craik, Dinah Maria (Mulock)
Munford, Robert 1737(?)-1783 LC 5
See also DLB 31
Mungo, Raymond 1946- CLC 72
See also CA 49-52; CANR 2
Munro, Alice 1931- CLC **6, 10, 19, 50, 95;**
DAC; DAM MST, NOV; SSC 3; WLCS
See also AITN 2; CA 33-36R; CANR 33, 53;
DLB 53; MTCW 1; SATA 29
Munro, H(ector) H(ugh) 1870-1916
See Saki
See also CA 104; 130; CDBLB 1890-1914; DA;
DAB; DAC; DAM MST, NOV; DLB 34, 162;
MTCW 1; WLC
Murasaki, Lady CMLC 1
Murdoch, (Jean) Iris 1919-CLC **1, 2, 3, 4, 6, 8,**
11, 15, 22, 31, 51; DAB; DAC; DAM MST,
NOV
See also CA 13-16R; CANR 8, 43, 68; CDBLB
1960 to Present; DLB 14, 194; INT CANR-
8; MTCW 1
Murfree, Mary Noailles 1850-1922 SSC 22
See also CA 122; DLB 12, 74
Murnau, Friedrich Wilhelm
See Plumpe, Friedrich Wilhelm
Murphy, Richard 1927- CLC 41
See also CA 29-32R; DLB 40
Murphy, Sylvia 1937- CLC 34
See also CA 121
Murphy, Thomas (Bernard) 1935- CLC 51
See also CA 101
Murray, Albert L. 1916- CLC 73
See also BW 2; CA 49-52; CANR 26, 52; DLB
38
Murray, Judith Sargent 1751-1820 NCLC 63
See also DLB 37, 200
Murray, Les(lie) A(llan) 1938-CLC **40; DAM**
POET
See also CA 21-24R; CANR 11, 27, 56
Murry, J. Middleton
See Murry, John Middleton
Murry, John Middleton 1889-1957 TCLC 16
See also CA 118; DLB 149
Musgrave, Susan 1951- CLC **13, 54**
See also CA 69-72; CANR 45
Musil, Robert (Edler von) 1880-1942 T C L C
12, 68; SSC 18
See also CA 109; CANR 55; DLB 81, 124
Muske, Carol 1945- CLC 90
See also Muske-Dukes, Carol (Anne)
Muske-Dukes, Carol (Anne) 1945-
See Muske, Carol
See also CA 65-68; CANR 32, 70
Musset, (Louis Charles) Alfred de 1810-1857
NCLC 7
See also DLB 192

My Brother's Brother
See Chekhov, Anton (Pavlovich)
Myers, L(eopold) H(amilton) 1881-1944
TCLC 59
See also CA 157; DLB 15
Myers, Walter Dean 1937- CLC **35; BLC 3;**
DAM MULT, NOV
See also AAYA 4, 23; BW 2; CA 33-36R;
CANR 20, 42, 67; CLR 4, 16, 35; DLB 33;
INT CANR-20; JRDA; MAICYA; SAAS 2;
SATA 41, 71; SATA-Brief 27
Myers, Walter M.
See Myers, Walter Dean
Myles, Symon
See Follett, Ken(neth Martin)
Nabokov, Vladimir (Vladimirovich) 1899-1977
CLC **1, 2, 3, 6, 8, 11, 15, 23, 44, 46, 64;**
DA; DAB; DAC; DAM MST, NOV; SSC
11; WLC
See also CA 5-8R; 69-72; CANR 20; CDALB
1941-1968; DLB 2; DLBD 3; DLBY 80, 91;
MTCW 1
Nagai Kafu 1879-1959 TCLC 51
See also Nagai Sokichi
See also DLB 180
Nagai Sokichi 1879-1959
See Nagai Kafu
See also CA 117
Nagy, Laszlo 1925-1978 CLC 7
See also CA 129; 112
Naidu, Sarojini 1879-1943 TCLC 80
Naipaul, Shiva(dhar Srinivasa) 1945-1985
CLC **32, 39; DAM NOV**
See also CA 110; 112; 116; CANR 33; DLB
157; DLBY 85; MTCW 1
Naipaul, V(idiadhar) S(urajprasad) 1932-
CLC **4, 7, 9, 13, 18, 37, 105; DAB; DAC;**
DAM MST, NOV
See also CA 1-4R; CANR 1, 33, 51; CDBLB
1960 to Present; DLB 125; DLBY 85;
MTCW 1
Nakos, Lilika 1899(?)- CLC 29
Narayan, R(asipuram) K(rishnaswami) 1906-
CLC **7, 28, 47; DAM NOV; SSC 25**
See also CA 81-84; CANR 33, 61; MTCW 1;
SATA 62
Nash, (Frediric) Ogden 1902-1971 CLC **23;**
DAM POET; PC 21
See also CA 13-14; 29-32R; CANR 34, 61; CAP
1; DLB 11; MAICYA; MTCW 1; SATA 2,
46
Nashe, Thomas 1567-1601(?) LC 41
See also DLB 167
Nashe, Thomas 1567-1601 LC 41
Nathan, Daniel
See Dannay, Frederic
Nathan, George Jean 1882-1958 TCLC 18
See also Hatteras, Owen
See also CA 114; DLB 137
Natsume, Kinnosuke 1867-1916
See Natsume, Soseki
See also CA 104
Natsume, Soseki 1867-1916 TCLC **2, 10**
See also Natsume, Kinnosuke
See also DLB 180
Natti, (Mary) Lee 1919-
See Kingman, Lee
See also CA 5-8R; CANR 2
Naylor, Gloria 1950-CLC **28, 52; BLC 3; DA;**
DAC; DAM MST, MULT, NOV, POP;
WLCS
See also AAYA 6; BW 2; CA 107; CANR 27,
51; DLB 173; MTCW 1

Neihardt, John Gneisenau 1881-1973 **CLC 32**
See also CA 13-14; CANR 65; CAP 1; DLB 9, 54

Nekrasov, Nikolai Alekseevich 1821-1878
NCLC 11

Nelligan, Emile 1879-1941 **TCLC 14**
See also CA 114; DLB 92

Nelson, Willie 1933- **CLC 17**
See also CA 107

Nemerov, Howard (Stanley) 1920-1991 **CLC 2, 6, 9, 36; DAM POET; PC 24**
See also CA 1-4R; 134; CABS 2; CANR 1, 27, 53; DLB 5, 6; DLBY 83; INT CANR-27; MTCW 1

Neruda, Pablo 1904-1973 **CLC 1, 2, 5, 7, 9, 28, 62; DA; DAB; DAC; DAM MST, MULT, POET; HLC; PC 4; WLC**
See also CA 19-20; 45-48; CAP 2; HW; MTCW 1

Nerval, Gerard de 1808-1855 **NCLC 1, 67; PC 13; SSC 18**

Nervo, (Jose) Amado (Ruiz de) 1870-1919
TCLC 11
See also CA 109; 131; HW

Nessi, Pio Baroja y
See Baroja (y Nessi), Pio

Nestroy, Johann 1801-1862 **NCLC 42**
See also DLB 133

Netterville, Luke
See O'Grady, Standish (James)

Neufeld, John (Arthur) 1938- **CLC 17**
See also AAYA 11; CA 25-28R; CANR 11, 37, 56; CLR 52; MAICYA; SAAS 3; SATA 6, 81

Neville, Emily Cheney 1919- **CLC 12**
See also CA 5-8R; CANR 3, 37; JRDA; MAICYA; SAAS 2; SATA 1

Newbound, Bernard Slade 1930-
See Slade, Bernard
See also CA 81-84; CANR 49; DAM DRAM

Newby, P(ercy) H(oward) 1918-1997 **CLC 2, 13; DAM NOV**
See also CA 5-8R; 161; CANR 32, 67; DLB 15; MTCW 1

Newlove, Donald 1928- **CLC 6**
See also CA 29-32R; CANR 25

Newlove, John (Herbert) 1938- **CLC 14**
See also CA 21-24R; CANR 9, 25

Newman, Charles 1938- **CLC 2, 8**
See also CA 21-24R

Newman, Edwin (Harold) 1919- **CLC 14**
See also AITN 1; CA 69-72; CANR 5

Newman, John Henry 1801-1890 **NCLC 38**
See also DLB 18, 32, 55

Newton, Suzanne 1936- **CLC 35**
See also CA 41-44R; CANR 14; JRDA; SATA 5, 77

Nexo, Martin Andersen 1869-1954 **TCLC 43**

Nezval, Vitezslav 1900-1958 **TCLC 44**
See also CA 123

Ng, Fae Myenne 1957(?)- **CLC 81**
See also CA 146

Ngema, Mbongeni 1955- **CLC 57**
See also BW 2; CA 143

Ngugi, James T(hiong'o) **CLC 3, 7, 13**
See also Ngugi wa Thiong'o

Ngugi wa Thiong'o 1938- **CLC 36; BLC 3; DAM MULT, NOV**
See also Ngugi, James T(hiong'o)
See also BW 2; CA 81-84; CANR 27, 58; DLB 125; MTCW 1

Nichol, B(arrie) P(hillip) 1944-1988 **CLC 18**
See also CA 53-56; DLB 53; SATA 66

Nichols, John (Treadwell) 1940- **CLC 38**
See also CA 9-12R; CAAS 2; CANR 6, 70; DLBY 82

Nichols, Leigh
See Koontz, Dean R(ay)

Nichols, Peter (Richard) 1927- **CLC 5, 36, 65**
See also CA 104; CANR 33; DLB 13; MTCW 1

Nicolas, F. R. E.
See Freeling, Nicolas

Niedecker, Lorine 1903-1970 **CLC 10, 42; DAM POET**
See also CA 25-28; CAP 2; DLB 48

Nietzsche, Friedrich (Wilhelm) 1844-1900
TCLC 10, 18, 55
See also CA 107; 121; DLB 129

Nievo, Ippolito 1831-1861 **NCLC 22**

Nightingale, Anne Redmon 1943-
See Redmon, Anne
See also CA 103

Nightingale, Florence 1820-1910 **TCLC 85**
See also DLB 166

Nik. T. O.
See Annensky, Innokenty (Fyodorovich)

Nin, Anais 1903-1977 **CLC 1, 4, 8, 11, 14, 60; DAM NOV, POP; SSC 10**
See also AITN 2; CA 13-16R; 69-72; CANR 22, 53; DLB 2, 4, 152; MTCW 1

Nishida, Kitaro 1870-1945 **TCLC 83**

Nishiwaki, Junzaburo 1894-1982 **PC 15**
See also CA 107

Nissenson, Hugh 1933- **CLC 4, 9**
See also CA 17-20R; CANR 27; DLB 28

Niven, Larry **CLC 8**
See also Niven, Laurence Van Cott
See also AAYA 27; DLB 8

Niven, Laurence Van Cott 1938-
See Niven, Larry
See also CA 21-24R; CAAS 12; CANR 14, 44, 66; DAM POP; MTCW 1; SATA 95

Nixon, Agnes Eckhardt 1927- **CLC 21**
See also CA 110

Nizan, Paul 1905-1940 **TCLC 40**
See also CA 161; DLB 72

Nkosi, Lewis 1936- **CLC 45; BLC 3; DAM MULT**
See also BW 1; CA 65-68; CANR 27; DLB 157

Nodier, (Jean) Charles (Emmanuel) 1780-1844
NCLC 19
See also DLB 119

Noguchi, Yone 1875-1947 **TCLC 80**

Nolan, Christopher 1965- **CLC 58**
See also CA 111

Noon, Jeff 1957- **CLC 91**
See also CA 148

Norden, Charles
See Durrell, Lawrence (George)

Nordhoff, Charles (Bernard) 1887-1947
TCLC 23
See also CA 108; DLB 9; SATA 23

Norfolk, Lawrence 1963- **CLC 76**
See also CA 144

Norman, Marsha 1947- **CLC 28; DAM DRAM; DC 8**
See also CA 105; CABS 3; CANR 41; DLBY 84

Normyx
See Douglas, (George) Norman

Norris, Frank 1870-1902 **SSC 28**
See also Norris, (Benjamin) Frank(lin, Jr.)
See also CDALB 1865-1917; DLB 12, 71, 186

Norris, (Benjamin) Frank(lin, Jr.) 1870-1902
TCLC 24

See also Norris, Frank
See also CA 110; 160

Norris, Leslie 1921- **CLC 14**
See also CA 11-12; CANR 14; CAP 1; DLB 27

North, Andrew
See Norton, Andre

North, Anthony
See Koontz, Dean R(ay)

North, Captain George
See Stevenson, Robert Louis (Balfour)

North, Milou
See Erdrich, Louise

Northrup, B. A.
See Hubbard, L(afayette) Ron(ald)

North Staffs
See Hulme, T(homas) E(rnest)

Norton, Alice Mary
See Norton, Andre
See also MAICYA; SATA 1, 43

Norton, Andre 1912- **CLC 12**
See also Norton, Alice Mary
See also AAYA 14; CA 1-4R; CANR 68; CLR 50; DLB 8, 52; JRDA; MTCW 1; SATA 91

Norton, Caroline 1808-1877 **NCLC 47**
See also DLB 21, 159, 199

Norway, Nevil Shute 1899-1960
See Shute, Nevil
See also CA 102; 93-96

Norwid, Cyprian Kamil 1821-1883 **NCLC 17**

Nosille, Nabrah
See Ellison, Harlan (Jay)

Nossack, Hans Erich 1901-1978 **CLC 6**
See also CA 93-96; 85-88; DLB 69

Nostradamus 1503-1566 **LC 27**

Nosu, Chuji
See Ozu, Yasujiro

Notenburg, Eleanora (Genrikhovna) von
See Guro, Elena

Nova, Craig 1945- **CLC 7, 31**
See also CA 45-48; CANR 2, 53

Novak, Joseph
See Kosinski, Jerzy (Nikodem)

Novalis 1772-1801 **NCLC 13**
See also DLB 90

Novis, Emile
See Weil, Simone (Adolphine)

Nowlan, Alden (Albert) 1933-1983 **CLC 15; DAC; DAM MST**
See also CA 9-12R; CANR 5; DLB 53

Noyes, Alfred 1880-1958 **TCLC 7**
See also CA 104; DLB 20

Nunn, Kem **CLC 34**
See also CA 159

Nye, Robert 1939- **CLC 13, 42; DAM NOV**
See also CA 33-36R; CANR 29, 67; DLB 14; MTCW 1; SATA 6

Nyro, Laura 1947- **CLC 17**

Oates, Joyce Carol 1938- **CLC 1, 2, 3, 6, 9, 11, 15, 19, 33, 52, 108; DA; DAB; DAC; DAM MST, NOV, POP; SSC 6; WLC**
See also AAYA 15; AITN 1; BEST 89:2; CA 5-8R; CANR 25, 45; CDALB 1968-1988; DLB 2, 5, 130; DLBY 81; INT CANR-25; MTCW 1

O'Brien, Darcy 1939-1998 **CLC 11**
See also CA 21-24R; 167; CANR 8, 59

O'Brien, E. G.
See Clarke, Arthur C(harles)

O'Brien, Edna 1936- **CLC 3, 5, 8, 13, 36, 65; DAM NOV; SSC 10**
See also CA 1-4R; CANR 6, 41, 65; CDBLB 1960 to Present; DLB 14; MTCW 1

O'Brien, Fitz-James 1828-1862 **NCLC 21**

See also CA 53-56; CANR 27, 47, 65; MTCW 1

Ozick, Cynthia 1928- **CLC 3, 7, 28, 62; DAM NOV, POP; SSC 15**
See also BEST 90:1; CA 17-20R; CANR 23, 58; DLB 28, 152; DLBY 82; INT CANR-23; MTCW 1

Ozu, Yasujiro 1903-1963 **CLC 16**
See also CA 112

Pacheco, C.
See Pessoa, Fernando (Antonio Nogueira)

Pa Chin **CLC 18**
See also Li Fei-kan

Pack, Robert 1929- **CLC 13**
See also CA 1-4R; CANR 3, 44; DLB 5

Padgett, Lewis
See Kuttner, Henry

Padilla (Lorenzo), Heberto 1932- **CLC 38**
See also AITN 1; CA 123; 131; HW

Page, Jimmy 1944- **CLC 12**

Page, Louise 1955- **CLC 40**
See also CA 140

Page, P(atricia) K(athleen) 1916- **CLC 7, 18; DAC; DAM MST; PC 12**
See also CA 53-56; CANR 4, 22, 65; DLB 68; MTCW 1

Page, Thomas Nelson 1853-1922 **SSC 23**
See also CA 118; DLB 12, 78; DLBD 13

Pagels, Elaine Hiesey 1943- **CLC 104**
See also CA 45-48; CANR 2, 24, 51

Paget, Violet 1856-1935
See Lee, Vernon
See also CA 104; 166

Paget-Lowe, Henry
See Lovecraft, H(oward) P(hillips)

Paglia, Camille (Anna) 1947- **CLC 68**
See also CA 140; CANR 72

Paige, Richard
See Koontz, Dean R(ay)

Paine, Thomas 1737-1809 **NCLC 62**
See also CDALB 1640-1865; DLB 31, 43, 73, 158

Pakenham, Antonia
See Fraser, (Lady) Antonia (Pakenham)

Palamas, Kostes 1859-1943 **TCLC 5**
See also CA 105

Palazzeschi, Aldo 1885-1974 **CLC 11**
See also CA 89-92; 53-56; DLB 114

Paley, Grace 1922- **CLC 4, 6, 37; DAM POP; SSC 8**
See also CA 25-28R; CANR 13, 46; DLB 28; INT CANR-13; MTCW 1

Palin, Michael (Edward) 1943- **CLC 21**
See also Monty Python
See also CA 107; CANR 35; SATA 67

Palliser, Charles 1947- **CLC 65**
See also CA 136

Palma, Ricardo 1833-1919 **TCLC 29**
See also CA 168

Pancake, Breece Dexter 1952-1979
See Pancake, Breece D'J
See also CA 123; 109

Pancake, Breece D'J **CLC 29**
See also Pancake, Breece Dexter
See also DLB 130

Panko, Rudy
See Gogol, Nikolai (Vasilyevich)

Papadiamantis, Alexandros 1851-1911 **TCLC 29**
See also CA 168

Papadiamantopoulos, Johannes 1856-1910
See Moreas, Jean
See also CA 117

Papini, Giovanni 1881-1956 **TCLC 22**
See also CA 121

Paracelsus 1493-1541 **LC 14**
See also DLB 179

Parasol, Peter
See Stevens, Wallace

Pardo Bazan, Emilia 1851-1921 **SSC 30**

Pareto, Vilfredo 1848-1923 **TCLC 69**

Parfenie, Maria
See Codrescu, Andrei

Parini, Jay (Lee) 1948- **CLC 54**
See also CA 97-100; CAAS 16; CANR 32

Park, Jordan
See Kornbluth, C(yril) M.; Pohl, Frederik

Park, Robert E(zra) 1864-1944 **TCLC 73**
See also CA 122; 165

Parker, Bert
See Ellison, Harlan (Jay)

Parker, Dorothy (Rothschild) 1893-1967 **CLC 15, 68; DAM POET; SSC 2**
See also CA 19-20; 25-28R; CAP 2; DLB 11, 45, 86; MTCW 1

Parker, Robert B(rown) 1932- **CLC 27; DAM NOV, POP**
See also BEST 89:4; CA 49-52; CANR 1, 26, 52; INT CANR-26; MTCW 1

Parkin, Frank 1940- **CLC 43**
See also CA 147

Parkman, Francis, Jr. 1823-1893 **NCLC 12**
See also DLB 1, 30, 186

Parks, Gordon (Alexander Buchanan) 1912- **CLC 1, 16; BLC 3; DAM MULT**
See also AITN 2; BW 2; CA 41-44R; CANR 26, 66; DLB 33; SATA 8

Parmenides c. 515B.C.-c. 450B.C. **CMLC 22**
See also DLB 176

Parnell, Thomas 1679-1718 **LC 3**
See also DLB 94

Parra, Nicanor 1914- **CLC 2, 102; DAM MULT; HLC**
See also CA 85-88; CANR 32; HW; MTCW 1

Parrish, Mary Frances
See Fisher, M(ary) F(rances) K(ennedy)

Parson
See Coleridge, Samuel Taylor

Parson Lot
See Kingsley, Charles

Partridge, Anthony
See Oppenheim, E(dward) Phillips

Pascal, Blaise 1623-1662 **LC 35**

Pascoli, Giovanni 1855-1912 **TCLC 45**

Pasolini, Pier Paolo 1922-1975 **CLC 20, 37, 106; PC 17**
See also CA 93-96; 61-64; CANR 63; DLB 128, 177; MTCW 1

Pasquini
See Silone, Ignazio

Pastan, Linda (Olenik) 1932- **CLC 27; DAM POET**
See also CA 61-64; CANR 18, 40, 61; DLB 5

Pasternak, Boris (Leonidovich) 1890-1960 **CLC 7, 10, 18, 63; DA; DAB; DAC; DAM MST, NOV, POET; PC 6; SSC 31; WLC**
See also CA 127; 116; MTCW 1

Patchen, Kenneth 1911-1972 **CLC 1, 2, 18; DAM POET**
See also CA 1-4R; 33-36R; CANR 3, 35; DLB 16, 48; MTCW 1

Pater, Walter (Horatio) 1839-1894 **NCLC 7**
See also CDBLB 1832-1890; DLB 57, 156

Paterson, A(ndrew) B(arton) 1864-1941 **TCLC 32**
See also CA 155; SATA 97

Paterson, Katherine (Womeldorf) 1932- **CLC 12, 30**
See also AAYA 1; CA 21-24R; CANR 28, 59; CLR 7, 50; DLB 52; JRDA; MAICYA; MTCW 1; SATA 13, 53, 92

Patmore, Coventry Kersey Dighton 1823-1896 **NCLC 9**
See also DLB 35, 98

Paton, Alan (Stewart) 1903-1988 **CLC 4, 10, 25, 55, 106; DA; DAB; DAC; DAM MST, NOV; WLC**
See also AAYA 26; CA 13-16; 125; CANR 22; CAP 1; DLBD 17; MTCW 1; SATA 11; SATA-Obit 56

Paton Walsh, Gillian 1937-
See Walsh, Jill Paton
See also CANR 38; JRDA; MAICYA; SAAS 3; SATA 4, 72

Patton, George S. 1885-1945 **TCLC 79**

Paulding, James Kirke 1778-1860 **NCLC 2**
See also DLB 3, 59, 74

Paulin, Thomas Neilson 1949-
See Paulin, Tom
See also CA 123; 128

Paulin, Tom **CLC 37**
See also Paulin, Thomas Neilson
See also DLB 40

Paustovsky, Konstantin (Georgievich) 1892-1968 **CLC 40**
See also CA 93-96; 25-28R

Pavese, Cesare 1908-1950 **TCLC 3; PC 13; SSC 19**
See also CA 104; DLB 128, 177

Pavic, Milorad 1929- **CLC 60**
See also CA 136; DLB 181

Payne, Alan
See Jakes, John (William)

Paz, Gil
See Lugones, Leopoldo

Paz, Octavio 1914-1998 **CLC 3, 4, 6, 10, 19, 51, 65; DA; DAB; DAC; DAM MST, MULT, POET; HLC; PC 1; WLC**
See also CA 73-76; 165; CANR 32, 65; DLBY 90; HW; MTCW 1

p'Bitek, Okot 1931-1982 **CLC 96; BLC 3; DAM MULT**
See also BW 2; CA 124; 107; DLB 125; MTCW 1

Peacock, Molly 1947- **CLC 60**
See also CA 103; CAAS 21; CANR 52; DLB 120

Peacock, Thomas Love 1785-1866 **NCLC 22**
See also DLB 96, 116

Peake, Mervyn 1911-1968 **CLC 7, 54**
See also CA 5-8R; 25-28R; CANR 3; DLB 15, 160; MTCW 1; SATA 23

Pearce, Philippa **CLC 21**
See also Christie, (Ann) Philippa
See also CLR 9; DLB 161; MAICYA; SATA 1, 67

Pearl, Eric
See Elman, Richard (Martin)

Pearson, T(homas) R(eid) 1956- **CLC 39**
See also CA 120; 130; INT 130

Peck, Dale 1967- **CLC 81**
See also CA 146; CANR 72

Peck, John 1941- **CLC 3**
See also CA 49-52; CANR 3

Peck, Richard (Wayne) 1934- **CLC 21**
See also AAYA 1, 24; CA 85-88; CANR 19, 38; CLR 15; INT CANR-19; JRDA; MAICYA; SAAS 2; SATA 18, 55, 97

Peck, Robert Newton 1928- **CLC 17; DA;**

DAC; DAM MST
See also AAYA 3; CA 81-84; CANR 31, 63;
CLR 45; JRDA; MAICYA; SAAS 1; SATA
21, 62

Peckinpah, (David) Sam(uel) 1925-1984 **C L C 20**
See also CA 109; 114

Pedersen, Knut 1859-1952
See Hamsun, Knut
See also CA 104; 119; CANR 63; MTCW 1

Peeslake, Gaffer
See Durrell, Lawrence (George)

Peguy, Charles Pierre 1873-1914 **TCLC 10**
See also CA 107

Peirce, Charles Sanders 1839-1914 **TCLC 81**

Pena, Ramon del Valle y
See Valle-Inclan, Ramon (Maria) del

Pendennis, Arthur Esquir
See Thackeray, William Makepeace

Penn, William 1644-1718   **LC 25**
See also DLB 24

PEPECE
See Prado (Calvo), Pedro

Pepys, Samuel 1633-1703 **LC 11; DA; DAB; DAC; DAM MST; WLC**
See also CDBLB 1660-1789; DLB 101

Percy, Walker 1916-1990 **CLC 2, 3, 6, 8, 14, 18, 47, 65; DAM NOV, POP**
See also CA 1-4R; 131; CANR 1, 23, 64; DLB 2; DLBY 80, 90; MTCW 1

Percy, William Alexander 1885-1942 **TCLC 84**
See also CA 163

Perec, Georges 1936-1982   **CLC 56**
See also CA 141; DLB 83

Pereda (y Sanchez de Porrua), Jose Maria de 1833-1906   **TCLC 16**
See also CA 117

Pereda y Porrua, Jose Maria de
See Pereda (y Sanchez de Porrua), Jose Maria de

Peregoy, George Weems
See Mencken, H(enry) L(ouis)

Perelman, S(idney) J(oseph) 1904-1979 **C L C 3, 5, 9, 15, 23, 44, 49; DAM DRAM; SSC 32**
See also AITN 1, 2; CA 73-76; 89-92; CANR 18; DLB 11, 44; MTCW 1

Peret, Benjamin 1899-1959   **TCLC 20**
See also CA 117

Peretz, Isaac Loeb 1851(?)-1915 **TCLC 16; SSC 26**
See also CA 109

Peretz, Yitzkhok Leibush
See Peretz, Isaac Loeb

Perez Galdos, Benito 1843-1920   **TCLC 27**
See also CA 125; 153; HW

Perrault, Charles 1628-1703   **LC 2**
See also MAICYA; SATA 25

Perry, Brighton
See Sherwood, Robert E(mmet)

Perse, St.-John
See Leger, (Marie-Rene Auguste) Alexis Saint-Leger

Perutz, Leo 1882-1957   **TCLC 60**
See also DLB 81

Peseenz, Tulio F.
See Lopez y Fuentes, Gregorio

Pesetsky, Bette 1932-   **CLC 28**
See also CA 133; DLB 130

Peshkov, Alexei Maximovich 1868-1936
See Gorky, Maxim
See also CA 105; 141; DA; DAC; DAM DRAM, MST, NOV

Pessoa, Fernando (Antonio Nogueira) 1898-1935   **TCLC 27; HLC; PC 20**
See also CA 125

Peterkin, Julia Mood 1880-1961   **CLC 31**
See also CA 102; DLB 9

Peters, Joan K(aren) 1945-   **CLC 39**
See also CA 158

Peters, Robert L(ouis) 1924-   **CLC 7**
See also CA 13-16R; CAAS 8; DLB 105

Petofi, Sandor 1823-1849   **NCLC 21**

Petrakis, Harry Mark 1923-   **CLC 3**
See also CA 9-12R; CANR 4, 30

Petrarch 1304-1374 **CMLC 20; DAM POET; PC 8**

Petrov, Evgeny   **TCLC 21**
See also Kataev, Evgeny Petrovich

Petry, Ann (Lane) 1908-1997   **CLC 1, 7, 18**
See also BW 1; CA 5-8R; 157; CAAS 6; CANR 4, 46; CLR 12; DLB 76; JRDA; MAICYA; MTCW 1; SATA 5; SATA-Obit 94

Petursson, Halligrimur 1614-1674   **LC 8**

Peychinovich
See Vazov, Ivan (Minchov)

Phaedrus 18(?)B.C.-55(?)   **CMLC 25**

Philips, Katherine 1632-1664   **LC 30**
See also DLB 131

Philipson, Morris H. 1926-   **CLC 53**
See also CA 1-4R; CANR 4

Phillips, Caryl 1958- **CLC 96; BLCS; DAM MULT**
See also BW 2; CA 141; CANR 63; DLB 157

Phillips, David Graham 1867-1911 **TCLC 44**
See also CA 108; DLB 9, 12

Phillips, Jack
See Sandburg, Carl (August)

Phillips, Jayne Anne 1952- **CLC 15, 33; SSC 16**
See also CA 101; CANR 24, 50; DLBY 80; INT CANR-24; MTCW 1

Phillips, Richard
See Dick, Philip K(indred)

Phillips, Robert (Schaeffer) 1938-   **CLC 28**
See also CA 17-20R; CAAS 13; CANR 8; DLB 105

Phillips, Ward
See Lovecraft, H(oward) P(hillips)

Piccolo, Lucio 1901-1969   **CLC 13**
See also CA 97-100; DLB 114

Pickthall, Marjorie L(owry) C(hristie) 1883-1922   **TCLC 21**
See also CA 107; DLB 92

Pico della Mirandola, Giovanni 1463-1494 **LC 15**

Piercy, Marge 1936- **CLC 3, 6, 14, 18, 27, 62**
See also CA 21-24R; CAAS 1; CANR 13, 43, 66; DLB 120; MTCW 1

Piers, Robert
See Anthony, Piers

Pieyre de Mandiargues, Andre 1909-1991
See Mandiargues, Andre Pieyre de
See also CA 103; 136; CANR 22

Pilnyak, Boris   **TCLC 23**
See also Vogau, Boris Andreyevich

Pincherle, Alberto 1907-1990   **CLC 11, 18; DAM NOV**
See also Moravia, Alberto
See also CA 25-28R; 132; CANR 33, 63; MTCW 1

Pinckney, Darryl 1953-   **CLC 76**
See also BW 2; CA 143

Pindar 518B.C.-446B.C.   **CMLC 12; PC 19**
See also DLB 176

Pineda, Cecile 1942-   **CLC 39**
See also CA 118

Pinero, Arthur Wing 1855-1934   **TCLC 32; DAM DRAM**
See also CA 110; 153; DLB 10

Pinero, Miguel (Antonio Gomez) 1946-1988 **CLC 4, 55**
See also CA 61-64; 125; CANR 29; HW

Pinget, Robert 1919-1997   **CLC 7, 13, 37**
See also CA 85-88; 160; DLB 83

Pink Floyd
See Barrett, (Roger) Syd; Gilmour, David; Mason, Nick; Waters, Roger; Wright, Rick

Pinkney, Edward 1802-1828   **NCLC 31**

Pinkwater, Daniel Manus 1941-   **CLC 35**
See also Pinkwater, Manus
See also AAYA 1; CA 29-32R; CANR 12, 38; CLR 4; JRDA; MAICYA; SAAS 3; SATA 46, 76

Pinkwater, Manus
See Pinkwater, Daniel Manus
See also SATA 8

Pinsky, Robert 1940- **CLC 9, 19, 38, 94; DAM POET**
See also CA 29-32R; CAAS 4; CANR 58; DLBY 82

Pinta, Harold
See Pinter, Harold

Pinter, Harold 1930- **CLC 1, 3, 6, 9, 11, 15, 27, 58, 73; DA; DAB; DAC; DAM DRAM, MST; WLC**
See also CA 5-8R; CANR 33, 65; CDBLB 1960 to Present; DLB 13; MTCW 1

Piozzi, Hester Lynch (Thrale) 1741-1821 **NCLC 57**
See also DLB 104, 142

Pirandello, Luigi 1867-1936 **TCLC 4, 29; DA; DAB; DAC; DAM DRAM, MST; DC 5; SSC 22; WLC**
See also CA 104; 153

Pirsig, Robert M(aynard) 1928- **CLC 4, 6, 73; DAM POP**
See also CA 53-56; CANR 42; MTCW 1; SATA 39

Pisarev, Dmitry Ivanovich 1840-1868 **N C L C 25**

Pix, Mary (Griffith) 1666-1709   **LC 8**
See also DLB 80

Pixerecourt, (Rene Charles) Guilbert de 1773-1844   **NCLC 39**
See also DLB 192

Plaatje, Sol(omon) T(shekisho) 1876-1932 **TCLC 73; BLCS**
See also BW 2; CA 141

Plaidy, Jean
See Hibbert, Eleanor Alice Burford

Planche, James Robinson 1796-1880 **NCLC 42**

Plant, Robert 1948-   **CLC 12**

Plante, David (Robert) 1940- **CLC 7, 23, 38; DAM NOV**
See also CA 37-40R; CANR 12, 36, 58; DLBY 83; INT CANR-12; MTCW 1

Plath, Sylvia 1932-1963 **CLC 1, 2, 3, 5, 9, 11, 14, 17, 50, 51, 62, 111; DA; DAB; DAC; DAM MST, POET; PC 1; WLC**
See also AAYA 13; CA 19-20; CANR 34; CAP 2; CDALB 1941-1968; DLB 5, 6, 152; MTCW 1; SATA 96

Plato 428(?)B.C.-348(?)B.C. **CMLC 8; DA; DAB; DAC; DAM MST; WLCS**
See also DLB 176

Platonov, Andrei   **TCLC 14**
See also Klimentov, Andrei Platonovich

Platt, Kin 1911-   **CLC 26**
See also AAYA 11; CA 17-20R; CANR 11;

JRDA; SAAS 17; SATA 21, 86

Plautus c. 251B.C.-184B.C. **CMLC 24; DC 6**

Plick et Plock
See Simenon, Georges (Jacques Christian)

Plimpton, George (Ames) 1927- **CLC 36**
See also AITN 1; CA 21-24R; CANR 32, 70; DLB 185; MTCW 1; SATA 10

Pliny the Elder c. 23-79 **CMLC 23**

Plomer, William Charles Franklin 1903-1973 **CLC 4, 8**
See also CA 21-22; CANR 34; CAP 2; DLB 20, 162, 191; MTCW 1; SATA 24

Plowman, Piers
See Kavanagh, Patrick (Joseph)

Plum, J.
See Wodehouse, P(elham) G(renville)

Plumly, Stanley (Ross) 1939- **CLC 33**
See also CA 108; 110; DLB 5, 193; INT 110

Plumpe, Friedrich Wilhelm 1888-1931 **TCLC 53**
See also CA 112

Po Chu-i 772-846 **CMLC 24**

Poe, Edgar Allan 1809-1849 **NCLC 1, 16, 55; DA; DAB; DAC; DAM MST, POET; PC 1; SSC 1, 22; WLC**
See also AAYA 14; CDALB 1640-1865; DLB 3, 59, 73, 74; SATA 23

Poet of Titchfield Street, The
See Pound, Ezra (Weston Loomis)

Pohl, Frederik 1919- **CLC 18; SSC 25**
See also AAYA 24; CA 61-64; CAAS 1; CANR 11, 37; DLB 8; INT CANR-11; MTCW 1; SATA 24

Poirier, Louis 1910-
See Gracq, Julien
See also CA 122; 126

Poitier, Sidney 1927- **CLC 26**
See also BW 1; CA 117

Polanski, Roman 1933- **CLC 16**
See also CA 77-80

Poliakoff, Stephen 1952- **CLC 38**
See also CA 106; DLB 13

Police, The
See Copeland, Stewart (Armstrong); Summers, Andrew James; Sumner, Gordon Matthew

Polidori, John William 1795-1821 **NCLC 51**
See also DLB 116

Pollitt, Katha 1949- **CLC 28**
See also CA 120; 122; CANR 66; MTCW 1

Pollock, (Mary) Sharon 1936- **CLC 50; DAC; DAM DRAM, MST**
See also CA 141; DLB 60

Polo, Marco 1254-1324 **CMLC 15**

Polonsky, Abraham (Lincoln) 1910- **CLC 92**
See also CA 104; DLB 26; INT 104

Polybius c. 200B.C.-c. 118B.C. **CMLC 17**
See also DLB 176

Pomerance, Bernard 1940- **CLC 13; DAM DRAM**
See also CA 101; CANR 49

Ponge, Francis (Jean Gaston Alfred) 1899-1988 **CLC 6, 18; DAM POET**
See also CA 85-88; 126; CANR 40

Pontoppidan, Henrik 1857-1943 **TCLC 29**

Poole, Josephine **CLC 17**
See also Helyar, Jane Penelope Josephine
See also SAAS 2; SATA 5

Popa, Vasko 1922-1991 **CLC 19**
See also CA 112; 148; DLB 181

Pope, Alexander 1688-1744 **LC 3; DA; DAB; DAC; DAM MST, POET; WLC**
See also CDBLB 1660-1789; DLB 95, 101

Porter, Connie (Rose) 1959(?)- **CLC 70**

See also BW 2; CA 142; SATA 81

Porter, Gene(va Grace) Stratton 1863(?)-1924 **TCLC 21**
See also CA 112

Porter, Katherine Anne 1890-1980 **CLC 1, 3, 7, 10, 13, 15, 27, 101; DA; DAB; DAC; DAM MST, NOV; SSC 4, 31**
See also AITN 2; CA 1-4R; 101; CANR 1, 65; DLB 4, 9, 102; DLBD 12; DLBY 80; MTCW 1; SATA 39; SATA-Obit 23

Porter, Peter (Neville Frederick) 1929- **CLC 5, 13, 33**
See also CA 85-88; DLB 40

Porter, William Sydney 1862-1910
See Henry, O.
See also CA 104; 131; CDALB 1865-1917; DA; DAB; DAC; DAM MST; DLB 12, 78, 79; MTCW 1; YABC 2

Portillo (y Pacheco), Jose Lopez
See Lopez Portillo (y Pacheco), Jose

Post, Melville Davisson 1869-1930 **TCLC 39**
See also CA 110

Potok, Chaim 1929- **CLC 2, 7, 14, 26, 112; DAM NOV**
See also AAYA 15; AITN 1, 2; CA 17-20R; CANR 19, 35, 64; DLB 28, 152; INT CANR-19; MTCW 1; SATA 33

Potter, (Helen) Beatrix 1866-1943
See Webb, (Martha) Beatrice (Potter)
See also MAICYA

Potter, Dennis (Christopher George) 1935-1994 **CLC 58, 86**
See also CA 107; 145; CANR 33, 61; MTCW 1

Pound, Ezra (Weston Loomis) 1885-1972 **CLC 1, 2, 3, 4, 5, 7, 10, 13, 18, 34, 48, 50, 112; DA; DAB; DAC; DAM MST, POET; PC 4; WLC**
See also CA 5-8R; 37-40R; CANR 40; CDALB 1917-1929; DLB 4, 45, 63; DLBD 15; MTCW 1

Povod, Reinaldo 1959-1994 **CLC 44**
See also CA 136; 146

Powell, Adam Clayton, Jr. 1908-1972 **CLC 89; BLC 3; DAM MULT**
See also BW 1; CA 102; 33-36R

Powell, Anthony (Dymoke) 1905- **CLC 1, 3, 7, 9, 10, 31**
See also CA 1-4R; CANR 1, 32, 62; CDBLB 1945-1960; DLB 15; MTCW 1

Powell, Dawn 1897-1965 **CLC 66**
See also CA 5-8R; DLBY 97

Powell, Padgett 1952- **CLC 34**
See also CA 126; CANR 63

Power, Susan 1961- **CLC 91**

Powers, J(ames) F(arl) 1917- **CLC 1, 4, 8, 57; SSC 4**
See also CA 1-4R; CANR 2, 61; DLB 130; MTCW 1

Powers, John J(ames) 1945-
See Powers, John R.
See also CA 69-72

Powers, John R. **CLC 66**
See also Powers, John J(ames)

Powers, Richard (S.) 1957- **CLC 93**
See also CA 148

Pownall, David 1938- **CLC 10**
See also CA 89-92; CAAS 18; CANR 49; DLB 14

Powys, John Cowper 1872-1963 **CLC 7, 9, 15, 46**
See also CA 85-88; DLB 15; MTCW 1

Powys, T(heodore) F(rancis) 1875-1953 **TCLC 9**

See also CA 106; DLB 36, 162

Prado (Calvo), Pedro 1886-1952 **TCLC 75**
See also CA 131; HW

Prager, Emily 1952- **CLC 56**

Pratt, E(dwin) J(ohn) 1883(?)-1964 **CLC 19; DAC; DAM POET**
See also CA 141; 93-96; DLB 92

Premchand **TCLC 21**
See also Srivastava, Dhanpat Rai

Preussler, Otfried 1923- **CLC 17**
See also CA 77-80; SATA 24

Prevert, Jacques (Henri Marie) 1900-1977 **CLC 15**
See also CA 77-80; 69-72; CANR 29, 61; MTCW 1; SATA-Obit 30

Prevost, Abbe (Antoine Francois) 1697-1763 **LC 1**

Price, (Edward) Reynolds 1933- **CLC 3, 6, 13, 43, 50, 63; DAM NOV; SSC 22**
See also CA 1-4R; CANR 1, 37, 57; DLB 2; INT CANR-37

Price, Richard 1949- **CLC 6, 12**
See also CA 49-52; CANR 3; DLBY 81

Prichard, Katharine Susannah 1883-1969 **CLC 46**
See also CA 11-12; CANR 33; CAP 1; MTCW 1; SATA 66

Priestley, J(ohn) B(oynton) 1894-1984 **CLC 2, 5, 9, 34; DAM DRAM, NOV**
See also CA 9-12R; 113; CANR 33; CDBLB 1914-1945; DLB 10, 34, 77, 100, 139; DLBY 84; MTCW 1

Prince 1958(?)- **CLC 35**

Prince, F(rank) T(empleton) 1912- **CLC 22**
See also CA 101; CANR 43; DLB 20

Prince Kropotkin
See Kropotkin, Peter (Alekseievich)

Prior, Matthew 1664-1721 **LC 4**
See also DLB 95

Prishvin, Mikhail 1873-1954 **TCLC 75**

Pritchard, William H(arrison) 1932- **CLC 34**
See also CA 65-68; CANR 23; DLB 111

Pritchett, V(ictor) S(awdon) 1900-1997 **CLC 5, 13, 15, 41; DAM NOV; SSC 14**
See also CA 61-64; 157; CANR 31, 63; DLB 15, 139; MTCW 1

Private 19022
See Manning, Frederic

Probst, Mark 1925- **CLC 59**
See also CA 130

Prokosch, Frederic 1908-1989 **CLC 4, 48**
See also CA 73-76; 128; DLB 48

Prophet, The
See Dreiser, Theodore (Herman Albert)

Prose, Francine 1947- **CLC 45**
See also CA 109; 112; CANR 46; SATA 101

Proudhon
See Cunha, Euclides (Rodrigues Pimenta) da

Proulx, Annie
See Proulx, E(dna) Annie

Proulx, E(dna) Annie 1935- **CLC 81; DAM POP**
See also CA 145; CANR 65

Proust, (Valentin-Louis-George-Eugene-) Marcel 1871-1922 **TCLC 7, 13, 33; DA; DAB; DAC; DAM MST, NOV; WLC**
See also CA 104; 120; DLB 65; MTCW 1

Prowler, Harley
See Masters, Edgar Lee

Prus, Boleslaw 1845-1912 **TCLC 48**

Pryor, Richard (Franklin Lenox Thomas) 1940- **CLC 26**
See also CA 122

See also DLB 21

Reade, Hamish
See Gray, Simon (James Holliday)

Reading, Peter 1946- **CLC 47**
See also CA 103; CANR 46; DLB 40

Reaney, James 1926- **CLC 13; DAC; DAM MST**
See also CA 41-44R; CAAS 15; CANR 42; DLB 68; SATA 43

Rebreanu, Liviu 1885-1944 **TCLC 28**
See also CA 165

Rechy, John (Francisco) 1934- **CLC 1, 7, 14, 18, 107; DAM MULT; HLC**
See also CA 5-8R; CAAS 4; CANR 6, 32, 64; DLB 122; DLBY 82; HW; INT CANR-6

Redcam, Tom 1870-1933 **TCLC 25**

Reddin, Keith **CLC 67**

Redgrove, Peter (William) 1932- **CLC 6, 41**
See also CA 1-4R; CANR 3, 39; DLB 40

Redmon, Anne **CLC 22**
See also Nightingale, Anne Redmon
See also DLBY 86

Reed, Eliot
See Ambler, Eric

Reed, Ishmael 1938-**CLC 2, 3, 5, 6, 13, 32, 60; BLC 3; DAM MULT**
See also BW 2; CA 21-24R; CANR 25, 48; DLB 2, 5, 33, 169; DLBD 8; MTCW 1

Reed, John (Silas) 1887-1920 **TCLC 9**
See also CA 106

Reed, Lou **CLC 21**
See also Firbank, Louis

Reeve, Clara 1729-1807 **NCLC 19**
See also DLB 39

Reich, Wilhelm 1897-1957 **TCLC 57**

Reid, Christopher (John) 1949- **CLC 33**
See also CA 140; DLB 40

Reid, Desmond
See Moorcock, Michael (John)

Reid Banks, Lynne 1929-
See Banks, Lynne Reid
See also CA 1-4R; CANR 6, 22, 38; CLR 24; JRDA; MAICYA; SATA 22, 75

Reilly, William K.
See Creasey, John

Reiner, Max
See Caldwell, (Janet Miriam) Taylor (Holland)

Reis, Ricardo
See Pessoa, Fernando (Antonio Nogueira)

Remarque, Erich Maria 1898-1970 **CLC 21; DA; DAB; DAC; DAM MST, NOV**
See also AAYA 27; CA 77-80; 29-32R; DLB 56; MTCW 1

Remizov, A.
See Remizov, Aleksei (Mikhailovich)

Remizov, A. M.
See Remizov, Aleksei (Mikhailovich)

Remizov, Aleksei (Mikhailovich) 1877-1957 **TCLC 27**
See also CA 125; 133

Renan, Joseph Ernest 1823-1892 **NCLC 26**

Renard, Jules 1864-1910 **TCLC 17**
See also CA 117

Renault, Mary **CLC 3, 11, 17**
See also Challans, Mary
See also DLBY 83

Rendell, Ruth (Barbara) 1930- **CLC 28, 48; DAM POP**
See also Vine, Barbara
See also CA 109; CANR 32, 52; DLB 87; INT CANR-32; MTCW 1

Renoir, Jean 1894-1979 **CLC 20**
See also CA 129; 85-88

Resnais, Alain 1922- **CLC 16**

Reverdy, Pierre 1889-1960 **CLC 53**
See also CA 97-100; 89-92

Rexroth, Kenneth 1905-1982 **CLC 1, 2, 6, 11, 22, 49, 112; DAM POET; PC 20**
See also CA 5-8R; 107; CANR 14, 34, 63; CDALB 1941-1968; DLB 16, 48, 165; DLBY 82; INT CANR-14; MTCW 1

Reyes, Alfonso 1889-1959 **TCLC 33**
See also CA 131; HW

Reyes y Basoalto, Ricardo Eliecer Neftali
See Neruda, Pablo

Reymont, Wladyslaw (Stanislaw) 1868(?)-1925 **TCLC 5**
See also CA 104

Reynolds, Jonathan 1942- **CLC 6, 38**
See also CA 65-68; CANR 28

Reynolds, Joshua 1723-1792 **LC 15**
See also DLB 104

Reynolds, Michael Shane 1937- **CLC 44**
See also CA 65-68; CANR 9

Reznikoff, Charles 1894-1976 **CLC 9**
See also CA 33-36; 61-64; CAP 2; DLB 28, 45

Rezzori (d'Arezzo), Gregor von 1914-1998 **CLC 25**
See also CA 122; 136; 167

Rhine, Richard
See Silverstein, Alvin

Rhodes, Eugene Manlove 1869-1934**TCLC 53**

Rhodius, Apollonius c. 3rd cent. B.C.- **CMLC 28**
See also DLB 176

R'hoone
See Balzac, Honore de

Rhys, Jean 1890(?)-1979 **CLC 2, 4, 6, 14, 19, 51; DAM NOV; SSC 21**
See also CA 25-28R; 85-88; CANR 35, 62; CDBLB 1945-1960; DLB 36, 117, 162; MTCW 1

Ribeiro, Darcy 1922-1997 **CLC 34**
See also CA 33-36R; 156

Ribeiro, Joao Ubaldo (Osorio Pimentel) 1941- **CLC 10, 67**
See also CA 81-84

Ribman, Ronald (Burt) 1932- **CLC 7**
See also CA 21-24R; CANR 46

Ricci, Nino 1959- **CLC 70**
See also CA 137

Rice, Anne 1941- **CLC 41; DAM POP**
See also AAYA 9; BEST 89:2; CA 65-68; CANR 12, 36, 53

Rice, Elmer (Leopold) 1892-1967 **CLC 7, 49; DAM DRAM**
See also CA 21-22; 25-28R; CAP 2; DLB 4, 7; MTCW 1

Rice, Tim(othy Miles Bindon) 1944- **CLC 21**
See also CA 103; CANR 46

Rich, Adrienne (Cecile) 1929-**CLC 3, 6, 7, 11, 18, 36, 73, 76; DAM POET; PC 5**
See also CA 9-12R; CANR 20, 53; DLB 5, 67; MTCW 1

Rich, Barbara
See Graves, Robert (von Ranke)

Rich, Robert
See Trumbo, Dalton

Richard, Keith **CLC 17**
See also Richards, Keith

Richards, David Adams 1950- **CLC 59; DAC**
See also CA 93-96; CANR 60; DLB 53

Richards, I(vor) A(rmstrong) 1893-1979**CLC 14, 24**
See also CA 41-44R; 89-92; CANR 34; DLB 27

Richards, Keith 1943-
See Richard, Keith
See also CA 107

Richardson, Anne
See Roiphe, Anne (Richardson)

Richardson, Dorothy Miller 1873-1957**TCLC 3**
See also CA 104; DLB 36

Richardson, Ethel Florence (Lindesay) 1870-1946
See Richardson, Henry Handel
See also CA 105

Richardson, Henry Handel **TCLC 4**
See also Richardson, Ethel Florence (Lindesay)
See also DLB 197

Richardson, John 1796-1852 **NCLC 55; DAC**
See also DLB 99

Richardson, Samuel 1689-1761**LC 1, 44; DA; DAB; DAC; DAM MST, NOV; WLC**
See also CDBLB 1660-1789; DLB 39

Richler, Mordecai 1931-**CLC 3, 5, 9, 13, 18, 46, 70; DAC; DAM MST, NOV**
See also AITN 1; CA 65-68; CANR 31, 62; CLR 17; DLB 53; MAICYA; MTCW 1; SATA 44, 98; SATA-Brief 27

Richter, Conrad (Michael) 1890-1968**CLC 30**
See also AAYA 21; CA 5-8R; 25-28R; CANR 23; DLB 9; MTCW 1; SATA 3

Ricostranza, Tom
See Ellis, Trey

Riddell, Charlotte 1832-1906 **TCLC 40**
See also CA 165; DLB 156

Riding, Laura **CLC 3, 7**
See also Jackson, Laura (Riding)

Riefenstahl, Berta Helene Amalia 1902-
See Riefenstahl, Leni
See also CA 108

Riefenstahl, Leni **CLC 16**
See also Riefenstahl, Berta Helene Amalia

Riffe, Ernest
See Bergman, (Ernst) Ingmar

Riggs, (Rolla) Lynn 1899-1954 **TCLC 56; DAM MULT**
See also CA 144; DLB 175; NNAL

Riis, Jacob A(ugust) 1849-1914 **TCLC 80**
See also CA 113; 168; DLB 23

Riley, James Whitcomb 1849-1916**TCLC 51; DAM POET**
See also CA 118; 137; MAICYA; SATA 17

Riley, Tex
See Creasey, John

Rilke, Rainer Maria 1875-1926**TCLC 1, 6, 19; DAM POET; PC 2**
See also CA 104; 132; CANR 62; DLB 81; MTCW 1

Rimbaud, (Jean Nicolas) Arthur 1854-1891 **NCLC 4, 35; DA; DAB; DAC; DAM MST, POET; PC 3; WLC**

Rinehart, Mary Roberts 1876-1958**TCLC 52**
See also CA 108; 166

Ringmaster, The
See Mencken, H(enry) L(ouis)

Ringwood, Gwen(dolyn Margaret) Pharis 1910-1984 **CLC 48**
See also CA 148; 112; DLB 88

Rio, Michel 19(?)- **CLC 43**

Ritsos, Giannes
See Ritsos, Yannis

Ritsos, Yannis 1909-1990 **CLC 6, 13, 31**
See also CA 77-80; 133; CANR 39, 61; MTCW 1

Ritter, Erika 1948(?)- **CLC 52**

Rivera, Jose Eustasio 1889-1928 **TCLC 35**

See also CA 162; HW

Rivers, Conrad Kent 1933-1968   **CLC 1**
See also BW 1; CA 85-88; DLB 41

Rivers, Elfrida
See Bradley, Marion Zimmer

Riverside, John
See Heinlein, Robert A(nson)

Rizal, Jose 1861-1896   **NCLC 27**

Roa Bastos, Augusto (Antonio) 1917-CLC 45;
DAM MULT; HLC
See also CA 131; DLB 113; HW

Robbe-Grillet, Alain 1922-CLC 1, 2, 4, 6, 8, 10,
14, 43
See also CA 9-12R; CANR 33, 65; DLB 83;
MTCW 1

Robbins, Harold 1916-1997   **CLC 5; DAM
NOV**
See also CA 73-76; 162; CANR 26, 54; MTCW
1

Robbins, Thomas Eugene 1936-
See Robbins, Tom
See also CA 81-84; CANR 29, 59; DAM NOV,
POP; MTCW 1

Robbins, Tom   **CLC 9, 32, 64**
See also Robbins, Thomas Eugene
See also BEST 90:3; DLBY 80

Robbins, Trina 1938-   **CLC 21**
See also CA 128

Roberts, Charles G(eorge) D(ouglas) 1860-1943
TCLC 8
See also CA 105; CLR 33; DLB 92; SATA 88;
SATA-Brief 29

Roberts, Elizabeth Madox 1886-1941 **T C L C
68**
See also CA 111; 166; DLB 9, 54, 102; SATA
33; SATA-Brief 27

Roberts, Kate 1891-1985   **CLC 15**
See also CA 107; 116

Roberts, Keith (John Kingston) 1935-CLC 14
See also CA 25-28R; CANR 46

Roberts, Kenneth (Lewis) 1885-1957TCLC 23
See also CA 109; DLB 9

Roberts, Michele (B.) 1949-   **CLC 48**
See also CA 115; CANR 58

Robertson, Ellis
See Ellison, Harlan (Jay); Silverberg, Robert

Robertson, Thomas William 1829-1871NCLC
35; DAM DRAM

Robeson, Kenneth
See Dent, Lester

Robinson, Edwin Arlington 1869-1935T C L C
5; DA; DAC; DAM MST, POET; PC 1**
See also CA 104; 133; CDALB 1865-1917;
DLB 54; MTCW 1

Robinson, Henry Crabb 1775-1867NCLC 15
See also DLB 107

Robinson, Jill 1936-   **CLC 10**
See also CA 102; INT 102

Robinson, Kim Stanley 1952-   **CLC 34**
See also AAYA 26; CA 126

Robinson, Lloyd
See Silverberg, Robert

Robinson, Marilynne 1944-   **CLC 25**
See also CA 116

Robinson, Smokey   **CLC 21**
See also Robinson, William, Jr.

Robinson, William, Jr. 1940-
See Robinson, Smokey
See also CA 116

Robison, Mary 1949-   **CLC 42, 98**
See also CA 113; 116; DLB 130; INT 116

Rod, Edouard 1857-1910   **TCLC 52**

Roddenberry, Eugene Wesley 1921-1991

See Roddenberry, Gene
See also CA 110; 135; CANR 37; SATA 45;
SATA-Obit 69

Roddenberry, Gene   **CLC 17**
See also Roddenberry, Eugene Wesley
See also AAYA 5; SATA-Obit 69

Rodgers, Mary 1931-   **CLC 12**
See also CA 49-52; CANR 8, 55; CLR 20; INT
CANR-8; JRDA; MAICYA; SATA 8

Rodgers, W(illiam) R(obert) 1909-1969CLC 7
See also CA 85-88; DLB 20

Rodman, Eric
See Silverberg, Robert

Rodman, Howard 1920(?)-1985   **CLC 65**
See also CA 118

Rodman, Maia
See Wojciechowska, Maia (Teresa)

Rodriguez, Claudio 1934-   **CLC 10**
See also DLB 134

Roelvaag, O(le) E(dvart) 1876-1931TCLC 17
See also CA 117; DLB 9

Roethke, Theodore (Huebner) 1908-1963CLC
1, 3, 8, 11, 19, 46, 101; DAM POET; PC 15**
See also CA 81-84; CABS 2; CDALB 1941-
1968; DLB 5; MTCW 1

Rogers, Samuel 1763-1855   **NCLC 69**
See also DLB 93

Rogers, Thomas Hunton 1927-   **CLC 57**
See also CA 89-92; INT 89-92

Rogers, Will(iam Penn Adair) 1879-1935
TCLC 8, 71; DAM MULT
See also CA 105; 144; DLB 11; NNAL

Rogin, Gilbert 1929-   **CLC 18**
See also CA 65-68; CANR 15

Rohan, Koda   **TCLC 22**
See also Koda Shigeyuki

Rohlfs, Anna Katharine Green
See Green, Anna Katharine

Rohmer, Eric   **CLC 16**
See also Scherer, Jean-Marie Maurice

Rohmer, Sax   **TCLC 28**
See also Ward, Arthur Henry Sarsfield
See also DLB 70

Roiphe, Anne (Richardson) 1935-   **CLC 3, 9**
See also CA 89-92; CANR 45; DLBY 80; INT
89-92

Rojas, Fernando de 1465-1541   **LC 23**

**Rolfe, Frederick (William Serafino Austin
Lewis Mary)** 1860-1913   **TCLC 12**
See also CA 107; DLB 34, 156

Rolland, Romain 1866-1944   **TCLC 23**
See also CA 118; DLB 65

Rolle, Richard c. 1300-c. 1349   **CMLC 21**
See also DLB 146

Rolvaag, O(le) E(dvart)
See Roelvaag, O(le) E(dvart)

Romain Arnaud, Saint
See Aragon, Louis

Romains, Jules 1885-1972   **CLC 7**
See also CA 85-88; CANR 34; DLB 65; MTCW
1

Romero, Jose Ruben 1890-1952   **TCLC 14**
See also CA 114; 131; HW

Ronsard, Pierre de 1524-1585   **LC 6; PC 11**

Rooke, Leon 1934-   **CLC 25, 34; DAM POP**
See also CA 25-28R; CANR 23, 53

Roosevelt, Theodore 1858-1919   **TCLC 69**
See also CA 115; DLB 47, 186

Roper, William 1498-1578   **LC 10**

Roquelaure, A. N.
See Rice, Anne

Rosa, Joao Guimaraes 1908-1967   **CLC 23**
See also CA 89-92; DLB 113

Rose, Wendy 1948-CLC 85; DAM MULT; PC
13
See also CA 53-56; CANR 5, 51; DLB 175;
NNAL; SATA 12

Rosen, R. D.
See Rosen, Richard (Dean)

Rosen, Richard (Dean) 1949-   **CLC 39**
See also CA 77-80; CANR 62; INT CANR-30

Rosenberg, Isaac 1890-1918   **TCLC 12**
See also CA 107; DLB 20

Rosenblatt, Joe   **CLC 15**
See also Rosenblatt, Joseph

Rosenblatt, Joseph 1933-
See Rosenblatt, Joe
See also CA 89-92; INT 89-92

Rosenfeld, Samuel
See Tzara, Tristan

Rosenstock, Sami
See Tzara, Tristan

Rosenstock, Samuel
See Tzara, Tristan

Rosenthal, M(acha) L(ouis) 1917-1996   C L C
28
See also CA 1-4R; 152; CAAS 6; CANR 4, 51;
DLB 5; SATA 59

Ross, Barnaby
See Dannay, Frederic

Ross, Bernard L.
See Follett, Ken(neth Martin)

Ross, J. H.
See Lawrence, T(homas) E(dward)

Ross, John Hume
See Lawrence, T(homas) E(dward)

Ross, Martin
See Martin, Violet Florence
See also DLB 135

Ross, (James) Sinclair 1908-   CLC 13; DAC;
DAM MST; SSC 24
See also CA 73-76; DLB 88

Rossetti, Christina (Georgina) 1830-1894
**NCLC 2, 50, 66; DA; DAB; DAC; DAM
MST, POET; PC 7; WLC**
See also DLB 35, 163; MAICYA; SATA 20

Rossetti, Dante Gabriel 1828-1882 NCLC 4;
DA; DAB; DAC; DAM MST, POET; WLC
See also CDBLB 1832-1890; DLB 35

Rossner, Judith (Perelman) 1935-CLC 6, 9, 29
See also AITN 2; BEST 90:3; CA 17-20R;
CANR 18, 51; DLB 6; INT CANR-18;
MTCW 1

Rostand, Edmond (Eugene Alexis) 1868-1918
**TCLC 6, 37; DA; DAB; DAC; DAM
DRAM, MST**
See also CA 104; 126; DLB 192; MTCW 1

Roth, Henry 1906-1995   **CLC 2, 6, 11, 104**
See also CA 11-12; 149; CANR 38, 63; CAP 1;
DLB 28; MTCW 1

Roth, Philip (Milton) 1933-CLC 1, 2, 3, 4, 6, 9,
15, 22, 31, 47, 66, 86; DA; DAB; DAC;
DAM MST, NOV, POP; SSC 26; WLC**
See also BEST 90:3; CA 1-4R; CANR 1, 22,
36, 55; CDALB 1968-1988; DLB 2, 28, 173;
DLBY 82; MTCW 1

Rothenberg, Jerome 1931-   **CLC 6, 57**
See also CA 45-48; CANR 1; DLB 5, 193

Roumain, Jacques (Jean Baptiste) 1907-1944
TCLC 19; BLC 3; DAM MULT
See also BW 1; CA 117; 125

Rourke, Constance (Mayfield) 1885-1941
TCLC 12
See also CA 107; YABC 1

Rousseau, Jean-Baptiste 1671-1741   **LC 9**

Rousseau, Jean-Jacques 1712-1778LC 14, 36;

DA; DAB; DAC; DAM MST; WLC

Roussel, Raymond 1877-1933   **TCLC 20**
See also CA 117

Rovit, Earl (Herbert) 1927-   **CLC 7**
See also CA 5-8R; CANR 12

Rowe, Elizabeth Singer 1674-1737   **LC 44**
See also DLB 39, 95

Rowe, Nicholas 1674-1718   **LC 8**
See also DLB 84

Rowley, Ames Dorrance
See Lovecraft, H(oward) P(hillips)

Rowson, Susanna Haswell 1762(?)-1824
    NCLC 5, 69
See also DLB 37, 200

Roy, Arundhati 1960(?)-   **CLC 109**
See also CA 163; DLBY 97

Roy, Gabrielle 1909-1983 **CLC 10, 14; DAB;
    DAC; DAM MST**
See also CA 53-56; 110; CANR 5, 61; DLB 68;
    MTCW 1

Royko, Mike 1932-1997   **CLC 109**
See also CA 89-92; 157; CANR 26

Rozewicz, Tadeusz 1921-   **CLC 9, 23; DAM
    POET**
See also CA 108; CANR 36, 66; MTCW 1

Ruark, Gibbons 1941-   **CLC 3**
See also CA 33-36R; CAAS 23; CANR 14, 31,
    57; DLB 120

Rubens, Bernice (Ruth) 1923-   **CLC 19, 31**
See also CA 25-28R; CANR 33, 65; DLB 14;
    MTCW 1

Rubin, Harold
See Robbins, Harold

Rudkin, (James) David 1936-   **CLC 14**
See also CA 89-92; DLB 13

Rudnik, Raphael 1933-   **CLC 7**
See also CA 29-32R

Ruffian, M.
See Hasek, Jaroslav (Matej Frantisek)

Ruiz, Jose Martinez   **CLC 11**
See also Martinez Ruiz, Jose

Rukeyser, Muriel 1913-1980**CLC 6, 10, 15, 27;
    DAM POET; PC 12**
See also CA 5-8R; 93-96; CANR 26, 60; DLB
    48; MTCW 1; SATA-Obit 22

Rule, Jane (Vance) 1931-   **CLC 27**
See also CA 25-28R; CAAS 18; CANR 12; DLB
    60

Rulfo, Juan 1918-1986   **CLC 8, 80; DAM
    MULT; HLC; SSC 25**
See also CA 85-88; 118; CANR 26; DLB 113;
    HW; MTCW 1

Rumi, Jalal al-Din 1297-1373   **CMLC 20**

Runeberg, Johan 1804-1877   **NCLC 41**

Runyon, (Alfred) Damon 1884(?)-1946**T C L C
    10**
See also CA 107; 165; DLB 11, 86, 171

Rush, Norman 1933-   **CLC 44**
See also CA 121; 126; INT 126

Rushdie, (Ahmed) Salman 1947-   **CLC 23, 31,
    55, 100; DAB; DAC; DAM MST, NOV,
    POP; WLCS**
See also BEST 89:3; CA 108; 111; CANR 33,
    56; DLB 194; INT 111; MTCW 1

Rushforth, Peter (Scott) 1945-   **CLC 19**
See also CA 101

Ruskin, John 1819-1900   **TCLC 63**
See also CA 114; 129; CDBLB 1832-1890;
    DLB 55, 163, 190; SATA 24

Russ, Joanna 1937-   **CLC 15**
See also CANR 11, 31, 65; DLB 8; MTCW 1

Russell, George William 1867-1935
See Baker, Jean H.

See also CA 104; 153; CDBLB 1890-1914;
    DAM POET

Russell, (Henry) Ken(neth Alfred) 1927-**C L C
    16**
See also CA 105

Russell, William Martin 1947-   **CLC 60**
See also CA 164

Rutherford, Mark   **TCLC 25**
See also White, William Hale
See also DLB 18

Ruyslinck, Ward 1929-   **CLC 14**
See also Belser, Reimond Karel Maria de

Ryan, Cornelius (John) 1920-1974   **CLC 7**
See also CA 69-72; 53-56; CANR 38

Ryan, Michael 1946-   **CLC 65**
See also CA 49-52; DLBY 82

Ryan, Tim
See Dent, Lester

Rybakov, Anatoli (Naumovich) 1911-**CLC 23,
    53**
See also CA 126; 135; SATA 79

Ryder, Jonathan
See Ludlum, Robert

Ryga, George 1932-1987**CLC 14; DAC; DAM
    MST**
See also CA 101; 124; CANR 43; DLB 60

S. H.
See Hartmann, Sadakichi

S. S.
See Sassoon, Siegfried (Lorraine)

Saba, Umberto 1883-1957   **TCLC 33**
See also CA 144; DLB 114

Sabatini, Rafael 1875-1950   **TCLC 47**
See also CA 162

Sabato, Ernesto (R.) 1911-**CLC 10, 23; DAM
    MULT; HLC**
See also CA 97-100; CANR 32, 65; DLB 145;
    HW; MTCW 1

Sa-Carniero, Mario de 1890-1916   **TCLC 83**

Sacastru, Martin
See Bioy Casares, Adolfo

Sacher-Masoch, Leopold von 1836(?)-1895
    NCLC 31

Sachs, Marilyn (Stickle) 1927-   **CLC 35**
See also AAYA 2; CA 17-20R; CANR 13, 47;
    CLR 2; JRDA; MAICYA; SAAS 2; SATA 3,
    68

Sachs, Nelly 1891-1970   **CLC 14, 98**
See also CA 17-18; 25-28R; CAP 2

Sackler, Howard (Oliver) 1929-1982 **CLC 14**
See also CA 61-64; 108; CANR 30; DLB 7

Sacks, Oliver (Wolf) 1933-   **CLC 67**
See also CA 53-56; CANR 28, 50; INT CANR-
    28; MTCW 1

Sadakichi
See Hartmann, Sadakichi

Sade, Donatien Alphonse Francois, Comte de
    1740-1814   **NCLC 47**

Sadoff, Ira 1945-   **CLC 9**
See also CA 53-56; CANR 5, 21; DLB 120

Saetone
See Camus, Albert

Safire, William 1929-   **CLC 10**
See also CA 17-20R; CANR 31, 54

Sagan, Carl (Edward) 1934-1996**CLC 30, 112**
See also AAYA 2; CA 25-28R; 155; CANR 11,
    36; MTCW 1; SATA 58; SATA-Obit 94

Sagan, Francoise   **CLC 3, 6, 9, 17, 36**
See also Quoirez, Francoise
See also DLB 83

Sahgal, Nayantara (Pandit) 1927-   **CLC 41**
See also CA 9-12R; CANR 11

Saint, H(arry) F. 1941-   **CLC 50**

See also CA 127

St. Aubin de Teran, Lisa 1953-
See Teran, Lisa St. Aubin de
See also CA 118; 126; INT 126

Saint Birgitta of Sweden c. 1303-1373**C M L C
    24**

Sainte-Beuve, Charles Augustin 1804-1869
    NCLC 5

**Saint-Exupery, Antoine (Jean Baptiste Marie
    Roger) de** 1900-1944**TCLC 2, 56; DAM
    NOV; WLC**
See also CA 108; 132; CLR 10; DLB 72;
    MAICYA; MTCW 1; SATA 20

St. John, David
See Hunt, E(verette) Howard, (Jr.)

Saint-John Perse
See Leger, (Marie-Rene Auguste) Alexis Saint-
    Leger

Saintsbury, George (Edward Bateman) 1845-
    1933   **TCLC 31**
See also CA 160; DLB 57, 149

Sait Faik   **TCLC 23**
See also Abasiyanik, Sait Faik

Saki   **TCLC 3; SSC 12**
See also Munro, H(ector) H(ugh)

Sala, George Augustus   **NCLC 46**

Salama, Hannu 1936-   **CLC 18**

Salamanca, J(ack) R(ichard) 1922-**CLC 4, 15**
See also CA 25-28R

Sale, J. Kirkpatrick
See Sale, Kirkpatrick

Sale, Kirkpatrick 1937-   **CLC 68**
See also CA 13-16R; CANR 10

Salinas, Luis Omar 1937-   **CLC 90; DAM
    MULT; HLC**
See also CA 131; DLB 82; HW

Salinas (y Serrano), Pedro 1891(?)-1951
    TCLC 17
See also CA 117; DLB 134

Salinger, J(erome) D(avid) 1919-**CLC 1, 3, 8,
    12, 55, 56; DA; DAB; DAC; DAM MST,
    NOV, POP; SSC 2, 28; WLC**
See also AAYA 2; CA 5-8R; CANR 39; CDALB
    1941-1968; CLR 18; DLB 2, 102, 173;
    MAICYA; MTCW 1; SATA 67

Salisbury, John
See Caute, (John) David

Salter, James 1925-   **CLC 7, 52, 59**
See also CA 73-76; DLB 130

Saltus, Edgar (Everton) 1855-1921   **TCLC 8**
See also CA 105; DLB 202

Saltykov, Mikhail Evgrafovich 1826-1889
    NCLC 16

Samarakis, Antonis 1919-   **CLC 5**
See also CA 25-28R; CAAS 16; CANR 36

Sanchez, Florencio 1875-1910   **TCLC 37**
See also CA 153; HW

Sanchez, Luis Rafael 1936-   **CLC 23**
See also CA 128; DLB 145; HW

Sanchez, Sonia 1934-   **CLC 5; BLC 3; DAM
    MULT; PC 9**
See also BW 2; CA 33-36R; CANR 24, 49; CLR
    18; DLB 41; DLBD 8; MAICYA; MTCW 1;
    SATA 22

Sand, George 1804-1876**NCLC 2, 42, 57; DA;
    DAB; DAC; DAM MST, NOV; WLC**
See also DLB 119, 192

Sandburg, Carl (August) 1878-1967**CLC 1, 4,
    10, 15, 35; DA; DAB; DAC; DAM MST,
    POET; PC 2; WLC**
See also AAYA 24; CA 5-8R; 25-28R; CANR
    35; CDALB 1865-1917; DLB 17, 54;
    MAICYA; MTCW 1; SATA 8

Scott, Duncan Campbell 1862-1947 **TCLC 6; DAC**
See also CA 104; 153; DLB 92
Scott, Evelyn 1893-1963 **CLC 43**
See also CA 104; 112; CANR 64; DLB 9, 48
Scott, F(rancis) R(eginald) 1899-1985**CLC 22**
See also CA 101; 114; DLB 88; INT 101
Scott, Frank
See Scott, F(rancis) R(eginald)
Scott, Joanna 1960- **CLC 50**
See also CA 126; CANR 53
Scott, Paul (Mark) 1920-1978 **CLC 9, 60**
See also CA 81-84; 77-80; CANR 33; DLB 14; MTCW 1
Scott, Sarah 1723-1795 **LC 44**
See also DLB 39
Scott, Walter 1771-1832 **NCLC 15, 69; DA; DAB; DAC; DAM MST, NOV, POET; PC 13; SSC 32; WLC**
See also AAYA 22; CDBLB 1789-1832; DLB 93, 107, 116, 144, 159; YABC 2
Scribe, (Augustin) Eugene 1791-1861 **N C L C 16; DAM DRAM; DC 5**
See also DLB 192
Scrum, R.
See Crumb, R(obert)
Scudery, Madeleine de 1607-1701 **LC 2**
Scum
See Crumb, R(obert)
Scumbag, Little Bobby
See Crumb, R(obert)
Seabrook, John
See Hubbard, L(afayette) Ron(ald)
Sealy, I. Allan 1951- **CLC 55**
Search, Alexander
See Pessoa, Fernando (Antonio Nogueira)
Sebastian, Lee
See Silverberg, Robert
Sebastian Owl
See Thompson, Hunter S(tockton)
Sebestyen, Ouida 1924- **CLC 30**
See also AAYA 8; CA 107; CANR 40; CLR 17; JRDA; MAICYA; SAAS 10; SATA 39
Secundus, H. Scriblerus
See Fielding, Henry
Sedges, John
See Buck, Pearl S(ydenstricker)
Sedgwick, Catharine Maria 1789-1867**N C L C 19**
See also DLB 1, 74
Seelye, John (Douglas) 1931- **CLC 7**
See also CA 97-100; CANR 70; INT 97-100
Seferiades, Giorgos Stylianou 1900-1971
See Seferis, George
See also CA 5-8R; 33-36R; CANR 5, 36; MTCW 1
Seferis, George **CLC 5, 11**
See also Seferiades, Giorgos Stylianou
Segal, Erich (Wolf) 1937- **CLC 3, 10; DAM POP**
See also BEST 89:1; CA 25-28R; CANR 20, 36, 65; DLBY 86; INT CANR-20; MTCW 1
Seger, Bob 1945- **CLC 35**
Seghers, Anna **CLC 7**
See also Radvanyi, Netty
See also DLB 69
Seidel, Frederick (Lewis) 1936- **CLC 18**
See also CA 13-16R; CANR 8; DLBY 84
Seifert, Jaroslav 1901-1986 **CLC 34, 44, 93**
See also CA 127; MTCW 1
Sei Shonagon c. 966-1017(?) **CMLC 6**
Selby, Hubert, Jr. 1928-**CLC 1, 2, 4, 8; SSC 20**
See also CA 13-16R; CANR 33; DLB 2

Selzer, Richard 1928- **CLC 74**
See also CA 65-68; CANR 14
Sembene, Ousmane
See Ousmane, Sembene
Senancour, Etienne Pivert de 1770-1846 **NCLC 16**
See also DLB 119
Sender, Ramon (Jose) 1902-1982**CLC 8; DAM MULT; HLC**
See also CA 5-8R; 105; CANR 8; HW; MTCW 1
Seneca, Lucius Annaeus 4B.C.-65 **CMLC 6; DAM DRAM; DC 5**
Senghor, Leopold Sedar 1906- **CLC 54; BLC 3; DAM MULT, POET**
See also BW 2; CA 116; 125; CANR 47; MTCW 1
Serling, (Edward) Rod(man) 1924-1975 **C L C 30**
See also AAYA 14; AITN 1; CA 162; 57-60; DLB 26
Serna, Ramon Gomez de la
See Gomez de la Serna, Ramon
Serpieres
See Guillevic, (Eugene)
Service, Robert
See Service, Robert W(illiam)
See also DAB; DLB 92
Service, Robert W(illiam) 1874(?)-1958**TCLC 15; DA; DAC; DAM MST, POET; WLC**
See also Service, Robert
See also CA 115; 140; SATA 20
Seth, Vikram 1952-**CLC 43, 90; DAM MULT**
See also CA 121; 127; CANR 50; DLB 120; INT 127
Seton, Cynthia Propper 1926-1982 **CLC 27**
See also CA 5-8R; 108; CANR 7
Seton, Ernest (Evan) Thompson 1860-1946 **TCLC 31**
See also CA 109; DLB 92; DLBD 13; JRDA; SATA 18
Seton-Thompson, Ernest
See Seton, Ernest (Evan) Thompson
Settle, Mary Lee 1918- **CLC 19, 61**
See also CA 89-92; CAAS 1; CANR 44; DLB 6; INT 89-92
Seuphor, Michel
See Arp, Jean
Sevigne, Marie (de Rabutin-Chantal) Marquise de 1626-1696 **LC 11**
Sewall, Samuel 1652-1730 **LC 38**
See also DLB 24
Sexton, Anne (Harvey) 1928-1974**CLC 2, 4, 6, 8, 10, 15, 53; DA; DAB; DAC; DAM MST, POET; PC 2; WLC**
See also CA 1-4R; 53-56; CABS 2; CANR 3, 36; CDALB 1941-1968; DLB 5, 169; MTCW 1; SATA 10
Shaara, Michael (Joseph, Jr.) 1929-1988**C L C 15; DAM POP**
See also AITN 1; CA 102; 125; CANR 52; DLBY 83
Shackleton, C. C.
See Aldiss, Brian W(ilson)
Shacochis, Bob **CLC 39**
See also Shacochis, Robert G.
Shacochis, Robert G. 1951-
See Shacochis, Bob
See also CA 119; 124; INT 124
Shaffer, Anthony (Joshua) 1926- **CLC 19; DAM DRAM**
See also CA 110; 116; DLB 13
Shaffer, Peter (Levin) 1926-**CLC 5, 14, 18, 37,**

60; DAB; DAM DRAM, MST; DC 7
See also CA 25-28R; CANR 25, 47; CDBLB 1960 to Present; DLB 13; MTCW 1
Shakey, Bernard
See Young, Neil
Shalamov, Varlam (Tikhonovich) 1907(?)-1982 **CLC 18**
See also CA 129; 105
Shamlu, Ahmad 1925- **CLC 10**
Shammas, Anton 1951- **CLC 55**
Shange, Ntozake 1948-**CLC 8, 25, 38, 74; BLC 3; DAM DRAM, MULT; DC 3**
See also AAYA 9; BW 2; CA 85-88; CABS 3; CANR 27, 48; DLB 38; MTCW 1
Shanley, John Patrick 1950- **CLC 75**
See also CA 128; 133
Shapcott, Thomas W(illiam) 1935- **CLC 38**
See also CA 69-72; CANR 49
Shapiro, Jane **CLC 76**
Shapiro, Karl (Jay) 1913- **CLC 4, 8, 15, 53**
See also CA 1-4R; CAAS 6; CANR 1, 36, 66; DLB 48; MTCW 1
Sharp, William 1855-1905 **TCLC 39**
See also CA 160; DLB 156
Sharpe, Thomas Ridley 1928-
See Sharpe, Tom
See also CA 114; 122; INT 122
Sharpe, Tom **CLC 36**
See also Sharpe, Thomas Ridley
See also DLB 14
Shaw, Bernard **TCLC 45**
See also Shaw, George Bernard
See also BW 1
Shaw, G. Bernard
See Shaw, George Bernard
Shaw, George Bernard 1856-1950**TCLC 3, 9, 21; DA; DAB; DAC; DAM DRAM, MST; WLC**
See also Shaw, Bernard
See also CA 104; 128; CDBLB 1914-1945; DLB 10, 57, 190; MTCW 1
Shaw, Henry Wheeler 1818-1885 **NCLC 15**
See also DLB 11
Shaw, Irwin 1913-1984 **CLC 7, 23, 34; DAM DRAM, POP**
See also AITN 1; CA 13-16R; 112; CANR 21; CDALB 1941-1968; DLB 6, 102; DLBY 84; MTCW 1
Shaw, Robert 1927-1978 **CLC 5**
See also AITN 1; CA 1-4R; 81-84; CANR 4; DLB 13, 14
Shaw, T. E.
See Lawrence, T(homas) E(dward)
Shawn, Wallace 1943- **CLC 41**
See also CA 112
Shea, Lisa 1953- **CLC 86**
See also CA 147
Sheed, Wilfrid (John Joseph) 1930-**CLC 2, 4, 10, 53**
See also CA 65-68; CANR 30, 66; DLB 6; MTCW 1
Sheldon, Alice Hastings Bradley 1915(?)-1987
See Tiptree, James, Jr.
See also CA 108; 122; CANR 34; INT 108; MTCW 1
Sheldon, John
See Bloch, Robert (Albert)
Shelley, Mary Wollstonecraft (Godwin) 1797-1851**NCLC 14, 59; DA; DAB; DAC; DAM MST, NOV; WLC**
See also AAYA 20; CDBLB 1789-1832; DLB 110, 116, 159, 178; SATA 29
Shelley, Percy Bysshe 1792-1822 **NCLC 18;**

DA; DAB; DAC; DAM MST, POET; PC
14; WLC
See also CDBLB 1789-1832; DLB 96, 110, 158
Shepard, Jim 1956- **CLC 36**
See also CA 137; CANR 59; SATA 90
Shepard, Lucius 1947- **CLC 34**
See also CA 128; 141
Shepard, Sam 1943- CLC 4, 6, 17, 34, 41, 44;
DAM DRAM; DC 5
See also AAYA 1; CA 69-72; CABS 3; CANR
22; DLB 7; MTCW 1
Shepherd, Michael
See Ludlum, Robert
Sherburne, Zoa (Morin) 1912- **CLC 30**
See also AAYA 13; CA 1-4R; CANR 3, 37;
MAICYA; SAAS 18; SATA 3
Sheridan, Frances 1724-1766 **LC 7**
See also DLB 39, 84
Sheridan, Richard Brinsley 1751-1816N C L C
5; DA; DAB; DAC; DAM DRAM, MST;
DC 1; WLC
See also CDBLB 1660-1789; DLB 89
Sherman, Jonathan Marc **CLC 55**
Sherman, Martin 1941(?)- **CLC 19**
See also CA 116; 123
Sherwin, Judith Johnson 1936- **CLC 7, 15**
See also CA 25-28R; CANR 34
Sherwood, Frances 1940- **CLC 81**
See also CA 146
Sherwood, Robert E(mmet) 1896-1955T C L C
3; DAM DRAM
See also CA 104; 153; DLB 7, 26
Shestov, Lev 1866-1938 **TCLC 56**
Shevchenko, Taras 1814-1861 **NCLC 54**
Shiel, M(atthew) P(hipps) 1865-1947TCLC 8
See also Holmes, Gordon
See also CA 106; 160; DLB 153
Shields, Carol 1935- **CLC 91, 113; DAC**
See also CA 81-84; CANR 51
Shields, David 1956- **CLC 97**
See also CA 124; CANR 48
Shiga, Naoya 1883-1971 **CLC 33; SSC 23**
See also CA 101; 33-36R; DLB 180
Shilts, Randy 1951-1994 **CLC 85**
See also AAYA 19; CA 115; 127; 144; CANR
45; INT 127
Shimazaki, Haruki 1872-1943
See Shimazaki Toson
See also CA 105; 134
Shimazaki Toson 1872-1943 **TCLC 5**
See also Shimazaki, Haruki
See also DLB 180
Sholokhov, Mikhail (Aleksandrovich) 1905-
1984 **CLC 7, 15**
See also CA 101; 112; MTCW 1; SATA-Obit
36
Shone, Patric
See Hanley, James
Shreve, Susan Richards 1939- **CLC 23**
See also CA 49-52; CAAS 5; CANR 5, 38, 69;
MAICYA; SATA 46, 95; SATA-Brief 41
Shue, Larry 1946-1985CLC 52; DAM DRAM
See also CA 145; 117
Shu-Jen, Chou 1881-1936
See Lu Hsun
See also CA 104
Shulman, Alix Kates 1932- **CLC 2, 10**
See also CA 29-32R; CANR 43; SATA 7
Shuster, Joe 1914- **CLC 21**
Shute, Nevil **CLC 30**
See also Norway, Nevil Shute
Shuttle, Penelope (Diane) 1947- **CLC 7**
See also CA 93-96; CANR 39; DLB 14, 40

Sidney, Mary 1561-1621 **LC 19, 39**
Sidney, Sir Philip 1554-1586 LC 19, 39; DA;
DAB; DAC; DAM MST, POET ·
See also CDBLB Before 1660; DLB 167
Siegel, Jerome 1914-1996 **CLC 21**
See also CA 116; 151
Siegel, Jerry
See Siegel, Jerome
Sienkiewicz, Henryk (Adam Alexander Pius)
1846-1916 **TCLC 3**
See also CA 104; 134
Sierra, Gregorio Martinez
See Martinez Sierra, Gregorio
Sierra, Maria (de la O'LeJarraga) Martinez
See Martinez Sierra, Maria (de la O'LeJarraga)
Sigal, Clancy 1926- **CLC 7**
See also CA 1-4R
Sigourney, Lydia Howard (Huntley) 1791-1865
NCLC 21
See also DLB 1, 42, 73
Siguenza y Gongora, Carlos de 1645-1700L C
8
Sigurjonsson, Johann 1880-1919 **TCLC 27**
Sikelianos, Angelos 1884-1951 **TCLC 39**
Silkin, Jon 1930- **CLC 2, 6, 43**
See also CA 5-8R; CAAS 5; DLB 27
Silko, Leslie (Marmon) 1948-CLC 23, 74, 114;
DA; DAC; DAM MST, MULT, POP;
WLCS
See also AAYA 14; CA 115; 122; CANR 45,
65; DLB 143, 175; NNAL
Sillanpaa, Frans Eemil 1888-1964 **CLC 19**
See also CA 129; 93-96; MTCW 1
Sillitoe, Alan 1928- **CLC 1, 3, 6, 10, 19, 57**
See also AITN 1; CA 9-12R; CAAS 2; CANR
8, 26, 55; CDBLB 1960 to Present; DLB 14,
139; MTCW 1; SATA 61
Silone, Ignazio 1900-1978 **CLC 4**
See also CA 25-28; 81-84; CANR 34; CAP 2;
MTCW 1
Silver, Joan Micklin 1935- **CLC 20**
See also CA 114; 121; INT 121
Silver, Nicholas
See Faust, Frederick (Schiller)
Silverberg, Robert 1935- CLC 7; DAM POP
See also AAYA 24; CA 1-4R; CAAS 3; CANR
1, 20, 36; DLB 8; INT CANR-20; MAICYA;
MTCW 1; SATA 13, 91
Silverstein, Alvin 1933- **CLC 17**
See also CA 49-52; CANR 2; CLR 25; JRDA;
MAICYA; SATA 8, 69
Silverstein, Virginia B(arbara Opshelor) 1937-
CLC 17
See also CA 49-52; CANR 2; CLR 25; JRDA;
MAICYA; SATA 8, 69
Sim, Georges
See Simenon, Georges (Jacques Christian)
Simak, Clifford D(onald) 1904-1988CLC 1, 55
See also CA 1-4R; 125; CANR 1, 35; DLB 8;
MTCW 1; SATA-Obit 56
Simenon, Georges (Jacques Christian) 1903-
1989 **CLC 1, 2, 3, 8, 18, 47; DAM POP**
See also CA 85-88; 129; CANR 35; DLB 72;
DLBY 89; MTCW 1
Simic, Charles 1938- **CLC 6, 9, 22, 49, 68;
DAM POET**
See also CA 29-32R; CAAS 4; CANR 12, 33,
52, 61; DLB 105
Simmel, Georg 1858-1918 **TCLC 64**
See also CA 157
Simmons, Charles (Paul) 1924- **CLC 57**
See also CA 89-92; INT 89-92
Simmons, Dan 1948- **CLC 44; DAM POP**

See also AAYA 16; CA 138; CANR 53
Simmons, James (Stewart Alexander) 1933-
CLC 43
See also CA 105; CAAS 21; DLB 40
Simms, William Gilmore 1806-1870 **NCLC 3**
See also DLB 3, 30, 59, 73
Simon, Carly 1945- **CLC 26**
See also CA 105
Simon, Claude 1913-1984 **CLC 4, 9, 15, 39;
DAM NOV**
See also CA 89-92; CANR 33; DLB 83; MTCW
1
Simon, (Marvin) Neil 1927-CLC 6, 11, 31, 39,
70; DAM DRAM
See also AITN 1; CA 21-24R; CANR 26, 54;
DLB 7; MTCW 1
Simon, Paul (Frederick) 1941(?)- **CLC 17**
See also CA 116; 153
Simonon, Paul 1956(?)- **CLC 30**
Simpson, Harriette
See Arnow, Harriette (Louisa) Simpson
Simpson, Louis (Aston Marantz) 1923-CLC 4,
7, 9, 32; DAM POET
See also CA 1-4R; CAAS 4; CANR 1, 61; DLB
5; MTCW 1
Simpson, Mona (Elizabeth) 1957- **CLC 44**
See also CA 122; 135; CANR 68
Simpson, N(orman) F(rederick) 1919-CLC 29
See also CA 13-16R; DLB 13
Sinclair, Andrew (Annandale) 1935- CLC 2,
14
See also CA 9-12R; CAAS 5; CANR 14, 38;
DLB 14; MTCW 1
Sinclair, Emil
See Hesse, Hermann
Sinclair, Iain 1943- **CLC 76**
See also CA 132
Sinclair, Iain MacGregor
See Sinclair, Iain
Sinclair, Irene
See Griffith, D(avid Lewelyn) W(ark)
Sinclair, Mary Amelia St. Clair 1865(?)-1946
See Sinclair, May
See also CA 104
Sinclair, May 1863-1946 **TCLC 3, 11**
See also Sinclair, Mary Amelia St. Clair
See also CA 166; DLB 36, 135
Sinclair, Roy
See Griffith, D(avid Lewelyn) W(ark)
Sinclair, Upton (Beall) 1878-1968 CLC 1, 11,
15, 63; DA; DAB; DAC; DAM MST, NOV;
WLC
See also CA 5-8R; 25-28R; CANR 7; CDALB
1929-1941; DLB 9; INT CANR-7; MTCW
1; SATA 9
Singer, Isaac
See Singer, Isaac Bashevis
Singer, Isaac Bashevis 1904-1991CLC 1, 3, 6,
9, 11, 15, 23, 38, 69, 111; DA; DAB; DAC;
DAM MST, NOV; SSC 3; WLC
See also AITN 1, 2; CA 1-4R; 134; CANR 1,
39; CDALB 1941-1968; CLR 1; DLB 6, 28,
52; DLBY 91; JRDA; MAICYA; MTCW 1;
SATA 3, 27; SATA-Obit 68
Singer, Israel Joshua 1893-1944 **TCLC 33**
Singh, Khushwant 1915- **CLC 11**
See also CA 9-12R; CAAS 9; CANR 6
Singleton, Ann
See Benedict, Ruth (Fulton)
Sinjohn, John
See Galsworthy, John
Sinyavsky, Andrei (Donatevich) 1925-1997
CLC 8

See also CA 85-88; 159

Sirin, V.
See Nabokov, Vladimir (Vladimirovich)

Sissman, L(ouis) E(dward) 1928-1976 **CLC 9, 18**
See also CA 21-24R; 65-68; CANR 13; DLB 5

Sisson, C(harles) H(ubert) 1914-   **CLC 8**
See also CA 1-4R; CAAS 3; CANR 3, 48; DLB 27

Sitwell, Dame Edith 1887-1964 **CLC 2, 9, 67; DAM POET; PC 3**
See also CA 9-12R; CANR 35; CDBLB 1945-1960; DLB 20; MTCW 1

Siwaarmill, H. P.
See Sharp, William

Sjoewall, Maj 1935-   **CLC 7**
See also CA 65-68

Sjowall, Maj
See Sjoewall, Maj

Skelton, Robin 1925-1997   **CLC 13**
See also AITN 2; CA 5-8R; 160; CAAS 5; CANR 28; DLB 27, 53

Skolimowski, Jerzy 1938-   **CLC 20**
See also CA 128

Skram, Amalie (Bertha) 1847-1905 **TCLC 25**
See also CA 165

Skvorecky, Josef (Vaclav) 1924- **CLC 15, 39, 69; DAC; DAM NOV**
See also CA 61-64; CAAS 1; CANR 10, 34, 63; MTCW 1

Slade, Bernard   **CLC 11, 46**
See also Newbound, Bernard Slade
See also CAAS 9; DLB 53

Slaughter, Carolyn 1946-   **CLC 56**
See also CA 85-88

Slaughter, Frank G(ill) 1908-   **CLC 29**
See also AITN 2; CA 5-8R; CANR 5; INT CANR-5

Slavitt, David R(ytman) 1935-   **CLC 5, 14**
See also CA 21-24R; CAAS 3; CANR 41; DLB 5, 6

Slesinger, Tess 1905-1945   **TCLC 10**
See also CA 107; DLB 102

Slessor, Kenneth 1901-1971   **CLC 14**
See also CA 102; 89-92

Slowacki, Juliusz 1809-1849   **NCLC 15**

Smart, Christopher 1722-1771   **LC 3; DAM POET; PC 13**
See also DLB 109

Smart, Elizabeth 1913-1986   **CLC 54**
See also CA 81-84; 118; DLB 88

Smiley, Jane (Graves) 1949-**CLC 53, 76; DAM POP**
See also CA 104; CANR 30, 50; INT CANR-30

Smith, A(rthur) J(ames) M(arshall) 1902-1980 **CLC 15; DAC**
See also CA 1-4R; 102; CANR 4; DLB 88

Smith, Adam 1723-1790   **LC 36**
See also DLB 104

Smith, Alexander 1829-1867   **NCLC 59**
See also DLB 32, 55

Smith, Anna Deavere 1950-   **CLC 86**
See also CA 133

Smith, Betty (Wehner) 1896-1972   **CLC 19**
See also CA 5-8R; 33-36R; DLBY 82; SATA 6

Smith, Charlotte (Turner) 1749-1806 **NCLC 23**
See also DLB 39, 109

Smith, Clark Ashton 1893-1961   **CLC 43**
See also CA 143

Smith, Dave   **CLC 22, 42**
See also Smith, David (Jeddie)

Smith, David (Jeddie) 1942-
See Smith, Dave
See also CA 49-52; CANR 1, 59; DAM POET

Smith, Florence Margaret 1902-1971
See Smith, Stevie
See also CA 17-18; 29-32R; CANR 35; CAP 2; DAM POET; MTCW 1

Smith, Iain Crichton 1928-   **CLC 64**
See also CA 21-24R; DLB 40, 139

Smith, John 1580(?)-1631   **LC 9**
See also DLB 24, 30

Smith, Johnston
See Crane, Stephen (Townley)

Smith, Joseph, Jr. 1805-1844   **NCLC 53**

Smith, Lee 1944-   **CLC 25, 73**
See also CA 114; 119; CANR 46; DLB 143; DLBY 83; INT 119

Smith, Martin
See Smith, Martin Cruz

Smith, Martin Cruz 1942-   **CLC 25; DAM MULT, POP**
See also BEST 89:4; CA 85-88; CANR 6, 23, 43, 65; INT CANR-23; NNAL

Smith, Mary-Ann Tirone 1944-   **CLC 39**
See also CA 118; 136

Smith, Patti 1946-   **CLC 12**
See also CA 93-96; CANR 63

Smith, Pauline (Urmson) 1882-1959**TCLC 25**

Smith, Rosamond
See Oates, Joyce Carol

Smith, Sheila Kaye
See Kaye-Smith, Sheila

Smith, Stevie   **CLC 3, 8, 25, 44; PC 12**
See also Smith, Florence Margaret
See also DLB 20

Smith, Wilbur (Addison) 1933-   **CLC 33**
See also CA 13-16R; CANR 7, 46, 66; MTCW 1

Smith, William Jay 1918-   **CLC 6**
See also CA 5-8R; CANR 44; DLB 5; MAICYA; SAAS 22; SATA 2, 68

Smith, Woodrow Wilson
See Kuttner, Henry

Smolenskin, Peretz 1842-1885   **NCLC 30**

Smollett, Tobias (George) 1721-1771   **LC 2**
See also CDBLB 1660-1789; DLB 39, 104

Snodgrass, W(illiam) D(e Witt) 1926- **CLC 2, 6, 10, 18, 68; DAM POET**
See also CA 1-4R; CANR 6, 36, 65; DLB 5; MTCW 1

Snow, C(harles) P(ercy) 1905-1980 **CLC 1, 4, 6, 9, 13, 19; DAM NOV**
See also CA 5-8R; 101; CANR 28; CDBLB 1945-1960; DLB 15, 77; DLBD 17; MTCW 1

Snow, Frances Compton
See Adams, Henry (Brooks)

Snyder, Gary (Sherman) 1930-**CLC 1, 2, 5, 9, 32; DAM POET; PC 21**
See also CA 17-20R; CANR 30, 60; DLB 5, 16, 165

Snyder, Zilpha Keatley 1927-   **CLC 17**
See also AAYA 15; CA 9-12R; CANR 38; CLR 31; JRDA; MAICYA; SAAS 2; SATA 1, 28, 75

Soares, Bernardo
See Pessoa, Fernando (Antonio Nogueira)

Sobh, A.
See Shamlu, Ahmad

Sobol, Joshua   **CLC 60**

Socrates 469B.C.-399B.C.   **CMLC 27**

Soderberg, Hjalmar 1869-1941   **TCLC 39**

Sodergran, Edith (Irene)
See Soedergran, Edith (Irene)

Soedergran, Edith (Irene) 1892-1923 **TCLC 31**

Softly, Edgar
See Lovecraft, H(oward) P(hillips)

Softly, Edward
See Lovecraft, H(oward) P(hillips)

Sokolov, Raymond 1941-   **CLC 7**
See also CA 85-88

Solo, Jay
See Ellison, Harlan (Jay)

Sologub, Fyodor   **TCLC 9**
See also Teternikov, Fyodor Kuzmich

Solomons, Ikey Esquir
See Thackeray, William Makepeace

Solomos, Dionysios 1798-1857   **NCLC 15**

Solwoska, Mara
See French, Marilyn

Solzhenitsyn, Aleksandr I(sayevich) 1918- **CLC 1, 2, 4, 7, 9, 10, 18, 26, 34, 78; DA; DAB; DAC; DAM MST, NOV; SSC 32; WLC**
See also AITN 1; CA 69-72; CANR 40, 65; MTCW 1

Somers, Jane
See Lessing, Doris (May)

Somerville, Edith 1858-1949   **TCLC 51**
See also DLB 135

Somerville & Ross
See Martin, Violet Florence; Somerville, Edith

Sommer, Scott 1951-   **CLC 25**
See also CA 106

Sondheim, Stephen (Joshua) 1930- **CLC 30, 39; DAM DRAM**
See also AAYA 11; CA 103; CANR 47, 68

Song, Cathy 1955-   **PC 21**
See also CA 154; DLB 169

Sontag, Susan 1933-**CLC 1, 2, 10, 13, 31, 105; DAM POP**
See also CA 17-20R; CANR 25, 51; DLB 2, 67; MTCW 1

Sophocles 496(?)B.C.-406(?)B.C.   **CMLC 2; DA; DAB; DAC; DAM DRAM, MST; DC 1; WLCS**
See also DLB 176

Sordello 1189-1269   **CMLC 15**

Sorel, Julia
See Drexler, Rosalyn

Sorrentino, Gilbert 1929-**CLC 3, 7, 14, 22, 40**
See also CA 77-80; CANR 14, 33; DLB 5, 173; DLBY 80; INT CANR-14

Soto, Gary 1952-   **CLC 32, 80; DAM MULT; HLC**
See also AAYA 10; CA 119; 125; CANR 50; CLR 38; DLB 82; HW; INT 125; JRDA; SATA 80

Soupault, Philippe 1897-1990   **CLC 68**
See also CA 116; 147; 131

Souster, (Holmes) Raymond 1921-**CLC 5, 14; DAC; DAM POET**
See also CA 13-16R; CAAS 14; CANR 13, 29, 53; DLB 88; SATA 63

Southern, Terry 1924(?)-1995   **CLC 7**
See also CA 1-4R; 150; CANR 1, 55; DLB 2

Southey, Robert 1774-1843   **NCLC 8**
See also DLB 93, 107, 142; SATA 54

Southworth, Emma Dorothy Eliza Nevitte 1819-1899   **NCLC 26**

Souza, Ernest
See Scott, Evelyn

Soyinka, Wole 1934-**CLC 3, 5, 14, 36, 44; BLC 3; DA; DAB; DAC; DAM DRAM, MST,**

See also CA 85-88; 143; CANR 38, 60; MTCW
1

Thomas, Paul
See Mann, (Paul) Thomas

Thomas, Piri 1928-   **CLC 17**
See also CA 73-76; HW

Thomas, R(onald) S(tuart) 1913- **CLC 6, 13,
48; DAB; DAM POET**
See also CA 89-92; CAAS 4; CANR 30;
CDBLB 1960 to Present; DLB 27; MTCW 1

Thomas, Ross (Elmore) 1926-1995   **CLC 39**
See also CA 33-36R; 150; CANR 22, 63

Thompson, Francis Clegg
See Mencken, H(enry) L(ouis)

Thompson, Francis Joseph 1859-1907**TCLC 4**
See also CA 104; CDBLB 1890-1914; DLB 19

Thompson, Hunter S(tockton) 1939- **CLC 9,
17, 40, 104; DAM POP**
See also BEST 89:1; CA 17-20R; CANR 23,
46; DLB 185; MTCW 1

Thompson, James Myers
See Thompson, Jim (Myers)

Thompson, Jim (Myers) 1906-1977(?)**CLC 69**
See also CA 140

Thompson, Judith   **CLC 39**

Thomson, James 1700-1748   **LC 16, 29, 40;
DAM POET**
See also DLB 95

Thomson, James 1834-1882 **NCLC 18; DAM
POET**
See also DLB 35

Thoreau, Henry David 1817-1862**NCLC 7, 21,
61; DA; DAB; DAC; DAM MST; WLC**
See also CDALB 1640-1865; DLB 1

Thornton, Hall
See Silverberg, Robert

Thucydides c. 455B.C.-399B.C.   **CMLC 17**
See also DLB 176

Thurber, James (Grover) 1894-1961   **CLC 5,
11, 25; DA; DAB; DAC; DAM DRAM,
MST, NOV; SSC 1**
See also CA 73-76; CANR 17, 39; CDALB
1929-1941; DLB 4, 11, 22, 102; MAICYA;
MTCW 1; SATA 13

Thurman, Wallace (Henry) 1902-1934**T C L C
6; BLC 3; DAM MULT**
See also BW 1; CA 104; 124; DLB 51

Ticheburn, Cheviot
See Ainsworth, William Harrison

Tieck, (Johann) Ludwig 1773-1853 **NCLC 5,
46; SSC 31**
See also DLB 90

Tiger, Derry
See Ellison, Harlan (Jay)

Tilghman, Christopher 1948(?)-   **CLC 65**
See also CA 159

Tillinghast, Richard (Williford) 1940-**CLC 29**
See also CA 29-32R; CAAS 23; CANR 26, 51

Timrod, Henry 1828-1867   **NCLC 25**
See also DLB 3

Tindall, Gillian (Elizabeth) 1938-   **CLC 7**
See also CA 21-24R; CANR 11, 65

Tiptree, James, Jr.   **CLC 48, 50**
See also Sheldon, Alice Hastings Bradley
See also DLB 8

Titmarsh, Michael Angelo
See Thackeray, William Makepeace

**Tocqueville, Alexis (Charles Henri Maurice
Clerel Comte)** 1805-1859   **NCLC 7, 63**

Tolkien, J(ohn) R(onald) R(euel) 1892-1973
**CLC 1, 2, 3, 8, 12, 38; DA; DAB; DAC;
DAM MST, NOV, POP; WLC**
See also AAYA 10; AITN 1; CA 17-18; 45-48;

CANR 36; CAP 2; CDBLB 1914-1945; DLB
15, 160; JRDA; MAICYA; MTCW 1; SATA
2, 32, 100; SATA-Obit 24

Toller, Ernst 1893-1939   **TCLC 10**
See also CA 107; DLB 124

Tolson, M. B.
See Tolson, Melvin B(eaunorus)

Tolson, Melvin B(eaunorus) 1898(?)-1966
CLC 36, 105; BLC 3; DAM MULT, POET
See also BW 1; CA 124; 89-92; DLB 48, 76

Tolstoi, Aleksei Nikolaevich
See Tolstoy, Alexey Nikolaevich

Tolstoy, Alexey Nikolaevich 1882-1945**T C L C
18**
See also CA 107; 158

Tolstoy, Count Leo
See Tolstoy, Leo (Nikolaevich)

Tolstoy, Leo (Nikolaevich) 1828-1910**TCLC 4,
11, 17, 28, 44, 79; DA; DAB; DAC; DAM
MST, NOV; SSC 9, 30; WLC**
See also CA 104; 123; SATA 26

Tomasi di Lampedusa, Giuseppe 1896-1957
See Lampedusa, Giuseppe (Tomasi) di
See also CA 111

Tomlin, Lily   **CLC 17**
See also Tomlin, Mary Jean

Tomlin, Mary Jean 1939(?)-
See Tomlin, Lily
See also CA 117

Tomlinson, (Alfred) Charles 1927-**CLC 2, 4, 6,
13, 45; DAM POET; PC 17**
See also CA 5-8R; CANR 33; DLB 40

Tomlinson, H(enry) M(ajor) 1873-1958**TCLC
71**
See also CA 118; 161; DLB 36, 100, 195

Tonson, Jacob
See Bennett, (Enoch) Arnold

Toole, John Kennedy 1937-1969 **CLC 19, 64**
See also CA 104; DLBY 81

Toomer, Jean 1894-1967**CLC 1, 4, 13, 22; BLC
3; DAM MULT; PC 7; SSC 1; WLCS**
See also BW 1; CA 85-88; CDALB 1917-1929;
DLB 45, 51; MTCW 1

Torley, Luke
See Blish, James (Benjamin)

Tornimparte, Alessandra
See Ginzburg, Natalia

Torre, Raoul della
See Mencken, H(enry) L(ouis)

Torrey, E(dwin) Fuller 1937-   **CLC 34**
See also CA 119; CANR 71

Torsvan, Ben Traven
See Traven, B.

Torsvan, Benno Traven
See Traven, B.

Torsvan, Berick Traven
See Traven, B.

Torsvan, Berwick Traven
See Traven, B.

Torsvan, Bruno Traven
See Traven, B.

Torsvan, Traven
See Traven, B.

Tournier, Michel (Edouard) 1924-**CLC 6, 23,
36, 95**
See also CA 49-52; CANR 3, 36; DLB 83;
MTCW 1; SATA 23

Tournimparte, Alessandra
See Ginzburg, Natalia

Towers, Ivar
See Kornbluth, C(yril) M.

Towne, Robert (Burton) 1936(?)-   **CLC 87**
See also CA 108; DLB 44

Townsend, Sue   **CLC 61**
See also Townsend, Susan Elaine
See also SATA 55, 93; SATA-Brief 48

Townsend, Susan Elaine 1946-
See Townsend, Sue
See also CA 119; 127; CANR 65; DAB; DAC;
DAM MST

Townshend, Peter (Dennis Blandford) 1945-
CLC 17, 42
See also CA 107

Tozzi, Federigo 1883-1920   **TCLC 31**
See also CA 160

Traill, Catharine Parr 1802-1899 **NCLC 31**
See also DLB 99

Trakl, Georg 1887-1914   **TCLC 5; PC 20**
See also CA 104; 165

Transtroemer, Tomas (Goesta) 1931-**CLC 52,
65; DAM POET**
See also CA 117; 129; CAAS 17

Transtromer, Tomas Gosta
See Transtroemer, Tomas (Goesta)

Traven, B. (?)-1969   **CLC 8, 11**
See also CA 19-20; 25-28R; CAP 2; DLB 9,
56; MTCW 1

Treitel, Jonathan 1959-   **CLC 70**

Tremain, Rose 1943-   **CLC 42**
See also CA 97-100; CANR 44; DLB 14

Tremblay, Michel 1942- **CLC 29, 102; DAC;
DAM MST**
See also CA 116; 128; DLB 60; MTCW 1

Trevanian   **CLC 29**
See also Whitaker, Rod(ney)

Trevor, Glen
See Hilton, James

Trevor, William 1928-   **CLC 7, 9, 14, 25, 71;
SSC 21**
See also Cox, William Trevor
See also DLB 14, 139

Trifonov, Yuri (Valentinovich) 1925-1981
CLC 45
See also CA 126; 103; MTCW 1

Trilling, Lionel 1905-1975   **CLC 9, 11, 24**
See also CA 9-12R; 61-64; CANR 10; DLB 28,
63; INT CANR-10; MTCW 1

Trimball, W. H.
See Mencken, H(enry) L(ouis)

Tristan
See Gomez de la Serna, Ramon

Tristram
See Housman, A(lfred) E(dward)

Trogdon, William (Lewis) 1939-
See Heat-Moon, William Least
See also CA 115; 119; CANR 47; INT 119

Trollope, Anthony 1815-1882**NCLC 6, 33; DA;
DAB; DAC; DAM MST, NOV; SSC 28;
WLC**
See also CDBLB 1832-1890; DLB 21, 57, 159;
SATA 22

Trollope, Frances 1779-1863   **NCLC 30**
See also DLB 21, 166

Trotsky, Leon 1879-1940   **TCLC 22**
See also CA 118; 167

Trotter (Cockburn), Catharine 1679-1749**L C
8**
See also DLB 84

Trout, Kilgore
See Farmer, Philip Jose

Trow, George W. S. 1943-   **CLC 52**
See also CA 126

Troyat, Henri 1911-   **CLC 23**
See also CA 45-48; CANR 2, 33, 67; MTCW 1

Trudeau, G(arretson) B(eekman) 1948-
See Trudeau, Garry B.

See also CA 81-84; CANR 31; SATA 35

Trudeau, Garry B.   **CLC 12**
See also Trudeau, G(arretson) B(eekman)
See also AAYA 10; AITN 2

Truffaut, Francois 1932-1984   **CLC 20, 101**
See also CA 81-84; 113; CANR 34

Trumbo, Dalton 1905-1976   **CLC 19**
See also CA 21-24R; 69-72; CANR 10; DLB 26

Trumbull, John 1750-1831   **NCLC 30**
See also DLB 31

Trundlett, Helen B.
See Eliot, T(homas) S(tearns)

Tryon, Thomas 1926-1991   **CLC 3, 11; DAM POP**
See also AITN 1; CA 29-32R; 135; CANR 32; MTCW 1

Tryon, Tom
See Tryon, Thomas

Ts'ao Hsueh-ch'in 1715(?)-1763   **LC 1**

Tsushima, Shuji 1909-1948
See Dazai Osamu
See also CA 107

Tsvetaeva (Efron), Marina (Ivanovna) 1892-1941   **TCLC 7, 35; PC 14**
See also CA 104; 128; MTCW 1

Tuck, Lily 1938-   **CLC 70**
See also CA 139

Tu Fu 712-770   **PC 9**
See also DAM MULT

Tunis, John R(oberts) 1889-1975   **CLC 12**
See also CA 61-64; CANR 62; DLB 22, 171; JRDA; MAICYA; SATA 37; SATA-Brief 30

Tuohy, Frank   **CLC 37**
See also Tuohy, John Francis
See also DLB 14, 139

Tuohy, John Francis 1925-
See Tuohy, Frank
See also CA 5-8R; CANR 3, 47

Turco, Lewis (Putnam) 1934-   **CLC 11, 63**
See also CA 13-16R; CAAS 22; CANR 24, 51; DLBY 84

Turgenev, Ivan 1818-1883   **NCLC 21; DA; DAB; DAC; DAM MST, NOV; DC 7; SSC 7; WLC**

Turgot, Anne-Robert-Jacques 1727-1781 **L C 26**

Turner, Frederick 1943-   **CLC 48**
See also CA 73-76; CAAS 10; CANR 12, 30, 56; DLB 40

Tutu, Desmond M(pilo) 1931-**CLC 80; BLC 3; DAM MULT**
See also BW 1; CA 125; CANR 67

Tutuola, Amos 1920-1997**CLC 5, 14, 29; BLC 3; DAM MULT**
See also BW 2; CA 9-12R; 159; CANR 27, 66; DLB 125; MTCW 1

Twain, MarkTCLC 6, 12, 19, 36, 48, 59; SSC 6, 26; WLC
See also Clemens, Samuel Langhorne
See also AAYA 20; DLB 11, 12, 23, 64, 74

Tyler, Anne 1941- **CLC 7, 11, 18, 28, 44, 59, 103; DAM NOV, POP**
See also AAYA 18; BEST 89:1; CA 9-12R; CANR 11, 33, 53; DLB 6, 143; DLBY 82; MTCW 1; SATA 7, 90

Tyler, Royall 1757-1826   **NCLC 3**
See also DLB 37

Tynan, Katharine 1861-1931   **TCLC 3**
See also CA 104; 167; DLB 153

Tyutchev, Fyodor 1803-1873   **NCLC 34**

Tzara, Tristan 1896-1963   **CLC 47; DAM POET**

See also CA 153; 89-92

Uhry, Alfred 1936-   **CLC 55; DAM DRAM, POP**
See also CA 127; 133; INT 133

Ulf, Haerved
See Strindberg, (Johan) August

Ulf, Harved
See Strindberg, (Johan) August

Ulibarri, Sabine R(eyes) 1919-**CLC 83; DAM MULT**
See also CA 131; DLB 82; HW

Unamuno (y Jugo), Miguel de 1864-1936
TCLC 2, 9; DAM MULT, NOV; HLC; SSC 11
See also CA 104; 131; DLB 108; HW; MTCW 1

Undercliffe, Errol
See Campbell, (John) Ramsey

Underwood, Miles
See Glassco, John

Undset, Sigrid 1882-1949**TCLC 3; DA; DAB; DAC; DAM MST, NOV; WLC**
See also CA 104; 129; MTCW 1

Ungaretti, Giuseppe 1888-1970**CLC 7, 11, 15**
See also CA 19-20; 25-28R; CAP 2; DLB 114

Unger, Douglas 1952-   **CLC 34**
See also CA 130

Unsworth, Barry (Forster) 1930-   **CLC 76**
See also CA 25-28R; CANR 30, 54; DLB 194

Updike, John (Hoyer) 1932-**CLC 1, 2, 3, 5, 7, 9, 13, 15, 23, 34, 43, 70; DA; DAB; DAC; DAM MST, NOV, POET, POP; SSC 13, 27; WLC**
See also CA 1-4R; CABS 1; CANR 4, 33, 51; CDALB 1968-1988; DLB 2, 5, 143; DLBD 3; DLBY 80, 82, 97; MTCW 1

Upshaw, Margaret Mitchell
See Mitchell, Margaret (Munnerlyn)

Upton, Mark
See Sanders, Lawrence

Upward, Allen 1863-1926   **TCLC 85**
See also CA 117; DLB 36

Urdang, Constance (Henriette) 1922-**CLC 47**
See also CA 21-24R; CANR 9, 24

Uriel, Henry
See Faust, Frederick (Schiller)

Uris, Leon (Marcus) 1924- **CLC 7, 32; DAM NOV, POP**
See also AITN 1, 2; BEST 89:2; CA 1-4R; CANR 1, 40, 65; MTCW 1; SATA 49

Urmuz
See Codrescu, Andrei

Urquhart, Jane 1949-   **CLC 90; DAC**
See also CA 113; CANR 32, 68

Ustinov, Peter (Alexander) 1921-   **CLC 1**
See also AITN 1; CA 13-16R; CANR 25, 51; DLB 13

U Tam'si, Gerald Felix Tchicaya
See Tchicaya, Gerald Felix

U Tam'si, Tchicaya
See Tchicaya, Gerald Felix

Vachss, Andrew (Henry) 1942-   **CLC 106**
See also CA 118; CANR 44

Vachss, Andrew H.
See Vachss, Andrew (Henry)

Vaculik, Ludvik 1926-   **CLC 7**
See also CA 53-56; CANR 72

Vaihinger, Hans 1852-1933   **TCLC 71**
See also CA 116; 166

Valdez, Luis (Miguel) 1940-   **CLC 84; DAM MULT; HLC**
See also CA 101; CANR 32; DLB 122; HW

Valenzuela, Luisa 1938- **CLC 31, 104; DAM MULT; SSC 14**
See also CA 101; CANR 32, 65; DLB 113; HW

Valera y Alcala-Galiano, Juan 1824-1905
TCLC 10
See also CA 106

Valery, (Ambroise) Paul (Toussaint Jules) 1871-1945   **TCLC 4, 15; DAM POET; PC 9**
See also CA 104; 122; MTCW 1

Valle-Inclan, Ramon (Maria) del 1866-1936
TCLC 5; DAM MULT; HLC
See also CA 106; 153; DLB 134

Vallejo, Antonio Buero
See Buero Vallejo, Antonio

Vallejo, Cesar (Abraham) 1892-1938**TCLC 3, 56; DAM MULT; HLC**
See also CA 105; 153; HW

Vallette, Marguerite Eymery
See Rachilde

Valle Y Pena, Ramon del
See Valle-Inclan, Ramon (Maria) del

Van Ash, Cay 1918-   **CLC 34**

Vanbrugh, Sir John 1664-1726 **LC 21; DAM DRAM**
See also DLB 80

Van Campen, Karl
See Campbell, John W(ood, Jr.)

Vance, Gerald
See Silverberg, Robert

Vance, Jack   **CLC 35**
See also Kuttner, Henry; Vance, John Holbrook
See also DLB 8

Vance, John Holbrook 1916-
See Queen, Ellery; Vance, Jack
See also CA 29-32R; CANR 17, 65; MTCW 1

Van Den Bogarde, Derek Jules Gaspard Ulric Niven 1921-
See Bogarde, Dirk
See also CA 77-80

Vandenburgh, Jane   **CLC 59**
See also CA 168

Vanderhaeghe, Guy 1951-   **CLC 41**
See also CA 113; CANR 72

van der Post, Laurens (Jan) 1906-1996**CLC 5**
See also CA 5-8R; 155; CANR 35

van de Wetering, Janwillem 1931-   **CLC 47**
See also CA 49-52; CANR 4, 62

Van Dine, S. S.   **TCLC 23**
See also Wright, Willard Huntington

Van Doren, Carl (Clinton) 1885-1950 **TCLC 18**
See also CA 111; 168

Van Doren, Mark 1894-1972   **CLC 6, 10**
See also CA 1-4R; 37-40R; CANR 3; DLB 45; MTCW 1

Van Druten, John (William) 1901-1957**TCLC 2**
See also CA 104; 161; DLB 10

Van Duyn, Mona (Jane) 1921- **CLC 3, 7, 63; DAM POET**
See also CA 9-12R; CANR 7, 38, 60; DLB 5

Van Dyne, Edith
See Baum, L(yman) Frank

van Itallie, Jean-Claude 1936-   **CLC 3**
See also CA 45-48; CAAS 2; CANR 1, 48; DLB 7

van Ostaijen, Paul 1896-1928   **TCLC 33**
See also CA 163

Van Peebles, Melvin 1932- **CLC 2, 20; DAM MULT**
See also BW 2; CA 85-88; CANR 27, 67

Vansittart, Peter 1920-   **CLC 42**
See also CA 1-4R; CANR 3, 49

Van Vechten, Carl 1880-1964   **CLC 33**

See also CA 89-92; DLB 4, 9, 51

Van Vogt, A(lfred) E(lton) 1912- **CLC 1**
See also CA 21-24R; CANR 28; DLB 8; SATA 14

Varda, Agnes 1928- **CLC 16**
See also CA 116; 122

Vargas Llosa, (Jorge) Mario (Pedro) 1936-
CLC 3, 6, 9, 10, 15, 31, 42, 85; DA; DAB; DAC; DAM MST, MULT, NOV; HLC
See also CA 73-76; CANR 18, 32, 42, 67; DLB 145; HW; MTCW 1

Vasiliu, Gheorghe 1881-1957
See Bacovia, George
See also CA 123

Vassa, Gustavus
See Equiano, Olaudah

Vassilikos, Vassilis 1933- **CLC 4, 8**
See also CA 81-84

Vaughan, Henry 1621-1695 **LC 27**
See also DLB 131

Vaughn, Stephanie **CLC 62**

Vazov, Ivan (Minchov) 1850-1921 **TCLC 25**
See also CA 121; 167; DLB 147

Veblen, Thorstein B(unde) 1857-1929 **TCLC 31**
See also CA 115; 165

Vega, Lope de 1562-1635 **LC 23**

Venison, Alfred
See Pound, Ezra (Weston Loomis)

Verdi, Marie de
See Mencken, H(enry) L(ouis)

Verdu, Matilde
See Cela, Camilo Jose

Verga, Giovanni (Carmelo) 1840-1922 **TCLC 3; SSC 21**
See also CA 104; 123

Vergil 70B.C.-19B.C. **CMLC 9; DA; DAB; DAC; DAM MST, POET; PC 12; WLCS**

Verhaeren, Emile (Adolphe Gustave) 1855-1916 **TCLC 12**
See also CA 109

Verlaine, Paul (Marie) 1844-1896**NCLC 2, 51; DAM POET; PC 2**

Verne, Jules (Gabriel) 1828-1905**TCLC 6, 52**
See also AAYA 16; CA 110; 131; DLB 123; JRDA; MAICYA; SATA 21

Very, Jones 1813-1880 **NCLC 9**
See also DLB 1

Vesaas, Tarjei 1897-1970 **CLC 48**
See also CA 29-32R

Vialis, Gaston
See Simenon, Georges (Jacques Christian)

Vian, Boris 1920-1959 **TCLC 9**
See also CA 106; 164; DLB 72

Viaud, (Louis Marie) Julien 1850-1923
See Loti, Pierre
See also CA 107

Vicar, Henry
See Felsen, Henry Gregor

Vicker, Angus
See Felsen, Henry Gregor

Vidal, Gore 1925-**CLC 2, 4, 6, 8, 10, 22, 33, 72; DAM NOV, POP**
See also AITN 1; BEST 90:2; CA 5-8R; CANR 13, 45, 65; DLB 6, 152; INT CANR-13; MTCW 1

Viereck, Peter (Robert Edwin) 1916- **CLC 4**
See also CA 1-4R; CANR 1, 47; DLB 5

Vigny, Alfred (Victor) de 1797-1863**NCLC 7; DAM POET**
See also DLB 119, 192

Vilakazi, Benedict Wallet 1906-1947**TCLC 37**
See also CA 168

Villa, Jose Garcia 1904-1997 **PC 22**
See also CA 25-28R; CANR 12

Villaurrutia, Xavier 1903-1950 **TCLC 80**
See also HW

Villiers de l'Isle Adam, Jean Marie Mathias Philippe Auguste, Comte de 1838-1889 **NCLC 3; SSC 14**
See also DLB 123

Villon, Francois 1431-1463(?) **PC 13**

Vinci, Leonardo da 1452-1519 **LC 12**

Vine, Barbara **CLC 50**
See also Rendell, Ruth (Barbara)
See also BEST 90:4

Vinge, Joan (Carol) D(ennison) 1948-**CLC 30; SSC 24**
See also CA 93-96; CANR 72; SATA 36

Violis, G.
See Simenon, Georges (Jacques Christian)

Virgil
See Vergil

Visconti, Luchino 1906-1976 **CLC 16**
See also CA 81-84; 65-68; CANR 39

Vittorini, Elio 1908-1966 **CLC 6, 9, 14**
See also CA 133; 25-28R

Vizenor, Gerald Robert 1934-**CLC 103; DAM MULT**
See also CA 13-16R; CAAS 22; CANR 5, 21, 44, 67; DLB 175; NNAL

Vizinczey, Stephen 1933- **CLC 40**
See also CA 128; INT 128

Vliet, R(ussell) G(ordon) 1929-1984 **CLC 22**
See also CA 37-40R; 112; CANR 18

Vogau, Boris Andreyevich 1894-1937(?)
See Pilnyak, Boris
See also CA 123

Vogel, Paula A(nne) 1951- **CLC 76**
See also CA 108

Voigt, Cynthia 1942- **CLC 30**
See also AAYA 3; CA 106; CANR 18, 37, 40; CLR 13,48; INT CANR-18; JRDA; MAICYA; SATA 48, 79; SATA-Brief 33

Voigt, Ellen Bryant 1943- **CLC 54**
See also CA 69-72; CANR 11, 29, 55; DLB 120

Voinovich, Vladimir (Nikolaevich) 1932-**CLC 10, 49**
See also CA 81-84; CAAS 12; CANR 33, 67; MTCW 1

Vollmann, William T. 1959- **CLC 89; DAM NOV, POP**
See also CA 134; CANR 67

Voloshinov, V. N.
See Bakhtin, Mikhail Mikhailovich

Voltaire 1694-1778 **LC 14; DA; DAB; DAC; DAM DRAM, MST; SSC 12; WLC**

von Daeniken, Erich 1935- **CLC 30**
See also AITN 1; CA 37-40R; CANR 17, 44

von Daniken, Erich
See von Daeniken, Erich

von Heidenstam, (Carl Gustaf) Verner
See Heidenstam, (Carl Gustaf) Verner von

von Heyse, Paul (Johann Ludwig)
See Heyse, Paul (Johann Ludwig von)

von Hofmannsthal, Hugo
See Hofmannsthal, Hugo von

von Horvath, Odon
See Horvath, Oedoen von

von Horvath, Oedoen
See Horvath, Oedoen von

von Liliencron, (Friedrich Adolf Axel) Detlev
See Liliencron, (Friedrich Adolf Axel) Detlev von

Vonnegut, Kurt, Jr. 1922-**CLC 1, 2, 3, 4, 5, 8, 12, 22, 40, 60, 111; DA; DAB; DAC; DAM**

MST, NOV, POP; SSC 8; WLC
See also AAYA 6; AITN 1; BEST 90:4; CA 1-4R; CANR 1, 25, 49; CDALB 1968-1988; DLB 2, 8, 152; DLBD 3; DLBY 80; MTCW 1

Von Rachen, Kurt
See Hubbard, L(afayette) Ron(ald)

von Rezzori (d'Arezzo), Gregor
See Rezzori (d'Arezzo), Gregor von

von Sternberg, Josef
See Sternberg, Josef von

Vorster, Gordon 1924- **CLC 34**
See also CA 133

Vosce, Trudie
See Ozick, Cynthia

Voznesensky, Andrei (Andreievich) 1933-
CLC 1, 15, 57; DAM POET
See also CA 89-92; CANR 37; MTCW 1

Waddington, Miriam 1917- **CLC 28**
See also CA 21-24R; CANR 12, 30; DLB 68

Wagman, Fredrica 1937- **CLC 7**
See also CA 97-100; INT 97-100

Wagner, Linda W.
See Wagner-Martin, Linda (C.)

Wagner, Linda Welshimer
See Wagner-Martin, Linda (C.)

Wagner, Richard 1813-1883 **NCLC 9**
See also DLB 129

Wagner-Martin, Linda (C.) 1936- **CLC 50**
See also CA 159

Wagoner, David (Russell) 1926- **CLC 3, 5, 15**
See also CA 1-4R; CAAS 3; CANR 2, 71; DLB 5; SATA 14

Wah, Fred(erick James) 1939- **CLC 44**
See also CA 107; 141; DLB 60

Wahloo, Per 1926-1975 **CLC 7**
See also CA 61-64

Wahloo, Peter
See Wahloo, Per

Wain, John (Barrington) 1925-1994 **CLC 2, 11, 15, 46**
See also CA 5-8R; 145; CAAS 4; CANR 23, 54; CDBLB 1960 to Present; DLB 15, 27, 139, 155; MTCW 1

Wajda, Andrzej 1926- **CLC 16**
See also CA 102

Wakefield, Dan 1932- **CLC 7**
See also CA 21-24R; CAAS 7

Wakoski, Diane 1937- **CLC 2, 4, 7, 9, 11, 40; DAM POET; PC 15**
See also CA 13-16R; CAAS 1; CANR 9, 60; DLB 5; INT CANR-9

Wakoski-Sherbell, Diane
See Wakoski, Diane

Walcott, Derek (Alton) 1930-**CLC 2, 4, 9, 14, 25, 42, 67, 76; BLC 3; DAB; DAC; DAM MST, MULT, POET; DC 7**
See also BW 2; CA 89-92; CANR 26, 47; DLB 117; DLBY 81; MTCW 1

Waldman, Anne (Lesley) 1945- **CLC 7**
See also CA 37-40R; CAAS 17; CANR 34, 69; DLB 16

Waldo, E. Hunter
See Sturgeon, Theodore (Hamilton)

Waldo, Edward Hamilton
See Sturgeon, Theodore (Hamilton)

Walker, Alice (Malsenior) 1944- **CLC 5, 6, 9, 19, 27, 46, 58, 103; BLC 3; DA; DAB; DAC; DAM MST, MULT, NOV, POET, POP; SSC 5; WLCS**
See also AAYA 3; BEST 89:4; BW 2; CA 37-40R; CANR 9, 27, 49, 66; CDALB 1968-1988; DLB 6, 33, 143; INT CANR-27;

Weller, Paul 1958-   **CLC 26**
Wellershoff, Dieter 1925-   **CLC 46**
  See also CA 89-92; CANR 16, 37
Welles, (George) Orson 1915-1985**CLC 20, 80**
  See also CA 93-96; 117
Wellman, John McDowell 1945-
  See Wellman, Mac
  See also CA 166
Wellman, Mac 1945-   **CLC 65**
  See also Wellman, John McDowell; Wellman,
  John McDowell
Wellman, Manly Wade 1903-1986   **CLC 49**
  See also CA 1-4R; 118; CANR 6, 16, 44; SATA
  6; SATA-Obit 47
Wells, Carolyn 1869(?)-1942   **TCLC 35**
  See also CA 113; DLB 11
Wells, H(erbert) G(eorge) 1866-1946**TCLC 6,
  12, 19; DA; DAB; DAC; DAM MST, NOV;
  SSC 6; WLC**
  See also AAYA 18; CA 110; 121; CDBLB 1914-
  1945; DLB 34, 70, 156, 178; MTCW 1;
  SATA 20
Wells, Rosemary 1943-   **CLC 12**
  See also AAYA 13; CA 85-88; CANR 48; CLR
  16; MAICYA; SAAS 1; SATA 18, 69
Welty, Eudora 1909- **CLC 1, 2, 5, 14, 22, 33,
  105; DA; DAB; DAC; DAM MST, NOV;
  SSC 1, 27; WLC**
  See also CA 9-12R; CABS 1; CANR 32, 65;
  CDALB 1941-1968; DLB 2, 102, 143;
  DLBD 12; DLBY 87; MTCW 1
Wen I-to 1899-1946   **TCLC 28**
Wentworth, Robert
  See Hamilton, Edmond
Werfel, Franz (Viktor) 1890-1945   **TCLC 8**
  See also CA 104; 161; DLB 81, 124
Wergeland, Henrik Arnold 1808-1845 N C L C
  5
Wersba, Barbara 1932-   **CLC 30**
  See also AAYA 2; CA 29-32R; CANR 16, 38;
  CLR 3; DLB 52; JRDA; MAICYA; SAAS 2;
  SATA 1, 58
Wertmueller, Lina 1928-   **CLC 16**
  See also CA 97-100; CANR 39
Wescott, Glenway 1901-1987   **CLC 13**
  See also CA 13-16R; 121; CANR 23, 70; DLB
  4, 9, 102
Wesker, Arnold 1932-   **CLC 3, 5, 42; DAB;
  DAM DRAM**
  See also CA 1-4R; CAAS 7; CANR 1, 33;
  CDBLB 1960 to Present; DLB 13; MTCW 1
Wesley, Richard (Errol) 1945-   **CLC 7**
  See also BW 1; CA 57-60; CANR 27; DLB 38
Wessel, Johan Herman 1742-1785   **LC 7**
West, Anthony (Panther) 1914-1987 **CLC 50**
  See also CA 45-48; 124; CANR 3, 19; DLB 15
West, C. P.
  See Wodehouse, P(elham) G(renville)
West, (Mary) Jessamyn 1902-1984**CLC 7, 17**
  See also CA 9-12R; 112; CANR 27; DLB 6;
  DLBY 84; MTCW 1; SATA-Obit 37
West, Morris L(anglo) 1916-   **CLC 6, 33**
  See also CA 5-8R; CANR 24, 49, 64; MTCW 1
West, Nathanael 1903-1940   **TCLC 1, 14, 44;
  SSC 16**
  See also CA 104; 125; CDALB 1929-1941;
  DLB 4, 9, 28; MTCW 1
West, Owen
  See Koontz, Dean R(ay)
West, Paul 1930-   **CLC 7, 14, 96**
  See also CA 13-16R; CAAS 7; CANR 22, 53;
  DLB 14; INT CANR-22
West, Rebecca 1892-1983   **CLC 7, 9, 31, 50**

  See also CA 5-8R; 109; CANR 19; DLB 36;
  DLBY 83; MTCW 1
Westall, Robert (Atkinson) 1929-1993**CLC 17**
  See also AAYA 12; CA 69-72; 141; CANR 18,
  68; CLR 13; JRDA; MAICYA; SAAS 2;
  SATA 23, 69; SATA-Obit 75
Westlake, Donald E(dwin) 1933-   **CLC 7, 33;
  DAM POP**
  See also CA 17-20R; CAAS 13; CANR 16, 44,
  65; INT CANR-16
Westmacott, Mary
  See Christie, Agatha (Mary Clarissa)
Weston, Allen
  See Norton, Andre
Wetcheek, J. L.
  See Feuchtwanger, Lion
Wetering, Janwillem van de
  See van de Wetering, Janwillem
Wetherald, Agnes Ethelwyn 1857-1940**TCLC
  81**
  See also DLB 99
Wetherell, Elizabeth
  See Warner, Susan (Bogert)
Whale, James 1889-1957   **TCLC 63**
Whalen, Philip 1923-   **CLC 6, 29**
  See also CA 9-12R; CANR 5, 39; DLB 16
Wharton, Edith (Newbold Jones) 1862-1937
  **TCLC 3, 9, 27, 53; DA; DAB; DAC; DAM
  MST, NOV; SSC 6; WLC**
  See also AAYA 25; CA 104; 132; CDALB 1865-
  1917; DLB 4, 9, 12, 78, 189; DLBD 13;
  MTCW 1
Wharton, James
  See Mencken, H(enry) L(ouis)
Wharton, William (a pseudonym) CLC 18, 37
  See also CA 93-96; DLBY 80; INT 93-96
Wheatley (Peters), Phillis 1754(?)-1784**LC 3;
  BLC 3; DA; DAC; DAM MST, MULT,
  POET; PC 3; WLC**
  See also CDALB 1640-1865; DLB 31, 50
Wheelock, John Hall 1886-1978   **CLC 14**
  See also CA 13-16R; 77-80; CANR 14; DLB
  45
White, E(lwyn) B(rooks) 1899-1985 **CLC 10,
  34, 39; DAM POP**
  See also AITN 2; CA 13-16R; 116; CANR 16,
  37; CLR 1, 21; DLB 11, 22; MAICYA;
  MTCW 1; SATA 2, 29, 100; SATA-Obit 44
White, Edmund (Valentine III) 1940-**CLC 27,
  110; DAM POP**
  See also AAYA 7; CA 45-48; CANR 3, 19, 36,
  62; MTCW 1
White, Patrick (Victor Martindale) 1912-1990
  CLC 3, 4, 5, 7, 9, 18, 65, 69
  See also CA 81-84; 132; CANR 43; MTCW 1
White, Phyllis Dorothy James 1920-
  See James, P. D.
  See also CA 21-24R; CANR 17, 43, 65; DAM
  POP; MTCW 1
White, T(erence) H(anbury) 1906-1964 **C L C
  30**
  See also AAYA 22; CA 73-76; CANR 37; DLB
  160; JRDA; MAICYA; SATA 12
White, Terence de Vere 1912-1994   **CLC 49**
  See also CA 49-52; 145; CANR 3
White, Walter F(rancis) 1893-1955   **TCLC 15**
  See also White, Walter
  See also BW 1; CA 115; 124; DLB 51
White, William Hale 1831-1913
  See Rutherford, Mark
  See also CA 121
Whitehead, E(dward) A(nthony) 1933-**CLC 5**
  See also CA 65-68; CANR 58

Whitemore, Hugh (John) 1936-   **CLC 37**
  See also CA 132; INT 132
Whitman, Sarah Helen (Power) 1803-1878
  NCLC 19
  See also DLB 1
Whitman, Walt(er) 1819-1892   **NCLC 4, 31;
  DA; DAB; DAC; DAM MST, POET; PC
  3; WLC**
  See also CDALB 1640-1865; DLB 3, 64; SATA
  20
Whitney, Phyllis A(yame) 1903-   **CLC 42;
  DAM POP**
  See also AITN 2; BEST 90:3; CA 1-4R; CANR
  3, 25, 38, 60; JRDA; MAICYA; SATA 1, 30
Whittemore, (Edward) Reed (Jr.) 1919-**CLC 4**
  See also CA 9-12R; CAAS 8; CANR 4; DLB 5
Whittier, John Greenleaf 1807-1892**NCLC 8,
  59**
  See also DLB 1
Whittlebot, Hernia
  See Coward, Noel (Peirce)
Wicker, Thomas Grey 1926-
  See Wicker, Tom
  See also CA 65-68; CANR 21, 46
Wicker, Tom   **CLC 7**
  See also Wicker, Thomas Grey
Wideman, John Edgar 1941-   **CLC 5, 34, 36,
  67; BLC 3; DAM MULT**
  See also BW 2; CA 85-88; CANR 14, 42, 67;
  DLB 33, 143
Wiebe, Rudy (Henry) 1934-   **CLC 6, 11, 14;
  DAC; DAM MST**
  See also CA 37-40R; CANR 42, 67; DLB 60
Wieland, Christoph Martin 1733-1813**N C L C
  17**
  See also DLB 97
Wiene, Robert 1881-1938   **TCLC 56**
Wieners, John 1934-   **CLC 7**
  See also CA 13-16R; DLB 16
Wiesel, Elie(zer) 1928- **CLC 3, 5, 11, 37; DA;
  DAB; DAC; DAM MST, NOV; WLCS 2**
  See also AAYA 7; AITN 1; CA 5-8R; CAAS 4;
  CANR 8, 40, 65; DLB 83; DLBY 87; INT
  CANR-8; MTCW 1; SATA 56
Wiggins, Marianne 1947-   **CLC 57**
  See also BEST 89:3; CA 130; CANR 60
Wight, James Alfred 1916-1995
  See Herriot, James
  See also CA 77-80; SATA 55; SATA-Brief 44
Wilbur, Richard (Purdy) 1921-**CLC 3, 6, 9, 14,
  53, 110; DA; DAB; DAC; DAM MST,
  POET**
  See also CA 1-4R; CABS 2; CANR 2, 29; DLB
  5, 169; INT CANR-29; MTCW 1; SATA 9
Wild, Peter 1940-   **CLC 14**
  See also CA 37-40R; DLB 5
Wilde, Oscar (Fingal O'Flahertie Wills)
  1854(?)-1900**TCLC 1, 8, 23, 41; DA; DAB;
  DAC; DAM DRAM, MST, NOV; SSC 11;
  WLC**
  See also CA 104; 119; CDBLB 1890-1914;
  DLB 10, 19, 34, 57, 141, 156, 190; SATA 24
Wilder, Billy   **CLC 20**
  See also Wilder, Samuel
  See also DLB 26
Wilder, Samuel 1906-
  See Wilder, Billy
  See also CA 89-92
Wilder, Thornton (Niven) 1897-1975**CLC 1, 5,
  6, 10, 15, 35, 82; DA; DAB; DAC; DAM
  DRAM, MST, NOV; DC 1; WLC**
  See also AITN 2; CA 13-16R; 61-64; CANR
  40; DLB 4, 7, 9; DLBY 97; MTCW 1

CAAS 22; CANR 54; DLB 130; INT 117

Wolfram von Eschenbach c. 1170-c. 1220
CMLC 5
See also DLB 138

Wolitzer, Hilma 1930- **CLC 17**
See also CA 65-68; CANR 18, 40; INT CANR-18; SATA 31

Wollstonecraft, Mary 1759-1797 **LC 5**
See also CDBLB 1789-1832; DLB 39, 104, 158

Wonder, Stevie **CLC 12**
See also Morris, Steveland Judkins

Wong, Jade Snow 1922- **CLC 17**
See also CA 109

Woodberry, George Edward 1855-1930
TCLC 73
See also CA 165; DLB 71, 103

Woodcott, Keith
See Brunner, John (Kilian Houston)

Woodruff, Robert W.
See Mencken, H(enry) L(ouis)

Woolf, (Adeline) Virginia 1882-1941 **TCLC 1, 5, 20, 43, 56; DA; DAB; DAC; DAM MST, NOV; SSC 7; WLC**
See also CA 104; 130; CANR 64; CDBLB 1914-1945; DLB 36, 100, 162; DLBD 10; MTCW 1

Woolf, Virginia Adeline
See Woolf, (Adeline) Virginia

Woollcott, Alexander (Humphreys) 1887-1943
TCLC 5
See also CA 105; 161; DLB 29

Woolrich, Cornell 1903-1968 **CLC 77**
See also Hopley-Woolrich, Cornell George

Wordsworth, Dorothy 1771-1855 **NCLC 25**
See also DLB 107

Wordsworth, William 1770-1850 **NCLC 12, 38; DA; DAB; DAC; DAM MST, POET; PC 4; WLC**
See also CDBLB 1789-1832; DLB 93, 107

Wouk, Herman 1915- **CLC 1, 9, 38; DAM NOV, POP**
See also CA 5-8R; CANR 6, 33, 67; DLBY 82; INT CANR-6; MTCW 1

Wright, Charles (Penzel, Jr.) 1935- **CLC 6, 13, 28**
See also CA 29-32R; CAAS 7; CANR 23, 36, 62; DLB 165; DLBY 82; MTCW 1

Wright, Charles Stevenson 1932- **CLC 49; BLC 3; DAM MULT, POET**
See also BW 1; CA 9-12R; CANR 26; DLB 33

Wright, Jack R.
See Harris, Mark

Wright, James (Arlington) 1927-1980 **CLC 3, 5, 10, 28; DAM POET**
See also AITN 2; CA 49-52; 97-100; CANR 4, 34, 64; DLB 5, 169; MTCW 1

Wright, Judith (Arandell) 1915- **CLC 11, 53; PC 14**
See also CA 13-16R; CANR 31; MTCW 1; SATA 14

Wright, L(aurali) R. 1939- **CLC 44**
See also CA 138

Wright, Richard (Nathaniel) 1908-1960 **C L C 1, 3, 4, 9, 14, 21, 48, 74; BLC 3; DA; DAB; DAC; DAM MST, MULT, NOV; SSC 2; WLC**
See also AAYA 5; BW 1; CA 108; CANR 64; CDALB 1929-1941; DLB 76, 102; DLBD 2; MTCW 1

Wright, Richard B(ruce) 1937- **CLC 6**
See also CA 85-88; DLB 53

Wright, Rick 1945- **CLC 35**

Wright, Rowland
See Wells, Carolyn

Wright, Stephen 1946- **CLC 33**

Wright, Willard Huntington 1888-1939
See Van Dine, S. S.
See also CA 115; DLBD 16

Wright, William 1930- **CLC 44**
See also CA 53-56; CANR 7, 23

Wroth, LadyMary 1587-1653(?) **LC 30**
See also DLB 121

Wu Ch'eng-en 1500(?)-1582(?) **LC 7**

Wu Ching-tzu 1701-1754 **LC 2**

Wurlitzer, Rudolph 1938(?)- **CLC 2, 4, 15**
See also CA 85-88; DLB 173

Wycherley, William 1641-1715 **LC 8, 21; DAM DRAM**
See also CDBLB 1660-1789; DLB 80

Wylie, Elinor (Morton Hoyt) 1885-1928
TCLC 8; PC 23
See also CA 105; 162; DLB 9, 45

Wylie, Philip (Gordon) 1902-1971 **CLC 43**
See also CA 21-22; 33-36R; CAP 2; DLB 9

Wyndham, John **CLC 19**
See also Harris, John (Wyndham Parkes Lucas) Beynon

Wyss, Johann David Von 1743-1818 **NCLC 10**
See also JRDA; MAICYA; SATA 29; SATA-Brief 27

Xenophon c. 430B.C.-c. 354B.C. **CMLC 17**
See also DLB 176

Yakumo Koizumi
See Hearn, (Patricio) Lafcadio (Tessima Carlos)

Yanez, Jose Donoso
See Donoso (Yanez), Jose

Yanovsky, Basile S.
See Yanovsky, V(assily) S(emenovich)

Yanovsky, V(assily) S(emenovich) 1906-1989
CLC 2, 18
See also CA 97-100; 129

Yates, Richard 1926-1992 **CLC 7, 8, 23**
See also CA 5-8R; 139; CANR 10, 43; DLB 2; DLBY 81, 92; INT CANR-10

Yeats, W. B.
See Yeats, William Butler

Yeats, William Butler 1865-1939 **TCLC 1, 11, 18, 31; DA; DAB; DAC; DAM DRAM, MST, POET; PC 20; WLC**
See also CA 104; 127; CANR 45; CDBLB 1890-1914; DLB 10, 19, 98, 156; MTCW 1

Yehoshua, A(braham) B. 1936- **CLC 13, 31**
See also CA 33-36R; CANR 43

Yep, Laurence Michael 1948- **CLC 35**
See also AAYA 5; CA 49-52; CANR 1, 46; CLR 3, 17; DLB 52; JRDA; MAICYA; SATA 7, 69

Yerby, Frank G(arvin) 1916-1991 **CLC 1, 7, 22; BLC 3; DAM MULT**
See also BW 1; CA 9-12R; 136; CANR 16, 52; DLB 76; INT CANR-16; MTCW 1

Yesenin, Sergei Alexandrovich
See Esenin, Sergei (Alexandrovich)

Yevtushenko, Yevgeny (Alexandrovich) 1933-
CLC 1, 3, 13, 26, 51; DAM POET
See also CA 81-84; CANR 33, 54; MTCW 1

Yezierska, Anzia 1885(?)-1970 **CLC 46**
See also CA 126; 89-92; DLB 28; MTCW 1

Yglesias, Helen 1915- **CLC 7, 22**
See also CA 37-40R; CAAS 20; CANR 15, 65; INT CANR-15; MTCW 1

Yokomitsu Riichi 1898-1947 **TCLC 47**

Yonge, Charlotte (Mary) 1823-1901 **TCLC 48**
See also CA 109; 163; DLB 18, 163; SATA 17

York, Jeremy
See Creasey, John

York, Simon
See Heinlein, Robert A(nson)

Yorke, Henry Vincent 1905-1974 **CLC 13**
See also Green, Henry
See also CA 85-88; 49-52

Yosano Akiko 1878-1942 **TCLC 59; PC 11**
See also CA 161

Yoshimoto, Banana **CLC 84**
See also Yoshimoto, Mahoko

Yoshimoto, Mahoko 1964-
See Yoshimoto, Banana
See also CA 144

Young, Al(bert James) 1939- **CLC 19; BLC 3; DAM MULT**
See also BW 2; CA 29-32R; CANR 26, 65; DLB 33

Young, Andrew (John) 1885-1971 **CLC 5**
See also CA 5-8R; CANR 7, 29

Young, Collier
See Bloch, Robert (Albert)

Young, Edward 1683-1765 **LC 3, 40**
See also DLB 95

Young, Marguerite (Vivian) 1909-1995 **C L C 82**
See also CA 13-16; 150; CAP 1

Young, Neil 1945- **CLC 17**
See also CA 110

Young Bear, Ray A. 1950- **CLC 94; DAM MULT**
See also CA 146; DLB 175; NNAL

Yourcenar, Marguerite 1903-1987 **CLC 19, 38, 50, 87; DAM NOV**
See also CA 69-72; CANR 23, 60; DLB 72; DLBY 88; MTCW 1

Yurick, Sol 1925- **CLC 6**
See also CA 13-16R; CANR 25

Zabolotsky, Nikolai Alekseevich 1903-1958
TCLC 52
See also CA 116; 164

Zamiatin, Yevgenii
See Zamyatin, Evgeny Ivanovich

Zamora, Bernice (B. Ortiz) 1938- **CLC 89; DAM MULT; HLC**
See also CA 151; DLB 82; HW

Zamyatin, Evgeny Ivanovich 1884-1937
TCLC 8, 37
See also CA 105; 166

Zangwill, Israel 1864-1926 **TCLC 16**
See also CA 109; 167; DLB 10, 135, 197

Zappa, Francis Vincent, Jr. 1940-1993
See Zappa, Frank
See also CA 108; 143; CANR 57

Zappa, Frank **CLC 17**
See also Zappa, Francis Vincent, Jr.

Zaturenska, Marya 1902-1982 **CLC 6, 11**
See also CA 13-16R; 105; CANR 22

Zeami 1363-1443 **DC 7**

Zelazny, Roger (Joseph) 1937-1995 **CLC 21**
See also AAYA 7; CA 21-24R; 148; CANR 26, 60; DLB 8; MTCW 1; SATA 57; SATA-Brief 39

Zhdanov, Andrei Alexandrovich 1896-1948
TCLC 18
See also CA 117; 167

Zhukovsky, Vasily 1783-1852 **NCLC 35**

Ziegenhagen, Eric **CLC 55**

Zimmer, Jill Schary
See Robinson, Jill

Zimmerman, Robert
See Dylan, Bob

Zindel, Paul 1936- **CLC 6, 26; DA; DAB; DAC; DAM DRAM, MST, NOV; DC 5**
See also AAYA 2; CA 73-76; CANR 31, 65;

CLR 3, 45; DLB 7, 52; JRDA; MAICYA;
MTCW 1; SATA 16, 58, 102
Zinov'Ev, A. A.
See Zinoviev, Alexander (Aleksandrovich)
Zinoviev, Alexander (Aleksandrovich) 1922-
CLC 19
See also CA 116; 133; CAAS 10
Zoilus
See Lovecraft, H(oward) P(hillips)
Zola, Emile (Edouard Charles Antoine) 1840-
1902**TCLC 1, 6, 21, 41; DA; DAB; DAC;
DAM MST, NOV; WLC**
See also CA 104; 138; DLB 123
Zoline, Pamela 1941-   **CLC 62**
See also CA 161
Zorrilla y Moral, Jose 1817-1893   **NCLC 6**
Zoshchenko, Mikhail (Mikhailovich) 1895-1958
TCLC 15; SSC 15
See also CA 115; 160
Zuckmayer, Carl 1896-1977   **CLC 18**
See also CA 69-72; DLB 56, 124
Zuk, Georges
See Skelton, Robin
Zukofsky, Louis 1904-1978**CLC 1, 2, 4, 7, 11,
18; DAM POET; PC 11**
See also CA 9-12R; 77-80; CANR 39; DLB 5,
165; MTCW 1
Zweig, Paul 1935-1984   **CLC 34, 42**
See also CA 85-88; 113
Zweig, Stefan 1881-1942   **TCLC 17**
See also CA 112; DLB 81, 118
Zwingli, Huldreich 1484-1531   **LC 37**
See also DLB 179

Literary Criticism Series
Cumulative Topic Index

This index lists all topic entries in Gale's *Classical and Medieval Literature Criticism, Contemporary Literary Criticism, Literature Criticism from 1400 to 1800, Nineteenth-Century Literature Criticism,* and *Twentieth-Century Literary Criticism.*

CMLC Cumulative Nationality Index

CMLC Cumulative Title Index

CMLC Cumulative Critic Index

Abu'l-'Addus, Yusuf
Al-Jahiz **25**:314

'Abdul Hakim, Khalifa
Rumi, Jalal al-Din **20**:345

Abe Akio
Sei Shonagon **6**:299

Abusch, Tzvi
Epic of Gilgamesh **3**:365

Adams, Charles Darwin
Demoshenes **13**:148

Adams, Henry
The Song of Roland **1**:166

Adcock, F. E.
Thucydides **17**:288

Addison, Joseph
Aeneid **9**:310
Iliad **1**:282
Ovid **7**:292
Sappho **3**:379
Sophocles **2**:293

Adler, Mortimer J.
Plato **8**:342

Adlington, William
Apuleius **1**:6

Ahmad, S. Maqbul
Al-Biruni **28**:123

Aiken, Conrad

Murasaki, Lady **1**:423

Aili, Hans
St. Birgitta **24**:97

Albert, S.M.
Albert the Great **16**:33

Alford, John A.
Rolle, Richard **21**:378

Alighieri, Dante
Aeneid **9**:297
Bertran de Born **5**:4
Seneca, Lucius Annaeus **6**:331
Sordello **15**:323

Ali-Shah, Omar
Khayyam **11**:288

Allen, Archibald W.
Livy **11**:334

Allen, Harold J.
Presocratic philosophy **22**:42

Allen, Hope Emily
Rolle, Richard **21**:308

Allen, Richard F.
Njals saga **13**:358

Allinson, Francis G.
Menander **9**:204

Allison, Rev. William T.
The Book of Psalms **4**:371

Al-Nadim
Arabian Nights **2**:3

Alphonso-Karkala, John B.
Kalevala **6**:259

Alter, Robert
The Book of Psalms **4**:451
Song of Songs **18**:283

Ambivius, Lucius
Terence **14**:302

Ames, Roger T.
Confucius **19**:88

Amis, Kingsley
Beowulf **1**:112

Anacker, Robert
Chretien de Troyes **10**:144

Anderson, David
St. John **27**:83

Anderson, Earl R.
Cynewulf **23**:86

Anderson, George K.
Beowulf **1**:98
The Dream of the Rood **14**:245

Anderson, J. K.
Xenophon **17**:342

Anderson, William S.
Juvenal **8**:59
Plautus **24**:255

Andersson, Theodore M.
Hrafnkel's Saga **2**:103

Annas, Julia
Epicurus **21**:201

Anthes, Rudolf
Eastern Mythology **26**:113

Apuleius, Lucius
Apuleius **1**:3

Aquinas, St. Thomas
Augustine, St. **6**:5
Averroes **7**:3
Plato **8**:217

Arberry, A. J.
Rumi, Jalal al-Din **20**:364

Arendt, Hannah
Augustine, St. **6**:116

Aristophanes
Aeschylus **11**:73

Aristotle
Aeschylus **11**:73
Greek Historiography **17**:13
Hesiod **5**:69
Iliad **1**:273
Plato **8**:202
Sophocles **2**:291

Armstrong, A. H.
Presocratic philosophy **22**:29

Arnold, E. Vernon